Zambia

the Bradt Travel Guide

Chris McIntyre

edition
6

www.bradtguides.com

Bradt Travel Guides Ltd, UK
The Globe Pequot Press Inc, USA

CALGARY PUBLIC LIBRARY

NOV   2016

D0174319

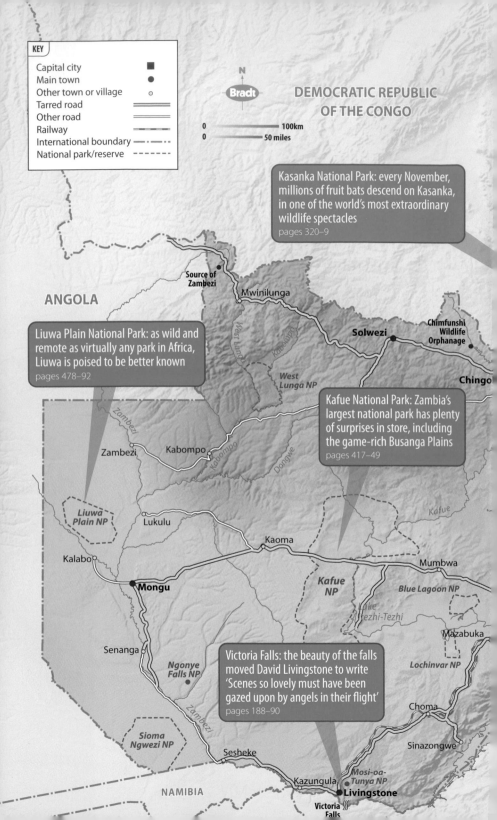

KEY

- Capital city   ■
- Main town   ●
- Other town or village   ○
- Tarred road
- Other road
- Railway
- International boundary
- National park/reserve

N

Bradt

0   100km
0   50 miles

DEMOCRATIC REPUBLIC OF THE CONGO

Kasanka National Park: every November, millions of fruit bats descend on Kasanka, in one of the world's most extraordinary wildlife spectacles
pages 320–9

ANGOLA

Source of Zambezi

Mwinilunga

West Lunga

Kabompo

Solwezi

Chimfunshi Wildlife Orphanage

Chingo

Liuwa Plain National Park: as wild and remote as virtually any park in Africa, Liuwa is poised to be better known
pages 478–92

West Lunga NP

Kafue National Park: Zambia's largest national park has plenty of surprises in store, including the game-rich Busanga Plains
pages 417–49

Zambezi

Kabompo

Zambezi

Kabompo

Dongwe

Kafue

Liuwa Plain NP

Lukulu

Kaoma

Mumbwa

Blue Lagoon NP

Kalabo

Mongu

Kafue NP

Lake Itezhi-Tezhi

Mazabuka

Senanga

Ngonye Falls NP

Lochinvar NP

Victoria Falls: the beauty of the falls moved David Livingstone to write 'Scenes so lovely must have been gazed upon by angels in their flight'
pages 188–90

Choma

Zambezi

Sioma Ngwezi NP

Sesheke

Kazungula

Mosi-oa-Tunya NP

Sinazongwe

NAMIBIA

Livingstone

Victoria Falls

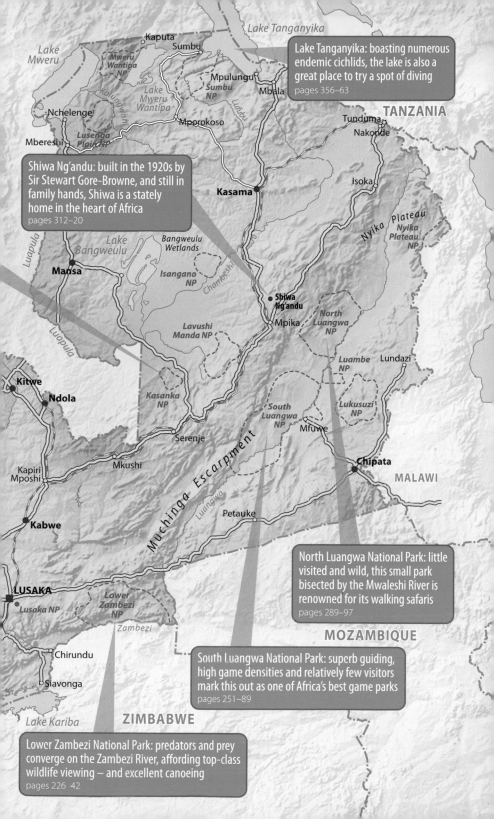

Lake Tanganyika: boasting numerous endemic cichlids, the lake is also a great place to try a spot of diving pages 356–63

Shiwa Ng'andu: built in the 1920s by Sir Stewart Gore-Browne, and still in family hands, Shiwa is a stately home in the heart of Africa pages 312–20

North Luangwa National Park: little visited and wild, this small park bisected by the Mwaleshi River is renowned for its walking safaris pages 289–97

South Luangwa National Park: superb guiding, high game densities and relatively few visitors mark this out as one of Africa's best game parks pages 251–89

Lower Zambezi National Park: predators and prey converge on the Zambezi River, affording top-class wildlife viewing – and excellent canoeing pages 226–42

Lake Tanganyika

TANZANIA

Lake Mweru

Kaputa

Sumbu

Mweru Wantipa NP

Mpulungu

Sumbu NP

Mbala

Tunduma

Nakonde

Nchelenge

Lake Mweru Wantipa

Mporokoso

Kalungwishi

Lufubu

Mbereshi

Lusenga Plain

Isoka

Kasama

Nyika Plateau

Nyika Plateau NP

Luapula

Lake Bangweulu

Bangweulu Wetlands

Isangano NP

Chambeshi

Shiwa Ng'andu

Mpika

North Luangwa NP

Mansa

Lavushi Manda NP

Luambe NP

Lundazi

Luapula

Kasanka NP

South Luangwa NP

Lukusuzi NP

Kitwe

Mfuwe

Ndola

Serenje

Chipata

MALAWI

Kapiri Mposhi

Mkushi

Muchinga Escarpment

Luangwa

Kabwe

Petauke

LUSAKA

Lusaka NP

Lower Zambezi NP

Zambezi

MOZAMBIQUE

Chirundu

Siavonga

ZIMBABWE

Lake Kariba

Zambia
Don't
miss...

Birdlife

Zambia is a superb birding
destination, with 757
different species — including
the grey-crowned crane

(SS) pages 32–3

Victoria Falls

The spectacular Victoria Falls are
1,688m wide and average just over
100m in height

(SS) pages 188–90

National parks
Lower Zambezi National Park is just one of 20 national parks in Zambia
(AZ) pages 35–7

Shiwa Ng'andu
Shiwa Ng'andu is one of the subcontinent's most extraordinary memorials to British colonial rule
(TII) pages 312–20

Wildlife
Zambia's native fauna comprises classic big game found throughout east and southern Africa, as well as endemic subspecies such as Thornicroft's giraffe
(AZ) pages 32–3

Zambia in colour

above   Many homes boast traditional patterns, but this colourful house in Northern Province is unusual (TH) page 347

right   Buying locally made souvenirs and produce will help the whole community (SS) page 75

below   Fisherman with traps, Bangweulu Wetlands; the wetlands are often described as one of Africa's last great wilderness areas (SS) pages 336–45

above   One of Zambia's biggest attractions is its walking safaris, which are among the best in Africa (SS) pages 105–7

left   Guided canoeing is a great way to experience the Zambezi River up close (AZ) page 199

below left   The Zambezi, below Victoria Falls, is one of the world's most renowned stretches of river for white-water rafting (SS) pages 199–201

AUTHOR

Chris McIntyre went to Africa in 1987, after reading physics at Queen's College, Oxford. He taught with VSO in Zimbabwe for almost three years and travelled around extensively, mostly with a backpack. In 1990 he co-authored the UK's first guide to Namibia and Botswana, published by Bradt, before spending three years as a shipbroker in London.

Since then, Chris has concentrated on what he enjoys most: Africa. He wrote the first guidebook to Zambia for Bradt in 1996, the first edition of their Namibia guide in 1998, a new Botswana guide in 2003, and co-authored a guide to Zanzibar in 2006. Whilst keeping these guidebooks up to date, his day job is managing director of Expert Africa – a specialist tour operator that organises high-quality trips throughout Africa for individual travellers from around the world. It probably sends more travellers on safaris to Zambia than any other company.

Chris maintains a keen interest in development and conservation issues, acting as advisor to various NGOs and projects associated with Africa. He is a Fellow of the Royal Geographical Society and contributes photographs and articles to various publications, including *The Times*, *Wanderlust*, *BBC Wildlife* and *Travel Africa*. Now based in Surrey, Chris and his wife, Susan, still regularly travel and research in Africa. Chris can usually be contacted by email on chris.mcintyre@expertafrica.com or through his website www.expertafrica.com.

Call the author

No bias, no hard sell: for real insight, call an Expert

This book's author, **Chris McIntyre** runs specialist tour operator Expert Africa.

See **www.expertafrica.com** for the most detailed information on Zambia safaris, then call us to help you plan your own superb trip.

UK: +44 (0) 20 8232 9777

USA/Canada (toll-free): 1-800-242-2434

Australia (toll-free): 1-800-995-397

info@expertafrica.com
www.expertafrica.com

EXPERT AFRICA

NAMIBIA · SOUTH AFRICA · BOTSWANA · ZIMBABWE · ZAMBIA · MOZAMBIQUE
MALAWI · TANZANIA · KENYA · RWANDA · SEYCHELLES

ABTA
The Travel Association
ABTA No. Y1608

AITO assured

PUBLISHER'S FOREWORD   *Hilary Bradt*

When this book was first published, an American bookseller wrote to tell us that it was '… the most comprehensive and well-organised book of the bunch and I also believe it is one of the best travel books ever published.'

Over the years, Chris has expanded his guide in line with continuing developments in Zambia's tourism. This ensures that both first-time visitors and those who have a long familiarity with the country will find insightful comments about all that is new in the context of the detailed background text that is the hallmark of the book.

Sixth edition published June 2016
First published 1996
Bradt Travel Guides Ltd
IDC House, The Vale, Chalfont St Peter, Bucks SL9 9RZ, England
www.bradtguides.com
Print edition published in the USA by The Globe Pequot Press Inc,
PO Box 480, Guilford, Connecticut 06437-0480

Text copyright © 2016 Chris McIntyre
Maps copyright © 2016 Bradt Travel Guides Ltd Includes map data © OpenStreetMap contributors
Photographs copyright © 2016 Individual photographers (see below)
Project manager: Claire Strange
Cover research: Pepi Bluck, Perfect Picture

The author and publisher have made every effort to ensure the accuracy of the information in this book at the time of going to press. However, they cannot accept any responsibility for any loss, injury or inconvenience resulting from the use of information contained in this guide. All rights reserved. No part of this publication may be reproduced, stored in a retrieval system, or transmitted in any form or by any means, electronic, mechanical, photocopying, recording or otherwise without the prior consent of the publisher. Requests for permission should be addressed to Bradt Travel Guides Ltd in the UK (print and digital editions), or to The Globe Pequot Press Inc in North and South America (print edition only).

ISBN: 978 1 78477 012 9 (print)
e-ISBN: 978 1 78477 157 7 (e-pub)
e-ISBN: 978 1 78477 257 4 (mobi)

British Library Cataloguing in Publication Data
A catalogue record for this book is available from the British Library

Photographs FLPA: Philip Perry (PP/FLPA), Malcolm Schuyl (MS/FLPA), Chris & Tilde Stuart (C&TS/FLPA); Bob Hayne (BH); Tricia Hayne (TH); Chris McIntyre (CM); Chris Meyer (CMeyer); Will-Burrad-Lucas/Nature Picture Library (WBL/NPL); Shutterstock: Philip Allaway (PA/S), David Havel (DH/S), Martin Mecnarowski (MM/S), Natalia Paklina (NP/S); SuperStock (SS); Ariadne Van Zandbergen (AZ); Eleanor Walkingshaw (EA)

Front cover Lion (*Panthera leo*) (WBL/NPL)
Back cover Walking on safari (SS); A gorge on the Zambezi River (SS)
Title page Carmine bee-eater (*Merops nubicoides*) (SS); souvenir shop (SS); giraffe (*Giraffa camelopardis*) (SS)

Illustrations Annabel Milne
Maps David McCutcheon FBCart.S; Colour map relief base by Nick Rowland FRGS

Typeset from the author's disk by Ian Spick and Wakewing, Chesham
Production managed by Jellyfish Print Solutions; printed and bound in India
Digital conversion by www.dataworks.co.in

Major Contributors

This book, just as much as the previous editions, has been a team effort, and many have devoted their energy to it. Largest amongst the contributions to this sixth edition are those from the following.

Tricia and Bob Hayne updated much of the text for this edition, having worked extensively on the previous three editions, and helped Chris to update his other guides to Botswana, Namibia and Zanzibar. Formerly editorial director of Bradt Travel Guides, Tricia is now a freelance travel writer, and a member of the British Guild of Travel Writers. When not getting lost in Zambia, she and Bob are more likely to be found toting backpacks on long-distance hikes.

Freddie Sutton has always had a passion for two things, travel and wildlife. After leaving school he spent time exploring Tanzania, discovering that Africa was the perfect continent for combining these interests. After reading zoology at the University of Bristol and working as a research assistant in the Udzungwa Mountains, Freddie now works at Expert Africa, where he specialises in Zambia. For this edition he updated the Luangwa Valley, Kafue River Basin and Livingstone chapters.

Sue Watt (*www.suewatt.co.uk*) and her partner **Will Whitford** first travelled to Zambia in 2004 as part of an eight-month tour of Africa. They've returned many times since, drawn by its wide open spaces and sense of wilderness. Sue is now an experienced travel writer specialising in Africa and regularly published in UK national press and magazines including *The Telegraph, The Independent* and *Travel Africa*. Will's photography accompanies her features. For this edition, they travelled to Liuwa Plains National Park and Bangweulu Wetlands.

Eleanor Walkingshaw's love of travel started with three months' marine research off Tanzania's Pemba Island and a further six months travelling in southern Africa. During her summers, whilst reading history at Newcastle University, she made time for trips to Asia and Central America, but the African bug had bitten. So, after another year exploring east Africa, she joined Expert Africa where she now specialises in Zambia, Tanzania, Rwanda and Mozambique.

LIST OF MAPS

Contents

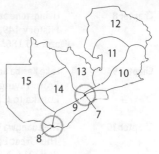

Acknowledgements

The sixth edition of this book has been built on the first five – and, like those, has been a team effort. For this edition (and in many cases for help with several earlier editions, too), we would particularly like to thank the Wilderness team in Kafue and Livingstone; the team at KaingU; Phil and Tyrone at Musekese in the Kafue; Jess Salmon at Flatdogs; John and Carol Coppinger and Remote Africa's team; Derek, Jules and Izzy from Shenton Safaris; Andy and the team from Bushcamps; all at RPS; Chris Liebenberg and the Chongwe team; Grant, Lindsay and the team from Chiawa; Jason and everyone at Sausage Tree; all at Anabezi; Sabine, Debbie and Ben at Baines' River Camp; Kim at Jollyboys in Livingstone; and Chris Meyer at Kasanka.

Several people dropped everything to check various sections of the text, or kindly provided bits of the jigsaw. These include Grant Gatchell from Voyagers' in the Copperbelt (who generously kept us on the road, too); Mike and Lari Merrett; Charlie and Jo Harvey; Craig Zytkow at Ndole Bay Lodge; and Claire Powell at Thorn Tree Safaris. Thanks, too, to Heather Chalcraft, for kindly allowing us access to reprint articles from *The Lowdown*.

Many others went out of their way to help with the research for earlier books, including Judi Helmholz and Arthur Sonnenberg in Livingstone; Christina (Gid), Abraham and the NCS crew; Jo and Robin Pope at RPS; Babette and Phil Berry at Kuyenda; Bryan Jackson for great walking, and pulling my Land Rover through a few rivers; Lynn, Pete and Paul Fisher; Charlie Rae; Pete Leonard, who kindly shared information from his encyclopaedic Zambian bird atlas; and Philip Briggs, for the kind use of his writings as the basis for the wildlife appendix.

Zambia's top birding expert, the late Bob Stjernstedt, kindly reviewed the birding comments, making a number of very helpful additions and contributions. Anna Weyher of the Kasanka Baboon Project made similarly valuable comments on the baboon text. Ilse Mwanza's help over the years has been invaluable. And I still owe huge thanks to John Coppinger, not only for unstinting hospitality, but also for his time and many emails in the past about the Luangwa's history, wildlife and environment.

Many readers of earlier editions have helped with their news and views, and countless Expert Africa travellers have generously provided valuable feedback on their trips. These have given me hundreds of extra pairs of eyes and ears in Zambia every year – constantly updating me on the latest news and views of the various camps, lodges and offbeat corners. We couldn't list everyone here if we tried; most will, I hope, forgive me for not mentioning them.

Colleagues at Expert Africa know the country so well themselves that without their help with news and research, and support from them and the whole team there, I'd be unable to continue writing these guides.

Bradt's whole team have, as ever, been superb – including Claire Strange and David McCutcheon. I am particularly grateful to Rachel Fielding for the hours that she spent meticulously checking facts for some of the least-visited areas of Zambia which, for this edition, we were unable to visit. That which is good and correct owes much to their care and attention; errors and omissions are my own.

Finally my love and thanks to Susie, for company on the road, generous help in writing, map-making and proofing, and for continuous good humour over many years and many books.

AUTHOR'S STORY

In 1995 I crossed the Zambezi with trepidation. I left behind me prosperous Zimbabwe, which I knew well; I'd lived in the rural areas there for nearly three years. Ahead was the unknown: Zambia. I had been able to find little about the country's attractions, and I expected problems, but backpacking around I found kindness and friendliness in a great country. I marvelled at the Victoria Falls; ventured into the national parks; canoed on the Zambezi; and dined under the stars. The result was the first travel guide to Zambia. Since then, I have returned often, initially with my backpack, but latterly driving a 4x4 and occasionally taking to the air. With Zambia's more inaccessible places within reach, I explored further, discovering hidden waterfalls, private reserves, the colonial extravagance of Shiwa Ng'andu, and the superb birding of Liuwa Plain.

Over the years, I have grown to love the country and have been lucky enough to share it with the visitors that I send there. In updating this guide for the sixth edition, my hope is that you, too, will find it by turns spectacular, challenging and intriguing.

KEY TO SYMBOLS

― · ― · ―	International boundary	⌂	Hotel/inn, etc
═══	Tarred road (regional)	▲	Campsite
═ ═ ═	4x4 track	☆	Nightclub/casino
··········	Footpath	✕	Restaurant
━ ─ ━	Railway	♀	Bar
▭	Railway station	⌸	Café
✈ ✈	Airport (international/domestic)	⊖	Internet café
✝	Airstrip (light aircraft)	†	Church/cathedral
⛽	Filling station/garage	☾	Mosque
🚌	Bus station, etc	▶	Golf course
✕―✕	Park gate	⤲	Bird sanctuary
⊣―⊢	Border post	∭	Waterfall
ⓘ ⓘ	Tourist information office/kiosk	⊕	GPS location
Ⓔ	Embassy	⌇	Radio mast
⛰	Museum/art gallery	⚘	Stadium
☻	Theatre/cinema	▲	Summit (height in metres)
⚲	Statue/monument		Marsh
$	Bank/bureau de change		National park/protected area
⊠	Post office		Urban park
⊞	Hospital/clinic, etc		Market
✚	Pharmacy/dentist		Shopping centre/mall

Introduction

Zambia may be becoming increasingly well known, yet the country still retains its essence: that authentic feeling of a wilderness which is wild, beautiful and slightly unpredictable. It is to these remote, scarcely touched areas that, along with the glories of the Victoria Falls, most visitors are drawn – and that is why we have adjusted the focus of this sixth edition. While we have retained coverage of the country's least-visited areas, such as the far north, and the industrial heartland of the Copperbelt, we have cut these sections back in favour of Zambia's overarching attractions.

For those in the know, Zambia remains *the* place for walking safaris. In its three main safari areas – the Luangwa Valley, the Lower Zambezi and northern Kafue – you'll find top, owner-run camps, superb game and some of the continent's best guides. In all of these you'll see few other visitors; most Zambian camps are still tiny and remote. You'll travel around using small, open-sided 4x4s seeing few, if any, other vehicles. Throughout Africa there are khaki-uniformed chauffeurs who drive through the bush, but here you still find expert guides to trust with your life.

In 1999, I introduced the second edition of this guide with the comment that Zambia was a country for the cognoscenti, and especially those who knew about walking safaris – it wasn't a place for everyone. Ten years later, I was forced to reassess. A lot has changed in the intervening years and the options for visitors have broadened. Zambia now offers more than simply superb bushcamps: there is increasing variety – from cultural offerings to family-friendly safaris and luxury lodges. Transport is becoming much easier: internal flights make more areas accessible, whilst old Africa hands are starting to make mini-expeditions here in self-contained 4x4s. National parks that had been written off are coming back to life, as pioneers open up original camps in more offbeat areas. Levels of both quality and choice have generally increased.

Meanwhile, new places to stay and new areas to visit are starting up outside the old, established circuits. Gradually, the rest of this huge country (twice the size of Zimbabwe) is opening up, and its less famous attractions are coming to light. Many of these lesser-known areas are gems. Consider Kafue National Park: this is a wilderness area the size of Wales, yet it receives only a scattering of visitors. The far south of this park is ideal not only for adventurers equipped to camp, but also for visitors to a handful of rustic safari camps. It is less than a day's drive from the busy hub of Livingstone, yet most of its bush tracks were, until the last few years, becoming overgrown.

In the centre of Zambia lies the huge Lake Bangweulu, surrounded by the swamp that defeated Livingstone – his heart is buried nearby. This land of islands and waterways is a permanent wetland, home to the rare shoebill stork and an endemic species of antelope, the black lechwe. It's now easy to fly here, and the proximity of other destinations makes it more attractive: Kasanka National Park and Mutinondo Wilderness are both close by. So, also, is Shiwa Ng'andu, which remains one of the subcontinent's most extraordinary memorials to British colonial rule. Here an English aristocrat carved out a utopian estate from the untamed bush, whilst helping Zambia to achieve its own independence. Although Africa gradually defeated his dream, Shiwa, like Zambia, has been re-invented – and now tells a new story of how sheer determination can re-shape a place in the wilderness into a world-class attraction for a handful of fortunate visitors.

Far to the west, Liuwa Plain National Park is the venue for one of Africa's last great wildlife migrations: blue wildebeest in their thousands, plus zebra, tsessebe and buffalo, all converging on a vast open plain for the rains. Liuwa is one of the most amazing reserves that I've ever visited in Africa, yet it receives only a few hundred visitors per year. Getting there once required an expedition, but following considerable but sensitive investment, this is changing.

HOW TO USE THIS GUIDE

AUTHOR'S FAVOURITES
Finding genuinely characterful accommodation or that unmissable off-the-beaten-track café can be difficult, so the author has chosen a few of his favourite places throughout the country to point you in the right direction. These 'author's favourites' are marked with a ✳.

MAPS
Keys and symbols Maps include alphabetical keys covering the locations of those places to stay, eat or drink that are featured in the book. Note that regional maps may not show all hotels and restaurants in the area: other establishments may be located in towns shown on the map.

Grids and grid references Several maps use gridlines to allow easy location of sites. Map grid references are listed in square brackets after the name of the place or sight of interest in the text, with page number followed by grid number, eg: [124 C3].

Landmarks On occasion, hotels or restaurants that are not listed in the guide (but which might serve as alternative options if required or serve as useful landmarks to aid navigation) are also included on the maps; these are marked with accommodation 🏠 or restaurant ✕ symbols.

WEBSITES Although all third party websites were working at the time of going to print, some may cease to function during this edition's lifetime. If a website doesn't work, you might want to check back at another time as they often function intermittently. Alternatively, you can let us know of any website issues by emailing info@bradtguides.com.

EXCHANGE RATES Where sterling and US dollar equivalents are given in this guide, I have assumed a notional rate of around £1 for K11.50, or US$1 for K7.50, corresponding to rates that prevailed at the time of research. Despite fluctuations in the value of the kwacha, US dollar prices remain relatively constant, making them a more stable gauge for visitors than the local currency.

Surrounding Liuwa, in the remote west of the country, is the ancient Lozi kingdom of Barotseland, where the landscape has changed little since Livingstone's day. The rich cultural heritage of a monarch and his people survived colonialism almost unscathed. Their seasonal rhythm is still followed, as the whole kingdom moves by boat from the rich floodplains to higher ground in February or March, making one great, grand traditional flotilla. Now the maps and GPS locations in this guide will enable you to navigate around these areas, and explore a very lovely and remote region that's been largely unvisited by travellers.

Zambia is an amazing country if you can get to its heart. Its government encourages tourism, and foreign exchange is desperately needed to alleviate the poverty of many of its people. But for such logic, this guide might have remained unwritten. Many would prefer Zambia to stay as it is – a favourite place to visit, with superb wildlife, fascinating culture, few other visitors, and Zambians who still treat travellers with kindness and hospitality.

So now, having committed more of Zambia's secrets to paper, I again ask those who use this guide to do so with respect. Zambia's wild areas need great care to preserve them. Local cultures are easily eroded by a visitor's lack of sensitivity, and hospitality once abused is seldom offered again. Enjoy – but be a thoughtful visitor, for the country's sake.

USEFUL INFORMATION

NOTE ON DATUM FOR GPS CO-ORDINATES For all the GPS co-ordinates in this book, note that the datum used is WGS 84 – and you must set your receiver accordingly before copying in any of these co-ordinates.

All GPS co-ordinates in this book have been expressed as degrees, minutes, and decimal fractions of a minute. For further details see page 60.

NOTE ON ACCOMMODATION LISTINGS here a small group of lodges or hotels come under the same umbrella organisation within a similar area, these have been grouped together. For ease of recognition, the typography used for the 'parent' lodge is as for other lodges, but subsidiaries within the group are noted in small capital letters, with a grey symbol. For example:

⌂ **Kafunta**
⌂ ISLAND BUSHCAMP

FEEDBACK REQUEST AND UPDATES WEBSITE

At Bradt Travel Guides we're aware that guidebooks start to go out of date on the day they're published – and that you, our readers, are out there in the field doing research of your own. You'll find out before us when a fine new family-run hotel opens or a favourite restaurant changes hands and goes downhill. So why not write and tell us about your experiences? Contact us on ☏ 01753 893444 or e info@bradtguides.com. We will forward emails to the author who may post updates on the Bradt website at www.bradtupdates.com/zambia. Alternatively you can add a review of the book to www.bradtguides.com or chrismcintyre@expertafrica.com.

ACCOMMODATION AND RESTAURANT PRICE CODES

Rates at places to stay in this guide have been coded. For urban establishments, and others offering B&B accommodation, rates are based on the cost of a double room with breakfast. Single supplements average around 20%, but may be significantly higher. VAT may be charged extra.

B&B double

$$$$$	£165+; US$250+; K1,875+
$$$$	£100–165; US$150–250; K1,125–1,875
$$$	£50–100; US$80–150; K600–1,125
$$	£25–50; US$40–80; K300–600
$	up to £25; up to US$40; up to K300

For **all-inclusive** places, such as safari lodges and camps, rates are based on a double room including full board and activities (FBA).

LLLLL	US$2,000+; £1,330+
LLLL	US$1,300–2,000; £865–1,330
LLL	US$600–1,300; £400–865
LL	US$250–600; £165–400
L	up to US$250; up £165

Restaurant price codes are based on the average cost of a main course, which usually exclude VAT (currently 16%) and service of around 10%. For specialities such as seafood, you can expect to pay considerably more.

$$$$$	£9+; US$13+; K100+
$$$$	£7–9; US$10.50–13; K80–100
$$$	£5.50–7; US$8–10.50; K60–80
$$	£3.50–5.50; US$5–8; K40–60
$	up to £3.50; up to US$5; up to K40

ZAMBIA ONLINE

For additional online content, articles, photos and more on Zambia, why not visit www.bradtguides.com/zambia.

Part One

GENERAL INFORMATION

Location Landlocked in the tropics at the northern edge of the region referred to as 'southern Africa'

Size 752,610km^2

Climate December–April hot and wet, with torrential downpours in the afternoon; May–August dry, and fairly cool; September–November dry, but progressively hotter.

Status Republic

Population 13,046,508 (2010 census), 15.02 million (2015 estimate, World Bank)

Population growth per year 3% (2014 estimate, World Bank)

Life expectancy at birth 58 years (2013, World Bank)

Capital Lusaka (provincial population 2,191,225, 2010; city population 1.8 million)

Other main towns Livingstone, Kitwe, Ndola, Kabwe

Economy Minerals (principally copper and cobalt), agriculture, hydro-electricity, tourism

Natural resources Copper, cobalt, gemstones

GDP US$27.97 billion (2014, World Bank)

GDP growth rate 6% (2014, World Bank)

Currency Kwacha (K)

Rate of exchange £1 = K13.17, US$1 = K9.22, €1 = K10.44, ZAR1 = K0.64 (February 2016)

Language English, numerous ethnic languages

Religion Christianity, Islam, indigenous beliefs

International telephone code +260

Time GMT +2

Electricity 220v, delivered at 50Hz; British-style plugs with three square pins

Weights and measures Metric

Flag Bright green background; panel lower right of three vertical bands of red, black and orange, surmounted by an orange eagle in flight.

Motto 'One Zambia, One Nation'

Public holidays 1 January, Youth Day (March), Good Friday, Holy Saturday, 1 May, 25 May, Heroes' Day (July), Unity Day (July), Farmers' Day (August), Independence Day (end October), 25–6 December. See pages 42–3.

Tourist board www.zambiatourism.com

1

History, Politics and Economy

HISTORY

ZAMBIA'S EARLIEST INHABITANTS Palaeontologists looking for evidence of the first ancestors of the human race have excavated a number of sites in Zambia. The earliest remains yet identified are stone tools dated to about two million years ago recovered from gravel deposits in the Luangwa Valley and probably also from Victoria Falls. It is thought that these probably belong to the *Homo erectus* species, whose hand-axes in Ethiopia have been dated to 1.75 million years. These were hunter-gatherer people, who could use fire, make tools, and had probably developed some simple speech.

Experts divide the Stone Age into the middle, early and late Stone Ages. The transition from early to middle Stone-Age technology – which is indicated by a larger range of stone tools often adapted for particular uses, and signs that these people had a greater mastery of their environment – was probably in progress around 300,000 years ago in Zambia, based on recent excavations near Lusaka and at Kalambo Falls near Mbala.

The famous 'Broken Hill Man' lived around this time. His skull and other bones and stone artefacts were unearthed from about 20m underground during mining operations near Kabwe in 1921. He has been described as being from a species called *Homo rhodesiensis*, but is more generally attributed to *Homo heidelbergensis*, the common ancestor of *Homo sapiens* in Africa, and of the Neanderthals in Europe. (His name comes from the fact that Kabwe's old name was Broken Hill.)

The late Stone Age in Zambia is normally characterised by a distinctive tradition of geometric rock art; by the use of composite tools, those made of wood and/or bone and/or stone used together; and by the presence of a revolutionary invention: the bow and arrow. This first appeared in Zambia about 25,000 years ago. Skeletons found around the Kafue Flats area indicate that some of these late Stone-Age hunters had a close physical resemblance to the modern San/Bushmen people, whose culture, relying on a late Stone-Age level of technology, survived intact in the Kalahari Desert until the middle of the 20th century.

THE IRON AGE Around 3000BC, late Stone-Age hunter-gatherer groups in Ethiopia, and elsewhere in north and west Africa, started to keep domestic animals, sow seeds and harvest the produce: they were among the world's first farmers.

By around 1000BC these new pastoral practices had spread south into the equatorial forests of what is now the Democratic Republic of Congo (DRC), to around Lake Victoria, and into the northern area of the Great Rift Valley, in northern Tanzania. However, agriculture did not spread south into the rest of central/southern Africa immediately. Only when the technology, and the tools, of iron-working became known did the practices start their relentless expansion southwards.

The spread of agriculture and Iron-Age culture seems to have been rapid. It was brought south by Africans who were taller and heavier than the existing small inhabitants. The ancestors of the San/Bushmen people, with their simple Stone-Age technology and hunter-gatherer existence, just could not compete with these Iron-Age farmers, who became the ancestors of virtually all the modern black Africans in southern Africa.

This major migration occurred around the first few centuries AD, and since then the San/Bushmen of southern Africa have gradually been either assimilated into the migrant groups, or effectively pushed into areas which could not be farmed. Thus the older Stone-Age cultures persisted in the forests of the north and east of Zambia – which were more difficult to cultivate – much longer than they survived in the south of the country.

MORE IMMIGRANTS By the 4th or 5th century AD, Iron-Age farmers had settled throughout much of southern Africa. As well as iron-working technology, they brought with them pottery, the remains of which are used by archaeologists to work out the migrations of various different groups of these Bantu settlers. These migrations continued, and the distribution of pottery styles suggests that the groups moved around within the subcontinent: this was much more complex than a simple north–south influx.

THE ORIGINS OF TRADE In burial sites dating from the latter half of the first millennium, occasional 'foreign' objects start to occur: the odd cowrie shell, or copper bangles in an area where there is no copper. This indicates that some small-scale bartering with neighbouring villages was beginning to take place.

In the first half of the second millennium, the pace and extent of this trade increased significantly. Gold objects appear (as well as the more common copper, iron and ivory) and shells from the Indian Ocean. The frequency of these indicates that trade was gradually developing. We know from European historical sources that Muslim traders (of Arab or possibly African origin) were venturing into the heart of Africa by around AD1400, and thus trade routes were being established.

As trade started, so the second millennium also saw the development of wealth and social structures within the tribes. The evidence for this is a number of burial sites that stand out for the quantity and quality of the goods that were buried with the dead person. One famous site, at Ngombe Ilede, near the confluence of the Lusitu and Zambezi rivers, was occupied regularly over many centuries. There is evidence that its inhabitants traded from the 14th century with people further south, in Zimbabwe, exporting gold down the Zambezi via traders coming from the Indian Ocean. Indications of cotton-weaving have also been found there, and several copper crosses unearthed are so similar that they may have been used as a simple form of currency – valuable to both the local people and traders from outside.

By the middle of the second millennium, a number of separate cultures seem to have formed in Zambia. Many practised trade, and a few clearly excelled at it. Most were starting to develop social structures within the group, with some enjoying more status and wealth than others.

THE CHIEFS From around the middle of the second millennium, there is little good archaeological evidence that can be accurately dated. However, sources for the events of this period in Zambia's history are the oral histories of Zambia's people, as well as their current languages and social traditions. The similarities and differences between the modern Zambian languages can be extrapolated by linguistic experts to point to the existence of about nine different root languages, which probably existed in Zambia in the 15th century.

The latter half of the second millennium AD saw the first chiefs, and hence kingdoms, emerge from Zambia's dispersed clans. The title 'chief' can be applied to anyone from a village headman to a god-like king. However, this was an era of increasing trade, when the groups with the largest resources and armies dominated local disputes. Thus it made sense for various clans to group together into tribes, under the rule of a single individual, or chief.

One of the oldest groups is thought to have been that of the Chewa people, led by the Undi, who came to the Luangwa area from the southern side of Lake Malawi in the 16th century. By the end of that century the Ng'andu clan (clan of the crocodile) established a kingdom amongst the Bemba people. These lived mostly in woodland areas, practising simple slash-and-burn types of agriculture. Perhaps because of the poverty of their lifestyle, they later earned a reputation as warriors for their raids on neighbouring tribes.

In the latter part of the 17th century the first recorded Lozi king (or Litunga, as he is known) is thought to have settled near Kalabo, in the west of Zambia, starting a powerful dynasty which lasts to the present day. Early in the 18th century Mwata Kazemba established a kingdom around the southern end of Lake Mweru in the Luapula Valley.

THE GROWTH OF TRADE As various cohesive kingdoms developed, their courts served as centres of trade, and their chiefs had the resources to initiate trade with other communities. Foodstuffs, iron, copper, salt, cotton, cloth, tobacco, baskets, pottery and many other items were traded within Zambia, between the various tribes.

From around the 14th century, Zambia had a trickle of trade with non-Africans: mostly Muslims exporting gold through the east coast of Africa. (This trade had started as early as the 10th century on the Limpopo River, south of Zimbabwe's gold-fields.) However, by the early 17th century the Muslims had been supplanted by the Portuguese, and by the latter half of the 17th century these Portuguese merchants were operating out of Mozambique, trading gold, ivory and copper with Zambia.

Trade with the outside world escalated during the 18th century, as more and more tribes became involved, and more foreigners came to the table. Some chiefs started to barter their commodities for weapons, in attempts to gain advantage over their neighbours. Those vanquished in local conflicts were certainly used as sources of slaves – an increasingly valuable trading commodity. These and other factors increased the pressure on Zambians to trade, and the influx of foreign traders made the picture more complex still.

By the early 19th century, both traders and slavers were visiting Zambia with increasing frequency. These were responding to the increasing consumer demands of newly industrialised Europe and America. More trade routes were opening up, not just through Mozambique and Angola, but also to the north and south. Internal conflicts were increasing, as both the means to conduct these, and the incentives for victory, grew.

WESTERN REQUIREMENTS During the 19th century, the West (western Europe and North America) had traded with the native Africans to obtain what they wanted – commodities and slave labour – without having to go to the trouble of ruling parts of the continent. However, as the century progressed, and the West became more industrialised, it needed these things in greater quantities than the existing tribal structures in Africa could supply. Further, there was demand for materials that could be produced in Africa, like cotton and rubber, but which required Western production methods.

Given that the West wanted a wider range and greater quantity of cheaper raw materials, the obvious solution was to control the means of supply. African political organisation was widely regarded as primitive, and not capable of providing complex and sustained trade. Inward investment would also be needed, but would be forthcoming only if white enterprises were safe from African interference. Hence the solution to Western requirements was to bring Africa, and the Africans, under European rule.

Another reason for considering the acquisition of African territory was that the world was shrinking. There were no inhabitable continents left to discover. Staking a nation's claim to large chunks of Africa seemed prudent to most of the Western powers of the time, and growing competition for these areas meant they could always be traded for one another at a later date.

LIVINGSTONE'S CONTRIBUTION David Livingstone's *Missionary Travels and Researches in South Africa* excited great interest in England. This account of his journeys across southern Africa in the 1840s and '50s had all the appeal that undersea or space exploration has for us now. Further, it captured the imagination of the British public, allowing them to take pride in their country's exploration of Africa, based on the exploits of an explorer who seemed to be the epitome of bravery and righteous religious zeal.

Livingstone had set out with the conviction that if Africans could see their material and physical well-being improved – probably by learning European ways, and earning a living from export crops – then they would be ripe for conversion to Christianity. He was strongly opposed to slavery, but sure that this would disappear when Africans became more self-sufficient through trade.

In fact Livingstone was almost totally unsuccessful in his own aims, failing to set up any successful trading missions, or even to convert many Africans permanently to Christianity. However, his travels opened up areas north of the Limpopo for later British missionaries, and by 1887 British mission stations were established in Zambia and southern Malawi.

THE SCRAMBLE FOR AFRICA British foreign policy in southern Africa had always revolved around the Cape Colony, which was seen as vital to British interests in India and the Indian Ocean. Africa to the north of the Cape Colony had largely been ignored. The Boers were on the whole left to their farming in the Transvaal area, and posed no threat to the colony.

However, Germany annexed South West Africa (now Namibia) in 1884, prompting British fears that they might try to link up with the Boers. Thus, to drive a wedge through the middle of these territories, the British negotiated an alliance with Khama, a powerful Tswana king, and proclaimed as theirs the Protectorate of Bechuanaland – the forerunner of modern Botswana.

Soon after, in 1886, the Boers discovered large gold deposits in the Witwatersrand (around Johannesburg). The influx of money from this boosted the Boer farmers, who expanded their interests to the north, making a treaty with Khama's enemy, the powerful Lobengula. This in turn prompted the British to look beyond the Limpopo, and to back the territorial aspirations of a millionaire British businessman, Cecil Rhodes. By 1888 Rhodes, a partner in the De Beers consortium, had control of the lucrative diamond-mining industry in Kimberley, South Africa. He was hungry for power, and dreamt of linking the Cape to Cairo with land under British control.

His wealth enabled Rhodes to buy sole rights to mine minerals in Lobengula's territory. Thence he persuaded the British government to grant his company – the British South Africa Company – the licence to stake claims to African territory with the authority of the British government. In 1889 Rhodes sent out several expeditions to the chiefs in the area now comprising Zimbabwe, Zambia and Malawi, to make treaties. These granted British 'protection and aid' in return for sole rights to minerals in the chiefs' territories, and assurances that they would not make treaties with any other foreign powers. This effective strategy was greatly helped by the existing British influence from the missions, which were already established in many of the regions. By 1891 the British had secured these areas (through Rhodes's British South Africa Company) from the other European powers, and confirmed their boundaries in treaties with the neighbouring colonial powers.

By the closing years of the 19th century, Zambia – or Northern Rhodesia as it was called – was clearly under British rule. However, this had little impact until local administrations were set up, and taxes started to be collected.

THE MINES In the early years of the 20th century, Rhodes's British South Africa Company did little in Northern Rhodesia. Its minerals were not nearly as accessible or valuable as those in Southern Rhodesia, and little protection or aid actually materialised. It became viewed by the colonials as a source of cheap labour for the mines of South Africa and Southern Rhodesia.

To facilitate this, taxes were introduced for the local people, which effectively forced them to come into the cash economy. Virtually the only way for them to do this was to find work in one of the mines further south. By 1910 a railway linked the mine at Kimberley, in South Africa, with Victoria Falls and beyond, making long-distance travel in the subcontinent more practical.

Meanwhile the cost of administering and defending the company's interests was rising, and in 1923 Southern Rhodesia became self-governing. In 1924 the British Colonial Office took over administration of Northern Rhodesia from the British South Africa Company, though the mining rights remained with the Company. The Colonial Office then set up a legislative council to advise on the government of the province, though only a few of its members came from outside the administration.

Shortly afterwards, in 1928, huge deposits of copper were located below the basin of the upper Kafue, under what is now known as the Copperbelt. Over the next decade or so these were developed into a number of large copper mines, working rich, deep deposits of copper. World War II demanded increased production of base metals, and by 1945 Northern Rhodesia was producing 12% of the non-communist world's copper. This scale of production required large labour forces. The skilled workers were mostly of European origin, often from South Africa's mines, whilst the unskilled workers came from all over Northern Rhodesia.

Wages and conditions were very poor for the unskilled miners, who were treated as migrant workers and expected to go home to their permanent villages every year or so to 'recover'. Death rates among them were high. Further, the drain of men to work the mines inevitably destabilised the villages, and poverty and malnutrition were common in the rural areas.

WELFARE ASSOCIATIONS As early as 1929 welfare associations had formed in several of the territory's southern towns, aimed at giving black Africans a voice and trying to defend their interests. These associations were often started by teachers or clerks, the more educated members of the communities. They were small at first, far too small to mount any effective challenge to the establishment, but they did succeed in raising awareness amongst the Africans, all of whom were being exploited.

In 1935 the African mineworkers first organised themselves to strike over their pay and conditions. By 1942 the towns of the African labourers in the Copperbelt were forming their own welfare associations, and by 1949 some of these had joined together as the Northern Rhodesian African Mineworkers' Union. This had been officially recognised by the colonial government as being the equal of any union for white workers. In 1952 the union showed its muscle with a successful and peaceful three-week strike, resulting in substantial wage increases.

The unions remain a force in Zambia, especially in the state sector. In February 2004, a coalition of unions organised the country's first national strike in 16 years, protesting against tax hikes and wage freezes which were being imposed on government employees.

CENTRAL AFRICAN FEDERATION The tiny European population in Northern Rhodesia was, on the whole, worried by the growth of the power of black African mineworkers. Most of the white people wanted to break free from colonial rule, so that they could control the pace and direction of political change. They also resented the loss of vast revenues from the mines, which went directly to the British government and the British South Africa Company, without much benefit for Northern Rhodesia.

During the 1930s and 1940s the settlers' representation on Northern Rhodesia's Legislative Council was gradually increased, and calls for self-rule became more insistent. As early as 1936 Stewart Gore-Browne (founder of Shiwa Ng'andu; see pages 312–20) had proposed a scheme for a Central African Federation, with an eye to Britain's future (or lack of one) in Africa. This view gained ground in London, where the government was increasingly anxious to distance itself from African problems.

In 1948 the South African Nationalist Party came to power in South Africa, on a tide of Afrikaner support. The historical enmity between the Afrikaners and the British in South Africa led the British colonials in Southern and Northern Rhodesia to look to themselves for their own future, rather than their neighbours in South Africa. In 1953 their pressure was rewarded and Southern and Northern Rhodesia were formally joined with Nyasaland (which is now Malawi), to become the independent Central African Federation.

The formation of the Federation did little to help the whites in Northern Rhodesia, though it was strongly opposed by the blacks, who feared that they would then lose more of their land to white settlers. Earlier, in 1948, the Federation of African Societies – an umbrella group of welfare associations – changed its name at an annual general meeting into an overtly political Northern Rhodesian Congress. This had branches in the mining towns and the rural areas, and provided a base upon which a black political culture could be based. A few years later, it was renamed as the Northern Rhodesia African National Congress.

INDEPENDENCE Despite the Federation, Northern Rhodesia actually remained under the control of the Colonial Office. Further, the administration of the Federation was so biased towards Southern Rhodesia that the revenues from its mines simply flowed there, instead of to Britain. Thus though the Federation promised much, it delivered few of the settlers' wishes in Northern Rhodesia.

A small core of increasingly skilled African mineworkers gained better pay and conditions, whilst poverty was rife in the rest of the country. By the 1950s small improvements were being made in the provision of education for black Zambians, but widespread neglect had demonstrated to most that whites did not want blacks as their political or social equals. Thus black politics began to focus on another goal: independence.

In 1958 elections were held, and about 25,000 blacks were allowed to vote. The Northern Rhodesia African National Congress was divided about whether to participate or not, and eventually this issue split the party. Kenneth Kaunda, the radical secretary general, and others founded the Zambia African National Congress (ZANC). This was soon banned, and Kaunda was jailed during a state of emergency.

Finally, in 1960, Kaunda was released from jail, and greeted as a national hero. He took control of a splinter party, the United National Independence Party (UNIP), and after a short campaign of civil disobedience forced the Colonial Office to hold universal elections. In October of 1962, these confirmed a large majority for UNIP. In 1963 the Federation broke up, and in 1964 elections based on universal adult suffrage gave UNIP a commanding majority. On 24 October 1964 Zambia became independent, with Kenneth Kaunda as its president.

ZAMBIA UNDER KAUNDA President Kenneth Kaunda (usually known as just 'KK') took over a country whose income was controlled by the state of the world copper market, and whose trade routes were entirely dependent upon Southern Rhodesia, South Africa and Mozambique. He also inherited a 50 million kwacha national debt from the colonial era, and a populace which was largely unskilled and uneducated. (At independence, there were fewer than one hundred Zambians with university degrees, and fewer than a thousand who had completed secondary school.)

In 1965, shortly after Zambia's independence, Southern Rhodesia made a Unilateral Declaration of Independence (UDI). This propelled Zambia's southern neighbour further along the path of white rule that South Africa had adopted. Sanctions were then applied to Rhodesia by the rest of the world. Given that most of Zambia's trade passed through Rhodesia, these had very negative effects on the country's economy.

As the black people of Rhodesia, South Africa and South West Africa (Namibia) started their liberation struggles, Kaunda naturally wanted to support them. Zambia became a haven for political refugees, and a base for black independence movements. However ideologically sound this approach was, it was costly and did not endear Zambia to its economically dominant white-ruled neighbours. As the apartheid government in South Africa began a policy of destabilising the black-ruled countries around the subcontinent, so civil wars and unrest became the norm in Mozambique and Angola, squeezing Zambia's trade routes further.

The late 1960s and early 1970s saw Zambia try to drastically reduce its trade with the south. Simultaneously it worked to increase its links with Tanzania – which was largely beyond the reach of South Africa's efforts to destabilise. With the help of China, Tanzania and Zambia built excellent road and rail links from the heart of Zambia to Dar es Salaam, on the Indian Ocean. However, as a trading partner Tanzania was no match for the efficiency of South Africa, and Zambia's economy remained sluggish.

During these difficult years Zambia's debt grew steadily. The government's large revenues from copper were used in efforts to reduce the country's dependence on its southern neighbours, and to improve standards of living for the majority of Zambians. Education was expanded on a large scale, government departments were enlarged to provide employment, and food subsidies maintained the peace of the large urban population. Kaunda followed Julius Nyerere's example in Tanzania in many ways, with a number of socialist policies woven into his own (much promoted) philosophy of 'humanism'.

In retrospect, perhaps Kaunda's biggest mistake was that he failed to use the large revenues from copper either to reduce the national debt, or to diversify Zambia's export base – but his choices were not easy.

By 1969, the Zambian government was receiving about three-quarters of the profits made by the mining industries in taxes and duties. Because of this, they were reluctant to invest further. With the stated aim of encouraging expansion in the industry and investment in new mines, the government started to reform the ownership of the copper mines. A referendum was held on the subject and the government took control of mining rights throughout the country. It then bought a 51% share in each of the mines, which was paid for out of the government's own dividends in the companies over the coming years. Thus began ZCCM (Zambia Consolidated Copper Mines).

In the early 1970s, the world copper price fell dramatically. Simultaneously the cost of imports (especially oil) rose, the world economy slumped and the interest rates on Zambia's debt increased. These factors highlighted the fundamental weaknesses of Zambia's economy, which had been established to suit the colonial powers rather than the country's citizens.

The drop in the price of copper crippled Zambia's economy. Efforts to stabilise the world copper price – through a cartel of copper-producing countries, similar to the oil-producing OPEC countries – failed. The government borrowed more money, betting on a recovery in copper prices that never materialised.

In the 1970s and 1980s Kaunda's government became increasingly intertwined with the International Monetary Fund (IMF) in the search for a solution to the country's debt. None was found. Short-term fixes just made things worse, and the country's finances deteriorated. The West did give Zambia aid, but mostly for specific projects that usually had strings attached. What Zambia most needed was help with the enormous interest payments that it was required to make to the West.

Various recovery plans, often instituted by the IMF, were tried. In 1986 food subsidies were sharply withdrawn, starting with breakfast meal, one of the country's staple foods. This hit the poor hardest, and major riots broke out before subsidies were hastily re-introduced to restore calm. In 1988 Zambia applied to the United Nations for the status of 'least-developed nation' in the hope of obtaining greater international assistance. It was rejected. By the end of the decade Zambia's economy was in tatters. The official exchange rate bore little relation to the currency's actual worth, and inflation was rampant. Zambia was one of the world's poorest countries, with a chronic debt problem, a weak currency and at times very high inflation. A reputation for corruption, reaching to the highest levels of the government, did little to encourage help from richer nations.

Despite Kaunda's many failures with the economy, his policies did encourage the development of some home-grown industries to produce goods which could replace previously imported items. It also created systems for mass education, which were almost entirely absent when he came to power.

EARLY 20TH CENTURY These economic problems, and the lack of obvious material benefits for the majority of Zambians, gradually fomented opposition. UNIP's tendency to become authoritarian in its demands for unity also led to unrest. Kaunda's rule was finally challenged successfully by the capitalist Movement for Multiparty Democracy (MMD) led by Frederick Chiluba. This received widespread support during the late 1980s, on a platform of liberalisation and anti-corruption measures.

Kaunda agreed to an election, apparently certain that he would win. In the event, UNIP was resoundingly defeated by the MMD (16% to 84%), and Chiluba became Zambia's second elected president, in November 1991. Kaunda accepted the results, at least at face value. However, he later claimed that the elections were unfair because many of Zambia's older people, whom he regarded as his natural constituency, didn't vote. He continued to head UNIP until 2000, and he still lives in Zambia – which, in itself, is a rare and encouraging co-existence in the volatile world of modern African politics.

When elected, Frederick Chiluba faced enormous economic problems, which he attempted to tackle. He succeeded in liberalising and privatising much of the economy, resulting in a freely floating market for the kwacha, and policies to attract inward investment. However, in 1995 the country's debt stood at US$6.25 billion, and debt service payments were some 40% of the gross national product – equivalent to about US$600/£400 per capita per annum. Zambia owed US$3.1 billion to the World Bank and the IMF alone.

Initially Chiluba gained the confidence of Western donors when he came to power in 1991. However, his reforms were long term, and much of their success depended on the continued willingness of international donors to help him. Many allege that corruption grew during his time in power.

Certainly the general attitude of Zambians towards visitors changed under Chiluba: Zambia became a more welcoming country than it was under Kaunda's reign. Tourism began to be recognised as a direct and helpful source of jobs and foreign currency, and the climate of suspicion prevailing in Kaunda's Zambia was replaced with a warmer welcome.

LATE 20TH CENTURY Presidential elections were held in 1996. However, using his enormous majority, Chiluba changed the constitution to include a clause that 'no person born of non-Zambian parents can be president'. Kenneth Kaunda, as is well known, was born of Malawian parents, and so this was a clear move to exclude him from running for the office. It was not the only such move, and caused endless furore.

As head of UNIP, KK called for all UNIP candidates to boycott the elections, believing that they could not be fair. In the event, several UNIP candidates split off and stood as independent candidates, but the overall result was another resounding win for Chiluba. (MMD won about 132 of 150 seats.) It's widely thought that he would have won anyhow, even in a fair election, so it seems a pity that he resorted to dubious tactics to achieve the victory.

With poetic justice, it later transpired that Chiluba himself was of illegitimate birth and uncertain national origin. *The Post* newspaper claimed to have researched and verified that his own parents were of DRC/Zairean descent, which led to a long-running persecution of the paper by the government for 'being disrespectful' and 'insulting' the president – both of which are punishable offences in Zambia. (Travellers take note!)

THE COUP At the end of October 1997, a small group of soldiers briefly took over the state-run radio station. They were led by Stephen Lungu, the self-styled 'Captain Solo', who claimed to represent the 'National Redemption Council'. (Neither he nor the council had been heard of before.) He announced that the group had launched 'Operation Born-again' and ousted the MMD government and Chiluba, saying later in a short broadcast that he had seen 'an angel and the message was that the Government had to be overthrown'.

Although this group transpired to have been little more than a few drunken soldiers, Chiluba used the incident as an excuse to institute a state of emergency for five months. He detained more than 70 civilians and soldiers, including opposition leaders and the former president, KK. Some detainees claimed that torture was used during interrogations, allegations which were later substantiated by the government's own human rights commission headed by Supreme Court judge, Lombe Chibesakunda. The clampdown by the state attracted heavy criticism from human rights groups and affected the international donor community's willingness to release funds for debt relief.

A year later the case against many was dropped for lack of evidence, and some sued the state for wrongful arrest. Nevertheless, 44 were convicted and sentenced to death, although within months their sentences were commuted by the president to between ten and 20 years of hard labour.

THE END OF CHILUBA'S REGIME Many regarded President Chiluba's presidency as a disappointment, yet looking at conditions in neighbouring Zaire and Zimbabwe, most agreed that the situation in Zambia could have been much worse. Chiluba avoided any military involvement in the conflict in neighbouring Democratic Republic of Congo (DRC) – which had already sucked in Zimbabwe, Angola, Namibia, Chad, Uganda and Rwanda – and instead played a high-profile role in brokering various peace talks.

However, he continued KK's habit of regularly reshuffling ministers (thus ensuring that none developed their own power base), was slow to take decisions and proved unable to control corruption. Despite vowing that he would stand by the constitution, he tried his best to arrange a third term for himself. It was only tremendous pressure from the people, and from within the MMD, that forced him to step down in 2001.

THE 21ST CENTURY In 2001 the MMD's candidate and Chiluba's chosen successor, Levy Patrick Mwanawasa, was narrowly declared the victor with just 29% of the vote, but the elections were criticised by international observers, and three of the opposition parties challenged the results in the High Court.

A lawyer by profession, Mwanawasa was almost universally respected for his integrity. With his mandate of 'Continuity with Change', he launched an anti-corruption campaign which resulted in the prosecution of Chiluba, and many of the ex-president's supporters. Yet despite the allegations of misappropriating some US$500,000 of government funds, Chiluba was finally cleared of all charges in 2009. He died on 18 June 2011.

Mwanawasa himself was re-elected in 2006 with a rather more convincing 43% of the vote, but he died from a stroke in 2008. His vice-president, Rupiah Banda, took over the reins – albeit with a similarly shaky mandate – but it was not to last. In September 2011, following a fiercely contested and at times violent election, the MMD met defeat at the hands of the Patriotic Front (PF), led by the charismatic Michael Sata. The 74-year-old Sata, nicknamed King Cobra, had significant experience, having served with both UNIP and the MMD before setting up the PF in 2001. Indeed, he was only narrowly defeated in the 2008 presidential by-election. The failure of the MMD to hold on to power was in part due to Sata himself, a more colourful character than his presidential adversary, but other factors included a public reaction against the state-controlled section of the media, and increasing concern at the perceived lack of benefit to Zambia from the privatised mining industry.

Once again, however, fate intervened. The new president was already rumoured to be suffering from ill health when he was sworn in, and following medical treatment in several countries, he died in the UK on 28 October 2014. His deputy, Guy Scott, stepped into the breach as interim president, but the 70-year-old white Zambian was ineligible to run for president. Following a by-election on 20 January

2015, Sata's Patriotic Front colleague, Edgar Chagwa Lungu, was voted into office, winning by the narrowest of margins: just 1.66%.

Described on his website as 'officer, gentleman, lawyer and politician', Lungu held ministerial roles in the areas of home affairs and defence during the Sata administration. He was also secretary-general of the PF, a position from which he was notably ousted by Scott, albeit for just one day. Although the early days of Lungu's presidency were also marked by ill health, he is, at 58, considerably younger than his predecessor. His promise of lower interest rates and promotion of human rights suggests a liberal approach, as does his appointment of a female vice-president, but his is no long-term tenure: under Zambia's constitution, the presidency is contested every five years, with the next election scheduled for 11 August 2016.

STORM CLOUDS OVER THE 2016 ELECTIONS Whether or not Lungu remains in power after the elections, there's a lot at stake, particularly in the context of Zambia's recent political past. For the past couple of decades, Zambia has been a real democracy. The party in government has been changed peacefully twice, via a ballot box. That's very impressive: it's as many times as this has happened in the rest of post-independence southern Africa put together.

However, the commodity-fuelled economic boom of the past decade has encouraged complacency from successive governments, coupled with a degree of economic mismanagement and corruption. During this time, Zambia's debt has grown from its (post-write-off) US$500 million in 2005 to nearly US$5 billion by 2016. Now, as the boom is over and the country faces major economic challenges, the ruling Patriotic Front (PF) party faces a tough election contest against the opposition United Party for National Development (UPND).

Worrying evidence is coming to light that PF hardliners, desperate to hold onto power, are planning a very undemocratic strategy – including curbs on the press, violence and intimidation. Their admiration for Robert Mugabe's one-party state is no secret, and Zambia's Chinese sponsors certainly value 'stability' above 'democracy'. How prevalent these factions are will heavily influence the outcome of this election, and the kind of governance that Zambia has into the future.

GOVERNMENT AND ADMINISTRATION

The chief of state and the head of government is the president, who appoints cabinet ministers from members of the National Assembly, a chamber of 150 elected representatives, plus a further eight nominated by the president. Elections are held every five years, with all Zambian citizens of 18 years and over eligible to vote in a first-past-the-post system.

The country is divided into ten provinces for administrative purposes: Central, Copperbelt, Eastern, Luapula, Lusaka, Muchinga, Northern, North-Western, Southern and Western.

The judicial system was set up according to a British model, based on English common law and customary law. Legislative acts receive judicial review in an ad hoc constitutional council.

ECONOMY

Zambia's economy is totally dependent upon its mining sector, and particularly its copper mines, although agriculture, industry and tourism all make their contribution, and the government is committed to diversification. The country's high, well-watered plateau means that it has about 40% of southern Africa's water resources. Hydro-electric schemes, which provide most of the country's power, make it self-sufficient in energy, and Zambia already exports power to neighbouring countries.

Despite recent improvements in the economy and the write-off of most external debt, Zambia remains among the world's poorest countries. While its mineral wealth has brought considerable economic dividends over the years, heavy reliance on that sector also serves to make the country very vulnerable to fluctuations in world markets. In the last few years, world growth, and thus demand for raw materials such as copper and cobalt, has been largely triggered by China. Now, the slowdown in Chinese growth is in turn having serious consequences for Zambia.

RECENT ECONOMIC HISTORY Zambia's recent economic history has been a bumpy ride. In the mid 1990s, prospects looked good. GDP growth was about 6.5%; inflation was down to 24% (from 187% in 1993); a decline in manufacturing had been reversed; non-traditional exports were expanding at a rate of 33% a year; and the privatisation programme was being hailed as one of Africa's most successful. Even the kwacha had been stabilised and a surge in foreign investment was being reported.

By 1998, however, the reversal of Zambia's economic fortunes was stark. GDP growth was minimal, manufacturing output was again in a downturn, and inflation was slowly rising. While the breakdown in the privatisation of Zambia Consolidated Copper Mines (ZCCM) was a major cause of this reversal (pages 16–17), part of the problem stemmed from the coup attempt in late 1997. On both counts, Western donors withheld aid to Zambia.

A year later, when the signs improved, aid and debt relief were again forthcoming, and there was optimism that Zambia's economy could continue to improve. Privatisation of the government-owned copper mines relieved the government from covering mammoth losses generated by the industry and greatly improved the chances for copper mining to return to profitability and spur economic growth.

THE BURDEN OF DEBT For years, Zambia was visibly crippled by its burden of debt. At around US$500 per person, the country had one of the highest levels of per-capita debt in the world, but a GNI (gross national income) of only around US$340 per capita. About two-thirds of all Zambians lived on less than US$1 per day, a figure that remains largely unchanged.

For most of the 1990s, Zambia followed a programme of economic reforms largely dictated by the IMF and World Bank. This scheme, known as the Enhanced Structural Adjustment Facility (ESAF), allowed the world's poorest nations to pay lower interest rates on the money that they owed. In 1995, with assistance from ESAF, Zambia embarked on a series of far-reaching reforms. These centred on trade liberalisation, deregulation and exchange-rate reform. Pivotal to the whole programme was a greater role for the private sector, and the sale of state-owned enterprises, thus encouraging direct foreign investment. The Zambia Privatisation Agency (ZPA), now the Zambia Development Agency, was set up to oversee privatisation.

Having largely followed the dictates of the IMF and World Bank, Zambia found itself in the 'good books' of its donors. However the social consequences were onerous: rising unemployment, increased prices for basic necessities (including the staple mealie-meal) and cuts in healthcare and education. All of these tended to foster an increase in social unrest.

By the late 1990s, Zambia's annual debt repayments were equivalent to about a third of the value of its exports of goods and services. To put this in perspective,

Zambia was spending five times more on its interest repayments than it did on education, and three times as much as on healthcare. The consequences were clear: literacy declined and the percentage of infant deaths doubled from 1992 to 1999. Despite this, Zambia managed to remain current on its debt-service payments and even to clear some of its arrears – although such commitments were clearly a major constraint on economic development. Zambia relied on foreign donors for 35% of its budget, but for every dollar Zambia received in aid, it repaid US$3 to service its debt.

Debt write-offs and HIPC status In 1999, the Finnish government announced that it was writing off US$7.5 million of Zambia's debt, and the IMF gave Zambia a much-needed boost with US$14 million of its new US$349-million ESAF loan. Also, the World Bank promised US$65 million, despite continuing problems in selling the mines. These were crucial signals to other donors, and on 16 April of the same year the Paris Club agreed to write off US$670 million of Zambian debt, and restructure the repayments of about US$330 million of the rest. Another major step towards helping the country was to confer on Zambia the status of highly indebted poor country (HIPC), which would open the door to the World Bank and other donors relieving more of the debt.

Optimists hoped that these payments would mark the start of concerted efforts by the international community to alleviate Zambia's crippling debt, and that moves to liberalise Zambia's economy would bear fruit. However this optimism was tempered with more realism. Though Zambia had taken most of the economic medicine prescribed for it, trade liberalisation was tough on the country in the short term. A report by the World Development Movement, *Zambia: Condemned to Debt* (page 527), accused the IMF-backed reforms of being undemocratic and unfair and of undermining development – as well as of being counter-productive and unsuccessful. In 2003 the donors' 'Balance of Payment support' was frozen, on account of the country's weak fiscal management and inability to institute a new Poverty Reduction and Growth Facility strategy (PRGF) proposed by the IMF. Successful implementation of this PRGF strategy was one of the crucial milestone indicators needed by the IMF and World Bank before Zambia could reach the 'completion point' under the HIPC initiative that would trigger debt relief. Meanwhile, Zambia's debt repayments continued to cripple the economy.

In 2005, it was agreed at the G8 summit to write off US$40 billion of debt owed by 18 of the worlds HIPCs, of which Zambia was one. Following a write-off of US$7 billion, the country was left with a residual external debt of US$500 million. The Zambian government pledged to invest the proceeds in health and education, and in 2006 restored free health care to those living in rural areas. Borrowing continues, however, and by 2015, the country's external debt stood at US$4.8 billion, or about 18.5% of GDP.

THE ECONOMY TODAY In 2014, GDP rose by around 6%, with inflation remaining in single figures at 7.8%. In the same year, exports – largely to Switzerland, China, the DRC and South Africa – fell by almost 10% over 2013, to US$9,688 million, but imports also fell slightly, to US$9,539 million.

Although the kwacha has stabilised in recent years, its rates against the US dollar and UK pound have varied greatly over the last decade or so, providing an interesting context to the present economic climate (see box, page 16). With inflation under control, the Zambian government rebased the kwacha in 2013 with a view to restoring 'the intrinsic value of the currency as a medium of exchange by bringing normalcy to the numeration of the local currency'. However, the

EXCHANGE RATES 1995–2015

Date	To US$	To British £	To SA rand	To euro
1995: July	925	1,480	255	–
1996: July	1,270	1,970	289	–
1997: July	1,310	2,180	287	–
1998: July	1,945	3,200	310	–
1999: July	2,500	4,000	415	2,630
2000: July	3,083	4,656	448	2,710
2001: July	3,585	5,208	453	2,480
2002: July	4,720	7,340	470	4,690
2003: July	4,930	8,020	655	5,600
2004: July	4,775	8,800	785	5,870
2007: July	3,978	8,081	560	5,453
2011: July	4,880	7,725	707	6,788
2015: July*	7.50	11.50	0.59	8.26
2016: Apr*	9.22	13.17	0.64	10.44

Kwacha 'rebased' 2013, since when Kw1,000 old = K1 new.

downturn in the price of raw materials, together with has had a dramatic impact on the kwacha, causing it to fall from K7.50 to K12.59 against the US dollar between June and November 2015.

Zambia's mining industry

Mining as a whole accounts for around 80% of Zambia's export earnings and about 12% of its GDP. Investment in recent years from countries as diverse as Brazil, South Africa and – most importantly – China has resulted from a combination of high copper prices and changes in regulations that have attracted considerable overseas interest in the sector. However, the slowdown in China's growth, which has been instrumental in the declining value of copper since 2011, has combined with a recent increase in governmental taxation to put heavy pressure on the industry.

Copper is easily the country's most important natural resource, with cobalt second; it also has small but significant reserves of gold and other minerals and gemstones.

Copper Zambia has large, high-quality deposits of copper ore, and is the world's eighth-largest producer of copper. In 2013, production totalled 790,007 tonnes, a marginal increase on the previous year, and 12.3% up on 2012 figures. While the opening of several new mines in the last few years has contributed to a boom in Zambia's industrial heartland, the Copperbelt region, the impact of the more recent fall in prices has in turn created big problems both for business and the workforce.

Before 2000, all the mines were controlled by the parastatal Zambia Consolidated Copper Mines (ZCCM), which had long been viewed as the jewel of Zambia's economic crown. Of these, Nchanga and Nkana mines alone accounted for 65% of Zambia's total copper production. However, disuse and mismanagement caused Zambia's mines to degenerate, and by the late 1990s they were recording losses of around US$15–20 million per month. In 2000 they were eventually privatised, and bought by a consortium led by Anglo American – which, ironically, owned the mines before they were nationalised. Today, the country's mining base has expanded beyond the Copperbelt into the Northwestern Province, with a third large mine in that area, Kalumbila, coming onstream in 2015 to join the Kansanshi and Lumwana mines. A subsidiary of ZCCM retains a holding share of between ten and 20% in most large mines.

Cobalt Zambia is the world's second-largest producer of cobalt, responsible for around 20% of the world's total output of this valuable, strategic metal. Cobalt is usually produced as a by-product of copper or nickel mines. Indeed, in one Zambian deal, a private mining company that was granted rights to extract cobalt and copper from Nkana's slag heap estimated that this still contained about 56,000 tonnes of cobalt and 86,000 tonnes of copper.

Coal Zambia's main coal mine is the former state-owned open-pit mine at Maamba, near Lake Kariba. Since 2009, when a controlling share in the mine was bought by a Singapore-based company, production has risen to hit almost 150,000 tonnes in 2013. Total combined reserves of low- and high-grade coal are estimated at more than 170 million tonnes.

Other mineral resources Zambia has natural resources of amethyst, fluorite, feldspar, gypsum, aquamarine, lead, zinc, tin and gold – as well as a variety of gemstones. All are on a small scale, and few are being commercially exploited. An exception is emeralds, which are said to be among the highest quality in the world. These are being mined to the order of about US$200 million per year, with the Kagem Emerald Mine in the Copperbelt responsible for about half the country's gems, or 20% of global production: 30 million carats in 2013. Despite that, about half the country's emeralds are thought to be smuggled out of the country, so the real amounts remain uncertain.

Other industrial sectors
Zambia's manufacturing industry is focused primarily on construction, chemicals, textiles and fertiliser production, with steel and cement coming to the fore in recent years. In 2013, the sector accounted for about 10% of national GDP, but the domestic market is small, and high costs mean that it isn't very competitive regionally.

Agriculture
Agriculture represents less than 20% of Zambia's GDP, but employs perhaps 60% of its workforce. Although most farming is still done by small-scale subsistence farmers, large commercial farms are becoming more important, often financed by private investors. The country's varied topography encourages a wide diversity in the crops cultivated. The main commercial crops are maize (the staple food for most people), sugar, tobacco, cotton and coffee, with sorghum, rice, peanuts, soya beans, sunflowers and cassava also grown, and cattle, goats, beef, poultry and eggs produced. The amount of land given over to maize has been increased following good harvests over the last decade, giving an added boost to the economy, but production declined in 2013.

Tourism
Zambia has the (arguable) benefit of a late-developing tourism industry, which should allow it to learn from the mistakes of others. Hopes for the development of tourism lie firmly with the private sector, and the government is happy for private investors to buy into the industry. Since the mid 1990s tourism has been expanding very steadily – which is by far the best way for a tourism industry to move if it is to stay on a sustainable basis – and increasingly there is a focus on the development that tourism can bring to local communities.

Until around 2000, Zambia's annual visitor influx could still probably have been counted in the low thousands. Then came political turmoil in Zimbabwe, which resulted in the rapid demise of that country's tourism industry. Livingstone, meanwhile, experienced significant developments in its tourist infrastructure (albeit not without considerable pressure for unsustainable development from some sectors). As a result, the town for many years took on the mantle of regional tourism capital, formerly held by its neighbour, the Zimbabwean town of Victoria Falls. Although the situation is now more balanced, Livingstone remains a big focus for Falls tourism, and makes a significant contribution to Zambia's tourist industry.

While tourism remains one of Zambia's least-developed sectors, generating in total an estimated 5.2% of GDP in 2013, it continues to grow. In the same year, the industry supported 23,300 jobs, a figure that is anticipated to rise to 38,000 within the next ten years. It is estimated that in 2014, the country welcomed 941,000 tourists, an increase of around 17% since the last peak in 2007.

The praises of Zambia's national parks are sung elsewhere in this book, but here it's worth noting that the country's best camps command prices (and standards) to match their equivalents in Tanzania, Zimbabwe or Botswana. What's more, Zambia still has vast tracts of pristine wilderness, which is exactly what is needed for new safari destinations. Most importantly, visitors to Africa realise that top wildlife guides, like those found in Zambia, are few and far between.

2

People and Culture

POPULATION OVERVIEW

Zambia's 2010 census puts the country's population at just over 13 million, a figure that was estimated to have risen to 15 million by 2014. Almost two-thirds of the people live below the poverty line, with nearly half surviving on less than US$1.25 a day. The vast majority of people are of black African (Bantu) descent, though there are significant communities whose ancestors came from Europe and India. Zambia is a large country, and its population density – around 20 people per square kilometre – is relatively low: just over half that of Zimbabwe, or about a quarter of the population density of Kenya.

Zambia's urban population is about 40% of the total, with the capital, Lusaka, home to some 17% of the whole, and a further 15% or so residing in the Copperbelt Province. Conversely, rural areas generally have a low population density, and the country retains large tracts of wilderness.

Statistics indicate that almost half the population is under 14 years of age, and the population growth rate is about 3% per annum. Infant mortality continues a slow decline, to 8.7% in 2013, while the average life expectancy for a Zambian at birth has risen to 58 years. This marks a significant increase over recent years, and at least in part reflects the decline in incidence of HIV/AIDS: it is estimated that the number of people between the ages of 15 and 49 who are affected by AIDS has stabilised at 13% since 2007.

However, the statistics say nothing of the warmth that the sensitive visitor can encounter. If you venture into the rural areas, take a local bus, or try to hitchhike with the locals; you will often find that Zambians are curious about you. Chat to them openly, as fellow travellers, and you will find most Zambians to be delightful. They will be pleased to assist you where they can, and as keen to help you learn about them and their country as they are interested in your lifestyle and what brings you to Zambia.

ETHNIC GROUPS

AFRICAN LANGUAGE GROUPS English is the official language in Zambia, and most urban Zambians speak it fluently. In rural areas it is used less, though only in truly remote settlements will you encounter problems communicating in English.

The main vernacular languages are Bemba, Kaonde, Lozi, Lunda, Luvale, Nyanja and Tonga – though more than 72 different languages and dialects are spoken in the country. Of these, the most widely recognised and understood are Nyanja and Bemba. For basic words and phrases, see pages 524–6.

Below are detailed some of the major language groups, arranged alphabetically. This is only a rough guide to the languages and dialects of Zambia's people.

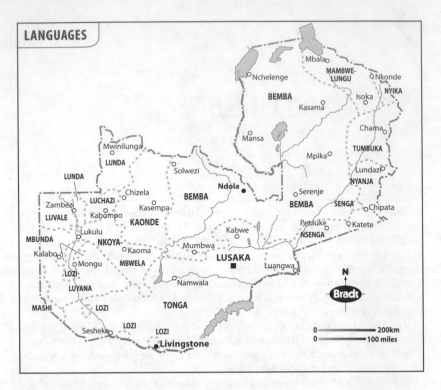

LANGUAGES

Mbala

Nchelenge   MAMBWE-   Nkonde
             LUNGU
                              NYIKA
BEMBA   Isoka
         Kasama

                        Chama

Mwinilunga   TUMBUKA
                  Mpika
LUNDA

LUNDA   Solwezi   Lundazi
                              NYANJA
         Chizela   Ndola
LUCHAZI   BEMBA   Serenje
Zambezi   Kasempa   BEMBA   SENGA   Chipata
LUVALE   Kabompo
         KAONDE   Petauke   Katete
Lukulu   Kabwe   NSENGA
MBUNDA   NKOYA
         Kaoma   Mumbwa
Kalabo   LUSAKA
    Mongu   MBWELA   Luangwa   N
    LOZI
LUYANA   Namwala

MASHI   LOZI   TONGA

         LOZI
Seseke   LOZI
         Livingstone

Although these different language groupings do loosely correspond to what many describe as Zambia's tribes, the distinctions are blurred further by the natural linguistic ability of most Zambians. Whilst it is normal to speak English plus one local language, many Zambians will speak a number of local languages fluently.

When the colonial powers carved up Africa, the divisions between the countries bore only a passing resemblance to the traditional areas of these various ethnic groups. Thus many of the groups here are split between several countries. Note that the estimates of populations quoted below are based on surveys done during the 1980s, and average estimated population growth rates since then.

Bemba Bemba is the first language of about two and a quarter million Zambians: almost a quarter of the country's population. It is spoken in the rural areas of northern Zambia, from the Luapula River eastwards to Mpika, Kasama and beyond. Because people from these areas were the original workers in the mines of the Copperbelt, Bemba has subsequently achieved the status of *lingua franca* in the major urban areas of the Copperbelt and Lusaka.

It is recognised for administration and education purposes within Zambia, whilst outside its borders Bemba is also spoken by over 150,000 people in the Democratic Republic of Congo, and around 37,000 in Tanzania.

Kaonde Kaonde-speakers live mostly around the northern side of Kafue National Park, centring on the area around Kasempa, and extending southeast as far as Mumbwa. They are one of Zambia's larger language groups, and probably number about 200,000.

A NOTE ON 'TRIBES'

The people of Africa are often viewed, from abroad, as belonging to a multitude of culturally and linguistically distinct tribes – which are often portrayed as being at odds with each other. Whilst there is certainly an enormous variety of different ethnic groups in Africa, most are closely related to their neighbours in terms of language, beliefs and way of life. Modern historians eschew the simplistic tag of 'tribes', noting that such groupings change with time.

Sometimes the word 'tribe' is used to describe a group of people who all speak the same language; it may be used to mean those who follow a particular leader or to refer to all the inhabitants of a certain area at a given time. In any case, 'tribe' is a vague word which is used differently for different purposes. The term 'clan' (blood relations) is a smaller, more precisely defined, unit – though rather too precise for our broad discussions here.

Certainly, at any given time, groups of people or clans who share similar language and cultural beliefs do band together and often, in time, develop 'tribal' identities. However, it is wrong to then extrapolate and assume that their ancestors will have had the same groupings and allegiances centuries ago.

In Africa, as elsewhere in the world, history is recorded by the winners. Here the winners, the ruling class, may be the descendants of a small group of intruders who achieved dominance over a larger, long-established community. Over the years, the history of that ruling class usually becomes regarded as the history of the whole community, or tribe. Two 'tribes' have thus become one, with one history – which will reflect the origins of that small group of intruders, and not the ancestors of the majority of the current tribe.

Zambia is typical of a large African country. Currently historians and linguistics experts can identify at least 16 major cultural groupings, and more than 72 different languages and dialects are spoken in the country. As you will see, there are cultural differences between the people in different parts of the country. However, these are no more pronounced than those between the states of the USA, or the different regions of the (relatively tiny) UK.

There continues to be lots of inter-marriage and mixing of these peoples and cultures – perhaps more so than in the past, due to the efficiency of modern transport systems. Generally, there is very little friction between these communities (whose boundaries, as we have said, are indistinct) and Zambia's various peoples live peacefully together.

Lozi There are about 500,000 Lozi-speakers in Zambia, concentrated in the Western and Southern provinces, around Barotseland and Livingstone. The centre of Lozi culture is the rich agricultural floodplain around the Upper Zambezi River – and it is here that the Kuomboka (see *Festivals*, pages 24–6) takes place each year.

Luchazi This language has only a small number of speakers, perhaps 70,000 in the west of Zambia – less than 1% of the country's population. There are thought to be a similar number of Luchazi-speaking people in Angola.

Lunda Not to be confused with Luunda, which is a dialect of Bemba, Lunda is the first language of about 230,000 Zambians and is spoken in areas of the Copperbelt, as well as nearby DRC and Angola. It is officially taught in primary schools, and can occasionally be heard on the radio or seen in newspapers in the area.

Luvale Luvale is an important language in Angola, where it is spoken by almost one million people. In Zambia there are only about 215,000 people whose first language is Luvale, and they live in the North-Western and Western provinces.

Luyana The Luyana-speaking people are a small group, perhaps numbering 130,000 in total. Their language has not been well documented, though it is spoken in Zambia, Angola, Namibia and also Botswana. In Zambia it is found almost exclusively in the Western Province.

Mambwe-Lungu These are other languages that need further study – so far they appear to differ from each other only slightly, as dialects would. In total about 280,000 Zambians count them as their first language – about 3% of the population. Their stronghold is in the northeast of the Northern Province, south of Lake Tanganyika. As you might expect, they are also spoken in Tanzania.

Mashi Mashi seems to be spoken by only a tiny number of Zambians, perhaps only 25,000 people, who are often nomadic within a southwestern area of the Western Province. Little has been documented about this language – though it has been noted that virtually all the native speakers of Mashi follow traditional religious practices, rather than the more recently introduced Christian beliefs.

Mbunda The first language of about 130,000 Zambians, Mbunda is spoken in the north of Barotseland and the northern side of western Zambia – as well as in Angola.

Nkoya-Mbwela Nkoya and Mbwela are two closely related languages. Mbwela is often referred to as a dialect of Nkoya, though here we have grouped them together as equals. They also have only a tiny number of speakers – around 80,000 people – who are found around the Mankoya area, in Zambia's Western and Southern provinces.

Nsenga There are thought to be over 330,000 people speaking Nsenga as their first language, of whom the vast majority live in Zambia. These are clustered around the area of Petauke – near to the borders with Zimbabwe and Mozambique, across which the language is also spoken.

Nyanja Nyanja is the Bantu language most often encountered by visitors in Zambia. It is widely used in much of the country, including the key cities of Lusaka and Livingstone. Nyanja is sometimes described as not being a language *per se*, but rather a common skill enabling people of varying tribes living in eastern, central and southern parts of Zambia and Malawi to communicate without following the strict grammar of specific local languages. In other words, like Swahili and other 'universal' languages, Nyanja is something of a *lingua franca* for Zambia.

Nyanja is certainly the official language of the police, and is widely used for administrative and educational purposes. About a million Zambians use Nyanja as their first language – mostly in the eastern and central areas of the country – and there may be double that number using the language in Malawi. Then there are around 330,000 Nyanja-speakers in Zimbabwe, and perhaps 500,000 in Mozambique. A total of approaching four million people in the subcontinent speak Nyanja as a first language.

Nyika Also known as Nyiha, or more precisely as Chi-Nyika, Nyika is spoken most widely in Tanzania, and also in Malawi. In Zambia it is used around the Isoka and Chama areas, across to the Malawi border. (It is closely related to the language known as Ichi-Lambya in Tanzania and Malawi.)

Tonga Tonga is the language of a small minority of Zimbabweans, many of whom were displaced south by the creation of Lake Kariba (pages 214–15). However, in Zambia it is the first language of around one million people, about 11% of the country's population, and is widely used in the media. Tonga is distributed throughout the south of the country, with its highest concentration in the middle Zambezi Valley.

Tumbuka Zambia has about 430,000 people who speak Tumbuka as a first language, mostly living on the eastern side of the country. Outside Zambia many Tumbuka-speakers live in Malawi and Tanzania, bringing the total number to about two million.

OTHER ETHNIC GROUPS

White Zambians There are a small number of white Zambians, very different from the expat community (see below) who are often white but simply working in the country on a temporary basis. Many white Zambians will trace their families back to colonial immigrants who came over during British rule, but most will regard themselves as Zambian rather than, say, British. This is generally an affluent group of people, and many of the country's businesses and especially the safari companies, are owned and run by white Zambians.

Asian Zambians Like the white Zambians, many people of Asian origin came here during the colonial period. When the British ruled African colonies like Zambia as well as India, there was movement of labour from Asia to Africa. Now, like the white Zambians, this is generally an affluent group. On the whole, Zambians of Asian descent retain a very strong sense of Asian identity and culture, and many are traders or own small shops.

Expatriates Distinct from Zambians, there is a large expat community in Zambia. These foreigners usually come to Zambia for two or three years, to work on short-term contracts, often for either multi-national companies or aid agencies. Most are highly skilled individuals who come to share their knowledge with Zambian colleagues – often teaching skills that are in short supply in Zambia.

In the 1990s there was a migration of trained Zambian teachers and lecturers to neighbouring countries, where they are paid better, but this has now stabilised.

RELIGION

It has been estimated that there are some 200 different Christian churches in Zambia, of which the most active in the community is considered to be the Catholic Church. However, as in many other sub-Saharan African countries, many people will also subscribe to some traditional African religious practices and beliefs.

EDUCATION

While some 61% of adult Zambians are considered literate, the figure masks considerable variation in terms of age and sex. For men between the ages of 15 and 24, it rises to 70%, whereas for women in the same age group, it's closer to 59%.

In theory, primary education has been free to all children in Zambia since 2002, and statistics suggest that all children do indeed go to school. In practice, however, this is only half the story. Parents still need to find the means to pay for school uniform and books and pencils, or their children will be turned away, and the 'voluntary contribution' so beloved of state schools in the West becomes a crippling burden to impoverished Zambian families. An annual 'fee' equivalent to US$10.50/£7 for each primary-age child is not unusual, with penalties levied, for instance, if a parent fails to turn up at a school meeting. At secondary level, fees are around US$42/£28.

Typically, primary schools are run on a shift pattern, with children spending 3 hours in the classroom each day; the first are in school at 07.00, finishing at 10.00, when the next group starts. The secondary school day normally runs from 07.00 to 13.00. There are also 'basic' schools, which serve a wider age range than primary in areas where there is no secondary school. Class sizes are large, frequently exceeding the expected norm of 45 children, and lessons are often disrupted by strike action on the part of the teachers.

Zambia's first university, the University of Zambia, was established in Lusaka as recently as 1966, shortly after independence. It has since been joined by several more in both the public and private sectors.

FESTIVALS

Zambia has several major cultural festivals which, on the whole, are rarely seen by visitors. If you can get to any, then you will find them to be very genuine occasions, where ceremonies are performed for the benefit of the local people and the participants, and not for the odd tourist who is watching.

Cultural celebrations were strongly encouraged during Kenneth Kaunda's reign, as he favoured people being aware of their cultural origins. 'A country without culture is like a body without a head', was one of his phrases. Thus during the 1980s one group after another 'discovered' old traditional festivals. Most are now large local events, partly cultural but also part political rally, religious gathering and sports event.

Bear in mind that, like most celebrations worldwide, these are often accompanied by the large-scale consumption of alcohol. To see these festivals properly, and to appreciate them, you will need a good guide: someone who understands the rituals, can explain their significance, and can instruct you on how you should behave. After all, how would you feel about a passing Zambian traveller who arrives, with curiosity, at your sibling's wedding (a small festival), in the hope of being invited to the private reception?

Photographers will find superb opportunities at such colourful events, but should behave with sensitivity. *Before* you brandish your camera, remember to ask permission from anyone who might take offence.

FEBRUARY: THE NC'WALA On 24 February there is a festival at Mutenguleni village, near Chipata to celebrate the first fruit. This large celebration was recently revived, after 80 years of not being practised. It consists of two parts. First the chief tastes the first fruit of the land – usually sugarcane, maize and pumpkins. Then there is the ritual rebirth of the king (involving the king being locked up in his house) and the blessing of the fruit – which consists of a fairly gory spearing of a black bull whose blood the king has to drink. It's all accompanied by traditional dancing and beer-drinking.

EASTER: THE KUOMBOKA The most famous of Zambia's ceremonies takes place in the Western Province. It used to be around February or March, often on a Thursday, just before full moon. The precise date would be known only a week or so in advance, as it was decided upon by the Lozi king. Now that the ceremony attracts more visitors, it is usually held at Easter, though if water levels are not high enough, it will not take place at all.

The Lozi kingdom is closely associated with the fertile plains around the Upper Zambezi River. When dry, this well-defined area affords good grazing for livestock, and its rich alluvial soil is ideal for cultivation. It contrasts with the sparse surrounding woodland, growing on poor soil typical of the rest of western Zambia. So for much of the year, these plains support a dense population of subsistence farms.

However, towards the end of the rains, the Zambezi's water levels rise. The plains then become floodplains, and the settlements gradually become islands. The people must leave them for the higher ground, at the margins of the floodplain. This retreat from the advancing waters – known as the Kuomboka – is traditionally led by the king himself, the Litunga, from his dry-season abode at Lealui, in the middle of the plain. He retreats with his court to his high-water residence, at Limulunga, on the eastern margins of the floodplain.

The Litunga's departure is heralded by the beating of three huge old royal war drums – Mundili, Munanga and Kanaono. These continue to summon the people from miles around until the drums themselves are loaded aboard the royal barge, the *nalikwanda*, a very large wooden canoe built around the turn of the century and painted with vertical black-and-white stripes. The royal barge is then paddled and punted along by 96 polers, each sporting a skirt of animal skins and a white vest. Their scarlet hats are surmounted by tufts of fur taken from the mane of unfortunate lions.

The royal barge is guided by a couple of 'scout' barges, painted white, which search out the right channels for the royal barge. Behind it comes the Litunga's wife, the Moyo, in her own barge, followed by local dignitaries, various attendants, many of the Litunga's subjects, and the odd visitor lucky enough to be in the area at the right time. The journey takes most of the day, and the flotilla is accompanied by an impromptu orchestra of local musicians.

John Reader's excellent book, *Africa: A Biography of the Continent* (page 527), comments:

> When the Litunga boards the *nalikwanda* at Lealui he customarily wears a light European-style suit, a pearl-grey frock coat and a trilby hat; when he leaves the barge at Limulunga he is dressed in a splendid uniform of dark-blue serge ornately embroidered with gold braid, with matching cockade hat complete with a white plume of egret feathers.

In fact, Chapter 47 of this book contains the fascinating story of some of the first Europeans to see the original Kuomboka, and the sad narration of the gradual European subjugation of the Lozi kingdom. It also includes details of the Litunga's trip to London, in 1902, for the coronation of King Edward VII. It was here that the problem arose of what the Litunga should wear. Reader reports:

> By happy coincidence, the king [Edward VII] took a particular interest in uniforms; he was an expert on the subject and is even said to have made a hobby of designing uniforms. Doubtless the king had approved the design of the new uniforms with which Britain's ambassadors had recently been issued. Certainly he was aware that the introduction of these new outfits had created a redundant stock of the old style, which were richly adorned with gold braid. Lewanika [the Litunga] should be attired in one of those, the king ordained. And thus the Litunga acquired the uniform which has become part of the Kuomboka tradition. Not an admiral's uniform, as is often reported, but a surplus dress uniform of a Victorian ambassador; not a gift from Queen Victoria, but the suggestion of her son ...

When the royal barge finally arrives at Limulunga, the Litunga steps ashore in the ambassador's uniform to spend an evening of feasting and celebrations, with much eating, drinking, music and traditional dancing.

JULY: MUTOMBOKO (also Umutomboko) This is nothing to do with the Kuomboka, described above. It is an annual two-day celebration, performed during the last weekend of July, whereby the paramount chief celebrates the arrival of the Luunda people, the 'crossing of the river'. It is held in a specially prepared arena, close to the Ng'ona River, at Mwansabombwe.

On the first day the chief, covered in white powder, receives tributes of food and drink from his subjects – the cause for much feasting and celebration by all. On the second day an animal (often a goat) is slaughtered and the highlight is the chief's dance with his sword. See also box, page 374.

AUGUST: LIKUMBI LYA MIZE The Luvale people of western Zambia have an annual 'fair' type of celebration, which takes place for four or five days towards the end of August. 'Likumbi Lya Mize' means 'Mize day' and the event is held at the palace of the senior chief – at Mize, about 7km west of Zambezi. This provides an opportunity for the people to see their senior chief, watch the popular Makishi dancers, and generally have a good time. There is also lots of eating and drinking, plus people in traditional dress, displays of local crafts, and singing.

SEPTEMBER/OCTOBER: SHIMUNENGA This traditional gathering is held on the weekend of a full moon, in September or October, at Maala on the Kafue Flats – about 40km west of Namwala. Then the Ila people (whose language is closely related to Tonga) gather together, driving cattle across the Kafue River to higher ground. It used to be a lechwe hunt, but that is now forbidden.

OTHER FESTIVALS The above list of festivals is by no means exhaustive; others include:

February: Lwiinda A ceremony celebrated by Chief Mokuni, of the Toka Leya people near Livingstone, around February. The people honour their ancestors and offer sacrifices for rain.

May: Kufukwila A celebration led by the chief of the Kaonde people, held in the Solwezi area of northwestern Zambia.

July: Malaila A ceremony to honour past chiefs, held by the Kunda people. It is currently celebrated by Chieftainess Nsefu, near Mfuwe in the Luangwa Valley.

August: Kulamba Also a thanksgiving ceremony for the Chewa people. It's held in the Katete Province, in eastern Zambia, and here you'll be able to see lots of fascinating Nyao (secret society) dancers.

August: Lukuni Luzwa Buuka A celebration of past conquests by the Toka people in the Southern Province, usually held in August.

October: Tuwimba A thanksgiving festival for the Nsenga people.

3

The Natural Environment

PHYSICAL ENVIRONMENT

TOPOGRAPHY Zambia lies landlocked between the Tropic of Capricorn and the Equator, far from both the Atlantic and the Pacific oceans. It is at the northern edge of the region referred to as 'southern Africa', while sharing many similarities with its neighbours in east and central Africa. Shaped like a giant butterfly, it covers about 752,610km², slightly smaller than the UK and France combined, and slightly larger than California plus Nevada. In comparison with its neighbours, it is almost double the size of Zimbabwe, but only two-thirds that of South Africa.

Most of the country is part of the high, undulating plateau that forms the backbone of the African continent. Typically, it has an altitude of between 1,000m and 1,600m, deeply incised by the great valleys of the Zambezi, the Kafue, the Luangwa and the Luapula that lie below 500m.

There are several large lakes on Zambia's borders: Tanganyika and Mweru in the north, and the manmade Kariba in the south. Lake Bangweulu, and its swamps and floodplain, dominate a large area of the interior.

GEOLOGY Zambia's oldest rocks, known as the Basement Complex, were laid down at an early stage in the pre-Cambrian era – as long as 2,000 million years ago. These were extensively eroded and covered by sediments which now form the Katanga system of rocks, dating from around 1,000 to 620 million years ago. These are what we now see near the surface in most of northeast and central Zambia, and they contain the important mineral deposits of the Copperbelt. Later still, from about 300 to 150 million years ago, the karoo system of sedimentary rocks was deposited: sandstones, mudstones, conglomerates and even coal. Towards the end of this era, molten rock seeped up through cracks in the crust, and covered areas of western Zambia in layers of basalt – the rock that is seen cut away by the Zambezi River in the gorges below Victoria Falls.

About 150 million years ago, during the Jurassic era of the dinosaurs, Africa was still part of Gondwana – a super-continent which included South America, India, Australasia and Antarctica. Since then Zambia's highlands have been eroded down from an original altitude of over 1,800m (Nyika Plateau is still at this altitude) to their present lower levels.

Very recently, perhaps only a few million years ago, the subcontinent had a dry phase. Then the sands from the Kalahari Desert blew far across southern Africa, covering much of western Zambia with a layer of Kalahari sand – as becomes abundantly clear the moment you try to drive in the region.

CLIMATE Situated squarely in the tropics, Zambia gets a lot of strong sunlight, though the intense heat normally associated with the tropics is moderated in most

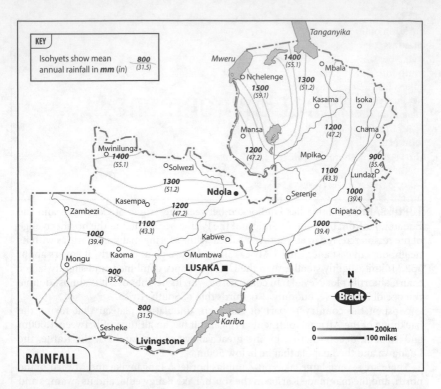

KEY

Isohyets show mean annual rainfall in **mm** (*in*) **800** (*31.5*)

RAINFALL

places by the country's altitude and its rainfall. The climate is generally moderate; only in the great valleys does it feel oppressive. It can be summarised broadly into three periods: from December to April it is hot and wet, with torrential downpours often in the late afternoon; from May to August it is dry, and becomes increasingly cool; and from September to November it remains dry, but gets progressively hotter.

This follows a similar pattern to that in most of southern Africa, with rainfall when the sun is near its zenith from November to April. The precise timing and

CLIMATE STATISTICS: LUSAKA

	Temp °C		Temp °F		Humidity %		Rainfall
	max	min	max	min	am	pm	mm
Jan	26	17	78	62	84	71	231
Feb	26	17	78	62	85	80	191
Mar	26	17	78	62	83	56	142
Apr	26	15	78	59	71	47	18
May	25	12	77	52	59	37	3
Jun	23	10	73	50	56	32	0
Jul	23	9	73	48	54	28	0
Aug	25	12	77	53	46	26	0
Sep	29	15	84	59	41	19	0
Oct	31	18	87	64	39	23	15
Nov	29	18	84	64	57	46	91
Dec	27	17	80	62	76	61	150

duration of this is determined by the interplay of three airstreams: the moist 'Congo' air-mass, the northeastern monsoon winds, and the southeastern trade winds. The water-bearing air is the Congo air-mass, which normally brings rain when it moves south into Zambia from central Africa. This means that the northern areas, around Lakes Tanganyika and Mweru, receive the first rainfall – often in late October or November. This belt of rain will then work south, arriving in southern Zambia by the end of November or the start of December.

As the sun's intensity reduces, the Congo air-mass moves back north, leaving southern Zambia dry by around late March, and the north by late April or May. Most areas receive their heaviest rainfall in January, though some of the most northerly have two peaks: one in December and one in March. This twin-peak cycle is more characteristic of central and eastern Africa. The heaviest total rainfall is found in the north, and the lightest in the south. It's worth adding a caveat here. Zambia, as elsewhere, is experiencing fluctuations in its traditional weather patterns, so while the traditional pattern remains a good guide, be prepared for variations from the norm.

Lusaka's climate statistics (see box, page 28) are typical of the pleasant climate found in the higher areas of southern and central Zambia. The lower-lying valleys, including the Luangwa and Lower Zambezi, follow the same broad pattern but are considerably hotter throughout the year. In October, which is universally the hottest month, temperatures there often reach over 45°C in the shade.

FLORA AND FAUNA

Zambia has many large national parks and game management areas (GMAs) where conservation and sustainable utilisation of the native wildlife are encouraged.

Miombo woodland – a mixture of grassland dotted with trees and shrubs – makes up about 70% of Zambia's natural environment, with *mopane* woodland dominating the lower-lying areas. The native fauna is classic big game found throughout east and southern Africa. Amongst the predators, leopard do exceptionally well here; lion are common but cheetah are not. Wild dog are uncommon, though seem to have increased in numbers in recent years, and there are many smaller predators. Zambia's antelope are especially interesting for the range of subspecies that have evolved. Giraffe, wildebeest, waterbuck and, especially, lechwe are notable for this – each having subspecies endemic to the country.

With rich vegetation and lots of water, Zambia has a great variety of both resident and migrant birds, over 750 species in total. Wetland and swamp areas attract some specialised waterfowl, and Zambia is on the edge of the range for both southern African and east African species.

FLORA As with animals, each species of plant has its favourite conditions. External factors determine where each species thrives, and where it will perish. These include temperature, light, water, soil type, nutrients, and what other species of plants and animals live in the same area. Species with similar needs are often found together, in communities which are characteristic of that particular environment. Zambia has a number of different such communities, or typical 'vegetation types', within its borders – each of which is distinct from the others. The more common include:

Woodlands Where they haven't been destroyed or degraded by people, woodlands cover the vast majority of Zambia, with miombo being especially common. Because the canopies of the trees in a woodland area don't interlock, you'll generally find them lighter and more open than the country's relatively few forested areas. The main types of woodland are:

Miombo woodland Without human intervention, the natural vegetation of most of Zambia (about 70%) is miombo woodland and its associated *dambos* (page 31). This exists on Zambia's main plateau and its adjacent escarpments, where the acid soils are not particularly fertile and have often been leached of minerals by the water run-off.

Miombo woodland consists of a mosaic of large wooded areas and smaller, more open spaces dotted with clumps of trees and shrubs. The woodland is broadleafed and deciduous (though just how deciduous depends on the available water), and the tree canopies generally don't interlock. The dominant trees are *Brachystegia*, *Julbernardia* and *Isoberlinia* species – most of which are at least partially fire-resistant. There is more variation of species in miombo than in mopane woodland, but despite this it is often known simply as 'brachystegia woodland'. The ground cover is also generally less sparse here than in mopane areas.

Mopane woodland The dominant tree here is the remarkably adaptable mopane (*Colophospermum mopane*), which is sometimes known as the butterfly tree because of the shape of its leaves. It is very tolerant of poorly drained or alkaline soils, and those with a high clay content. This tolerance results in the mopane having a wide range of distribution throughout southern Africa; in Zambia it occurs mainly in the hotter, drier, lower parts of the country, including the Luangwa and Zambezi valleys.

Mopane trees can attain a height of 25m, especially if growing on rich, alluvial soils. These are often called cathedral mopane, for their height and the graceful arch of their branches. However, shorter trees are more common in areas that are poor in nutrients, or have suffered extensive fire damage. Stunted mopane will form a low scrub, perhaps only 5m tall. All mopane trees are semi-deciduous. The leaves turn beautiful shades of yellow and red before falling between August and October, depending on their proximity to water (the closer the water, the later the leaves fall). Fresh new leaves start unfurling from late October.

Ground cover in mopane woodland is usually sparse, just thin grasses, herbs and the occasional bush. The trees themselves are an important source of food for game, as the leaves have a high nutritional value – rich in protein and phosphorus – which is favoured by browsers and is retained even after they have fallen from the trees. Mopane forests support large populations of rodents, including tree squirrels (*Peraxerus cepapi*), which are so typical of these areas that they are known as 'mopane squirrels'.

Munga woodland The word 'munga' means thorn, and this is the thorny woodland which occurs when open grassland has been invaded by trees and shrubs – normally because of some disturbance like cultivation, fire or overgrazing. *Acacia*, *Terminalia* (bearing single-winged seeds) and *Combretum* (bearing seeds with four or five wings) are the dominant species, but many others can be present. Munga occurs mainly in the southern parts of Zambia.

Forests In most equatorial areas further north in Africa, where rainfall is higher, forests are the norm. However, there are a few specific ecological niches in Zambia where you will find forests – distinguished from woodlands by their interlocking canopy. These are:

Teak forest In a few areas of western and southwestern Zambia (including the southern part of Kafue National Park), the Zambezi teak (*Baikaea plurijuga*), forms dry semi-evergreen forests on a base of Kalahari sand. This species is not fire-resistant, so these stands occur only where slash-and-burn cultivation methods have never been used. Below the tall teak is normally a dense, deciduous thicket of vegetation usually referred to as *mutemwa*, interspersed with sparse grasses and herbs in the shadier spots of the forest floor.

Moist evergreen forest In areas of higher rainfall (mostly in the north of Zambia), and near rivers, streams, lakes and swamps, where a tree's roots have permanent access to water, dense evergreen forests are found. Many species occur, and this lush vegetation is characterised by having three levels: a canopy of tall trees, a sub-level of smaller trees and bushes, and a variety of ground-level vegetation. In effect, the environment is so good for plants that they have adapted to exploit the light from every sunbeam.

This type of forest is prevalent in the far north of the country, especially in the Mwinilunga area. However, three more localised environments can give rise to moist evergreen forests in other areas of the country.

Riparian forests (often called riverine forests) are very common. They line many of Zambia's major rivers and are found in most of the national parks. Typical trees and shrubs here include ebony (*Diospyros mespiliformis*), mangosteen (*Garcinia livingstonei*), wild gardenia (*Gardenia volkensii*), sausage tree (*Kigelia africana*), Natal mahogany (*Trichilia emetica*) and various species of figs. But walk away from the river, and you'll find riparian species thinning out rapidly.

Montane forests are found on the lower slopes of mountains, where the rainfall is high. The Zambian slopes of Nyika Plateau are probably the best example of this kind of vegetation.

Finally *swamp* forest occurs near to some of Zambia's permanent swamps. Kasanka National Park probably has the country's best, and most accessible, examples of this.

Grasslands and open areas

Dambo A 'dambo' is a shallow grass depression, or small valley, that is either permanently or seasonally waterlogged. It corresponds closely to what is known as a 'vlei' in other parts of the subcontinent. These open, verdant dips in the landscape often appear in the midst of miombo woodlands and support no bushes or trees. In higher valleys amongst hills, they sometimes form the sources of streams and rivers. Because of their permanent dampness, they are rich in species of grasses, herbs and flowering plants, like orchids – and are excellent grazing (if a little exposed) for antelope. Their margins are usually thickly vegetated by grasses, herbs and smaller shrubs.

Pan Though not an environment for rich vegetation, a pan is a shallow, seasonal pool of water with no permanent streams leading into or out of it. The bush is full of small pans in the rainy season, most of which will dry up soon after the rains cease. Sometimes there's only a fine distinction between a pan and a dambo.

Floodplain Floodplains are the low-lying grasslands on the edges of rivers, streams, lakes and swamps that are seasonally inundated by floods. Zambia has some huge areas of floodplain, most obviously beside the Kafue River, in the Barotseland area around the Zambezi, and south of the permanent Bangweulu Swamps. These often contain no trees or bushes, just a low carpet of grass species that can tolerate being submerged for part of the year. In the midst of some floodplains, like the Busanga Plains, you'll find isolated small 'islands' of trees and bushes, slightly raised above the surrounding grasslands.

Montane grassland More common in other areas of Africa, montane grassland occurs on mountain slopes at higher altitudes where the precipitation is heavy and the climate cool. Zambia's best examples of this are on Nyika Plateau, and here you'll find many species of flora and fauna that occur nowhere else in Zambia.

FAUNA See also pages 507–23, for an introductory field guide to some of Zambia's larger animals.

Mammals
Zambia's large mammals are typical of the savannah areas of east and (especially) southern Africa. The large predators here are lion, leopard, cheetah, wild dog and spotted hyena, although cheetah and wild dog are relatively uncommon.

Elephant and buffalo occur in large herds in protected national parks, and in small, furtive family groups where poaching is a problem. Black rhino were probably, sadly, extinct in Zambia until they were re-introduced into North Luangwa National Park in 2003. There are also white rhino in the small, well-protected, Mosi-oa-Tunya National Park at Livingstone, re-introduced from South Africa.

Antelope are well represented, with puku and impala numerically dominant in the drier areas. There are several interesting, endemic subspecies found in Zambia, including the Angolan and Thornicroft's giraffe, Cookson's wildebeest, Crawshay's zebra, and two unusual subspecies of lechwe – the black and the Kafue lechwe – which occur in very large numbers in some of the country's bigger marshy areas.

Because Zambia is a wet country, with numerous marshy areas, its natural vegetation is lush and capable of supporting a high density of game. The country has a natural advantage over drier areas, and this accounts for the sheer volume of big game to be found in its better parks.

Birds
Much of Zambia is still covered by original, undisturbed natural vegetation, and hunting is not a significant factor for most of the country's birds. Thus, with a range of verdant and natural habitats, Zambia is a superb birding destination, with 757 different species recorded by 2010. BirdWatch Zambia – formerly the Zambian Ornithological Society – has a checklist on their website (*www.birdwatchzambia. org*), and – in partnership with BirdLife International – has designated a total of 42 'important bird areas' (IBAs), covering 14% of the country. For details, see Peter Leonard's *Important Bird Areas in Zambia*, page 528).

Whilst the animal species differ only occasionally from the 'normal' species found in southern Africa, the birds are a much more varied mix of those species found in southern, eastern and even central Africa. The obvious celebrity is the ungainly shoebill stork, which breeds in the Bangweulu Swamps, and only one or two other places in central Africa. A lesser-known attraction is the Zambian or Chaplin's barbet, Zambia's only endemic bird species, found in southern Zambia around the south side of Kafue National Park. However, there are many other unusual, rare and beautifully coloured species that attract enthusiasts to Zambia, from the collared barbet to the black-cheeked lovebird, Heuglin's robin and Schalow's turaco.

In addition to its resident bird species, Zambia receives many migrants. In September and October the Palaearctic migrants (those that come from the northern hemisphere – normally Europe) appear, and they remain until around

April or May. This is also the peak time to see the intra-African migrants, which come from further north in Africa.

The rains from December to April see an explosion in the availability of most birds' food: seeds, fruits and insects. Hence this is the prime time for birds to nest, even if it is also the most difficult time to visit the more remote areas of the country.

FIELD GUIDES Finding good, detailed field guides to plants, animals and birds in Zambia is becoming much easier. There are now very comprehensive guides on the flora and fauna of southern Africa, which remain invaluable in Zambia. For total coverage there are also many smaller guides, published in Zambia by the Wildlife and Environmental Conservation Society of Zambia (page 51), covering snakes, trees, wild flowers, birds and the like, and ideal for general game viewing and birdwatching. There's even a guide to the Zambian bird species that have been excluded from the southern Africa guides, and – at the other end of the scale – a heavy but very comprehensive guide to the birds of sub-Saharan Africa. See pages 527–9 for more details.

CONSERVATION

A great deal has been written about the conservation of animals in Africa, much of it over-simplistic and intentionally emotive. As an informed visitor you are in the unique position of being able to see some of the issues at first hand, and to appreciate the perspectives of local people. So abandon your preconceptions, and start by considering the complexities of the issues involved. Here I shall try to develop a few ideas common to most current thinking on conservation, ideas to which the rest of the book only briefly alludes.

First, conservation must be taken within its widest sense if it is to have meaning. Saving animals is of minimal use if the whole environment is degraded, so we must consider conserving whole areas and ecosystems, not just the odd isolated species.

Observe that land is regarded as an asset by most societies in Africa, as it is elsewhere. To 'save' the land for the animals, and use it merely for the recreation of a few privileged foreign tourists, is a recipe for huge social problems – especially if the local people remain excluded from benefit and in poverty. Local people have hunted animals for food for centuries. They have always killed game that threatened them, or ruined their crops. If we now try to protect animals in populated areas without addressing the concerns of the people, then our efforts will fail.

The only pragmatic way to conserve Zambia's wild areas is to see the development of the local people, and the conservation of the animals and the environment, as interlinked goals.

In the long term, one will not work without the other. Conservation without development leads to resentful locals who will happily, and frequently, shoot, trap and kill animals. Development without conservation will simply repeat the mistakes that most developed countries have already made: it will lay waste a beautiful land and kill off its natural heritage. Look at the tiny areas of undisturbed natural vegetation that survive in the UK, the USA or Japan. See how unsuccessful we in the northern hemisphere have been at long-term conservation over the past 500 years.

As an aside, the local people in Zambia are sometimes wrongly accused of being the only agents of degradation. Many would like to see 'poachers' shot on sight, and slash-and-burn agriculture banned. But observe the importation of tropical hardwoods by the West to see the problems that our demands place on the natural environment in the developing world.

In conserving some of Zambia's natural areas and assisting the development of its people, the international community has a vital role to play. It could effectively encourage the Zambian government to practise sustainable long-term strategies, rather than grasping for the short-term fixes which politicians seem universally to prefer. But such solutions must have the backing of the people themselves, or they will fall apart when the foreign-aid budgets eventually wane.

In practice, to get this backing from the local communities it is not enough for a conservation strategy to be compatible with development. Most Zambians are more concerned about where they live, what they can eat and how they will survive, than they are about the lives of small, obscure species of antelope that taste good when roasted.

To succeed in Africa, conservation must not only be compatible with development, it must actually promote it. It must actively help the local people to improve their own standard of living. If that situation can be reached, then local communities can be mobilised behind long-term conservation initiatives.

Governments are the same. As Luangwa's late conservationist Norman Carr once commented, 'governments won't conserve an impala just because it is pretty'. But they will work to save it if they can see that it is worth more to them alive than dead.

The best strategies tried so far on the continent attempt to find lucrative and sustainable ways to use the land. They then plough much of the revenue back into the surrounding local communities. Once the local communities see revenue from conservation being used to help them improve their lives – to build houses, clinics and schools, and to offer paid employment – then such schemes rapidly get their backing and support.

Carefully planned, sustainable tourism is one solution that can work effectively. For success, the local communities must see that the visitors pay because they want

FIRE! *Tricia Hayne*

Somewhere – at any given time of the year – part of Zambia burns. Sometimes these are forest fires, spontaneously setting the bush alight as they have for millennia. Often, however, they are set deliberately. The reasons for this are many and varied, and not all are negative; fire is considered a mixed blessing by both agriculturalists and conservationists.

At worst, fires are set by poachers, or even traditional hunters, to drive animals out into the open. Subsistence farmers, too, employ destructive slash-and-burn techniques in order to create new plots of agricultural land from scrub or forest. More positively, fire is an important tool in the conservation armoury. Burning off the old grass before it is totally dry, for example, encourages the growth of new sweet shoots, which in turn attract grazers such as wildebeest. At a more local level, villagers will often set fire to long grass to create an open space around houses or to clear paths, thus discouraging rats and snakes. And sometimes controlled fires may be used to clear an area in order to create a firebreak as an insurance against greater damage.

Many of the tree species that make up the classic miombo woodland which covers large tracts of Zambia have evolved over time to become at least partially fire-resistant – and this in turn may help to explain their dominance in areas where fires are a regular part of the annual cycle. Other miombo species, however, as well as numerous indigenous trees such as mopane and teak, exhibit no such resistance. Thus, while the benefits are there, the risk of fire resulting in long-term environmental damage is a real threat.

the wildlife. Thus, they reason that the existence of wildlife directly improves their income, and they will strive to conserve it.

It isn't enough for people to see that the wildlife helps the government to get richer; that won't dissuade a local hunter from shooting a duiker for dinner. However, if he is directly benefiting from the visitors, who come to see the animals, then he has a vested interest in saving that duiker.

It matters little to the Zambian people, or ultimately to wildlife species, whether these visitors come to shoot the wildlife with a camera or with a gun. The vital issue is whether the hunting is done on a sustainable basis (ie: only a few of the oldest 'trophy' animals are shot each year, so that the size of the animal population remains largely unaffected).

Photographers may claim the moral high ground, but should remember that hunters pay far more for their privileges. Hunting operations generate large revenues from few guests, who demand minimal infrastructure and so cause little impact on the land. Photographic operations need more visitors to generate the same revenue, and so generally cause greater negative effects on the country.

Conservation of Zambian wildlife and the environment falls within the remit of the Ministry of Tourism (see below), whereas the body responsible for heritage conservation is the National Heritage Conservation Commission (NHCC; *Old Lusaka Boys' School, Dedan Kimathi Rd, Lusaka*). The commission publishes a biannual magazine, *Zambia Heritage*.

NATIONAL PARKS AND GMAS A considerable area of Zambia is protected by national parks. Of these, the latest to be gazetted is Lusaka National Park, close to the capital, which opened in June 2015 and will add further protection in a more urban area. These parks are designated for photographic visitors; here no hunting is allowed. Around the parks are large areas designated as game management areas (GMAs). Within these are villages and hence small-scale farms, and hunting is (at least in theory) controlled and practised sustainably. Both local and overseas hunters use the GMAs, and the latter usually pay handsomely for the privilege.

Integral to this model is that the GMAs provide a buffer between the pristine national park and the land outside where uncontrolled hunting is allowed. This should serve to protect the national park's animals from incursions by poachers, whilst the park acts as a large gene pool and species reservoir for the GMA.

The theory of GMAs is good, but their administration has many practical difficulties. In some of them hunting by the local people has been uncontrolled, and in a few much of the game has been wiped out – resulting in no income from the wildlife, and so more pressure to hunt unsustainably. Many have projects that aim to reverse this trend, to regenerate their game resources and then set the communities off on a sustainable path. However, much more work needs to be done if a long-term effect is to be felt across the country.

In 2015, responsibility for both national parks and GMAs was removed from the semi-independent Zambia Wildlife Authority (ZAWA), to be incorporated back into a government department within the Ministry of Tourism. ZAWA had more autonomy and greater financial independence than its predecessor, the National Parks and Wildlife Service (NPWS), and there is concern that the move may result in greater political interference on environmental issues. Given the likely speed of change, however, we have retained all references to ZAWA in this guide while we await developments.

One initiative instigated during ZAWA's tenure was the establishment of community partnership parks (CPPs), the first of which is in the Bangweulu Wetlands. Broadly, such parks are owned by the local community rather than by the

3

NATIONAL PARKS

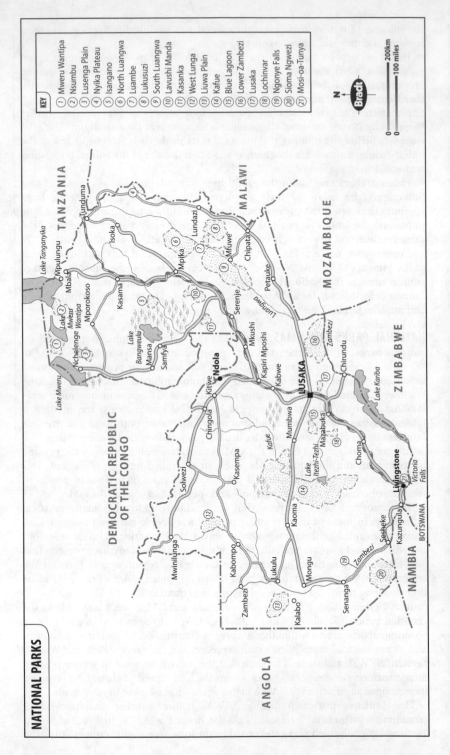

KEY

1. Mweru Wantipa
2. Nsumbu
3. Lusenga Plain
4. Nyika Plateau
5. Isangano
6. North Luangwa
7. Luambe
8. Lukusuzi
9. South Luangwa
10. Lavushi Manda
11. Kasanka
12. West Lunga
13. Liuwa Plain
14. Kafue
15. Blue Lagoon
16. Lower Zambezi
17. Lusaka
18. Lochinvar
19. Ngonye Falls
20. Sioma Ngwezi
21. Mosi-oa-Tunya

0   200km
0   100 miles

state, and are to be managed by a partner within the private sector in cooperation with ZAWA.

TOURISM Zambia lies in the heart of sub-Saharan Africa. To the northeast lie the 'original' safari areas of east Africa: Kenya and Tanzania. Some of their best parks are now rather crowded, though their wildlife spectacles are still on a grand scale. South of Zambia are the more subtle attractions of Zimbabwe, Botswana and Namibia. Each country draws its own type of wildlife enthusiasts, and all have an element of wilderness that can seem difficult to find in east Africa today.

All have embraced tourism in different ways. Zambia is fortunate in having addressed this question later than the others, with the chance to learn from the mistakes of its neighbours. It is hoped that sustainable tourism can be a saviour of Zambia's economy as well as its wildlife, though there is a long way to go before tourism contributes a sizeable slice of the country's revenue.

Nevertheless, tourism is helping Zambia – both in economic terms and with conservation. It is providing employment and bringing foreign exchange into the country, which gives the politicians a reason to support the preservation of the parks. Increasingly Zambia's small-scale safari operators have mobilised themselves behind local development objectives, and in recent years we're seeing very positive initiatives for tourism to help development and sustainable land use, both inside and outside of Zambia's national parks.

The visitor on an expensive safari is generally, by his or her mere presence, making a financial contribution to development and conservation in Zambia. When on safari, one very simple thing that you can do to help is to ask your safari operator:

- Besides employment, how do local people benefit from this camp?
- How much of this camp's revenue goes directly back to the local people?
- What are you doing to help the people living near this reserve?
- How much control do the local people have over what goes on in the area where these safaris operate?

If more visitors did this, it would make a huge difference. That said, most operators do have programmes to help their local communities. They've already realised that the mass of Zambian people must benefit more (and more directly) from tourism if conservation is going to be successful in Zambia.

For ways in which you can support small local charities which directly help the people of Zambia, see *Travelling positively*, pages 81–2.

HUNTING Big-game hunting, where visiting hunters pay large amounts to kill trophy animals, is practised on a number of private ranches and hunting areas. It is also a valuable source of revenue in the long term for people living in the country's GMAs. In some this is already working, whilst in others development agencies, including the World Wide Fund for Nature (WWF), are working to start up sustainable schemes.

Poaching After tales of government corruption and complicity with poachers, those travellers who have not ventured into Zambia can be forgiven for asking, 'Is there any game left in Zambia?' The answer is a definitive 'Yes'.

The 1970s and especially the 1980s saw rampant hunting in the GMAs, and considerable poaching in Zambia's national parks – partly small-scale hunting for food by local people, and partly large commercial poaching operations. The government reaction to this was a mixture of indifference and, allegedly, complicity. The only national park with an appreciable number of foreign visitors, South Luangwa, was effectively defended from all but the most persistent infiltrations of specialist rhino-poachers. Other parks were, to various extents, neglected. Most still suffer from the results of that past neglect even now, and in some of the smaller parks, the battle can feel lost.

However, various parks and GMAs are now firmly on the way up, and a real attraction for visitors. With that development comes a reason to protect the parks (as well as a financial motivation – see pages 33–7). Kafue's game populations are almost back to normal, as are those in the Lower Zambezi National Park. Both Kasanka and North Luangwa are being effectively protected with the help of two very different private conservation initiatives, Liuwa Plain has embraced that model, and more recently the Bangweulu Wetlands has followed suit. The WWF has long been working hard to help the local people earn an income from the sustainable utilisation of wildlife around the Bangweulu Swamps. Camps are opening up along the upper reaches of the Zambezi.

So the message from Zambia is upbeat. The main parks have excellent game populations and many more are gradually recovering. Unlike much of Africa, Zambia has not generally been ravaged by overgrazing, and so even the parks that have suffered from poaching have usually retained their natural vegetation in pristine condition. This gives hope that good game populations can be re-established, and that large tracts of Zambia will once again be returned to their natural state.

TO GET THE WHOLE PICTURE ON ZAMBIA & THE NICEST CAMPS AND LODGES TO VISIT; AND FIND THE BEST WAY TO DO IT, WHY NOT CALL US?

AFRICA EXPLORER
TELEPHONE: 020 89 87 87 42
www.africa-explorer.co.uk

4

Planning and Preparation

Tourists generally come to Zambia in small numbers, and for the most part restrict themselves to a few of the main towns and national parks. Away from these centres, visitors are regarded with mild curiosity and often shown great warmth and hospitality. Zambia is a genuinely friendly country which (perhaps Lusaka excepted) has not yet had enough bad experiences of visitors to lower its opinion of them.

Zambia's attitude to tourism has changed considerably over the past few years, and visitors are now generally seen as good for the country because they spend valuable foreign currency and create employment. Tourism is helping both Zambia's economy and – by making a major contribution to the preservation of the national parks – its conservation policy.

WHEN TO GO AND HIGHLIGHTS

WEATHER See the section on *Climate*, pages 27–9, for a detailed description of the weather that can be expected, and note that Zambia's rainy season occurs around December to April (slightly different every year).

Dry season Many of Zambia's tourists come during the dry season, with the peak being August to early October. Zambia's small camps and lodges ensure that it never feels busy, even when everywhere is full. Others visit early or late in the season – May to July or November – because the camps are quieter and often costs are lower. The dry season (May to November), when you are unlikely to meet rain and can expect clear blue skies, is the easiest time to travel. It is ideal if this is your first trip to Africa, or if seeing lots of big game is top of your wish list.

June to August are the coolest months, then from September onwards the heat gradually builds up. Note, though, that where the altitude is relatively low – like the Luangwa, the Lower Zambezi Valley or Lake Tanganyika – the temperature is always higher. These places, especially, can get very hot towards the end of October, and occasions of over 40°C in the shade in the middle of the day have earned October the tag of 'suicide month' amongst the locals.

November is a variable month, but many days can be cooler than October, as the gathering clouds shield the earth from the sun. On some days these bring welcome showers; on others they simply build, and with them come tension and humidity. It's always an interesting month.

Wet season A small but increasing number of visitors come during what's known as the 'emerald season', from December to April. While the likelihood of rain means that this isn't for everybody, it remains a fascinating time of year to visit. The camps that open then will often be quiet for days. Their rates can be much lower, and they're often far more flexible about bringing children on safari.

At this time of year, the days can vary enormously from one to the next. Even within a day, skies will often change from sunny to cloudy within minutes and then back again. Downpours are usually heavy and short, and often in the late afternoon. Even in the lower valleys, temperatures are pleasant, rising to only around 30°C, and the nights only slightly cooler (typically down to perhaps 15°C). You will need a good waterproof for the rainy season, but it seldom rains for long enough to really stop you doing anything. Except travelling on bush roads …

Travelling Travelling around Zambia in the dry season often has its challenges – but in the wet season it's a totally different game. Most untarred roads become quagmires; many are completely impassable. The rivers swell to bursting, often beyond, as their surging brown waters undermine trees and carry them downstream like Pooh-sticks. Streams that were ankle-deep in October become potential rafting challenges. Many rural areas are cut off for a few months, so getting anywhere away from the main routes can be tricky.

However, if you are planning to fly into a national park for a safari, you'll find that only a few camps remain open. The South Luangwa has a network of all-weather roads for driving safaris. If you've often been to Africa in the dry season, then this is a fascinating time to visit – like being introduced to a different side of an old friend.

VEGETATION During the wet season, the foliage runs wild. The distinctive oxbow lagoons of the Luangwa and Lower Zambezi fill, while trees everywhere are deeply green. The open sandy plains become verdant meadows, often with shallow pools of water. It's a time of renewal, when a gentler light dapples Zambia's huge forests and areas of bush.

When the rains end, the leaves gradually dry and many eventually drop. More greys and browns appear, and good shade becomes harder to find. Eventually, by late September and October, most plants look dry and parched, coloured from straw-yellow to shrivelled brown.

GAME From the point of view of most herbivores, the wet season is a much more pleasant time to visit. Those in national parks live in enormous salad bowls, with convenient pools of water nearby. It's a good time to have their young and eat themselves into good condition. Val and Bob Leyland were the first visitors for whom I ever organised a trip during the rains. On returning, they commented that 'having [previously] visited Africa last dry season, there's something special about seeing all the animals when they aren't struggling with thirst and a lack of vegetation … It gives a sense of luxuriance which isn't there in the dry season.'

Visiting South Luangwa in the wet season you will see game, but probably less of it. On my last trip during the rains I went on two night drives. On the first we saw a good range of antelope (including some wonderful sightings of young animals), a few elephant and buffalo and a leopard at the end of the evening. The next we found a hyena on a kill, and later followed three lionesses hunting for several hours. The birding was consistently phenomenal, far better than during the dry season.

However, if game viewing is your priority, or this is one of your first trips to Africa, then the animals are much easier to spot when it's dry, as no thick vegetation obscures the view. Further, they are forced to congregate at well-known water points, like rivers, where they can be observed. Many more tracks are navigable in the bush, and so more areas can be explored by vehicle. So if you want to see large numbers of animals, then do come to Zambia in the dry season – and later rather than earlier if possible.

A few specific animal highlights include:

- **February–May** Most of the herbivores are in their best condition, having fed well on the lush vegetation.
- **May–August** Leopard are generally easier to see, as they come out more during the twilight hours. Later in the year they often come out later in the evening, waiting until it is cool.
- **September–October** Buffalo groups tend to amalgamate into larger, more spectacular herds. (They splinter again just before the rains.) Lion sightings become more frequent, as they spend more time near the limited remaining water sources.
- **October–December** Crocodiles are nesting, so are found on or near exposed sandbanks.
- **November** The great wildebeest gathering masses on Liuwa Plain, in western Zambia. It's still accessible by 4x4 at this time of year, but you'll need a small expedition to witness it.
- **November–March** Baby warthogs and impala start to appear in November, followed by most of the mammals that calve sometime during the rainy season.

BIRDLIFE The birdlife in Zambia is certainly best when the foliage is most dense, and the insects are thriving: in the wet season. Then many resident birds are nesting and in their bright, breeding plumage. This coincides to a large extent with the 'summer' period, from around October to March, when the Palaearctic migrants from the northern hemisphere are seen. Certainly in terms of waterbirds – storks, herons, ducks, geese and the smaller waders – the rainy season (and just after) is an infinitely better time to visit.

The birding calendar's highlights include:

- **March–July** Large breeding colonies of storks and herons gather to breed. The only sites I know are in the Nsefu Sector of the South Luangwa National Park.
- **August–October** 'Fishing parties' of herons, egrets and storks will arrive at pools as they dry up, to feed on the stranded fish.
- **September–November** Carmine bee-eaters form large nesting colonies in the soft sand of vertical riverbanks.
- **October–November** Pennant-winged nightjars are in resplendent breeding plumage.
- **November–April** Most of the weavers are in breeding plumage.
- **February–April** Fire-crowned bishop birds, yellow-billed storks and the spectacular paradise whydahs have their breeding plumage on display.
- **April–June** Resident African skimmers are nesting.

PHOTOGRAPHY I find the light clearest and most spectacular during the rainy season. Then the rains have washed the dust from the air, and the bright sunlight can contrast wonderfully with dark storm clouds. The vegetation's also greener and brighter, and the animals and birds often in better condition. However, it will rain occasionally when you're trying to take shots, and the long periods of flat, grey light through clouds can be very disappointing. Sometimes it can seem as if you're waiting for the gods to grant you just a few minutes of stunning light, between the clouds.

A more practical time is probably just after the rains, around April to June, when at least you are less likely to be interrupted by a shower.

The dry season's light is reliably good, if not quite as inspirational as that found during the rains. You are unlikely to encounter any clouds, and will get better sightings of game to photograph. Try to shoot in the first and last few hours of the day, when the sun is low in the sky. Otherwise, use a filter (perhaps a polariser) to guard against the strength of the light leaving you with a camera full of washed-out shots.

WALKING SAFARIS For safe and interesting walking, you need the foliage to be low so that you can see through the surrounding bush as easily as possible. This means that the dry season is certainly the best time for walking. Walking in the wet season, through shoulder-high grass, is possible – but I'd only go with a very experienced guide and it is harder than during the dry season. My favourite months for walking are June to September, as October can get hot on longer walks.

FISHING The best times to fish in Zambia depend on the area. In the north, on Lake Tanganyika, the rainy season is ideal, between November and March, but in most other areas of the country much of that period is off limits for fishing. On Zambia's great rivers, such as the Zambezi, Kafue and Luangwa, fishing is at its best when the waters are clear. This usually happens from around May to June and lasts until the end of November. Although it is cold during those months the fish are there and will usually fall to bait and spinner, and even fly.

There is a ban on fishing during the months of December to February in all Zambian waters, with the exception of Lake Tanganyika, Lake Kariba, and private dams.

TOURIST INFORMATION

The Zambia Tourism Board (\ *0211 229087;* e *ztb@zambiatourism.org.zm, info@ zambiatourism.org.zm; www.zambiatourism.com*) offers consumer and general information, and visa advice to potential travellers. It has a good website, and three offices overseas:

South Africa 570 Ziervogel St, Arcadia, Pretoria; \ +27 12 326 1847/1854; e tourism@ zambiapretoria.net, zambiatourism@iburst.co.za
UK 2 Palace Gate, London W8 5NG; \ 020 7589 6655; e info@zambiahc.org.uk

USA 2200R St, Washington, DC 20008 (temporary address); \ +1 202 265 9717; e embzambia@ aol.com

For details of other websites offering tourist information, see page 530.

PUBLIC HOLIDAYS

Aside from the private lodges and large hotels, much of Zambia effectively shuts down on public holidays. Independent travellers in particular may need to plan ahead, especially in terms of changing money and finding fuel.

New Year's Day	1 January
Youth Day	around 11–13 March
Good Friday	around March/April
Holy Saturday	day following Good Friday
Labour Day	1 May
Africa Freedom Day	25 May
Heroes' Day	first Monday of July

Unity Day	first Tuesday of July
Farmers' Day	first Monday of August
Independence Day	24 October (plus a holiday on the nearest Monday)
Christmas Day	25 December
Boxing Day	26 December

ORGANISING A SAFARI

Most visitors who come to Zambia for few weeks' safari stay at some of the small safari camps. Combinations of time in the Kafue, the Luangwa Valley, the Lower Zambezi and a few days around Victoria Falls would be typical.

WHEN TO BOOK If you have favourite camps, or a tight schedule, then book as far ahead as you can; eight to ten months in advance is perfect. Bear in mind that most camps are small, and thus easily filled. They organise their logistics with military precision and so finding space at short notice, especially in the busier months, can be tricky. (The exception to this rule is usually the rainy season.)

If you are looking to travel in the next few months, then one or two of your chosen camps may be full; you'll have to accept alternatives.

HOW MUCH? Safaris in Zambia are not cheap. Expect to pay US$4,000/£2,600 per person sharing per week, plus international airfares. This would include a few of your internal transfers or flights, camp transfers, meals, activities, laundry, park fees and even drinks.

HOW TO BOOK It's best to arrange everything together, using a reliable, independent tour operator. Many operators sell trips to Zambia, but few know the country well. Insist on dealing directly with someone who does. Zambia is changing fast, so up-to-date local knowledge is vital in putting together a trip that runs smoothly and suits you. Make sure that whoever you book with is bonded, so your money is protected if they go broke. If you're unsure, pay with a credit card. Never book a trip from someone who hasn't spent time there – you are asking for problems. Ask the person you're dealing with specifically, 'Have you been to this camp or place?'

Booking directly with most Zambian camps is easily possible; the camps are the easy bit. Once they are organised, you need to piece together the jigsaw puzzle of transfers, internal flights and stopovers to link them into your trip. Without local knowledge, this can be tricky – and you will have little recourse if anything goes wrong.

European, US and local operators usually work on commission for the trips that they sell, which is deducted from the basic cost that the visitor pays. Thus you should end up paying the same whether you book through an overseas operator, or talk directly to a camp in Zambia.

Perhaps because of the UK's historical links, or the high number of British safari-goers, there seems to be more competition amongst UK tour operators than elsewhere. Hence they've a reputation for being generally cheaper than US operators for the same trips.

TOUR OPERATORS Zambia is something of a touchstone for tour operators to southern Africa: those who know Zambia well are the small core of Africa specialists. Most operators can send you to Cape Town with ease. But ask them where to visit in Zambia, and you'll rapidly sort those that know southern Africa from those that haven't got a clue.

Don't let anyone convince you that there are only three first-class safari camps in Zambia, as it's rubbish. If your operator doesn't know most of the camps in this book – and offer a wide choice to suit you – then use one that does.

Here I must, as the author, admit a personal interest in the tour-operating business. I run Expert Africa (page i), which is currently the leading operator to Zambia. With offices in London, New Zealand and Cape Town, we organise trips to Zambia for travellers from all over the world. Our website has detailed original maps, the widest choice of Zambian lodges and camps, and extensive reviews from many of our travellers. Booking your trip with a tour operator like us will always cost you the same as or less than if you contacted Zambia's camps directly – plus you get independent advice, full financial protection, and experts to organise it for you. Our safaris are completely flexible; they cost from about US$3,000/£2,000 per person for a week, including accommodation, meals and game activities, and excluding international flights.

For a fair comparison, international tour operators featuring Zambia include the following. (Tour operators based in Zambia are listed in the relevant chapters.)

UK

Aardvark Safaris Aspire Business Centre, Ordnance Rd, Tidworth, Hants SP9 7QD; 01980 849160; e info@aardvarksafaris.com; www. aardvarksafaris.com. Small, reliable upmarket safari specialist to Africa, Mauritius & Seychelles. Also has US office.

Abercrombie & Kent St George's Hse, Ambrose St, Cheltenham, Glos GL50 3LG; 01242 547760; e info@abercrombiekent.co.uk; www. abercrombiekent.co.uk. Worldwide individual & group holidays to upmarket destinations with upmarket price tags.

Acacia Adventure Holidays 23a Craven Terr, London W2 3QH; 020 7706 4700; e info@acacia-africa.com; www.acacia-africa.com. Adventure holidays & overland/camping safaris throughout Africa.

Africa Explorer 5 Strand on the Green, London W4 3PQ; 020 8987 8742; e john@africa-explorer.co.uk; www.africa-explorer.co.uk. Tiny but knowledgeable company run by the jovial John Haycock. See ad on page 38.

Africa Travel 227 Shepherds Bush Rd, London W6 7AS; 020 7843 3500; e info@africatravel. co.uk; www.africatravel.co.uk. General operator offering trips across Africa & the Indian Ocean.

Audley Travel New Mill, New Mill La, Witney, Oxon OX29 9SX; 01993 838505; e info@ audleytravel.com; www.audleytravel.com. Large tailor-made operator offering trips worldwide from Burma to New Zealand, including Africa.

Cazenove & Loyd Argon Hse, Argon Mews, London SW6 1BJ; 020 3773 1538; e info@ cazloyd.com; www.cazloyd.com. Top-end

tailor-made operator with worldwide options, including Africa.

Exodus Grange Mills, Weir Rd, London SW12 0NE; 0845 869 8282; e sales@exodus.co.uk; www. exodus.co.uk. Worldwide guided group specialists, with safari & canoe trips in Zambia.

Expert Africa Upper Sq, Old Isleworth, Middx TW7 7BJ; 020 8232 9777; e info@expertafrica. com; www.expertafrica.com. Africa specialists with the most comprehensive website on Zambia safaris & a very wide range of options. Run by this book's author.

Extraordinary Africa 0207 097 1801; e info@ extraordinary-africa.com; www.extraordinary-africa.com. New, small tailor-made operator featuring East and Southern Africa, inc Zambia, plus Seychelles & Mauritius. See ad on page 82.

Gane & Marshall 118 Collier Row Rd, Romford, Essex RM5 2BB; 01822 600600; e info@ ganeandmarshall.com; www.ganeandmarshall. com. Tailor-made operator with worldwide destinations that include Africa.

Hartley's Safaris The Old Chapel, Chapel La, Hackthorn, Lincs LN2 3PN; 01673 861600; e info@hartleysgroup.com; www.hartleys-safaris. co.uk. Long-established tailor-made specialists to east & southern Africa & Indian Ocean islands.

Journeys by Design Africa Hse, Brunswick Row, Brighton BN1 4JZ; 01273 623790; e info@ journeysbydesign.com; www.journeysbydesign. com. Small tailor-made operator (ground arrangements only) featuring east & southern Africa.

Okavango Tours & Safaris White Lion Hse, 64A Highgate High St, London N6 5HX; 020 8347 4030; e info@okavango.com; www.okavango.

com. Tailor-made specialists to Africa & Indian Ocean islands, with a good knowledge of Zambia.

Original Travel 21 Ransome's Dock, 35–37 Parkgate Rd, London SW11 4NP; ☎020 3740 7842; e ask@originaltravel.co.uk; www.originaltravel. co.uk. Upmarket holidays including to Africa.

Rainbow Tours 2 Waterhouse Sq, 138–140 Holborn, London, EC1N 2ST; ☎020 7666 1276; e enquiries@rainbowtours.co.uk; www. rainbowtours.co.uk. Once pure Africa specialists, now part of the larger Western & Oriental travel group.

Safari Club 4 Littlebrook Av, Burnham, Bucks SL2 2NN; ☎0845 054 5889; e info@safari-club. co.uk; www.safari-club.co.uk. Small independent operator offering tailor-made trips to Africa & Indian Ocean islands. See ad on page 244.

Safari Consultants Africa Hse, 2 Cornard Mills, Mill Tye, Great Cornard, Suffolk CO10 0GW; ☎01787 888590; e info@safari-consultants.com; http:// safari-consultants.com. Long-established tailor-made specialists to east & southern Africa, & Indian Ocean islands, with a good knowledge of Zambia. See ad in 3rd colour section.

Safari Drive The Trainer's Office, Windy Hollow, Sheepdrove, Lambourn, Berks RG17 7XA; ☎01488 71140; e info@safaridrive.com; www.safaridrive. com. Specialising in self-drive 4x4 trips across southern & East Africa. See ad on page 94.

Scott Dunn World Riverbank Hse, 1 Putney Bridge Approach, London SW6 3JD; ☎020 3432 5704; e africa@scottdunn.com; www.scottdunn. com. Worldwide coverage, with itineraries & tailor-made trips to Zambia.

Steppes Africa 51 Castle St, Cirencester, Glos GL7 1QD; ☎01285 601756; e enquiry@steppestravel. co.uk; www.steppestravel.co.uk. Upmarket tailor-made operators to destinations worldwide.

Tribes Travel The Old Dairy, Wood Farm, Ipswich Rd, Otley, Suffolk IP6 9JW; ☎01473 890499; e enquiries@tribes.co.uk; www.tribes.co.uk. Worldwide travel on fair-trade principles; particularly strong on cultural trips. See ad on page 148.

Wildlife Worldwide Capitol Hse, 12–13 Bridge St, Winchester, Hants SO23 0HL; ☎01962 302086; e reservations@wildlifeworldwide.com; www. wildlifeworldwide.com. Worldwide operator offering tailor-made & small-group wildlife holidays.

Zambezi Safari & Travel Company Africa Hse, Poundwell St, Modbury, Devon PL21 0QJ; ☎01548 830059; e info@zambezi.com; www.zambezi.com. Specialist safari planners with offices in Zimbabwe & UK, concentrating on small, owner-run operators throughout Africa.

France
Makila Voyages 4 place de Valois, 75001 Paris; ☎01 42 96 80 00; www.makila.fr

Africa
Malawian Style e info@malawianstyle.com; www.southluandwasafaris.com. Relatively new Malawi-based operator offering both conventional & volunteering holidays in Malawi, & safaris in Zambia. See ad on inside front cover.

Land & Lake Safaris ☎+265 (0)175 7120; e info@ landlake.net; www.landlake.net. Based in Lilongwe, this operator focuses on Malawi, with some trips to Zambia. See ad on page 18.

Pulse Africa ☎+27 (0)11 325 2290; e info@ pulseafrica.com; www.pulseafrica.com. Long-standing, reputable & highly bespoke operator based in South Africa, run by knowledgeable Sandy Wood. Offers East & Southern Africa. See ad on page 93.

North America
Africa Adventure Company 2601 E Oakland Park Blvd, Suite 600, Fort Lauderdale, FL 33306; ☎954 491 8877, 1 800 882 9453; e safari@ africanadventure.com; www.africa-adventure.com

Geographic Expeditions 1008 General Kennedy Av, San Francisco, CA 94129-0902; ☎888 570 7108; www.geoex.com

OAT ☎1 800 955 1925; www.oattravel.com. Typically OAT takes over entire camps for a minimum of a year. They appeal to more mature US-based clients with highly structured activities at low prices.

Australasia
The Classic Safari Company 124A Queen St, Woollahra, NSW 2025, Australia; ☎1300 130 218; www.classicsafaricompany.com.au

Expert Africa 11 Brightwater Cres, Totara Park, Upper Hutt 5018, New Zealand; ☎04 976 7585; e info@expertafrica.com; www.expertafrica.com

SUGGESTED ITINERARIES Those backpacking and driving themselves around Zambia need time but have great flexibility, and part of the adventure of such a trip is having no itinerary. However, most visitors have a much shorter time available.

Although Zambia's tourism infrastructure is developing fast, proper facilities for people with mobility problems are still rare. But don't let this put you off; depending on your ability and sense of adventure, most obstacles are surmountable and Africans are used to finding solutions for practical problems: if you need help, you will receive it.

PLANNING AND BOOKING Most mainstream operators listed in this guide (pages 44–5) will listen to your needs and try to create an itinerary suitable for you. In Zambia, there are two operators that specialise in catering to disabled travellers (see below). For the more independent traveller, it is possible to limit potential surprises by contacting local operators and establishments by email in advance.

ACCOMMODATION Some of Zambia's international-standard hotels have adapted rooms, including the Radisson Blu and the Southern Sun Ridgeway in Lusaka, and Livingstone's Avani Victoria Falls Resort and Royal Livingstone. We have yet to hear of completely accessible accommodation in any of Zambia's national parks, but many lodges are making efforts to improve access for those with limited mobility, including the provision of level paths, and ramps rather than steps.

TRANSPORT
Air travel Both Lusaka and Livingstone international airports have assistance, wheelchairs and aisle chairs for those who need help entering or leaving the aircraft. Livingstone also has accessible toilets and this feature is part of the plan for Lusaka's airport, too.

Buses and trains There is no effective legislation in Zambia to facilitate disabled travellers' journeys by public transport; therefore, if you cannot walk at all then both of these options are going to be difficult. You will need to ask for help from fellow passengers to lift you to your seat, it will often be crowded and it is unlikely that there will be an accessible toilet.

By car Distances are great and roads are often bumpy, so if you are prone to skin damage you need to take extra care. Place your own pressure-relieving cushion on top of (or instead of) the original car seat and if necessary, pad around knees and elbows. If you're not sticking to the main roads, you will need to use a 4x4 vehicle, which will be higher than a normal car making transfers more difficult. Drivers/guides are normally happy to help, but are not trained in this skill, so you must thoroughly explain your needs and always stay in control of the situation. In Livingstone, Hemingways (see *Specialist operators*, below) can provide wheelchair-accessible transfers.

Fly-in trips If you're flying in, then getting your itinerary right and arranging it carefully in advance is important. For most visitors to Zambia, the four main areas of attraction are the Luangwa Valley, Kafue National Park, the Lower Zambezi Valley and Livingstone. All these parks are worth visiting for a week (less than three nights in a park is really too short), and there's often a slight saving if you spend at least a week exclusively with one operator. For most people, a visit to Livingstone takes two to three nights.

HEALTH AND INSURANCE Doctors will know about 'everyday' illnesses, but you must understand and be able to explain your own particular medical requirements. Zambian hospitals and pharmacies are often basic, so it is wise to take as much essential medication and equipment as possible with you, and it is advisable to pack this in your hand luggage during flights in case your main luggage gets lost. Zambia can be hot; if this is a problem for you then try to book accommodation with fans or air conditioning. A useful cooling aid is a plant-spray bottle.

Most insurance companies will insure disabled travellers, but it is essential that they are made aware of your disability. In the UK, both Age UK (\ *0800 389 4852; www.ageuk.org.uk*) and Free Spirit (\ *0800 170 7704; www.free-spirit.com*) offer travel insurance for people with pre-existing medical conditions.

SECURITY For anyone following the usual safety precautions (pages 90–2) the chances of robbery are greatly reduced. In fact, as a disabled person I often feel more 'noticed' when in public places, and therefore a less attractive target for thieves. But the opposite may also apply, so do stay aware of where your bags are and who is around you, especially during car transfers and similar activities.

SPECIALIST OPERATORS
Hemingways \ +260 0213 323097; m +260 977 866492/870232; e info@hemingwayszambia.com; www.hemingwayszambia.com. Livingstone-based operator offering transfers using wheelchair-accessible vehicle. See page 157.
Endeavour Safaris 23 Lark Cres, Table View, 7441 Cape Town, South Africa; \ +27 (0)21 556 6114; m +27 (0)73 206 7733; e info@endeavour-safaris.com; www.endeavour-safaris.com. Specialists in Botswana, South Africa & Namibia who also cover Livingstone.

Disability Travel (*www.disabilitytravel.com*) is a comprehensive US site written by travellers in wheelchairs who have been researching disabled travel full-time since 1985. There are many tips and useful contacts (including lists of travel agents on request) and articles, including pieces on disabled travelling worldwide.

Global Access News (*www.globalaccessnews.com/index.htm*) provides general travel information, reviews and tips for disabled travellers.

The **Society for Accessible Travel and Hospitality** (*www.sath.org*) provides some general information.

Other useful websites include: **Enable Holidays** (*www.enableholidays.com*), **Disabled Holidays** (*www.disabledholidaydirectory.co.uk*), **Access Travel** (*www.access-travel.co.uk*) and **Disabled Access Holidays** (*www.disabledaccessholidays.com*).

When designing a trip, bear in mind that:

- Keen walkers would usually include the Luangwa, and some of the smaller 'walking bushcamps' in their trip.
- Visit the Lower Zambezi or the Kafue for water-based activities.
- If you want to visit North Luangwa, then first spend a few days in the South Park, then perhaps 3–5 nights in North Luangwa.

Ten years ago, taking children on safari in Zambia might have been considered unusual, but things are changing, and the country's lodges and camps haven't been slow to pick up on the trend.

The idea of taking a child on safari might at first seem obvious. You'll be out in a wilderness environment, with plenty of animals to watch, and seemingly non-stop entertainment. But that, of course, is part of the problem. The 'entertainment' cannot be guaranteed, so during a typical three-hour game drive, there's often time when things that might fascinate you – colourful birds, the construction of a termite mound, last night's hyena tracks, even a(nother) herd of puku – will be of little interest to a child. And when big game is spotted, instead of being able to leap up and down with excitement, your child is expected to be absolutely quiet and still. Then there's the often unspoken concern of a sensitive child witnessing a kill.

Add to this the rather exclusive make-up of many safari camps, the safety issues within camp (wildlife, high walkways, rivers and unguarded pools being just a few), and the lack of opportunity for letting off steam, and the considerations mount up.

So how can it work? Although many lodges still maintain a very adult atmosphere, designating a high minimum age for children, several offer some form of 'family' accommodation. Sometimes that's simply a room with an extra bed or two, rather than anything particularly child friendly; at others, it's a suite of rooms, either sharing a bathroom or with each of them en suite, and occasionally with their own lounge area. More specifically, a handful of places have built entirely separate houses that are exceptionally well suited to families – including Chongwe River House and Kasaka's Hippo Pod in the Lower Zambezi, Robin's House and Luangwa River House in the

- Shiwa Ng'andu works really well for 3–4 nights, ideally as part of a trip that passes through South Luangwa (the closest place for flights is Mfuwe).
- Kasanka, Bangweulu and Shiwa Ng'andu work well together, usually in that sequence.

Some combinations that work well are:

Short trips
- 7 nights South Luangwa, or Lower Zambezi, or Kafue
- 2–3 nights Livingstone plus 5–6 nights Kafue, or vice versa

Slightly longer trips
- 5–6 nights South Luangwa plus 4 nights North Luangwa
- 5–6 nights South Luangwa plus 3–4 nights Shiwa Ng'andu
- 5–6 nights Kafue plus 4 nights Lower Zambezi
- 5–6 nights Kafue or Lower Zambezi or South Luangwa, plus 2–3 nights Livingstone

Two weeks If you've got about two weeks, then the obvious option is to devote a week each to two of the main three parks. Alternatively, for something a bit more offbeat, consider:

South Luangwa, and Tangala House in Livingstone – with space to run around, and your own chef so that you can eat at times that suit your family rather than other guests. Mealtimes in many lodges can be a trial for children, though some will prepare meals early, so that you can dine with the other guests while a member of staff (not a qualified childminder) babysits for you.

One further option would be to base yourself in a family-friendly hotel in Livingstone, where you'll be rewarded with the Victoria Falls, as well as wildlife in the Mosi oa Tunya National Park and boat trips on the Zambezi River, without feeling cooped up the rest of the time.

When lodges do accept families, many insist that those with children under, say, eight years old reserve a private vehicle and guide. If this at first seems draconian, consider too that this is for the benefit of the children, as well as for other guests. With your own guide, you select where you stop and spend time, and if your children want to ask questions, that's fine.

In accordance with national parks' regulations, children under the age of 12 cannot go on canoe safaris or bush walks, for very good safety reasons. Some camps have imposed their own, higher, age limits, such as 14 at Musekese in the Kafue, and 16 at Lion Camp in the South Luangwa. However, all camps and guides will assess the maturity of individual children before embarking on these activities. Some camps, among them Kafunta in the South Luangwa, and Kasaka River Lodge in the Lower Zambezi, will offer a member of staff to look after your children while you do these activities, perhaps taking them fishing, or on a short nature walk around the camp grounds.

Whatever your decision, be aware that if you opt for a conventional safari trip, you will need to take plenty to occupy your offspring when in camp. Bored children are likely to be the bane of everyone's life on safari, including yours.

- 3 nights Kasanka, 3 nights Bangweulu (especially green season), 4 nights Shiwa Ng'andu, 4 nights South Luangwa

4x4 trips If you're an experienced Africa hand, driving in your own self-contained vehicle in the dry season, then the choices are much wider. All such trips are long; they're effectively mini-expeditions. The country is your oyster, but there are two obvious routes, and a third that's rather more offbeat, each taking at least three weeks:

Western circuit Livingstone – Upper Zambezi – Mongu – Liuwa Plain – Mongu – Lukulu – Kafue (from northern tip right through to southern tip) – Livingstone

Eastern circuit Lusaka – Kasanka – Lake Waka Waka – Bangweulu – Mutinondo Wilderness – Shiwa Ng'andu – transit through North Luangwa – Luambe – South Luangwa – Lusaka

Northern circuit This suggestion, perhaps for those who have already visited some of the country's highlights, could take you north, visiting some of the lesser-known waterfalls and the Lake Tanganyika area: Lusaka – Kasanka – Bangweulu – Luapula River – Nsumbu National Park – Kasama – Shiwa Ng'andu – Mutinondo Wilderness – Lusaka.

NATIONAL PARKS

Head office For many years, almost all Zambia's national parks have fallen under the control of the Zambia Wildlife Authority (ZAWA; *Private Bag 1, Chilanga;* ❧ *0211 278129, 278482, 279080*). ZAWA have set the rules and administered the parks from their head office, about 20km south of Lusaka. In 2015, however, this changed and responsibility for the parks reverted to a government-run body within the Department of National Parks and Wildlife Services. Until the new situation has been formalised and bedded in, we would suggest that if you want to do anything unusual, such as filming or some form of research, you first approach the staff at Chilanga or, failing that, contact the Zambia Tourism Board (page 42).

Park entry fees Most organised trips include park entry fees in their costs, but if you are travelling on your own then you must pay these directly, either at one of the ZAWA offices or at the park gates – or, very occasionally, at individual lodges. Park offices are normally open 06.00 to 18.00. When paying your fees, you will need to state the gate from which you will be leaving the park. This is ostensibly for security reasons – though don't bank on anyone coming to find you if you come unstuck.

Park fees are officially payable per day (06.00–18.00), rather than per 24 hours, but the ZAWA head office acknowledges that those staying overnight have until 08.00 the following morning to leave the park without paying that day's park fees. However, if you are staying overnight and leaving any later than that, then you will have to pay for two days, as well as the overnight levy. There is a scale of entry fees, with additional charges for taking a vehicle into the parks, and for staying overnight. Fees vary, not just between parks, but according to the visitor, with international visitors paying significantly higher rates than those from southern Africa (SADC), who in turn pay more than Zambian citizens. In 2015, national park fees for international visitors were as follows, per person, per day:

South Luangwa	US$25 (self drive US$30)
Lower Zambezi	US$25 (self drive US$30)
North Luangwa	US$20 (self drive US$25)
Kafue	US$20
Liuwa Plain	US$40
Luambe	US$15
Mosi-oa-Tunya	US$10 (self drive US$15)
Blue Lagoon, Kasanka, Lochinvar, Nsumbu, Lavushi Manda	US$10
Other parks	US$5

The fee for taking a **vehicle** (up to 3 tonnes/50 hp) into the parks is the same in all cases: US$15 (K94) per day, or K17 a day for a Zambian-registered vehicle (which includes local hire cars). In most parks, an additional bed levy of around US$10 is charged per person per night, a fee that is almost always included in the rates at individual lodges. For campers, however, there is a camping levy of US$5 that is payable at the park gate, on top of any campsite rates.

All park fees are payable in cash – US dollars or kwacha – and you are strongly advised to have the correct money as change can be a problem. Do check the documentation carefully, and retain all receipts as these may be required both at lodges and at your exit gate.

Guides For more adventurous trips to remote parks, hire a game scout from the nearest camp to act as your guide – or, better, arrange this in advance through ZAWA. For around US$30 per day, this can be an inexpensive way to get a local guide who may be able to add a whole new dimension to your trip. It can also save wasted driving time, and probably personal anguish over navigational puzzles. Nowadays, guides normally have their own tents and food.

WECSZ The Wildlife and Environmental Conservation Society of Zambia (*4435 Kumoyo Rd, off Los Angeles Bd, Lusaka;* \ *0211 251630;* e *wecsz@coppernet.zm; www.conservationzambia.org;* ⊕ *08.00–17.00 Mon–Fri; membership K100pp/year*) supports environmental education and awareness in Zambia. It sponsors various conservation activities, organises monthly talks for Lusaka members, and runs innovative children's clubs, like the Chongololo and Chipembele conservation clubs, and the related Chongololo Club of the Air (broadcast on Radio 2 each Sunday). It also publishes a number of good, inexpensive field guides specific to Zambia (pages 527–8).

The WECSZ owns three very simple camps in the national parks: Kafwala and Chibila camps in Kafue, and the Wildlife Camp at Mfuwe, as well as Chembe Bird Sanctuary in the Copperbelt. They are managed by others, but some of the revenue still comes back to the society. All are for members only, and may be booked either in writing or in person at the Lusaka office. The society's books can also be bought in Lusaka or at one of the bookshops in town, as can its bi-annual magazine, *Black Lechwe* (*free to members*), which is well written with plenty of interesting articles.

GETTING THERE

BY AIR However you get to the subcontinent, if you don't fly directly to Lusaka then do book your flight to Africa and any scheduled internal links between countries (eg: Nairobi–Lusaka or Johannesburg–Lusaka flights) at the same time. Booking the whole trip together is almost certain to save you money. Sometimes the airline taking you to Africa will have cheap regional flights within Africa; for example Johannesburg–Lusaka with South African Airways is usually much cheaper if booked with an SAA flight from London to Johannesburg, than it is if booked alone. At other times the tour operator you book through will have special deals if you book all the flights with them. And most importantly, if you book all your flights together then you'll be sure to get connecting ones, so you have the best schedule possible.

A US$25 **departure tax** is levied on all international flights. While this is almost always pre-paid on your ticket nowadays, it might be wise to ensure that you have sufficient US dollars in cash as a precaution; credit cards are not accepted.

From Europe With the withdrawal in 2013 of British Airways' flights from the UK to Lusaka, there are no longer direct flights from western Europe, but in 2015 Turkish Airlines started operating a new route between Istanbul and Lusaka. Otherwise, passengers must now transit through one of the major African hubs, usually Nairobi, Addis Ababa or Johannesburg, or via the Middle East and Dubai.

These routes are mainly for business traffic and pre-booked holidays; finding cheap tickets online is usually difficult (if not impossible). Expect to pay about £750–900/US$1,200–1,400 for a return flight. Tour operators (pages 43–5) can sometimes have access to slightly cheaper seats, but you will only be able to buy these if you are buying a complete holiday from them. However, many airlines now save their cheapest fares for online sales, so it's wise to shop around.

If you want a cheap flight, but don't mind spending longer travelling, then consider using one of the nearby regional centres and connecting through to Zambia (see *From within Africa*, below). It used to be cheaper to fly to Harare than to Lusaka, but there is no longer any advantage in taking that route. Johannesburg and Nairobi are some of the busiest airports on the continent, and most of the world's larger airlines have flights there, or at least connections.

From within Africa Several operators have regular flights linking regional cities with both Lusaka and other Zambian towns. From Johannesburg (JNB), **South African Airways** (SAA; *www.flysaa.com*) flies into Lusaka (LUN), Livingstone (LVI) and Ndola (NLA), and both **Kenya Airways** (*www.kenya-airways.com*) and BA's subsidiary **Comair** (*www.comair.co.za*) cover Livingstone and Lusaka.

Among other airlines servicing Lusaka, **Kenya Airways** (*www.kenya-airways. com*) has daily flights from Nairobi (NBO), codesharing with KLM. **Ethiopian Airlines** (*www.ethiopianairlines.com*) has daily flights to Addis Ababa (ADD), and daily flights to and from Guangzhou (ZGGG) in China. (It's worth noting that Ethiopia is one of the few African countries from which the US government allows direct flights to and from the USA.) There are also **Air Botswana** (*www. airbotswana.co.bw*) flights between Gaborone and Lusaka twice a week, on Wednesday and Sunday, and weekly flights between Luanda and Lusaka every Saturday, operated by **TAAG** (*www.taag.com*). **Emirates** (*www.emirates.com*) have daily flights to and from Dubai, with connections in Dubai onto a wide variety of destinations in Europe, North America, India and Asia.

Low-cost airlines are breaking into the scene with newcomer **fastjet** (*www.fastjet. com*) – based in Tanzania and under the same ownership as British airline easyJet – connecting Lusaka with Dar es Salaam.

The only Zambian airline operating within the region is **Proflight** (*proflight-zambia.com*), which has three flights a week from Lusaka to Durban, and to Johannesburg.

From North America If you are coming from the US, you will probably need to stop in London, Johannesburg or Dubai to make connections to Zambia. There are no direct flights. Booking everything in the US may not save you money; investigate the flight prices in comparison with those available in London. Increasingly visitors from America are discovering that UK operators offer better-value safaris than their competitors in America. So consider buying a cheap ticket across the Atlantic, and then organising your Zambian trip through a reliable UK operator.

OVERLAND Most overland border posts open from about 06.00 to 18.00, although this is less rigidly adhered to at the smaller, more remote posts. The paperwork required can be lengthy and time consuming, so allow plenty of time – and in some cases, such as at Kazungula on the border with Botswana, several hours.

To/from South Africa or Namibia The South African Intercape Mainliner (*www.intercape.co.za*) has a regular bus between Windhoek and Livingstone/ Victoria Falls.

CR Holdings (📞 *0211 286255, 221784, 225633*; 📱 *0978 960517, 621148*, e *crholdingslimited@gmail.com*) operates a service between Lusaka and Johannesburg every Monday, Wednesday and Friday.

For self drivers, there is a high-level bridge across the Zambezi at Sesheke (page 462).

To/from Zimbabwe Zambia's greatest flow of visitors comes from Zimbabwe, over the Livingstone–Victoria Falls border. Many visitors come for just a day trip and locals come to shop, so this is usually a very relaxed and swift border crossing. The crossings over the Kariba Dam and at Chirundu are also straightforward, and the latter is especially good for hitchhiking on long-distance lorries, which ply the route from Harare to Lusaka.

To/from Botswana Despite their territories only meeting at a point, Botswana does have one border crossing with Zambia: a reliable if somewhat chaotic ferry across the Zambezi linking Kazungula with the corner of Botswana, which costs about US$25. Long-standing rumours of a bridge at this point look as though they may now be coming to fruition, though it's likely to be many years before it materialises.

To/from Angola Parts of northern Angola are still not regarded as safe to visit, so do check with the Foreign and Commonwealth Office (*www.fco.gov.uk*) if you're planning to use this route. The easiest border post with Angola is near Chavuma, northwest of Zambezi town. Elsewhere in western Zambia there is a danger of accidentally wandering into Angola, as the border has few markings.

To/from Democratic Republic of Congo (formerly Zaire) There are numerous crossings between Zambia and the DRC, especially around the Copperbelt. Otherwise there is a good track leading into DRC reached via Mwinilunga and Ikelenge. However, the DRC remains an unstable and potentially dangerous place to visit; you should check on the latest security situations before crossing the border, and be careful not to stray across by accident if you're in the Copperbelt region or heading east near Mkushi.

To/from Tanzania Many visitors from Tanzania enter Zambia by ferryboat across Lake Tanganyika into Mpulungu. The main alternative is the land border, either by road crossing or by Tanzania Zambia Railway Authority (TAZARA) train, crossing east of Tunduma. See *Chapter 13*, and the section on *Kapiri Mposhi* (pages 388–90), for more details of TAZARA's important rail link between Zambia and Dar es Salaam. There should also be good hitchhiking opportunities as there are plenty of long-distance lorries plying the route, as well as Zambian drivers picking up Japanese cars in Dar es Salaam.

To/from Malawi The main crossing between Zambia and Malawi is east of Chipata. This would also be the swiftest way to reach the Nyika Plateau, as the roads in Malawi are better than those to Nyika in Zambia.

To/from Mozambique There is a land crossing between Zambia and Mozambique south of Katete, which itself is southwest of Chipata, though this is not often used. A more common route would be via Malawi or Zimbabwe.

RED TAPE

VISAS AND ENTRY REQUIREMENTS Zambia's visa rules appear, on reading them, to be very complex, so it is probably essential to ask at your nearest Zambian embassy or high commission (*www.zambiaimmigration.gov.zm*), as they will know the latest news and how the rules are generally being interpreted.

Most visitors, including nationals of Great Britain and the USA, require a visa to enter Zambia. The current fee is US$50 for single entry and US$80 for a double entry, regardless of nationality. However, those staying for less than 24 hours – for example in transit to Botswana from Livingstone Airport – pay just US$20.

Most visas can be obtained on arrival at border posts on payment of the correct fee in US dollars cash, online from www.evisa.zambiaimmigration .gov.zm, or overseas from your local Zambian diplomatic mission. Applications for multiple-entry visas (*also US$80 pp*) must be made in advance at the nearest Zambian embassy or high commission (below). You must have at least six months left on your passport, and at least three blank pages. You may also be asked to show an onward ticket, or at least demonstrate that you can support yourself as you pass through the country (credit cards are invaluable), but this is unusual.

In 2014 a year-long trial started, offering travellers to both Zambia and Zimbabwe a dual visa, known as the KAZA Univisa, with 40 countries being eligible to receive one on arrival for a cost of US$50. This was available from Livingstone, Lusaka, Harare and Victoria Falls airports, and also from the land borders at Kazungula (with Botswana), and Victoria Falls, although acquiring one was less reliable here. The visa lasted 30 days, provided that you stayed within Zambia and Zimbabwe, and allowed 24 hours in Botswana. The visa expired in late 2015 after the trial period ended, but it is hoped that it will be reinstated permanently in order to make cross-border travel between the two countries much easier and cheaper. There are longer term plans to extend it to include all southern African countries.

In the 1980s, during KK's rule, visitors were routinely treated with suspicion but nowadays the prevailing attitude amongst both the government and the people is very welcoming. Visitors are seen as good for the country because they spend valuable foreign currency; if you look respectable you should not have any difficulty entering Zambia.

Visa extensions Visas can be extended by personal application to the Immigration Office in Lusaka (*Kent Bldg, Haile Selassie Rd*; ✎ *0211 251725/252669*; m *0955 659493, 0962 172550, 0971 718499*; e *zambiavisa@zambiaimmigration.gov.zm*; *www. zambiaimmigration.gov.zm*). You'll need two completed application forms (each with a passport photo), a valid passport and proof of sufficient funds to cover your stay. If it's a business application then you'll also need an explanatory letter with some good reasons. Your application will take at least three working days to process.

Zambia's diplomatic missions abroad The following is a selection of Zambia's embassies and high commissions. For a complete list, see www.zambiaimmigration. gov.zm/index.php/missions. For foreign embassies in Zambia, see page 141.

Angola (embassy) PO Box 1496, Luanda; ✎ 0222 441763; e zamemblua@netangola.com
Belgium (embassy) 469 Av Molière, 1050 Brussels; ✎ 02 343 5649; e zambianbrussels@ brutele.be; www.zebru.org
Botswana (high commission) PO Box 362, Gaborone; ✎ 0385 1951, 0395 3952; e zambico@ mega.bw
Canada (high commission) 151 Slater St, Suite 205, Ottawa, Ontario K1B 5H3; ✎ 0613 232 4400/4410; www.zambiahighcommission.ca

China (embassy) Dongsijie, San Li Tun, Beijing; ✎ 065 321554
Democratic Republic of Congo (embassy) BP 1144, Kinshasa; ✎ 09 999437; e amcazambia@ ic.cd
Ethiopia (embassy) PO Box 1909, Addis Ababa; ✎ 011 371 1302; e za.emb@telecom.net.et
France (embassy) 63 rue Pierre Charron, 75003 Paris; ✎ 01 56 88 12 72
Germany (embassy) Axelspringerstr 54A, 10117 Berlin; ✎ 030 206 2947; e zambianbonn@t-online.de

India (high commission) C-79 Anand Niketan, New Delhi; ☏0112 410 1289/1520; e zambiand@nde.vsnl.net

Italy (embassy) Via Ennio Quirino Visconti 8, 00193 Rome; ☏0636 006903/002590/088824; www.zambianembassy.it

Japan (embassy) PO Box 1 738, Tokyo 142-0063; ☏33 491012

Kenya (high commission) PO Box 48741, Nairobi; ☏020 724796/710664; e zambiacom@swiftkenya.com

Malawi (high commission) PO Box 30138, Lilongwe 3; ☏01 772635/772114; e zambia@malawi.net

Mozambique (high commission) PO Box 4655, Maputo; ☏021 492452/493292; e zhcmmap@zebra.uem.mz

Namibia (high commission) PO Box 22882, Windhoek; ☏061 237610/228162; e zahico@iway.na

South Africa (high commission) PO Box 12234, Pretoria; ☏012 326 1847/1897; e hc@zambiapretoria.net; www.zambiapretoria.net

Sweden (embassy) Gardsvagen 18, Box 3056, SE-169 03 Solna; ☏08 679 9040; www.zambiaembassy.se

Tanzania (high commission) PO Box 2525, Dar es Salaam; ☏022 212 5529; e zhcd@raha.com

UK (high commission) 2 Palace Gate, London W8 5NG; ☏020 7589 6655, 7581 0546; www.zambiahc.org.uk

USA (embassy) 2200 R St, NW Washington, DC 20008; ☏202 265 9717; www.zambiaembassy.org

Zimbabwe (embassy) PO Box 4698, Harare; ☏04 773777/82; e zambiae@mweb.co.zw

WHAT TO TAKE

This depends on how you intend to travel and exactly where you are going. If you are flying in for a short safari holiday then you need not pack too ruthlessly – provided that you stay within your weight allowance. However, note that smaller, privately chartered planes may specify a maximum weight of 10–12kg for hold luggage, which must be packed in a soft, squashable bag. Once you see the stowage spaces in a small charter plane, you'll understand the importance of not bringing along large or solid suitcases.

If you are backpacking then weight becomes much more important, and minimising it becomes an art form. Each extra item must be questioned: is its benefit worth its weight?

If you have your own vehicle then neither weight nor bulk will be as vital, and you will have a lot more freedom to bring what you like. Here are some general guidelines.

CLOTHING For most days all you will want is light, loose-fitting cotton clothing. Pure cotton, or at least a cotton-rich mix, is cooler and more absorbent than synthetic materials, making it more comfortable in the heat. A squashable hat and a robust pair of sunglasses with a high UV-absorption are essential.

No matter what your plans, you'll need something warmer, such as a thick fleece, for evenings during the cooler winter months – roughly from April until August. And in the rainy season, don't forget an umbrella if you want to avoid getting drenched; a waterproof jacket, while occasionally useful, is rarely up to the task.

Zambia's dress code is generally conservative. For men, shorts (not too short) are fine in the bush, but long trousers are more socially acceptable in towns and villages. (You will rarely see a respectable black Zambian man wearing shorts outside a safari camp.) For women, a knee-length skirt, culottes or loose trousers are ideal. A woman wearing revealing clothing in town implies that she is a woman of ill repute, whilst untidy clothing suggests a poor person, of low social standing.

These rules are redundant at safari camps, where dress is casual, and designed to keep you cool and protect skin from the sun. Green, khaki and dust-brown cotton

Before you read this tale, it must be emphasised that the overwhelming majority of lodges and their owners in Zambia are honest and reliable, with a real commitment to good practice and responsible tourism. The events described below refer to an extreme exception, rather than the rule. Dave and Louise tell me it's a true account, and only the names have been changed.

The story revolves around a young English couple – Dave and Louise – who fell in love with Africa on holiday. Nothing unusual there. Further trips heightened their affection, until the two were dreaming of swapping their England life for a new life in Africa. Neither being doctors, engineers or teachers – the professions needed most in Africa – their chances of employment seemed meagre. Until, that is, they met Stuart.

Stuart was a South African with fingers in many pies, including the construction of a safari camp. He didn't have time to supervise this, but – with their qualifications in business, finance and management, and with David also a professional chef – it seemed that Louise and David were the answer to his prayers, and vice versa. Before long, the pair had taken a year off, with a view to a permanent move if things worked out, packed their bags and flown to Zambia to oversee the building work. With qualified local builders, the couple's lack of knowledge of construction didn't seem to be a problem.

Initially, Dave and Louise had agreed to work for free, with a view to managing the camp when it was finished. Stuart promised that they would be provided with a 4x4, radio communication, a weapon, food, fuel and a tent at the camp/construction site. However, when the pair were finally dumped at the camp, 90km from the nearest town, things began to look a little less rosy. A few days after arriving, the owners of a nearby lodge warned them that Stuart was not a man to be trusted.

True, they were in the heart of Africa, in an idyllic spot overlooking the Zambezi with an abundance of the local fauna, including elephants, hippos, hyenas, lions,

---

is *de rigueur* at the more serious camps (especially those offering walking trips) and amongst visitors out to demonstrate how well they know the ropes. The same cognoscenti are usually to be found wearing old and well-worn items, rather than anything straight out of the box; charity shops in the UK can be a great source of safari wear! At the less serious camps you'll see a smattering of brighter-coloured clothes amongst many dull bush colours, the former usually worn by first-time visitors who are less familiar with the bush. On a practical note, women may want to consider a sports bra for safaris in bumpy game-drive vehicles.

Note that washing is done daily at virtually all safari camps, so few changes of clothes are necessary.

FOOTWEAR If you plan to do much walking, either on safari or with a backpack, then lightweight walking boots (with ankle support if possible) are essential. This is mainly because the bush is not always smooth and even, and anything that minimises the chance of a twisted ankle is worthwhile. Secondly, for the nervous, it will reduce still further the minute chance of being bitten by a snake, or other creepy-crawly, whilst walking.

Because of the heat, take the lightest pair of boots you can find – preferably canvas, or a breathable material such as Gore-tex. Leather boots are too hot in October, but thin single-skin leather is bearable for walking in July and August.

leopards, snakes and even the odd poacher for company. However, the promised vehicle, weapon and radio communication all failed to materialise, and the allowance to pay for their upkeep proved entirely inadequate. They were not even given enough to cover the cost of the building materials, or to buy sufficient food. Trips back to the city to see Stuart proved fruitless – he always seemed to be 'away on business'.

Though their dreams were crumbling, Dave and Louise remained determined, and resourceful. They set up an impromptu campsite to raise cash, and with the income generated they bought food to supplement the fish that Dave caught from the Zambezi.

Details were sketchy, but what Louise and Dave found out about Stuart wasn't proving positive. It involved allegations of smuggling: cobalt, diamonds and even ivory were mentioned. Stuart appeared to be using three different aliases, each with a different passport. The final straw came when a group of besuited heavies arrived at the camp, demanding money for their involvement with the 'big bwana' – Stuart's nickname. Dave and Louise successfully sent them away, but next time the couple visited Lusaka, they were arrested at a roadblock and had their visas revoked. It seemed that Stuart was behind this too. The pair were now visa-less and without work permits. They eventually fled Zambia, poorer, perhaps more cynical – but infinitely wiser.

Looking back, Dave doesn't regret the experience. He's philosophical, preferring to concentrate more on the positive aspects of the whole farrago, and the opportunity it gave them to live in the wilds of the world's most beautiful continent. Their decision to leave their jobs merely for a year proved to be a good one, and as Dave wrote at the end of his letter: 'I sincerely hope that our experience will act as some kind of warning to anyone else who is looking for the same dream.'

Never bring a new pair, or boots that aren't completely worn in. Always pack several pairs of thin socks – two thin pairs of socks are more comfortable than one thick pair, and will help to prevent blisters.

CAMPING EQUIPMENT If you are on an organised safari, then even a simple bushcamp will mean walk-in chalets with linen, mosquito nets and probably an en-suite shower and toilet. However, if you're planning any camping, then note that little equipment is available in Zambia, and see *Camping equipment* (pages 102–3) for ideas of what to take.

ELECTRICAL ITEMS The local voltage is 220V, delivered at 50Hz. Sockets fit plugs with three square pins, like the current design in the UK. Even the most remote safari camp nowadays can usually arrange for you to charge a camera battery, but if this is important, do make sure to check facilities in advance.

OTHER USEFUL ITEMS Obviously no list is comprehensive; only travelling will teach you what you need, and what you can do without. Here are a few of my own favourites and essentials, just to jog your memory.

For visitors embarking on an organised safari, camps will have most things but useful items include:

- Sunblock and lipsalve – for vital protection from the sun
- Binoculars – totally essential for game viewing
- A small pocket torch (see *Camping equipment*, pages 102–3)
- 'Leatherman' tool – never go into the bush without one, but always pack it in your check-in bag; never in your hand luggage
- A small water bottle, especially on flights (see *Camping equipment*, pages 102–3)
- Electrical insulating tape – remarkably useful for general repairs
- Camera – long lenses are vital for good shots of animals
- Basic sewing kit – with at least some really strong thread for repairs
- Cheap waterproof watch (leave expensive ones, and jewellery, at home)
- Couple of paperback novels
- Large plastic 'bin-liner' (garbage) bags, for protecting luggage from dust
- Simple medical kit (page 84) and insect repellent

And for those driving or backpacking, useful extras are:

- Concentrated, biodegradable washing powder
- Long-life candles (Zambian candles are often soft, and burn quickly)
- Nylon 'paracord' – bring at least 20m for emergencies and washing lines
- Hand-held GPS navigation system, for expeditions to remote areas
- Good compass and a whistle
- More comprehensive medical kit

WHAT NOT TO TAKE There are several things worth leaving behind. In particular, avoid anything which looks military; wearing camouflage patterns anywhere in Africa is asking for trouble. You are very likely to be stopped by the genuine military, or at least the police, who may assume that you are a member of some militia – and question exactly what you are doing in Zambia. Few will believe that this is a fashion statement elsewhere in the world.

Even if you're going on the most expensive of safaris, leave any jewellery that you don't usually wear all day, every day, at home. It'll take a load off your mind not to have to worry about its security.

MAPS AND NAVIGATION

MAPS For general purposes, there are several reasonable road maps of Zambia, of which the best is currently the 1:1,500,000 sheet published in Germany by **Ilona HupeVerlag**, and available at bookshops in Lusaka. In addition to good road and topographical detail, it features fuel stations, campsites and GPS co-ordinates – though the last (and the distances) aren't always entirely reliable. There are also inset overview maps of Lusaka and Livingstone, and the major national parks.

Other commercially produced maps, available both in Zambia and overseas, include those published by International Travel Maps, Globetrotter (New Holland), both at 1:1,500,000, and Macmillan (1:2,200,000). The **International Travel Map** shows contours and the parks, with surrounding text boxes covering topics from wildlife to Zambia's history and geography. Road detail is good, with many of the pontoons (flat, open-sided ferry boats) carefully marked, though coverage of the main points of tourist interest is less detailed. The illustrated **Globetrotter** map incorporates several regional and national park maps at a larger scale, as well as town plans of Livingstone and Lusaka, and climate charts. The smaller-scale **Macmillan** map is less detailed, but better at marking the points of interest for visitors, and on the reverse are many excellent 'inset' maps of the main parks, plus plans of Lusaka and Livingstone.

For **more detail**, Zambia has an excellent range of 'Ordnance Survey'-type maps available cheaply in Lusaka, from the Ministry of Lands in Mulungushi House (page 120). A wide range of maps is kept here, including the useful 1:250,000 series, a number of town plans, some 'tourist' maps of the parks – including an excellent 1989 map of South Luangwa's landscape and vegetation – and many more detailed maps of selected areas. Some are always out of print, and many are out of date – but you can usually find at least some sort of map to cover most areas. If you are planning to drive yourself around, then buy the maps for your trip at the start.

Navigation by any of these maps becomes more difficult as your location becomes more remote, when expecting any of them to be entirely accurate is unrealistic. Thus if you're heading into the wilds, get what maps you can and compare them with reality as you go.

Many overland travellers with a GPS (see below) would be lost – sometimes quite literally – without **Tracks4Africa** (*www.tracks4africa.com*), a digital mapping software package that covers the whole continent. More prescriptively, **Open Africa** (*www.openafrica.org*) is a non-profit organisation linking a network of tourism routes across the continent, including several in Zambia, with the aim of encouraging visitors to explore further afield and to benefit local communities.

GPS SYSTEMS If you are heading into one of the more remote parks in your own vehicle, then consider investing in a small GPS: a global positioning system. These can fix your latitude, longitude and elevation to within about 10m, using a network of American military satellites that constantly pass in the skies overhead. They will work anywhere on the globe.

What to buy Commercial hand-held GPS units cost from around US$150/£80 in Europe or the USA. As is usual with high-tech equipment, their prices are falling and their features are expanding as time progresses.

I have been using a variety of Garmin GPS receivers for years now. The early ones ate batteries at a great rate and often took ages to 'fix' my position; more recent models not only have endless new functions and far better displays, but also use fewer batteries, fix positions much more quickly, and usually even work when sitting on the car's dashboard. Whatever make you buy, you don't need a top-of-the-range machine.

A GPS should enable you to store 'waypoints' and build a simple electronic picture of an area, as well as working out basic latitude, longitude and elevation. So, for example, you can store the position of your campsite and the nearest road, making it easier to be reasonably sure of navigating back without simply retracing your steps. This can be invaluable in remote areas with lots of bush and no signposts, but it comes with a warning: a GPS takes no account of bends in the road, or indeed of natural hazards, so both directional arrows and distances may appear to be misleading at times.

Although a GPS may help you to recognise your minor errors before they are amplified into major problems, note that it is no substitute for good map work and navigation. Try not to rely on it too much, or you will be unable to cope if it fails, and always have a back-up plan in case it stops working. Note, too, that all these units use lots of battery power, so bring spares with you and/or a cigarette-lighter adaptor.

GPS positions in this book You'll note that I've given almost all of the GPS locations in this book a six-letter name. These were simply the names that I assigned to them in my system, as I recorded them, and I've used them throughout for ease of reference. All GPS co-ordinates have been expressed as degrees, minutes, and decimal fractions of a minute.

I hope that their inclusion may enable more adventurous and experienced readers to venture safely out to Zambia's lesser-known corners, although my points don't remove the need to take up-to-date local advice on safety and conditions.

Important note For all the GPS co-ordinates in this book, note that the datum used is WGS 84; you must set your receiver accordingly before copying in any of these co-ordinates. Many maps in Zambia used the ARC 1950 datum – so you should expect a slight discrepancy between points estimated from such maps, and your GPS unit.

PHOTOGRAPHY AND OPTICS

Don't expect to find any reasonably priced or reasonably available optical equipment in Zambia – so bring everything that you will need with you.

Pictures taken around dawn and dusk will have the richest, deepest colours, whilst those taken in the middle of the day, when the sun is high, will seem pale and washed-out by comparison. Beware of the very deep shadows and high contrast that are typical of tropical countries – cameras just cannot capture the range of colours and shades that our eyes can. If you want to take pictures in full daylight, and capture details in the shadows, then you will need a good camera, and to spend some time learning how to use it fully. By restricting your photography to mornings, evenings and simple shots you will get better pictures and encounter fewer problems.

The bush is very dusty, so bring plenty of lens-cleaning cloths, and a blow-brush. Take great care not to get dust into the back of any camera, as a single grain on the back-plate can be enough to make a long scratch which ruins every frame taken.

CAMERA INSURANCE Most travel insurance policies are poor at covering valuables, including cameras. If you are taking valuable camera equipment abroad, then include it in your house insurance policy, or cover it separately with a specialist.

BINOCULARS For a safari holiday, especially if you are doing much walking, a good pair of binoculars is essential. They will bring you far more enjoyment than a camera, as they make the difference between merely seeing an animal or bird at a distance, and being able to observe its markings, movements and moods closely. Do bring one pair per person; one between two is just not enough.

There are two styles: the small 'pocket' binoculars, perhaps 10–12cm long, which account for most modern sales, and the larger, heavier styles, double or triple that size, which have been manufactured for years. Both styles vary widely in cost and quality. If you are buying a pair, then consider getting the larger style. The smaller ones are fine for spotting animals, but are difficult to hold steady, and very tiring to use for extensive periods. You will only realise this when you are out on safari, by which time it is too late.

Around 8 x 30 is an ideal size for field observations, as most people need some form of rest, or tripod, to hold the larger 10 x 50 models steady. Get the best-quality ones you can for your money. The cheapest will be about £40/US$60, but to get a reasonable level of quality spend at least £250/US$400. If you use binoculars regularly, as against for just one holiday, then try to stretch your budget above the £500/US$900 barrier. Once you do this, makes like Swarovski, Zeiss and Leica, which are considerably better than cheaper models, come within reach – and will hugely enhance your experience of viewing wildlife.

MONEY AND BUDGETING

CURRENCY Zambia's unit of currency is the kwacha (K), which was 'rebased' on 1 January 2013. At that time, the new Zambian kwacha replaced the old at a rate of 1 new kwacha to 1,000 old kwacha. At the same time, three new coins were introduced, in denominations of one kwacha, and 10 and 50 ngwee.

Theoretically each kwacha is divided into 100 ngwee, although until the introduction of the new currency, one ngwee was worth so little that these subdivisions were never used. Today, although almost all currency still comes in the form of notes, there are three new coins, in denominations of one kwacha, 50 ngwee and 10 ngwee.

EXCHANGE RATES Over the years, the kwacha has devalued steadily in line with the country's inflation rate. Then, in the last decade or so, the rate of devaluation slowed and it became more stable. The old practices of strict exchange control and unrealistic exchange rates were gone – as was the black market for currency that these policies created. As the kwacha strengthened, hotels and lodges were expected to quote their prices in kwacha, rather than the US dollar, and in 2012, payment in US dollars and other foreign currency were no longer permitted until, following fierce lobbying by many businesses, including those in the tourism sector, the decision was revoked in 2013. International-based organisations may now accept payment in US dollars, South African rand and euros.

During 2015, however, with Zambia suffering from the impact of plunging commodity prices, pressure on the currency has resulted in a sharp fall in the value of the kwacha, making US dollar prices a more stable gauge for visitors.

Despite this, payments made in Zambia, except to tourism providers, are most likely to be made in kwacha. Thus prices in this guide are generally given in kwacha, with those quoted in US dollars usually for lodges and operators whose clientele comes primarily from overseas and pays in one of the international currencies.

Where sterling and US dollar equivalents are given in this guide, I have assumed a notional rate of around £1 for K11.50, or US$1 for K7.50, corresponding to rates that prevailed in June 2015, though bear in mind that the value of the kwacha fell rapidly in late 2015. In April 2016 exchange rates against the kwacha were:

£1 = K13.17
US$1 = K9.22
€1 = K10.44
ZAR1 = K0.64

BUDGETING Zambia is not a cheap country to visit, especially if you want to see some of the national parks. This isn't because of high park fees: on the contrary, US$5–40/£3.50–25 per day is reasonable by African standards. Rather, costs are high because most safari camps are small and seasonal, and their supply logistics are difficult and costly. However, you do generally get what you pay for: camps in remote locations and pristine environments tend to set very high standards.

To make up a trip using such camps, which are the easiest and most practical way for visitors to Zambia, budget for an all-inclusive cost of about US$300–1,000/£200–670 per person per day when staying in a camp. Internal flights cost varying amounts, but US$260/£175 per leg would be a good approximation.

At the other end of the spectrum, if you travel through Zambia on local buses, camping and staying in the occasional local (sometimes seedy) resthouse, then Zambia is not expensive. A budget of US$40–60/£20–30 per day for food, accommodation and transport would suffice. However, most backpackers who undertake such trips are simply 'in transit' between Malawi and Zimbabwe. They see little of Zambia's wildlife or its national parks, missing out on even its cheaper attractions.

If you have your own rugged 4x4 with equipment *and* the experience to use it, then you will be able to camp and cook for yourself, which can cut costs for four people down to around US$35–50/£25–35 per person per day including camping and park fees, but excluding fuel (which is expensive in Zambia). However, to hire such a vehicle and supply it with fuel would cost upwards of another US$60/£40 per person per day.

The cost of food depends heavily on where you buy it, as well as what you buy. If you can shop in Lusaka or one of the bigger towns for your camping supplies then you will save money and have a wider choice than elsewhere. Imported foods are inevitably more expensive than locally produced items. If you are sensible, then US$12–25/£8–16 per day would provide the supplies for a good, varied diet, including the odd treat. In any event, it will be cheaper than eating out.

In Lusaka and the main cities the bigger hotels are about US$200–350/£135–233 for a double room, whilst a good guesthouse will cost around US$65–100/£45–65. Camping at organised sites on the outskirts of the cities is, again, a good bet if you have the equipment and transport. It will cost from around US$5/£3 per person per night.

Restaurant meals in the towns are still relatively inexpensive, although costs have risen in recent years: expect to pay US$15–30/£10–20 for a good evening meal, including a local beer or two. Imported beers are more expensive than local beer (which is perfectly adequate), and South African wines are more costly again.

European wines and spirits, as you might expect, are ridiculously priced (and so make excellent gifts if you are visiting someone here). You will pay well over US$110/£75 for a bottle of champagne in Lusaka!

Finally, do be aware that prices in Zambia – as anywhere else – can and do rise, as can VAT (which is currently 16%). Rates quoted in this guide were correct at the time of research in 2015, but many will change during the life of the guide, so please do be sensitive to any increases.

HOW TO TAKE YOUR MONEY Although both US dollars and UK pounds sterling are easily changed at a bank, in practice US dollars are far more useful to the visitor. You will normally need to have US dollars in cash to pay for visas at the border, and for any tax due at the airport, and they're usually required for national parks' fees, too. Occasionally you may be able to pay for the larger hotels and other services in US dollars (small-denomination notes) too, although this becomes less common away from the bigger towns, so don't rely on it.

If you're going to more offbeat locations, kwacha are essential – although in case of need, some places will accept cash in low denominations of US dollars. If you're driving yourself, however, it is crucial that you allow sufficient cash (in kwacha) to pay for fuel; with only one or two notable exceptions in Lusaka, credit cards will not be accepted, and neither will US dollars.

In addition to kwacha, I travel with mostly US$1, US$5, US$10 and US$20 bills (and a few £10 or £20 notes). Because of the risk of forgeries, people are sometimes suspicious of larger-denomination notes; conversely, some places offer a lower exchange rate for smaller-denomination notes. US$100 and even US$50 bills are often rejected in shops and even some banks.

In the Western Province near the Namibian border, South African rand may occasionally be accepted; elsewhere they're virtually useless.

Most of the larger hotels and shops, and some safari camps, accept the major **credit and debit cards** (Visa and MasterCard), but bear in mind that a 3–5% commission may be levied, so be sure to enquire, prior to using your card, about any charges. Don't expect to be able to pay park fees, or for fuel, by card. It is advisable to take at least two cards, ideally a Visa and a MasterCard, though note that many banks – with the notable exception of Stanbic – will accept Visa but not MasterCard. Do remember to notify your bank of your travel plans in advance of departure, in case of any attempted fraud (and thus a block on your account) while you're travelling.

Some travellers still prefer to take some of their money as **travellers' cheques.** While these may be preferable from a security point of view, as they are refundable if stolen, they are less flexible, and they cannot be used as cash as they are in the USA. (Note that Amex travellers' cheques are not always welcomed, and their charge cards are seldom of use in Zambia.)

CHANGING MONEY AND BANKING   Almost all banks will exchange US dollars, but to change foreign currency, receive bank drafts, or do any other relatively complex financial transactions, then banks in the larger cities (ideally Lusaka) are your best option. Typically, banking hours are around 08.30–15.30, Monday to Friday, although in smaller towns they may close earlier, or – crucially – be open only on certain days. A few of the bigger banks also open around 09.00–11.00 on Saturdays. Note that in 2015, Barclays announced that they plan to sell their branches in Africa, but no change is anticipated for at least two to three years.

ATMs are widely available in the major towns, but are not the norm elsewhere. Even where they do exist, they are not entirely reliable, so carry plenty of cash as a back up. At a number of banks (including Barclays, Standard Chartered and Stanbic) you can use European debit cards bearing the Maestro or Visa logo to withdraw cash, up to around K2,000 per day.

If you are changing money at one of the main banks, in Lusaka or Livingstone, there is minimal difference in the rates between travellers' cheques and pounds sterling or US dollars in cash. At a bureau de change, however, you'll usually get better rates for cash.

The once relatively wide 'black market' in foreign currency, with US dollars worth much more if changed surreptitiously with a shady (and illegal) street dealer rather than at a bank, was effectively wiped out when financial reforms enabled the kwacha to float at a free-market rate. Now the shady characters on the street who hiss 'Change money' as you pass are more likely to be conmen relying on sleight of hand than genuine money-changers. Give them a very wide berth.

TIPPING   Tipping is a difficult and contentious topic – worth thinking about carefully. Read the section on *Local payments*, page 110, and realise that thoughtlessly tipping too much is just as bad as tipping too little.

Faced with rising concern over wages, the Zambian government has introduced a compulsory 10% service charge to be added to all bills in tourism-related service industries, including lodges, hotels and restaurants. Elsewhere, ask locally what's appropriate; here I can give only rough guidance. Helpers with baggage might expect K1–2/US$0.25–0.50, someone looking after your car around K1.50–2.50/US$0.30–0.50, depending on the time you're away, whilst sorting out a problem with a reservation would be K4.50–12/US$1–2.50. Given that restaurants must now add a 10% service charge to the bill, it is difficult to decide whether or not you

4

should add anything further. Certainly for the most part it would not be the norm. Tipping a taxi driver is not normally expected.

At safari camps, tipping is not obligatory, despite the assumption from some visitors that it is. If a guide has given you really good service then a tip of about US$5–10 per day per guest would be a generous reflection of this. If the service hasn't been that good, then don't tip.

Always tip at the end of your stay, not at the end of each day or activity. Do not tip after every game drive. This leads to the guides only trying hard when they know there's a tip at the end of the morning. Such camps aren't pleasant to visit and this isn't the way to encourage top-quality guiding. It's best to wait until the end of your stay, and then give what you feel is appropriate in one lump sum.

However, before you do this find out if tips go into one box for all of the camp staff, or if the guides are treated differently. Ask the managers as you're about to leave. Then ensure that your tip reflects this – with perhaps as much again divided between the rest of the staff.

GETTING AROUND

BY AIR   For those who want to fly internally in Zambia, the number of possibilities is increasing. Although only Proflight operates a scheduled service, offering internet booking with payment by credit card, several other local companies provide very reliable charters. None of the others is featured on any of the global flight reservations systems, so outside of Zambia (and even inside sometimes) most travel agents won't have a clue about the intricacies of Zambia's internal flights. You are strongly advised to book your internal flights through an experienced tour operator, who uses them regularly. (As an aside, this means that if the airline goes bust the tour operator loses money; you don't.) If you want to arrange something whilst you are in Zambia, or need to get in touch with an airline in a hurry, see the contact details below and on pages 51–3.

The services that I have encountered are high-quality operations, so you need have few worries about safety. On the whole, the smaller charter operations are very reliable, and more flexible for individual passengers, than the larger airlines.

However, if you book an internal flight a long time in advance, be aware that its timings (and indeed existence) may change. Cancellation at short notice is unlikely, though taking a philosophical attitude towards this possibility would be wise. A good operator will always be able to make a back-up plan for you.

Note that internal flights are subject to both a US$16 **departure tax**. This cost is included in the ticket price for scheduled flights with Proflight, but will need to be paid in cash upon departure for any other company.

There are an increasing number of scheduled internal flights offered by Proflight (see below), but for other destinations you will have to **charter** your own plane. This isn't for the backpacker's budget, but if you plan to stay at private safari camps then short charters may be within your price range.

It's possible to charter planes seating from three passengers up to 29. Costs vary according to the size of plane, but you can expect to pay from around US$5.40 per kilometre for a single-engine plane seating 3–5 passengers. or US$8.40/km for a seven seater. Use these figures as a rough guide only, as the rates fluctuate significantly according to the route travelled, the individual companies and the (increasingly high) price of fuel. When making your calculations, remember to include any mileage to/from the aircraft's base, and when booking remember that tour operators who book these trips every day will be given much better rates than

ONE-WAY FLYING DISTANCES (KM)

	Bangweulu	Kafue	Kalabo	Kasanka	Livingstone	Zambezi	Lusaka	Mfuwe	Nchila	Shiwa Ng'andu
Bangweulu		490	885	70	810	410	435	235	650	185
Kafue (Lunga)	490		405	465	410	385	255	610	400	670
Kalabo	885	405		865	455	750	610	1,015	450	1,070
Kasanka	70	465	865		760	350	380	195	670	220
Livingstone	810	410	455	760		480	390	840	750	980
Zambezi (Jeki)	410	385	750	350	480		140	365	750	545
Lusaka	435	255	610	380	390	140		455	635	600
Mfuwe	235	610	1,015	195	840	365	455		860	230
Nchila	650	400	450	670	750	750	635	860		810
Shiwa Ng'andu	185	670	1,070	220	980	545	600	230	810	

individuals interested in a one-off charter. And if you do decide to charter, it's important to be aware that on most flights there is a maximum luggage allowance of 12kg per person (15kg on Proflight, or 20kg on a 12-passenger Caravan), to be carried in soft bags only.

For rough one-way distances, in kilometres, see box above.

Scheduled airlines

✈ **Proflight** 📞 0211 252476/252452/251550; m 0977 335563; e reservations@proflight-zambia.com; www.flyzambia.com. Proflight has regular scheduled flights linking Lusaka with Livingstone (*US$82–302*), Mfuwe (*US$112–326*) &, in season, the Lower Zambezi (*US$72–222*); all fares are pp one way. Other internal destinations are Ndola, Kitwe, Solwezi & Kasama, while international flights connect Lusaka with Johannesburg, Durban, Lilongwe & Luwumbashi.

Charter airlines

✈ **Proflight** In addition to its scheduled service, Proflight (see above) operates charter flights nationwide.

✈ **Royal Air Charters** m 0971 251493; e reservations@royalaircharters.com; www.royalaircharters.com. A relatively new company linked to Royal Zambezi Lodge on the Lower Zambezi.

✈ **Sky Trails** m 0967 867812/867840/867848; e reservations@skytrailszambia.com; www.skytrailszambia.com. Founded in 2003, Sky Trails operates throughout Zambia & neighbouring countries, with bases in Livingstone, Lusaka, Kafue NP & – in season – Kasanka NP. Their planes, seating between 3 & 8 passengers, include a sgl-engine C206, taking 4–5 passengers, & costing US$5.40/km, & they also have a helicopter. As experts in wildlife aerial surveys & anti-poaching work, they have high-wing aircraft that offer good views, a real boon for scenic flights.

✈ **Wilderness Air** 📞 0213 321578–80; m 0966 770485; e reservations@wilderness-air.com; www.wilderness-air.com. Operates all of Wilderness Safaris' flights & private charters into various lodges across Zambia.

BY RAIL There are two totally separate rail systems in Zambia: ordinary trains and TAZARA (Tanzania Zambia Railway Authority) trains. Zambia's **ordinary rail network** was privatised in 2003 and is now run by RSZ (Railway Systems of Zambia) on a 20-year contract – but only now is the system beginning to show indications of improvement. Passenger trains run on only one line, linking Livingstone with Lusaka; the journey north to the Copperbelt has for now been discontinued. Once painfully slow, and rarely used by travellers – one local described the journey as 'like signing a death warrant' – it is now a weekly overnight service and is relatively competitive with buses on the same route. For details, see page 119.

In contrast, the **TAZARA** service has long been very popular with backpackers. It connects Kapiri Mposhi with the Indian Ocean, at Dar es Salaam in Tanzania. This is a reliable international transport link which normally runs to time and is by far the fastest way between Zambia and Tanzania with the exception of flying. See *Kapiri Mposhi*, pages 388–90, for details of this useful service.

For rail aficionados, there's an occasional third option in the form of the luxury train operated by the South African Rovos Rail (\ *+27 12 315 8242;* e *reservations@ rovos.co.za; www.rovos.com*) between Cape Town and Dar es Salaam. It's a 15-day journey, crossing into Zambia at the Victoria Falls Bridge near Livingstone, and joining the TAZARA line at Kapiri Mposhi before entering Tanzania. Prices start from around US$11,850 per person sharing.

BY BUS AND COACH Zambia's **local buses** are cheap, frequent and a great way to meet local people, although they can also be crowded, uncomfortable and noisy. In other words they are similar to any other local buses in Africa, and travel on them has both its joys and its frustrations. In the main bus stations, there are essentially two different kinds: the smaller minibuses, and the longer, larger 'normal' buses. Both will serve the same destinations, but the smaller ones tend to go faster and stop less. They may also be a little more comfortable. Their larger relatives will take longer to fill up before they leave the bus station (because few buses ever leave before they are full), and then go slower and stop at more places. For the smaller, faster buses there is usually a premium of about 20% on top of the price. Be aware, too, that even buses said to be running to a timetable may not depart until they are full, so check carefully what service you can expect – and ideally take a look at the bus on which you'll be travelling too. A broken windscreen hints at poor overall maintenance.

Then there are a few **postbuses** which operate between the post offices in the main towns, taking both mailbags and passengers as they go. These conform to a more fixed schedule, and standards have improved in recent years. Tickets are booked in advance at the nearest post office. For details, see pages 118–19.

Various luxury **coach services** connect most major towns and the smaller towns in between. See individual chapters for details of those that are running at the time of writing.

BY TAXI Taxis are common and very convenient in Lusaka, Livingstone and the main towns of the Copperbelt, and are starting to appear in smaller towns; Tom Kok reports that even Kaoma has several taxis. (Elsewhere they are uncommon or don't formally exist.) They can be hailed in the street, though foreign travellers may be best advised to book one through a reliable source or through your hotel. Meters are non-existent, but all drivers should have typed sheets of the 'minimum' rates to and from various local places – though charges can be higher if their customers appear affluent. Rates should always be agreed before getting into the vehicle. If you are unsure of the route then rates per kilometre, or per hour, are easy to negotiate.

BY POSTBOAT Rather like the postbuses, postboats used to operate on the Upper Zambezi and the waters of Lake Bangweulu during the rainy season, transporting cargo, passengers and even vehicles. However, this service has now been subcontracted, with information sketchy and none too reliable, even at the individual ports themselves. For the most part it's best to ask advice locally.

DRIVING Driving in Zambia is on the left, based on the UK's model. However, the standard of driving is generally poor, matched only by the quality of the roads. Most roads in the cities, and the major arteries connecting these, are tar. These vary from silky-smooth recently laid roads, to pot-holed routes that test the driver's skill at negotiating a 'slalom course' of deep holes, whilst avoiding the oncoming traffic that's doing the same. Inconveniently, the smooth kind of road often changes into the holed variety without warning, so speeding on even the good tar is a dangerous occupation. Hitting a pot-hole at 40–60km/h will probably just blow a tyre; any faster and you risk damaging the suspension, or even rolling the vehicle.

As an additional hazard, even the tar roads are narrow by Western standards, often with steep sides designed to drain off water during the rains. As a result, it's all too easy, faced with a sharp bend or an oncoming lorry, to veer off the road, a fact borne out by the regular sight of a truck lying on its side in the ditch, or to damage the sump of the vehicle. Finally, watch out for speed humps that may occur without warning, even on major roads. You often find these at the entrance and exit of a town (Kapiri Mposhi, for example), but also sometimes as you approach a level crossing.

Away from the main arteries the roads are gravel or just dirt and usually badly maintained. During the dry season these will often need a high-clearance vehicle: a 4x4 is useful here, but not vital. (The exceptions are areas of western Zambia standing on Kalahari sand, which always require 4x4.) During the wet season Zambia's gravel roads are less forgiving, and they vary from being strictly for 4x4s to being impassable for any form of vehicle. Travel on anything except the tar roads is very difficult during the rains. For more details, and particularly if you intend to hire a vehicle, read the important section on driving in *Chapter 6*, pages 95–101.

Most overseas visitors may drive on a national licence for up to 90 days. Speed limits are 120km/h on main roads and 50km/h in towns, but there are significant local variations, particularly in the approach roads to Lusaka, where they tend to be strictly enforced. Beware of speed humps, often without warning, at the approach to a town or school, in both directions.

All vehicles should carry two warning triangles for use in case of an accident or breakdown (although you'll often see brushwood laid out on the road at strategic intervals for the same purpose). They should also display reflective tape: white at the front, and red at the rear. Failure to comply with these regulations may result in a fine.

Police (and immigration) roadblocks are an occupational hazard of driving, and you can expect to be stopped regularly. They are usually indicated in advance by oil drums or traffic cones placed in the middle of the road, but some are very poorly marked, so keep an eye out for them, and do stop! Note that driving using a mobile phone when at the wheel is illegal, and infringement of the drink-driving laws now incurs a mandatory prison sentence. For more on this subject, see *Chapter 6*, pages 96–7.

Fuel Availability of fuel can be a problem, so it is important to top up whenever you can rather than to let the tank run low. Fuel stations may be prominent in towns and cities, but they're thin on the ground outside major centres, and supplies can be erratic, especially in outlying areas.

Distances in kilometres (approx)
Note that distances between towns are only one part of the equation when calculating travelling times. More important are the type of road (tar, gravel, dirt), and the conditions, both of which must be taken into consideration.

	Chipata	Chirundu	Kapiri Mposhi	Kasama	Kitwe	Livingstone	**Lusaka**	Mansa	Mbereshi	Mongu	Mpika	Mporokoso	Mpulungu	Mwinilunga	Seseke	Solwezi
Chipata																
Chirundu	695															
Kapiri Mposhi	780	346														
Kasama	1475	996	644													
Kitwe	990	498	150	796												
Livingstone	1080	608	682	1332	834											
Lusaka	**560**	**136**	**210**	**860**	**362**	**472**										
Mansa	1400	926	650	350	800	1262	**790**									
Mbereshi	1600	1126	850	386	1000	1462	**990**	200								
Mongu	1210	760	834	1484	986	525	**624**	1414	1614							
Mpika	1269	839	493	221	643	1175	**703**	559	759	1327						
Mporokoso	1635	1156	804	160	954	1492	**1020**	307	181	1644	381					
Mpulungu	1679	1210	864	210	1014	1576	**1074**	517	560	1698	431	370				
Mwinilunga	1470	1020	674	1324	501	1356	**884**	1324	1524	780	1167	1478	1538			
Seseke	1260	741	872	1522	1024	190	**662**	1452	1652	335	1311	1682	1736	1115		
Solwezi	1210	744	398	1042	225	1080	**608**	1048	1248	896	891	1202	1262	292	1231	
Zambezi	1650	1156	810	1454	658	1150	**1020**	1460	1660	625	1303	1614	1674	396	960	515

The price of fuel is extremely high by southern African standards, which is largely a reflection of high government taxes. Despite the country's distance from the nearest port, transportation is less of an issue: crude oil is brought by pipeline from Dar es Salaam to Ndola, where it is refined then distributed both within Zambia and to the DRC. In the past, the cost of transporting the oil was reflected in widely varying prices, but the price that you'll pay at the pumps is now fixed by the energy authorities. In summer 2015, petrol cost K8.74/US$1.16 a litre, with diesel at K7.59/US$1. That said, in parts of the country, such as the Western Province, where supplies at the pumps often run dry, you could well find yourself paying far more to fill your tank on the black market.

Vehicle hire With difficult roads, which seem to vanish completely in some of the more remote areas, driving around Zambia away from the main arteries is not easy. The big car-hire firms do have franchises in Lusaka, but most concentrate on businesspeople who need transport around the city. Even now, some will insist that foreigners hiring cars also hire a chauffeur, and only the specialists are geared up for visitors in search of recreation.

Hiring a 2WD A mid-range model like a Ford Focus from, say, Europcar (*www.europcarzambia.com*) will cost around US$116/£77 per day with fully comprehensive insurance, 100km 'free' per day, and a 35¢/24p charge per kilometre after that. While this is an improvement on rates even a few years ago, just add up the distances on a map and you'll realise that it still isn't viable for most trips. Further, a standard saloon vehicle just wouldn't stand up to the pot-holes found on most of the main highways, never mind the state of the dirt tracks beyond, so for exploring beyond the major towns you'll be needing either a high-clearance 2WD or – better – a 4x4.

See *Car hire* in the chapters on Lusaka (page 121), Livingstone (pages 156–7), and the Copperbelt (pages 391, 402, 405 and 411) for contact details of the various car-hire agencies.

Hiring a 4x4 Until recently, it wasn't possible to hire reliable 4x4 vehicles in Zambia so the only option was to bring them in from outside, or arrange for a safari company to take you around on a mobile safari. While, this has changed, and there are now a few options within Zambia itself, it may still be cheaper to organise a vehicle through one of the specialists in South Africa or Namibia such as Britz (*www.britz.co.za*) or Kwenda Safari (*www.kwendasafari.co.za*).

That said, it's important to realise that self-drive trips around Zambia are not for the inexperienced; I think that they're suitable only for those who have previously taken several in Africa, including at least one self-drive 4x4 trip (a 4x4 trip around Botswana makes a perfect precursor). And if you have any doubts, read the box *Lessons in bush travel* on pages 270–1, then think hard about what you're planning. Bear in mind, too, that self-drive trips are expensive; it can often be cheaper to fly between major cities before collecting a vehicle.

There are a few obvious candidates for hiring a 4x4; the best choice depends on the route you're taking.

Safari Drive (page 45) If you're thinking of a self-drive trip around Zambia, then this UK-based company has a small fleet of Land Rover Defender 110 & Toyota Land Cruiser 79 vehicles based in Livingstone, from about £2,500 pp for a 14-day bespoke safari. All come extremely well equipped with practical & sturdy kit for bush camping, including long-range fuel tanks, rooftop tents,

If you drive carefully in Zambia, during the day, and stick to the speed limits and sensible speeds (maximum 100–120km/h on good tar, much less on gravel or pot-holed tar), then you should never have an accident here. However, traffic – especially around Lusaka – is increasing fast, and animals and people (especially cyclists) on the road can be a nightmare, so don't be shy about using your horn a lot, and well in advance, particularly in busy towns.

If you're unfortunate enough to be involved in an accident, you need to think clearly. If you've hit a dog, a goat or a chicken, then you do not have to stop. It would be courteous to compensate the owner – although you may end up in a heated situation which becomes very difficult. If you hit a wild animal, you should report it to the local ZAWA office, or police station. Always check the vehicle, too; if you have hit a goat, for example, the impact could damage the coolant system and cause a leak.

If you hit a person, then the accident must be reported. Your natural instinct will be to stop – but most Zambians will tell you that you should not to do so, for fear of being seriously assaulted by friends or relatives of the injured person. That said, if the person is injured then you may be able to help to get him or her to hospital. I've never had to make this choice, and hope I never have to. (Should you be in this situation, and decide to help, do remember to wear plastic gloves and glasses to minimise the risk of HIV infection, and don't attempt mouth-to-mouth resuscitation without a protective mask.) In any case, you must go directly to the nearest police station, or police roadblock. If a death has occurred then you will be expected to hand over your passport to the police.

In order to make an insurance claim in Zambia you will need to obtain a police report, for which you'll be expected to pay.

portable fridges & satellite phone, as well as the relevant paperwork for crossing any borders.
Hemingways (page 157) Limo Hire Zambia
m 0977 743145; e limohirezambia@gmail.com, info@limohire-zambia.com; www.limohire-zambia.com. From its base south of Lusaka, this company offers a wide range of vehicles, including 4x4 Toyota Land Cruisers with rooftop tents. Reports suggest that equipment is adequate if sometimes a little tired.

HITCHHIKING Hitchhiking is a practical way to get around Zambia – especially in the more remote areas. Most of Zambia's poorer citizens hitchhike, and view buses as just a different form of vehicle. Either way, lifts are normally paid for.

Hitching has the great advantage of allowing you to talk one-to-one with a whole variety of people, from local businesspeople and expats, to truck drivers and farmers. Sometimes you will be crammed in the back of a windy pick-up with a dozen people and as many animals, while occasionally you will be comfortably seated in the back of a plush Mercedes, satisfying the driver's curiosity as to why you are in Zambia at all. It is simply the best way to get to know the country, through the eyes of its people, though it is not for the lazy or those pressed for time.

Waiting times can be long, even on the main routes, and getting a good lift can take 6 or 8 hours. Generally, on such occasions, the problem is not that lots of potential vehicles refuse to take you. The truth is that there are sometimes very few people going your way with space to spare. If you are in a hurry then combining hitchhiking with taking the odd bus can be a quicker and more pragmatic way to travel.

The essentials for successful hitching in Zambia include a relatively neat, conservative set of clothes, without which you will be ignored by some of the more comfortable lifts available. A good ear for listening and a relaxed line in conversation are also assets, which spring naturally from taking an interest in the lives of the people that you meet. Finally, you must always carry a few litres of water and some food with you, both for standing beside the road, and for lifts where you can't stop for food.

Dangers of drink driving Unfortunately, drinking and driving is common in Zambia. It is more frequent in the afternoon/evening, and towards the end of the month when people are paid. Accepting a lift with someone who is drunk, or drinking and (simultaneously) driving, is foolish. Occasionally your driver will start drinking on the way, in which case you would be wise to start working out how to disembark politely.

An excuse for an exit, which I used on one occasion, was to claim that some close family member was killed whilst being driven by someone who had been drinking. Thus I had a real problem with the whole idea, and had even promised a surviving relative that I would never do the same ... hence my overriding need to leave at the next reasonable town/village/stop. This gave me an opportunity to encourage the driver not to drink any more; and when that failed (which it did), it provided an excuse for me to disembark swiftly. Putting the blame on my own psychological problems avoided blaming the driver too much, which might have caused a difficult scene.

Safety of hitchhiking Notwithstanding the occasional drunk driver, Zambia is generally a safe place to hitchhike for a robust male traveller, or a couple travelling together. It is safer than the UK, and considerably safer than the USA; but hitchhiking still cannot be recommended for single women, or even two women travelling together. This is not because of any known horror stories, but because non-Zambian women, especially white women, hitching would evoke intense curiosity amongst the local people. Local people might view their hitching as asking for trouble, whilst some would associate them with the 'promiscuous' behaviour of white women seen on imported films and television programmes. The risk seems too high. Stick to buses.

ACCOMMODATION

Zambia boasts the full range of accommodation, from top-class safari lodges and international hotels to simple guesthouses and campsites, with an equally diverse range of standards and prices. Pricing can appear complex at first, since many of the better establishments have a two- or even three-tier structure. Typically, there will be two rates: one for local visitors, the other for international guests. In some cases, the 'local' rate will be further divided into Zambian citizens and Zambian residents; in others, these two may be lumped together, but a further category introduced: visitors from within southern Africa.

Prices quoted in this guide are for the most part international rates – those payable by visitors from Europe, America and other Western countries. While prices were correct at the time of research, inevitably many will rise during the life of the guide.

HOTELS Traditionally, hotels in Zambia have tended to fall into two categories, all geared to the business market: large concrete blocks with pretensions to an 'international' standard, or small, run-down places catering to Zambians who are

ACCOMMODATION PRICE CODES

Rates at places to stay in this guide have been coded. For urban establishments, and others offering **B&B accommodation**, rates are based on the cost of a double room with breakfast. Single supplements average around 20%, but may be significantly higher. VAT may be charged extra.

B&B double

$$$$$	£165+; US$250+; K1,875+
$$$$	£100–165; US$150–250; K1,125–1,875
$$$	£50–100; US$80–150; K600–1,125
$$	£25–50; US$40–80; K300–600
$	up to £25; up to US$40; up to K300

For **all-inclusive** places, such as safari lodges and camps, rates are based on a double room including full board and activities (FBA).

LLLLL	US$2,000+; £1,330+
LLLL	US$1,300–2,000; £865–1,330
LLL	US$600–1,300; £400–865
LL	US$250–600; £165–400
L	up to US$250; up to £165

not very particular about quality. They're a very uninspiring bunch on the whole, and most visitors spend as little time in them as possible. Things started to change when Sun International opened two hotels near Victoria Falls in Livingstone in 2001, and since then other investors have seized the initiative. The South African Protea chain is gradually increasing its presence in Zambia, and such influences are impacting on standards nationwide.

The larger hotels are found mostly in Lusaka, Livingstone and the Copperbelt. They generally have clean modern rooms, good communications and all the facilities that international businesspeople expect. Their prices (increasingly dynamic) reflect this, at around US$140–325/£95–215 for a double room. Most still have little to distinguish them from each other, but again, this is changing, and in Lusaka, the odd specialist boutique hotel is adding to the mix.

Zambia's smaller and cheaper hotels vary tremendously, but very few are good and many seem over-priced.

GUESTHOUSES In the last few years Zambia's larger towns, and especially Lusaka, have seen a proliferation of small guesthouses of varying quality spring up throughout the more spacious suburbs. These are not very practical if you need a courtesy bus to the airport, room service, or a telephone beside your bed – but they are often full of character and can be good value. Expect them to cost US$$65–100/£45–65 for a double room, or upwards of US$40–60/£25–45 for a single. Typically rates will include a continental breakfast, which is usually just a roll or a couple of slices of bread and a cup of tea, but could be a substantial meal complete with eggs.

GOVERNMENT RESTHOUSES These are dotted around the country in virtually every small town: a very useful option for the stranded backpacker. The town or district council usually runs them and, although a few have degenerated into brothels, others are adequate for a brief overnight stop. Most have rooms with private facilities that are normally clean (as are the sheets), though rarely spotless or in mint condition.

LODGES AND BUSHCAMPS Zambia's lodges and bushcamps are a match for the best in Africa. As befits a destination for visitors who take their game viewing and birdwatching seriously, the camps are very comfortable but concentrate on good guiding rather than luxury *per se*. En-suite showers and toilets are almost universal, the accommodation is fairly spacious, the organisation smooth and food invariably good to excellent. However, a few forget that their reputations are won and lost by the standards of their individual guides.

Aside from a few larger lodges, you can usually expect a maximum of ten to 18 guests, and close personal care. But beware: if you seek a safari for its image, wanting to sleep late and then be pampered in the bush; or expect to dine from silverware and sip from cut-glass goblets ... then perhaps Zambia isn't for you after all.

FOOD AND DRINK

FOOD Zambia's native cuisine is based on *nshima*, a cooked porridge made from ground maize. (In Zimbabwe this is called *sadza*, in South Africa *mealie-pap*.) Nshima is usually made thin, perhaps with sugar, for breakfast, then eaten thicker – the consistency of mashed potatoes – for lunch and dinner. For these main meals it will normally be accompanied by some spicy relish, perhaps made of meat and tomatoes, or dried fish. Do taste this at some stage when visiting. Safari camps will often prepare it if requested, and it is always available in small restaurants in the towns. Often these will have only three items on the menu: nshima and chicken; nshima and meat; and nshima and fish – and they can be very good.

Camps, hotels and lodges that cater to overseas visitors serve a very international fare, and the quality of food prepared in the most remote bushcamps amazes visitors. Coming to Zambia on safari, your biggest problem with food is likely to be the temptation to eat too much.

If you are driving yourself around and plan to cook, it makes sense to stock up at a supermarket in Lusaka or one of the larger towns, where you'll find pretty well all that you will need. While supermarkets are beginning to put in an appearance in the smaller towns, supplies here may be limited to products that are popular locally. These include bread, flour, rice, soups and various tinned vegetables, meats and fish, though locally grown produce such as tomatoes, bananas, watermelon or

RESTAURANT PRICE CODES

Price codes are based on the average cost of a main course, which usually exclude VAT (currently 16%) and service of around 10%. For specialities such as seafood, you can expect to pay considerably more.

$$$$$	£9+; US$13+; K100+
$$$$	£7–9; US$10.50–13; K80–100
$$$	£5.50–7; US$8–10.50; K60–80
$$	£3.50–5.50; US$5–8; K40–60
$	up to £3.50; up to US$5; up to K40

RECIPE FOR FRIED TERMITES   *Judi Helmholz*

November typically marks the beginning of the rainy season in Zambia. The first rains bring vast swarms of termites out of their nests to find mates and reproduce. Termites are a once-a-year delicacy not to be missed for culinary adventurers. And capturing them is half the fun!

Termites are attracted to light, so it's easiest to catch them when they are swarming around in the evening. Get a large bowl and fill it with water. Catch live termites with your hand as they fly around and drop them into the water (which keeps them from flying or crawling out). Or you can wait until the morning and collect them off the ground after they have dropped their wings (then you don't have to pull the wings off yourself). Gather as many as you need, live ones only.

PREPARATION Remove any wings from termites and throw wings away. Place wingless termites in a colander or bowl and rinse them under running water. Heat a frying pan with a dash of cooking oil until sizzling temperature. Drop in live termites and sauté until they are crisp and golden brown (about one minute). Add salt to taste. Serve in a bowl as you would peanuts. *Bon appétit!*

sweet potatoes will be available in season. This is fine for nutrition, but you may get bored with the selection in a week or two.

DRINK
Alcohol
Like most countries in the region, Zambia has two distinct beer types: clear and opaque. Most visitors and more affluent Zambians drink the **clear beers**, which are similar to European lagers and best served chilled. Mosi, Castle and Carling Black Label are the lagers brewed by South African Breweries' Zambian subsidiaries. They are widely available and usually good.

Note that most beer produced in Zambia has a deposit on its bottles, like those of soft drinks. If you want to avoid this, buy non-returnable bottles or cans instead. The contents will cost about US$0.60/K7.50 from a supermarket, or around US$1.25/K15 in a hotel bar or restaurant. Imported lagers such as Windhoek, Holsten and Amstel may cost considerably more than this.

Less-affluent Zambians usually opt for some form of the **opaque beer** (sometimes called *chibuku*, after the market-leading brand). This is a commercial version of traditional beer, usually brewed from maize and/or sorghum. It's a sour, porridge-like brew, an acquired taste, and is much cheaper than lager. Locals will sometimes buy a bucket of it, and then pass this around a circle of drinkers. It would be unusual for a visitor to drink this, so try some and amuse your Zambian companions. Remember, though, that traditional opaque beer changes flavour as it ferments and you can often ask for 'fresh beer' or 'strong beer'. If you aren't sure about the bar's hygiene standards, stick to the pre-packaged brands of opaque beer like Chibuku, Chinika, Golden, Chipolopolo or Mukango.

A word of caution: if you're planning to drive, stay well clear of alcohol. Aside from the obvious safety reasons, drink-driving in Zambia carries a mandatory jail sentence.

Soft drinks
Soft drinks are available everywhere, which is fortunate when the temperatures are high. Choices are often limited, though the ubiquitous Coca-Cola is usually there at around US$1/K12 – perhaps a little cheaper in a supermarket,

and a little more in a decent café. Diet drinks are rarely seen in the rural areas – which is no surprise for a country where malnutrition is a problem.

Until recently, all soft drinks were sold in glass bottles, though increasingly plastic bottles are in use. If you're faced with glass, try to buy up at least one actual bottle (per person) in a city before you go travelling: it will be invaluable. Because of the cost of bottle production, and the deposit system (typically around US$0.30/K1,500 per bottle), you will often be unable to buy full bottles of soft drinks in rural areas without swapping them for empty ones in return. The alternative is to stand and drink the contents where you buy a drink, and leave the empty behind you. This is fine, but can be inconvenient if you have just dashed in for a drink while your bus stops for a few minutes.

Water Water in the main towns is usually purified, provided there are no shortages of chlorine, breakdowns or other mishaps. The locals drink it, and are used to the relatively innocuous bugs that it may harbour. If you are in the country for a long time, then it may be worth acclimatising yourself to it – though be prepared for some days spent near a toilet. However, if you are in Zambia for just a few weeks, then try to drink only bottled, boiled or treated water in town – otherwise you will get stomach upsets. Bottled water can be bought almost anywhere, although if you want it cold you may often find it's frozen! Expect to pay around US$0.60/K7 for a half-litre in a supermarket, more in a smaller outlet or garage.

Out in the bush, most of the camps and lodges use water from boreholes. These underground sources vary in quality, but are normally free from bugs so the water is perfectly safe to drink. Sometimes it is sweet, at other times a little alkaline or salty. Ask locally if it is suitable for an unacclimatised visitor to drink, then take their advice.

SHOPPING

CURIOS Zambia's best bargains are handicrafts: carvings and baskets made locally. The curio stall near Victoria Falls close to the Zimbabwean border has a good selection, but prices are lower if you buy away from tourist areas, in Lusaka (try Kabwata Cultural Centre, pages 144–5), or at some of the roadside stalls.

Wherever you buy handicrafts, don't be afraid to bargain gently. Expect an eventual reduction of about a quarter of the original asking price and always be polite and good-humoured. After all, a few cents will probably make more difference to the person with whom you are bargaining than it will mean to you.

Note that you will often see carvings on sale in the larger stalls which have been imported from Kenya, Tanzania, DRC and Zimbabwe. Assume that they would be cheaper if purchased in their countries of origin, and try to buy something Zambian as a memento of your trip.

Occasionally you will be offered 'precious' stones to buy – rough diamonds, emeralds and the like. Expert geologists may spot the occasional genuine article amongst hoards of fakes, but most mere mortals will end up being conned. Stick to the carvings if you want a bargain.

For a more practical and much cheaper souvenir get a *chitenje* for about K40–50 – there are shops in the smallest of towns. You will see these 2m-long sections of brightly patterned cotton cloth everywhere, often wrapped around local women. Whilst travelling use them as towels, sarongs, picnic mats or – as the locals do – simply swathed over your normal clothes to keep them clean. When back home, you can cut the material into clothes, or use them as wall-coverings or tablecloths. Either way, you will have brought a splash of truly African colour back home with you.

ABOUT CIGARETTES AND BEER   *Willard Nakutonga and Judi Helmholz*

There are several types of beer or *mooba* ('beer' in Nyanja) produced in Zambia. If you're after a bottle of the standard lager, such as Rhino, you can ask for it in Nyanja by saying '*Nifuna mooba wa Rhino*' – 'I want Rhino beer'. The cheaper opaque beer or *chibuku* is a favourite among more traditional Zambians. It is also known as Shake-Shake – appropriate since it resembles an alcoholic milkshake.

Don't confuse this with the main illicit beer, *kachusu* – akin to 'moonshine'. It is brewed in villages or at shebeens, and best avoided. Not only is it illegal, so you may be arrested just for drinking it, but it may also damage your liver and kidneys.

Cigarettes, or *fwaka* in Nyanja, can be purchased almost anywhere. In local markets, you can find big bins of raw tobacco, or tobacco shavings, for those who like to roll their own. The most popular cigarette brand available is Peter Stuyvesant, affectionately referred to as 'Peters'. Don't even think about trying *mbanje* or *dagga* (marijuana); if you're arrested there is no bail, and the penalty is five years in prison with hard labour.

Imports and exports There is no problem in exporting normal curios, but you will need an official export permit from the Department of National Parks to take out any game trophies. Visitors are urged to support the letter and the spirit of the CITES bans on endangered species, including the ban on the international trade in ivory. This has certainly helped to reduce ivory poaching, so don't undermine it by buying ivory souvenirs here. In any case, you will probably have big problems when you try to import them back into your home country.

SUPPLIES Since 1996, Zambia's shops have emerged from a retailing time-warp, where cramped corner shops had the monopoly. Until then, most of the country's residents were innocent of consumer-friendly hypermarkets where wide, ergonomically designed aisles are lined with endless choice. Then, in 1996, Shoprite/Checkers arrived, promoting a largely alien practice of high-volume, low-margin superstores using good levels of pay to reward honest employees. This rocked Lusaka's existing, mainly Asian, shop-owning community who had always gone for the high-margin corner-shop approach. Rumours were rife of the ways in which Shoprite's arrival was resisted, and even blocked by the capital's existing business community. Now, though, Shoprite has found a very solid footing, with stores in most of Zambia's major towns, and some smaller ones, that are normally the best and cheapest places to shop for supplies.

However, all is not rosy. To many it seems that while the state is dismantling many of its own monopolies, the private sector is being allowed to generate new ones. Several aggressive South African companies, such as Shoprite and Game, have moved into Zambia and their increasing dominance causes resentment from local businesspeople, who fear that they are losing out. Critics say the success of these is down to South Africa's policy of lucrative tax breaks, which effectively subsidise exports. They point to the import bills generated by such stores, which often source more of their stock from outside Zambia than from inside. However, supporters cite the increased availability of goods, and the small Zambian businesses that are improving their standards and starting to supply these stores.

Whatever the arguments, you can now buy most things in Zambia (and in kwacha) at a price, and if you have the money then this will seem like a good thing. Perhaps the best advice for the careful visitor is to try to buy Zambian products wherever possible, for the sake of the local economy.

COMMUNICATIONS AND MEDIA

POST The post is neither cheap nor fast, though it is fairly reliable for letters and postcards. It's worth noting that Zambia has some lovely stamps for sale, a favourite of stamp collectors.

The best way to send mail quickly within Zambia is via EMS (Expedited Mail Service), a reasonably priced service where letters are hand delivered (no postbox mail). It is also available to overseas destinations and is generally less expensive than a courier company. For express mail services, there are several choices, some of which also offer phone, fax and internet as well. With any you can send letters, parcels and small packets to destinations within Zambia and worldwide. This is costly but reliable. If you need important documents sent from overseas, couriers such as DHL or FedEx (pages 140 and 184 for contact details in Lusaka and Livingstone) are the quickest way to be assured of them reaching you safely. Packages take about a week from Europe or the USA.

Post offices in large towns are normally open Monday to Friday, 08.00–17.00, Saturday 08.00–12.30, but you can expect shorter hours in more out-of-the-way places.

TELEPHONE The Zambian telephone system, operated by Zamtel, is overloaded and has difficulty coping, despite an overhaul in 2007 and its more-recent privatisation. It is still common for companies to have several different numbers, although increasingly both business and personal users rely on mobile phones.

The old payphones may have given way to cardphones, but these too are increasingly hard to find, and those that remain are none too reliable. In theory, phonecards are available from Zamtel offices and other outlets from around K10. You can dial internationally from these, and there is no time limit placed on their use.

Telephone codes To dial into the country from abroad, the international access code for Zambia is +260. From inside Zambia, you dial 00 to get an international line, then the country's access code (eg: 44 for the UK, or 1 for the USA).

Since 2007, all regional codes have been prefixed with the numbers 021, each broadly incorporating the following towns:

0211	Central: Chilanga, Chirundu, Chisamba, Chongwe, Kafue, Luangwa, Lusaka, Mumbwa, Namalundu Gorge, Siavonga
0212	Copperbelt and Luapula: Chililabombwe, Chingola, Itimpi, Kalulushi, Kawambwa, Kitwe, Luanshya, Mansa, Masaiti, Mufulira, Mwense, Nchelenge, Ndola, Samfya
0213	South-central: Choma, Gwembe, Itezhi-Tezhi, Kalomo, Kazungula, Livingstone, Maamba, Mazabuka, Monze, Namwala, Pemba, Zimba
0214	Northeast: Chambeshi, Chinsali, Isoka, Kasama, Luwingu, Mbala, Mpika, Mporokoso, Mpulungu, Mungwi, Nakonde
0215	North-central: Chibombo, Kabwe, Kapiri Mposhi, Mkushi, Serenje
0216	East: Chadiza, Chama, Chipata, Katete, Lundazi, Mfuwe, Nyimba, Petauke
0217	West: Kalabo, Kaoma, Lukulu, Mongu, Senanga
0218	Northwest: Kabompo, Kasempa, Mufumbwe, Mwinilunga, Solwezi, Zambezi

When dialling from a landline within the same area, there is no need to dial the code. However, if – like most Zambians – you're using a mobile phone, then you *will* need to include the area code.

Mobile phones The use of mobile phones, or 'cells' as they're usually called in Zambia, has grown very rapidly to counter the problems with the country's still-unreliable landline network. Coverage is surprisingly widespread, although in rural areas you can expect it to be patchy at best, or non-existent. The major networks are Airtel (which has the widest coverage) and MTN, as well as the state-owned Zamtel. All Zambian mobile-phone numbers are prefaced 09, and consist of ten digits.

Top-up cards for each of the mobile networks are available in even the smallest towns, or from touts at major road junctions. If you're in the Livingstone area, be careful of picking up Zimbabwean networks, as prices may be based on official Zimbabwean exchange rates, and hence be much more expensive than their Zambian equivalents.

If you're planning to use your own mobile phone in Zambia, it's almost certainly going to be cheaper to buy a local SIM card for the duration of your visit. Note, however, that for security reasons, all SIM cards must now be registered, so allow plenty of time for this, and make sure you take along some form of ID, such as a passport. Expect to pay around K10 (about £1/US$1.50) for a SIM card, including K5 talk-time. As elsewhere, there are numerous packages, so do ask before you buy. Whatever you select, call charges to other Zambian mobiles are exceptionally reasonable by Western standards, and international texts shouldn't break the bank either.

EMAIL AND THE INTERNET Wi-Fi access is broadening rapidly, even in the most remote safari camp, and despite ongoing issues with speed and outdated hardware. Yet while the email community in Zambia is quite large, far fewer people have access to the internet. If you're emailing someone in Zambia and don't get a reply within 48 hours, it would be wise to re-send the email. There are fairly reliable and high-speed internet cafés in Lusaka and many of the bigger towns.

MEDIA
The press The main daily papers are *The Post* (*www.postzambia.com*), which is privately owned and fairly independent, and the *Times of Zambia* (*www.times.co.zm*) and the *Daily Mail*, both of which are owned by the government. The *Financial Mail* is part of the *Daily Mail*, as are the *Sunday Mail* and the *Sunday Times*. On the whole, *The Post* is the most outspoken and interesting paper. It's well worth having a look at the various websites before you go; some of the stories can be fascinating. For an online digest, consider also www.lusakatimes.com, which is free to access.

There are also several weekly papers, including the *National Mirror, Monitor* and *Mail & Guardian*, which despite its independent status tends to be strongly pro-government. Monthlies worth reading include *The Bulletin & Record* and the long-running Lusaka-based guide, *The Lowdown* (*www.lowdownzambia.com*).

Zambia claims to have a free press, and most issues are debated openly. However, when the more sensitive ones are skirted around, only *The Post* tries to take a more investigative approach. Often this is respected, but see *20th century*, page 11, for an example of an incident when the authorities were less than respectful in their approach.

Various publications are targeted directly at the visitor. Of these, the bi-monthly *Zambian Traveller* (*www.thezambiantraveller.com*) is distributed through hotels and lodges in Zambia as well as being available to download. It features a range of articles covering everything from mining and conservation to hotel reviews. There's also *Zambezi Traveller* (*www.zambezitraveller.com*), a tourist newspaper with a strong environmental bent. The popular *Travel Zambia* (*http://ta-emags.com*) is now available only online.

Radio and television Radio is limited, as Zambia National Broadcasting Corporation (ZNBC) runs three channels which are all used as government communication tools: Radio 1, Radio 2 and Radio 4. (Radio 4 used to be the rather fun Radio Mulungushi, until it was swallowed up.)

There is some good news though, as in the cities – especially Lusaka – you'll find smaller commercial stations. The obvious one is Radio Phoenix, which broadcasts popular music and Zambian news, though it's worth scanning the airwaves for others. Outside of the large cities, you'll find little, although those with short-wave radios can always seek the BBC World Service, the Voice of America and Radio Canada.

Two public television stations are also run by ZNBC. They stick to the official party line on most issues, but do tune in – some of their panel debates can be fascinating. There's also Muvitv (*www.muvitv.com*), which tends to focus on local productions. Most hotels with in-room televisions subscribe to satellite channels such as DSTV, often including BBC World, CNN and/or the South African cable network, M-Net, with its multitude of sports and movie channels.

CULTURAL GUIDELINES

Comments here are intended to be a general guide, just a few examples of how to travel more sensitively. They should not be viewed as blueprints for perfect Zambian etiquette. Cultural sensitivity is a state of mind, not a checklist of behaviour – so here we can only hope to give the sensitive traveller a few pointers in the right direction.

When we travel, we are all in danger of leaving negative impressions with local people. It is easily done – by snapping that picture quickly, whilst the subject is not looking; by dressing scantily, offending local sensitivities; by just brushing aside the feelings of local people, with the high-handed superiority of a rich Westerner. These things are easy to do, in the click of a shutter, or flash of a dollar bill.

You will get the most representative view of Zambia if you cause as little disturbance to the local people as possible. You will never blend in perfectly when you travel – your mere presence there, as an observer, will always change the local events slightly. However, if you try to fit in and show respect for local culture and attitudes, then you may manage to leave positive feelings behind you.

One of the easiest, and most important, ways to do this is with **greetings**. African societies are rarely as rushed as Western ones. When you first talk to someone, you should greet them leisurely.

So, for example, if you enter a bus station and want some help, do not just ask outright, 'Where is the bus to ...' That would be rude. Instead you will have a better reception (and better chance of good advice) by saying:

Traveller: 'Good afternoon.'
Zambian: 'Good afternoon.'
Traveller: 'How are you?'
Zambian: 'I am fine, how are you?'
Traveller: 'I am fine, thank you.' (*Pause*) 'Do you know where the bus to ...'

This goes for approaching anyone – always greet them first. For a better reception still, learn these phrases of greeting in the local language (pages 526–8). English-speakers are often lazy about learning languages, and, whilst most Zambians understand English, a greeting given in an appropriate local language will be received with delight. It implies that you are making an effort to learn a little of their language and culture, which is always appreciated.

Occasionally, in the town or city, you may be approached by someone who doesn't greet you. Instead s/he tries immediately to sell you something, or even hassle you in some way. These people have learned that foreigners aren't used to greetings, and so have adapted their approach accordingly. An effective way to dodge their attentions is to reply to their questions with a formal greeting, and then politely – but firmly – refuse their offer. This is surprisingly effective.

Another part of the normal greeting ritual is **handshaking**. As elsewhere, you would not normally shake a shop-owner's hand, but you would shake hands with someone to whom you are introduced. Get some practice when you arrive; there is a gentle, three-part handshake used in southern Africa which is easily learnt.

Your **clothing** is an area that can easily give offence. Most Zambians frown upon skimpy or revealing clothing, especially when worn by women. Shorts are fine for walking safaris, otherwise dress conservatively and avoid short shorts, especially in the more rural areas. Respectable locals will wear long trousers (men) or long skirts (women).

Homosexuality is illegal in Zambia, although no-one – as far as I know – has ever been prosecuted, and same-sex relationships have never been a problem for guests in safari camps. While it's not at all unusual in traditional societies to see two men – or two women – casually holding hands, public **displays of affection** between two people (gay or straight) may create tension and are best avoided.

Photography is a tricky business. Most Zambians will be only too happy to be photographed – provided you ask their permission first. Sign language is fine for this question: just point at your camera, shrug your shoulders, and look quizzical. The problem is that then everyone will smile for you, producing the type of 'posed' photograph that you may not want. However, stay around and chat for 5 or 10 minutes more, and people will get used to your presence, stop posing, and you will get more natural shots of them (a camera with a quiet shutter is a help). Note that special care is needed with photography near government buildings, bridges and similar sites of strategic importance. You must ask permission before photographing anything here, or you risk people thinking that you are a spy.

If you're **seeking directions**, don't be afraid to stop and ask. Most people will be polite and keen to help – so keen that some will answer 'Yes' to questions if they think that this is what you want to hear. So try to avoid asking leading questions. For example, 'Yes' would often be the typical answer to the question, 'Does this road lead to …?' And in a sense the respondent is probably correct – it will get you there. It's just that it may not be the quickest or shortest way. To avoid misunderstandings, it is often better to ask open-ended questions like, 'Where does this road go to?' or 'How do I drive to …?'

The specific examples above can only be taken so far – they are general by their very nature. But wherever you find yourself, if you are polite and considerate to the Zambians you meet, then you will rarely encounter any cultural problems. Watch how they behave and, if you have any doubts about how you should act, then ask someone quietly. They will seldom tell you outright that you are being rude, but they will usually give you good advice on how to make your behaviour more acceptable.

TRAVELLING POSITIVELY

If you ask locally you'll often find projects that need your support. Many lodges and camps also assist with community or wildlife projects, and will be able to suggest a good use for donations. Alternatively, there are several ideas below. All welcome donations – so make a resolution now to help at least one of them as an integral part of the cost of your trip.

HELPING ZAMBIA'S POORER COMMUNITIES Visiting Zambia, especially the rural agricultural areas and the towns, many visitors are struck by the poverty and wish to help. Giving to beggars and those in need on the street is one way. It will alleviate your feelings of guilt, and perhaps some of the immediate suffering, but it is not a long-term solution.

There are ways in which you can make a positive contribution, but they require more effort than throwing a few coins to someone on the street.

Habitat for Humanity Zambia (HFHZ)
42 Kudu Rd, Kabulonga, Lusaka; ✆0211 251087; e hfhzm@habitatzambia.org; www.habitatzambia.org. Part of a wider Christian NGO, not-for-profit HFHZ works towards solving the housing problems of the poor. Since 1984 they have built more than 2,700 houses in different projects throughout the country, using largely volunteer labour, some from overseas. Families may be eligible for a loan, which is then repaid into a revolving fund, enabling more houses to be built in the same community.

ZOCS (Zambia Open Community Schools)
20 Tito Rd, Rhodes Park, Lusaka; ✆0211 253841/3; e zocs2008@gmail.com; www.zambiaopencommunityschools.org. My favourite project, ZOCS provides a basic education to orphaned & vulnerable young Zambians, & those with special needs, who would not otherwise be able to go to school. Education is vital for Zambia's future, while in the present it gives children some hope. Deaths from AIDS have left increasing numbers of orphans, many of whom end up on the streets. This project is making a difference on a local level, currently supporting 524 schools through individual communities.

ENVIRONMENT AND WILDLIFE Of the numerous worthwhile conservation initiatives in Zambia, these two are involved in areas most visited by tourists – so seem particularly apt. Both are committed to working with the local community and wildlife authorities to promote the conservation and sustainable use of the area's natural resources through a programme of environmental protection, education and community development.

Conservation Lower Zambezi (CLZ)
e eleanor@conservationlowerzambei.org; http://conservationlowerzambezl.org. See page 230.

South Luangwa Conservation Society (SLCS)
m 0979 180452; www.slcszambia.org. See pages 262–3.

VOLUNTEERING Zambia, like many African countries, hasn't been slow to take advantage of the upsurge in volunteering holidays. To set the ball rolling, contact **The Book Bus** (*11 The Orchard, Montpelier Rd, London W5 2QW, UK;* ✆ *020 8099 9280;* e *info@thebookbus.org; www.thebookbus.org*), which takes volunteers to help operate their mobile library and reader mentoring service in Livingstone, Mfuwe and Kitwe.

Meanwhile there are many pitfalls for unwary volunteers, so be sure to do your homework – especially if you are trying to get involved with a local community. An excellent place to start is www.ethicalvolunteering.org, which also has a

4

downloadable pamphlet entitled *The Ethical Volunteering Guide*. Some of the many issues to consider include:

- For every bona fide organisation there will be others who are willing to take your cash without delivering on their side of the deal.
- Try to be realistic about what your skills are; they will probably define what you can usefully contribute. Zambian communities don't need unskilled hobbyists; they need professionals. To teach skills properly takes years of volunteering, not weeks. (How long did *you* take to learn those skills?) So, for example, if you're not a qualified teacher or builder in your home country, then don't expect to be let loose to do any teaching or building in Zambia.
- Most volunteers will learn much more than the members of the communities that they come to 'help'; be aware of this when you describe who is helping whom.
- Make sure that what you are doing isn't effectively taking away a job from a local person.

Time in Zambia will do you lots of good; make sure it's not to the detriment of your hosts.

EXTRAORDINARY
AFRICA

Personal service, straightforward advice, endless imagination. *Visit www.extraordinary-africa.com or call our Zambia expert Alex on +44 (0) 207 097 1801*

5

Health and Safety

There is always great danger in writing about health and safety for the uninitiated visitor. It is all too easy to become paranoid about exotic diseases that you may catch, and all too easy to start distrusting everybody you meet as a potential thief – falling into an unjustified us-and-them attitude towards the people of the country you are visiting.

As a comparison, imagine an equivalent section in a guidebook to a Western country – there would be a list of possible diseases and advice on the risk of theft and mugging. Many Western cities are very dangerous, but with time we learn how to assess the risks, accepting almost subconsciously what we can and cannot do.

It is important to strike the right balance: to avoid being either excessively cautious or too relaxed about your health and your safety. With experience, you will find the balance that best fits you and the country you are visiting.

HEALTH with Dr Felicity Nicholson

Zambia, like most parts of Africa, is home to several tropical diseases unfamiliar to people living in more temperate and sanitary climates. However, with adequate preparation, and a sensible attitude to malaria prevention, the chances of serious mishap are small. To put this in perspective, your greatest concern after malaria should not be the combined exotica of venomous snakes, stampeding wildlife, gun-happy soldiers or the Ebola virus, but something altogether more mundane: a road accident.

PREPARATIONS Sensible preparation will go a long way to ensuring your trip goes smoothly. Particularly for first-time visitors to Africa, this includes a visit to a travel clinic to discuss matters such as vaccinations and malaria prevention. A full list of travel clinic websites worldwide is available at www.itsm.org, and other useful websites for prospective travellers include travelhealthpro.org.uk (formerly Nathnac) and www.netdoctor.co.uk/travel. The Bradt website now carries a page to help travellers prepare for their African trip, elaborating on most points raised below (*www.bradtguides.com/articles/africa-health-updates*), but the following summary points are worth emphasising:

- Don't travel without comprehensive medical **travel insurance** that will fly you home or to another country in an emergency.
- Make sure all your **immunisations** are up to date. On the whole Zambia is no longer considered a yellow fever endemic area, although there remains a very low risk of the disease in the northwest of the country. Vaccination may therefore be recommended for travellers to that part of the country. Otherwise, under International Health Regulations (2005), a certificate of yellow fever

vaccination is required from travellers over 9 months of age arriving from countries with a risk of yellow fever transmission and for travellers having transited for more than 12 hours through an airport of a country with a risk of yellow fever transmission. Zambia considers that the yellow fever vaccine lasts for life. South Africa is no longer asking for a yellow fever certificate from Zambia as they do not consider Zambia to be a yellow fever endemic country. Please take advice from a Yellow Fever Registered Centre.

- It is unwise to travel in the tropics without being up to date with immunisation against measles, mumps and rubella (MMR), tetanus, polio and diphtheria (now given as an all-in-one vaccine, Revaxis), hepatitis A and typhoid. Immunisation against rabies, hepatitis B, and possibly TB may also be recommended.
- The biggest health threat is **malaria**. There is no vaccine against this mosquito-borne disease, but a variety of preventative drugs is available, including mefloquine, atovaquone/proguanil (Malarone) and the antibiotic doxycycline. Malarone and doxycycline need only be started two days before entering Zambia, but mefloquine should be started two to three weeks before. Doxycycline and mefloquine need to be taken for four weeks after the trip and Malarone for seven days. It is as important to complete the course, as it is to take it before and during the trip. The most suitable choice of drug varies depending on the individual (their health and age) and the countries in which they are travelling, so visit your GP or a specialist travel clinic for medical advice. If you will be spending a long time in Africa, and expect to visit remote areas, be aware that no preventative drug is 100% effective, so carry a cure too. It is also worth noting that no homeopathic prophylactic for malaria exists, nor can any traveller acquire effective resistance to malaria. Those who don't make use of preventative drugs risk their life in a manner that is both foolish and unnecessary.
- Though advised for everyone, a **pre-exposure course of rabies vaccination**, involving three doses taken over a minimum of 21 days, is particularly important if you intend to have contact with animals, or are likely to be 24 hours away from medical help. If you have not had this then you will almost certainly need to evacuate for medical treatment, as it is possible that Zambia will not have all the necessary treatment.
- Anybody travelling away from major centres should carry a **personal first-aid kit**. Contents might include a good drying antiseptic (eg: iodine or potassium permanganate), Band-Aids, suncream, insect repellent, aspirin or paracetamol, antifungal cream (eg: Canesten), ciprofloxacin or norfloxacin (for severe diarrhoea), antibiotic eye drops, tweezers, condoms or femidoms, a digital thermometer and a needle-and-syringe kit with accompanying letter from healthcare professional. For a full list of recommended items, visit Bradt's website (*www.bradtguides.com/articles/africa-health-updates*).
- Bring any **drugs or devices relating to known medical conditions** with you. That applies both to those who are on medication prior to departure, and those who are, for instance, allergic to bee stings, or are prone to attacks of asthma. However, always check with www.gov.uk/foreign-travel-advice/zambia/local-laws-and-customs, which provides information on the Zambia Pharmaceutical Authority who can identify any restricted medications. Allow plenty of time in case you need to apply for a licence to import your medication into Zambia. Carry a copy of your prescription and a letter from your GP explaining why you need the medication.
- Prolonged immobility on long-haul flights can result in **deep-vein thrombosis** (DVT), which can be dangerous if the clot travels to the lungs to cause

pulmonary embolus. The risk increases with age, and is higher in obese or pregnant travellers, heavy smokers, those taller than 6ft/1.8m or shorter than 5ft/1.5m, and anybody with a history of clots, recent major operation or varicose veins surgery, cancer, a stroke or heart disease. If any of these criteria apply, consult a doctor before you travel.

COMMON MEDICAL PROBLEMS

Malaria This potentially fatal disease occurs throughout Zambia all year round. Since no malaria prophylactic is 100% effective, one should take all reasonable precautions against being bitten by the nocturnal *Anopheles* mosquitoes that transmit the disease (see box, page 87). Malaria usually manifests within two weeks of transmission, but it can be as little as seven days and anything up to a year. Any fever occurring after seven days should be considered as malaria until proven otherwise. These typically include a rapid rise in temperature (over 38°C), and any combination of a headache, flu-like aches and pains, a general sense of disorientation, and possibly even nausea and diarrhoea. The earlier malaria is detected, the better it usually responds to treatment. So if you display possible symptoms, *get to a doctor or clinic immediately*. (In the UK go to accident and emergency and say that you have been to Africa). A simple test, available at even the most rural clinic in Africa, is usually adequate to determine whether you have malaria. You need 3 negative tests to be sure it is not malaria. And while experts differ on the question of self-diagnosis and self-treatment, the reality is that if you think you have malaria and are not within easy reach of a doctor, it would be wisest to start treatment.

Travellers' diarrhoea Many visitors to unfamiliar destinations suffer a dose of travellers' diarrhoea, usually as result of imbibing contaminated food or water. Rule one in avoiding diarrhoea and other sanitation-related diseases is arguably to wash your hands regularly, particularly before snacks and meals. As for what food you can safely eat, a useful maxim is: PEEL IT, BOIL IT, COOK IT OR FORGET IT. This means that fruit you have washed and peeled yourself should be safe, as should hot cooked foods. However, raw foods, cold cooked foods, salads, fruit salads prepared by others, ice cream and ice are all risky. It is rarer to get sick from drinking contaminated water but it happens, so stick to bottled water, which is widely available.

If you suffer a bout of diarrhoea, it is dehydration that makes you feel awful, so drink lots of water and other clear fluids. These can be infused with sachets of oral rehydration salts, though any dilute mixture of sugar and salt in water will do you good, for instance a bottled soda with a pinch of salt. If diarrhoea persists beyond a couple of days, it is possible it is a symptom of a more serious sanitation-related illness (typhoid, cholera, hepatitis, dysentery, worms, etc), so get to a doctor. If the diarrhoea is greasy and bulky, and is accompanied by sulphurous (eggy) burps, one likely cause is giardia, which is best treated with tinidazole (four x 500mg in one dose, repeated seven days later if symptoms persist).

Bilharzia Also known as schistosomiasis, bilharzia is an unpleasant parasitic disease transmitted by freshwater snails most often associated with reedy shores where there is lots of water weed. It cannot be caught in hotel swimming pools or the ocean, but should be assumed to be present in any freshwater river pond, lake or similar habitat, even those advertised as 'bilharzia free'. The most risky shores will be within 200m of villages or other places where infected people use water, wash clothes, etc. Ideally, however, you should avoid swimming in any fresh water other than an artificial pool. If you do swim, you'll reduce the risk by applying DEET insect repellent first, staying in the water for under 10 minutes, and drying off vigorously with a towel. Bilharzia is often asymptomatic in its early stages, but some people experience an intense immune reaction, including fever, cough, abdominal pain and an itching rash, around four to six weeks after infection. Later symptoms vary but often include a general feeling of tiredness and lethargy. Bilharzia is difficult to diagnose, but it can be tested for at specialist travel clinics, ideally at least six weeks after likely exposure. Fortunately, it is easy to treat at present.

Rabies This deadly disease can be carried by any mammal and is usually transmitted to humans via a bite, a scratch that breaks the skin and saliva on skin or other mucous membranes such as eyes, nose or mouth. Beware village dogs and monkeys, but assume that *any* mammal can carry rabies, even if it looks healthy. First, scrub the affected area with soap under a running tap for a good 10–15 minutes, or while pouring water from a jug, then pour on a strong iodine or alcohol solution, which will guard against infections and might reduce the risk of the rabies virus entering the body. Whether or not you underwent pre-exposure vaccination, it is vital to obtain post-exposure prophylaxis as soon as possible after the incident. The post-exposure treatment is highly unlikely to be available in Zambia. Evacuate as soon as you can. Death from rabies is probably one of the worst ways to go, and once you show symptoms it is too late to do anything – the mortality rate is virtually 100%.

Tetanus Tetanus is caught through deep dirty wounds, including animal bites, so ensure that such wounds are thoroughly cleaned. Immunisation protects for ten years, provided you don't have an overwhelming number of tetanus bacteria on board. If you haven't had a tetanus shot in ten years, or you are unsure, get a booster immediately.

HIV/AIDS Rates of HIV/AIDS infection are high in most parts of Africa, and other sexually transmitted diseases are rife. Condoms (or femidoms) greatly reduce the risk of transmission.

Tick bites Ticks in Africa are not the rampant disease transmitters that they are in the Americas, but they may spread tickbite fever along with a few dangerous rarities. They should ideally be removed complete as soon as possible to reduce the chance of infection. The best way to do this is to grasp the tick with your finger nails as close to your body as possible, and pull it away steadily and firmly at right angles to your skin (do not jerk or twist it). If possible douse the wound with alcohol (any spirit will do) or iodine. If you are travelling with small children, remember to check their heads, and particularly behind the ears, for ticks. Spreading redness around the bite and/or fever and/or aching joints after a tick bite imply that you have an infection that requires antibiotic treatment, so seek advice.

Skin infections Any mosquito bite or small nick is an opportunity for a skin infection in warm humid climates, so clean and cover the slightest wound in a good drying antiseptic such as dilute iodine, potassium permanganate or crystal (or gentian) violet. Prickly heat, most likely to be contracted at the humid coast, is a fine pimply rash that can be alleviated by cool showers, dabbing (not rubbing) dry and talc, and sleeping naked under a fan or in an air-conditioned room. Fungal infections also get a hold easily in hot moist climates so wear 100%-cotton socks and underwear and shower frequently.

Eye problems Bacterial conjunctivitis (pink eye) is a common infection in Africa, particularly for contact-lens wearers. Symptoms are sore, gritty eyelids that often stick closed in the morning. They will need treatment with antibiotic drops or ointment. Lesser eye irritation should settle with bathing in salt water and keeping the eyes shaded. If an insect flies into your eye, extract it with great care, ensuring you do not crush or damage it, otherwise you may get a nastily inflamed eye from toxins secreted by the creature.

Sunstroke and dehydration Overexposure to the sun can lead to short-term sunburn or sunstroke, and increases the long-term risk of skin cancer. Wear a T-shirt and waterproof sunscreen when swimming. On safari or walking in the direct sun, cover up with long, loose clothes, wear a hat, and use sunscreen. The glare and the dust can be hard on the eyes, so bring UV-protecting sunglasses. A less direct effect of the tropical heat is dehydration, so drink more fluids than you would at home.

Other insect-borne diseases Although malaria is the insect-borne disease that attracts the most attention in Africa, and rightly so, there are others, most too uncommon to be a significant concern to short-stay travellers. These include dengue fever and other arboviruses (spread by day-biting mosquitoes), sleeping sickness (tsetse flies), and river blindness (blackflies). Bearing this in mind, however, it is clearly sensible, and makes for a more pleasant trip, to avoid insect bites as far as possible (see box below). Two nasty (though ultimately relatively harmless) flesh-eating insects associated with tropical Africa are *tumbu* or *putsi* flies, which lay eggs, often on drying laundry, that hatch and bury themselves under the skin when they come into contact with humans, and jiggers, which latch on to bare feet and set up home, usually at the side of a toenail, where they cause a painful boil-like

AVOIDING MOSQUITO AND INSECT BITES

The *Anopheles* mosquitoes that spread malaria are active at dusk and after dark. Most bites can thus be avoided by covering up at night. This means donning a long-sleeved shirt, trousers and socks from around 30 minutes before dusk until you retire to bed, and applying a DEET-based insect repellent to any exposed flesh. It is best to sleep under a net, or in an air-conditioned room, though burning a mosquito coil and/or sleeping under a fan will also reduce (though not entirely eliminate) bites. Travel clinics usually sell a good range of nets and repellents, as well as Permethrin treatment kits, which will render even the tattiest net a lot more protective, and helps prevents mosquitoes from biting through a net when you roll against it. These measures will also do much to reduce exposure to other nocturnal biters. Bear in mind, too, that most flying insects are attracted to light: leaving a lamp standing near a tent opening or a light on in a poorly screened hotel room will greatly increase the insect presence in your sleeping quarters.

It is also advisable to think about avoiding bites when walking in the countryside by day, especially in wetland habitats, which often teem with diurnal mosquitoes. Wear a long loose shirt and trousers, preferably 100% cotton, as well as proper walking or hiking shoes with heavy socks (the ankle is particularly vulnerable to bites), and apply a DEET-based insect repellent to any exposed skin.

swelling. Drying laundry indoors and wearing shoes are the best way to deter this pair of flesh-eaters. Symptoms and treatment of all these afflictions are described in greater detail on Bradt's website (*www.bradtguides.com*).

Tsetse flies are slightly larger than a housefly and have pointed mouth-parts designed for sucking blood; they hurt when they bite. They thrive in broad-leaved woodland across Zambia but are highly localised. They are also said to be attracted to the colour blue and moving vehicles. Locals will advise on where they are a problem and where they transmit sleeping sickness. Bites are nasty, and the vast majority will swell up and turn red – that is a normal allergic reaction to any bite. However, if the bite develops into a boil-like swelling after five or more days, and a fever starts two or three weeks later, then seek immediate medical treatment to avert permanent damage to your central nervous system. The name 'sleeping sickness' refers to a daytime drowsiness which is characteristic of the later stages of the disease.

WILD ANIMALS Don't confuse habituation with domestication. Most wildlife in Africa is genuinely wild, and widespread species such as hippo or hyena might attack a person given the right set of circumstances. Such attacks are rare, however, and they almost always stem from a combination of poor judgement and poorer luck. A few rules of thumb: never approach potentially dangerous wildlife on foot except in the company of a trustworthy guide; never swim in lakes or rivers without first seeking local advice about the presence of crocodiles or hippos; never get between a hippo and water; and never leave food (particularly meat or fruit) in the tent where you'll sleep. For further information see pages 104–7.

SNAKE AND OTHER BITES Snakes are very secretive and bites are a genuine rarity, but certain spiders and scorpions can also deliver nasty bites. In all cases, the risk is minimised by wearing closed shoes and trousers when walking in the bush, and watching where you put your hands and feet, especially in rocky areas or when gathering firewood. Only a small fraction of snakebites deliver enough venom to be life-threatening, but it is important to keep the victim calm and inactive, and to seek urgent medical attention; head to the nearest farm, camp or town.

If bitten, you are unlikely to have received venom; keeping this fact in mind may help you to stay calm. Many so-called first-aid techniques do more harm than good: cutting into the wound is harmful; tourniquets are dangerous; suction and electrical inactivation devices do not work. The only treatment is anti-venom. In case of a bite that you fear may have been from a venomous snake:

- Try to keep calm – it is likely that no venom has been dispensed.
- Prevent movement of the bitten limb by applying a splint.
- Keep the bitten limb BELOW heart height to slow the spread of any venom.
- If you have a crêpe bandage, wrap it around the whole limb (eg: all the way from the toes to the thigh), as tight as you would for a sprained ankle or a muscle pull.
- Evacuate to a hospital that has the relevant anti-venom.

And remember:

- NEVER give aspirin; you may take paracetamol, which is safe.
- NEVER cut or suck the wound.
- DO NOT apply ice packs.
- DO NOT apply potassium permanganate.

If the offending snake can be captured without risk of someone else being bitten, take this to show the doctor – but beware since even a decapitated head is able to bite.

CAR ACCIDENTS Dangerous driving is probably the biggest threat to life and limb in most parts of Africa. On a chauffeured tour, don't be afraid to tell the driver to slow or calm down if you think he is driving too fast or being reckless. See pages 67–70 for information on driving.

ASSISTANCE
Hospitals and dentists Zambia's public-health system is overstretched and under-funded, presenting a risk of coming away with something worse than you had when you arrived. In the main cities – Lusaka, Livingstone and the Copperbelt – there are better-funded private hospitals that cater for both affluent Zambians and expats/diplomatic staff. These are much better, and will accept payment from genuine travel health insurance schemes.

For situations that are more serious, and may require immediate evacuation, **Specialty Emergency Services (SES)** (m *0962 740300, 0977 770302; http://ses-zambia.com*) operates throughout Zambia, with bases in Lusaka, Livingstone and Kitwe. If offers ambulances and in-patient care, as well as emergency cover. SES can also arrange short-term insurance cover for visitors, either prior to arriving in Zambia or at their local offices. Most tour operators, and many lodges, include SES cover in their rates, but it's important to have good travel insurance – costs for evacuation are extremely high.

Pharmacies Pharmacies in main towns have a basic range of medicines, often at considerably lower prices than in their Western counterparts; they also stock malaria-test kits. That said, not all of these outlets are reliable, so stick to one that has been recommended.

As you might expect, specific brands are often unavailable, so bring with you all that you will need, as well as a repeat prescription for anything that you might run out of. Outside of the main centres, you will be lucky to find anything other than very basic medical supplies. Thus you should carry a very comprehensive medical kit if you are planning to head off independently into the wilds.

STAYING HEALTHY Rural Zambia is often not a healthy place to be. However, visitors using the better hotels, lodges and camps are unlikely to encounter any serious problems. The standards of hygiene in even the most remote bushcamps are generally at least as good as you will find at home.

The major dangers in Zambia are car accidents (see above) and sunburn. Both can also be very serious, yet both are within the power of the visitor to avoid.

The following is general advice, applicable to travelling anywhere, including Zambia.

Food and storage Throughout the world, most health problems encountered by travellers are contracted by eating contaminated food or drinking unclean water. If you are staying in safari camps or lodges, or eating in restaurants, then you are unlikely to have problems in Zambia.

However, if you are backpacking and cooking for yourself, or relying on local food, then you need to take more care. Tins, packets and fresh green vegetables (when you can find them) are least likely to cause problems – provided that clean water has been used in preparing the meal. In Zambia's hot climate, keeping meat or animal products unrefrigerated for more than a few hours is asking for trouble.

Water and purification Whilst piped water in the major towns is unlikely to harbour any serious pathogens, it will almost certainly cause upset stomachs for overseas visitors. In more rural areas, the water will generally have had less treatment, and therefore will be even more likely to cause problems. Hence, as a general rule, ensure that all water used for drinking or washing food in Zambia is purified.

To purify water yourself, first filter out any suspended solids, perhaps passing the water through a piece of closely woven cloth, or something similar. Then bring it to the boil, or sterilise it chemically. Boiling is much more effective, provided that you have the fuel available.

Tablets sold for purification are based on chlorine dioxide. Iodine is no longer recommended for use and is not sold in the UK and the rest of Europe as there have been concerns over its safety.

Returning home Many tropical diseases have a long incubation period, and it is possible to develop symptoms weeks after returning home (this is why it is important to keep taking anti-malaria prophylaxis for the prescribed duration after you leave a malarial zone). If you do get ill after you return home, be certain to tell your doctor where you have been. For more information check Bradt's Africa health web pages: www.bradtguides.com/articles/africa-health-updates.

SAFETY

Zambia is not a dangerous country. If you are travelling on an all-inclusive trip and staying at lodges and hotels, then problems of personal safety are exceedingly rare. There will always be someone on hand to help you. Even if you are travelling on local transport, perhaps on a low budget, you will not be attacked randomly just for the sake of it. A difficult situation is most likely to occur if you have made yourself an obvious target for thieves, perhaps by walking around, or driving an expensive 4x4, in town at night. The answer then is to capitulate completely and give them what they want, and cash in on your travel insurance. Heroics are not a good idea.

The British Foreign and Commonwealth Office currently advises caution when travelling in rural parts of the country bordering the Democratic Republic of Congo (DRC), especially after dark, a reflection of ongoing cross-border raids. The advice does not relate to main roads, or to towns along the routes, including those between Kapiri Mposhi and Serenje, Serenje and Mansa, and the main routes through the Copperbelt. However, those proposing to travel north from Ndola to Mufulira should be cautious.

For women travellers, especially those travelling alone, it is doubly important to learn the local attitudes, and how to behave acceptably. This takes some practice, and a certain confidence. You will often be the centre of attention but, by developing conversational techniques to avert over-enthusiastic male attention, you should be perfectly safe. Making friends of the local women is one way to help avoid such problems.

THEFT Theft is a problem in Zambia's urban areas. Given that a large section of the population is living below the poverty line and without any paid work, it

When attention becomes intrusive, it can help if you are wearing a wedding ring and have photos of 'your' husband and children, even if they are someone else's. A good reason to give for not being with them is that you have to travel in connection with your job – biology, zoology, geography, or whatever. (But not journalism – that's risky.)

Pay attention to local etiquette, and to speaking, dressing and moving reasonably decorously. Look at how the local women dress, and try not to expose parts of yourself that they keep covered. Think about body language. In much of southern Africa direct eye-contact with a man will be seen as a 'come-on'; sunglasses are helpful here.

Don't be afraid to explain clearly – but pleasantly rather than as a put-down – that you aren't in the market for whatever distractions are on offer. Remember that you are probably as much of a novelty to the local people as they are to you; and the fact that you are travelling abroad alone gives them the message that you are free and adventurous. But don't imagine that a Lothario lurks under every bush: many approaches stem from genuine friendliness or curiosity, and a brush-off in such cases doesn't do much for the image of travellers in general.

Take sensible precautions against theft and attack – try to cover all the risks before you encounter them – and then relax and enjoy your trip. You'll meet far more kindness than villainy.

is surprising that the problem is not worse. Despite Lusaka's reputation, in my experience theft is no more of an issue here than it is in Harare – while the centre of Johannesburg is significantly more dangerous than either. However, car jacking is on the increase, so it is wise to take sensible precautions to protect your vehicle – and you.

How to avoid it Thieves in the bigger cities usually work in groups – choosing their targets carefully. These will be people who look vulnerable and who have items worth stealing. To avoid being robbed, try not to fit into either category – and certainly not into both. Observing a few basic rules, especially during your first few weeks in Zambia's cities, will drastically reduce your chances of becoming a target. After that you should have learnt your own way of assessing the risks, and avoiding thefts. Until then:

- Try not to carry anything of value around with you.
- If you must carry cash, then use a concealed money-belt for your main supply – keeping smaller change separately and to hand.
- Try not to walk around alone. Move in groups. Take taxis instead.
- Try not to look too foreign. Blend in to the local scene as well as you can. Act like a streetwise expat rather than a tourist, if you can. (Conspicuously carrying a local newspaper may help with this.)
- Rucksacks and large, new bags are bad. If you must carry a bag, choose an old battered one. Around town, a local plastic carrier bag is ideal.
- Move confidently and look as if you know exactly what you are doing, and where you are going. Lost foreigners make the easiest targets.
- Never walk around at night – that is asking for trouble.

If you have a vehicle then don't leave anything in it, and avoid leaving it parked outside in a city. One person should always stay with it, as vehicle thefts are common, even in broad daylight. Armed gangs doing American-style vehicle hijacks are on the increase, though still rare – and their most likely targets are new 4x4 vehicles. When driving in urban areas, and especially at night, keep the doors locked, and ensure that you're not using a mobile phone within easy reach of a passer-by. Scams to get you to stop include faking an accident, so be on the alert. And if you are held up then just surrender: you have little choice if you want to live.

Reporting thefts to the police If you are the victim of a theft then report it to the police – they ought to know. Also try to get a copy of the report, or at least a reference number on an official-looking piece of paper, as this will help you to claim on your insurance policy when you return home. Some insurance companies won't act without it. But remember that reporting anything in a police station can take a long time, and do not expect any speedy arrests for a small case of pick-pocketing.

ARREST To get arrested in Zambia, a foreigner will normally have to try quite hard. During the Kaunda regime, when the state was paranoid about spies, every tourist's camera became a reason for suspicion and arrest. Fortunately that attitude has now vanished, though as a precaution you should still ask for permission to photograph near bridges or military installations. This simple courtesy costs you nothing, and may avoid a problem later.

One excellent way to get arrested in Zambia is to try to smuggle drugs across its borders, or to try to buy them from 'pushers'. Drug offences carry penalties at least as stiff as those you will find at home – and the jails are a lot less pleasant. Zambia's police are not forbidden to use entrapment techniques or 'sting' operations to catch criminals. Buying, selling or using drugs in Zambia is just not worth the risk.

Failing this, arguing with any policeman or army official – and getting angry into the bargain – is a sure way to get arrested. It is essential to control your temper and stay relaxed when dealing with Zambia's officials. Not only will you gain respect, and hence help your cause, but also you will avoid being forced to cool off for a night in the cells.

If you are careless enough to be arrested, you will often only be asked a few questions. If the police are suspicious of you, then how you handle the situation will determine whether you are kept for a matter of hours or for days. Be patient, helpful, good-humoured and as truthful as possible. Never lose your temper; it will only aggravate the situation. Avoid any hint of arrogance. If things are going badly after half a day or so, then start firmly, but politely, to insist on seeing someone in higher authority. As a last resort you do, at least in theory, have the right to contact your embassy or consulate, though the finer points of your civil liberties may be overlooked by an irate local police chief.

BRIBERY Bribery is a fact of life in Zambia, though it is a difficult subject to write about. If you're visiting on an organised holiday, then it's unlikely to become an issue – you'll not come across any expectation of bribes. However, independent travellers ought to think about the issue before they arrive, as they are more likely to encounter the problem, and there are many different points of view on how to deal with it.

Some argue that it is present already, as an unavoidable way of life, and so must be accepted by the practical traveller. They view using bribery as simply practising one of the local customs. Others regard paying bribes as an unacceptable step towards condoning an immoral practice; thus any bribe should be flatly refused, and requests to make them never acceded to.

Whichever school of thought you favour, bribery is an issue in Zambia that you may need to consider. It is not as widespread, or on the same scale, as countries further north – but on a low level is not uncommon. A large 'tip' is often expected for a favour, and acceptance of small fines from police for traffic offences often avoids proceedings which may appear deliberately time-consuming. Many pragmatic travellers will only use a bribe as a very last resort, and only then when it has been asked for repeatedly.

Never attempt to bribe someone unsubtly, or use the word 'bribe'. If the person involved hasn't already dropped numerous broad hints to you that money is required, then offering it would be a great insult. Further, even if bribes are being asked for, an eagerness to offer will encourage any person you are dealing with to increase their price.

Never simply say, 'Here's some dollars, now will you do it?' Better is to agree, reluctantly, to pay the 'on-the-spot-fine' that was requested; or to gradually accept the need for the extra 'administration fee' that was demanded; or to finally agree to help to cover the 'time and trouble' involved ... provided that the problem can be overcome.

Use our expertise to realise your African dreams.

Contact www.pulseafrica.com Email: info@pulseafrica.com

Pulse Africa
SELECT DESTINATIONS

The ultimate way to explore Zambia

Safari Drive has been organising tailor-made, self drive safaris in Zambia since 1993.

With expert knowledge of the roads, driving conditions and routes, Safari Drive gives you the freedom and security to embark on an adventure of a lifetime. Self drive safaris offer versatile, independent travel with the freedom to explore at your own pace.

Personal itineraries are tailored to your time frame, level of 4x4 driving experience and budget.

Choose from a range of accommodation from luxury lodges to camping.

Safari Drive trips include:

- Expedition equipped 4x4s for up to five people
- In-country briefing & backup
- Satellite phone
- Handbook
- Roof tent
- Water tanks
- Satellite navigation with Tracks 4 Africa
- All camping equipment

+44 (0)1488 71140 | info@safaridrive.com

www.safaridrive.com

ABTOT

6

In the Wilds

DRIVING

Driving around Zambia isn't for the novice, or the unprepared. Long stretches of the tarred roads are extensively pot-holed, most of the secondary gravel roads are in very poor repair, and many areas rely on bush tracks maintained only by the passage of vehicles. If you plan on exploring in the more rural areas, and remote parks, then you will need at least two sturdy, fully equipped 4x4 vehicles. It says something of the roads in general that until very recently most of Zambia's car-hire companies would rent vehicles only if you took a local driver – and even then only for use in towns.

Those planning to drive themselves around Zambia should read this section in conjunction with the general details on driving in *Chapter 4*, pages 67–70.

EQUIPMENT AND PREPARATIONS
Fuel and fuel consumption Petrol and diesel are available in most of the towns (pages 67–9), but elsewhere diesel is generally more widely available. Although shortages are relatively rare, they do still occur – especially in the more remote west – and you'll need to be prepared for them. For travel into the bush in particular you will need long-range fuel tanks, and/or a large stock of filled jerrycans. It is essential to plan your fuel requirements well in advance, and to carry more than you expect to need.

Remember that using the vehicle's 4x4 capability, especially in low-ratio gears, will significantly increase your fuel consumption. Similarly, the cool comfort of a vehicle's air conditioning will burn your fuel reserves swiftly.

Spares Zambia's garages do not generally have a comprehensive stock of vehicle spares – though bush mechanics can effect the most amazing short-term repairs, with remarkably basic tools and raw materials. Spares for the more common makes are easiest to find, so most basic Land Rover and Toyota 4x4 parts are available somewhere in Lusaka, at a price. If you are arriving in Zambia with a foreign vehicle, it is best to bring as many spares as you can, though be aware that you could be charged import duty. Spares for both Toyota and Ford are available in Lusaka and Kitwe, Southern Cross in Lusaka and Chingola stock Mercedes and Jeep parts. For more general spares, there are branches of Autoworld in several major cities, including Lusaka and Ndola.

Navigation See the section on *Maps and navigation*, pages 58–60, for detailed comments, but there are good if old survey maps available from the Surveyor General's office in Mulungushi House, in Lusaka. You should seriously consider taking a GPS system if you are heading off the main roads in the more remote areas of the country.

COPING WITH ZAMBIA'S ROADS

Tar roads Many of Zambia's tar roads are excellent, and a programme of tarring is gradually extending these good sections. However, within them there are occasional patches of pot-holes. These often occur in small groups, making some short stretches of tar very slow going indeed. If you are unlucky, or foolish, enough to hit one of these sections after speeding along a smooth stretch of tar, then you are likely to blow at least one tyre and in danger of a serious accident. For this reason, if for no other, even tar roads that look good are worth treating with caution. It is wiser never to exceed about 80km/h.

If you're coming into a town, or approaching a roadblock, or near a school, you're likely to come across some form of traffic-calming measure. Typically these take the form of speed humps of varying degrees of efficacy and height, and some can do considerable damage to a vehicle if hit at even a modicum of speed. They can also slow traffic down to a crawl, which can be immensely frustrating.

At the beginning of the rainy season, in October and November, take particular care. During the dry season there can be a considerable build-up of diesel and oil

POLICE ROADBLOCKS

Often in Zambia you'll come across a police or immigration roadblock. You'll find them on all the main roads around the larger towns, and randomly placed on other tar roads and arteries also. It's vital that you stop for them, and it'll speed your journey if you know how to deal with them. I usually slow down on my approach, turn off any music or air conditioning, take off my sunglasses and roll down my window. Then greet the officer with a broad smile and a traditional greeting, or at least a polite 'Good morning, how are you?' (See *Cultural guidelines*, pages 79–80, for more on these.)

Foreigners will often be waved through. Sometimes you'll be asked a few questions – typically about where you are going and what you are doing. Keep your answers simple, honest and clear. You may be asked to test your lights, or indicators, or to show your insurance or identification, so it's important to have your passport, driving licence and vehicle documentation to hand. Answer politely with good humour and keep cool.

Like any country, Zambia has occasional radar traps, and there are rules of the road; if you contravene these, then you may be fined. If so, then it's best to fill out the official forms, pay the official fine as swiftly as possible, and keep the receipt. Fines vary from K300 for driving without a seatbelt or with a defective tyre to K450 for using a hand-held mobile phone.

SPURIOUS CHARGES The vast majority of roadblocks are fair and friendly, but occasionally you may find one where the officers are really looking to levy a fine. This is rare, but it happens! Then the officers will either find a problem, or make one up, to try to get you to pay an on-the-spot fine – and they won't be using official forms.

Some of their favourite excuses may be the finer, real or fictitious, points of the law of the road. These might include claiming that you haven't got two six-inch white strips of reflective tape on your front bumper, or two in red on the back bumper; or that you should have two steel triangles that are easy to get at (a favourite is to fine people with plastic ones!); or that your reversing lights don't work. Another ploy is to charge a fine, but one that's lower than it should be – if on tar roads, so after the first rains water tends to lie on this layer and can create a surface akin to black ice.

Strip roads Occasionally there are roads where the sealed tar surface is only wide enough for one vehicle. This becomes a problem when you meet another vehicle travelling in the opposite direction … on the same stretch of tar. Then local practice is to wait until the last possible moment before you steer left, driving with two wheels on the gravel adjacent to the tar, and two on the tar. Usually, the vehicle coming in the opposite direction will do the same, and after passing each other both vehicles veer back on to the tar. If you are unused to this, then slow right down before you steer on to the gravel.

Gravel roads Gravel (or dirt) roads can be very deceptive. Even when they appear smooth, flat and fast (which is not often), they still do not give vehicles much traction. You will frequently put the car into small skids, and with practice at slower speeds you will learn how to deal with them. Gravel is a less forgiving

you're asked for, say, K25 for driving without a seatbelt, the likelihood is that no receipt will be forthcoming.

Whatever the charge, however unreasonable, it's vital that you keep your cool, take your time, and don't appear at all bothered. Act as if you've all the time in the world, keep smiling and stay helpful and cheerful. Never get angry; always keep it amiable. However, do politely insist on a few of Zambia's basic road laws:

- You should always, very pleasantly and politely, record the officer's name and number – I'd be casual about this – but make it clear that you have done it.
- Note that higher police officers and authorities try hard to stamp out this sort of corrupt behaviour. For this reason you should always find a way to report dodgy behaviour to a higher officer at the local station, though obviously don't imply that the officer(s) in question is doing anything wrong.
- You never need to give your car keys or licence to a police officer; they have the right to see your licence – but not to take it off you.
- If you are charged with anything, then you have the right to insist that the officer accompanies you to the local police station, to discuss the charge with his superior. So, basically, you say politely that you're happy to pay the fine … but you wish to do so at the local police station.
- Never threaten to 'report' an officer – but instead you might innocently insist that you need a receipt with a stamp – and you'll have to take it to the station for one, even after they let you go.
- Finally, I'd never admit to being late, or having to be anywhere too quickly; it's tantamount to admitting that you'll be willing to pay a bribe to get away faster.
- If you willingly pay bribes then your corruptness is perpetuating the practice. Don't do it.

Stick to these rules, take your time, remain patient and they'll eventually let you go – or at least the price of the 'fine' will reduce to being insignificant!

surface on which to drive than tar. The rules and techniques for driving well are the same for both, but on tar you can get away with sloppy braking and cornering which would prove fatal on gravel.

Further, in Zambia you must always be prepared for the unexpected: an animal wandering onto the road, a rash of huge pot-holes, or an unexpected corner. So it is verging on insane to drive over about 60km/h on any of Zambia's gravel roads. Other basic driving hints include:

Slowing down If in any doubt about what lies ahead, always slow down. Road surfaces can vary enormously, so keep a constant lookout for pot-holes, ruts or patches of soft sand which could put you into an unexpected slide. If you do find the vehicle wandering having hit a corrugated section, always steer into the direction in which you are travelling.

Passing vehicles When passing other vehicles travelling in the opposite direction, always slow down to minimise both the damage that stone chippings will do to your windscreen, and the danger in driving through the other vehicle's dust cloud.

Using your gears In normal driving, a lower gear will give you more control over the car – so keep out of high 'cruising' gears. Rather stick with third or fourth, and accept that your revs will be slightly higher than they normally are.

Cornering and braking Under ideal conditions, the brakes should only be applied when the car is travelling in a straight line. Braking whilst negotiating a corner is dangerous, so it is vital to slow down before you reach corners. Equally, it is better to slow down gradually, using a combination of gears and brakes, than to use the brakes alone. You are less likely to skid.

DRIVING AT NIGHT Never drive at night unless you have to. Both wild and domestic animals frequently spend the night by the side of busy roads, and will actually sleep on quieter ones. Tar roads are especially bad as the surface absorbs all the sun's heat by day, and then radiates it at night – making it a warm bed for passing animals. A high-speed collision with any animal, even a small one like a goat, will not only kill the animal, but also cause very severe damage to a vehicle, with potentially fatal consequences. A word of caution about other road users, too: there's a prevalence for both drivers and pedestrians to be under the influence of alcohol at night. Finally, watch out for drivers with poorly maintained vehicles, who tend to drive between dawn and dusk to avoid contact with the police.

4X4 DRIVING TECHNIQUES You will need a high-clearance 4x4 to get anywhere in Zambia that's away from the main arteries. However, no vehicle can make up for an inexperienced driver – so ensure that you are confident of your vehicle's capabilities before you venture into the wilds with it. You really need extensive practice, with an expert on hand to advise you, before you'll have the first idea how to handle such a vehicle in difficult terrain. Finally, driving in convoy (preferably with some reasonably strong people) is an essential precaution in the more remote areas, in case one vehicle gets stuck or breaks down. Some of the more relevant techniques include:

Driving in sand If you're in a 4x4 and are really struggling in deep sand, then stop on the next fairly solid area that you come to. Lower your tyre pressure until there is a small bulge in the tyre walls (having first made sure that you have the means to re-inflate them when you reach solid roads again). A lower pressure will help your traction greatly, but increase the wear on your tyres. Pump them up again before you drive on a hard surface at speed, or the tyres will be badly damaged.

Where there are clear, deep-rutted tracks in the sand, don't fight the steering wheel – just relax and let your vehicle steer itself. Driving in the cool of the morning is easier than later in the day because when sand is cool it compacts better and is firmer. (When hot, the pockets of air between the sand grains expand and the sand becomes looser.)

If you do get stuck, despite these precautions, don't panic. Don't just rev the engine and spin the wheels – you'll only dig deeper. Instead stop. Relax and assess the situation. Now dig shallow ramps in front of all the wheels, reinforcing them with pieces of wood, vegetation, stones, material or anything else which will give the wheels better traction. Lighten the vehicle load (passengers out) and push. Don't let the engine revs die as you engage your lowest-ratio gear. That probably means using '4x4 low' rather than '4x4 high'. Use the clutch to ensure that the wheels don't spin wildly and dig themselves further into the sand.

Sometimes rocking the vehicle backwards and forwards will build up momentum to break you free. This can be done by the driver intermittently applying the clutch and/or by getting helpers who can push and pull the vehicle at the same frequency. Once the vehicle is moving, the golden rule of sand driving is to keep up the momentum: if you pause, you will sink and stop.

Navigation note Remember that your fuel consumption when driving in sand is much higher than on harder surfaces. Also, when navigating on sandy roads observe that your wheels slip and spin, and so your milometer will register a much greater distance than you have actually travelled. I've generally used a GPS to track distances for this book – not a vehicle's milometer.

Driving through high grass
After the rains, many of Zambia's tracks are often knee-high in seeding grass. As your vehicle drives through, stems and especially seeds can build up in front of and inside the radiator, and get trapped in crevices underneath the chassis. This is a major problem in the less-visited areas of Kalahari sand. It's at its worst in March to June, after the rains, and in western Zambia and Kafue.

This causes a real danger of overheating (pages 100–1) and fire. First, the build-up of seeds and stems over the radiator insulates it. Thus, if you aren't watching your gauges, the engine's temperature can rocket. It will swiftly seize up and catch fire. Secondly, the grass build-up itself, if allowed to become too big, can catch fire due to its contact with the hot exhaust system, underneath the vehicle.

In addition to the obvious precaution of carrying a fire extinguisher, there are several strategies to minimise these dangers; best apply them all. Firstly, before you set out, buy a few square metres of the tightly woven window-meshing gauze material used in the windows of safari tents. Fix one large panel of this on the vehicle's bull-bars, well in front of the radiator grill. Fix another much closer to it, but still outside of the engine compartment. This should vastly reduce the number of seeds reaching your radiator.

Secondly, watch your vehicle's engine-temperature gauge like a hawk when you're travelling through areas of grassland.

Thirdly, stop every 10km or so (yes, really, that often) and check the radiator and the undercarriage for pockets of stems and seeds. Pay special attention to the hot areas of the exhaust pipe; you should not allow a build-up of flammable material there. Use a stick or piece of wire to clean these seeds and stems out before you set off.

When driving through the grass, take particular care to avoid hidden obstacles, which can inflict considerable damage to your vehicle. Watch out too, for bush fires, which can move rapidly and make some roads impassable for a while.

Driving in mud This is difficult, though the theory is the same as for sand: keep going and don't stop. That said, even the most experienced drivers get stuck. Many areas of Zambia (like large stretches of the Kafue, Luangwa and Lower Zambezi valleys) have very fine soil known as 'black-cotton' soil, which becomes impassable when wet. This is why many of the camps close down for the rains, as the only way to get there would be to walk.

Mud can also have the same overheating effect as grass seed, so it's important to wash it away from the radiator once you stop.

Push-starting when stuck If you are unlucky enough to need to push-start your vehicle whilst it is stuck in sand or mud, there is a remedy. Raise up the drive wheels, and take off one of the tyres. Then wrap a length of rope around the hub and treat it like a spinning top: one person (or more) pulls the rope to make the axle spin, whilst the driver lifts the clutch, turns the ignition on, and engages a low gear to turn the engine over. This is a very difficult equivalent of a push-start, but it may be your only option.

On rocky terrain Have your tyre pressure higher than normal and move very slowly. If necessary, passengers should get out and guide you along the track to avoid scraping the undercarriage on the ground. This can be a very slow business, but often applies in some of Zambia's mountainous areas.

Crossing rivers The first thing to do is to stop and check the river. You must assess its depth, its substrate (type of riverbed) and its current flow; and determine the best route to drive across it. This is best done by wading across the river (whilst watching for hippos and crocodiles, if necessary). Beware of water that's too deep for your vehicle, or the very real possibility of being swept away by a fast current and a slippery substrate.

If everything is OK then select your lowest gear ratio and drive through the water at a slow but steady rate. Your vehicle's air intake must be above the level of the water to avoid your engine filling with water. It's not worth taking risks, so remember that a flooded river may subside to safer levels by the next morning.

Many rivers in Zambia have pontoon crossings capable of ferrying vehicles across. Traditionally these are hand-operated wooden platforms tied on top of buoyant empty oil cans and kept in line by steel cables stretched across the river. Nowadays, on the busier crossings, such structures are often motorised, with a steel superstructure, but in many cases the cables remain. The pontoons are usually manned by local people for either a large official charge (K56 per vehicle is fairly average) or – occasionally – a handsome tip. You need to take great care (everybody out, use first gear) when driving on and off these, and make sure that the pontoon is held tightly next to the bank on both occasions.

Overheating If the engine has overheated then the only option is to stop and turn it off. Don't open the radiator cap to refill it until the radiator is no longer hot to the touch. Even then, keep the engine running and the water circulating while you refill the radiator – otherwise you run the risk of cracking the hot metal by suddenly cooling it. Flicking droplets of water onto the outside of a running engine will cool it. And see *Driving through high grass* above.

DRIVING NEAR BIG GAME The only animals which are likely to pose a threat to vehicles are elephants – and generally only elephants which are familiar with vehicles. So, treat them with the greatest respect and don't 'push' them by trying to move ever closer. Letting them approach you is much safer, and they will feel far less threatened and more relaxed. Then, if the animals are calm, you can safely turn the engine off, sit quietly, and watch as they pass you by.

If you are unlucky, or foolish, enough to unexpectedly drive into the middle of a herd, then don't panic. Keep your movements, and those of the vehicle, slow and measured. Back off steadily. Don't be panicked, or overly intimidated, by a mock charge – this is just their way of frightening you away. Professionals will sometimes switch their engines off, but this is not for the faint-hearted.

BUSH CAMPING

Many 'boy scout'-type manuals have been written on survival in the bush, usually by military veterans. If you are stranded with a convenient multi-purpose knife, then these useful tomes will describe how you can build a shelter from branches, catch passing animals for food, and signal to the inevitable rescue planes which are combing the globe looking for you – whilst avoiding the attentions of hostile forces.

In Zambia, bush camping is usually less about survival than comfort. You're likely to have much more than the knife: probably at least a bulging backpack, if not a loaded 4x4. Thus the challenge is not to camp and survive, it is to camp and be as comfortable as possible. With practice you'll learn how, but a few hints may be useful for the less experienced.

WHERE YOU CAN CAMP In frequently visited national parks, there are designated campsites that you should use, as directed by the local game scouts. Elsewhere the rules are less obvious, though it is normal to ask the scouts, and get their permission, for any site that you have in mind.

Outside of the parks, you should ask the local landowner, or village head, if they are happy for you to camp on their property. If you explain patiently and politely what you want, then you are unlikely to meet anything but warm hospitality from most rural Zambians. They will normally be as fascinated with your way of life as you are with theirs. Company by your campfire is virtually assured.

CHOOSING A SITE Only experience will teach you how to choose a good site for pitching a tent, but a few points may help you avoid a lot of problems:

- Avoid camping on what looks like a path through the bush, however indistinct. It may be a well-used game trail.
- Beware of camping in dry riverbeds: dangerous flash floods can arrive with little or no warning.
- In marshy areas camp on higher ground to avoid cold, damp mists in the morning and evening.
- Camp a reasonable distance from water: near enough to walk to it, but far enough to avoid animals which arrive to drink.

- If a lightning storm is likely, make sure that your tent is not the highest thing around.
- Finally, choose a site which is as flat as possible – you will find sleeping much easier.

CAMPFIRES Campfires can create a great atmosphere and warm you on a cold evening, but they can also be damaging to the environment and leave unsightly piles of ash and blackened stones. Deforestation is a major concern in much of the developing world, including parts of Zambia, so if you do light a fire then use wood as the locals do: sparingly. If you have a vehicle, consider buying firewood in advance from people who sell it at the roadside.

If you collect it yourself, then take only dead wood, nothing living. Never just pick up a log: always roll it over first, checking carefully for snakes or scorpions.

Experienced campers build small, highly efficient fires by using a few large stones to absorb, contain and reflect the heat, and gradually feeding just a few thick logs into the centre to burn. Cooking pots can be balanced on the stones, or at the point where the logs meet and burn. Other campers will use a small trench, lined with rocks, to similar effect. Either technique takes practice, but is worth perfecting. Whichever you do, bury the ashes, take any rubbish with you when you leave, and make the site look as if you had never been there.

Don't expect an unattended fire to frighten away wild animals – that works in Hollywood, but not in Africa. A campfire may help your feelings of insecurity, but lion and hyena will disregard it with stupefying nonchalance.

Finally, do be hospitable to any locals who appear. Despite your efforts to seek permission for your camp, you may effectively be staying in their back gardens.

USING A TENT (OR NOT) Whether to use a tent or to sleep in the open is a personal choice, dependent upon where you are. In an area where there are predators around (specifically lion and hyena) then you should use a tent – and sleep *completely* inside it, as a protruding leg may seem like a tasty takeaway to a hungry hyena. This is especially true at organised campsites, where the local animals are so used to humans that they have lost much of their inherent fear of man.

Outside game areas, you will be fine sleeping in the open, or preferably under a mosquito net, with just the stars of the African sky above you. On the practical side, sleeping under a tree will reduce the morning dew that settles on your sleeping bag. If your vehicle has a large, flat roof then sleeping on this will provide you with peace of mind, and a star-filled outlook. (Hiring a vehicle with a built-in rooftop tent would seem like a perfect solution, until you want to take a drive whilst leaving your camp intact.)

CAMPING EQUIPMENT If you are taking an organised safari, you will not need any camping equipment at all. However, for those travelling independently very little kit is available in Zambia. So buy high-quality equipment beforehand as it will save you a lot of time and trouble once you arrive. Here are a few comments on various essentials.

Tent During the rains a good tent is essential in order to stay dry. Even during the dry season one is useful if there are lion or hyena around. If backpacking, invest in a high-quality, lightweight tent. Mosquito-netting ventilation panels, allowing a good flow of air, are essential. (Just a corner of mesh at the top of the tent is not enough for comfort.) Don't go for a tent that's small; it may feel cosy at home, but will be hot and claustrophobic in the heat.

I have been using the same Spacepacker tent, manufactured by Robert Saunders Ltd (*Five Oaks Lane, Chigwell, Essex IG7 4QP, UK; www.robertsaunders.co.uk*) for over ten years. It's a dome tent with fine mesh doors on either side which allow a through draught, making all the difference when temperatures are high. The alternative to a good tent is a mosquito net, which is fine unless it is raining or you are in a big game area.

Sleeping bag A lightweight, 'three-season' sleeping bag is ideal for Zambia, unless you are heading up to the Nyika Plateau in winter where the nights freeze. Down is preferable to synthetic fillings for most of the year, as it packs smaller, is lighter, and feels more luxurious to sleep in. However, when down gets wet it loses its efficiency, so bring a good synthetic bag if you are likely to encounter much rain.

Ground mat A ground mat of some sort is essential. It keeps you warm and comfortable, and it protects the tent's groundsheet from rough or stony ground. (Do put it underneath the tent!) Closed cell foam mats are widely available outside Zambia, so buy one before you arrive. The better mats cost double or treble the price of the cheaper ones, but are stronger, thicker and warmer – well worth the investment. Therm-a-Rests, the combination air-mattress and foam mats, are strong, durable and also worth the investment – but take a puncture repair kit with you just in case of problems.

Sheet sleeping bag Thin, pure-cotton sheet sleeping bags are small, light and very useful. They are easily washed and so are normally used like a sheet, inside a sleeping bag, to keep it clean. They can, of course, be used on their own when your main sleeping bag is too hot.

Stove 'Trangia'-type stoves, which burn methylated spirits, are simple to use, light, and cheap to run. They come complete with a set of light aluminium pans and a very useful all-purpose handle. Often you'll be able to cook on a fire with the pans, but it's nice to have the option of making a brew in a few minutes while you set up camp. Methylated spirits is cheap and widely available, even in the rural areas, but bring a tough (purpose-made) fuel container with you as the bottles in which it is sold will soon crack and spill all over your belongings.

Petrol- and kerosene-burning stoves are undoubtedly efficient on fuel and powerful – but invariably temperamental and messy. Gas stoves use pressurised canisters, which are not allowed on aircraft and are difficult to buy in Zambia.

Torch (flashlight) This should be on every visitor's packing list – whether you're staying in upmarket camps or backpacking. Find one that's small and tough, and preferably water- and dust-proof. Headtorches leave your hands free (useful when cooking or mending the car) and the latest designs are relatively light and comfortable to wear. Consider one of the new generation of super-bright LED torches; the LED Lenser range is excellent.

Water containers For everyday use, a small two-litre water bottle is invaluable, however you are travelling. If you're thinking of camping, you should also consider a strong, collapsible water-bag – perhaps 5–10 litres in size – which will reduce the number of trips that you need to make from your camp to the water source. (Ten litres of water weighs 10kg.) Drivers will want to carry a number of large containers of water, especially if venturing into the Kalahari sand in western Zambia, where good surface water is not common.

See pages 57–8, for a memory-jogging list of other useful items to pack.

ANIMAL DANGERS FOR CAMPERS Camping in Africa is really very safe, though you may not think so from reading this. If you have a major problem whilst camping, it will probably be because you did something stupid, or because you forgot to take a few simple precautions. Here are a few general basics, applicable to anywhere in Africa and not just Zambia.

Large animals Big game will not bother you if you are in a tent – provided that you do not attract its attention, or panic it. Elephants will gently tiptoe through your guy ropes whilst you sleep, without even nudging your tent. However, if you wake up and make a noise, startling them, they are far more likely to panic and step on your tent. Similarly, scavengers will quietly wander round, smelling your evening meal in the air, without any intention of harming you. Bear the following precautions in mind:

- Remember to use the toilet before going to bed, and avoid getting up in the night if possible.
- Scrupulously clean everything used for food that might smell good to scavengers. Put these utensils in a vehicle if possible, suspend them from a tree, or pack them away in a rucksack inside the tent.
- Do not keep any smelly foodstuffs, like meat or citrus fruit, in your tent. Their smells may attract unwanted attention.
- Do not leave anything outside that could be picked up – like bags, pots, pans, etc. Hyenas, amongst others, will take anything. (They have been known to crunch a camera's lens, and eat it.)
- If you are likely to wake in the night, then leave the tent's zips a few centimetres open at the top, enabling you to take a quiet peek outside.

Creepy-crawlies As you set up camp, clear stones or logs out of your way with great caution: underneath will be great hiding places for snakes and scorpions. Long moist grass is ideal territory for snakes, and dry, dusty, rocky places are classic sites for scorpions.

If you are sleeping in the open, it is not unknown to wake and find a snake lying next to you in the morning. Don't panic: your warmth has just attracted it to you. You will not be bitten if you gently edge away without making any sudden movements. (This is one good argument for using at least a mosquito net!)

Before you put on your shoes, shake them out. Similarly, check the back of your backpack before you slip it on. Just a curious spider, in either, could inflict a painful bite.

WALKING IN THE BUSH

Walking in the African bush is a totally different sensation from driving through it. You may start off a little unready – perhaps even sleepy – for an early morning walk, but swiftly your mind will awake. There are no noises except the wildlife, and you. So every noise that isn't caused by you must be an animal, or a bird, or an insect. Every smell and every rustle has a story to tell, if you can understand it.

With time, patience and a good guide you can learn to smell the presence of elephants, and hear when a predator alarms impala. You can use oxpeckers to lead you to buffalo, or vultures to help you locate a kill. Tracks will record the passage of animals in the sand, telling what passed by, how long ago and in which direction.

Eventually your gaze becomes alert to the slightest movement, your ears aware of every sound. This is safari at its best: a live, sharp, spine-tingling experience that's hard to beat and very addictive. Be careful: watching game from a vehicle will never be the same again for you.

WALKING TRAILS AND SAFARIS One of Zambia's biggest attractions is its walking safaris, which can justly claim to be amongst the best in Africa. The concept was pioneered here, in the Luangwa Valley, by the late Norman Carr. He also founded Nsefu Camp and Kapani Lodge, and trained several of the valley's best guides. It was he who first operated walking safaris for photographic guests, as opposed to hunters. The Luangwa still has a strong tradition of walking – which, in itself, fosters excellent walking guides. Several of the camps are dedicated to walking safaris, and guiding standards are generally very high.

One of the reasons behind the valley's success is the stringent tests that a guide must pass before he, or she, will be allowed to take clients into the bush. Walking guides have the hardest tests to pass; there is a less demanding exam for guides who conduct safaris from vehicles.

The second major reason for excellence is Zambia's policy of having a safari guide and an armed game scout accompany every walking safari. These groups are limited (by park rules) to a maximum of seven guests, and there's normally a tea-bearer (carrying drinks and refreshments) as well as the guide and armed scout.

If a problem arises with an aggressive animal, then the guide looks after the visitors – telling them exactly what to do – whilst the scout keeps his sights trained on the animal, just in case a shot is necessary. Fortunately such drastic measures are needed only rarely. This system of two guides means that Zambia's walks are very safe. Few shots are ever fired, and I can't remember hearing of an animal (or a person) ever being injured.

Contrast this with other African countries where a single guide (who may, or may not, be armed) watches out for the game *and* takes care of the visitors at the same time. The Zambian way is far better.

Etiquette for walking safaris If you plan to walk then avoid wearing any bright, unnatural colours, especially white. Dark, muted shades are best; greens, browns and khaki are ideal. Hats are essential, as is sunblock. Even a short walk will last for 2 hours, and there's no vehicle to which you can retreat if you get too hot.

Binoculars should be immediately accessible – one pair per person – ideally in dust-proof cases strapped to your belt. Cameras too, if you decide to bring any, as they are of little use buried at the bottom of a camera bag. Heavy tripods or long lenses are a nightmare to lug around, so leave them behind if you can (and accept, philosophically, that you may miss shots).

Walkers see the most when walking in silent single file. This doesn't mean that you can't stop to whisper a question to the guide; just that idle chatter will reduce your powers of observation, and make you even more visible to the animals (who will usually flee when they sense you).

With regard to safety, your guide will always brief you in detail before you set off. S/he will outline possible dangers, and what to do in the unlikely event of them materialising. Listen carefully: this is vital.

Face-to-face animal encounters Whether you are on an organised walking safari, on your own hike, or just walking from the car to your tent in the bush, it is not unlikely that you will come across some of Africa's larger animals at close quarters. Invariably, the danger is much less than you imagine, and a few basic guidelines will enable you to cope effectively with most situations.

First of all, don't panic. Console yourself with the fact that animals are not normally interested in people. You are not their normal food, or their predator. If you do not annoy or threaten them, you will be left alone.

If you are walking to look for animals, then remember that this is their environment and not yours. Animals have evolved in the bush, and their senses are far better attuned to it than yours. To be on less unequal terms, remain alert and try to spot them from a distance. This gives you the option of approaching carefully, or staying well clear.

Finally, the advice of a good guide is far more valuable than the simplistic comments noted here. Animals, like people, are all different. So whilst we can generalise here and say how the 'average' animal will behave, the one that's glaring at you over a small bush may have had a really bad day, and be feeling much grumpier than normal.

That said, here are a few general comments on how to deal with some potentially dangerous situations.

Buffalo This is probably the continent's most dangerous animal to hikers, but there is a difference between the old males, often encountered on their own or in small groups, and large breeding herds.

The former are easily surprised. If they hear or smell something amiss, they will charge without provocation – motivated by a fear that something is sneaking up on them. Buffalo have an excellent sense of smell, but fortunately they are short-sighted. Avoid a charge by quickly climbing the nearest tree, or by side-stepping at the last minute. If adopting the latter, more risky, technique then stand motionless until the last possible moment, as the buffalo may well miss you anyhow.

The large breeding herds can be treated in a totally different manner. If you approach them in the open, they will often flee. Sometimes though, in areas often used for walking safaris, they will stand and watch, moving aside to allow you to pass through the middle of the herd.

Neither encounter is for the faint-hearted or inexperienced, so steer clear of these dangerous animals wherever possible.

Black rhino If you are both exceptionally lucky to find a black rhino, and then unlucky enough to be charged by it, use the same tactics as you would for a buffalo: tree climbing or dodging at the last second. (It is amazing how even the least athletic walker will swiftly scale the nearest tree when faced with a charging rhino.)

Elephant Normally elephants are a problem only if you disturb a mother with a calf, or approach a male in musth (state of arousal). So keep well away from these. Lone bulls can usually be approached quite closely when feeding. If you get too close to any elephant it will scare you off with a 'mock charge': head up, perhaps shaking – ears flapping – trumpeting. Lots of sound and fury. This is intended to be frightening, and it is. But it is just a warning and no cause for panic. Just freeze to assess the elephant's intentions, then back off slowly.

When elephants really mean business, they will put their ears back, their head down, and charge directly at you without stopping. This is known as a 'full charge'. There is no easy way to avoid the charge of an angry elephant, so take a hint from the warning and back off very slowly as soon as you encounter a mock charge. Don't run. If you are the object of a full charge, then you have no choice but to run – preferably round an anthill, up a tall tree, or wherever.

Lion Tracking lion can be one of the most exhilarating parts of a walking safari. Sadly, they will normally flee before you even get close to them. However, it can be a problem if you come across a large pride unexpectedly. Lion are well camouflaged; it is easy to find yourself next to one before you realise it. If you had been listening, you would probably have heard a warning growl about 20m ago. Now it is too late.

The best plan is to stop, and back off slowly, but confidently. If you are in a small group, then stick together. *Never* run from a big cat. First, they are always faster than you are. Secondly, running will just convince them that you are frightened prey, and worth chasing. As a last resort, if they seem too inquisitive and follow as you back off, then stop. Call their bluff. Pretend that you are not afraid and make loud, deep, confident noises: shout at them, bang something. But do not run.

John Coppinger, one of Luangwa's most experienced guides, adds that every single compromising experience that he has had with lion on foot has been either with a female with cubs, or with a mating pair, when the males can get very aggressive. You have been warned.

Leopard Leopard are very seldom seen, and would normally flee from the most timid of lone hikers. However, if injured, or surprised, then they are very powerful, dangerous cats. Conventional wisdom is scarce, but never stare straight into the leopard's eyes, or it will regard this as a threat display. (The same is said, by some, to be true with lion.) Better to look away slightly, at a nearby bush, or even at its tail. Then back off slowly, facing the direction of the cat and showing as little terror as you can. As with lion – loud, deep, confident noises are a last line of defence. Never run from a leopard.

Hippo Hippo are fabled to account for more deaths in Africa than any other animal (ignoring the mosquito). Having been attacked and capsized by a hippo whilst in a dugout canoe, I find this very easy to believe, but see *Appendix 1* (page 518) for an alternative comment on this. Visitors are most likely to encounter hippo in the water, when paddling a canoe (pages 108–9) or fishing. However, as they spend half their time grazing on land, they will sometimes be encountered out of the water. Away from the water, out of their comforting lagoons, hippos are even more dangerous. If they see you, they will flee towards the water – so the golden rule is never to get between a hippo and its escape route to deep water. Given that a hippo will outrun you on land, standing motionless is probably your best line of defence.

Snakes These are really not the great danger that people imagine. Most flee when they feel the vibrations of footsteps; only a few will stay still. The puff adder is responsible for more cases of snakebite than any other venomous snake in Zambia because, when approached, it will simply puff itself up and hiss as a warning, rather than slither away. This makes it essential to always watch where you place your feet when walking in the bush.

Similarly, there are a couple of arboreal (tree-dwelling) species which may be taken by surprise if you carelessly grab vegetation as you walk. So don't.

Spitting cobras are also encountered occasionally, which will aim for your eyes and spit with accuracy. If one of these rears up in front of you, then turn away and avert your eyes. If the spittle reaches your eyes, you must wash them out *immediately* and thoroughly with whatever liquid comes to hand: water, milk, even urine if that's the only liquid that you can quickly produce.

CANOEING

The Zambezi – both above the Victoria Falls and from Kariba to Mozambique – is in constant use for canoeing trips. Paddling along this beautiful, tropical river is as much a part of Zambia's safari scene in the Lower Zambezi as are open-top Land Rovers. Generally you either canoe along the river for a set number of days, stopping each night at a different place, or paddle for a short stretch from one of the camps – as an alternative activity to a walk or a game drive.

Rather than traditional *mekoro* (dug-out canoes, singular *mokoro*), most operators use large, two- or three-person Canadian-style fibreglass canoes. Three-person canoes usually have a guide in the back of each, while two-person canoes are often paddled in 'convoy' with a guide in just one of the boats. Less confident (or lazier) paddlers might prefer to have a guide in their own canoe, while the more energetic usually want to have the boat to themselves.

ZAMBEZI CANOE GUIDES Most of the Zambezi's specialist canoeing operations are run by large companies on a very commercial basis. On these you can expect to join a party of about seven canoes, one of which will contain a guide. S/he should know the stretch of river well and will canoe along it regularly. The actual distances completed on the two-/three-night trips are quite short. All the trips run downstream and a day's canoeing could actually be completed in just 3 hours with a modicum of fitness and technique.

Like other guides, the 'river guides' must possess a professional licence in order to be allowed to take paying guests canoeing. Note that only a few of the best river guides also hold licences as general professional guides (ie: are licensed to lead walking safaris). These all-rounders generally have a far deeper understanding of the environment and the game than those who are only 'river guides'.

However, their greater skill commands a higher wage – and so they are usually found in the smaller, more upmarket operations. Given the inexperience of some of the river guides, I would always be willing to pay the extra. Although the safety record of river trips is good, accidents do happen occasionally.

THE MAIN DANGERS

Hippo Hippos are strictly vegetarians, and will usually attack a canoe only if they feel threatened. The standard avoidance technique is first of all to let them know that you are there. If in doubt, bang your paddle on the side of the canoe a few times (most novice canoeists will do this constantly anyhow).

During the day, hippopotami will congregate in the deeper areas of the river. The odd ones in shallow water – where they feel less secure – will head for the deeper places as soon as they are aware of a nearby canoe. Avoiding hippos then becomes a fairly simple case of steering around the deeper areas, where the pods will make their presence obvious. This is where experience, and knowing every bend of the river, becomes useful. Problems arise when canoes inadvertently stray over a pod of hippos, or when a canoe cuts a hippo off from its path of retreat into deeper water. Either is dangerous, as hippos will overturn canoes without a second thought, biting them and their occupants. Once in this situation, there are no easy remedies. So – avoid it in the first place.

Crocodiles Crocodiles may have sharp teeth and look prehistoric, but are rarely a danger to a canoeist while in the boat, although the larger, wilier animals can pose a serious threat. If you find yourself in the water, the situation is considerably worse. Then the more you struggle and the more waves you create, the more you will attract their unwelcome attentions. There is a major problem when canoes are overturned by hippos – then you must get out of the water as soon as possible, either into another canoe or onto the bank.

When a crocodile attacks an animal, it will try to disable it, normally by getting a firm, biting grip, submerging, and performing a long, fast barrel-roll. This will disorient the prey, drown it, and probably twist off the limb that has been bitten. In this dire situation, your best line of defence is probably to stab the reptile in its eyes with anything sharp that you have. Alternatively, if you can lift up its tongue and let the water into its lungs whilst it is underwater, then a crocodile will start to drown and will release its prey.

Jo Pope reports that a man survived an attack in the Zambezi when a crocodile grabbed his arm and started to spin backwards into deep water. The man wrapped his legs around the crocodile, to spin with it and avoid having his arm twisted off. As this happened, he tried to poke his thumb into its eyes, but with no effect. Finally he put his free arm into the crocodile's mouth, and opened up the beast's throat. This worked. The crocodile left him and he survived with only a damaged arm. Understandably, anecdotes about tried and tested methods of escape are rare.

MINIMUM IMPACT

When you visit, drive through, or camp in an area and have 'minimum impact' this means that that area is left in the same condition as – or better than – when you entered it. Whilst most visitors view minimum impact as being desirable, spend time to consider the ways in which we contribute to environmental degradation, and how these can be avoided.

DRIVING Use your vehicle responsibly. If there's a road, or a track, then don't go off it – the environment will suffer. Driving off-road can leave a multitude of tracks that detract from the 'wilderness' feeling for subsequent visitors. Equally, don't speed through towns or villages: remember the danger to local children, and the amount of dust you'll cause.

HYGIENE Use toilets if they are provided, even if they are basic longdrop loos with questionable cleanliness. If there are no toilets, then human excrement should always be buried well away from paths, or groundwater, and any tissue used should be burnt and then buried.

If you use rivers or lakes to wash, then soap yourself near the bank, using a pan for scooping water from the river – making sure that no soap finds its way back into the water. Use biodegradable soap. Sand makes an excellent pan-scrub, even if you have no water to spare.

RUBBISH Biodegradable rubbish can be burnt and buried with the campfire ashes. Don't just leave it lying around: it will look very unsightly and spoil the place for those who come after you.

Bring along some plastic bags with which to remove the remainder of your rubbish, and dispose of it at the next town. Items that will not burn, like tin cans, are best cleaned and squashed for easy carrying. If there are bins, then use them, but also consider when they will next be emptied, and also if local animals are likely to rummage through them first. Carrying out all your own rubbish may still be the sensible option.

HOST COMMUNITIES Whilst the rules for reducing impact on the environment have been understood and followed by responsible travellers for years, the effects of tourism on local people have only recently been considered. Many tourists believe it is their right, for example, to take intrusive photos of local people – and even become angry if the local people object. They refer to higher prices being charged to tourists as a rip-off, without considering the hand-to-mouth existence of those selling these products or services. They deplore child beggars, then hand out sweets or pens to local children with outstretched hands.

Our behaviour towards 'the locals' needs to be considered in terms of their culture, with the knowledge that we are the uninvited visitors. We visit to enjoy ourselves, but this should not be at the expense of local people. Read *Cultural guidelines*, pages 79–80, and aim to leave the local communities better off after your visit.

LOCAL PAYMENTS If you spend time with any of Zambia's poorer local people, perhaps camping in the bush or getting involved with one of the community-run projects, then take great care with any payments that you make.

First, note that most people like to spend their earnings on what *they* choose. This means that trying to pay for services with beads, food, old clothes or anything else instead of money isn't appreciated. Ask yourself how you'd like to be paid, and you'll understand this point.

Second, find out the normal cost of what you are buying. Most community campsites will have a standard price for a pitch and, if applicable, an hour's guided activity, or whatever. Find this out before you sleep there, or accept the offer of a walk. It is then important that you pay about that amount for the service rendered – no less, and not too much more.

As most people realise, if you try to pay less you'll get into trouble – as you would at home. However, many do not realise that if they generously pay a lot more, this can be equally damaging. Local rates of pay in rural areas can be very low, and a careless visitor can easily pay disproportionately large sums. Where this happens, local jobs can lose their value overnight. (Imagine working hard to become a game scout, only to learn that a tourist has given your friend the equivalent of your whole month's wages for just a few hours guiding. What incentive is there for you to carry on with your regular job?)

If you want to give more – for good service, a super guide, or just because you want to help – then either buy some locally made produce (at the going rate) or donate money to one of the organisations working to improve the lot of Zambia's most disadvantaged (page 81).

SEND US YOUR SNAPS!

We'd love to follow your adventures using our *Zambia* guide – why not send us your photos and stories via Twitter (@BradtGuides) and Instagram (@bradtguides) using the hashtag #zambia. Alternatively, you can upload your photos directly to the gallery on the Zambia destination page via our website (*www.bradtguides.com*).

Part Two

THE GUIDE

FOLLOW BRADT

For the latest news, special offers and competitions, subscribe to the Bradt newsletter via the website www.bradtguides.com and follow Bradt on:

f www.facebook.com/BradtTravelGuides
@BradtGuides
@bradtguides
www.pinterest.com/bradtguides

7

Lusaka

Despite the assertions of the tourist board, Lusaka is not high on Zambia's list of major attractions. Its wide, tree-lined boulevards can be pleasant, but as the city grows the traffic is increasingly chaotic and many of the suburbs are sprawling and dirty. However, Lusaka is no worse than London, New York or any number of other big cities. Like them, it has a fascination because it is unmistakably cosmopolitan, alive and kicking. Now home to almost one in five of Zambia's people, it has a discernible heartbeat which smaller or more sanitised cities lack. So if you go to Zambia with an interest in meeting a cross-section of its people, Lusaka should figure on your itinerary.

In my experience, the city's bad reputation has been exaggerated. Walking around at night is stupid and potentially dangerous, and during the day pickpockets will strike if you keep valuables obvious or accessible – as they will in any big city. However, as Lusaka has grown and security measures have increased, especially around the ever-rising number of malls, the perceived risks at least have lessened. Visitors to Lusaka who allow their paranoia to elevate the city's dangers to the dizzy heights of Lagos are deluding themselves. It isn't that dangerous, if you are careful.

HISTORY

Lusaka's status as a capital city dates only from 1935. Until then, the capital of Northern Rhodesia was Livingstone, but as Zambia's mines were developed it was felt that the town was too far away from the country's industrial heartland in the Copperbelt.

The site of the new capital was chosen both for its central location and for its position high on a plateau, resulting in a relatively cool climate. There was already a permanent settlement here: Lusaka owes its establishment to construction of the railway at the beginning of the 20th century, when a camp was needed for the workers. The decision to site the new state buildings on the ridge a couple of kilometres to the east of the railway was linked to the frequency with which the lower-lying land was flooded during the rains. While it was anticipated that Lusaka's heart would eventually shift east, the capital remained firmly divided, with its spacious new administrative area contrasting with the bustle of the business area focused on Cairo Road. Now commercial developments have combined with increasing levels of affluence to shift the focus once again – blurring the traditional divides and opening up new areas both close to the centre and out towards the suburbs.

GETTING THERE AND AWAY

BY AIR Now that British Airways no longer flies between the UK and Lusaka (airline code LUN), most visitors from Europe and the USA use Nairobi or

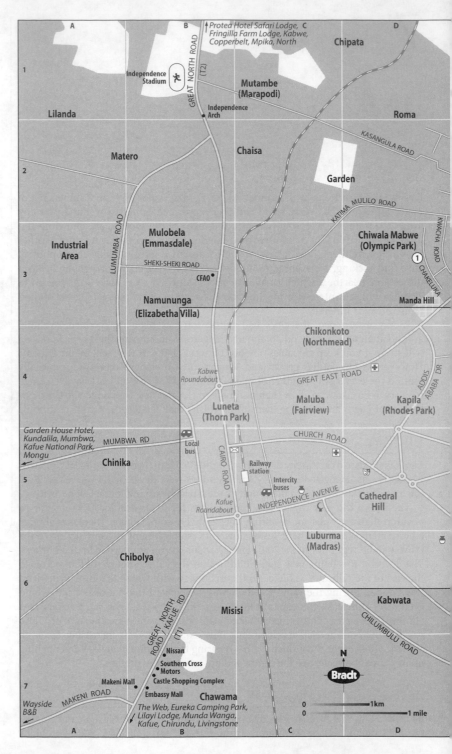

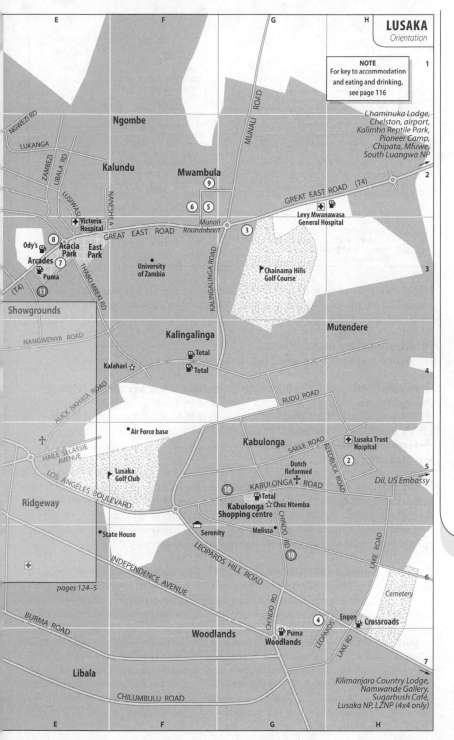

NOTE
For key to accommodation
and eating and drinking,
see page 116

Chaminuka Lodge,
Chelston, airport,
Kalimba Reptile Park,
Pioneer Camp,
Chipata, Mfuwe,
South Luangwa NP

Ngombe

Kalundu

Mwambula

GREAT EAST ROAD (T4)

NGWEZI RD

LUKANGA

ZAMBEZI

LIBALA RD

LUSWISI

NANESHILA

Victoria
Hospital

GREAT EAST ROAD

Munali
Roundabout

Levy Mwanawasa
General Hospital

Ody's

Acacia
Park

East
Park

Arcades

Puma

THABO MBEKI RD

University
of Zambia

KALINGALINGA ROAD

MUNALI ROAD

Chainama Hills
Golf Course

Mutendere

Showgrounds

NANGWENYA ROAD

Kalingalinga

Kalahari

Total

Total

RUDU ROAD

ALICK NKHATA ROAD

Air Force base

Kabulonga

SAILLE ROAD

REEDBUCK ROAD

Lusaka Trust
Hospital

HAILE SELASSIE
AVENUE

Lusaka
Golf Club

Dutch
Reformed

KABULONGA ROAD

Dil, US Embassy

LOS ANGELES BOULEVARD

Ridgeway

State House

Total

Kabulonga
Shopping centre

Chez Ntemba

Serenity

Melissa

CHINDO RD

LAKE ROAD

pages 124–5

INDEPENDENCE AVENUE

LEOPARDS HILL ROAD

CH NDO RD

Cemetery

BURMA ROAD

Woodlands

Puma
Woodlands

Engen

Crossroads

LEOPARDS

LAKE RD

Libala

CHILUMBULU ROAD

Kilimanjaro Country Lodge,
Namwande Gallery,
Sugarbush Café,
Lusaka NP, LZNP (4x4 only)

Johannesburg as a hub to the continent. See pages 51–2 for more details of the best routes and fares to Zambia, and pages 64–5 for local airlines, and general comments on getting around the country by air.

International airlines

International airlines represented in Lusaka include:

✈ **Emirates** ✆0211 258484, 271360/1, 334400; www.emirates.com

✈ **Ethiopian Airlines** ✆0211 236401–3, 235761; www.ethiopianairlines.com

✈ **Kenya Airways/KLM** ✆0211 271412; www.kenya-airways.com

✈ **South African Airways** ✆0211 254350; www.flysaa.com

✈ **TAAG-Angola Airlines** ✆0211 222401, 238633/4; www.taag.com

Local airlines and charter companies
The charter companies and local airlines based in Lusaka have had a chequered past, with companies forming and disappearing with monotonous regularity. The current contenders – of which Proflight is by far the largest and most organised – wisely stick mainly to domestic routes. For details of these and other operators, see pages 64–5.

Kenneth Kaunda International Airport
The airport is well signposted, if isolated, off the Great East Road, 20km east of Arcades, or 25km from the city's government district and three of the large hotels. Transport there is either by shuttle bus from one of the big hotels, by private taxi, or via the Platinum Shuttle (m *0979 069571, 0968 652729*). The Platinum service runs up to six times a day between the airport and the Cresta Golfview, Arcades and Downtown, with one-way fares at K50 per person. This slightly undercuts the hotel shuttles which cost about US$20 per person one way. A taxi for the same journey should cost around US$50 for up to four passengers (though this is the route for which the drivers will charge most imaginatively). At weekends, the journey takes only about 20 minutes, but during the week – and especially at peak periods – you should allow at least double that time because of the traffic.

If you're driving yourself, note that the speed limit between Lusaka and the airport is 80km/h, rising to 100km/h, and there are frequent speed traps. Parking at the airport is free for the first 20 minutes in the short-term car park, but thereafter you'll pay from K12 for the next 40 minutes. There's a fuel station at the airport, useful if you need to refuel a hire car, though keep the receipt to prove that you've done so.

Despite much talk of a new airport building, it could still be some years before this becomes reality. For now, the terminal remains distinctly low key. In addition to offices for all the main airlines, facilities at the airport include a post office, and desks for the major car-hire companies: Avis and Voyagers (representing Europcar). There are also two banks with ATMs, a few shops selling confectionery, newspapers, curios and the like, and a casual café.

In the departure lounge upstairs it's well worth the cost of a drink to take advantage of the comfortable seating in the bar/café. Also on hand are various duty-free and gift shops, including an outlet for Jackal & Hide.

BY BUS
Long-distance coaches and buses Zambia's buses fall broadly into two categories. Comfortable, long-distance coaches, often with air conditioning, ply the longer routes, operating to a timetable and generally keeping good time. Rather less well-maintained vehicles may cover the same ground, but may wait until they're full before leaving. Both now operate out of the **Intercity Bus Terminal** [124 B5], on the western side of Dedan Kimathi Road, near the railway station. It's a noisy, bustling station sheltering under a large purpose-built roof, and is the place to catch a bus to virtually any of Zambia's provincial or district capitals, even those that are quite isolated.

Locals are paranoid about thieves who frequent the area, so expect warnings about safety. It is certainly not a place to go idly strolling at night, or to display your valuables, but if you keep your wits about you, and keep a firm eye on your belongings, then you should have no problems. Be aware, though, that ticket touts can be quite aggressive in their bid for your custom, so be firm if you haven't made up your mind.

Despite the apparent confusion that greets you, there is some order to the terminal's chaos. The buses sitting in bays are grouped roughly by their eventual destinations, as indicated on the boards displayed next to the driver. If you can't see the name you want, then ask someone – most people will go out of their way to help, and the staff on the 24-hour information desk (\ *0211 226676*), something of an oasis in the centre of the terminal, are usually very helpful. While in theory you can phone for details of buses, in practice it's far better to turn up in person.

Coach operators Operators tend to come and go, so it's best to ask around the city's travel agents or at the bus station for the latest news, including details of services to South Africa. Carriers include the usually reliable Mazhandu Family Buses (m *0977 806060, 489414*), and Juldan Motors (m *0955 776315, 0965 732016*; e *info@juldanmotors.com; www.juldanmotors.com*). CR Holdings (m *0978 621148, 960517*), Euro-Africa (m *0977 772025, 311565*) and RPS are also major operators, but there are numerous regional variations, some better than others. The best are well maintained and comfortable, with air conditioning, and they tend to reach their destinations in good time – albeit sometimes at high speed.

Tickets For some (but not all) long-distance buses, it is best to buy a **ticket** at the terminus in advance. There are often different prices for any given place, depending on the company, the standard of the bus, and the speed of service, and the cost of a return ticket may differ from that of the outward journey. Expect about a 20% premium for the better companies. Tickets are on sale at the bus station the day beforehand, but some may also be purchased online at www.busticketszambia.com or at branches of PostNet at Arcades, Manda Hill and Kabulonga (m *0975 274224, 0968 010415*).

Schedules The larger companies, and postbuses (see below) run their buses to a timetable, but those operated by smaller companies may not leave until they are full, which can take hours. If this is the case, try to avoid paying until the bus has started on its way, as you may want to swap buses if another appears to be filling faster and hence is likely to depart earlier.

Buses to some destinations leave frequently, others weekly, according to demand. The best way to find out is to go to the bus station and ask. There are regular services between Lusaka and Livingstone, and Lusaka and the Copperbelt, as well as east to Chipata. The first departures tend to be early in the morning, around 05.00, and are fairly punctual; it's advisable to be there half an hour ahead of the listed departure time. Just a few of the many options, with approximate one-way fares (which can vary considerably), include:

To/from Livingstone Several buses a day run between Livingstone and Lusaka. The journey takes about six hours, and a one-way ticket costs about K110, depending on the speed and standard of service. Operators change regularly, so ask locally before you travel. The best is Mazhandu, but others include Shalom and Khondwani.

To/from the Copperbelt and beyond Several buses a day, mostly in the morning and early afternoon, head from Lusaka to Kitwe via Kabwe, Kapiri Mposhi and Ndola, taking approximately six hours. Some services then continue on to Chingola and Solwezi. Approximately K60 to Kapiri Mposhi, K75 to Ndola, K80 to Kitwe.

To Chipata Up to eight buses a day. Reliable operators are Johabbee & Kobs, departing at 06.00 and 07.00 daily. K130 one way.

To Kashikishi Via Kabwe, Kapiri Mposhi, Serenje, Samfya, Mansa and Nchelenge; also to Kawambwa. Bus operators include Juldan Motors. Up to five buses a day, departing around 14.00. Serenje K115, Mansa K155, Kashikishi K180.

To Mongu Normally eight buses per day, at 09.30 and 13.30, operated by Shalom, Khondwani and Red Bomber. K150.

To Mpulungu Four buses a day via Kasama and Mbala. Operators include the recommended Juldan Motors. Depart around 16.00. K180.

To Sesheke Departures at 06.30 and 19.30 with Mazhandu, Shalom and CR. K105–125.

A few **international buses** also leave from Lusaka, travelling to Johannesburg, Harare, Lilongwe and Blantyre in Malawi, and Dar es Salaam.

Postbuses The post office operates a scheduled passenger bus service, on which vehicles stop only at post offices, though this has been curtailed in recent years and no longer covers Livingstone. Postbuses, some of them almost brand-new vehicles, run to a timetable, so are generally quicker than the normal buses, and they tend to be less crowded too.

The ticket office in Lusaka is tucked behind the main post office on Cairo Road [124 B4] (⊕ *05.00–17.00 Mon–Fri, 06.00–14.00 Sat–Sun*), but tickets are also available at post offices along the various routes. Tickets may in theory be bought on the day of departure, but they're available up to seven days ahead, and it's often advisable to pre-book. Boarding starts half an hour prior to departure. Postbuses stop only at designated post offices, and cannot be hailed from the roadside.

Services are limited to the following routes, returning to Lusaka the following day; the Livingstone service has been discontinued. Fares quoted here are for the full journey; if you alight at a town *en route*, fares are reduced proportionately.

Lusaka to Chipata Lusaka – Luangwa – Nyimba – Petauke – Sinda – Katete – Chipata. Depart 06.00 Tuesday, Thursday and Saturday, arriving in Chipata about 15.30. K130 one way.

Lusaka to Ndola Lusaka – Kabwe – Kapiri Mposhi – Ndola. Depart 07.30, 11.30, 13.00 daily, taking four hours. K70 one way.

Lusaka to Kasama Lusaka – Mkushi – Serenje – Mpika – Kasama. Depart 06.00 Monday, Wednesday and Friday, arriving at Kasama at about 17.00. K140 one way.

BY TRAIN Lusaka's railway station [124 B4] (Dedan Kimathi Rd) is just north of the bus station, so convenient for Levy Park, Cairo Road and various hotels and backpackers' places. Ordinary passenger trains have for many years been far too slow and totally impractical for travellers, but slowly the situation may be improving. While there are not at present any passenger trains to the Copperbelt, the introduction of the Golden Jubilee Express, a weekly overnight service between Lusaka and Livingstone, has certainly improved that route. Trains leave Lusaka at 18.00 on Friday, arriving in Livingstone at 06.00 the next morning. The return train runs to the same times, departing from Livingstone on Sunday evening and reaching Lusaka early on Monday morning. One-way fares in different classes are K90, K110, K135 and – for a sleeper – K145.

The regular TAZARA trains to Tanzania have long been more efficient. They leave from Kapiri Mposhi, not Lusaka (pages 389–90 for details), but tickets are also available with rather less hassle in Lusaka at Tazara House [124 B5] (*Independence Av; www.tazarasite.com;* ⊕ *07.30–16.30 Mon–Fri*); the entrance gate is on Dedan Kimathi Road. The current timetable is usually displayed on a noticeboard outside, to the left of the door, but if not, take a look in the office on the second floor.

DRIVING FROM LIVINGSTONE For details of getting to Lusaka by road from Livingstone, see *Chapter 9*, pages 209–10.

ORIENTATION

Lusaka is very spread out, so get hold of a good map when you first arrive (see *Maps*, page 120). Its business heart was once the axis of Cairo Road, which runs roughly north–south: 4km long, about six lanes of traffic wide, and with an island running like a spine down its centre. Parallel to Cairo Road, to the west, is Chachacha Road – a terminus for numerous local minibuses and home to the lively Central Market, while west again, on Lumumba Road, is the larger New City Market.

As the west of the city has become increasingly congested, many businesses have upped sticks and moved their head offices to the east, clustering around the modern shopping mall at the Arcades, some 4km away, and near the more diffuse government area.

This 'government area', linked to Cairo Road by Independence Avenue, and to Manda Hill/the Arcades by Addis Ababa Drive, is centred on Cathedral Hill and Ridgeway. Here you will also find three of the big international-standard hotels, as well as many of the government departments and embassies. It has a different atmosphere from the bustle of Cairo Road and the malls: the quiet and official air that you often find in diplomatic or administrative corners of capitals around the world.

MAPS A limited selection of Zambia's most commonly used maps can be found at one of the city's bookshops (page 138), which – more importantly – also sells the recommended street atlas of Lusaka and Livingstone, published by Streetwise at K100.

Detailed maps covering the whole of Zambia can be bought cheaply from the main government map office at the Ministry of Lands (*basement of Mulungushi Hse, cnr Independence Av & Nationalist Rd;* \0211 252288, 253640; ⊕ 08.30–noon, 14.00–16.30 Mon–Fri*). Prices are around K20–30 per map. Aside from the normal 'Ordnance Survey'-type maps, special tourist maps are available on request. To see what's in stock, browse through the maps in the entrance area before choosing. The detailed street map of Lusaka held by the office has now been superseded by commercial mapping, but for trips venturing beyond Lusaka, and particularly off the main roads, you'll simply have to come here and buy up a selection of the 1:250,000 series, or for serious expeditions, the more detailed 1:50,000 sheets. They're generally very good, though their information is inevitably dated.

GETTING AROUND

If you don't have your own vehicle you'll probably need to use taxis, and/or the small minibuses that ply between the outer suburbs/townships and the centre. If you are careful, then these are very useful and quite safe. The other possibility is to hire a car with a driver – which is the norm – then the driver can act as a convenient guide for a short trip. As the number of vehicles on the road has increased, traffic congestion has become a major problem, especially in the mornings and evenings. Pick your journey times carefully.

BY TAXI Lusaka's taxis were traditionally small, decrepit Datsuns, held together by remarkable roadside mechanics and lots of improvisation; today, however, they are largely rather less run-down Toyota Corollas. The licensed ones are light blue and white in colour, with a large number painted on their side, but even these have no meters. When taking a taxi, you should agree a rate for the journey before you get into the vehicle; expect to pay around K8.5 per kilometre. If you know roughly what it should cost, then most drivers recognise this and don't try to overcharge. As a last resort when bargaining, all licensed taxis should have a rate-sheet, giving the 'standard' prices for waiting time and various common journeys – though drivers will not admit to having one if the bargaining is going their way. Typical fares are:

K50	between Ridgeway (international hotels) and Manda Hill/ Arcades
K50	between Ridgeway and Cairo Road
K200	between the airport and Ridgeway
K50	between Arcades and Levy Park/Cairo Road
K100	between Crossroads and Manda Hill/Arcades

K50–60   between the centre of town (bus station) and the inner suburbs
K30   per hour of additional waiting time

If you need a vehicle all day, then consider hiring a taxi with its driver. Start by making a clear deal to pay by the hour or the kilometre, and record the time or the mileage reading. Around K60 per hour, or K8.5 per kilometre, is fair, though a tough negotiator would pay less. Drivers inevitably change, but there's one consistent taxi service that can be booked by phone:

Dial a Cab   m 0966 222222, 0977 773937

BY MINIBUS   These are the packed transport used by Lusaka's poorer commuters to travel between the outer, satellite suburbs and the city centre. Demarcated by prominent orange side stripes, they weave through the traffic scene, fanning out from their bases at City Market [124 A4], the Kulima Tower on Freedom Way [124 A4], and Downtown, by the Kafue roundabout [124 B5]. The buses are all privately owned, and cover many different routes, so competition between them is fierce. Minibuses are a good way to reach the farther-flung suburbs, or to get a lift along one of the main routes out to a practical hitching spot. Fares are relatively low, reflecting the cramped seating and general lack of timetable – for the most part, buses leave town only when they are full. There is a minimum fare of K2.50. You can expect to pay around K3 for a journey between Cairo Road and the international hotels, or K4 to Manda Hill. Minibuses usually have regular stops, but if you're lucky they can sometimes just be flagged down if they're not full.

CAR HIRE   See *Vehicle hire* in *Chapter 4*, pages 69–70, for advice and a guide to typical rates. Lusaka's car-hire companies cater more for businesspeople visiting the city than for tourists. Some offer only chauffeur-driven vehicles, and may have only time-and-mileage rates rather than the 'unlimited-mileage' rates normally expected by those hiring cars for fly-drive trips. (Which makes sense as you'd have to be insane to hire a 2WD for a fly-drive trip around Zambia.) The larger companies, including some offering 4x4 hire, are:

🚗 **Avis Airport** ✆ 0211 271020, 323122; 24hr emergency ✆ +27 11 387 8432; e reservation@avis.co.za; www.avis.co.za. Min age 23.
🚗 **Juls Africa**   5507 Libala Rd, Kalundu; ✆ 0211 291712, 292942, 292979, 293972; e juls.travel@travelport.co.zm; www.julstravelzambia.com. From saloon cars to 4x4s, either self drive or chauffeur-driven.
🚗 **Limo Hire**   21 Lilayi Rd; ✆ 0211 278628; m 0977 743145; e limohirezambia@gmail.com;

www.limohire-zambia.com. Options include saloon cars, 4x4s & camping kit.
🚗 **Voyagers/Europcar**   6941 Suez Rd; ✆ 0211 375700, airport ✆ 0211 271221–3; m 0977 860648; e rentals@voyagerszambia.com; www.voyagerszambia.com, www.europcarzambia.com. Reliable franchisee for Europcar, with both 2WD & 4x4 vehicles, with or without a driver. For 4x4 hire, see page 70. See ad in 3rd colour section.

DRIVING YOURSELF   Traffic in and around Lusaka can be chaotic, especially at the beginning and end of a working day, and accidents are not infrequent. Speed limits on the roads around the city are strictly enforced, with an on-the-spot fine of about K180 for infringements. Watch out for speed traps, especially along the Great East Road towards the airport where the limit gradually decreases from the initial 100km/h. In the city centre, though, most drivers would be hard pushed to get anywhere near the urban limit of 50km/h.

Parking on the streets is not a good idea unless you leave someone trustworthy in charge of the vehicle. Far more sensible is to use one of the guarded private car parks. Most hotels and guesthouses have secure free parking, as do shopping complexes, including Levy Park, Manda Hill and the Arcades, and many restaurants. In the Cairo Road, there's parking behind the post office for K2/hr, or in front of Shoprite (K2/hr).

It is not advisable to drive at night in or around the city. Aside from the risk of car-jackings, you're likely to encounter vehicles without lights (especially around the time of the full moon), and even people sleeping on the warm tarmac, a hazard that's said to be particularly common on the Great North Road.

There are numerous fuel stations throughout the city and more springing up on every corner. Several now have ATMs on site, and one or two are starting to accept card payments. Nowadays shortages of fuel are relatively rare.

⌂ WHERE TO STAY

There is an increasing level of choice between Lusaka's international hotels, with improving standards of service and design, although they can often be soulless. You might ask yourself if you need to be near the centre, or can afford to stay beyond the suburbs, at somewhere like Lilayi, Pioneer, Protea Safari Lodge, or Chaminuka (pages 131–3). These are more pleasant than being in town, but transport (with the exception of Pioneer, which is close to the airport) can be a costly issue. A good balance is to head for the boutique Eight Reedbuck Hotel or the new Latitude 15.

Those on a budget should choose their lodgings with care. Price is often a poor guide and the quality of the budget hotels and guesthouses varies considerably. Ask around if you can, as new places are opening all the time. If your budget is very tight then head for a backpackers' hostel or a campsite. Lusaka's cheap hostels are often seedy.

A word of warning: if you plan to make international phone calls from any hotel, find out their charges first, or – better – buy a local SIM card. Hotel phone bills can run into hundreds of dollars for just a few minutes.

If you're passing through Lusaka, perhaps between flights, or are here for a few days' business, then one of the top international hotels may fit the bill. Three of these have been established in Lusaka's central area for many years, while a fourth – the Radisson – opened in 2011. For those seeking something less corporate, the arrival on the scene of a couple of contemporary boutique hotels opens up an entirely different option. While one or two of Lusaka's mid-range hotels have been here for years, others of very different styles have capitalised on the rapidly growing business and conference market, with the South African Protea Chain opening a number of hotels in and around the centre.

Even 'budget' hotels and guesthouses aren't that cheap in Lusaka, but if you have upwards of K375 (US$50) per night to spend on a double room, then there is a choice within this range. However, many are used extensively for conferences and few shine. Most visitors prefer the city's smaller guesthouses, which are often much friendlier and start at the same kind of price, though the range is considerable. The last few years have seen a real boom in the numbers, and the quality, of such guesthouses throughout Zambia, but especially in Lusaka. Some are simply restaurants that offer a few rooms for guests as a legal convenience, others are dedicated entirely to their guests, with prices to match. A few are old favourites, but beware of the speed with which these open up and then close down again.

If you're visiting on a tight budget, then look towards one of the backpackers' hostels in the centre, or – often better – one of the campsites on the edge of town, which are surprisingly attractive. Excellent camping is also available at Pioneer Camp, just east of the airport (pages 131–2).

If you've more than a night and want somewhere to relax away from the city, then try one of lodges outside town. All have lots of space and are set in large areas of greenery, often stocked with game. Because of this, they are out of the centre, so communications can be less easy. Also, because they are smaller, most of them organise transfers to/from the airport (or the city) on an individual basis, and this is reflected in their rates or in transfer charges. However, for an extended stay all are very pleasant and worth seeking out.

TOP END $$$$–$$$$$

🏠 Eight Reedbuck Hotel [115 H5] (10 suites) 8 Reedbuck Rd, Kabulonga; ☎0211 264788/264733; m 0966 740004; e info@tribehotels.co.zm, reservations@tribehotels.co.zm; www.tribehotels.co.zm. The brainchild of Clive Shamwana, a genial & cosmopolitan Zambian with years of experience in the UK service industry, Eight Reedbuck is a small, quality guesthouse, & was Lusaka's first, & for a long time only, boutique hotel. It's always had an authentically Zambian feel, with slightly haphazard but incredibly friendly & personal service.

When we last visited the hotel it was undergoing a complete, & much needed, refurbishment. Each of the large suites is named after a Zambian tribe, & they are subtly furnished with the appropriate art & fabrics to represent this. Two are slightly larger & more expensive than the others, but all enjoy broadly similar facilities: satellite TV, a proper fridge, safe, tea-/coffee-making facilities, AC, an in-house phone & free Wi-Fi access (albeit a little slow). Most have king-size beds, & there's usually space for an extra child bed. The en-suite bathrooms, with shower & separate bath, are as different as the suites. Those on the ground floor have a glass roof above the shower – with bushes & trees around it outside – & some even have a jacuzzi. Smokers should ask for a ground-floor room with a private garden.

As a reflection of the hotel itself the restaurant serves Zambian dishes alongside those with a Zambian twist, but with an overseas palate in mind. The garden has several shaded sitting areas & a very big, clear & inviting swimming pool. **$$$$$**

🏠 Hotel InterContinental [125 F4] (204 rooms, 20 suites) Haile Selassie Av; ☎0211 250000; e reservations.iclusaka@ihg.com; www.ichotelsgroup.com. The InterCon has suffered over the years from inconsistent standards of service, which is unfortunate. Rooms are reasonably big, with space for a couch & a desk, & are kitted out with DSTV, fridge & phone. For meals, the Savannah Grill & Restaurant has both a buffet & a daily à-la-carte menu, served either indoors or on a pleasant covered terrace over the pool. More upmarket is Rosso, a Mediterranean-style venue (🕐 dinner only, Mon–Sat). There's also a rather soulless bar, typical of those in large hotels.

The InterCon's lobby has huge windows looking out to the front, making it feel well lit & airy. It includes some comfy seating, a café with food served all day, & a smattering of African artwork, but otherwise it's largely anonymous. There are some smart gift shops, though, & the more active can take advantage of the hotel's gym & attendant health facilities, attractive oval swimming pool & floodlit tennis courts. There's also a 24hr business centre, & a substantial spa on site. **$$$$$**

🏠 Latitude 15 [115 G6] (18 rooms) 35F Leopards Lane, Kabulonga; ☎0211 268802–4; e 15@thelatitudehotels.com; www.thelatitudehotels.com. Opened in Oct 2014, Latitude 15 has taken Lusaka's hotel (& restaurant) scene by storm. The functional Corbusier-style building gives no hint of what to expect inside: classy, contemporary & colourful, it's a feast for the eyes & very much the place to be seen. Rooms – with AC, sofa, coffee machine & fridge – are airy & light, their silver & grey décor enlivened by photos & vibrant artwork, while larger suites have a balcony overlooking the pool. A further 20 rooms were in the pipeline in 2015. In the communal areas, African artefacts jostle for space with creative modern pieces, old Zanzibari

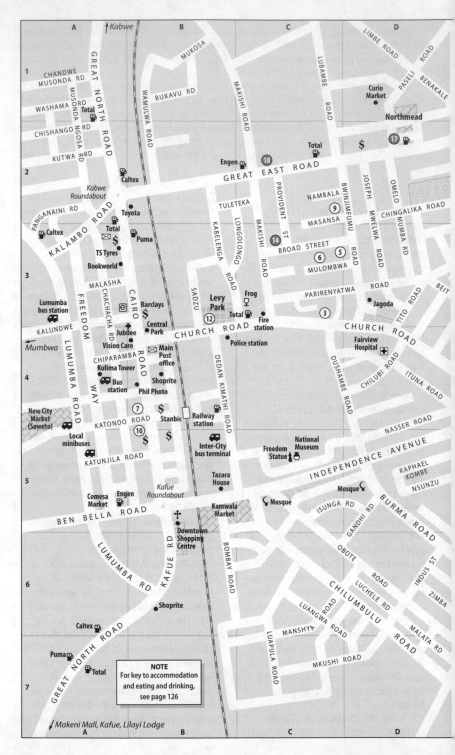

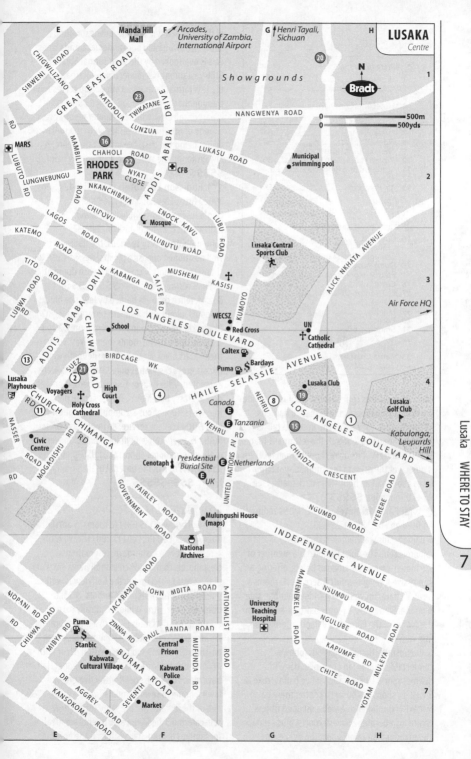

Manda Hill
Mall

Arcades,
University of Zambia,
International Airport

Henri Tayali,
Sichuan

Showgrounds

N

Bradt

0 ———————— 500m
0 ———————— 500yds

NANGWENYA ROAD

1

CHIGWILIZANO ROAD

SIBWENI ROAD

GREAT EAST ROAD

KATOPOLA

TWIKATANE

LUNZUA

ADDIS ABABA DRIVE

23

MAMBILIMA ROAD

RD

LUBUTO RD

LUNGWEBUNGU

MARS

16

CHAHOLI ROAD

RHODES PARK

22

NYATI CLOSE

CFB

LUKASU ROAD

Municipal
swimming pool

2

NKANCHIBAYA

ROAD

CHIPOVU ROAD

LAGOS ROAD

KATEMO ROAD

ENOCK KAVU

Mosque

NALUBUTU ROAD

LUBU ROAD

Lusaka Central
Sports Club

ALICK NKHATA AVENUE

TITO ROAD

LUBWA ROAD

RD

KABANGA RD

SAISE RD

MUSHEMI

KASISI

Air Force HQ

3

ADDIS ABABA DRIVE

CHIKWA ROAD

LOS ANGELES BOULEVARD

School

WECSZ

Red Cross

KUMOYO

UN

Catholic
Cathedral

13

Lusaka
Playhouse

SUEZ RD

BIRDCAGE WK

Caltex

Puma

Barclays

HAILE SELASSIE AVENUE

Lusaka Club

19

Lusaka
Golf Club

4

2

21

Voyagers

High
Court

4

Canada

NEHRU RD

8

15

1

LOS ANGELES BOULEVARD

Kabulonga,
Leopards
Hill

CHURCH RD

11

NASSER ROAD

Holy Cross
Cathedral

Tanzania

Netherlands

CHISIDZA CRESCENT

NYERERE ROAD

CHIMANGA RD

MOGADISHU RD

Civic
Centre

P

NEHRU

AV

UNITED NATIONS AV

Cenotaph

Presidential
Burial Site

UK

NGUMBO ROAD

5

RD

FAIRLEY ROAD

GOVERNMENT ROAD

Mulungushi House
(maps)

National
Archives

INDEPENDENCE AVENUE

MANENEKELA ROAD

6

MOPANI RD ROAD

RD

CHIBWA ROAD

MIBYA RD

JACARANDA ROAD

JOHN MBITA ROAD

NATIONALIST ROAD

NSUMBU ROAD

NGULUBE ROAD

MULEVA ROAD

Puma

Stanbic

ZINNIA RD

PAUL BANDA ROAD

University
Teaching
Hospital

KAPUMPE ROAD

7

Kabwata
Cultural Village

BURMA ROAD

Central
Prison

Kabwata
Police

MUFUNDA RD

CHITE ROAD

YOTAM

DR AGGREY ROAD

KANSOKOMA ROAD

SEVENTH

Market

doors do service as coffee tables, & sofas lie inside & out by a proper pool in tree-shaded gardens. At the cool bar, they'll mix you up a cocktail as fast as pouring you a beer, & the restaurant (page 134) is in a class of its own. The suburban location is quiet, yet the drive to the international airport takes about half an hour along back roads. Free Wi-Fi throughout. **$$$$$**

⌂ **Taj Pamodzi Hotel** [125 E4] (193 rooms) Addis Ababa Dr; ☎ 0211 254455; e pamodzi.lusaka@tajhotels.com; www. tajhotels.com. The large Pamodzi is a member of the Indian-owned Taj group of hotels, offering an impressive level of comfort & service. Its rooms have AC, bath/shower, DSTV, fridge/minibar, safe & phone. Some have a proper balcony, & those on the higher of the Pamodzi's 9 floors afford some fine views.

Downstairs, there's a spacious lobby, a comfortable lounge, an open-plan bar with discreet sports TV & occasional live bands, cake & jewellery shops & a business centre; there's also free Wi-Fi throughout. A well-equipped fitness centre incorporates 2 squash courts, plus sauna, steam room, hair salon & spa; the gym is one

of the best in town. Outside, lawns surround a good-size swimming pool under jacaranda trees. This is overlooked by the semi-formal Steak & Grills restaurant (⌚ *dinner only*). Alternatively, the less formal Jacaranda Coffee Shop serves food throughout the day. A good, varied buffet b/fast is part of the deal, while the dinner menu covers a range of international dishes, with the Indian dishes being the best. I've often stayed here, & always found the staff to be courteous & helpful. **$$$$$**

⌂ **Radisson Blu Hotel** [115 E3] (142 rooms) 19029 Great East Rd; ☎ 0211 368900; e info.lusaka@radissonblu.com; www. radissonblu.com/hotel-lusaka. Light, contemporary & very spacious, the Radisson is well positioned opposite the Arcades, so close to shops, restaurants & cafés. The stylish dome of its Filini restaurant (dinner **$$$–$$$$**), bar & conference centre is backed by low-rise blocks of rooms, along with a superb terraced pool, a fitness centre with sauna & steam rooms, a spa & a poolside bar. The rooms themselves, with their smart black-&-white floor tiles balanced by soft greys & splashes of red, are huge & well-appointed, with twin or king-size beds, a proper desk & classy bathrooms. There's secure parking, free Wi-Fi throughout & computers for guest use. With excellent service, an impressive b/fast buffet & a very convenient location 20km west of the international airport (taxi US$30 pp), the Radisson is one of the best of Lusaka's upmarket hotels. **$$$–$$$$$**

MID RANGE $$$–$$$$

⌂ **Golfview** [115 G3] (78 rooms, 5 apts) 10247 Great East Rd; ☎ 0211 290718/290770; e resgolfview@cresta.co.zm, reservations@ crestahotels.com; www.crestagolfview.com. Part of the Cresta hotel group, the Golfview is well placed some 16km from the airport, & 13km from the city centre. While technically a 3-star establishment, its rates put it in a higher bracket. It's an earthy terracotta & cream complex with en-suite dbl & twin rooms of neutral décor with AC, minibar, tea/coffee facilities & a phone. Half have views over the pool & attractive green lawns, home to several impala, so do ask for one of these: rates are the same for all. New self-catering 3-bedroom apartments are ideal for families or long-stay visitors. If the entrance is rather soulless, this doesn't extend to the bar & traditional restaurant which overlook the pool, enclosing a small courtyard with umbrella shade. There's also a business centre, as well as a well-equipped gym with AC & a spa, both open to non-guests. The hotel is affiliated to the adjacent Chainama Hills Golf Club, where residents can play free of charge except for club rental & caddy fees. **$$$$**

🏠 **Protea Hotel Lusaka** [115 E3] (100 rooms) Arcades, Great East Rd; ☎0211 254664, 375800; e reservations@phlusaka.co.zm; www.proteahotels.com/lusaka. With direct access to the Arcades, & a stone's throw from Acacia Park, the Protea is within a short stroll of shops, cafés & several good restaurants. Spacious dbl & twin rooms all have AC & come equipped with the standard business accoutrements, which here include DSTV, safe, hairdryer & free Wi-Fi. While the entrance lobby – & the splash pool located on a small balcony – are rather uninspiring (why did they hide an attractive water feature behind the lift?), the restaurant & bar are pleasant, & the standard of service from a young team is impressive. Airport shuttle US$20 pp. **$$$$**

🏠 **Protea Hotel Lusaka Tower** [115 E3] (137 rooms) Arcades, Great East Rd; ☎0211 375800; e reservations@phlusakatower.co.zm; www.proteahotels.com/lusakatower. Opened in 2014, Lusaka Tower is the newest of the Protea developments. Close to the Protea Hotel Lusaka, the hotel is located within the Arcades, with direct access to the shops & restaurants. As standard rooms come equipped with DSTV, safe, hairdryer & free Wi-Fi, with 'club' & 'executive' rooms offering extra space. The pleasant restaurant serves à la carte buffets for all meals, & the late-opening bar on the 9th floor has good views across the city, as does the rooftop swimming pool. Airport shuttle US$20. **$$$$**

🏠 **Southern Sun Ridgeway** [125 E4] (155 rooms) Cnr Independence Av & Church Rd; ☎0211 251666; e res@southernsun.co.zm; www. tsogosunhotels.com. The former Holiday Inn is close to the InterCon, & though its rooms show little more imagination, the service is friendly & the atmosphere more relaxed. Functional rooms have twin or king-size beds, with AC, phone, DSTV, & tea-/coffee-making facilities.

On the ground floor the Musuku restaurant serves buffet lunch & dinner (*K155 & K185*

respectively) or à-la-carte meals from b/fast through to dinner. Alongside is Zango Pub (⊙ *10.00–22.00*), which offers salads & more substantial pub grub against a backdrop of TV screens featuring an unrelenting diet of news & sport – a cool, dark retreat from the heat. However, instead of gazing into your pint here, try stepping outside into the central courtyard & studying the colony of masked weavers nesting in a tree over the ornamental pond, where a few small crocs bask on the sheltered rocks. The hotel also has an inviting pool set in its shady garden & an adjacent gym. In front of the entrance you'll find the offices of South African Airways & Proflight, a curio shop, & a useful Barclays ATM. **$$$$**

🏠 **Protea Hotel Cairo Road** [124 B4] (75 rooms) Cairo Rd; ☎0211 238360; e reservations@phcairoroad.co.zm; www. proteahotels.com/cairoroad. While it won't win any prizes for design, the 7-storey Protea on Cairo Rd has certainly raised the standard for business hotels in the area, & has the bonus of some good views of the city from its top floors. Sgl, dbl or twin rooms & dbl suites are clean, smart & functional, & are kitted out in much the same way as its sister hotel above. The ground-floor restaurant is in the same mould – light & airy – & the internet centre (⊙ *08.00–22.00*) has some of the best rates in town; there's also free Wi-Fi. Crucially, the hotel has its own secure multi-storey car park. Airport shuttle US$20 pp. **$$$–$$$$**

🏠 **Chrismar Hotel** [125 H4] (47 rooms) Los Angeles Bd; ☎0211 253036; e book@ chrismarhotels.com; www.chrismarhotels.com. In extensive grounds next to the Lusaka Club, with secure parking, the established Chrismar had a makeover in 2015. The contemporary style of the new-look foyer & cool, calm brasserie is echoed in the latest room design, where dark furniture & wooden floors are lightened by white linen. Cheaper but more spacious rooms have an African touch, with leopard-print covers & colourful wall hangings. Some overlook the courtyard, others the swimming pool, but all have AC, phone & a kettle.

Outside a rather over-elaborate stone bridge leads across a fish pool with fountain, half hidden by an overgrown bamboo. Umbrella-shaded tables surround the large swimming pool with its own bar, next to the popular Cattleman's Grill (page 135), a w/end venue for live bands. Indoors, there's a cool, calm brasserie & a lounge bar where cocktails are a hit with Lusaka's ladies. Fitness fanatics can use the gym, there's a children's play area, & there's free Wi-Fi throughout. **$$$**

🏠 **City Lodge** [125 E4] (8 rooms) 6942 Suez Rd; 📞 0211 253588; e reservations@ citylodgelusaka.com; www.citylodgelusaka.com. Alongside the Smugglers Bar (page 135), but now operated separately, City Lodge opened in 2013. Small, functional & conveniently located, it offers clean, compact en-suite rooms with AC, safe, fridge, tea station & free Wi-Fi. B/fast is available at the adjacent Four Seasons Bistro (page 134), & the pool at the Smugglers Inn may be used by guests. **$$$** exc b/fast

🏠 **stayeasy** [124 B3] (130 rooms) Church Rd; 📞 0211 372000; e res@stayeasylusaka.co.zm; www.tsogosun.com. Right alongside Levy Park mall, so convenient for the west of the city, the new stayeasy is a lot nicer inside than its drab exterior would suggest. The feel of a business hotel is offset by the virulent green & orange décor of the restaurant/bar area, which is toned down to splashes of lime green in compact twin & dbl rooms. The lines are clean, the bathrooms contemporary, the Wi-Fi free, & AC, TV, safe & a coffee station are standard. Outside, there's a small pool with lawns & shaded tables. **$$$**

BUDGET $–$$$
Centre and Cairo Road

🏠 **Lusaka Hotel** [124 B4] (80 rooms) Cairo Rd; 📞 0211 229049/221833; m 0969 229049; e lushotel@zamnet.zm; www.lusakahotel. com. Several decades ago the Lusaka Hotel was the only hotel in Lusaka, right at the centre of town, convenient for buses & trains, but not the airport. Now competition is fierce, not least from the newer Protea Hotel opposite. The décor & furnishings remain dated, & service is on the slow side, but the old hotel has secure parking, & the en-suite rooms now have simple tiled floors, AC, tea/coffee makers, TV, phone & fridge. Downstairs there's a bar, & the restaurant – whose menu includes traditional Zambian dishes – spills outside alongside a small swimming pool. **$$–$$$**

🏠 **Fairview Hotel** [124 C3] (31 rooms) Church Rd; 📞 0211 222604/5, 239634; e hotel@ httifairview.co.zm; www.fairview.co.zm. The Fairview is a hotel training centre, so you can

expect attentive & cheerful service from its young personnel. En-suite rooms with heavy wooden bedsteads & ornate mirrors, feel rather old-fashioned, and are in need of a full refurbishment, but they're spotlessly clean, & flat-screen TVs plus a fridge & tea/coffee facilities add a more modern touch. The public rooms include a terrace bar overlooking Church Rd, & a restaurant that serves traditional Zambian food at lunchtime during the week ($–$$) with a Western à-la-carte menu in the evenings. There's limited Wi-Fi access & a small business centre with internet. Outside is a beer garden, & secure parking. **$$**

🏠 **Ndeke Hotel** [125 G4] (47 rooms) Chisidza Cres; 📞 0211 251734/60; e gardengroup@ zamtel. zm; www.gardengroupzambia.com. Hidden behind a high inner wall, Ndeke is a smart &, mostly, modern hotel near the roundabout of Haile Selassie Av & Los Angeles Bd. Its spacious entrance is enlivened by original artwork & wooden sculptures, while rooms are in a 2-storey terracotta-painted block at the back, some overlooking a good swimming pool. The newer ones have cane furniture & cream paintwork, but some of the older-style rooms remain too. (Rates are the same, so asking for a new room makes sense.) Most have TV & en-suite toilet & bath, but 4 sgls have en-suite showers, & share a toilet. At the front is a slightly sunken dining area with a lounge above, & outside is a courtyard with secure parking. **$$**

🏠 **Nena's Guest House** [124 C2] (4 rooms) 126 Masansa Cl, Rhodes Pk; 📞 0211 239541; m 0977 773213; e nenaguesthouse@zamnet.zm; www.nenaguesthouse.co.zm. Yugoslavian-born Nena's eponymous guesthouse offers clean, en-suite dbl or twin rooms with DSTV & AC, some with showers & some baths. Outside is a grassy courtyard, available for camping. Guinea fowl & hens forage in the garden around a large pool with its own terrace & a nearby bar, & there's secure parking. The restaurant ($$$; ⊕ 06.00–09.00, noon–22.00), open to allcomers, specialises in Yugoslav dishes, with a spit roast on Fri evening & Sun. Free Wi-Fi is available throughout. **$$** Camping K25 pp.

East towards the airport

🏠 **Chita Lodge** [114 D3] (10 rooms) 25 Chakeluka Rd; 📞 0211 293779; m 0979 561276 e chitalodge@chita.co.zm; www.chita.

co.zm. Stylish & professionally run, Chita Lodge is friendly, modern & well looked after. To find it, turn left immediately after Manda Hill onto Kwacha Rd, take the 2nd left, then the 1st right & it's on the left; the lodge has secure parking. Indoors, a wildlife theme is reflected in the décor & touches of original artwork. Dbl & twin rooms are spacious, with smart tiled floors & comfy chairs; each has a phone, AC/heating, fridge, hot drinks facility, DSTV, & a DVD. Alongside a crystal-clear swimming pool with soft grassy surround there's a shaded terrace with a bar & dining tables. The restaurant serves both light lunches & dinner, when the à-la-carte menu ranges from Indian dishes through traditional Zambian fare such as oxtail & fried bream to a range of grills ($$–$$$). **$$$**

🏠 **Mika Lodge** [115 F2] (29 rooms) 106 Central St (cnr 1st St), Jesmondine; ☏0211 291494; m 0961 876570; e reservations@mikagroupofhotels.com; www. mikagroupofhotels.com. The juxtaposition of cool, tiled entrance with heavy armchairs & arrangements of fresh flowers suggests a modern approach tempered with tradition – a reflection of Mika Lodge as a whole. Each cream-painted room, with tiled floor & dbl bed, has a good desk, AC, TV, Wi-Fi (for your own computer) & en-suite shower. A central patio has a small swimming pool, & there's a bright, modern restaurant serving buffet meals ($$–$$$) with red tablecloths & roses on the tables. The atmosphere is one of businesslike efficiency: definitely more of a small hotel than a guesthouse but good value & immaculately maintained. **$$$**

🏠 **Reed Mat Lodge** [115 F2] (15 rooms, 5 chalets) 9718 5th St, Munali; ☏0211 293426; m 0977 7854768, 9180339; e info@ reedmatlodge.com; www.reedmatlodge.com. This Zambian-run lodge with a strong cultural ethic is about 30mins from the airport. Catering more towards backpackers, rooms have either en suite or shared facilities, set in attractive gardens & decorated with local crafts. Two lounges have DSTV, & Wi-Fi access is on hand. Children are particularly welcome, with cots & play equipment available, & there's an 8-bed private chalet with 2 bedrooms & its own lounge. Home-cooked meals are served in the restaurant, or guests can use the kitchen themselves. The lodge has a small but deep swimming pool, & a well-equipped gym. Free Wi-Fi is available throughout. **$$–$$$**

🏠 **Mwambula Garden Lodge** [115 F2] (10 rooms) Mwambula Rd; ☏0211 292826/9; m 0977 897020, 0979 343229; e mwambulagardenlodge@yahoo.com. Beyond the unprepossessing entrance & the garden gnomes, you'll find a friendly welcome at this small guesthouse. Turn north off the Great East Rd just before the Munali roundabout, then take the first left; it's on the right. Attractive gardens with an enormous stand of bamboo & a pool form the focus of the lodge, with 5 more rooms under construction around the edge. The rooms are a bit rough around the edges, but are perfectly clean, with heavy wooden furniture, TVs, fans & mosi nets, & adequate en-suite showers. Wicker chairs on the veranda make for a peaceful place to relax – peaceful, that is, except on the occasional BBQ night, open to allcomers. **$$**

Southeast: Kabulonga and Leopards Hill

🏠 **Kilimanjaro Country Lodge** [off map, 115 H7] (15 rooms) Leopards Hill Rd; m 0955 611779; e info@kilimanjarozambia.com; www. kilimanjarozambia.com. Next to the café of the same name, this occupies a tranquil, relatively rural spot some 7.5km along Leopards Hill Rd, on the right-hand side. Transfers to the airport (30 mins) & Manda Hill, & free Wi-Fi access. Dbl, twin & family rooms are divided across 3 buildings, each with a communal tea station. Embroidered bedding, quirky tables & beaded lampshades add a touch of individuality, while pleasant lawned gardens give plenty of space for children to run around, to play badminton, or simply to relax. With the on-site café offering b/fast, lunch & dinner, this could be a good option for the first or last night of a safari, too. Airport transfers US$60/4 people. **$$$**

South along the Kafue Road

🏠 **Wayside B&B** [off map, 114 A7] (8 rooms) 39 Makeni Rd; ☏0211 273439; m 0966 765184/860494; e info@wayside-guesthouse. com; www.wayside-guesthouse.com. This oasis of calm has been run with care & attention to detail by Beverley Horn since 1998. Take the Kafue Rd for about 4.5km, go past the Castle shopping complex, then turn right at the traffic lights, opposite the Cosmopolitan Mall, onto Makeni Rd; Wayside is on the left after about 2km.

A row of en-suite rooms, each with a covered porch & garden furniture outside, fronts a beautiful garden, while another 3 are tucked away in a separate cottage, 2 of them linked by a fully equipped kitchen/dining room & private garden. Solid wood furniture, Zambian wall-hangings & curtains of local fabric give a sense of place; amenities include AC, a fan, fridge, tea/coffee facilities, safe, DSTV & free Wi-Fi. Rates are the same for all, but 2 larger rooms have a small study. B/fast (& dinner on request) is served in a cosy dining room, while a separate room offers a large TV, DVD player, dining table, comfy chairs & small library, ideal for groups or families to get together. Luggage can be stored for those heading out of town for a few days. Gardening is Beverley's passion, & it shows – in the flowers & shrubs, the well-tended lawns, the walled garden encompassing a sparkling pool, & the tranquil parkland area beyond, woven with paths & big enough for jogging should you be so inclined. **$$$**

West towards Mumbwa & Kafue National Park

🏠 **Garden House Hotel** [off map, 114 A5] (50 rooms) Mumbwa Rd; ☎0211 213004; m 0977 667170 e gardengroup@zamtel.zm; www.gardengroupzambia.com. About 6km west of the city, this is well situated if you arrive late from Kafue National Park. The institutional feel of the corridors is relieved by original Zambian artwork on the walls. Dbl or twin rooms have DSTV, fridge, en-suite shower or bath, & AC. The restaurant caters for all meals, & there's a pool in the otherwise unadorned gardens. The hotel is noteworthy as the place where the MMD political party was started in 1990. **$$**

HOSTELS AND CAMPING

🏠 **Kalulu Backpackers** [124 C3] (9 rooms, 3 dorms, camping) 20 Broad St; ☎0211 231486, m 0955 761533; e info@backpacklusaka.com; www.backpacklusaka.com. Relatively new on the scene, Kalulu is central, relaxed & friendly, despite the tatty furniture. The kitchen is modern & clean, the pool good, the water hot & the free Wi-Fi fast. Zambian & international meals are available & there's also a bar (🕐 noon–20.30). Accommodation varies from en-suite dbls through dorms (2 x 6 beds, 1 x 9) & a small camping area. Airport transfer US$30. Safaris can be booked.

Dorm bed K85; camping K40 pp; dbl/family sharing bathroom K280–463; en suite K375/dbl.

🏠 **Lusaka Backpackers** [124 C3] (26 dorm beds, 4 dbl rooms, 2 cabins, chalet) 161 Mulombwa Cl; m 0977 805483; e lusakabackpackers@gmail.com; www.lusakabackpackers.com. Still known by taxi drivers as Chachacha, Lusaka's long-established backpackers is a relaxed, slightly rambling place, though a facelift is long overdue. A taxi from the bus station will cost about K30, or from the airport around K200 (up to 4 people).

Clean dorms have 6 or 8 beds, while for a little more privacy there are en-suite rooms in the main house, or rather jaded cabins or an A-frame chalet in the garden, sharing facilities. As well as free Wi-Fi access, there are safes for your valuables, & a fully equipped kitchen, though meals are also available (b/fast K20–40, lunch/dinner K25–45). The outside bar with pool table & a small pool is a good spot to discuss your travels or just put the world to rights, & if you're planning to explore, they can organise a number of trips within Zambia & will store your backpack free of charge. *Dorm bed US$12; cabin/chalet US$40; en suite US$55.*

🏠 **Pioneer Lodge and Camp** See page 131 for details of this popular campsite, which now offers smart chalets too.

🏕 **Eureka Camping Park** [off map, 114 A7] (camping, 4 A-frames, 13 chalets, 5-bed cottage, 26 dorm beds) Kafue Rd; ☎0211 272351; e eurekacamp.zm@gmail.com; www.eurekacamp.com. Lusaka's best campsite, Eureka has long been considered the city's best place for budget travellers, too. Owned & run since 1992 by Henry & Doreen van Blerk, it is on a private farm within a game area, protected by an electric fence. Expect to see the ghostly stripes of zebra by moonlight, or to be woken by impala browsing the trees. The site is clearly signposted on the eastern side of Kafue Rd, opposite Baobab College, about 10km south of the Kafue Rd roundabout. If you're coming from the south, you'll need to drive about 2km beyond the turning to the next roundabout, then turn back, as you can no longer cross the central reservation. If you don't have a vehicle, take a Chilanga bus from Kulima Tower bus station [124 A4] & ask to be dropped at Eureka; the fare is about K5. To return to town, just wait for a minibus outside the gates. A taxi from the bus station will cost about K50 pp.

For campers, there's an extensive area of beautiful lawn under trees, with electric hook-ups available. If you don't fancy camping, consider a simple thatched A-frame chalet, with 2 or 3 beds, sharing well-kept toilets & showers with the campers. More privacy comes with en-suite 2- or 3-bed chalets, which are worth booking in advance. There's also a 5-bed cottage with toilet & shower, & a large, 6-room bunkhouse aimed primarily at school groups.

Most people bring their own food, using the camp's kitchen & communal fridge/freezer, but you can get b/fast, good burgers & pies at the bar, as well as fresh meat for the braai, wood & charcoal. Here you'll also find easy chairs, a dartboard, pool table & DSTV. A fenced swimming pool & a volleyball court offer more active pastimes. *Camping US$7 pp (overlanders & backpackers US$3.50 pp); A-frame US$40/45 2-bed/3-bed; chalet US$60/75 2-bed/3-bed; cottage US$125; dorm bed US$20 pp.*

LODGES OUTSIDE TOWN
North and northeast
🏠 **Chaminuka Lodge** [off map, 115 H2] (30 suites; 4 villas) 📞0211 840883/254146; e information@chaminuka.com, reservations@ chaminuka.com; www.chaminuka.com. Chaminuka is about 50km northeast of town, & about half that distance from the airport. Many guests are effectively in transit, & the lodge usually provides transfers; it also caters for day visitors. From the airport, it is 28km along a gravel road, a ½ hr drive, or slightly longer during the rains, when you will need a 4x4. To find it, head towards the airport, go under the arch, then turn left straight after the police roadblock; the lodge is signposted. Once the private home of one of Lusaka's most affluent citizens, the lodge stands atop a small rise overlooking Lake Chitoka. This is one of 4 small, manmade lakes in the 100km² Chaminuka Nature Reserve, which has a variety of different woodland & savannah habitats, lots of wetlands, & plenty of game. Buffalo, lion & hyena are kept in their own fenced enclosures.

Chaminuka is said to house the country's largest collection of traditional & contemporary Zambian art. From a spacious lounge, adorned with original art & leather sofas, large sliding glass doors lead onto a wide terrace. It's all very grand, with a corporate feel to it, amplified by the 3 conference centres on site. Around the main building are square, red-brick chalets, with en-suite facilities & lots of space. Rooms have solid wood queen- or king-size beds, TVs, minibars, quick Wi-Fi, AC & patio doors onto the surrounding lawns. More self-contained are 4 villas, with their own lounge, kitchen & dining room, sleeping up to 8 people in 4 en-suite bedrooms. There are a few *insakas* (small lounges), a dining room, a small library including a section on African history & a TV, & a snooker room (with full-size table). Outside are 2 swimming pools, with adjacent terrace, table tennis, tennis court & a new spa with sauna & jacuzzi. Activities are flexible. In addition to 4x4 game drives, walks, birdwatching & fishing sorties on the lakes, tours around local villages and churches can be arranged. Airport transfer US$50 pp return. *US$288 pp sharing FBA, inc drinks/house wine & tours. Day visitor US$132 inc b/fast, activities & use of all facilities.* **LL**

🏠 **Fringilla Farm Lodge** [off map, 114 B1] (71 rooms, 5 chalets, 3 flats, 2 houses, camping) Great North Rd, Chisamba; m 0968 626896; e fringill@zamnet.zm; www.fringillalodge.com. Situated about 50km north of Lusaka towards Kabwe. See page 384.

🏠 **Pioneer Lodge and Camp** [off map, 115 H2] (11 chalets, 2 tents, cottage, camping) Palabana Rd; m 0966 432700; e mail@pioneercampzambia.com; www. pioneercampzambia.com. Run by owner Paul Barnes, Pioneer is located in a wooded area just outside Lusaka, only 20 minutes drive from the airport. To get there, drive east on the Great East Rd, then turn right 1km after the turn-off to the airport, just after the roadblock. It's a further 5km from there on gravel roads, although these are due to be tarmacked. If you don't have transport, take a minibus from Manda Hill to Chelston, by the water tower (approx K4), then take a taxi for about K50. Transfers into Lusaka, or to the airport, can be arranged in camp for US$40 each way per vehicle.

The accommodation at Pioneer is closer to that of a safari lodge than the city hotels, with 2 safari-style walk-in tents with a thatch covering, 2 basic chalets, a couple of 3-bed thatched chalets sharing a toilet & shower; 2 family chalets of a similar standard with their own facilities; a large, self-contained 2-bedroom cottage sleeping up to 6; & 7 twin 'luxury' chalets, located on the edge of the site

& facing east to catch the sunrise. These last are a cut above the others: spacious & well designed, each with an en-suite bathroom; one is built of natural stone under high thatch, cool & dark, with a toilet & stone bath discreetly tucked behind a solid screen of the same material. Campers remain welcome, with a large shady campsite with a clean ablution block, & a small, fenced pool – all in about 12ha of woodland surrounded by a discreet electric fence, beyond which is a 6km walking trail. The camp's rural location means that you'll wake to the sound of Heuglein's robin rather than the blare of a horn.

The large, thatched bar area is the focus for a real mix of travellers, which makes for plenty of interesting conversation. There are comfy chairs aplenty, & a small satellite TV. Snacks & meals are on hand, with a full b/fast (*around US$5*), & dinner (*US$10*), with the huge steaks being a speciality. Fridge/freezer space is available, as are laundry facilities. With its rural location close to the airport, Pioneer is a good choice for the first or last night of a safari holiday. *'Safari' chalet US$60 pp sharing B&B, or US$160 DBB, inc airport transfers; 3-bed chalet US$80 pp B&B. Cottage US$200 (6 people, exc b/fast). Camping US$10 pp.* **$$** See ad in 3rd colour section.

🏠 **Protea Hotel Safari Lodge** [off map, 114 B2] (60 rooms) Chisamba; ☎0211 212843; e reservations@phsafarilodge.co.zm; www. proteahotels.com. This safari-style Protea stands in a 12km² private game reserve of rolling bush about 45km north of Lusaka. To get there, take the Great North Rd for about 38km, then turn right & follow the signs for a further 7km along a recently graded track.

A large, curved, thatched roof shelters the lounge, bar & restaurant, which extends out onto a large terrace overlooking the gardens. The food is good, popular amongst Lusaka's more affluent residents for the buffet Sun lunch (all you can eat K185); at other times there's either a buffet or an à-la-carte menu. In one corner there's a business centre with 2 computers & a printer; in another, a comfy sofa & chairs. A smaller 'sister' building hosts a cosy bar with plenty of seating for relaxing with a beer in hand. The lodge has free Wi-Fi throughout.

The original bedrooms are stunning: high, thatched ceilings, lots of style & space, & views across the lawns from a private veranda. All have en-suite bathrooms with marble tops, bath &

separate (powerful) shower, as well as phones, tea/coffee makers, safes & DSTV. Mosi nets cover the king-size dbls or twins. Larger suites or family rooms are constructed in pairs, each with 2 bunks in a separate area, & with the option of interlinking the rooms as required. These are more conventional but still very comfortable, their colourful headboards & mirror frames embellished with zany African patterns.

Outside, beautiful herbaceous borders surround a patio & swimming pool area with plentiful sunloungers, as well as a network of lawns. Beyond lies a wilderness area, including a lake (in the rainy season), which is home to a wide range of wildlife. I've watched a memorable flock of Abdim's stork during the wet season here, but the grass was too high (& lunch too good) to go out searching for game, though you'd expect to find zebra, warthogs, reedbuck, puku, kudu & impala amongst other common game. More surprising is the presence of Lichtenstein's hartebeest, tsessebe, oribi, sable, Kafue lechwe, eland & sitatunga. Clearly it's worth exploring during the dry season, either on a game drive (*US$16 pp*) or by quad bike (US$25 pp), or on one of 2 short walking trails. A large lion enclosure houses 2 resident lions, a male & a female, while even more prominent are various hand-reared antelope, including a bushbuck. **$$$$**

South of Lusaka
🏠 **Lilayi Lodge** [off map, 125 A7] (12 chalets) ☎0211 840435/6; m 0971 002010; e reservations@lilayi.com; www.lilayi.com. Situated on a 650ha farm criss-crossed with game-viewing roads, Lilayi is one of the most pleasant of the more upmarket options close to Lusaka, though you'll need your own transport. To get there, head south from the Kafue roundabout at the end of Cairo Rd for about 11km. Turn left at the signpost, right at the T-junction (where the police training college is in front of you), then immediately left; this leads straight to the lodge, which is about 9km off the main road.

Lilayi means 'place of rest', & the name is apt: cool green lawns are dotted with comfortable, well-furnished brick chalets. Ten of these are suites, with a bedroom, spacious lounge, & en-suite bath, shower & toilet; the others have 2 en-suite bedrooms off a small, shared lounge. The main building has a good-sized bar & restaurant overlooking a large pool, plus an upstairs lounge. The à-la-carte menu (**$$$$**) includes daily specials such as venison, & is sometimes complemented by an outdoor braai.

The farm has been well stocked with most of Zambia's antelope, including some of the less common species like roan, defassa waterbuck, tsessebe & giraffe, & boasts a good range of bird species. So if you failed to sight something in one of the parks, walk around here for a few hours or ask to be taken on a game drive or guided walk

(*US$25/10 adult/child*). For experienced riders, horseriding is an option, by prior arrangement (*US$50 pp/hr; hard hats available*). The lodge is also home to the Lilayi Elephant Nursery, which is linked to the Elephant Orphanage in Kafue (pages 447–9). At 11.30am each day, visitors can view the elephants from a platform near the lodge, & once a week, up to 4 guests may tour the nursery, help to prepare the milk, & watch from 15m as the elephants are fed (US$100 pp). *US$350 dbl B&B; US$465 pp sharing FBA.* **$$$$$, LLL**

✖ WHERE TO EAT AND DRINK

The gradual evolution that was Lusaka's eating scene has speeded up in the last few years as the ever-increasing number of shopping malls vie for business. Levy Park and Manda Hill are arguably the best places for fast food, with the likes of Nandos and Subway among other imports jostling for position – though Cairo Road and the various fuel stations offer their own variations.

For more classy fare, the Arcades and adjacent Acacia Park are the better bet, but there are several more individual restaurants dotted around the city that are well worth seeking out.

With quite a high turnover of restaurants, it's inevitable that my recommendations are soon obsolete, so ask around for what's new. Do note that menu prices are frequently quoted without VAT (currently 16%) and a now-compulsory service charge of 10%.

If you're on a tight budget, and catering for yourself, see *Shopping: food and supplies* (page 138) for details of the various shopping options. Some of the supermarkets, such as Spar in the Arcades, serve ready-made dishes at lunchtime, catering for the local office trade. The surprising lack of street-food stalls is the result of a controversial policy introduced in 1999 banning all vendors from the streets of the city (though that doesn't stop the proliferation of touts braving the traffic to offload anything from newspapers and mobile-phone cards to maps of Zambia and leather belts).

RESTAURANTS In the last ten years, the number and variety of restaurants in Lusaka has all but exploded, with almost every ethnic cuisine catered for (frequently in the same venue), and a range of standards to match. If you're looking for somewhere special, then a consensus of informed opinion gives Lusaka's top spots for foodies as Marlin and – new on the scene – Latitude 15 and the Four Seasons Bistro.

For competent but unimaginative food, the big **hotels** – the InterCon, Taj Pamodzi, Southern Sun Ridgeway and Radisson – all have their own restaurants. The Taj Pamodzi also does a good line in Indian cuisine, while Italians in search of authentic food from home make for the Radisson's **Filini** restaurant. The location and generally good service of these hotels make them an easy option for visitors, but there are often more interesting alternatives within relatively easy reach.

For the visitor, Acacia Park [115 E3] is a good place to start. Adjacent to the Arcades, it has four separate restaurants with tables both inside and out, against an incongruous backdrop of palm trees and bank buildings.

The Showgrounds, near Manda Hill on the Great East Road [125 G1], is worth an evening visit in its own right, when its restaurants and bars come to life.

Surprisingly, those in search of Zambian cuisine may be best advised to stick to the hotels, which are well used to catering to the city's business population, especially at lunchtime. In particular, the two Protea hotels and the Lusaka Hotel serve Zambian cuisine on request, but there's also the simpler Broads on Broad Street.

Nobody walks in Lusaka at night, so unless you're staying at the Radisson or the Protea Arcades, you'll need either to dine at your hotel or take a taxi. In this case, arrange with your driver to collect you at the end of the evening as well. For those with their own vehicle, most restaurants and shopping complexes offer secure or guarded parking. Finally, do remember that restaurants can get very busy, so at the classier places – especially on Friday and Saturday nights – it's wise to book.

✗ **Latitude 15** [115 G6] See pages 123–6; ⏱ 06.00–10.30, noon–15.00, 18.00–22.00 daily. The restaurant at Latitude 15 shares some of the whackiness of the hotel – check out the dreadlock light fittings! – but the menu is altogether more serious. From tables inside & out on tree-shaded lawns, indulge in the likes of spice-rubbed pork fillet with tzatziki, romesco sauce, roast potatoes & seasonal veg. There are plenty of innovative salads, too, some home grown, as well as cosmopolitan takes on fish, steak & chicken, & options such as Thai jungle curry. Service is friendly, if rather erratic. $$$$–$$$$$

✗ **Chicago's** [125 F1] Manda Hill; m 0977 760647; ⏱ 09.00–23.00 Sun–Thu, 09.00–03.00 Fri/Sat. Al Capone wouldn't look out of place at this dark & trendy venue, Lusaka's take on gangsterland. In the food stakes, it offers all the standards, plus an unlikely sushi menu. It's also a popular late-night drinking den. $$$–$$$$$

✗ **Four Seasons Bistro** [125 E4] Suez Rd; m 0973 151933; www.fourseasonsbistro.net; ⏱ 07.00–10.00 daily, noon–15.00 Mon, noon–21.30 Tue–Thu, noon–22.30 Fri/Sat, noon–21.00 Sun. Simple wooden tables & chairs are the setting for Lusaka's latest foodie hotspot, where chef/owner Jamey Townsend concentrates on fresh, local, sustainable produce. The seasonal menu has a strong emphasis on game (think zebra steak or bushpig *potjie*), but vegetarians are rewarded with home-grown organic salads & veggies, & offerings such as chick-pea melt. Is this the start of Lusaka's slow-food movement? $$$–$$$$$

✗ **Rhapsody's** [115 E3] Arcades; ☎ 021 256705/6; www.rhapsodys.co.za; ⏱ noon–late daily. With its large circular bar, varnished brickwork, & open girders, Rhapsody's is often buzzing – especially on Fri nights. The restaurant, set slightly higher than the bar, is fronted by a semi-covered courtyard with its own bar. Options

on lunch & dinner menus range through steaks, salads, fish, sushi & veggie dishes, with sufficient innovation (such as spicy butternut fajitas) to lift it above Lusaka's norm. No shorts after 18.00. Credit cards accepted. $$$–$$$$$

✗ **Le Triumph Dolphin** [124 D2] Paseli Rd, Northmead; ☎ 0211 292133; m 0977 774954; ⏱ 10.00–15.00 & 18.00–22:00 Mon–Sat. Old favourites belting out on the sound system & kitsch decoration contrast with Le Triumph's slightly sleazy atmosphere. Service is good, & the food's not bad either – especially the steaks. Creole dishes & (pricey) seafood are specialities. If karaoke's not your thing, come on a Monday or before 21.00. $$$–$$$$$

✗ **Chang Thai** [115 E3] Acacia Park; ☎ 0975 835999; ⏱ noon–22.30 Sun–Thu, noon–23.00 Fri/Sat. An unlikely find in Lusaka, Chang Thai is at its best in the evening when soft lighting & candles illuminate the warmth of the interior. The food is surprisingly good, the staff efficient & friendly, & there's a takeaway service too. $$$–$$$$

✳ ✗ **Marlin** [125 G4] Lusaka Club, nr cnr of Los Angeles Bd & Haile Selassie Av, Longacres; ☎ 0211 252206; m 0966 765462, 0979 627546; ⏱ noon–14.30, 18.30–22.00 Mon–Sat. At the back of the old sports club, this apparently uninspiring place serves some of the best (& best-value) food in town. The sizeable pepper steaks are renowned (ask for a 'lady's steak' if you're not up for it), or try the superb crab tom yam soup. Salads, chow meins & stir fries are always good, & the service is professional & discreet. Booking strongly advised. $$$–$$$$

✗ **Mike's Kitchen** [115 E3] Arcades; m 0978 711555; ⏱ 10.00–21.30 Sun–Thu, 10.00–22.30 Fri/Sat. With booths, black-&-white checked floors, sports TV & a menu like a glossy magazine, Mike's is an all-American diner. Classic grills & burgers jostle with more esoteric offerings: snails, sweet-&-sour pork & South African boerwors. There's a great selection of milkshakes, but service is slow. $$$–$$$$

Χ News Café [115 E3] Acacia Park; 0211 258215; www.newscafe.co.za; ⏰ 07.30–23.00 Sun–Tue, 07.30–01.30 Wed/Thu, 07.30–14.00 Fri/Sat. Gourmet shakes & 'bubble tea' enliven the menu of this trendy spot, popular for fancy b/fasts & sharing platters, but its greater reputation is for late-night drinks. $$$–$$$$

Χ Royal Dil [115 E3] Acacia Park; 0211 841015; m 0974 566878; ⏰ noon–23.00 daily. Under the same ownership as the Dil ([off map, 115 H5] 153 Ibex Hill Rd; 0211 262391/262691), the Royal is more central for visitors, with welcoming if slightly erratic service, and a rather divided style: the veranda area is comfortable but inside it's like a canteen. Large portions of predominantly Indian dishes are fresh & tasty, albeit on the pricy side. $$$–$$$$

Χ Cattleman's Grill [125 H4] Chrismar Hotel, Los Angeles Bd; 0211 253036; ⏰ noon–22.00 daily. Strictly for carnivores, this thatched outdoor restaurant has African friezes decorating the walls. Fri & Sat nights are particularly busy, with regular live bands. $$$

Χ Dong Fang [125 G4] 275 Dunduza Chisidza Ct, Longacres; 0211 254328; ⏰ 11.30–14.30, 18.00–22.00 daily. In a quiet area of the city, but now in larger premises, the pleasant Dong Fang offers large portions of traditional Chinese fare. $$$

Χ Gerritz [125 E2] 26 Chaholi Rd, Rhodes Pk; 0211 253639; www.gerritzrestaurant.com; ⏰ noon–22.00 Mon–Fri, noon–17.00 Sun; closed Sat. This German restaurant is owned & run by the eponymous chef, who serves reliable & original dishes from a mixed menu. The atmosphere is casual, the food generally hearty. $$$

Χ Muskaan [115 G5] Kabulonga Rd; 0211 265976. Muskaan's Indian cuisine is rated highly by locals both for quality & value for money. Also at Chindo Rd; 0211 262078. $$$

Χ Smugglers Bar [124 E4] Suez Rd; m 0973 151933; ⏰ noon–15.00 Mon, noon–21.30 Tue–Thu, noon–22.30 Fri/Sat, noon–21.00 Sun. The poolside pub next to City Lodge features food from the Four Seasons kitchen, so freshness is a given. Zebra burgers & crayfish rub shoulders with a delicious favourite: smoked pork medallion & pineapple salsa. $$$

Χ Zoran Café [124 B3] Levy Park; m 0966 060347, 0979 060374; ⏰ 09.00–22.00 daily. Upstairs in Levy Park, with more tables on the balcony, the Karaleic family brings Serbian cuisine to a cosmopolitan menu. Daily specials such as Serbian *muchkalica* (slow-cooked pork). $$$

Χ Sichuan [115 E3] Showgrounds, Great East Rd; 0211 253842; ⏰ 10.00–22.00. One of numerous Chinese restaurants in the city – & recommended, if a little hard to find. Once inside the large warehouse building, however, you'll find good-value authentic Chinese food. $$–$$$$

Χ Mint Lounge [115 E3] Acacia Park; 0975 071505. Lusaka's buzzword for healthy eating, Mint Lounge is a great lunchtime venue, & a good spot for sundowners, though less inviting in the evening. Informal, cool & with inside & outside seating, it's a must for salads, wraps, cakes or a late b/fast. $$–$$$

Χ O'Hagans [115 G7] Woodlands; 0211 262156/7; ⏰ 10.30–late, last food orders 22.30; occasional happy hours. The popular O'Hagans moved every last table & beer tap to its new suburban home – & you'd hardly know the difference. The menu boasts a range of specials from beef trinchado to eisbein, but if it's the staples you're craving, never fear: mains of fish & chips or steaks continue to dominate. $$–$$$

Χ Portico [125 G1] Showgrounds, Great East Rd; 0211 250111. Overlooking the Lusaka Polo Grounds, Portico is vying with the Radisson's Filini for Italian foody credentials. A wood-fired oven produces excellent pizzas, & the steaks are reported to be great. It gets busy at the weekend so it's worth booking, & there's live music on Wed & at the w/end. $$–$$$

Χ Broads [124 C3] Broad St; ⏰ 06.00–22.00 daily. Broads focuses exclusively on local cuisine &, judging by the number of diners when we visited, it's pretty popular. $–$$

Χ Mahak [124 C2] 61 Great East Rd; 0211 229002. A great Indian restaurant, where an all-you-can-eat vegetable thali offers amazing value for money & the butter chicken is said to be 'fantastic'. $

CAFÉS, PUBS AND LIGHT MEALS

Kilimanjaro Café [off map, 115 H7] Leopards Hill Rd; 0211 250527; m 0955 611779; ⏰ 06.00–20.00 daily. If Kilimanjaro has lost a little of its freshness, it's still worth the trip for its hallmark colourful crafts, Wi-Fi access & tables that spill onto a wide veranda fronted by grassland dotted with trees. With b/fast, salads & light lunches, or burgers, steaks & curry, there's something for any time of day. See Kilimanjaro Country Lodge, page 129, for directions. $$–$$$

⌨ **Zebra Crossings** [125 F1] Ababa Hse, Twikatane Rd; ☏ 0211 257148; ⏰ 07.00–17.00 Mon–Sat. A seasonal menu with salads, soups & daily specials make this open-sided venue a lunchtime favourite. Come for b/fast, smoothies or coffee & cakes, too, & check out the artwork from Ababa House's latest exhibition (page 139) that adorn the café. It's creative & colourful, & there's a Wi-Fi hotspot too. $$–$$$

⌨ **Bush Buzz** [115 H6] Crossroads, Leopards Hill Rd; ☏ 0211 268339; ⏰ 08.00–late daily. The colourful café at Crossroads does a decent line in b/fast, burgers, sandwiches, pasta & grills. $$

⌨ **La Mimosa** [115 E3] Arcades; ⏰ 07.30–22.30. This conventional coffee shop with sports TV has tables inside and out under umbrellas. As well as b/fasts, baguettes, crêpes & salads, it serves good coffee – including decaffeinated choices. $$

⌨ **Mint Café** [115 E3] Arcades; m 0965 900800; ⏰ 08.00–21.00 Sun–Thu, 08.00–21.30

Fri/Sat. This stylish little café is modern & minimalist. Stop for light meals such as salads, wraps & sandwiches as well as smoothies & fresh juices – or head for its more grown-up sibling, Mint Lounge, at Acacia Park. $$

⌨ **Sugarbush Café** [off map, 115 H7] Leopards Hill Rd; m 0950 500487; ⏰ 08.00–17.00 Tue–Sun. One of the new generation of out-of-town cafés, Sugarbush invites leisurely lunches. Spilling out from the Jackal & Hyde leather shop, it's set in mature gardens with a regularly changing menu: from pancakes & calamari to salads & steaks. $–$$

✳ ⌨ **The Zambean Coffee Co** [125 F2] 6 Nyati Cl; ⏰ 09.00–16.00 Mon–Sat. Tables inside & out in a quiet garden offer a relaxed setting for this unassuming café, opened in Oct 2014. Enjoy a freshly ground coffee or a glass of South African wine, with tasting notes, backed up by 'gourmet' sandwiches (think smoked chicken with honey wholegrain mustard, rocket, pecan nuts & avocado). Delicious cakes – especially the carrot cake – add to the treats, & there's free Wi-Fi. $–$$

⌨ **Vasilis** [125 F1] Manda Hill; ⏰ 08.00–20.00 daily. Take a break from shopping for coffee & cakes or pizza & baguettes at this modern café-cum-bakery. $

ENTERTAINMENT AND NIGHTLIFE

BARS AND NIGHTCLUBS The period that a nightclub remains in fashion, and hence remains in business, is even shorter than the life of most restaurants, so recommendations in this section will, by their very nature, be out of date quickly. It's better to ask the locals about the best places, and follow their suggestions. Always be mindful of your safety: don't take much cash to a club with you, and don't linger anywhere that feels uncomfortable.

Consistently popular are the bars at **Rhapsody's** and **O'Hagans**, which open till late and attract a mixed, fairly upmarket crowd. More clubby in style are the **News Café** and **Chicago's** at Manda Hill. See above for details of these.

For live music, top of the current list is **Kalahari** [115 F4] (*Alick Nkhata Rd*), where local music is a regular feature. More sedate is the Chrismar's **Cattleman's Grill** [125 H4] (see above), and **Portico** [125 G1] (see above) where there's a live band on Friday and Saturday nights. The easy-going **Frog Pub & Grill** [124 C3] *Kabelenga Rd;* m 0961 548833; ⏰*10.00–23.00 Mon–Thu, Fri–Sat 10.00–03.00)* usually has a band Thursday to Saturday (*entrance K5–10*), & you can mop up the drink with nshima & beef, goat or chicken. Then there's **The Web** out on the Kafue Road [off map, 114 A7] (m 0978 630843; *entry K100*), another popular venue for live music, especially blues, & with food on tap too

There's dancing at **Room 101** by the casino in the Arcades [115 E3] (*entry K50*), and – in Kabulonga – at **Chez Ntemba** [115 G5] (*Chindo Rd;* ⏰ *21.00–06.00 Wed, Fri & Sat; K30*), which has a small cover charge and plays mainly rumba. The bar is good, and on Friday and Saturday nights partying continues until dawn – but there's no food available. If karaoke's your thing, head straight for **Le Triumph Dolphin** (page 134) after 21.00, any night except Monday.

ENTERTAINMENT Lusaka's first permanent **cinema in the Arcades** [115 E3] (*0211 256719; m 0965 172128) is a modern five-screen multiplex. Films are mostly fairly up to date, and tickets cost K35, or half price from Monday to Thursday. Competition has arrived, though, at Levy Park [124 B3] (m 0974 107361) and Manda Hill [125 F1] (m 0974 745548), each of which boasts six screens, and shows Zambian as well as international films. Tickets at both cost K20 for 2D or K35 for 3D from Monday to Thursday, and K35–50 Friday to Sunday.

The Lusaka Playhouse, opposite the Southern Sun Ridgeway and Taj Pamodzi hotels [125 E4] (*cnr Nasser & Church rds*), features a variety of local **theatre** productions. For details, check the current edition of *The Lowdown,* or just turn up to see what's on. Tickets are typically K10–30. Note, though, that parking in the area isn't great, so you'd be well advised to leave your vehicle in the car park of the Southern Sun.

If the city is hosting a **concert**, the most likely venue is the Mulungushi International Conference Centre, opposite the Arcades [115 E3] (*Great East Rd*).

SHOPPING

Lusaka's main shopping centre used to be Cairo Road which, before 1996, was full of small, cramped private trader's shops where it was very difficult to find the right place to buy what you wanted. Then Shoprite opened its flagship store in the centre, followed shortly afterwards by the city's first shopping mall. Since then, the city's shopping opportunities have marched on apace, leaving Cairo Road feeling rundown and in places rather sleazy.

While Lusaka's traditional, vibrant **markets** (page 144) continue to thrive, and are well worth a visit if you have the time, it is the malls that now take centre stage in the retail sector.

The complex at **Manda Hill** [125 F1] (*www.shopmandahill.com*), on the Great East Road, revolutionised shopping in Lusaka when it was first opened. Modern and clean, with plenty of parking and a conspicuous security presence, it became the preferred place to shop for both visitors and many local people. It now offers two-storey parking and feels exactly like any shopping mall in the West. Come on a Saturday afternoon and you'll see Lusaka's fashionistas seeking out the latest trends alongside mothers doing the week's grocery shopping and plenty of young men wandering around looking cool.

A stone's throw to the east, on the other side of the road, the **Arcades** complex [115 E3] (*www.arcades.co.zm*) has more of an entertainments and restaurant bias, but it still offers a range of shops, including music and video stores and a SuperSpar supermarket. There's also a filling station and round-the-clock guarded parking for up to 750 vehicles.

New on the scene, and one of the most central of the malls, is **Levy** [124 B3] (*www. levy.co.zm*), widely known as Levy Park, which – with its mix of shops, restaurants, cafés, cinema and hotel – is breathing new life into the western side of the city.

In the wealthier suburbs, smaller shopping complexes include **Crossroads** at Leopards Hill [115 H6], the new **Woodlands** shopping centre [115 G7], and the more established **Kabulonga** [115 G5]. To the south, the recently opened **Makeni Mall** [114 B7] is already on the verge of expansion, and is soon to face competition from the new Cosmopolitan Mall [114 B7] opposite.

Shops at Lusaka's malls are usually open Monday to Friday, from around 09.00 to 18.00, but at weekends, most shops close earlier, especially on Sunday when midday or early afternoon is the norm. Shops elsewhere in the city are usually closed on a Sunday.

FOOD AND SUPPLIES Most of Lusaka's visitors now stick to one of the large **supermarkets**, which are similar to those found in Europe or America. The original Shoprite [124 B4], on the eastern side of Cairo Road, with guarded parking was their pioneering store in Zambia. Now, however, such supermarkets have proliferated, first at Manda Hill [125 F1], then at the Arcades [115 E3], and more recently at the new Levy Park [124 B3]. As shopping malls continue their inexorable spread through the suburbs, so the supermarkets have strengthened their hold, from Pick 'n' Pay at Woodlands [115 G1], Makeni Mall [off map, 114 B7] and East Park to a large SuperSpar at Crossroads mall [115 H6] on Leopards Hill Road. Of the smaller alternatives, Food Lover's Market at Levy Park is a good bet, with fresh vegetables, bread and hot food to take away. Melissa minimarket [124 D1] (*Great East Rd, Northmead*) is one of the best. It isn't cheap compared with its larger rivals, but several delis and a bakery or two have sprung up around it, and opposite it is a small craft market. There's another branch on Chindo Road, near Kabulonga shopping centre [115 G5].

Fresh fruit and vegetables can of course be picked up from one of the local markets (page 144), as well as from various street-sellers.

BOOKS AND MUSIC
Book Cellar [125 F1] Manda Hill; ✆ 0211 255475/6. Stocks books on Zambia, wildlife, plus new novels, maps & reference books of all kinds.
Bookworld [125 F1] Manda Hill; [124 A3] Cairo Rd; [115 G5] Kabulonga; [115 H6] Crossroads; Makeni [114 B7]; ✆ 0211 225282, 268329, 274591, 255470. This is the place for a wider range of literary interests, including Zambian literature & poetry.
Planet Books [115 E3] Arcades; ✆ 0211 256715. Similar stock to the Book Cellar.
Sounds [115 E3] Arcades & [115 H6] Crossroads. A reasonable selection of music CDs.

CAMPING AND OUTDOOR EQUIPMENT Most of the basic outdoor equipment can be found at Game [125 F1] (*Manda Hill*), but for gas canisters you could also try the Mica hardware store [115 E3] (*Arcades*), or possibly Shoprite [124 B4] (*Cairo Rd*). For fishing tackle and a range of outdoor essentials, there's Tackle & Pet Haven at Manda Hill [125 F1]. Walking shoes and boots are stocked by branches of Shortys in the Arcades [115 E3], Levy Park [124 B3] and Manda Hill [125 F1].

CAR SPARES See page 141.

CRAFTS, CURIOS AND GIFTS For typical African carvings, basketware and curios, you probably won't get better value or a wider selection than at Kabwata Cultural Centre, on Burma Road [125 E7] (pages 144–5), although there's a good range of baskets at the shop in the National Museum [124 C5]. Every Sunday a regular outdoor curio market is held at the Arcades [115 E3], or you could try the small craft market at the back of the outdoor market at Northmead [124 D1], opposite Melissa minimarket (park at the supermarket), which sells some good malachite bracelets, necklaces and a wide selection of carvings.

Specialist shops afford the opportunity to browse at leisure, without the hassle of bargaining. Or how about combining retail therapy with lunch? Try Ababa House [125 F1], Kilimanjaro Café [115 H7] or Sugarbush Café [off map, 115 H7]. The expensive shops at some of the big hotels showcase gems and jewellery, though don't expect any bargains; Jagoda might be a better bet.

For a much cheaper souvenir in the form of a *chitenje* (page 75), try one of the smaller local shops such as Safique's, or take a trip to one of the markets (page 144). Even if you come away empty-handed, you'll have seen a far more authentic side to Zambian shopping culture than that offered by upmarket shops.

Ababa House [125 F1] Twikatane Rd; ☎0211 257148; m 0977 415391; ⊕ 08.00–17.00 Mon–Fri, 08.00–14.30 Sat. In a converted private house, Serena Ansley showcases the work of more than 80 artists & craftworkers, from AIDS orphans & the Malambo Women's co-operative at Monze to professionals. Much of their work is very affordable – & transportable. Browsing through the pottery, sculptures, furniture, jewellery, textiles & more makes for a very enjoyable hour or so, & can be combined with coffee or lunch in the adjacent Zebra Crossings café. An outlet for wickedly delicious homemade chocolates is an added bonus. An art exhibition is held at 17.30 on the 1st Thu of each month, with snacks & a cash bar; the month's art is then displayed in the café.

J&S [115 H6] Crossroads, Leopards Hill Rd. Along with the crafts at this market-style shop is a tailoring & repair service, covering shoes as well as clothes.

Jackal & Hide [115 H7] Sugarbush Farm, Leopards Hill Rd; ☎0211 213841; m 0977 874771; e gillie@tribaltextiles.co.zm; www. jackalandhide.net; ⊕ closed Mon. Hand-crafted leather handbags may not be cheap, but they are unusual, & designs can be made up to order. Find it 10.4km beyond Crossroads, on the right (there's a café here, too), & at the airport.

Jagoda [124 D3] 1 Luano Rd; ☎0211 220814; www.jagodagems.com

Kilimanjaro Café [off map, 115 H7] Leopards Hill Rd; ☎0211 250527; m 0955 611779. Inject some fun into your shopping at this out-of-town café, which is decked out with a colourful array of toys, carvings, paintings & textiles, all for sale. For directions, see Kilimanjaro Country Lodge, page 129.

Kubu Crafts [125 F1] Manda Hill; ☎0211 256644. Curios & crafts make this a souvenir-hunter's favourite, but it's no longer a place for serious art.

Safique's [124 B5] Independence Av; ☎0211 228449. Next to Tazara House, this fabric emporium is a great place to pick up a good-quality *chitenje*, though bargaining isn't part of the deal.

OPTICIANS As Lusaka grows, so opticians are becoming more prominent. Most easily found are:

Phil Opticians [124 B4] Cairo Rd; ☎0211 225572; also at Arcades [115 E3],Crossroads [115 H6] & Woodlands [115 G7]. Same ownership as Phil Photo (see below).

Vision Care Opticians [124 B4] Cairo Road ☎0211 230475/6; also at Levy Park [124 B3] & Makeni Mall [114 B7].

PHARMACIES These are dotted all over the city. Recommended are:

Jubilee Chemist ☎0211 255556/7, 265331/238216. Branches at Cairo Rd [124 A4], Manda Hill [125 F1], Crossroads [115 H6] & Kabulonga [115 G5]

Link ☎0211 231124. Branches at Manda Hill [125 F1], Arcades [115 E3], Levy Park [124 B3], Woodlands [115 G7] & East Park [115 F3]. More expensive than Jubilee, but arguably with better stock.

PHOTOGRAPHIC AND COMPUTER SUPPLIES

Phil Photo [124 B4] Cairo Rd; ☎0211 225572; branches at Manda Hill [125 F1]; Arcades [115 E3] & Crossroads [115 H6]. Formerly Phoenix Photographics, Phil's sells cameras, memory cards etc, & offers a printing service.

HiFi Corp [125 F1] Manda Hill. Phones, cameras & other electronic devices.

BANKS AND CHANGING MONEY

BANKS Although the main banks traditionally had their head offices along Cairo Road, many have now moved further east towards less congested areas of the city. For most visitors, though, the banks and ATMs at Manda Hill, the Arcades, Levy Park and almost all other shopping complexes are far more relevant, and security here is far better than on Cairo Road. There is also a well-guarded Barclays ATM at the Southern Sun Ridgeway.

CHANGING MONEY Use a bank or bureau de change to change money wherever possible; otherwise stick to a hotel – though these generally offer poor rates of exchange, or charge steep commissions.

Wherever you change money, don't forget to take some ID with you. When changing travellers' cheques, you may – somewhat controversially – need to take the 'proof of purchase' slip that you were given when you bought the cheques.

Bureaux de change Bureaux de change are to be found in shopping complexes across the city, including in the Spar supermarket at the Arcades [115 E3] and at Levy Park [124 B3]. You may get slightly lower rates than in similar establishments on Cairo Road, but with these comes a conspicuous improvement in security. Bureaux de change usually deal only with cash and will not exchange travellers' cheques.

COMMUNICATIONS

INTERNET In the last few years, Wi-Fi has taken off in Lusaka, and is available free of charge in most of the better hotels and guesthouses, as well as restaurants and cafés. Some of the larger hotels have dedicated business centres with internet facilities, too, though connections can be erratic and the service slow.

The same goes for internet cafés, which often suffer from outdated hardware. Your best options are at the various shopping malls – the central trio of Manda Hill, Arcades and Levy Park – as well as the more outlying complexes such as Woodlands and Crossroads, and at the main post office (see below).

POST AND TELEPHONE Lusaka's busy main **post office** is in the centre of Cairo Road [124 B4]. Responsibilities range from savings to postal matters, each handled at separate desks, and long queues are the norm. If you're just looking for stamps, it's probably quicker to go to one of the smaller post offices around the city. There's parking behind the post office (*K2*), though you can expect a bit of hassle from touts here.

Both the main post office and the one at Ridgeway have a philatelic counter for purchasing Zambia's colourful stamps, including first-day issues and blocks. Upstairs you will find a bureau de change where rates are on a par with those of the banks.

The major **mobile-phone** providers have countless branches throughout the city. Top-up cards are easily available from shops, garages and street vendors at major road junctions.

COURIERS If you need to send something valuable, a courier is far more reliable than the postal service. Lusaka's main couriers are:

DHL (Zambia) ✆0211 229768/71; www.dhl.co.zm
FedEx ✆0211 226680, 252065, 252191, 252585; www.fedex.com/zm

Mercury Express/UPS ✆0211 257361/4/5; www.ups.com
TNT Express ✆0211 256461; www.tnt.com

OTHER PRACTICALITIES

CAR REPAIRS AND SPARES As spare parts have become more readily available, so vehicle repairs have become more straightforward to arrange. Specialists include:

CFAO (Vehicle Centre Zambia) [114 B3] Sheki-Sheki Rd; 📞0211 243112/240767–9; www. cfao-automotive.com. Agents for several major brands, including Ford.

Southern Cross Motors [114 B7] Kafue Rd; 📞0211 844778/9, 844780, 844887; www. southerncross.co.zm. Mercedes & Mitsubishi.
Toyota Zambia [124 A2] Cairo Rd; 📞0211 229109/13. The main Toyota centre for parts, sales & service.

For **tyres and more general spares**, consider one of the many fuel stations, including Total [124 A7] on the Kafue Road, or try:

Autoworld [124 A5] Freedom Way; 📞0211 223207, 237716/9; www.autoworldzm.com. Also at Downtown shopping centre, Kafue Rd [124 B5]; Woodlands [115 G7]. Some outlets handle basic repairs.

Impala Service Station [124 A2] 15 Great North Rd; 📞0211 238275, 238284. Just north of the Kabwe roundabout at the top of Cairo Rd.
TS Tyre Services [124 A3] Cairo Rd 📞0211 235901; [115 E3] opp Arcades

EMBASSIES AND HIGH COMMISSIONS IN LUSAKA The following is a selection of Lusaka's diplomatic missions in Lusaka. For a complete list, see www.zambiatourism. com/travel/listings/foreign or look in the front of the telephone directory.

🇪 **Angola (embassy)** 8660 Mumana Rd, Olympia Pk; 📞0211 263697/203627
🇪 **Botswana (high commission)** 5201 Pandit Nehru Rd; 📞0211 252895/250555
🇪 **Canada (high commission)** 5119 United Nations Av; 📞0211 250833
🇪 **DRC (Zaire) (embassy)** 1124 Parirenyatwa Rd; 📞0211 235679/229045
🇪 **European Union** 4899 & 4987 Los Angeles Bd; 📞0211 250711/251140/255585
🇪 **Finland (embassy)** Haile Selassie Av (opp Ndeke Hse), Longacres; 📞0211 251988/251234; www.finland.org.zm
🇪 **France (embassy)** 74 Independence Av; 📞0211 251322; www.ambafrance-zm.org
🇪 **Germany (embassy)** 5209 United Nations Av; 📞0211 250644
🇪 **India (high commission)** 1 Pandit Nehru Rd; 📞0211 253159–60
🇪 **Ireland (embassy)** 6663 Katima Mulilo Rd, Olympia Pk Ext; 📞0211 291124/ 291298/291234/290650; www.dfa.ie/irish-embassy/zambia
🇪 **Italy (embassy)** 5211 Embassy Pk, Diplomatic Triangle; 📞0211 250781/55; www. amblusaka.esteri.it

🇪 **Kenya (high commission)** 5207 United Nations Av; 📞0211 250722/42/51; www. kenyamission.org.zm
🇪 **Malawi (embassy)** 5th Flr, Woodgate Hse, Cairo Rd; 📞0211 228296–8
🇪 **Mozambique (high commission)** 9592 Kacha Rd, Northmead; 📞0211 220333/239135
🇪 **Namibia (high commission)** 508 Mutende Rd, Woodlands; 📞0211 211407/8
🇪 **Nigeria (embassy)** 2503 Haile Selassie Av; 📞0211 253177/253265
🇪 **Norway (embassy)** cnr Birdcage Wk, Haile Selassie Av; 📞0211 389000, 389020/1; www. norway.org.zm
🇪 **South Africa (embassy)** D26 Cheetah Rd, Kabulonga; 📞0211 263944/262119
🇪 **Sweden (embassy)** Haile Selassie Av; 📞0211 251711; www.swedenabroad.com
🇪 **Tanzania (embassy)** Ujamaa Hse, 5200 United Nations Av; 📞0211 253222/253323–4
🇪 **UK (high commission)** 5210 Independence Av; 📞0211 251133/423200
🇪 **USA (embassy)** Kabulonga Rd, Ibex Hill; 📞0211 250955; http://zambia.usembassy.gov
🇪 **Zimbabwe (embassy)** 11058 Haile Selassie Av; 📞0211 254006/12/18

7

EMERGENCIES AND HEALTH CARE

Emergencies In the event of an accident, or for a serious medical condition, see pages 85–90, don't hesitate to use the emergency number given with your medical insurance. Note, too, that many adventure/safari companies, lodges and camps subscribe to an emergency medical evacuation service. Good travel insurances will also cover you for use of their service, although authorisation for this in an emergency can take time. Their regional offices are:

✚ **Specialty Emergency Services** 770302/0962 740300 general ☏ 0211 273302;
(SES) Emergency control centre ☏ 0977   sales@ses-zambia.com; www.ses-zambia.com

The government-run **University Teaching Hospital** [125 G6] (*Nationalist Rd;* ☏ *0211 251451; www.uth.gov.zm*) has a department for emergencies, but it is sadly overstretched and best avoided if possible. More up to date is the new **Levy Mwanawasa General Hospital** [115 G2] (*Great East Rd;* ☏ *0211 285464;* m *0968 769140*), also a public hospital, which was opened in 2011 with the aid of Chinese finance, and has its own casualty department.

General health care For less life-threatening conditions, either your embassy or hotel should be able to recommend a doctor or clinic. A sick foreign traveller will usually be accepted by one of the well-equipped clinics used by the city's more affluent residents without too many questions being asked at first, though proof of comprehensive medical insurance will make this all the more speedy. Some are affiliated to specific insurance companies, so it would be wise to check this first if you can. Among the most well-known are:

✚ **Care for Business (CFB)** [125 F2] 4192 Addis Ababa Dr; ☏ 0211 252917, 254396/8; m 0979 700100; www.cfbmedic.com.zm. 24hr service.
✚ **Corpmed Medical Centre** [124 B3] 3236 Cairo Rd (behind Barclays Business Centre); ☏ 0211 222612/236643; www.corpmedzambia. com

✚ **Fairview Hospital** [124 D4] Chilubi Rd; ☏ 0211 373000; www.medicare-zambia.net
✚ **Lusaka Trust Hospital** [115 H5] 2191 Nsumbu Rd, Woodlands; ☏ 0211 252190/253481/254702; m 0977 472214; www.lusakatrusthospital.com
✚ **Victoria Hospital** [115 E3] 5498 Lunsenfwa Rd; ☏ 0211 290985. Close to the Arcades. 24hr service.

RELIGIOUS SERVICES Lusaka is well served both for churches and mosques. The city's Anglican Cathedral of the Holy Cross is close to the international hotels in the Ridgeway district [125 E4]. Regular services are held here every Sunday at 08.00, 10.00 and 17.00, while those on weekdays vary; for details, see the noticeboard outside the church. The Catholic Cathedral is off Kumoyo Road [125 G4].

TRAVEL AGENTS There's no shortage of travel agents in the capital, but attentive and efficient service isn't as common, and at present only a few, such as Voyagers, are used to the demands of overseas clients. In addition, many have their own favourite properties or trips, and will recommend those, regardless of what would suit you best.

Most safari arrangements are best made as far in advance as possible. Unless you are travelling totally independently (driving or hiking, and camping everywhere), you should ideally book with a good specialist tour operator before you leave home (pages 43–5). This will also give you added consumer protection, and recourse from home if things go wrong. By booking ahead, you also have the best chance of getting into the places you want to visit.

If you do choose to book locally, try one of Lusaka's better travel agents – or one for which you have a reliable personal recommendation. Several readers have been defrauded by rogue Zambia-based travel agents in recent years, so always pay by credit card as it will give your money some degree of protection.

Bush Buzz ☎0211 265827/256992; e info@ bush-buzz.com; www.bush-buzz.com
Juls Africa [115 E2] 5507 Libala Rd, Kalundu; ☎0211 291712, 292942, 292979, 293972; e juls. travel@travelport.co.zm; juls.travel@travelport. co.zm; www.julstravelzambia.com
The Travel Shop Zambia [115 E3] Arcades; ☎0211 255559; [125 F1] Manda Hill; e tsmarketing@microlink.zm

Tikuya Travel & Tours [124 B3] Levy Park; ☎0211 324099; m 0978 717524. Also at Woodlands [115 G6]. Flights & travel within Zambia.
Voyagers [125 E4] Suez Rd; ☎0211 375700; m 0977 860648; e tours@voyagerszambia.com; www.voyagerszambia.com. Lusaka office of this well-recommended travel agent, with its own car-hire division. See ad in 3rd colour section.

FURTHER INFORMATION

There are few really useful sources of information about Lusaka, except for the excellent monthly *The Lowdown* (*www.lowdownzambia.com*). Each issue of this reliable magazine has topical articles, letters and occasional travel features, and a sprinkling of humour, as well as invaluable listings for what's on. It's available online, or – at K10 per issue – at hotels, supermarkets, service stations, craft and bookshops in Lusaka and Shoprite outlets across the country.

SPORT AND ACTIVITIES

The bigger **hotels** have their own fitness suites, featuring gyms, saunas and spas, as well as some very good pools, some just for their own guests. The city also has an Olympic-size **municipal swimming pool** [125 G2] (*Nangwenya Rd;* ⊕ *usually Oct–Apr; admission around K20*).

Lusaka has all the normal sports clubs, including the **rugby** club at the Showgrounds, and **golf** clubs both at Longacres [115 F5] and at Chainama [115 G3], towards the airport. The National Sports Development Centre in the Showgrounds [125 G1] has the city's cheapest and best **squash** courts (glass-backed), as well as **tennis** courts and a bar.

WHAT TO SEE AND DO

Perhaps the most fun to be had around town is simply people-watching, and talking with those who live here. From the poor street vendors (when the police haven't chased them away!) to taxi drivers and the aid-agency expats in the larger hotels, you'll find that people are usually happy to chat. They will comment freely on politics and the issues of the day, and probably ask you how you view things as a foreigner.

These conversations can be fascinating, but be mindful that there aren't debating points to be earned, just new points of view to learn. Try not to expound your prejudices and you'll have much longer and more interesting conversations. Other ways to spend your time in Lusaka include:

MARKETS AND BAZAARS Several of the markets (⏱ *06.00–18.00 Mon–Sat*) are fascinating to wander around, but pay attention to your safety and don't take anything valuable with you. Think twice before wandering around with a backpack, which is inviting theft, and if you have a safe place to leave your money-belt, then don't take that either.

Most of the market stalls concentrate on vegetables and fresh and dried fish, plus new and second-hand clothes. There'll be plenty of others, though, selling everything from baskets to tobacco, bicycle parts to an assortment of hardware. Of particular interest may be the traditional-healer stalls, tinsmiths and furniture makers.

The more relaxed of the two main markets for visitors is **Kamwala Market** on Independence Avenue [124 B5]; if you're heading west, it's just before the railway on the left-hand side of the road. Stalls here are predominantly owned by the city's Chinese and Lebanese communities, and have a reputation for poor quality, though the difference between this and other markets is none too clear to the casual observer.

On the western side of Cairo Road, the **New City Market** – widely known as 'Soweto' Market although the location and name were changed some years ago – is on Lumumba Road [124 A4], which in itself is lined with street vendors peddling their wares. This is the city's biggest market, lively and interesting – it's even popular with adventurous expats on Saturday mornings. Here in particular it's important to dress down for a visit, and don't even think of taking those valuables with you.

There are two other large markets in the centre, both smaller than the New City Market. The **Central Market** is near the Kulima Tower on Chachacha Road [124 A4], and **Comesa** (or Luburma) Market is off Independence Avenue near the Kafue Road fly-over bridge [124 A5]. Comesa is the preserve of traders from across the region, importing goods from Botswana, Zimbabwe, Namibia, Mozambique and Angola. In all of these you'll find clothing donated by charities from the West, with shoes piled up in great heaps. This trade, known as *salaula*, has badly affected Zambia's indigenous clothes industry – which previously thrived on the production and sale of printed cotton fabrics, like the common *chitenjes*. This is why *salaula*'s long-term value as a form of aid is hotly debated.

Many visitors will find the Sunday **street market** at the Arcades [115 E3] (⏱ *10.00–17.00*) less daunting, though bargaining here is as important as in the bigger markets.

Somewhat different in character is the genteel bazaar held on the last Saturday of each month at the **Dutch Reformed Church** [115 G5] (*Kabulonga Rd;* ⏱ *08.00–14.00*). It's a good place for gifts and crafts, from jewellery to handmade clothing and carvings from all over central Africa. It's also a friendly and relaxed place to have coffee and cakes, to savour Chinese and Indian snacks, or to find good biltong.

MUSEUMS AND CULTURE
Kabwata Cultural Centre [125 E7] (Burma Rd; ⏱ *07.00–18.00*) The rondavels of the Kabwata Cultural Village are all that remain of 300 similar huts, which were built in the 1930s and '40s by the colonial government to house Lusaka's black labour force. They were designed with just one room, to house single men whose families were expected to remain in the rural areas rather than become permanent urban settlers.

Between 1971 and '73 the government demolished most of the huts to construct the flats now seen nearby. Fortunately, in 1974, 43 rondavels were saved and turned into a 'cultural centre' with the aim of preserving the country's cultural heritage. Today, many of the rondavels house artists from all over Zambia, who live and work here. In addition to wood- and stone-carvers, you'll find jewellery and other crafts, much of it the work of a women's co-operative based at the centre, as well as some interesting textiles. Sadly, the centre isn't in a great state of repair, and plans to upgrade and revitalise it have so far come to nothing. Nevertheless, it is probably the city's best spot for buying hand-carved crafts and curios. Large wooden hippos are generally cheaper than equivalent carvings at the craft centre near Victoria Falls in Livingstone.

National Museum [124 C5] (*Independence Av;* ⏰ *09.00–16.30 daily, exc Christmas & New Year's Day; entry K25/15 adult/child; no photography*) Lusaka National Museum officially opened its doors to the public in 1996, more than ten years after its inception. It was to have been part of the UNIP Party complex on Independence Avenue but, after Kaunda's electoral defeat in 1991, the plans came to naught and the complex remained an unfinished eyesore until the government stepped in.

The museum houses several galleries on two storeys, and is well worth a visit. Upstairs is the museum proper, currently in the throes of a major and ongoing reorganisation, subject to securing appropriate funding. The eventual aim is to focus individually on Zambia's history, rural culture and urban culture, with a separate children's corner. Already there's a life-size rural village complete with rondavels and model people, set against a painted mural, all depicting traditional village life. It's well thought out and executed, and bodes well for the future. A section on urban culture awaits completion.

For now, the rest of the museum has sections devoted to archaeology and ethnography, political and social history, and an area where artwork by children is displayed. Of these, the ethnography section is probably the most interesting, with exhibits of the material culture of various Zambian ethnic groups, including musical instruments, pottery and basket work, and a popular display of artefacts relating to witchcraft and initiation ceremonies. Don't miss the display of masks, particularly the Makishi masks of the North-Western Province. By contrast, the archaeology section is very small, essentially showing only a cast of 'Broken Hill Man', Zambia's contribution to early hominid finds. The political-history displays feature colonial, independence-era and present-day leaders, with the emphasis on Kaunda's liberation struggle.

On the ground floor, changing exhibitions feature work by contemporary Zambian painters and sculptors, while in the central area a handful of traders have jewellery and clothes for sale. This is also where short-term exhibitions take place, as well as occasional special functions like book launches or film premieres (for details check the local press). Students of Zambian history will find the small library useful, but visitors may be more likely to head for the well-stocked shop selling a good range of baskets and other crafts, and a few relevant books. There's also a simple snack bar.

Freedom Statue [124 C5] (*Independence Av*) This memorial to fallen freedom fighters is just west of the National Museum. The statue, of a man breaking his chains, symbolises Zambia's liberation from the colonial yoke.

Presidential Burial Site [125 F5] (*Embassy Park, Independence Av;* ⏰ *08.30–17.00 daily; US$15/7 adult/child*) Opened to the public in 2012, this burial complex is designed to honour the memory of Zambia's recent presidents. While it is envisaged that there will one day be five presidents interred here, there are at present just three: Levy Patrick Mwanawasa, who died in 2008, his predecessor in office, Frederick Chiluba, who died in 2011, and the most recent incumbent, Michael Sata who died in 2014.

It's ironic that the first two men, once united within the MMD party, and now reunited, should have ended their lives in conflict when Mwanawasa brought a corruption case against his former colleague and president that was to last six bitter years (pages 12–13).

Each of the presidents to be buried here will be acknowledged by an individual memorial be designed to reflect his character, his policies and his time in office. Thus for Mwanawasa, the architect has incorporated a traditional stool to represent that he was a sitting president, with four legs to denote his four keynote policies, and eight steps, one for each of his years in office. For Chiluba's memorial, the ten pillars, for his ten years in office, are beneath a roof topped with a cross, indicating his Christian beliefs. A memorial for President Sata, who was buried here after his death in 2014, has yet to be constructed.

Henry Tayali Visual Arts Centre [125 G1] (☏ 0211 254440; ⊕ 08.00–17.00 Mon–Fri, 10.00–16.30 Sat–Sun) In the middle of the Agricultural Showgrounds, opposite Manda Hill, this interesting art gallery has permanent as well as changing exhibitions of contemporary Zambian art. Items on display are for sale, at prices negotiated with the artist. The centre is probably the best place in Lusaka from which to buy paintings, and sometimes carvings and sculptures. Note, though, that opening hours can be somewhat erratic.

The Showgrounds [125 G1] (*Great East Rd*) Known more formally as the Agricultural Society Showgrounds, this enclosed area is just past Manda Hill. Every August, its network of roads fills to overflowing with visitors to stalls and displays for an annual exhibition of many aspects of Zambian industry and commerce. For most of the rest of the year it's reduced to an eclectic mix of restaurants, bars and businesses, from Barclays Bank to a canine vet and a primary school to fast-food outlets. Note that many of its entrances and exits close around sunset.

OUTSIDE THE CITY
Namwande Art Gallery [off map, 115 H7] (*Leopards Hill Rd*; m 0977 796443; ⊕ *closed Mon*) Those interested in Zambian painting and sculpture might also try this gallery. Expect oil paintings by prominent Zambian artists as well as watercolours, wood and stone carvings, and some delicate ceramics by over 150 Zambian practitioners. There are also pieces from other African artists.

Getting there Follow Leopards Hill Road for about 15km southeast of Lusaka centre, and the gallery is just past the American School on the left.

Kalimba Reptile Park [off map, 115 H2] (☏ 0211 213272/847190; m 0967 213272; ⊕ 09.00–17.00 Mon–Fri, 09.00–18.00 Sat–Sun; entry K25/15 adult/ child under 14) This well-established park has good displays of crocodiles, snakes, chameleons and tortoises, including the rare African slender-nosed crocodile (*Crocodilus cataphractus*). These occur from the DRC to west Africa, but are endangered because of the degradation of their habitat and because they are hunted for food in the DRC. In Zambia, *C. cataphractus* are found only in the Luapula River system, where they were (erroneously) thought to be extinct until recently.

Kalimba also has fishing ponds for anglers, stocked with bream, as well as crazy golf, a children's playground and a volleyball court. Drinks and snacks are available, with croc-burgers – derived from farmed animals – a major attraction.

Getting there Head out of town on the Great East Road, then turn left onto District Road at the Caltex station, about 1km before the Chelston water tower. Follow this road, the D564, for about 11km to a T-junction, turn right and the park is about 1km later on the right. (There's also an alternative access road that's clearly signposted from the airport.)

Lusaka National Park [off map, 115 H7] (☉ 06.00–18.00 daily; entry K30/15 adult/child) Some 16km southeast of the city from Crossroads shopping mall, along Leopards Hill Road, Zambia's newest national park was unveiled by President Lungu on 4 June 2015 with the aim of introducing city dwellers to some of Zambia's natural wildlife. Incongruously close to a zone earmarked for commercial development, it covers an area of just 46km², making it also the smallest of the parks, bar the tiny Ngonye Falls.

The land enclosed for the park has suffered over the years from deforestation, and is now largely scrub with rocky outcrops, few mature trees and no natural water. Tree shade is limited too, and poaching has been a problem since the first animals arrived a few years ago. Despite that, the park has been stocked with a range of herbivores, including wildebeest, eland, hartebeest, sable antelope, zebra and kudu – though whether or not they can be spotted from a vehicle is largely a matter of luck. Pride of place in their own heavily protected enclosure is given to two white rhino.

Visitors are not permitted to enter the park on foot, so you'll need a vehicle to explore the game loops. On the main roads a standard saloon car should be fine, but elsewhere you'll need a high-clearance vehicle to negotiate the rocks – and potentially a 4x4 in the rainy season. There are toilets at the entrance gate, and at the large picnic site some 8km from the gates, where there are also a couple of viewing platforms, but signage is poor, so ask at the gate to see a map before you set off.

Initially, entry fees will be the same across the board, but it's likely to be only a matter of time before there is an increase for overseas visitors. In the first few months since it opened, the park proved popular with locals at weekends, but whether that will translate into a regular stream of visitors, which will in turn justify the upkeep of the park, remains to be seen. And that, in turn, will affect how the authorities protect such a tempting source of fresh meat so close to an industrial heartland.

Getting there As yet there is no public transport to Lusaka National Park, so you'll need your own vehicle. Head out of town on the Leopards Hill Road. Just after the checkpoint, turn right onto Chifwema Road; there is a small sign, but it's dominated by a larger one for the industrial estate. From here it's a further 6km or so to the gate. Follow the road just over 2km, watching out for speed bumps, to a big security gate. It's then almost 4km to the park entrance: take the first left, then continue straight on to a junction, where you turn left again for the gate.

Munda Wanga Wildlife Park and Sanctuary [off map, 114 A7] (*Kafue Rd, Chilanga;* \ *0211 278614;* e *mundawanga@iconnect.zm; www.mundawanga.com;* ☉ *08.00–17.00 daily; entry K25/15 adult/child*) At least 20-minutes' drive south of the city, depending on the traffic, Munda Wanga's botanical gardens and wildlife sanctuary are now back on the map.

After privatisation in 1998, both the sanctuary and botanical gardens were revitalised with the help of volunteers and NGOs such as the Born Free Foundation, although in 2013 it was repossessed by the government, and standards seem to be slipping again. Parts of the park are starting to look overgrown or rundown, but the animals still seem to be properly cared for. The emphasis of the park is still on education, with the aim of helping Lusaka's citizens (and the wider public) to understand and appreciate the importance of their natural heritage.

The park has a number of native Zambian species, such as Kafue lechwe, which share a combined wetland and grassland habitat with puku, impala and waterbuck. Predators such as cheetah, wild dogs and lions are housed in their own natural enclosures, and there's also a small selection of exotic species such as camels, mostly rescued from the exotic pet trade.

On Friday–Sunday and public holidays, feeding time at 14.00 is particularly popular – and it's suggested that you should arrive at noon to take full advantage of this. There's also a bird sanctuary that's home to illegally traded or damaged birds, such as African grey parrots and black kites.

Alongside the animal park, the botanical gardens have been redeveloped with an interpretation centre. The work of young Zambian sculptors – all for sale – is displayed in a natural setting in the gardens, which are a super venue for a picnic (drinks and snacks are available) or a laze in the sun. Children, though, are likely to head for the recreational village, with its swimming pool and waterslide. Nearby is a licensed bar where lunch is served.

Getting there To get there, follow the Kafue Road south for about 15km (and watch your speed – there's a limit of 80km/h along this road). The park is on the right. For visitors without transport, take a local bus from the Kulima Tower depot on Freedom Way ([124 A4] *K5 one way*).

TRIBES
TAILORMADE TRAVEL

• Independent award-winning sustainable travel company since 1998

• We share our expert knowledge so you get the experience you really want

Lodge to lodge safaris ● Expert-led walking mobile safaris ● Combines well with Victoria Falls

Exciting tailor made safaris to Zambia

www.tribes.co.uk   01473 890499

AFRICA | SOUTH AMERICA | ASIA & THE MIDDLE EAST

AITO ssured

PROTECTED

8

Livingstone and the Victoria Falls

Livingstone is probably better oriented towards visitors than any other corner of Zambia. In spite of this, visitors travelling north from Zimbabwe are attracted simply by the Victoria Falls. Until relatively recently the town of Livingstone often remained unseen. In the past, some have even viewed it with suspicion, being bigger and less well known than the small Zimbabwean town which shares the name of the waterfall. As a result of Zimbabwe's recent political instability, however, Livingstone has developed rapidly over the last decade or so. Indeed, the town now plays host to a number of tour operators and lodge owners who cut their teeth across the border – so Zimbabwe's loss is very much Livingstone's gain. Additionally, Livingstone hosted the UNWTO General Assembly in 2013, resulting in an impressive push to develop local infrastructure and improve the cleanliness of the city.

The Zambian and Zimbabwean sides offer different views of the Falls, and if you have time it is worth seeing both sides to appreciate the whole waterfall. It's worth noting, though, that at present Livingstone is the preferred destination for most people visiting the Victoria Falls. Historians might note that most adventure activities like rafting, bungee jumping and microlighting originally started on the Zambian side of the Falls, before being taken over by more commercial Zimbabwean companies.

HISTORY

We can be sure that the Falls were well known to the native peoples of southern Africa well before any European 'discovered' them. After the San/Bushmen hunter-gatherers, the Toka Leya people inhabited the area, and it was probably they who christened the Falls Shongwe. Later, the Ndebele knew the Falls as the aManza Thunqayo, and after that the Makololo referred to them as Mosi-oa-Tunya.

However, their first written description comes to us from Dr David Livingstone, who approached them in November 1855 from the west – from Linyanti, along the Chobe and Zambezi rivers. Livingstone already knew of their existence from the locals, and wrote:

> I resolved on the following day to visit the Falls of Victoria, called by the natives Mosioatunya, or more anciently Shongwe. Of these we had often heard since we came into the country: indeed one of the questions asked by Sebituane [the chief of the Makololo tribe] travelling was, 'Have you the smoke that sounds in your country?' They did not go near enough to examine them, but, viewing them with awe at a distance, said, in reference to the vapour and noise, 'Mosi oa tunya' (smoke does sound there). It was previously called Shongwe, the meaning of which I could not ascertain. The word for a 'pot' resembles this, and it may mean a seething cauldron; but I am not certain of it.

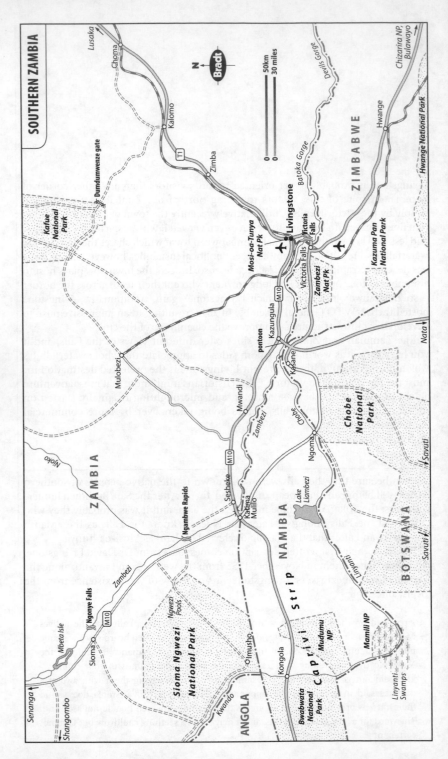

Bradt

50km
30 miles

0
0

Livingstone continues to describe the river above the Falls, its islands and their lush vegetation, before making his most famous comment about sightseeing angels, now abused and misquoted by those who write tourist brochures to the area:

> Some trees resemble the great spreading oak, others assume the character of our own elms and chestnuts; but no one can imagine the beauty of the view from anything witnessed in England. It had never been seen before by European eyes; but scenes so lovely must have been gazed upon by angels in their flight. The only want felt is that of mountains in the background. The Falls are bounded on three sides by ridges 300 or 400 feet in height, which are covered in forest, with the red soil appearing amongst the trees. When about half a mile from the Falls, I left the canoe by which we had come down this far, and embarked in a lighter one, with men well acquainted with the rapids, who, by passing down the centre of the stream in the eddies and still places caused by many jutting rocks, brought me to an island situated in the middle of the river, on the edge of the lip over which the water rolls.

From the autobiographical *Journeys in South Africa*.

Those who bemoan the area's emphasis on tourism should note that there must have been sightseeing boat trips ever since David Livingstone came this way.

Being the most eastern point reachable by boat from the Chobe or Upper Zambezi rivers, the area of the Falls was a natural place for European settlement. Soon more traders, hunters and missionaries came into the area, and by the late 1800s a small European settlement had formed around a ferry crossing called the Old Drift, about 10km upstream from the Falls. However, this was built on low-lying marshy ground near the river, buzzing with mosquitoes, so malaria took many lives.

By 1905 the spectacular Victoria Falls Bridge had been completed, linking the copper deposits of the Copperbelt and the coal deposits at Wankie (now Hwange) with a railway line. This, and malaria, encouraged the settlers to transfer to a site on higher ground, next to the railway line at a place called Constitution Hill. It became the centre of present-day Livingstone, and many of its original buildings are still standing. A small cemetery, the poignant remains of Old Drift, can still be made out on the northern bank of the Zambezi within the Mosi-oa-Tunya National Park.

In 1911 Livingstone became the capital of Northern Rhodesia (now Zambia), which it remained until 1935, when the administration was transferred to Lusaka.

GEOLOGY

The Falls are, geologically speaking, probably a very recent formation. About a million years ago, the Zambezi's course is thought to have been down a wide valley over a plateau dating from the karoo period, until it met the Middle Zambezi rift – where the Matetsi River mouth is now.

Here it fell about 250m over an escarpment. However, that fast-falling water would have eroded the lip of the waterfall and gouged out a deeper channel within the basalt rock of the escarpment plateau – and so the original Falls steadily retreated upstream. These channels tended to follow some existing fissure – a crack or weakness, formed when the lava first cooled at the end of the karoo period. At around the Batoka Gorge these fissures naturally run east–west in the rock, parallel to the course of the valley.

By around the Middle Pleistocene period, between 35,000 and 40,000 years ago, this process had formed the Batoka Gorge, carving it out to within about 90km of the present Falls.

However, as water eroded away the lip of the Falls, its valley gradually turned north, until it was almost at right angles to the basalt fault lines which run east–west. Then the water began to erode the fissures and turn them into walls of rock stretching across the valley, perpendicular to it, over which gushed broad curtains of water.

Once such a wall had formed, the water would wear down the rock until it found a fault line behind the wall, along which the water would erode and cause the rock subsequently to collapse. Thus the new fault line would become the wall of the new Falls, behind the old one. This process resulted in the eight gorges that now form the river's slalom course after it has passed over the present Falls. Each gorge was once a great waterfall.

Today, on the eastern side of the Devil's Cataract, you can see this pattern starting again. The water is eroding away the rock of another fault line, behind the line of the present Falls, which geologists expect will form a new waterfall a few thousand years from now.

LIVINGSTONE

GETTING THERE AND AWAY

By air Livingstone's international airport, code LVI, is just 5km northwest of the town centre on Airport Road. A US$2 million programme of upgrading and development was carried out to improve infrastructure for the 2013 UNWTO General Assembly, with an extended runway allowing for larger flights from South Africa and Kenya, although direct routes from Europe are yet to be established.

The entrance foyer has pleasant waiting rooms, airline offices, a bank (⊕ 08.00–16.00 Mon–Fri, 08.15–14.30 Sat) with ATM, a post office, several car-hire kiosks and a desk for Bushtracks Africa. You can also buy sundries such as sweets and postcards, and there are curio shops for last-minute purchases. If you're after extra security for your luggage, there's a wrapping service for US$10 per bag, located in the same cavernous hall as the check in desks.

A simple snack bar (⊕ 08.00–18.00 daily) serves substantial local dishes, but once you've passed through passport control, neither the bar nor the shops offer anything more substantial than snacks. As if in recompense, though, there's now a duty-free shop and a couple more curio outlets, including Kubu Crafts and Jewel of Africa. Free Wi-Fi is available throughout.

Airlines The airport is served by a number of scheduled airlines and charter companies.

International airlines Both Comair and South African Airways have daily flights between Johannesburg and Livingstone, typically departing Johannesburg mid-morning, and returning early afternoon; the flight time is around 1½ hours. New to the route is the low-cost 1time which, with flight schedules running slightly earlier, operates every day except Tuesday and Saturday. One-way fares between Livingstone and Johannesburg are from around US$140 with 1time, or US$240 with the traditional airlines.

Kenyan Airways has started a new route between Nairobi and Livingstone, operating on Wednesdays, Fridays and Sundays. The flights typically depart early afternoon, returning early evening, with the duration of the flight ranging between 3–5 hours, depending on whether the flight stops over in Harare. One-way fares between Livingstone and Johannesburg are from around US$400.

✈ **1time Airline** ✆+27 21 468 4300; m 0861 878; www.1time.co.za
✈ **British Airways/Comair** ✆0213 322827; www.comair.co.za
✈ **South African Airways** ✆0213 323031/3; www.flysaa.com
✈ **Kenyan Airways** ✆0211 271042; www.kenya-airways.com

Internal and charter airlines Of the local airlines that fly into Livingstone, the following have offices in the town. Other charter companies do fly to the city, but it's rare for them to have an aircraft based in Livingstone, so the cost of chartering a flight to anywhere apart from Lusaka is extremely high.

✈ **Proflight** ✆0211 252452/476; m 0977 335563; e reservations@proflight-zambia.com; www.flyzambia.com. A reliable company offering scheduled & charter flights. The only direct scheduled flights are to Lusaka, but these are timed to connect onto Proflight's transfers to other areas, as well as international flights wherever possible.

✈ **Wilderness Air** ✆0213 321578–80; m 0966 770485; e ashleighb@wilderness-air.com; www. wilderness-air.com. Operates all of Wilderness Safaris' flights from neighbouring countries and within Zambia. The only flights operated from Livingstone are up to the Busanga Plains in the Kafue National Park.

By bus Construction has been underway for some years now on a major new bus station on Kafubu Road. However, even though this was supposed to have been completed in time for the UNWTO 2013 General Assembly, it's still very much work in progress. In the meantime the main bus terminus is at the end of Airport Road, on the corner with Chimwemwe Way [158 C1], although one of the town's most reliable companies is currently Mazhandu Family Bus Service which is based on Mutelo St, just down from the Spa [158 B2]. Buses gather in the early morning, most heading towards Lusaka. This trip takes around six hours, depending on the company, with a one-way fare costing around K100–110. Ticket prices for some companies may be lower, but check out the state of the bus first; a cracked windscreen doesn't instil much confidence.

If you want to go west to Kazungula or Sesheke your best bet is to board the daily Mazhandu Family Bus that goes to Mongu via both towns.

Expect the first buses to leave at around 06.00, with others to follow according to demand (and note that music played may be at ear-splitting levels). Tickets can usually be bought on the bus, but when demand is high – especially early in the morning, when touts are around – bus stations can be chaotic, so it's wise to buy tickets the day before. It's also advisable to be at the bus station at least half an hour before departure, since buses may leave early if they're full.

🚐 **FM Travellers** [124 B2] m 0976 751925. Operates from the main bus terminus, with the first departure at 07.00, & the last at 21.00. Tickets to Lusaka cost K120, & can be booked online via www.busticketszambia.com.
🚐 **CR Carriers** [158 B1] ✆0211 288425; m 0977 861063. An established company but with very mixed standards. 5–6 buses a day to Lusaka between 06.30 & 20.00 from the corner of Mosi-oa-Tunya Rd & Akapelwa St, opposite Barclays Bank. There are also onward services to Ndola (4–5hrs) & Kitwe (5–6hrs).

🚐 **Mazhandu Family Bus Services** [158 B2] m 0977 806060, 489414. Livingstone's most reliable bus company operates from outside the Spa on the corner with Mutelo St. Regular daily departures to Lusaka start at 06.00, with the last bus at 22.30. Services also run to Kazungula (K50) & on to Sesheke (K70). On 'business class' buses (09.00 daily), which have AC, fares from Lusaka are K130, against the economy fare of K120. Tickets can be booked online via www.tamangatickets.net.
🚐 **Shalom** [158 B2] m 0977 747013. Operates from Town Centre Market, with the 1st bus to Lusaka at 06.30, & the last at 22.00.

8

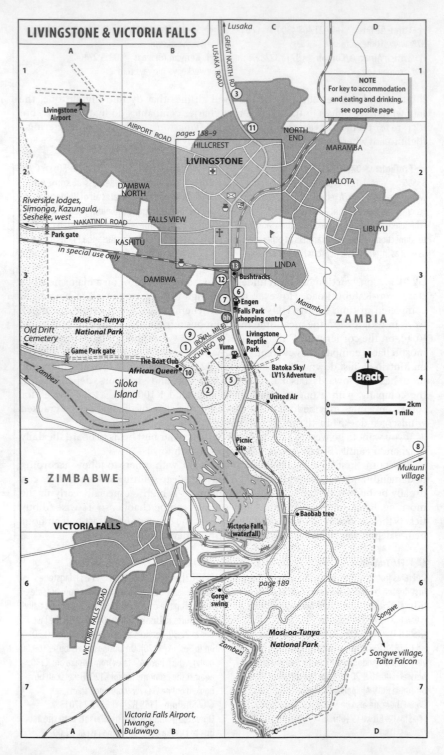

LIVINGSTONE & VICTORIA FALLS

↑ Lusaka

C   D

NOTE
For key to accommodation
and eating and drinking,
see opposite page

Livingstone Airport

AIRPORT ROAD   pages 158–9

HILLCREST

LIVINGSTONE

NORTH END

MARAMBA

MALOTA

DAMBWA NORTH

Riverside lodges,
Simonga, Kazungula,
Sesheke, west

FALLS VIEW

LIBUYU

NAKATINDI ROAD

Park gate

KASHITU

in special use only

LINDA

DAMBWA

Bushtracks

Marambo

ZAMBIA

Engen
Falls Park
shopping centre

**Mosi-oa-Tunya
National Park**

Old Drift
Cemetery

Livingstone Reptile Park

Game Park gate

The Boat Club
African Queen

Zambezi

Siloka
Island

Sichango RD

Vuma

(ROYAL MILE)

Batoka Sky/
LV1's Adventure

N

Bradt

United Air

0   2km
0   1 mile

Picnic
site

Mukuni
village

ZIMBABWE

Baobab tree

VICTORIA FALLS

Victoria Falls
(waterfall)

page 189

Gorge
swing

Songwe

**Mosi-oa-Tunya
National Park**

Songwe village,
Taita Falcon

Zambezi

VICTORIA FALLS ROAD

Victoria Falls Airport,
Hwange,
Bulawayo

A   B   C   D

In addition to these, **Intercape Mainliner** (*www.intercape.co.za*) runs a return service from Windhoek in Namibia to Livingstone and on to Victoria Falls town. Buses arrive in Livingstone at South End Travel, next to Barclays Bank [158 B1]. Tickets must be booked in advance, either online or at the Intercape Mainliner offices in Windhoek. Prices start from around ZAR730 one way.

By train The railway station [159 D7] is well signposted about 1km south of the town centre on the way to the Falls, on the eastern side of Mosi-oa-Tunya Road. Most trains nowadays are geared towards freight with passenger trains being infrequent. However, with the introduction of the Golden Jubilee Express, an overnight service between Lusaka and Livingstone, the passenger trains that do run are becoming quicker and more reliable. Trains leave Lusaka at 18.00 on Friday, arriving in Livingstone at 06.00 the next morning. The return train runs to the same times, departing Livingstone on Sunday evening and reaching Lusaka early on Monday morning. One-way fares in different classes are K90, K110, K135 and K145 for a sleeper. Historically the train has been the slowest and least reliable method of transport between the two cities, and although this does appear to be improving, the bus is still likely to offer you greater flexibility and reliability.

Driving For details of driving between Livingstone and Lusaka, see pages 209–10.

Those heading **west**, into Namibia's Caprivi Strip, Botswana or western Zambia, should take the Nakatindi Road – signposted as the M10 – past the lodges by the river. After about 70km this comes to the Zambezi River at Kazungula – where Namibia, Botswana, Zimbabwe and Zambia all meet at a notional point. Here you can continue northwest within Zambia to Sesheke, or take the ferry across the Zambezi into Botswana, near Kasane. The drive from Livingstone to Sesheke takes about 2½ hours. Note that the last 40km section from Kazungula to Sesheke has more potholes than tarmac.

GETTING AROUND

Orientation Livingstone town itself is fairly compact and surrounded by several small township suburbs, sprawling out from its centre. Much bigger than the Zimbabwean town of Victoria Falls, on the other side of the river, the town has two main business areas concentrated along the all-important Mosi-oa-Tunya Road. Sections of this are lined with classic colonial buildings with

Livingstone and the Victoria Falls LIVINGSTONE

8

corrugated-iron roofs and wide wooden verandas, some restored and others in a state of disrepair.

The larger and busier central business district begins atop a small hill just past the museum, while in the lower part of town is a smaller but growing retail area known as '217'. Developments further south have introduced a new shopping area between Livingstone and the Falls. Navigation is easy, even without a map, though signposts are often missing or may point to establishments no longer in existence.

Drive north out of the city, and the main street leading to the capital becomes Lusaka Road. Head south for about 10km and you reach the Zambezi River and the Victoria Falls themselves, and the border post to cross into Zimbabwe via Victoria Falls Bridge. Many visitors choose to stay close to the Falls at one of Sun International's two hotels, but there are now several new options on this side of town.

Travel west from town on the M10 Nakatindi Road and you'll find yourself driving parallel to the north bank of the Zambezi upstream towards Kazungula and the ferry to Botswana. Signposts to the left point to small, exclusive lodges perched at picturesque spots on the river's bank.

A good street atlas covering both Livingstone and Lusaka is published by Streetwise and is available locally.

By taxi or with a tour operator Livingstone town is small enough to walk around, as is the Falls area. However if you are travelling between the two, or going to the airport, or in a hurry, then use one of the plentiful – if battered – light-blue taxis that congregate near the old Shoprite at the main taxi stand [158 B2] or on Mosi-oa-Tunya Road opposite the curio market in the park [158 E3]. All taxis are supposed to carry a fare chart, though you will be lucky to see one. A taxi between town and either the Falls or the airport will cost around K50–55/US$9–10 for up to four passengers. A taxi out to the riverside lodges will cost from around K80/US$15, depending on the location; some are a considerable distance from town. Competition amongst taxi drivers can be fierce, so be sure to negotiate for the best deal and agree on the price in advance.

While you can negotiate to hire a taxi for the day to take you around town, to the Falls and to outlying areas, you'll have a more informative trip with one of the licensed and more knowledgeable tour operators. For details, see pages 186–8.

By bus Minibuses run to the Falls from the Town Centre Market in the centre of Livingstone throughout the day. The buses only depart when they are full, so expect the 10-minute journey to be cramped. Expect to pay around K5 for the journey.

Driving yourself Driving in Livingstone is pretty straightforward, though watch out for the none-too-subtle speed humps along Mosi-oa-Tunya Road.

Most lodges and hotels have secure parking, as do many restaurants. If you're parking on the street in town, you're likely to come across any number of volunteers to look after your car or to wash it for you. There's nothing organised about this, and you're under no obligation to accept their help, but if you're prepared to trust someone then – in spite of considerable protestations to the contrary – a tip of about K2–3/US$0.30–0.50 is about right, depending on the length of time you're away.

There are several 24-hour fuel stations on the main Mosi-oa-Tunya Road. Nowadays, the price of fuel, both diesel and unleaded, is the same nationwide (see page 69).

Car hire If you don't have a vehicle and wish to explore the area at your own pace, you can hire a car with or without a driver – the former can even be a cheaper option.

Alternatively, you can rent a 4x4 with full kit if you wish to do a self-drive safari, although this can be a very expensive option.

🚗 **Hemingways** ☎0213 323097; m 0977 866492, 870232; e info@hemingwayszambia. com; www.hemingwayszambia.com. Specialist vehicle hire, with or without a driver, for day tours, transfers or independent safaris. Their fleet consists of 8 Toyota Hilux double-cab vehicles which are fully equipped for camping, including rooftop tents, long-range fuel tanks & fridge.

🚗 **Arma Investments Ltd** [159 D7] Mosi-oa-Tunya Rd; ☎0213 320437; m 0974 612010; e armainvestments1@gmail.com; www. armazambia.com; ⊕ 08.00–20.30 Mon–Sat, 13.00–20.30 Sun). Well signposted north of the railway station, Arma rents cars, 4x4s &

minibuses, & can arrange taxis, other transport & tours.

🚗 **Voyagers** [154 A4] ☎0213 322753; m 0977 860648; e rentals@voyagerszambia. com, livingstone@voyagerszambia.com; www. voyagerszambia.com, www.europcarzambia.com. From its base at the airport, and also on Mosi-oa-Tunya Rd south of the train station [159 D8] Voyagers Rentals is the franchisee for Europcar, with self-drive & chauffeur-driven vehicles in all price ranges & styles. They can also arrange trips throughout the region, including transfers from Kazungula & into Botswana, Zimbabwe & Namibia. See ad in 3rd colour section.

By bicycle Guided bike tours can be arranged with Oliver Sikatumba (m *0977 747837, 0978 171547;* e *oliversikatumba@rocketmail.com*). A 4-hour guided tour costs US$25 pp, and can include riverside rides to the Falls, market and village tours, and a visit to the small school started by 'Cowboy' Cliff Sitwala, the founder of the company. The profits from the tours go towards supporting this school.

You can also rent bikes from **Jollyboys**, or from **Livingstone Urban Adventures** (m *0977 545754*) costing US$15 pp for the day, and US$10 for a half day.

WHERE TO STAY Since the late 1990s, Livingstone has experienced a boom in tourism and now offers a great variety of places to stay for all types of travellers and budgets. Whereas accommodation used to be of widely varying standards, now you will find excellent choices in all price ranges, with many providing the service, standards and amenities that international visitors have come to expect. If the choice is overwhelming, knowing the options in advance will make finding the right place much easier. Most of the larger establishments accept credit cards.

Numerous bush lodges occupy lovely situations along the Zambezi River, some close enough to easily take advantage of the attractions and activities of the Falls, others further upstream and more remote. Closer to town, and to the Falls, an increasing number of upmarket hotels, some on the river, and others in a more urban setting, offer Western creature comforts. At the cheaper end of the market, staying in a guesthouse or in-town lodge, where you may meet African travellers or volunteers from overseas, can add a multi-cultural dimension to your visit, while backpacker accommodation tends to cater strictly to the international budget traveller.

In town Hotels in Livingstone itself are still relatively spread out, with some in town, and others on the road south towards the Falls. Establishments listed here are roughly in order of price.

Even the most unobservant visitor in Livingstone can't help but notice the multitude of signs pointing to **guesthouses** all over town, but standards vary immensely. Many are new to tourism and others cater to the local market rather than to overseas visitors. One thing is for certain: the Western image of a guesthouse – a charming and personal B&B – is not to be found here … yet.

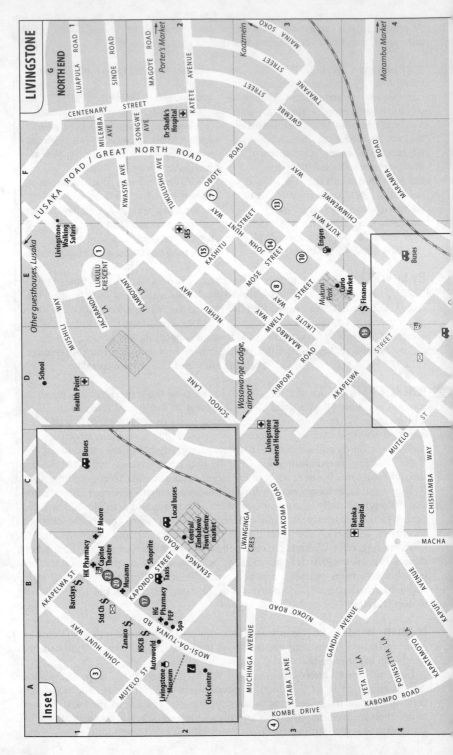

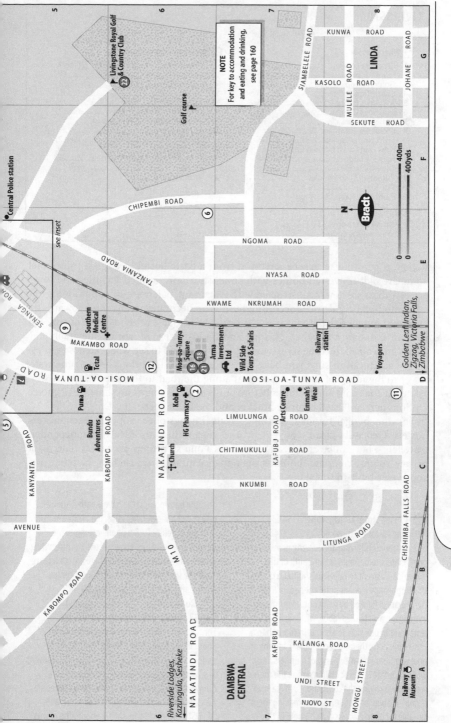

NOTE
For key to accommodation and eating and drinking, see page 160

Livingstone Royal Golf & Country Club

Golf course

Central Police station

see inset

CHIPEMBI ROAD

TANZANIA ROAD

SENANGA ROAD

Southern Medical Centre

MAKAMBO ROAD

MOSI-OA-TUNYA ROAD

Puma

Total

Mosi-oa-Tunya Square

Arma Investments Ltd

Wild Side Tours & Safaris

Railway station

Voyagers

NGOMA ROAD

NYASA ROAD

KWAME NKRUMAH ROAD

MOSI-OA-TUNYA ROAD

Golden Leaf Indian, Zigzag, Victoria Falls, Zimbabwe

SIAMBELELE ROAD

KUNWA ROAD

KASOLO ROAD

MULELE ROAD

SEKUTE ROAD

JOHANE ROAD

LINDA

400m
400yds

N
Bradt

Bundu Adventures

KABOMPO ROAD

NAKATINDI ROAD

Church

Kobil

HG Pharmacy

LIMULUNGA ROAD

CHITIMUKULU ROAD

NKUMBI ROAD

KAFUBU ROAD

Arts Centre

Emmah's Wear

ROAD

LITUNGA ROAD

CHISHIMBA FALLS ROAD

KANYANTA ROAD

AVENUE

KABOMPO ROAD

M10

NAKATINDI ROAD

Riverside Lodges, Kazungula, Sesheke

DAMBWA CENTRAL

KAFUBU ROAD

KALANGA ROAD

UNDI STREET

NJOVO ST

MONGU STREET

Railway Museum

159

LIVINGSTONE

For listings, see pages 160–5 & 177–81

Rather, a 'guesthouse' can be anything from a basic hostel to a quasi mini-hotel. Some are old, converted homes with smallish rooms, limited facilities and lower prices; others are newly constructed with restaurant, bar, pool, air conditioning and other mod-cons, and priced accordingly. Interior decoration leans either towards the basic and functional, perhaps with the odd ethnic touch, or tends to be overblown, with an abundance of velvet, chrome and multi-patterned fabrics. Inevitably new places crop up all the time so it's worth looking around to see what catches your eye and which location suits you best; there are numerous options around the water tower to the north of town, and several along the road to the airport, too. Always ask to see the room and facilities before booking in, as there's no shortage of choice. Options here are listed by price bracket and then alphabetically.

For the budget-minded, nothing beats Livingstone's popular **backpackers'** hostels. Generally clean, convenient and cheap, they are ideal for independent travellers – but can be crowded at times. As a one-stop shop, they offer shared and private rooms, camping, booking agency, restaurant, bar, kitchen, laundry, pool and even a built-in social life.

Hotels

🏠 **Protea Hotel Livingstone** [154 C3] (80 rooms) Mosi-oa-Tunya Rd; 📞 0213 324630; e reservations@phlivingstone.co.zm; www. proteahotels.com. About 0.5km south of the railway, & adjacent to Falls Park shopping centre, this surprisingly elegant hotel opened in 2008. From the entrance, flanked by giant pots overflowing with water, a wide tiled lobby, with a formal restaurant to one side, leads in turn through to a courtyard. Here, there's a rectangular swimming pool with its own bar & plenty of loungers. Dark-wood furniture & classic styling define the rooms, some of which face the courtyard. Each features a king-size bed, or 2 of queen size, making them suitable for up to 2 adults & 2 children. In the

en-suite bathroom, some have a bath & shower, others just a shower. AC, safes, tea-/coffee-making facilities, satellite TV & a phone complete the picture. The hotel has its own activity centre, while for the more work orientated, there are conference facilities, free Wi-Fi access & a business centre. There's also a secure car park. **$$$$**

🏠 **Road Lodge** [154 C3] (17 rooms) 📞 0977 324646; e roadlodge@zamtel.zm. Formerly known as Fallsway Lodge & located south of the town, opposite the Protea, Road Lodge is a mid-market place, with lawned gardens & a swimming pool that has a children's area. Single, twin, dbl & family rooms, all en suite, are classified as 'small' or 'large', and all come with AC, DSTV, fridge, kettle, safe & phone. The rooms were modern, but unfortunately in a slight state of disrepair, & in need of refurbishment. The marble-floored halaal restaurant overlooks the garden & serves local & Western cuisine, though guests can also cater for themselves. 2-for-1 cocktails are served in the bar on Wed & Fri, 19.00–20.00. As well as having Wi-Fi hot spots, the hotel has a room where guests can surf the internet for 30 mins without charge. **$$$**

🏠 **Kaazmein Lodge** [159 G3] (34 rooms, camping) Maina Soko; m 0977 32 2244, 0977 32 2244; e info@kaazmeinlodge.com; www. kaazmeinlodge.com. Whatever you may think of this lodge, opened in 2007, it's certainly different. Set in some 8ha, it features a series of manmade lakes, complete with artificial islands & bridges over narrow streams, & the green lawns are grazed by a couple of resident zebras. At its heart is a huge, 2-storey domed structure that houses both a restaurant & conference facilities. There is a non-alcoholic bar across the lake, near to a blue thatched gazebo set up like a bandstand for seating, & a pool table a short walk away. Accommodation is set well apart from this area with 12 chalets overlooking a water feature, 10 hotel-style rooms overlooking the lawns, & 12 self-contained A-framed rooms. All have AC, a TV & an en suite with décor on the ornate side. Budget travellers can camp & have their own ablution block. Finally, there's a pool & secure parking. Rates have fallen considerably since the lodge was first opened. **$$$** *Camping US$8 pp.*

🏠 **Ngolide Lodge** [159 D8] (16 rooms) 110 Mosi-oa-Tunya Rd; 0213 321091/2; e info@ ngolidelodge.com; www.ngolidelodge.com. On the south side of town, as the main road leaves Livingstone for the Falls, this thatched lodge is fronted by a secure car park. It's actually more of a mini-hotel than a lodge, well built & compact, if a bit dark. A central quadrangle is surrounded by a water feature & incorporates a small lounge with a satellite TV. The reception area is located at one end, with a sunny grass square at the other. Small but comfortable rooms surround the perimeter, decorated with ethnic fabrics. Each has tiled floors, en suite bathrooms, twin or dbl beds with mosi nets, AC, tea/coffee maker, safe & satellite TV & a fridge. There is a bar licensed to be open from 14.30, & the lodge also runs the Golden Leaf Restaurant just across the street. There's Wi-Fi access across the whole site. **$$$**

🏠 **Wasawange Lodge** [158 D3] (22 rooms, 2 apts) Airport Rd; 0213 324066/324078; e waslodge@yahoo.com/wasofice@zamnet.zm. Situated 2km from the town centre & the same distance from the airport, Wasawange Lodge is a comfortable small hotel with a rather austere reception area & a few ethnic touches. Its spacious dbl & twin rooms are individual rondavels with en-suite facilities, AC, a fridge/minibar, in-room coffee/tea, mosquito repellent & satellite TV. Clean & well serviced, they have high wooden ceilings, large mirrors & rugs to cover nice stone floors. The place has a good restaurant, bar, swimming pool & sauna, & its conference rooms are popular with business visitors. Transfers & all activities can be arranged. **$$$**

🏠 **New Fairmount Hotel & Casino** [158 E3] (104 rooms) Mosi-oa-Tunya Rd; 0213 320723/8, 322630, 320075; e nfhc@zamnet.zm; www. newfairmounthotel.co.zm. In the centre of town, between Mose & Mwela streets, this large old hotel of Moorish design in sparkling white plaster was once the town's focal point, & remains good value. En-suite rooms – ranging from 'singles' (with a dbl bed) to executive suites – are clean & traditional in style, with AC, fridge, kettle, satellite TV & even a DVD/video player. These are set around white-painted concrete courtyards at the back, where there's a swimming pool (open to non-residents) & plenty of shady seating. The hotel has an air-conditioned restaurant serving Zambian & international dishes, plus a nightclub popular at w/ends. The hotel also has a casino, but at time of research in 2015 this was disused, with little sign that it would be operating again soon. A cavernous lobby contains a white piano, & a reception desk where external activities can easily be arranged. Wi-Fi is available throughout the hotel at an extra cost of K30 for 24hrs. In front is ample covered parking under the watchful eye of 24hr security. **$–$$**

🏠 **Golden Chopsticks Hotel** [158 A1] (40 rooms); John Hunt Way; e goldenchopsticks@ microlink.zm. Located in the centre of town, only minutes from the Livingstone museum, Golden Chopsticks is a Chinese-owned hotel built in 2014. It's a modern hotel, & with all of the fixtures imported from China, it's catering heavily to the Chinese market, which can make communications difficult for those not familiar with the language. Each of the en-suite guestrooms have twin or dbl beds, AC, DSTV & free Wi-Fi. The staff are friendly

& the hotel is impeccably clean, & there is also a restaurant on site. $-$$

Guesthouses

⌂ **Olga's Guesthouse** [158 D6] (9 rooms) Nakatindi Rd; ☏ 0213 324160; e info@ olgasproject.com; www.olgasproject.com. Although the rooms at this small guesthouse were only built in 2012, the associated Italian restaurant is well established. The 9 thatched en-suite rooms are constructed using traditional local materials, & while they are on the small side they are charming & comfortable. The guesthouse finances the Youth Community Training Centre, who constructed all of the teak furniture for the rooms. The rooms surround a small enclosed garden, & there is also a good restaurant & a bar, although these close at 22.00 to avoid disturbing guests. Discounts are available for NGO workers & members of the clergy. $$$$$

⌂ **Chanters Lodge** [158 E1] (11 rooms) Lukulu Cres; ☏ 0213 323412; e richardchanter@ gmail.com; www.chanters-livingstone.com. Run by former Lusaka hotelier Richard Chanter, Chanters was one of the first guesthouses in Livingstone. It stands in a leafy residential area off Obote Av, about 1km north of town. Lukulu Cres is the 4th right turn & is well signposted.

Comfortable en-suite rooms – some with bath & shower, others with just a shower – vary in size from 'singles' (with a dbl bed) to family accommodation, but all have AC, satellite TV & fridge. The public rooms are pleasant, with tables & chairs extending onto a patio & garden at the back around a small pool. There's also secure parking. Free Wi-Fi is available in the public areas. The restaurant (page 179) is open all day until 21.30. $$

⌂ **Green Tree Lodge** [158 A3] (5 chalets, camping) 2015 Kombe Dr; ☏ 0213 322631; m 0977 630159; e greentreelodge@livingstonezambia. com; www.greentreelodgezambia.com. Individual en-suite chalets with secure parking alongside make this an attractive proposition for the self driver. The chalets are set among fruit trees, & each boasts dbl or twin beds, AC, fridge, TV, Wi-Fi & kettle, as well as its own veranda. It's also possible to camp on the grass, close to the pool & bar, where meals are available. $$ *Camping US$6 pp.*

⌂ **Limbo Lodge** [154 C1] (12 chalets) 7671/7673 Lusaka Rd; ☏ 0213 322096; m 0955 78 0330; e reservations@limbolodge.com; www.

limbolodge.com. A tranquil option in a lovely garden, Limbo offers warm hospitality & good value. You'll find it 100m to the right of the road heading north out of town. Grass-thatched chalets are spread across green lawns, & have been constructed incorporating local rocks. Each chalet has 2 rooms, which can interconnect to form a family room, each with its own en suite & decorated with ethnic décor matching the style of the structures. Modern amenities include mosi nets, minibar, coffee/tea facilities, satellite TV & AC. In addition, there's a restaurant & bar, a swimming pool, & a brand new conference room, as well as secure parking. $$

⌂ **Rite Inn** [158 E3] (10 rooms) 301 Mose St; ☏ 0213 323264, m 0972 811181; e riteinn@ gmail.com. In a small, secure courtyard within walking distance of town, Rite Inn has clean, attractive rooms that are both functional & comfortable. Both twin and dbl rooms, & a family room decorated in an African motif, have tiled bathrooms, AC, fridges, coffee/tea service, digital safes & satellite TVs. The family room, sleeping 4 people, also has a jacuzzi bath in the bathroom. These & the reception area are adjacent to a sparkling swimming pool, surrounded by a tiled patio. The street-side carport is patrolled around the clock, or you can park inside the courtyard on request. There is a small bar & restaurant serving local & western food. $$

⌂ **Wane Guest Lodge** [154 C2] (7 rooms, house) Lusaka Rd; ☏ 0213 324058; e info@ waneguestlodge.com, www.waneguestlodge. com. Another lodge on 'guesthouse row'; look for the sign on the main road & the name on the entrance gate. The lodge was refurbished in 2014, so the en-suite bedrooms & separate, self-catering family house (sleeping 5) are modern, clean & well appointed, each with tiled floors, new bedclothes, AC, satellite TV, fridge & tea/ coffee station. As well as a full restaurant (*K55*) & bar, serving international & Zambian dishes, there's 24hr room service, a small pool, round-the-clock security & a conference centre seating up to 30 people. $$

⌂ **Zambezi Ultima Guesthouse** [158 E2] (14 rooms) 36 Likute Way; ☏ 0213 323435, m 0972 008779. Situated on a large plot in the residential section of town, this guesthouse has dbl & twin rooms, & 2 suites that can be used for families – all painted in the same colour as Livingstone's blue taxis. Even so the newer 'superior' rooms in the garden area are nice enough, & are worth the small additional cost to upgrade from the 'standard' rooms. The hotel has an outside pool that was being renovated in 2015, & an outside bar, dining room, satellite TV, kitchen facilities, & free Wi-Fi in the communal areas. All rooms are en suite with AC & mosi nets. **$$**

🏠 **Zigzag** [154 B3] (12 rooms) Industrial Rd; ☎0213 322814; m 0977 681741; e info@zigzagzambia.com, www.zigzagzambia. com. Signposted down a side road off Mosi-oa-Tunya Rd, near the railway crossing, Zigzag is on the edge of town & has secure parking. From its origins as a coffee house, restaurant & craft market (page 180), it has expanded to include a block of triple, twin, dbl & family rooms in its 0.5ha garden complex. These are nicely furnished with AC, tiled bathrooms & ethnic décor, & there's a lounge with satellite TV & free Wi-Fi. The leafy, shaded garden houses an enticing pool & a children's play area with swings & a jungle gym. The lodge is run by the owners Lynne & Vasco lending it a good amount of character, & it's worth asking them about the philanthropic work they do in the Livingstone area. **$$**

🏠 **Pumulani Livingstone** [158 F3] (6 rooms) Mosi-oa-Tunya Rd; ☎0213 320981; m 0964 017019, 0954 516518; e pumulanizambia@yahoo. com. Conveniently located on the main road with secure parking, this guesthouse works well for self drivers. With a grass courtyard & high boundary walls it's also surprisingly peaceful. Converted from a house, each room is decorated with a mixture of traditional & modern African décor, although they are close together & can lack privacy. Each room has tea/coffee making facilities, fridge, DSTV & Wi-Fi. **$$**

🏠 **La Residence** [158 F2] John Hunt Way (5 rooms) ☎0213 320875; m 0955 892460, 0977 474140; e gakapelwa@gmail.com; www. laresidence.co.zm. This simple guesthouse, just north of the centre, is contained within a colonial style building, & feels more like someone's home than a hotel, although the service is pleasant & helpful. Each room has a sgl, dbl or king-size bed, as well as AC, fridge, Wi-Fi & DSTV. The restaurant uses many fresh ingredients from the on-site garden, & serves traditional Zambian meals. **$$**

🏠 **Likute Guesthouse** [158 E3] (14 rooms) 62 Likute Way; ☎0213 323264; m 0927 811181;

e likuteguest@zamnet.zm, likuta_guest_ house@yahoo.com. This clean guesthouse is conveniently located in a small walled complex behind the Fairmount Hotel. En-suite rooms have AC, mosi nets, satellite TV, kettle & fridge, & there's a pleasant lounge. Renovations were being carried out in 2015 to smarten up the main areas. There's a bar, & meals are available on request. Secure parking. **$**

Backpackers

🏠 **Fawlty Towers** [158 D6] (34 dorm beds, 24 rooms, camping) 216 Mosi-oa-Tunya Rd; ☎0213 323432, m 0972 250154; e ahorizon@ zamnet.zm; www.adventure-africa.com. Just south of the turn-off to Nakatindi/Kazungula Rd, you can't miss this popular international backpackers' place – just look for the white wrought-iron burglar bars shaped like rising suns.

This large hostel feels very spacious, & a bit more upmarket then the other backpacker options in Livingstone, but the dorm rooms, reasonable prices & lively bar mean that it certainly hasn't forgotten its backpacker roots. Enter through the large gates covered by straw mats, & you come to a smart reception area with an impressively stocked bar, lounge, satellite TV & pool table, which is decorated with pictures of local Zambian people on one wall, & the cast of the eponymous television show.

Upstairs in the main building are 4 dorms sleeping 6, one sleeping 4, & both a trpl & a twin room, all sharing toilets & showers. There's also a reading lounge, self-catering kitchen & dining room serving a full English b/fast for about US$4. All these areas are tastefully decorated with wooden tables, Persian rugs & comfy armchairs, making them vaguely reminiscent of an old English study. Below the restaurant there is also a new spa offering a range of treatments including a full body massage (K100).

Behind the main building, you'll find a spacious private garden shaded by mango trees & coloured with bougainvillea where lawns fringe an inviting pool. Campers on the lawns share clean toilets & showers. Also in the garden area are a further 6-bed dorm, plus 4 twins & a dbl, all sharing showers & toilets; & – in a separate complex, 9 twin, 8 dbls & 2 4-bed en-suite rooms. There is also a second communal kitchen (all accessories provided). Everything is neat & clean, all rooms come with mosi nets, desk fans & bed linen, &

showers have hot & cold running water. Tea & coffee are on hand all day, & free pancakes are offered poolside each afternoon. There's even a laundry service at US$10 per bag.

Fawlty Towers is quiet, secure, well run & tremendously convenient for the centre of Livingstone. The atmosphere is informal & lively, & it's a great place to meet other travellers, but the bar closes early so you can still get a reasonable night's sleep. There is free Wi-Fi available throughout the hostel & they offer free transport & transfers to Victoria Falls daily at 10.00. To help with organising your stay there's also an in-house booking office (☉ 07.30–16.30 Mon–Fri, 07.30–13.00 Sat). **$–$$** *exc b/fast. Dorm bed US$12; en suite room US$55; shared ablutions room US£45, camping US$6 pp.*

✳ 🏠 **Jollyboys Backpackers** [159 C5] (14 en-suite rooms, 11 with shared ablutions, 50 dorm beds, camping) 34 Kanyanta Rd; ✆ 0213 324229/322086; e enquiries@backpackzambia. com; www.backpackzambia.com. The ever-popular Jollyboys occupies a tree-shaded site just behind the museum, a 2-min walk from the town centre. Owner-operated & managed by the helpful & friendly Kim, Sue & John, its reputation as the quintessential backpackers' lodge remains undimmed.

The main facilities are set within a large, central thatched courtyard, with the dorms, reception area & ablutions around the perimeter. There are also 14 en-suite twin & dbl rooms with AC & mosi nets, 3 of which are positioned around the quad. Mixed dorms come with 4 beds, 8 beds (& AC!), or – the cheapest – 16 beds, all with bedding included, fans & sharing a good-sized toilet & shower block with endless hot water. In the back garden are 2-bed A-frame thatched chalets & some camping space, both sharing ablution facilities.

In the middle of the 'quad' is a wonderful sunken lounge with firepit & pillows – a perfect spot to chill out, read & meet fellow travellers. Above is a wooden deck from which you can see the spray from the Falls. A covered sitting area has comfy seating & table tennis, & looks out to an enticing rock swimming pool, lawns & gardens. Adjacent are the open-plan bar with satellite TV, & the restaurant, where you can enjoy a home-cooked meal at reasonable prices – the burgers here are particularly good. There's also a separate self-catering kitchen. Internet is available through Wi-Fi or a computer in the main area; both are free to use. Bikes can

be hired (US$5/10 ½/full day), & there's a laundry service, book exchange (K2 per book, with proceeds to charity), secure parking & short- & long-term baggage storage. There's also a free pick-up service from the airport, by arrangement. Kim & Sue offer friendly, first-hand advice on what to see & do; there are free lifts to the Falls at 10.00 daily, & they can book any & all activities. The atmosphere is relaxed & unpretentious, if busy, & with the bar shut by 23.00 noise isn't a major issue. **$–$$**, *exc b/fast. 4/8/16-bed dorm US$18/15/12 pp; en suite room US$65; shared ablutions room US$45. Camping US$9 pp.*

🏠 **Jollyboys Camp** [159 E6] (24 dorm beds, 9 en-suite rooms, 6 twin chalets, camping) 80 Chipembi Rd; ✆ 0213 324756; e enquiries@ backpackzambia.com; www.backpackzambia. com. This offshoot of Jollyboys, owned & run by the same people, is close to the golf course, less than 10mins' walk to the centre of town. It has all the hallmark offerings of its well-known parent, but with a greater focus on family accommodation. This comes in the form of twin & dbl en-suite rooms, including a family room, 6 twin chalets, & 4- & 6-bed dorms with shared ablutions. For campers, there are spaces both for tents & – with power points, water & lights – for 4x4 vehicles with rooftop tents. All guests can use the bar where sports are typically shown on satellite TV, self-catering kitchen, braai facilities, Wi-Fi, short- & long-term baggage storage, secure off-street parking, swimming pool, & free pick up from the airport. Evenings around the firepit offer the chance to mull over the day's activities, kids are catered for with their own jungle gym. **$–$$** *exc b/fast. En-suite room US$65; shared ablutions room US$45; dorm bed US$12–15; camping US$9 pp.*

⚑ **Jungle Junction** [off map, page 154] Bovu Island; m 0978 725282; e stay@junglejunction. info; www.junglejunction.info. This island camp outside of Livingstone remains a favourite amongst the backpacker & volunteer community. For details, see page 172.

🏠 **Livingstone Backpackers** [159 D5] (6 rooms, 84 dorm beds, camping) 559 Makambo Rd; ✆ 0213 324730; e info@ livingstonebackpackers.com; www.livingstonebackpackers.com. Having been taken over by new owners in 2012, Livingstone backpackers is now family run & offers budget accommodation in the form of 12 dorm rooms with 4 or 6 beds, & 6 private rooms, some with en suites & some using the same ablutions as the dorms. Limited camping is also offered on a small grass patch within the grounds, but you will need to bring your own equipment.

A tall wall, painted on the inside with bright African murals, surrounds the secure property. Adding to the colour of the lodge, the main buildings are painted bright orange & blue, & armchairs in the open-sided library & sun loungers surrounding the pool are covered in brightly patterned *chitenje* material.

The main facilities are positioned around the perimeter of the site, and include a well-stocked thatch bar in one corner, & a restaurant serving cheap but cheerful food, although there is also a well-equipped open-sided kitchen surrounded by wind chimes, which allows for self-caterers. Next to the grassy area for the campers there is also a covered games area with pool & beer pong tables.

With a plethora of open, breezy areas, with plenty of green vegetation, the hostel can feel quite relaxing, and it's often quiet during the day. However, with room for 96 travellers it can fill up quickly, and it can get quite lively during the evenings, particularly around the weekend.

Included in the cost of the stay is the Wi-Fi available in the communal areas, as well as the rooms, and also transfers to the airport & the Falls. Helpful staff are often on hand at reception to discuss activities with you, and arrange all the necessary details. **$–$$** *exc b/fast. Room US$20/30 pp shared ablutions/en suite; dorm US$12; camping US$9 pp.*

Beside the Zambezi: Upriver

Livingstone's riverside lodges are for the most part spread along the shores of the Zambezi leading west from the town off Nakatindi Road. As well as the more exclusive lodges, there are now a few more accessible offerings further upstream, including a couple of campsites. The following are listed from east to west.

⌂ **Toka Leya** [off map, page 154] (12 tented chalets) Contact Wilderness Safaris, page 422; ☺ All year. Set within the national park, some 5km from Livingstone, Toka Leya's green canvas, natural wood decking & walkways defined by rope handrails, blends into the riverine environment. Although each tented chalet faces the river, some lie well back, glimpsing the water through the trees rather than affording a panoramic view. From wide wooden verandas, with a sunken seating area as well as wicker chaises lunges, glass sliding doors lead through to the bedroom. Here, 4-poster dbl or twin beds flanked by smart table lamps are enveloped by mosi nets; there's also a desk, a couple of comfy chairs, plus AC/heating, fan, & a hairdryer. At the back are a roomy dressing area, twin basins, separate toilet & shower, & a further outside shower & bath. (3 family rooms have an entirely separate twin room at the back, too.) It's airy & spacious but not cavernous, with Persian-style rugs & brightly coloured lamps enlivening an otherwise neutral décor.

The understated style runs through to the main lounge & restaurant area, segmented into 'rooms' by squashy sofas, with linking walkways to a bar, tree-shaded deck where steps lead down to a small sandy section of beach – a wonderful place to have dinner when the water is low. Nearby, wicker sunloungers surround a small infinity pool, & by the river is a simple spa, a relaxing spot with 2 rooms for massages, manicures, body wraps & more, or for the more energetic there's a riverside gym with AC. Dinner is often taken at a group table, though it can be served privately on your own deck, & there are individual tables during the day. Particularly popular at lunchtime is pizza, freshly prepared out of a wood-fired oven. There's also free Wi-Fi throughout the camp.

Boat trips from the lodge's jetty, 2hr game drives & 1½hr birding/nature walks are all possible, as are trips to the Falls, museum & market; most other activities can be booked. Environmental issues are high on the agenda, with a filtration system for drinking water, solar geysers for hot water, & a worm farm for kitchen waste; guests can even plant a tree as part of a project to replace lost specimens along the river. *US$697/746 Nov–14 Jun/15 Jun–Oct pp sharing/sgl FB, inc local drinks, laundry, 2 activities/ day, exc spa treatments.* **LLLL**

⌂ **Sussi & Chuma** [off map, page 154] (12 chalets, 2 houses) Contact Sanctuary Retreats, page 265. Named after the Zambian bearers who carried David Livingstone's body from Zambia to Dar es Salaam after his death, Sussi & Chuma lies within the national park, just 15mins' drive from Livingstone. Set amongst riverine forest & constructed high up on wooden platforms, from the outside Sussi & Chuma's chalets are reminiscent of tree houses. Inside though, the rooms are a lot smarter with a modern feel to them. Although, polished wooden floors & furniture, the high thatched ceiling with exposed rafters, cream walls & natural fabrics mean that these styles complement each other nicely. The room is furnished with a walk-in mosquito net around the bed(s), a writing desk, tea & coffee making station & a couple of comfy armchairs. A powerful shower surrounded by a glass screen is in the corner of the open plan room, just next to a large bath tub (complete with candles & bath salts); only the toilet is private. Wooden doors with large glass windows at the front of the chalet open out onto an elevated wooden deck, where a couple of wicker armchairs allow you to admire the views of the Zambezi. The ultimate in privacy comes with the 2-bedroom Chuma houses, each with en-suite bathrooms, a private plunge pool, & a chef & butler.

Raised walkways connect the chalets to a large 2-storey thatched central area, which mirrors the circular design of the rooms. Upstairs, a sitting room with comfortable sofas & a bar have views over the river. Below, the dining area extends onto a circular deck where meals may be taken with other guests, or individually, as you prefer. The lodge has its own wine cellar, but can order specific wines on request. A short walkway leads to a sheltered bend of the river, the location of an infinity pool & a sundowner deck with fire pits. Spa treatments are available using Africology products, also sold in the gift shop. Reliable Wi-Fi is available in all of the rooms, but not in the main areas.

Activities include game drives or walking safaris, which can easily be combined with a rhino walk allowing a close up experience with Mosi-oa-Tunya's small population of white rhino. Also on offer is boat cruises at sunrise & sunset, fishing, a village tour, & visits to the Falls. *US$650–720 pp sharing FB, inc local drinks, laundry, 2 guided activities/day. House US$809–990 pp. Children under 4 in houses only.* ☺ *all year.* **LLLL**

⌂ **Thorntree River Lodge** [off map, page 154] (9 rooms) ☏ +27 21 701 0270; e info@africanbushcamps.com; www.africanbushcamps.

com. Thorntree is 15km from the Falls on private land within the broader confines of the national park, about 10 mins from town & clearly signposted. The camp was purchased in 2015 by African Bush Camps, an owner-run safari company with a number of established camps in Botswana & Zimbabwe. The lodge is being completely redeveloped, heading for completion in 2016, with the concept to have accommodation reflecting the company's tented camps, but with a more substantial feel to it. There are plans to include both a spa & a gym facility, with the main area to have a split-level deck overlooking the Zambezi.

Set a little way along the river (though entirely separate from the lodge) is a thatched boma with ethnic decoration, the base for SafPar's (page 203) elephant-back safaris where guests can meet the resident herd. River cruises are planned to be operated from the lodge, & numerous other activities offered. **LLL**

⌂ **Bushbuck River House** [off map, page 154] (8 rooms, camping) Contact Nomad African Travel, page 187. Situated 16km from town, Bushbuck lies just outside the national park. Take the first left after leaving the main road, cross the railway, turn sharp left following the railway line back, then turn towards the river for about 1km. A traditional thatched farmhouse & a smaller thatched cottage, added in 2013, are both in a quiet spot with good river views & reportedly excellent home-cooked meals. The main house has 4 en-suite rooms, whilst the 'Waterbuck Cottage' contains 2 suites, each with 2 bedrooms & a shared bathroom. One of the suites also has a self-catering kitchen downstairs. The accommodation here is comfortable & affordable, & is very much in the style of a shared house rather than the other lodge-style properties on the river, which may afford you slightly more privacy. Both camping & self catering are further options. Relax in the attractive poolside boma, watch the river from a high viewing platform, or chill in the lounge with DSTV, including Sky Sports. *Main house US$80/90 pp sharing/sgl BB; Waterbuck Cottage US$180/160 for 2 ppl, or US$260/240 for 3–4 ppl downstairs/upstairs room only, meals at the main house can be booked in advance; camping US$15 pp.* **LL**

⌂ **The River Club** [off map, page 154] (11 chalets) ☏ 0213 327457; m 0962 650138; reservations: ☏ +27 72 517 4880; e reservations@theriverclubzambia.com; www.

theriverclubafrica.com. Perched on a rise beside the Zambezi, The River Club is an expansive restored 1940s homestead with a distinctly colonial atmosphere, & has the décor & service to match. It's an exclusive & intimate lodge, set in securely fenced grounds with green lawns, organic vegetable gardens & even its own helipad. Most guests are transferred from Livingstone by boat, a scenic 10-min ride, but for those who wish to drive the turning off Nakatindi Rd is clearly signposted.

Large, thatched chalets are built on stilts amidst indigenous riverside trees, with stunning views over the Zambezi below. All boast teak furniture & quality fabrics, though the beautifully polished floors tend to be slippery, so be careful. Creature comforts include duvets, AC/heating, a ceiling fan inside the canopied mosquito nets, a fridge, international electric sockets, a hairdryer & a digital safe. In most, the main bathroom with claw-foot tub is on a lower level, with a 2nd basin & loo by the bedroom. Of similarly high standard are 2 suites that carry the same amenities, but also have their own decks & plunge pools set in small private gardens. One of these suites is wheelchair accessible, & both are ideal for honeymooners. A family suite shares these features, but with the addition of a second bedroom with twin beds & an en suite. Secluded at the far end of the lodge, the Princess Mary Suite is a double storey unit that can accommodate 4 adults in 2 en-suite bedrooms, one on the ground floor & the other upstairs with a viewing deck overlooking the Zambezi. With its own garden, lounge area, bar & dining area it can act autonomously from the main lodge, although guests are still more than welcome to use the communal facilities.

The colonial style runs through to the main building, with magnificent river views from its wide verandas. Here you can enjoy traditional afternoon tea, or watch the sun slip beneath the horizon with a cocktail in hand. Inside are the reception, a small gift shop, cloakrooms, a formal dining room (with a magnificent teak table), a comfortable lounge, a massive double-sided fireplace & a well-stocked library. Antiques, colonial pictures & many decorator touches add to the Edwardian ambience, while Wi-Fi access throughout brings a touch of the 21st century. Meals prepared in the fully kosher kitchen are elegant affairs featuring pre-set dinner menus that change daily. Typically guests dine together, but individual tables can be arranged, & for absolute privacy there's a classy riverside 'gazebo'. Opposite the main building, & built in the same style, is a 'summerhouse', ideal for small groups with its own lounge & dining table, plus a snooker room with AC & a small library.

Overlooking the river is a stunning infinity pool surrounded by sunloungers shaded by over-sized umbrellas. Walkways, illuminated at night, cross the sweeping lawns, while palms, brightly coloured bougainvillaea & gardens complete the picture. Croquet, boules & bush golf are on hand, & for the more active, there's an all-weather tennis court & a 2.5km nature-walk/running track around the 20ha property. A wellness centre provides the perfect venue for massages & other treatments, while below is a small gym, with a sauna & jacuzzi. Included in the rates are a choice of fishing, sundowner boat trips, game-park drives, Falls visits, & trips to a local village. All other activities can be booked direct from the lodge. *Suite US$662/695, luxury suite US$761/799, Princess Mary suite US$1,005/1,056 all pp sharing, low/high season (11 Jan–14 Jun & 1 Nov–19 Dec/15Jun–31 Oct & 20 Dec–10 Jan), FBA, inc local drinks, laundry, exc transfers, park fees. 25% sgl suppt high season.* **LLLL–LLLLL**

🏠 **Tongabezi** [off map, page 154] (5 cottages, 6 houses) 📞0213 327450; 📱 0979 312766/0968 237785; e reservations@tongabezi.com; www. tongabezi.com. Set on a sweeping bend of the Zambezi, 15km west of the town centre, Tongabezi opened in the 1990s & remains one of the most exclusive lodges on the north side of the Zambezi. Its setting is matched by excellent service from a team of first-class local staff.

Overlooking the river are 5 beautiful & tastefully decorated thatched cottages with king-size or twin beds, large tiled en-suite bathrooms with river-view bathtubs, & private sitting areas. Even more exclusive are the individually designed houses with one side completely open to the river: the Bird House, the Tree House, & the Honeymoon House (once cited as 'worth getting married for'). Each has a king-size bed & impressive en-suite bathroom with inviting tub. The fully enclosed Nut House has large folding French doors & its own infinity plunge pool at the top of the cliff. Down closer to the river the Dog House has 2 bedrooms with king-size beds surrounded by concertina glass doors, & connected by a large wooden deck with an infinity pool, lounger area & bar. Then, tucked away from the river in its own private enclosure, is the Garden Cottage. Ideal for families or 2 couples sharing, it comprises 3 separate buildings – 2 en-suite dbl rooms & a lounge with fireplace & French windows – set in a rough horseshoe around a private plunge pool with decking; perfect for outdoor dining. Each of Tongabezi's houses is carefully secluded from its neighbours, & has the services of a dedicated private valet.

A riverside thatched boma, shaded by ebony trees hung with trailing creepers, incorporates the bar, dining room & 2 intimate lounge areas, one with a fireplace. Right on the river are 2 thatched lounge areas with comfy chairs. One, aptly named Look Out, has stunning views from its upper storey, & also has a small library, desks, a computer with internet access & even a private dining area (which must be pre-booked), it's an attractive place to relax. Further relaxation comes in the form of in-room massages, manicures & pedicures. There's a good swimming pool, too, set against a rock wall under a tumbling waterfall, with sunloungers on a large wooden deck over the Zambezi.

Towards sunset, everyone gathers outside around a roaring campfire for sundowners & hors d'oeuvres. Meals are sumptuous affairs, cooked to a high standard & served on the riverside deck, in the dining room, or even in your own cottage. By special arrangement & when the water isn't too high, couples can dine under the stars on Tongabezi's floating 'sampan', with each course hand delivered by canoe – a romantic & memorable occasion.

The lodge's ethos is confirmed by its school, Tujatane, run for around 160 children of Tongabezi staff & from local villages. School visits are popular with guests, & many contribute to the school & the children's future education.

Guided sunrise & sunset boat trips from the lodge's jetty, canoeing, birdwatching trips, fishing, game drives (to Mosi-oa-Tunya National Park), island picnics, village visits, shopping excursions, museum tours & gorge walks are all included (exc park fees & museum entrance). Mountain bikes are available to visit Simonga village & explore the surrounding area. With advance notice, & at extra cost, guests may also sleep on Sindabezi Island (see below), or have a meal on Livingstone Island (page 191), beside the Falls. *Cottage US$655/775, house US$755/875, Nut House & Dog House US$875/995, all pp sharing, low/high season (Nov–May/Jun–Oct), FBA, inc local drinks, laundry, levies,*

exc transfers, park fees. 40% sgl suppt high season, no children under 7. **LLLL**

❋ 🏠 **Sindabezi Island** (5 chalets) Contact via Tongabezi, above. A short, 2km boat (or canoe) trip downstream from Tongabezi, Sindabezi Island offers barefoot luxury on an island retreat, just a stone's throw across the water from Zimbabwe's Zambezi National Park. Sindabezi was built with a strong focus on the environment, with all waste water recycled & hot water from solar geysers; it's widely regarded to be one of the most environmentally friendly properties on the river. Its individually designed en-suite chalets are carefully spaced around the shore of the sandy island for maximum privacy. With solid wood furniture & copper basins, these are beautifully appointed; 2 – designated for honeymooners – have outdoor baths, & one even has its own beach. All are raised on decks & are open on 3 sides, with canvas roll-down walls for protection from the elements. There's a campfire for relaxing over a drink, & a deck high in the ebony trees offers a cool retreat, with commanding views of the river. A relaxed open-sided dining area with teak decking is just one of the settings for meals prepared by the island's own chef. While the rooms now have subtle battery lighting, paraffin lanterns maintain the sense of remoteness. Game is often sighted on the river banks, & there's often a hippo sleeping behind the camp's kitchen. With your own guide, you can explore the river & surrounding islands by boat or canoe, or go walking, fishing & birdwatching, as well as take part in all activities run at Tongabezi itself. *Chalet US$520/595, honeymoon chalet US$566/676, both pp sharing low/high season (Nov–May/Jun–Oct) FBA, inc drinks, laundry, transfers to/from island. 4 or more people booking together can reserve the whole island for their exclusive use (max US$607/728 pp).* **LLL–LLLL**

🏠 **Tangala House** (sleeps up to 8) Contact via Tongabezi, above. Right on the Zambezi about 1km from Tongabezi, this luxury private house is worth considering for families (not least because it's well protected against insects), or for those seeking a greater degree of privacy & freedom than is possible in a lodge. Accommodation for 4–8 people is in 4 en-suite bedrooms. Of these, 3 – including a twin, a dbl & a larger master suite – overlook the river; the 4th has a garden view. Beautifully furnished & equipped living

& dining areas lead out onto a large swimming pool overlooking the Zambezi, with views in both directions. The house is the residence for the owners of Tongabezi when it's not being rented out, so has a very personal & homely feel to it, & also comes with a couple of friendly dogs. It's available for bookings on a FBA basis as at Tongabezi, but with a chef, waiters, housekeeping staff, pool attendant, private guide & even a trained nanny provided, plus private use of vehicles & boats. *US$756 pp, inc use of boat & vehicle, & friendly dogs; children under 14 US$378 pp. Min 4 adults, 3 nights.* **LLLL**

🏠 **Natural Mystic Lodge** (10 chalets)
m 0977 408024; **e** naturalmysticlodge@ gmail.com; www.naturalmysticlodge.com. The statue at the entrance to Natural Mystic, of Namatama (Mother Earth) with her water pot, depicts the philosophy that underpins this lodge: that the source of life comes from the earth. The low-lying, often wet site, some 20km from Livingstone, is crossed by a walkway with strategic points from which visitors can watch visiting hippos or the occasional elephant. After several unfortunate years when the lodge was looking in a rather unkempt state, new owners took over in 2014, and were in the process of much-needed renovations at time of research.

The simple thatched chalets are grouped close together, 4 of them fronting the river (although you can see the river only when the door is open). With 2 double beds & a floor fan in each, they're quite cramped. Some have a bath & shower, others just a shower, & all have a small porch area. The lodge's best feature is a large decked bar/ restaurant area (*dinner US$13*), right on the river & open to non-residents. There's also a small swimming pool with stone surround, & a lounge with satellite TV & free Wi-Fi access. The usual activities such as river cruises & game drives can be organised, & you can arrange to attend a local church service. **$$$** *Extra guest US$30 (max 4).*

🏠 **Chundukwa River Lodge**
(5 chalets, 1 cottage) **m** 0969 641797; **e** chundukwariverlodge@gmail.com, chundukwa@zamnet.zm; www. chundukwariverlodge.com, www.ridezambezi. com. Situated 25km from Livingstone, Chundukwa is owner run by the Zambian-born Doug & Gail, who are both incredibly friendly & passionate hosts. It was fully refurbished

in 2015, and offers en-suite thatched chalets raised on stilts along the river bank. The chalets, each named after a local bird, are open fronted allowing views of the river, which can flow under the chalets during high water. Each room has a full-sized mosi net, fan & electric blankets for the winter. At the edge of the lodge is a self-contained cottage that sleeps 4 adults & 2 children & has its own swimming pool: perfect for families. In the thatched main area is the lounge & dining room, the lodge prides itself on the quality of its home-cooked food, & nearby there's a rock plunge pool. In keeping with the theme this area is open plan with views across the river to Chundu Island & Zimbabwe's Zambezi National Park beyond. Chundukwa is also the home of the Livingstone Polocrosse Club (pages 195–6), evidenced by the pitches (& the horses) next to the entrance road. Horseriding can be arranged (*1½ hr horse trail around US$55*) for both novices & more experienced riders, although other activities can also be organised through the lodge. **$$$$**

🏠 **Kayube Estate** (4 rooms, 1 house) **** 0213 323726; **m** 0978 323726; **e** karien.kermer@ outlook.com; www.kayubezambeziriverhouse. com. Kayube Estate is comprised of an eclectic mixture of accommodation located on a private 90ha estate, well signposted on the main road about 26km outside of Livingstone. Owned & run by Karien Kermer, the owner of Wild Side Safaris who has her own home on the estate, there are 3 kinds of accommodation outfitted for self-catering, independent travellers.

The most basic kind of rooms are the 3 air-conditioned bungalows raised on stilts along the river bank, each well spaced & completely private. With large glass sliding doors facing the river the bungalows feel secure while still allowing views of the river. They are well furnished with a small kitchen & lounge area, separate bedroom & bathroom. There is also a fire pit for outdoor cooking, with wood provided. With an emphasis on functionality rather than style they feel quite homely, & are well suited to independent travellers looking for a longer stay.

By far the most interesting accommodation choice is the 'Mama Out of Africa'. Originally the mobile dressing room for the film *Out of Africa*, this odd vehicle spent time being used for mobile safaris before ending up in its current stationary location under a large thatch roof on the river bank. Sleeping a cosy 4 people, the caravan is equipped with 2 dbl beds, a small kitchen & some comfy seating. Extra seating is available outside the caravan under the thatch roof, including an elevated viewing platform furnished with the rear seats from an old Audi.

The final accommodation option is the Zambezi River House. This is a large wood-framed house with 2 bedrooms, sleeping a maximum of 6 people. The house also has a large lounge area & a small library, & outside on the river bank is a pentagonal swimming pool. The house is owned by a German countess, who typically occupies the property in February, March & November of most years, but outside of these months the house can be rented out to visitors. *Bungalow US$135; River House US$360; 'Mama Out of Africa' US$150, all per room, 2 pp sharing, self catering.* See ad on page 207. **$$$$**

✳ 🏠 **Waterberry Zambezi Lodge** (7 chalets) 📞 0213 327455; enquiries +44 (0)1379 873474; e reservations@waterberrylodge.com; www. waterberrylodge.com. Named for the waterberry tree, Waterberry Lodge is set in a secluded position on the banks of the Zambezi, about 35 minutes' drive from Livingstone. It's an understated place, offering style, comfort and service well worth its modest price tag. Constructed of brick & thatch, Waterberry's rooms are dotted around the landscaped gardens, which include a lagoon & nature trail around the grounds, making this a wonderful spot for birdlife.

The rooms themselves, all named after local birds, aren't big but they are comfortable & clean. Polished concrete floors (which are nicer than they sound) & significant use of natural materials characterise the buildings, from dbl, twin or family thatched chalets to the 2-storey main lodge. Rooms all have en-suite bathrooms, fans & mosi nets. Most are grouped around the main building & swimming pool, but 2 larger rooms are set further back, with a private deck over the lagoon, & a secluded honeymoon suite sits at the river's edge. The 2-storey family room next to the main area is spacious & can sleep up to 6 people, but parents should keep in mind that the site is open, & frequented by hippos, so a degree of caution is needed with children. An additional option for families is Waterberry's River Farmhouse. Opened in 2013, it's a 5-minute walk from the main lodge & sleeps up to 8, with the option of coming with its own chef.

The 2-storey central building has a dining area & ground-floor terrace, while upstairs the main bar & lounge are open under deep thatch, with magnificent views over the river & Zambezi National Park beyond. Here there is plenty of seating, a few reference books, & a well-stocked bar. Meals – tailored to fit around individual activities – are served in the dining area, on the sundeck, or on the terrace overlooking the pool, & there are island picnics & traditional bush dinners, too.

Activities offered are very flexible ranging from sunset & daytime cruises to birding, fishing, a tour of the Falls, & village & market visits. *US$415 pp FBA, inc drinks, laundry, airport transfers.* **LLL**

🏠 **Kubu Cabins** (6 cabins, 1 villa, camping) m 0973 048830; e reservations@kubucabins. com; www.kubucabins.com. Although currently owned by Camp Nkwazi, Kubu Cabins have been in a serious state of disrepair for some years, and they are currently not open for business. However, it's rumoured that new owners are about to take over & carry out some major renovations on the property. If you are interested in staying here it would be wise to find out in advance the state of the property, & whether it's open for guests.

🏠 **Camp Nkwazi** (10 chalets, camping); m 0973 048830; e info@campnkwazi.com; www. campnkwazi.com. Situated on the banks of the Zambezi, shaded by riverine forest, Camp Nkwazi opened for business in 2013. Its en-suite chalets are well spaced out, some with a river view, & others overlooking a lagoon at the rear of camp. Each stands slightly elevated off the ground & is constructed from canvas walls on a wooden frame, with a brick bathroom at the back & a private wooden deck at the front. Inside the rooms are smart & modern, with polished wooden floors & dbl or twin beds covered by walk-in mosi nets. Each chalet has a private parking spot, an outside braai, & a small kitchen with an electric hob, kettle, microwave & fridge, so they serve the independent traveller well. However, if guests prefer they can eat in the camp's restaurant, located in the main area, a redbrick structure with a canvas roof that also incorporates a fully stocked bar, comfortable lounge, & a wooden deck projecting over the river.

This main area is accessible via ramps, & two of the chalets are also set up for wheelchairs, with ramps, larger bathrooms & handrails in the shower

& next to the toilet, meaning this is one of the few lodges in the area that caters well for travellers with mobility problems.

Across from the lagoon several camping areas have been cut out of the thick bush, but retaining plenty of privacy. This is certainly one of the better-designed campsites in the area. Smaller pitches for 3 or 4 vehicles & larger areas for overlanders each have their own ablution blocks, with free electricity provided. Boat trips are offered on site, & the camp can book activities in town or at the Falls. *US$140/195 pp self catering/FB; exc laundry, airport transfers. Camping US$30 pp.* **LL**

🏠 **Islands of Siankaba** (6 chalets, 1 honeymoon/VIP chalet) 📞0213 327490; e info@siankaba.net; www.siankaba.net; reservations 📞0211 260279; m 0977 720530. Siankaba is an exclusive lodge that offers considerable attention to detail & superb cuisine. It is 35km from Livingstone, followed by a 7km track through open bush & a 5-min boat ride. The mood is set as you leave the jetty with its small gift shop & chug along a peaceful back channel of the Zambezi before joining the main river. Shortly upstream, Siankaba lies on 2 separate islands linked by suspension bridges (great fun to walk across). On one, spacious chalets reached along raised wooden walkways nestle like bird hides among the trees that overhang the banks, their decks an ideal place to watch the river in complete privacy. In contrast to the half-canvas walls & roof, everything about the accommodation oozes luxury & comfort. Polished teak furniture sits on polished teak floors, offset by thick oriental rugs. Stately comfortable beds with an integral ceiling fan are hung like 4-posters with pristine white mosquito nets, & good reading lights complement the otherwise subdued lighting. Set on a platform to the rear are a regal claw-footed bathtub & twin pedestal basins with views towards the river, as well as a modern shower & separate toilet. Tucked discreetly away, a safe & fridge are almost incidental. For even greater luxury or privacy, the honeymoon/VIP chalet boasts its own deck with views across the river & loungers in the shade of a pergola, as well as a minibar, games compendium, 'his & hers' aromatherapy bath products & reference bookcase. Private meals can be set up on the deck & b/fast in bed is offered as standard.

The adjacent island serves as the epicentre of the camp. Here you'll find the spacious restaurant & comfortable bar/lounge area, with natural décor & tables out on the terrace for al-fresco dining. Among the trees is a secluded pool with stylish sunloungers, & nearby there's a small spa offering a range of treatments from hot-stone treatments to full-body massages. In addition to the treatment rooms in the spa, massages are available outside by the pool, or on the privacy of your room's deck. A 1.5km nature trail also runs around the island, providing ample opportunities for birdwatching. Activities include a sundowner cruise, birding & fishing excursions, & a mokoro trip among the islands. Sustainably sourced bamboo mountain bikes are supplied for guests' use, & village walks – taking in a visit to the local school & returning by mokoro – are popular, too. The school, Mandia, is a government-run establishment that – along with other community projects like tree planting & a clinic – is supported by a trust fund operated by the lodge. *Chalet US$520/635 pp sharing/sgl; honeymoon chalet US$580 pp sharing, all FB, inc drinks, transfers to/from Livingstone airport, & their own activities. No children under 10.* **LLL**

🏠 **Royal Chundu River Lodge** (10 chalets) lodge: 📞0213 327060; reservations: 📞 +27 13 751 1038; e reservations@royalchundu.com; www.royalchundu.com. About 63km from Livingstone, or just over 1hr's drive from the Falls, Royal Chundu is a firmly upmarket lodge on a peaceful, wooded stretch of the river. Two sets of rapids ensure that this is practically a private section of the river for the lodge, visited by just the occasional canoeist from the nearby village, & a haven for birds.

Solid thatched chalets are stretched along the riverbank, enfolded by waterberry & water-pear trees. Concertina doors at the front of the chalets provide views of the river, & open up onto a short but smart wooden deck. Inside, mosi nets envelop the king-size bed & side tables, fronted by comfortable chairs. Bathrooms have twin showers, twin basins, a separate toilet & bidet. The rooms are light & airy, with colourful artwork & African fabrics brightening up the area. With a dressing area, safe, Wi-Fi, mini bar & tea & coffee making station it feels like a very smart hotel room.

At the heart of the lodge, linked to the chalets by wide wooden walkways, a large, sparkling infinity pool overlooks the river, bordered by neat lawns & with shaded day beds for R&R. B/fast is usually served out on the expansive deck, while dinner may be either in the firelit boma – perhaps with entertainment from the local villagers – or in the formal dining room. Ingredients for the meals are impressively all sourced from a 3km radius of the lodge, with traditional Zambian ingredients incorporated into the meals; there's even a very interesting Zambian cultural tasting menu available. Meals can be accompanied by a good selection of (rather pricy) fine wines available from the cellar, & cigars are also available.

There's a large, open-sided lounge/bar next door, with plenty of books (including railway memorabilia belonging to owner Hugh O'Mahoney's father), squashy sofas & coffee tables, while above – carefully shielded for noise – are a TV lounge, small library & computer room, with more comfy chairs. (There's also Wi-Fi throughout – but no mobile phone coverage.) A new floating riverside spa has added a further level of luxury to this already swanky lodge.

The lodge has good links with the local village, which guests can visit, & where many of the items in the curio shop are made. Other activities include boat cruises, fishing, canoeing & bush walks. While it's too far from the Falls for easy access, the lodge operates full-day trips combining the Falls with lunch on Livingstone Island & an evening on the *Royal Livingstone Express*. *US$574 pp FB, inc airport transfers, river cruise; US$868 pp FBA, inc airport transfers, drinks, 2 activities/day.* ⊕ *All year.* **LLL–LLLL**

🏠 **Royal Chundu Island Lodge** (4 suites) Contact via Royal Chundu, above. Just a short boat trip upstream of Royal Chundu Rover Lodge, its exclusive sister-lodge is set on its own 1km² private wooded island, overlooking the Katombora Rapids. It is staffed with its own chef & guide, & equipped with a boat, ensuring that activities, too, are exclusive. Standards are on a par with those at the main lodge, but the suites here are even closer to the river & boast a wider frontage, with an outdoor, lamplit bath on the deck, a shower that's open on 2 sides, & a more spacious sitting area to one side of the room. The main building incorporates 2 colonial-style lounges with contemporary comforts & a fireplace each side, & a dining area for full silver-service dinners. Boma dinners are an alternative option, with b/fast usually taken on the deck, where a small infinity pool looks across to Zimbabwe. A 3–4km nature trail takes in the huge jackalberries, baobab trees & python creepers that

characterise the island, or you can participate in any activities offered by the main lodge. *US$662 pp FB, inc airport transfers sundowner cruise; US$975 pp FBA, inc airport transfers, drinks, 2 activities/day.* ⊕ *All year.* **LLLL**

🅰 **Jungle Junction** (4 chalets, 5 huts, camping) Bovu Island; m 0978 725282; e stay@ junglejunction.info; www.junglejunction.info. About 1hr's drive from Livingstone, this popular backpackers' hang-out is based on its own island in the Zambezi. Just a 10 min mokoro ride from the shore, its launch site is suitable only for 4x4s & can be difficult to find; it isn't signposted. It's therefore essential to book in advance via email, & transfers can be easily arranged to the lodge from Livingstone, or from the Victoria Falls or Kazungula border posts.

Facilities are still rustic, but the setting is splendid: indigenous shade trees, sandy beaches & sweeping river views. Large, reed-walled chalets are built on stilts with wood floors, mesh windows, mosi nets & a veranda with river views. Five smaller 'fisherman's huts' are simple A-frame structures with raised wooden floors, & are constructed from local reed & thatch. They are very simple, & without walls, windows or doors they are very open to the environment. The huts come furnished with beds, all bedding & mosquito nets. Both of these room types share a basic ablution block, with flush loos & hot showers, which is also used by the campsite. Here, there's plenty of space to pitch a tent on the sandy shore, & there's a kitchen with utensils, charcoal & essentials provided. Hot water is provided in the showers from a wood boiler, & there are also propane-powered fridges & a solar-power system is available for recharging batteries.

The barefoot bar with its river views is undoubtedly the most popular place to hang out in camp, & in the adjacent dining room & library, books line shelves made of mekoro. The restaurant serves fairly standard fare such as chicken curry, spaghetti Bolognese & beef stew, served with fresh vegetables & salads (⊕ *all day; full b/fast or lunch US$7; dinner to US$12*). A small shop sells curios & clothing made from colourful African *chitenje* material, which can be made to fit by the resident tailor.

A one-off charge of US$25 pp covers activities for the duration of your stay. These include fishing, nature walks, village visits & trips taking you hippo watching or to a secluded swimming spot. Think twice before venturing into crocodile-infested waters, though, no matter how safe it is deemed; crocs quickly become habituated to people & may lurk in the shadows. Fashioning your own fishing rod out of a reed pole is quite novel, or you can hire tackle (*approx US$15/day*). The lodge has built, & is still heavily involved with, a community school opposite the island on the mainland, & guests are welcome to visit. Transfers & all boat activities are by mokoro, which are fun but potentially perilous. *Hut US$35 pp; chalet US$45. Camping US$10 per tent per night.* **$–$$**

Game park, Falls and Gorge environs
The development by Sun International of a prime spot close to the Falls has introduced a whole new style of accommodation to Livingstone. Other accommodation to the south of town has in recent years been augmented by lodges built away from the river, affording the advantages of open bush but without the high prices associated with a riverside location. Many of the following are actually much closer to the Falls than those situated on the upper river to the west of Livingstone, and are listed as if heading south from Livingstone towards the Falls, then out towards the gorges.

⌂ Chrismar Hotel [154 B4] (109 rooms) Sichango Rd; ✆0213 323141; e booklvn@ chrismarhotels.com; www.chrismarhotels.com. Opened in 2006, this mid-market hotel near the entrance to the national park is well thought out & offers good value for money. While it is not on the river, its bush setting is enhanced by numerous fountains & water features, including the largest swimming pool in town, complete with a sunken bar in the middle. Dbl & twin rooms, in a range of styles up to executive suites, are set around spacious grounds, & wouldn't disgrace a hotel of far better quality – despite the faux-fur fabrics. An interesting design feature is a window between the bedroom & en-suite bathroom, which boasts a shower & jacuzzi bath, while cool tiled floors, AC, TV, Wi-Fi access, a safe, hairdryer & a fridge are all important extras. As you'd expect, there are a couple of restaurants, as well as an activity centre, with a gym & conference centre. **$$$$**

⌂ The Bushfront Lodge [154 B4] (14 chalets, camping) Sichango Rd; ✆0213 322446; e info@bushfront.com. Bordering the national park, Bushfront Lodge is a few km upriver from the Falls, & about 5km from town. The thatched en-suite chalets are set amongst indigenous vegetation with abundant birdlife. This natural theme continues in the bathrooms of the chalets which are decorated with potted plants, & some with rock walls with water cascading off a small ledge that serves as the shower tap. For campers there are 3 individual pitches with modern ablutions & a braai area. The main lodge area is well designed & maintained, with satellite TV, free Wi-Fi, a large bar/lounge & a restaurant. All meals are served here, & snacks are always available. Guests can relax by the small pool or explore Livingstone – all activities can be booked at the lodge. **$$$** *Camping US$10 pp.*

⌂ Victoria Falls Waterfront [154 B4] (23 rooms, 24 tents, camping) off Sichango Rd; ✆0213 320606–08; m 0968 320606; e waterfront@safpar.com; www. thevictoriafallswaterfront.com. This large, secure & affordable riverside complex, within the unfenced area of Mosi-oa-Tunya National Park is only 4km upstream from the Falls, & is both well equipped & positioned to take advantage of the array of activities on offer in the Livingstone area. The main thatch-&-pole building contains the reception, booking office, internet café & a small souvenir shop. A spacious restaurant & teak bar (with satellite TV) both have plenty of seating indoors, & on a large open-air deck where you can often see the spray from the Falls; it's one of the best places to watch the sunset over the Zambezi. Outside, amongst palm trees, is a sunken pool surrounded by teak decking, with lounge chairs overlooking the river. Eight large A-frame thatched chalets house individual rooms that are comfortable, light & airy, with teak furniture, quality fabrics & ethnic touches. At ground level are individual en-suite dbl or twin rooms with a patio, & river or garden views. The upper level comprises larger suites with a queen bed, separate lounge area, good-size bathroom, & deck offering sweeping river views. Also up here are spacious family rooms with 4 sgl beds & a deck, overlooking the garden.

Beyond the main building is the Adventure Village with a large natural-style rock pool, another bar & a thatched auditorium where daily activity briefings are given & rafting videos are shown in the evening, accompanied by a BBQ. In the gardens here, permanent tents are perched on wooden platforms, each with 2 beds with bedding & linen (or bring your own). Nearby ablutions are clean & spacious, with flush toilets & hot & cold showers. Further along, a separate grassed camping area has its own ablutions, BBQ & washing-up area; taking about 75 campers, it gets pretty noisy when it's busy with overland trucks. SafPar's activity centre is located upstairs in the main area, offering a full range of activities & excursions, many that they operate themselves (page 187); you will often begin & end your activities at the Waterfront, even if staying elsewhere in Livingstone). Among these are 2 boats offering b/fast, lunch or sunset cruises (*US$55 pp inc snacks, unlimited drinks & park fees*) from the Waterfront's own jetty. The larger Mukambi takes up to 100 people & tends to draw a more lively crowd, while the more upmarket Mabushi takes up to 25 passengers, & is perfect for families or those wanting a quieter cruise. *Chalet room* $$$$; *tent US$36 pp; camping US$7 pp.*

🏠 **David Livingstone Safari Lodge & Spa** [154 B4] (77 rooms) ☎0213 324601; e lodge@dlsandspa.com; www.thedavidlivingstone.com. This efficient 5-star hotel under steep thatch occupies an impressive spot on the Zambezi, and makes the most of its wide river frontage. The entrance lobby, restaurants, rooms & even a good-sized infinity pool command excellent views of the river, where the *Lady Livingstone* (page 191) awaits passengers to cruise along the Zambezi. Huge basketwork lampshades & wooden sculptures dominate the décor, conveying a strong sense of Africa. Concrete walkways with rustic pole railings lead across the sprawling site to tastefully appointed rooms, each furnished in dark wood with AC, large, flat-screen TV, safe & walk-in mosi nets (helpfully encompassing bedside lights & a phone). Glazed folding doors lead to a small balcony with a couple of chairs, while behind lies a modern bathroom with separate toilet & shower. Two rooms are specifically designed for paraplegics, while 5 suites each have a lounge/bar area & a private jacuzzi. There's Wi-Fi throughout.

In addition to the 1st-floor Kalai Restaurant & the Ujiji bar, a waterside terrace serves drinks, snacks & light lunches (food, drinks & services are subject to 10% service charge). Other facilities include an award-winning spa, a gym, gift shop, & the Safari Par Excellence activity centre. $$$$$ *inc 1 activity/day (sunset cruise or Vic Falls tour).*

🏠 **Maramba River Lodge** [154 C4] (10 chalets, 26 tents, camping) ☎0213 324189; m 0976 587511; e reservations@marambariverlodge.com; www.maramba-zambia.com. This well-established lodge & campsite, founded in 1991, lies 4km from the Falls, down a short, bumpy track just south of Livingstone Reptile Park. Situated within the national park on the banks of the Maramba River, it is a real oasis in the bush, with green lawns & mature trees, hippos, elephants & birds aplenty. The lodge has a relaxed atmosphere, & with a large pool, children's play area & several family rooms it works well for families. It's important to note though that wildlife does walk through the grounds, so children still need to be supervised at all times. The lodge is well appointed with an activity booking office, craft shop, fully licensed riverside bar, simple restaurant, & free Wi-Fi is available in the communal areas.

There are 4 types of accommodation. The thatched en-suite chalets (with 2 or 4 beds) are bright & airy, in a pretty location under mopane & mahogany trees. Each has treated mosquito nets & ceiling fans. 9 spacious luxury tents combine lodge comfort with the pleasures of camping. They are en suite (with tiled bathroom & open-air shower) & have handcrafted furniture, including a dbl & a sgl bed under walk-in mosi nets & a small veranda. Simpler accommodation comes in the form of 10 twin-bedded safari tents under thatch, with chairs, clothes storage, electricity & en-suite facilities. Simpler still, there are 7 small dome tents, fitted with twin beds & a lockable drawer. They have a dedicated ablution block, & a covered main area overlooking the river. The small campsite is very popular, so it's wise to book in advance; campers share an ablution block with hot showers & laundry facilities. $$$ *Camping US$20 pp, & US$3 per vehicle if power required. Luxury mtent & chalet US$123, safari tent US$97, dome tent US$55; all B&B inc morning & afternoon tea.*

🏠 **Livingstone Safari Lodge** [map, page 154] (9 chalets, camping) m 0965 634954. This rambling 'love-it-or-hate-it' lodge (emphatically not to be confused with David Livingstone Safari Lodge!) is set amid 8.5ha of open bush near the Maramba River, on a securely fenced site 6km from the centre of Livingstone, & a similar distance from the Falls. To get there, follow Mosi-oa-Tunya Rd towards the Falls, & turn left after the Reptile Park. From here, take the 1st left-hand track, then it's clearly signposted, almost 1.5km on a level sandy road.

The lodge changed owners in 2012, & is unfortunately feeling a bit run down & in need of some attention. The main area still includes the rustic bar with pool table & braai area, with a scattering of working xylophones & drums. However, the kitchen is now closed, making it necessary to head into town for lunch & dinner. A large, secluded swimming pool is set away from the main area, although at time of research it was not in use & had no water in it.

Asphalt paths link the main building to some decidedly quirky en-suite chalets dotted around the grounds. Secluded & cooled by a through breeze, most have high thatched roofs & colourful stencilled walls, mosquito nets, coffee/tea facilities, & private verandas. Some have 2 dbl beds; others have a 2nd upstairs bedroom with bunk beds. Campers can choose from 2 pitches with private showers & toilets, or the main campsite, which has electric hook-ups & plenty of water points. Ablution & laundry facilities are tiled & clean, with hot & cold showers. **$$$** *Camping US$10/15 pp standard/en-suite.*

🏠 **Royal Livingstone** [map, page 189] (173 rooms) Mosi-oa-Tunya Rd; m 0978 777044/45/46/47; reservations ✆ +27 11 780 7810; e zambia.reservations@suninternational. com; www.suninternational.com. Opened in 2001, this opulent 5-star hotel situated in extensive grounds is owned by the South African Sun International group. If its broad, low, white frontage is rather disappointing at first glance, inside all is spacious & elegant, with an old-world attention to detail & service. Step outside onto extensive verandas, where sweeping lawns lead to an unparalleled frontage along the Zambezi, the 'smoke' from the Falls rising tantalisingly close. A 15-min walk along the river brings you to the Falls themselves via the direct access point that is the preserve of the two Sun International hotels, or guests can be escorted by porters in pith helmets on one of the hotel's 'club cars' (golf-cart style).

The hotel is in the national park; zebra, impala & giraffe are often seen grazing in the grounds.

All rooms have twin or king-size beds & are fitted with AC, satellite TV, radio, blu-ray DVD player, minibar, safe & phone; 2 rooms are fully equipped for the disabled. Tasteful & comfortable, if on the small side, each room has its own private balcony, & benefits from the services of a butler. Should all this not be sufficient, there are also 4 suites.

Meals are served either in the excellent à-la-carte restaurant where live piano music is often played in the evenings (pages 178–9), or outside on the veranda, while for a special occasion private candlelit dinners on the lawns can be arranged at extra cost. The long, wood-panelled bar has a relaxed, colonial air. A sundeck built on stilts over the Zambezi makes a pleasant spot to enjoy a sundowner drink, & when the spray from the Falls is visible in high water the view is spectacular, although the deck can get incredibly busy in the evenings. There's also a smaller, private deck nearby that can be reserved for groups. A grand swimming pool overlooks the river, & makes a great place to relax in the afternoon. The Royal Livingstone has a well-equipped & air-conditioned gym, while those in search of pampering can visit the Royal Spa (page 196) with its white massage tents spread along the riverbank.

No activities are included in the cost of the hotel, but the concierge can help to organize any of the activities in the Livingstone area, & the hotel even has its own helipad should you wish to arrive & depart in style.

Considerably more expensive than the adjacent Avani, the Royal Livingstone caters for a very different market – those seeking traditional standards of décor & service in a truly gracious setting. If you'd like to indulge without the high price of accommodation, consider sundowners on their magnificent riverside deck, or a highly civilised afternoon tea in the lounge (about US$25 pp). **$$$$$**

🏠 **Avani Victoria Falls Resort** [map, page 189] (212 rooms) 393 Mosi-oa-Tunya Rd; ✆ 0213 321122; m 0978 777044–7; e victoriafalls@ avanihotels.com; www.avanihotels.com. Known as the Zambezi Sun until Minor International took over a controlling share in 2014, Avani is the lively 3-star sibling of the Royal Livingstone, & what a contrast. Crenellated walls are more reminiscent of a north African mosque than of southern Africa, their deep desert red contrasting with the Zambian sky. Vervet monkeys, the bane of the staff, cavort through the colourful grounds as if through a children's playground. Although the hotel is only 5 mins' walk from the Falls there are no views of the river. Instead balconies from each room overlook the extensive lawns where impala, zebra & giraffes freely wander amongst the ironwork animal statues dotted around the grounds. Well designed, if rather compact, the rooms are very comfortable – the standard of a good international business hotel – but with considerably more flashes of colour & individuality. Each has AC, satellite TV, free Wi-Fi, safe & phone, with a bath & shower en suite. 2 rooms are adapted for paraplegics.

In addition to the extensive buffet restaurant (*US$40 pp*), there's a relaxed al-fresco grill beside the pool that snakes through the grounds, often accompanied by a live band or dancers, or – adjacent to The Falls activity centre – both Squire's Grillhouse & a simple café. If you want something more formal it's possible to eat in the Royal Livingstone's restaurant, which is similarly priced, but you will need to book in advance, & its dress code requires trousers rather than shorts. You can use the Royal's spa, too – although on-site massages can be organised here. The complex also includes a children's club & playground, & business & conference centres. Ultimately, though, everything hinges on the location. Just a few hundred metres' walk from the lip of the Falls & the curio market, & with unrestricted access, the hotel's position is unbeatable. **$$$$$**

🏠 **Stanley Safari Lodge** [154 D5] (10 cottages) Contact Robin Pope Safaris, pages 264–5. Set some distance back from the river & bordering the Mosi-oa-Tunya National Park, Stanley Safari Lodge was taken over by Robin Pope Safaris in 2011. Positioned at the top of a hill, the lodge enjoys sweeping views down towards the Zambezi, & spray from the Falls is often visible when the river is in full flow. It's best suited as a place to chill out, relax & unwind. Advance reservations are essential, with almost all clients arriving by air & collected at the airport. Should you be driving yourself, turn east off the main road to the Falls almost opposite the Royal Livingstone & continue past a large baobab on your right, bearing sharp right after 500m, then following the road towards Mukuni village for a further 2km. The turning

(✦ 17°54'1.45 S, 25°53'39.32 E) is on the rise of a hill, on the left, just after the sign for Munali Farm.

The lodge is set behind a high electric fence, but once inside all is calm & spacious. Large, fairly formal gardens with a central infinity pool face west towards the Zambezi. The main building is a beautifully designed thatched affair with an open-aspect lounge, bar & dining area, & the 'map room' (with a laptop & free Wi-Fi) deserves to be popular with guests. Above is a further sitting area, while below, a wine cellar allows candlelit tastings of a range of South African, French & Italian wines. Permutations for serving dinner are many – including the option of a dining table *in* the infinity pool!

Five stylish open 'cottages', each slightly different but most with an open front & a view towards the Zambezi, are built in a half-moon shape, with king-size or twin beds, a 'loo with a view' & an outside shower & bath; a closed cottage has a similar layout but with a solid front. The Honeymoon Suite is an open suite with its own plunge pool & fireplace, while the family suite, which is also open fronted, is 2 bedroomed, & works well for children. It has a shallow paddling pool, & a bucket shower set outside around a tree, giving younger children the opportunity to experience in safety the fun of living in the bush. There are also 2 closed suites, Livingstone & Stanley, decorated in a colonial style with a lounge, fireplace, covered terrace, & private plunge pool. The Stanley Suite has 2 en-suite bedrooms so it also works well for families.

Throughout, the décor is both stylish & comfortable, with good use of wood, stone & natural fabrics, & plenty of space. Activities offered by the lodge include mountain biking, rhino tracking in the national park, & village & museum tours. The lodge can easily arrange external activities around Livingstone. *Cottage US$405/450/510, open suite US$450/510/600, closed suite US$510/625/665 Nov–21 May/ 22May–Jun/Jul–Oct, all FBA; inc local drinks, laundry, airport transfers.* **$$$$$**

🏠 **Taita Falcon Lodge** (7 chalets, camping) lodge ✆ 0213 327046, reservations ✆ 0213 321850; e taita-falcon@microlink.zm; www. taitafalcon.com. ✦ 17°58.879'S, 25°54.654'E. Perched on the very edge of Batoka Gorge, with the raging waters below, Taita's view is breathtaking to say the least. It is a 45-min drive from Livingstone, for which you'll need a high-clearance vehicle, & a 4x4 during the rains. The lodge has its own helipad, but drivers should follow the main road from town towards the Falls, take the well-signposted left turn opposite the entrance to the Royal Livingstone, then go right at the baobab tree. From here, follow the signs for about ½hr along 11km of long, winding track, passing through Songwe village.

The lodge is named after the rare Taita falcon that frequents cliffs & gorges, especially in the Zambezi Valley – & this area is one of the best in Africa for spotting them. They are small (less than 30cm long) with cream to brown underparts – no bars or markings – & a strong, fast style of flight. Look for them especially in the evenings, perhaps trying to catch swallows or bats on the wing. Verreaux's (black) eagles, peregrine falcons & many other raptors & small birds are also resident, numbering among the 234 bird species recorded here.

Run by Faan & Anmarie Fourie, the lodge is pleasant & informal surrounded by indigenous gardens & with personable service. Its en-suite chalets are constructed of stone, timber & reeds under thatch. Rebuilt & enlarged a few years ago, they retain their rustic idiosyncrasy, with pull-down rush 'windows', a simple sliding door, & locally made beds, tables & chairs. With a shower, basin & toilet at the back, & a separate outside shower in a garden area at the front, they're open in design, but entirely private. Two can be made up as family rooms, sleeping up to 5; the rest are dbls or trpls. Electricity is from a generator.

Narrow pathways, accessible by wheelchair, weave through the bush parallel to the cliff, linking the chalets to the bar & restaurant. In front of the bar, overlooking the gorge & Rapids 16 & 17, downstream of the Falls, is a great place both to spot birds & to watch the rafters down below. That said, & although the chalets are set back from the precipice, I'd be wary of letting children run wild here. There's a nice small pool for a dip, encompassed by a tiled patio with adjacent small lawn.

A couple of kilometres from the lodge is a small campsite with 3 pitches, set well apart with their own ablution blocks but with no river view. Campers can use the lodge's bar & restaurant if they book in advance, but not the pool.

Included in some of the lodge rates are a tour of Songwe village & one of 4 activities: a game drive, a sunset cruise, a town tour, or a visit to the Falls. Other activities include guided bush & bird walks, hiking trails in & around the gorge (equipped hikers can do 2–3-day hikes) & fishing (for the fit – it's a steep walk!). Taita Falcon Lodge is a relaxing place in a remote spot – albeit only 12km from the Falls. Adrenalin junkies, though, could feel cut off from the epicentre of things. *US$165 pp FB; US$284 FB, inc airport transfers, village tour & a bush & bird walk. Camping US$15 pp.*

✕ WHERE TO EAT

Takeaways and fast food There are several takeaways in town, including Wonderbake, one of the best and most popular, and the Hungry Lion on the corner with Kapondo Street [158 B2]. For a few kwacha, these serve the usual fare of pre-packaged chips, burgers, samosas, sandwiches and soft drinks. All are in the centre of town, along Mosi-oa-Tunya Road. Falls Park shopping centre [154 C3] and Mosi-oa-Tunya Square [159 D6] are useful sources of fast food, too, with branches of Steers, Hungry Lion and Debonair's Pizza along one side and sharing an outside seating area. Most are open every day until around 21.00.

⌨ Wonderbake [158 B1] Mosi-oa-Tunya Rd, ⊕ 08.00–21.00 Mon–Sat, 08.00–20.00 Sun. One of the few cafes in the area with Wi-Fi, this is a convenient location for a quick snack & a great spot to rendezvous, though it's often crowded. Expect fresh bread, samosas & pies, drinks, chicken, cakes, sandwiches & ice cream; plus espressos & cappuccinos should you need a jolt of caffeine. **$**

⌨ Munali Café [158 B1] Mosi-oa-Tunya Rd, 08.00–21.00 Mon–Sat, 08.00–20.00 Sun. Another pleasant café in the centre of Livingstone, it makes a good alternative to Wonderbake if that's too crowded. Serving the usual pastries, samosas, sandwiches & basic hot food, it's a good place for a cheap & quick meal, & the coffee is as good as any that you'll find in Livingstone. **$**

Restaurants In the last decade, several independent restaurants have opened up in Livingstone, offering a wider variety (Indian, Chinese, seafood, etc) than the hotels at fairly decent prices. Don't expect to find haute cuisine, as food tends more towards standard pub fare and sustenance rather than fine dining. Here's a small selection of the current favourites, though it's also worth remembering restaurants in those hotels that are not listed, which often cater to foreign tastes and may have more to offer, albeit at higher prices.

✕ **Avani Victoria Falls Resort** [map, page 189] Mosi-oa-Tunya Rd; ☎ 0213 321122. The buffet dinner here is wide ranging with a selection of grilled kebabs, burgers, omelettes to order, salads & desserts, though at US$45 pp it's not cheap. Alternatively, there's an al-fresco restaurant serving Western food alongside the entertainment area at the pool, ideal for light lunches, snacks or a full evening meal. Tables are set inside & out around a large pool, & the atmosphere is lively, especially in the afternoons.

When there's live music, it's good value for an evening out, but don't expect cordon bleu standards. Within the same complex are Squire's (see below) & a small café serving drinks & snacks. $$$$$

✕ **Royal Livingstone** [map, page 189] Mosi-oa-Tunya Rd; m 0978 777044/45/46/47. Sun's flagship hotel has a fabulous restaurant with surprisingly reasonable prices, particularly when compared with the Avani next door. The setting is lovely – old-world elegance & comfort – the

THE LEGACY OF LIVINGSTONE'S JEWISH COMMUNITY *Peter Jones*

Among the earliest white settlers north of the Zambezi were many Jews from the Baltic states of Lithuania and Latvia, then part of the Russian empire. From the 1880s onwards, they came in large numbers to the goldfields of South Africa, both as economic migrants, and as refugees fleeing religious and political persecution. Some more adventurous souls, including Elie and Harry Susman, moved on north to Bulawayo and then, attracted by the cattle stocks of Barotseland, crossed the Zambezi shortly before the Cape-to-Cairo railway reached the Victoria Falls in 1904.

Jewish traders played an important role at the Old Drift on the Zambezi river bank and then in the new town of Livingstone, which was laid out in 1905. A Hebrew Congregation was established in 1910 and the foundation stone of the synagogue was laid in 1928. In the late 1930s, Livingstone's Jewish population was reinforced by a new influx of German Jewish refugees from Nazism. Then, during World War II, there was an even larger influx of Polish, and mainly Christian, refugees.

After the war, Indian traders began to replace their Jewish counterparts in the retail trade, but Jewish businesses branched out into the development of secondary industry. The Susman Brothers & Wulfsohn group either took over or established both Zambezi Saw Mills, with its famous railway, and Zambia Textiles, while the Tow Brothers established an iron foundry. The most prominent Jewish families in the town were the related Susmans and Grills, and the Kopelowitzes.

While there is no longer a Jewish presence in the town, their influence can be seen in its colonial architecture. It was, for example, the Grill family who built the remarkable **Capitol Theatre** [158 B1] on Mosi-oa-Tunya Road in the early 1930s. (This was fully renovated in 2009, but sadly its new lease of life was short, and it has once more closed.) Others places of interest that can be visited include:

* The **Synagogue** on Likute Way (formerly Highway), now the Church of Christ. The first synagogue in Northern Rhodesia, its foundation stone was laid by Eli Susman in 1928. The church elders are very happy to open the doors to allow

service excellent, & the food the best in town. However, be sure to book in advance; if the hotel is full they don't take outside reservations. If you feel like a bit of refined luxury, try the very genteel afternoon tea (about US$25), with sandwiches & cakes – though be warned: vervet monkeys might try to steal your food. $$$$$

✗ **Squire's Grillhouse & Action Bar** [map, page 189] The Falls, Mosi-oa-Tunya Rd; ☏0213 323351; ⏰ noon–22.00 daily. This branch of the South African restaurant chain next to the Avani Victoria Falls Resort serves decent but standard fare, mostly grilled meat, chicken & fish, as well as burgers & pizzas. It's on the expensive side, & the beer is extortionate, but they do have some better-value lunch specials. The unprepossessing location is a drawback, & there's noise from the road, but the service is friendly & efficient. $$$–$$$$

✗ **Victoria Falls Waterfront** [154 B4] Sichango Rd; ☏0213 320606–08. The magnificent setting of SafPar's riverside complex makes this a good place to dine. You can enjoy b/fast, lunch or dinner (or a snack) overlooking the Zambezi at affordable prices. The food is good & plentiful with the usual variety of chicken dishes, burgers & chips, soups, sandwiches & daily specials served by friendly staff. There is also a full bar. While it is out of town, it's the kind of place you might go for a meal & stay for hours to savour the riverside ambience. $$$–$$$$

✗ **Chanters** [158 E1] Lukulu Cres; ☏0213 323412; www.chanters-livingstone.com; ⏰ 07.00–21.30 daily. Chanters has a varied & comprehensive menu, with a good selection of local specialities such as braised oxtail & a range of pasta & vegetarian dishes. The food is good, & the garden setting attractive. $$$

you to look inside. The 'Sefer Torah' was removed to Lusaka when one of the last Jewish families, the Iljons, left the area in 1972. Nickie Iljon's name still adorns the building that housed his shop on Mutelo Street, formerly Codrington Street.

- The **clock** at the Livingstone Museum, donated by the Susman brothers in 1951 to commemorate the 50th anniversary of their arrival north of the Zambezi.
- **Stanley House,** on the main Mosi-oa-Tunya Road next to the Capitol Theatre, which housed the elegant stores of the wealthy Harry Sossen, who was married to Bella Grill.
- The **Zambezi Saw Mills** office in the industrial area, now the Railway Museum. In the cabinet it is still possible to read the guards' reports which show that bales of cloth belonging to Susman Brothers & Wulfsohn, and destined for their Western and North-Western Province stores, were pilfered at various intervals!
- The **old cemetery** on the outskirts of town, which incorporates a small walled-off section for the Jewish community.

Less visible, but no less interesting, is the history behind two roads. Susman Drive, now called Kapufi Avenue, was originally named after Eli Susman and all the good work that he did for the community. And the town's central crossroads was once known to the locals as 'Ficks, Flax and Aufochs' corner after the three shops at the intersection. Sam Fix was a tailor, Flax ran a haberdashery and the Aufochs family had a trading store on the opposite corner. After independence, Mainway and Sackville Street became Mosi-oa-Tunya Road and Akapelwa Street respectively.

Further information on the Jewish community in Zambia can be found in Hugh Macmillan and Frank Shapiro's *Zion In Africa: the Jews of Zambia* and Macmillan's *An African Trading Empire: the story of Susman Brothers & Wulfsohn, 1901–2005* (see *Appendix 3*, page 527).

✗ **Ocean Basket** [159 D6] 82 Mosi-oa-Tunya Rd; ☏0213 321274; www.oceanbasket.com; ⏲ noon–22.00 daily. A branch of the South African chain, this fish restaurant is located in a restored historical building near the junction of Kazungula Rd. If you have a hankering for fish or prawns in this landlocked country, this is the place. They even do good sushi. Set inside a large secure courtyard with sprawling lawn & ample parking, it offers dining either inside or out on the wide veranda. Staff are efficient & very friendly & the food, served in large frying pans, is good. $$–$$$$$

✗ **Golden Leaf Indian Restaurant** [off map, 159 D8] Mosi-oa-Tunya Rd; ☏0213 321266, m 0974 321266; ⏲ 07.00–10.00, 12.30–14.00, 18.15–22.00. Originally part of Ngolide Lodge, but now based in its own establishment just down the road, this small Indian restaurant is one of the better places to eat in town. On offer are a variety of dishes, from fish masala to kadai chicken, & there are also plenty of veggie options. You can order a takeaway or eat in, although due to its popularity it's advisable to book in advance. $$–$$$

✗ **O'Driscoll's** [159 D6] Mosi-oa-Tunya Rd (behind Fawlty Towers); ☏0213 323432; ⏲ 11.00–22.00 daily. Popular with both visitors & local tour operators, who come to unwind after a hard day's rafting, touring or guiding. Expect an unpretentious bar with a distinctly Irish feel & Guinness behind the bar. Tables are set under a gigantic thatched roof & an open-plan main area with cushioned seating. And there's satellite TV, often tuned in to international sports. $$–$$$

✗ **Old Drift Restaurant & Bar** [159 G6] Livingstone Royal Golf & Country Club; ☏0213 323052; m 0978 170791; ⏲ 08.00–22.00 daily. The à-la-carte restaurant & bar in the golf club's colonial-style clubhouse has a beautiful setting overlooking the course. Excellent food is served throughout the day, with pizzas, sandwiches, burgers, steaks & samosas at lunch. Dinners are more extravagant & slightly more expensive but good value overall. There are free snacks & happy-hour prices 17.30–18.30 every Fri. $$–$$$

✳✗ **Olga's** [159 D6] Nakatindi Rd; ☏0213 324160; www.olgasproject.com; ⏲ 07.00–22.00 daily. Close to the Catholic church, this is the place for pizzas cooked in a traditional wood-fired oven, as well as pasta dishes & salads. A thatched eating area incorporates crafts & furniture made by members of the Local Youth Community

Training Centre & a school for disadvantaged youngsters, with profits from the restaurant fed back to the centre. The restaurant has free Wi-Fi, & takeaway is available. $$–$$$

✳✗ **Zigzag** [154 B3] Industrial Rd; ☏0213 322814; ⏲ 07.00–21.00 Sun–Wed, 07.00–23.00 Thu–Sat. Zigzag is a welcome respite from the hustle & bustle of town. Large & inviting, with shady guava, lemon & mango trees, it's a popular place for an extensive b/fast, coffee & cakes, lunch, or an evening meal. There's also a children's menu, a range of desserts & milkshakes, & a fully licensed bar. There's also an enticing pool with grassy surround, a changing area & a children's play area, useful if you want to keep the kids entertained as you sip your cappuccino, or surf the net courtesy of free Wi-Fi access. $$–$$$

✗ **Kubu Café** [159 D6] Mosi-oa-Tunya Sq; m 0975 689114; e kubucafe@zamnet.zm. Affiliated with the Kubu Crafts curio shop, this café/restaurant is located in the corner of Mosi-oa-Tunya Square next to Shoprite. There is ample seating both inside & outside, including a collection of comfy sofas & armchairs in one corner. The café serves milkshakes & coffees that go well with a slice of one of their homemade cakes. More substantial meals such as burgers, pizzas & steaks are also available, & there's a reasonably stocked bar. Wi-Fi is available to paying customers. $–$$$$

✗ **Golden Chopsticks** [158 A1] John Hunt Way; ⏲ 11.00–21.00. Set behind the sadly diminished Laughing Dragon, Golden Chopsticks opened with it's associated hotel in 2014. The probable cause of decline of its nearby competitor, it serves good-quality Chinese food in generous helpings, & due to the Chinese expat owners, it's the most authentic Chinese food you'll get in Zambia. $–$$

✗ **Fez Bar** [159 D6] Mosi-oa-Tunya Rd; m 0978 667555; ⏲ 10.00–23.00 daily. This popular evening hang-out just next to Ocean Basket is a favourite among the local community & has a distinctly Mexican flair. If you have a taste for tequila & dancing into the early hours, this is the place to be, with its impressive pop-art murals, sunken couches & outside seating. There's a large-screen satellite TV & even DJs at the w/end. Mexican food, standard fare of chicken, steaks & chips, & their 'famous' burger (generally considered to be the best in Livingstone) are all available. $–$$

above   **Hippo (*Hippopotamus amphibias*)**
(SS) page 518

right   **African elephant (*Loxodonta africana*)**
(TH) page 517

below   **Herd of buffalo (*Syncerus caffer*)**
(AZ) pages 518–19

above **Leopard (*Panthera pardus*)** (EW) pages 507–8

left **Lion cub (*Panthera leo*)** (CM) page 507

below **African wild dog (*Lycaon pictus*)** (CM) page 509

above   Side-striped jackal (*Canis adustus*) (MS/FLPA) page 510

below   Spotted hyena (*Crocuta crocuta*) (MM/S) page 510

above left **Plains zebra (*Equus quagga*)** (CM) page 519

above centre **Black lechwe (*Kobus leche smithemani*)** (CM) page 516

above right **Oribi (*Ourebia ourebi*)** (CM) page 517

centre **Puku (*Kobus vardoni*)** (CM) page 516

below left **Roan antelope (*Hippotragus equinus*)** (CM) page 512

above left   **Greater kudu** (*Tragelaphus strepsiceros*) (AZ) pages 513–14

above right   **Blue wildebeest** (*Connochaetes taurinus*) (CM) page 513

centre   **Waterbuck** (*Kobus ellipsiprymnus*) (SS) pages 512–13

below left   **Lichtenstein's hartebeest** (*Alcelaphus lichtensteini*) (AZ) page 513

below right   **Bushbuck** (*Tragelaphus scriptus*) (CM) page 514

above	**Warthogs** (*Phacochoerus aethiopicus*) (CM) page 519
left	**Tree hyrax** (*Dendrohyrax arboreus*) (SS) page 522
below left	**Yellow baboon** (*Papio cynocephalus cynocephalus*) (SS) page 510
below right	**Vervet monkey** (*Cercopithecus aethiops*) (MS/FLPA) page 511

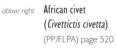
above right **African civet**
(*Civettictis civetta*)
(PP/FLPA) page 520

right **Large-spotted genet**
(*Genetta tigrina*)
(SS) page 520

below **White-tailed mongoose**
(*Ichneumia albicauda*)
(PP/FLPA) page 520

above **Miombo woodland** (C&TS/FLPA) page 30

left **Leopard orchid (*Ansellia africana*)** (TH)

below left **Protea** (TH)

below right **Blood lily (*Scadoxus multiflorus*)** (TH)

✕ Laughing Dragon [158 A1] John Hunt Way; ☎0977 610557; ⏱ 11.00–23.00 daily. Set behind the museum, Laughing Dragon serves authentic Szechuan Chinese food, has a full alcohol licence & also does takeaways. The menu depends on what's available in Livingstone that day, but the food is good, & the quantities generous. Although the food has always been reported to be good, the restaurant was looking rather run down on our last visit. $–$$

✕ Mukamba/Ann's Steak House [158 D4] 97 John Hunt Way. Down the road from Jollyboys, this is a great place to chill out with some cheap Zambian or German food & drinks, often accompanied by live, local music or sports on one of the many large satellite TVs. $–$$

ENTERTAINMENT AND NIGHTLIFE Livingstone's **nightlife** centres largely around dancing and drinking, although the bars at various restaurants offer a pleasant atmosphere if you simply want to relax and chat. For sundowners, join the crowd at the Victoria Falls Waterfront [154 B4], overlooking the river. The Fez Bar [159 D6] & B' Hive [154 C3] are lively venues most nights – favourite hangouts for local expats letting off steam after a tough day looking after visitors. Another popular options is Mukamba [158 D4].

For live music, there's a band at Avani [map, page 189] most evenings and at weekends. Mukamba (see above) often features live local bands, too. Traditional dancing can be seen at The Waterfront, though you'll need to check times and dates with them.

Those in search of dancing should try Eat Rite's open-air disco on Kapondo Street, which later moonlights as a nightclub – Steprite Sounds. A cover charge is made when there's a band playing. The New Fairmount Hotel [158 E3] has the dark and popular Club Fairmount (☎ *0213 320723; ⏱ normally 20.00–04.00 Thu–Sat, but phone to confirm*), that's generally jam-packed at weekends.

SHOPPING With both the Falls Park shopping centre [154 C3] and Mosi-oa-Tunya Square [159 D6] (commonly referred to as the 'Shoprite Centre'), options for shopping in Livingstone have improved considerably in recent years. There are also a couple of markets, and several shops along the main Mosi-oa-Tunya Road. Opening hours are usually around 09.00–17.00 Monday to Friday, and Saturday mornings, unless otherwise stated.

Food and drink Although you can find most things in Livingstone, you may still have to visit several shops, and imported gourmet items are harder to come by and expensive.

Of the **supermarkets**, the newer Shoprite [159 D6] (*Mosi-oa-Tunya Sq; ⏱ 08.00–20.00 daily*) is the largest and has the best selection (The original Shoprite on Kapondo Street [a162 B2] is an entirely different affair, so don't get them confused!), although the new branch of Spar Super Store on the corner of Mutelo St [158 B2] (*Mosi-oa-Tunya Rd; ⏱ 07.00–20.00 daily*) is also useful and well stocked.

For somewhere less corporate, for fruit and vegetables, try the Zambian open-air **markets**. Positioned around town, these have fresh tomatoes, onions and other basic fruits and vegetables, and are generally cheaper than the supermarkets, although some haggling may be required. If it's just **meat** you're after, cross Mosi-oa-Tunya Road to Pama Meats for a selection of beef, poultry and pork, or try Shopper's Butchery [158 B1] (*John Hunt Way, behind post office*). Wonderbake and Munali Café [158 B1] sell good fresh-baked **bread** and pastries.

Books and magazines Several of the curio shops stock wildlife reference books and regional travel guides. Kubu Café has a small second-hand bookshop selling books (*K5*) and slightly out of date magazines (*K2*). Jollyboys (page 164) has a book-exchange system, as do many other places to stay in town. Current magazines may be harder to come by. Your best bet is the Spar in the centre [158 B2] or Shoprite at Mosi-oa-Tunya Sq [159 D6] – though be warned, magazines are expensive and tend to be several months old, so be sure to check the issue date. Oddly, the street vendors in front of the Capitol Theatre [158 B1] often have more recent ones at much lower prices, but this is very hit or miss.

Clothes You can pick up clothing essentials at the PEP store [158 B2] (*Mosi-oa-Tunya Rd, opposite Zanaco*), or at Power Sales, a few doors down from the same bank, though you'll need to be selective. There are also plenty of shops selling a hotchpotch of stuff that includes assorted clothing, mostly from China – so it can become rather a mission (or adventure) to find what you seek. For more fashionable wear try the clothing stores at Falls Park shopping centre [154 C3] or at the Avani Victoria Falls Resort [map, page 189], though these will be pricier. For shoes, there's Bata, by Barclays Bank [158 B1], though both the selection and sizes are rather limited.

Despite its shortcomings on fashion, Livingstone is a great place to find African wear – brightly coloured shirts, skirts and dresses, some complete with matching caps or headscarves – and garments can often be made to order with a few days' notice. *Chitenje*, the colourful lengths of traditional African cloth, can be found at most of the small Indian shops on the main road and on Kuta Way, parallel to the main road, or at any of the local markets (page 181). Clothes can be made up at Emmah's Wear (below) from your own fabrics or theirs.

Crafts, curios and gifts If you like bargaining and have lots of patience, then try one of the craft markets (page 194), either in town or next to the Falls. Alternatively, look out for the informal craft market in the car park at Falls Park shopping centre [154 C3], where curio vendors lay out their goods on a more ad hoc basis.

If time isn't on your side, or you don't fancy the hassle of bargaining, one of the following might suit you much better.

Bobbili Gems [159 D6] Mosi-oa-Tunya Sq; ✆0213 323210; m 0976 446240; ◷ 09.00–18.00. If bling is your thing, look no further. Bobbili Gems designs its own jewellery – necklaces, earrings & other items – much of it fashioned from Zambian silver, beads, semi-precious stones & gemstones. Friendly staff are on hand to answer your questions & help you find that special souvenir, or the resident artisan will work with you to create your own signature piece. There is also a smaller store at the airport for last-minute gifts.

Emmah's Wear [159 D7] 121 Mosi-oa-Tunya Rd; ✆0213 322254; e emmahwear@gmail.com; ◷ 08.00–17.00 Mon–Fri, 08.00–12.30 Sat. Just north of the railway station, Emmah's can tailor-make anything from clothing to tablecloths, quickly & affordably. Bring your own fabric (bought at a local market or an Indian shop in town) or choose one at their shop, & expect to pay from K45 for a simple skirt. There's also a small craft shop here.

Mosi-oa-Tunya Arts Centre [159 D7] 123 Mosi-oa-Tunya Rd. Just next to Emmah's Wear on the main road, the Arts Centre is an open-sided shop that looks like a small market. It sells a range of art from life-size iron sculptures of bulls, to more practical items like paintings & locally made jewellery. You can expect to engage in some haggling to get a reasonable price, but it's less pushy than some of the larger craft markets.

Kubu Crafts [158 E3] Livingstone Airport & Mosi-oa-Tunya Sq; ✆0213 320230; e kubucrafts@zamnet.zm, www.kubucrafts.com. Although the flagship store of Livingstone's most established curio shop has now closed, 2 smaller branches remain. Though they're very tourist orientated, crafts from all over Africa – textiles, wood carvings, pottery, metal sculptures & more – afford plenty of choice, & browsing is hassle free.

Zambezi Jewels [map, page 189] 147 Mosi-oa-Tunya Rd; ✆0213 324567; ⊕ 09.00–18.00. Located just next to Avani's activity centre, Zambezi Jewels has an interesting collection of handcrafted jewellery from across Zambia. The staff are helpful & it's a non-pressured environment for souvenir shopping.

Livingstone Trading Company [154 C3] The Falls, Mosi-oa-Tunya Rd; ✆0213 323864; ⊕ 08.00–18.00 daily. Next to the Avani, this is a good option for everything from children's & ladies' clothes to books, cards & basic toiletries.

Museum Curio Shop & Art Gallery [159 A2] Livingstone Museum. The museum's curio shop showcases Zambian handicrafts & basketware. A wide selection of Zambian paintings & other art by local artists is for sale – everything from wildlife to people to abstract.

Women in Mining [map, page 189] The Falls, Mosi-oa-Tunya Rd; ⊕ 08.00–18.00 daily. If it's gemstones or jewellery you're after, this shop linked to the Association of Zambian Women in Mining (AZWIM) could be the place to find it.

Pharmacies For cosmetics, toiletries or medicines there are several good pharmacies stocking a selection of items including insect repellents, beauty products, suncreams, medical supplies, baby supplies, batteries, film and more. Each has a trained pharmacist, who can also offer advice on medications and fill prescriptions. Otherwise, the Spar Super Store in the centre [158 B2] and Shoprite in Mosi-oa-Tunya Square [159 D6] sell a variety of beauty products and the basics.

Health & Glow Pharmacy [158 B2 & 159 D6] Mosi-oa-Tunya Rd; ✆0213 322249; e saketravel@yahoo.com ⊕ 08.00–18.30 Mon–Fri, 08.00–14.00 Sat, 09.30–13.00 Sun. Next to Fawlty Towers, opposite Shoprite & next to PEP in the centre, these well-stocked shops have helpful, knowledgeable staff.

HK Pharmacy & Photo Studio [158 B1] Mosi-oa-Tunya Rd, next to Capitol Theatre; ✆0213 324296; ⊕ 08.30–19.00 Mon–Fri, 08.00–14.00 Sat. Get your prescriptions filled & photos digitally printed at the same time. They also have a wide selection of beauty products.

L F Moore Chemists [158 C1] 133 Akapelwa St; ✆0213 321640; ⊕ 08.00–18.00 Mon–Fri, 08.00– 13.00 Sat, 09.30–12.30 Sun/public holidays. Established in 1936, L F Moore is a Livingstone institution. It remains one of the best-stocked chemists in town, with friendly staff who will go out of their way to help.

Link Pharmacy [159 D6] Mosi-oa-Tunya Sq; ✆0213 324222; ⊕ 09.00–18.00 Mon–Fri, 09.00–17.00 Sat, 09.00–13.00 Sun. If this well-stocked chemist doesn't have what you want, they can usually get it from their Lusaka store.

Musamu Chemist [158 B1] 141A, cnr Kuta Way & Zambezi St; ✆0213 323226; after hours m 0979 276839; ⊕ 08.00–20.00 Mon–Fri, 08.00–18.00 Sat, 09.00–13.00 Sun

Other supplies Basic **camera supplies** can be found at the various chemists (see above), but a better bet is Konica Photo Express [158 C1] (*Mosi-oa-Tunya Rd, nr Airport Rd*), which offers one-hour photo processing, enlargements and passport photos, and stocks film and related supplies. Also recommended are the convenient HK Photo Studio [158 B1] (*nr Capitol Theatre*), and Kodak Express [158 E4] (*Liso Hse, next to Finance Bank*).

For cassette tapes and DVDs of popular **music**, including many African selections, try Zimbabwe or Town Centre Market at the bottom of Kapondo Street [158 B2]. They have a wide selection of cheap (probably bootlegged) cassette tapes, DVDs and videos. Follow your ears for blaring music and you'll find a kiosk selling tapes! Often goods will be brought direct to you from one of the many roving salesmen in town selling cassettes, DVDs and other sundries. A more recent alternative is Sounds [159 D6] (*Mosi-oa-Tunya Sq*).

If you have **computer** trouble, Falcon Technologies (*Linda Rd, past Zigzag*; ✆0213 322676*) offers repair and service and also sells new and used computers.

BANKS AND CHANGING MONEY Livingstone has several major banks and various bureaux de change dotted throughout town. Most of the banks have ATMs, for which you'll generally need a Visa card rather than MasterCard. More convenient, but with the least favourable exchange rate, is to change money at a hotel or lodge.

Unless you are very savvy or very desperate, avoid the freelance 'money-changers' who tend to congregate around the Capitol Theatre and at the border. No matter how carefully you watch, they always take advantage of unsuspecting (and even suspicious) tourists by short-changing them somehow.

The major **banks** are situated around the post office area, parallel to the main Mosi-oa-Tunya Road [158 D4]. Typically they open Monday to Friday 08.00–16.00, and sometimes on Saturday mornings, but get there early if you want to avoid long queues. The spacious air-conditioned interior and more private exchange facilities of Zanaco make it preferable to the generally crowded Barclays.

$ Bank ABC Mosi-oa-Tunya Sq; ✆0213 320681

$ Barclays Mosi-oa-Tunya Rd; ✆0213 323525/526/527. Also small branch with ATM at The Falls [map, page 189].

$ Finance John Hunt Way; ✆0213 320122. The main branch has an ATM & Moneygram office; smaller branch at Mosi-oa-Tunya Sq [159 D6].

$ Stanbic Mosi-oa-Tunya Sq; ✆0213 324350/1

$ Standard Chartered ✆0213 220489. Also at Falls Park, inc ATM [154 C3].

$ Zanaco Cnr Mutelo St & Mosi-oa-Tunya Rd; ✆0213 321901/320171/320995

$ NSBC Maina Soko; ✆0213 322649. Also at airport, inc ATM.

Many of the **bureaux de change** are close to or opposite Barclays Bank, with others at Falls Park shopping centre. You can also exchange money at the post office, though rates are likely to be lower than at the private bureaux de change.

$ Fx Africa [158 B1] Mosi-oa-Tunya Rd, nr Capitol Theatre; ✆0213 320154; ⊕ 08.00–16.30 Mon–Fri, 08.00–11.30 Sat

$ Zampost [158 B1] Mosi-oa-Tunya Rd, in post office complex; ✆0213 322472; ⊕ 08.00–16.30 Mon–Fri, 08.00–12.30 Sat

$ Zampost [154 C3] Falls Park; ✆0213 324797; ⊕ 09.00–12.30, 12.45–17.00 Mon–Fri, 08.00–12.30 Sat

COMMUNICATIONS

Internet Driven by increasing expectations from international travellers the majority of accommodation, and many restaurants, now offer free Wi-Fi access and/or computers with internet access. As such the number of internet cafes in Livingstone has declined in recent years, although there is still a reliable one at PostNet near the Capitol Theatre [158 B1] (⊕ 08.00–18.00 Mon–Fri, 08.00–13.00 Sat). While rates are low and comparable, at around K1–2/hour, the standard of computers, speed and service varies; high-speed service in Livingstone is pretty rare, and the service often goes down during the common power outages. For those with a laptop, Wonderbake [158 B1] is a Wi-Fi hot zone, so a good place for a cappuccino while you check your emails.

Post and courier You can't miss Livingstone's post office [158 B2] (✆0213 324797; ⊕ 08.00–noon, 14.00–16.30 Mon–Fri, 08.00–12.30 Sat) in the centre of town in a sprawling complex of banks and shops, adjacent to the main road.

DHL Mosi-oa-Tunya Hse; ✆0211 376400. Located on the bottom floor of this high-rise building.

FedEx John Hunt Way (opp St Andrew's Church); ✆0213 220247. In addition to the courier service, this is also an agent for Western Union.

PostNet Stanley Hse, Mosi-oa-Tunya Rd; ✆ 0213
200044. The new PostNet is an agent for DHL &
Western Union, & offers internet access too.

Telephone If you can't make phone calls where you are staying, try one of the
internet cafés or shops advertising a telephone service, such as PostNet [158
B1], or the post office itself [158 B2]. Many visitors will find it more convenient
to purchase a local SIM card. Those for both Airtel and the state-owned Zamtel
are easily obtainable from numerous outlets across town; look out for their signs
at shopping malls and on Mosi-oa-Tunya Road, including next to Wonderbake.
Expect to pay around K5 a SIM card, with top-up cards available from K3.

OTHER PRACTICALITIES
Car repairs and spares
The two biggest workshops in town are Foley's Africa
(*Industrial Rd;* ✆ *0213 320888;* e *info@foleysafrica.com; www.foleysafrica.com*),
which caters for Land Rovers; and Bennett Engineering, also known as Harry's
workshop [154 C3] (✆ *0213 321611, 322380,* m *0978 308936;* e *hbennett@iconnect.
zm*), opposite Falls Park. Bennett services most of the tour operators' vehicles in
town and is your best bet for more serious problems.

For more basic repairs, contact Channa's Motors (*Mosi-oa-Tunya Rd;* ✆ *0213
320468*), just across the railway line. Their facilities are somewhat limited and
service can be slow but they can often help get you moving again, barring
major problems. For punctures and tyre repairs try the Total fuel station, on the
right side of Mosi-oa-Tunya Road as you head up towards the centre of town
[159 D5], or the Kobil fuel station next to Fawlty Towers [159 D6]. If it's parts or
vehicle accessories that you need, the most central place is Autoworld [158 A2]
(*Mosi-oa-Tunya Rd;* ✆ *0213 320264;* e *autoworld@zamtel.zm*), about 50m south
of Barclays Bank.

Emergencies
Medical facilities are limited in Livingstone, and the local hospitals
are not up to the standard of those in the West, but in the event of an emergency
contact:

✚ **SES** [159 E2] Speciality Emergency Services,
cnr Likute Way & Obote Rd; ✆ 0213 322330;
emergency control centre ✆ 0977 770302/0962
740300; m 0977 740306/8;
e livingstoneparamedics@ses-zambia.com;
www.ses-zambia.com. The local base is staffed
with South African-trained paramedics.

✚ **Dr Shafik's Hospital** [158 G2] Katete Av;
✆ 0213 321130 (24hrs); m 0955/0966/0977
863000; e shafikhosp@rocketmail.com
✚ **Health Point (Dr Shanks)** [158 D1] Mushili
Way; m 0978 100666; e shanks@zamnet.zm
✚ **Southern Medical Centre** [159 D5]
Makambo Rd; ✆ 0213 323547; m 0977 777017;
e sanjaysouthmed@gmail.com

Should you need an **optician**, head for Falls Park shopping centre [154 C3] or try
Sunbird Opticians ([158 B1] *Mosi-oa-Tunya Rd, nr Barclays Bank*). For pharmacies,
see page 183.

Tourist information
The Zambia Tourism Board [158 A2] (*Mosi-oa-Tunya
Rd;* ✆ *0213 321404/87;* e *ztb@zambiatourism.org.zm; www.zambiatourism.com;*
⊕ *08.00–17.00 Mon–Fri, 09.00–noon Sat*), has an office at the tourist centre next to
the Livingstone Museum, easily spotted for the two-seater plane outside. Here you
can expect pleasant, friendly staff working with limited resources. You can pick up

brochures and get referrals, but agents and tour operators (pages 43–5) are usually better geared to assist you with actual bookings.

Travel agents For international airline tickets and fares, your best choice is:

Southend Travel [158 E4] Liso Hse, nr Finance Bank, Mosi-oa-Tunya Rd; ✆0213 320773/320241; e southend@zamnet.zm; ⏱08.00–17.30 Mon–Fri, 08.00–13.00 Sat.) Agents for SAA, British Airways, Kenya Airways, Lufthansa & Ethiopian Airways, amongst others. Able to advise on special air fares, & also for the Intercape Mainliner bus service (page 52).

WHAT TO SEE AND DO

The area around Victoria Falls has been a major crossroads for travellers for over a hundred years. From the early missionaries and traders, to the backpackers, overland trucks and package tourists of the last few decades – virtually everyone passing through the region from overseas has stopped here. Recently this has created a thriving tourism industry and, apart from simply marvelling at one of the world's greatest waterfalls, there are now lots of ways to occupy yourself for a few days. Some of these are easily booked after you arrive; one or two are better pre-arranged.

The past decade has witnessed a huge shift in the area's atmosphere. Visitors used to be from southern Africa, with perhaps the odd intrepid backpacker and the fortunate few who could afford an upmarket safari. Now the sheer volume of visitors to the Falls has increased massively. This increase, especially noticeable in the proportion of younger visitors, has fuelled the rise of more active, adventurous pursuits like white-water rafting, bungee jumping, river-boarding and other thrill-based pastimes.

A genteel cocktail at a luxury hotel is no longer the high point of a visit for most people. You are more likely to return home with vivid memories of the adrenalin rush of shooting rapids in a raft, or the buzz of accelerating head-first towards the Zambezi with only a piece of elastic to save you.

TOUR OPERATORS In a town where tourism is such big business, almost everyone – from hoteliers to car-hire companies to taxi firms – can handle bookings for individual activities. Those listed here are the specialists. For flight operators, see page 197.

Many companies offer **guided sightseeing tours** around Livingstone, including visits to traditional villages, local markets, museums, the Falls, game park and historical sites. While some activities can be organised without notice, others need to be pre-booked, so it's as well to be organised if you don't want to be disappointed. Rates almost always include transfers from your accommodation, within a reasonable radius.

If you are staying in one of the lodges, sightseeing tours for guests using their own guides and vehicles are generally included. Bushtracks Africa, Wild Side Tours & Safaris and Safari Par Excellence are popular operators, although there are many others (page 187). Of these, Wild Side is run by people who have lived in Livingstone for years, and who understand the place well; it can personalise tours to suit individual requirements, while the larger Bushtracks runs set trips aimed largely at guests at many of the top hotels and lodges. Several other specialist operators have combined under the marketing umbrella of the Livingstone's Adventure Group, making a convenient one-stop shop for their activities. In all cases, trips are professionally run with competent guides. Most tours can be either stand-alone or in combination with others.

Abseil Zambia [159 D6] aka **The Zambezi Swing**; Fawlty Towers; 📞0213 321188; ℮ theswing@zamnet.zm; www.thezambeziswing. com. Gorge swinging, abseiling, highwiring & rap-jumping activities at their site atop the 5th gorge on the Zambian side, some 5km from the Falls.

African Queen/African Princess [154 B4] Contact Livingstone's Adventure (opposite column). Two luxury catamarans operating b/fast, lunch & dinner trips.

Angle Zambia 📞0213 327489; m 0977 707829/586353; ℮ anglezam@microlink.zm; www.zambezifishing.com. Half-day, full-day & multi-day fishing trips with experienced guides. Also owns Barotse Tiger Camp on the Barotse Floodplain (pages 491–2).

Batoka Sky Adventures [154 B4] Maramba Aerodrome, off Sichango Rd; contact Livingstone's Adventure. Microlights & helicopters for scenic flights over the Falls, game park & upper river.

Bundu Adventures [159 C5] The Gem Stone Lounge, 1364 Kabompo Rd; m 0978 203988; ℮ info@bunduadventures.com; www. bunduadventures.com. Based in a new restaurant serving Mediterranean-style cuisine, Bundu offers rafting, riverboarding, kayaking, canoeing & the new 'spray view' tour (Aug–Jan) which gives a unique perspective of the falls, from right beneath them. See ad in 3rd colour section.

Bushtracks Africa [154 C3] Mosi-oa-Tunya Rd; 📞0213 323232; ℮ victoriafalls@bushtracksafrica. com; www.bushtracksafrica.com. One of the best & most reliable tour operators in Livingstone, Bushtracks is located just south of the railway station, where the railway line crosses the road. It's an effective one-stop shop for everything from game drives & river cruises to day trips to Botswana, as well as operating the *Royal Livingstone Express*.

Gwembe Safaris [154 C4] Livingstone Reptile Park, Mosi-oa-Tunya Rd; 📞0213 321733/321648; ℮ gwemsaf@iconnect.zm; www.gwembesafaris. com. Booking agents, tour operators, & owners of the reptile park.

Jet Extreme Zambia 📞0213 321375; m 0977 388465; ℮ info@jetextremezambia.com. Runs jet boat trips in the Batoka Gorge, & operates the cable car out of the gorge at rapid 25.

Kayak the Zambezi m 0966 607478; ℮ kayak@ thezambezi.com; www.thezambezi.com. The kayaking specialists for novice & experienced

paddlers alike. Will help you plan day trips & longer expeditions as well as offering the latest craze (commercially speaking at least) at Rapid 11: river surfing (for experienced riders only).

Livingstone's Adventure [154 B4] 4023 Sichango Rd; 📞0213 323589; m 0978 770175; ℮ reservations@livingstonesadventure.com; www.livingstonesadventure.com. This umbrella organisation with good insurance coverage groups together a variety of activities: the *African Queen*, Batoka Sky (helicopter & microlights), Livingstone Quad Company, Makora Quest (canoeing), Victoria Carriage Company (horseriding) & Victoria Falls River Safaris. Booking several trips attracts a discount. To experience the Zambezi from 2 angles, their 'combo' follows a river safari with a more sedate river cruise.

Livingstone Quad Company [154 B4] Maramba Aerodrome, off Sichango Rd; contact Livingstone's Adventure (above). Quadbike excursions either from the aerodrome on an 'eco-trail' or on a local 'village trail'.

Livingstone Walking Safaris [158 F1] 4 Nakambala La; 📞0213 322267; m 0977 450716, 0977 712496; ℮ gecko@zamnet.zm; www. livingstonerhinosafaris.com. Guided walks in Mosi-oa-Tunya NP with ½-day activities taking in the usual walking safari or tracking the national park's star attraction – the resident white rhino.

Makora Quest Contact Livingstone's Adventure (above). Livingstone's most established canoe operator, with extensive local knowledge & friendly service.

Nomad African Travel Zambia
📞0213 327769; m 0977 846164/755429; ℮ info@nomadafricantravel.co.uk; www. nomadafricantravel.co.uk. Local transfers & booking service, plus guided, tailormade & self-drive safaris throughout southern Africa.

Ride Zambezi Chundukwa River Lodge; m 0979 549558; ℮ chundukwahorse@microlink.zm; www. ridezambezi.com. Organises various guided rides depending on preference & experience, using horses from the stables at Chundukwa River Lodge.

Safari Par Excellence [154 B4] Zambezi Waterfront & Activity Centre, Sichango Rd; 📞0213 320606; m 0968 320606; ℮ zaminfo@safpar. com; www.safpar.com. One of Livingstone's larger tourism enterprises, 'SafPar' is a one-stop shop for everything you need. The company also operates the *Lady Livingstone* as well as the lion & elephant encounters at Thorntree.

8

Shearwater Adventures ✆ +263 134 4471; m +263 773 461716; e reservations@ shearwatervf.com; www.shearwatervictoriafalls. com. Bungee jumping, gorge swing & bridge slide.

Taonga Safaris [154 B4] Sichango Rd, next to the Boat Club; ✆ 0213 322508; m 0977 878065; e info@taonga-safaris.com; www.taonga-safaris.com. Booze cruises catering mainly to backpackers.

Thorn Tree Safaris www.thorntreesafaris.com. With a house planned in Livingstone in 2016, Thorn Tree are expanding from their traditional base in the north. For full details, see pages 347–8.

United Air Charters ✆ 0213 323095; e info@ uaczam.com; www.uaczam.com. Operates a fleet of helicopters for scenic & charter flights from its spectacular base on Baobab Ridge, to the east of Mosi-oa-Tunya Rd.

Victoria Carriage Co Contact Livingstone's Adventure (page 187). Horse-drawn carriage trips on Sun International property & horseriding in the bush near the Falls.

Victoria Falls River Safaris Contact Livingstone's Adventure (page 187). Aluminium 'safari' boats with shade, akin to the 4x4 of the river, can go far beyond the reach of conventional craft.

Wild Side Tours & Safaris [159 D7] 131 Mosi-oa-Tunya Rd; ✆ 0213 323726; m 0978 323726; e wild@iconnect.zm. Located in a restored railway house in the 217 area; look for the big 'i' sign indicating tourist information. Owner operated, & one of Livingstone's long-time tour companies, Wild Side offers a full service including village & town tours, game drives, cultural tours, activities & transfers, as well as online accommodation booking.

VICTORIA FALLS The Falls are 1,688m wide and average just over 100m in height. Around 550 million litres (750 million during peak months) cascade over the lip every minute, making this one of the world's greatest waterfalls. Closer inspection shows that this immense curtain of water is interrupted by gaps, where small islands stand on the lip of the Falls. These effectively split the Falls into smaller waterfalls, which are known as (from west to east) the Devil's Cataract, the Main Falls, the Horseshoe Falls, the Rainbow Falls and the Eastern Cataract.

Around the Falls is a genuinely important and interesting rainforest, with plant species (especially ferns) rarely found elsewhere in Zimbabwe or Zambia. These are sustained by the clouds of spray, which blanket the immediate vicinity of the Falls. You'll also find various monkeys and baboons here, whilst the lush canopy shelters Livingstone's lourie amongst other birds.

The flow, and hence the spray, is greatest just after the end of the rainy season – around March or April, depending upon the rains. It then decreases gradually until about December, when the rains in western Zambia will start to replenish the river. During low water, a light raincoat (available for rent on site) is very useful for wandering between the viewpoints on the Zimbabwean side, though it's not necessary in Zambia. However, in high water a raincoat is largely ineffective as the spray blows all around and soaks you in seconds. Anything that you want to keep dry must be wrapped in several layers of plastic or, even better, zip-lock plastic bags.

The Falls never seem the same twice, so try to visit several times, under different light conditions. At sunrise, both Danger Point and Knife-edge Point are fascinating – position yourself carefully to see your shadow in the mists, with three concentric rainbows appearing as halos. (Photographers will find polarising filters invaluable in capturing the rainbows on film, as the light from the rainbows at any time of day is polarised.)Moonlight is another fascinating time, when the Falls take on an ethereal glow and the waters blend into one smooth mass which seems frozen over the rocks.

On the Zambian side (*entry US$20 pp, vehicle US$5; gate ⊕ 06.00–19.00 daily*), viewing the Falls could not be easier, and every season brings a reason to visit. For photographers, the area is best explored in the early morning, when the sun is still

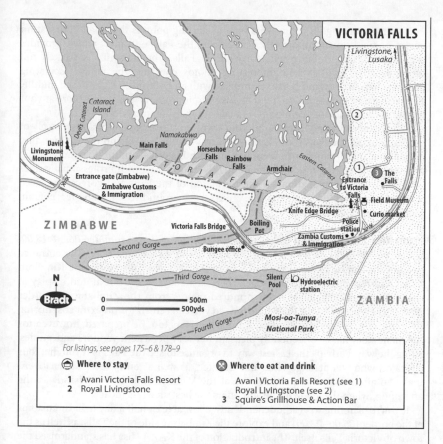

For listings, see pages 175–6 & 178–9

Where to stay
1 Avani Victoria Falls Resort
2 Royal Livingstone

Where to eat and drink
Avani Victoria Falls Resort (see 1)
Royal Livingstone (see 2)
3 Squire's Grillhouse & Action Bar

behind you and illuminates the Falls, or in the late afternoon when you may catch a stunning sunset. If you visit when the river is at its lowest, towards the end of the dry season, then the channels on the Zambian side may have dried up. Yet, while the Falls will be less spectacular then, their fascinating geology, normally obscured by spray, is revealed. In recent years, the diversion of water to generate power has been curtailed so the flow of water is more constant, and there is generally some water flowing over the edge on the Zambian side.

The main path leads along the cliff opposite the Falls, then across the swaying knife-edge bridge, via scenic points, photo stops and a good vantage point from which to watch bungee jumpers. This finishes at the farthest west of the Zambian viewpoints.

A third path descends right down to the water's edge at the Boiling Pot, which is used as a raft launch-site during the main rafting season. It is a beautiful (but steep) hike down, first navigating big cement steps, then through palm-fringed forest and finally scrambling over boulders, but well worth the long, hot climb back as long as you have good footwear. Take a picnic and relax by the river if you've time (and if you notice a smell of urine, it's probably from the monkeys!).

Viewing the Falls by moonlight (*US$25 pp*) is possible for four days at full moon, including two days before and one day after. Watch for a lunar rainbow at this time, too; it's an amazing sight. It's best not to go alone, as elephants occasionally wander about.

If you are touring on your own a helpful starting point is the small information centre or **field museum**, directly across from the Falls entrance, which provides a good overview of the origins of Victoria Falls. The museum is packed full of informative exhibits and interesting photos covering the area's fascinating geology, archaeology and history, complete with an excavation right in the middle. Knowledgeable guides are on hand to answer questions, or you can explore at your leisure. Snacks and cold drinks are available in the shop next door.

While you can easily explore on your own, most tour operators offer excellent guided tours of the Falls (both Zimbabwe and Zambia sides) and the surrounding area, either stand-alone or in combination with historical, cultural, game-viewing and other sightseeing tours. These are highly informative with professional guides offering detailed explanations of the formation of the Falls and gorges, the river, local history and flora and fauna. Tours cost around US$25–35 per person, including entrance fees.

From the Zimbabwean side *(entry US$30 pp; gate ⊕ summer 06.00–18.00, winter 06.30–18.00 daily)* Viewing the Falls is more regulated here. The entrance to the Falls can be reached via paths from the Victoria Falls Hotel, the Kingdom Hotel and just opposite Ilala Lodge. There is a small ticket booth and display at the entrance gate, which is a few hundred metres from the Zimbabwean border post. Tickets are valid for the whole day, so you can return for no extra cost during the same day. There's also a car park for self drivers too. Be prepared, however, for the mandatory hassle of generally pleasant but very persistent vendors and 'guides' along the way. Perhaps the easiest way to organise to see the Falls is through a tour operator, who will arrange visas and transfers as well as entry fees. Alternatively, make an afternoon of it and have tea at the Victoria Falls Hotel. Visiting in the afternoon, when the angle of the sun offers the best views, is ideal.

If you're planning to visit independently, allow at least half a day to clear customs at the border *(06.00–22.00)* and explore the Zimbabwe side of the Falls, as well as the town of Victoria Falls itself. The introduction of the KAZA Visa has standardised the cost of a visa for both Zambia and Zimbabwe to US$50 for citizens of 40 countries including many European countries, America, Canada and Australia. As well as negating the need to buy two separate visas, and thus reducing the cost of visiting the two countries, it has also helped to streamline the process of crossing the border, and it now rarely takes more than half an hour to clear both customs posts.

Technically this area is within the Victoria Falls National Park – and you will find a map of the paths at the entrance. Start at the western end, by Livingstone's statue – inscribed with 'Explorer, Missionary and Liberator', and overlooking the Devil's Cataract.

Visiting the viewpoints in order, next is the Cataract View. If water levels are low, and the spray not too strong, after clambering down quite a steep stairway you will be greeted by views along the canyon of the Falls. Climbing back up, wander from one viewpoint to the next, eastwards, and you will eventually reach the slippery-smooth rocks at Danger Point.

Few of these viewpoints have anything more than brushwood fences and low railings to guard the edges – so going close to the edge is not for those who suffer from vertigo. Viewing the Falls by moonlight is possible by special arrangement.

If you are keen to visit the Town of Victoria Falls it's just a short taxi ride away. Taxis are readily available from the border post and car park opposite the Falls, and the one-way trip into the town centre should cost you US$5–10, depending on your willingness to haggle.

LIVINGSTONE ISLAND (*Prices inc transfers & park fees: breakfast US$95; lunch US$155; afternoon tea US$130*) Livingstone Island (also known as Namakabwa Island) lies in the middle of the great waterfall, and is the island from which Dr Livingstone first viewed the Falls. Trips are run exclusively by Tongabezi (pages 167–8) between July and March (subject to water levels), with guests transferred to the island from the Royal Livingstone launch site by boat. There you'll have the opportunity to take in the scene – gazing over the edge, perhaps chancing a thrilling dip in the Devil's Pool right on the Falls edge, and having a gourmet meal in an exclusive setting. Several trips are offered daily; choose either morning (called 'breezer'), with a full English breakfast, gourmet lunch, or afternoon high tea with a full bar and hors d'oeuvres.

When the water's at its lowest, around October and November, you can sometimes walk across the top of the Falls, climbing over rocks, exploring pot-holes and crossing small streams along the way – it's even possible to swim at the very edge of the Falls at the right time of year. These activities are now permitted only if booked through Tongabezi. (Aside from the fact that the island is private, there is a risk of being stuck on top of the Falls should water levels unexpectedly rise. If you were to attempt the walk alone, you would almost certainly be turned back by ZAWA scouts.)

RIVER CRUISES Floating on the Upper Zambezi with a glass in one hand, and a pair of binoculars in the other, is still a pleasant way to watch the sun go down, even if nowadays booze-cruise boats operate round the clock (you can choose from breakfast, lunch, sunset or dinner cruises), and sometimes all congregate close together. Whatever type of boat you choose, taking a gentle look around the Zambezi's islands, surrounded by national parks on both sides of the river, is one of the region's highlights.

African Queen [154 B4] (*US$65 pp b/fast, mid morning or lunch cruise, US$75 pp sunset cruise; all inc open bar & a meal or canapés*) On the Zambian side, surely the most elegant and leisurely way to experience the river is aboard the *African Queen* or its sister boat, the *African Princess*. These old-style double-decker riverboats complete with gleaming brass cruise regally upriver from their dock on the aptly named but sadly dilapidated Royal Mile. (The name is derived directly from royalty, for it was from here that George VI and his entourage took a launch onto the river during their visit in 1947. Today it is known more prosaically as Sichonga Road.) In the rarified atmosphere on board, guests sip cocktails or soft drinks to the rhythmic accompaniment of xylophones, or marimba, that sound the vessel's imminent departure. As the boat makes its stately way upstream, you may spot the odd hippo, crocodile or elephant – or even, if you're very lucky, a white rhino – not to mention numerous birds. Such luxury doesn't come cheap, but the price includes an open bar (with a charge for premium and imported brands) and a substantial finger buffet. Breakfast, lunch and dinner cruises are also available.

Lady Livingstone [154 B4] (*SafPar Sunset US$75 pp, inc drinks & snacks, exc park fees US$10; b/fast cruise US$75; lunch cruise US$80 pp*) Based at David Livingstone Safari Lodge, the Lady Livingstone takes up to 144 passengers on three decks. While it is similar in design to the *African Queen*, it's clearly more modern. The bar is at one end, giving the passengers more room to circulate, and the choice of drinks is generally wider than on its rival. Snacks are served as three courses during the course of the cruise, ending with 'delicious chocolate truffles' and brownies. The most popular excursion is the 2–2½-hour sunset cruise, departing between 16.00 and 16.30, but there are also lunch and breakfast cruises.

Other boats (*US$50 pp; SafPar dinner cruise US$55*) On the Zambian side, smaller craft plying the same route are organised by Victoria Falls River Safaris, Safari Par Excellence and Taonga Safaris. All have an open bar and are generally popular with backpackers. Typically cruises last around 2½ hours. Most of the lodges along the upper stretches of the Zambezi offer boat cruises away from the crowded waters near the falls, usually as one of their inclusive activities. Here you can cruise in solitude, taking in the scenery, prolific birdlife and wildlife along the banks of the Zambezi National Park. Hippos, elephants and crocodiles are commonly seen as well as waterbuck, bushbuck and even buffalo.

Victoria Falls River Safaris uses specialised propeller-free aluminium boats, which can get within 200m of the Falls, and to stretches of the Zambezi unreachable by other boats (*US$100 pp, min 2 passengers*).

FISHING EXCURSIONS (*Angle Zambia: US$145/295 ½/full day inc lunch; multi-day trips on request*) Among the angling fraternity, the Zambezi River is synonymous with great fishing for prized tigerfish and Zambezi bream. If you dream of hooking a 'tiger' then a memorable day on the river with a knowledgeable guide can help make it come true. Angle Zambia, with their excellent local knowledge and friendly, personalised service, has been in operation since 2000 and is highly recommended. Owner-operated by Gerard and Viv Simpson, it runs half- and full-day fishing trips on the Upper Zambezi, about 30km from Livingstone. Catering to both novice and experienced anglers as well as fly-fishermen, the company has three 6m aluminium boats complete with fish finders, sunshades and radio communications to their base. Trips include fishing tackle, boat hire, fuel, transfers, a qualified guide and refreshments.

ROYAL LIVINGSTONE EXPRESS (*Bushtracks; dep winter 16.30, summer 17.00 Wed & Sat, or other days if demand is high enough; US$170 pp, inc transfers, dinner & drinks; not recommended for children under 12*) The whistle of a steam loco rarely fails to stir a frisson of excitement, and Livingstone's foray into steam has proved a considerable success since its inaugural journey in late 2007. A joint venture between Bushtracks and Sun International, the train brings Zambia's railway history to life. It is pulled by one of two locomotives, the first of which – the 10th class *Princess of Mulobezi*, built in Glasgow in 1924 for Rhodesian Railways – until recently took pride of place in Livingstone's Railway Museum. The second, Loco 204, is a 12th-class locomotive originally built in 1924. Both have been restored with meticulous attention to detail by Ben Costa, a Zimbabwean railway engineer with a passion for the iron horse, the locos and attendant wooden carriages are polished until they gleam. Many of the train's staff have the railways in their blood, some tracing their railway ancestry back three or more generations.

The train starts its 15km journey in a purpose-built station next to the Bushtracks office, getting up steam as it passes excited children and families gathering for the evening meal, heading to the Victoria Falls Bridge in time to witness the sun set behind the falls. Wine, beer and soft drinks are served in air-conditioned comfort, with a cash bar on board for those who prefer spirits. Large windows, as well as an observation car, ensure good visibility for all, with game such as elephants and antelope often spotted en route to the bridge. For a photo opportunity of the train itself the best time is at the Palm Grove Run Around, where passengers are able to disembark and watch as the locomotive detaches itself from the front of the train and attached itself to the opposite end. After a 20-minute sundowner on the bridge itself, an unhurried five-course dinner is served as the train makes its way back towards

Livingstone, prepared and served by staff from the Royal Livingstone Hotel, in an atmosphere enhanced by soft lighting and classical music. The train no longer runs scheduled journeys through Mosi-oa-Tunya National Park on the Mulobzi Line, but this can still be arranged on non-scheduled days for a minimum of 30 people.

CULTURAL ATTRACTIONS AND TOURS

Museums Given its fascinating history, it is no surprise that Livingstone has several good museums. The main Livingstone Museum is the most important of these, and certainly one of the best in the country.

Tours (1½hrs, inc entry fees & transfers, US$47 pp Bushtracks) can be organised to visit the Livingstone Museum or the Railway Museum, or both. Although you can readily visit on your own, an organised tour is an easy alternative, especially as part of a full day's sightseeing trip, with transfer included.

Livingstone Museum [158 B2] (*Mosi-oa-Tunya Rd; US$5/2 adult/child. ⊕ 09.00–16.30 daily*) In a prime position in the centre of town, Livingstone's main museum more than justifies a visit. To start with, there's an excellent three-dimensional map showing how the Zambezi River flows over Victoria Falls and downstream into the gorges, which puts everything into good perspective. There are several galleries focusing on the origins of humans in Zambia, the history of man in the country up to the modern age, the natural history of the area and an impressive gallery on traditional village life including a life-size village household. Watch out, too, for the David Livingstone gallery, with a unique collection of the famous explorer's personal possessions, including many of his letters: it's a must.

The museum often has special exhibitions, including an interesting comparison of traditional villages to modern towns. Sculpture and paintings by Zambian artists are also displayed and available for sale, as are local handicrafts and curios. The staff are friendly and knowledgeable and guided tours are included.

Railway Museum [159 A8] (*National Heritage Conservation Commission; Chishimba Falls Rd; US$20/10 pp adult/child; ⊕ 08.30–16.30 daily*) Located on the site of the Zambezi Saw Mills, this collection of beautifully preserved old steam locomotives and memorabilia, and displays on railway history, originally belonged to the artist David Shepherd. It celebrates the iron horse's history in Livingstone since the 3ft 6in narrow-gauge railway was built by the British in 1905. Sadly a serious fire took its toll on the collections, and the museum building itself is looking a bit rundown, but the engines themselves are in good condition, and will be of interest to railway buffs. Fortunately, the 1924 10th Class 156 out of Glasgow that used to take pride of place has now been put to work hauling the *Royal Livingstone Express* (page 192). There is also a small but informative Jewish museum on the site.

Field Museum [map, page 189] Directly across from the entrance gate to Victoria Falls, next to the curio market, this is signed as an information centre, but is more of a small interpretation centre. It's well worth a visit for an understanding of the geology, archaeology and history of the Falls.

Markets Livingstone has many colourful local markets. In addition to the large and fascinating Maramba Market [off map, 158 G4], there is also Porters' Market, further north [off map, 158 G2]. For something smaller and closer to town, try Zimbabwe, Central or Town Centre Market (take your pick of the names!), down the road from Shoprite and next to the minibus station [158 B2].

At the heart of Livingstone's community, these markets offer everything from fresh produce to second-hand clothes (called *salaula*), from hand-fashioned metal pots to live chickens, from *chitenjes* (the traditional African cloth) to hand-crafted wood furniture and more. A company called Bushtracks runs 1½-hr **market tours** (*US$35 pp*).

Craft markets Just inside the Zambian border, by the entrance to the Falls, is an outstanding curio market [map, page 189]. The carvers and traders come mostly from Mukuni village, though the goods come from as far as the Democratic Republic of Congo and Malawi. In town itself there's Mukuni Park Curio Market [158 E3] (⊕ *06.00–20.00 daily*), where local artisans, craftsmen and traders sell their wares from newly constructed permanent stalls along the edge of the park. Both of these are excellent places to buy wood and stone carvings, handicrafts, chessboards, masks, drums, baskets and the like, and are open during daylight hours throughout the week. There are usually about 20 or 30 individual traders, laying out their wares separately, and competing with one another for your business. The best buys are *makenge* baskets (these come exclusively from Zambia's Western Province), malachite and heavy wood carvings: hippos, elephants, rhinos, giraffes and smaller statues, often made out of excellent-quality, heavy wood. However, do consider the ethics of encouraging any further exploitation of hardwoods. Note, too, that some wooden items, especially wooden salad bowls and tall giraffes, are prone to cracking once you get them home due to changes in climate, and that very rarely are 'antiques' sold at craft markets anything other than fakes. Unless you have the expertise to tell the difference, it's better to buy such artefacts from a reputable shop in town.

Vendors will vie hard for your attention, and you can expect to bargain hard, hearing all sorts of prefabricated stories as to why you should pay more. When you start to pay, you will realise how sophisticated the traders are about their currency conversions, reminding you to double-check any exchange rates. Traders will accept most currencies and sometimes credit cards.

For something rather less demanding, there's an ad-hoc craft and curio market in the car park at the Falls Park shopping centre [154 C3]. Buying items from street traders, however, is illegal, so stick to the designated markets.

Village visits (*Mukuni Village: Bushtracks US$40, SafPar US$50.*) While some of the lodges organise independent visits to local villages for their guests, there are also several organised trips to different locations. Most popular among these is **Mukuni village,** a settlement of about 7,000 Leya people to the east of the Falls. An organised tour here, lasting around 2½ hours, will give you a glimpse of how local people live and work in a traditional setting along with informative explanations. You can visit local huts, view villagers at work, watch curio making and even sample traditional beer and food. However, Mukuni village, with its proximity to the Falls and popularity with tour operators, relies heavily on the tourist trade, so tends towards a commercial, rather than authentic, feel, with often relentless though friendly pressure to buy curios made there.

Some operators organise less commercial tours which involve clients going to smaller villages, perhaps visiting local markets to buy food which they then prepare in the village and eat with the locals while having some language lessons (and of course a walk around the village).

Further afield is **Songwe village**, about a 40-minute drive through the bush, and less commercial as it receives fewer tourists. The Livingstone Quad Company also offers guided quadbike excursions to villages and the bush (page 187). Alternatively, if your heart is set on a more remote village off the beaten path and you have the time, Bwaato Adventures offer a day trip some 45km upriver to one of the rural villages along the Zambezi.

Simonga village (m 0977 870548; *overnight K75 pp FBA, exc transport; day visitor K20; ⊙ all day*) This traditional village some 15km from Livingstone has been welcoming day visitors since 2001, with three traditional huts renovated for tourist accommodation. During a tour of the village, a guide will explain about daily life: culture, housing, agriculture, water supply and medical care. You can see the basic school, watch cultural performances and visit the traditional healer, as well as meet the head lady. For those staying overnight, traditional food is served at breakfast, lunch and dinner, and the village has its own water supply.

To get there from Livingstone, go to Mingongo station along the Kanzungula Road (*taxi around K15*), then hitchhike or take a minibus/taxi to the turn off for Simonga Basic School. The fare should be K5, though *mzungus* may be asked to pay double or more; stand firm! A taxi all the way from Livingstone will cost K30–40. In the village ask for Aston or the head lady, Inonge.

Historical tour of Livingstone (*Bushtracks 1½hrs US$35 pp; Wild Side 2½ hrs US$60 pp*) Livingstone, the capital of Northern Rhodesia from 1907 to 1935, has a fascinating history marked by many old historical buildings and accented by colourful characters, intriguing tales and a once-vibrant social life. A guided historical tour through town – on foot and by vehicle – will trace the town's history from frontier town to modern-day tourist capital, including the first hospital, school, library, churches, sports clubs, shopping districts, the old North Western Hotel and other historical sites.

African heritage tour (*Bushtracks ½ day; US$137 pp, inc park fees & bottled water, min 4 people*) Dubbed the 'Mists of Time' tour, this trip takes in the Victoria Falls and one of the local villages. In the hands of Russell Gammon, whose family history in Africa dates back to the 19th century, the aim is to bring these sites to life through the stories of those who have left their mark on Livingstone over the years.

Music and dance The opportunity to see local dance theatre is offered by the Livingstone Performing Arts Foundation (\ 0977 371700; e *lipafzm@yahoo. com; www.lipaf.org*). The group's *Dancing Around Zambia* (*US$20*) is performed regularly at Avani (pages 175–6) and features traditional dancing and drumming in a celebration of Zambia's diverse culture, although they are always coming up with new shows. For details of performances and venues, contact them direct.

SPORTS AND SPAS Many of Livingstone's hotels and lodges have small gyms or even tennis courts for their guests to use, or trained massage therapists on hand, but some facilities are open to all, and are worthy of specific mention. The Zambezi River Regatta is sporadically held in the area, with alumni from Oxford and Cambridge rowing teams taking part alongside prestigious universities from Zimbabwe, South Africa and the USA, with the last race taking place in 2013.

Polocrosse Not surprisingly in a town with such a rich colonial history, horseriding is popular locally. Polocrosse is a fast-paced mix of polo and lacrosse that Zambia excels at, even participating in the 2011 World Cup in England. The home of the Livingstone Polocrosse Club is a little way out of town at Chundukwa

River Lodge (page 169), whose stables house many of the club's horses. Lodge owner Doug Evans is also a Zambian National Polocrosse Coach, and has coached for the world cup. During the season, which runs from April to September, the sport attracts a good following locally.

Golf The Livingstone Royal Golf and Country Club [159 G6] (✆ *0213 320440; green fees US$15/30 9/18 holes; caddy fees US$5/18 holes; club hire (left- & right-handed) US$10),* established in 1908, was once a popular social and sports club, complete with tennis and lawn bowling. Re-opened in 2006, it is the second-oldest golf club in Zambia and designated as a national monument. To get to the club from the centre of town, turn onto Akapelwa Street, cross the railway line, turn left at the junction towards the central police station, and then immediately right. Follow the signs.

Once visited by royalty and the site of many tournaments, the club fell into a state of disrepair, but both the course and the clubhouse have now been fully renovated. The 18 holes of the par-72, 6,205m parkland-type golf course have been entirely re-landscaped, the fairways and greens replanted with Bermuda and hybrid Bermuda grass, respectively. The clubhouse itself was renovated with great care to preserve its teak woodwork and many historical features, and the result speaks for itself – a stunning colonial-style building with restaurant and bar, in a genteel setting in the heart of Livingstone.

The club also houses an excellent **gym and fitness centre** with personal trainer in residence. For the kids there are a trampoline, boules and a wooden climbing frame with swings. A training swimming pool was completed in 2009 and two lawn tennis courts are planned for the future. Both members and non-members are welcome to play a round of golf, enjoy a meal in the clubhouse, or simply relax, drink in hand, on its sweeping veranda.

Massages and pampering With accommodation from backpacking hostels such as Jollyboys and Fawlty Towers, to top-end lodges like Sussi & Chuma and Toka Leya opening their own spas, it's never been easier to get relief from the exhaustion from all the sightseeing, shopping and adventure activities. Some of the better spas that welcome walk-in guests are detailed below.

Royal Spa [map, page 189] Royal Livingstone Hotel; m 0978 777044/45/46/47; e zambia. reservations@suninternational.com; ⊕ 10.00–19.00 Mon–Fri, 08.00–19.00 Sat–Sun. If your idea of the ultimate massage is in a billowing white tent on the banks of the Zambezi with spray from the Falls & hippos as backdrop, then this is the place to go. It offers diverse riverside massages in stylish tented gazebos, each with 1 side open to the river & 2 massage beds. Such divine pampering isn't cheap: expect to pay upwards of US$122 pp. Also available within the salon itself are all the usual spa services: manicures, pedicures, facials, waxing, basic hair

care & beauty products, all catering to foreign visitors & priced accordingly.
David Livingstone Safari Lodge & Spa [154 B4] ✆0213 324601; e camelot@dsllandspa. com; ⊕ 09.00–20.00 daily. Up there with the best – & the most expensive.
Salon Namel [154 C3] Falls Park; ✆0213 324272; e namelslodge@zamnet.zm. This more affordable salon offers hair & beauty care including massages, manicures, pedicures, facials, haircuts, etc. Despite the rather plain & uninspiring design, the services are generally good & offer value for money.

THRILLS AND SPILLS The Falls area is indisputably *the* adventure capital of southern Africa. There is an amazing and seemingly endless variety of ways to get your shot of adrenalin: white-water rafting, canoeing, bungee jumping, kayaking, abseiling, gorge swinging, riverboarding or simply a flight over the Falls.

None comes cheaply. Most are upwards of US$100 per activity, which adds up quickly. If you wish to do multiple activities, check out the many combination packages on offer. These can be slightly cheaper than booking individually. There are also choices of operator for most of these, so if you book locally, shop around to find something that suits you before you decide. Prices won't vary much, but you will find the true range of what's available. Whatever you plan, expect to sign an indemnity form before your activity starts.

On the Zambian side there is a single cable car at Rapid 25 to bring clients out of the gorge after rafting trips, with the cost included in the activity price.

Flight of Angels Named after Livingstone's famous comment, 'Flight of Angels' describes any sightseeing trip over the Falls by microlight or helicopter. This is a good way to get a feel for the geography of the area, and is surprisingly worthwhile if you really want to appreciate the Falls. If you're arriving from Kasane, or leaving for there, consider combining a sightseeing flight and an air transfer. Otherwise any of these trips can be readily booked by agents in the area.

Microlight ([154 B4] *Batoka Sky Adventures US$170 pp/15 mins, US$340/½hr, inc transfers from Livingstone & Victoria Falls town; weight limit 100kg unless notified in advance*) This is a totally different experience from a light aircraft: essentially sightseeing from a propeller-powered armchair 500m above the ground; it's the closest you can come to soaring like a bird over the Falls.

Microlights take only one passenger plus the pilot. Because the passenger sits next to the propeller, cameras cannot be carried for safety reasons. However, for US$20 you can arrange to be photographed above the Falls from a camera fixed to the wing. Flights are operated out of Batoka Sky's Maramba Aerodrome and within five minutes are over the Zambezi. A 15-minute flight takes in a circle over the Falls and the islands in the river. The longer flight then continues upstream before crossing over the national park. Microlights are affected by the slightest turbulence, so if you book in advance, it's best to specify early morning or late afternoon, when conditions are ideal.

Helicopter (*Typically US$180/250/360 pp for 15/22/30 mins, inc transfers from either Livingstone or Victoria Falls*) This is the most expensive way to see the Falls, but it is tremendous fun. A 15-minute trip takes in the Falls and the national park. Longer trips, lasting between 22 and 30 minutes, will also include a sweep down into the Batoka Gorge, flying down the river just above the rapids. The 30-minute trip also passes over local villages and the town of Victoria Falls on the Zimbabwe side, or some aerial game viewing over Mosi-oa-Tunya National Park. At extra cost, you can stop in the gorge at Rapid 22, 'Bobo Camp', for a 1- or 2-hour picnic (min six people). Alternatively, if you plan to raft, riverboard or ride a jet boat, you can get an exhilarating lift out of the gorge by helicopter – at extra cost of course, but including a scenic flight over the Falls and Zambezi gorges. Flights are operated by United Air Charters, in four- and six-seater helicopters from the aptly named Baobab Ridge just south of town, and Batoka Sky, based at the Maramba Aerodrome, in three-, four- or six-seater craft. All are designed to give each passenger a good view, though it's difficult to guarantee the best view at the window seats as passengers are placed in the helicopter according to weight and balance safety requirements. Note that Batoka Sky will fly with just two people.

Bungee jumping (*US$160 per jump; no refund if you change your mind. Min age 14, but under-18s require attendance of parent or guardian & their signature on the indemnity form. Min/max client weight 40/120kg (88/265lb). ⊕ 9.30–17.00, or from 10.00 at high water due to spray from Falls*) There's only one company organising bungee jumping: African Extreme, part of Shearwater Adventures and an offshoot of the original New Zealand pioneers, Kiwi Extreme. Solo or tandem, you jump from the middle of the main bridge between Zambia and Zimbabwe, where the Zambezi is 111m below you. It is among the highest commercial bungee jumps in the world, and not for the nervous.

You can book in advance, either direct or through a tour operator, or simply turn up at the bridge and pay there. There's a bar on site, and digital photos and videos of your jump are available.

Bridge walks (*US$65 pp 1½ hour tour, min 2 people*) There's no-one better positioned to show you the ins and outs – no, make that ups and downs – of the Victoria Falls Bridge than the bungee folks, whose intimate bridge knowledge will not only fascinate you but have you clambering around and underneath the bridge like a monkey. With safety harness on and accompanied by guide, you have the opportunity to explore the bridge's superstructure while hearing all about its construction and riveting history. While not as adrenalin-charged as bungee jumping, it's still bound to get your heart beating faster as you navigate your way high above the Zambezi.

Abseiling, high-wiring, gorge swing and slide (*Abseil Zambia US$140/160 pp ½/full day, inc insurance, transfers, drinks & snacks. Gorge swing only US$120/95 dbl/sgl. Flying fox or cable slide only US$55. Shearwater Adventures swing/tandem swing US$160/205; slide/tandem slide US$45/70; 'big air experience' US$210*) A very popular addition to the adventure menu is the Zambezi swing, a cable swing set across the gorge which, together with a 90m-high cable slide (flying fox), abseiling (rappelling) and 'rap' jumps (rappelling forwards) down the side of the gorge, offers daring fun for all ages. These are currently offered by both Abseil Zambia at the top of the fifth gorge on the Zambian side, and Shearwater Adventures from their site on the bridge (see above).

At Abseil Zambia, the swing is a fixed 135m cable spanning the gorge. Participants are harnessed to ropes attached to the cable's sliding pulley and, after stepping off the cliff face, experience a heart-stopping 53m, three-second free-fall, followed by an exhilarating pendulum-like swing across the gorge, accelerating up to 140km/h (with a pull of roughly 2.5 times gravity) for some two minutes before being lowered to the ground. Described by participants as 'even more thrilling than bungee jumping', it's definitely not for the faint-hearted, though participants as young as eight and as old as 76 have braved it. It's even possible to try it out in tandem.

A slightly tamer alternative is the high wire or flying fox, set on another static cable stretched across the gorge. With harness and pulley, you leap off a platform and 'fly' (slide) across the gorge some 90m above the ground. It can be done in either a sitting or a flying position, and is suitable for children.

Except for the flying fox, be prepared to hike some 30 minutes out of the gorge after each go.

A full day's activity allows you to go up, down and over the gorge to your heart's content. Lunch, beer and cool drinks are included and sundowners are offered. Videos or disks of your activities are available at extra cost. It's also possible to spend just a half day, or to do any activities on their own.

The site is 5km from the Falls. If you're driving yourself, turn off the main road to the Falls just before the Avani Victoria Falls Resort, and follow the signposts.

Canoeing on the Upper Zambezi *(Canoeing US$116/140 ½/full day inc b/fast or lunch; overnight US$215, floating US$50, elephant encounter US$155; min age 12)* Canoeing down the Upper Zambezi is a cool occupation on hot days, and the best way to explore the upper river, its islands and channels. Zimbabwe's Zambezi National Park stretches all along the western shore providing ample opportunity for game viewing, while lodges, farms, villages and bush dot the Zambian side as you head downstream to the upper reaches of the Mosi-oa-Tunya National Park. The silence of canoes makes them ideal for floating up to antelope drinking, elephants feeding or crocodiles basking. Birdlife is prolific – you may hear the cry of the African fish eagle or see pied kingfishers hover and dive. The large number of hippos that call this stretch of the river home can provide excitement, but the river is wide and you need to show them respect by giving them plenty of space. If you follow the instructions of your guide they shouldn't cause you any problems.

A variety of options is available, from half- to full-day excursions, combo canoeing and game drives, and even overnight camping trips with the evening spent under the stars. You'll find any of them generally relaxing, although paddling becomes a bit more strenuous if it's windy. All canoe trips are accompanied by a licensed river guide, and sometimes also a motorboat for additional safety. Canoes range from two-seater open-decked kayaks to inflatable 'crocodiles'.

There are some sections of choppy water if you'd like a little more excitement, though it's possible to avoid most of these easily if you wish. Trips concentrating on these shouldn't be confused with the white-water rafting beneath the Falls (below).

For those who'd like the experience but don't want to paddle, canoe operators also run guided 'float' trips known as the Livingstone Drift on the Upper Zambezi. Participants can paddle when they feel like it or simply float downstream on a raft.

No prior canoeing experience is necessary, and once you are used to the water, the better guides will encourage you to concentrate on the wildlife. Lunch is typically served on an island. Trips are run by Makora Quest, Bundu Adventures and Safari Par Excellence, with the latter two also running float trips using rafts. At Tongabezi, canoeing for guests is included in the rates. SafPar offers an 'Elephant Encounter' trip combining a half-day canoeing safari, riverside brunch and an opportunity to interact with their elephants used for elephant-back safaris. A further option is a half-day's canoeing (or floating) followed by lunch and a drive in the game park.

White-water rafting The Zambezi below the Falls is one of the world's most renowned stretches of white water. It was the venue for the 1995 World Rafting Championships, and rafting is now very big business here, with keen competition for tourist dollars. (About 50,000 people now go down the river every year, paying about US$160–180 each. You can do the sums.)

Experienced rafters grade rivers from I to VI, according to difficulty. Elsewhere in the world, a normal view of this scale would be:

- Class I   No rapids, flat water.
- Class II   Easy rapids, a float trip. No rafting experience required.
- Class III   Intermediate to advanced rapids. No rafting experience required.
- Class IV   Very difficult rapids. Prior rafting experience highly recommended. No children.

- Class V   For experts only. High chance of flips or swims. No children or beginners.
- Class VI   Impossible to run.

The rapids below the Falls are mostly graded IV and V. This isn't surprising when you realise that all the water coming slowly down the Zambezi's 1.7km width is being squeezed through rocky gorges that are often just 50–60m wide.

Fortunately for the rafting companies, most of the rapids here may be very large, but the vast majority of them are not 'technical' to run. This means that they don't need skill to manoeuvre the boat while it is within the rapids, they just require the rafts to be positioned properly before entering each rapid. Hence, despite the grading of these rapids, they allow absolute beginners into virtually all of the rafts. That said, you should think very carefully about committing yourself if you have no experience. Boats do flip over, and the consequences can be severe. It's also important to ensure that your chosen operator will give a thorough safety briefing before departure, explaining what to do in the event of a capsize.

High or low water, and which side of the river? Rafting is offered from both Zambia and Zimbabwe by a wide range of companies.

From July to January, when the water is low, full- or half-day trips leave from the Boiling Pot just below the Falls: a spectacular start to the day. This period, when the river's waves and troughs (or 'drops') are more pronounced, is probably the best time to experience the Zambezi's full glory.

In high-water months (February to July), only half-day trips are offered, starting below Rapid 9 on both sides of the river. Note that when the river is highest its rapids may seem less dramatic, but it is more dangerous, due to the strong whirlpools and undercurrents. If the water is too high, rafting is suspended until it recedes to a safer level.

The trips A typical rafting trip will start with a briefing, covering safety/health issues, giving the plan for the day and answering any questions. Once you reach the 'put-in' at the river, you will be given a short safety/practice session to familiarise yourself with the raft, techniques and commands that will be used to run the rapids. Half-day trips typically run from rapid 1 to 10 in the morning (the more extreme of the rapids), and 11 to 25 in the afternoon, which are of a lower grade (II-IV) and therefore slightly less challenging. A full day's rafting is needed to get all the way from rapid 1 to 25. Lunch and cool drinks are included. It's also possible to organise a multi-day trip of between one and five days with SafPar.

The climb up and out of the gorge at the end of the trip can be steep and tiring, especially in hot weather, but on the Zambian side, a cable car at Rapid 25 has made this a thing of the past – albeit at a price (though the cost of the lift is included in SafPar's rates). Alternatively, most companies offer a heli–raft combo, whereby you can opt to fly out instead at additional cost. Beyond the obvious advantage of 'taking the easy way out', the heli flight is an exhilarating end to an exciting day, zipping you out of the gorge with a bird's-eye view of the rapids you've just run and the Falls as well.

A trained river guide pilots every raft, but you need to decide whether you want to go in an oar boat or in a paddle boat. In an oar boat expect to cling on for dear life, and throw your weight around the raft on demand – but nothing more. Oar boats are generally easier and safer because you rely on the skills of the oarsmen to negotiate the rapids, and you can hang onto the raft at all times.

Only occasionally will you have to 'highside' (throw your weight forward) when punching through a big wave.

In a paddle boat the participants provide the power by paddling, while a trained rafting guide positions the boat and yells out commands instructing you what to do. You'll have to listen, and also paddle like crazy through the rapids, remembering when and if you are supposed to be paddling. You can't just hang on! In paddle boats you are an active participant and thus are largely responsible for how successfully you run the rapids. The rafting guide calls commands and positions the boat, but then it's up to you. If your fellow paddlers are not up to it, then expect a difficult ride. Paddle boats have a higher tendency to flip and/or have 'swimmers' (someone thrown out of the boat).

Originally, only oar boats were run on the Zambezi. However, nowadays paddle boats have become more popular as rafting companies compete to outdo each other in offering the most exciting rides. There is, of course, a very fine line between striving to be more exciting, and actually becoming more dangerous.

With either option, remember that people often fall out and rafts do capsize. Trips are always accompanied by a number of safety kayaks though, and safety records are usually cited as excellent. Serious injuries are said to be uncommon and fatalities rare.

Rafting operators (*US$160/180 pp ½/full day inc transfers & gorge lift or cable car at Rapid 25 if appropriate; min age 15*) All rafting companies offer broadly similar experiences. To gain a competitive edge, some now offer freebies like dinner and sundowners in their prices, so it's well worth asking around and comparing what's included, as this changes from time to time. The rapids are numbered from 1 to 25, starting from the Boiling Pot, so it's easy to make a rough comparison of the trips on offer.

Zambian operators include Bundu Adventures and Safari Par Excellence. Special options include breakfast, lunch, sundowners and barbecue dinner. All offer videos and photos of your trip at a rather extortionate additional cost. A shorter, three-hour trip from rapids 1 to 7 is also available through Bundu Adventures, at US$138 per person.

In addition to day trips, there are four day expeditions as far as the proposed Batoka Gorge Dam site, while seven-day expeditions reach the mouth of the Matetsi River. These offer more than the adrenalin of white water, and are the best way to see the remote Batoka Gorge, though trips are few and far between.

Riverboarding (*US$68 pp; riverboard & raft combo US$190/220 half/full day pp inc transfers, light b/fast, lunch & sundowner; min age 15*) For a more up-close and personal encounter with the Zambezi rapids, adrenalin junkies can try their hand at riverboarding (also known as boogie-boarding) or combo riverboarding and rafting. After donning your fins, lifejacket and helmet, you and your foam board (the size of a small surfboard) will have an opportunity to 'surf' the big waves of the Zambezi, after being taught basic skills in a calmer section of the river. A raft accompanies each trip and takes you downstream to the best spots of the day. Here you can try finding the best 'standing waves' where you can stay still and surf as the water rushes beneath you. Experts can stand, but most will surf on their stomachs. It's thrilling for the fit who swim strongly, but not for the faint of heart. Trips are offered by both Bundu Adventures and Safari Par Excellence.

White-water kayaking (*Kayak the Zambezi: experienced kayakers US$100/180 pp ½/full day, inc lunch & transfers; tandem US$185 pp*) Yet another option for white-water enthusiasts is kayaking in the gorge. Those without experience can try tandem kayaking in Topolino Duo kayaks; a qualified guide sits in the back, piloting and manoeuvring the kayak through rapids, while you sit in front and assist with paddle power. In all cases you must be a confident swimmer; kayaks, smaller and lighter than rafts, may capsize in bigger rapids, and although your guide will attempt to right it by executing an 'Eskimo roll', you (and your guide) may have to swim the rest of the rapid.

There are also four-day courses for experienced kayakers and fully outfitted multi-day expeditions by special arrangement.

Jet boating *(Jet Extreme US$116 pp, inc transfers, drinks & cable car.)* Another adrenaline activity on the river, but on the flatter sections of water between rapids 23 and 27. Undertaken in a 22-seater, 700-horsepower jet boat, the trip up and down the river reaches speeds of up to 90km/h, with 30 minutes of sharp turns and swift navigation of the small rapids ensuring that all occupants of the boat get suitably wet. The trip also includes a tour of Mukuni village on the way to the activity, as well as the 8-minute, 220m trip down into the gorge, and back out again at the end.

WILDLIFE ENCOUNTERS
Mosi-oa-Tunya National Park *(Park entry US$10 (self drive US$15) pp/day; vehicle US$15/day; guided game drive US$50 pp; game walk US$80 pp)* Much of the Zambian area around the Falls is protected within the Mosi-oa-Tunya National Park, until 2009 the smallest national park in Zambia, which now has a fenced off area of 66km². The original area, about half this size and known as 'the game park', lies in the middle, and this is where walks and game drives take place. The newer area stretches along the river in both directions. Visitors can also see the cemetery at Old Drift, the site of Livingstone's first settlement.

Getting there and around You can drive yourself around easily, or go with one of the many operators (pages 186–8) who run 4x4 trips into the park. The three lodges inside the park – Toka Leya, Sussi & Chuma and Thorntree River Lodge – also offer their guests guided drives or walks from the lodge. For the more adventurous there are 3-hour walking safaris, led by licensed safari guides from Livingstone Walking Safaris (*US$80*). Beyond the excitement of tracking game on foot, these are an excellent way to learn about the flora and fauna. The best time to go for birds is early in the morning, but walks also take place in the afternoon.

Flora and fauna The park boasts tracts of riverine vegetation, dry mixed woodland and mopane trees. A few hours' driving could yield sightings of most of the common antelope and some fine giraffe, as well as buffalo, elephant and zebra. Although outside of the historical range of the white rhino, several attempts have been made to establish a population in the park. The first attempts failed due to poaching, but the latest attempt, with the introduction of four individuals from South Africa, appears to have been successful, with several new calves bringing the population up to seven in 2015. Always protected by armed rangers, they can sometimes be spotted from game drives, but a rhino walk with Livingstone Walking Safaris (*US$80*) will give you a much better chance of a sighting, and a much closer experience. Even wild dog are present: a pack recently crossed the river from Zimbabwe. There are, however, no lion, leopard or other cats present.

For birdlife, see below.

Birdwatching Birdwatching isn't normally regarded as an adrenalin sport, but with the outstanding avifauna to be found in and around the Falls, serious 'twitchers' might disagree.

Even the casual visitor with little interest will often see fish eagles, Egyptian geese, lots of kingfishers, numerous different bee-eaters, Hadeda and sacred ibis, and various other storks, egrets and herons. Meanwhile, avid twitchers will be seeking the more elusive birds like the rare Taita falcon, as Batoka Gorge is one of the best sites to look for them. Rock pratincoles have almost as restricted a distribution (just following the Zambezi), but can often be seen here balancing on boulders by the water's edge and hawking for insects, while African skimmers can be found nesting upon sandy shores of islands. Look in the riverine forest around the Falls and you may spot a collared palm thrush rummaging around; again, these are really quite rare birds recorded in only a few areas. In contrast, African finfoot occur throughout sub-Saharan Africa, but are always shy. They prefer slow water, overhung with leafy branches, and they find the upper sections of the Zambezi perfect, so are often seen there if you look when it's quiet. Back on land, keep an eye out for birds of prey; on a recent visit, a martial eagle was spotted surveying our early-morning walk from on high.

Birdwatching excursions are an offered activity at many of the lodges along the river, often included in the nightly rate. Experienced guides can take you out either on foot or on the river. Alternatively, you can arrange to go out with a member of Bird Watch Zambia, formerly known as the Zambian Ornithological Society (*US$50; \0211 239420; e birdwatch.zambia@gmail.com; www.birdwatchzambia.com.*)

Elephant riding (*SafPar: US$165 pp ½ day inc light snacks & drinks plus US$10 park fees; no children under 10*) Zambezi Elephant Trails, based at Thorntree River Lodge, offer the only elephant-back safaris in Zambia. Here you and your *nduna* (elephant guide) will ride African elephants through the bush and along the river in the upper reaches of the Mosi-oa-Tunya National Park, where you may encounter a variety of game. In addition to the hour-long ride, guests are encouraged to interact with the elephants close up.

We are assured that all the elephants were originally orphaned, or were born to individuals already used for the encounters. We are also assured that the elephants are comfortable around people, and have been trained with positive reinforcement methods as opposed to the controversial methods associated with Asian elephants – we have no reason not to believe this.

Horseriding and horse-drawn carriages (*1½ hr ride US$60; ½ day with lunch US$110; full-day ride with lunch US$160; overnight ride inc drinks & meals US$350*) Riding along the Zambezi and through the bush is a wonderful way to experience nature up close. Trips for all levels are offered by Ride Zambezi, using horses from the stables at Chundukwa River Lodge where the thoroughbred horses are used either for local polocrosse teams or the riding trails along the Zambezi and through the national park. Trips can last a few hours (including a champagne breakfast or a picnic lunch), the whole day, or over several days, stopping to sleep under the stars on the banks of the river. There are also pony trails led by a guide on foot close to the stables for younger children. Hard hats are supplied and are mandatory.

Victoria Carriage Company also offers half- and full-day horse rides in the park and along the river, and also more sedate transport in the form of Victorian horse-drawn carriages, which depart every half an hour from the Royal Livingstone and make a tour around the Sun International complex near the Falls.

Livingstone Reptile Park ([154 C4] *Gwembe Safaris: entry US$15/10 adult/child.* ☺ *All year*) Just to the south of Livingstone, the Reptile Park (still signposted 'Livingstone Crocodile Park') offers the opportunity to see some huge crocs at close quarters – from behind the safety of a chain-link fence or from covered walkways – and to get some great photographs. Well-informed and friendly guides offer explanations about the behaviour and history of the animals, and feeding times (usually early afternoon) are posted at the entrance. The park plays a valuable role in

THE ETHICS OF WALKING WITH LIONS

There are now several operations in Africa which offer visitors the opportunity to pay to touch, stroke and walk with baby lions. All cite their 'projects' as part of larger conservation initiatives to 'save lions', some with the backing of charities (often small charities, very closely linked with the projects). The problem with this for conservationists is two-fold: first, what happens to the cubs when they grow older; and second, are these projects really doing valuable conservation work?

WHAT HAPPENS TO ALL THE BABY LIONS? When lion cubs reach about 18 months old, they become too large and dangerous to be mixed with people. Lions typically live for about 16 years in the wild and up to 25 in captivity. If they have spent time as cubs mixing with people, then they cannot be released into an unfenced area, because sooner or later they'd probably come across local villagers – and with no fear of humans they'd be likely to kill.

Most of Africa's national parks and really wild areas are unfenced. It doesn't take much to do the maths and estimate the number of adult lions that each of these projects will produce every year. These will all need to be housed in fenced areas stocked with game for them to eat. Many conservationists claim that there just aren't enough such areas, and they point out that 'lions breed like rabbits' when given the right conditions.

Considerable controversy was stirred up by a *Sunday Times* article by Chris Haslam in February 2008 entitled 'African lion encounters: a bloody con'. This looked at one such operation and alleged that, once adult, the original lion cubs were likely to be used for 'canned hunting' on farms in South Africa. The paper was unable to prove that farms in South Africa which had received lions from the project in question had definitely used the lions for canned hunting, and hence issued a retraction. However, you only have to search the internet to realise that there's great debate over the ethics of such operations.

VALUABLE CONSERVATION? Many leading lion conservationists question if there is any conservation value at all in most of these projects.

They argue that habitat destruction and human encroachment are the real conservation issues that need to be addressed for conserving Africa's lions, and observe that there is little evidence of these commercial operations doing any meaningful work of this type. They also question the wisdom of randomly mixing lion populations, which risks introducing deleterious genes or diseases into established lion populations.

So I'd urge you to think carefully about the ethics of your actions and to try to look beyond the fine words of the commercial concerns involved. Your few hours of fun may come at a hefty price.

the local community, capturing and housing snakes and crocodiles that could pose a danger to the public, and also running education trips with visiting groups from local schools and the wider community learning about these dangerous creatures, and in many cases developing a new-found respect for them. Picnic tables are set in the landscaped grounds and there's a café serving the park's signature 'Croc Bite'. The park also features some of Zambia's snakes, housed in glass cages. It, hopefully, will be your only chance to see Africa's most dangerous snakes – black mamba, cobra, puff adder – up close and personal; you can even hold the 'safe' snakes to get a feel for them. There is also an activity centre here where visitors can book any of a wide range of activities or go on one of Gwembe's game drives in the Mosi-oa-Tunya National Park (in which case you get free entrance to the Reptile Park).

Walking with lions (*SafPar Lion Encounter: US$150 pp ½ day, inc transfers within Livingstone, b/fast or snacks, drinks; exc US$10 park fees; 1¼ hr walks at 06.15 & 15.00; min age 15; min height 1.5m. Mukuni Big 5 Safaris: US$120 pp/½ day, inc transfers within Livingstone*) For visitors, the appeal of this encounter is the opportunity to walk with lion cubs, which are bred specially for the programme. Clearly this is very appealing to some people and is also unusual. (See box opposite for more on the controversy surrounding this activity.) Mukuni also offers the chance to walk with cheetah and visit their 'research centre'.

OTHER ACTIVITIES
Quadbikes (*Eco Trail US$80; village trail US$140, inc transfers. Other destinations & tailormade trips also available*) Guided quadbike (four-wheel motorbike) excursions are operated by the Livingstone Quad Company. Choose from a 1-hour 'eco-trail' at Batoka Land (starting at Maramba Aerodrome), consisting of 17ha in and around the unfenced portion of the national park, or a 2-hour trip venturing out into the bush to explore African villages and the landscape by the Zambezi gorges. Participants are given an introduction and a chance to practise before heading out on the trail of their choice.

Segway tours (e *victoriafalls@bushtracksafrica.com; general tour US$52, falls tour US$60, sundowner tour US$42, multi-terrain tour US$58, all pp*) If your idea of fun is to glide along laid-out trails to observe wildlife such as giraffe, baboons, zebra, impala and monkeys, this is for you. No experience is necessary, since coaches are on hand to teach the basics of riding the two-wheeled, stand-on segway. Operated by Bushtracks on Sun International property.

SAFARIS AROUND THE FALLS AREA

Livingstone is well placed for day trip safaris, both in Zambia's Mosi oa Tunya National Park (see above) and in Victoria Falls and Zambezi national parks across the river in Zimbabwe.

If you are seeking a four- or five-day excursion from the Falls area, there are several superb game parks within easy reach. Some of the local operators (pages 186–8) run trips from Livingstone, and for backpackers there are usually a few operators running buses or trucks to Windhoek, Maun or even Harare. Like cut-down overland trips, these often stop at parks on the way.

VICTORIA FALLS NATIONAL PARK, ZIMBABWE Like the northern side of the river, a good section of Zimbabwe's land around the Falls is protected – though only the rainforest area, criss-crossed by footpaths to viewing points, is actually fenced off. If you are feeling adventurous, then follow the riverbank upstream from Livingstone's statue. (If the gate is closed beyond the statue, then retrace your steps out of the entrance to the rainforest; and turn right, then right again, down Zambezi Drive, to reach the outside of that gate.)

This path runs next to Zambezi Drive for a while. After almost 2km, Zambezi Drive leaves the river and turns back towards town, passing a famous baobab tree called the Big Tree. From there the path continues for about 8km upstream until it reaches A'Zambezi River Lodge, just outside the gate to the Zambezi National Park. This is a very beautiful, wild walk but, despite its innocent air, you are as likely to meet hippo, elephant or buffalo here as in any other national park. So take great care as you admire the view across the river. You may also want to plan ahead and arrange a pick-up from A'Zambezi back into town, or alternatively just ask the hotel on arrival.

ZAMBEZI NATIONAL PARK, ZIMBABWE This park borders the Zambezi River, starting about 6km from Victoria Falls and extending about 40km upstream. You cannot walk here (without a professional guide), so you need a vehicle, but there are several Zimbabwean operators running morning and afternoon drives through the park who will collect you from any of the main hotels.

The park is actually bisected by the main road from Victoria Falls to Kazungula/Kasane (which has long been an unlikely, but favourite, spot for sightings of wild dogs). Better game viewing is to be had from the roads designed for it: the Zambezi River Drive, or the Chamabondo Drive.

The former is easily reached by driving out of town along Park Way, past the Elephant Hills Hotel and the Victoria Falls Safari Lodge. This road follows the river's course almost to the end of the park, and there are plenty of loop roads to explore away from the river.

The Chamabondo Drive has a separate entrance on the road to Bulawayo. Take a right turn just before the road crosses the Massive River, about 7km out of town. This leads past several pans and hides until it terminates at Nook Pan, from where you must retrace your steps as there are no loop roads.

The park has good populations of elephant, buffalo and antelope – especially notable are the graceful sable which thrive here. The riverfront is beautiful, lined with classic stands of tall winterthorn trees, *Acacia albida*. Note that when wet this park is often impossible to drive through in a 2WD, and when dry some of the roads remain in poor condition.

KAFUE NATIONAL PARK, ZAMBIA Geographically speaking, the southern side of Kafue is quite close to Livingstone, but the practicalities of getting to the park are trickier than they look. The area is remote and relatively underdeveloped, and it can take 4½ hours just to reach the park gate, and another 2 hours along weather-dependent roads to reach the first lodge. To get here you will need a fully kitted 4x4, a GPS and some off-road driving experience, or the help of a local tour operator. This is not a day trip from Livingstone. For details, see *Chapter 14*.

CHOBE NATIONAL PARK, BOTSWANA This is often suggested as a day trip from the Falls, but is really too far to be worthwhile. (You end up arriving after the best of the morning's game viewing is finished, and leaving before the afternoon cools down sufficiently for the game to re-appear!) However, the Chobe riverfront, around Serondela, probably has higher wildlife densities than any of the other parks mentioned here. So if you can cope with the sheer number of vehicles there, it may be worth a trip for a few days. Its luxurious lodges (and high park fees) mean that northern Chobe is always expensive. In spite of that, day trips with some of the major operators are extremely popular. A typical trip with Wild Side (*US$180 pp*) will incorporate a game drive, boat cruise and lunch at one of the hotels. Bushtracks includes a morning riverboat on the Chobe River, with an afternoon game drive (*US$195 pp*). Longer trips are also available. Jollyboys offers a full-day excursion (*US$160 pp*) which includes all transfers, a light breakfast, lunch and a game drive and boat cruise along the river.

There are regular transfers between Victoria Falls and Kasane (in Botswana, beside the park) which take around 2 hours. Then stay at Chobe Game Lodge, Chobe Chilwero or Elephant Valley Lodge – the three lodges in that section of the park. Either can easily be arranged by a good tour operator before you arrive, or by a travel agent in Livingstone. The lodges in Kasane, outside the park, don't compare (though Impalila Island Lodge or Ichingo Chobe River Lodge on the opposite bank of the river are little-known options that are both excellent value, and cheaper).

Alternatively, if you have a good 4x4 then you can drive yourself around and (advance reservations essential) camp at the basic, unfenced site at Ihaha. Take all your food and equipment with you, and watch for the baboons.

HWANGE NATIONAL PARK, ZIMBABWE Zimbabwe's flagship national park has three established public camps that provide excellent value, basic accommodation and camping. It also has several more basic camping spots at picnic sites.

Alternatively there are a few more expensive private lodges in the park, most of them towards the south side of the park's road network in an area of Kalahari sandveld.

CHIZARIRA NATIONAL PARK, ZIMBABWE One of Zimbabwe's wildest and least visited parks, Chizarira requires patience, lots of driving skill, and a 4x4 – and that's just to get there. Unfortunately this isolated and cash-starved park was hit heavily by poaching, and the wildlife is now scarce and skittish, but the wilderness experience is excellent.

There are no lodges operating in the area, but there are a number of campsites that can be used as self-driving bases, although you will need to bring all your own supplies, including water. Alternatively, Leon Varley and his team run walking safaris here and have been doing so for years. They're a first-class operation.

KAZUMA PAN NATIONAL PARK, ZIMBABWE This small, little-visited national park borders Botswana between the Zambezi and Hwange national parks. It is used for walking safaris more than for driving, though the environment is very different. It consists of a huge, almost flat depression – a grass-covered pan surrounded by forests that are dominated by the familiar mopane and teak trees.

Only a few groups are allowed into the park at any time, each requiring a fully licensed walking guide – which effectively limits access to organised operators.

KAYUBE ESTATE *Zambezi River*

Your 'Out of Africa' Dream

karien.kermer@outlook.com
www.kayubezambeziriverhouse.com
+260 978 323726

Victoria Falls – Zambia

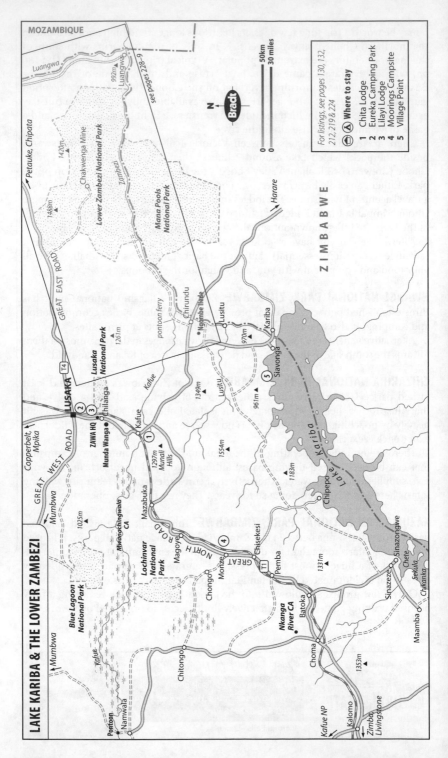

LAKE KARIBA & THE LOWER ZAMBEZI

MOZAMBIQUE

see pages 228–9

0   50km
0   30 miles

N
Bradt

Where to stay

For listings, see pages 130, 132, 212, 219 & 224

1 Chita Lodge
2 Eureka Camping Park
3 Lilayi Lodge
4 Moorings Campsite
5 Village Point

ZIMBABWE

Luangwa

Lower Zambezi National Park

Mana Pools National Park

992m

1420m

1488m

Chakwenga Mine

Zambezi

Petauke, Chipata

Harare

GREAT EAST ROAD

Chirundu

pontoon ferry

Ngombe Ilede

Lusitu

Kariba

970m

Siavonga

5

961m

Lake Kariba

1183m

Chipepo

Sinazongwe

Chete

Sekula

Chikanka

Maamba

Zimba, Livingstone

Kalomo

Kafue NP

1353m

Choma

Batoka

Nkanga River CA

Pemba

1331m

Chisekesi

T1

Monze

4

Chongo

Magoye

GREAT NORTH ROAD

Chitongo

Namwala

Pontoon

Kafue

Blue Loon National Park

1025m

Lochinvar National Park

Mwanachingwala CA

Mumbwa

Mazabuka

1297m

Munali Hills

1554m

Lusitu

1349m

Kafue

Kafue

1

Munda Wanga

ZAWA HQ

Chilanga

LUSAKA

2
3

Lusaka National Park

1261m

Lusitu

Lusitu

T4

Copperbelt, Mpika

GREAT WEST ROAD

Mumbwa

9

Lake Kariba and the Lower Zambezi

Zambia's border with Zimbabwe is defined by the course of the Zambezi as it slowly meanders towards the Indian Ocean. Below the Victoria Falls, it flows east, sometimes northeast, and today's biggest features of this river are artificial: Lake Kariba, between Zambia and Zimbabwe, and Lake Cabora Bassa, in Mozambique.

Zambia's attractions on Lake Kariba are limited to a few islands in the lake, accessed from Sinazongwe, and perhaps Siavonga, which is a pleasant place to relax. Of the islands, Chete is large enough to be a credible wilderness destination with some good wildlife on it, but its lodge has been closed for some years. Chikanka, however, remains accessible to those on a mid-range budget. Below the wall of Kariba Dam, the Zambezi continues through the hot, low-lying Lower Zambezi Valley amid some of the best game viewing in the country. On both sides of the river – Zambian and Zimbabwean – are important national parks. This is also the place to canoe down one of the world's great rivers, whilst game spotting and avoiding the hippos.

FROM LIVINGSTONE TO LUSAKA

(see also map *Southern Zambia*, page 150)
This main tar road is only 473km, but it seems longer. Despite its many sections that are faultlessly smooth, particularly as far as Mazabuka, there are some rough patches to negotiate, and speed humps in the towns, so allow about 6 or 7 hours for the journey if you're driving yourself, and stick to a safe 80km/h or so. Better still, stop along the way and explore, including Choma's small museum on your list. If you've more time, then detour to Sinazongwe and on to one of Kariba's islands.

Those brave few hitchhikers will find it one of the easiest roads in the country: lots of towns, regularly spaced, and plenty of traffic. The buses are frequent if you get stuck.

Here I've arranged a few brief comments on what you'll find if you're heading towards Lusaka from Livingstone. If you're planning to stop overnight, your best bets are in Chomba or Mazabuka or – even if you don't have your own camping gear – the super Moorings Campsite (page 212).

ZIMBA Zimba is the first town reached from Livingstone, after about 76km. It's around 397km to Lusaka and really notable only for a large local market close to the main road. Aside from a post office, a church and a few small shops, there's little else to detain you here.

KALOMO This small town, about 126km from Livingstone and 347km from Lusaka, marks the turn-off from the main road towards the Dumdumwenze gate into the southern section of Kafue National Park. The turning is clearly signposted. See pages 436–8, for details of this route, and note that a 4x4 is essential to drive in the park.

There's a **fuel** station (✦ KAFUEL 17°01.673'S, 26°29.259'E) on the main road, just south of the Kafue turn-off, but don't bank on it; fuel may not always be available. There are also branches of both Barclays and Finance **banks**, the former with an ATM, plus a district hospital, a chemist, and Catholic and Anglican churches. Should you need somewhere to stay, there's an old hotel set back from the main road, and a couple of small guesthouses.

Excursions from Kalomo

Administrator's House (*US$5/3 adult/child*) Some 6km from the tar road, between the centre of Kalomo and its main suburb/township, this national monument dates to around 1903–04. It was built for the Administrator of Northwestern Rhodesia, as appointed by the British South Africa Company. Then Kalomo was the 'capital' of the territory, and the house is said to be the first non-traditional brick house built in Northern Rhodesia.

Kalundu Mound About 3km north of Kalomo, on the main road, is a slightly raised mound of earth (a matter of just a few metres) through which the road passes. This marks the site of an Iron-Age village, and the mound is the accumulated debris of many centuries of occupation.

It was excavated in the late 1950s and early 1960s when the road was being built, and the archaeologists estimated that it might have been occupied as early as the 4th century AD, although it was certainly full of people from about AD800–1300. (Note that the occupants during this latter period are sometimes referred to by Zambian archaeologists as following the 'Kalomo Tradition'.)

CHOMA
Choma (✦ 16°48.547'S, 26°59.302'E) is another small, friendly town, about 285km from Lusaka and 188km from Livingstone. The main road between the two, here called Livingstone Road, runs through the centre of the town, and on (or just off) it you'll find all the amenities of small-town life: shops, market, cafés, post office, internet facilities, a couple of fuel stations, and branches of several major banks, as well as a good Spar supermarket. Perhaps more surprisingly, there's a super little museum (see page 211). North of the town, roadside craft stalls mingle with those of the charcoal sellers, and you may also see local fishermen touting their catch by waving it aggressively in the face of passing cars.

🏠 **Where to stay** Unfortunately, one of the better places to stay near Choma, Kozo Lodge, was destroyed by fire in October 2015, and it remains to be seen whether or not it will be rebuilt. Of the others, there's the New Choma Hotel (below) and numerous smaller guesthouses, including the following, all with similarly simple facilities: **Leon's Lodge** (*12 rooms;* ✆ *0213 220156;* **$$**); and **Crystal Lodge** (*17 rooms;* ✆ *0213 220271;* **$**) behind Barclays Bank.

With your own transport, you could also consider the lodge or campsite within Nkanga River Conservation Area (page 211).

🏠 **New Choma Hotel** (19 rooms) ✆ 0213 220836; m 0974 955286; e chomahotel@ gmail.com. In the centre of town, this helpful if uninspiring hotel with a restaurant, beer garden, & secure parking, is convenient for an overnight stop. Sgl, dbl & twin rooms have AC, TV & fridge. **$**

✗ **Where to eat** Meals and snacks are served at the museum and at the New Choma Hotel. Elsewhere, try Wonderbake behind Spar for fresh-baked goodies, or the supermarket itself for takeaway dishes.

What to see and do The popular Choma **Museum and Crafts Centre** (m *0979 323929;* e *chomamuseumartgallery.webbly; www.museumszambia.org/CHOMA_ MUSEUM.html;* ⊕ *08.00–17.00 daily; admission US$2/1 adult/child*) is on the main road through town. In addition to a collection of regional artefacts related to the Tonga people, the centre focuses on contemporary crafts and – to a lesser extent – art, showcasing the work of rural craftspeople throughout the area. There's a café on site, as well as a craft shop.

NKANGA RIVER CONSERVATION AREA (*Entry US$15 pp*) About 5km north of
Choma there's a signpost to Nkanga, 20km away on a dirt road; it is also easily reached on the tarred road from Namwala. Here you'll find a conservation area that incorporates three local farms, and protects antelope including sable, eland, puku, hartebeest, wildebeest, kudu, tsessebe and many other species. The area is also one of Zambia's important bird areas (IBA), with a total of 439 species noted. These include Zambia's only endemic bird, the Zambian (Chaplin's) barbet.

As it's a conservation area that sustainably manages its populations of native game, some hunting is also conducted, though this does not interfere with the photographic visitors. Visitors may not walk around the farm without first obtaining permission.

⌂ Where to stay

⌂ **Masuku Lodge** (6 rondavels) `0213 225225;` m 0966 763172; e bedrockafrica@ gmail.com; masukulodge@gmail.com, www. bedrockafrica.com. Overlooking a dam within the conservation area, Masuku Lodge is managed by Rory McDougall, a specialist birding guide who runs birding safaris throughout the country, & Doris Glasspool. Guests at the lodge stay in thatched, en-suite rondavels with twin beds, & dine at one table in a central lounge/dining area. The setting is particularly suited to birding, but much of the farm's game can be spotted during the summer months too, including sable, kudu, zebra, eland & bushbuck There are some good walks, & game drives (*US$20 pp*) can also be arranged for guests. *US$135 pp DBB, exc conservancy fee.* ⊕ *All year; advance booking essential.* **$$$**

Å **Nkanga River Conservation Area** (camping) `0213 225592;` m 0977 863873/ 766260; e nansaibm@gmail.com. In a separate riverbank location is a basic campsite, the domain of bushbuck, Cape clawless otter & countless birds. There's a communal shelter here, with firewood & the facility for BBQs, plus cold showers, toilets & electric lights. Note that it can become cold by the river, especially May–Jul, & do bring mosquito protection. Activities include guided game & birding walks, & fishing for bream & barbel. Nkanga also runs valuable educational bushcamps Apr–Oct for groups (min 14) of children aged 7–16, covering bush knowledge, skills & outdoor activities. *Camping US$15 pp, exc conservancy fee.* ⊕ *All year; advance booking essential.*

BATOKA Little more than a market-lined road with a small post office, Batoka is significant for visitors as the turn-off for Sinazongwe and Lake Kariba, which is signposted to the east of the road. It's almost the midway point between Livingstone (222km) and Lusaka (251km).

PEMBA Another small town, scarcely more than a dot on the map, Pemba is about 261km from Livingstone.

CHISEKESI The linear community of Chisekesi, 270km from Livingstone, boasts a useful fuel station. Just to the north is the **Mayfair Guesthouse**.

Chisekesi is the turn-off to Chipepo Harbour and some of the non-commercial Kariba islands, at a distance of 92km. This is one of the settlement areas of the Tonga people who were displaced when the dam was constructed (Siavonga/Lusitu is another).

After the dam was built, ZESCO was committed to restoring the road that connects Siavonga with Sinazongwe and southwest to Sianzovo with its amethyst mines and market, but this remains inconsistent and rough going in parts. (As an aside, stones have in the past been sold illegally here by Senegalese traders known as the Masenesene.) Beyond Sianzovo a rough road continues to Syagulula, and on a further 15km to Devil's Gorge. You'll need some large-scale maps of the area, but the scenery is rewarding. A similarly poor road connects Sianzovo market back to Kalomo.

MONZE Monze (MONZE ⊕ 16°15.436'S, 27°28.588'E) is another small town with little of note except a useful fuel station, but north of the town is an excellent spot to spend the night.

🏠 **Where to stay** *See map, page 208.*

⋏ Moorings Campsite (3 chalets, camping) m 0977 521352; e enquiries@ mooringscampsite.com; www.mooringscampsite. com. Clearly signposted to the east of the main road, about 11km north of Monze, this is probably the best place to camp between Livingstone & Lusaka. The campsite is set in a grassy field on a mixed 2,600ha farm, supplementing the income from cattle, maize & soya. The site is also well placed for Lochinvar National Park, about 2hrs' drive away. Do ask managers James & Kim about the birding; keen birders may spot the Zambian (Chaplin's) barbet here.

Campers pull up alongside one of a number of open-sided thatched rondavels that are dotted about the field, each with electric light & space for a large open fire, with wood available. You can hire a tent if you don't have your own, & for non-campers there are small, en-suite brick-built chalets, 1 suitable for a family. The ablution block is spotlessly clean & visitors may use the small

kitchen – with a limited menu available if you don't fancy cooking; there's also a large, airy bar area with plenty of chairs.

Visitors to the campsite are welcome to look around. Owner Thea Savory originally came to Monze from the Netherlands to work in the local hospital. Now she runs a medical clinic which is free for the farm's permanent workers & their families; other patients pay a small fee. The farm effectively has its own primary school, too, & partially funds secondary education.

Finally, there is the Malambo Women's Centre & Craft Shop, where local women come together to make & sell the quilts, cushion covers & other items. The centre is also home to adult education classes, with English lessons followed by a topic such as cookery or gardening. It all adds up to so much more than a campsite so it's well worth breaking your journey. *Camping US$8 pp (US$15 pp to include tent hire); chalet US$25/30 pp sharing/sgl. ⊕ All year.* **$$** *exc b/fast*

Excursions from Monze

Fort Monze *(Entry US$5/2 adult/child; vehicle US$5/day)* About 16km to the west of the town is the site of Fort Monze, which was one of the first police posts established in Zambia by the colonial powers. (Access is now only possible in the dry season, and the track is in very poor condition. It's signposted from town.) This post was founded in 1898 by the British South Africa police, led by Major Harding, who was subsequently buried in the cemetery here. The post was demolished soon after, in 1903, by which time the colonial authorities had a much firmer grip on the country. Now all that's left is a rather neglected graveyard and a monument in the shape of a cross.

Lochinvar National Park Lochinvar National Park, northeast of Monze, has been designated as a wetland of international importance for its very special environment. It's about 48km from Monze, and if you have an equipped 4x4 and some time to explore, then it could be worth a visit. See pages 451–3 for details.

MAZABUKA This large, bustling, tree-lined town, 349km from Livingstone and 124km from Lusaka (⊕ 15°51.489'S, 27°45.747'E), is at the centre of a very prosperous commercial-farming community. The huge Zambia Sugar company (locally referred to as the Nakambala Sugar Estates) dominates the area, and you'll see their fields of mono-culture sugarcane lining the main road either side of town.

Where to stay Although Mazabuka has a wide range of simple guesthouses there is little to choose between many of them. Among the larger and better-quality options are:

Lodge Benoni (15 rooms) Chachacha Rd; 0213 230784; m 0967 886769; e lodgebenoni@yahoo.com. To find this welcoming lodge, the former Linga Longa, pass Shoprite on your left, go over a crossroads & take the first right onto Chachacha Rd. En-suite rooms have AC, DSTV & fridge. Meals, including a cooked English b/fast, are available ($$). Outside, there's a shaded garden & secure parking. **$$**

Golden Pillow (11 rooms) Livingstone Rd; 0213 231026; e goldenpillowlodge@yahoo.co.uk. With en-suite rooms, AC, DSTV, fridge & tea/coffee facilities, this, too, is at the top of the hill – behind a small bus stop on the left as you travel to Lusaka. There is also a bar, restaurant & lounge with TV. **$–$$**

Where to eat Both the supermarkets have their own fast-food outlets and bakeries, and several other fast-food joints serve snacks and larger meals, too, among them a branch of the pizza chain **Debonairs**.

Other practicalities Along with Choma, Mazabuka is the most developed of the towns between Livingstone and Lusaka. Aside from a number of **fuel** stations, it has branches of several major **banks** with ATMs, a couple of **internet cafés** and a **pharmacy**. There is a major branch of **Shoprite** in the centre of town, and the **Kontola Hypermarket** on the roundabout leading from the town towards Livingstone. For vehicle spares, try Autoworld, also in the centre of town.

Around Mazabuka
Mwanachingwala Conservation Area This conservation area on the Kafue Flats, some 25km north of Mazabuka, covers about 470km² beside the Kafue River, northeast of Lochinvar, and just south of the river. It combines land contributed by the local community of Chief Mwanachingwala with some of the private commercial farms in the area, and is rich in birdlife. The area is also home to the Kafue lechwe and the shy sitatunga.

Those who make the journey are welcome to walk, fish, or hire a mokoro to explore the area's hidden lagoons. It may also be possible to meet Chief Mwanachingwala and to visit his village, or a large, semi-permanent fishing village. Any income generated in this way is ploughed back into the local community.

For access, in the dry season only, you'll need a 4x4. Head south of Mazabuka towards Livingstone for around 5km, then turn right on Ghana Road, cross the Kaleya Stream, then after 3km or so take another right to Etebe School. A further 3–4km brings you to a turn off to Mamba Fishing Camp; you're then on the Kafue Flats.

In theory, information about the area is available at the municipal offices in Mazabuka, near Shoprite, and this is where arrangements to visit should be made.

However, there's no guarantee that the office will be staffed, so be prepared to ask around and allow plenty of time.

MAZABUKA TO LUSAKA This final stretch of the journey between Livingstone and Lusaka covers a distance of 131km. Potholes come and go, so as always, it's best not to exceed 80km/h.

The road passes through the Munali Hills, where – 56km north of Mazabuka – there's a sign to **Munali Hills historic site**, a stone cairn 1km along the Munali Pass road commemorating Livingstone's passage through the hill pass that separates the Lusaka high plateau from the Kafue Flats. (Munali, meaning 'you have been' or 'you have passed through', was the nickname given to Livingstone.)

Further north, you come to the small town of **Kafue**, which is the turn-off to Chirundu and the Lower Zambezi, and to Siavonga on Lake Kariba. Look out at the junction for roadside stalls selling baskets, from small decorative items to large linen numbers. For details of this road and the town itself, see *From Lusaka to Chirundu*, pages 224–6.

The final 50km of the route, from Kafue to Lusaka, is fairly plain sailing as far as Chilonga, but from here the steadily increasing level of traffic spreading out from the capital has the potential to cause delays.

LAKE KARIBA

Lake Kariba was created by the construction of a huge dam, started in November 1956 and completed in June 1959. It was the largest dam of its time – 579m wide at its crest, 128m high, 13–26m thick – and designed to provide copious hydro-electric power for both Zimbabwe and Zambia. It was a huge undertaking that turned some 280km of the river into around 5,200km^2 of lake. It has six 100,000kW generators on the Zimbabwean side, and five on the Zambian side – although the electricity generated here is promptly sold to Zimbabwe. The total construction cost was £78 million.

In human terms, construction of the dam immediately displaced thousands of BaTonga villagers, on both sides of the border, and took the lives of 86 workers in the process – around 18 of whom are entombed within the dam's million cubic metres of cement. It has opened up new industries relying on the lake, just as it closed off many possibilities for exploiting the existing rich game areas in that section of the Zambezi Valley.

It inevitably drowned much wildlife, despite the efforts of Operation Noah to save and relocate some of the animals as the floodwaters rose. However, the lake is now home to rich fish and aquatic life, and several game reserves (and lodges) are thriving on its southern shores.

For the visitor, Zambia's side of the lake is less well developed than Zimbabwe's and lacks a national park. Only on its islands, Chete and Chikanka, will you find much game. However, the fishing is very good and the small resorts of Siavonga and Sinazongwe make pleasant places to relax, or to base yourself for outings onto the lake.

A commercial ferry (*www.karibaferries.com*) runs the length of the lake on the Zimbabwean side between Kariba and Mlibizi; otherwise the only way to go on the lake is rent a boat or houseboat, or to visit one of the islands (pages 219–20 and 222–4).

HEALTH AND SAFETY AROUND THE LAKE

Bilharzia Bilharzia is found in Lake Kariba, but only in certain parts. Unfortunately, it isn't possible to pinpoint its whereabouts exactly, but shallow, weedy areas that suit the host snail are likely to harbour the parasites; you're unlikely to contract bilharzia whilst in deep water in the middle of the lake.

See pages 85–6 for more detailed comments on this disease. Local people who engage in watersports consider it an occupational hazard, and are regularly treated to expel the parasites from their bodies (those who can afford the treatment, that is).

Animal dangers The lake contains good populations of crocodiles, and a few hippos. Both conspire to make bathing and swimming near the shore unsafe. However, it is generally considered safe to take quick dips in the middle of the lake – often tempting, given Lake Kariba's high temperatures and humidity. The crocodiles have apparently not yet learned how to catch water-skiers.

SIAVONGA
Approaching Siavonga
The road to Siavonga (⊕ 16°32.371'S, 28°42.545'E) leaves the main Lusaka–Chirundu road (pages 224–6) a few kilometres west of the Chirundu Bridge over the Zambezi. It's marked by a police checkpoint, and a motley selection of corrugated metal craft stalls. From that turn-off, it is some 71km of rolling tarred road to the roundabout in Siavonga, mostly through areas of subsistence farming. From Lusaka to Siavonga takes around 2½ hours. The area is relatively densely populated, largely the result of 'forced migration' when the dam was built and entire villages, such as Lusitu (⊕ 16°08.050'S, 28°44.329'E), which now lies along this road, were relocated. You can expect animals wandering over the road, so drive slowly. While straight after the rains this makes an attractive drive, enhanced by some marvellous ancient baobabs, during a visit I made at the end of the dry season, the problems of erosion and overgrazing seemed especially bad. Numerous gullies cut through the powdery red soil, there was little green grazing to be seen anywhere, and even the goats were looking thin. It is, though, a good route for roadside stalls – selling baskets in a range of sizes, as well as numerous pieces of quartz, for which you'll need to be prepared to bargain very hard. (And be aware, too, that some of these 'gemstones' are broken pieces of insulation glass.)

About 15km after the turning off the main road, there's a track to the left (⊕ 16°07.948'S, 28°44.290'E) leading to **Ngombe Ilede** (*US$15/7 adult/child; vehicle US$5/day*), some 13km away. Designated a national monument, the flat, square, sacred stone – the name translates 'the cow that is lying down' – lies in a stark landscape devoid of all but baobabs. More details can be found in D W Phillipson's book, *National Monuments of Zambia* (page 529).

Nearing Siavonga, the road winds its way around the hills in steep spirals, affording some superb views, before finally dropping down into the town, on the edge of Lake Kariba.

Like Kariba, its Zimbabwean neighbour over the dam, Siavonga has a strange layout as the result of being built on the upper sections of three or four hills – the lake's artificially created shore. What started out as a camp for the builders working on the dam in the 1950s eventually developed into a quiet holiday resort. There are a few things to do here, mainly focusing on the lake. The one thing that everyone should try is the local fresh fish (mainly *tilapia* bream) from the dam that is offered by all hotels and lodges.

Getting there and away
Minibuses ply the route between here and Lusaka each day, costing about K70 one way. Alternatively, you could take a minibus between Lusaka and Chirundu, then hitch from the junction.

According to legend, the name of Kariba should be *kariwa*, 'the trap', for long ago a lake behind the hills broke through and the violent torrent tore out the gorge; when the water subsided it left behind a massive stone slab, the *kariwa*, until it collapsed.

The real trapping of the river took place on 2 December 1958, when the peaceful course that the Zambezi had run for centuries was stopped in its stride. This was the day on which the gap in the wall was closed. Less than 100 years ago, the Kariba Gorge was considered an obstacle to river navigation, for in its 26km the river ran fast. In 1912, a district commissioner visiting from Southern Rhodesia (now Zimbabwe) reported on the potential dam site with a view to irrigation of the Zambezi Valley. Ten years later, it was suggested as a source of hydro-electric power but, as in 1912, there was no money available for this. By 1937 it was recognised that the potential of Zambia's copper mines could not be realised without cheap electrical power but it was only in 1951 that Kariba was recommended as a suitable site for the construction of a dam.

The project was dogged by controversy. A similar scheme had already been suggested on the Kafue River, but the experts backed Kariba as it was the bigger of the schemes. When the announcement was made in March 1955 that the dam was to be built at Kariba there was outrage north of the Zambezi where politicians called it the 'Great Betrayal'.

Finance for the dam, a total of £80 million, came from a variety of sources, including the World Bank, the Colonial Development Corporation, the British South Africa Company and the Rhodesian Federal Government. The closing date for tenders was 17 April 1956 and one tender arrived in Salisbury (now Harare) with only 10 minutes to spare – the aircraft with the courier from Italy had been delayed due to a technical fault. Three months later, the main contract for the construction of the dam and south-bank power station was awarded to an Italian firm – Impresit South Africa – at a value of over £25 million. Another Italian-controlled firm, Rhodesia Power Lines, was awarded the contract for the transmission lines at a value of nearly £10 million. The British companies that had tendered for the job were outraged.

Getting around The small town is quite spread out, and the roads curve incessantly, sticking to the sides of the hills on which the town is built. Each of the hotels is tucked away in a different little cove or inlet, and to get from one to another usually involves several kilometres of up-and-down, winding roads. So while you could walk everywhere, you'll find it much easier with your own transport.

Where to stay and eat Siavonga has a surprising amount of accommodation considering its size and relatively few attractions (though the lake itself is a powerful draw). The reason is its proximity to Lusaka – normally just 2½ hours' drive away – which makes it very convenient for conferences, the stock trade for almost all Siavonga's hotels. That, in turn, means that most of the hotels accept credit cards.

Because the town is used to the 'packaged' conference trade, check the rates for dinner, bed and breakfast, and full board, rather than just B&B; these are often good value, especially as there are no sparkling local restaurants to compete. On a quiet night, you can find a good bed at a reasonable price. Campers have less choice, but are well catered for at the refurbished Eagle's Rest, although those with their

One of the earliest contracts awarded, to Costain, was for the construction of Kariba township, where those involved in the building of the dam would live for the duration. Original estimates were that the township would take two years to complete, but this was cut down by a third. Work went on for 18 hours a day, seven days a week, with temperatures sitting at 43°C at 22.00 and 32°C at 05.00. Fitters took to carrying tools in buckets of water to prevent them becoming too hot. Houses, from foundations to door locks, were being completed at the rate of three every two days. A bank was built from start to finish in nine days.

The building of the dam was an outstanding engineering feat. A great river which could in the space of a few hours become a raging torrent had to be tamed; the site was remote with no roads leading to or from it; the gorge in which they had to work was narrow; and the temperatures and humidity were high. In November 1956, the first skip of concrete, two tons of it, was poured. This was only the first of nearly three million tons used in the wall – enough to pave a road from Zambia to Russia. On 22 June 1959 the last skip of concrete was released on the curve of the wall by the federal Prime Minister, Sir Roy Welensky – ten months ahead of schedule despite the floods of 1957 and 1958 when the Zambezi did its best to fight man's intentions.

Meanwhile virgin bush was being cleared to the north for the transmission lines – a job which was started in 1955 and was to take four years. The trees, which would be covered with water, were being pulled down and work was commencing on the south-bank power station. For those who worked at Kariba, they needed no references or testimonials – they only had to say 'I worked at Kariba' and the job was theirs. But there were human tragedies too – a number of people lost their lives during the construction of the dam; some are still buried within the wall. Eight of Chief Chipepo's people who were forcibly being moved to higher ground were killed during violent clashes with the police. And the human tragedies continue for those displaced people …

First published in The Lowdown, *January 2004*

own transport could consider heading out to Sandy Beach. On the lake, there are boats for hire by the day or for overnight excursions (pages 218–19).

To rent a **houseboat** on Lake Kariba, try Lake Kariba Inns or Eagle's Rest (see pages 218–9), or the specialist Lake Kariba Houseboats (+263 4291 2027; e *maureen@karibahouseboats.com; www.karibahouseboats.com*). As a taster, three of the many options are outlined below.

West of Siavonga, there are various simple lodges along the lake shore, reached by taking the turning to the west about 2km north of town (16°24.290'S, 28°43.763'E). It's a very rough track, for which a high-clearance vehicle is essential, and a 4x4 in the rainy season. For the more westerly lodges, it's more sensible to arrange a boat transfer with the lodge concerned than to drive yourself.

Lakeside
Lake Safari Lodge [map, page 218]
(70 rooms) 0211 511148; m 0978 659584; e lakesafari@gmail.com; www.lakesafari.com. This attractive hotel is perched on a headland

slightly above the lake, about 1km from Siavonga market. Rooms, spread out between the main building & a slipway into the water, come as standard or executive, & have a view of the lake or gardens. All are en suite with AC, fridge, kettle,

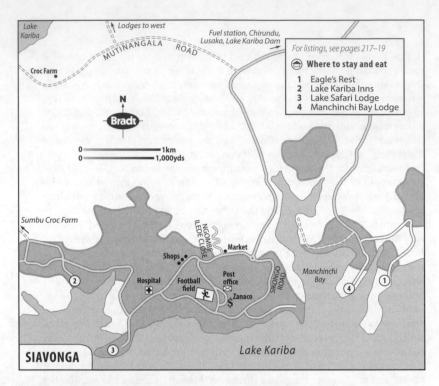

For listings, see pages 217–19

Where to stay and eat
1 Eagle's Rest
2 Lake Kariba Inns
3 Lake Safari Lodge
4 Manchinchi Bay Lodge

SIAVONGA

Lake Kariba

flat-screen TV & free Wi-Fi. Inside, the restaurant has an à-la-carte menu & buffet, & there's a late-night bar & lounge. For the energetic, the lodge has a gym & 2 excellent swimming pools. Several boats, moored at its own slipway, can be hired by the hour, from the open-topped 9-seater Bacardi (K350) to an 80-person pontoon boat, Rigi (K1,000), or you could try the faster 8-seater, Makali One (K1,500). $$$$

Lake Kariba Inns [map, page 218] (50 rooms) ☎0211 511249; m 0977 770480; e info@karibainns.com; www.karibainns.com. With its pleasant gardens that afford good views, & a range of facilities, the efficient Lake Kariba Inns is arguably the best of Siavonga's options, though it's often full of convention participants. All rooms have en-suite shower, AC, & cable TV, while in executive rooms you can expect a small entrance hall, space for 2 children's beds if needed, & a veranda – some overlooking the lake. There are also 7 villas with their own private pools. As an added bonus, zebra & impala roam the adjacent hill.

Along with a large bar & restaurant are 4 swimming pools & a gym. Guests may use these & the pedal boats free of charge, but other water-based activities, including boat trips, fishing & kapenta rig tours, are extra, as is the beauty salon. A steep set of stairs leads down to the water, many metres below, where the inn's pontoon boat, the 30-person Chipembere, & its houseboat, the Takamaka (page 219), are usually moored. $$$

Manchinchi Bay Lodge [map, page 218] (30 rooms) ☎0211 511218/511283; m 0955 849814, 0976 849814; e info@manchinbaylodge. com; http://manchinbaylodge.com. In its heyday, this was Siavonga's plushest place, with the best gardens in town thanks to its extensive manicured lawns, shrubby borders, & a main swimming pool with an adjacent shallow one for children. Then standards slipped & the place went to seed, but now, thanks to a new owner, it seems to be back on track. Sgl, twin & dbl rooms remain slightly dated, but all have been refurbished with en-suite shower, AC, DSTV, kettle & a veranda with a view of the lake. Dining is poolside or in their restaurant, & cruises on the Manchinchi MV is a great way to watch the sunset. $$$

Eagle's Rest [map, page 218] (12 chalets, camping) m 0967 688617, 0978 869126;

e info.eagles@siavonga-zambia.com (hotel), eagles@siavonga-zambia.com (boats); www. eaglesrestresort.com. Eagle's Rest is less than 10km from the Kariba Dam wall. To find it, turn left at the gate to Manchinchi Bay Lodge, & follow the winding road for about 1km. The only place in Siavonga itself to be geared more to tourists than to conferences, it has seen marked improvements in recent years. Each of its compact chalets has a dbl or twin beds, with some suited to families. AC, fridge & en-suite shower & toilet come as standard, as does a sheltered outside area for preparing food, with a sink, & a BBQ overlooking the bay. The adjacent tree-shaded campsite is beautifully located, with ablutions block & points for electricity & water, & 2-person tents to rent if you don't have your own (K100/night). There's a modest restaurant/bar for b/fast, lunch & evening meals ($$–$$$), but much nicer is the lively thatched beach bar. With its pool & beach volleyball the place is popular with families, who can also canoe on the lake (*K20 pp/hr*) or take part in dam wall cruises (*K550 up to 12 people*) & sunset cruises (*K750/12 people*). Boats can also be hired for fishing trips (*from K500/hr up to 4 people*), with fishing tackle available to rent. For houseboat cruises on the *Bateleur*, see opposite column. River canoe safaris & hikes can also be organised. *Chalet US$75 dbl B&B; camping K100 pp.* $$

Houseboats
▬▬▬ *Southern Belle* (22 cabins) Contact Lake Kariba Houseboats (page 217). The sweeping staircase from the central salon adds a touch of glamour to this 55m houseboat, based in Manchinchi Bay following a US$1 million refit in 2010. Dbl, twin & 1 trpl en-suite cabins boast AC & satellite TV. There's a separate restaurant, 2 bars, a conference room & a plunge pool with sunloungers on deck, & passengers can enjoy fishing trips, bush

walks & cultural tours. As well as lake cruises the boat is open as a restaurant when it's in harbour. Rates on application.
▬▬▬ *Takamaka* (8 berth) Contact Lake Kariba Inns (page 218). This 2-storey pontoon-style houseboat has 4 cabins sharing 2 bathrooms, a plunge pool, a bar (stocked on request), & the option of self-catering or fully catered accommodation. You'll be accompanied by a small crew, & a tender boat is brought along to allow for fishing expeditions & forays to the shore. *US$700/ night inc fuel; full board US$40 pp/day*
▬▬▬ *Bateleur* (10 berth) Contact Eagle's Rest (page 218). A relatively large boat offering overnight trips sleeping up to 10 passengers, 6 of them on the upper deck. *US$60–75 pp/day based on 10/8 passengers, plus US$40 pp/day for catering.*

West of Siavonga
⌂ **Village Point** [map, page 208] (4 chalets, 3 huts, camping) reservations ☏ +44 (0)1952 877163; m +44 (0)7582 472386; e sharonvlewis84@gmail.com; lodge m 0966 289005; e nessylewis@yahoo.co.uk. This upmarket lodge geared to more hedonistic bush lovers is set in 20ha on a peninsula in Lotri Bay, some 40km west of Siavonga. The transfer by speedboat takes about 30mins. Tall chalets are perched above the lake with an open-fronted upper storey under thatch to make the most of the breeze – & the views. For the more budget minded, there's Mango Grove, designed in the style of a Zambian village, with both dbl-bedded huts & a larger one containing 4 beds. There's also a campsite, & 2-man tents can be hired. Dinner is served outside under the stars. To balance the opportunities for fishing, walking & birding, the lodge prides itself on its village tours. *US$60 pp FB, exc drinks. Camping US$15, or US$30 with hired tent.* $$

Other practicalities Siavonga is quite a sleepy, relaxed place but it does have a **post office**, a few shops and a **Zanaco Bank** with an ATM. These, together with the civic centre (where you'll find the police station and a courtroom), form the 'town centre' which is perched on one of the hills. The fuel station here has closed, but there are two options close to the turn-off to Siavonga from Lusaka.

For **shopping**, a simple supermarket and a bakery stock the basics, while fresh produce can be found at one of the town's two markets.

What to see and do
On the lake Most of the activities in Siavonga revolve around the lake: boating, fishing and watersports such as windsurfing, tubing and waterskiing (though note

the comments on safety on pages 232–3). Canoeing trips are available through Eagle's Rest.

Lake cruises are offered by all the hotels and lodges, from around K60 per person, depending on the type of boat and the numbers on board. They are also able to organise longer boat trips, perhaps to do a spot of fishing, or to visit the dam wall.

Visiting the dam Lake cruises to visit the dam wall can be organised through various hotels, including Eagle's Rest. It's also possible for visitors to take a walk over the dam wall. If you have your own transport, simply present your passport to the customs office at the Zambian border post, then drive down the border road to the car park. From here, you can walk along the wall, enjoying an east–west view of lake and gorges, huge spillgates, and Zam and Zim's power stations.

Note that both Zimbabwe and Zambia are acutely aware of the vulnerability of the dam to damage or terrorist attack. So don't appear 'suspicious', and always ask before taking photographs – it may be just a wall to you, but it's of vital importance to them.

Kapenta rig tour Kapenta are small, sardine-like fish, similar to whitebait, that were introduced on commercial grounds into Kariba in the 1960s (see box,

THE FOOD OF THE PAINTED WOMEN   *Heather Chalcraft*

Fishing for kapenta (*Limnothrissa miodon*) is an important commercial enterprise on Lake Kariba, giving a living to a significant number of people around the lake. It first came to the towns and cities of Zambia from Lake Tanganyika, although as early as 1860 the explorer Richard Burton had described the use of circular nets lowered from a canoe to catch fish attracted by the light of an *mbaula* (a wood-fired brazier). Today, kapenta rigs have enormous lights on the surface and are fitted with the same circular nets, although they are much larger, and the lights are lowered into the water. The lights attract the fish and, when there are sufficient numbers, the net is lifted to the surface with the catch.

The possibility of introducing kapenta into Lake Kariba was considered as early as 1956, although the first experimental attempts began in 1952. Under the supervision of Dr George Coulter, Senior Fisheries Officer in the then Northern Rhodesia, a brood of sardine fry of the genus *Limnothrissa* was netted near Mpulungu and placed into two galvanised-iron transport tanks. They all died within 5 hours. A second method, whereby the fry were caught in a large polythene net and placed in polythene bags, resulted in a greater survival rate, although mortality was still high. However, some individual fry survived and were growing beyond the maximum transportation size, so a trial run to Kariba of 350 fry was attempted. These were transported by road to Abercorn (now Mbala) Airport, by air to Kariba Airport and by road to the lakeshore.

At Kariba, 7½ hours after capture, 45% of the fry had survived. Half of these were introduced immediately to a lakeside storage dam where they all died within a few minutes, possibly because of a difference in water temperatures. The next day only 14 of the original 350 were still alive. These were placed in a keep-net in the lake where they lived and grew for more than three months until a storm wrecked the net and the fry escaped into the lake. Albeit accidentally, the first introduction of sardines to Lake Kariba had taken place.

But it was still not known whether they would find conditions suitable for breeding, nor which of the two species involved would be the better. Investigations below). Since then, fishing for them has become an important new industry around the lake, in both Zimbabwe and Zambia. When dried, kapenta are tasty, high in protein, and very easy to transport: an ideal food in a country where poorer people often suffer from protein deficiency.

Look out over the lake at night and watch the fishing rigs use powerful lights to attract the fish into their deep nets. These are then brought back to shore in the early morning, sun-dried on open racks (easily smelled and seen), and packaged for sale. Short tours lasting a couple of hours in the early evening can be arranged to one of these rigs through the hotels in Siavonga, and you'll bring back fresh kapenta to eat.

Crocodile farms Siavonga boasts a couple of private crocodile farms, both open to the public: Kaliolio, located on the Mutinangala Road, and Kandilo, which is visited by Manchinchi Bay Lodge.

SINAZONGWE Zambia's second small town on Lake Kariba is roughly equidistant between Livingstone and Siavonga. It is a typical small Zambian town, originally built as the fishing and administrative centre for the southern lakeshore area, and is

were carried out and by September 1966 it was decided that *Limnothrissa miodon*, the larger, less specialised species, would be the one. *Limnothrissa miodon* was known to grow to 17cm in Lake Tanganyika and did not require such deep water for laying its eggs as the other species. Further experiments on the catching, handling, keeping and transportation of the sardines were undertaken until, in 1969, fish of varying sizes were caught in Lake Kariba and identified as kapenta, suggesting that they had not only survived but also bred in their new environment. The Kariba kapenta grew much smaller than the Tanganyika ones, reaching sexual maturity before a length of 5cm and rarely growing beyond 6cm.

The first attempts to catch the kapenta were made using banana boats, lights and scoop, and lift nets. The catches were not spectacular but large numbers of fish could be seen under the lights, and by the end of the first year some had been caught 64km east of Sinazongwe. It was not until 1976 that commercial fishing of kapenta started on the Rhodesian (Zimbabwean) side of the lake, followed by the Zambian side in the early 1980s, after Zimbabwe's independence. At night one can see the flickering lights across the dark waters of Lake Kariba. These are the fishing rigs at work. Catches are seasonal as during the summer months the kapenta move inshore to breed in protected bays. Commercial catches rise again after March when the adults return to open waters. However, if the rain has been poor, there is less food for them, which means poor harvests for fisherfolk (and for the fish and birds which feed on them).

But it is not only on Lake Kariba that man, fish and birds benefit from this 'silver gold'. These hardy little fish are sucked into the turbines and spewed into the stilling pool below the dam. They survive, only to fall prey to the hundreds of tern and kingfishers that are waiting for their dazed emergence at the dam's tailrace. Survivors have even made the 220km journey through a river devoid of plankton and infested with predators, to establish new shoals in Lake Cahora Bassa in Mozambique.

From an article first published in The Lowdown, *January 2004* used mainly as an outpost for kapenta fishing. Despite the town's location, its centre is actually up the hill away from the lake, with a couple of simple restaurants, a small hospital and the appropriately named Budget Guest House, while Sinazongwe post office is actually a couple of kilometres further inland, at Sinazeze.

When the lake was first flooded Sinazongwe was a much busier harbour, and even had the only lighthouse on the lake. Although its prosperity has faded somewhat, it is well placed to become the hub of operations for Zambian tourism to Lake Kariba, and its first campsite has now been developed into attractive self-catering chalets.

Getting there and away There's a good tar road from Batoka, signposted to Maamba Mines, on the main Lusaka–Livingstone road (30km northeast of Choma), to within 17km of Sinazongwe, and then the rest is a reasonable, all-weather gravel road. Hitching is certainly a possibility, and shouldn't be that difficult. Driving time to/from Lusaka is approximately 4 to 5 hours, or from Livingstone 3 to 4 hours.

Sinazongwe lies almost directly beneath the flight-path between Livingstone and the Lower Zambezi National Park – between which there are occasional direct charter fights. Organising a seat on these would be tricky, but may be possible; check with a knowledgeable tour operator.

Where to stay The closure of Kariba Bush Club in 2016 has left quite a gap in accommodation options around Sinazongwe, although there is still one pleasant lakeside lodge.

Lakeview Lodge (3 chalets) m 0962 667752, 0976 667752; e reservations@lakeview-zambia.com, lakeviewzambia@gmail.com; www.lakeview-zambia.com. Signposted about 1km from Sinazongwe, this tranquil lodge is an ideal place to unwind, with just lizards & kingfishers for company. Overlooking the lake from their secluded, airy terraces are cream-painted chalets, simply but attractively furnished with dbl & sgl beds beneath mosquito nets, en-suite showers, & ceiling fans to help out the breeze off the lake. Lawns lead down to the reed-fringed lakeshore, backed by large boulders that shelter a small sandy beach. There's an attractive dining room & tables on the veranda, with stone pots & cooling ceiling fans. Work is in hand to upgrade the rooms, with a further 6 dbl rooms to be added, & there are plans for a licensed restaurant & bar, & a swimming pool with entertainment area. Activities feature day trips to Chikanka Island (*K1,400/up to 6 people, exc lunch*; sunset cruises (*K135 pp*); & guided walks on Chete Island (*K300 pp*). For details of Chikanka & Chete islands, see below and page 223. **$$$**

ISLANDS ON LAKE KARIBA Of the numerous islands on Lake Kariba, only two are currently inhabited, Chikanka and Maaze (see above); Chete's lodge has been closed for some years.

Chete Island Chete is the largest island on the lake, and after a quick glance at the map you'll realise that it's much nearer to the Zimbabwean mainland (150m) than it is to Zambia (15km). This is because the border is defined as the deepest part of the Zambezi's old river course, not a line through the middle of the lake. In fact, the island lies just offshore from Zimbabwe's Chete Safari Area – so it's no surprise that it's become recognised under Zambia's national parks system as a private wildlife reserve and bird sanctuary.

Chete is in a remote southern part of the lake, isolated except for the distant nocturnal lights of the kapenta rigs. The island's game isn't tame, nor as dense as you'll find in the Luangwa or the better areas of the Kafue, but there is a sense of solitude and wilderness such as only a wild island like this can give. Its closest point of contact is really Sinazongwe, 17km away across Lake Kariba.

Much of the bigger game migrates to and fro between Zimbabwe and the island. This is especially true of the elephant bulls, but there's also a resident breeding herd of around 50 elephants on the island. A small pride of lion frequents the island, too. Then there are perhaps half-a-dozen leopard, a herd of eland, and plenty of waterbuck, bushbuck, impala and some magnificent kudu. Not forgetting the many crocodile and hippo that surround the shores, and a wide variety of birds – some 161 species have been counted on Chete and the neighbouring Sikula Island. Vultures circle in the thermals over the high ground, and a solitary martial eagle may be spotted over the centre of the island, while lower down, numerous smaller birds come to the fore, including little bee-eaters and colourful blue waxbills.

Typically, a guided walk across the centre of the island takes around 2 hours. The landscape is very varied, similar in parts to Zimbabwe's Chizarira and Matusadonna national parks. Areas of dense cover, rugged interior woodlands and gorges contrast with lightly wooded clearings criss-crossed with game tracks; nearer the shore, the terrain opens up into expansive floodplains. There are no roads here, and now that the lodge is closed, the island is totally deserted.

Chikanka Island
Chikanka Island is now strictly an archipelago of three islands due to a rise in the level of the lake since it was formed, although at the end of the dry season, you can sometimes walk between the three. It lies about 8km from the Zambian mainland, 10km west–southwest of Chete and 18km southwest of Sinazongwe. Covering 240ha (2.4km²), it is smaller than Chete, and is also privately owned.

The islands are mostly wooded, with mopane trees, marulas and the occasional baobab contrasting with the stark skeletons of drowned trees in the surrounding lake. Rock figs display their intricate root system; wild purple morning glory entwines its way through the waterplants along the shoreline, and dwarf plated lizards flash their brilliant blue tails as they dart among the rocks.

Chikanka has some plains game, including kudu, impala and bushbuck, and elephants occasionally visit too. Not surprisingly, there are also hippos and crocodiles around the shores, so it's not sensible to swim, but guided game walks are offered. The channels between the islands boast a good variety of fish, including bream, tiger fish, Cornish jack and bottlenose.

Where to stay

Chikanka Island Fishing & Game Lodge (8 chalets) Contact via Lakeview Lodge (page 222). Reached by boat from Lakeview Lodge, & under the same ownership, Chikanka is a lovely spot to spend a night or two. En-suite chalets have been built on one of the islands, each in a peaceful & secluded spot on a low cliff, looking east over the lake towards Zimbabwe, so the view at dawn is truly memorable. Stone clad, with a Tonga-thatched roof, each is gauzed to deter insects & furnished with dbl beds (plus mosquito nets). Lighting is powered by a generator. There's a honeymoon suite, too, & a 'double' chalet (2 twin chalets with space for an extra bed) with a private pool & deck. The thatched dining area is fronted by a terrace that leads down to the lake, & a good-size pool is a welcome new addition. Fishing is the big appeal here (*from K450/1/2 day up to 4 people*), but there are also game cruises by boat (*K135 pp*), & walks on Chete Island (*K300 pp*), all minimum 2 people. *K1,350/750 dbl/sgl FB (min 4 guests), exc drinks, transfers & fishing.* **LLLL** *exc activities.*

FROM LUSAKA TO CHIRUNDU

It takes at least 20 minutes to slough off the increasing urban sprawl of Lusaka before you're on an open road, beyond Chilanga. Some 50km south of the city, you'll come to the town of Kafue and, shortly before the busy turning to Livingstone (marked by a police checkpoint), cross over the wide and slow Kafue River that is also heading to join the Zambezi. From here the road gradually, consistently and occasionally spectacularly, descends. It leaves the higher, cooler escarpment for the hot floor of the Zambezi Valley, before passing the turn-off to Siavonga and crossing the busy bridge at Chirundu into Zimbabwe.

This tar road is an important commercial artery, so is kept in reasonably good repair, though you can expect some outbreaks of pot-holes on the lower sections of the escarpment. Between Kafue and Chirundu, lumbering trucks struggle to negotiate the steep, sharp bends, with breakdowns common and accidents all too frequent.

Occasional stalls set up on the side of the road sell seasonal fruit and vegetables, but the best spot for carved wooden animals, drums, baskets and other crafts is at the turn-off to Livingstone, just south of Kafue town. If you decide to buy, and you're flying home, remember that large carvings such as giraffes have to be put in the plane's hold, so make sure that they are very carefully packed.

KAFUE This rapidly growing but straggling industrial town lies close to the Norwegian-built hydro-electric dam on the Kafue River (see box, pages 216–17). It seems to have the most rumble strips of any town in Zambia, a dubious honour that causes no end of traffic delays.

The new Kafue Mall, under construction in 2015, is likely to revolutionise services in the town, which already has a post office and a bus station, two **banks** with ATMs, and several **fuel** stations. One of these is located towards Chirundu, just after the turn-off to Livingstone.

Where to stay and eat Options in town are limited to a clutch of small guesthouses that predominantly serve the town's industries, of which one of the better options is the aptly named **House of Excellence Guesthouse** (signposted off the main road, with en-suite rooms, a restaurant and secure parking). As you're entering the town from Lusaka, the Rose Food Court Bar and Restaurant on the right looks promising, too, though we haven't stopped there.

On the river outside town, some 5km to the south, you'll find the smart new Chita Lodge, and a small community campsite. See map, page 208.

Chita Lodge (24 chalets, camping) Great North Rd; 0211 293779; m 0979 306840; e chitalodge@gmail.com. ⊕ CHITAK 15°48.382'S, 28°12.632'E. About 5km south of Kafue, the old River Motel to the west of the main road changed hands in 2013, & was officially re-opened in summer 2015. Smart contemporary styling with a hint of Africa characterises the big, cool restaurant with a large shaded terrace by the pool (open to non-residents, K50). A good spot to break a journey

(⊕ daily 06.00–21.00; $$$–$$$$), the restaurant offers Zambian dishes such as oxtail casserole & nshima as well as a range of grills. Spread among the trees across expansive grounds are a series of small but clean en-suite chalets, geared to the conference trade. Each has a dbl bed, AC, kettle, fridge, & flat-screen TV; in time they will number around 100, & there will be camping again, too. The site has access to the river from where, in time, activities will again be organised. $$$

CHIRUNDU BORDER AREA A few kilometres before Chirundu, just 500m after the turn-off to Siavonga and Kariba and another police checkpoint, is the **Chirundu**

Fossil Forest (*entry US$15/7 adult/child*), a small area around the road where the remnants of petrified trees can be seen strewn on the ground.

The approach to Chirundu is lined with truck parks harbouring lorries waiting to get across the border to Zimbabwe. In Chirundu itself, there's a garage that hasn't had **fuel** for some years (the nearest supply is at Gwabi River Lodge), a selection of basic **shops**, a few **banks**, a **post office** and a good mission **hospital**. The imminent arrival of Shoprite in the town could well bring fuel too, but for now there is a slightly seedy, unsafe feel typical of a town where many people come and go, but few ever stay. As a result, Chirundu is a promising place to look for a lift if you are hitchhiking.

Getting to the Lower Zambezi

By car The unsignposted dirt road to Gwabi River Lodge and the Lower Zambezi branches east from the main road about 200–300m from the border. To find it, turn left at the entrance to the town itself, opposite the sign to the Zanaco Bank, and continue past the bus station. After about 2km you'll pass the sign for Machembere on your right, followed some 3.5km later by one for Zambezi Breezers, then a further 6.5km on is the Gwabi turn-off, to the left. From here, after another 2km, the road heads towards the Kafue River where a 2km stretch of tar heralds a modern bridge. Much as the old pontoon across the river could be time consuming, there's no denying that it had considerably more character than the stark new construction, complete with incongruous urban streetlights, that has recently replaced it.

By public transport The Juldan Motors **bus** between Lusaka and Harare passes through Chirundu and will stop on request. If you'd like to get a taste of the Zambezi River, ask the driver to let you off in Chirundu, then you can take a taxi to one of the riverside lodges (see below). Alternatively you can get a minibus to Chirundu, costing about K55 per person from Lusaka, or consider a taxi from Lusaka, which at K600–700 might be worth it for a group.

Where to stay Despite a handful of cheap lodgings in Chirundu itself, the town is no place to linger. Far better is to consider one of the three options on this side of the Kafue River. All can be reached by taxi; expect to pay around K30 to get as far as Machembere, or K60 to Zambezi Breezers.

Machembere [228 A4] (5 chalets, camping) m 0977 758691/412246, 0986 625471; e harrylully@hotmail.com (⊕ MACHEM 16°01.100'S, 28°51.228'E). Down a bumpy 1.5km track about 2km from Chirundu, Machembere is notable for its wide river frontage & lush gardens, the pride of owner Hilary Vlahakis. The deeply shaded main area with TV faces the river, with tables & benches where you can dine on pizzas, steaks & sometimes goat stew (**$$$**). Rooms are very low key, with a dbl bed (an extra bed can be added), mosquito nets, print fabrics, ceiling fan, fridge & TV. Nicer is the tree-shaded campsite by the river; bring your own tent, or rent one of theirs with bedding. The ablution block overlooks a big riverside pool, which was under construction in 2015, & canoeing is an option for visitors. *K450/500 sgl/*

dbl B&B; camping K100 pp, or K50 pp own tent. ⊕ All year. **$$**

Zambezi Breezers [228 A4] (10 tented chalets, 7 rooms, camping) m 0977 628120, 0979 279468; e zambezibreezers@gmail.com; http:// sites.google.com/site/zambezibreezers (⊕ 7AMBR7 15°59.112'S, 28°52.833'E). Right on the banks of the Zambezi River, this Dutch-owned camp is about 7km from Chirundu. To get there, follow the directions above, then turn right on to a good 2WD track for the final 2km. It's an open, riverside site with neatly cut grass, backed by an open-fronted bar & restaurant where relaxed chat is the order of the day. The menu (**$$–$$$**) ranges from toasties to fresh bream & steak; veggie options to local dishes. Tented twin, dbl & family chalets on low wooden decks have been cleverly designed to give a wide river vista, extra height to increase the flow of air, & mosi nets that curtain off the whole bedroom. All but one are en suite. Cheaper are basic twin rooms which share clean ablutions with plenty of hot water at the spacious, grassy campsite. It's all simple & unpretentious, but very well maintained & with mains electricity & free Wi-Fi. As well as a small pool, there's a jetty over the river, ideal for a casual lunch or sunset drink. Activities focus on fishing & game viewing by boat (*US$60 ½ day, plus fuel*), with some rods & tackle for hire. *Chalet US$60/70 pp sharing/sgl B&B; room US$18/25 exc b/fast; camping US$10 pp.* ⊕ *All year.* **$$**

🏠 **Gwabi River Lodge** [228 B4] (11 chalets, 8 tents, camping) ☎ 0211 515078; m 0966 345962/870222, 0961 560350; e gwabilodgezambia@gmail.com; www. gwabiriverlodge.com (⊕ GWABI 15°55.889'S, 28°52.266'E). Self-styled 'the gateway to the Lower Zambezi', this established lodge is now in the hands of Ann & Tony Weber, who are continuing its steady upward trend. Some 12km from Chirundu, it is set on an undulating site on the Kafue River, 3km from its confluence with the Zambezi. Something of a one-stop shop for independent travellers, Gwabi has its own fuel station (petrol & diesel), a workshop for minor repairs, including tyres, & parking (US$4/ night). For those without transport, a bus can be organised from Lusaka (US$302 up to 4 people,

then US$14 pp), as can boat transfers to other riverside lodges.

Varied & versatile accommodation ranges from smart new river-view chalets with contemporary styling, & refurbished older chalets, all en suite with stone floors, AC, mains electricity & DSTV, to simpler en-suite chalets above the campsite, & a couple of basic 'stone tents' with half-stone walls, gauze windows & metal roofs. Camping – with your own kit or in pre-erected twin-bedded tents – is along the river, on a well-lit, tree-shaded site with ablution block, BBQ & electricity, & nightly entertainment from a percussion band of painted reed frogs. There's a great pool overlooking the river (some distance below) with superb sunset views from the deck, & a cool bar with pool table, sports TV & Wi-Fi. A-la-carte menus incorporate everything from toasties to T-bones (**$–$$$$$**).

Small game can be found on the property, with elephant & hippo often seen from the river, but for more wildlife there are full-day excursions to the national park by boat then 4x4. River-based activities include boat cruises, fishing (*boat hire US$70/125 ½/full day plus fuel*), with rods & tackle available for hire, & you can also rent a speedboat with driver. Guided day & overnight canoe trips can be organised, with costs depending on numbers. There are village walks, too. *Chalet US$46–83/52–95 pp sharing/sgl B&B; tent US$35/44 exc b/fast; stone tent US$20 pp exc b/fast; camping US$14 pp.* ⊕ *All year.* **$–$$$**

LOWER ZAMBEZI VALLEY

The Lower Zambezi Valley, from the Kariba Dam to the Mozambique border, has a formidable reputation for big game – leading UNESCO to designate part of the Zimbabwean side as a World Heritage Site. The Lower Zambezi National Park protects a large section of the Zambian side. Across the river, much of the Zimbabwean side is protected by either Mana Pools National Park or various safari areas. This makes for a very large area of the valley devoted to wildlife, and a terrific amount of the bigger game, notably elephants and buffalo, actually cross the river regularly.

However, take a look at a map of the Zambian bank and you'll realise that the land up to 55km east from the Kafue River (from Gwabi River Lodge) is not in the national park at all; the river defines the border with the Chiawa Game Management Area (GMA), which is owned by the operators within the area, obtained with permission from the chieftainess. Only to the east of the Chongwe River are you in the national park.

As you might expect, the game densities increase as you travel east, with the best game in the national park, and fewer animals on the privately owned land nearer to Chirundu. The situation is similar on the other bank of the river, in Zimbabwe, so if you want good game viewing then do get into the park if you can, or at least near to it.

GEOGRAPHY From Chirundu to the Mozambique border, the Zambezi descends 42m, from 371m to 329m above sea level, over a distance of over 150km. That very gentle gradient (about 1:3,500) explains why the Zambezi flows so slowly and spreads out across the wide valley, making such a gentle course for canoeing. From the river, look either side of you into Zambia and Zimbabwe. In the distance you will spot the escarpment, if the heat haze doesn't obscure it. At around 1,200m high, it marks the confines of the Lower Zambezi Valley and the start of the higher, cooler territory beyond which is known as the 'highveld' in Zimbabwe.

The valley is a rift valley, similar to the Great Rift Valley of east Africa (though probably older), and it shares its genesis with the adjoining Luangwa Valley. The original sedimentary strata covering the whole area are part of the karoo system, sedimentary rocks laid down from about 300 to 175 million years ago. During this time, faulting occurred and volcanic material was injected into rifts in the existing sediments. One of these faults, the wide Zambezi Valley, can still be seen. In geologically recent times, the Zambezi has meandered across the wide valley floor, eroding the mineral-rich rocks into volcanic soils and depositing silts which have helped to make the valley so rich in vegetation and wildlife. These meanders have also left old watercourses and oxbow pools, which add to the area's attraction for game.

So look again from one side of the valley to the other. What you see is not a huge river valley: it is a rift in the earth's crust through which a huge river happens to be flowing.

FLORA AND FAUNA

Flora Most of the park, made up of higher ground on the sides and top of the escarpment, is thick bush – where game viewing is difficult. This is broadleafed miombo woodland, dominated by brachystegia, *julbernardia*, *combretum* and *terminalia* species. Fortunately, there's little permanent water here, so during the dry season the game concentrates on the flat alluvial plain by the river.

Acacia species and mopane dominate the vegetation on the richer soils of the valley floor, complemented by typical riverine trees like leadwood (*Combretum imberbe*), ebony (*Diospyros mespiliformis*) and various figs (*Ficus* species). Here the riverine landscape and vegetation are very distinctive: similar to the Luangwa Valley, but quite different from other parks in the subcontinent.

Perhaps it is the richness of the soils which allows the trees to grow so tall and strong, forming woodlands with carpets of grasses, and only limited thickets of shrubs to obscure the viewing of game. The acacia species include some superb specimens of the winterthorn (*Faidherbia albida*, which used to be known as *Acacia albida*), and the flat-topped umbrella thorn (*Acacia tortilis*). Both of these produce seedpods which the game love, the former looking like apple-rings, the latter being tightly spiralled seedpods which are very nutritious (19% protein, 26% carbohydrate, 5% minerals). It all results in a beautiful, lush landscape that can support a lot of game, and is excellent for the ease of viewing which it allows.

Mammals The Lower Zambezi has all the big game that you'd expect, with the exceptions of rhino (due to poaching), giraffe and cheetah. Buffalo and elephant are very common, and can often be seen grazing on the islands in the middle of the river, or swimming between Zimbabwe and Zambia. It is normally safe to get quite close by drifting quietly past these giants as they graze.

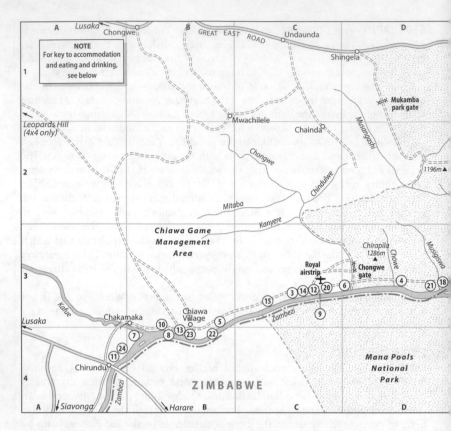

NOTE
For key to accommodation and eating and drinking, see below

The antelope in the valley are dominated by large herds of impala, but good populations of kudu, waterbuck, bushbuck, zebra and the odd duiker or grysbok also occur. Giraffe are notable for their absence – in fact, there's no record of them ever having lived here.

Lion, leopard and spotted hyena are the major predators, and in 2015 wild dog had re-appeared in the valley. There have long been plans to re-introduce cheetah but these have not yet come to fruition. On my first visit, back in 1995, lion were very visible, with one marvellous pride having in excess of 30 animals – and the game viewing has improved a lot since then. The lion prides, though, are separating out, perhaps in part due to a predominance of males. Many of the larger trees have branches that seem made-to-measure for leopards, which are sometimes seen on night drives, and increasingly during the day, too.

In the river, crocodile and hippo are always present, but look also for the large water monitor lizard, or *leguvaan*, and the entertaining Cape clawless otter, which both occur frequently though the latter are very seldom seen.

Birds Around 350 species of bird have been recorded in the valley. By the river you will find many varieties of water-loving birds like pied, giant, woodland, malachite and brown-hooded kingfishers, to name the more common of the species. Similarly, darters, cormorants, egrets and storks are common, and fish eagles are always to be found perching on high branches that overlook the river. Less common residents include ospreys, spoonbills, Pels' fishing owl and African skimmers, and the river

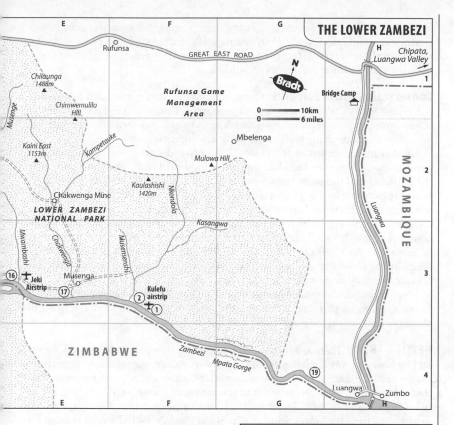

Rufunsa

GREAT EAST ROAD

N

Bradt

Chipata,
Luangwa Valley

Chilaunga
1488m ▲

Rufunsa Game
Management
Area

Bridge Camp

0 ▬▬▬ 10km
0 ▬▬▬ 6 miles

Chimwemulilo
Hill ▲

Mbelenga

Kaini East
1153m ▲

Kampetauke

Mulowa Hill ▲

M
O
Z
A
M
B
I
Q
U
E

Chakwenga Mine

Kaulashishi
1420m ▲

Nkondola

Luangwa

LOWER ZAMBEZI
NATIONAL PARK

Kasangwa

Mwamboshi

Chakwenga

Musensenshi

16 ✛ Jeki
Airstrip

Musenga

17

Kulefu
2 airstrip
✈ 1

ZIMBABWE

Zambezi
Mpata Gorge

19

Luangwa
Zumbo

Lake Kariba and the Lower Zambezi   LOWER ZAMBEZI VALLEY

9

is rich in waders, both resident and migrant, including squacco heron.

CONSERVATION
Poaching In the 1940s, due to numerous severe outbreaks of sleeping sickness, several villages were evacuated from this area, which became a hunting concession from the 1960s. Although the valley was classified as a national park in 1983, in the mid-1980s, commercial poaching for ivory and rhino horn completely wiped out the park's black rhino population, and threatened to do the same to the elephants. Fortunately, the CITES ban on the world ivory trade did much to stop this; the elephant population in the park is now good, and the Lower Zambezi's game is generally in good shape. That said, as in most national parks, three types of poaching still occur

in the Lower Zambezi: commercial ivory, commercial bushmeat and subsistence (mostly snaring). However, ZAWA teams stationed around the park, with the assistance of Conservation Lower Zambezi, carry out law-enforcement patrols on a daily basis to minimise the impact on wildlife.

Conservation Lower Zambezi Committed to the conservation and sustainable use of the valley's wildlife and natural resources, Conservation Lower Zambezi (CLZ; *http://conservationlowerzambezi.org*) focuses on wildlife protection, education and supporting local community development.

Funded by the camps in the Lower Zambezi and concerned individuals and companies, CLZ provide logistical support – food, fuel and communications – to the ZAWA patrol teams, mounts aerial patrols and facilitates research projects. It is also responsible for the park's guide training scheme. On the community front, schoolchildren from the surrounding communities are able to learn about their local wildlife through visits to the activity centre, and CLZ is also addressing the concerns of human–wildlife conflict in the surrounding GMA.

Supporting CLZ helps to protect the wildlife and environment in this area from illegal killing and degradation, both through short-term law enforcement and long-term community involvement.

More recent is the establishment of the Lower Zambezi Conservation Trust (e *info@lzct.org*), a partnership between the local community and tour operators to conserve wildlife and the environment within the eastern GMA.

GETTING THERE There are three means of getting into this area: by road, by air and by boat – or any combination of these. Most visitors stay at one of the private camps as a base, and go for game-viewing drives, walks and trips on the river from there. Arriving by air is certainly the fastest means of transport. Planes land at one of several airstrips in the valley, including Royal Zambezi, Jeki and Kulefu, with the drive to and from the lodges being an activity in itself. A few lodges can arrange for transfers by road and river from Lusaka, though this tends to be very expensive.

More economical, for those with their own vehicle, is to drive to Gwabi River Lodge (page 226) and arrange to be collected from there by boat; again, this is an experience that is an intrinsic part of a trip. Alternatively, the well equipped can drive themselves all the way (see below), but this is neither an easy nor a fast option.

Finally, there are popular canoe safaris (pages 232–4) that run along the river, using simple temporary fly-camps at night.

Visiting independently The adventurous and well equipped can drive in with their own vehicles, either staying at lodges or camping – which usually involves bringing all supplies as well as camping gear. Note that the only fuel available within the whole area is to be found at Gwabi River Lodge (page 226), which also offers minor repairs, including tyres.

The roads into the park need a 4x4 vehicle (ideally two, for safety's sake) but are not difficult driving in the dry season, though the going can be very slow. Get detailed maps of the whole valley before you leave Lusaka, and pack a compass and GPS. Getting lost among the labyrinth of game-drive loops is all too easily done.

From Chirundu As you enter Chirundu from the north, turn left onto a dirt road signposted to Zambezi Breezers and Gwabi River Lodge, and follow this road for about 8km to the smart new bridge across the Kafue River (⊕ CHIAWP

15°56.667'S, 28°52.500'E). Once across the bridge you'll be in the Chiawa GMA. The tarmac runs out almost immediately and at this point the road splits; take the right fork (the left one leads to a Zambeef installation) then it's largely a case of sticking close to the river, and following the main track. As far as Chiawa village, this runs alongside fertile fields, where maize, paprika, bananas, mangoes and beans are the staple crops, and passes numerous small homesteads. About 16km from the bridge, a sign for Chiawa Cultural Village (⊕ CHIACV 15°50.230'S, 29°07.061'E) marks a fork; for the national park, bear right here, towards Chiawa village.

The western entrance to the national park, Chongwe gate, lies about 46km from here, or 62km from the bridge. The route is pretty clear as far as Royal airstrip, which you'll pass on your right. However, about 3km beyond the airstrip you come to a fork (⊕ FKAIR 15°43.046'S, 29°19.308'E). Bear left here, and another 4km or so will bring you to the Chongwe River. Depending on the crossing point, which can vary, you'll come to the Chongwe gate into the national park (⊕ CHONGG 15°42.093'S, 29°20.045'E) after 2km or 4km.

Once inside the national park itself, the terrain is dominated by broad plains, dotted with baobab trees and inhabited only by plains animals and birds, before eventually dropping down into *albida* forest where shallow lagoons among the trees attract brightly coloured saddle-billed storks.

From the Great East Road For those heading for the eastern side of the park, there's a little-known access road that starts from the Great East Road, some 100km east of Lusaka. It's rough, slow going, and easy to get lost; travelling in convoy is a must and a GPS essential. To find the start of the road, go past Chongwe village, then turn right shortly after the village of Shingela (⊕ TUSHIN 15°14.188'S, 29°10.032'E). From here, follow the road to the Mukanga gate (⊕ MUKANG 15°21.015'S, 29°17.135'E). Shortly after the gate there's another checkpoint marking the entrance to the Chakwenga Mine. The road then drops over the escarpment, a steep descent culminating in a series of sandy riverbeds, and the main game-viewing area on the valley's floor in the Kulefu area, eventually coming out at ⊕ TUCHMN 15°36.577'S, 29°40.167'E, between Jeki airstrip and Old Mondoro. You'll need to allow at least 5 hours from the Great East Road to Kulefu.

From Lusaka Another equally poor 4x4 track starts from Leopards Hill Road in Lusaka, and gradually deteriorates as it winds its way steeply down the escarpment. Back-up is essential as very little passes this way, and there's a real danger of rolling your vehicle. The track finally emerges at ⊕ EXLEOP 15°55.880'S, 28°57.205'E, opposite cultivated fields and close to Chiawa village.

ACTIVITIES Most of the lodges along the river offer similar activities, concentrating primarily on drives, boat trips, walking safaris, canoeing and fishing, but each has its own individual atmosphere and areas of expertise, and some specialise. Outside the park, some of the lodges also offer village visits, or trips to Chiawa Cultural Village.

Game drives Day and night drives, both in the Chiawa GMA and into the Lower Zambezi National Park (⏱ *Jun–Oct*), are high on the list of priorities for most visitors. They are offered by almost all camps, whether they're located inside or outside the park – though it's worth remembering that the further you are from the national park, the less game you're likely to see; game drives on the west of the GMA can be uneventful.

Walking safaris Walking safaris with a professional guide, and an armed scout, are also widely available, affording the opportunity to get closer to the wildlife on their terms. There are now strict exams, organised by the CLZ (page 230), for potential guides which match the quality and scope of those in the Luangwa Valley. I would never go walking with an unqualified guide. Most walks last between 2 and 4 hours, and are done as an activity from a lodge or camp.

Birdwatching Birdwatching is usually built into most walks, drives or boating trips if you're interested. With a range of habitats the region is a great place for birdwatching at any time, but especially from September to March, when migrants from central Africa can be spotted in the area.

Fishing Fishing on the Zambezi – primarily for tiger fish – is offered by most outfits. It is at its best when the waters are clear, from around May to June until towards the end of the year, with the prime season for tiger fishing around September and October. Catch and release is obligatory in the national park, and is practised by most lodges/camps within the GMA. Fishing permits are normally obtained by the lodge on behalf of their guests. There's a ban on fishing between December and February.

Canoeing Canoeing on the Zambezi is a firm favourite for the more adventurous. It's a terrific way to relax in the open air and see the river, whilst doing some gentle exercise and game viewing at the same time.

Most operators use stable Canadian-style fibreglass canoes which are 5.7m long, and large enough for two people plus their camping equipment and personal belongings. Trips are usually limited to a maximum of five canoes led by a fully qualified canoe guide; while this means that the guide has control over the group, you could still occasionally find yourself closer to a pod of hippos than to your trusty guide.

Broadly there are two different ways to go canoeing. You can opt for this as an activity from a lodge or camp, or you can paddle from A to B, sleeping on islands or at points on the bank along the way.

Canoeing guides and safety In the 1990s the question asked about these trips was always 'Which section should we canoe?' Now it is more usually 'How qualified is the guide?' This is important both for safety reasons and to help you make the most of your trip.

Canoe safaris were started on the Zimbabwean side of the river in the early 1980s, led by qualified canoe guides who had to pass national parks' examinations. In the early 1990s, with the emergence of the Lower Zambezi National Parks Wildlife Protection Programme, Zambia also started canoe safaris. Today's canoeing guides on the Lower Zambezi are fully qualified wildlife guides with further stringent training in canoeing and water safety.

You should understand from the outset that canoeing on this river, including the channels, has a risk attached to it that no guide can ever take away. Even with the very best of guides, it's possible to get into dangerous, even life-threatening, situations with both hippos and crocs. Although the safety record among the best canoe operators is exceptional, situations when these animals injure or even kill visitors are not unknown. That said, the vast majority of such encounters are with local Zambian fishermen, making theirs a particularly hard and dangerous life. For the visitor, canoeing with, and listening to, a good guide who knows the river will give you the best chance of avoiding dangerous situations, and of escaping those that prove unavoidable.

Short trips from a camp or lodge Most of the lodges/camps along the Lower Zambezi offer canoeing as a morning or afternoon activity, typically taking about 3 to 4 hours, and occasionally extended to a whole day.

Depending on the location of the lodge, you'll either be driven upstream with the canoes, and will then paddle back to the lodge, or you will paddle downstream, and be returned to your lodge by boat or on a game-drive vehicle. Increasingly, rather than use the main river, lodges are focusing on a couple of narrower side channels that are more sheltered and tend to offer more in the way of game. These include the Nkalangi Channel and, further east, the beautiful Chifungulu Channel, deep inside the national park.

Canoeing from a lodge has several advantages. First, there's no hurry, so your guide can build in time to stop and investigate the game along the river; second, if you're at a good lodge then you're probably spending all your canoeing time in a prime game area, within or close to the park; third, you're not committing yourself to more than 3 or 4 hours paddling; and finally, you've got a comfortable bed lined up for the night back at camp.

Longer overnight trips: from point to point On these trips you put all your kit in the canoe, and paddle downstream for a number of days. Typically, you'll carry tents and food, and camp along the way.

Physically, you will feel tired at the end of a day, but canoeing downriver is not excessively strenuous (unless you meet a strong headwind), and no previous experience is demanded. To some extent that feeling of exertion often leads to a feeling of achievement at the end of the trip, which increases with the length of the trip and the distance covered.

Costs normally include basic camping kit, food (and wine with the evening meal), guide, canoes, paddles etc. Transfers are extra.

Which section to canoe? Broadly, canoe safaris vary according to the length of time available. Typically the shortest, taking two nights/three days, covers the section of the river from Chirundu to around Mvuu Lodge. The second, from Chirundu to the mid-Mana Pools region, features larger numbers of game and birdlife due to the proximity of national parks on both sides of the river, and takes three nights/four days. Slightly longer, at four nights/five days, is to paddle as far as the Chongwe River on the borders of the Lower Zambezi National Park. Undoubtedly the wildest option runs the whole length of the two national parks, from the Chongwe River, passing through floodplains and the spectacular Mpata Gorge, and ending at the confluence of the Luangwa River some 163km downstream; for this, allow at least five nights/six days.

Canoeing operators Although most lodges offer canoeing as an activity from camp, there isn't the choice of trips, or operators, doing longer canoe trips here that there was in the early 1990s. Both Kiambi Lower Zambezi (pages 234–5) and Gwabi River Lodge (page 226) organise expeditions lasting from one to four nights. There is also one dedicated specialist:

Zambezi River Adventures aka River Horse Safaris m +263 772 235311/ 235340, 773   523848; e info@riverhorsesafaris.com; www. zambezicanoeing.com. River Horse operates canoeing safaris on both sides of the Lower Zambezi, from Kariba to the Mozambique border, for individuals, families & groups. On the Zambian side, these are run from their base close to Chiawa Cultural Village, & range from the 2-night/3-day Zambezi Short (*US$510 pp*), to the 5–6-night/6–7-day Great Zambezi Canoe Safari (*US$1,245–1,450 pp, min 4*); both exc park fees. Trips can also be tailormade, & can also be combined with local community projects. There's normally a maximum of 5 18ft 2-man Canadian-style canoes per safari. No children under 15 unless by prior arrangement.

Chongwe Falls (⊕ CHONGF 15°41.173'S, 29°18.581'E)

These accessible falls on the Chongwe River, which forms the western boundary of the Lower Zambezi National Park, make a beautiful picnic spot with some good birding. You can clamber up the rocks to see the falls from above, or try your hand at fishing, but don't be beguiled by the still waters; there are large crocs lurking in there so a cooling dip is out of the question.

Cultural tourism Several of the lodges at the western end of the valley offer village trips. Some arrange these on an informal basis, but others take in **Chiawa Cultural Village** [228 B3] (⊕ CHIACV 15°50.230'S, 29°07.061'E; *admission K50 pp*), which is about 25km east of the bridge and clearly signposted. Access is either by boat, or by road. If you're driving, ask for directions shortly after the signpost, and you'll probably find a gaggle of children vying with each other to show you the way.

The village was established with funds from the African Wildlife Foundation to showcase the cultural traditions of the local Goba people, and at the same time to raise funds for orphans and other vulnerable people within the community. In this way, people from the villages around the national park get the chance to benefit from the conservation of wildlife and the not-inconsiderable wealth that tourists bring to the area.

Visitors who come by appointment are usually greeted by a group of dancers, an interactive display that can be considerable fun. A guide is on hand to explain the history of the Goba people and to look at many aspects of traditional village life: from cooking and medicinal herbs to clothes, toys and weapons. There are full-size village huts, an interesting museum/interpretive centre, a curio shop, and even a look-out post for elephants (with a great view of the river). If you just turn up, it's very much more low key, and although you can camp here, facilities are rudimentary in the extreme.

WHERE TO STAY There are several lodges in the valley and a few campsites as well. Almost all are good, but their styles vary widely, from traditional thatched and/or tented lodges to more permanent structures with something of a hotel feel. For the most part, power is either solar generated or supplied by battery, so needs to be used sparingly. With advance booking and a 4x4, you can drive yourself into any of these, but most people arrange for a transfer by road or charter flight. Establishments to the west of the national park are in the Chiawa GMA. All overnight visitors in the park are required to pay a levy of US$10 per person per night towards Conservation Lower Zambezi (page 230), an organisation committed to the protection of the wildlife and habitat of the national park and the Chiawa GMA. Looking at the various establishments from west to east:

Outside the national park in the Chiawa GMA

🏠 **Kiambi Lower Zambezi** [228 B3] (6 chalets, 8 Meru tents, 2 cottages, camping) reservations m 0966 655878, 0977 876003/186106; e info@ kiambi.com; www.kiambi.com. ⊕ KIAMBI

15°56.170'S, 28°55.520'E. The first lodge that you come to in the GMA, Kiambi lies on an 11ha site at the confluence of the Zambezi & Kafue rivers, with views across to Kanyemba Island. It is clearly signposted 12km from the Kafue bridge, with transfers possible from Chirundu (*US$55/boat*) or from Lusaka (*US$400 return/4 people*) With relatively easy access & reasonable rates, the camp is popular with w/enders & can get very busy. Power is supplied by mains electricity, & fuel, firewood, charcoal & ice are available.

High over the river, next to a young baobab, the main camp's lounge/bar has great views from the stone terrace. The cool, thatched dining area behind it is surrounded by reed walls, although dinner is normally served around the fire. There's also a small pool.

The original Meru tents under thatch are erected on polished wooden platforms with a large veranda, some with a river view. Inside are dbl or twin beds (with space for a further 2) & a reed-enclosed shower, toilet & washbasin. More upmarket are solidly built en-suite chalets, well-designed with AC, lounge area & TV. Then there are 2 self-catering cottages sleeping up to 6 or 8 people respectively, each with a bathroom, fully equipped kitchen & a fireplace/BBQ area. Finally, there's a flat, grassy campsite, where 8 separate pitches have their own fireplace & braai, & the ablution block has hot showers privately enclosed by reed & wooden walls. The campsite has its own pool, & an air-conditioned bar with snooker table & DSTV. Snacks are available here, or campers may eat at the lodge if space is available (*dinner US$24*).

Kiambi specialises in canoeing, from 3hr trips (*US$40 pp; included for those staying 3 nights*) to guided overnight expeditions with a crew to set up camp & cook (*US$189 pp/night FB*). Ideally these should be prebooked. Fishing is a prime attraction, too, from *US$93/½ day inc 10 litres fuel*, with rod & reels for hire (*US$7/day*), & some tackle for sale. Other activities include cruises in canopied flat-bottomed motorboats, taking up to 8 people. *Apr–Nov & Xmas/New Year chalet US$190/231, tent US$153/208, both pp sharing/ sgl FB; self-catering cottage US$208–254 (up to 6–8); Dec–Mar chalet US$143/173, tent US$115/156; self-catering cottage US$156–191. Camping US$12 pp; 2-man tent/bedding US$20 pp.* ⊕ *All year.* **$$**

🏠 **Kanyemba Lodge** [228 B4 (6 rondavels, 1 family unit) m 0977 755720; e info@ kanyemba.com; www.kanyemba.com. ⊕ KANYEM 15°56.265'S, 28°55.919'E. Just 1km from Kiambi, Kanyemba was opened in 2002 by Zambian-born Italian Riccardo Garbaccio, & refurbished in 2011 & 2015. From its bougainvillea-adorned entrance to the expanses of green lawns along the river, it's an attractive, well-run place – & foodies will appreciate the Italian-influenced cuisine.

Cool, spacious stone-&-thatch rondavels (1 of them a honeymoon suite with plunge pool & garden) are tasteful & stylish, with locally made solid wood furniture that includes king-size or twin beds under walk-in mosquito nets; there's also a walk-in wardrobe area & safe, an en-suite shower, & a wooden veranda facing the river. For families, the rondavels can take an extra 2 beds, or there's a larger house with 3 entirely separate en-suite rooms: 2 dbls & 1 with 4 beds. The understated décor runs through the thatched & partially open-sided central restaurant/bar, rebuilt in 2015 to create a cool, airy space with its own pizza oven. Above, chunky leather sofas furnish the lounge area, where the rafters afford a superb triangular view of the river below. To the front, a stone terrace is shaded by a wild mango tree, & chaises longues are set by a small pool near the river. There's a good gift shop, including Tribal Textiles products, & the lodge is connected to mains electricity.

Activities include game walks on the private Kanyemba Island, where the birding is good & you might encounter wildlife such as elephant, waterbuck, bushbuck & even buffalo. There are also boat trips, canoeing, fishing (tackle included), village walks & sunset cruises. Full-day trips to the national park can be organised (& are included for those staying 3 nights or more); these take a boat to the gate, then driving from there. Unusually for this area, Kanyemba is open almost all year. *US$410/470 pp sharing/sgl Jun–Oct, US$330/385 rest of year, all FBA, inc most drinks, park fees.* ⊕ *Closed mid Jan–Feb.* **LLL**

🏠 **Kanyemba Island Bushcamp** [228 B4] (4 chalets) Contact Kanyemba, above. The largest island on the Zambezi, some 7km long & 2km wide, is privately owned by Kanyemba Lodge, & home to their exclusive bushcamp. It's a rather romantic affair, this, its secluded reed-walled chalets raised high on stilts with canvas flaps opening on to tree-shaded decks over the river & private bathrooms on a platform in the trees. Even the LED 'fairy lights' have a slightly romantic quality! More prosaically, there's a radio on hand in case of emergency. Meals – to the same standard as those at the lodge – are served in an open thatched dining area above the river. There's a firepit here, too, as well as a simple bar & a small plunge pool.

With a resident elephant population & good birding, the island is the base for Kanyemba's bush walks; these & all other activities are as at the lodge. *US$450/500 pp sharing/sgl Jun–Oct, US$330/385 rest of year, all FBA, inc most drinks, park fees. No children under 12.* ☺ *Mar–Dec.* **LLL**

🏠 **Mukuyu** [228 B4] (1 tent, 1 rondavel, camping) m 0977 851361; e mkuyucampingsite@gmail.com. ✤ 15°49.937'S, 29°07.680'E. Mukuyu has an open site down a 1.5km track with hippo-cropped lawns sloping down to the river. There's no vehicle access to the tiny camping area so cars must be parked at the entrance. A traditional thatched shelter & simple bar is matched by a similarly styled shower/toilet for campers, & a small en-suite chalet built of heavy poles & thatch. The owner, Kennedy, will serve meals by arrangement; it's all very low key. *Boat trip K200/hr. Chalet US$25 pp B&B; camping US$10pp.* ☺ *All year.* **$**

🏠 **Wildtracks** [228 B4] (4 tents, 3 chalets, camping) m 0977 349418; e info@wildtracks-zambia.com; www.wildtracks-zambia.com. ✤ WILDT 15°56.463'S, 29°00.288'E. Well maintained & very family friendly, the simple Wildtracks is clearly signposted 15km east of the bridge, down a 3.3km track. It's a family-run place with the emphasis on environmental education, & reservations are essential. Safari tents & chalets come in various sizes & configurations (2–6 beds), most sharing ablutions, though the secluded 'honeymoon' chalet by the river has its own bathroom. You need to bring all your own food & drink, but staff are on hand to prepare your meals, & there's a new dining area as well as an attractive 2-storey boma. At the campsite, where 2 of the 4 pitches are on the river, cooking is down to you, so bring everything you need except firewood & charcoal.

Wildtracks is popular with school groups, which explains a large swimming pool, child-focused walks, an obstacle course, geocaching & superb climbing on an old baobab tree (*all K100 pp*). Sundowner cruises (from *K230/2hrs*) & fishing (*K460/½ day*) round off the options, both including 20 litres of fuel, with rods available for hire. *En-suite chalet K1,035 dbl B&B; tent K630 pp sharing (max 4) exc b/fast, chalet K1,380/2,070 4/6 beds. Camping K60 pp.* **$$$**

🏠 **Tsika Island Camp** [228 B4] (3 chalets) Contact via Chongwe River Camp. ✤ TSIKA 15°51.205'S, 29°06.583'E. Chongwe's rustic bushcamp is on a small island, 2.5km x 1.5km, about 35km upstream from its parent lodge. It's an unspoiled spot, shaded by winterthorn trees with sandy paths leading to the rather quirky riverfront chalets, with painted ferro walls under thatch, & pole-framed 'windows' & reed blinds. Furnished with a dbl or twin beds under mosi nets, & with solar lighting, each has a pole walkway leading to a toilet, basin & bucket shower. (One chalet can take 2 extra beds.) It's a simple camp, with a thatched dining shelter & riverside firepit; a small plunge pool is the only modern luxury present. The island offers good birding, & is a permanent home to a couple of porcupines. Elephant & hippo sometimes wander onto the island though, so a scout is needed to walk the perimeter. Boat trips & fishing are on offer, as are visits to the cultural village that's almost opposite. Transfers to Chongwe are often by canoe, a pleasant day's drift downstream. *US$500 pp Apr–Jun, US$600/850 pp sharing/sgl Jul–Oct, all FBA, inc most drinks, laundry, park fees. No children under 7.* ☺ *Jul–mid Nov.* **LLL**

🏕 **Chiawa Cultural Village** (camping) [228 B3] ✤ CHIACV 15°50.230'S, 29°07.061'E. The valley's cultural village (page 234) will accommodate campers on a dusty site by the river beneath a couple of sausage trees. You'll need to bring all your own supplies (even the water here is sporadic), & ablutions are basic in the extreme. There are without doubt better options. *US$15 pp.*

🏠 **Mvuu Lodge** [228 C3] (11 tents, camping) lodge m 0966 363762; res m +27 79 524 8709; e info@mvuulodge.com; www.mvuulodge. com. ✤ MVUU 15°45.913'S, 29°13.122'E. This laidback & flexible lodge is particularly popular with the angling fraternity. It's 18km west of the national park, & visitors either drive themselves here or arrive by boat from Gwabi River Lodge.

There's a generator for power, but lighting is largely provided by paraffin or battery lamps.

Wooden hippos roam the deck above the river, in front of a three-sided central area with a proper bar & bar stools, & Wi-Fi access. Squashy leather sofas & cane chairs complement wooden tables set up for individual dining. There's a firepit by the river & a pool bubbling on the lawns. Paths through the grass link to the en-suite twin-bedded walk-in tents (1 for families) & the campsite. Eight of the tents have partially open stone-walled bathrooms & wooden terraces, some looking across to the river. The others, in the camping area, are set up for self-catering, with their own fire, braai & cooking equipment; you just bring the food. Camping is pricy but it comes with an element of luxury: each of the 7 pitches – 4 on the river – has its own braai area, firepit, private shower & flush toilet, with an attendant to provide firewood & clean pots & pans. Bliss! With advance notice, campers may also dine in the restaurant (*dinner US$35 pp + VAT*), & you can hire a dome tent, too (*US$10*). Activities (all exc VAT) include sundowner cruises (*US$38 pp*), fishing (*US$75/125 ½/full day exc fuel*), ½-day canoe trips (*US$88 pp*) & game drives (from *US$48 pp*). *US$184–266 pp sharing HB; US$251/329 dbl/ family self catering. Camping US$26–28 pp. 25% sgl supplement.* ⊕ *Mar–Dec.* **$**

🏠 **Baines' River Camp** [228 C3] (8 chalets, 1 family cottage) \+27 33 342 7498; m +27 82 806 4074; e reservations@bainesrivercamp. com; www.bainesrivercamp.com. ⊕ BAINES 15°45.743'S, 29°13.913'E. Rebuilt on the wide riverfront site of the earlier Kiubo Camp, Baines' is just 16km west of the national park, & about 50km from the bridge, although most guests arrive by plane at the nearby Royal airstrip. With its soft-grey metal roofs, cream-painted walls & glazed windows, it looks solid & cool, akin to a smart club, with professional yet friendly service to match.

As you step down into the main area, the first impression is of space, oodles of it: in the lounge with its large fireplace & leather sofas, in the rather masculine bar, even in the 'boardroom' that doubles as a library & study centre. There's Wi-Fi in the main area, & computer stations with laptops in the lounge. Step outside & you'll find a firepit tantalisingly close to the river, & a narrow 11m pool.

Sharing the river views are colonial-style chalets with comfortable dark-wood furniture & private verandas. Expect AC, glazed windows (backed by netting), carpeted floors, king-size or twin beds beneath ceiling fans, & a smart bathroom with separate toilet; each chalet (2 of them smaller than the others) boasts a minibar, hairdryer & safe, & 2 feature outdoor showers. Baines' Cottage has 2 en-suite bedrooms with a dining/lounge/kitchen area.

Activities are many, but there is no structure, though recommendations of the best times to fish, canoe along a channel of the Zambezi, laze on the river or do a game drive (in the GMA or national park) are happily forthcoming. With 24hrs notice, walking is an option, or you can indulge in a private spa treatment on your veranda (30min session included for FBA guests). There are also opportunities to participate in professionally run fly-fishing clinics, or 5-day workshops: one on photography; a 2nd focusing on elephants: their breeding habits & the threats they face. Birding courses are a further option. There are special rates for non-participating partners, & a group of 14 will get exclusive use of the lodge. *Jul–Oct chalet US$650–720/775–845 pp sharing/sgl, cottage US$645/770; rest of year chalet US$520–580/645– 705, cottage US$795/920, all FBA, inc most drinks, laundry, airstrip transfers; exc park fees, fishing tackle, spa treatments. Min stay 2 nights. No children under 8.* ⊕ *Mar–mid Dec.* **LLL–LLLL**

🏠 **Munyemeshi River Lodge** [228 C3] (9 rooms) \0211 231466; m 0977 789786; www.munyemeshi.co.zm. ⊕ MUNYEM 15°45.437'S, 29°15.309'E. Visitors to this self-catering camp some 10km west of the national park need to bring their own food (for their chef to prepare & serve at the central dining table), their own drink (there's no bar), & their own fishing gear. The lodge itself, though, is substantial, its stone central building under thatch matched by its chalets. These are all en suite, pleasantly fitted out with twin, dbl or 4 beds, & the newer ones share a separate kitchen & dining area. Activities comprise game drives (*K600–700/½ day exc park fees*) & boat cruises (*K100/hr plus fuel*), with a pool under construction in 2015. Walking can be arranged with a ZAWA scout. *K300 pp self-catering.* **$$**

🏠 **Msaku Mbezi** [228 C3] (5 chalets) e lana@myriad-holdings.com; www.myriad-holdings.com/msaku-mbezi-lodge. ✪ MSAKU 15°44.554'S, 29°15.815'E. Nearing completion in 2015, this traditional thatched lodge occupies a sloping site with neat sandy paths through the grass. Though the 1km entrance road was pretty tortuous when we visited, it may well have improved since then. In similar vein to the neighbouring Munyemeshi, it's a self-catering option, with several beds in each of its stone-built en-suite cottages, a kitchen & dining area. Game drives, fishing, boat cruises & other activities can be arranged. Rates on application.

🏠 **Kasaka River Lodge** [228 C3] (8 tented chalets, family house) www.kasakariverlodge. com; contact via Chongwe River Camp, below. ✪ KASAKA 15°44.242'S, 29°17.982'E. Taken into the Chongwe fold in 2010, Kasaka is just 5km west of the national park. It's a family-friendly place, set high above the river, & almost 2 lodges in one. On the 'tame side', en-suite tented chalets on stone-clad platforms sit among neat lawns & facing a small pool. Dirt paths & a wooden bridge lead over an ornamental pool past the lounge, bar & dining area to the 'wild side', where more chalets are connected by suspended wooden walkways, ending at the secluded honeymoon suite with an open-air bath, looking across the river to Zimbabwe. En-suite bathrooms surrounded by head-height walls, ringed with thorny acacia branches to keep the baboons out, include plumbed-in showers & toilets. For families, there's an entirely separate 2-bedroom unit, the 'Hippo Pod', with its own pool, firepit & deck. Cut into the steep hillside is a further lounge area with a deck over the river below.

Alongside day & night game drives & safari walks in the GMA & national park are river cruises, canoeing & fishing trips & cultural visits; the lodge is actively involved with local schools. Those seeking privacy can indulge in bush picnics, private dinners or lunch on Nyamangwe Island, while families are unusually well catered for, with children's menus, games and an entire 'Bush Kids' programme. *US$500 pp Nov–Jun, US$600/850 pp sharing/sgl Jul–Oct, all FBA inc most drinks, laundry, park fees. No children under 7. Hippo Pod US$500 pp Nov–Jun, US$690 pp Jul–Oct, (max 6 people; min 4 adults).* ⊙ *Jul–mid Nov.* LLL–LLLL

🏠 **Royal Zambezi Lodge** [228 C3] (15 tented chalets) m 0979 486618; e reservations1@royalzambezilodge.com; www.

royalzambezilodge.com. ✪ ROYAL 15°43.641'S, 29°18.876'E. Just 4km west of the national park, with a full 3km of river frontage, Royal Zambezi is linked to Royal Air Charters, & many guests fly into Royal airstrip; alternatively, leave your vehicle at Gwabi River Lodge & transfer by boat, taking about 1½hrs.

Imposing gates set the scene for the main building, where lounge & dining areas, each with outsize fireplaces, lead off from a huge lobby. Bare walls jar slightly against the formality of the setting, but the service is good, the welcome friendly, & there's free Wi-Fi. Meals, at individual tables, are served from an à-la-carte menu, with a pizza oven a popular feature. Outside, a wide terrace offers more relaxed seating & dining options, & a walkway leads to the bar, built around the trunk of a large sausage tree (*Kigelia africana*). En-suite tented chalets under thatch are accessed along a concrete path at the back of the lawned site, separated by rough pole screens for privacy. Inside, cream bed linen on twin or dbl beds & the soft lines of mosquito netting draping the walls add a lightness of touch, & wooden doors open on to a porch facing the river. There are 4 'deluxe' chalets with a private pool & outside bathroom, & at the far end 3 'presidential' suites (2 of them interlinked for families) come with outside bathrooms, their own pools, & thatched 'salas' at the end of a private deck.

Royal is very much a holiday place, with unstructured activities allowing you to do as much or as little as you like. Chill out in camp by the pool or at the spa, browse in the gift shop, or take part in activities both in the GMA & the park: day & night game drives, walks, picnics, bush dinners, fishing, canoeing along a channel of the Zambezi & 3hr hikes into the mountains are all on the agenda; they'll even take guests running on the 2km airstrip! With a large team of guides, they aim for private guiding, but this isn't guaranteed. *US$898/1,015/1,089 Jul–Nov, US$505/585/646 Dec–Mar, US$615/744/818 Apr–Jun all classic/ deluxe/presidential pp sharing FBA, inc most drinks, exc park fees, spa, fly fishing. Sgl suppt US$184.44. Min stay 2 nights.* ⊙ *All year.* LLL–LLLLL

🏠 **Chongwe River Camp** [228 D3] (8 tents, 2 suites) 📞 0211 841051/2; m 0973 965851 e reservations@chongweriver.net; www.chongwe. com. ✪ CHONRC 15°42.911'S, 29°20.287'E. Set right on the Chongwe River that marks the boundary between the GMA & the national park, at its confluence with the Zambezi, Chongwe has an enviable location, with the escarpment making an impressive backdrop to the camp. Concentrations of game, while not as good as within the park itself, are greater here than further west, but without the high charges levied by the park's authorities. Most visitors arrive on scheduled flights at Royal airstrip, or occasionally by boat.

Meru-style tents are set up on platforms along the river, each with dbl or twin beds, a small shaded porch & a semi-open bathroom with ochre-painted ferro walls. To cool off, there's a large pool surrounded by a ferro wall behind the tents. At the south end of camp, right on the confluence of the Chongwe and the Zambezi Rivers, are Chongwe's 2 suites, enclosed by funky free-form walls. The Albida is the larger, with 2 en-suite octagonal tents linked by a canvas-canopied lounge/dining area. The Cassia Suite has just one large tent, with a private lounge & dining area, perfect for honeymooners. Both have private plunge pools, & guests may dine here in privacy, or in the central sandy dining area, shaded by an old winterthorn (*Faidherbia albida*), its pods beloved of the local elephant population. There's an informal lounge/bar, too, decked out with cushions on ochre-coloured benches beneath a couple of canvas canopies.

Traditionally popular with fishing groups, Chongwe offers all the standard activities, plus the option of walking upstream to return by canoe – or canoeing downstream from its bushcamp on Tsika Island. There's good birding as well, explained in part by the proximity of the Lower Zambezi escarpment. The atmosphere is informal & friendly, with knowledgeable & informative staff & good guiding. *Standard tent US$550 pp Apr–Jun, US$740/990 pp sharing/sgl Jul–Oct; suites US$700pp Apr–Jun, US$900/1150 pp sharing/sgl, all FBA, inc most drinks,*

laundry, park fees. No children under 7. ☺ *Jul–mid-Nov.* **LLL–LLLL**

✳ 🏠 **Chongwe River House** [228 D3] www.chongeriverhouse.com. Contact via Chongwe, page 238. ☍ CHONRH 15°42.488'S, 29°20.259'E. At the end of a massive winterthorn grove (*Faidherbia albida*), this unique, 4-bedroom private retreat lies on the banks of the peaceful Chongwe River, with a spectacular view of the nearby mountainous escarpment. The entire house is built of ferro walls & wild wood, so its structure follows the natural lines of the branches used. There is not a straight line to be seen! The main room looks out over the deck & a large pool to the river & mountains beyond. Furniture in the living area has been carved from a single huge fallen winterthorn tree, as if it had come to rest across the room, while embedded in the ceilings are pastel-coloured pebbles from the river. Each of the ground-floor bedrooms is entered through a tunnel, rather like walking through a cave; the curved entrance gives privacy without the need for doors. Their bathrooms have water pouring out of the stone ceiling instead of the normal shower rose, & upstairs the showers are waterfalls. There are wooden 'taps', & the basins have been carved out of wood & white marble by the Zambian artist, Eddie Mumba. From the bedrooms, the sitting room & the deck you will have game in view, feeding & watering; even the unusual baths in the upstairs bedrooms afford a view across the bush, inc the huge elephants attracted by the house's winterthorn trees. The house is completely autonomous, with its own chef, safari guide & vehicle, giving groups complete flexibility over their activities. *US$700 pp Apr–Jun, US$900 pp Jul–Oct; FBA, inc most drinks, laundry, park fees. Min 4 adults.* ☺ *Jul–mid Nov.* **LLLL**

Within the Lower Zambezi National Park (Park fees US$25 pp/day; self drivers US$30 pp/day plus US$15 per vehicle/day; local vehicles K17/day; ☺ sunrise–sunset Jun–Oct)

✳ 🏠 **Chiawa Camp** [228 D3] (9 tented chalets) ☎0211 261588; m 0977 767433; e res@chiawa.com; www.chiawa.com.
☍ CHIAWA 15°41.058'S, 29°24.829'E. Small, friendly & highly efficient, the oldest camp in the valley is set beneath a grove of mahogany trees, about 8km (30 mins' drive) inside the national

park. Most guests fly in to Royal airstrip, followed by a short drive, & a boat ride to the lodge. Private flights from elsewhere, including the Luangwa, can be organised.

Being in the park, Chiawa is open only during the dry season, so is largely built of wood, canvas & reeds. Though the setting remains rustic, the camp itself has become considerably more stylish over the years. Six of its rooms are well-spaced, insect-proof, Meru-style tents on raised timber decks facing the river. With smart, dark-wood furniture, king-size or twin beds enveloped in mosquito nets, a bath, indoor & outdoor showers, & twin washbasins, they're large, airy, comfortable & well appointed. Two newer tented chalets under thatch have white interiors to give a lighter, brighter feel. And then there's the honeymoon suite, with its bathtub on the split-level deck, & seating down below. Every chalet has 12v lighting & 220v power for charging batteries, & there's free Wi-Fi throughout.

Central to the camp is a comfortable riverside structure with a proper bar & a well-designed lounge area with plenty of books & magazines; stairs lead up to a 2nd seating & viewing area above. Most meals are taken in a separate dining shelter, overlooking the river, & kitted out with a spotting scope, but other venues feature too: their 'barge lunch' out to the islands is particularly special. There's even a gift shop for a touch of retail therapy.

From walking safaris & 4x4 trips (inc night drives), to motorboat excursions & canoe trips along the river or the Nkalangi Channel: activities are exceptionally flexible here. Game-drive vehicles have bean bags for camera kit, & window seats for all. Few visitors just want to fish, but Chiawa has also maintained a top reputation for serious fishing trips for tiger fish (all catch & release). Right in camp, a solid hide towers above an area where elephants come to drink, while a reed hide downstream is accessed by boat, & a third, behind the camp, by vehicle. For those after a cooling dip, there's a large, secluded pool backed by decking & sunloungers, with a gym under construction in 2015.

As part of its commitment to the development of conservation education, Chiawa & its guests fund the education of 140 children in local village schools, & it is a top contributor to the funding of anti-poaching, environmental education programmes & conservation in the area. Chiawa is run by a family team along with professional staff & good guides, & has carved out a reputation as one of Zambia's top camps. *US$1,200/875/655 pp Jul–Oct/Jun–mid-Jul & early Nov/mid-Apr–May, all FBA, inc local drinks, laundry, exc park fees. No children under 8.* ⊕ *15 Apr–15 Nov.* **LLLL–LLLLL**

✳ 🏠 **Sausage Tree Camp** [228 D3] (8 chalets) 📞 0211 845204; 📱 0977 455448; 📧 info@sausagetreecamp.com; www. sausagetreecamp.com. ⊕ SAUSTR 15°40.675'S, 29°28.692'E. In a beautiful riverside position, Sausage Tree is usually accessed by a short flight to either Jeki or (closer) Royal airstrip. The sausage tree for which the camp was named has long since been washed away, but mature Natal mahoganies give plenty of shade, & sandy paths add a very natural, bush feel.

The camp is privately owned & professionally staffed & run, with first-class food & attentive service. Personal attention extends to private guiding, & each chalet is the responsibility of an individual *muchinda* or butler, though the camp is less formal than this might suggest. Five large, very comfortable reed-walled chalets with billowing cream-canvas roofs have ochre-painted bedheads & floors, topped with Persian-style rugs. Steps lead down to matching open-air bathrooms, cleverly built around indigenous trees, while sliding gauze doors open on to small verandas. Larger & more open are 2 honeymoon suites, their baths by the window, their showers beneath the trees, & their own infinity pools fronting the river. In the same mould is Kigelia House (*min 3 guests*), its 2 en-suite bedrooms (one dbl, one twin) with indoor bathrooms flanking a central lounge/diner with bar & fridge that opens on to the pool deck. Solid teak furniture, top-class ivory fabrics & linen sheets add further quality, & each chalet is equipped with binoculars & an emergency radio. Generator power is giving way to solar, with 24hr electricity & no ill effects on the hot water supply! There's also Wi-Fi throughout.

The cream canvas roofs extend to the living & dining areas, & matching umbrellas that shade tables & chairs on the wooden deck. Most meals are taken here or by the firepit, but they may turn up in some surprising venues. Almost out of sight behind a canvas wall is a magnificent 25m infinity pool, with a river view that justifies swimming a length or two. Out of camp you'll typically do 2 activities a day, to include game drives (day & night), canoeing, walking, boating or fishing, but it's very flexible; midday activities can be organised, as can full-day drives with a picnic. One of the camp's main assets is the proximity of a lovely backwater, the Chifungulu Channel, which runs parallel to the main river for about 14km & makes a great area for a gentle paddle. It's popular with the local hippo population, too, not to mention elephants & buffalo & some wonderful birdlife. As an aside, *chifungulu* is the local name for *Combretum microphyllum*, the 'flame creeper' that grows up winterthorn trees here. In his book on the Luangwa's flora, Smith observes that local people used to grind up the roots of this creeper, mix them with dog turds, & burn the mixture – using the ashes as a cure for lunacy. Back at camp, it colours the trees blood red during July. *US$1,140 pp Jul–mid Nov, US$980 pp Jun, US$760 Apr–May, all FBA inc drinks, exc park fees; honeymoon US$1,240/1,080/860 pp.* ⊕ *Apr–Nov.* **LLLL–LLLLL**

🏠 **Potato Bush Camp** [228 D3] (4 tented chalets) www.potatobushcamp.com; contact via Sausage Tree, above. A short walk from Sausage Tree, Potato Bush has a simpler, more contemporary feel than its sibling, the broad canvas roofs of its central area & chalets lending a hint of the east. Low, open-sided wooden walkways and chalets set on plinths mean that the camp can enjoy a longer season than Sausage Tree, as rises in water levels are less crucial.

Cream canvas stretched over rosewood frames creates the walls & roofs of the chalets & the main area, instilling a sense of light & space. The chalets are entered from the back, but bifold wooden doors open to a river view, with a 2-person hammock swinging by each private plunge pool. Inside are twin or king-size beds draped in walk-in mosquito nets, cream-coloured couches, & an open-fronted bathroom with twin basins, shower & bath. A 2-bedroom family chalet is set further back than the others at the end of camp, with a dbl-sized plunge pool. All have fans & 24hr electricity. In the central area, solid-wood furniture runs to a beautiful rosewood dining table, balanced by a couple of intimate seating areas looking out towards the firepit by the river.

With a strong professional team linked to that of Sausage Tree, & the same range of activities, this is a small, relaxed camp that benefits from very high standards. *US$855 pp Jul–Oct, US$735 pp Jun & Nov–early Jan, US$650 Apr–May, all FBA inc drinks, exc park fees.* ⊕ *Apr–early Jan.* **LLLL**

🏠 **Mwambashi River Lodge** [228 C3] (9 tents, 1 chalet) UK m +44 (0)7927 534647; e nigel@adventurewildsafaris.com; www.

mwambashiriverlodge.com. ⊕ MWAMRL 15°38.392'S, 29°34.681'E. Mwambashi occupies a well-shaded site in a bend in the river with large *albida* trees, typical of this riverine environment. Most visitors arrive by plane at Jeki airstrip. It is now run exclusively for groups of up to 22 people, who arrive on Sat & stay for 7 nights, & cannot be booked by individual travellers.

Its large, walk-in tents are built on wooden platforms with verandas overlooking the river, & canvas shadecloths. Each has a dbl or twin beds with mosquito-netted walls & a large en-suite bathroom at the back. A rather grand honeymoon chalet, open fronted & constructed of wood under thatch, has its own plunge pool. Central to the lodge is a wide thatched structure, with a bar & dining area flanking a substantial lounge; it's light, open & airy, with good river views. With day & night game drives, walking safaris, canoeing, boat trips & fishing, there's plenty to keep a large group occupied. There's even an 'exercise area' to work off excess energy, & a lovely riverside pool to cool off afterwards. *US$34,000–77,000/wk (18 guests) FBA inc park fees, exc alcoholic drinks. Additional guest US$240/day.* ⊕ *Apr–Oct.* **LL–LLL**

✳ 🏠 **Old Mondoro** [228 E3] (5 chalets) www.oldmondoro.com; contact via Chiawa (page 239). ⊕ OLDMON 15°37.839'S, 29°41.423'E. This remote riverside camp surrounded by open woodland remains the only bushcamp in the Lower Zambezi National Park – although recent refurbishments – including 24hr electricity – have served to reinvent the term 'bushcamp'! Today, it is owned & run by Chiawa Camp, & staffed by an experienced team. Unless booked by a sgl group, there is a maximum of eight guests in camp.

A smart canvas-roofed central area with plenty of cushioned wicker chairs, a dining table & a firepit looks across to the Zambezi, as do 4 of the well-spaced chalets. These are set on temporary concrete platforms with reed walls that are low enough to give views of the river, & canvas sides that can be rolled down for greater warmth or privacy. Inside are comfortable dbl or twin beds & teak chairs, plus a basin & curtained toilet; outside there's a proper hot shower & a huge riverside bath that doubles as a plunge pool, while on the veranda a daybed complements the usual chairs. It may look rustic, but there's everything you could want, from sockets for charging batteries & running computers to gas geysers for hot water, fans & good bedside lights. Away from the others, next to the managers' house, is a family chalet, its 2 en-suite rooms (1 dbl, 1 twin) with an interlinking door.

The camp focuses on walking, day & night game drives, game viewing by boat, canoe trips & fishing. We're told that there's an increasing presence of leopard locally – & certainly this is borne out by experience. Despite a considerable upgrade, the remote & open location means that this is still very much a bushcamp experience for those seeking an emphasis on guiding & wildlife, though the standard of food & service remains very high. *US$1,120/1,512 sgl/pp sharing mid Jul–Oct, US$760 pp Jun & early Nov, US$610 pp end Apr–May, all FBA, inc most drinks, laundry; exc park fees. No children under 12.* ⊕ *May–Oct.* **LLL–LLLLL**

🏠 **Anabezi** [228 F3] (11 chalets) m 0967 786398; e res@anabezi.com; www.anabezi.com. ✪ 15°36.630'S, 29°46.192'E. On the site of the former Mushika Camp & Ana Tree Lodge, Anabezi was opened in 2014, just 4km from Kulefu airstrip. Originally built as one camp, Anabezi stretches along almost 500m of raised wooden walkways. Now, however, it has been split into two: Anabezi, with 7 chalets closer to the Zambezi, & Little Anabezi, with 4, looking out to the Mushika floodplain. Each has its own bar, seating & dining areas (with individual rather than communal tables), as well as a pool & firepit, & Wi-Fi in the communal areas. Guests at the smaller camp are welcome to use the facilities of the larger, whose main area looks across to the Zambezi River. It's a good way of getting some exercise, too.

The chalets here are simply huge: canvas-roofed structures with reed walls, fronted by a series of sliding glass doors. These open onto a long shaded deck with day beds & a plunge pool. At one end there's an open-air shower, toilet & basin; in the centre, a second indoor bathroom complete with bathtub. Twin or king-size beds with bedside tables are enveloped in mosquito nets, & there's a

substantial sitting area with solid-wood furniture & a proper sofa. Extra beds can be added for children.

Activities take in the range of game drives (day & night), walking, fishing, canoeing & boat trips, led by a very good guiding team which aims for flexibility. While private guiding isn't always possible, all guests have a 'window' seat in very comfortable game-drive vehicles. It'll take time for Anabezi to settle into the comfortable mould of more established operators in the valley, but it has the makings of a solid camp in a good location for wildlife. *US$750 pp Apr–Jun, US$980 pp Jul–Oct, US$870 pp early Nov, all FBA inc most drinks, exc park fees.* ⊕ *Apr–mid Nov.* **LLLL**

🏠 **Amanzi** [228 F3] (4 chalets) Contact via Anabezi, above ✪ 15°36.516'S, 29°47.163'E. Ranged along a low rise above a tranquil channel of the Zambezi, just a 5min drive from Kulefu airstrip, Amanzi opened in summer 2015. Under the same ownership as Anabezi, it is smaller & more intimate, with a rustic touch that feels more in keeping with the environment. In the central area, raised up on stilts, the open sides are complemented by wooden decking fitted around the existing trees, the outdoors feel enhanced by wicker & canvas chairs & simply crafted tables. Should protection from the elements prove necessary, roll-down blinds are ready & waiting. Down below, sunloungers sit alongside a small pool, & closer to the river there's a firepit.

The chalets – each of them long & narrow – are designed to make the best of the location, with a wall of gauzed picture windows facing the river. Amanzi might be simpler than its sibling, but creature comforts are plentiful: dbl or twin 4-poster beds with a fan inside the mosquito net; a comfy lounge area; a dressing room with a big shower & separate loo with a view; & its own deck with swinging chairs. Two of the chalets are built closer together with a linking walkway, so would work well for families. Activities are as at Anabezi, with the same degree of flexibility. *US$600 pp Apr–Jun, US$700 pp Jul–Oct, US$650 pp early Nov, all FBA inc most drinks, exc park fees.* ⊕ *Apr–mid Nov.* **LLL–LLLL**

East of the national park There are normally a few small camps operating east of the national park and the Mpata Gorge. These are usually accessed from the village of Luangwa, or Luangwa boma, which is some 85km from the Great East Road (page 245), or can be reached by charter flight from Lusaka. At present, the most reliable is:

Redcliff Zambezi Lodge [228 G4] (6 chalets) ☏ +27 82 856 6272; m 0979 587822; e info@redcliff-lodge.com; www.redcliff-lodge.com. Redcliff Zambezi is tucked away in a GMA between the dramatic scenery of the Mpata Gorge & the village of Luangwa on the Mozambique border. Access is by 45min boat transfer from Luangwa boma.

Accommodation is in en-suite tented chalets, with 2 or 4 beds, the latter layout designed for families. An 'entertainment area' encompasses a TV lounge, dining room & bar, with a pool, campfire & deck overlooking the river. There's limited mobile phone reception & Wi-Fi in case you can't manage without! The lodge is particularly popular for fishing, with a strict catch-&-release policy except for the occasional fish dinner. Also on the agenda are sunset cruises, birding, guided walks, cultural trips, & game viewing in the national park. *US$275 pp sharing FBA; exc bar, transfers.* ⊕ *All year.* **LL**

You've got the guide, now make the call

This book's author, **Chris McIntyre** runs specialist tour operator Expert Africa.

See **www.expertafrica.com** for the most detailed information on Zambia safaris, then call us to help you plan your own superb trip.

No bias, no hard sell: for real insight, call an Expert

UK: +44 (0) 20 8232 9777

USA/Canada (toll-free): 1-800-242-2434

Australia (toll-free): 1-800-995-397

info@expertafrica.com
www.expertafrica.com

EXPERT ✦ AFRICA

NAMIBIA · SOUTH AFRICA · BOTSWANA · ZIMBABWE · ZAMBIA · MOZAMBIQUE
MALAWI · TANZANIA · KENYA · RWANDA · SEYCHELLES

ABTA
The Travel Association
ABTA No. Y1608

AITO Assured

SAFARI CLUB

African specialists who have been creating journeys of a lifetime for over 10 years

- Visit some of Africa's finest authentic safari camps and pristine game reserves with superb guiding

- Private luxury tours to South and North Luangwa, Lower Zambezi and Kafue national parks and Victoria Falls

- Our UK-based expert safari consultants will design your tailor-made safari holiday in Zambia

- Call us and talk to people who have lived and worked in Zambia for free, unbiased advice

- Our tours represent excellent value for money

- Visit our website and check out our flexible sample itineraries

e: info@safari-club.co.uk
w: www.safari-club.co.uk
t: 01664 464 228 / 0845 054 5889

10

The Luangwa Valley

This lush rift valley, enclosed by steep escarpment walls, is one of the continent's finest areas for wildlife. Four national parks protect parts of the area: South Luangwa, North Luangwa, Luambe and Lukusuzi. Separating these are game management areas (GMAs), which also contain good populations of game. This entire valley is remote but, for the enthusiast, the wildlife is well worth the effort made to get here.

For most visitors, South Luangwa National Park (known locally as just 'the South Park') is by far the most practical park to visit in the valley. This is the largest of the parks, with superb wildlife and many excellent camps. Organising a trip to South Luangwa is not difficult, and its infrastructure is easily the best. However, it is still a very remote park, and so most visitors arrive on trips organised outside Zambia. A few arrive independently and, though this is possible, it does limit their accommodation and activity choices.

The more intrepid may also organise a safari from the South Park into North Luangwa, which is even more remote and exclusive. Its wildlife is now flourishing, thanks to some intensive conservation efforts over the past decade, and the few safaris that do run concentrate on taking small groups for purely walking trips.

Luambe National Park is much smaller than either the South or the North parks, and there's one camp there that makes a good stopover if you're heading that way. The birdwatching is good, as with the other parks, though there is less game.

Finally, Lukusuzi National Park is something of an unknown quantity. Few people have even visited this park and there are currently no facilities or camps there.

THE GREAT EAST ROAD

The Great East Road leads from Lusaka to Chipata, the Luangwa's 'gateway', and just over the border from Malawi. It's a long drive: about 555km of tar which is good in places, and pot-holed in others and now under a slow but ongoing reconstruction programme. Alternatively, there are regular buses – though you'll need to take a coach from Lusaka early in the morning to be sure of getting to Chipata by evening. There's relatively little *en route* bar a few fuel stations and some useful places to stop for a meal or to sleep, but beyond Chipata is the little-visited town of Lundazi, notable mainly for its anachronistic castle.

LUANGWA RIVER AREA The impressive suspension bridge over the Luangwa is some 225km east of Lusaka, or 329km west of Chipata. Just 1.9km west of this is a turning to the village of Luangwa (or Luangwa boma), which lies at the confluence of the Luangwa and the Zambezi rivers, close to the border with both Mozambique and Zimbabwe. Near the turning is a small market where there are baskets for sale.

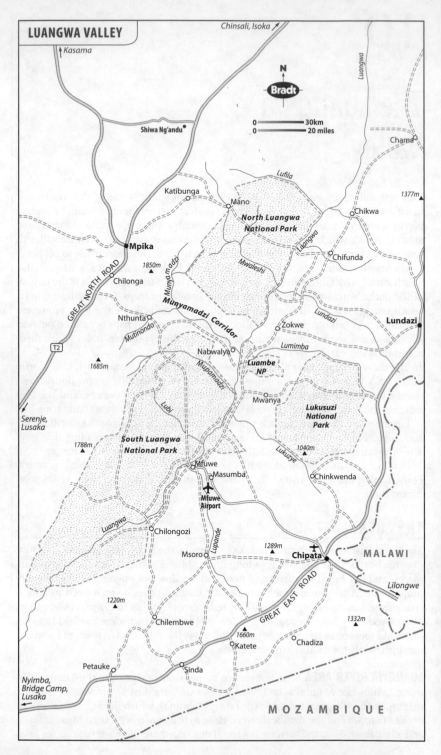

LUANGWA VALLEY

Chinsali, Isoka

Kasama

N

Bradt

0   30km
0   20 miles

Chama

Shiwa Ng'andu

Luangwa

Lufila

1377m

Katibunga

Mano

North Luangwa
National Park

Chikwa

Mpika

Luangwa

Chifunda

Chilonga

1850m

Mwaleshi

Munyamadzi

Munyamadzi Corridor

Lundazi

Nthunta

Mutinondo

Zokwe

Lundazi

GREAT NORTH ROAD

T2

Nabwalya

Lumimba

1685m

Mupamadzi

Luambe
NP

1788m

Lubi

Mwanya

Lukusuzi
National
Park

Serenje,
Lusaka

South Luangwa
National Park

1040m

Lukuzye

Mfuwe

Masumba

Mfuwe
Airport

Chinkwenda

Luangwa

Chilongozi

Msoro

Lupande

1289m

Chipata

MALAWI

1220m

GREAT EAST ROAD

Lilongwe

Chilembwe

1660m

1332m

Katete

Chadiza

Petauke

Sinda

Nyimba,
Bridge Camp,
Lusaka

MOZAMBIQUE

The lodge near the start of this road is the obvious place to stay between Lusaka and Chipata (or Malawi).

Where to stay and eat

Bridge Camp [map, page 228] (10 chalets, camping) Feira Rd; m 0977 395037, 0979 180507; e brldgecamp@gmail.com; www.bridgecampzambia.com. ✪ 15°00.191'S, 30°12.547'E. This budget camp built on a hill overlooking the Luangwa River is on Feira Rd just 3km from the Great East Rd towards Luangwa boma, & clearly signposted. It offers a range of simple stone chalets, variously furnished with sgl, dbl or twin beds. All are thatched with gauze windows, & generator-powered electrics. Some are en suite; others share toilets & showers. There is also a tree-shaded, level campsite within the grounds of the main lodge, with BBQ facilities & separate ablution blocks, & charcoal & wood provided. The bar & restaurant, with an à-la-carte menu, are open to passing visitors, & there's a pool.

Changa Changa Adventures run hiking, canoeing & floating trips from the camp: guided hikes (*US$20/40, ½/full day*) &, in the dry season only, guided canoe trips (*US$50–90 per canoe ½/full day – or US$30 pp for a sundowner trip*). Options include overnight hiking to the confluence of the Lunsemfwa & Luangwa, followed by canoeing back the following morning (*US$170 per boat/day*), & 3–5 nights' trekking in the Lunsemfwa Gorge (*US$170 per group/ day*). Overnight trips are self-catering, & you'll need your own equipment, though the camp will prepare lunch boxes & you can hire tents & sleeping bags. *Chalet US$70 shared facilities, US$90–105 en suite, both 2 people sharing; camping US$8 pp.* **$$–$$$**

NYIMBA Some 98km east of the Luangwa Bridge, huge speed humps announce the presence of this small town, which has both a **fuel** station and a **bank** with an ATM. There's also a small market, a bus station and a **post office**.

Where to stay and eat Along the road about 2km further east there's a prominent restaurant and bar, **Thula**. Serving everything from nshima and chicken to T-bone steak, it's a handy option for a break during a long drive. Nearby the relatively recent **Tatiana Lodge** has a number of chalets (but to date we have been unable to obtain further details).

PETAUKE Little more than a dot on the map, Petauke nevertheless has a **fuel** station, **banks**, a market and guesthouses including, **Chimwemwe Executive Lodge** (*2260m Boma Road;* \0216 371543; m 0966 247674/0979 326955; e info@chimwemwelodge. com; www.chimwemwelodge.com; *$$*) which has been expanded considerably over the past couple of years and now has 40 rooms in thatched chalets as well as a campsite and restaurant. More reports welcome.

KATETE Another fairly nondescript town some 79km west of Chipata, Katete is home to a large mosque, a useful **filling station**, a **Finance Bank**, **post office**, and half-a-dozen grocery **shops**. There's also a Catholic church on the southern side of the road at the western end of town and the St Francis Mission Hospital. If you're interested in volunteering, or in cultural tourism, check out Tiko Lodge (see below). If you are catching the bus from Lusaka, the journey to Katete is about 7 hours long and you can ask the bus to drop you at Tiko Lodge or take a taxi there (about 5 minutes) from Katete bus station.

Where to stay

Tiko Lodge (17 rooms, 14 dorm beds, 1 African hut) Great East Rd; \021 6252122;

m 0979 176960; e tikoeducation@gmail.com; www.tikondane.org. Next to the hospital, about

2km west of Katete, this lodge was set up to raise funds for the Tikondane Community Centre, which brings together skills training, early childhood & adult education programmes (in particular the '19 steps out of poverty' programme for subsistence farmers). Guests are welcome to get involved at several levels: teaching their own subject, perhaps joining classes for drumming or dancing, learning the local language or helping make peanut butter or soap. A structured programme of longer voluntary work means that even those with just a few weeks can contribute to the project. Computer skills, fundraising, basic teaching & reading are much valued, but the list is seemingly endless!

Volunteering packages cost $225 a week including meals & accommodation & run from 8 days to 12 weeks. In order to help foster local traditions, the lodge works with 3 villages, & organises a number of 'cultural safaris'. One option features a visit by oxcart to watch the Chewa initiation rites: Chinamwali for women & Gule Wamkulu, the 'ghost dance', for men. You are invited into homes in the village & a vegetarian meal is included. Accommodation in the lodge varies from en-suite family or double rooms to simple dormitories, & there is also campground & a restaurant with a license. *$20 en suite with fridge; dorm bed $6; camping $5 pp.* **$**

CHIPATA

Chipata (✪ CHIPAT 13°38.557'S, 32°38.796'E) is a relatively small but busy town that is more than just a gateway to South Luangwa; it is also a border town just 30km from Malawi. Known in colonial days as Fort Jameson, and now the capital of Eastern Province, Chipata stands in a valley, surrounded by quite a fertile area of subsistence farms with low bush-covered hills around. To the east of town is an attractive mosque.

Getting there and away

Note that there is an ongoing programme of reconstruction work on the roads into and out of Chipata.

By bus There are regular coach services between Chipata and Lusaka – reliable operators include Johabie, Kobbs. Johabie buses depart daily at 05.00 and 06.00 and 9.00 taking around 7 to 8 hours to reach Lusaka; tickets cost around K150 one way. In the other direction, there are buses to Lilongwe in Malawi on Sunday and Wednesday, departing at around 11.00; the fare is K70 one way. The town's bus station is a little way off the main road, near the main township and market, and is not a place to be hanging around after dark.

Chipata is also the terminus of one of the postbus routes out of Lusaka, with buses departing from Lusaka every Tuesday, Thursday and Saturday at 06.00, arriving in Chipata at 15.30; the fare is K130 one way.

Local minibuses ply between Chipata and Mfuwe, leaving only when they're full and costing from K70 one way; alternatively, there are taxis available.

Where to stay and eat

Map, page 249. Most visitors continue to the Mfuwe area, down in the Luangwa Valley, if they can. However, if you arrive late then staying in Chipata is a wise move, and hitchhikers could easily end up here for a night or two due to lack of lifts. There are several good places to lay your head or get a meal, of which Mama Rula's is probably the most geared to travellers rather than the business market.

🏠 **Protea Hotel Chipata** (40 rooms) Great East Rd; ☎ 0216 222905; e reservations@ phchipata.co.zm; www.proteahotels.com/chipata. Just 2km west of town, 300m from the turn-off to Mfuwe the Protea has all the accoutrements of a good modern mid-range hotel for corporate as well as leisure travellers – twin & dbl rooms with TV, AC, phone, tea station, safe & free Wi-Fi, plus a restaurant & lounge. Outside, against a backdrop of the Kanjala Hills, the restaurant spills out onto a terrace where there's a good-sized pool in gardens, with a bar & umbrella shade. **$$$**

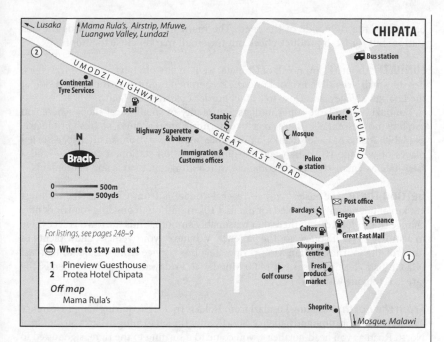

Lusaka · Mama Rula's, Airstrip, Mfuwe, Luangwa Valley, Lundazi

UMODZI HIGHWAY

Continental Tyre Services

Total

Highway Superette & bakery

Immigration & Customs offices

Stanbic $

GREAT EAST ROAD

Mosque

Police station

Market

KAFULA RD

Bus station

N

Bradt

0 —— 500m
0 —— 500yds

For listings, see pages 248–9

⊖ **Where to stay and eat**
1 Pineview Guesthouse
2 Protea Hotel Chipata
Off map
  Mama Rula's

Barclays $

Caltex

Shopping centre

Golf course

Fresh produce market

Shoprite

Post office

Engen

$ Finance

Great East Mall

Mosque, Malawi

🏠 **Mama Rula's** (12 rooms, camping)
m 0977 790226/0965 790225; e mamarula@
iwayafrica.com; www.mamarulas.com. In a quiet
location, Mama Rula's is well signposted north
of town, about 6km down the main Mfuwe road.
It's run by Andrea Breitenbach, whose passion
for plants shows in the colourful, lush gardens.
The campsite (*US$9 pp*), with its own bar & TV,
spreads across a large lawn under a canopy of
marvellous red mahogany (*Khaya anthotheca*)
trees & the odd banana or papaya. The ablutions
are clean (although reports indicate could do with
an update), & the simple twin rooms here – some
sharing facilities, some en suite – are spotless.
Dotted around are more en-suite 'executive'
rooms with twin beds & there's a tree-shaded
pool that's exclusively for guests. There is a well-
stocked bar & dining room; full English breakfast

is served & group meals on request with advance
warning; there is a limited menu but the steaks
are highly rated. Andrea can arrange trips to the
Luangwa & Luambe national parks & offer advice
& information on Malawi, from crossing the border
with a vehicle to currency exchange. **$–$$**
🏠 **Pineview Guesthouse** (35 rooms) 📞 0216
221633; m 0977 232735; e pineview@coppernet.
zm. Clearly signposted opposite Shoprite, this is
one of several guesthouses on a quiet street. Even
the simplest rooms are fine – with mosquito nets
on twin beds, polished floors, en-suite bath or
shower, a TV & fan; a little more buys a dbl bed
& tiled bathroom. There are tables & a bar in the
pleasant garden & secure parking. Good food
although you may have to wait depending on the
electricity supply. **$–$$**

Other practicalities As you arrive by road from Lusaka, the first of several **fuel**
stations is on your right, well placed for those continuing north to Mfuwe. The heart
of the town, however, is a couple of kilometres beyond this, past the police station
and around a sharp bend. There are various **banks**: Barclays and FNB amongst
others have ATMs. Watch out for money sharks, though, especially around the fuel
stations; if you need to change Malawian kwacha, contact Andrea at Mama Rula's
for advice on the best place to go.

For **supplies**, start at the large, very well-stocked Spar in the Great East Mall
(⏰ *07.30–20.00 daily*). Further southeast there's also a branch of Shoprite, set

The Luangwa Valley THE GREAT EAST ROAD

10

back from the right side of the road. The main market is out towards the bus station, but for fresh produce check out the small market close to Shoprite.

LUNDAZI About 180km north of Chipata, well off any obvious route for travellers, lies the small, friendly town of Lundazi. It's perched high above the eastern side of the Luangwa Valley, and close to a quiet border crossing to Malawi.

Lundazi has no large supermarkets, but plenty of small, local **shops** where you can buy most essentials. There are a lot of farming areas around, so fresh produce is available. It also has a few **banks**, a **post office**, a police station, an airstrip, assorted places of worship (Christian and Muslim), a mission station, a convent – and a fairy-tale Norman-style castle complete with a dungeon, turrets and battlements.

Getting there The easiest way to reach Lundazi is from Chipata. Then it's just 180km of tar, heavily pot-holed for the first 10km (although ongoing roadwork may change this in future), but thereafter reasonably smooth. Thus the town is accessible in a sturdy 2WD if you've got the patience. Whatever your vehicle, allow plenty of time for the journey. Juldan Motors operate a bus service from Lusaka to Lundazi (via Chipata) leaving Lusaka at 14.00 Monday to Friday and 13.00 at weekends; the fare is K180 one way.

From the north Reaching Lundazi from Isoka is trickier, requiring a high-clearance 4x4 and even more time and patience. Shortly after the left turning to Isoka on the Great North Road as you head northeast, you come to a turning to the right, signposted to the 'airport bar'. Take this turning, which will lead you through Ntendere and up into the mountains. After about 75km, there's a fork and you turn right, heading almost south to reach Muyombe 50km later. It's a rocky road on the escarpment with many gullies, but the scenery is beautiful. From Muyombe, continue south towards Nyika Plateau and the border with Malawi, dropping down from the mountains as you do so. After around 25km, just before the Malawi border, turn right (southwest) onto a dirt road. This is generally good, though sandy in parts. After shadowing the border for some 70km, there's a fork and Lundazi is signposted to the left, whilst Chama is about 35km away if you take the right turn. Lundazi is now about 110km south of you; making the whole journey a very full day's drive from Isoka.

From the Luangwa Valley Both of the two roads from the Luangwa Valley are impassable during the rains, and even in the dry season require hours of hard 4x4 travel. The better of them leaves the main road on the east side of the valley about 20–25km north of Luambe National Park. It then climbs up the escarpment directly to Lundazi, about 130km away. It's a 4- to 5-hour drive.

The second turns eastwards around the northern boundary of South Luangwa National Park and then cuts up the escarpment through Lukusuzi National Park. It then joins the Chipata–Lundazi road some 60km south of Lundazi (120km north of Chipata).

⌂ **Where to stay** There's only one place of choice (though it's pretty basic). If the castle's full then the town has several other small, basic resthouses, including the **Tigone**, where all the rooms are en suite.

⌂ **Lundazi Castle Hotel** (17 rooms) m 0978 4131988; http://lundazicastlehotel.com. Dick Hobson's excellent *Tales of Zambia* (page 527) tells of how the district commissioner in the late 1940s, Errol Button, needed to build a resthouse here. Tourism was then taking off & visitors needed to stop between Nyika Plateau & the Luangwa Valley (the same could be said today!). Button designed & had built a small castle in Norman style, with thick walls & narrow slits for archers, overlooking a lake. It has a dungeon, high turrets at each corner & battlements all around. It was christened 'Rumpelstiltskin' after a fairy-tale character favoured by his daughter, & cost a mere £500 at the time. The castle quickly became very popular, & was extended in 1952 to accommodate more visitors.

The castle today is a basic hotel, very cold in winter but with a good atmosphere & often fully booked. All but 4 of the clean but poorly maintained rooms share bathrooms, though running water is not always available – & only the more expensive rooms have hot showers. There is a lounge with DSTV, a cash bar & a restaurant. Simple traditional & Western dishes are served. **$**

SOUTH LUANGWA NATIONAL PARK

(*Park fees US$25 pp/day; self drivers US$30 pp/day plus US$15 per vehicle/day or K17 if Zambian registered; bed levy US$20/night*) There are many contenders for the title of Africa's best game park. The Serengeti, Amboseli, Ngorongoro Crater, Etosha, Kruger, Moremi and Mana Pools would certainly be high on the list. South Luangwa has a better claim than most. Some of these other areas will match its phenomenally high game densities. Many others – the lesser known of Africa's parks – will have equally few visitors. One or two also allow night drives, which open up a different, nocturnal world to view, allowing leopards to be commonly seen and even watched whilst hunting.

However, few have South Luangwa's high quality of guiding together with its remarkable wildlife spectacles, day and night, in the isolation of a true wilderness. These elements, perhaps, are how the contenders ought to be judged, and on these the South Luangwa Park comes out as one of the highest on the list.

HISTORY
Note on prehistory Some of the earliest evidence of humans in south-central Africa is currently emerging from excavations in and around the South Luangwa National Park. Stone tools dating to at least two million years ago have been found, and all other periods of the Stone Age are represented in the park. There is also evidence emerging of early farmers in the valley, appearing by AD400. As yet there are no sites accessible to the public, but plans have been afoot for some years to build a museum at Mfuwe, on the site of the old cultural centre at Nsendamila, to showcase the valley's rich prehistory.

From the 8th century
With thanks to John Hudson OBE for his help in preparing this text
With the Zambezi established as a trade route by the 8th century, it seems reasonable to assume that small settlements were also appearing on the neighbouring Luangwa River, though it is harder to navigate and was, at that time, probably used mainly to reach the abundant game of the valley, rather than for any trading purposes. Records tell us that Zumbo, on the eastern banks of the Luangwa, was founded in 1546 by the Portuguese – their first settlement in what is now Zambia – and one can only surmise that Luangwa township itself, situated at the strategically important confluence of the Luangwa and Zambezi rivers, must have been founded at around that time too. Both these settlements were subsequently abandoned and resettled, until about 1763 when Zumbo was recorded as having 200 Portuguese families living within its boundaries.

In the 19th century the area was crossed by many European explorers who came to hunt, trade, bring the Gospel or simply to satisfy their curiosity. Around 1810–20, a trading post was opened at Malambo, some 100km north of Mfuwe. This was on the main trade route from Tete to Lake Mweru, which had first been established by Lacerda as early as 1798.

In his last book, *Kakuli*, Norman Carr quotes a Portuguese captain, Antonio Gamitto, as writing of the Luangwa in around 1832:

Game of all kinds is very abundant at this season of drought; great numbers of wild animals collect here, leaving dry areas in search of water … we can only say that this district appears to be the richest in animal life of any we have seen.

Later, in December 1866, when Livingstone crossed the Luangwa at Perekani (a place north of Tafika and south of Chibembe), he was just one of many Europeans exploring the continent. He commented:

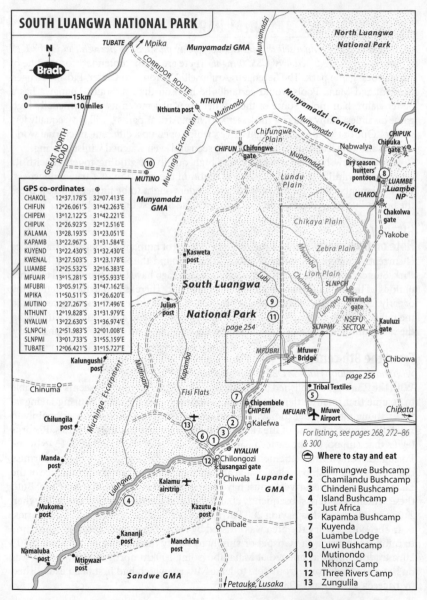

SOUTH LUANGWA NATIONAL PARK

0 —————15km
0 —————10 miles

GPS co-ordinates ⊕	
CHAKOL	12°37.178'S 32°07.413'E
CHIFUN	12°26.061'S 31°42.263'E
CHIPEM	13°12.122'S 31°42.221'E
CHIPUK	12°26.923'S 32°12.516'E
KALAMA	13°28.193'S 31°23.051'E
KAPAMB	13°22.967'S 31°31.584'E
KUYEND	13°22.430'S 31°32.430'E
KWENAL	13°27.503'S 31°23.178'E
LUAMBE	12°25.532'S 32°16.383'E
MFUAIR	13°15.281'S 31°55.933'E
MFUBRI	13°05.917'S 31°47.162'E
MPIKA	11°50.511'S 31°26.620'E
MUTINO	12°27.267'S 31°17.496'E
NTHUNT	12°19.828'S 31°31.979'E
NYALUM	13°22.630'S 31°36.974'E
SLNPCH	12°51.983'S 32°01.008'E
SLNPMI	13°01.733'S 31°55.159'E
TUBATE	12°06.421'S 31°15.727'E

For listings, see pages 268, 272–86 & 300

Where to stay and eat

1 Bilimungwe Bushcamp
2 Chamilandu Bushcamp
3 Chindeni Bushcamp
4 Island Bushcamp
5 Just Africa
6 Kapamba Bushcamp
7 Kuyenda
8 Luambe Lodge
9 Luwi Bushcamp
10 Mutinondo
11 Nkhonzi Camp
12 Three Rivers Camp
13 Zungulila

I will make this land better known to men that it may become one of their haunts. It is impossible to describe its luxuriance.

In 1904 a Luangwa Game Park was declared on the eastern bank of the river. However, this was not maintained, hunting licences were given out to control allegedly marauding elephants, and the park came to mean little. Then on 27 May 1938 three parks were defined in the valley: the North Luangwa Game Reserve, the Lukusuzi Game Reserve and the South Luangwa Game Reserve – which corresponded roughly to the present park, though without the Chifungwe Plain or the Nsefu Sector.

In the following year, Norman Carr and Bert Schultz were appointed as game rangers and villages within the reserves were moved outside its boundaries. Initially Norman Carr recommended that hunting safaris be started, but over the coming decade he realised that visitors would also come for what are now called 'photographic safaris'.

In 1949 the Senior Chief Nsefu, prompted by Norman Carr, established a private game reserve on the Luangwa's eastern bank, between the Mwasauke and Kauluzi rivers. A safari camp was started here which sent some of its income directly back to the local community. (Norman Carr was ahead of his time!) This soon moved to the site of the present-day Nsefu Camp. The chief's reserve became the Nsefu Sector, which was absorbed into the boundaries of the present park – along with the Chifungwe Plain, north of the Mupamadzi River – when new legislation turned all game reserves into national parks on 15 February 1972.

In the later years of his life, Norman Carr lived at Kapani Safari Lodge, having played a pivotal role in the history of the valley by pioneering commercial walking safaris, upon which South Luangwa has founded its reputation. He remained an important and highly outspoken figure to the end, and devoted much energy in his latter years to development projects designed to help the surrounding local communities to benefit from the park. He was especially involved with local school projects, encouraging the next generation of Zambians to value their wildlife heritage.

His excellent example is increasingly being followed by many of the more forward-thinking safari operators. More and more operators are taking their role in the community seriously, often by sponsoring schools and clinics in the surrounding countryside. Kawaza Village (pages 288–9) is a highly visible tourism venture run by and for one of the local communities.

GEOGRAPHY The South Park now covers about 9,050km^2 of the Luangwa Valley's floor, which varies from about 500m to 800m above sea level. The western side of the park is bounded by the Muchinga Escarpment, and from there it generally slopes down to the eastern side of the park, where, except in the extreme south, it is bordered by the wide meanders of the Luangwa River.

Near the banks of the Luangwa the land is fairly flat, and mostly covered with mature woodlands. There are few dense shrubberies here, but many open areas where beautiful tall trees stand perhaps 10–20m apart, shading a mixture of small bushes and grassland. Occasionally there are wide, open grassland plains. The largest are Mutanda Plain in Nsefu, Lion Plain just opposite Nsefu, Chikaya Plain north of there, Ntanta around the Mupamadzi's confluence with the Luangwa, the huge Chifungwe Plain in the far north of the park, and the little-known Lundu Plain, south of the Mupamadzi River. These are not Serengeti-type plains with short grass; instead they usually boast tall species of grasses and often bushes. It is their lack of trees that makes them open.

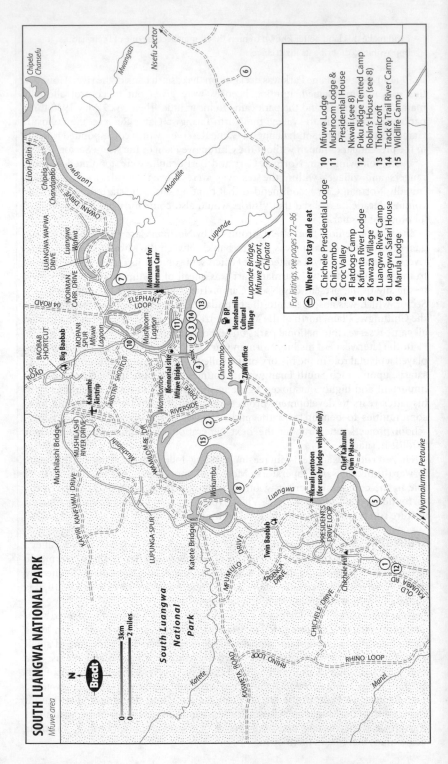

SOUTH LUANGWA NATIONAL PARK
Mfuwe area

N

Bradt

0   3km
0   2 miles

South Luangwa National Park

Where to stay and eat

For listings, see pages 272–86

1   Chichele Presidential Lodge
2   Chinzombo
3   Croc Valley
4   Flatdogs Camp
5   Kafunta River Lodge
6   Kawaza Village
7   Luangwa River Camp
8   Luangwa Safari House
9   Marula Lodge

10   Mfuwe Lodge
11   Mushroom Lodge &
      Presidential House
      Nkwali (see 8)
12   Puku Ridge Tented Camp
      Robin's House (see 8)
13   Thornicroft
14   Track & Trail River Camp
15   Wildlife Camp

Understandably, the highest density of animals (and hence camps) is around the Luangwa River. However, increasingly camps are being set up elsewhere in the park. The trio of bushcamps run by Norman Carr Safaris is located along the Lubi (or Luwi) River, one of the Luangwa's smaller tributaries, while temporary walking camps run by Robin Pope Safaris are sited beside the Mupamadzi River rather than the Luangwa.

The Luangwa River For the visitor, perhaps the most notable feature of the Luangwa Valley is the pristine river that runs through it. Take a close look at it: very few rivers of this size in Africa (or anywhere else!) have been so unaffected by man. There are no dams on it, no commercial agriculture along its banks, and incredibly little pollution. Hence here you can still see the seasonal fluctuations of water levels and flooding which lead to the dynamic nature of a river in a really natural state. It's not only beautiful but also textbook geography.

Note how the river's twisting curves cut easily through the valley's fertile soil, leaving a sprinkling of crescent-shaped oxbow lakes, or *wafwas*, in their wake. Every year new sandbanks arise as its original banks are cut back and the river's course changes with the floods. Just look at the number of riverside camps and lodges that, over the years, have either moved or gradually been swallowed up by river erosion.

GEOLOGY The Luangwa Valley is a rift valley, similar to the Great Rift Valley of east Africa, though probably older, and it shares its genesis with the adjoining Lower Zambezi Valley. The original sedimentary strata covering the whole area is part of the karoo system, sedimentary rocks laid down from 175 to 300 million years ago.

During this time, faulting occurred and volcanic material was injected into rifts in the existing sediments. One of these faults is the wide valley that the Luangwa now occupies. In geologically recent times, the Luangwa meandered extensively across the wide valley floor, eroding the volcanic rocks and depositing mineral-rich silts. These meanders also left behind them old watercourses and oxbow pools. The most recent of these can still be seen, and they are an important feature of the landscape near the present river.

FLORA AND FAUNA
Vegetation To understand the Luangwa Valley's vegetation, the base of its productive ecosystem, consider the elements that combine to nurture its plants: the water, light, heat and nutrients. Rainfall in the valley is typically 800–1,100mm per annum – which is moderate, but easily sufficient for strong vegetation growth. Occupying a position between 12° and 14° south of the Equator, the valley lacks neither light nor heat. (Visit in October and you may feel that it has too much of both.)

However, the key to its vegetation lies in the nutrients. The Luangwa's soils, being volcanic in origin, are rich in minerals, and the sediments laid down by the river are fine, making excellent soils. Thus with abundant water, light, heat and nutrient-rich soils, the valley's vegetation has thrived: it is both lush and diverse.

Unlike many parks, the 'bush' in the Luangwa is very variable, and as you drive or walk you'll pass through a patchwork of different vegetation zones. See *Flora and Fauna*, pages 29–33, for more detail, but the more obvious include some beautiful mature forests of 'cathedral mopane'. South of Mfuwe, just outside the national park on the way to the salt pans south of Nkwali, is one area where the mopane are particularly tall.

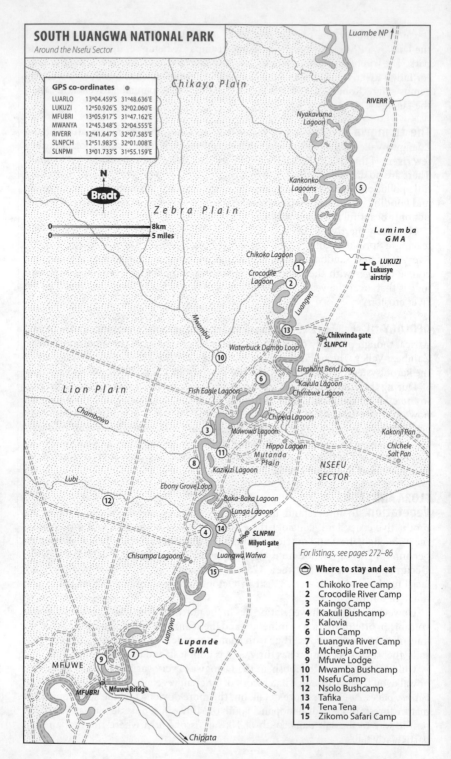

Luambe NP

Chikaya Plain

Nyakavuma
Lagoon

RIVERR

GPS co-ordinates ⊕
LUARLO   13°04.459'S 31°48.636'E
LUKUZI   12°50.926'S 32°02.060'E
MFUBRI   13°05.917'S 31°47.162'E
MWANYA   12°45.348'S 32°04.555'E
RIVERR   12°41.647'S 32°07.585'E
SLNPCH   12°51.983'S 32°01.008'E
SLNPMI   13°01.733'S 31°55.159'E

Kankonko
Lagoons

N

Bradt

Zebra Plain

0   8km
0   5 miles

Lumimba
GMA

⊕ LUKUZI
Lukusye
airstrip

Chikoko Lagoon

①

Crocodile
Lagoon

②

Luangwa

⑬

Chikwinda gate
SLNPCH

Waterbuck Dambo Loop

⑩

Elephant Bend Loop

Mwamba

⑥

Kavula Lagoon

Lion Plain

Fish Eagle Lagoon

Chimbwe Lagoon

Chambowo

Chipela Lagoon

Kakonji Pan

③

Muwowo Lagoon

Chichele
Salt Pan

⑪

Hippo Lagoon

⑧

Mutanda
Plain

NSEFU
SECTOR

Kazikizi Lagoon

Lubi

Ebony Grove Loop

⑫

Baka-Baka Lagoon

Lunga Lagoon

④ ⑭

SLNPMI
Milyoti gate

Chisumpa Lagoons

Luangwa Wafwa

⑮

For listings, see pages 272–86

⊖ Where to stay and eat

1   Chikoko Tree Camp
2   Crocodile River Camp
3   Kaingo Camp
4   Kakuli Bushcamp
5   Kalovia
6   Lion Camp
7   Luangwa River Camp
8   Mchenja Camp
9   Mfuwe Lodge
10 Mwamba Bushcamp
11 Nsefu Camp
12 Nsolo Bushcamp
13 Tafika
14 Tena Tena
15 Zikomo Safari Camp

Luangwa

Lupande
GMA

⑨ ⑦

MFUWE

MFUBRI   Mfuwe Bridge

Chipata

Along the Luangwa's tributaries, which are just rivers of sand for most of the year, you'll find lush riverine vegetation dominated by giant red mahogany trees (*Khaya anthotheca*, formerly known as *Khaya nyasica*) and *Adina microsephala*. Sometimes you'll also find Natal mahoganies (*Trichilia emetica*), and African ebony trees (*Diospyros mespiliformis*). There are several locations in the park where the latter form dense groves, casting a heavy shade on the sparse undergrowth. Look for such groves where the tributaries meet the Luangwa; there's one beside Mchenja Camp, and another near Kaingo.

Elsewhere are large, open grassland plains. Chief amongst these are probably the plains in the Nsefu Sector. These surround some natural salt springs, which attract crowned cranes in their thousands.

Antelope and other herbivores With its rich vegetation, the Luangwa supports large numbers of a wide variety of animals. Each species has its own niche in the food chain, which avoids direct competition with any other species. Each herbivore has its favourite food plants, and even species that utilise the same food plants will feed on different parts of those plants. This efficient use of the available vegetation – refined over the last few millennia – makes the wildlife far more productive than any domestic stock would be if given the same land. It also leads to the high densities of game that the valley supports.

The game includes huge herds of buffalo, commonly hundreds of animals strong, and seemingly endless family groups of elephants; both are particularly spectacular if encountered whilst you are on foot. Despite Zambia's past poaching problems, South Luangwa's elephants are generally neither scarce nor excessively skittish in the presence of people. Just north of Mfuwe Lodge, you'll find an open plain with few trees, just the skeletal trunks of an old cathedral mopane forest. This has always been attributed to elephant damage from the 1970s, before ivory poaching became a problem, when there were around 56,000 elephants in the park (100,000 in the whole Luangwa Valley) – though very recent research suggests that soil changes and even heart rot disease may have contributed to the trees' demise.

The park's dominant antelope species are puku and impala. Whilst impala are dominant in much of southern Africa, including the Zambezi Valley and throughout Zimbabwe, puku are rare south of the Zambezi. They form small breeding groups which are exceedingly common in their favourite habitat – well-watered riverine areas. Groups are dominated by a territorial male adorned with the characteristic lyre-shaped horns.

Luangwa has a number of 'specialities' including the beautiful Thornicroft's giraffe (*Giraffa camelopardalis thornicroftii*). This rare subspecies differs from the much more common southern giraffe, found in Mosi-oa-Tunya National Park, south of the Zambezi, and throughout southern Africa, in having a different (and more striking) coloration. Thornicroft's have dark body patches and lighter neck patches; their colour patches don't normally extend below the knees, leaving their lower legs almost white; and their faces are light or white. Fortunately, around the Mfuwe area there is a widespread traditional belief that people who eat giraffe meat will get spots like those of a giraffe. Hence giraffe are rarely hunted by the local people, and are even very common in the GMA to the east of the river, outside the national park.

Cookson's wildebeest (*Connochaetes taurinus cooksoni*), a subspecies of the blue wildebeest found throughout sub-Saharan Africa, are endemic to the valley. They are more common in more northerly areas of the valley, such as the North Luangwa, and Norman Carr's wildlife guide (page 528) maintains that they also

10

The success of safaris in the Luangwa Valley is due in no small measure to one man: Norman Carr. Originally a ranger within the newly formed game reserves in the valley, Carr was quick to spot the potential of tourism as a lucrative source of income for the park. Although originally an advocate of hunting safaris, Carr soon recognised that there was an alternative – and one that didn't involve hunting down and killing the local fauna.

By 1950, Carr had persuaded Senior Chief Nsefu to establish a private reserve on the eastern bank of the Luangwa River. (Interestingly, a reliable local historian maintains that the colonial provincial commissioner was nervous about this. He feared that ultimately the local people would lose both their land and their access to collect salt at the pans in the centre of the Nsefu Sector. His concerns proved valid when, 20 years later, the Nsefu Sector was combined into the national park.) In partnership with the chief, Norman founded Nsefu Camp in 1952. The camp was close to the present-day Nsefu Camp (it's still visible on the Nsefu Luangwa Wafwa), though it was subsequently moved when the river changed its course.

In 1961, Carr set up his own wilderness safaris, based out of another camp, Kapani. This had been established in 1960, when he was warden of the Luangwa Valley, and it was here that he stayed with Big Boy and Little Boy, the two lions that he famously kept as companions. Kapani Camp lay just north of the Nsefu Sector, close to today's Tafika. In 1961, Carr leased what was later known as Old Lion Camp, close to Kapani Camp but on the opposite (western) bank of the Luangwa River.

In those days the whole operation was basic, with Carr wading across the Luangwa every morning to fetch his clients from Old Lion Camp before taking them on a walking safari. Further camps were tried by the lower Kapamba River in 1963, and the Mwaleshi in the north of the reserve, but none was commercially viable. The venture to Mwaleshi, in North Luangwa, ended with the sad death of one of the guides, Peter Hankin, who was killed by a lioness.

Norman was more successful with his next venture. In 1965, he started walking safaris out of Chibembe Camp, just north of the Chibembe/Luangwa confluence (close to the now closed Zebra Plains camp). With this as a hub, he established a circuit of several small pole-and-grass bushcamps, with his clients walking from camp to camp. Nine years later, he built Chibembe Lodge on the east bank; as this was larger and built of permanent materials, it had to be sited outside the park. With this as his main base, he continued to use the old Chibembe Camp as a walking bushcamp. This modus operandi of a number of small, temporary walking bushcamps working like satellites for one more-permanent lodge is still used by several of the valley's more traditional operations today.

Norman's clientele in those early days came mainly from the UK, with a few from Southern Rhodesia, South Africa and America. The expense of travelling to and from Zambia ensured that such safaris were a very expensive, elite activity.

Two years after Chibembe Lodge, Mwamba Bushcamp was constructed on the East Mwamba River, close to present-day Crocodile Bushcamp. This was the first exclusive bushcamp, a place where clients could hire the whole six-bed camp and have their own vehicle and guide. Other camps and lodges followed, including Chikoko and Kasansanya (1974). In 1977 Norman founded Chinzombo, on the same site as the present day Chinzombo, which could be reached all year (Chibembe had always been inaccessible during the rains), then later came Kakuli, in 1984, and finally Kapani Safari Lodge in 1986.

NORMAN CARR'S LEGACY Nsefu Camp was the valley's first camp for photographic visitors. From the outset, one of its founding principles was that the indigenous people, the traditional owners of the wildlife, should benefit from the visitors. This mirrors the approach to conservation and development that has been adopted only recently by most of those working in this sector. (In the jargon, it is now called 'community-based natural-resource management'!) Norman Carr was a conservationist far ahead of his time.

Not only did Norman start a number of these camps, he also implemented education projects in the valley, and worked alongside and helped to train many of those who are now the valley's most experienced guides. These include:

- **Phil Berry**, who came to the Luangwa in 1963, and in 1973 joined the Zambian National Tourist Bureau to manage walking safaris, in competition with Norman's safari operations. Three years later they joined forces to start Chibembe. Phil is now the valley's most senior guide, and still leads some walks from his small bushcamp, Kuyenda. He's widely respected not only for his guiding, but also for his meticulous keeping of flora and fauna records, and work with Thornicroft's giraffe.
- **Robin Pope** came into the valley in 1976, working with Phil and Norman at Chibembe and then Nsefu Camp. Tena Tena started around 1983 as one of Nsefu's walking bushcamps, then Robin took it over in 1986 – and branched off to start perhaps the valley's most successful safari operation, Robin Pope Safaris. In 2010 Robin stepped back from the day-to-day running of the safari company and camps, although he still guides some trips, including the mini-expeditions that visit Liuwa Plains.
- **John Coppinger** started as a guide at Nsefu in 1984, whilst Robin was manager. He managed Nsefu for a few years, and then became general manager of Wilderness Trails – which then ran Chibembe, Nsefu, Big Lagoon and a travel agency in Lusaka. Eventually he left there is 1994, to start his own operation, Remote Africa Safaris, based out of Tafika.
- **Isaac Zulu** originally studied as an agriculturalist, but was trained by Norman from 1974. He guided in the valley for many years, including at Chibembe in the late 1980s. Eventually he left the valley in 1989 and worked with Tongabezi in Livingstone, until returning to the valley in 2001 with Chilongozi Safaris (now defunct). Currently he's again guiding with John at Remote Africa Safaris.
- **Abraham Banda** was trained by Norman in 1989, having come straight from the Kapani School (set up by Norman to offer local children the chance of a good education). Now Abraham is one of the leaders of the new generation of Luangwa guides; based at their new flagship camp Chinzombo, he manages the safari operation at Norman Carr Safaris. In addition, he runs a very successful charity to support Yoseffe School, and a number of other community projects.

The way that the Luangwa Valley's safari business has created opportunities for an increasing number of locally born people like Abraham, both in education and tourism, is part and parcel of why Norman Carr started safaris in the Luangwa over 60 years ago. Perhaps his greatest legacy is not the wealth of high-quality walking safaris here, but the impressively strong conservation and development ethics which underpin virtually all of the better, long-standing safari operations in the valley.

seem to favour the east side of the river, rather than the west. That said, in South Luangwa you've also a fair chance of seeing them in the Nsefu Sector, and on Lion Plain, and particularly around Mwamba Bushcamp area. They differ from the blue wildebeest in having cleaner colours, including slightly reddish bands, and being a little smaller and more compact.

Another special of the Luangwa Valley is Crawshay's zebra (*Equus quagga crawshaii*), a subspecies of the more common plains zebra, which is found in much of the subcontinent. Crawshay's zebra occur east of the Muchinga Escarpment – in the Luangwa Valley and on Nyika Plateau – and lack the brown shadow-stripe that plains zebra usually have between their black stripes.

In contrast to these examples, it is the common waterbuck (*Kobus ellipsiprymnus*) that is found in the valley, rather than its rarer subspecies, the defassa waterbuck (*K. e. crawshayi*), which is found over most of the rest of Zambia. The common waterbuck has the characteristic white 'toilet seat' ring on its rump, whereas the defassa has a white circular patch.

Other antelope in the park include bushbuck, eland and kudu. The delicate oribi occur occasionally in the grassland areas (especially Chifungwe Plain), while grysbok are often encountered on night drives. Reedbuck and Lichtenstein's hartebeest also occur, but not usually near the river, whilst sable are occasionally seen in the hills near the escarpment. Like sable, roan antelope seem to be most frequently seen in the hills – often on the roads south of Chichele, although in the late dry season there are frequent sightings in the Chikoko area, on the fringes of Chifungwe Plain, and in the 'corridor' area between the North and South parks.

A special mention must go to the hippopotami (and crocodiles) found in the rivers, and especially in the Luangwa: their numbers are remarkable. Look over the main bridge crossing the Luangwa at Mfuwe – sometimes there are hundreds of hippo there. Towards the end of the dry season, when the rivers are at their lowest, is the best time to observe such dense congregations of hippo. Then these semi-aquatic mammals are forced into smaller and smaller pools, and you'll appreciate their sheer numbers. These congregations reach their peak in October and November when, for example, you'll find a concentration of 1,000 hippo in just 2km of river, in the Changwa Channel, north of Chibembe.

Predators The main predators in the Luangwa Valley are typical of sub-Saharan Africa: lion, leopard, spotted hyena and wild dog. During the day, the visitor is most likely to see lion (*Panthera leo*), the park's most common large predator whose population was given a boost by a ban on hunting in the surrounding GMAs between 2013 and 2015. Their large prides are relatively easily spotted, at least in the dry season when the grass is low, and to witness one of their hunting trips makes a gripping spectacle.

South Luangwa has made a name for itself amongst the safari community as an excellent park for leopard (*Panthera pardus*). This is largely because leopard hunt nocturnally, and Zambia is one of the few African countries to allow operators to go on spotlit game drives at night. Estimates made whilst filming a BBC documentary about leopards in the park suggest an average leopard density of one animal per 2.5km^2 – roughly twice the density recorded in South Africa's Kruger National Park. So perhaps the reputation is justified. In my experience, night drives in Luangwa with experienced guides do consistently yield excellent sightings of these cats – at a frequency that is difficult to match elsewhere on the continent. In contrast to this, there have been no reports of cheetah in the park for a number of decades, and are highly likely to be extinct in the park.

Wild dog are also uncommon, though their population seems to oscillate over a period of years. A study of wild dogs in Zambia by Kenneth Buk in 1994 (page 528) suggested that the Luangwa holds Zambia's second-largest wild dog population, even though this was badly depleted by an outbreak of anthrax in 1987. Since the late 1990s, wild dog have gradually been making more appearances. They're now regularly seen, with a particularly high incidence of sightings south of Mfuwe, near the Nkwali pontoon, from around February to May. Recent research suggests that their numbers are building up (see box, page 262).

Birds The Luangwa boasts the rich tropical birdlife that you would expect of such a fertile valley. This includes species that prefer a dry habitat of plains and forests, and those that live close to water. It is difficult to mention more than a few of the Luangwa's 400 species, but several books listed in *Appendix 3* (page 527–9) cover the region's birds. As the Luangwa is situated between southern and east Africa, keen birdwatchers may want to arrive with two field guides, each describing birds from one region, so that between them they will cover the full range of species encountered in the valley. Better still, bring a good guide to southern Africa's birds, like Newman's guide, and buy Aspinwall and Beel's Zambian guide locally (see *Appendix 3*, which explains the logic of this). Alternatively, get hold of a single guide to the birds of sub-Saharan Africa or the more concise Collins Illustrated Checklist to the *Birds of Southern Africa*. Many bird guides, such as Newman's and Sasol's come with apps for smartphones and tablets, which can aid with easy identification and include bird calls.

Species of note include flocks of crowned cranes occurring on the marshes of the Nsefu Sector; the colonies of iridescent carmine bee-eaters that nest in sandy riverbanks in September and October; the African skimmers found along the river; and the giant eagle owls which are sometimes picked out by the spotlight on night drives.

The best time for birds is the summer: the rainy season. The birds' food supply is then at its most abundant, and the summer migrants are around. Just drive into the park during the rains and it becomes immediately apparent that both the vegetation and the birdlife are running riot. Dry plains have sprouted thick, green vegetation mirrored all around in shallow water. Flocks of egrets, herons and storks wade through this, around feeding geese and ducks.

Many species breed here, including storks that often form impressive colonies. There are several sites of tall trees in the Nsefu Sector which, when surrounded by shallow water, regularly become breeding colonies. The most amazing of these has half-a-dozen huge trees filled with nests of yellow-billed storks in their spectacular pink breeding plumage. This is one of the Luangwa's most remarkable sights.

CONSERVATION IN THE LUANGWA
Hunting and poaching South Luangwa has always been Zambia's 'most favoured park'. Over the years it has been given a disproportionately large share of the resources allotted to all of the country's national parks. Many would argue that this has been to the detriment of the other parks, though it did enable it to fight the plague of commercial poaching, which hit the country in the 1980s, with some success. The poachers came for rhino horn – which is sold to make dagger-handles in the Middle East and Chinese medicines for the Far East – and, of course, for ivory.

Sadly the valley's thriving black rhino population was wiped out, with the last confirmed sightings in the Luangwa in 1987, and being declared extinct in Zambia in 1998. (One or two sources suggest that a couple of individual animals may be left in the wild, but this is probably just wishful thinking.) However, the good news is

CARNIVORES IN ZAMBIA'S NATIONAL PARKS

Because large threatened carnivores such as African wild dog, lion and cheetah are naturally wide-ranging and low density they require immense areas to survive, and are therefore very susceptible to human impacts such as habitat loss, disease and persecution. Consequently the presence of these species is synonymous with large relatively intact ecosystems, and Zambia's national parks are a case in point.

With nearly one-third of the country managed for wildlife through national parks and adjacent game management areas (GMAs), Zambia is home to a number of threatened large carnivore species (many of whose populations extend into neighbouring countries such as Malawi). Of these, the African wild dog, or painted dog, once found throughout most of sub-Saharan Africa, is now one of the continent's most endangered carnivores, with Zambia one of only six countries to have a viable population. The immense Kafue National Park is thought to have the country's largest number of wild dogs, followed by the Luangwa Valley.

Intensive conservation work on these dogs was initiated in 1999 in the Lower Zambezi National Park with the formation by Dr Kellie Leigh of African Wild Dog Conservation. This has since broadened into the Zambian Carnivore Programme (ZCP) which, working in collaboration with ZAWA, is focused on conserving Zambia's large carnivores and the ecosystems on which they depend. Fully field-based and operating in eastern Zambia, Kafue and Liuwa Plain the ZCP uses an interdisciplinary approach of research, conservation and education to ensure the best chances of survival for Zambia's large carnivores. In addition, because cheetah and wild dog can be individually identified by their coat patterns, any photographs you take of these sightings in Zambia can be invaluable to research and conservation efforts; please submit yours to ZCP direct (e *zambiacarnivores@gmail.com; www.zambiacarnivores.org*).

that a project to reintroduce black rhino into a specially protected area within the North Luangwa National Park is progressing well, with a small population having been established. This is a long-term project though, and it's likely to be decades before the South Luangwa sees its own rhino population again.

Fortunately, the valley's elephant populations didn't fare as badly as the rhino; they were only reduced. In recent years, thanks in part to the CITES ban on the ivory trade, they have bounced back – and South Luangwa, especially, has very healthy, large herds of relaxed elephants.

Today there is minimal poaching in the park, as demonstrated by the size of the animal populations, and certainly no lack of game. Only in the nervous elephant populations of North Luangwa does one get any echo of the poaching problems of the past.

South Luangwa Conservation Society (e *rachel@slcszambia.org; www. slcszambia.org*) Formed in 2003 in order to support the Zambia Wildlife Authority and Community Resource Boards, the South Luangwa Conservation Society pulled together the work initially undertaken by the honorary rangers and volunteers in the valley. Now with its own premises just outside the national park, it continues to focus on the original aspect of its work, supported by many of the camps in the park, as well as membership fees and donations. The society directly employs many local people, providing them with salaries, accommodation, rations, equipment, incentives and ongoing training.

In addition, the society is actively involved in education programmes with the local community. An ongoing anti-snaring programme helps to make both adults and children aware of the impact of poaching and snaring on the wildlife and on the local environment, while a darting programme helps to rescue animals that have been snared by poachers. From another angle, the introduction of chilli fences (see box, page 323) is helping farmers whose crops are threatened by wildlife.

Conservation and development in Lupande GMA
South Luangwa has always been protected from poaching in a way that Zambia's other parks were not. This wasn't always 100% effective, but it was a lot better than elsewhere. Several years ago a project was started in sections of the Lupande GMA, which is immediately adjacent to the national park, to distribute direct cash benefits from the park to the local people. This has worked very well beside the river (ie: alongside the park), where the animals are plentiful and the hunting income has been very good. Certainly one of the local chiefs has a very nice brick-built palace with satellite television and an impressive new twin-cab Land Cruiser parked in front.

However, further from the park the hunting isn't as good, and the fees have certainly been less. Locals comment that the influx of people into the Mfuwe Bridge area over the last decade has been very noticeable. Even I can see that there are now far more people around that when I first visited in 1995.

Much of the cause of this may be simply the employment prospects generated directly (and indirectly), by the lodges. However, this influx means that the GMA's revenues are being effectively divided among more people. It also puts more strain on the area's agriculture, and areas used for cultivation encroach further towards, and into, the GMAs each year, which will inevitably lead to a reduction in the GMA's game densities.

This is another Gordian knot for those working on conservation and development in the area to tackle. See pages 33–5 for a more general discussion of these issues.

LOCAL SAFARI OPERATORS
When choosing a camp or local operator, it's important that you pick a good and reliable one. You're in such a remote area that you can't afford to have problems. One safeguard is to seek advice from a good, independent overseas tour operator. For all except the budget camps, you should find that booking your trip through them will be cheaper than booking directly with the camps.

Perhaps also check out Expert Africa's website, www.expertafrica.com (even if you're not arranging a trip with them), as I will be posting updates there for all to see. Many of the smaller one- or two-camp operations are excellent. Meanwhile, here are the contact details and selected snippets of background information on a few of the higher-profile safari operators, in alphabetical order:

Bushcamp Company ✆0216 246041; m 0978 770055; e info@bushcampcompany.com; www. bushcampcompany.com. The Bushcamp Company was formed in 2000 from 2 very old bushcamps (Chamilandu & Kuyenda), both originally owned by Chinzombo, & 2 new ones (Bilimungwe & Chindeni), which were originally owned by Mfuwe Lodge – which is now the hub of their operations.

A 5th camp, Kapamba, was added In 2005, & Zungulila in 2008. The company is still run by Andy Hogg, its main founding director, although in 2010 it was bought by a US-based billionaire philanthropist, Paul Allen.

Bushcamp Company has carved out a niche by offering small, remote, high-quality bushcamps. Each camp is different & each offers day & night

CHIPEMBELE WILDLIFE EDUCATION CENTRE

Chipembele (0216 246108; e info@chipembele.org; www.chipembele.org; ⊕ CHIPEM 13°12.122's, 31°42.221'E) came about through the determination of Steve and Anna Tolan, who retired from the British police force in 1998 to invest in their dream of educating children in conservation matters. With a passion for African wildlife born of years of travelling and reading, they set about building an education centre, which was finally opened on the eastern bank of the Luangwa River, about 16km southwest of Mfuwe, in 2001. The centre has a large interpretive room complete with displays and exhibits, and visitors are welcome by prior arrangement.

Chipembele's work focuses on teaching through active involvement and fun. Children come for the day from schools all over the area, spending time *en route* spotting game that many of them may never have seen before.

From this central project, Anna has branched out into an extensive conservation outreach programme in the local schools, school improvement projects and a pupil sponsorship scheme, while Steve has taken on anti-poaching work and forestry protection. Rehabilitation of orphaned and injured animals is a further aspect of their work, together with an active involvement from other conservation organisations in the area.

drives in the park, although walking is the main focus at several of the camps. Note that it's possible to walk from Chamilandu to Chindeni to Bilimungwe to Kapamba to Zungulila.

Norman Carr Safaris ⬄0216 246025 / 015; e bookings@normancarrsafaris.com; www. normancarrsafaris.com. Norman Carr himself lived at Kapani until his death in 1997, & his son & daughter still live at the lodge. Although no longer open to guests, the lodge functions as the company headquarters where operations encompass 4 bushcamps used for walking trips & game drives: Nsolo, Luwi, Kakuli & Mchenja. If you want to walk between different bushcamps, going from one to the next every few days, then the walk down the dry Luwi River is difficult to beat. A more recent addition is the incredibly stylish Chinzombo, offering levels of luxury not previously seen in the park. All are excellent camps & Norman Carr Safaris rightly retains one of the best reputations of any company in the valley. It is currently 1 of only 2 companies to organise regular river safaris in the park (pages 287–8).

Remote Africa Safaris ⬄0216 246185; e reservations@remoteafrica.com; www. remoteafrica.com. Founded by John & Carol Coppinger, Remote Africa Safaris is a small but high-quality operator with truly innovative ideas. They run 4 excellent camps: Tafika in South Luangwa,

plus the Chikoko Trails walking camps (Chikoko & Crocodile), & Mwaleshi in the North Park; all are regularly refurbished. John used to run Wilderness Trails in the valley, & is regarded as one of the most experienced guides in the region. His guides include Bryan Jackson & Isaac Zulu, who are experts in their own right. John is one of the very few people to have canoed the length of the Mwaleshi & Luangwa rivers & was the first to run river safaris in the valley. Remote Africa is unquestionably another of the valley's very best operators. See ad on page 301.

Robin Pope Safaris ⬄+265 (0)179 4491/ 5483; e info@robinpopesafaris.net; www. robinpopesafaris.net, www.robinpopecamps. com. This excellent & highly reliable company was founded by Robin Pope, who was raised in Zambia, trained by Norman Carr, & is another of the top wildlife guides in the valley. His English wife, Jo, was the first woman to qualify as a walking guide in the valley – but it is her efficiency with the marketing & business side of the operation that make her legendary. Together with a very good team they built up what is probably the valley's most complex set of camps & trips, including Tena Tena, Nkwali & Nsefu, river safaris, & a range of different walking safaris (including some true mobiles, the valley's first true bush-camping, & various 'special-interest' safaris in & beyond the valley). In 2010 Robin & Jo handed over the helm of RPS to a Malawi-based Dutch couple, Ton & Margeaux do Rooy – although Robin continues to lead interesting safaris, & Jo's marketing skills are in demand, not least by the Zambia Tourism Board. RPS is unusual in the valley in having no single supplement for most of their camps – although others will often waive this.

Sanctuary Retreats ☏+27 (0)11 438 4650; e reservations.safrica@sanctuaryretreats.com; www.sanctuaryretreats.com. Sanctuary entered the Zambian market in 2007, taking over several camps from the former Star of Africa. Two of these – Chichele Presidential Lodge & the neighbouring Puku Ridge Camp – are in the South Luangwa, & they also own Sussi & Chuma in Livingstone.

Owned by Abercrombie & Kent, Sanctuary also owns a number of small, luxury properties in Botswana, South Africa & east Africa.

Shenton Safaris ☏(May–Oct only) 0216 246064; e info@kaingo.com; www.kaingo.com. Established by Derek Shenton, Shenton Safaris runs Kaingo Camp & Mwamba, both classic, small camps in a good game area with a strong focus on good guiding & photography. Derek was later joined by Juliet leading to a rise in service & comfort. Although they are now raising their family in Lusaka, they frequently visit both the camps. Notable are the value they place on using game hides, & a keenness to organise 3 activities a day. The family also owns Forest Inn, near Mkushi (page 304).

GETTING THERE

By air Most visitors to the South Luangwa fly in to Mfuwe, which during the main safari season, from June to the end of October, is one of the easiest places in Zambia to reach by air. Currently it is regularly serviced by Proflight (page 391), who schedule up to three flights a day throughout the year. Expect a one-way trip between Lusaka and Mfuwe to cost around US$282 per person; double that for a return.

Proflight no longer operate direct transfers between Mfuwe and the Lower Zambezi, but these transfers can now be arranged on a chartered basis by Remote Africa Safaris (page 264).

With its location close to Zambia's eastern border, it's simple and quick to fly into Mfuwe from Lilongwe, and vice versa, either on a chartered flight with Robin Pope Safaris, or a scheduled flight with Ulendo Airlink.

Ulendo Airlink ☏+265 (0) 179 4638; m +265 (0)992 961201; e reservaions@flyulendo.com; www.flyulendo.com. A small but reliable airline offering scheduled & charter international flights between Mfuwe & Lilongwe, departing late morning & early afternoon, as well as internal connections within Malawi.

Mfuwe Airport Mfuwe Airport (✪ MFUAIR 13°15.281'S, 31°55.933'E) is an international airport, with customs and immigration, but it feels like a small, local one. There's one terminal building, and if you're on one of the smaller flights in and out of the valley, then you're likely to have the pilot coming to find you.

Inside the terminal are toilets, a few small shops and two ATMs, one of which is a Barclays. Just outside you'll find the labelled parking spaces where 4x4s from the lodges wait for their pre-booked incoming passengers. A few yards away is a small café worth investigating:

✦**Mukula Café** ⊕ normally 08.00–17.00 all year. Situated beside the airport, Mukula Café is more comfortable than the terminal building, and it's a relaxed place to have a drink or a bite to eat as you arrive, or before you leave. The menu includes sandwiches, samosas, & more filling options such as steak, bream or chicken with a side of nshima, chips or salad. Prices are in Kwacha but you can pay in dollars. $

Driving Approaching from Chipata is by far the easiest way to reach the park now that tarring has been completed along this stretch of road, and the drive typically

10

PROJECT LUANGWA

Initiated by Jo Pope, many of the lodges in South Luangwa have brought their various community projects under one umbrella: Project Luangwa (www.projectluangwa.org). The project aims to improve the long-term economic prospects of the community whilst avoiding negative impacts on the natural environment, in part by developing and improving education in the area. This includes raising the standards of more than 20 schools that have previously had little or no support and – more ambitiously – to increase the number of children who attend school in the first place. A specific focus is education for girls, aiming to address why so few attend, and why those who do so often fall behind the boys.

But the project isn't just focused on children. They plan to work with youngsters to develop vocational training both in order to improve their employment prospects and to enable some to start their own small businesses. More broadly, there are moves to help with provision of clean water sources and to address conservation issues such as deforestation through exploring alternatives to firewood.

There are numerous ways of becoming involved. Just check out their website!

takes about 2 hours. The road is easily passable in all seasons, although a vehicle with good suspension is still advisable.

Driving from the north, or Mpika, is a totally different story: it requires a small expedition of at least two well-equipped 4x4 vehicles, driven by experienced bush drivers with a high degree of self-reliance.

From Chipata The turn-off to Mfuwe is clearly signposted just west of Chipata. Now that tarring has been completed this is a smooth, easy and quick road that winds down from the high escarpment and into the valley. The views are spectacular, and you will pass many small villages on the way. Keep the windows open and you will feel both the temperature and the humidity rise as you descend.

After around 65km you will pass the Chisengu turn-off (⊕ TUSLNP 13°18.131'S, 32°13.234'E) to the right, where a rough track leads to the Kauluzi and Chikwinda gates. This is part of an old district road which used to connect Chipata and Lundazi, though sections of it further north have not been passable for many years, so it's unlikely to be re-opened.

Continuing straight on, the road leads to Jumbe after about 16km, and then over Mpata Hill. (⊕ HILL2 13°26.728'S, 32°20.489'E). Another 15km brings you to a tarmac T-junction. Turn left for 3–4km to reach Mfuwe Airport (⊕ MFUAIR 13°15.281'S, 31°55.933'E), or right for Mfuwe Bridge (⊕ MFUBRI 13°5.917'S, 31°47.162'E) and the park. From Chipata it's about 95km to Mfuwe Airport, or about 115km to the main bridge into the park, over the Luangwa River.

From Petauke Fully-equipped 4x4 vehicles coming from Lusaka might be tempted to take an earlier turn off the Great East Road, and approach the south side of the park via a turn-off from Petauke. I haven't driven this road; it's very rarely used and is much slower and more difficult than the Chipata road (above), though also more scenic and interesting. It's about 150km to the park's southern gate at Chilongozi, then a further 40km to Mfuwe, during which time you're unlikely to see any other vehicles.

For those who have the back-up and want to try this, here are some old directions and GPS waypoints. Turn off the Great East Road to Petauke (✪ PETAUK 14°17.730'S, 31°20.253'E) next to the Oryx fuel station (last fuel-up before Mfuwe). It's 4km until you pass the police station, on the right. Then turn left and continue up the hill, taking a left fork after about 200m (✪ PETS01 14°14.982'S, 31°20.280'E). Head for Ukwimi which is about 50km of ungraded track, following this route:

✪ PETS02 13°56.842'S, 31°36.867'E	✪ PETS08 13°37.398'S, 31°34.609'E
✪ PETS03 13°50.448'S, 31°35.188'E	✪ PETS09 13°34.183'S, 31°34.183'E
✪ PETS04 13°48.282'S, 31°34.699'E	✪ PETS10 13°31.152'S, 31°34.360'E
✪ PETS05 13°47.971'S, 31°34.555'E	✪ PETS11 13°25.981'S, 31°33.354'E
✪ PETS06 13°46.096'S, 31°35.789'E	✪ PETS12 13°26.011'S, 31°33.593'E
✪ PETS07 13°38.386'S, 31°34.774'E	✪ PETS13 13°22.746'S, 31°36.775'E

This brings you to the Chilongozi area and the now-defunct Nyamaluma pontoon (✪ NYALUM 13°22.630'S, 31°36.974'E). From here you now have to continue roughly northeast, shadowing the east bank of the Luangwa, and you'll eventually emerge into Mfuwe just east of the bridge.

From Mpika via the Corridor Road and '05' Driving south from Mpika, down into the Luangwa Valley between the North and South parks, and then crossing the Mupamadzi into South Luangwa, is possible only in the dry season – but it's probably the trickiest of the ways to get here. See the section on getting to Luambe National Park, entitled *From Mpika via the Corridor Road*, on pages 299–300, for the start of the route. After turning east from the Great North Road (✪ TUBATE 12°6.421'S, 31°15.727'E) about 40km south of Mpika, you will need to follow the road in a south easterly direction for 37km before you pass Nthunta scout camp (✪ NTHUNT 12°19.447'S, 31°32.232'E) and then drop over the escarpment and eventually reach the Mutinondo River. About 8.8km after crossing this, there's a left turning which leads to Nabwalya village and the Luangwa River (though the pontoon across the river is no longer operational).

To reach the national park, don't turn left to Nabwalya but continue straight on, then after a further 7.3km you will reach the Chifungwe gate (✪ CHIFUNG 12°26.061'S, 31°42.263'E), just before the Mupamadzi River. This is the boundary to South Luangwa National Park, reached about 69km from the Great North Road. The community campsite here (✪ MUNYAM 12°22.410'S, 31°35.779'E) has unfortunately closed, but you can still free camp here, and it's a beautiful spot. Crossing the Mupamadzi (which should only be attempted when low) is tricky, but then it's a simple, if long, journey to head due south.

About 3km after the Mupamadzi crossing you reach a junction (✪ MUNYAM 12°26.778'S, 31°43.791'E): to the right is a seldom-used road that skirts round the western boundary of the park before ending up near Bilimungwe Bushcamp 140km later, the road quality is poor and there's nowhere to stop off along the way; to the left is the '05' road (see also box, pages 270–1) which is also little used but will take you right across the heart of the park, skirting the western side of Zebra Pans. About 55km after the Mupamadzi, you will reach the deep sand of the Luwi River (✪ 05LUWI 12°56.381'S, 31°45.468'E) near Nsolo Bushcamp, and then some 10km after that you join the network of all-weather roads in the Mfuwe area, just north of the 'Big Baobab' and Mfuwe Lodge (see map, page 254).

From Luambe See page 299 for details of this route in reverse, and backtrack.

By bus/taxi With an increasing population in Mfuwe there are now small minibuses which ply between Chipata and Mfuwe. These cost from K60 one way (though as a tourist you could expect to pay considerably more) and usually won't leave until full. Small groups of travellers may be able to hire a vehicle for a reasonable rate; make sure you agree on Mfuwe Airport as the drop-off location.

Hitchhiking With plenty of water and stamina, getting to Mfuwe from Chipata is possible. Start hitching early at the turn-off. (There's a basic motel nearby so you can always sleep there if necessary.) Don't accept local lifts going just a few kilometres; there's no point – better to wait for a vehicle going at least to Mfuwe Airport. Some of the camps have trucks doing supply runs to Chipata, there are occasional tourists (though fewer with space to spare) and there is a small amount of local traffic. I took 5 hours just to get a lift from here one October morning, so expect a long wait.

AROUND THE MFUWE AREA If you are driving (or hitching) to the South Luangwa, then you may be aiming for a dot on the map marked 'Mfuwe'. On the ground, however, this is far from clear. In spirit, the centre of Mfuwe is probably the airport (page 265), where most of the valley's visitors arrive and depart, and thus frequented by vehicles from the valley's camps.

For the most part, though, the focus of Mfuwe is increasingly the area around the Mfuwe Bridge (⊕ MFUBRI 13°5.917'S, 31°47.162'E) over the Luangwa River. This is 25km northwest of the airport, and is the main entrance to the park's all-weather road network; most visitors entering or leaving the national park pass this way. Here you'll find a fuel station that has increased in reliability, meaning it only runs out of fuel for days rather than weeks, along with a very unreliable Zanaco ATM and some basic shops.

As you approach the bridge, there's a tar road to the left towards Kafunta, Nkwali and the lodges and camps on the southern side of Mfuwe. Then, a little further on the right, is the turning to various lodges including Marula Lodge and Track and Trail, and finally there's a turning to the left to Flatdogs.

Along the D104 road between the airport and the bridge you will pass the occasional farm stalls selling vegetables, as well as a school, a church and a clinic – but there is no big town here. There are, though, more small shops, including the well-stocked **Mayana** which sells good cuts of meat as well as milk, eggs, crisps, etc. There's also a small hotel, and the main outlet for Tribal Textiles.

⌂ Where to stay near the airport *Map, page 268.*

⌂ **Just Africa** (7 rooms) m 0979 696503; e justafrica.lodge@yahoo.com; www.just-africa. com. ⊕ 13°12.123'S, 31°54.949'E. Some 3km from the airport, Just Africa is owned by an engaging, entrepreneurial local woman, Misozi Kadewele, who is also responsible for the 'Snarewear' range of jewellery made locally from wire snares. Recommended for those on a tight budget, Just Africa has 4 chalets & 3 bedrooms, most of which have an en-suite shower (water heated by wood-fired boilers) & toilet. These are basic but clean, the beds have mosi nets & there's electricity for charging – including an unexpected solar-&-battery inverter system in the chalets. Game drives & village visits can be organised. Self-catering is possible although dinner – typically nshima & relish (*US$6–10 pp*) & even drinks are available for residents. **$**

Tribal Textiles (e *marketing@tribaltextiles.co.zm; www.tribaltextiles.co.zm;* ⊕ 13°12.052'S, 31°54.803'E) About 5km from the airport, this well laid-out shop to the right of the road is marked by large, painted pillars. Started to create local employment, it sells perhaps Zambia's best hand-painted textiles. Prices are reasonable (credit cards accepted) and a guide is on hand to explain how the fabrics are made and to take you round the factory. Don't miss it.

GETTING AROUND
In your own vehicle South Luangwa's network of roads is not as extensive as you might expect. A few all-weather roads (mostly graded gravel) have been built in the park around the Mfuwe area – accessible over the main bridge into the park. There's also an isolated network around the camps owned by the Bushcamp Company, in the south of the park. These are the only roads that can be relied upon during the wet season.

Elsewhere, the park has seasonally passable roads that are (optimistically) marked on some of the maps. Such tracks follow both banks of the Luangwa, north and south of Mfuwe, and a few penetrate westwards into the park. In the areas near camps, there are numerous 'loop' roads, which leave these main tracks and return to them. These are just side roads for game viewing, and trying to be precise about their position is pointless – they are usually made simply by the passage of a few vehicles, and will disappear again very swiftly once the vehicles stop.

Note that if you are driving your own vehicle around the park then you are limited to being in the park from dawn to dusk. You are not allowed to stay in and drive around after dark; only local safari companies have licences to conduct night drives. (Note also that the Nkwali pontoon marked on many maps is not for use by private vehicles.)

Without a vehicle If you have organised your camps and lodges in advance then you can relax. A vehicle will be waiting to take you to camp, and there's no need to think ahead. If you haven't done so before you arrive, then you may be limited to a handful of budget options based in the Mfuwe area. If your budget is higher, then you might consider taking advantage of the cell reception at the airport to phone a few of the more upmarket camps (or ask one of the safari vehicles usually waiting outside the airport to radio for you) to see if they have any space left. This is unusual, and don't expect bargains (you won't find any), but it is a real waste to get all the way here and then not make the most of the park. So if you can, splash out on the best place that you can afford. There is one other possibility:

The Personal Touch m 0978 459965, 0979 306826; e info@tptouch.com. Owner Ben Koobs rents out 4x4 open Land Rover safari vehicles with 9 seats, geared to game drives within or around the park. An accompanying guide can be arranged on request. Airport/lodge transfers within the South Luangwa NP & trips to Kawaza & other community projects are also possible. *US$125/24 hrs, exc park fees.*

Maps Accurate, up-to-date maps of the South Luangwa are difficult to come by but a couple may be available in Lusaka. One showing South Luangwa and Luambe national parks was compiled for the national tourist board, and is useful in giving the general scheme of the area's roads. Otherwise the information on its reverse side is fairly dated, and so not very valuable.

A second, very different map concentrates on just the South Luangwa National Park. This was produced in 1989 using aid donations and shows the landscape and vegetation in considerable scientific detail; it's a scholarly work. Its reverse side details the various land systems in the area: the different combinations of land form, rock, soil and vegetation in the park. This is a fascinating map, but the camps and roads are long out of date, and will be of very little use for navigation.

In early November 2002, two German visitors borrowed a brand-new 4x4 to explore the South Luangwa. The car was a small, low-slung saloon, one of the latest models and very much state-of-the-art. It had on-board computers to control much of the vehicle, from the engine to the suspension.

Coming from Mpika, they entered the Luangwa Valley by the tricky 'corridor' road, successfully reaching the remote Chifungwe game scouts' camp. They planned to take the road known locally as the '05', which passes near the old site of Zebra Pans Bushcamp, before eventually reaching a crossroads near Nsolo Bushcamp, and then the heart of the Mfuwe area. It's a dead straight road (with a bearing of about 5°), mostly through thick bush. It's used very little, and was sure to be very quiet then as all the valley's bushcamps close at the end of October.

All went smoothly until they were crossing the Mupamadzi River, about 3km after the scouts' camp. Halfway across, they got stuck. Then the driver realised that he hadn't locked his hubs (some 4x4 vehicles require one to physically turn a switch on the wheels), so he got out in the river and turned the hubs. Surprisingly, they managed to drive to the other side.

All seemed well and the pair continued south, but 25km further along the road, the car died. Water had got into the wiring; the car's computer had shut down and with it the engine. If the car had broken down in the river, the two men would have been only 3km from the scouts' camp. Now they were 28km away. As is normally wise, they decided to wait with their car for a passing vehicle to summon help. Unfortunately, 24 hours later, not one vehicle had passed by. The '05' is one of many bush roads in Africa which may see only a handful of vehicles per year; just because it's marked on the maps, it is a mistake to assume that it's used frequently!

The men were starting to feel desperate. They had told nobody local what their plans were; nobody was expecting them anywhere. Nobody would raise an alarm. All they had with them was some fruit juice, water, butter and cheese, and the water was running out fast, They decided to walk to find help – southwards towards Mfuwe. After 25km, the elder of the two men, sore and tired, could walk

In the unlikely event that you need to navigate yourself in the park, the Hupe Zambia Road Map includes a detailed map of the South Luangwa National Park, and is best used as a physical back up for a GPS loaded with the Tracks4Africa (*www.tracks 4africa.co.za*) GPS maps of the area, which would be essential for visitors to Luambe or Lukusuzi.

⌂ **WHERE TO STAY** I've seen the park several ways over the years – I've hitchhiked here and camped, I've driven myself around, and I've flown in with advanced bookings at lodges and small bushcamps. I think that much of the Luangwa's magic is about being guided by some of Africa's best guides – in a vehicle, or especially on foot. These guys know this area, and its flora and fauna, like the back of their hands.

Upmarket camps and lodges Most of South Luangwa's camps aim at upmarket visitors from overseas. Given the park's remote location, this is not surprising. They incur great difficulties (and costs) in communicating, organising supplies and actually getting their clients into the valley. Then remember that most of them no further. They agreed that he should stop there, whilst the younger, fitter man would continue.

Then their fortunes turned: it rained. The older man, who had been sitting in temperatures of 43°C during the day, took off his clothes and lay on the ground to soak up the water. At 16.00 the next day, he was discovered at the side of the road by a scout patrol. He was naked and approaching delirium; the scouts estimated that he was about 3 to 4 hours from death.

Meanwhile, the younger man had continued walking through the night, but lost the main road whilst avoiding a small herd of elephants. Miraculously, in the morning he stumbled across Nsolo Bushcamp. Being November, everything had just closed down for the rains, but a rummage through the bins uncovered tin cans, while the dry river nearby yielded water where the elephants had dug up the bed with their tusks. Boiling the water in the cans on an open fire, the man felt better. The next morning, the scout patrol who had found his friend followed his tracks to Nsolo, and found him there. He was relatively well, although concerned by the two lionesses who had been watching him closely.

Both men were very lucky and now safe – but what of the car? It took 9 hours to tow it northwards and back across the river. Then it rained for two days, and the river flooded – making the road impassable. Anyone who knows the area would have told them that November was a crazy time to drive across that river.

Meanwhile, a mechanic flew up to attempt repairs. Plugging his laptop into the car, he restarted its computer and had it working in minutes. Apparently it just needed resetting! Later the men learnt that it would have been possible to shut down the computer entirely.

There are many lessons to draw from this, but the big picture is clear. Unless you're an experienced old Africa hand with a good network of local contacts, unless you take good advice, and drive a vehicle that you know, then driving yourself around the more remote corners of Zambia is asking for trouble. Just because this book indicates GPS positions and bush tracks, it does not mean that these routes are suitable for drivers who aren't experienced in remote African travel.

can operate for only for five or six months of the year, after which they pack up, returning to rebuild their camps after every rainy season. Thus, they have some very good reasons to be costly.

The rates at these camps, generally including all meals and activities, and often your bar bill and park fees too, are around US$450–900 per person per day. Most offer a special 'safari rate', typically about 5–10% cheaper than the normal rate, if you stay in camps run by just one operator for seven nights or more. This can be very convenient and is certainly recommended. It will provide a welcome continuity whilst you visit totally different camps. Such combinations include Chinzombo and Norman Carr's bushcamps; Nkwali, Tena Tena and Nsefu; Tafika and its bushcamps, including Mwaleshi; and Mfuwe Lodge and the camps of the Bushcamp Company.

A few offer discounts in the quieter parts of the season if you are a resident of Zambia, but the best deals are usually available from overseas operators (pages 43–5) who specialise in Zambia; their volumes of business give them access to significant discounts.

Note that although many of the camps cost around a similar level, their atmospheres and styles differ greatly – so choose carefully. The valley's camps, in alphabetical order, include:

🏠 **Bilimungwe Bushcamp** [map, page 252] (4 chalets) Contact Bushcamp Company, pages 263–4; ✪ BILIMU 13°23.295'S, 31°34.198'E. Some 46km (as the eagle flies) southeast of Mfuwe, Bilimungwe (which means 'chameleon' in the local Kamanga tongue) stands about 100m from the Luangwa, slightly upstream of its confluence with the Kapamba River. Although the camp dates back to 1996, it was completely rebuilt in 2011 with a modern style, while keeping enough rustic design choices for it to still suit the environment. The central area has been beautifully designed as a raised wooden deck & a tall thatch roof intertwined around the trunks & branches of natal mahogany & winterthorn trees. Comfy chairs, a bar & a dining table occupy the main space, while on a lower deck colourful scatter cushions enliven the bench seating & just a stone's throw away there's a sandy firepit in the open. Overlooking a permanent waterhole, it's a wonderful spot to relax & watch wildlife.

Very comfortable thatched chalets have walls of cane & reeds topped with mosquito gauze. Concertina doors open on to an extensive deck, allowing views of the waterhole from the twin dbl or king-size beds, & giving the huge rooms a light & airy feel. With plentiful wood incorporated into the design, plus an ingenious stone-enclosed outdoor shower in addition to the indoor bathroom, the rooms manage to feel both modern & natural in design.

The camp focuses on both walking safaris & game drives, with some flexibility built into guests' choice of activities, who often combine a stay at Bilimungwe with other Bushcamp Company camps, some of them within walking distance. Otherwise, the 3-hr transfer from Mfuwe is mainly through miombo woodlands (look out for roan antelope & tsetse flies!). *US$530/705 Nov–Dec, 17–31 May, US$550/740 Jun, Oct, US$720/945 Jul–Sep; all pp sharing/sgl FBA, inc bar, laundry, airport & inter-camp transfers, exc park fees.* ☉ *17 May–Dec.* **LLLL**

🏠 **Chamilandu Bushcamp** [map, page 252] (3 chalets) Contact Bushcamp Company, pages 263–4. ✪ CHAMIL 13°19.023'S, 31°38.526'E. About 2hrs' drive southwest of Mfuwe, Chamilandu is set up as a bushcamp for walking safaris, & is one of the more rustic properties in this area of the park. The camp is set on the banks of the Luangwa facing the Nchindeni Hills, which look beautiful in the late afternoon sun & the rooms, set on high

wooden decks, make full advantage of the views. The reed & thatch chalets are smartly furnished king-size or twin ¾ beds under mosquito nets, and are completely open to the front. En-suite bathrooms have open-air showers, dbl washbasins & flush toilets. At night, solar-powered lights augment the light from the moon & stars.

The camp's central area is close to the river, while a short walk brings you to an old hide – now a smart thatched building whose deck overlooks 1 of 7 oxbow lagoons that surround the camp; a great spot for lunch or to watch game. Game drives are offered as an alternative to the usual walks. There is only one resident guide, but several floating guides who work for Bushcamp Company bring some flexibility to the activities. Walking between Chamilandu, Chindeni, Bilimungwe & Zungulila – with your luggage taken ahead for you – can usually be arranged as there's only about 10km between each camp. *US$550/740 Jun, Oct, US$720/945 Jul–Sep; all pp sharing/sgl FBA, inc bar, laundry, airport & inter-camp transfers, exc park fees.* ☉ *Jun–Oct.* **LLLL**

🏠 **Chichele Presidential Lodge** [map, page 254] (10 suites) Contact Sanctuary Retreats, page 265. ✪ CHICHE 13°10.008'S, 31°42.605'E. About 15km southwest of Mfuwe Lodge, Chichele was built in 1972 as President Kaunda's private lodge in the Luangwa. High up atop President Hill, it's in an area where the Luangwa River starts to come much closer to the escarpment, & it's got a great view! Around it are a variety of environments including miombo woodland & mopane glades, on soil that varies from patches of gravel/sand to patches of black-cotton soil. Having passed from the government & through several private safari operators, it's now owned by Sanctuary Retreats. Although it was completely rebuilt in 2007 there was an obligation to keep many of Chichele's original buildings for their alleged historical value, so the design has taken these into account, & the place feels very different from anything else in the park. It retains a grand, rather colonial feel; The communal areas are huge, including a large dining area with candelabra, ceiling fans & even a cappuccino maker, while outside is a relaxing pool & a panoramic view of the surrounding area. It's not difficult to picture a president entertaining his guests here.

Each of its elegant rooms, which include a sgl room & an interleading family room, boasts a veranda, minibar, AC, hairdryer, tea-/coffee-making facilities, & a mosquito net that's part of the bed's canopy, while en-suite facilities comprise a glass-fronted shower room, bath & twin washbasins.

Activities comprise game drives day & night, & guided walks. Small groups or conferences can also be accommodated, in combination with the nearby Puku Ridge. *US$490/735 15 Jun–31 Oct, 21–31 Dec, US$390/490 Jan–14 Jun, Nov–20 Dec; all pp sharing/sgl FBA, inc bar, laundry, park fees, airport & inter-camp transfers. ⊕ All year.* **LLL**

🔺 **Chikoko Trails** (2 camps) Contact Remote Africa Safaris, page 264. These 2 small bushcamps operate slightly upstream of their parent camp, Tafika, on the opposite bank of the Luangwa. This is around the spot where David Livingstone crossed the Luangwa in 1866, & little seems to have changed since then; it's still a beautiful corner of the valley with excellent game densities.

Being in a wilderness area, there is only one road used for emergencies, all your luggage & supplies are carried by porters. From Tafika this means a brief drive along the river, followed by a quick crossing by canoe & then a short walk. At both you'll find a very simple but relaxed air, with solar lighting & a simple dining shelter. But to focus on the camps themselves is to miss the point; Remote Africa's guides are amongst the valley's most experienced – so though simple, these are amongst the valley's very best bushcamps in wonderful wilderness areas. *US$660 Aug–Sep, US$625 May–Jul, Oct; all FBA, inc bar, laundry, current park fees, airport & inter-camp transfers. Sgl suppt US$280.* **LLLL**

🔺 CHIKOKO TREE CAMP [map, page 256] (3 chalets) Only about 10 mins' walk from the Luangwa, beside the small, seasonal Chikoko Channel, Chikoko's simple, grass-walled chalets are more like tree houses. Reached by wooden stairs, & raised about 3m off the ground, their bedrooms have low sides & are open to the front, providing a good vantage point for spotting wildlife but with the height giving the nervous an added sense of security. There's a canvas shade above the dbl or twin beds to keep off the sun & any rain, & downstairs is a private flush toilet & shower (hot on request). ⊕ *May–Oct.*

🔺 CROCODILE RIVER CAMP [map, page 256] (3 chalets) Further from the river, about a 40-min walk, Crocodile is in a great location, beneath a row of ebony trees overlooking a large & usually dry oxbow lagoon. Flashes of vivid colour enliven its dbl or twin rondavels, which are all at ground level, with half walls at the front, & en-suite flush toilet & shower (hot on request), open to the air. ⊕ *May–Oct.*

🔺 **Chindeni Bushcamp** [map, page 252] (4 tents) Contact Bushcamp Company, pages 263–4. ✦ CHINDE 13°22.056'S, 31°36.426'E. About 7km further upstream than Bilimungwe, Chindeni is also about 3hrs' drive south of Mfuwe. It stands on the banks of a large, semi-permanent lagoon, which stretches away from it on both sides. The main river is about 1km away, & in the near distance rise the Nchindeni Hills, overlooking the park's eastern boundary.

Chindeni's large, well-spaced tents are raised up on hardwood decks, hidden in the vegetation. They're lined with soft-brown canvas, rising to 3 pinnacles, like a trio of miniature big tops. Beneath the centre are twin or dbl beds, flanked by an en-suite shower, loo & twin basins; & open basketwork chairs with cushioned footstools. Outside, twin hammocks on a private shaded veranda invite you to laze away the afternoon. It's all very light: lots of polished, light wood & neutral fabrics give the rooms a modern, minimalist feeling. At the heart of the camp a sturdy split-level deck overlooks the lagoon, furnished with low wicker armchairs and deckchairs made from cow hide. Ebony & tamarind trees provide shade, while shelter for the separate dining & lounge areas comes from 2 large canvas-topped 'gazebos' held up by heavy poles. Lighting is from paraffin lamps.

It's usual to combine time here with stays at Bilimungwe, or the company's other camps. Here, too, day & night game drives & walks are available, with some flexibility over activities. *US$530/705 Nov, US$550/740 Jun, Oct, US$720/945 Jul–Sep; all pp sharing/sgl FBA, inc bar, laundry, airport & inter-camp transfers, exc park fees. ⊕ Jun–Nov.* **LLLL**

🔺 **Chinzombo** [map, page 254] (6 villas) Contact Norman Carr Safaris, page 264. ✦ 13°6.334'S, 31°45.733'E. Situated just outside of the park, overlooking a wide bend in the Luangwa River, Chinzombo is the newest camp in the South Luangwa from Norman Carr Safaris. Opened in 2013, it's built on the site of one the valley's first safari camps, from which Chinzombo gets its name.

This latest incarnation of Chinzombo has been designed by top safari camp architects Silvio Reach & Lesley Corstens, who designed some of

Botswana's top camps as well as the iconic North Island in the Seychelles. The design is luxurious & stylish, & it's quite unlike any other camp operating in the valley. It more closely matches Botswana's safari camps than Zambia's.

The minimalist structure of the main area is comprised of a metal frame & white-washed wooden decking, cleverly built around existing trees, leaving the sides completely open. Lots of leather, canvas & wooden fittings in the lounge & bar give the camp a very colonial atmosphere, but there are also plenty of modern amenities such as a Nespresso coffee machine & a swimming pool towards the river. A firepit perched on the river bank provides a great spot to eat breakfast & watch the sun rise.

Chinzombo has 6 spacious villas, one of which has 2 bedrooms for families, which closely match the design & décor of the main area. They have king-size or twin beds complete with full-size mosi nets & 'evening breeze' AC units, which quietly & effectively cool the air around the beds. Through a curtain is an open-plan en-suite with a shower (hot & cold), twin basins, & a large bath. Mains electricity allows amenities in the rooms such as a mini-bar, tea- & coffee-making station & Wi-Fi. The gauze panels at the front of the villas can be rolled up, leading to a private deck with a plunge pool & ample comfortable seating.

Private guiding is included as standard for each booking, giving complete freedom over your choice of activities; these include drives & walks in the park, privately accessed by a short boat trip across the river from camp.

Chinzombo has overseen the training of several local women & offers a range of spa treatments in the privacy of your own villa. This adds to the comfort & luxury of the lodge, making it a good place to end your safari, usually after spending time at Norman Carr's bushcamps. However, the area around Chinzombo is much busier with other vehicles compared to the more remote areas of the park. *US$1,250/1,500 pp sharing/sgl Jun–Oct, US$900 pp Jan–May, Nov–Dec; all FBA inc drinks, exc park fees.* ⏲ All year. **LLLLL**

🏠 **Kafunta River Lodge** [map, page 254] (10 chalets) 📞 0216 246046; e bookings@ luangwa.com; www.luangwa.com. ⊕ KAFUNT 13°9.785'S, 31°44.360'E. Kafunta is about 9km from the main road between Mfuwe Airport & the bridge. To get there, turn left before the bridge, signposted to Kafunta, Nkwali & other lodges.

Then around where the tar ends, there's a left fork signposted to Kafunta. Believe it or not, this is the main road that runs southwest outside the park & follows the river downstream. There are then 3 clearly signposted right turns: to the Wildlife Camp, to Nkwali Camp, & finally to Kafunta.

On a spacious site beside the river, Kafunta was built from scratch in 1998 by a team including Ron & Anke Cowan, who now own & run the camp. Its central dining/bar area under a huge thatched roof is very impressive – built around a wild mango tree. Dinner is often served by candlelight on an open-air deck to the front, with great views over the floodplains. (There's a small wildlife hide cleverly built into the underneath of this deck.) Beside the bar is an infinity pool, & a hot tub supplied by a natural hot spring, discovered when the camp was drilling for their borehole. Set behind the main area there's even a small bush spa.

Kafunta's rooms are thatched chalets with cool grey stone walls, elevated 1m off the ground. Paned windows are set into each of the walls, & a set of double doors at the front lead onto a private veranda. Each of the 8 'standard' chalets has 2¾ beds under a large, walk-in mosquito net; 2 'luxury suites' have more space, including an upper deck which can act as a viewing platform or an extra bedroom for 1–2 children. All chalets have a minibar, kettle & ceiling fan – powered by mains electricity – as well as a shower (hot & cold), twin basins & flush toilet. The suites also have large bath tubs.

Walking safaris are possible, but activities centre around 4x4 game drives (day & night). Kafunta is 9km from the Mfuwe Bridge, but its drives normally access the park across the Nkwali pontoon, which is only about 1.5km from the lodge. *US$550 Jun–Oct, US$405, 25 Mar–May, Nov–Dec; all pp sharing FBA, inc bar, laundry, park fees, airport & inter-camp transfers. Sgl suppt US$90. Suite suppt US$50.* ⏲ 25 Mar–Dec. **LLL** See ad on page 301.

🏠 **Island Bush Camp** [map, page 252] (5 chalets) Contact Kafunta River Lodge (above). About 2hrs' drive south of Kafunta. It stands on the banks of the Luangwa River, in the remote south of the park, where the river no longer forms the border of the national park but rather runs though it. Guests are normally driven from Kafunta, aong a dirt track, a journey that can take 2–3 hours. With its twin chalets raised up on platforms, reed walls open to the river & en-suites with bucket showers, it offers a truly rustic add-on to Kafunta, in an area primarily reserved for walking. *US$550/640 pp sharing/sgl FBA, inc drinks, park fees.* ⊕ *25 May–Oct.* **LLL**

🏠 **Three Rivers Camp** [map, page 252] (5 tents) Contact Kafunta River Lodge (page 274). Kafunta Safaris are currently constructing a new bush camp at the confluence of the Luangwa, Luzngazi & Kapamba rivers at the southern end of the park. Opening of the camp is planned for mid 2016, with the camp consisting of a main area & 5 luxury tents. Activities will focus on safari drives & walks, with it being possible to walk the 7km south to Island Bush Camp. *US$535/625pp sharing/ sgl FBA, inc drinks, park fees.* ⊕ *25 May–Oct.* **LLL**

🏠 **Kaingo Camp** [map, page 256] (6 chalets) Contact Shenton Safaris, page 265. ✥ KAINGO 12°55.370'S, 31°55.441'E. Where the seasonal Mwamba River meets the main Luangwa River, this small camp looks over the water towards the Nsefu Sector from beneath an old grove of mahogany & ebony trees. The open-sided sitting room cum dining area is a large thatched *chitenge*, with an amazing bar made from an old leadwood tree trunk. Outside, a deck extends over the river – perfect for game viewing & afternoon tea. Each of the chalets, too, has its own shaded deck over the river, where lunch is served in complete privacy. The thatched chalets are constructed from rendered brick covered with an orange-red plaster reminiscent of the local soil on the outside. Stable-style doors lead in to en-suite rooms where gauzed skylights give a view of the stars as you drift off to sleep. Solid, hand-crafted wood sets the tone – in the headboards backing king-size or twin beds, in the mirror frames, in the wardrobes. There's also a separate daybed, plus solar lights, & a lockable box. The new addition of an outside bath also allows you to bathe under the stars.

Close to the camp are 3 hides – the 'elephant' & 'hippo' hides, & the seasonal 'carmine bee-eater' hide – as well as several mobile hides. These are fairly unusual in the Luangwa, & have been widely used by film-crews from both the BBC & *National Geographic*. If you're too active for a late-morning snooze, or are keen on photography, this is the place to keep watch; in fact, photographers are particularly well catered for, with camera dust covers & bean bags provided, & with a maximum of 6 people per vehicle guests are guaranteed an outside seat.

Derek Shenton, who owns & runs the operation with his wife Jules, is quiet & unassuming, which has perhaps helped the lodge to attain a solid, established & yet very calm air. It's been open since 1993 & its head guide, Patrick Njobvu, has over 20 years' experience of guiding in this area. As well as the usual walking safaris & day & night drives, there are picnics in the bush & hide trips; many guests take in 3 activities a day. It's possible to arrange camping trips from Kaingo, geared towards fit people looking for a minimalist set up (*extra US$464/2 people*), as well as nights in the elephant hide next to the river, & on the Numbu Platform in a vast open savannah (*both extra US$174/2 people*). Note that the Shenton family also own Forest Inn, near Mkushi (page 304). *US$874 Aug–Sep, US$816 Jul, Oct, US$752 May–Jun; all pp sharing FBA, inc drinks, current park fees. Sgl suppt US$290.* ⊕ *20 May–Oct.* **LLLL**

🏠 **Kakuli Bushcamp** [map, page 256] (4 chalets) Contact Norman Carr Safaris, page 264. A camp was first started here in 1984 by Norman Carr, overlooking a wide bend in the Luangwa. *Kakuli* is the local word for an old buffalo bull which has left the main herd, & by association was also Norman Carr's nickname amongst the local people before he died.

Kakuli Bushcamp is linked to Nsolo & Luwi camps, respectively 15km & 20km away, by the seasonal Luwi River, which makes 3-day walks between these 3 sister camps a very interesting option.

Its chalets are rebuilt every year, when their design is often tweaked a little. When last visited, each had a large thatched roof covering its cream-coloured tent (complete with full mosquito-net lining, king-size or twin ¾ beds & solar-powered hurricane lamps) & polished deck at the front. A curtain separates each bedroom from a spacious, covered en-suite bathroom surrounded by reed walls. As well as plentiful storage there's a twin washbasin, & the flush toilet & shower are hidden from view.

The dining-room/bar area is simple & comfortable: a thatched, reed-walled structure with 2 open sides, a sprinkling of cushioned chairs & a good bookshelf. A suspended deck with built in fireplace overlooks the floodplain.

The camp seldom takes more than 8 guests, & it concentrates on both walking & driving, though night drives are possible in the area. If 8 guests are in camp, it usually has 3 guides resident; if

10

there are 6 guests, then expect 2 guides. Either way there is some flexibility over activities. A stay here is usually combined with some of its sister bushcamps, Luwi, Nsolo & Mchenja, & also Chinzombo for those looking to add some luxury into their trip. *US$800/1,050 pp sharing/sgl Jun–Oct, US$695 pp 20 Jan–4 Apr, 20–31 May, 1–7 Nov; all FBA inc drinks, exc park fees.* ⊕ *20 May–7 Nov, & 20 Jan–4 Apr for river safaris.* **LLLL**

🏠 **Kapamba Bushcamp** [map, page 252] (4 chalets) Contact Bushcamp Company, pages 263–4. ✵ KAPAMB 13°22.967'S, 31°31.584'E. This one of the Bushcamp Company's camps, a 3½hr drive from Mfuwe, is quite different from the rest. Unencumbered by a 4th wall, each of Kapamba's stone-walled chalets (with dbl or twin beds) is open fronted, with sweeping views of a floodplain around the Kapamba River – which is shallow enough to paddle through barefoot or even to sit in during the dry season for a sundowner or intimate dinner. Wrought-iron gates span the front of each chalet, offering protection from unwanted visitors & creating a spider-web effect against the African sky. Inside, each chalet is colourful & stylish, with bright colours & a clear north African influence in its design. En-suite bathrooms are twin showers above a bath the size of a small plunge pool (a happy accident, resulting from a specification given in centimetres, which the builders assumed was in inches!). The rooms are more stylish & modern than a traditional bushcamp, but they have been done well & still fit in with the surrounding area.

Activities include walking, driving & night drives in the area around camp, which has plentiful wildlife but few other vehicles. Similarly to Bushcamp's other properties, if the camp is full then there will be 2 resident guides; if not there will be 1 while the company's floating guides provide guests with some flexibility over their choice of activities. *US$ 530/705 May, Nov–Dec, US$550/740 Jun, Oct, US$720/945 Jul–Sep, all pp sharing/sgl FBA, inc bar, laundry, airport & inter-camp transfers, exc park fees.* ⊕ *Apr–Jan.* **LLLL**

🏠 **Kuyenda** [map, page 252] (4 rondavels) Contact Bushcamp Company, pages 263–4. ✵ KUYEND 13°22.430'S, 31°32.430'E. About 75 mins' drive south of Mfuwe, this small, very traditional bushcamp concentrates on walking safaris with the occasional drive. It overlooks the Manzi River, a sand-river tributary of the main Luangwa.

Much of the guiding here is done by Phil Berry – the valley's most experienced guide with a legendary reputation for his knowledge of the area's wildlife. Though Phil no longer leads all the walks, he still spends most of the season at the camp guiding many of the walks & sharing his extensive knowledge of the bush. In the evening, the conversation over dinner can be particularly interesting & convivial, especially when Phil & his partner, Babette, are in camp. The round chalets, made of thatch & reeds, have en-suite toilets & showers open to the sky (hot water is brought on request). Inside are twin queen-size beds, or a king-size dbl, veiled by mosquito netting, & with atmospheric paraffin lanterns. It's understated, nicely finished & very peaceful.

Though walking is the main focus here, drives are also possible – & night drives are always a feature of your time here. Returning to the camp when it's dark is a great pleasure as the whole camp is lit by romantic hurricane lamps which look magical as you approach across a wide sand river. *US$530/705 Jun, Oct, US$720/945 Jul–Sep, all pp sharing/sgl FBA, inc bar, laundry, airport & inter-camp transfers, exc park fees.* ⊕ *Jun–Oct.* **LLLL**

🏠 **Lion Camp** [map, page 256] (10 chalets) ☎ 0216 246024, 📱 0965 156181; 📧 info@ lioncamp.com; www.lioncamp.com. ✵ LIONCA 12°53.089'S, 31°58.032'E. All Africa is here in this large lodge that's a riot of colour, from the cushions of Zambian *chitenje* cloth to beaded Nigerian belts. Situated inside the park around 2½hrs' drive from Mfuwe, it stands on the edge of an oxbow lagoon, or *wafwa*, overlooking an open plain. Having fallen into disuse, it was rebuilt in 2003, & has since been renovated to a standard that wouldn't disgrace a smart hotel.

At the heart of the camp, seating areas under thatch form a horseshoe around a central fireplace. Parallel to the lagoon, a narrow ribbon of deck edges a similarly narrow infinity pool. At the back, the walls lined with black-&-white wildlife photos, are a large bar & a full-size billiard table; a separate lounge with TV for wildlife DVDs & Wi-Fi, & a well-stocked curio shop. Dining is flexible – with tables moved from one meal to the next.

High wooden walkways lead to the chalets, themselves on wooden platforms with French windows leading onto decks overlooking the lagoon. They're solid, spacious structures under thatch with wood-clad canvas walls, canvas flaps over gauze windows & stylish interiors: polished wood floors, king-size dbl or twin beds with walk-in mosquito nets, a fan, en-suite shower & separate toilet, & a day bed for afternoon relaxation. There's 220V inverter power in each chalet, & locks on the doors – a rarity in the Luangwa!

Activities revolve around game drives & walking safaris, & there are photographic safari weeks with Patrick Bentley 3 times a year. It's a professionally run lodge in a wildlife rich, yet remote, area of the park. The facilities are impressive & it has a much more solid structure than some of the more traditional properties in the area, so it may not suit people looking for a simple bushcamp. *US$560/710 pp sharing/sgl Aug–Sep, US$525 pp Jul, Oct, US$470 pp 25 May–Jun, all FBA, inc bar, laundry, airport & inter-camp transfers, exc park fees.* ⊕ *25 May–Oct.* **LLL**

⚠ Luangwa Bushcamping See *Fly-camping,* page 287, for details.

🏠 Luangwa River Camp [map, page 254] (5 chalets) Contact Robin Pope Safaris, pages 264–5. ⊕ LUARLO 13°04.459'S, 31°48.636'E. In a riverside setting 10km northeast of Mfuwe, overlooking the South Park, Luangwa River Camp is a well-established property that was taken over & refurbished by Robin Pope Safaris in 2011. The new design retains the lodge's former solidity, and has a double-level infinity pool sunk into the tiered wooden deck along the front of the lodge, overlooking a manicured lawn & the river beyond. Palm panelling forms the backdrop for both the substantial open-plan lounge & dining area & the en-suite bathrooms in the spacious brick & thatch chalets, which come complete with showers, toilets, & huge sunken baths (soon to be replaced with claw-footed baths). Mains electricity enables the use of spotlights, hairdryers, fans & other 'luxuries', making the lodge a good introduction to a safari holiday.

Aside from walking safaris & game drives, usually in the national park, there are boat trips when the river is sufficiently high, & cultural trips are easily within range, too, including visits to Chipembele Wildlife Education Centre (box, page 264), Kawaza Village (pages 288–9), & various other craft & village projects. It's all very flexible – right down to the option of a holistic massage! *US$590 Jul–Oct, US$490 22 May–Jun, US$450 22 Jan–21 May, Nov, all pp FBA, inc drinks, laundry, airport & inter-camp transfers, exc park & community fees.* ⊕ *22 Jan–Nov.* **LLL**

🏠 Luangwa Safari House [map, page 254] (4 bedrooms) Contact Robin Pope Safaris, pages 264–5. Built in 2005 near to Nkwali (see below), this large & traditional-looking house has a carefully crafted structure based around the trunks of 25 ancient leadwood trees. From the front entrance, a huge pivoted door opens into the spacious main room, some 12m high, with comfy sofas, large marble dining table & full-height views of the bush through 1 open wall.

There are 4 grand bedrooms, each individually styled & reflecting a different material from copper to glass. Open-tread wooden staircases made from massive reclaimed slabs of wooden banana tree lead to 2 of these rooms; both with balconies supported like drawbridges. All are highly original & styled on a grand scale, with king-size or twin beds & very large en-suite bathrooms.

Despite that, the focus is on the outdoors. Terraces lead to an infinity pool, & a wooden jetty extends away from the house to an open-sided lounge deck constructed around a group of huge ebony trees in the middle of an often-dry lagoon. Nearby a waterhole attracts families of elephants, which can be easily observed from a sunken hide. During the day, a double-storey wall of the lounge, & a section of each bedroom wall, are opened up completely, turning the outside into a continuation of the living space inside. At night a clever system of insect-proof mesh, wrought-iron grills &, if necessary, waterproof panels slot into place to close up the house & keep it cosy.

The house can only be booked in its entirety by a single group, & comes with a private chef, house manager, safari guide & game-viewing vehicle, giving guests complete flexibility over their schedule. Although often referred to as a 'family house', Luangwa Safari House really best suits small groups of adults, or at least adults & older children, who will appreciate the openness of its design & the complete flexibility of its high-quality activities. *US$3,800 Nov–mid Jan & mid Mar–21 May, US$4,000 22 May–Jun, US$4,200, rate for house per day FBA, inc drinks, laundry, airport transfers, exc park & community fees. Min 4 adults; no children under 7.* ⊕ *Mid Mar–mid Jan.* **LLLL**

🏠 Luwi Bushcamp [map, page 252] (4 chalets) Contact Norman Carr Safaris, page 264. A further 10km up the Luwi (or Lubi) River from its sister camp, Nsolo, Luwi is at least as rustic.

It is set under a group of tall shady trees (*Vitex, Breonadia & Khaya anthotheca*), looking out over a small plain. The chalets, which can be twin or dbl, are similarly of reed & thatch, with grass matting covering their polished floors, mosquito nets, storm lanterns, solar lights & a small veranda. All have en-suite facilities, with flush toilets, hot showers & washbasin under the stars.

A very short walk leads to a large, permanent lagoon at a bend in the river (usually frequented by a pod of about 60 hippos). This is purely a camp for walking: either for day walks based here, or for walks linking with Nsolo, Kakuli & Mchenja bushcamps. It's not a camp for game drives – although there's always a vehicle in camp to investigate interesting noises at dusk – & the camp seldom takes more than 7 guests. Luwi is often combined with its sister bushcamps, allowing a mixture of walks & drives in different areas of the park. *US$800/1,050 pp sharing/sgl Jun–Oct, US$695 pp 20–31 May, all FBA inc drinks, exc park fees.* ☉ *20 May–Oct.* **LLLL**

✴ 🏠 **Mchenja Camp** [map, page 256] (5 chalets) Contact Norman Carr Safaris, page 264. Mchenja has been run by Norman Carr Safaris since about 1995. It stands in one of the very best locations of any camp in the valley, beside the Luangwa River at the end of a serenely beautiful grove of African ebony trees (*Diospyros mespiliformis*, which are known as *muchenja* in the local ChiNyanja dialect).

The unusual octagonal chalets all have thatched roofs supported on wooden poles, & each is lined with a light green canvas. Bedouin-style drapes cover the shade-mesh windows & the double-doors which lead onto a veranda at the front. Inside are a king-size bed, or twin ¾ beds, plenty of wicker furniture on a polished floor, & a feeling of airy space. Part of the bathroom – with ball-&-claw bath – is inside the tent, next to the bedroom, linked to an open-air reed-enclosed toilet, washbasin & shower with a view.

The airy dining area & small lounge are under thatch, & there is a little slate-grey freshwater plunge-pool set into the deck. Food & activities are reliably good, & the camp usually has at least 2 guides resident when there are more than 4 guests, giving a real choice to the activities.

About 30km from Mfuwe, Mchenja stands opposite the Nsefu Sector, between Nsefu Camp &

Tena Tena. It makes a good last stop at the end of a walking safari, being an easy 10km walk (3–4hrs) from either Nsolo or Kakuli. *US$850/1,100 pp sharing/sgl Jun–Oct, US$695 pp 20–31 May, 1–7 Nov, all FBA inc drinks, exc park fees.* ☉ *20 May– 7 Nov.* **LLLL**

🏠 **Mfuwe Lodge** [map, page 254] (18 chalets) Contact Bushcamp Company, pages 263–4. ⊕ MFUWEL 13°4.725'S, 31°47.441'E. Following a significant makeover in 2010, this long-established lodge has emerged stylish & smart. Now the hub of the Bushcamp Company operations, it stands in a prime location overlooking the picturesque Mfuwe Lagoon in the centre of the park's all-weather road network, where the game is prolific & relaxed. The lodge's history dates back many years, having been rebuilt from scratch in the 1990s by the Bizzaro family, owners of the successful Club Makokola in Malawi. It was, & remains, relatively big in the context of the Luangwa's tiny camps.

Each of Mfuwe's painted brick-&-thatch chalets overlooks a lagoon from a broad veranda, complete with wicker hanging chair. Inside are dbl or large twin beds encased in walk-in mosquito nets & cooled by a fan, plus a writing desk, safe, tea/coffee maker, comfy chairs & coffee table. The contemporary bathroom has dual washbasins, a separate toilet, & a shower with a view. Larger family rooms & suites are split level, some with a bath.

It's as well that Mfuwe has a vast lobby, for at the end of the dry season it's the scene of an extraordinary sight: a whole family of elephants coming through to feast on the wild mango trees beyond. For most guests, a large pool, squashy sofas, huge fireplaces & an open-air dining area with pizza oven are the greater draw! The food is good & the bar well stocked. Added bonuses are a proper library with leather chairs, a good curio shop, internet access – & its own lagoon-side spa (box, page 280). Morning & afternoon/night drives are in Land Rovers with 3 rows of individual seats, & walks are also possible, though keen walkers would be best to combine a stay here with time at one or more of the bushcamps. *US$385/520 Nov– May, US$445/595 Jun, Oct, US$545/725 Jul–Sep, all pp sharing/sgl FBA, exc drinks, park fees. Suites US$60 pp suppt.* ☉ *All year.* **LLL**

🏠 **Mushroom Lodge & Presidential House** [map, page 254] (12 chalets) ☎0211258184/5; 📱 0977 758056; 📧 info@mushroomlodge.com;

www.mushroomlodge.com. The historic Mushroom Lodge overlooking Mfuwe Lagoon was built in the early 1970s for President Kaunda & his guests, & remained in use until the fall of UNIP in 1991. In the ensuing years, the house fell into disrepair, but it has now been redeveloped as a safari lodge, & was fully refurbished in 2007. To get there from the main park gate, follow the road for about 2km, then turn right as signposted for a further 1.2km.

The substantial en-suite chalets are painted a deep red & shaded under thatch. Each has both a dbl & a sgl bed, its own lounge area with wicker furniture, a minibar, safe, fan, kettle & hairdryer, & a private veranda fronted by the lagoon. Children are particularly welcome, with special meals & games laid on for them, & a babysitting service available. Central to the lodge are a restaurant, lounge & bar area with an extensive veranda & a swimming pool, while nearby is an open-sided *nsaka* where massages are offered. There's extensive Wi-Fi coverage, too. In addition to morning & evening game drives & walks, guests can also take part in tours to Mfuwe & the surrounding villages. *US$450 Jun–Oct, US$340 Nov–May, all pp FBA, laundry, airport & inter-camp transfers, exc park fees, bar.* ⊕ *All year.* **LLL**

✳ 🏠 **Mwamba Bushcamp** [map, page 256] (4 chalets) Contact Shenton Safaris, page 265. ⊕ MWAMBA 12°52.973'S, 31°55.940'E. About 6km north of Kaingo, only a morning's walk away, lies Kaingo's satellite bushcamp Mwamba, located at the confluence of the East Mwamba & main Mwamba rivers. The approach to the camp is lovely as the rivers are usually dry & sandy, & the banks open & green. There's an area of mopane forest nearby, as well as ebony groves & grasslands. The camp itself is shaded within a grove of ebonies (*Diospyros mespiliformis*), where there are some particularly beautiful trees. Simple reed-&-thatch chalets have gauze skylights, enabling guests to enjoy the stars from their beds – as they can from the open-air, en-suite bathrooms (with hot bucket shower & flush toilet). There's a comfy dining area by the river, & a well-placed anthill makes a great sundowner spot. The camp has its own hide, too, focused on a waterhole that regularly attracts wildlife. Walking & driving safaris, & hide trips are on offer – & with 2 guides generally in camp, it's very flexible. It's one of South Luangwa's best spots for Cookson's wildebeest, & eland are sometimes spotted in the area. *US$822 Aug–Sep, US$764 Jul, Oct, US$706 Jun,*

all pp sharing FBA, inc drinks, current park fees. Sgl suppt US$290. ⊕ *Jun–Oct.* **LLLL**

🏠 **Nkwali** [map, page 254] (6 rooms, Robin's House, Luangwa Safari House) Contact Robin Pope Safaris, pages 264–5. ⊕ NKWALI 13°6.989'S, 31°44.414'E. Nkwali is the main base for Robin Pope Safaris. It overlooks the Luangwa & the park beyond from the Lupande GMA which encompasses some beautiful tall acacia & ebony woodlands, a favourite haunt for giraffe & elephant. As you turn left just before the main bridge at Mfuwe, Nkwali is well signposted. Take the road for about 5km, then turn left just before the end of the tarmac. Take this for about 2km, then turn right for a further 4km.

Each of Nkwali's comfortable rooms has a high thatched roof resting on 3 creamy-white walls, leaving the front completely open with views of the river. The chalets are furnished with dbl or twin beds surrounded by a walk in mosi net. In the en-suite at the back the shower is open to the sky while the toilet & two basins are under cover. Five of the chalets are the same size, while the 6th is larger & can act as a family room with the extra beds. All are on mains power with a back-up generator.

The camp feels rustic, but very stylishly so, & the high level of attention to detail is clear. Its bar is spectacularly built around an ebony tree, & there's a small swimming pool behind the dining room. The proximity to the river & a nearby water hole often attracts game close to camp. The food is very good, & you'll usually find exceedingly smooth standards of service.

Note that nearby are 2 private safari houses: the child-friendly 2-bedroom Robin's House (page 281) & the rather more stylish 4-bedroom Luangwa Safari House (page 277). Both are close to Nkwali, but they run with their own autonomous chefs & guides, so don't impact upon the character of Nkwali at all.

Most activities from Nkwali are drives into the park, which is accessed either by boat across the river, or over the conveniently close Nkwali pontoon. Walks are led into both the park & in the surrounding GMA; often you'll just cross the river by boat & walk from there. The camp has permission to run walking safaris throughout the year.

It's usual to combine time here with time at Tena Tena &/or Nsefu camps, further north – when Nkwali often works best as the first camp on the itinerary. *US$650 Jul–Oct, US$510 22 May–Jun, US$450 Jan–21 May, Nov–Dec, all pp FBA, inc drinks,* laundry, airport & inter-camp transfers, exc park & community fees. ☺ All year. **LLL**

* 🏠 **Nsefu Camp** [map, page 256] (6 rondavels) Contact Robin Pope Safaris, pages 264–5. ◈ NSEFU 12°56.236'S, 31°55.289'E. Nsefu is superbly situated on the Luangwa River, in the middle of the Nsefu Sector. It was first opened in 1951 by Norman Carr – making it Zambia's oldest safari camp – & moved to its present location in 1953. Then the camp consisted of raised brick rondavels that were entered via a few steps.

In recent years these deteriorated until, in late 1998, the camp was bought by Robin Pope Safaris, who completely rebuilt & refurbished it. (Robin himself had guided there for many years before starting up his own company, so had always been closely connected with Nsefu.) Now it is once again one of the best camps in the valley.

Nsefu's original row of round rondavels has been retained, but each now has a shady wooden veranda at the front. Inside twin or dbl beds are cooled by a very gentle & quiet AC system that operates within the mosqi nets surrounding the beds. Large windows look out over the river, stylishly curtained. At the back, each rondavel has had an en-suite shower & toilet added – complete with old-style bath taps (but efficient hot water) – which is partially open to the outside.

The camp has been furnished with taste & elegance, in the style of the 1950s – complete with wind-up gramophone & traditional silver service. The whole effect is impressive &, despite the camp's creature comforts, it has retained an old, solid feel of history.

Nsefu's bar stands under a thatch roof beside a huge termite mound, & a nearby hide overlooks a small lagoon. Excellent food is served in a separate thatched dining area where the atmosphere is relaxed – although the tables are often laid beside the riverbank, or elsewhere under the skies. A stay here is often combined with Nkwali, Tena Tena, or one of Robin Pope's walking safaris. *US$795 Jul–Oct, US$660 22 May–Jun, US$560 22 Jan–Mar, 1–20 Nov, all pp FBA, inc drinks, laundry, airport & inter-camp transfers, exc park & community fees.* ☺ *22 May–20 Nov, & 22 Jan–Mar for river safaris.* **LLLL**

🏠 **Nsolo Bushcamp** [map, page 256] (4 chalets) Contact Norman Carr Safaris, page 264. Set on a sweeping bend of the seasonal Luwi River, with a permanent waterhole to the front, Nsolo focuses on a central *chitenje* in the shade of mahogany & sausage trees. This is an airy thatched room with a separate open-air seating area & a good library – including the *Nsolo Journals*, written by Craig & Janelle Doria when they managed the camp in the 1990s. Meals are normally taken here, but on special occasions the table is laid in the sand river, lit by the soft glow of hurricane lamps.

The large chalets were designed by Shadrack (Shaddy) Nkhoma, a long-serving guide with

---

SPA SAFARI

The Bush-Spa at Mfuwe Lodge (m *0979 306826, 0974 514030; www.bush-spa. com.* ☺ *08.00–17.00 daily; from US$45/75 ½/1hr*) must be the most unlikely location for a full-scale spa. Overlooking a lagoon are three treatment rooms – two singles and a double – set within a large, thatched structure which also features a wet deck area and a jacuzzi. Watching elephant while having a massage must be for some the ultimate in game-viewing!

The brainchild of Nathalie Zanoli, the award-winning spa was opened in 2007, and offers a chance for local women to work within the tourist industry, which is otherwise largely dominated by men. Nathalie trains them in a range of techniques using indigenous products, such as those extracted from the sausage tree (*Kigelia africana*) or the baobab (*Adansonia digitata*), and taking on board African holistic practices. Massages or wraps, facials or pedicures, hydrotherapy or reflexology: there are numerous options, all priced by the hour rather than according to the treatment.

The spa is open to all comers. The team visits lodges in the Mfuwe area to offer in-room treatments, but they can also arrange free transfers to the spa itself from camps in the vicinity.

Norman Carr Safaris. Built simply on wooden decks with reed walls & high thatched roofs, each has either twin beds or a dbl under a walk-in mosquito net. En-suite bathrooms are open to the stars with a flush toilet & shower with a view. A dbl door opens onto a tree- or thatch-shaded private deck, with comfortable chairs & a great view over the river. Solar lights are used in the evenings.

The camp was named for the *nsolo* or honeyguide bird (*Indicator indicator*). It lies 9–10km inside the park from the main Luangwa River, directly west of the Nsefu Sector in a sandy area dominated by mopane trees, with veins of shady riparian forest. Though short game drives are possible, walking is the major attraction. On my first visit to Nsolo in 1995 the ranger for our walks was Rice Time, a sprightly Zambian hunter who strode through the bush with speed & confidence – despite being over 70 years of age. Sadly he died in 2006, but there is a memorial for him in camp, & his stories are still told & re-told. A stay here is usually combined with visits to Nsolo's sister camps, and with Luwi 10km to the east, & 15km west to Kakuli & Mchenja, a few days spent walking down the sand river between the camps makes a great trip. *US$800/1,050 pp sharing/ sgl Jun–Oct, US$695 pp 20–31 May, all FBA inc drinks, exc park fees.* ☺ *20 May–Oct.* **LLLL**

🏠 **Puku Ridge Tented Camp** [map, page 254] (7 tents) Contact Sanctuary Retreats, page 265. Barely a kilometre from its sister lodge, Chichele, Puku Ridge opened in 2003, & has since been taken over by Sanctuary Retreats. It stands on the side of a rocky outcrop, overlooking a lovely floodplain on the south side of the park.

Unlike Chichele, the smart Puku Ridge was designed with the safari market in mind, & has a more contemporary, bush feel. Each of its safari tents has a private veranda, whilst inside are a king-size or twin beds, surrounded by a walk-in mosquito net with a ceiling fan above the bed. Each private bathroom has twin washbasins & flush toilet, indoor & outdoor showers & a bath, and they have plans to build a swimming pool – demonstrating a relatively high level of luxury by Luangwa standards. Morning tea or coffee are delivered by your room steward. Activities include walks & day or night game drives. *US$450/562 Apr–14 Jun, Nov–20 Dec, US$680/1,020 15 Jun– Oct, 21–31 Dec, sharing/sgl FBA, inc bar, laundry, park fees, airport & inter-camp transfers.* ☺ *Apr–Dec.* **LLLL**

🏠 **Robin's House** [map, page 254] (2 bedrooms) Contact Robin Pope Safaris, pages 264–5. The private, 5-bed Robin's House stands on the riverbank near Nkwali, under a grove of large ebony trees. Originally the home of Robin & Jo Pope themselves, it's homely & functional rather than stylish, but it's still comfortable & tastefully decorated. It has a central sitting room & 2 large bedrooms (a dbl & a trpl), each with its own bathroom. Large windows give great views across the river, & there's a grassy garden complete with small swimming pool. It's all relatively child-friendly, even for small children, & comes complete with a small bookcase full of books. The house has a private guide, hostess & chef, so it's ideal for families &/or those seeking more privacy. Those with older children, & larger groups, might consider Luangwa Safari House (above) as a more appropriate alternative. *US$700 Jul–Oct, US$605 22 May–Jun, US$555 Jan–21 May, Nov–Dec, all pp FBA, inc drinks, laundry, airport transfers, exc park & community fees. Min 2 adults, 1 child.* ☺ *All year.* **LLLL**

☀🏠 **Tafika** [map, page 256] (6 chalets) Contact Remote Africa Safaris, page 264. ⊕ TAFIKA 15°51.250'S, 31°59.811'E. Tafika stands on the bank of the Luangwa, overlooking the national park, & is perhaps the smallest of the valley's main camps. It was founded by John & Carol Coppinger, who managed Chibembe for years until they started Tafika on their own around 1995. John's years of experience in the valley are augmented by the experience of several other top guides working here, including Bryan Jackson & Isaac Zulu; thus Tafika's guiding is amongst the best in the valley.

Four of the reed-&-thatch chalets have 2 dbl beds in each, surrounded by separate walk-in mosquito nets. The family chalet, built around the trunk of a stunning sausage tree (*Kigelia africana*), has 2 rooms, while the new honeymoon suite is very similar to the standard rooms, but has a king-size bed, dbl showers & a private hammock. All have en-suite facilities, including a flush toilet, washbasin, & excellent shower that is open to the skies. Lighting is by solar-powered storm lanterns. The bar/dining area has comfortable chairs & large, circular dining tables, though dinner is a relaxed affair, often eaten together outside. Tafika is not flash or luxurious in any forced sense, though it is very high quality: the food is superb, the atmosphere friendly & unpretentious, & the guiding truly expert.

10

Game activities include day & night drives, as well as walking safaris. It's also possible to do a mountain-bike safari, cycling through the local village & then into the park itself. Alternatively, you could cycle to the school & clinic supported by Tafika (as you might expect, the camp is closely connected to the local community, which it supports extensively). With such a large guiding team at Tafika there are almost never more than 4 guests per vehicle, & it would be very unusual for the camp not to be able to arrange the activity of your choosing.

During the dry season, Tafika acts as the hub for Chikoko Trails (page 273), which use 2 walking bushcamps, Chikoko & Crocodile, just over the river in a wilderness area of the park, & also with Mwaleshi Camp's walking safaris in North Luangwa National Park (page 296). *US$1,010 Aug–Sep, US$830 Jul, Oct, US$725 May, Jun, Nov, all FBA, inc bar, laundry, current park fees, airport & inter-camp transfers. Sgl suppt US$280.* ☼ *May–Nov.* **LLLLL**

⌂ **Tena Tena** [map, page 256] (5 tents) Contact Robin Pope Safaris, pages 264–5. ✦ 12°59,089'S, 31°53,655'E. Having moved 1km upstream from its original site in 2012 (due to river erosion threatening the camp), Tena Tena now overlooks a stretch of the Luangwa River at the southern end of the Nsefu sector of the park, about 20km northeast of the bridge at Mfuwe. Tena Tena is not only a widely recognised name in safari circles, it's also one of the park's best camps. Its large comfortable safari tents are under canvas roofs & are completely insect proof. Each is set on a solid base with twin or dbl beds, & have an en-suite shower & toilet at the rear. They are all spaced well apart in quite thick vegetation, & the front of the tents can roll up to give views of the river.

The main area at Tena is split over 2 levels, built under a large tented roof supported by rustic poles overlooking the river. The upper level has a well-stocked bar, a comfortable lounge, & a large dining table with director's chairs. The lower level has seating built into the banks of the Luangwa River with ample cushions, a good spot for relaxing & watching wildlife just on the edge of camp.

Activities concentrate on morning & afternoon walks, & game drives (including night drives). The guiding, like everything else here, is first-class – it ranks with the best in Africa. A stay here is often combined with Nkwali, Nsefu (camp or bush camping), or one of Robin Pope's walking safaris. *US$795 Jul–Oct, US$660 22 May–Jun, all pp FBA, inc drinks, laundry, airport & inter-camp transfers, exc park & community fees.* ☼ *22 May–Oct.* **LLLL**

⌂ **Zungulila** [map, page 252] (4 chalets) Contact Bushcamp Company, pages 263–4. ✦ ZUNGUL 13°21.117'S, 31°30.928'E. Situated in an untouched part of the park, Zungulila focuses on exploring some of the most untamed sections of bush on foot (though drives are possible). Routes include the Hippo Pools trail along the Kapamba River, or guests can walk to or from its sister camp, Bilimungwe. With its dark wood furniture & kilim-style floor rugs, the camp itself is redolent of the days of the old explorers, though solar lighting augments the paraffin lamps & comfy sunloungers on the deck bring a 21st-century twist. Its large tents, unusually turned sideways with views of the river from the deck or dbl/twin beds, boast many comforts, from partially open-air bathrooms with a separate toilet to a tiny private plunge pool. You can even cool off with a sundowner in the river! Access is usually by 3½hr transfer from Mfuwe Lodge, but there's also an airstrip close by. *US$530/705 May & Nov–10 Jan, US$550/740 Jun & Oct, US$720/945 Jul–Sep, all pp sharing/sgl FBA, inc bar, laundry, airport & inter-camp transfers, exc park fees.* ☼ *May–10 Jan.* **LLLL**

Budget and mid-range camps

South Luangwa National Park is not an ideal safari destination for the impecunious backpacker. Hitchhiking into the park from Chipata is difficult (flying is the best way to arrive 'independently'), and there are no touts selling cheap safaris. There are a few budget camps as well as a lot of smaller, more exclusive ones (with all-inclusive rates). The latter don't cater well for unexpected visitors; they're best booked in advance.

If you want to be independent, then come in your own fully equipped 4x4 – as then you can see the park for yourself. That said, although driving yourself around is fun, it's a pale shadow of the experience that you get at one of the better small lodges. Note, too, that self-drive vehicles may not be driven in the national park when it's dark; only registered guides can conduct night drives. Make sure that you bring supplies of food (fresh vegetables and other limited provisions can be bought locally), and the best maps that you can buy in Lusaka.

Most budget travellers who come to the Luangwa arrive in overland trucks. These travel between Malawi and Zimbabwe, stopping here and in Lusaka. They usually stay, together with a few backpackers and independent travellers, at one of Luangwa's less expensive camps, most clustered around the Mfuwe Bridge area.

🏠 **Croc Valley** [map, page 254] (6 chalets, 8 tents, 10 backpacker beds, camping) ✆0216 246074; m 0977 175172; e crocvalleycamp@ iwayafrica.com; www.crocvalley.com. Upstream of the main Mfuwe Bridge, this leafy & bustling camp has beautifully maintained gardens shaded by Natal mahogany, ebony & sausage trees. To find it, turn right onto a dirt road just before entering the park, in the same direction as Marula Lodge & Track & Trail Rivercamp. When the road splits, follow it to the right; the camp is well signposted. The extensive river frontage looks over hippos & a healthy crocodile population on the sandbanks, & is dominated by 6 spacious safari tents & the open-fronted bar area. Other accommodation incorporates 2 more safari tents set back from the river, 2 en-suite chalets with small kitchens overlooking the bush, 2 family rooms & 3 backpacker rooms with AC (1 twin, 1 dbl & one 6-bed) sharing an outdoor 'bush' bathroom. There's a 'hippo-friendly' paddling pool (with sloping sides so that bathing hippos can get out), gym, volleyball net, table tennis, a small kitchen for self-caterers & a spacious lounge & bar. If it feels rather crowded in high season, it is still well designed & attractive. Activities comprise walking safaris (US$50pp) & 4x4 game drives (US$40pp). River tent US$200/240, standard tent US$75/90, chalets US$110/170 Nov–Jun/Jul–Oct, all pp FB; dorm bed US$10; camping US$6.50–12. Park fees extra. ⊕ All year. **L–LL**

❋ 🏠 **Flatdogs Camp** [map, page 254] (10 tents, 6 chalets, 1 treehouse, 1 family chalet, 1 family tent) ✆0216 246038; e info@ flatdogscamp.com; www.flatdogscamp.com. ⊕ FLATDO 13°6.298'S, 31°46.546'E. The local nickname for the crocodile, 'flatdog' was an apt choice when the original campsite was opened in 1992 at the old crocodile camp near the Mfuwe Bridge. In 2000, Flatdogs was moved to its present site on about 100ha of land beside the river, just to the left of the bridge. It's a lovely spot, with

plenty of shade from winterthorn, *Faidherbia albida*, & mahogany, *Trichelia emetica*. A lot of game wanders through the area, including a good population of giraffe, attracted by the acacia trees.

Flatdogs today is an extensive & imaginatively designed camp. It includes an open-plan bar; satellite TV & internet café; a swimming pool; a shop for crafts, bush clothes & toiletries; & an à-la-carte restaurant serving meals (including vegetarian food) all day. The bar & restaurants are open to non-residents, & are sociable in the evenings. That said, the camp doesn't get as lively as it used to, & the rooms are well spaced & private.

Three thatched, 2-storey units are each split into 2 rooms, although they each easily combine to suit groups & families. Each has a communal kitchenette (self-catering equipment provided) & en-suite bathroom; downstairs is a dbl room with fan & a wraparound veranda, while upstairs is a twin room with a view of the river. A 4th chalet is slightly larger, with 2 sgl beds on a mezzanine floor with viewing deck, 1 room with 3 sgl beds, & 1 with a dbl & sgl, as well as a separate kitchen. All beds have mosquito nets. The innovative Jackalberry Treehouse has 2 en-suite bedrooms & a completely open sitting room on a platform overlooking a small dambo. The Crocs Nest is a large tented house & is another lovely addition. It has 2 en-suite rooms (a dbl & a twin) joined by a large living & dining area, & a large deck outside has a private pool overlooking the river.

There are also 3 'standard' & 7 'luxury' permanently en-suite safari tents. The luxury are larger, and on the riverbank; whilst the smaller standard tents have a bush view. As a radical departure in 2011, Flatdogs decided to close its campsite completely.

Activities include day & night drives in the park (max 6 people per 4x4 vehicle), walking safaris, & all-day drive/walks (US$50 per activity, exc park fees). The camp is excellently run & well

10

suited to those on a tighter budget, especially as accommodation & activities can be booked separately. *Chalet US$60–95 pp room only, US$300–395 pp FBA, inc park fees. Standard/ luxury tents: US$40–50/US$60–95 pp room only, US$250–325/US$300–390 pp FBA, inc park fees. Treehouse & Croc Nest; US408–455 pp (2 sharing) FBA, inc park fees.* ⊕ *Apr–mid Nov.* **L–LLL**

🏠 **Kawaza Village** [map, page 254] (6 huts) For details of this cultural village, see pages 288–9.

🏠 **Marula Lodge** [map, page 254] (11 rooms, 6 tents, 10 backpacker beds) \ 0216 246 073; m 0974 595838; e info@marulalodgezambia.com; www. marulalodgezambia.com. In a classic position just upstream from the main Mfuwe Bridge, Marula is just before Croc Valley & Track & Trail Rivercamp; when the dirt road splits, continue straight to reach Marula Lodge. Despite its beautiful position, this is a very simple camp, used mostly by local groups & businesspeople, as well as those on budget safaris from Malawi, though also receiving some international guests.

Marula's en-suite chalets, are dotted over well-kept lawns. All chalets have high ceilings, concrete floors, mosquito nets & a ceiling fan. 7 of the chalets (5dbl, 2 twin) are smaller with louvered windows, which may add a sense of security for a more nervous traveller, but may feel rather restrictive to others. Close by 2 newer rooms are more spacious & have an airy feel to them. Lined along the river bank are 6 dome tents with a communal bathroom, & another 2-storey building has a dormitory with 10 beds upstairs, & an office below. The camp has mains electricity, with both Wi-Fi & cell reception available.

The camp's focal point is a large thatch dining area with open sides & a bar. Wholesome food is served in the à-la-carte restaurant, although guests are also welcome to self-cater. Fridges & freezers are available on site, & the camps chefs are more than happy to help you cook. Game drives & walks are offered (*US$45pp*), & there's a pool near the river. *Chalets US$190/225 Jul–Oct, US$130/140 Nov–Jun pp sharing/sgl, inc FB & 2 game activities/day; US$40/50 Jul–Oct, US$30/40 Nov–Jun pp sharing/sgl self-catering; tents/dorms US$13 pp self catering. Park fees extra.* ⊕ *All year.* **L–LL**

✳ 🏠 **Nkhonzi Camp** [map, page 252] (4 tents) m 0978 733265; e info@jackalberry.

net; www.jackalberrysafaris.net. ⊕ 12°58.615′S 31°44.988′E'. Located along the banks of the seasonal Mushilashi River deep inside the park, Nkhonzi is the only camp within the park itself that can accurately be described as a budget/mid-range option. Opened in 2015, the camp has a strong focus on sustainability, with a borehole being the only permanent fixture of the camp. When combined with the budget approach this gives the camp a very basic (but comfortable) style without the luxury touches, or high prices, of the upmarket camps & lodges in the park.

The camps 4 walk-in tents are small, but can still fit a dbl bed. Gauze windows & canvas flaps at the entrance allow light & a breeze into the tents, but also make them largely mosquito proof. At the back of each tent open-air bathrooms are surrounded by reed walls & contain a bucket shower & a composting toilet.

The communal area is incredibly basic with no main structure, just a table for meals & a cool-box set out under the shade of a large ebony tree. Reed walls conceal the simple bush-kitchen & an array of solar panels that power the camp. The focus at Nkhonzi is very much on a simple, affordable wilderness experience away from the busy Mfuwe area where most of the other budget camps are located.

Walking safaris are the main focus of the camp, which are often led by owner Gavin Opie who has years of experience guiding & running safari camps in Zambia. However, day & night game drives are also possible. While there is plentiful wildlife in the area, its true draw is the isolation from other camps & the wilderness experience. The camp typically offers 3, 4 or 5 day all-inclusive package safaris, but it's also possible to stay on a per night basis. *US$255/295 1 nt, US$445/495 3 nts, US$745/825 4 nts, US$795/995 5 nts Mar–May/Jun–Oct, all pp FBA, inc airport transfers, laundry & park fees, exc bar.* ⊕ *Mar– Oct.* **LL**

🏠 **Thornicroft** [map, page 254] (9 chalets) \ 0216 246247; e info@thornicroft-lodge.com; www.thornicroft-lodge.com. 1km downstream of the confluence of the Luangwa & the Lupande rivers, Thornicroft aims at both the local market & international visitors – & is more mid range than budget. Each solid chalet here has stones & wood inset into its walls, with large mesh windows to allow the breeze in & keep the chalets cool during the summer, & a large thatch roof providing insulation during the colder winter nights. Inside is en suite, with comfortable beds & white linen inside a walk-in mosquito net, plus a desk & hanging space. Outside a veranda overlooks the Luangwa, which is eating away at the bank to get closer every year. At the heart of the lodge is a quirky swimming pool in the shape of Zambia, & nearby a huge thatched building incorporates the restaurant, bar & lounge area, where tea & coffee is available all day. Morning & afternoon/night game drives are offered as standard, & all day drives (*US$50*), walks (*US$20*) & village excursions (*US$25*) are chargeable extras available on request. *US$230/280 Jul–Oct, US$200/240 Nov–Jun, all pp sharing /sgl FBA, exc drinks, airport transfers & park fees.* ⊕ *All year.* **LL**

🏠 **Track & Trail River Camp** [map, page 254] (9 chalets, camping) \0216 246020; m 0977 600556; e info@trackandtrailrivercamp.com; www.trackandtrailrivercamp.com. ⊕ 13°09.979'S, 31°79.261'E. Track & Trail is a Dutch-owned, mid-range camp just 5 mins' drive from the park entrance. Right next to Croc Valley, it overlooks the river, & is reached along the same track. Thatched en-suite chalets of a split-level design each have a private veranda & a narrow balcony allowing guests to take advantage of the river views. The rooms are tastefully decorated with African artwork, & dbl beds downstairs are supplemented by 2 single beds on the upper level, all of which are surrounded by large mosi nets. Towards the back of the property, the shady campsite offers individual pitches with water, electricity & BBQ facilities. All campers share a central ablution block. Campers can eat in the main camp; the food is reported to be very good & there's an excellent coffee machine behind the bar. There's an unusual above-ground pool to keep cool, an open-sided gym rondavel to provide an opportunity for some exercise, & a spa offering a range of aromatherapy & massage treatments.

In addition to guided safaris on foot & in an open game vehicle, this is a good place to pick up photography tips from owner-photographer Peter Geraerdts, who also runs photographic workshops from the camp. *Chalet US$147/207 pp sharing FB Nov–Jun/Jul–Oct or US$310/370 FBA, inc park fees, airport transfer, laundry. Sgl suppt US$49–85. Camping US$12.50 pp.* ⊕ *All year.* **LL**

🏠 **Wildlife Camp** [map, page 254] (9 chalets, 7 safari tents, camping, bushcamp) \0216 246026; e info@wildlifezambia.com; www.wildlifezambia.com. ⊕ WILDLI 13°6.320'S, 31°45.133'E. This popular, buzzing camp, still large by Luangwa standards, has been leased & run from the WECSZ (page 51) by the helpful Herman Miles since 1992. As the lease fee goes towards conservation/development projects, by staying here you are contributing to a good cause. The camp makes a good base if you have your own vehicle, or you can arrange to be collected from Mfuwe Airport (*US$30 pp/min 2*). If you're driving, pass the airport & turn left just before the main Mfuwe Bridge, following the signs to Nkwali, the Wildlife Camp & others. Routes differ slightly in the dry season, but in the wet season you pass the entrance to Kapani, now closed to guests, then carry on through mopane woodland for about 3km until you see the Wildlife Camp signs; the camp is shortly after that.

Each of the chalets (with 2–4 beds) & twin-bedded safari tents is en suite; all are clean & pleasant, but not luxurious. For those with their own kit, there's a huge campsite within a large grove of mopane trees, with plenty of shaded spots along the river to set up camp. As with any big-game location, don't even think about sleeping outside without a closed tent. In addition to an ablution block, the campsite has thatched shelters, & its own pool & bar. Basic kitchen equipment is available both for the chalets & at the campsite, or with 24hrs notice you can arrange for staff to cook for you (*US$15/day per tent/chalet*). Either way, you'll need to bring your own food; there are a few shops in Mfuwe where you can pick up supplies. Note that there are monkeys in camp, so don't leave food lying around.

The bar/restaurant is often busy & always relaxed. It overlooks a floodplain & the main Luangwa River beyond, & serves both à-la-carte meals & snacks. There are exceedingly popular day & night game drives (*US$50 pp/min 3*) &, between Jun & Nov, walking safaris (*US$45–55 pp/min 3*) on WECSZ land & in the park; the 4-tent bushcamp (about 2–3km from the main camp) makes a great overnight walking safari option (*US$250 pp all inc*). If you have your own vehicle you can drive yourself into the park during the day, though only licensed guides are allowed to conduct night drives. Village tours are also possible (*US$30 pp*). *Chalet US$68/85 Jul–Oct, US$45–55 Nov–Jun, pp sharing/sgl room only;*

10

US$250/280 Jul–Oct, US$165/200 Nov–Jun FBA, inc airport transfers & laundry. Safari tent US$45/55 Jul–Oct, US$30/35 Nov–Jun pp sharing/sgl room only; US$200/220 Jul–Oct, US$155/180 Nov–Jun FBA, inc airport transfers & laundry. Camping US$12 Jul–Oct, US$8 Nov–Jun. Park fees & drinks extra. Discounts for WECSZ members. ⊕ All year. **L–LL**

🏠 **Zikomo Safari Camp** [map, page 256] (9 chalets, camping) 📞 0216 246202/201; 📱 0973 741708; info@zikomosafari.com; www.zikomosafari.com. ⊕ ZIKOMO 13°01.400'S, 31°53.646'E Zikomo, meaning 'thank you' in the Chichewa language, is a new camp that opened in 2012 on the border of the Nsefu sector of the park. The camp is owned & run by David & Victory Wallace, a couple from the States. To get to the camp, head north on the road from Mfuwe to Luambe & the turning to Zikomo is well signposted approximately 14km from the turning in Mfuwe.

Zikomo is spread out under a section of riverine forest along the eastern bank of the Luangwa. Although it's situated in the GMA, its proximity to the Nsefu sector means it has easy access to some excellent areas of the park for walks & game drives. Also, there's often plenty of wildlife around camp. The main area in the centre of the camp is raised slightly from the ground, with completely open sides & a high thatch roof covering a dining area, modest bar & lounge area with plenty of wicker furniture. Close by is a small swimming pool, with several sunloungers overlooking the river.

The chalets at Zikomo come in 2 styles, with 4 being raised chalets with timber frames, reed walls & high thatch roofs, & 5 chalets with walls constructed from local sand & soil. Both of these rooms are comfortably furnished with both dbl & single beds, & are decorated with plentiful African fabrics from Tribal Textiles. Being constructed entirely from natural materials, these rooms feel quite rustic, but they come with modern amenities such as flushing toilets & hot showers in the en-suite bathrooms, & power sockets in the rooms. There is also Wi-Fi available in the main area. The shady campground is also on the riverbank, with 5 separate pitches & shared ablution blocks. Campers are welcome to make use of the facilities at the main lodge. *US$210 pp FB; US$445/495 May–Jun & Oct–Nov/Jul–Sep pp FBA; inc park fees, bar, airport transfers. Camping US$15. ⊕ May–Nov.* **LLL**

Campsites around the South Luangwa

🔺 **Kalovia** [map, page 256] (Camping) Contact Remote Africa Safaris, page 264. ⊕ KALOVI 12°45.354'S, 32°04.579'E. Utilising the same site as the old Mwanya Bushcamp, Kalovia sits on elevated ground just outside the national park, surrounded by floodplains & the old channel of the Luangwa River. To get here, drive north on the main road from Mfuwe & through the Nsefu sector of the park. Continue 18km north from the Chikwinda Gate, & turn left at the well signposted turning. (⊕ KALOTU 12°45.675'S, 32°04.809'E.) Nearby lagoons often draw wildlife to the area around the camp, & a game viewing track runs from the campsite & north along the Luangwa. The campsite is equipped with a flush toilet, wash basin & bucket shower, & there are always a couple of caretakers on site. *US$70 whole camp. ⊕ Jun–Oct.*

Other types of trips/accommodation

Mobile safaris There's a lot of hype about mobile walking safaris. Perhaps images of Livingstone or Stanley striding through deepest Africa with an entourage of trusty porters and guides are to blame. I don't know. But these days, let's be honest, it is somewhat different. The term 'mobile safari' is overused.

It used to mean that you set off with all your kit on the backs of porters and camped where you stopped. Think, for a moment, of the consequences of this. You'll realise that it resulted in either very basic camping stops with few facilities, or more comfortable camps requiring a safari of enormous cost. It also required total freedom to camp where you liked, which is now limited and controlled by ZAWA for very good reasons.

Although the term 'mobile safari' is often abused, there is one operation in South Luangwa National Park that comes close to running a proper mobile operation:

Robin Pope's Mobile Safaris Contact Robin Pope Safaris, pages 264–5. Between mid Jun & Sep, RPS organises about 22 mobile walking safaris along the Mupamadzi River, in the far north of the park. The trip itself lasts 6 days & 5 nights; participants also spend at least 1 night prior to the trip at Nkwali, & 1 at the end at Nsefu – though a few more days either side would be ideal.

The walks are about 10km per day & a truly mobile camp is used, moved by the back-up vehicle to meet you. The camp has comfortable walk-in tents (each with twin beds), shared hot & cold showers, shared long-drop toilets, & a staff of 8 or 9. Typically they'll use 3 different sites for the 5 nights, & the choice depends on the game & the walkers' interests.

Trips are organised on fixed dates each year, & take a max of 6 people. They are always oversubscribed, & sometimes booked up a year or 2 in advance. The real attraction of these trips is, firstly, that they are just walking in a wilderness area. There's no driving, & you are away from everything but the bush. Secondly, you're in a small group that stays together with just 1 guide. You get to know each other & have a lot of time with one of the valley's best guides. They're very relaxing. (As there is no sgl supplement whilst walking, these trips are popular amongst sgl people.) *US$575 Jun, US$697 Jul–early Oct, all pp per night, inc costs of Nkwali & Nsefu, exc park fees.* ☉ *Mid Jun–early Oct.*

Fly-camping In Africa, the term 'fly-camp' usually means a simple campsite with a campfire and a small, very simple tent – or possibly just a mosquito net. This is obviously a far cry from the luxurious en-suite tents of most modern safari camps – but camping like this out in the bush, with nothing around you apart from the darkness, does have a real appeal for many cosseted travellers. They're ideal for the thrill of no-frills camping in the bush – expect a bucket shower under a tree and a long-drop toilet – but there's certainly no better way to feel close to the wildlife at night.

Lodges have operated fly-camps in some areas of Africa for years – most notably the Selous Game Reserve in southern Tanzania – but they're still new to the Luangwa. The main companies offering them are:

- **Robin Pope Safaris** (pages 264–5), which terms them 'Bush Camping', and offers them as individual nights, or for 2 to 3 days as you walk between Tena Tena and Nsefu.
- **Norman Carr Safaris** (page 264), which offers what it terms 'Luwi River sleepouts' – usually for just one night, for a maximum of four people, and as part of a walk between their bushcamps.
- **Shenton Safaris** (page 265) have a less well-known option called 'camp-outs' available for guests residing at Mwamba – they go north of the camp for one night with a maximum of four guests.

Robin Pope Safaris uses small, walk-in tents for these nights, whilst Norman Carr and Shentons usually use mosquito nets.

River safaris River safaris are only possible around February to April, depending on the water level in the Luangwa River; then, this is the only way to get around most of the park. See pages 39–40, for more comment on the wet season – but from that you'll realise that the rain is usually in short, sharp, late-afternoon bursts. The rest of the day is often sunny – for photographers the clarity and quality of the light is extraordinary. So if you've been on safari quite a bit, but only seen the Luangwa (or southern Africa) in the dry season, you should aim to make a trip during the rains. You won't see the density of animals that you'll find in October, but the place comes alive with animals and plants you just don't see in the dry season, and the birdlife is phenomenal.

For ten months of the year most of the river's tributaries are sand rivers, but for just a few months they fill with water. Often they are lined by tall old hardwood trees. In a few areas the trees open out onto wide, shallow floodplains, usually dotted with egrets, waders or geese, while in the middle are several nesting colonies for storks and herons, of which the most well known are those in the Nsefu Sector of the park. These rely on a high water level, and the birds won't nest unless the area is flooded. (This is probably a protection mechanism against nest raiders who would be deterred by the water at the foot of the trees.) The main one of these is a huge colony for yellow-billed storks, which take on a beautiful, delicate pink hue when breeding and collectively make for an amazing sight.

Two operations, Norman Carr Safaris (page 264) and Robin Pope Safaris (pages 264–5) currently run river trips during the rainy season:

Norman Carr Safaris Their 'Rivers & Rainbows Safari' is a 6-night trip, visiting Kakuli for 4 nights & Chinzmobo for 2. *US$3,240/4,370 pp sharing FBA on 6 night/9 night trip, inc bar, laundry, local transfers & park fees.*

Robin Pope Safaris Their 'River Journeys' safari typically spends 7 nights between Luangwa River Camp, Nsefu & Nkwali camps. *US$2,961/3,927 pp sharing/sgl FBA, inc bar, laundry & local transfers, exc park fees.*

CULTURAL TOURISM Though wildlife is often the main draw of the Luangwa Valley, increasing numbers of visitors are enjoying meeting the local people and learning more of their traditional lifestyles. Cultural tourism is gradually taking off. Currently this has two main points of focus:

Kawaza Village [map, page 254] (*Contact Robin Pope Safaris, pages 264–5. Day visit US$20 pp inc lunch; overnight min US$70 pp. Robin Pope Safaris charges US$165 pp per night, of which 50% is paid into Kawaza's school fund, & the rest goes to the village*). Jointly developed between Robin Pope Safaris and local villagers, and now part of the wider Project Luangwa, Kawaza is an efficient and viable small business for the village which involves visitors staying either for an afternoon, or (much better) overnight. Here they can spend time with people from this Kunda community and learn more of their daily ways of living, traditions and culture.

It started as an effort to end the villagers' feeling of exclusion. Some of the communities around Mfuwe felt that many overseas visitors arrive and leave without any meaningful form of social contact with them. They also wished to get involved in tourism, to raise funds for their school and to support vulnerable members of their community (orphans and the elderly). The scheme is run by a committee of villagers, with Felix John Kalubu, headmaster of the adjacent school, as secretary. His predecessor, David Mwewa, explained to me that the objectives were 'to provide an authentic Zambian experience and raise money for the community'.

Kawaza is a real village and visitors are encouraged to participate in its normal everyday life – to help the women cook nshima and relish, to visit the local traditional healer, to tend the crops, to try fishing, or to visit the local school, church or clinic. Villagers will tailormake an agenda to suit your interests and time – with an overnight stay (see below) the best option.

The effects of the project on the community are gradually showing. Some of the villagers are learning more English in order to communicate better with visitors. David commented, 'When the visitors first came the villagers could not imagine dancing together with a white person or eating together. But when guests come to the village they join in all the activities … when they see the villagers putting up a roof they join them … The visitors like it that way.' Further, the community is benefiting directly, as a proportion of the income goes towards financially supporting orphans and elderly people in the community, as well as providing the local school with text books, computers, and transport for pupils and staff.

The village is a 30–45-minute drive from the Mfuwe Bridge, depending on the time of year and the route taken. Transfer costs vary between operators, but expect to pay from US$80 per trip.

⌂ Where to stay

⌂ (6 huts) A handful of rondavels has been built just for visitors: small, clean huts of traditional design with thatched roofs. These have mattresses on simple wooden bedsteads, with spotlessly clean sheets & mosquito nets. Visitors also have their own separate long-drop toilets & rondavels for bathing (using a large tin bowl & a scoop for the water). The food is grown locally & prepared in the village – including tasty cassava for breakfast, with coffee, tea & milk.

Activities are really just taking part in whatever is going on when you are there, & whatever you are interested in. That might mean going into the bush to the village's plots of arable land, collecting local plants & herbs, preparing the food, or even going to help teach a class at the school. Depending on the time of year, you may be allowed to see some (though not all) of the initiation ceremonies for the young people. (As you'd expect, men attend only the men's ceremonies & women only the women's.)

Of special interest, usually arranged on request, would be a visit to a traditional healer, or a local clinic, or a meeting with the area's senior chief Nsefu – the paramount chief of the 6 local chiefs. In the evening, the community's elders tell traditional stories or sing songs around the campfire.

If you've never really tried to put yourself in a totally different culture, then spend a night here. It'll make you think about your own culture as much as Kawaza's, & you'll remember it long after you've forgotten the animals.

Guests staying at most camps in the Luangwa can add a night at Kawaza to their itinerary, with rates depending on the individual camp & the cost of transfers (see above).

Nsendamila Cultural Village [map, page 254] Very close to the hub of the Mfuwe area, Nsendamila village has been closed for several years, but now offers a small selection of curios for sale. It is easily found by turning left towards Nkwali just before the Mfuwe Bridge, followed shortly by another turning to the left. The village was originally built by the local communities, with funding from various charities and NGOs, its traditional rondavels laid out to demonstrate a local village's way of life. Further plans – for a cultural and heritage centre with drama productions, and for a small museum to house prehistoric artefacts from the Luangwa Valley – have yet to come to fruition. The village is also the site of Uyoba Community School, built and sponsored by the SLCS, at which visitors are welcome.

NORTH LUANGWA NATIONAL PARK

(*Park fees US$20 pp/day; self drive US$25 pp/day & vehicle US$15/day; bed levy US$20 pp per night*) North Luangwa National Park (known usually as 'the North Park') covers about 4,636km² of the Luangwa Valley; it's half the size of the South Luangwa National Park (aka the 'South Park'). It shares the same origin as the South Park, being part of the same rift valley, and its eastern boundary is also the Luangwa River. It has the same geology, soil types and vegetation as South Luangwa, and so its landscapes are very similar.

However, unlike the South Park, which is basically bounded by the steep Muchinga Escarpment to the west, the North Park takes in a lot of this within its protection.

About 24% of North Luangwa lies within the escarpment, compared with about 5% of South Luangwa. This means that North Luangwa has a more diverse range of habitats, which is especially interesting for birdwatchers, although there are also mammals found on the hill which aren't normally seen on the valley floor.

From a conservation point of view, it also means that much of the catchment area of North Luangwa's main rivers falls within the boundaries of the park – giving the park authorities more control of its rivers and habitats.

For visitors to the wilderness camps, perhaps the park's most important natural feature is the Mwaleshi River – which is unlike the Luangwa or any of its tributaries in the South Park (except, possibly, stretches of the Mupamadzi). It's a permanent river that flows even in the heat of the dry season, when it's generally very clear and shallow.

THE PARK'S ZONES For the visitor, it's important to understand that North Luangwa is now 'zoned'. Most of the southern side of the park is strictly reserved as a wilderness area. It has very few roads and is currently used only by two small camps, which concentrate on walking safaris. The only way to visit this is to arrange your trip with one of these operators, and stay in one of these tiny camps. If you're not staying at a camp, then you cannot even pass through this area; you'll find clear signs and even booms across the tracks.

However, north of this is a 'zone' that was opened to wider access in 2002. Now it's possible for experienced travellers to bring fully equipped vehicles into the park, and drive through from east to west, or vice versa. Access is strictly restricted to the more northerly zone, which has one main track across it and several side-tracks. This is a new way to see parts of this remote park, whilst getting between Luambe National Park and the Great North Road. It also opens up the possibility of an interesting (if challenging) circular drive around eastern Zambia.

HISTORY
Before the mid 1980s Without the conservation efforts and funds that were devoted to South Luangwa, the country's premier game park, the North Luangwa National Park has until recently been a 'poor relation'. Poachers hunting rhino and elephant met less resistance there, and local people crossed its boundaries freely in search of food. The impact on the game was inevitable.

North Luangwa remained a wilderness area for many years, officially accessible only to the Game Department, until 1984 when Major John Harvey and his wife Lorna (daughter of Sir Stewart Gore-Browne, of Shiwa Ng'andu) started to run walking safaris here. They were the first safari operators here and their son, Mark Harvey, runs one of the three camps currently in the North Park (*Buffalo Camp*, page 296).

The Owens' ideal In 1986 a couple of American zoologists – Mark and Delia Owens – visited the park in search of an African wilderness in which to base their animal research, and returned in October '87 to base themselves here. They came from a project in Botswana's Central Kalahari Game Reserve, with an uncompromising reputation for defending the wildlife against powerful vested interests. They also had behind them an international best-selling book about their experiences – *The Cry of the Kalahari*. This had brought conservation issues in Botswana to a popular audience, which earned them considerable financial backing for high-profile conservation efforts, including the vital support of the Frankfurt Zoological Society (FZS).

Their presence here was to have a profound impact upon the park. In the early 1980s, elephant poaching was estimated at about 1,000 animals per year. Their second best-seller, the highly readable *Survivor's Song* (called *The Eye of the Elephant* in the US; see *Appendix 3*, page 529), relates their struggles to protect this park from the poachers, and their efforts to find alternatives for the local people so that they would support the anti-poaching work.

Read it before you arrive, but don't be alarmed: the place is much safer now. Also be aware that their book has been written to sell. It's an exciting yarn, but does describe events as if they were a personal campaign. It doesn't mention any real contribution to education, development or anti-poaching from anyone apart from Mark and Delia. Others involved with the park have long maintained that this was not a true picture, and that the Owens' book simply ignored the 'bigger picture' of all the efforts which were going on at the time. Whatever the truth, it's worth reading.

With the dedication of the Owens, and the vital financial assistance that they could attract, poaching has been virtually eliminated. The park's game scouts were paid well and properly housed, and became the most zealous and effective in the country. Local education and development programmes were initiated in villages around the park, aiming to raise awareness of conservation and to provide alternatives for people who relied upon poaching for food.

However, Mark and Delia left Zambia in a hurry in 1996. This followed an alleged incident in which forceful anti-poaching actions went too far. It was precipitated by a documentary screened in the US by the ABC television network, *Deadly Game: The Mark and Delia Owens Story*, in which an alleged poacher appeared to be executed. Mark and Delia have never returned to Zambia.

NORTH LUANGWA CONSERVATION PROJECT Perhaps the real, lasting legacy of Mark and Delia is that they introduced the Frankfurt Zoological Society (FZS) to North Luangwa. The FZS's constant financial support over more than 30 years has done an amazing amount to safeguard this terrific park. Thanks to them, and other important donors, the privately financed North Luangwa Conservation Project continues to support the park and its authorities.

The NLCP's input has concentrated on support for the law enforcement effort, through training and the supply of essential field equipment, rations, vehicles and the building of houses for the field staff. Thus the park's scouts continue to be keen, well trained and well motivated. They also help to conduct regular aerial surveys of large mammals, records of which stretch all the way back to the late 1980s, and to maintain and gradually expand the road network – as well as other aspects of the park's management and conservation.

Various programmes continue to support the communities around the park. These vary from a conservation education programme, with material that is specific to this area, to work on land-use plans – to get the nearby communities to think critically about their future and how they can generate income, whilst safeguarding some of their natural resources for the future.

The rhino Meanwhile, the game goes from strength to strength. In 2003 five black rhino were reintroduced, and I was lucky enough to be there to watch as these first animals were fitted with a radio transmitter prior to their release into a large, fenced off, intensive protection zone at the heart of the park. A further ten were added in 2006, five more in 2008, and a final five in 2010. There have been several setbacks, such as the unfortunate deaths of six rhinos from disease and intraspecific fighting in 2011, but also huge successes such as the birth of a number of calves, and never losing an individual to poaching. The total population stood at 34 by 2015, a real achievement for conservation in the valley.

10

These are now probably the only black rhino in the country; their presence is a strong sign of how secure the North Luangwa is, and that the park expects to enjoy the long-term support of the FZS. It's worth noting that while there are 4x4 tracks through the protection zone, no-one is currently allowed to stop within the fenced area. Other animals, however, can get under or over the fencing; it is only the rhino that are kept within the zone.

The future for North Luangwa seems bright – and Zambia's positive experience of having a national park run with the strong support of a donor-funded private organisation has helped it to look to the future in places like Liuwa Plain, where an analogous project is progressing well, and in the Bangweulu Wetlands.

FLORA AND FAUNA In general, the flora and fauna of the North Park are the same as those found in South Luangwa (pages 255–61). However, the inclusion of the escarpment in the park certainly brings a new dimension to the flora here. An excellent example is the road from Mano down from the escarpment, which is about 12km long. This brings you from the two-storey woodlands of the upper and plateau escarpment, with a lightly closed canopy of semi-evergreen trees 15–20m high, and down through the miombo woodlands on the hills to vegetation more typical of the valley as most people know it.

Often there are bird species here that aren't usually found on the valley floor, and sometimes sable antelope, bushpig or blue monkeys. In the dry season, look also for signs of elephant, which often move into the mountains.

On the valley floor, the ecosystems of the two parks, and the native game species found therein, often seem virtually identical. The North Park has some east African bird species that don't occur further south – like the chestnut-mantled sparrow weaver, the white-winged starling and especially the yellow-throated longclaw – but the differences in species are minor.

However, several differences are apparent. You're more likely to see Cookson's wildebeest (*Connochaetes taurinus cooksoni*), one of the valley's endemic subspecies. The population seems much larger in the north of the valley than in the south. However, you won't find any giraffes here, as they don't seem to occur much north of the Mupamadzi River. (Phil Berry has reliable records of a few sightings here until about the mid '80s. John Coppinger comments that in his years operating to the North Park since 1990, he's only ever received a report of one giraffe ... and that was probably lost!)

Eland, the largest of the antelope, are more common here, and hartebeest are also seen more often than in the South Park. Given their long lifespan, and slow regeneration after poaching, elephant are skittish in the North Park and still relatively scarce. The population is growing, but it'll take a long time before they are as numerous, or as relaxed, as they are around Mfuwe. Buffalo herds seem to be even larger than those in the South Park, and there are some very strong prides of lion. Hyena are also common; those in the North Park seem to hunt more than those in the South, and have developed a tactic of chasing puku into the Mwaleshi River in order to catch them. Those in the South Park tend perhaps to do a little more scavenging, and less hunting. Then, of course, there are the re-introduced black rhino – see pages 291–2.

GETTING THERE Prior to 2002, the only way for visitors to see North Luangwa was to come to one of the few camps for walking safaris within the park. That's still the way that most people visit, and certainly the way to get the most out of the park. Typically a three- to five-night stay at one of the walking camps is perfect. Most visitors (and there are only a total of a few hundred in the average year) combine a walking trip here with some time in the South Park, and fly between the two. For the cognoscenti, it's one of Africa's top safari destinations.

By air Transfers to and from North Luangwa are normally organised as part of your safari package, on small four- to six-seater light aircraft. A short hop here by light aircraft from Lukuzi or Mfuwe (both in South Luangwa) takes about 20–45 minutes and costs in the region of US$255 per person.

Driving The adventurous and experienced may now drive themselves through the north side of the park. Although the access roads from the Mpika area are graded,

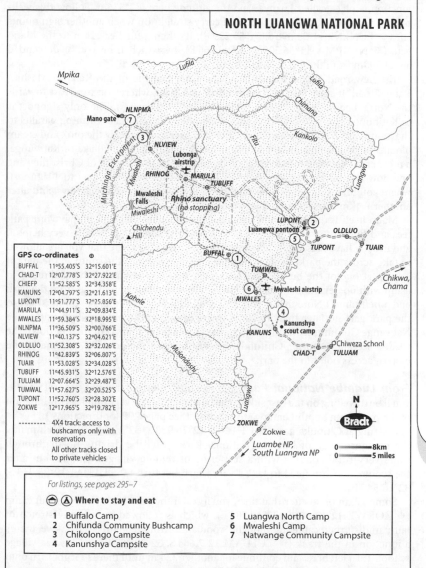

NORTH LUANGWA NATIONAL PARK

GPS co-ordinates ⊕

BUFFAL	11°55.405'S	32°15.601'E
CHAD-T	12°07.778'S	32°27.922'E
CHIEFP	11°52.585'S	32°34.358'E
KANUNS	12°04.797'S	32°21.613'E
LUPONT	11°51.777'S	32°25.856'E
MARULA	11°44.911'S	32°09.834'E
MWALES	11°59.384'S	32°18.995'E
NLNPMA	11°36.509'S	32°00.766'E
NLVIEW	11°40.137'S	32°04.621'E
OLDLUO	11°52.308'S	32°32.026'E
RHINOG	11°42.839'S	32°06.807'S
TUAIR	11°53.028'S	32°34.028'S
TUBUFF	11°45.931'S	32°12.576'E
TULUAM	12°07.664'S	32°29.487'E
TUMWAL	11°57.627'S	32°20.525'S
TUPONT	11°52.760'S	32°28.302'E
ZOKWE	12°17.965'S	32°19.782'E

------ 4X4 track: access to bushcamps only with reservation

All other tracks closed to private vehicles

For listings, see pages 295–7

⊖ Ⓐ **Where to stay and eat**

1　Buffalo Camp
2　Chifunda Community Bushcamp
3　Chikolongo Campsite
4　Kanunshya Campsite
5　Luangwa North Camp
6　Mwaleshi Camp
7　Natwange Community Campsite

10

and even those within the park are reasonably well maintained, it's a very remote and wild area, so you'll need two fully equipped 4x4 vehicles, the expertise to use them, and a high degree of self-sufficiency. Read *Lessons in bush travel* box, on pages 270–1, before you even consider this! Then directions are as follows:

From Mpika via Mano gate There are now two roads to North Luangwa National Park from the Mpika area, the new route being considerably closer to Mpika. The established route, a turning off the Great North Road (✪ TUNLNP 11°26.378'S, 31°44.307'E), is well signposted just over 60km northeast of Mpika, and 28km south of the turning to Shiwa Ng'andu. There are a few buildings at the junction, a place called Luanya, and the altitude here is 1,556m. Follow this well-maintained track for about 32km, and carry straight on when another sign points left (✪ TUNLN2 11°35.698'S, 31°55.229'E). It's then a further 11km to the Mano gate (✪ NLNPMA 11°36.509'S, 32°00.766'E), by which time you've descended about 390m from the Great North Road.

The new road, opened in 2010, glories in the name of the Kalenga Mashitu Range Road. It starts just over 5km north of Mpika, where you turn east towards the North Luangwa (✪ TU2NLP 11°47.056'S, 31°27.663'E). The only signpost is to Katibunga High School. This, too, is a graded road, initially running parallel to the mountains through woodland, enlivened here and there by the pink and cream blooms of protea flowers. After 38km, you'll go through the village of Katibunga, a prosperous-looking mission station dominated by the Church of Christ the King and now run by Tanzanian monks. A further 21km will bring you to a signpost, where you turn right to the national park. From here the road narrows, and after another 9.4km brings you to the Mano gate.

Mano itself is outside of the park, but this is where you sign in, pay your park fees and find out about the latest park news. The staff are generally very helpful, and usually have reasonably accurate maps charting the route that you are allowed to take across the park. (Self drivers are only allowed into the south of the park if staying at one of the bushcamps, and must stick to the road, driving directly to camp with no deviations. Breaking these rules can result in removal from the park and a hefty fine!) Note that if you're driving to one of the lodges, you must get to the park gate no later than 16.00. If you're camping, the obvious first stop is the Natwange Community Campsite (opposite), not more than 1km further down the road; a second campsite, Chifunda, lies just beyond the pontoon that marks the eastern access point to the park.

From Luambe National Park Approaching North Luangwa from Luambe, you'll be travelling on the east side of the Luangwa River – very much a continuation of the road from South Luangwa to Luambe. (See page 299 for directions.)

Starting at Chipuka gate (✪ CHIPUK 12°26.923'S, 32°12.516'E), which marks the northern edge of Luambe National Park, you'll be driving north through some very rural country with a scattering of remote villages. About 9km after the scout camp you need to take a very sharp left turn (✪ TULUA1 12°25.313'S, 32°16.547'E).

Some 17km or so after that turn, you'll reach the very basic Zokwe scout camp (✪ ZOKWE 12°17.965'S, 32°19.782'E), which is followed by a lovely stretch of fairly undisturbed cathedral mopane woodland. Around 30km after Zokwe, there's a junction in the track (✪ TULUAM 12°7.664'S, 32°29.487'E) at Chiweza village school. Turn left here, and continue for another 2.9km until there's a right turn onto another track at ✪ 12°07.778'S, 32°27.922'E.

(Continuing straight on would lead to a crossing of the Luangwa near the old Kanunshya gate, but this entry to the park is exclusive to the operators who work there, and there is no public right of access.)

Hence take a right turn at ✪ CHAD-T (✪ 12°07.778'S, 32°27.922'E) and continue north and slightly east for about 28km until you cross an airfield. Just beyond this, turn left (west) at ✪ TUAIR 11°53.028'S, 32°34.028'E. After another 5km you pass a place called Old Luelo Camp (✪ OLDLUO 11°52.308'S, 32°32.026'E), and then about 8.5km later, take a right turn (✪ TUPONT 11°52.760'S, 32°28.302'E). The road ahead is a game track. After almost 7km you'll pass the entrance to Chifunda Bushcamp (✪ CHIFBC 11°51.645'S, 32°26.066'E), then another 0.4km brings you to a T-junction. Turn right for 200m or so to reach the manual pontoon across the Luangwa (✪ LUPONT 11°51.777'S, 32°25.856'E; *no charge*) into the North Park. Note that the pontoon takes one vehicle only and is normally operated from 1 June until the end of October, but it's always wise to check in advance. The pontoon is usually monitored by the park's very sharp scouts. In case of vehicle problems they can arrange for help, but a substantial vehicle recovery fee will be payable.

🏠 **WHERE TO STAY** *See map, page 293.*

Northern zone The only permanent camp currently in the northern zone is Luangwa North Camp. However, for those who are self-sufficient and driving themselves through the northern zone of the park, there are three simple community camps, two to the west, by the Mano gate, the second close to the Luangwa pontoon in the east of the park. Alternatively, you can camp at Luambe Lodge (pages 300–1) in Luambe National Park.

🏠 **Luangwa North Camp** (4 chalets)
m 0973 105189; e info@feelingafrica.com; www. feelingafrica.com. We received mixed reports about this camp under its previous name of Delia Camp, which closed in 2011 before being taken over by Feeling Africa, a Spanish-owned tour operator based in Livingstone. It is built beside the Luangwa River, to the east of the national park, between Chifunda gate & the Mwaleshi River. From the turn off to camp (✪ TUDELC 11°50.956'S, 32°25.573'E), it's a further 10km.

As it stands, the camp receives the occasional guest to stay in one of their open-fronted twin chalets with en-suite facilities, all built of reed & thatch, & raised up on stilts. In similar style, & linked by walkways, the central area has a veranda where meals are taken overlooking the river. There are plans to refurbish the camp, converting it into a luxury-tented camp. *US$680pp FBA, inc bar, park fees; exc premium wines.* ☺ *Jun–Oct.*

Southern wilderness area Being very remote, and only accessible for part of the year, the park's southern zone – the walking wilderness area – is a difficult place for a safari company to operate. Hence for many years there have been only two or three camps here, all of which concentrate on walking rather than driving. North Luangwa offers an experience that is even more remote and isolated than the rest of the valley, and you can guarantee that you won't be disturbed by anyone else whilst walking here.

Both of the park's bushcamps stand on the banks of the Mwaleshi, one of the few sources of water for the game, which consequently gravitates to it. It is shallow enough to be easily crossed on foot, allowing you to follow game back and forth across the river. This isn't usually an option beside the main Luangwa, but is easy here. Certainly in the heat of October I relished the cool of paddling across it and even the chance to just sit down in the middle with a drink at sundown. Having such a convenient, cool stream next to camp does make a big difference to both your comfort in the heat and your game viewing.

If you're driving yourself, you will have to leave the park by either the Mano gate or the Chifunda gate. If the latter, do be aware that the road that runs north, parallel to the Luangwa River, is very rarely used, so be prepared for fallen trees, and give yourself plenty of time.

Buffalo Camp (6 chalets) m 0976 970444; e kapishya@shiwasafaris.com, mathew@ shiwasafaris.com; www.shiwasafaris.com. ⊕ BUFFAL 11°55.405'S, 32°15.601'E. Situated close to the Mwaleshi River, surrounded by plains, this small camp is set under some welcome shade. Simple, reed-&-thatch chalets along the river are rebuilt each year, complete with en-suite toilets & hot showers. They're no-frills affairs, but spacious & comfortable, with twin or dbl beds & a low reed wall giving an open view of the river & plains beyond. Relax in a hammock during the heat of the day, or simply cool off in the river; when it's colder, there's a firepit backed by a simple dining shelter.

Buffalo is good value & more offbeat than the other camps in the park; having a laid-back attitude to your time here is a prerequisite to enjoying it! Predominantly a walking camp, it's owned & run by Mark Harvey, who was born & brought up at Shiwa Ng'andu & speaks several local languages; he's a very experienced, knowledgeable & entertaining guide – though note that he isn't always in camp as he also runs Kapishya Hot Springs at Shiwa.

The camp offers the flexibility to book on a room-only basis as an alternative to a fully inclusive package. As a result, travellers can self-cater, with the option of adding activities when they want (*walking US$25, game drive US$40*), offering a more independent style of travel suitable for self-drives; although it's worth phoning ahead to confirm this. It is also possible to fly in, but there is a US$25 landing fee. *US$100/265 pp room only/FBA, exc drinks, park fees, bed levy.* ⊕ *Mid Jun–31 Oct.* **L–LL**

✳ Mwaleshi Camp (4 chalets) Contact Remote Africa Safaris, page 264. ⊕ MWALES 11°59.384'S, 32°18.995'E. John Coppinger set up Mwaleshi Camp for Wilderness Trails in 1989, then retained control of it when he set up his own operation, Remote Africa Safaris. Almost all visitors fly between South & North Luangwa national parks; it's a 35min hop from Lukuzi Airstrip, near Tafika, or 45mins from Mfuwe. A minimum stay of 3 nights is sensible.

Mwaleshi is a delightfully simple yet well-equipped bushcamp whose reed-&-grass chalets are set on the southern bank of a scenic stretch of the Mwaleshi River. Each has a flush toilet & hot shower en suite, under the stars. There's an attractive thatched dining & bar area, also overlooking the river, & a small riverside shelter so you can cool off in the heat of the day. The permanent manager/guide is one of the experienced team from Remote Africa Safaris – so it's a top-class operation & one of my favourite bushcamps in Africa. Walking really is the activity here (very convenient, given the amount you'll be tempted to eat of their excellent food), & the first time you get on a vehicle from camp may well be when you're leaving. That said, the presence of a vehicle enables walks further afield, a day trip to Mwaleshi Falls, or even the occasional night drive. *US$645 15 Jun–Jul & Oct, US$680 Aug–Sep, all pp FBA inc bar, current park fees, exc premium wines.* ⊕ *Mid Jun–31 Oct.* **LLLL**

Campsites around the North Luangwa

⚑ Natwange Community Campsite (Camping) m 0972 607672, 0967 834910; e info@natwange.org; www.natwange. org. ⊕ NLNPMA 11°36.509'S, 32°00.766'E. Opened in 2002 with the help of the North Luangwa Conservation Project, Natwange is run by the local Mukungule community, & all the proceeds go into a fund that benefits the community. It's an ideal place to camp on the western boundary of the park. The campsite is set in beautiful thick *mushitu* forest on the banks of the Mwaleshi River, just 1km or so inside the Mano gate. Individual pitches have flush toilets, hot-water showers & fireplaces for BBQs, & there's a central shelter. Dome tents can be hired (*US$5/night*), with water & firewood provided, but otherwise you'll need all your own supplies.

You can walk along the river from here, arrange a visit to one of the local villages, or perhaps do a little birding or fishing (*guided birding US$5 pp/hr*). Look out for Ross's turaco &

the uncommon green twinspot. *US$15 pp.*
☺ *May–mid Dec.*

⚔ Chifunda Community Bushcamp
(3 chalets, camping) ☏0216 246127; m 0978
014706; e bushcamp@itswild.org; www.itswild.
org. ⊕ CHIFbc 11°51.645'S, 32°26.066'E. This
thriving community bushcamp on the Luangwa
River, just 0.6km from the Luangwa pontoon, is
the only survivor of 3 set up under an initiative
sponsored by Community Markets for Conservation
(COMACO), each employing local people – some of
them ex-poachers – & with profits shared between
local villages.

Surrounded by tall, shady trees, Chifunda is an
attractive, well-maintained site overlooking the
national park. As well as camping, there are simple
but spacious thatched chalets, each with large twin
beds, solar lighting, open-air toilet & a big shower
area. There's a central dining shelter where meals
can be provided (*b/fast US$10, lunch/dinner US$15
pp*) or, if you bring your own food, they'll help
with preparation. Guided walks (*US$15 pp*) can be
organised, as can game drives in your own vehicle
(*US$10 pp*), both exc park fees. Village visits (*US$10
pp*) are a further option. *Camping US$12 pp; chalet
US$42 pp.* ☺ *12 Jun–Oct.*

⚔ Chikolongo Campsite (Camping) Contact
Remote Africa Safaris, page 264. ⊕ CHIKOL
11°37.288'S, 32°02.273'E. Clearly signposted
4km after the Mano Gate, this campsite is run
& managed by Remote Africa Safaris, & can
be prebooked on an exclusive basis. It's in a
picturesque location in the escarpment, in an area

of miombo woodland close to the source of the
Mwaleshi, where it's possible to take a paddle in
the river after a quick check for crocodiles.

The camp has a communal ablutions block
with flush toilets & bucket showers, with hot
water available on request. You will need to bring
all of your own equipment, although the camp
caretakers are available to help with some of the
camp chores for a small, previously negotiated
price. *US$70 whole camp.* ☺ *Jun–Oct.*

⚔ Kanunshya Campsite (Camping) Contact
Remote Africa Safaris, page 264. ⊕ KANUNS
12°02.937'S, 32°22.286'E. Another campsite run
by Remote Africa Safaris, Kanunshya is on the
east side of the park, & is also available only for
exclusive bookings. To get here from Luambe, see
the section on getting to North Luangwa from
Luambe on pages 294–5 for the start of the route.
Once you've reached the junction at ⊕ 12°07.778'S,
32°27.922'E, continue straight on & proceed to the
Kanunshya Gate, where you'll need to pick up a
scout. After 700m, take the right-hand fork
(⊕ KANTUR 12°04.368'S, 32°21.551'E), & cross the
Lundazi River 1.6km later, which should be dry from
July. From here the track is indistinct & ephemeral,
so the scout will need to escort you to the campsite.

Opposite the confluence of the Mwaleshi &
Luangwa rivers, the campsite is situated on a shady,
sandy riverbank, although here the abundance
of crocodiles & hippos make paddling in the river
unsafe. The site is equipped with flush toilets &
bucket showers, & is looked after by a couple of
caretakers. *US$70 whole camp.* ☺ *Jun–Oct.*

LUAMBE NATIONAL PARK

(*Park fees US$15 pp/day; vehicle US$15/day; full fees payable in transit between
North & South parks*) This small park, just 254km², is situated between North and
South Luangwa national parks and can be reached only between about May and
October. The first serious rains turn the area's powdery black-cotton soil into an
impassable quagmire – impossible even in the best 4x4. Even in the dry season the
roads are not great, as the black-cotton soil sets into a series of hard bumps. The
good news, though, is that these – including some self-drive game loops – are re-
graded each year.

The park is administered by ZAWA, but the concession for the park was won by
Luambe Conservation Ltd, a German-owned Zambia-based company with a mixture
of German & Zambian management who run the only lodge within the park.

FLORA AND FAUNA Luambe is mostly riverine forest, and stretches of mopane
woodland; some of this is beautiful, tall cathedral mopane with lots of space between
the trees and very little undergrowth. There are also areas of miombo woodland and

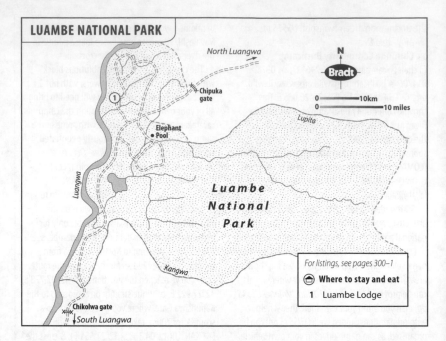

LUAMBE NATIONAL PARK

North Luangwa

Chipuka gate

Elephant Pool

Lupita

Luambe National Park

Luangwa

Kangwa

Chikolwa gate
South Luangwa

For listings, see pages 300–1

⊘ **Where to stay and eat**
1 Luambe Lodge

grasslands – including the open Chipuka Plains that are criss-crossed by streams and lagoons, and regularly visited on game drives.

Although the ecosystem is virtually identical to that of the North and South Luangwa parks, Luambe is a small park in the middle of a large GMA, where controlled hunting is allowed. Thus game densities are lower, and the game tends to be a bit more skittish than in the larger parks. That being said, game densities have recovered significantly under the auspices of the German NGO Communities for Conservation Society Cologne (although they no longer operate in the park). On my last trip through here in June, I saw a sprinkling of small antelope – especially around the lodge and near the river: puku, impala, bushbuck, kudu, and waterbuck are common, and both the shy oribi and the endemic Cookson's wildebeest are occasionally seen. In addition to the huge numbers of resident hippo, the elephant population is rising, and there are also reports of increased sightings of predators such as lions, leopards and wild dog. With a bird count of around 400 species, it would be well worth investigating further.

GETTING THERE Many of the park's visitors are adventurous 4x4ers passing through, heading to or from the North Park.

If you are not driving, you'll probably need to charter a five-seater **plane** (pilot plus four passengers) from Mfuwe, which will cost around US$860 for a one-way trip to either airstrip. Alternatively, Luambe Lodge can arrange transfers from Mfuwe, which cost US$250 for up to four people. Luambe Lodge can also arrange transfers to other locations on request. There are a couple of airstrips (Waka Waka and Luawata) approximately 45 minutes' drive from Luambe Lodge, the transfer from Luawata including a short river crossing.

Driving Do read *Lessons in bush travel*, page 270, before you attempt to get to this remote corner by yourself! When you've taken heed of this, the directions are as follows.

From South Luangwa Approaching Luambe or North Luangwa from the South Park, you'll be travelling on the east side of the river. From Mfuwe, head north through the Nsefu Sector, and finally exit the park from Chikwinda gate (✪ SLNPCH 12°51.983'S, 32°1.008'E). It is then about 3 hours' drive to Luambe, and perhaps seven to the edge of North Luangwa.

On this road, especially near the start, there are a number of small tributaries of the Luangwa to cross. Between about mid June and the end of October these will usually be fairly easy; outside of that they can be very tricky. About 26km after Chikwinda gate, one of the more notable of these is the Lukusuzi River (✪ RIVERR 12°41.647'S, 32°7.585'E). I know from experience that this is easier to cross going south–north than north–south, as the southern bank stopped me for about 5 hours on one muddy night in early June. Fortunately, virtually the whole of the nearby village soon appeared – many helped to push and manoeuvre, while some just came for the entertainment. I hope it was better than TV for the villagers, as their unstinting help certainly saved us from a wet and uncomfortable night in the river.

The turning east to the Lukusuzi National Park is (at least in theory) on the south bank of this river, although in practice very, very few people ever venture that way.

About 10km after the river you'll come to the Chakolwa gate (✪ CHAKOL 12°37.178'S, 32°7.413'E), the entry into Luambe National Park. The road through Luambe is primarily thick black-cotton soil so is often hard and bumpy when dry, and impassable when wet.

It's re-graded each year, but was particularly bad when I last travelled this way shortly after the rainy season; leaving second gear was a novelty.

Some 18km later (✪ TULUA2 12°28.869'S, 32°9.486'E) you'll pass a left turning to Luambe Lodge (page 300), which is almost 3km away. Continuing north, a further 7km will bring you to Chipuka gate (✪ CHIPUK 12°26.923'S, 32°12.516'E), which marks the northern edge of Luambe National Park.

From North Luangwa See pages 294–5 for the route from Luambe to North Luangwa, and back-track along that.

From Lundazi There's a 4x4 route from Lundazi to Luambe that is passable in the dry season only. It's a scenic drive of 140km or so, but not to be rushed, particularly when going down the escarpment.

From Mpika via the Corridor Road There is in theory a very difficult route into the Luangwa Valley which leaves the Great North Road south of Mpika, and involves the 'Corridor pontoon' across the Luangwa River, but it's a serious undertaking. Even in a good year it's viable only in the dry season – and unless the pontoon is operating, then only in September or October when the river is very low.

The 'Corridor' is the area between the North and South parks, usually used by professional trophy hunters (hunting on a sustainable basis). They have a few simple camps there, they make the roads, and they usually ensure that the pontoon across the Luangwa is working. But if there's no hunting in any given year, then many of the tracks through here will be impassable.

That said, in a normal year you can turn east from the Great North Road about 40km south of Mpika, at ✪ TUBATE 12°6.421'S, 31°15.727'E – on the track that passes the old Bateleur Farm after 26km. The next landmark is Nthunta Scout Camp (✪ NTHUNT 12°19.828'S, 31°31.979'E). About 46km from the main road you reach the Nthunta Escarpment, with its breathtaking view over the whole Luangwa Valley.

THE GOUGH MEMORIAL

High on the Nthunta Escarpment, near the Nthunta scout post, stands a small memorial to Mary Gough. Memories of the origins of this are hazy, but it's said that she was a woman who went (against all advice) to camp alone and unprotected for a long time on the Chifungwe Plain in the 1970s. Some remains of her body and clothing were found, from which it was deduced that she had been eaten by lions – and hence she was buried here.

I'm told that a few years later, during the height of Zimbabwe's war for independence, her son from Rhodesia (now Zimbabwe) came here to revisit the memorial. Local sources allege that he was a spy, who fed back information to the Rhodesian armed forces – resulting in the bombing of several bridges along the Great North Road. However, it seems he was never caught or charged with this – so the truth is uncertain.

Perhaps a reader could confirm or refute this rough history, so that I can expand on the facts and stories around this memorial in another edition!

The road is very rough as it descends down the escarpment, but after about 11km (it feels longer) you will reach the Mutinondo River. Cross this, and after 8km there's a turning to the left which takes you to Nabwalya village, in the middle of the Munyamadzi GMA. In the dry season, the hunters usually keep a pontoon across the Luangwa, just south of here (near Nyampala Hunting Camp), which links up with the track between Luambe and the South Park. Unless the river is very low, it's absolutely essential to check that this is operating before you even consider embarking upon this route – since otherwise you cannot get through.

If you were to carry straight on, instead of turning towards Nabwalya, you would be heading directly over the Mupamadzi River into the South Park. For those directions, see the section on getting to South Luangwa on page 267.

🏠 **WHERE TO STAY** *Map, page 252.*

🏠 **Luambe Lodge** (4 tents, camping) 📞0978 823331 e info@luambe-lodge.com; www.luambe-lodge.com. ✤ LUAMBE 12°25.532'S, 32°16.383'E. Just 3km from the road that links North & South Luangwa, Luambe Lodge is currently the only lodge in the park, & is an ideal stopover for those driving between the 2 parks. Whilst few overseas visitors will fly over the camps in the South Park to get here, there is a nearby airstrip, & the area can be seen as a destination in its own right.

Built on the site of the now closed Luangwa Wilderness Lodge, Luambe sits in the cool & dense shade of the thick riverine vegetation, overlooking a deep section of the Luangwa River where hippos congregate in their hundreds as the water levels drop. Opened in 2015, the campsite has space for approximately 10 vehicles & tents, sharing a bathroom & cooking area. Scheduled to open in mid 2016, the main lodge will consist of 4 safari tents along the riverbank, each with a private veranda,

allowing guests to take advantage of the river views, & an open-air, en-suite bathroom allowing guests to shower under the stars. Power for the lodge will come from solar panels, while a mixture of solar geysers & wood boilers will supply hot water for the rooms.

Activities at Luambe Lodge include day & night game drives, usually in the Chipuku plains area of the park. Walks are also possible, as are guided bird tours where you can try & spot some of the parks more notable avian species such as Grimwood's Longclaw, or colonies of Bocage's weaver.

Luambe has a strong relationship with the local village of Chitungulu, located approximately 15km to the north, & the lodge purchases much of its poultry, eggs, vegetables & building materials from the village. In partnership with the Chitungulu Foundation, a local sustainable development charity, Luambe runs tours to the village where you can learn about daily life, & the conservation issues facing this isolated community.

US$440/530 pp sharing/sgl FBA, inc laundry, drinks, exc park fees; US$340/430 pp sharing/sgl FB.

Camping US$15 pp, inc hot showers & firewood, exc park fees. ☺ May–Oct. **LLL**

LUKUSUZI NATIONAL PARK

This remote park is on the eastern side of the Luangwa Valley, slightly higher in altitude than the other parks in the valley. There are no facilities here at all, and despite rumours of its privatisation it has seen no development. There's a manned scouts' post near the gate, and an exceedingly poor track leading through the park. It's uncertain how much wildlife has survived the poaching, though it is thought that the dominant predator here is the spotted hyena, rather than the lion. The vegetation is mostly miombo woodland, dotted with grassland.

GETTING THERE Visiting the park requires a major expedition. There is a track that turns east from the South Luangwa–Luambe track, and then continues through Lukusuzi National Park until it reaches the Great East Road. This track east to the Lukusuzi National Park starts (at least in theory) on the south bank of the Lukusuzi River (✪ RIVERR 12°41.647'S, 32°7.585'E). See *From South Luangwa*, page 299, for more directions, but don't expect this turning to be very clear or well marked.

This track is bound to be impassable during the rains. The easiest approach to the park would be to take the Great East Road to Chipata, then turn north towards Lundazi. About 110km beyond Chipata there is a track on the left to Lukusuzi. It's strongly advisable to stop at the game scouts' camp at the park's entrance, and ask them about the condition of the roads. I haven't driven on either of these routes myself.

zambia • luangwa • 1995
REMOTE AFRICA
Safaris

TAFIKA CAMP • CHIKOKO TRAILS • MWALESHI CAMP
walking safaris | game drives | cultural visits | cycling | hides
www.remoteafrica.com | reservations@remoteafrica.com
Zambia | North Luangwa | South Luangwa

Kafunta
SAFARIS
The best South Luangwa has to offer!
Kafunta River Lodge
Island Bush Camp
Three Rivers Camp
www.luangwa.com
Email:bookings@luangwa.com

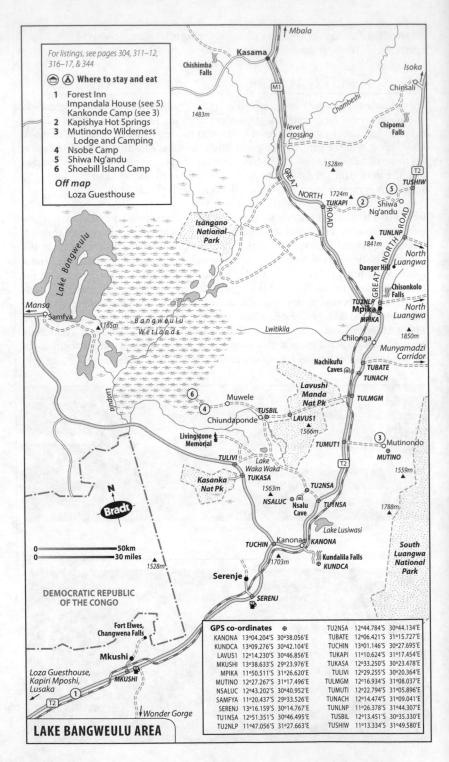

11

Bangweulu Area

The spectacular Bangweulu Wetlands are, after the rains, a fascinating water-wilderness similar in size to Botswana's Okavango Delta. A huge wetland area with its own endemic species of antelope, the black lechwe, it is also a breeding place for one of Africa's strangest and rarest birds: the shoebill.

Nearby Kasanka National Park is a jewel of a reserve, proving beyond doubt that small can be beautiful, while the manor house and estate at Shiwa Ng'andu are a must for anyone seeking an insight into Zambia's colonial history. Meanwhile Mutinondo is a relatively new area, ripe for modern adventurers to explore. Hardcore safari enthusiasts may also want to venture into the stunning and remote North Luangwa National Park (pages 289–97), which can be accessed by road from these areas. Apart from these main attractions there are numerous fascinating stops – from waterfalls to caves and old colonial monuments – in the area where David Livingstone, literally, left his heart.

If you want to explore Zambia beyond the obvious trio of great game parks (Luangwa, Lower Zambezi and Kafue) then this is perhaps the first area that you should visit. The region is perfect for adventurous self-driving visitors with fully equipped 4x4s, but most of the main highlights here can also be visited on fly-in trips using light aircraft for transport.

THE GREAT NORTH ROAD

Access to much of the region is via the Great North Road out of Lusaka. For the most part this is a good tar road, almost pot-hole-free as far as Serenje, though beyond here watch out for some significant lapses in maintenance. From the turn-off at Kapiri Mposhi, the road passes Mkushi and Serenje, then on to Mpika further north. None of these towns is a really attractive destination for most visitors, but all can be useful bases for the area's real draws: Kasanka, Bangweulu, Mutinondo and Shiwa Ng'andu.

MKUSHI Some 92km from Kapiri Mposhi, Mkushi (✛ MKUSHI 13°38.633'S, 29°23.976'E) is 1km north of the Great North Road, across the railway. Far from being just another stop on the TAZARA line, it's a thriving little town, the centre of a prosperous farming area, with a number of large commercial farms in the vicinity keeping cattle and cultivating cash crops. There is a **fuel** station on the main road, and another in town, where there are also plenty of **shops**, a **post office**, three **banks** (and ATMs) and a police post.

Getting there Several of the **buses** heading north stop in Mkushi, including the postbus that plies between Lusaka and Kasama. Mkushi is also a stop for **trains** on the TAZARA line between Kapiri Mposhi and Dar es Salaam (page 306).

🏠 **Where to stay and eat** Alongside a couple of places in Mkushi itself are three more interesting options within easy reach, with **Forest Inn,** 30km to the west, particularly geared to the needs of passing travellers.

In Mkushi

🏠 **Motel Mariana** (4 rooms, 10 chalets) ✆0215 362513; m 0977 194252. On the left as you enter Mkushi, the neat thatched chalets in well-tended lawns have the air of a model village & there is a pleasant pool. Twin rooms have TVs & en-suite showers; dbl-bedded chalets also have fridges. There's a simple bar & separate restaurant, where fish, steak or chicken (**$**) are served every evening. **$** exc b/fast.

🏠 **Nindo Country Lodges** (10 rondavels) Great North Rd; m 0977 573653/ 573563; e nindocountrylodges@gmail.com. The name may have changed from 'Blu Bubbles', but the bright pink rondavels here remain, ranged along a low grassy hill close to the turn-off to Mkushi, & interspersed with animal sculptures. All are en suite, & there's a restaurant/bar serving local dishes. **$**

Beyond Mkushi

🏠 **Forest Inn** [map, page 302] (11 chalets, camping) Great North Rd; ✆0215 353003; e forestinn@iwayafrica.com; www.forestinn-zambia.com. About 62km from Kapiri Mposhi, or 30km west of Mkushi, Forest Inn is to the south of the main road, & is clearly signposted. The 4hr drive from Lusaka makes it a convenient place to stop for lunch or overnight for those heading towards Kasanka, Mutinondo or Shiwa Ng'andu.

The inn's thatch-on-brick en-suite chalets, refurbished in 2015, have rustic wooden furniture & electric lights. They are secure, clean & functional rather than opulent, but set in large grounds, with cultivated plants & trees, cut grass, & even an old steam engine. The grassy campsite has its own well-lit shelter with BBQ facilities, & a sizeable, if basic, ablution block. The gate is kept closed, but there's a gatekeeper & guard on 24hr duty.

The restaurant (⏰ *06.00–20.00*), a good place to stop if you're driving through, serves good, farm-fresh produce, including excellent steaks (**$$–$$$**). Entertainment in the form of a pool table & darts is in the bar, while the lounge comes complete with a TV & a log fire on winter evenings. Signposted trails lead along short woodland walks, where birding highlights include Boehm's flycatcher & chestnut mantled sparrow weaver, & a family of flying squirrels has recently taken up residence. *Camping K60 pp.* **$$**

🏠 **Loza Guesthouse** [off map, 302] (10 rooms) ✆0215 352170; m 0965 353170; e loza@zamtel.zm. ✪ 13 43.515'S, 29 13.455'E. Some 26km southwest of Mkushi, or 78km from Kapiri Mposhi, is a signpost along a 10km gravel track to this converted farmhouse with a slightly Italianate feel. Loza has its own vegetable garden, a vineyard (the farm produces its own grappa), restaurant (**$$–$$$$**) & a pool. The rooms are simply but personally decorated, each with a dbl or twin beds draped with mosquito netting; most have en-suite bath or shower, & 2 are family rooms. There's also Wi-Fi access. Loza is set on a working farm, which guests are welcome to explore. **$$** *exc b/fast*

🏠 **ATB Lodge** (17 rooms) ✆0215 352410; m 0966 359791/0954 183250/0955 521246/0979 956129; e Atblodgemkushi@gmail.com. This old house in well-maintained grounds has been in the family since 1973. It's popular with Peace Corps volunteers, who appreciate Agnes's cooking – & the DSTV! – as well as the dark, comfortable lounge with big fireplace. En-suite rooms with mosi nets are clean & pleasant. To find it, head 5km northeast of Mkushi, then follow the signs towards Wonder Gorge for a further 5km. *Camping K40pp.* **$–$$**

Excursions from Mkushi There are two interesting sites to the north of Mkushi, and one to the south, though you'll need a self-sufficient 4x4 to reach any of them. If heading north, note the proximity of the sites to the border with the DRC (ex Zaire), and check the security situation locally before you go. Make sure that you don't inadvertently drive too far, which would be surprisingly easy to do. Explaining an illegal entry into the DRC might not be fun.

Finally, if you are staying here, you're also within reach of Nsalu Cave and the Kundalila Falls, both covered under *Around Kasanka and Bangweulu* on pages 331–8.

Changwena Falls This is a very pretty waterfall, near to Fort Elwes and Mount Mumpu. It's about 2 hours north of Mkushi, accessible along a bush track through a forest reserve. These tracks are highly seasonal, so do ask for local directions from Mkushi before you set off. Camping is allowed.

The falls themselves are where a small stream leaves its dambo and cascades through a series of three rock pools. The rocks around are a very attractive copper colour, helping to make this remote spot particularly beautiful. From here you can climb Mumpu and visit Fort Elwes (see below).

Fort Elwes Almost on the border with the DRC, Fort Elwes lies about 40km northeast of Mkushi at an altitude of 1,600m. The tracks to get there are in poor condition and it's not easy to find; ask locally for directions before you embark upon this trip.

The fort was built around 1896–97 by Europeans who came to seek gold in the area west of the Luangwa Valley. They feared reprisals from the local Ngoni people, if (as planned) the British attacked them near Chipata and the Ngoni were forced west.

It's an impressive place, with superb views of the hills in the surrounding area. Four huge drystone walls, some 2m thick and 3m high, form a rectangular building, which originally had a single entrance under one of them. Today it's disintegrating, but a few remnants of the original wooden structures still survive. The *National Monuments of Zambia* booklet (page 529) attributes the building to Frank Smitheman.

Lunsemfwa Wonder Gorge This spectacular 300m-deep gorge marks the point where the Mkushi River meets the Lunsemfwa, and both cut into the sedimentary rocks of the Muchinga Escarpment. It is in an extremely remote area, east of Kabwe and about 130km south of Mkushi, further south than what is known as Old Mkushi. Although the road is signposted near the ATB Lodge just northeast of Mkushi, the gorge is more easily accessed from Kabwe; see page 388 for details.

SERENJE Set in a valley in undulating countryside about 3km north of the main Great North Road, Serenje is 110km northeast of the turn-off to Mkushi. An increasing level of agricultural activity in the vicinity is likely to benefit the town, which currently has a **fuel** station, a **bank**, a Catholic mission, a teacher training college, a **post office**, a police station and a small hospital.

Getting there If you're **driving** yourself, turn off the main road at the Puma fuel station (✪ SERENJ 13°16.159'S, 30°14.767'E). At the noisy and busy **bus** station, several buses a day stop between Lusaka (*from K115 one way*) and Kashikishi on Lake Mweru, while the Lusaka–Kasama **postbus** stops at the post office three times a week in both directions. Serenje is also a station on the **TAZARA** line (page 306).

Where to stay and eat Of Serenje's selection of guesthouses, one – the Mapontela – has long shone out above the others; it's also the best restaurant in town. There's competition, though, both from **Villa Mbanandi** (m *0977 192844/0966 140096*) further down the road, and from the Salala, as well as from MU's restaurant and bakery next door.

Salala Executive Lodge (10 rooms) Ng'answa Rd; m 0799 95010; e salalalodge@ gmail.com. Close to the junction with the Great North Rd. Rather grand rooms at the back sport DSTV, a fridge, & bath or shower en suite. In the evening, sit down in the pleasant dining room to a plate of meat or chicken with potatoes, pasta, rice or nshima. **$$**

Mapontela Village Inn (8 rooms) 515 Ng'answa Rd, m 0979 587262. Serenje's established favourite is on the right as you enter the town, beyond the police station. It's a small warren of a place, run by a charming Zambian matriarch, Anna Mulenga, & her husband Steve Luker, a retired builder who came to Zambia with the Peace Corps. It has a smart exterior, umbrella-shaded restaurant veranda & spotlessly clean rooms & secure parking. It's a good spot to overnight or for lunch; the menu ranges from sandwiches to omelette & chips to nshima & steak (**$–$$**). Most of the rooms, each with dbl (or 3) beds, bath or shower, TV, fan & mosquito net, are brick built & lead off a courtyard; the older 2 are slightly smaller (& cheaper) with no fan. **$–$$** exc b/fast.

Excursions from Serenje There are various waterfalls in the area, including the narrow but pretty cascades of **Mulembo Falls** (⊕ MULEMB 13°13.067'S, 30°25.809'E). This is reached by turning off the main road 12km northeast of the Serenje turn-off, towards Kalwa Farm (where the Baptist mission has a guesthouse and campsite). From there drive 4km, then turn left just before the guesthouse, and immediately right. Just over 5km brings you to a rounded, domed rock, and a further 6.2km to the falls themselves. The right track leads to the falls, whilst straight on will take you to the river.

A little further afield are the beautiful **Kundalila Falls** (pages 330–1).

MPIKA Though no bigger than Mkushi or Serenje, Mpika (⊕ MPIKA 11°50.511'S, 31°26.620'E) is a busy crossroads of a place which has an increasing air of affluence. Here the Great North Road forks: one branch goes to Kasama, Mbala, and Mpulungu on Lake Tanganyika; the other heads directly for the Tanzanian border at Nakonde. It is about a day's travel from Lusaka, Mpulungu or the Tanzanian border, which perhaps explains why one often ends up stopping here overnight.

Getting there Getting to Mpika is easy, with a choice of public transport if you are not driving.

By bus Daily local bus services link Mpika with Lusaka, Mbala and (to a lesser extent) northeast to Isoka and Nakonde. Depending on the operator, buses stop either next to the fuel station on the main road through town, or on the opposite side of the road. Sometimes, they will pick you up if you wave them down on the side of the road, but don't bank on it. The town is also serviced by the thrice-weekly postbus between Lusaka and Kasama.

By train Mpika is one of the stops between Kapiri Mposhi and Dar es Salaam, in Tanzania, on the TAZARA railway. Tickets on the express train between Mpika and Kapiri Mposhi cost K94 in first class, K72 in second and K51 in third.

The TAZARA station is about 5–6km out of town, along a turning off the road towards Kapiri Mposhi. Private pick-up trucks operate shuttle runs between there and the central boma in Mpika, fitting as many people onto the vehicles as they can carry. The train rarely arrives on time so be prepared. If you arrive in the early hours of the morning then your options are to get one of these shuttles quickly, or to sleep rough on the station until daybreak and then try to get one. At times like this, the station is crowded but fairly clean and safe.

Hitchhiking With clear roads and a reasonable amount of traffic, hitching is a very practical form of transport to and from Mpika. There is probably more traffic going towards Mbala than towards Nakonde, but if you're heading to Lusaka you can hitch around the Puma station where both roads join.

If you're going towards Kasama and Mbala, then hitch at the turn-off by the fuel station. Alternatively, and especially if it is late in the day, walk a further 2–3km down that tarred turn-off road, until you reach a smart, fenced compound on your right. This is known as the DDSP compound – it houses offices for various aid and semi-governmental groups, and small businesses. You may pick up a lift from one of its workers, who travel widely in the district. You'll certainly see them come and go in a variety of plush 4x4s, and if the worst happens and no lift appears then you can wander across the road and sleep at their simple resthouse.

Tourist information Based at Bayama's Lodge (below) the Mpika Tourism Association (MTA), a non-profit organisation founded with the help of Open Africa, offers local maps, a reservation service and information on local sights and tours.

Where to stay and eat

Mazingo Motel [map, page 308] (34 rooms, camping) Great North Rd; ☎0214 370314; m 0966 803919. ◈ 11°48.570'S, 31°27.091'E. West of the road, almost 3km northeast of Mpika on the way to Isoka, this secure motel lies in pleasant gardens within a quiet compound. It offers en-suite dbl, twin & sgl rooms furnished with solid wood furniture; all have a kettle & DSTV; some have fridges. Campsite now has separate showers. Lunch & dinner are served: choose from an à-la-carte menu, & there's Wi-Fi access. $–$$ exc b/fast.

Bayama's Lodge, Pub & Grill [map, page 308] (4 to 8 cottages, 3 rooms, camping); m 0977 410839/316143; e bayamakumpika@gmail.com; www.bayama.de; ◈ 11°50.733'S, 31°26.780'E. Just east of the Great North Rd at the Kasama turn-off, look out for Continental Filling Station & turn right for about 250m. Bayama (Bemba for 'uncle)' has 4 newly built cottages (soon to be extended to 8) with dbl beds (extra beds on request), hot showers, mosi nets, a sitting area & veranda & 3 budget dbl rooms; bar, restaurant (traditional & international fare inc pizza; $) camping & BBQ facilities, secure parking & tourist information (see above). Reports welcome as we have not visited yet. $ exc b/fast.

Fresh Air Lodge [off map 308] (12 rooms) Kasama Rd; ☎0214 370095; m 078 158100; e freshairlodge@yahoo.com. Hidden on the right behind peach-pink walls topped with razor wire, about 400m from the main road, Fresh Air Lodge is unmissable. En-suite rooms have dbl beds, mosi nets & a fan, while more exclusive rooms have fridges & DSTV. There's secure parking at the back. $

Tusha Safari Lodge [map, page 308] (chalets & camping) Great North Rd; m 0977 694535; ◈ 11°51.305'S, 31°26.344'E. Southwest of Mpika, about 1km north of the turn-off to the Tazara station, this modest 2-storey thatched building in extensive grounds promises a little more than it delivers. Accommodation in en-suite self-catering chalets is adequate; the traffic is noisy & 'safari lodge' is a misnomer. Campers may use toilets & showers in the chalets & the bar area. The lodge has a restaurant, bar & BBQ area. $ exc b/fast.

Chintu Mukulu Community Campsite [map, page 308] (3 chalets, camping) Great North Rd, Salamo Village; m 0978 064516; or contact Mutinondo (page 311). ◈ CHINTU 12°16.601'S, 31°2.515'E. This community-run site lies close to the road about 83km south of Mpika. It has both simple chalets with bedding, & conventional tent pitches, sharing ablutions. Walks & cultural tours to the local Mpumba community to sample the traditional Bisa lifestyle are on offer, plus farming demonstrations (Nov–Jul). $

CIMS Restaurant [map, page 308] Great North Rd. This clean, modern place opposite Melodies Lodge feels more US diner than Zambian restaurant, but the meals combine 'the best chicken & chips in Mpika' traditional with more adventurous offerings such as ifishimu – caterpillar. There's a selection of bread, cakes, pies & dairy produce too, making it a good place to put together a packed lunch. $

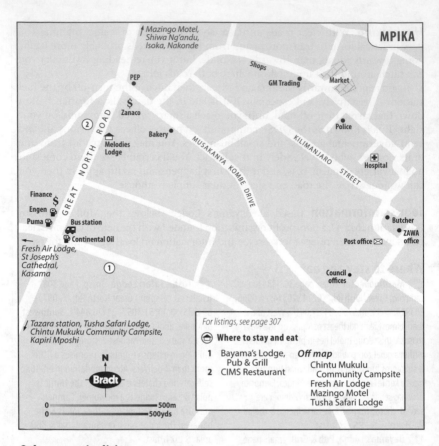

For listings, see page 307

🏠 **Where to stay and eat**

1	Bayama's Lodge, Pub & Grill	*Off map*
2	CIMS Restaurant	Chintu Mukulu Community Campsite
		Fresh Air Lodge
		Mazingo Motel
		Tusha Safari Lodge

Other practicalities There are three **fuel** stations near each other on the Great North Road, close to the turn-off to Kasama. The most conspicuous of these has an **ATM** – and there's another ATM at Zanaco near the turning into the town; there's also a branch of the Finance Bank in town. For **supplies**, GM Trading is worth a glance as is the slightly more expensive but very useful supermarket on the Great North Road. There's also a busy little market and a couple of bakeries.

For **communications**, there are a couple of post offices, one at the Mpika–Kasama junction and one in the southeast in Mpika Boma. Should you be in need of vehicle **repairs**, ask at Bayama's Lodge (page 307).

Excursions from Mpika There are a few interesting caves and waterfalls around Mpika, whilst both Mutinondo and Shiwa Ng'andu (see pages 309–12 and 312–20) are worthy of large sections of this chapter on their own. To go anywhere away from the main roads you'll really need a self-contained 4x4, even in the dry season.

Nachikufu Caves (⊕ NACAVE 12°13.939'S, 31°08.693'E; *entry US$10/5 adult/ child; vehicle US$5; camping US$15 pp inc entry*) The striking setting of this cave complex with it's geometric San/Bushman rock paintings may be worth a brief detour, though now that the admission fees have increased, that's debatable unless you're planning to camp. When excavated in the 1940s Nachikufu Cave was estimated to have been occupied intermittently for about the last 15,000 years. This is no surprise when you consider that all the essentials for survival are here: a regular supply of water from a nearby stream, shelter provided by the cave, firewood in abundance, grass for bedding and a good supply of game and vegetable food sources from the local environment. The cave is also the 'type' site of the Zambian Late Stone Age, which is known to archaeologists as the 'Nachikufan Industry' (25,000–2,000 years ago). A small display of artefacts is kept within the cave entrance and access is only with the official guide who is stationed on site.

Both the rock shelter and the cave look north over a wide plateau, and are formed from a ridge of quartzite rock – perfect for stone tools. There's also a perennial stream about 500m away from the cave. The paintings themselves are fairly simple: various figures silhouetted in black, including a couple of elephants, a beautifully drawn antelope, and human figures, some of whom are depicted with bows and arrows and one with a spear. It has to be said, however, that they are not brilliant.

The signposted turning (✪ TUNACH 12°14.474'S, 31°9.041'E) to Nachikufu is about 55km southwest of Mpika. This turning leads you north and west from the main road, over the TAZARA railway, and reaches the cave within about 2km.

Chipoma Falls (*Entry US$10/5 adult/child; vehicle US$5; camping US$15 pp inc entry*) About 20km south of Chinsali, the Lubu River drops 40m over a distance of 500m at this large set of rapids and cascades (✪ CHIPOM 10°44.998'S, 32°00.284'E). It's a lovely spot for exploring, and there are basic camping facilities here.

To reach the falls from Mpika, head north for Chinsali and Isoka and then turn left about 24km before you reach the turn-off for Chinsali (that's about 57km past the turning to Shiwa Ng'andu). Follow this road for around 6km, taking left turns at all the forks and junctions encountered, until you reach the caretaker's house by the falls. There's an entrance fee of a few dollars.

Chisonkolo Falls (*www.diompika.org/lwitikila-school/chisonkolo-falls;* ◷ *08.00– 22.00 daily.* Also known as the Lwitikila Falls, this is a good place for a dip and lunch, or simply to wander. The falls are pretty rather than spectacular, with scope for walking in the surrounding woodland and up to see the views. It lies in a community area, with local people responsible for the site who also sell drinks and snacks. There are even plans for a restaurant, botanic garden and simple accommodation. At present, though, it's quiet except in August when there are various youth camps here. All money raised goes to the school, and visits might be possible on request.

To get to the falls from Mpika, take the road to Chinsali and Isoka for about 20km, until you see a right turn signed to Lwitikila Girls' Secondary School (✪ TOLWIT 11°43.600'S, 31°28.572'E). Follow this track, which bends round slowly to the left and then goes uphill, until you see some houses on the right. In front of the first house, before the school, a smaller track to the right leads directly to the falls (✪ LWITIK 11°43.810'S, 31°29.674'E).

Danger Hill A little further north on the Lwitikila River is this tall rock and the falls beneath. There are some lovely views from the top.

AROUND MPIKA

MUTINONDO WILDERNESS AREA Mutinondo Wilderness is a private 100km^2 reserve, started and run by Mike and Lari Merrett. After spending more than 20 years in the area, they are now retired, and have handed over the reserve to the ecologists Inge Akerboom and Frank Willem, who previously lived and worked in the nearby Kasanka National Park. The area encompasses a pristine section of verdant miombo woodland near the edge of the Luangwa Escarpment, complete with huge granite whalebacks, crystal-clear rivers, stunning waterfalls, pristine woodlands and some small wetland areas. There are great plants and birds, which all make for a lovely ambience.

It's a lovely bit of Africa to explore on foot or on bike, as well as being terrific value; ideally you should spend at least three nights here. While Mutinondo is quite off the beaten track (if there is a beaten track in this part of Zambia?!), it does have its own airstrip.

History Although this area has been occupied for centuries, as witnessed by the Iron-Age workings about 6km from the lodge, Mutinondo was first really put on the visitors' map in 1994, when Mike and Lari started looking for a place suitable for both conservation and tourism. Even having obtained the permission of the local authorities and chief, it wasn't until 2001 that they were able to start development. Throughout the process, they seem to have made every effort to develop the area sensitively, with minimum impact and maximum use of renewable natural resources, such as solar and wind power.

Flora and fauna Mike and Lari have strong ties to the academic community, and offer generous 'research rates' at their lodge. As such, the area's smaller flora and fauna has been meticulously catalogued – including over 1,000 plants, confirmed with help from teams at the Royal Botanical Gardens at Kew, as well as dozens of butterflies and a good range of the varied birdlife.

Flora The main vegetation here is classic miombo woodland, which is in pristine condition with plenty of *Brachystegia* and *Julbernadia* species. This is interspersed with numerous lush, herby dambos, many of which drain into permanent rivers and streams on the reserve. This water, together with the shade of the established woodland, makes the atmosphere relatively moist – which helps to promote such lush plant growth, making this a wonderful spot for *Aloe* species. Beside the rivers, you'll also find thin strips of riverine forest, and occasional patches of moist evergreen forest (*mushitu*). Judging by the thick lichens on the rocks and 'old man's beard' (*Usnea*) hanging from the trees, the air is very clean, and looking into the night sky you'll be hard pressed to spot any light pollution at all.

There is an impressive array of flowering plants, especially during and at the end of the rains. Among these are several species of proteas and a great range of orchids; many of the latter have been carefully relocated around the chalets after they were rescued from the trees felled to build the lodge's access road. During one visit I found a huge cycad in the woodland. At the end of winter, in mid September, it's a magical place to witness the 'miombo flush', when the fresh new leaves bring a sea of colour across the woodland. If you're visiting during the rains, keep a look out for specimens of *Termitomyces titanicus,* which is the world's largest edible mushroom. The largest that Mike and Lari found had a diameter of about 85cm but they grow up to a metre in diameter. The local people have known about these for centuries; but it seems that they were first described to science as late as 1980.

Fauna Mutinondo is a good spot for birding and is one of Zambia's 'important bird areas', according to Birdlife International. The bird list available to visitors currently stands at 325 species, and is constantly growing. Obvious 'specials' include Anchieta's barbets, long-toed fluff tails, bar-winged weavers, half-collared kingfishers and Ross's turaco.

While Mutinondo is not primarily a game destination, if you spend enough time here you might find a variety of mammals, from duikers and klipspringer to sitatunga – though sightings are infrequent. As the area has remained protected, wildlife sightings are improving, with some of the larger antelope species like roan and sable sometimes seen grazing in the wetlands between September and November. Of much more interest really are the plants, flowers, trees, mushrooms and smaller wildlife, which also help to make walking here a real pleasure.

Getting there The Mutinondo turn-off on the Great North Road (✇ TUMUTI 12°22.794'S, 31°5.896'E) is a few hundred metres south of Kalonje railway station on the TAZARA railway. It's about 12km southwest of the turning to Lavushi Manda, and 77km southwest of Mpika, or 364km northeast of Kapiri Mposhi. From the signboard to the lodge is a further 25km along a level track, which is accessible by 2WD year-round.

Mutinondo's airstrip is just over 1km from the lodge (✇ MUTAIR 12°26.998'S, 31°16.954'E), useful for those on a fly-in trip. Its 900m runway is suitable only for single-engine aircraft. Alternatively, with advance notice, it is possible to arrive at Kalonje by train, and arrange for the team at the lodge to collect you.

Where to stay and eat For individual visitors there are three options: the lodge, the nearby campsite and the new self-catering camp, Kankonde. All are open year round, and share the same contact details. Activities available are detailed below. Note that special arrangements can be made for scientific, educational and school groups, which are warmly welcomed.

⌂ **Mutinondo Wilderness Lodge** [map, page 302] (4 chalets) m 0978 198198, 0979 862545; e info@mutinondozambia.com; www. mutinondozambia.com. ✇ MUTINO 12°27.267'S, 31°17.496'E. The lodge is a lovely spot to stay – though quite idiosyncratic in its way, with both the chalets & the bar & dining areas carefully built around the rocks, each some distance from the other. Every effort has been made to source the building materials locally, & to use local skills & labour in the lodge's construction. The handmade bricks, stone & thatch used were all manufactured, quarried or harvested locally, & all the woodwork, including the furniture, was constructed by a father & son carpentry team from the village of Salamo. As you'd expect, most of the staff are from the surrounding villages.

Each of the chalets is large & individually designed: solid, but not luxurious. One has a particularly spectacular balcony, while all have great views over the wilderness. The 'spacious chalets' are effectively suites, ideal for families with 2 'rooms' divided by a half wall, 3 beds & glass doors at the front. The 'standard' ones are smaller,

although still very roomy, & are totally open at the front. In each you'll find a wardrobe & some have a fireplace, for when it gets cold. (Given the altitude of about 1,400m, it can get very cold!) Three of the chalets have an en-suite shower & separate toilet, while the last, arguably the most spectacular, has a separate bathroom with a home-built bath as well as a shower & a 'loo with a view'. Water is heated by individual solar heaters & wood-burning boilers. The cash bar operates on the honour system, & the restaurant serves straightforward but substantial meals, including curries, casseroles & roasts. Limited Wi-Fi is available at the lodge, free of charge. *Standard US$145/260 sgl/dbl; spacious US$160/290 sgl/dbl, all FBA; extra bed US$90 pp.* **LLL**

▲ **Mutinondo Wilderness Camping** [map, page 302] (4 pitches) This is a lovely campsite, with raven-proof storage cupboards, good hot showers & clean long-drop toilets. As there are a limited number of pitches you should consider booking in advance if possible. The campsite is adjacent to the lodge; campers are welcome in the bar &, with advance notice, to dine here (*evening meal US$25*). The 1st bundle of firewood is free, then you'll pay K20/bundle. *US$15 own tent; US$95 sgl or dbl tent, inc bedding & meals.*

⚐ Kankonde Camp [map, page 302] (1 chalet, camping) ⊕ KANKON 12°24'S, 31°19'E. Some 11km from the main lodge & camp, 50m from a swimming area on the Mutinondo River, Kankonde offers the independent traveller a further degree of freedom. Its open-air grass chalet has 2 twin beds, & there's ample room for pitching tents. These share 2 long-drop loos, & 2 bucket showers (with staff to carry hot water). A thatched *nsaka* rounds off the amenities. Firewood is supplied, & water for bathing & drinking is sourced from the Mutinondo & is safe to drink or can be boiled if preferred. Otherwise you'll need to bring your own, along with all bedding, food, crockery, cutlery, etc, though a few basic ingredients are sold in the shop at the lodge. Visitors usually check in at the lodge first to collect a map & other information before heading for Kankonde. *Chalet US$30 pp; camping US$17 pp.*

What to see and do Mutinondo best suits those who feel comfortable exploring; it's a magical place for 'old Africa hands' who want to go off for hours on their own. It's less ideal for those who are new to the bush, although those with some degree of independence can hire one of the lodge's team to guide them around (*US$25/day*), and still have a great time. It's not the perfect place if you need your hand held all of the time, or if you're reluctant to abandon your vehicle, as there are relatively few motorable tracks (although there is one dry-season track which extends 25km to the escarpment). For lodge guests, activities are included in the rates; campers and those staying at Kankonde pay extra, as below.

Walking and cycling There's a good network of trails, and the country is hilly without being particularly strenuous. The huge granite whalebacks are great for scrambling up, giving you access to superb views of the surrounding country and, in the east, to the Luangwa Escarpment and beyond. It would be very easy to spend three or four days exploring the tracks and whalebacks alone. Trail maps are available at the lodge, and several of the hiking trails are signposted with arrows and distances, but I'd also suggest that you take a GPS.

Dedicated and totally self-contained hikers who want something more challenging can arrange longer hikes here, including bush-camping stops. These might encompass the adjacent community-based conservation area, some of the magnificent escarpment waterfalls, or possibly even a long walk down into the Luangwa Valley. It's necessary to give advance warning to the lodge so they can make the appropriate arrangements with the local community. If you would prefer some support on the longer hikes you can arrange porters (*K700/trek*) and ZAWA scouts (*K330/day*) at the lodge. If you prefer cycling, you can also rent mountain bikes.

On the water There's a network of very clear rivers and waterfalls, with no crocodiles, hippos or bilharzia. (Though *always* double-check the safety of such a comment locally before you swim, rather than trust any guidebook, even this one!) These have been re-stocked with indigenous fish: red-breasted, three-spot and green-headed bream – so fishing is possible, albeit on a strict catch-and-release policy.

There are two canoes stationed above one of the waterfalls, allowing you to float through the waterlilies along a tranquil, tree-lined section of the river. Alternatively you can just swim in the pools around the waterfalls. For campers, canoe hire is K60 per half day.

SHIWA NG'ANDU
Background
The early days Shiwa Ng'andu was the inspiration of Stewart Gore-Browne. Born in England in 1883, Gore-Browne first came to Africa in 1902, at the tail

end of the Boer War, and later returned in 1911 as a member of the Anglo-Belgian Congo Boundary Commission. On his way back to England, in 1914, one of his carriers guided him north towards Tanzania, passing beside Shiwa Ng'andu, the 'Lake of the Royal Crocodiles'. He intended to settle in Northern Rhodesia, so he negotiated with the local chief to buy the land around the lake – and then, after World War I, he returned to establish himself there. He borrowed money from his beloved Aunt Ethel, and began to build Shiwa.

Gore-Browne was uncomfortable with the colonial attitude towards the African people. He was determined to establish a utopian state, and in his hands Shiwa grew into a vast enterprise with schools and a hospital run with benevolent paternalism. By 1925, Shiwa Ng'andu was employing 1,800 local people.

Gore-Browne passed on skills to them, and together they built neat workers' cottages with tile roofs, as well as bridges and workshops and finally a magnificent manor house, set atop a hill overlooking the lake. Anything that could not be made locally was transported on the heads and backs of porters, along the arduous route from the nearest town, Ndola. At that time it took three weeks to reach Shiwa from Ndola: 70 miles on foot or horseback to the Luapula River, followed by a boat through the Bangweulu Wetlands, and a further ten-day walk from the Chambeshi River to Shiwa.

The heavy English-style furniture was made out of local wood; the large gilt-framed portraits and paintings, silver ornaments, and an entire library of books came from England. Everything came together to create an English country mansion in the heart of Africa – a testament to the determination with which Gore-Browne pursued his vision.

In 1927, when he was 44, Gore-Browne met and married Lorna Goldman, the 'ravishing' 18-year-old daughter of his first love, Lorna Bosworth-Smith. She came to Shiwa, threw herself into her husband's projects, and the estate and its inhabitants prospered. Gore-Browne built a distillery for the essential oils that he hoped to make into a profitable local industry. (Given Shiwa's remote location, the estate's produce had to be easily transportable: a non-perishable, valuable commodity of low bulk.) He had several failures, trying roses, geraniums, eucalyptus, peppermint and lemon grass with no success. Eventually, he succeeded with citrus fruit, which flourished and brought a good income into the estate ... until a *tristezia* virus killed off the fruit trees. This hit the estate hard, forcing Gore-Browne to turn to more conventional, less profitable, agriculture.

Regrettably, the stresses of the estate and Gore-Browne's constant travelling took a toll on his marriage; it resulted in his separation from Lorna, who had found it difficult spending such a great deal of time alone at Shiwa with their two daughters, Lorna and Angela. Lady Lorna returned to live in London in 1945. She came back to Shiwa once, in 1958, and then never again. Even in England she would rarely speak of Shiwa; in December 2001 she died, aged 93.

In the meantime, Gore-Browne had become a rare political figure in Northern Rhodesia: an aristocratic Englishman, with excellent connections in London, who commanded respect both in the colonial administration and from the African people. He had been elected to Northern Rhodesia's Legislative Council as early as 1935, and was the first member of it to argue that real concessions were needed to African demands for more autonomy. He was impatient with the rule of the Colonial Office, and resented the loss of huge amounts of revenue through taxation paid to Britain, and 'royalties' paid to the British South Africa Company.

He was knighted by George VI and became mentor to Zambia's first president, Kenneth Kaunda, who, in 1966, appointed him the first ever Grand Officer of the Companion of the Order of Freedom, the highest honour ever bestowed on a white man in Zambia. He died, an octogenarian, in 1967, and today I believe that he remains the only white man in Africa to have been given a full state funeral. He is buried on a hill overlooking the lake at Shiwa – an honour only bestowed on the Bemba chiefs. In the words of Kaunda, 'He was born an Englishman and died a Zambian. Perhaps if Africa had more like him, the transition from colonial rule to independence would have been less traumatic.'

A highly readable and very successful historical account of the life and times of Stewart Gore-Browne and Shiwa Ng'andu, *The Africa House*, was first published in 1999 (page 527), although note that reservations have been expressed by the family about the historical accuracy of the book.

After Sir Stewart   On Sir Stewart's death, the estate at Shiwa passed to his daughter Lorna and her husband, John Harvey, who lived in the house with their four children, Penny, Charlie, Mark and David. However, with the very poor agricultural soils, both the farm estate and the manor house proved difficult to run and maintain. In 1967 the Harveys bought a dairy farm near Lusaka, where both John and Lorna were murdered in 1992. On their deaths, the estate passed to three of Gore-Browne's grandchildren. Initially David took over its management, and by 1995 there were moves to turn the manor house into a museum. Finally, in 2000, Charlie Harvey bought the estate from his siblings and now runs it with his wife, Jo, and their two children, Tom and Emma.

Shiwa reinvented   Until 2000, Shiwa typified an old English-style country estate that was gradually slipping back into the African bush. In 2001, Charlie and Jo sold their property and literally 'picked up' their entire farming business just north of Lusaka and translocated it 750km north to Shiwa. Together they brought endless farm equipment, 800 cattle, 600 sheep, 500 assorted wild game animals, eight horses, five cats and five dogs. It was a massive undertaking: for the cattle it was a three-day train ride, followed by a ten-day trek through the bush. With them came two large buses carrying the families – women and children – of the 34 men who had elected to follow the Harveys north.

Soon the house became a hum of activity, with builders and renovators raising much dust and gradually restoring Shiwa's past glory. When I visited Shiwa in 2003, some eight years after I'd first been there, the transformation was startling and impressive. The stranglehold of a slow, tropical decay had been arrested by sheer determination – and the whole feeling of the place had changed. Now it's a thriving family estate, combining a strong sense of history with a vibrant present and a solid future.

Before 2001, Shiwa's only real story – and the only reason to visit – was its history: Gore-Browne and the estate's past glories. Shiwa had been reduced to a curious anachronism in the African bush. By contrast, Shiwa's history is now just that: history. A visit here today will look at the past, but also explore the present: Shiwa's people, its animals and its environment – and how these are developing and changing. At one point during a stay here I saw a young carpenter making one of the internal windows over the courtyard. He was doing a good job, clearly deep in concentration. I asked him if he had also made some of the freshly painted windows on the outside of the house. 'No,' he replied, without pausing, 'my grandfather made those.'

So by all means come to Shiwa to wonder at its past, and the story of Sir Stewart; but expect to leave enthralled by the present – and intrigued by the apparently seamless continuity between the two.

Shiwa today

The manor house As you approach from the main road, the rectangular cottages built for farm workers come into view first, their whitewashed walls and tiled roofs saying more of England than of Africa. Then a red-brick gatehouse appears, its design of Italian influence. An old clock tower rises above its tiled roof, and through its main arch is a long straight avenue, bordered by eucalyptus, leading to the stately manor house.

Climbing up, the avenue leads through typically English gardens – designed on several levels with bougainvillea, frangipani, jacaranda and neatly arranged cypresses. These gardens have been restored with beautiful flowers and well-maintained lawns, though their maintenance represents a continuing battle with bushpigs and the increasing herds of antelope.

Above the front door is a small carving of a black rhino's head, a reminder that Gore-Browne had earned the local nickname of Chipembele, black rhino. At the centre of the manor is the square tiled Tuscan courtyard, surrounded by arches, overlooking windows and a red tiled roof. Climbing one of the cold, stone-slab staircases brings you into an English manor house, lined with old paintings and its wooden floors covered with old rugs.

Much of the old heavy wooden furniture remains here, including the sturdy chests; together with muskets and all manner of memorabilia, such as pictures of old relatives and regiments. Two frames with certificates face each other. One is from King George VI, granting 'our trusty and well-beloved Stewart Gore-Browne, esq' the degree, title, honour and dignity of Knight Bachelor. Opposite, President Kaunda appoints 'my trusted, well-beloved Sir Stewart Gore-Browne' as a Grand Officer of the Companion of the Order of Freedom, second division; it is dated 1966.

The library remains the manor's heart, with three huge walls of books, floor to ceiling, which tell of Gore-Browne's interests – Frouede's *History of England* in at least a dozen volumes, *Policy and Arms* by Colonel Repington and *The Genesis of War* by the Right Honourable H H Asquith. His wife was very keen on poetry: there is a classic collection of works by Byron, Shelley, Coleridge, Eliot and others. Gore-Browne left behind a wealth of diaries and personal papers, and much work is in progress cataloguing and archiving these. Central to the room is a grand fireplace, surmounted by the Latin inscription: *Ille terrarum mihi super omnes anculus ridet* – 'This corner of the earth, above all others, smiles on me'.

It's now possible to stay in the manor house; see page 316, for details.

Shiwa estate The working estate extends to include a farm, a well-stocked game-ranch, a lake, stables and all the support necessary for almost total self-sufficiency – directly employing a permanent staff of around 80, with another 120 or so working on a casual basis. It covers just over 100km² of land, and encompasses the domestic livestock, including about 15,000 laying hens, 1,200 cattle, 40 dairy cows, 700 sheep, 20 pigs and 52 Saanan goats, imported from the USA, whose milk is used to raise orphaned children. Ten years after the move, the game farm has expanded considerably, with over 1,500 head of assorted game, and these are being continuously augmented to improve the bloodlines of the existing herds, and increase the numbers; Shiwa boasts one of the largest breeding herds of pure-bred Boran cattle in Zambia (originally imported from Kenya), its own abattoir in Mpika, as well as a butchery on the farm, where guests are welcome to buy their own meat. Pasture crops are grown largely to feed the livestock but the workers and their wives are encouraged to cultivate vegetable gardens and blocks of maize for their own consumption and for sale on and to the farm.

Gore-Brown's hospital has been brought back to life, thanks in part to grants from the British and German embassies – whilst smaller grants from diplomatic and private sources have enabled it to complete a very good maternity ward. The two government schools are now thriving once more, supplemented by tuition in IT from visiting international students.

Getting there Shiwa Ng'andu is reasonably well signposted off the main road to Isoka and Nakonde; the turn-off (⊕ TUSHIW 11°13.334'S, 31°49.580'E) is about 87km northeast of Mpika. The manor house (⊕ SHIWAH 11°11.924'S, 31°44.289'E) is about 13km from this turn-off. The road then continues westwards to Kapishya Hot Springs and onto the Mpika–Kasama road.

Alternatively Shiwa can be reached directly from the Mpika–Kasama road; again turn off about 87km from Mpika (⊕ TUKAPI 11°10.624'S, 31°17.454'E). It's then a little over 30km to Kapishya, and about half of that again to the manor house.

Shiwa also has its own airstrip, so can easily be reached via charter flight from Lusaka or Mfuwe – a quick but expensive option.

⌂ **Where to stay** There are three very different places to stay on the estate:

⌂ **Shiwa Ng'andu Manor House** [map, page 302] (6 rooms) m 0973 311246; e shiwa@shiwangandu.com; www.shiwangandu.com. ⊕ SHIWAH 11°11.924'S, 31°44.289'E. Charlie & Jo Harvey accept paying house guests, & make engaging & energetic hosts. Their guest rooms, hung with paintings from the Shiwa collection, retain many original features, including fireplaces in which fires are lit every night in winter. Traditional hardwood furniture is complemented by new 4-poster bedsteads made on the estate, while en-suite bathrooms add a touch of modernity – but only a touch; some have huge old metal baths rather than modern showers, & an aura of Edwardian style prevails. Meals are very simple farm fare, much of it sourced on the farm, but served with style in the grand setting of a formal dining room. It's very much like staying in an English stately home in Africa – which you'll realise isn't a contradiction in terms when you visit.

Jo & Charlie are very generous with the time that they give to their guests – but there is also a house manager on hand, & a professional guide to take you around the estate. Days are very full, with plenty of activities – you can choose what you'd like to do from a wide range of possibilities (pretty much as below).

Most people come to Zambia on safari, then wonder about adding on Shiwa as an afterthought. That's sad, as I found my last stay here to be among the most interesting & engaging few days that I've spent anywhere in Zambia – a view backed up by the visitors that I've sent here since. If you do come, then allow at least 3 or 4 nights; any fewer would be far too frustrating for you! *US$360 pp, fully inclusive.* ☉ *All year.* **LL**

⌂ **Impandala House** [map, page 302] (4-bedroom house) Originally built by Gore-Browne in 1933, to house missionaries translating the Bible from English to Bemba, this quaint & simple farmhouse was renovated by the Harveys & opened to visitors in mid 2009. A 20-min drive from the main house, it, too, retains a sense of colonial times. Its bedrooms – 2 en suite & 2 sharing a bathroom – are set on 2 levels. The comfortable lounge, dining room & wraparound veranda are furnished simply but appropriately, with some items brought from the main house. Though not as grand as the main house, it still has its fair share of history, & lays claim to being the site of the final signings of the Declaration of Independence of Zambia back in 1964. The house is ideal for families or friends travelling together, & makes a good, low-cost alternative to the main house. It's usually self-catering, but for international guests, with advance notice, the estate can supply groceries & cook. Fish, milk & bread can also be bought from local shops, & local farmers will often bring their home-grown vegetables around for sale. The house is fully staffed, including housekeepers & a local guide. *US$480 per night self catering; US$220 pp FBA, exc horseriding & access to Shiwa House.* ☉ *All year.* **LL**

🏠 **Kapishya Hot Springs** [map, page 302] (6 chalets, camping) m 0976 970444; e mark@ shiwasafaris.com; www.shiwasafaris.com. ⊗ KAPISH 11°10.263'S, 31°36.057'E. Kapishya is run by Mark Harvey, Sir Stewart's second grandson, a mine of local information & a top local guide. The camp lies on the Manshya River, set amongst picturesque gardens where individual plants are labelled with common & scientific names.

The thatched brick chalets are simple but comfortable, each sleeping 4, & with its own porch & brick floors covered with reed mats. Mosquito-netted windows & en-suite facilities that include large showers are standard. Two of the chalets are dbl-storey, with a particularly good view of the river from the top & their own firepit. The restaurant serves a fusion of international & Zambian dishes, with many of the ingredients sourced from Kapishya's own vegetable garden, with local meat. A rustic cash bar nearby is well stocked, & a small pool with a lounging deck is set next to a miniature set of rapids on the river. Also close to the river is Kapishya's campsite, with good, hot showers & clean, flushing toilets, as well as a dining shelter & BBQ areas. All visitors can use the communal facilities, with a 3-course dinner costing US$25, or can cater for themselves (chalet guests can use the camp's kitchen). To spice up the self-catering option, homemade jams & chutneys are for sale.

Kapishya Springs themselves are a great attraction, as is the birding on the property (Ross's turaco is a relatively common visitor), but guests here can also take part in most of the activities on the Shiwa estate; US$20 pp will cover a game drive or a lake trip. Alternatively, there are some lovely waterfalls nearby to explore yourself – see pages 319–20 – & a number of mountain-bike trails in the area, with bikes available for rent (*K50*). In 2011, a horde of 60,000-year-old rock paintings was discovered, & it's possible to walk the 20mins from camp with Mark to see them. Additional cave paintings have been discovered since, although these are estimated to date back only 1,000 years. For those looking for a slower pace, Kapishya also has a spa, located at the edge of its gardens. Kapishya combines well with a visit to Buffalo Camp (page 296) in North Luangwa National Park, also run by Mark. With lots of advance notice, it's sometimes possible to pre-arrange vehicle transfers between the 2. *US$75/130/165 pp self catering/DBB/FB; camping US$15 pp.* ⊕ *All year.* **L**

What to see and do Shiwa's a great place for a surprising variety of activities, so there's no question of being bored. For those staying at the manor house, these are generally included; for guests at Kapishya they're optional extras. Always bear in mind that numbers of visitors here are fairly small, so where I refer to a 'tour' you should generally visualise half-a-dozen visitors or fewer! Here are just a few of Shiwa's highlights.

Kapishya Hot Springs About 20km from Shiwa Ng'andu, the hot springs in the Manshya River at Kapishya were always a favourite spot of Gore-Browne's and a great place to unwind. Within a shallow part of the cool, rocky river, surrounded by *combretum* bushes and gently curving raffia palms (*Raphia farinifera*) is an inviting pool of hot spring water. It makes a great site for bathing. Those not staying overnight on the Shiwa estate can visit for the day (*K50 pp*).

Boating and rafting There are several activities possible on the water. It's lovely to take a slow boat trip around the edges of the lake, looking out for wildlife, from birds and otters to crocodiles, and it's also possible to do this by traditional mokoro (dugout canoe). During the fishing season, you can bring a rod and reel.

Alternatively, take a full-day trip around the lake, and then from there down the Manshya River to Kapishya, or from Kapishya to the Chusa Waterfall. These routes go over some small (Grade II) rapids, and are particularly good spots for birdlife (though do remember to protect any belongings in waterproof containers in case they should be thrown out).

Nature walks and drives Much of Shiwa estate is now a game area, so early morning walks or game drives can be very much a feature of staying here. Those not staying at the estate can self-drive around the area (*US$20*). It's a particularly good place to spot the elusive blue duiker, whilst the more common game includes puku, kudu, defassa waterbuck, Kafue lechwe, Lichtenstein hartebeest, common duiker, oribi, zebra, bushbuck, reedbuck, impala, yellow baboon, vervet monkey, grysbok and wildebeest.

The lechwe and the wildebeest are of a different subspecies than you'll find elsewhere in this part of northern Zambia; they're unlike those in the Luangwa and Bangweulu areas. With patience, sitatunga can usually be spotted from the hide, whilst bushpig, wild cat, civet, genet and clawless otters are around but often less visible. As in many of Zambia's isolated kopjes, there's a resident population of fairly elusive klipspringers.

One of the estate's natural highlights occurs in November, at the start of the rains, when thousands of straw-coloured fruit bats return to Shiwa to roost. For details of a similar spectacle at Kasanka, see page 324.

Guided walks The Shiwa estate, and the area around it, is a lovely place for scenic walks, with a number of stunning hills and sites of interest. It's as easy to have a good hour's walk alone as it is to stay out for the day with a local guide,

One notable spot is Nachipala Bareback Hill – a large granite whaleback which affords stunning panoramic vistas and a magnificent view of the lake. This is an energetic 3-hour walk from the manor house, and on the top a small cairn marks the spot where, on his last journey in 1867, Dr David Livingstone took compass bearings in his final attempt to find the source of the Nile.

Kapishya has developed a series of short, self-guided walking trails of 4–7km in length, some up and around the local hills, and one mostly along village paths by the river, through Bemba villages and fields, before finishing at the Chusa Falls. Maps with the routes are available at Kapishya, and guides, although not required, are available (*K50*).

Birdwatching Shiwa has been identified as a priority site for conservation and is listed as one of 31 'important bird areas' in Zambia (pages 32–3). You can stroll around the estate and game ranch with or without a guide (there aren't usually any lion, buffalo or elephant here, so this is fairly safe), and some of the walks lead through beautiful raffia palm forests.

In total, over 380 species of birds have been seen on the estate. Birding highlights include palm-nut vultures, bat hawks, Ross's turacos, white-cheeked bee-eaters, white-tailed and blue flycatchers, Stanley's bustards, African finfoot, black-rumped buttonquail, long-toed flufftail, greater snipe, grass owls, black-chinned quail finch and a veritable kaleidoscope of different sunbirds. Down by the water, the swamps, rivers and lakes offer a haven for a variety of waterbirds, including pygmy geese; cormorants; yellow-billed, knob-nosed and white-faced teal; giant and lesser egrets; blue, grey, night and goliath herons; Fülleborn's and rosy-breasted longclaws; malachite, half-collared, giant and pied kingfishers; golden-rumped tinkerbird; splendid starlings; black-bellied seed cracker; Bocage's robin; bar-throated apalis; and white-headed saw-wing. Fish eagles and even ospreys may be spotted, as well as transient flocks of pelicans and flamingos.

Around the estate If you've time to spare then take a slow wander around the estate, and perhaps down to the lake, ideally with a guide. You will find an exceedingly positive atmosphere, with the local people very welcoming and friendly, and usually happy to talk about what they are doing.

The farm itself is run on commercial lines, but methods are far from the intensive farming beloved of the West. The environment is a key factor, and nothing is left to waste. This is no place for shiny new gadgets; spending an hour or so watching the sort of machinery usually confined to a museum being coaxed into life can be fascinating in itself. There are numerous community initiatives going on, too, from fish-farming to bee-keeping and bio-gas projects – as well as a variety of projects within the estate's hospital and school.

Tours of the manor house Guided tours of the manor house are by prior arrangement only. If you're staying at the manor house then this is merely a case of asking Jo and Charlie to show you around; it's delightfully informal and totally fascinating.

If you're staying at Kapishya, or just dropping in for the day, the only way to see some of the interior of the house is to book on to a daily 'tour' (*Mon–Sat 09.00–11.00; the fee of US$20 pp goes towards the community fund*). Within the house the tour is limited to the lower floors; the upper floors are strictly for the family and their guests. (Remember that this is a family home first, and a small exclusive guesthouse second, and you'll realise that neither the family, nor their guests, will want a steady stream of visitors looking throughout the house.) Also included are a game drive and a historical guided tour of the estate.

Shiwa's archives Putting Gore-Browne's extensive collection of diaries, letters and papers into an ordered archive has been a long-term project for Jo, and is still not complete. Guests interested in the manor house can have some access to this, on request; it's fascinating to read some of Gore-Browne's old diaries even if you're not an amateur historian. Then there's the enormous library, and Gore-Browne's collection of early records!

Historical tours on the estate Jo is a trained archaeologist, and has been in the forefront of excavating some of the older sites on the estate – already uncovering the kilns that were built to make the bricks and the tiles for the manor house, and the locations of an old summerhouse.

There are a number of other spots of historical interest, including the old hospital, the essential oils distillery, the traction engine and the graveyard – and any can easily be integrated into a historical tour of the estate.

Excursions from Shiwa Shiwa is really a destination in itself, and isn't often used as a base for excursions, although Kapishya makes quite a good base for visiting a few local waterfalls, detailed below. If you ask the team at the springs, they could probably arrange for a guide to go with you to make locating them easier.

Chusa Falls Chusa Falls (✪ CHUSAF 11°09.353'S, 31°33.093'E) are the closest to Kapishya, making a good day trip. On foot, they're a distance of 7km away, or 10km by road. The falls are quite clearly a short series of three steps, each being several metres high.

Senkele Falls These falls (✪ SENKEL 11°06.150'S, 31°21.922'E) are a 15m drop on the Mansha River. The turn-off to them from the Mpika–Kasama Road is at ✪ TUSENK 11°11.712'S, 31°18.903'E, about 3.5km north of the turning to Kapishya and Shiwa. From there the track turns north and continues for 10km. Continue north where the road forks, then after about 2km of high grass, stop at the deserted house; the falls are 100m from here. This might be a lovely place to bush-camp.

Namundela Falls Finally, the stunning double Namundela Falls (✿ 11°06.760'S, 31°27.606'E) are about 2 hours' drive from Kapishya, followed by a 90-minute walk to the falls along the Mansha River. To get to them, head 28km west from Kapishya, turning north at Chilombo School (✿ CHILOM 11°13.525'S, 31°24.624'E). Follow this track about 13km north and slightly east to the Anderson Farm (✿ ANDERS 11°07.861'S, 31°26.542'E), and then further to the Kapololwe Homestead, marking the start of the walk along the river.

KASANKA NATIONAL PARK

(*Park fees US$10 pp/day; vehicle US$15/day; local registration K15.30/day*) This small park is the first privately managed national park in Zambia. It is run by a charity, the Kasanka Trust (*http://kasankanationalpark.com*), and the much-needed proceeds from tourism go directly into conservation and development of the park and its surrounding communities. Park fees are payable by all visitors, whether or not they are staying overnight, with the exception of those staying at the conservation centre, which is just outside the park boundary.

At just 390km² in area, Kasanka is one of Zambia's smallest national parks, but it encompasses a wide variety of vegetation zones: from dry evergreen forests, or *mateshe*, to various types of moist forest and permanent papyrus swamps. It's a delightful place to spend a relaxing few days at any time, when sitatunga are readily seen in the early morning and keen birdwatchers will find many pressing reasons to visit. In the later months of the year, Kasanka hosts a truly extraordinary wildlife spectacle: the annual bat migration.

HISTORY Kasanka was made a national park in 1972, but it was poorly maintained and poaching was rife until the late 1980s. Then an initiative was started by the late David Lloyd, a former district officer, and Gareth Williams, a local commercial farmer. With the approval of the National Parks and Wildlife Department and the local community, they started to put private money into revitalising the park.

In 1990 the National Parks Department signed a management contract with the Kasanka Trust, giving the latter the right to manage the park and develop it for tourism in partnership with the local community. The Trust, which is linked to a registered charity based in the UK and Netherlands, has trailblazed a model for the successful private management of a Zambian national park. It has been fortunate in gaining financial backing from various donors, but now relies almost entirely on tourism income to fund its activities.

The Kasanka Trust aims to manage the area's natural resources for the benefit of both the wildlife and the local people, and so it closely supports and consults with a locally elected community resource board.

GEOGRAPHY Kasanka is on the southern fringes of the Bangweulu Wetlands, and just 30km from the border with the DRC. It is almost completely flat and, lying at an altitude of about 1,200m, it gets a high rainfall during the wet season (about 1,200mm) which results in a lush cover of vegetation.

The park is dissected by two main rivers, the Kasanka and the Luwombwa, with a third, the Mulembo, on its northern boundary, but several smaller rivers and streams, and the evenness of the land, have resulted in an extensive marsh

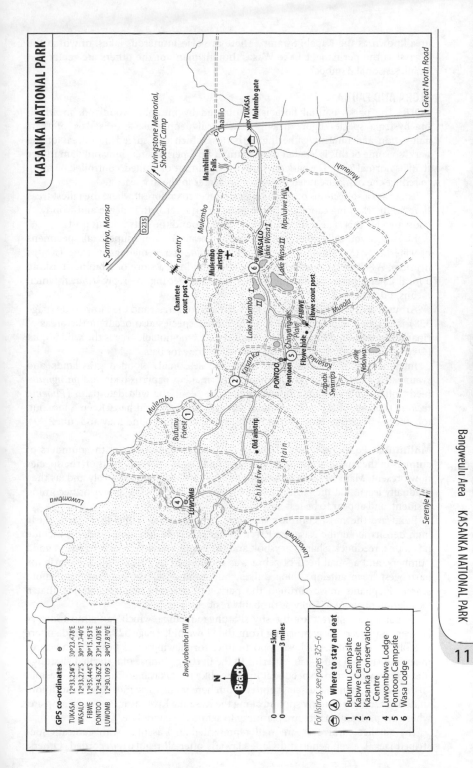

GPS co-ordinates ⊕

TUKASA	12°33.250'S	30°23.478'E
WASALO	12°33.272'S	30°17.740'E
FIBWE	12°35.444'S	30°15.153'E
PONTOO	12°34.362'S	33°14.098'E
LUWOMB	12°30.109'S	30°07.870'E

N

Braai

0			5km
0		3 miles	

For listings, see pages 325–6

Ⓐ **Where to stay and eat**

Ⓘ
1 Bufumu Campsite
2 Kabwe Campsite
3 Kasanka Conservation Centre
4 Luwombwa Lodge
5 Pontoon Campsite
6 Wasa Lodge

Samfya, Mansa

D235

Livingstone Memorial, Shoebill Camp

Chalilo

TUKASA
Mulembo gate

Ma mbilima Falls

Mulembo

Chantete scout post

no entry

Mulembo airstrip

WASALO
Lake Wasa I

Lake Wasa II

Mpululwe Hill

Lake Kalamba I

II

FIBWE
Fibwe scout post

Chinyangale Plain

Musola

PONTOO
Pontoon

Fibwe hide

Lake Ndolwa

Kasanka

Kapabi Swamps

Bufumu Forest

Mulembo

Old airstrip

Chikufwe Plain

LUWOMB

Luwombwa

Bwalyabemba Hill

Luwombwa

Serenje

Muluishi

Great North Road

area known as the Kapabi Swamp. There are also numerous lakes, of which the biggest is the permanent Lake Wasa, though many of the others are really just small, seasonal dambos.

FLORA AND FAUNA

Flora The park's natural flora is dominated by miombo woodland, in which brachystegia species figure heavily. The local people use fire as part of their cultivation and hunting/gathering activities, which can spread into areas of the park, so some of this is less tall than it might be – perhaps reaching only 5m rather than its normal 20m. The park operates a programme of limited, controlled burning to reduce the damage caused by hotter fires later in the dry season.

There are also sections of much taller dry evergreen forest, where the tallest trees have an interlocking canopy, and the *mateshi* undergrowth is dense and woody. A good area for this is near the Mulembo River around the Katwa scout post.

Elsewhere you will find evergreen swamp forest, with some superb tall specimens of waterberry (*Syzygium cordatum*) and *mululu*, or red mahogany, trees (*Khaya nyasica*). As an aside, one of the guides here told me a story of a biologist asking a local Chewa person the name of this tree, and getting the reply '*Khaya*', which means 'I don't know'!

Around the Fibwe scout post is one such area of forest, and the Fibwe hide (page 328) is perched in a huge *mululu* tree. Similar species also occur in the areas of riparian forest found by Kasanka's small rivers. One notable tree is the wild loquat (*Oxyanthus speciosus*), whose fruit is a major draw for bats.

Interspersed in these forested areas are seasonally flooded grasslands and swamps. The latter include large areas of permanent papyrus beds and *phragmites* reeds, often with very little open water to be seen. The wild date palm (*Phoenix reclinata*) is one of the most common species of tree found here. Keep a lookout, too, for the large tree-proteas that bloom spectacularly around May and June.

Mammals Poaching in the 1970s and '80s drastically reduced the numbers of animals in the park, but this seems to have had few long-term effects on the species now present. Many of these move into and out of the park quite freely and, as they gradually learn that the park is a safe haven, they are staying longer or becoming resident, and appear to be less shy.

Puku are the most common antelope here, and are found in a particularly high density along the Kasanka River. Other relatively common residents include bushbuck, reedbuck, Sharp's grysbok and the common duiker. Sable occur in good numbers, and a small herd of zebra was introduced in 2012, while Lichtenstein's hartebeest, roan antelope, blue duiker, buffalo and defassa waterbuck are more scarce. Elephants move through the park, but a recent count suggested that a population of about 35–50 was probably resident here.

Of particular interest are the shy sitatunga antelope, which can almost always be seen in the very early morning from the Fibwe hide (page 328). This hide offers one of the subcontinent's best opportunities for viewing these beautiful creatures in an undisturbed state – far superior to the fleeting glimpse of a startled sitatunga that you may get from a speedboat in places like the Okavango Delta. On occasion, 70 different animals have been spotted from here in the early morning. In addition, sitatunga are also regularly spotted along the Kasanka River near Pontoon campsite, where the park authorities are planning to set up a second hide.

The smaller carnivores are well represented in Kasanka, with caracal, side-striped jackal, civet, genet and Cape clawless otter all regularly recorded. Others,

CHILLI FENCES

One of the greatest problems facing the successful operation of a national park is managing the conflict between conservation and community. Kasanka is no exception: with a small elephant population in an unfenced park, and a number of arable farms in the vicinity, problems are almost inevitable. Villagers understandably object to elephants trampling their valuable maize and cassava crops, but keeping the animals at bay is rarely straightforward.

In 2000, two researchers in Zimbabwe came up with a simple idea: chilli fences. The aim was to create a barrier that would repel the elephants without resorting to costly and often ineffective barricades or electric fencing. Based on the premise that elephants have a strong aversion to the smell of chillies, they had set up the Chilli Pepper Development Project (now the Elephant Pepper Development Trust, www.elephantpepper.org). Using cheap, easily available materials, they created a fence made of wooden posts linked by sisal rope and hung with strips of cloth that had been doused in used engine oil and chillies. Their results were impressive.

Taking their research as a base, Victoria Paterson, a research student from Glasgow University, spent much of 2007 at Kasanka studying the potential of chilli fences for the villages around the national park. With a focus across five sites, she set up a series of fences, with control experiments to check the efficacy of the combination of materials, and worked with local farmers to explain the methods. Despite considerable resistance, some of the farmers have taken the suggestions on board, with very positive results for their crops.

One method of reinforcing the fences is to create a buffer zone between the precious maize crop and the elephant's forest habitat, by growing a secondary crop around it. The European potato, for example, doesn't find favour with elephants, so sowing this between the forest and the maize can help to persuade the elephant to look elsewhere rather than wading through a field of unappealing fare.

To mitigate the costs, villagers have been encouraged to use fibre for rope, and to grow chillies as one of their crops. Here, water is a huge factor, but if the chillies are grown alongside another, profitable crop that requires irrigation, such as rape, then a successful outcome is more likely.

Now, though, the elephants – thwarted of their free meal – have taken to heading for village grain stores, and so the cycle continues.

including leopard, serval, spotted hyena, honey badgers and the African wildcat, are more rarely seen. Lion are occasional visitors from the neighbouring Lavushi Manda National Park.

Mongooses are well represented: the water (or marsh), slender, white-tailed, banded, dwarf and large grey mongoose are all found here.

Given the park's proximity to the DRC, species that are typical of those equatorial rainforests (but rare for southern Africa), can also be spotted in Kasanka. For example, the blue monkey is often sighted in the *mushitu* forest, occurring together with the area's more common vervet monkeys. The baboons at Kasanka are unusual, too, a species known as the Kinda baboon that is smaller and more sociable than its better-known cousin in Zambia, the yellow baboon, and is the subject of a study by the Kasanka Baboon Project (*http://kasankababoonproject.com*).

Bats Without doubt the most spectacular sight in Kasanka occurs around the start of the rains, in November and December, when an enormous colony of straw-coloured fruit bats (*Eidolon helvum*) converges on the park to roost in the *mushitu* forest. Sometimes known as flying foxes, each evening they pour out of their resting-place just after sunset, filling the sky as they fly in search of food. The bats have wingspans of up to 85cm, making a grand spectacle that is best observed from the area of the Fibwe hide; for details, see page 328.

Riverine animals In the lakes, rivers and swamps, hippo and crocodiles are common. It is also said that the slender-snouted crocodile, a typical resident of DRC's tropical rainforest rivers, occurs here – though it has not been spotted for many years and may no longer be present.

Birds Kasanka has lush vegetation with a wide range of habitats, including three large rivers, five natural lakes, a papyrus swamp (Kapabi) and real moist evergreen swamp forest. In this small area, some 477 bird species had been identified by mid 2015, including many 'specials', and the number continues to rise – so it's a very good place for quiet, undisturbed birdwatching.

The rivers, lakes and wetland areas have excellent populations of ibis, storks, herons, kingfishers and bee-eaters as well as many waterfowl. Water rails, greater and lesser jacanas, white-backed ducks and pygmy geese are common. Reed cormorants and African darters are easily spotted on the more open stretches of water, and larger birds include wattled cranes and saddle-billed storks. Around Lake Ndolwa and Wasa there have even been two sightings of the rare shoebill, which breeds in the Bangweulu Wetlands to the north, but this is exceptionally unusual.

Many species common in east or central Africa occur here, on the edge of their range (South African bird books just won't be enough!), like the grey apalis, olive sunbird, red and blue sunbird (Anchieta's), green lourie, Boehm's flycatcher, Boehm's bee-eater, Sousa's shrike, black-backed barbet, Anchieta's tchagra, and both Schalow's and Ross's turacos (the latter also known as Lady Ross's lourie). Meanwhile, a quiet drift in a canoe down the Luwombwa River should produce sightings of finfoot, giant and half-collared kingfishers, narina trogons and yellow-throated leaflove, to name but a few.

The more common raptors in the area are the bateleur, martial, crowned, Ayre's, African hawk and steppe eagles, plus the snake eagles (black-breasted, western-banded and brown) and the chanting goshawks (pale and dark). Kasanka's fish eagles are often seen and crowned eagles breed here. There are also several pairs of Pel's fishing owls.

GETTING THERE

By road Coming from Kapiri Mposhi, head northeast for Serenje, where you should refuel as there's no fuel available in the park. Continue northeast for a further 38km, then take the main left turning along the D235, signposted to Samfya and Mansa. After another 55km, turn left for the park entrance, which is clearly signposted (⊕ TUKASA 12°33.250'S, 30°23.478'E).

The entrance to the park, close to the eastern border, is marked by the Mulembo gate, where you will need to register and pay your entrance fees. From here, most visitors should proceed to Wasa Lodge, bearing left at the fork after about 1km; should you be staying at the conservation centre, which is outside the park boundary, turn right here instead.

By air Those flying in will come to the park's Mulembo airstrip, which is close to Wasa Lodge. The original grass airstrip, on the Chikufwe Plain, is now overgrown and is no longer licensed for use.

GETTING AROUND During the dry season Kasanka's roads are generally good, and accessible with a high-clearance 2WD. The manually operated pontoon (✛ PONTOO 12°34.362'S, 30°14.008'E) across the Kasanka River has now been replaced by a narrow concrete bridge, thus improving access to the western side of the park.

Hardy 4x4 adventurers might consider the **Open Africa Nsobe Sitatunga Experience**, a route that takes in Kasanka, Lavushi Manda and Bangweulu to offer an interesting, if perhaps challenging drive.

GETTING ORGANISED Wherever you are going in the park, you should report first to Wasa Lodge. This is where you will book in for your accommodation, discuss meal requirements, arrange any activities, and get directions to other parts of the park.

WHERE TO STAY The Kasanka Trust (*satellite* ☏ *+873 762 067957;* e *res@ kasankanationalpark.com; http://kasankanationalpark.com*) runs all of the accommodation options in the park. Each operates slightly differently, particularly in terms of catering, and it's important to understand the implications before you decide where to stay. Although Kasanka can often accommodate 'drop-in' visitors who have their own food, booking in advance – for the campsites as well as the camps – is always a good idea.

Each of the **campsites** has flush toilets and bucket showers, with staff on hand to supply firewood, draw water, prepare hot showers, and give basic guidance to visitors. Campers need to bring all their own equipment and supplies, including drinking water.

Do remember that all visitors, irrespective of where they are staying, should report to Wasa Lodge before continuing further into the park.

Wasa Lodge [map, page 321] (3 chalets, 5 rondavels) ✛ WASALO 12°33.272'S, 30°17.740'E. The park's main camp is about 20 mins' drive from the main road, in a scenic spot on the shore of Lake Wasa. It's a fairly rustic set up, lit at night by small solar-powered lights, & all very low key. The 3 newer chalets are relatively spacious & comfortable, with a dbl & sgl beds, en-suite facilities with hot water (shower only) provided by donkey boilers, & a sheltered veranda facing the lake. The older rondavels are smaller, their bucket showers filled on request, & the family chalet has 2 rooms sharing a bathroom. All beds have mosquito nets.

Most visitors to Wasa Lodge stay on a full-board basis, with well-prepared meals served inside or on a covered veranda in the central area, where there's also a good-sized bar. Occasionally, guests may arrange to bring their own food, which is then cooked & served by the camp's staff, but this must be agreed in advance. A middle ground, again with advance notice, could be to take some meals

in Wasa's dining area, paying around US$15 for a cooked lunch, or US$19 for a 2-course dinner.

Wasa has its own tree hide, close to the chalets & a superb vantage point over the lake, where sitatunga are often spotted in the early morning. Game drives & escorted walks can be organised from camp, while water-based activities start & finish at Luwombwa, 1hr's drive through the park. *US$385 pp sharing FB, inc drinks, activities (best pre-arranged), laundry & park fees.* ⊕ *All year.* **LL**

Luwombwa Lodge [map, page 321] (3 chalets) ✛ LUWOMB 12°30.109'S, 30°0/.870'E. Smaller & more rustic still than Wasa Lodge, the remote so-called 'fishing lodge' sits on the bank of the Luwombwa River in the west of the park. It's about an hour's pleasant drive from Wasa Lodge, so if you're arriving in the afternoon, allow plenty of time to get here before dark. If you're driving yourself, you'll need a high-clearance vehicle, with a 4x4 during or after the rains. The thatched, A-frame chalets are built of brick & are

11

comfortable, if rather dark, with a small veranda over the river. Each has an en-suite toilet & shower (hot water on request), & a dbl & sgl bed beneath mosquito nets, while 2 of the chalets have an attic floor above with twin beds.

Most visitors to Luwombwa bring their own supplies, which are prepared & served by the camp's very helpful staff. Alternatively, you could make arrangements in advance to stay on a full-board basis. The simple bar & dining area is made of reeds & thatch, & is dominated by a huge & quite magnificent *mpundu* (or *mobola*) plum (*Parinari curatellifolia*), which also shelters the camp's firepit, while a second dining shelter on the riverbank offers a superb birdwatching venue out of the sun.

River trips in 3-seater canoes with a guide can be organised all year, while 4-seater motorboats are best when the river is higher. *US$60 pp sharing self catering, exc park fees; FB rates on request.* ⊕ *All year.* **L–LL**

🏠 **Kasanka Conservation Centre** [map, page 321] (4 rooms, 2 dormitories, camping) Accommodation at the conservation centre, about 2km from the park gate, is designed primarily for students or long-term researchers, but other visitors are welcome to stay here too. Rooms are small & basic, each with just enough space for twin beds with mosi nets; they are set up in pairs with a shared shower & toilet between them. A couple of 10-bed dormitories provides cost-effective accommodation for larger groups, and it's also

possible to camp. Some meals can be provided from the on-site kitchen or visitors can cook for themselves. *Room US$32 pp; dormitory US$19 pp; camping US$10 pp. No park fees applicable.* ⊕ All year. **$**

⛺ **Pontoon Campsite** [map, page 321] (3 pitches) xjzj ⊕ PONTOC 12°34.385'S, 30°14.073'E. Set under a beautiful shady stand of red mahogany or *mululu* trees (*Khaya nyasica*) near the Kasanka River bridge, this gently sloping campsite has views towards the river & plains. Each of the 3 separate pitches has a simple bucket shower & flush toilet, but they share 2 cooking shelters with BBQ stands. In 2015, there was talk of installing a sitatunga hide on one of the pitches, which would be quite a draw in the early morning. *US$15 pp.* ⊕ *All year.*

⛺ **Kabwe Campsite** [map, page 321] (1 pitch) ⊕ KABWEC 12°32.457'S, 30°12.690'E. Overlooking the Kasanka River plain, this is a smaller, secluded site for up to 6 people, with a shower & flush toilet that were spotlessly clean when we visited. *US$15 pp.* ⊕ *All year.*

⛺ **Bufumu Campsite** [map, page 321] (1 pitch) ⊕ BUFUMC 12°29.783'S, 30°11.763'E. With a beautiful view of the open plain, a good shelter & BBQ, plus a toilet & bucket shower, Kasanka's newest campsite is pretty idyllic. A short walk from here takes you to the tallest tree in Zambia (pages 328–9) in the Bufumu Forest. *US$15 pp.* ⊕ Mar–Dec.

Bat safaris During late November and early December, bat safaris are run by two safari operators. Robin Pope Safaris (pages 264–5) organises seven-night safaris which combine their Nkwali property in the South Luangwa (page 279) with three days at Wasa Lodge and a night in Lusaka (*US$5,019/5,594 pp sharing/sgl*). A similar trip is offered by Remote Africa Safaris (page 264) for their guests.

WHAT TO SEE AND DO

Activities Activities organised by the Kasanka Trust include escorted walks, day and night game drives, canoeing, motorboat trips and fishing. For those staying on an all-inclusive basis, these activities are included; for other guests, and for additional activities, see the rates below. All activities must be booked through Wasa Lodge.

Game drives and guided walks These can be organised with one of the park's own guides. Alternatively, you can drive yourself around the park, perhaps taking a guide with you if there is somebody free. A few places within the park are worth specific mention; see *Exploring the park*, below, for brief details. Specialist guides, such as expert birders, can also be organised with plenty of notice, a particular boon for the keen ornithologist. *Game drive US$40 pp (max 6 people); guide US$25/up to 3hrs.*

One of Kasanka's highlights is the magnificent tree-hide, perched high in a red mahogany tree overlooking the Kapabi Swamp. Most come here to spot sitatunga, but if you climb up on a late November afternoon, around the time the rains are beginning, then you'll also witness one of Africa's strangest wildlife spectacles. Between about 18.00 and 18.30, up to ten million straw-coloured fruit bats will take to the air above you. These large, fruit-eating bats have wingspans up to about a metre. They start by circling overhead like a vast, slow whirlwind. Gradually, individuals and groups break off and spread out over the forest in search of wild fruits. For an amazing 20–30 minutes the sky is filled, as far as you can see, with squadron upon squadron of bats, heading off into the twilight.

'They come to roost in the evergreen swamp forest, near the Musola River,' Edmund said, gazing down through the canopy. 'It's very unusual vegetation for Zambia – only found near rivers. Tremendously fragile and easily destroyed,' he added. 'During the day the bats occupy just a small area. They hang off the *mushitu* trees in such numbers that they pull off the branches, leaving just the woody skeletons to hang on to. This lets light on to the forest floor which, together with the inordinate amount of fertiliser that they drop, promotes very rich undergrowth. Imagine, eight million bats, weighing about 350g each … that's 2,800 tons of animals.' Edmund had clearly done his arithmetic before. 'The equivalent of a thousand elephants, hanging around in perhaps one hectare of forest, suspended from the trees,' he grinned.

Visiting this colony isn't for the faint-hearted, even during the day. Large crocodiles wander under the trees, far from the nearest water, scavenging for dead bats – along with vultures, gymnogenes and a host of other smaller predators. All of which provided further reasons why that high tree-hide was such a wonderful place to be. *Edited from an article by the author that first appeared in* Travel Africa, *and reproduced by kind permission.*

Boat trips Depending on the season, and thus the level of water, both motorboat and canoe trips can be organised on the Luwombwa River. I can highly recommend the excellent canoe trips: a magical way to spend a morning on the river. *Motorboat US$25 pp; canoe US$10 pp.*

Fishing Anglers should head for Luwombwa Lodge, as the best waters for fishing are normally those of the Luwombwa River. The main species found here are vundu catfish and large-mouth, small-mouth and yellow-belly bream and occasionally tigerfish. The camp's cooks will prepare your catch for dinner, if you wish, but note that strict park rules allow only large fish to be removed for eating.

Fishing tackle cannot be hired from the lodges, so you'll need to bring your own. You must also obtain a permit from Wasa Lodge before heading out to Luwombwa, where you can hire a boat with a guide (*US$25 pp*). No fishing is permitted between November and February.

Bat viewing Between October and December, Kasanka's *mushitu* forest is the focus of an extraordinary bat migration that sees millions of straw-coloured fruit bats descend on the park (see box, above). The bats are best seen near the Fibwe Hide, where public and exclusive viewing areas are opened especially for the season.

A guided bat experience (*US$50pp*) affords the opportunity to view the bats emerging at sunset or returning from their nightly forage from an exclusive bat hide or platform on the edge of the Bat Forest. As well as the bats, there's the chance of spotting the variety of raptors that prey on them as they return to their roosts in the mornings, including the crowned eagle.

Baboon walks By arrangement with Wasa Lodge, it's possible to join researchers from the Kasanka Baboon Project (*http://kasankababoonproject.com*) as they carry out their work monitoring the Kinda baboon. Walks (*US$50 pp, inc tea & snack*) take around 3 hours.

Conservation and community projects With advance notice, visitors may arrange to see aspects of some of Kasanka's community-based conservation projects, and to meet their participants, or to visit a local school.

Walking trips With plenty of notice, it is possible for fully equipped and self-sufficient campers to organise a walking trip through the park with an armed game scout, staying at the different campsites as they go. This offers the chance to see the many different vegetation types, insects, birds and animals, and to discuss the bush, the project, and anything else at leisure, but note that your scout will not be a trained guide. *US$25/3hrs.*

Scenic flights When there is a light aircraft stationed at Kasanka, usually between about May and November, it's possible to take a scenic flight over Kasanka and the Bangweulu Wetlands. The flight lasts about an hour, and costs US$600 for up to four passengers, or five with a child. Advance notice is normally required.

What to see
Conservation centre A visitor centre close to the entrance to the park showcases Kasanka's conservation work and acts as an interpretation centre, with posters, displays, information and videos of the annual bat migration. The centre is just outside the park boundary in the surrounding GMA, so visitors here do not have to pay park fees.

Fibwe hide A magnificent *mululu* or red mahogany tree (*Khaya nyasica*), near to the Fibwe scout post (✪ FIBWE 12°35.444'S, 30°15.153'E), can be climbed, using a basic ladder, to reach a platform some 18m above the ground. The views over a section of the Kapabi Swamp and the moist evergreen **Bat Forest** are excellent.

If you reach the hide in the early morning and climb quietly, your chances of seeing sitatunga are excellent. However, more leisurely risers should take heart: I have seen a number of sitatunga from here as late as midday. In short, this is probably the best place for seeing sitatunga in the wild anywhere in Africa – and so certainly one of the best tree-hides on the continent!

It's also a particularly productive birding spot, with specials such as Ross's and Schalow's turaco, Boehm's bee-eater, black-backed barbet, Anchieta's tchagra, speckled mousebirds and various sunbirds often visible in the nearby forest. And during the bat migration, the hide offers a superb vantage point, especially at dusk when millions of bats leave their roosts *en masse* to search for food in the surrounding miombo woodland.

Bufumu Forest This pocket of dry evergreen forest, or *mateshe*, is home to the 'Big Tree', which is considered to be the tallest tree in Zambia. Towering 65m over the surrounding forest, it's a semi-deciduous *mofu* tree (*Entandrophragma delevoyi*) that's estimated to be 400 years old. Its existence owes much to the presence of royal graves at its foot, giving rise to the name 'sacred forest'. The tree is easily found from the Bufumu campsite, about a 5-minute walk to the north; ask the campsite attendant to show you the way.

Chinyangale Plain and Kasanka River Between the bridge over the Kasanka River and the Fibwe hide, a game-viewing road winds through the open plain with palm clumps and plentiful puku. Another road runs along the western side of the river, going downstream from the crossing. There are often large herds of puku here, and you'll frequently spot bushbuck and warthog.

Chikufwe Plain The Chikufwe Plain (✛ CHIFUN 12°33.066'S, 30°09.645'E) is a large open area of seasonally flooded grassland on the western side of the park. The site of the old grass airstrip, it is a favourite place to spot sable, hartebeest and reedbuck. There is a loop road around the southern side of the plain.

Further afield Just outside the park's eastern boundary is a series of small rapids, the Mambilima Falls (not to be confused with the falls of the same name on the Luapula River). There is talk of cutting a road through the park to these, but for now, access is only from the main road between Kasanka and Mansa.

By prior arrangement, usually between May and November, day trips to Shoebill Island in the Bangweulu Wetlands (page 341) can be organised for guests staying at Kasanka. Typically you'll leave the park by light aircraft at about 07.45, returning around 17.00. The charter flight doesn't come cheap; expect to pay about US$720 return for up to four passengers (or five including a child). If Shoebill Island Camp is open, lunch can be arranged (*US$10 pp*) and a pick up from the airstrip with a game drive through the herds of black lechwe or to a shoebill nesting site (*US$40 pp*). Otherwise you'll need to take a packed lunch and drinks from Kasanka.

AROUND KASANKA AND BANGWEULU

There are several sites of interest in the area around Kasanka and Bangweulu, though you'll need a self-contained 4x4 to reach any of them, and local help for some.

LIVINGSTONE MEMORIAL A plain stone monument, under a simple cross, marks the place where David Livingstone's heart was buried in 1873, in the village of Chitambo. (The village has since moved, but Livingstone's heart – and the monument – remain.) After his death, from dysentery and malaria, his followers removed his heart and internal organs, and buried them under a *mpundu* tree that once stood where the monument is now.

In an amazing tribute, his two closest followers, Sussi and Chuma, then salted and dried his body before disguising it in a tree and carrying it over 1,000 miles to Bagamoyo (on Tanzania's coast). The journey took them about nine months. From there they took the body by ship to London, where Livingstone was finally buried with full honours in Westminster Abbey on 18 April 1874.

Twenty-five years later, in 1899, the Royal Geographical Society in London sent out a small expedition to cut down the *mpundu* tree and bring a section of its trunk, which had been engraved with the names of Livingstone and three of his party, to London, where it remains to this day.

The present Chief Chitambo, Freddy Chisenga, is the great grandson of the chief who received Livingstone. By appointment, the chief will receive visitors at his palace in Chaililo (sometimes spelled Cholilo or Chalilo) village, from where you can proceed to the memorial site.

Getting there The monument is clearly marked (if sometimes vaguely positioned) on most maps. The easiest route is to turn north off the Great North Road at ⊕ TUCHIN 13°1.146'S, 30°27.695'E towards Mansa and Samfya. After some 65km, or 10km beyond the sign for Kasanka National Park, turn right in Chaililo onto a dirt road. There is a signpost and a small market at this turning (⊕ TULIVI 12°29.255'S, 30°20.364'E), which is 27km from the memorial.

Follow the main track here for 1km, turning left at Chaililo School (there's a sign to the chief's palace). After 500m, bear right to avoid the chief's palace, or left if you want to visit the chief. Then continue straight on, passing Mupopolo Health Centre, for about a further 25km, till you get to a clinic on the left. Here you should sign the visitors' book and will sometimes be asked to pay a small entry fee. The memorial (⊕ LIVMEM 12°17.970'S, 30°17.580'E) is signposted a little way beyond the clinic, to the left, just before Chipundu School. There are toilets on site.

On your return, it's best to avoid forking left along the old road which is marked on many maps, as this takes a very long time to get back to the tarmac road. It is, however, a useful short cut if you're heading towards Lake Waka Waka or the Bangweulu Wetlands.

KUNDALILA (NKUNDALILA) FALLS (⊕ KUNDAC 13°09.260'S, 30°42.119'E. *Entry US$15/7 adult/child; camping US$15 pp*) Kundalila, which means 'cooing dove', is one of Zambia's most beautiful waterfalls. Set in an area of scenic meadows and forests on the edge of the Muchinga Escarpment, the clear stream drops 67m into a crystal pool below; it makes a great place for a picnic among the granite boulders. Look out for blue monkeys that are said to inhabit the forests here, and some cheeky white-necked ravens.

At the bottom of the parking area, there is an old bridge across the Kaombe River. The path then splits and the right branch leads you to the top of the gorge. The left takes you on a longer walk to the bottom, where there's a beautiful pool for swimming, if you can bear the water's chill. Take a close look at a good topographical map and you'll realise that you're in one of Zambia's highest areas, at an altitude of around 1,500m, so it's frequently cool, windy and pleasantly devoid of mosquitoes.

Campers have the choice of three separate pitches, sharing a new shelter and an ablution block with showers and flush toilets. Those with children will be pleased to know that fences have recently been erected on some of the paths around the falls, as protection against some very steep drops at the edge.

The caretaker may also be able to take you to the nearby Kaudina Falls, and possibly also direct you to the Chilindi Chipususha Falls, on the Musumpu River.

Getting there About 65km beyond Serenje, turn southeast off the Great North Road at the small settlement of Kanona (⊕ KANONA 13°4.204'S, 30°38.056'E), where a good dirt track is clearly signposted 'National Monument Kundalila Falls, 14km'. (If you were to take another right turn off this track almost immediately, you would reach the local ZAWA offices.)

Soon you'll cross the railway, then 6km further on there's a Kingdom Hall of Jehovah's Witnesses on the left, before finally reaching the falls. Generally you'll sign in with the caretaker, and pay your entry fee, either at the top of the track, or in the parking/camping area at the new shelter.

NSALU CAVE (*Entry US$10; camping US$15 pp, plus entry fees*) This huge semicircular cave, cut into Nsalu Hill, stands about 50m above the level of the surrounding plateau, and contains some excellent San/Bushmen rock paintings. Sadly a few years back the caves were vandalised, but since then the graffiti have been fading much faster than the paintings, so once again most of the paintings can still be seen.

Archaeological investigations have demonstrated occupation for at least 20,000 years, firstly by Middle and Late Stone-Age people, and later by Iron-Age settlers. The oldest paintings are in yellow and include parallel lines, circles and loops. Later drawings were executed in rust-coloured paint, and even later ones in red and white paints used together. The last paints applied appear as grey-white pigments and have been applied rather clumsily. They contain animal fats and are thought to have been the work of Iron-Age settlers within the last 2,000 years.

When you've finished looking at the paintings, the view from the cave's mouth over the surrounding countryside is great – and if you've lots of energy then a scramble to the top gives an even better view.

Getting there The cave is about half-an-hour's drive from the main road. Head northeast on the Great North Road to the signpost for Nsalu Cave and turn left (⊕ TU1NSA 12°51.351'S, 30°46.495'E). This is between Serenje and Mpika, about 30km northeast of Kanona (where you turn to Kundalila Falls) and 15km north of Chitambo Mission Hospital.

Follow this road north for about 14km and then turn left at the rather marvellous sign to 'National Nonument' (⊕ TU2NSA 12°44.784'S, 30°44.134'E). After a further 8km this track ends and the cave (⊕ NSALUC 12°43.202'S, 30°40.952'E) is visible about halfway up the hill, on which a walking trail is marked. If you continue north past the 'National Nonument' sign, then you're heading to Lake Waka Waka, Chiundaponde and the Bangweulu Wetlands.

LAKE WAKA WAKA If you're looking for some relatively untouched bush and a quiet setting, where you're very unlikely to encounter anyone else, you'll find a lovely tranquil spot by this lake. It's traditionally been good for walking, makes a convenient camping stop with basic facilities on the way to the Bangweulu Wetlands, and provides a pleasant lunch spot – though there are no facilities. The views from the surrounding hilltops are panoramic, and I'm reliably informed that the lake is safe to swim in, with no bilharzia, hippos or crocodiles – though I haven't done this myself. There are few settlements around here, and hence a scattering of game is present, including sitatunga and roan antelope, though both are skittish and scarce.

Getting there However you approach, you're really going to need a high-clearance 4x4 once you leave the main tarred roads – and even then you'll find travelling in the rainy season is a challenge.

From the west From the Great North Road, take the road north towards Mansa and Samfya for about 65km, turning right 10km after the sign to Kasanka National Park. (See the directions to the Livingstone Memorial, opposite.) About 1km from the tarmac, keep straight ahead at the Chaililo Basic School, rather than turning left to the Chief's Palace and Livingstone Memorial. Continue past Musangashi School for about 30km, before turning left (⊕ TUWAKA 12°31.524'S, 30°36.366'E) at a sign for Lake Waka Waka. Note that you'll need a high-clearance vehicle for this track at any time of year; it doesn't get much traffic, and is not maintained.

From the south There's a wonderful track from the Great North Road to Lake Waka Waka, but the more northerly sections of this are seldom used, so don't be lulled into taking half measures; you'll still need a high-clearance vehicle all year round, and a 4x4 during the rainy season.

Start by turning north at the signpost for Nsalu Cave (⊕ TU1NSA 12°51.351'S, 30°46.495'E), 30km northeast of Kanona. After 14km you'll pass the left turning to Nsalu Cave (⊕ TU2NSA 12°44.784'S, 30°44.134'E), but you continue heading north-northwest. This track basically follows a watershed, with the Lukulu to the east, which drains into Bangweulu, and tributaries of the Kasanka to the west, which drain into the park. Thus with no rivers crossing it, it should be passable even during the rains. When I journeyed in late May, this road was particularly beautiful, though I don't think that more than half-a-dozen cars had been through since the previous December. The grass was high, the miombo woodlands apparently untouched, and there were very few villages.

About 22km north of the Nsalu turning, the track bumps over a very rocky hill (⊕ WAKHIL 12°36.573'S, 30°39.333'E), and becomes quite indistinct in places. Carry on, and aim for the junction of this track with the 'main' track from Kasanka to Chiundaponde, at ⊕ TUWAKA 12°31.524'S, 30°36.366'E. This is barely a kilometre from the lake.

CHIUNDAPONDE Chiundaponde is a typical small Zambian village that lies at the heart of the area covered by this chapter. The inhabitants are mainly small-scale farmers from the Bisa tribe. In the fields around the village they grow cassava, finger millet, sorghum, maize and groundnuts as their staple crops. Finger millet and sorghum are also used to make beer for selling; groundnuts are grown as a cash crop. Some also keep goats and chickens, either for subsistence or to sell, and you'll often have to avoid these as they wander across the road in front of your vehicle. Chiundaponde isn't really a destination for most visitors, but you will go through it if you're visiting the Bangweulu Wetlands, and so it's useful to be able to navigate to/from here.

For directions from Chiundaponde to the Bangweulu Wetlands, see page 342.

Getting there and away
From the south or west Follow the directions (see opposite, *From the west* and *From the south*) from the Great North Road to the turning for Lake Waka Waka (⊕ TUWAKA 12°31.524'S, 30°36.366'E). From there, head on the track leading north – which bounces gently though miombo woodlands and, increasingly, small farming settlements. By 17km beyond the lake, you'll pass through a small village with a school where, like anywhere else here, you'll probably be the object of much curiosity and interest – if only from the local children. Although you'll be in third gear and the track is sandy in places, this isn't difficult driving.

After about 23km you'll cross a large dambo (⊕ DAMBO 12°21.947'S, 30°36.321'E), where the track follows a short causeway. A further 9km on and there's another large dambo to cross (⊕ DAMBO2 12°17.384'S, 30°35.407'E), and around 3km later there may be a sign to the new Nakapalayo village (see page 335) where you can stay. Some 6km after the second dambo, you reach Chiundaponde (⊕ CHSCHL 12°14.724'S, 30°34.741'E), where amongst other buildings you'll find a large school.

From the east Approaching from Mpika, leave the Great North Road about 65km from Mpika, and follow the directions given below to get across Lavushi Manda National Park. In the dry season it takes about 3 hours to reach Chiundaponde from the turn-off. In the wet season, the Lavushi Manda road is so bad that you should consider an alternative route – perhaps even going all the way to Kasanka, and approaching from the west.

Where to stay and eat Although many people will press on to reach Shoebill Camp, there's one option about 3–4km south of Chiundaponde that's worth considering:

Nakapalayo Village (6 local-style chalets, camping) ⊕ NAKAPA 12°16.542'S, 30°34.565'E. This community tourism project, started in early 2004, is signposted from the main track between Chiundaponde & Waka Waka. The village has built extra chalets in the traditional style: neat, rectangular structures made out of traditional mud bricks with smooth, small, arrow-shaped open windows, & twin or dbl beds with mattresses & mosquito nets. They share very clean long-drop toilets, & bathrooms that are simply reed shelters with showers – buckets on a high shelf from which you scoop water over yourself.

Nakapalayo's people have been trained by members of the Kawaza Village community, in South Luangwa, and offer a variety of activities. Most visitors will take a wander around the village with one of the local guides to see, learn & try everyday activities like drawing water, pounding cassava or cultivating the fields. There are also opportunities to visit the village headman, or local chief, to learn about the culture & history of the Bisa people; to visit Chiundaponde School, the rural health centre or one of the local churches; to meet the village's

traditional healer to learn about the medicinal uses of the area's flora; to take a bush walk to learn about traditional uses of the area's plants; & to enjoy dancing & storytelling around the fire. Locally made crafts are available to buy, & If you're staying, the villagers will also prepare tasty traditional meals for you. In return, you are asked to dress & behave modestly, with long trousers or skirts for women, & no public displays of affection, & not to give money or gifts to any individuals. I've had a glowing report from one visitor, who described the people as 'just the most lovely lot in the world'. Nakapalayo is worth supporting if you're passing through the area. Note, however, that contact with Nakapalayo is difficult. While efforts can be made through Kasanka to send a message via 'bush telegraph', this is not always reliable; it may be better to arrive unannounced and do things ad hoc. *Chalet US$60 pp FB, inc village tour & entertainment; US$50 pp DBB inc entertainment; US$40 inc entertainment but exc meals, camping US$20 pp inc activities, or US$10 without. Day visit US$20 pp, inc lunch & activities; lunch only US$10.* **L**

LAVUSHI MANDA NATIONAL PARK (*Park fees US$10 pp/day; vehicle US$15/*day) This park is potentially interesting for its hilly and very pleasant landscape, though sadly it lost some of its animals to poachers over the last few decades. Lavushi Manda's rocky, undulating land would make parts of it difficult to farm, and until tourism to Zambia is substantially bigger, there has been little incentive for anyone to try to rejuvenate its fortunes by restocking it with game.

The good news is that since 2011, the Kasanka Trust has handled the management of the park. Working as part of a donor funded development project, they started anti-poaching and roadbuilding immediately, and there has already been a significant reduction in poaching through better law enforcement and improved management. Visitor numbers are increasing slowly too, with three campsites now open and game-viewing loops created. That said, it's likely to take at least a few years before this wilderness area will have a complete road network and more accommodation options for visitors – but watch this space ...

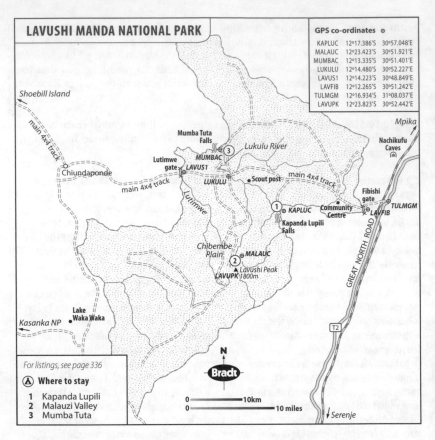

LAVUSHI MANDA NATIONAL PARK

GPS co-ordinates ⊕		
KAPLUC	12°17.386'S	30°57.048'E
MALAUC	12°23.423'S	30°51.921'E
MUMBAC	12°13.335'S	30°51.401'E
LUKULU	12°14.480'S	30°52.227'E
LAVUS1	12°14.223'S	30°48.849'E
LAVFIB	12°12.265'S	30°51.242'E
TULMGM	12°16.934'S	31°08.037'E
LAVUPK	12°23.823'S	30°52.442'E

Shoebill Island

Mpika

Nachikufu Caves

Mumba Tuta Falls

Lukulu River

Lutimwe gate MUMBAC **3**

Chiundaponde **LAVUS1**

LUKULU • *Scout post* main 4x4 track

Fibishi gate **TULMGM**

1 ⊕ **KAPLUC** Community Centre **LAVFIB**

Kapanda Lupili Falls

Chibembe Plain **2** ⊕ **MALAUC**

▲ *Lavushi Peak* 1800m
LAVUPK

Lake Waka Waka

Kasanka NP

GREAT NORTH ROAD

T2

For listings, see page 336

Ⓐ **Where to stay**
1 Kapanda Lupili
2 Malauzi Valley
3 Mumba Tuta

N

Bradt

0 ▬▬▬▬ 10km
0 ▬▬▬▬ 10 miles

Serenje

Geography Lavushi Manda is over three times the size of Kasanka, and covers 1,500km² including the Lavushi Hills. It is easily reached from the Great North Road, is almost equidistant from Serenje and Mpika, and the landscape is attractive and undulating. To the north the land slopes away, and the park's streams all drain into the Lulimala, Lukulu or Lumbatwa rivers and thence ultimately into the Bangweulu Basin.

Flora and fauna Miombo woodland covers most of the park, with some areas of riparian forest nearer the larger streams and many grassy dambos.

Mammals The park's history has left its mark on the wildlife, which remains relatively scarce and secretive. Nevertheless, remain it does, with antelope such as the common duiker, bushbuck, Sharpe's grysbok and southern reedbuck, although puku are thought to be extinct within the park. Unlike in Kasanka National Park, small groups of lion are resident in Lavushi Manda, as are leopard, side-striped jackal and spotted hyena. The Kinda baboon is widespread, especially near rock formations, and both vervet and blue monkeys are present. Hippo (and crocodile) are found in the rivers.

Birdlife By 2014, eminent ornithologist Frank Willems had catalogued a total of 352 birds in Lavushi Manda, though that number is likely to rise. Near the waterfalls, keep an eye out for African finfoot, long-tailed wagtail, black duck and other riverine species. Bohm's bee-eater, purple-throated cuckooshrike, olive-grey greenbul, Ross's turaco and black-backed barbet are among the many species that can be found in the evergreen forests along the rivers.

The Lavushi mountain range holds a range of rock-loving species. Verreaux's (black) eagle breeds near the peak and can be seen hunting the bush hyraxes and red rock rabbits that live here. Augur Buzzard, lazy cisticola, red-winged starling, mocking cliff chat, familiar chat and Reichard's seedeater are other typical species. The common sunbird on the bare parts of the mountains is eastern miombo double-collared sunbird, till very recently considered a subspecies but now thought to be a full species, while the western miombo double-collared sunbird is common in the surrounding woodlands. In the mountain gorges and elsewhere along streams, evergreen forests hold specials like black-bellied seedcracker and evergreen forest warbler.

The large dambos in the park hold many specials such as streaky-breasted and chestnut-headed flufftail, locustfinch, blue quail, black coucal, Fulleborn's longclaw and pale-crowned cisticola. Of special interest are the seasonal lakes Chibembe and Mikonko, where many interesting waterbirds have been recorded including jack snipe, a rare species this far south.

Almost all miombo woodland birds that occur in Zambia, can be found in Lavushi Manda. Relatively common are Anchieta's barbet (try the fig trees at Lutimwe Gate and Fibishi Community Centre), Anchieta's sunbird, Arnott's chat, Reichard's seedeater, miombo and rufous-bellied tit, yellow-bellied hyliota and black-necked eremomela. The ground hornbill is often seen as well.

Getting there Most easily accessed from the Great North Road, Lavushi Manda can also be reached from the western side at Chiundaponde. Driving through the park is a convenient route into the Bangweulu Game Management Area from the east, and makes an interesting diversion. There are park gates to both east and west, although park fees are not payable if you are travelling straight through.

From the east The turning to Lavushi Manda from the main Mpika–Serenje road (✦ TULMGM 12°16.934'S, 31°8.037'E) is about 141km northeast of the D235 turning to Mansa and Kasanka, and about 60km from Mpika. A large signboard with the African Parks' logo points the way to Lavushi Manda and the Bangweulu Wetlands.

This road goes across the TAZARA railway line, and enters the park via the 'new' Fibishi gate (✦ LAVFIB 12°17.533'S, 31°04.400'E), which is a few kilometres east of the old gate (now the community centre). Continuing west, you'll eventually come to a new concrete bridge, recently repaired following extensive flooding, over the lovely Lukulu River (✦ LUKULU 12°14.480'S, 30°52.227'E).

From the west There is only one good track which heads east from Chiundaponde, passing the turn-off to Bangweulu. A little over 20km later you'll enter Lavushi Manda at the Lutimwe gate (✦ LAVUS1 12°14.230'S, 30°46.856'E) – which is just above a crossing of the Lutimwe River. This is a little over 10km from the bridge over the Lukulu River (✦ LUKULU 12°14.480'S, 30°52.227'E) mentioned above.

Getting around For years, the main east–west road through the park has been dreadful. Driving is a challenge even in the dry season, with big muddy gullies and areas where the road has just been washed away; when I crossed the park in June some years back, I averaged about 15km/h. In the wet season, I'd expect this to be exceedingly time-consuming at best, and totally impassable at worst. That said, with the introduction of 91km of game-viewing loops, things are definitely changing, so don't be put off – but a 4x4 is still a must, and do proceed with caution.

🏠 **Where to stay** Since 2011, three campsites have been established in Lavushi Manda. Each site has space for just one group, with a long-drop toilet and a picnic table, but you'll need to bring all your food, water and equipment. Camping costs US$15 per person, per night, in addition to park fees.

If you want to camp, contact the Kasanka Trust (e *info@kasanka.com* or *res@ kasankanationalpark.com*) in advance, or ask at the park gate.

🏕 **Kapanda Lupili** [map, page 334] (◈ KAPLUC 12°17.461'S, 30°57.902'E) Perched on a ridge close to the Lukulu River, Kapanda Lupili has views across open plains. It's a short walk from the falls of the same name, which flow strongly during the rainy season. At other times, you may with care be able to pick your way across the rocks to the other side.

🏕 **Mumba Tuta** [map, page 334] (◈ 12°12.335'S, 30°51.401'E) Right by the Lukulu River bridge, the campsite has a view of the Mumba Tuta Falls. In theory it's possible to swim below the falls when the water's low, but there are crocodiles above – and hippos further downstream – so you'll need to be vigilant.

🏕 **Malauzi Valley** [map, page 334] (◈ 12°23.423'S, 30°51.921'E) By a stream near the Lavushi Peak, the newest of the sites looks over the palm-fringed plains of the valley, which support a fair amount of game.

What to see and do Organised activities in the park are in their infancy, and are dependent on the availability of guides, so a bit of forward thinking is essential if you want to make the most of your visit. In theory you can take part in game drives and guided walks, as well as canoeing or fishing on the Lukulu River (as at Kasanka, bring all your own tackle). More challenging is the possibility of climbing the 1,800m Lavushi Peak (◈ LAVUPK 12°23.823'S, 30°52.442'E), where you'll find klipspringer, bushy hyrax and white-necked ravens. Or consider a five-day hike across the eastern section of the park. Talk to the team at Kasanka if you're interested in any of these options, and allow plenty of time for them to be set up. Otherwise, Lavushi Manda might make a good area for exploration if you are a very dedicated hiker, though you'll probably want to arrange for one of the scouts from the gate to accompany you.

THE BANGWEULU WETLANDS

This area is often described, in clichéd terms, as one of Africa's last great wilderness areas. That might be overstating its case a little, but it is certainly a very large and very wild area, which very few people really know and understand.

Though most visitors' image of a wilderness area is an unpopulated, barren tract of land, the Bangweulu Wetlands encompasses numerous small villages. It remains home to some 90,000 local people, who still hunt and fish here, as their ancestors have done for centuries. They are as much a part of the landscape as the lily-strewn water channels and floodplains teeming with black lechwe. Bangweulu is one of those places that grows on you the more you get to know it, and is well worth visiting to see a different side to Zambia.

PROTECTION OF THE WETLANDS The old way of conserving an area by displacing the people and proclaiming a national park clearly hasn't worked in much of Zambia: witness the minimal game left in many of the lesser-known parks. Thus a more enlightened approach of leaving the people on the land, and encouraging them to develop through sustainable management of their natural resources, is a more modern way to attempt to preserve as much of the wildlife as possible. Despite this approach, the area's population was growing, illegal hunting was rife, and there were fears for the future of the wildlife.

The area was designated a Wetland of International Importance in 1991, and has also been defined as an Important Bird Area. When the WWF became involved in trying to help local communities to manage the area sustainably, the aim was to create a community partnership park (CCP) where illegal fishing would be stopped and the area intensively managed like a national park.

Then, in 2008, African Parks – already successful in turning round the management of Liuwa Plain National Park (pages 478–87) – was invited by the local chiefs and community representatives to take over responsibility for the park and to protect the region's resources in partnership with the community and ZAWA. The result was the declaration in 2010 of the Chikuni Community Partnership Park, an area of 2,900km² that is augmented by the 3,100km² of the surrounding Bangweulu GMA. Through education, training and law enforcement, it is aimed to restore and protect the environment, while monitoring fishing within the wetlands and implementing a seven-year programme of restocking the larger mammals. Over the years, African Parks have faced various challenges, from complex issues concerning revenues with ZAWA, which halted progress in the area pending resolution, to an initial waning in support from local communities as seasonal fishing bans were imposed in accordance with the national law. However, in 2015, Bangweulu is on the cusp of a new era. Management issues with the national parks' authorities have been resolved. And having benefited economically from more sustainable fishing practices and other income-generating projects introduced by African Parks, such as bee-keeping for honey production, communities are gradually coming on side. Other initiatives include improving healthcare and education facilities, the latest project involving the introduction of Zedupads (tablets featuring the Zambian school curriculum) to local schools.

GEOGRAPHY The low-lying basin containing Lake Bangweulu and its wetlands receives one of the highest rainfalls in the country – over 1,400mm per annum. On the northwestern edge of the basin is Lake Bangweulu itself, about 50km long and up to 25km wide. This is probably the largest body of water within Zambia's borders, and an excellent spot for watching the local fishermen but, apart from the lake's remarkable white, sandy beaches, is of little interest to most visitors. It is easily reached at Samfya, a small town on the main road from Serenje to Mansa. See also pages 370–1 for comments on Samfya and the surrounding area.

The more fascinating areas here are the vast wetlands to the southeast of the lake, which cover an area two to three times the size of the lake, and the seasonally flooded grasslands to the south of those wetlands.

The wetlands and grasslands are areas with few roads and lots of wildlife. It's one of the few regions of Zambia where the local communities are beginning to use the wildlife in their GMAs as a really sustainable source of income. There is little development here, just a small, tented lodge and a simple community-run camp for visitors who arrive on their own. The area still has many residents who continue to fish and eke out a living directly from the environment, but gradually the community development schemes are beginning to tap into tourism as a way to fund sustainable development.

FLORA AND FAUNA With access to the wetlands, the birdlife can be amazing and the animals impressive. However, choose the time of year for your visit very carefully: the type of fauna to be seen, and the activities required to see it, will vary hugely with the season.

Animals The speciality here is the black lechwe, an attractive dark race of the lechwe that is endemic to the Bangweulu area. The only other places where it has been recorded are the swamps beside Lake Mweru, where its status is now exceedingly questionable, and the Nashinga Swamps near Chinsali, where it has been re-introduced. It is much darker than the red lechwe found throughout southern Africa, or the race known as the Kafue lechwe which occur in the Lochinvar area. I think it's by far the most attractive of the three.

The current population in this area is estimated at 40,000 animals, and herds measured in their thousands are common on the dry floodplains around the wetlands. As well as these huge herds of black lechwe you'll find other animals including sitatunga, tsessebe, reedbuck, common duiker and oribi. Zebra are doing very well; about nine were released here at first, translocated from a game farm near Lusaka, and they have now bred up to a healthy herd which is often visible on the plains. Elephant and buffalo are frequently seen; predators are uncommon but hyena and leopard are sometimes observed. Often seen at dusk or dawn, or on a night drive, side-striped jackal are very common. White-tailed mongooses, civets and genets are also frequent nocturnal sightings. Relocations are still ongoing with plans to bring some 700 animals to the area around Nkondo by the end of 2015. At a later stage, African Parks may even consider reintroducing rhino.

Birds The Bangweulu area's big attraction is the unusual and rare shoebill (see box, page 339), a massive grey bird sometimes known as the whale-headed stork. The population of shoebills in Bangweulu is reckoned to be as high as 1,000, making this a vital refuge for this very threatened species. They do not migrate, and so are particularly sensitive to disturbance. They breed in the papyrus here, in May and June, and nowhere else in southern Africa – so visitors should be careful not to disturb them when they are sitting on their nests.

African Parks have initiated a successful 'Shoebill Guardian' project among the local fishing communities, offering them a financial incentive if they report shoebill nests and help protect them until the birds fledge. Don't be surprised if you see a shoebill near the staff house at Chikuni: rescued birds occasionally spend time here before, if possible, being released to the wild.

Aside from the elusive shoebill, the birdlife in the wetlands is amazing throughout the year, making it well worth the effort required to get here. The commoner birds include the little, cattle, black and great white egrets; black-headed, purple, squacco and grey herons; sacred, glossy and hadeda ibis; knob-billed, yellow-billed, fulvous and white-faced whistling ducks; open-billed storks, pygmy geese, pratincoles and grey-headed gulls. Plovers are well represented, with blacksmith, wattled, three-banded, crowned, Caspian and long-toed varieties – and recently there's also been an influx of spurwing plovers.

Migrants that stop here while the floodwaters are high include flamingos, whilst pelicans and spoonbills are normally resident. Meanwhile Bangweulu is a very important reserve for wattled cranes, which occur in large flocks and are readily seen. (There are greater numbers here than almost anywhere else, with the possible exception of the Kafue Flats.) The wetlands' shallow waters are ideal for smaller waders, like sandpipers, godwits and avocets. Other smaller birds worthy of particular note include the swamp flycatcher, lesser jacana, white-cheeked bee-eater (aka blue-breasted in east African literature) and Fülleborn's and rosy-breasted

With thanks to Stephanie Debere

The huge, rare and prehistoric-looking shoebill is found only in a few inaccessible spots between southern Sudan and northern Zambia – making it Africa's most sought-after species for birdwatchers.

Shoebills stand up to 1.4m tall, with a strong likeness to the dodo. They have always been named for their ungainly beaks, which resemble a wooden shoe, and older literature refers to them as whale-headed storks, whilst Arab traders knew them as *abu markub,* which means 'father of the shoe'. Their scientific name, *Balaeniceps rex,* means 'king whalehead'.

Shoebills can look rather sinister when viewed head-on, with their massive beaks and a frowning glare, but in profile they appear charmingly dolphin-like with a mouth that apparently smiles, and huge eyelashes. Despite this beguiling look, their mandibles are razor sharp; their upper bill ends in a curved hook that's used to pierce and hold their slippery prey. Their plumage is bluish slate-grey, with a slightly darker head which sports a small tuft of feathers that can be raised to form a crest. Their legs are long and dark, and their toes lack any webbing.

Shoebills inhabit a precise ecological niche: they specialise in feeding on large fish that live in poorly oxygenated waters of swamps and wetlands – particularly lungfish. They are usually seen standing motionless beside slow, deep-water channels, particularly in areas where fish concentrate – like the narrow channels where spreading waters spill out onto seasonally flooded areas. They remain still for hours, waiting for fish to surface for air, when they ambush with a swift and powerful strike. They will prey on species other than lungfish, and are also said to take amphibians, water-snakes, monitor lizards, terrapins, rats, young waterfowl and, some sources report, even young crocodiles.

Although they prefer to hunt in fairly open areas, where it's easy for them to take off if disturbed, they nest in large, flat nests found in denser vegetation – often papyrus. Between one and three eggs are laid, though only one chick usually survives. It takes about four and a half months for this silvery-grey chick to fledge and become independent, then a further three or four years until it first breeds.

Taxonomists have long debated if the shoebill is a member of the stork, the heron or the pelican family, as various characteristics suggest one or another. However, DNA studies now conclude that shoebills are closely related to pelicans, but in a family of their own.

Given their restricted and remote habit, shoebills are incredibly difficult to study and consequently relatively little is known about them. Estimates of the total world population seem to be around the 5,000–10,000 mark. We know that their main stronghold is in the Sudd, in southern Sudan, and that they are also found in Murchison Falls National Park in Uganda, the Moyowosi-Kigosi Swamp in western Tanzania, Manovo-Gounda-Saint Floris National Park in the Central African Republic, and, allegedly, in Akagera National Park in Rwanda (though nobody on the ground in Rwanda seems to know about them!).

We also know that they are, sadly, occasionally sold for meat by local people and for profit by foreign collectors – as shoebills are one of the most expensive birds in the trade. So if you are fortunate enough to see them, try to keep your distance and minimise any disturbance.

Bangweulu Area   THE BANGWEULU WETLANDS

11

longclaws (which is the local name for the birds known as pink-throated further south). There are plenty of raptors around, with fish eagles, marsh harriers and bateleur eagles particularly common. On the flat grass plains around the wetlands, Denham's bustards are frequently seen striding around.

WHEN TO GO There are many reasons to come to Bangweulu – only one of which is the birding. So choose your season carefully.

January and February are the heart of the rainy season, when the waters are rising. It's the worst time of year for the small, biting lechwe flies and other insects, so insect repellent is vital. Arriving with a head-net, covering your face and neck below your hat, would not be going too far.

This is a great time for birding, as many of the residents will be in breeding plumage, and there will be lots of migrants around – although shoebills usually arrive only at the end of February. The lechwe are in the swamps at this time, whilst other mammals have retreated to the woodlands on the margins of the water.

Water levels peak in **March**, though the rains draw to a close only around April. From **May** the water levels start slowly to recede and travelling begins to get easier by the end of the month. This is the best time to go for shoebills, which are often seen within sight of Shoebill Camp, along with countless other wading and water-loving species. Like many of these birds, visitors to Bangweulu will often spend a lot of time wading if they're keen to see shoebills at close range!

Towards the end of this period and into **June and July**, the waters pull back from the flat, seasonally flooded plains around the wetlands, exposing large areas of fertile, open grasslands – like the Chimbwi Plain. These attract huge herds of black lechwe along with tsessebe and other herbivores from the woodland margins. It's a great time for game drives, with night drives often yielding genets, side-striped jackals, civets and various mongooses. In the wetlands, the water has receded further and the shoebills have moved closer to the lake – so seeing them involves longer mokoro (dugout canoe) journeys from Shoebill Camp. That said, in early June I managed half-a-dozen sightings in one long day – and even later in July you are still almost guaranteed to see a shoebill if you apply enough effort. Though days are warm, the nights are very cold – with temperatures dropping to almost freezing.

In **August and September** the floodplains and outer reaches of the wetlands become even drier; Shoebill Camp is no longer an island, and most wildlife viewing is done on foot or by 4x4. The shoebills have retreated into the permanent swamps, and it takes a bit of determination (and a mini-expedition) to get close to them, though in recent years it has been very possible to see them at this time of year. The Lukulu River is the focus of much wildlife, whilst concentrations of storks and other birds form 'fishing parties' in the remnants of drying pools where fish and snails are stranded.

By **October** the land is parched and dusty everywhere except deep in the heart of the wetlands, far from Shoebill Camp. In **November and December** the first rains bring some relief, as well as a flush of new grass on the plains, which attracts massive herds of black lechwe back from the wetlands, and tsessebe in more moderate numbers from the woodlands.

GETTING THERE Getting to Bangweulu isn't always easy. You'll need to do one of the following:

- Organise a special 'mobile' trip here with an experienced safari company. (I know of none that regularly runs trips here – although the Kasanka team will sometimes organise 4x4 transfers to/from Bangweulu.)

- Fly into here, and then continue by flying out. This is how most people visit; although not cheap it is the easiest way to organise, and the most relaxing way to visit.
- Drive in here with your own fully equipped 4x4. This isn't easy or quick, but it can be fun if you've an adventurous streak and can be self-sufficient.

Organised trips There's only one company working on the ground in this area at present: the Kasanka Trust, who run Kasanka National Park and Shoebill Camp (page 344 for contact details, and http://kasankanationalpark.com for an informative website). You can book a trip with them directly or, more usually, arrange it through the tour operator (pages 43–5) who is organising the rest of your trip in Zambia for about the same price as booking direct.

Cycling tours African Parks and the Kasanka Trust are keen to encourage cycling in the Bangweulu area. It is an authentic, adventurous way to see the plains, with good paths to cycle, friendly guides and wide open spaces. You'll be sharing the paths with local people, for whom bicycles are central to their way of life.
The cycling 'season' is during the traditionally dry months, between June and December. At present there is no specific cycling product on offer, but routes can be tailor made. One recent group travelled from Kasanka, via Shoebill, all the way up to Shiwa N'gandu and then into the Luangwa valley. Another good route would be Kasanka National Park–Shoebill/Chikuni–Lavushi Manda National Park. Interested cyclists should contact Kasanka well in advance in order to arrange guides, park permits, river crossings and, if necessary, bush camping.

Fly-in trips These must be pre-arranged. You can fly in to Shoebill Camp, as there is an airstrip (called Chimbwe) at Chikuni, just 3km from the camp. You'll be transferred to the camp from there, and your activities will be arranged for you. There is currently no 'schedule' for these flight transfers, and so they are relatively costly for one person because you need to hire the whole plane. Consequently, the price becomes more economic for two or three passengers. Flying in will give you a view of the wetlands and surrounding plains that you can't get from the ground – it's fascinating!

Day trips These can be organised through Remote Africa Safaris (page 264) for guests staying more than four nights at their Tafika Camp in South Luangwa, using Tafika's own light aircraft to fly from Lukuzi airstrip to Chimbwe over the escarpment and Bangweulu's wetlands. Activities during the day include a guided game drive, a shoebill excursion in a fibreglass 'dug-out' canoe or banana boat, and a picnic lunch. For visitors short on time, this is an excellent way of combining Bangweulu with South Luangwa. The flights take a maximum of four people and cost from US$530, depending on numbers travelling.
With advance notice, it is also possible to organise a day trip for guests at Kasanka; see page 344.
In early May, Robin Pope Safaris (pages 264–5) operate a six-night 'Shoebill Safari' that combines a trip to Shoebill Camp with their Nkwali lodge in the South Luangwa and Kasanka National Park (*US$5,169 pp sharing FBA, inc transfers from Lusaka, for a minimum of four people*).

Driving yourself From around November to early May, driving yourself on any of these routes can be very challenging – not to say wet, muddy and very slow. If you don't know what you're doing, you're likely to get stranded. By contrast, in the dry season it is fine, although note that there are very few vehicles on some of these tracks, and you always need a fully equipped 4x4 – with your own food and supplies. See also page 325 for details of the Open Africa route that covers this region.

From Chiundaponde to Chikuni If you're approaching from Waka Waka, then to reach Bangweulu just continue straight through Chiundaponde, heading roughly north. After leaving the village, you'll find the track bends slowly round to the right before crossing a small bridge. Barely 500m after this bridge is a left turn (TUSBIL 12°13.451'S, 30°35.330'E) onto a track which is small and easy to miss; this leads northwest to Bangweulu. This turning is about 4km east of Chiundaponde, and a fraction under 2 hours' drive from Waka Waka.

Barely 100m north of the turning is a scout post – and it's always worth checking with the scouts here for the latest news and directions. (There's a fairly reliable radio here that's in close touch with Chikuni and, in case of problems, could even reach Kasanka.) Follow the track northwest, and after about 19km you'll pass Mwelushi Middle Basic School. In another 20km you'll reach Muwele village (TUMUWE 11°59.226'S, 30°22.850'E) where the track splits; the left fork leads in a more westerly direction towards Chikuni. At times this track resembles more of a footpath than a road, but don't give up!

About 6km after the village, the road forks (TUNSOB 11°59.098'S, 30°19.720'E), with the left turn going to Nsobe Camp. If you continue straight on, without turning to Nsobe, you will soon emerge from low scrub into a plain of open grass, stretching for as far as you can see. (Look around you – that dark reddish colour on the horizon may just be thousands of black lechwe!) Here you'll see the start of a long causeway leading to Chikuni, which has recently been repaired and raised. In recent years it has been better, in the dry season, to follow the vehicle tracks which run parallel to the causeway. In the wet season you really need experienced, up-to-date local advice – which, when levels are low, will generally be to splash through the water on existing tracks. During periods when water levels are very high, Chikuni has been inaccessible by vehicle.

However you are proceeding across the plains, about 8km after the turning to Nsobe, you reach the Chikuni Research Post (CHIKUN 11°58.097'S, 30°15.279'E). Chikuni literally stands out as it's on top of a small rise in the plains, marked very clearly by a tall eucalyptus tree. This is one of the few trees within sight on the plains; there is another at Kaleha, about 8km east along the Lukulu River.

If you're going to Shoebill Camp then you need to have pre-arranged your stay, and Chikuni is often the rendezvous point where you leave your vehicle, and continue by mokoro; in any case, you should stop, check with the scouts, and sign the register. The scouts here have a radio to contact Shoebill Camp (as well as the ZAWA scout post on the road from Chiundaponde). Somewhere beyond Chikuni, depending on water levels, the wetlands begin.

From Chikuni to Shoebill You should pre-book your time at Shoebill Camp, so take advice from the Kasanka team about how to get from Chikuni to Shoebill at the time of year when you are going. If the water's high (typically January to June) then you may need to leave your vehicle at Chikuni and reach the camp by mokoro (K105 pp).

Later in the year you should be able to drive, in which case you sign in with the scouts at Chikuni and then pass straight through. Follow the direction of the airstrip for part of its length, and then hit out at 30° to your right, where you should

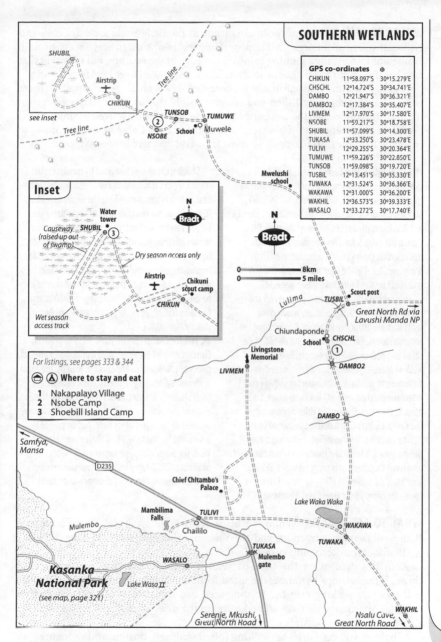

SHUBIL

Airstrip

Tree line

CHIKUN

TUNSOB

TUMUWE

NSOBE

School

Muwele

Tree line

see inset

Mwelushi
school

GPS co-ordinates	⊕	
CHIKUN	11°58.097'S	30°15.279'E
CHSCHL	12°14.724'S	30°34.741'E
DAMBO	12°21.947'S	30°36.321'F
DAMBO2	12°17.384'S	30°35.407'E
LIVMEM	12°17.970'S	30°17.580'E
NSOBE	11°59.217'S	30°18.758'E
SHUBIL	11°57.099'S	30°14.300'E
TUKASA	12°33.250'S	30°23.478'E
TULIVI	12°29.255'S	30°20.364'E
TUMUWE	11°59.226'S	30°22.850'E
TUNSOB	11°59.098'S	30°19.720'E
TUSBIL	12°13.451'S	30°35.330'E
TUWAKA	12°31.524'S	30°36.366'E
WAKAWA	12°31.000'S	30°36.200'E
WAKHIL	12°36.573'S	30°39.333'E
WASALO	12°33.272'S	30°17.740'E

Inset

Water
tower

Causeway
(raised up out
of swamp)

SHUBIL

3

N

Bradt

Dry season access only

Airstrip

Chikuni
scout camp

CHIKUN

Wet season
access track

N

Bradt

0 ———— 8km
0 ———— 5 miles

Lulima

TUSBIL

Scout post

Great North Rd via
Lavushi Manda NP

Chiundaponde

School

CHSCHL

1

DAMBO2

Livingstone
Memorial

LIVMEM

DAMBO

For listings, see pages 333 & 344

🏠 Ⓐ **Where to stay and eat**

1 Nakapalayo Village
2 Nsobe Camp
3 Shoebill Island Camp

Samfya,
Mansa

D235

Chief Chitambo's
Palace

Lake Waka Waka

Mambilima
Falls

TULIVI

Mulembo

Chaililo

WAKAWA

TUWAKA

TUKASA

WASALO

Mulembo
gate

**Kasanka
National Park**

(see map, page 321)

Lake Wasa II

Serenje, Mkushi,
Great North Road ↓

Nsalu Cave,
Great North Road ↘

WAKHIL

11

find the tracks of other vehicles to the Shoebill Island causeway. If in doubt, try scanning the flat horizon for Shoebill's distinctive rectangular water tower amongst a patch of small trees.

Facing the camp, you will need to bear slightly to the left in order to join the beginning of the causeway (or later on, depending on the water levels). However, the route varies a lot with the particular season, and so it's vital that you get directions from the team at Kasanka, or the scouts at Chikuni, before you try to drive here.

WHERE TO STAY There are two main camps in the Bangweulu area: Shoebill and Nsobe. If you're on an organised trip, or flying in, then you'll be staying at Shoebill. Nsobe was historically a hunting camp on the edge of the swamps, but now that that area has been afforded higher protection it has been taken over by African Parks.

If you're driving yourself in a self-contained 4x4 with all your supplies (there is no other sensible way!) then you could possibly stop at Nakapalayo village on the way to Bangweulu (the campsite at Muwele village is no longer recommended except in an emergency). However, note that Shoebill Camp is further into the wetlands than the other camps – so most trips end up there at some stage!

Shoebill Island Camp [map, page 343] (5 Meru-style tents, camping) Contact via Kasanka (page 326). ⊕ SHUBIL 11°57.099'S, 30°14.300'E. Shoebill Camp stands on a small, permanent island, just 2.5km northwest of Chikuni as the stork flies. During the rains & for a few months afterwards, this is within the wetlands, surrounded by channels & lagoons. Later in the year, it's left high & dry & accessible by 4x4 from Chikuni (see page 342).

Substantial refurbishment is planned for the camp until August 2016, possibly moving the tents to more attractive locations & improving the common areas. For now, though, it's an old-style safari camp, & facilities are simple. Each of the walk-in Meru-style tents has a private reed-walled bathroom at the back, with a bucket shower (hot water supplied on request) & a flush toilet, both open to the stars. During the drier months when the campsite isn't flooded, it is possible to camp.

The camp's other buildings, including a bar/dining area & a breakfast room-cum-lookout point, also have thatched roofs on grass walls. During your stay, do make the effort to climb the water tower for camp's best view over the swamps.

Shoebill Camp isn't luxurious by modern safari standards, but it is comfortable & remains by far the best option in this area, where the environment, flora & fauna are fascinating, & the activities (see below) can be excellent. This is a great destination for the adventurous who are keen on their wildlife, but it really needs to be booked in advance. US$65 pp sharing self catering; US$425 FB, inc activities (best pre-arranged), laundry, park fees. Note that rates may be subject to change following camp refurbishment. Camping US$20 pp. ⊕ All year when accessible, usually Mar–Nov. **L–LL**

Nsobe Camp [map, page 343] (6 pitches) Contact African Parks; e bangweulu@african-parks.org; www.africanparks.eu. Run by the local community, Nsobe is a pretty basic campsite with showers & toilets, but its location on the edge of the plains is a big plus. In time there may be reed-&-thatch chalets here, but at present it's purely for those with all their own camping kit & supplies, although firewood & water are available. US$10 pp plus US$10 pp conservation levy. ⊕ approx May–Oct depending on rains

WHAT TO SEE AND DO While the black lechwe are spectacular, the birdlife is Bangweulu's main attraction, and the ungainly shoebill (see box, page 339) is a particular favourite among visitors.

Activities depend on the time of year; if there isn't enough water to travel through the swamps by canoe, the usual form of water transport, then the guides will take you walking over the floating reed bed in search of shoebills and other wildlife. Alternatively, drives will take you to the drier areas of the plains and into the surrounding woodlands.

Whatever you do – driving, walking (often wading!), boating and canoeing – all activities should be done with a guide.

For those staying at Shoebill Camp on a full-board basis, this includes activities. For campers, however, and those who are self-catering, activities are charged extra: around US$30 per person for a half-day boat trip (up to 3 people), and US$40 pp for a half-day game drive (3–6 people).

As you might expect from an area which is seasonally flooded, and whose name translates as 'where the water meets the sky', Bangweulu is a largely trackless wilderness. It is easy to get lost if you simply head into it alone, and indiscriminate driving does much damage to both the soil structure and the ground-nesting birds. It is strongly recommended on safety and conservation grounds that 4x4 owners use one of the camps as a base for their explorations, and take local advice about where to go and how to minimise their environmental impact.

ISANGANO NATIONAL PARK

(*Park fees US$5 pp/day; vehicle US$15/day*) East of Lake Bangweulu, Isangano National Park covers 840km² of flat, well-watered grassland. The western side of the park forms part of the Bangweulu Wetlands, which are seasonally flooded.

While the park's ecosystem was originally the same as that of the Bangweulu GMAs, it is reliably reported that the game in Isangano has totally disappeared because of settlement, agriculture and the consequent subsistence hunting. There is no internal road network within the park at all, though there is quite a high density of subsistence farmers settled within its boundaries. With this in mind, it's very doubtful that Isangano will ever become a national park in anything but name. Visitors are advised to look toward the Bangweulu area if they want to visit this type of region. At least there is some infrastructure, and the local communities in the area will derive benefit from your visit.

SEND US YOUR SNAPS!

We'd love to follow your adventures using our *Zambia* guide – why not send us your photos and stories via Twitter (@BradtGuides) and Instagram (@bradtguides) using the hashtag #zambia. Alternatively, you can upload your photos directly to the gallery on the Zambia destination page via our website (*www.bradtguides.com*).

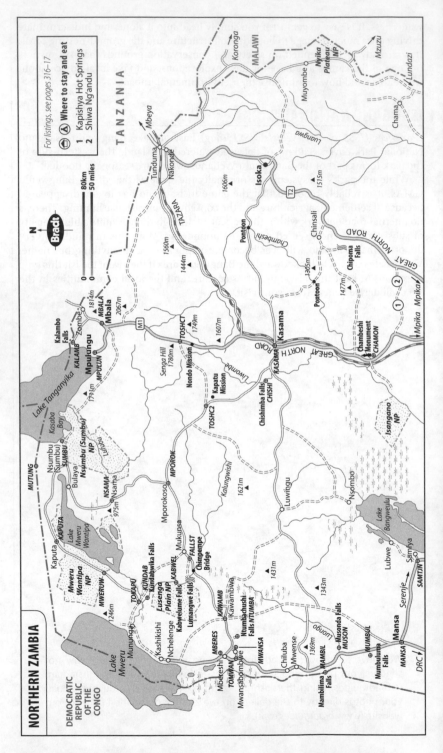

NORTHERN ZAMBIA

DEMOCRATIC
REPUBLIC
OF THE
CONGO

TANZANIA

MALAWI

For listings, see pages 316–17

Where to stay and eat
1 Kapishya Hot Springs
2 Shiwa Ng'andu

0   80km
0   50 miles

N

Bradt

12

Northern Zambia

To explore northern Zambia properly, and to visit the national parks here, requires some determination, or at least advance planning. All of the area's three main national parks have suffered from neglect over the years. However one, Nsumbu (also referred to as Sumbu), is hanging on with a couple of small lodges that could lead to a promising future. This large reserve is bounded by GMAs and Lake Tanganyika, one of the largest lakes in east Africa's Great Rift Valley, with a rich aquatic life found nowhere else. As well as more traditional safari pursuits, it offers snorkelling, diving and fishing, and it's a pleasant place to relax.

The north's other two parks, Mweru Wantipa and Lusenga Plain, may take more to get them back on the map, as neither has organised facilities for visitors, or good roads. Years of poaching have reduced the populations of game animals within them, and what animals are left remain shy and understandably wary of humankind. Outside the national parks, this part of northern Zambia is a fascinating area, and there are numerous sights and waterfalls at which to stop and wonder.

Finally, a word about Nyika, a high plateau that straddles the Malawi border and provides the Luangwa with many of its tributaries. There are national parks on both sides of the border. Nyika Plateau National Park, on the Zambian side, is unlike anywhere else in the country: high mountains clothed in rolling heathlands and often draped with mist. It's a great walking destination, a cool respite after the heat of the Luangwa Valley and home to numerous endemic species. However, it's easiest to access from the east, from Malawi, and so we are just mentioning it here and you can read more about it in our Malawi guide (page 381).

GETTING ORGANISED

Most tour operators based in Zambia specialise in wildlife safaris, but one specialises in northern Zambia (as well as further afield):

Thorn Tree Safaris m 0974 436267; e thorntreesafaris@yahoo.com; www. thorntreesafaris.com; https://www.facebook.com/ Thorn-Tree-Safaris-Zambia-458071970998498/. Run by Claire Powell, daughter of the owners of Thorn Tree Guesthouse, & her husband, Sean Van Niekerk, Thorn Tree Safaris is a mobile-safari operation that organises bespoke adventures, safaris & challenges country wide, but are specialists on Northern Zambia as Claire was born here & speaks the local language, Bemba,

fluently. All trips are tailor-made, & can combine such diverse activities as diving & dhow safaris on Lake Tanganyika, paddling a mokoro through the Bangweulu swamps, cycling through Zambia, Malawi, Botswana, Namibia &/or Tanzania, & tiger fishing on the Chambeshi River, with more conventional wildlife safaris. Claire & Sean are also heavily involved in charity work & organise cycle challenges (with their 60 imported mountain bikes, fleet of vehicles & overland truck) as often as monthly to raise funds for worldwide, as well as local, charities; contact them to ride or get involved with one of the many causes (& if this wasn't enough they also have a strong reputation as fixers should you need to shoot a film/documentary/or advert in Zambia).

THE GREAT NORTH ROAD TO MPULUNGU

The Great North Road stretches from Lusaka through Kapiri Mposhi to Mpika. Here it divides, with one fork going through Kasama and on to Mbala and Mpulungu – about 1,150km. This is the region's main artery, tarred all the way and – having been resurfaced in 2009/10 – now largely free of the pot-holes that have dogged it for years.

KASAMA Kasama is centrally located, about 860km from Lusaka. Visitors to northern Zambia will invariably end up spending some time here, even if only to refuel and buy a few soft drinks. It is a busy little town, the regional capital, with lots going on. As it acts as a supply centre for much of the north of the country, there are some well-stocked stores, and a relatively large amount of traffic coming into, and leaving, town.

Getting there

By air Kasama has a regular connection with Lusaka. Flights operated by Proflight (page 65) leave and return to Lusaka on Monday, Tuesday, Thursday and Friday depending on the time of year. For charter flights, the regional specialist is Sky Trails (page 65).

By train The TAZARA station is about 7km south of town, on the right as you enter from Mpika. This is your last chance to disembark at a major town before the

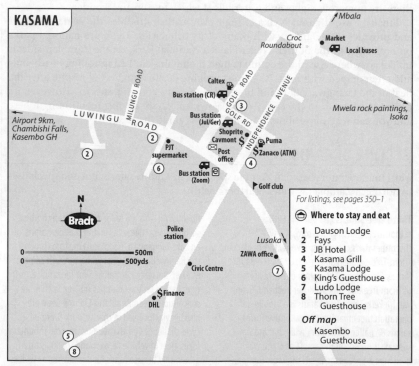

KASAMA

For listings, see pages 350–1

Where to stay and eat

1 Dauson Lodge
2 Fays
3 JB Hotel
4 Kasama Grill
5 Kasama Lodge
6 King's Guesthouse
7 Ludo Lodge
8 Thorn Tree Guesthouse

Off map
Kasembo Guesthouse

CHAMON	10°54.634'S, 31°05.344'E		MPULUN	08°45.907'S, 31°06.368'E
CHIMBR	09°33.082'S, 29°26.937'E		MUMBUL	10°55.801'S, 28°44.178'E
CHISHI	10°06.465'S, 30°55.100'E		MUSON	10°42.856'S, 28°48.858'E
FALLST	09°32.239'S, 29°27.874'E		MUTUNG	08°33.839'S, 30°12.405'E
KABWEL	09°31.432'S, 29°21.267'E		MWANSA	09°49.250'S, 28°45.350'E
KALAMB	08°35.831'S, 31°14.397'E		MWERUP	08°53.572'S, 29°28.878'E
KAPUTA	08°28.503'S, 29°39.990'E		NSAMA	08°53.448'S, 29°56.896'E
KASAMA	10°12.440'S, 31°11.290'E		NSUMBU	08°31.221'S, 30°28.629'E
KAWAMB	09°47.605'S, 29°04.675'E		NTUMBA	09°51.167'S, 28°56.652'E
KUNDAB	09°13.058'S, 29°18.258'E		SAMFYA	11°20.437'S, 29°33.526'E
MAMBIL	10°33.791'S, 28°48.858'E		SAMTJN	11°21.126'S, 29°29.453'E
MANSA	11°12.076'S, 28°53.451'E		TOKAPU	09°07.531'S, 29°12.996'E
MBALA	08°50.694'S, 31°22.325'E		TOMWAN	09°49.317'S, 28°45.474'E
MBERES	09°44.078'S, 28°47.350'E		TOSHCT	09°27.486'S, 31°13.136'E
MPOROK	09°21.831'S, 30°07.432'E		TOSHC2	09°40.270'S, 30°41.628'E

railroad turns east, away from Lake Tanganyika, towards the border at Tunduma. The express train from Kapiri Mposhi to Dar es Salaam passes through Kasama early on Wednesday at 03.09 and the slower train on Saturday at about 02.49, returning at 22.07 on Tuesday and 00.11 on Sunday respectively. For details, see pages 389–90.

By bus Kasama is an important regional hub for buses between Lusaka and the north, linking the town with Mbala and Mpulungu on Lake Tanganyika. Confusingly, each bus company has its own terminus, though the most reliable – Juldan Motors – is based on Golf Road.

Regular buses run from both Lusaka and the Copperbelt to Kasama and on to Mpulungu. Fares are K160 each way.

There is also a postbus to Kasama from Lusaka, arriving in the town every Monday, Wednesday and Friday at about 17.00. The one-way fare is K140.

For those heading west to Luwingu, the bus station is on the Luwingu Road towards the airport.

Going east is usually fairly straight forward. The road to Nakonde is pretty good, though it's worth checking the state of the roads at the end of the rainy season. If any of the pontoons are out of action, there's usually a sign on the way out of town saying so. An alternative option is to take the TAZARA train to Nakonde, at the border, then continue south by bus.

Hitchhiking Kasama is a good place for hitching. If you want to go north, to Mbala or Mpulungu, walk out beyond the roundabout with the crocodile statue, near the market, and start hitching there.

If you're heading south towards Mpika then you need to walk out past the TAZARA station, or perhaps a little further, hitching as you walk. There are some memorable speed humps on this road, which should slow down even the most ardent of speed-kings to a crawl.

Heading west or east is more difficult, as there is much less traffic. However, a traveller going in either direction is something of a rarity, so novelty value will encourage potential lifts. That said, most drivers will not have a clue where you're heading for.

12

CROSSING INTO TANZANIA AT TUNDUMA

Travellers on the TAZARA train will cross into Tanzania at Tunduma, some 245km northeast of Kasama. This is also a major crossing point for vehicles, with all the attendant queues and hassle that you might expect.

A Tanzanian visa, currently US$50, can be purchased at the border, but you'll need to pay in US dollars cash. There's a foreign exchange service at the bank near the immigration office.

To cross the border with a vehicle, you will require a temporary import permit (TIP) in place of a carnet, supplied on presentation of copies of your passport, the vehicle's registration document and the exit document from Zambia. A month's road tax costs a further US$25, also payable in US dollars cash, and you'll also need to purchase third party insurance.

Where to stay and eat There's no shortage of places to stay in Kasama, which boasts over 30 guesthouses. Of these, a few stand out, with Thorn Tree and Kasembo particularly recommended. Note that here more than ever price is no guide to quality.

In town

Kasama Lodge [map, page 348] (11 rooms) Zambia Rd; 0214 221039; e enquiries@zambiahostels.com; www. zambiahostels.com. Opposite Thorn Tree Guesthouse, & professionally run by the Hostels Board of Management, this small hotel has an airy location overlooking the escarpment. En-suite rooms are clean & modern, each with TV, kettle, mosi net & fan, & some with a sofa & fridge too. There's a bar & restaurant serving all meals (**$$**), & at the back is a pleasant courtyard. **$$–$$$**

Thorn Tree Guesthouse [map, page 348] (7 rooms, s/c 2-bed cottage) Zambia Rd; 0214 221615; e kansato@iconnect.zm. Hazel & Ewart Powell came to this area of Zambia to teach in 1969 & stayed on to combine teaching with running a coffee farm & guesthouse. Consequently they've a fund of knowledge on the local area & its people, & can help you get the best out of the region.

Thorn Tree lies about 1km southwest of town, on the edge of an escarpment with a great view; it's a 2-min drive or 10-min walk. Coming from Lusaka, turn left at the main crossroads & continue for about 300m. Pass a park on your right, the government offices on the left, & a police station on the right, then take the right-hand fork & carry on for a further 650m; the guesthouse is on the left. Alternatively, you can arrange for Ewart to collect you from the airport, station or buses.

Aside from a dbl room in the main house, rooms are in a purpose-built block overlooking the garden. All are en suite & have mosquito nets, fans, DSTV & Wi-Fi, & all share a lounge, bar & dining area. Good, family-style meals are served, with most of the ingredients – from oranges & limes to eggs, coffee & tea, & even the jams & peanut butter – produced on the farm. It's a very homely place, suitable for children, where you can easily feel part of the family.

Thorn Tree has a small plunge pool in the grounds, & if you want to play tennis or golf, or swim, or if you need transport to a local attraction such as Chishimba Falls or Mwela Rock Paintings, they can help. For trips farther afield, daughter Claire Powell runs a personal safari company, Thorn Tree Safaris (for details see pages 347–8). **$–$$**

Other reasonable guesthouses (**$–$$**) in town to try are **Dauson Lodge** (7 rooms; Luwingu Rd; 0214 221440), **JB Hotel** (30 rooms; Golf Rd; 0214 221452), **King's Guesthouse** (14 rooms; 2 Mulilansolo Cres; 0214 221028) and **Ludo Lodge** (9 rooms; Mpika Rd; 0214 221438). All are on the map on page 348.

Out of town

Kasembo Guesthouse [off map 348] (14 rooms) Luwingu Rd; 0214 230065/221158; e kasemboguest@gmail.com or kasembofarms@ gmail.com. ✿ KASEMB 10°13.714'S, 31°07.506'E.

Some 8km west of Kasama, Kasembo Guesthouse is on the farm of the same name. To get there, take Luwingu Rd east for about 750m beyond the airport, then turn left down a farm road (✪ TOKASE 10°13.239'S, 31°07.665'E), signposted to Kasembo Farms, & follow the signs for about 1km to the guesthouse.

Kasembo Farms was founded more than 50 years ago & is now owned & run by the Missionaries of Marianhill. It stretches for about 400ha, & keeps around 200 Friesian cows (40 are milked), 150 pigs, 2,000 hens for egg laying, & a few thousand chickens for the pot. The priests say that they leave things as natural as possible. 'Our vegetable garden has never seen a grain of fertiliser in its existence,' commented one. With most of the basic ingredients grown on the farm, it's no surprise that meals are a highlight here. Several types of local beer & a few spirits are on offer, too.

Accommodation for visitors (of any creed) consists of large rooms grouped in pairs around a grassy central area, shaded by indigenous trees, & near a good pool. Four are en suite & 2 of these have a private sitting room. Others share a toilet & separate shower. Each room has locally made pine furniture with a dbl or twin beds, mosquito nets, a fan, fridge & TV. It's a cool, tranquil spot, completely without hassle. About 80m away in a forest clearing a family house, originally belonging to the son of the former owner, has also been converted to take guests with 4 twin rooms (2 en suite, 2 sharing) & a small pool for children.

Discussions with the missionaries can give you an interesting insight into the area. If you arrive in town & want to stay then ask at the Kasembo Supermarket opposite the central market. **$** *exc b/fast.*

Bushcamping If you just want a quiet place in the bush to camp 'rough' around Kasama, then one very experienced old Zambian hand recommended the old (defunct) Kalungwishi State Ranch to me, about 2 hours' drive from town. He comments that it's a fantastic place to explore and is enormous with very few local people about and lots of nice habitat for birds, including good miombo woodlands and large dambos.

To get there take the Luwingu Road, then turn north before you reach Luwingu (about 20km). Drive past Chitoshi and aim for the headwaters of the Kalungwishi River. (You'll need a good map of the area!) Pass the trig-point tower (from which there is a good view, if you climb it) and take a left into the old ranch. There are two entrance roads to Kalungwishi, and at least one may still have a sign. We haven't had any recent reports about this area though so do check locally first.

The reality is that you can camp safely pretty well anywhere in this region – just be sure to ask if you are near a village.

✗ Where to eat For a bite to eat there are lots of small cafés including **Fays** on Luwingu Road. For something a bit more substantial, head for the **Kasama Grill** on Independence Avenue, close to the crossroads. Their locations are shown on the map on page 348.

If you are driving towards Mbala, you won't go hungry on the road, since 107km north of Kasama you come to a collection of **roadside stalls** near Senga Hill (✪ SENGA 09°21.968'S, 31°14.496'E). These sell all manner of fast food, including chicken and chips, fritters, and delicious potato samosas that almost justify a stop in their own right.

Other practicalities **Shoprite** on Golf Road has a vast array of foodstuffs and commodities.

There are a number of banks and fuel stops in town: Zanaco Bank on Independence Avenue has an ATM and there is a Puma petrol station round the corner on Golf Road. Should you need information on the national parks, there's a **ZAWA office**, next to Ludo Lodge, south of the Golf Club on the Lusaka road.

Excursions around Kasama

Mwela rock paintings (*Entry US$15/7 adult/child; vehicle US$5/day; camping US$15 pp, inc entry*) There are over 700 cave paintings outside Kasama, most of them to the east of the town, making this one of the richest areas for rock art anywhere in Africa. While a few of the images are representational, the tradition here is of enigmatic geometric designs that defy easy interpretation. The art is generally considered to be the work of the Twa people, around 2,000 years old, but has variously been dated to late Stone-Age peoples. The paintings are spread over a wide area across six recognised sites: Sumina, Mulundu and Changa are to the south of the road; Mwela and Muankole to the north; while Luimbo lies in the opposite direction, just beyond the airport on the left. To reach the main sites, take the road towards Isoka, east of Kasama, for about 6km until you see a sign indicating that this is a national monument. Sign in at the kiosk with the caretaker, and he will lead you around the paintings (and would appreciate a tip at the end).

While it's possible to spend hours here, for most casual visitors just a few paintings will suffice to give an idea of the style and scale of the work. Highlights include the *Lion at Sumina*, and a series of three paintings on the Mwela site (❂ MWELA 10°12.250'S, 31°13.958'E). An excellent book on the paintings, *Zambia's Ancient Rock Art: The Paintings of Kasama*, is available in Lusaka; for details, see page 529.

Chishimba Falls (*Entry US$15/7 adult/child; vehicle US$5/day; camping US$15 pp, inc entry*). The Luombe River at Chishimba is harnessed partially to run an unobtrusive hydro-electric station, but the water that is left makes for a super series of waterfalls: one artificial and the other two natural. The first, Mutumuna, has a drop of about 20m where it descends onto a rocky riverbed, and it's probably the prettiest of the three. In the centre, protected by a weir, is Kevala, more of a series of rapids than falls, with a large pool created by the weir. The third, Chishimba itself, is a short walk downstream. Here, water spouts over steep cliffs into a deep, rocky canyon that is, according to legend, inhabited by spirits. If you walk right down to the bottom you can stand behind the curtain of water with the rock face at your back and the water in front of you.

Close to the central weir are a sheltered picnic place and a campsite with flush toilets, and a visitor information centre. Walkways have been constructed between the falls, with thatched viewing shelters at strategic points, but note that at Chishimba Falls in particular there is a sheer drop that is not fenced, so it is important to take extra care. The helpful caretaker is usually happy to act as a guide.

To get to Chishimba (❂ CHISHI 10°06.465'S, 30°55.100'E), head west out of Kasama on the tarred Luwingu Road towards the airport. Continue along here for 25km, to the end of the tar, then turn right onto the wide gravel road to Mporokoso. Follow this for about 11km to a clear signpost to the falls (❂ TOCHIS 10°06.176'S, 30°55.694'E), where you turn left, then right again after about 200m, and continue for a further 500m to a parking area.

Chilambwe Falls (*Entry US$5/3 adult/child; vehicle US$5/day; camping US$10 pp*) About 72km from Kasama on the Mporokoso road, these attractive falls are worth a day trip – though there are no designated facilities for campers. Visitors can also hike to the top of the falls and follow the river through open fields.

Chambeshi Monument (*Entry US$10/5 adult/child; vehicle US$5/day; camping US$15 pp, inc entry*) At the north end of the bridge over the Chambeshi River, about

85km south of Kasama, is a monument beside the road (⊕ CHAMON 10°54.634'S, 31°05.344'E). It marks the place where General von Lettow-Vorbeck, Commander of the German forces in East Africa during World War I, surrendered to Hector Croad, the British District Commissioner, on 14 November 1918.

Von Lettow-Vorbeck and his forces had marched south from German East Africa (now Tanzania). They didn't realise that the war in Europe had been over for three days until told by Croad. Upon hearing the news from the British the Germans agreed to march back to Abercorn (now called Mbala) and there hand over their prisoners to the British. It seems as if it was all very civilised.

Part of the monument is a breech-loading field gun, made in 1890, which was the type that the German forces used during World War I.

Tiger fishing on the Chambeshi River One of Zambia's more remote fishing rivers, the Chambeshi offers tiger fishing in almost guaranteed isolation. Trips of two nights or longer are run between September and April by Thorn Tree Safaris (pages 347–8), using large canvas safari tents complete with hot bucket showers, and with three-course dinners served under the stars.

MBALA The small town of Mbala lies just off the road from Kasama to Mpulungu. From here, the road to Mpulungu descends into the merciless heat of the rift valley – so enjoy the relative cool whilst you can.

Known as Abercorn when the country was under British rule, Mbala was where the German General von Lettow-Vorbeck handed over his prisoners to the British at the end of World War I (see above). Today, it is a quiet backwater notable for the Moto Moto Museum, which is one of the country's best museums. It is also the access point by road for Kalambo Falls (page 354).

Mbala has a couple of **fuel stations**, **two banks**, a **post office** and even a small prison (the old prison building is now a historic monument). You can buy most things in the **shops**, including a decent selection of fresh fruit and vegetables.

Getting there and away Regular long-distance buses ply the route between Lusaka and Mpulungu, stopping at the bus station on Mbala's main street. Typically, southbound buses leave Mbala in the early hours of each morning. The one-way fare to Lusaka is around K180. There are also buses to Kitwe on most days.

Where to stay *Map, page 354.*

🏠 **Lake Chila Lodge** (20 rooms)
m 0977 795241/824499, 0968 503431;
e lakechilalodge@yahoo.com/lakechilalodge@
gmail.com; www.lakechilalodge.com.
⊕ 08°50.389'S, 31°23.085'E. Just 1km northeast of town & right on the perennial Lake Chila, this lodge is set in pleasant gardens. En-suite rooms are spacious with dbl or twin beds & a fridge. There's a bar & a restaurant – whose menu ranges from nshima to pasta & other Western-style dishes – & a boat for excursions on the lake. **$$**

🏠 **New Grasshopper Inn** (22 rooms)
Makanta Rd; 0214 450585. In a relatively peaceful location, but within walking distance of the centre, the New Grasshopper's rooms are pretty basic, but it's a friendly & reasonably secure place to stop for the night. Substantial meals such as chicken with nshima or potatoes are served in the simple restaurant, but the cavernous bar next door could become rowdy at w/ends. **$** *exc b/fast.*

What to see and do
Moto Moto Museum (⊕ MOTOMO 08°49.265'S, 31°21.416'E; ⊕ *09.00–16.45 daily exc Christmas & New Year; entry US$3/1 adult/child*) Opened in 1974, Moto

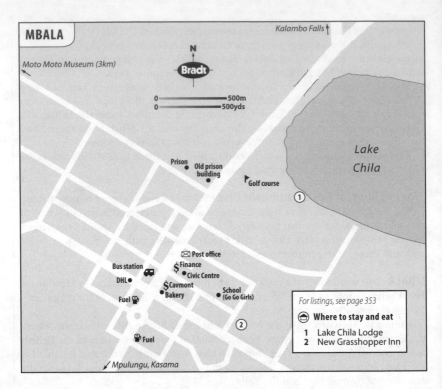

Kalambo Falls ↑

Moto Moto Museum (3km)

N

Bradt

0 ●━━━━━ 500m
0 ●━━━━━ 500yds

Prison ● Old prison
building ●
Golf course ↑

Lake
Chila

①

⊠ Post office
Bus station ⑂ Finance
● Civic Centre
DHL ● ⑂ Cavmont
Bakery ●
Fuel 🏠 School
(Go Go Girls) ●

② ⑭ Fuel

↙ Mpulungu, Kasama

For listings, see page 353
◉ **Where to stay and eat**
1 Lake Chila Lodge
2 New Grasshopper Inn

Moto is perhaps the best place in the country for Bemba history and artefacts. At its heart is an extensive and well-presented collection of tools, craft instruments and exhibits connected to traditional ceremonies and witchcraft, originally assembled by Father Jean-Jaques Corbeil, a French Canadian missionary stationed at the nearby Kayambi Mission. The museum takes its name, though, from Bishop Joseph Dupont, nicknamed Bwana Moto as he smoked a pipe and was renowned for calling for *moto* (KiSwahili for 'fire'). A large-scale reconstruction of a local village serves to put the various artefacts into context, while explanations of the traditional roles of a husband and wife, for example, add fascinating depth.

To get there, head north through Mbala, then turn left off the main road towards Kalambo Falls by the old prison. Continue along this road for about 3km, following the signposts; it's clearly signposted.

KALAMBO FALLS (◈ KALAMB 08°35.831'S, 31°14.397'E; ◷ *06.00–18.00 daily; entry US$15/7 adult/child, vehicle US$5/day, camping US$15 pp inc entry*) For a short distance the Kalambo River marks the boundary between Zambia and Tanzania. At the Kalambo Falls, it plunges over the side of the Great Rift Valley in one vertical drop of about 221m. This is the second-highest waterfall in Africa (after South Africa's Tugela Falls), about double the height of the Victoria Falls, and about the 12th-highest in the world.

The falls may have the impressive statistics, but the real appeal lies in the drama of the setting. On either side of the falls, sheer rock walls frame the river valley far below: Zambia to the south, Tanzania to the north. A large colony of marabou storks breeds in the cliffs during the dry season. The falls themselves are at their most spectacular towards the end of the wet season, in February or March, though are worth visiting at any time.

Archaeology Though few visitors realise it, the Kalambo Falls are also one of the most important archaeological sites in southern Africa. Just above the falls, by the side of the river, is a site that appears to have been occupied throughout much of the Stone Age and early Iron Age. The earliest tools and other remains discovered there may be over 300,000 years old, including evidence for the use of fire.

It seems that the earlier sites of occupation were regularly flooded by the river. Each time this occurred, a fine layer of sand was deposited, thus preserving each layer of remains, tools and artefacts in a neat chronological sequence. Much later, the river cut into these original layers of sand and revealed the full sequence of human occupation to modern archaeologists.

For years Kalambo provided the earliest evidence of fire in sub-Saharan Africa – charred logs, ash and charcoal have been discovered amongst the lowest levels of remains. This was a tremendously important step for Stone-Age humans as it enabled them to keep warm and cook food, as well as to use fire to scare off aggressive animals. Burning areas of grass may even have helped man to hunt. However, more recent excavations of older sites in Africa have discovered evidence of the use of fire before the time when we believe that the site at Kalambo was occupied.

The site is also noted for evidence of much later settlement, from the early Iron Age. Archaeologists even speak of a 'Kalambo tradition' of pottery, for which they can find evidence in various sites in northern Zambia. It seems that the early Iron-Age farmers may have gradually displaced indigenous hunter-gatherers from about the 4th century AD: no further Stone-Age remains are found after that date. However, oral history from northern Zambia, along with the extensive rock art around Kasama, speaks of a recent survival of hunter-gatherers alongside farming peoples.

Getting there
By boat-taxi The mouth of the Kalambo River is around 17km from Mpulungu, so adventurous backpackers can take a boat upstream to near the base of the falls, then return the following day. From the lake it is a fairly strenuous but enjoyable 2½-hour walk to the top of the falls, where camping is allowed. You will need to bring all your own food and equipment.

There's a regular boat service along this route (page 361), three times a week, taking 2 hours in each direction. Boats leave the village of Chipwa very early in the morning, returning from Mpulungu the same day at around midday; as a *mzungu* (white person), you can expect to pay around K25. Since the times are very approximate, you could end up walking into the falls after dark, so it may be better to negotiate a private trip with one of the fishermen in Mpulungu.

A better option by far is to bring all your provisions and stay at one of the lodges nearer the falls – Mishembe Bay or (if either is open) Kalambo or Isanga Bay. Then you can make a day trip to the falls, perhaps even walking there.

Alternatively, small boats that ply between Mpulungu and Kasanga, in Tanzania, can drop you off one day, and pick you up the next.

Driving The falls are about 38km from Mbala, along a graded track. In the dry season it should be possible to get through with a 2WD vehicle. Head north out of Mbala on the tar road towards Zombe and the Tanzanian border. Just past the golf club and lake to the right, the tar comes to an end. Beyond the bridge, take the left fork and continue to a clear signpost (✪ TOKALA 08°45.543'S, 31°06.884'E); turn left here – it's about 6km from Mbala. The road goes through villages and woodland, passing the currently impassable track to Isanga Bay Lodge (✪ TOIBL 08°41.634'S,

12

31°17.969'E) to the left. After 29km, you'll come to a fork (⊕ 08°36.619'S, 31°14.133'E); bear right and follow the road as it descends steeply to the entrance to the falls.

Because of Kalambo's border position, policing it has been difficult in the past, and vehicles left unattended have been likely targets for theft. While this is still a potential hazard, there is a caretaker on site in daylight hours, so the threat is now considerably less.

⋀ Where to stay You can camp here, with stunning views to the west across the rift valley. There's a caretaker on site all day, and a smart new shelter, as well as modern ablution facilities.

LAKE TANGANYIKA AND ENVIRONS

LAKE TANGANYIKA Lake Tanganyika is one of a series of geologically old lakes that have filled areas of the main East African Rift Valley. Look at a map of Africa and you will see many of these in a 'string' down the continent: lakes Malawi, Tanganyika, Kivu, Edward and Albert are some of the larger ones. Zambia just has a small tip of Tanganyika within its borders, but it is of importance to the country. Access to Lake Tanganyika grants Zambia a real port with transport links to a whole side of Tanzania and (during peaceable times) direct access to Burundi. It also makes this one corner of Zambia totally different from the rest of the country, with a mix of peoples and a 'tropical central Africa' feel.

There are some well-established lakeside lodges, those to the east within striking distance of Kalambo Falls, and two in the vicinity of the little-known but viable Nsumbu National Park.

Geography Lake Tanganyika is the deepest of the Rift Valley lakes of central/east Africa, with a maximum depth of about 1,470m, and is the second-deepest lake in the world. It has an area of around 34,000km² and is estimated to be about 10–15 million years old. The surface layers of water are a tropical 24–28°C and support virtually all of the known life in the lake.

Well below these, where it is too deep for the sun's light to reach, are separate, colder waters. Below about 200m, these are deprived of oxygen and hardly mix with the upper layers. They are currently the subject of much scientific study.

The lake has a variety of habitats around its 3,000km or so of shoreline, ranging from flat sands to marshy areas and boulder-strewn shores.

Flora and fauna
Flora The geology of the rocks around the lake has led to the water being unusually hard (between 7° and 11° dH), alkaline (average 8.4 pH) and rich in minerals for a freshwater lake. It is not an ideal environment for normal aquatic plants, so these are generally found near the entry of rivers into the lake but not elsewhere. Various species of algae have adapted to fill this ecological niche, and extensive 'lawns' of grass-like algae cover many of the lake's submerged rocks.

Animals The water's excellent clarity, the lack of cover and the rocky shores do not encourage either hippo or crocodiles, though both are more common around the relatively undisturbed shores of Nsumbu National Park. They are also seen regularly near the mouths of rivers, and their presence must always be considered before you swim. The lake is a reliable source of water for game, which often comes to drink during the dry season. Two reptiles are endemic to the lake: the fish-eating

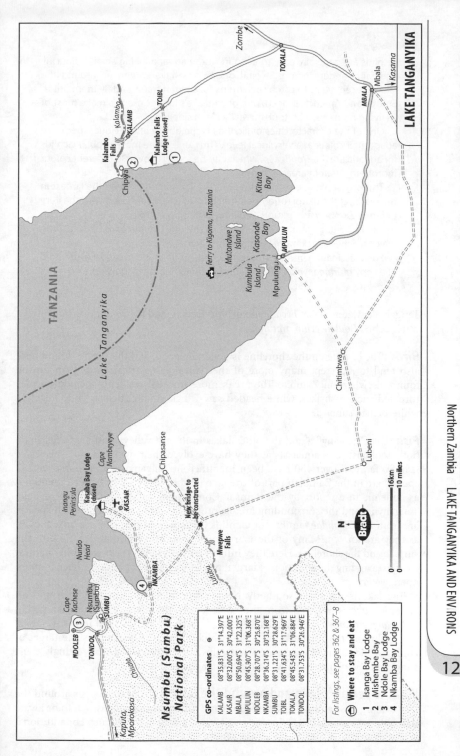

LAKE TANGANYIKA

Zombe

TOKALA

Kasama

Mbala

↓*Kasama*

MBALA

Kalambo

Kalambo
Falls

KALAMB

TOIBL

Kalambo Falls
Lodge (closed) ①

Chipwa ②

Kituta
Bay

Mutondwe
Island

ferry to Kigoma, Tanzania

Kasonde
Bay

MPULUN

TANZANIA

Lake Tanganyika

Kumbula
Island

Mpulungu

Mpulungu

Chitimbwa

Lubeni

Chipasanse

*Inangu
Peninsula*

Kasaba Bay Lodge
(closed)

KASAIR

*Cape
Nambeyeye*

New bridge to
be constructed

Mwewpe Falls

Lufubu

NKAMBA

NKAMBA

*Nundo
Head*

*Cape
Kachese*

Nsumbu
(Sumbu)

MDOLEB

TONDOL

SUMBU

SUMBU

*Kaputa,
Mporokoso*

Chisala

Nsumbu (Sumbu)
National Park

GPS co-ordinates ⊕

KALAMB	08°35.831'S	31°14.397'E
KASAIR	08°32.000'S	30°42.000'E
MBALA	08°50.694'S	31°22.325'E
MPULUN	08°45.907'S	31°06.368'E
NDOLEB	08°28.707'S	30°25.870'E
NKAMBA	08°36.214'S	30°32.168'E
SUMBU	08°31.221'S	30°28.629'E
TOIBL	08°41.634'S	31°17.969'E
TOKALA	08°45.543'S	31°06.884'E
TONDOL	08°31.753'S	30°26.946'E

For listings, see pages 362 & 367–8

ⓘ **Where to stay and eat**

1 Isanga Bay Lodge
2 Mishembe Bay
3 Ndole Bay Lodge
4 Nkamba Bay Lodge

Bradt

N

0   16km
0   10 miles

CICHLIDS

Cichlids are generally easy to keep in home aquaria, being small, colourful, and fairly undemanding. Several operations have sprung up around the lake in recent years to catch specimens for the pet trade, and fly them out to Europe and America. Indeed, one of the lake's lodges used to make most of its living from this, with tourism really just a sideline.

One of the characteristics of cichlids is the ability of individual species to adapt their colour at a very local level. Thus, one of the most popular cichlids for aquaria are the *Trophus sp*, which can be found in over 30 different colour morphs in different areas of the lake.

The largest of the cichlids found in Lake Tanganyika, indeed the largest in the world, is the nkupi (or emperor cichlid, to avoid confusion with the very different Zambezi fish, nkupi), *Boulengerochromis microlepis*, which grows up to 4kg in weight – in marked contrast to the tiny *Lamprologus multifaciatus*, which reaches a maximum length of just 1cm.

For a fascinating insight into the cichlids to be found in the lake, get hold of a copy of *Tanganyika Cichlids in their Natural Habitat* (page 528).

Tanganyika water-snake, *Lycodonomorphus bicolor*, and the venomous Tanganyika water cobra, *Boulengerina annulata*.

Birds The birdlife on the shoreline is generally good, and the species found here also tend to represent many more of the typical east African birds than can be found elsewhere in Zambia. The area's more unusual residents include purple-throated cuckoo-shrikes, white-headed saw-wings, stout cisticolas, and Oustalet's white-bellied sunbird.

Fish Lake Tanganyika and the other lakes in the rift valley continue to fascinate both zoologists and aquarists as they have evolved their own endemic species of fish. So far, well over 450 have been identified in Tanganyika, of which over 252 species are in the Zambian part of the lake (and of those, 82 have been identified as endemic in a report by the Ramsar Convention, under which much of Lake Tanganyika and the surrounding area is protected). Most of the lake's fish species are from the *Cichlidae* family – or cichlids (pronounced sick-lids; see box, above), as they are known. Many of these are small, colourful fish that live close to the surface and the shoreline. Here they inhabit crevices in the rocks and other natural cavities, avoiding the attention of larger, predatory fish that patrol the deeper, more open, waters.

The lake is the most southerly home of both the goliath tiger fish and an endemic species of perch from the *Lates* family, the silver or Tanganyika perch, *Lates angustifrons*. Three smaller species of perch are to be found in these waters, too, including the smallest, the buka, which along with kapenta is the target of commercial fishermen. There are also freshwater jellyfish which, interestingly, don't sting, and – very occasionally – a freshwater coelacanth is sighted.

What to see and do in and around the lake Most of the lodges around the lake can organise a range of watersports and fishing, though it's as well to be aware that if these involve a boat trip, costs will reflect the high cost of fuel. For additional activities around Nsumbu, see pages 370–2.

Swimming, snorkelling and diving Tanganyika is a marvellous lake in which to go snorkelling, or even scuba diving, as the numerous fish are beautifully coloured and there is seldom any need to dive deeply. Visibility depends on the state of the water, but can be as high as 10–20m in places. Halfway between Nsumbu and Mpulungu is a series of cliffs and drop-offs that are of particular interest to divers, while other popular diving spots include the area around Katete.

If you plan on any watersports, you must consider the *safety* issues. Both crocodiles and hippos are common in parts of the lake, but can be very localised. There is also the venomous if non-aggressive Tanganyika water cobra, which grows up to 2m. While it usually avoids swimmers as terrestrial snakes avoid walkers, you should still watch out for it. There is some doubt about the existence of bilharzia in the lake but you should be aware of the possibility (and see pages 85–6 for general guidelines). If you are considering taking a swim, ask advice from the locals about the precise place that you have in mind. They may not be infallible, but will give you a good idea of where is likely to be safe, and where is not.

Fishing Lake Tanganyika (and especially the Nsumbu area) has a first-class reputation in freshwater angling circles, because of the variety of fish that can be caught on rod and line. It is not unusual for visitors to catch a dozen different species in a single visit. The greatest appeal comes from the nkupi, the goliath tiger fish and the Nile perch, the last of which can reach an impressive 80kg in weight.

The best time for fishing is between November and March. Each March sees the annual fishing competition held at Nsumbu off the point near Nkamba Bay Lodge. Fly-fishing is becoming increasingly popular, particularly for nkupi and the perch species. Some of the tropical cichlids will also rise to a smaller fly.

There is considerable concern about the sustainability of commercial fishing on the lake, with the spotlight falling on both over-fishing and the impact of global warming on the breeding habits of the fish. Although fishing with nets is illegal within national park waters, the ban is regularly flouted by local fishermen. Nevertheless, commercial fishing is of significant importance, primarily for two species: the buka and the much smaller kapenta.

MPULUNGU Sitting in the heat of the rift valley, about 38km from Mbala, Mpulungu is Zambia's largest port and due to get a facelift over the next few years. It's a busy place and visited by many travellers, most of whom are Africans but with the odd backpacker thrown in too. The atmosphere is very international, a mix of various southern, central and east African influences all stirred together by the ferries which circle the lake from port to port.

There is a strong local fishing community and a small but thriving business community, complete with a small contingent of white Africans, expats and even aid workers. So though Mpulungu might seem like the end of the earth when you get off a bus in the pitch-black evening, it isn't.

Getting there and away
By bus Mpulungu is at the most northerly end of the main bus route from Lusaka, via Kabwe, Kapiri Mposhi, Mkushi, Serenje, Mpika and Kasama, and Mbala. Buses from Mbala tend to arrive around 07.00, and those heading south leave in the small hours. The fare to Lusaka is around K180. There are several operators on the route, of which the best is considered to be Juldan Motors.

12

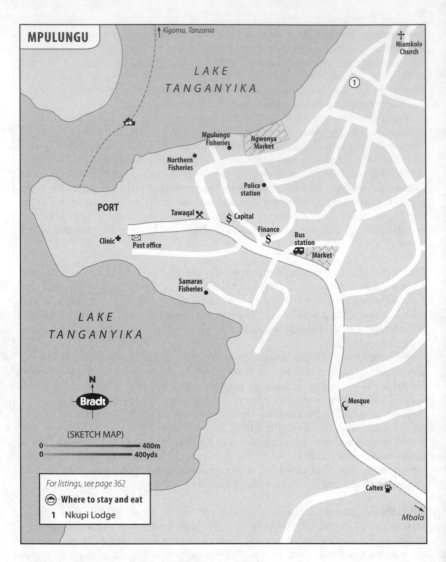

The 'terminus' is on the main road, beside the market – you cannot fail to go through it.

There are also buses to Kitwe every day except Monday, departing around midnight.

Driving Mpulungu is the final town on the Great North Road out of Lusaka. Long pitted with huge pot-holes, the descent from Mbala is now smooth tar and affords some great views of the lake. If you're transferring to one of the Nsumbu lodges, a taxi from Kasama airport to Mpulungu can be arranged for up to ten passengers, albeit at a hefty US$500 for the return trip.

Hitchhiking Hitching here from Mbala in the afternoon is very easy, with lots of lifts. However, getting out in the morning is virtually impossible. Everybody who has a little space in their vehicle goes to the bus terminus near the market and fills up with paying passengers, so few are interested in a stray hitchhiker walking away from the bus station. So, if you want to get out of Mpulungu, go with the crowd and hang around the main market area, quizzing any likely buses or vehicles. Because of the steep, twisting road out of the valley, heavy or under-powered vehicles can be painfully slow, so get a lighter, more powerful lift if you can.

By ferry Only one of the large international Tanganyika passenger ferries on Lake Tanganyika, the MV *Liemba*, is still operational. In theory it calls at Mpulungu every other Friday morning and leaves the same afternoon at around 16.00 – though actual times very much depend on the cargo. For precise dates, bookings and other information, contact either Thorn Tree Safaris (pages 347–8) or Nkupi Lodge (page 362).

From Mpulungu the ferry sails over the Tanzanian border to Kasanga, then to Kigoma in the north of Tanzania, with countless places in between. The journey takes up to two days, technically arriving in Kigoma on Sunday afternoon, and departing on Wednesday at about 16.00.

Ferry tickets fall into three classes. In first-class cabins there is a double bunk with a basin, while second-class cabins sleep four. Third-class passengers take pot luck of seating around the ship. There are also en-suite VIP and family cabins. Bikes may be taken on the ferry, but not cars. Tickets must be bought on the ship, but both the above can assist with bookings. Food and water are available on board.

By boat-taxi If you need a short trip out to one of the lodges on the lake then hire a boat-taxi from the beach-side market. You will need to make sure that the driver knows the lodge that you want, and exactly where it is, and you may want to bargain over the rate a little. Alternatively, if time is on your side, you can use one of the regular boat-taxis that go up the lakeside to the Kalambo River (a 2½-hour walk from Kalambo Falls) on Monday, Wednesday and Friday, stopping at several villages and taking around 2 hours in each direction. Boats leave the falls area very early in the morning, returning from Mpulungu the same day sometime after midday; one-way tickets should be K5, but a *mzungu* can expect to pay nearer K25.

Visitors to Nsumbu (pages 369–70) usually depart from Samaras Fisheries by prior arrangement with one of the lodges. To get there turn left down the gravel road opposite the bus station, which is about 1km after the Caltex garage. Boats usually arrive from Nsumbu on Monday, Wednesday and Friday morning, returning in the afternoon. All passengers must first report to the immigration authorities at the port to notify them of their destination.

No matter where you are heading, it's essential that you have a crystal-clear deal over the price for the trip, including you and all your baggage, before you set off from Mpulungu – as disagreements on arrival (or worse still, on the lake) are bad news for you and the person running the boat.

Getting organised To organise accommodation, or anything else in the area, your best bet is to speak to Claire Powell at Thorn Tree Safaris (pages 347–8). The company maintains a dhow on the lake at Mpulungu, and can organise transfers for up to 15 people, as well as accommodation and trips around the area.

Where to stay If you are backpacking through, or have arrived late in the day, staying in Mpulungu itself for a night or two is probably your best option. The established backpackers' favourite is Nkupi Lodge.

For those wishing to stay longer the choice is widened by a number of lakeside lodges, though these tend to come and go. Almost all are accessible only by boat.

In town

🏠 **Nkupi Lodge** [map, page 360] (9 rooms, camping) 📞 0214 455166; m 0977 456742, 0955 455166, 0966 69397; e nkupilodge@hotmail. com. This relaxed backpackers' retreat has become something of a legend with overlanders, largely because of its laid-back owner, Denish, & a lack of competition. To find it, follow the tar road past the main bus/market area almost to the port, then turn right & follow the coast road; Nkupi Lodge is on the right. While there are more direct roads leading from the market, it's a confusing area, & this is the clearest route. It's about 15–25 mins from town, or K20 by taxi.

Managed by the very helpful & knowledgeable Charity, the lodge has several large thatched rondavels with stone floors, mesh windows, mosi nets & a fan – on mains electricity. The campsite, & all except 1 room (a simple but spacious en-suite dbl), share clean hot showers & toilets. Beer is available, as is scrupulously boiled water. Self-catering is an option, or African & Indian meals can be ordered a couple of hours in advance ($–$$); particularly popular is *nkupi*.

Charity can organise all sorts of activities, from visits to Kalambo Falls to paddle-boat trips to one of the islands, to include a picnic & swimming. Just ask her! *camping K30 pp (own tent); K50 pp in room without bedding.* **$**

Lakeside lodges

🏠 **Isanga Bay Lodge** [map, page 357] (6 chalets, camping) m 0966 646991; e isangabay@gmail.com; www.isangabay. com. North of Mpulungu, about halfway to the Tanzanian border & within hiking distance of Kalambo Falls, Isanga Bay Lodge is usually reached by a ½–1hr boat transfer from Mpulungu (*US$100 return 8 people*); there is safe parking in the town at Samaras Fisheries. In theory you could drive in from the Kalambo Falls road north of Mbala, but the poor 26km track can't be recommended, even in a 4x4. 3 thatched wooden chalets stand on stilts on a beautiful white sandy beach, surrounded by coconut palms & indigenous vegetation. Each has a dbl bed & 2 sgls, all draped with mosquito nets, plus an en-suite shower & toilet, & a veranda facing the lake. Overlooking the rocks are a further 3 stone chalets, similarly equipped. The lodge uses solar power & there are no power points in the rooms but charging facilities for phones/laptops are available. There's also a campsite with hot showers, braai stands & firewood available, & campers can arrange to eat at the lodge. Very good meals are served in a central thatched *insaka*, where there's also a bar. Day visitors are welcome, with activities that include good snorkelling among the rocks, hikes to Kalambo Falls, kayaking, fishing, bird walks & even waterskiing or tubing. *Chalet beach view US$130/200 pp sharing/sgl FB; lake view US$100/160 pp sharing/sgl FB; camping US$20 pp.* **L–LL**

🏠 **Mishembe Bay** [map, page 357] Luke's Beach (3 chalets, camping) m 0976 664999/0967 664999; e mishembebay@gmail.com; https://www. facebook.com/mishembebayzambia. Mishembe is real Robinson Crusoe stuff – just a pure white sandy beach sheltered in its own bay – the last on the Zambian side of the shore. It is accessed in 30mins by private boat (*US$150 return, up to 8 people*), or by water-taxi from Mpulungu taking 1–3hrs (*Mon, Wed & Fri*). Hidden among the trees on wooden platforms overlooking the lake are simple open-sided chalets under thatch, built entirely of local materials & with roll-down canvas walls for protection against the rain. Inside are walk-in mosquito nets around twin or dbl beds, & an en-suite shower & flush toilet. Mishembe Bay s/c lodge is equipped for 6 with a fully kitted-out kitchen inc freezer & gas cooker (own generator/ice & gas/charcoal). Under the palm trees, amongst the baboons, monkeys & birds, there's space for campers, who may use the available equipment. It's a magical place, totally isolated & very good value.

There is very good snorkelling right in the bay, with visibility up to 10m, depending on the wind. The bay is also ideally situated for walks up to Kalambo Falls, about 2½hrs each way. On a more personal level, Mishembe has strong links with the local community, supporting schools in the nearby Miyamba villages, taking visitors to attend church services, & inviting local choirs to sing at the lodge. *Chalets US$25 pp s/c; camping US$10 pp; exclusivity (whole bay) US$250/day.* ⊕ *All year.* **L**

What to see

Just a few kilometres east of Mpulungu, beside the lake, you may see a tall, rectangular turret rising above the shoreline as you head to Kalambo Falls or one of the lodges in a water-taxi. This isn't a fort, but the remains of one of Zambia's oldest churches, Niamkolo Church. It was originally built by the London Missionary Society around 1893–96, but abandoned in 1902 because of health problems suffered by the missionaries. The original buildings were burned, but in 1962 the walls were restored to their former height and cemented into place. Now they're all there is to see. At 80cm thick in places, they may last for another century yet.

NSUMBU (SUMBU) NATIONAL PARK

(*Park fees US$10 pp/day; vehicle US$15/day; fishing US$30 pp/day*) Nsumbu (also referred to as Sumbu) National Park covers about 2,020km², and borders on Lake Tanganyika. It also covers a small part of the lake, which means that those boating in these waters are subject to park entry fees, as well as those on land. To the north- and southwest, the park is adjoined by the 360,000ha Kaputa GMA, while between this and the park to the west is the smaller Tondwa GMA, which is leased out to a small professional hunting operator. These two act as a very effective buffer for the park, keeping the local subsistence hunters/poachers out and giving the game numbers a chance to increase. Combined with the presence of two (and potentially three) lodges in this area, this has made Nsumbu's future look very promising indeed.

On another promising note, Nsumbu is one of several parks in Zambia that have been designated as being 'viable game parks' under a study funded by the EU. In 2012 several prominent conservationists helped Craig Zytkow from Ndole Bay set up a non-profit organisation to preserve and rejuvenate Nsumbu National Park and

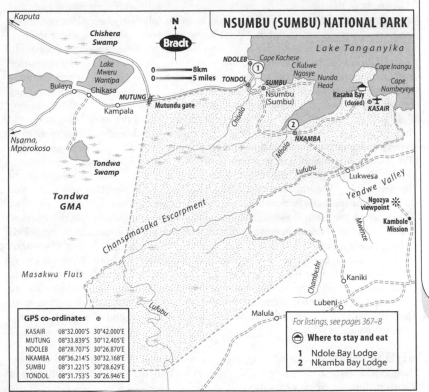

Lake Tanganyika: **Conservation Lake Tanganyika** (CLT) works in close cooperation with ZAWA to promote as well as protect the biodiversity in Nsumbu National Park and the surrounding area. This small NGO (*www.conservationtanganyika.org*) has become the best hope for Nsumbu to return to its former glory as a haven for wildlife through its support for wildlife protection and management. CLT has created the infrastructure for scout housing, provided field equipment for patrols as well as critical scout training and recruitment, and also operates a patrol boat on the waters of the park. Combatting poaching on land is already quite a challenge but nothing like as difficult as trying to clamp down on illegal fishing in an area where virtually everyone depends on fishing for their livelihood and many regard it as a divine right. Altering that perception is not an easy task but CLT are working with the local Community Resource Boards to ensure that the local community is part of the solution going forward, that local residents are involved and participate in the management of the park and GMA, are educated about conservation and, most importantly, can reap the benefits.

FLORA AND FAUNA Nsumbu protects populations of elephant, and a range of antelope including blue and yellow-backed duiker, roan, sable, bushbuck, waterbuck, sitatunga, the occasional zebra and a large number of puku; there are also reports of eland in the hills. Buffalo herds range up to about 400 individuals, and move around between Nsumbu and the neighbouring GMA. The park's main natural predators are lion and leopard, though numbers are uncertain. Although poachers continue to kill occasionally, the animal populations are increasing.

A study in the 1990s concluded that there were still wild dogs in the park and its surrounding GMAs, though there has been no follow-up, and their continued long-term survival was in doubt. I don't know of reports of wild dog since then.

Although Nsumbu cannot yet boast huge herds of the larger antelope, elephant or buffalo, there is sufficient game to make a trip to the park worthwhile. Its vegetation and environment are, on the whole, in pristine condition and offer a real Zambian wilderness experience The partnership between CLT and ZAWA has concentrated on protecting the remaining elephants in Nsumbu, now a much more common sight than in previous years – a measure of the success of the work being done and an indication of the resilience of these amazing animals. Breeding herds of up to 40 elephants are not uncommon now and Nsumbu remains the only place along Lake Tanganyika where elephants survive.

The birding is good, with 295 species recorded in the park and the adjacent Tondwa GMA. A number of east African species occur here that you won't find in the rest of southern Africa. Look out especially for the bare-faced go-away bird, common on the open floodplain areas; also a waxbill known as the red-cheeked cordon bleu, occasional ospreys, palmnut vultures and red-faced crombecs. Pel's fishing owl and bat hawks also occur, though not more commonly than elsewhere.

In the lake itself, there are plenty of hippos and a very healthy population of crocodile – including both Nile crocodile (*Crocodylus niloticus*) and its smaller, endangered cousin, the slender-snouted crocodile (*Crocodylus cataphractus* or *Mecistops cataphractus*). Some are sufficiently large to dissuade you from even thinking of dipping your toe in the water. For details of fish and other reptiles in the lake, see pages 356–58.

GETTING THERE Access has long been the main problem for visitors to the Lake Tanganyika area, and getting to Nsumbu is an added challenge. It's difficult, or time-consuming, or very expensive.

By air The 1,500m airstrip at Kasaba Bay (✈ KASAIR 08°32.00'S, 30°42.00'E) is being upgraded to international standards although work has stalled over the past few years. In time – and hopefully during 2016 – the new airport is expected to have customs and immigration facilities.

Limited amounts of AV-Gas are usually available from the lodges, by prior arrangement.

Normally both Ndole Bay and Nkamba Bay lodges will collect passengers from the airstrip by boat, taking about 30 minutes to Nkamba Bay, or 40 minutes to Ndole Bay, but Nkamba Bay also has its own airstrip and is now under new ownership, see pages 367–8 for more details. Ndole Bay charges US$150–250 per boat for return transfers from the Kasaba Bay airstrip.

Proflight has 4 scheduled flights a week between Lusaka and Kasama via Ndola, arriving in Kasama at 12.30 so that it's possible to get to Nsumbu the same day, by taxi to Mpulungu and then boat. Proflight offers some reasonable tickets: if you book in advance a return flight from Lusaka is about US$230. Expect this to reduce in 2016 as Kasama airport is being expanded and Proflight says they will put on bigger aircraft for better rates.

It is no longer possible to charter a flight from Kasama to Nsumbu, but charters can be arranged out of Ndola.

By boat Though they're at least 75km across the lake, the lodges in Nsumbu most commonly arrange to transfer their guests by boat from Mpulungu, where both use the harbour facilities of Samaras Fisheries (page 361). Each has different speeds and sizes of boat available, at different costs, but expect to pay around US$350 per boat each way. A 'banana boat' (a long, thin chug-chug motorboat with space for up to six people) will take about 4 hours to reach Nsumbu, whereas a traditional wooden dhow, although larger, can take up to 6 hours. Ndole Bay operates a large, high-speed catamaran that covers the distance in 2 hours, taking 2–10 passengers at US$750 return, with the option (by arrangement) of snorkelling/diving *en route* at Cape Chaitika.

Ferry A government-operated ferry now travels between Mpulungu and Nsumbu (near Ndole). The ferry *Stella* travels four times a week in each direction, from Mpulungu (from the old St George fishery) to Nsumbu on Mondays, Tuesdays, Thursdays and Fridays, heading back to Mpulungu on Mondays, Tuesdays, Wednesdays and Fridays. It departs from either point at 07.30 and takes about 6 hours. Ndole Bay offers free pickups and drop-offs to the harbour in Nsumbu for guests.

Transport boats Crowded transport boats ply up and down the lake with frequent stops, so if you don't have a transfer organised, these might be an option – though be prepared for a long wait (sometimes days). Expect to pay from about K80 for the trip, which takes between ten and 18 hours, depending on the number of stops. Alternatively, you could negotiate to hire the whole boat for around US$150 plus about 75 litres of fuel, but make it quite clear that you wish to go direct to your destination, or you could still find yourself stopping everywhere. Either way, ask around at Ngwenya Market in Mpulungu, or by the water taxis at the main market, or – in Nsumbu town – on the beach. Remember that the lake can be rough (and thus you could get wet), and that you'll need to take all food and water for the journey with you.

Driving Nsumbu National Park can be approached relatively easily in a 4x4 via Kaputa or Mporokoso, though neither is a fast option. There is also a 4x4 track from

Mbala as far as the Lufubu River, which defines the park's eastern boundary, with a new bridge supposedly under construction in 2016 to link it through to Nsumbu. It is possible to ford the river in the dry season in a 4x4.

From Mporokoso For the majority of drivers, the most direct approach to the park is from Mporokoso (✪ MPOROK 09°21.831'S, 30°07.432'E; see pages 379–80), a network of dirt roads that has been upgraded and is largely in good condition. Initially, the road heads more or less north through the village of Munyele and on towards Nsama (✪ NSAMA 08°53.448'S, 29°56.896'E), close to the eastern shores of Lake Mweru Wantipa, where there are a few shops, a secondary school and a Catholic church. Keen birdwatchers should note that just north of Nsama there's a patch of miombo woodland where the relatively uncommon white-winged starling is easily spotted. Beyond the town, there are numerous small villages lining the road, but nowhere of note. Despite mention of Bulaya on most maps, don't expect a town here: it's nothing more than a dot on the map.

About 135km from Mporokoso, and 39km before Nsumbu, you'll reach the Mutundu gate (✪ MUTUNG 08°33.839'S, 30°12.405'E), a game checkpoint that marks the beginning of the national park. This is also where the road from Kaputa (the area's administrative centre) joins the road from Mporokoso to Nsumbu.

From here the road runs along the northwestern edge of the park towards Nsumbu town (pages 369–70), with sweeping views over the bay as it descends from the plateau. Some 31km after the Mutundu gate, there's a left turn to Ndole Bay Lodge (✪ TONDOL 08°31.753'S, 30°26.946'E). To reach the national park gate, continue along the increasingly poor main road for a further 8km or so to the turn-off to Nsumbu town. This also marks the entrance to the national park, at Nsumbu gate, and is where you'll have to pay park fees. The road then continues to Nkamba Bay Lodge and Kasaba Bay, within the national park.

From Nchelenge via Kaputa For the first stretch of this route, see *The road to Mweru Wantipa and Kaputa*, pages 370–6.

Beyond Kaputa, the road widens, passing through numerous villages as it crosses the narrow strip between Lake Mweru Wantipa and the DRC border. The lake itself remains out of sight, although fishing nets laid out to dry indicate its proximity to the road. As the road descends, the land around becomes increasingly marshy, with papyrus beds and reeds, and pools dotted with purple water lilies. It's a haven for waterbirds, with reed cormorants, pied and malachite kingfishers, and African jacanas all easy to spot. Eventually, some 83km from Kaputa, you'll emerge onto the Mporokoso–Nsumbu road (see above) at the Mutundu gate (✪ MUTUNG 08°33.839'S, 30°12.405'E), marked on some maps as Kampela, where you turn left for Nsumbu.

Note that the dirt road from Mununga to Nsama (✪ NSAMA 08°53.448'S, 29°56.896'E) along the southern side of Lake Mweru Wantipa is very bad and becoming impassable.

Cross-country from Mbala For many years the poor track between Mbala and Nsumbu has ended abruptly at the Lufubu River, the park's southeastern boundary, with no bridge across. In 2011, however, the combined forces of a looming election and external finance resulted in work on grading the road, and the promise that the bridge would be rebuilt over the river – it may now happen in 2016 but do check locally first before setting out. From the Lufubu River west to Nsumbu a new road covers the remaining 50km. There is a very rough 1km-climb into the park after the river but the road in the park is reasonable.

The reinstatement of this link between the two sides of Lake Tanganyika will offer an attractive option in the dry season for experienced drivers with a strong sense of adventure.

According to Gerard Zytkow at Ndole Bay, 'the countryside is wonderful and the drop from the escarpment into the Yendwe Valley is breathtakingly beautiful.' Follow the sign to Lunzua power station, a new hydro-electricity project about 15km outside Mpulungu on the Mbala road. Go past the hydro plant to a T-junction with the Mbala–Yendwe road.

The turn-off is just 100m or so from the Mbala T-junction on the road towards Mpulungu, with a second access road from just outside Mpulungu.

GETTING AROUND THE PARK The network of roads in the park may have been extended in the last few years but these are largely only game tracks, devised by the lodges for their own use. For practical purposes, the only passable roads in the park are between Nsumbu Town and Nkamba Bay, then on to Kasaba Bay, or east to the Lufubu River. While these are open all year, you'll still need a 4x4 at any time.

Boat trips in national-park waters can be organised through one of the lodges (see below).

WHERE TO STAY Two lakeshore lodges, Nkamba Bay and Ndole Bay, are currently open – the first inside the national park; the second, more casual, just outside the park's northwestern boundary. (Nkamba Bay has changed ownership in 2015, and while open it is not yet clear if it will be operating in future as a full lodge or a private retreat.)

A third, Kasaba Bay Lodge on the Inangu Peninsula, has been closed for several years but once the airport project is completed it is now hoped that a private investor will take it over and set up new lodges. Historians will note that it was at the original lodge that Mozambique's president Samora Machel met regional leaders before catching his fatal flight in 1986 from the lodge's airstrip.

All three lodges have a chequered history. Originally, both those in the park were run by the government, but by the early 1990s both were in terminal decline: expensive yet poorly maintained. Eventually they were put up for tender in late 1995 and snapped up by private operators, although later fortunes have been mixed. Ndole Bay Lodge was originally privately owned, but was taken by the government in 1989, only to be closed in the early 1990s when its trade disappeared. Now it has reverted to its previous owners and is once again thriving.

🏠 **Ndole Bay Lodge** [map, page 363] (15 chalets, camping); m 0961 124917; e info@ ndolebaylodge.com; www.ndolebaylodge.com. ◈ NDOLEB 08°28.707'S, 30°26.870'E. Owned by Gerard & Barbara Zytkow, & run by their son, Craig, & his partner, Elise, Ndole Bay Lodge stands beside Lake Tanganyika in Cameron Bay, just northwest of the national park boundary, & offers the opportunity to swim, snorkel or fish from its private white-sand beach (which is considered to be perfectly safe).

Visitors usually arrive by boat, sometimes following a taxi transfer from Kasama airport. Drivers should take the well-signposted left turning as they approach Nsumbu, about 5km before the town (◈ TONDOL 08°31.753'S,

30°26.946'E). The lodge is 7km down a partly rocky track, for which you'll need a high-clearance vehicle at all times.

It's a lovely wild spot &, despite creature comforts such as mains electricity, still feels at one with the African bush. Both the chalets & the main central building are set back from the beach, well spaced among mature gardens on a gentle slope. The main area links the dining room with the bar & a library under a grand thatched roof, all surrounded by a low stone wall. It's a practical design – cool & airy. Under a thatched shelter, hammocks swing in the breeze, just the place to relax after a dip in the small pool, while over the water is a large, shaded wooden deck with more hammocks, sunbeds & steps into the lake. On a practical note, there's a shop for essential toiletries, local crafts & fishing lures, & Wi-Fi throughout the site.

The chalets are built of stone with thatched roofs, & most are en suite. They're large & comfortable, without being luxurious, some with space for extra beds. Four luxury rooms open onto the beach, 2 share a central lounge so are perfect for families or friends & 2 have a private deck & outdoor shower. Set to one side on the beach, beneath beautiful winterthorn trees, *Faidherbia albida*, is a campsite, equipped with running water, BBQ stands, & an ablution block with hot-water showers & flush toilets. Campers can book into the lodge for meals, & can use its facilities, provided they do not disturb other guests.

There's plenty to do, but don't come expecting to be organised; this is a laidback spot that is very much in tune with its location. You can hire various types of boat (*US$7–25/hr, or US$30–180/day plus fuel*), as well as snorkelling equipment & basic fishing tackle. As a qualified PADI instructor, Craig has established a PADI IRA resort at the lodge, the first on the lake, offering courses from 1-day try dives (*US$100 pp*) through to Rescue Diver. Other activities include game drives, nature walks, birding trips, lake cruises & waterskiing. Further afield, it's possible to visit some local hot springs, a traditional village (the lodge funds various community projects in Ndole village) & perhaps a village healer, or to organise a night trip to watch the operation of a kapenta fishing rig. A custom-built dhow, designed both for cruising & diving, allows extended trips such as a 5-night lake safari to Nsumbu NP and Kalambo Falls, or 4 nights in the park, to include the Lufubu River Valley. There's also a 1-night trip at a fly-camp near Nundo Head, including walks to the balancing boulders & Kampasa Rainforest, or the option of multi-day hikes up the Lufubu River. *En suite from US$125 pp sharing FB, inc snorkelling, kayaking & floating sunbeds from the lodge, guided walks, village visits, sunset paddle, laundry. Camping US$15 pp.* ☺ *All year.* **L**

🏠 **Nkamba Bay Lodge** [map, page 363] (9 rooms) e info@nkambabaylodge.com; or contact via Voyagers, page 396. ✆ NKAMBA 08°36.214'S, 30°32.168'E. Nkamba Bay has been taken over by new owners who are likely to invest heavily in the lodge but as we go to press it is unclear when they will open to clients (possibly late 2016) & whether or not it will be a full lodge or a private retreat. The description below is as it stands now before any refurbishment. This upmarket lodge is located on a low rise above the lake shore some 20km from the Nsumbu Park gate; there's a signpost indicating the turn-off. You'll need a 4x4 for this road, but most guests (& all in the rainy season) are transferred by boat from Mpulungu (2–4hrs). Nkamba Bay also has its own airstrip.

Accommodation currently consists of 4 spacious rooms built in a block around a couple of old fig trees overlooking the lake, & a further 5 chalets set further back with partial lake views. All have been stylishly renovated to be modern but comfortable, combining crisp white linen softened by fabrics & paintwork in more earthy tones. Each room has a king-size bed hung with walk-in mosquito nets on a minimalist concrete plinth, smart en-suite shower, & a wooden veranda that – in the lake-view rooms – is partially enclosed, a useful extra during the rains. Note that some rooms are quite high up, so are not suitable for children.

At the lodge's heart is a large, airy *insaka* sheltering a bar/dining area, hung with huge wooden masks & outsize baskets. To one side, squashy sofas & low *mukwa* tables are fronted by a small (but deep) pool – parents beware – & the lake beyond. The nearby conference room has become a cosy place to relax, with tea & coffee on tap, & a small library. There is also a small gift shop. Activities comprise game walks from the lodge or into the rainforest, game drives, beach dinners, boat trips, sundowner cruises, canoeing & fishing, for which tackle is available to hire. This is no place to swim, though – as attested by a quick glance at the crocodiles basking in the waters off the beach. It is possible to arrange a trip to local landmarks such as the waterfalls on the Lufubu River or a nearby beach, as well as to Chieftainess Chomba's village. Prices were around *US$420 pp FB, inc drinks (exc bottled wine & imported beers), airstrip transfers, & land-based activities. Boat US$150/day plus US$3 per litre of fuel. Park fees extra.* ☺ *All year.* **LLL**

WHAT TO SEE AND DO Ndola (and Nkamba Bay undoubtedly when it reopens) can organise a range of activities both on and off the water, but there are one or two local highlights that are worth singling out, detailed below. See also *Swimming, diving and snorkelling* and *Fishing* (page 359). Further afield, it's possible to organise excursions to Mpulungu (page 359) or Kalambo Falls (pages 354–6).

Balancing rocks One spot well worth an excursion is the balancing rocks (one large rock balancing on three small ones) that stand on the Nundo Head Peninsula – a favourite trail destination shrouded in local mystery. Each year around early June, a pre-fishing ceremony in honour of the spirit, Nundo, is held here to mark the beginning of the five-month period in which local fishermen can fish within a small area of national-park waters. Visitors can arrange to witness the ceremony through Ndole Bay Lodge.

Game viewing and birding As the lodges extend their influence and the number of animals increases, game viewing is increasingly drawing visitors up here. Apart from the ubiquitous puku, most antelope species are still re-establishing their populations; so although you won't see huge herds, you should see some good game here. The lodges have all worked to increase the road network for game drives, and the animals themselves are becoming much more relaxed as a result. Fortunately, with a large area and only a few lodges the roads are very quiet and other vehicles are a pleasant rarity. The birdwatching here has always been excellent: look out for Pel's fishing owl, palmnut vultures and numerous east African migrants.

Guided walks About 5km from Nkamba Bay Lodge and within the national park is the small Kampasa Rainforest, a favourite spot for guided walks. Trips usually involve a boat transfer, then a 3- to 4-hour walk from the beach, and are accompanied by an armed ZAWA scout.

The rainforest itself covers only about 300m² and is centred on an underground stream that bubbles up out of the ground most of the year. Mature woodland species such as sausage trees, *Kigelia africana*, and Natal mahogany, *Trichilia emetica*, grow alongside plants that include the flame creeper, *Gloriosa superba*. Before entering the forest, the trail leads past a dense reed bed where sitatunga are often seen. The area surrounding the reed beds is also rich in puku and is a well-used route for elephant, while the forest itself is regularly traversed by a pod of hippos on their way to the plains behind it. The park's lion frequent the area, too, and can often be heard from Nkamba Bay Lodge. Among the birds that are likely to be encountered are Pel's fishing owl, African broadbill, Angolan pitta and Narina trogon; crowned cranes are often seen on the plain, and during the rainy season the reed beds are the haunt of the black coucal.

A second walk option leads to the Muzinga Falls on a small stream to the east of Nsumbu town, about an hour's walk from the lake.

NSUMBU TOWN On the edge of Nsumbu National Park, about 8km east of the Ndole Bay turn off, Nsumbu town has grown considerably over the last few years and now has an estimated 20,000 residents, largely employed by the national parks, police, immigration or council – or in commercial fishing. As a result, there's talk of upgrading the status of the town, and there are even rumours of eventually tarring the road through to Kaputa. For now, though, a major improvement was the arrival of mains electricity in 2011.

While the town isn't nearly as cosmopolitan as Mpulungu (!) it can be fairly lively. In the town square, a short walk from the harbour, small shops and bars surround the water pump, alongside a popular pool table. It's possible to buy most things, including fresh fruit and milk, if you ask around, and simple meals such as nshima and chicken are to be had for around K25. If you're after a bed for the night, there are a couple of simple **guesthouses** charging around K80 a night: one in the market and a second at the harbour.

An open-air **market** for vegetables, dried fish and second-hand clothing spills from the square down to the harbour. There is also a government-run clinic, with a medical officer (but seldom any drugs), and a ZAWA post. **Fuel** – both petrol and diesel – is sometimes available in drums; just ask around in the square.

The Zambian military maintains a presence by the harbour, but now that the beached Congolese naval vessel has been returned to the DRC, their interest is largely in checking the ID of passengers off the transport boats from Mpulungu.

THE ROAD TO MWERU WANTIPA AND KAPUTA

The western side of this region, skirting the shores of Lake Bangweulu to Samfya then continuing up the Luapula River north to Lake Mweru, is known to only a handful of visitors, but offers plenty of rewards. The river is a draw in itself, as are the waterfalls that characterise much of this area, while the journey is enlivened by countless small villages, their square, brick houses topped with a mop of loose thatch and often decorated in striking geometric patterns.

If you're coming northeastward on the Great North Road from Kapiri Mposhi, it's wise to refuel at Serenje (see map, page 302). Then, after a further 36km, take the main left turning signposted to Samfya and Mansa (and Kasanka National Park). This is the artery that runs over some 580km of very good tar to Nchelenge, in the far northwest corner of the country.

The section of road up to the T-junction just west of Samfya used to be referred to as the 'Chinese road' because it was built, like the TAZARA railway, by the Chinese. After about 55km on this road you'll pass the entrance to Kasanka National Park (pages 320–9), then 10km later the right turn to the Livingstone Memorial (pages 329–30) and Bangweulu. Continuing north, the road crosses the impressive 3km-long Luapula Bridge, on the border with the DRC. During and after the rainy season, from around December to July, the river overflows onto the surrounding plain, which is dotted with miniature islands topped with palm trees. In the flooded fields, water lilies flower and water birds brighten the landscape. Permanent villages are augmented by temporary fishing camps, their inhabitants making the most of the months of plenty, and along the roadside fishermen tout their catch of bream or kasepa for sale.

Beyond the Luapula Bridge, watch out for the occasional pot-hole, although generally the road remains very good. About 350km from the Great North Road turn-off, or 115km from the Luapula Bridge, you'll reach a T-junction (⊕ SAMTJN 11°21.126'S, 29°29.453'E). Turn right here and a further 9km will bring you to the small town of Samfya.

SAMFYA With its location beside the powder-fine, white-sand beaches of Lake Bangweulu, Samfya seems to have the potential for a top resort. However, on closer inspection it's less tempting than it looks: accommodation could do with a serious shake up, strong winds blowing off the lake can be decidedly disruptive, and for the most part the lake is full of crocodiles, so this is really more of a stopover than a destination in its own right. (While people do bathe in the clear waters by the hotels, local advice is mixed; think carefully before wading in.)

On a more practical note, the town has a rather unpromising-looking **fuel station**, as well as a Finance **Bank**, a **post office**, a small **market** and a range of basic **shops**.

Getting there Several **buses** a day run between Lusaka and Kashikishi via Kabwe, Kapiri Mposhi, Serenje, Samfya, Mansa and Nchelenge. Those heading north stop at the market in Samfya at around 08.00, but southbound buses must be boarded at the T-junction 9km west of town, at a similar time.

Regular **postboats** used to ply Lake Bangweulu, collecting and delivering mail to the island communities on the lake. Like the postbuses, these would happily take paying passengers, but in recent years the service has been contracted out to private concerns, and information is patchy. Even in Samfya itself it is difficult to ascertain any form of timetable, but the boat used to depart every Thursday at 10.00, calling at Mbabala Island, Chisi Island and Muchinshi amongst others. To get to the port, turn left at the crossroads as you enter the town and follow this dirt road, with shops on either side, for about 300m to the end.

Where to stay and eat Samfya's accommodation options seem to come and go, but the addition of a new lakeside lodge broadens the choice for visitors.

Chita Lodge Samfya (21 chalets, 2 lodges, 5 s/c homes) `0211 293779; m` 0979 562176; e chitalodge@gmail.com; www.chita.co.zm. New to Samfya from the reputable Chita Lodges & Resorts, this lakeside hotel opened in December 2015. **$$$**

Kwacha Water Front Lodge (16 rooms) m 0973 045769, 0977 419675. Offers basic en-suite rooms with DSTV, fridge & view of the lake. **$**

LUBWE It would be worth exploring the road north of Samfya towards Lubwe, on the western side of the lake. Lubwe itself is home to a Catholic mission hospital built in 1926 and now run by the Sisters of Mercy. Active fundraising since 2000 has resulted in significant improvements, both at the hospital and in attendant projects to improve the lives of the local people; for details, see www.lubwezambiafund.org.

MANSA About 72km from the T-junction, or 81km from Samfya, Mansa is the capital of Luapula Province. It's a thriving provincial town, with tree-lined roads and an appealing air of prosperity.

Getting there and away Mansa's links to the rest of the region are enhanced by its position close to the Luapula River and the DRC border. A tarred road leads southwest to the border town of Chembe, where the 350m Chembe bridge has now been built over the river connecting to the Congo Pedicle road, a dirt highway across the DRC to Mufulira in the Copperbelt. Some of the Pedicle road has now been paved but reconstruction is ongoing.

By bus Long-distance buses are operated by several companies, including the reputable Juldan Motors. Most leave from Mulenshi Road in the centre of town, though each operator has its own departure and arrival point; some are based next to the Civic Hotel. Regular buses connect Mansa with Lusaka and Kashikishi on Lake Mweru, as well as to Kawambwa. Buses to Lusaka leave in the morning, taking about 9 hours to complete the journey. Typically, northbound buses load in the early hours (buy a ticket the day before) or mid afternoon. Fares to Lusaka are around K155 one way; to Samfya K115 and to Kawambwa K185.

Where to stay *Map, page 372.*

Mansa Hotel (30 rooms) President Av; `0212 821607 m` 0976 051571. Central & well

established, the Mansa is immediately next to Cavmont Bank & down the road from Shoprite.

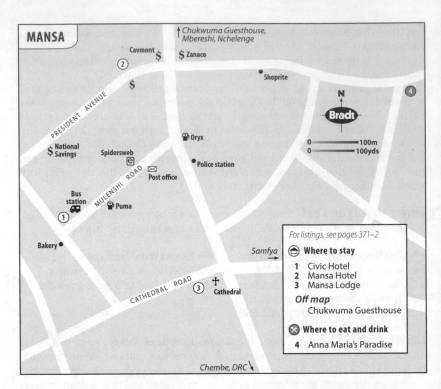

MANSA

↑ Chukwuma Guesthouse,
Mbereshi, Nchelenge

Cavmont $

$ Zanaco

• Shoprite

Bradt

PRESIDENT AVENUE

$

$ Oryx

N

0 ——— 100m
0 ——— 100yds

$ National
Savings

Spidersweb
e

• Police station

MULENSHI ROAD

Post office

Bus
station

Puma

Bakery •

Samfya →

Chembe, DRC ↘

CATHEDRAL ROAD

† Cathedral

For listings, see pages 371–2

🛏 **Where to stay**

1 Civic Hotel
2 Mansa Hotel
3 Mansa Lodge

Off map
   Chukwuma Guesthouse

✖ **Where to eat and drink**

4 Anna Maria's Paradise

Its brick-built rooms, arranged round a series of courtyards, are simply furnished but clean & pleasant; each has an en-suite toilet & bath, as well as TV, fridge, ceiling fan & mosi nets. The hotel also has a couple of well-stocked bars, & a restaurant serving b/fast, lunch & dinner (**$$**). Professionally run with helpful staff; even the president stayed here! **$$**

🏠 **Chukwuma Guesthouse** (12 rooms) 📞0212 821560; m 0977 240457. This pleasant guesthouse is just north of town; to find it, head north from Shoprite, go over the bridge, then turn right. Simple en-suite rooms built in a low block are fronted by a formal grassed area. Fans standard but A/C available in 4 rooms. Meals are available to residents. **$**

🏠 **Civic Hotel** (16 rooms) Mulenshi Rd; 📞0212 821930; m 0955 304765. Opened in 2006 in one of Mansa's oldest buildings, the Civic's exterior is a little unprepossessing, but solid wood & stone floors inside give a sense of permanence. Rooms (with 'sgl' beds – ie: small dbls – only) are off a long corridor, rather institutional in appearance but with en-suite showers, tea/coffee-making facilities, fans, mosquito nets & TV. The 1st-floor restaurant & bar, overlooking the road from a long veranda, serves à-la-carte meals all day. Unlikely extra facilities include a hairdresser, barber, 2 shops & an internet café. **$**

🏠 **Mansa Lodge** (17 rooms) Cathedral Rd; 📞0212 821301; e enquiries@zambiahostels. com; www.zambiahostels.com. ⊕ 11°12.132'S, 28°53.357'E. Just down the road from the main Catholic church, Mansa Lodge is run by the nationwide Hostels Board of Management. It's functional, very clean & efficient, if slightly soulless, with en-suite rooms in various categories. All have a bath & DSTV; executive rooms also have a fridge. All meals are available. **$**

✖ **Where to eat** Mansa's hotels have reasonable restaurants, and **Anna Maria's Paradise** (*President Av*) used to serve the best bream and chips in the region – now under different ownership; reports would be welcome.

Millions of fruit bats descend on Kasanka National
Park between October and December
(both CMeyer) page 324

top left	African fish eagle (*Haliaeetus vocifer*) (SS)
top right	Little bee-eater (*Merops pusillus*) (AZ)
above left	Giant kingfisher (*Megaceryle maxima*) (CM)
above right	Carmine bee-eater (*Merops nubicoides*) (SS)
left	Yellow-billed stork (*Mycteria ibis*) (CM)
below	Pelicans (*Pelecanus onocrotalus*) (CM)

above left   Wattled crane (*Bugeranus carunculatus*) (AZ)

above right   Shoebill (*Balaeniceps rex*) (NP/S) page 339

right   Three-banded courser (*Rhinoptilus cinctus*) (AZ)

below left   African darter (*Anhinga rufa*) (AZ)

below right   Giant eagle owl (*Bubo lacteus*) (AZ)

top **Nile crocodile (*Crocodylus niloticus*)** (CM) page 509

above left **Nile monitor lizard (*Varanus niloticus*)** (DH/S)

above right **Flap-necked chameleon (*Chamaeleo dilepis*)** (TH)

below **Pan-hinged terrapin (*Pelusios subniger*)** (SS)

Bundu
adventures

Since 1996

Email: info@bunduadventures.com
Mobile: ++260 978203988
www.bunduadventures.com
www.clickingbeetle.com

We offer:

- Swimming under the Victoria Falls
- White-water rafting (multi-day overnight rafting and day trips)
- Bespoke mobile safaris throughout Zambia and the region
- Photographic safaris with specially adapted vehicles
- Special interest safaris (entomological, ornithological, herpetological, botanical, zoological) throughout the region
- Logistical and administrative support for any project and event (scientific, outdoor, exploration, adventure, endurance sport)

We are passionate about nature and adventure!

Voyagers®

As a local, Zambian-based Destination Management Company, Voyagers® offers you unmatched convenience, service and security.

•

Corporate travel
Meet & greet at all airports
On-the-ground presence in Zambia
Extensive first-hand knowledge of Zambian hotels & lodges
Flights, car rental, hotels, transfers, buses, chauffeur hire

www.voyagerszambia.com • tours@voyagerszambia.com • +260 (0) 212 627800

Europcar
moving your way

DISCOVER ZAMBIA!

Car Rental • Transfers • Buses • Chauffeur Hire

www.europcarzambia.com • rentals@voyagerszambia.com • +260 (0) 977 860648

Zambia

South Luangwa, Lower Zambezi, Kafue,
Liuwa Plains, Livingstone and beyond....

Individually tailored safaris to East and Southern Africa, with expert advice and personal service

Contact us

T: +44 (0)1787 888590
E: info@safari-consultants.com
W: safari-consultants.com

HOME of the LEOPARD

Kafue has many special places to explore,
and one very special place to stay.
Come and enjoy our famous hospitality,
beautiful setting, expert guiding and
fabulous game viewing, especially leopards.

MAYUKUYUKU

Kafue National Park, Zambia
www.kafuecamps.com
info@kafuecamps.com

THE IDEAL START AND END TO ANY SAFARI

The gateway to Zambia, Pioneer is Lusaka's most relaxing lodge. Just 20 mins from the airport, it has a true safari feel.

PIONEER LODGE & CAMP
LUSAKA, ZAMBIA

Tel : +260 966 432 700
Email : mail@pioneercampzambia.com
Web : www.pioneercampzambia.com

Konkamoya

The only lodge on the Itezhi-Tezhi lake in the Kafue National Park

Konkamoya Lodge, Kafue National Park, Zambia
www.konkamoya.com - info@konkamoya.com

Other practicalities As you might expect in a regional capital, there are two all-important **fuel** stations (the last reliable source of fuel for several hundred kilometres if you're going north) and four **banks**, of which both Zanaco (opposite Cavmont) and Barclays have ATMs. The range of **shops** includes a branch of Shoprite (⊕ *08.00–19.00 Mon–Fri, 08.00–17.00 Sat, 09.00–13.00 Sun*); if you're heading north and self-catering, this is the last chance to stock up on anything other than the basics. For **internet** cafés, try Spidersweb on President Avenue, or the Civic Hotel.

NORTH OF MANSA Some 9km north of Mansa the road splits. The left turn leads to Mwense, Mbereshi and Nchelenge, while the road straight ahead is for Kawambwa. Both appear beautifully tarred, but don't be fooled; after the first 25km or so the Kawambwa road deteriorates rapidly into a bad dirt road, which is well worth avoiding, while the road to Nchelenge is pretty good tar for most of the way. Thus, if you're heading towards Kawambwa, take the road towards Nchelenge via Mwense, then turn right at Mbereshi for Kawambwa. It's both easier and quicker.

The Nchelenge road follows the verdant valley of the Luapula River as it flows north into Lake Mweru, forming the border with the DRC and widening all the way to the lake. A succession of villages lines the road, which crosses several rivers, all flowing west towards the Luapula from Zambia's higher ground in the east. It's an easy but interesting drive, particularly after the rainy season when the flooded plains attract temporary fishing camps, as further south. The route is further enhanced by views across the river to the DRC and the lure of several attractive waterfalls (see below), many of which offer a good spot for a picnic or to camp.

There are two fuel stations along this stretch, one at Mwense, 111km north of Mansa, the second 18km further north in the village of Chiluba, but neither is reliable, so do fill up in Mansa.

The Luapula waterfalls Along this route are numerous lovely waterfalls, many virtually unmarked, including the following:

Mumbuluma Falls (✪ MUMBUL 10°55.801'S, 28°44.178'E; *US$10/5 adult/child; vehicle US$5/day; camping US$15pp inc entry*) About 32km north of Mansa (167km from Mbereshi) there's a signposted turning to the left (✪ TOMUMB 10°55.536'S, 28°47.945'E), where there's a gate. After about 8.4km of rather bad track you'll reach the falls.

The water goes over a two-stage drop, about 30m across. There are attractive rapids in between and a deep pool at the bottom.

For campers, a new ablution block and circular shelter make camping at the falls a more attractive proposition than in the past.

Musonda Falls (✪ TOMUSO 10°42.2952'S, 28°48.784'E) About 60km north of Mansa (141km south of Mbereshi) you cross the Mwense Bridge over the Luongo River. There is a reasonable set of scattered cascades (✪ MUSON 10°42.856'S, 28°48.858'E) near here, but you first need to get permission to view them from the nearby hydro-electric power station; stop at the bridge and ask ZESCO security. This can be time-consuming, and there's not much to be seen as the river disappears into the power station.

Mambilima Falls (*US$10/5 adult/child; vehicle US$5/day; camping US$15pp inc entry*) About 90km north of Mansa (111km from Mbereshi) there's a set of lovely rapids on the Luapula River which make a very pleasant spot for lunch.

MUTOMBOKO CEREMONY
Thomas Morrow

During the last week of July, the people of the lower Luapula Valley in northern Zambia gather in the village of Mwansabombwe to celebrate their Lunda traditions and their paramount chief, Mwata Kazembe. For days prior to the main event, bars serve bottled beer, much of it imported from the DRC, to quench the thirst of guests who have arrived in the hot, dusty village; women from different village sections deliver pots of millet beer to Mwata Kazembe's palace; and the youth organise special sports competitions and cultural events. Towards the weekend when the main festivities are to take place, provincial, and on occasion national, political and military dignitaries dressed in their suits and ties arrive. On Saturday afternoon, following the performance of certain rituals in the morning, chiefs, headmen, state dignitaries and the villagers crowd together in a stadium on the outskirts of Mwansabombwe. A dignitary delivers a speech that highlights the importance of culture and tradition for progress, development and national well-being. Listening to the national leadership's calls for the preservation of these traditions, the chiefs and headmen appear in the traditional Lunda garb of long *imikonso* skirts (singular, *umukonso*), leather *inshipo* belts and *ututasa* crowns (singular, *akatasa*). After the speeches, on the instruction of Mwata Kazembe, selected aristocrats and members of the royal family dance. The day's events culminate in Mwata Kazembe performing the Lunda dance of conquest, the Mutomboko.

For further information, see www.mutomboko.org.

These used to be called the Johnstone Falls and are scattered over a 5km stretch of the river. Turn off the main road about 5km south of Mambilima village, at a sign to the Christian Brethren Church Conference Centre (✪ TUMAMB 10°32.260'S, 28°40.037'E). From here, follow the track for about 3km to the centre, where you can gaze over at the DRC or walk along the river for close-ups of some of the larger rapids.

MWANSABOMBWE The village of Mwansabombwe (✪ MWANSA 09°49.25'S, 28°45.35'E), just to the east of the main road (✪ TOMWAN 09°49.317'S, 28°45.474'E) and 13km south of Mbereshi, is the focus of the colourful Mutomboko Ceremony – the Dance of Victory – that takes place every year on the last Saturday of July (see box, above), starting at 08.00. Visitors are welcome to watch, but photographers will need a pass costing about K140 for the day. A statue at the entrance to the village commemorates the event.

If you're heading east to Kawambwa, don't be tempted to take a 'short cut' before Mbereshi by turning off the road at Mwansabombwe; this may look promising at first, but quickly disappears into a series of tracks that aren't the easiest to follow; stick to the main road unless you've time to explore!

MBERESHI The importance of Mbereshi (✪ MBERES 09°44.078'S, 28°47.350'E) to the visitor is threefold. It has a **fuel** station, though the supply at Kawambwa is rather more reliable. It is also the junction where you turn off for Kawambwa, Lumangwe Falls and Mporokoso. And finally, just after you turn onto this road, there's a church to the left on the hill that is one of Zambia's earliest. It was built in the early 1900s by the London Missionary Society, which was responsible for several other buildings in the vicinity, the rest of which are now in varying states of disrepair.

There are some serious speed humps at each end of the village; if you're driving yourself, be warned.

NCHELENGE This small town near the shores of Lake Mweru is the base for an occasional ferry service out to the two populated islands in the lake: Kilwa and Isokwe. In addition to a **post office** and small **market**, there is **fuel** available, albeit not necessarily reliable.

Getting there and away Buses heading north from Lusaka via Samfya and Mansa stop in Nchelenge, continuing on to Kashikishi which marks the end of the tar road.

⌂ Where to stay

⌂ **Lake Mweru Water Transport Guest House** \0212 972064. Rooms at this waterfront guesthouse are clean with en-suite facilities, & meals are available. This is also the place to organise boat trips out to Isokwe & Kilwa, though you'll need your own tackle if you want to fish. **$**

What to see and do The area by Lake Mweru will seem just like a continuous series of lakeside fishing villages. The fishing is (apparently) excellent, but there's also an abundance of crocodiles.

Birdwatchers might like to take a detour, using the track to the shore next to Chabilikila Primary School, which is just south of Nchelenge. This will lead you to some areas of papyrus near the mouth of the Luapula – a promising spot for finding swamp-dwelling species.

BEYOND KASHIKISHI TO MWERU WANTIPA NATIONAL PARK Some 3km beyond Nchelenge, at Kashikishi, the tar road comes to an end and the road deteriorates dramatically, so if you're aiming to get to Kaputa, allow plenty of time. Continue north along the edge of Lake Mweru for a scenic 30km or so, towards the village of Mununga then follow the road as it veers away from the lake until you reach the Kalungwishi River.

At the village of Mununga, turn right, then after around 30km go left (⊕ TOKAPU 09°07.531'S, 29°12.996'E) towards Kaputa. There are often market traders at the junction, so it's a good place to pick up whatever produce is in season. The stretch of road from this junction through Mweru Wantipa National Park to Kaputa is stony but reasonably level; it was re-graded in 2007 and is far better than many would have you believe, though you'll still need to drive with care. After 44km you'll come to a barrier, which marks the entrance to the national park (⊕ MWERUP 08°53.572'S, 29°28.8/8'E). From here, continue straight through the national park and across the top of Lake Mweru Wantipa to Kaputa (page 376).

Mweru Wantipa National Park (*Park fees US$5 pp/day; vehicle US$15/day*) This is another large tract (3,134km²) of Zambia that was once a thriving national park, renowned for large elephant and crocodile populations. Now poaching has much reduced these, though reports suggest that some big game still lives here, and claims are made that sitatunga can be found among the dense papyrus beds on the lake shore. Sadly, though, to the casual observer the park appears to be singularly devoid of life; even the birds seem to have deserted the place.

That said, the whole area, including the lake, was designated a Ramsar site in 2007, at the same time as three other wetland areas in Zambia. Ramsar reports that the diversity of habitats along the lake, featuring riverine forest, wetlands and miombo woodland, attracts numerous waterbirds, including the wattled crane, black stork and Goliath's heron.

The road to Kaputa goes straight through the park, on the western side of Lake Mweru Wantipa, a sedimentary and highly seasonal lake which itself forms part of the national park. Along this road, you'll come to a ZAWA scout post (⊕ MWSCOP 08°47.807'S, 29°30.519'E). If you anticipate camping here, or even exploring away from the road, then ask if one of the scouts can accompany you.

KAPUTA Despite being the district capital, Kaputa (⊕ KAPUTA 08°28.503'S, 29°39.990'E) is a rather unattractive place, its main street strewn with rubbish, and with the dejected air of a border town. There's a bank, an internet café, a few shops and a **market** where you can pick up basic foodstuffs in town. The presence of a few simple guesthouses (all **$**) is unlikely to deter most visitors from pressing on towards Lake Tanganyika (pages 356–9).

FROM MBERESHI TO KASAMA

THE ROAD TO MPOROKOSO Turning east at Mbereshi, towards Mporokoso, you turn off the tar and onto a reasonable gravel road. Note that the pontoon across the Kalungwishi River at Chimpembe, about 86km from Mporokoso, has long since been replaced by a solidly constructed bridge.

Places of interest along and around this road include:

Ntumbachushi Falls (⊕ NTUMBA 09°51.167'S, 28°56.652'E; *US$15/7 adult/ child; vehicle US$5/day; camping US$15 pp inc entry*) These falls are very clearly signposted about 23km east of Mbereshi and 18km west of Kawambwa, and 20km from the valley turn-off (n 09°50.666'S, 28°56.450'E). They are just 1.2km south of the road along a good track, and surrounded by some beautiful thick *mishitu* forest.

The main falls drop about 40m into a dark pool, with a second cataract alongside. Don't swim in the main pool, as there are strong currents and undertows that can pull you under the falls themselves. However, both the pool at the foot of the second cataract and the gentle rapids above the first falls offer perfect places for a cooling dip or a proper swim. Clear footpaths lead from the car park in both directions.

In the rainy season, there is a further set of falls, the Witch Doctor's Falls a short walk away, so called because there used to be *ng'anga* shrines at its base, one containing millet, the other a model canoe carved from bone. If you'd like to visit, ask the caretaker to guide you there, and remember to offer him a tip.

🏠 ***Where to stay*** This has long been an idyllic spot to camp, and with facilities now including a new ablution block and attractive circular shelter, it should be more comfortable, too.

Kawambwa Rather smaller than most maps of Zambia might suggest, Kawambwa is a pleasant backwater 18.6km from Ntumbachushi Falls, with little to detain the visitor. It is, though, widely known for the large Kawambwa Tea Estate, east of the town, which was privatised in 1996. Production has slowed considerably in the last few years, giving added poignancy to a road sign proclaiming that Kawambwa will be 'poverty free by 2030'.

There's a reasonably reliable fuel station at the junction with the Mbereshi road, and a small market in town, as well as a range of shops and a branch of the Zanaco Bank.

Getting there A regular bus service operates every day except Monday between Lusaka and Kawambwa via Mansa, stopping next to the fuel station.

If you're driving straight through the town from Mbereshi, you'll come to a T-junction; to stay on track, turn left here (right takes you into Kawambwa), then almost immediately right (at ⊕ KAWAMB 038 09°47.605'S, 29°04.675'E). After a further 24km you'll come to the end of the tar, just by the tea estate.

🏠 Where to stay
There are a few guesthouses in Kawambwa, including:

🏠 **Lusenga Trust Hotel** (5 rooms) m 0976 566819. On the left as you enter town, this lodge offers clean en-suite rooms decked out in sunny paintwork. Each has dbl beds with DSTV, tea station & direct-dial phone. **$**

🏠 **St Mary's Guesthouse** (12 rooms) m 0979 648746. Off Mbereshi Rd, this simple but central establishment is linked to the Catholic church. Rooms have mosquito nets over the beds, & share bathroom facilities. **$**

Lusenga Plain National Park
(*US$5 pp/day; vehicle US$15/day*) Lusenga Plain was originally designated as a park to protect a large open plain, fringed by swamp and dry evergreen forest and surrounded by ridges of hills. On its northeastern side it is bordered by the Kalungwishi River, which passes over three beautiful waterfalls: Lumangwe, Kabwelume and Kundabwika.

Sadly, without enough support, Lusenga is now a park in name only. Poaching has reduced the game considerably and, with no internal roads in the park, there are few reasons to visit.

Perhaps the formation of the Lusenga Trust and a community resource board will eventually serve to turn round its fortunes and revitalise its once-abundant wildlife.

Getting there The park is usually approached from the Kawambwa–Mporokoso road, and you should be very well equipped for any attempt to reach it. Some visitors have had success in reaching the park by getting a game scout as a guide from the ZAWA in Kawambwa. Otherwise the park is hard to enter.

Falls on and around the Kalungwishi River
The Kalungwishi River forms the boundary between the Luapula and northern regions of Zambia, and also the eastern boundary of Lusenga Plain National Park. Along the river are three major waterfalls in relatively close succession: Lumangwe, Kabwelume and Kundabwika. While Lumangwe is the most straightforward to reach, and well worth the visit, the greater draw is Kabwelume, 5km further on and a must for anyone in the vicinity. Getting to Kundabwika is altogether more demanding.

In addition to the falls themselves, there are miles of pleasant walking upstream, so consider staying overnight to give time to explore the other falls further downstream.

Pressure for electricity in Zambia is likely to impact on the river, with plans for a hydro-electric power station between Lumangwe and Kundabwika falls.

🏠 Where to stay
There are **campsites** with flush toilets at Lumangwe, Kabwelume and Kundabwika Falls, but we have been unable to contact the owners of the self-

catering Cascade Cottage nearby. However, in case the situation should change, it is signposted from the Kawambwa–Mporokoso road about 300m from the Chimpempe bridge, then a further 2km down the track.

Lumangwe Falls (*US$15/7 adult/child; vehicle US$5/day; camping US$15 pp inc entry*) To reach these, turn left off the Kawambwa–Mporokoso road about 2km east of the Chimpempe bridge (⊕ CHIMBR 09°33.082'S, 29°26.937'E), which crosses the Kalungwishi River some 65km from Kawambwa and 86km from Mporokoso. There's a clear signpost to Lumangwe and Kabwelume Falls on the north side of the road, on the outside of a bend (⊕ FALLST 09°32.239'S, 29°27.874'E). The track is narrow, level and fairly straight, continuing for about 10km to a fork (⊕ LUMAFK 09°32.466'S, 29°23.296''E), where there's a new information centre. Bear left here; the falls are just 300m away, manned by a caretaker.

Lumangwe is a solid white-and-green wall of water, 100m across and 30m high. It's perhaps the most spectacular of the waterfalls in this region and bears comparison to Victoria Falls. The noise is deafening and the air is filled with fine mist. There are two viewing points, one overlooking the main falls from the front, and a second – much drier! – from the top of the falls where you can see how a large island splits the river's flow. The energetic might want to climb to the bottom of the falls in order to reach the end of the rainbow that's seen on most days. There are no pots of gold here though, and the climb comes with a warning: instead of steps, you'll be making your way down (and then up) a rope using the cliff side for balance.

You can camp at the falls in safety: an ablution block with flush toilets has been built close to the falls, with a campsite behind. In place of the former guesthouse is a new information centre, completed in 2014.

Kabwelume Falls (⊕ KABWEL 09°31.432'S, 29°21.267'E; *US$15/7 adult/child; vehicle US$5/day; camping US$15 pp inc entry*) These falls are 5km downstream from Lumangwe, which makes a pleasant walk for 2 or 3 hours through the forest. Ask for precise directions at Lumangwe. Alternatively you can drive yourself, provided that you have a good 4x4: the track is very poor in parts and it's slow going. Simply return to the fork close to Lumangwe Falls, then turn left and continue for 5km or so to a small parking area. There's also a new campsite with ablution block.

Unlike that around many of the area's waterfalls, the vegetation at Kabwelume has been left to grow wild, enhancing the approach to the fall – provided that you come prepared (this is no place for flip-flops!). The increasingly overgrown path takes you across the river on stepping stones (probably inaccessible in the rainy season), then through thick vegetation dotted with bright flowers and alive with butterflies, and finally down a steep, slippery slope. You'll emerge after 300m or so to a most magnificent waterfall – a curving curtain of water 20m high and 75m across. Below is a deep pool, which itself flows over a second fall of 20m. On the left are two cataracts falling the whole 40m; on the right water pours down the cliff face. Look about you and this makes 180° of water – with the cataract, the main waterfall and the waterspout. It's a truly beautiful sight, worth savouring.

Kundabwika Falls (⊕ KUNDAB 9°13.058'S, 29°18.258'E; *US$10/5 adult/child; vehicle US$5/day; camping US$15 pp inc entry*) These are the last major falls on the Kalungwishi before it flows into Lake Mweru. Despite that, they are accessed from a different road, which may be impassable after rain; ask for advice locally, perhaps from the caretaker at Ntumbachushi.

There are two routes to the falls, both requiring a 4x4. The normal route is from the Kawambwa–Mporokoso road. About 21km east of the Chimpempe Bridge (✛ KUNDTO 09°27.945'S, 29°36.447'E), or 63km west of Mporokoso, turn northwest onto a narrow, very poor track; it's just west of a road barrier and signposted to Chikwanda Basic School; some maps mark this as a place called Mukunsa. Continue along this track, which is deeply rutted and pot-holed, for about 50km. It passes through villages for about 30km, then descends into less populous woodlands. It's very slow going so allow around 2 hours to the turn-off. The turning towards the falls (✛ TOKUND 09°11.397'S, 29°19.890'E) is into woodland, and almost invisible when the grass is high, so ask one of the villagers to point it out. From here, there's a straightforward 5km track that leads to the river.

Approaching from the opposite direction, drive 65km north of Nchelenge to the village of Mununga, on the banks of Lake Mweru. From there it's 35km to the falls on a reasonable dirt road, turning south at ✛ TOKUND, as above.

The woodland track brings you out by a series of gentle rapids, known as the upper falls. An expanse of open grassland offers plenty of room to camp, with no villages nearby, and just the occasional fisherman for company. To reach the main falls, a further 1km downstream, involves clambering over boulders along the riverbank.

Kundabwika itself is a geometrical waterfall, a 25m-wide rectangular block of green-and-white water. It's not possible to get very close to the falls, but there are good long-distance views from the top of the rock outcrop.

As you approach the falls, about 3km from the road and to the left of the woodland track, there's a rocky outcrop where rock paintings can clearly be seen. You can explore yourself or, if you have time, ask if one of the villagers can take you to see them. A new if basic campsite at the site, with flush toilets, is a bonus after the long drive in.

Mumbuluma Falls II (✛ MUMBII 09°13.024'S, 29°20.681'E; *US$10/5 adult/ child; vehicle US$5/day*) These falls lie 3km from the Kundabwika Falls turn-off, between Nyausa and Lumpa villages. Just before Nyausa School and past Kakoma Stream there's a 1km winding path to the falls. To be honest, it's little more than a rapid (they're also known as Mwesa Rapids) but it's quite scenic, with views of the Lusenga Plain National Park.

Yangumwila Falls There is said to be another set of falls, Yangumwila, on the Itabu River. From Lumangwe Falls, head towards Mporokoso. The falls lie a 3-hour walk away from Chiwala Primary School. Ask around for details.

MPOROKOSO Mporokoso (✛ MPOROK 09°21.831'S, 30°07.402'E) is a useful small town in the heart of northern Zambia. It lies at a T-junction on the Kawambwa–Kasama road, and is also the main access point for Nsumbu National Park (pages 365–7 for directions to the park). The centre is to the west of the T-junction, along a wide, tree-lined avenue. Here you'll find a branch of the National Savings and Credit Bank, a police station, post office, shops and a small market – in short, a normal Zambian town.

The town's recent history is very much tied up with that of refugees from the war in the DRC. In early 1999, a number of refugees and loyalist Congolese troops fled across the border to Zambia, crossing around Kaputa and Nsumbu. They were looked after by the UNHCR, the Red Cross, Oxfam and other agencies at Mwange Camp, about 60km outside Mporokoso, on the way to Kawambwa. Many of the aid agencies retain a presence here, and there's also a fairly large government hospital (with doctors but generally poor medicines and equipment), serving a large area of the country.

Getting there and away Most people coming to Mporokoso will be on the main Kawambwa–Kasama road – although it's in pretty poor shape from Kawambwa – and only a little better from Kasama.

If you're approaching from Mpulungu or Mbala, there is a road that avoids Kasama, although it's over 70km long, and rough going (you'll need a 4x4) even in the dry season – so it's hardly a 'short cut'. To find it, head towards Kasama from Mbala. About 74km from Mbala you'll see a turning to the right (⊕ TOSHCT 09°27.486'S, 31°13.136'E). This joins up with the Kasama–Mporokoso road at ⊕ TOSHC2 09°40.270'S, 30°41.628'E, about 8km northwest of Kapatu Mission (81km southeast of Mporokoso).

For those heading to Luwingu, there's also a way to avoid Kasama. To find it, follow the road southeast to Kasama for around 55km to a right turning. Take this road, continuing southwest until it joins the Kasama–Luwingu road. It's not in superb condition, but is just passable in a normal car during the dry season, though you would certainly need a 4x4 when it's wet.

🏠 **Where to stay** If you wish to break your journey here, there are a few very simple guesthouses.

Waterfall excursions from Mporokoso

Kapuma Falls These small but delightful falls (⊕ KAPUM 09°23.235'S, 30°05.675'E), cascading over scattered wall-like rocks, make a pleasant half-day trip from town and are a great picnic spot. Around 7km southwest of Mporokoso, past the district hospital, turn left just before the Agricultural Training Centre, from where it's around 2km to the falls. The road ends on a private farm, so if somebody is home do ask permission to see the falls.

Pule Falls Also known as Chipulwe Falls, these (⊕ PULEF 09°30.573'S, 30°17.001'E) lie just off the road to the (other) Luangwa River. Take the dirt road southeast of Mporokoso for 24km, turning off east after the Luangwa bridge onto a motorable path for 1km. There's a 500m footpath through cassava fields and banana plantations to these scenic, but not very deep, falls (about 15m drop). They're worth the 2-hour trip from Mporokoso.

Mumbuluma Falls III These falls (⊕ MUMIII 09°33.211'S, 29°44.736'E) are surprisingly impressive; surprising, as neither they nor the river that spawns them, the other Luangwa, are well known. Sadly, although they offer good places for camping, with no villages nearby, access has been blocked in recent years. Should the situation change, you reach them by heading 33km west out of Mporokoso to Angelo village (⊕ ANGELO 9°26.771'S, 29°49.511'E). Turn south here for 14km, then west for 4km, where there's a footpath to the falls across the clearing.

Lupupa Falls These (⊕ LUPUPA 9°16.441'S, 29°46.910'E) make for a pleasant outing when combined with Mumbuluma Falls III, possibly by having lunch at the former and camping at the latter. To reach them, head west out of Mporokoso on the 28km fair dirt road to Njalamimba. From here, head on 10km to Chandalala, then take the 3km motorable footpath before finally crossing the bridge on foot. The main attractions are the views from the falls down the gorge along the Mukubwe, over the hills and into the pool itself.

MPOROKOSO TO KASAMA Perhaps surprisingly for what might appear to be a fairly important artery, the 196km road between Mporokoso and Kasama is for the most part very poorly maintained, so it's not a journey to rush; you should allow around 4 hours, without stops. There are few villages along this stretch, either, so little to alleviate the monotony of consecutive pot-holes and deep ruts.

After 106km you'll come to the Kapatu Mission (⊕ KAPATU 09°43.148'S, 30°43.845'E) on the left of the road, where there are also a few shops. A further 54km brings you to the turn-off to Chishimba Falls (page 352), shortly after crossing the picturesque Luombe River. The falls are close to the road and it's well worth stopping here for an hour or two. From the falls, it's just 11km to the tar road, then at last a smooth final 25km to the centre of Kasama (pages 348–51).

NYIKA PLATEAU NATIONAL PARK Nyika Plateau is a marvellous area for hiking, and has some unusual wildlife. It lies mostly in Malawi, with just a slim Zambian national park hugging the border, but it is best approached from the Malawian side. If you plan an extended visit to Malawi, then get hold of a copy of the excellent *Malawi: The Bradt Travel Guide* by Philip Briggs before you travel – it's the standard reference on travel in Malawi.

FOLLOW BRADT

For the latest news, special offers and competitions, subscribe to the Bradt newsletter via the website www.bradtguides.com and follow Bradt on:

f www.facebook.com/BradtTravelGuides
🐦 @BradtGuides
📷 @bradtguides
📌 www.pinterest.com/bradtguides

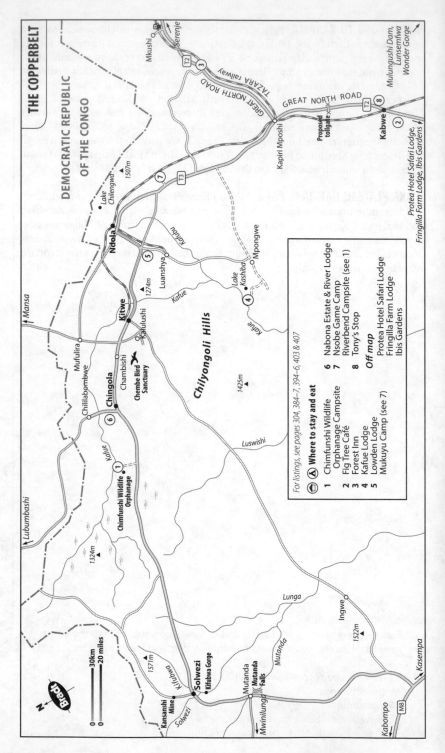

DEMOCRATIC REPUBLIC
OF THE CONGO

Chilyongoli Hills

For listings, see pages 304, 384–7, 394–6, 403 & 407

Where to stay and eat

1 Chimfunshi Wildlife
   Orphanage Campsite
2 Fig Tree Café
3 Forest Inn
4 Kafue Lodge
5 Lowden Lodge
   Mukuyu Camp (see 7)

6 Nabona Estate & River Lodge
7 Nsobe Game Camp
   Riverbend Campsite (see 1)
8 Tony's Stop

Off map

Protea Hotel Safari Lodge
Fringilla Farm Lodge
Ibis Gardens

Mulungushi Dam,
Lunsemfwa
Wonder Gorge

Protea Hotel Safari Lodge,
Fringilla Farm Lodge, Ibis Gardens

Serenje

Mkushi

TAZARA railway

GREAT NORTH ROAD

Proposed
tollgate

Kapiri Mposhi

GREAT NORTH ROAD

Kabwe

Lubumbashi

Mansa

Lake
Chilengwa

1507m

Ndola

Luanshya

Kafue

1274m

Kitwe

Kalulushi

Mufulira

Chililabombwe

Chingola

Chambishi

Chembe Bird
Sanctuary

Kafue

Mpongwe

Lake
Kashiba

Kafue

1425m

Luswishi

Chimfunshi Wildlife
Orphanage

1324m

Lunga

Ingwe

1522m

Kasempa

Kabompo

Mwinilunga

Mutanda

Mutanda
Falls

Mutanda

Solwezi

Kifubwa Gorge

1571m

Kansanshi
Mine

Kifubwa

Solwezi

N

30km

20 miles

13

The Copperbelt

The Copperbelt is Zambia's industrial base, a prosperous area around Ndola, Kitwe and Chingola dotted with mines: the area's production of copper and cobalt is of global importance. The population density here is high, and the environmental impact of so many people can clearly be seen. Despite this, the centres of the Copperbelt's cities are pleasant and not the sprawling industrial wastes that might be expected.

The area attracts few tourists, although there are many business travellers, so this chapter is deliberately concise. For simplicity's sake, this text also covers three of the main towns around the Copperbelt – Kabwe and Kapiri Mposhi to the south, and Solwezi to the west – even though these are outside the confines of the Copperbelt Province.

The region tends to have a higher level of rainfall than Lusaka, so bear this in mind if you are planning to travel in the rainy season. Note, too, that land in the Copperbelt is at a higher altitude than that further south – Ndola, for example, is 1,296m above sea level, and Solwezi higher still. As a result, it's generally cooler here than in the capital, so do remember to bring warmer clothes, especially for the evenings.

THE HISTORY OF THE COPPER

Zambia's rich copper deposits have been exploited since around the 6th or 7th century AD. There is evidence that the early Iron-Age inhabitants of Zambia mined, smelted and even traded copper with their neighbours – bracelets and bangles have been found at several sites.

However, large-scale exploitation of these reserves waited until the 20th century. Around the turn of the century, the old sites where native Africans had mined copper for centuries, like Bwana Mkubwa southeast of Ndola, were being examined by European and American prospectors. The demand for metals was stimulated from 1914 to 1918 by World War I, and small mines opened up to satisfy this need. They worked well, but these small-scale productions were only viable whilst the price of the raw materials remained high. Copper, zinc, lead and vanadium were among the most important of the minerals being mined.

Given Zambia's location, and the high costs of transporting any produce out of this land-locked country, it made economic sense to process the mineral ores there, and then export the pure metal ingots. However, this would require considerable investment and large-scale operations.

After the war, demand for copper continued to increase, fuelled by the expansion in the worldwide electrical and automotive industries. Large-scale mining became a more feasible option. In 1922 the British South Africa Company, who claimed to have bought all of the country's mining concessions in various tribal agreements, started to allocate large prospecting areas for foreign companies. Exploration skills from overseas flowed into the country, locating several large deposits of copper – well beneath the levels of the existing mining operations.

By the early 1930s, four large new mines were coming on stream: Nkana, Nchanga, Roan Antelope and Mufulira. These were to change Northern Rhodesia's economy permanently. Despite a collapse of the prices for copper in 1931, the value of the country's exports increased by 400% between 1930 and 1933 – leaving copper accounting for 90% of the country's exports by value. Thus began the mining industry which in 2012 accounted for about 12% of Zambia's GDP and 80% of Zambia's export earnings.

Over the last 15 years, the price of copper has fluctuated, first sending the Copperbelt's newly privatised industry into the doldrums, then elevating interest in the 'green rock' to goldrush levels, then plunging them once more into decline. At the same time, the industry has expanded beyond the traditional confines of the Copperbelt, first with the Kansanshi Mine at Solwezi and the huge Lumwana Mine another 65km to the west, followed in 2015 by the even bigger Kalumbila Mine.

LUSAKA TO KAPIRI MPOSHI

The Great North Road out of Lusaka, the T2, gradually slips off the city's dirty industrial belt for open bush and mile after mile of farmland, planted with everything from soya beans to maize and coffee. It's a good, tarred road, increasingly undulating beyond Kabwe, but traffic is rising fast. Now, the combination of slow-moving haulage trucks transporting goods to or from the region's mines and a plethora of police roadblocks can make for an exasperatingly slow journey, even at weekends. In 2015, signs indicated that a toll gate was being installed 40km south of Kapiri Mposhi, which could well exacerbate the problem.

At intervals along the roadside, local produce is offered for sale. Look out for **honey** in large plastic containers to the north of Kabwe, and various small **markets** that you'll pass in villages along the way.

WHERE TO STAY AND EAT If you're heading in this direction, but looking for somewhere to stop reasonably close to Lusaka, there are several options before the town of Kabwe. The best of these are listed below, from south to north.

Protea Hotel Safari Lodge (20 rooms, 20 chalets) Great North Rd, Chisamba; 0211 212843; e reservations@phsafarilodge.co.zm; www.proteahotels.com. Set in a private game reserve 45km north of Lusaka. For details, see page 132.

Fringilla Farm Lodge (71 rooms, 5 chalets, 3 flats, 2 houses, camping) Great North Rd, Chisamba; m 0968 626896; e fringillalodge@gmail.com; www.fringillalodge.com. Situated about 51km north of Lusaka towards Kabwe (look out for the sign on the east side of the road), Fringilla is part of a large, working farm that has expanded to include a butchery, a dairy, a clinic & even a post office; the bank that was on site is now further up the road.

Gone is the erstwhile small B&B, its place taken by a rather ramshackle selection of accommodation that capitalises primarily on the conference trade. The reception & conference room occupy the old farm building, but the restaurant & bar have moved to a spacious building centre stage ($$; ⊕ 06.30–21.30 daily). Dining here, or outside, concentrates on farm produce: sausages, steaks & chops, with excellent homemade pies (K40) & a braai at w/ends. That, plus an extensive children's playground, farm walks, & the option of horseriding (no hard hats provided), make it a good venue for day trips. Behind the restaurant is a complex of simple but well-kept rooms, all en suite (some with just a low partition) & with AC, fridge, kettle, nets & the obligatory TV. Well back again is a small shady campsite & basic ablution block, shared by 12, 2-bed chalets with fans. With friendly & helpful staff, the atmosphere is pleasant & relaxed. **$$–$$$** *b/fast K60. Camping K50 pp.*

🏠 **Ibis Gardens** (72 rooms) Great North Rd; m 0955 200400, 0966 200400, 0979 200400; e ibis@zamnet.zm; www.ibiszambia.com. East of the Great North Rd, some 74km from Lusaka, Ibis is set in 18ha grounds down a level 1km drive. With chalets neatly arranged across lawns dotted with banana & guava trees, the place has a rather suburban feel. The impression persists inside the dbl or twin rooms, with their white walls & simple but modern furnishings. Yet if it's quite corporate, it's also clean & pleasant. In each, AC/heater, safe, fridge & tea-/coffee-

GEOLOGY OF THE COPPERBELT   *Steven Lewis*

The Central African Copperbelt spans the border of northwestern Zambia and southern DRC and represents one of the largest copper provinces in the world. Known deposits falling within the Zambian Copperbelt contain approximately 88 million tonnes of copper.

Archaeological evidence for copper mining in Zambia dates as far back as the 4th century when malachite was mined and smelted into cross-shaped ingots known as *nsanshi*, which were used for trading. Large-scale copper production, however, didn't start until around the turn of the last century when early European explorers were shown the out-cropping copper deposits near present-day Ndola, Kitwe and Solwezi. As a result, commercial mines were opened shortly after the Cape-to-Cairo railway line reached Ndola from the south, and mining has continued to the present day.

However, the full story of the Zambian Copperbelt began around 877 million years ago, when the oldest rocks of the so-called Katangan Supergroup were deposited in a series of basins that now form the heart of the Copperbelt. The earliest rocks of this group are made up of conglomerates and sandstones that were deposited by rivers and deltas in a series of narrow troughs during the early stages of the evolution of the basins. As the basins developed and deepened, the character of the rocks changed in response to the changing depositional conditions, resulting in dolomite-dominated rocks that were deposited on platforms under fairly shallow water. In response to further basin deepening a later group of rocks, comprising a transition from dolomite, through a mixed series of dolomites and siltstones to a dominant siltstone were deposited, indicating an accumulation of material in a deep-water environment. At this point, a major change in the geological environment occurred, indicated by the presence of a thick unit of debris flows known as the 'Grand Conglomerate', with overlying siltstones. The Grand Conglomerate is a remarkable unit that can be traced for hundreds of kilometres and probably reflects the breaking up of the Rodinian Supercontinent around 740 million years ago.

The origin of the copper deposits contained in these rocks has long been debated by geologists studying the Copperbelt. Early theories leaned towards a 'syngenetic' origin, suggesting that the copper was deposited at the same time as the rocks in which it occurs. More recent research favours a longer, multi-stage 'diagenetic' origin, in which the copper was introduced into the rocks via major fault systems over a very long period of perhaps 300 million years or more, long after the rocks were deposited.

13

making facilities come as standard, as does a huge en-suite shower. Larger houses have 2 or 3 bedrooms, a lounge & a kitchenette. During the week this is very much a business venue, with conference rooms, restaurant & bar, but at w/ends it morphs into family mode, with pizzas & braais on offer, & sports facilities that include netball, volleyball, basketball, a gym & a large, free-form pool complete with its own island. Free Wi-Fi. **$$**

✕ Fig Tree Café Great North Rd; **m** 0968 652413; ⏰ 06.00–18.00 Mon–Sat. This excellent pit-stop between Lusaka & the Copperbelt is west of the road, some 10km south of Kabwe. Call in for what have been described as Zambia's best burgers, plus healthy wraps, tarts & excellent homemade cakes. You can eat indoors or out, or just drop in for a takeaway. **$–$$**

KABWE This bustling small town (⊕ KABWE 14°26.655'S, 28°26.717'E) is situated little more than 60km south of Kapiri Mposhi and about 142km north of Lusaka. It was built on the old colonial model of a central business area with a perpendicular road-grid, surrounded by pretty, spacious suburbs and with 'satellite' townships containing lots of high-density housing for poorer people. These divisions have melted a little, but the centre still has wide streets – albeit now lined with fuel stations, banks and fast-food outlets alongside the shops.

History Kabwe, when under colonial rule, was known as Broken Hill. In 1921 an almost complete human skull was unearthed here during mining operations, at a depth of about 20m. Together with a few other human bones nearby, it's estimated to be over 200,000 years old, making these the oldest human remains known from southern central Africa. Originally classified as *Homo rhodesiensis* by scientists, the remains are now generally attributed to *Homo heidelbergensis*, a large-brained species that was the common ancestor to *Homo sapiens* in Africa and the Neanderthals in Europe. However, to most people this human is best known as 'Broken Hill Man'.

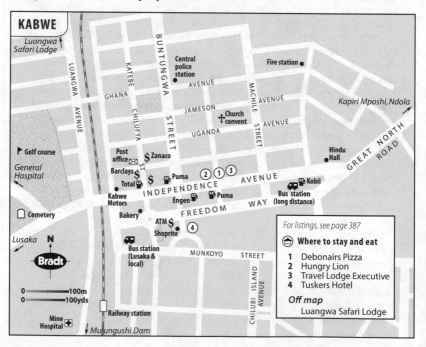

For listings, see page 387

Where to stay and eat
1 Debonairs Pizza
2 Hungry Lion
3 Travel Lodge Executive
4 Tuskers Hotel

Off map
Luangwa Safari Lodge

In more recent times, the town's economy has been closely linked with mining, most recently for zinc and lead (with very high-quality silver as a by-product). Although the mine, which was only about 2km south of the centre, was closed in 1994, there is ongoing interest in processing the tailings. Kabwe's large Chinese textiles factory, which was vandalised and closed several years ago, is anticipated to re-open under Tanzanian ownership

Getting there and away Regular long-distance **buses** connect Kabwe with both the Copperbelt and northern Zambia each day, as do **postbuses** on both the Lusaka–Ndola and Lusaka–Kasama routes. The Lusaka bus terminal is on Freedom Way, close to Tuskers Hotel; other buses use the area near the Kobil fuel station on Independence Avenue.

Where to stay and eat Most visitors to Kabwe are in transit, and accommodation is limited to one traditional hotel in the centre of town, the rather more individual Luangwa Safari Lodge, and several simple guesthouses – of which Travel Lodge Executive is not untypical.

Don't expect anything fancy in the food stakes, though **Tuskers** [map, page 386] does a reasonable line in barbecued steaks and fish, and their pizzas are said to be good. There are fast-food outlets near the fuel stations on Independence Avenue, so if you're passing through and in need of a quick break, it's a perfectly reasonable place to stop for a bite to eat. Out of town, the offerings are more promising. To the north, about 13km along the tar road, **Tony's Stop** [map, page 382] is a useful snack bar with a pleasant garden, and toilets, where you can sit with a drink and a homemade scone or fresh roll. To the south, altogether in another league, is the popular **Fig Tree Café** (page 386).

Luangwa Safari Lodge [map, page 386] (12 rooms) 8 Godetia St; ☎ 0215 225130; m 0977 601818; e sambiasafari@gmail.com. This pleasant guesthouse, on a quiet suburban street, opened in 2012. It may not fulfil 'safari' expectations, but it has an outdoors feel & the deeply thatched buildings are at least in keeping with the name. En-suite rooms come in 3 guises, all comfortably decorated with African print fabrics, a coolbox & TV. Sadly for those passing through, the restaurant (⊕ 14.00–21.00 daily; $$$$$) is not open at lunchtime, though you can stop for a drink by the small pool. **$$**
Tuskers Hotel [map, page 386] (35 rooms) Buntungwa St; ☎ 0215 222077; m 0966/0977 712909; e tuskers@zamnet.zm; www.

tuskerszambia.com. On the southern side of town, on the corner of Freedom Way, Kabwe's main hotel survives predominantly on the trade in local conferences. But the staff are helpful, & it's better than it looks at first glance. En-suite dbl & twin rooms are a decent size, with all that you'd expect from a small-town hotel, including AC, safe & fridge. The hotel has a bar & a cavernous restaurant (meats on the braai & pizza), but nicer is to have a drink on the terrace near a good-sized pool & pleasant garden. **$$**
Travel Lodge Executive [map, page 386] (8 rooms) 33A Independence Av; ☎ 0215 222885. Central, simple & perfectly adequate, the Travel Executive offers en-suite dbl rooms (& 1 family). There's a small garden with a bar, & meals such as nshima & chicken on offer for dinner. **$**

Other practicalities The main **shop** in town is the big Shoprite supermarket, just off Freedom Way, but there are other, smaller, shops – including a bakery – or you could try the large market, to the south of town near the railway line. Both Barclays and Zanaco have **ATMs** in town, including one near Shoprite. For motorists, there are a number of **fuel** stations on Independence Avenue, and should you be in need of spares, try Autoworld, just west of the Kobil fuel station, or perhaps Kabwe Motors at the Engen garage.

13

Excursions from Kabwe

Mulungushi Dam Some 60km southeast of town is the Mulungushi Dam – a 27km-long manmade lake that was formed in 1925 when the Lunsemfwa River was dammed to provide hydro-electricity for the mine in Kabwe. The **Mulungushi Boat Club** has a swimming pool over the lake, but at present, no boats. All the same, nature and bird walks can be arranged, and there's plenty of scope for exploring both by 4x4 and on foot – perhaps with a picnic. (Should you wish to stay in the chalets at the boat club or camp there, call m 0979 685349.) With care, it's possible to clamber down to the spillway, and on to the dam wall. With sufficient notice, you may even be able to get permission from the **Lunsemfwa Hydro Power Company** (\ 0215 224597) to view the powerhouse.

Getting there Entering Kabwe from the south, turn right just before you cross the railway. Follow this road parallel to the railway, cross a railway sidetrack, then swing left and cross a bigger railway crossing. On the other side are two roads; take the dirt track on the right – it may be signposted 'Mulungushi Boat Club 55km'.

Lunsemfwa Wonder Gorge (*Entry US$5/3 adult/child; vehicle US$5/day*) East of the dam, and about 80km from Kabwe as the pied crow flies (or 130km from Mkushi), is the spectacular and steep gorge marking where the Mkushi River meets the Lunsemfwa, as both cut 300m into the sedimentary rocks of the Muchinga Escarpment. This is a very rural, remote area so you'll need a reliable and sturdy 4x4, good maps of the area, and someone to come and look for you if you get stuck.

The best vantage point is **Bell Point**. It was apparently named after a Miss Grace Bell, a friend of the first European to see the gorge, who visited in 1913. The easiest approach is from the south. Bell Point is designated as a national monument but there are places you can camp. You can either scramble down to the bottom to keep exploring the gorge, or get to a vantage point and sit and enjoy. The latter is recommended.

Getting there Follow the directions for Mulungushi Dam, above. From here, continue across the Mulungushi, following the power lines northeast to Kampumba and on to Lunsemfwa. Crossing the bridge over the Lunsemfwa, take the RD204 to Old Mkushi. The turn for Bell Point, a track on the right that seems to head back the way you came, lies around 20km from Lunsemfwa (in a village confusingly also called Bell Point). Bell Point vantage point itself (⊕ 14°38.500'S, 29°08.600'E) is 35km away from this turning. After 1km there's a fork: take the right track. Ignore all turn-offs for 21km then, following an area of farmland, take a left onto a less used track. The last village on the route lies at 22km, after which the scenery grows ever more beautiful despite the presence of a car wreck at 32km (a casualty, so it is said, of the Rhodesian war).

KAPIRI MPOSHI
Kapiri Mposhi's main claim to fame is that it stands at one end of the TAZARA railway. Some 202km from Lusaka, it lies just south of the Nakonde Junction, where the Great North Road splits from the road to the Copperbelt. The constant flow of people, buses and trucks makes it feel lively, if sometimes slightly aggressive, with people around at all times of the day and night; be on your guard against opportunist thieves, especially if you're using the ATM at Barclays Bank.

There are several **fuel** stations in town, as well as a 24-hour Continental Oil station at the junction. With toilets, a shop and a fast-food restaurant, this seems to have lost some of its sleazy feel in the last few years, and most of the youths touting pirate DVDs have given way to people selling local produce. If you're in need of basic parts, try the branch of Autoworld to the south of town.

To the east of town you'll notice a small, rather incongruous-looking hill that gives the town its name: *kapiri* means 'mountain'. The town is the home of the glassworks KGP, which uses stone mined from the hill, and as you head north towards the Copperbelt you'll see traders selling glasses and mugs alongside the road.

Getting there and away Kapiri Mposhi is a linear town, but with its location just south of the junction where the Great North Road splits from the road to Ndola, it is effectively a major crossroads for those travelling northwards from Lusaka, with excellent links to the rest of the country.

By bus Kapiri Mposhi is easily reached by minibus, long-distance coach or postbus, as it stands on the main routes between Lusaka and both northern Zambia and the Copperbelt. There are very frequent arrivals and departures, especially to/from Lusaka and the Copperbelt; a ticket between here and Lusaka costs from around K60. The bus terminus is in the centre of town, on the left if you're travelling north, behind a variety of market stalls. The town is also on the postbus route between Lusaka and Ndola, with three buses a day in each direction.

By TAZARA train Heading north from Kapiri Mposhi, the road soon crosses a railway line. Just before this, turn right and continue for about 1km to reach the bustling and quite imposing TAZARA terminus.

If you did not buy one at the TAZARA office in Lusaka (page 119), this is the place to buy your ticket through to Dar es Salaam, 1,860km from Kapiri, or to stations *en route* within Zambia as far as Kasama and the border at Nakonde. The station becomes exceedingly busy around train departure times, and foreigners will encounter considerable hassle. To avoid this, arrive well before the train is due to depart and take great care of your belongings. If you need to buy a ticket, then allow at least an extra hour.

TAZARA services have long held a generally good reputation for time-keeping, though that's starting to look a little tarnished. Just two trains a week run on the route in each direction: the express on Tuesday, and a slower 'ordinary' train stopping at all stations on Friday. Both trains return the following day. Express trains leave Kapiri Mposhi at 16.00 on Tuesday, and arrive in Dar es Salaam at 12.35 on Thursday. The return leaves Dar at 16.00, also on a Tuesday, arriving back in Kapiri Mposhi on Thursday at 09.26. These trains stop at the major stations *en route*, including the Zambian towns of Mkushi, Serenje, Mpika, Kasama and Nakonde.

TAZARA TRAIN PRICES (IN KWACHA) FROM KAPIRI MPOSHI

Fares below are for the express service, one way. Fares on the slower 'ordinary' trains are about 20% cheaper.

To	1st class (sleeper)	2nd class (sleeper)	3rd class
Mkushi	30.60	19.20	18.40
Mpika	94.10	72.30	51.10
Kasama	129.40	107.00	86.10
Border (Nakonde/Tunduma)	157.50	130.80	110.70
Dar es Salaam	333.60	272.20	233.20

13

The slower, all-stations service departs from Kapiri Mposhi on Friday at 14.00, arriving in Dar es Salaam on Tuesday at 15.00; it returns on a Friday, leaving Dar at 13.00 and reaching Kapiri Mposhi on Sunday at 16.00.

Tickets are available in first, second and third classes. Both first- and second-class compartments are sleepers (although there are second-class seaters, too), accommodating four and six passengers respectively; in third class, it's seating only. Good food is available on the trains, as is bottled water, and in sleeper carriages you can expect to be provided with bedding, but you'll need to bring your own towels.

Remember to check in advance with the Tanzanian High Commission (page 55) if you'll need a visa to enter Tanzania. Travellers to Zambia can usually get their visa on the train, but again, do check your status first. (For details of visas, see pages 53–4.)

Hitchhiking Hitching to or from Kapiri Mposhi is fairly easy. Your best bet is to walk out of town for a kilometre or so until you find space. Alternatively ask around the truckers in town for a lift. If you are going north, then get a short lift or a taxi to take you the 2km or so to the Continental Oil fuel station, where the road to Ndola splits from the Great North Road to Mpika and beyond. This is an excellent hitching spot. (But do remember that hitching in Zambia is not a free ride; you will be expected to contribute to the cost of the journey.)

Where to stay and eat There are a few run-down hotels on the main road in town, mostly basic and noisy, and some with rooms rented by the hour as well as by the night. Better is **MaTwenty-two Lodge** next to the post office, near the junction, which boasts en-suite bathrooms, mosquito nets, TVs and a pool (**$**). This could be a good spot if you're heading out on the TAZARA train, but otherwise, Kapiri Mposhi is not a place to stay unless you have to.

Seasonal produce is available in the **market**, so expect tomatoes, peanuts and sweet potatoes at the end of the rainy season, followed by bananas and oranges in the middle of the year, then watermelon, tomatoes and butternut squash. There's a bakery opposite, and lots of takeaways, but for more varied supplies Kapiri boasts a branch of Shoprite, opposite the bus station.

NDOLA

About 325km north of Lusaka, Ndola is the provincial capital of the Copperbelt, but slightly smaller than its neighbour, Kitwe. It is a pleasant city with broad, leafy streets and little to indicate its industrial base. With the last boost in the price of copper, the town witnessed a parallel resurgence in prosperity, with several new guesthouses and restaurants in evidence. Today, the lime and cement industry is of increasing importance, giving a major boost to the town's economy, albeit with an increase in dust in the atmosphere.

As an aside, Ndola benefits from an unusually pure water supply, which explains why it is home to the large Mosi brewery.

GETTING THERE AND AROUND

By air Ndola's Simon Mwansa Kapwepwe International Airport is on the southern side of the centre of town, clearly signposted off to the right as you enter town from the south. It is well served by regional specialist Proflight, with several flights per day to Lusaka. There are also direct flights to Johannesburg with Airlink and South African Airways, to Nairobi with Kenya Airways, and to Addis Ababa with

Ethiopian Airlines. There are plans to relocate the airport to the west of the town, near the Dar Hammarskjöld Memorial, in order to accommodate increasing traffic.

The open-air café at the airport is one of the more pleasant places to while away time awaiting a flight. Inside, you'll find all you'd expect from a small-town airport: a bank, bureau de change and ATM (though this may not be the most reliable of machines), a curio shop, car-rental office, internet access, and offices for all the local airlines.

✈ **Airlink** ✆0212 612206; www.saairlink.co.za. Daily flights to Johannesburg.
✈ **Kenya Airways** ✆0212 620709; www. kenya-airways.com. Daily flights to Nairobi.
✈ **Proflight** ✆0212 611796; m 0977 207957; www.flyzambia.com. Scheduled flights between Lusaka & Ndola 3 times a day, twice on Sun.
✈ **South African Airways** ✆0212 620029; m 0973 096097; www.flysaa.com. Daily flights to Johannesburg.

✈ **Zambia Flying Doctor** ✆0216 11417/8; e zfdradio@zamnet.zm. The chief pilot can be contacted on m 0977 756989. This small outfit operates charter flights across northern Zambia. As ZFD is part of the medical emergency services, though, a charter booking might be subordinated to a medical incident.

By bus Ndola's central bus terminus is at the southern end of Chimwemwe Road, though most intercity buses, and coaches to Lusaka, start from around the Broadway Cinema area just north of the Savoy Hotel, or Buteko Avenue. There are very frequent links to Kitwe and the other towns of the Copperbelt and also Lusaka (*from K75*). To reach northern Zambia (accessed via the road through Mkushi and Serenje), take a southbound (probably to Lusaka) bus and change at Kapiri Mposhi.

A **postbus** service operates between Lusaka and Ndola three times a day, stopping in Kabwe and Kapiri Mposhi. The journey takes around 4 hours, with a one-way fare of K70.

By train The painfully slow passenger service between Kitwe and Livingstone via Ndola, stopping at all stations, has finally been suspended – which is of no loss to most travellers for whom the bus is far more efficient.

Car hire
🚗 **Voyagers/Europcar** [392 C3] 17–18 Arusha St; ✆0212 620314; airport m 0977 860648; e rentals@voyagerszambia.com; www. voyagerszambia.com; www.europcarzambia.com

🚗 **Interrent** www.interrent.com. Contact via Europcar, above. A low-cost rental company under the Europcar umbrella, using older vehicles maintained by Voyagers. Typically a saloon will cost US$35–40/day, inc the first 100km.

Hitchhiking Ndola is quite a big town, meaning that good hitching spots are a long walk from the centre – so consider getting a taxi for a few kilometres.

Until recently, it was considered far too dangerous to cross into the DRC, but driving this route may now be viable during daylight hours.

WHERE TO STAY The choice of hotels and guesthouses in Ndola is growing, all aimed at visiting businesspeople and with correspondingly high prices. For most visitors, the better guesthouses are generally a more appealing option than the town's hotels. That said, work has begun (September 2015) on a new Protea Hotel opposite the Levy Mwanawasa Stadium. There's also a new 50-room hotel opposite the golf club.

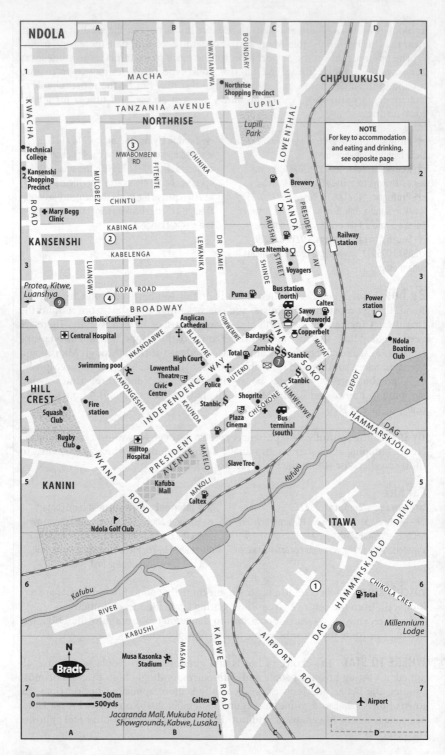

NDOLA

A — B — C — D

CHIPULUKUSU

MACHA

TANZANIA AVENUE

NORTHRISE

Northrise Shopping Precinct

Lupili Park

LUPILI

BOUNDARY

MWATIANWWA

LOWENTHAL

NOTE
For key to accommodation and eating and drinking, see opposite page

Technical College

Kansenshi Shopping Precinct

MWABOMBENI RD ③

Mary Begg Clinic

CHINTU

KABINGA ②

KANSENSHI

KABELENGA

MULOBEZI

FITENTE

CHINIKA

DR DAMIE

LEWANIKA

Brewery

VITANDA

ARUSHA STREET

SHINDE

PRESIDENT AV

Chez Ntemba ⑤

Voyagers

Railway station

Protea, Kitwe, Luanshya ←⑨

LUANGWA

KOPA ROAD

④

BROADWAY

Puma

Bus station (north)

Caltex ⑧

Power station

Catholic Cathedral ✝

Central Hospital

NKANDBWE

BLANTYRE

Anglican Cathedral ✝

CHINWEMWE

Barclays

MAINA

Savoy
Autoworld
Copperbelt

Ndola Boating Club

Swimming pool

High Court

Lowenthal Theatre

Civic Centre

Police

KANONGESHA

INDEPENDENCE WAY

KAUNDA

BUTEKO

Total

Zambia

Stanbic ⑦

Stanbic

SOKO

MOFFAT

DEPOT

HAMMARSKJÖLD

HILL CREST

Squash Club

Fire station

Rugby Club

Hilltop Hospital

Stanbic

Shoprite

Plaza Cinema

CHISOKONE

Bus terminal (south)

CHIMWEMWE

KANINI

NKANA ROAD

PRESIDENT AVENUE

MATELO

Kafuba Mall

MAKOLI

Caltex

Slave Tree

Kafubu

ITAWA

HAMMARSKJÖLD DRIVE

Ndola Golf Club

Kafubu

RIVER

KABUSHI

MASALA

KABWE ROAD

Musa Kasonka Stadium

①

⑥

Total

DAG

AIRPORT ROAD

CHIKOLA CRES

Millennium Lodge

N

Bradt

0 ——— 500m
0 ——— 500yds

Caltex

Jacaranda Mall, Mukuba Hotel, Showgrounds, Kabwe, Lusaka ↓

✈ Airport

Hotels

🏠 **Mukuba Hotel** [off map, 392 B7] (54 rooms) 📞 0212 651000/2/3; **m** 0954 920 921/ 0973 923 555/ 0962 229 933 **e** mukhotel@ microlink.zm, mukhotel@zamtel.zm; www. mukubahotel.com. If you want the amenities of a comfortable hotel, & can live with the 10-min drive from the centre of town, try the Mukuba about 6km south of town, adjacent to the Showgrounds. To get there, head towards Kabwe, then turn right into the industrial area onto Arkwright Rd, then Crompton Rd. A good-size floor rug softens the corporate effect in each room, where you'll find AC, tea/coffee maker, phone, DSTV & a fridge & free Wi-Fi. The hotel is built around a central courtyard where peacocks strut around the fishponds, while beyond roams a small resident herd of impala. There's a bar & restaurant, a gym & a pool. **$$$**

🏠 **Palace Hotel** [392 C3] (52 rooms) Cnr Vitanda St & Kabelenga Av; 📞 0212 621840; **e** thepalacehotelzambia@gmail.com. Under the same management as the Edinburgh Hotel in Kitwe, & at the heart of Ndola's business district, the Palace is quite an old hotel, having opened in the mid 1940s. Over the years it has had several different names, including the Coppersmith Arms, Naaznina, Travellers' Lodge &, more recently, the Royal Hotel. Its en-suite rooms are old-fashioned but adequate, each with satellite TV, direct-dial phone, minibar/fridge & tea/coffee machine. Downstairs there's a restaurant, a bar & secure parking. **$–$$$**

Guesthouses

🏠 **Michelangelo** [392 A3] (30 rooms) 126 Broadway; 📞 0212 620325; **m** 0966 780036; **e** michelangelo@m-lodge.com. This Italianate guesthouse comes with columns & cool tiles, & in the rooms arranged round the courtyard pool warm terracotta colours are offset by limed furniture & good, soft lighting. Each room is dominated by a large bed with all-round mosquito net, but there's still space for a desk with internet point, TV & hairdryer, & an en-suite bath & shower, & AC. There are 5 suites (inc one presidential) & most importantly 24-hr power thanks to the generator. The restaurant is warm & inviting, & the bar is popular in the evenings as well. Credit cards accepted. **$$$$**

🏠 **Chabanga Lodge** [392 C6] (18 rooms) Nakatindi Rd; 📞 0212 622353; **m** 0955 888195;

NDOLA
For listings, see pages 393–5

⬭ **Where to stay**
1 Chabanga Lodge C6
2 Kaps Villa A3
3 Katuba Guesthouse B2
4 Michelangelo A3
5 Palace C3
Off map
   Millennium Lodge D6
   Mukuba B7

✖ **Where to eat and drink**
6 Bei Tempi D6
7 Danny's C4
8 Leeja Palace C3
   Michelangelo .... (see 4)
9 Starscape A3

---

e chabangalodge@zamtel.zm. Down a narrow road close to the airport, Chabanga Lodge is well placed for travellers, though the yappy dogs may be off-putting to some. Light rooms have a modern feel, offset by wrought-iron furniture & tiled floors. Each has a dbl bed & is equipped with AC, mosquito nets, DSTV, kettle, phone & fridge. In the public rooms, ornate formality contrasts with a decidedly simple dining area, where very good evening meals are available on request (**$$$**). **$$–$$$**

🏠 **Millennium Lodge** [off map, 392 D6] (7 rooms) 3 Chikola Cres; 📞 0212 610940/1; **e** info@milleniumparklodge.com; http:// millenniumparklodge.com. With a swimming pool & jacuzzi surrounded by manicured green lawns, this is an attractive option. Modern, en-suite rooms have AC, DSTV, fridge & Wi-Fi access. A full English b/fast is served in the restaurant, where other meals are available on request, & there's also a bar. Free airport pick-up. **$$–$$$**

🏠 **Kaps Villa** [392 A3] (6 rooms) 2 Mulobwezi; 📞 0212 615765; **m** 0977 117747; **e** vkaps@yahoo. professional com. Mutale Kapoka brings a lively but approach to the management of her father's typical Zambian guesthouse. All rooms are en suite with TV, with larger ones having a kitchenette (& a higher price & only a continental b/fast). The small covered dining area has a TV & a bar which is open to the public & can get noisy on Fri nights & w/ends. Still a clean & relatively pleasant alternative to Ndola's more upmarket offerings. **$$**

🏠 **Katuba Guesthouse** [392 B2] (15 rooms, 2 cottages) Mwabombeni Rd; 📞 0212 671341;

m 0978 450245; e katubaguesthouse@gmail.com; www.katubaguesthouse.com. Neat gardens & mown lawns surround this well-maintained guesthouse in a quiet location north of the town centre. Most of the en-suite rooms are dbls, with one for families, & all boast a fan, & mosquito net, satellite TV, & tea/coffee station. The style is relatively modern, the parking secure & the welcome friendly. Meals are available on request. Wi-Fi. **$$**

Around Ndola

🏠 **Nsobe Game Camp** [map, page 382] (5 tents, 9 chalets, camping) \0212 671008/671097; e reservations@nsobe.com.zm; www.nsobegamecamp.com. Some 9km from the Great North Rd, the turn-off for Nsobe Game Camp is about 50km south of Ndola, or 62km north of Kapiri Mposhi; the track is accessible by 2WD all year. The camp is set on a 1,500ha game farm, Miengwe Farm, in predominantly miombo woodland, with 3 dams (manmade lakes), 15 species of antelope, including black lechwe, sable, eland & the rare sitatunga, & over 320 species of birds. The atmosphere is one of upmarket camping – & indeed there is a campsite at one end of the site, right on the lake with braais & hot-water showers, but no power. En-suite safari tents on raised wooden platforms have no frills, but everything you need, including a wooden veranda overlooking the lake; similar chalets sleep 2–4 guests. The nearby TV lounge & separate restaurant are especially popular at w/ends, when Nsobe is a favourite with local visitors. About 5–10 mins' walk away are 2 self-catering chalets, sleeping 6 or 8 people respectively. Food – much of it farm produce, from fresh orange juice & fish to venison & pork (& their own sausages) – is good & plentiful, & there's a shop selling their produce too. This is a working farm, with around 1,000 pigs, bream-stocked fishponds & a citrus orchard. Aside from farm visits, activities include fishing (2 of the dams are said to be croc free), bush walks, visits to their reptile park, & game drives in your own vehicle or theirs (this is no place for serious guiding, but there's a useful bird checklist & an identification sheet for the antelope). Day visitors can use braai sites, picnic tables & benches set near the water's edge. Or just chill in the grounds, swim in the pool, or take advantage of the jacuzzi or sauna. *Tent/chalet K550/500sgl/pp sharing DBB; self-catering chalet K1,300–1,700 6–8 people;*

camping K35 pp. Day entry K250. Game drive K50pp (min 3); self game drive K100. Weekday concessions. No credit cards. **$–$$**

🏠 **Mukuyu Camp** [map, page 382] (5 chalets) Contact via Nsobe, above. Some 10 mins' drive from Nsobe Game Camp, Mukuyu is a private, secluded camp that sleeps up to 10. With its thatched central dining/seating area & solar lighting, it is more upmarket than Nsobe, relaxing & comfortable without being luxurious. Everything was made on the premises, using locally sourced elephant grass for the walls & thatch, wood from the farm, & handmade clay bricks, while simple baskets adorn the walls. Square, thatched rooms have a small veranda overlooking a waterhole, & at the back is an open-air shower in a semi-open bathroom (1 has a sunken stone bath, too). With its own staff & kitchen, the camp is entirely self-contained, a perfect hideaway in the bush. In case the setting palls, there's a tiny plunge pool & night drives are on offer.

For something more romantic, try the private Miombo Woodland View. Perched on a rocky hill are an open-air dbl bedroom under thatch, a separate bathroom beneath the stars, & a dining area. *Bushcamp K650 pp FB; min 4, 1 group only. Miombo View K660 pp DBB.* **$$$**

🏠 **Lowden Lodge** [map, page 382] (13 rooms, camping) Luanshya Turn-off; \0212 515001; m 0966 701150/ 781105/904291/907154 ; e lowden@iwayafrica.com. Almost equidistant between Ndola & Kitwe, & about 1km off the main road in the direction of Luanshya, this small guesthouse with dbl, twin & sgl rooms is attractively set in gardens. Those in search of exercise will welcome the large pool, exercise room & jogging track, while others may find the sauna, bar & TV lounge more to their taste. Dinner, with home-grown produce, is available to guests, & there's free internet access. **$$$**

🏠 **Kafue Lodge** [map, page 382] (8 rooms) Book via Voyagers, page 396. ⊕ 13°22.127'S, 27°58.166'E. Some 2hrs' drive, or 92km, from Ndola, Kafue Lodge is popular with Copperbelt residents for a w/end break. Although it is just 32km from Mpongwe, a huge farming area northwest of Kapiri Mposhi, it is most easily accessed from the north. To get there, head towards Kitwe, then turn off to Luanshya after about 20km; continue through Luanshya & Mpongwe then, after a further 7km, turn right onto a dirt road & follow this for some 20km, bearing left after 1km; once you get to the airfield, turn left, continuing for a final 5km.

The lodge is on a 20km² game farm on the banks of the Kafue River, stocked with 12 species of antelope, including sable & kudu, & with excellent birding opportunities: The late Bob Stjernstedt, the Zambian birding expert, advised that it's a particularly good place to see Pel's fishing owl.

Relatively simple rooms have been built in pairs, 2 to a chalet. Each is en suite, with wrought-iron furnishings, twin beds, sliding windows, & rugs laid on the cement floor. Outside, to one side of the shared veranda, is a sink, crockery, cutlery & a tiny fridge (you'd need a coolbox & ice if you're self-catering), while on the other is a BBQ area. If self-catering doesn't appeal, there's a bar & restaurant (*lunch* $$$), with produce from the lodge's organic vegetable garden on the menu.

Walks & game-viewing tracks meander through tall miombo woodland & dambos, characteristic of this part of Zambia. It's also a popular spot for fishing, or for a cruise along the river, while close by is Lake Kashiba. $$ *exc b/fast.*

✖ **WHERE TO EAT** There are plenty of takeaways and fast-food joints around town, including the ubiquitous **Hungry Lion** near the police station on Blantyre Road [392 B4], and several outlets in both the **Kafubu** [392 B5] and **Jacaranda** [off map, 392 B7] **malls**. For more substantial meals, Mint Café in Jacaranda Mall is a relatively new option, as is the News Café in the Kafubu Mall; both have outlets in Lusaka. Kafubu also boasts a noisy pizza place, Bojangles, with a wood-fired oven and a DJ or occasional live music, and a branch of the South African steak restaurant, Spur. Of the hotels, the **Mukuba's** [off map, 392 B7] (page 393) restaurant is perfectly adequate, but at midday, the best place to head for is the recently refurbished **Boating Club** overlooking the river [392 D4].

✖ **Leeja Palace** [392 C3] Vitanda St; ✆ 0212 614361; m 0961 383871; ◷ 09.00–22.30 daily. Serves great Indian food as well as a mix of Chinese & Western cuisine. The upstairs restaurant has a veranda which is good for people watching, & with a well-stocked bar it is a pleasant place for a drink, too. $$$$$

✖ **Danny's** [392 C4] President Av; ✆ 0212 621828; ◷ noon–14.30, 19.00–22.30 daily. Refurbished with a good, predominantly Indian menu (but with more than a hint of other cuisines thrown in). $$$

✖ **Michelangelo** [392 A3] 126 Broadway; ✆ 0212 620325; ◷ 08.00–14.00 & 19.00–22.30 Mon–Sat; Sun residents-only dinner. As you might expect, the menu at Michelangelo is dominated by Italian fare, boasting freshly made ricotta cheese, & listing a big range of pizzas & pastas. At lunchtimes, the emphasis is on salads, stuffed pitta bread & omelettes. $$$

✖ **Starscape** [392 A3] Broadway Av; ✆ 0212 612248; ◷ Tue–Sun. Another Indian offering, now with accommodation as well. $$

☕ **Bei Tempi** [392 D6] Dag Hammarskjöld; ◷ 08.00–22.00 Tue–Sun. An unlikely find next to the Total garage, close to the airport, this is the place to seek out if you're craving a decent coffee or tea, or smoothies & shakes. The menu consists of meze, pancakes, stuffed pittas, quiches & salads. $$–$$$

NIGHTLIFE Most of Ndola's residents spend the evening at one of the town's restaurants or clubs, with the bar at the **Boat Club** a favourite. **Chabanga** [392 C6] and **Michelangelo** (see above) are pleasant after-dinner haunts. What the town's nightlife lacks in sophistication, it makes up for in sheer numbers. In addition to **Circles** and the **Garage**, there are at least five other clubs though these establishments are prone to change ownership and are not necessarily to be recommended. For more hard-core drinking, places such as **Chez Ntemba** [392 C3] are popular with locals.

SHOPPING Ndola isn't somewhere that you'd seek out for a shopping spree, but with a couple of shopping malls, things are looking up. New in town is the **Kafubu**

Mall [392 B5], where a big new branch of Shoprite eclipses their original branch on Chisokone Avenue [392 C4], and there's guarded parking.

Further south is the **Jacaranda Mall** [off map, 392 B7] (*Kabwe Rd*), reached by taking the first turning right after the Masala roundabout on your way south. Here you'll find a large branch of Pick 'n' Pay.

OTHER PRACTICALITIES

Banks   There are ATMs at Barclays and Stanbic banks, on President Avenue [392 C4].

Communications   Internet cafés are located both next to and opposite the Savoy Hotel on Buteko Avenue [392 C3], and opposite the Bank of Zambia on Broadway.

Health   The best clinic in Ndola is considered to be the Mary Begg Clinic [392 A2] (*Chintu Av*; \ *0212 612525/6/8*). There's also Ndola's Hilltop Hospital [392 B5] (*Independence Way*; \ *0212 611051/2*; m *0977 757272*). The town has several pharmacies, including Link in the Kafubu Mall, and Chemopharm on Chisokone Avenue, opposite Shoprite [392 C4].

Travel agents   If you're in town and need help with local arrangements either locally or around the region, contact:

Voyagers [392 C3] 17–18 Arusha St; \ 0212 627800; m 0977 860648; e nt@voyagerszambia. com; www.voyagerszambia.com. Ndola is the heartland of the generally highly regarded Voyagers, who have their head office in town. It's worth noting that they can collect travellers from the Kasumbalesa/Mokambo border post. See ad in 3rd colour section.

WHAT TO SEE AND DO   Most activities in the town centre around the local sports clubs: cricket, rugby, golf [392 A5] (with an 18-hole course) and sailing. There's also a swimming pool on Nkandabwe Avenue [392 B4] with a separate garden bar.

For the first-time visitor a walk to the top of the low, grassy **hill** in **Lupili Park** [392 C2], in a residential area just north of the centre, gives a good sense of location, with an excellent view across to the DRC – and the cement factories.

In town itself, the oft-overlooked **Copperbelt Museum** [392 C4] (*Buteko Av*) hosts small exhibitions on the geology and cultural history of the Copperbelt, with a rather unusual look at toys in the form of intricate wire models of mining machinery and the like, made by local children. Downstairs is a shop selling a range of baskets and other curios. There are still long-term plans for the museum to move to new premises on Independence Avenue, between the High Court and the Civic Centre, and to change its name to the Museum of Science and Technology. For now, though, the museum is of only passing interest.

Not far from the museum, the old **Slave Tree** on Makoli Avenue is of historical importance, though behind its locked gates it seems rather neglected, and taking photographs may not be welcome. The tree is a very old pod mahogany (*Afzelia quanzensis*, known locally as a *mupapa*), on which two species of figs are parasitic. In 1880 the Swahili slave-traders frequented this area and built a stockade, using the shade of the tree as a meeting place. It was also a place where slaves were bought and sold between the various traders. The slave trade was abolished in Zambia in the early 1900s, as the British established a colonial administration. Ndola was founded in 1904 and now just a representation of the tree features on its coat of arms, while a plaque at the foot of the tree reads:

DAG HAMMARSKJÖLD

The death of UN Secretary-General Dag Hammarskjöld in a plane crash on 17 September 1961 shocked the world, not least because the circumstances of the crash were steeped in controversy. Sixteen people died when the DC6 travelling *en route* from Congo to Ndola crashed into a tree on farmland just outside the town. Whether the crash was a result of pilot error, or whether the plane was shot down by mercenaries fighting on the side of the Congolese against the United Nations, has never been ascertained, although no evidence was ever found of foul play, or indeed of any mechanical failure. Attempts to find out the cause of the crash were hampered by looters who were at the scene before the arrival of the rescue services.

Mr Hammarskjöld was elected to the post of secretary-general in 1953, and takes the credit for introducing the idea of establishing a United Nations' peace-keeping force. At the time of his death, he had been taking part in talks in Leopoldville (now Kinshasa) to try to resolve the conflict, which by 1961 had been dragging on for a number of years. The talks ended in deadlock, and the delegates were travelling to neutral territory under cover of darkness, although stories of decoy planes and other spy-story antics are much exaggerated.

The memorial's former curator, M K Nasilele, has written a (somewhat controversial) account of the incident in *Crashed Hopes Revived*, published privately in 2006 and available at the Copperbelt Museum. To give the memorial a more lasting significance, Mr Nasilele was also involved in the establishment in 2002 of the nearby Dag Hammarskjöld Memorial School.

This plate has been placed on this mupapa tree to commemorate the passing of the days when, under its shade, the last of the Swahili traders, who warred upon and enslaved the people of the surrounding country, used to celebrate their victories and share out their spoils.

A second slave tree, Chichele Mofu Tree, lies in the centre of the dual carriageway to Kitwe, about 11km from Ndola – having fallen down in the last couple of years.

A couple of kilometres closer to Ndola, and signposted to the north of the road, the **Dag Hammarskjöld Memorial** (*US$15/7 adult/child*) commemorates the United Nations Secretary-General who was killed here in 1961 (see box, above). Designated a national monument, and a World Heritage Site, it lies along a 5km tarred road through farmland, lined in part with tall pine trees from the secretary-general's native Sweden. In addition to a stone cairn on the site, there is a memorial garden and a visitors' centre displaying information about Mr Hammarskjöld and his role in the UN, and documenting the circumstances leading up to the crash. Outside, pine trees at the memorial are laid out in the shape of a plane. It's slightly unnerving that the airport is to be relocated to land adjacent to the memorial.

EXCURSIONS FROM NDOLA Relatively near Ndola are two lodges which are destinations in their own right, and are often visited on long weekends from Lusaka or the Copperbelt: Nsobe Game Camp (page 394) and Kafue Lodge (pages 394–5).

Sunken lakes The landscape around Ndola and Kitwe features a series of water-filled limestone sinkholes which manifest themselves as lakes. Of these, two are particularly popular – and each tends to be known as simply 'the sunken lake'. The

The Copperbelt NDOLA

13

first, **Lake Chilengwa**, is about 16km southeast of Ndola, where fishing and boating make for a popular day trip.

Considerably further afield is the better-known **Lake Kashiba** (*US$10/5 adult/child; vehicle US$5/day*), also known as the 'sacred lake', a reflection of its status in traditional beliefs. Go for a picnic, to swim or simply just to explore. It's located 70km south of Ndola, to the southwest of Mpongwe, and near Kafue Lodge (pages 394–5).

KITWE

Situated a few kilometres southwest of the large Nkana Mine, Kitwe is 59km from Ndola, the two towns linked by a very good dual carriageway. The extensive pine forests lining the north side of the road extend as far as the border with the DRC, and were planted by President Kaunda as part of a timber export initiative. Kitwe is Zambia's second-largest town and relies for its prosperity on copper mining, whose presence is all too visible in the extensive slag heaps on the edge of town.

Like most of the Copperbelt towns, Kitwe was in the doldrums for several years with a steady decline in amenities, activities and general infrastructure. However, in the last few years it has seen a resurgence in prosperity following privatisation of the mines and a rapid rise in the value of copper on the world market. Today, it's a thriving town with plenty of amenities.

GETTING THERE AND AWAY

By bus Getting to or from Kitwe is easiest by bus. Kitwe's main bus terminus is in Martindale (shown on some maps as the 'second class trading area'), next to the main town centre. Here you'll find many departures for Ndola plus daily connections to Chingola Solwezi, and Lusaka (*K80*). There are also regular buses to the Luapula area and northern provinces, although buses on these long-distance routes will hang around until they fill, even if this takes a day or two.

By air The town's Southdowns Airport is about 25km to the west on the Kalulushi and then Kalengwa roads. In 2015, Proflight's link between Kitwe and Lusaka was reinstated, with flights twice a day from Wednesday to Friday and once on Saturday and Sunday. The region's main airport is at Ndola.

By train Kitwe used to be the end of the line for trains from Livingstone that pass through Ndola and Lusaka, but the service has been suspended. Fortunately the bus has long been a better option!

Hitchhiking Like Ndola, Kitwe is a large town, so good hitch spots are a long walk from the centre. It is best to get a taxi for a few kilometres.

WHERE TO STAY

In Kitwe When the first edition of this book was written, there was little choice of accommodation in Kitwe, and that which existed was poor value. However, that's all changed as small guesthouses such as the Mukwa seem to have sprung up everywhere, leaving the large old hotels like the Edinburgh with little choice but to reform radically or go out of business. That said, increased pressure on rooms in the town has seen many of the guesthouses expand, not always for the best.

Most of the following accept Visa and MasterCard credit cards.

🏠 **Africanza Lodge & Restaurant** [400 C1] (8 rooms) 11 Mushitu Cl, Parklands; \0212 221097; e africanza@copperbeltlodging.com; www. copperbeltlodging.com/africanza. In a garden setting, Africanza is centred on the restaurant formerly known as Arabian Nights but now owned by Copperbelt University (see below), but its rooms are no afterthought. All are en suite & the best of them, in the main house, are large & stylish, with AC, phone & fridge, DSTV & Wi-Fi. **$$$**

🏠 **Jasmin** [400 B2] (34 rooms) Jasmin Cl, off Poinsettia Dr, Parklands; \0212 215124; m 0966 192925; e jasmin@microlink.zm; www. copperbeltlodging.com/jasmin. Considerable expansion at Jasmin has resulted in lots of nooks & crannies, & some of the rooms spilling over across the road. If the communal areas feel a bit random in design, the en-suite rooms are all compact, modern & clean, with DSTV, phones & AC or fans. Accommodation ranges from sgl brick rondavels to 4-bed family units & 3 twin rooms within the main house. Outside is a swimming pool, overlooked by the restaurant & bar. Parking is outside the gate, under the supervision of a night watchman. **$$$**

🏠 **Mukwa Guest House** [400 C3] (13 rooms) 26–28 Mpezeni Av; \0212 224266/77; e mukwa@zamsat.net; www.mukwalodge. co.zm. The old colonial-style building at Mukwa is surrounded by attractive gardens with a swimming pool. Each of the spacious rooms has satellite TV, direct-dial phone, good Wi-Fi, fridge, complimentary fruit basket & a tea/coffee station. The lounge, with its Africa-centric décor, is notable for the absence of a TV, so makes a pleasant spot to read a book, but the greatest attraction is the smart Indian/Continental restaurant (page 401). **$$$**

🏠 **Sherbourne** [400 C3] (23 rooms, annexe, flats) 20–22 Pamo Rd; \0212 222168; m 0955 782778; e reservations@sherbourne.co.zm; www.sherbourne.co.zm. Sherbourne now has a range of accommodation on offer. In the Main Lodge & 4-room annexe at 14 Mpezeni Av, rooms each have twin or dbl beds, as well as satellite TV, minibar/fridge, internet access & phone. A swimming pool, fountains & playground are set in established gardens with tables on the lawn. The restaurant serves traditional & international cuisine. There are 3 self-catering family flats on Chibote Avenue & 14 modern apartments (12 2-bed & 2 studio, cont b/fast inc) at no.32, 3rd Nkana West. **$$$**

🏠 **Town House Lodge** [400 D1] (8 rooms) 65A Mabvuto Ct, off Freedom Av, Parklands; \0212 221855; e townhouse@coppernet.zm; www.copperbeltlodging.com/townhouse. If the corridors at this relaxed place feel rather old-fashioned, its rooms are modern & nicely appointed, with flashes of bright colour to enliven an otherwise neutral décor; the honeymoon suite, though, goes heavy on the leopard print. Each room has en-suite shower or bath, as well as AC, DSTV, minibar/fridge, safe, & kettle for tea & coffee. Guests can relax on a sunny veranda or in the TV lounge, & there's a small dining room or alfresco dining in the garden, too. **$$$**

🏠 **Pamo Lodge** [400 C3] (10 rooms) 2 Pamo Av; \0212 222769; e pamo@zamnet.zm. One of the town's less expensive offerings, Pamo Lodge makes a feature of mix 'n' match furniture & décor that's heavy on colour & frills. Rooms are clean, if dark, with en-suite shower or bath, & fan, fridge, DSTV & kettle. **$$**

✖ **WHERE TO EAT** Like Ndola, Kitwe has plenty of takeaways, with reliably hygienic standards – if not haute cuisine. The most notable include the **Hungry Lion** [400 C5] (opposite the main post office in the centre of town) for hamburgers and pies, and **After 10** [400 C4] (in Martindale – the 'second-class trading area') for snacks, sandwiches, pizzas, curries, Chinese and even Arabian dishes. The latter, predictably given its name, stays open late.

For a good evening meal you need to look more carefully. Try the following (and note that in addition to the restaurants listed here, both the **Jasmin** and **Sherbourne** guesthouses will accept non-residents for meals).

✖ **Africanza** [off map, 400 C1] 11 Mushitu Cl, Parklands; \0212 221097; ⊕ daily. Formerly Arabian Nights Africanza serves a variety of

international dishes. It's a classy place, sited both indoors & on a covered veranda, next to a series of fish pools with a fountain. It's dark &

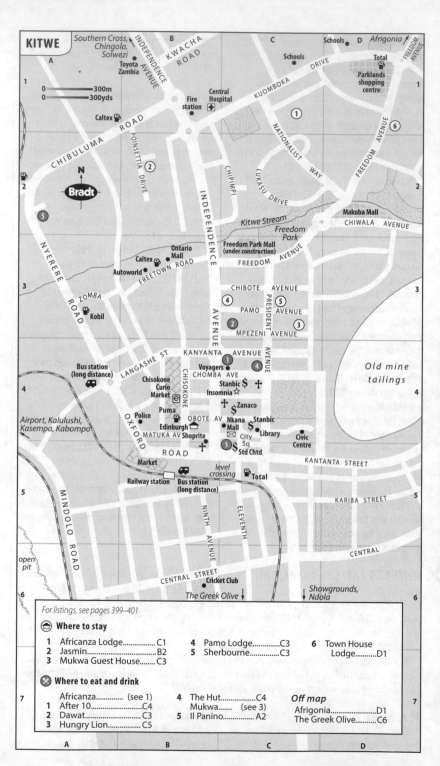

KITWE

Southern Cross,
Chingola,
Solwezi

Toyota
Zambia

Fire
station

Central
Hospital

Schools

Schools

Afrigonia

Total

Parklands
shopping
centre

Caltex

KWACHA ROAD

INDEPENDENCE AVENUE

CHIBULUMA ROAD

POINSETTIA DRIVE

KUOMBOKA DRIVE

NATIONALIST WAY

FREEDOM AVENUE

Bradt

NYERERE ROAD

Caltex

Ontario
Mall

Autoworld

ZOMBA

Kobil

Bus station
(long distance)

Airport, Kalulushi,
Kasempa, Kabompo

FREETOWN ROAD

INDEPENDENCE AVENUE

CHIPIMPI

LUKASU DRIVE

Kitwe Stream

Freedom
Park

Freedom Park Mall
(under construction)

FREEDOM AVENUE

Makuba Mall

CHIWALA AVENUE

CHIBOTE AVENUE

PAMO AVENUE

MPEZENI AVENUE

PRESIDENT AVENUE

Old mine
tailings

LANGASHE ST

CHISOKONE

KANYANTA AVENUE

Voyagers

CHOMBA AVE

Stanbic

Insomnia

Chisokone
Curio
Market

Police

Puma

Edinburgh

Matuka AV

Shoprite

OXFORD ROAD

OBOTE AV

Zanaco

Nkana
Mall

Stanbic

Library

City
Sq

Std Chtd

Civic
Centre

KANTANTA STREET

Market

Railway station

Bus station
(long distance)

level
crossing

Total

MINDOLO ROAD

NINTH AVENUE

ELEVENTH AVENUE

KARIBA STREET

CENTRAL

open
pit

CENTRAL STREET

Cricket Club

The Greek Olive

Showgrounds,
Ndola

0   300m
0   300yds

For listings, see pages 399–401

Where to stay

1   Africanza Lodge................C1
2   Jasmin................................B2
3   Mukwa Guest House........C3

4   Pamo Lodge..............C3
5   Sherbourne...............C3

6   Town House
      Lodge..........D1

Where to eat and drink

    Africanza............ (see 1)
1   After 10...........................C4
2   Dawat...............................C3
3   Hungry Lion.....................C5

4   The Hut...............C4
    Mukwa....... (see 3)
5   Il Panino................A2

Off map
Afrigonia.....................D1
The Greek Olive...........C6

atmospheric & the on-site guesthouse means you can stay over, too. $$$$–$$$$$

✗ **Afrigonia** [off map, 400 D1] Zambezi Way; m 0969 279251. Part Argentinian, part African, the popular Afrigonia adds a further dimension to Kitwe's dining scene. $$$$

✗ **The Hut** [400 C4] 69 Eno Chomba Av; m 0976 729978; www.thehutkitwe.com. One of Kitwe's best restaurants, The Hut serves Italian & Greek cuisine alongside steaks & more to give a varied menu in an informal setting. $$$$

✗ **Dawat** [400 C3] Independence Av; ☏0212 228281; ⊕ 09.00–22.00 Tue–Sun. Another good Indian restaurant, also serving steaks & fish. $$$$

✗ **Mukwa Restaurant** [400 C3] 26–28 Mpezeni Av (off President Av); ☏0212 224266;

⊕ 11.00–15.00, 18.00–21.30. Part of the guesthouse of the same name, Mukwa is an elegantly stylish restaurant serving a good variety of North Indian food, as well as more usual Continental fare. $$$–$$$$$

⊑ **Il Panino** [400 A2] 3044 Lilongwe Rd; ☏0212 212329; ⊕ 08.00–16.00 Mon–Fri. An unexpected find in the industrial area of Kitwe, this is a cool, modern place for b/fast or light meals, including pancakes & salads. There's a delicatessen on site, too, so you can top up on supplies at the same time. $$

⊑ **The Greek Olive** [off map, 400 C6] 14 Club St, Nkana West; ☏0212 227689; m 0976 526480. Lively taverna serving Greek food as well as pasta & pizza. $$

NIGHTLIFE As you might expect, many of the local restaurants are popular watering holes in the evenings. There are several nightclubs in town – though do take local advice as the current 'in' places change regularly. You could try Club Insomnia and Insomnia Chills [400 C4] on 49B Kabengele Avenue. All have pool tables, dance floors and disco music, tending to stick to rhumba and rhythm and blues.

As in other cities, these clubs are frequented almost exclusively by black Zambians, and they generally open until very late. Normally they have a very lively and friendly atmosphere, so overseas visitors should have no problems. If/when trouble develops, the owners of the clubs are generally quite good at sorting it out. You should, of course, take the standard precautions that apply in any such busy places to avoid the attention of thieves and pickpockets – by dressing down and not carrying valuables.

SHOPPING The large new Makuba Mall [400 D2] on Kitwe's Chiwala Avenue has transformed shopping in the town, complete with a big branch of Shoprite and another of Game. There's fast food aplenty, too. Another mall, Nkana Mall, is due to open in the heart of the city (on the corner of Obote and Independence avenues) in April 2016. Shoprite [400 B4] also has a branch just off Independence Avenue, near the Edinburgh Hotel. More interesting perhaps is the main **market** [400 B5], which runs alongside the railway, close to the Edinburgh Hotel. Adjacent to this, near the long-distance bus station, and right at the end of Obote Avenue past the Edinburgh Hotel, is the large Chisokone Curio Market [400 B4].

OTHER PRACTICALITIES
Car spares and repairs The best places for spares are: Autoworld [400 B3] (off Freetown Road, Takkies, Southern Cross, Vehicle Centre and Toyota Zambia [400 B1] (north on Independence Avenue towards Chingola on the left beyond Kwacha Road).

Communications There are various **internet cafés** around town, including one on the ground floor of the Edinburgh Hotel [400 B4]. One of the best is Botech [400 B3] (*Ontario Shopping Mall, Freetown Rd;* ⊕ 08.00–20.00). The main **post office** [400 C4] is just off Zambia Way, opposite Shoprite and Barclays Bank.

Health If you fall ill in or near Kitwe, contact the Mopani Copper Mines (Wusakile) Hospital (↑ *0212 249105*). To find it, take a left at the first set of traffic lights as you enter Kitwe from Ndola, and go past the mine. There are several pharmacies in the town.

For situations that are more serious, and may require immediate evacuation, contact Speciality Emergency Services on a toll-free, national, short code number – dial: 737. The call-centre is manned by paramedics.

Money and banking Most of the large banks have branches in the centre of town, around the junction of Oxford Road and Zambia Way.

Travel agents and car hire
Voyagers [400 C4] Enos Chomba Av;
↑ 0212 225056/229102–3; m 0977 860648;
e kt@voyagerszambia.com;
www.voyagerszambia.com

WHAT TO SEE AND DO In itself, Kitwe has few intrinsic attractions; as in Ndola, activities tend to centre around the local sports clubs. That said, the town is sufficiently close to Ndola for the two to share local attractions (pages 390–8). Nearer Kitwe itself, there are a number of places of interest, including the **crocodile ponds** at Chililabombwe – the last town to the north before the border with the DRC.

Chembe Bird Sanctuary This woodland reserve has been recently taken over by the government and handed over to ZAWA in a bid to restore it as a tourist attraction. The aim is to fence it and restock it with wild animals and different bird species. It is about half-an-hour's drive to the west of Kitwe, is just off the road between Kalulushi and Kasempa. Centred on a small lake, it has been a haven for birders, with over 300 of Zambia's listed birds recorded here; *chembe* is the local name for the African fish eagle, a regular visitor. Line fishing is permitted on the lake, where spotted-neck otters may be seen, but this is no place to swim: crocodiles are plentiful. Rather safer is the 7km Chinkamba Drive around the lake, offering a 2-hour walk or short drive: it's navigable by 2WD in the dry season.

In the same direction is **Mindolo Dam**, home of Kitwe Boat Club (where you can get drinks and snacks) and a good spot for picnics, boating and quadbikes.

CHINGOLA

Chingola lies at the western end of the Copperbelt, about 50km west of Kitwe on a good road with just the occasional pot-hole. Beyond here you either head west towards Solwezi and Mwinilunga, or proceed north towards Lubumbashi in the DRC. The town is dominated by the huge KCM open-pit mines – the largest in Zambia – that have gouged the landscape on the eastern side of the town. Signs of renewed prosperity are everywhere, with investment attracted from all over the world.

GETTING THERE AND AROUND Work started on a dual carriageway between Kitwe and Chingola, improving further the link between the two towns, although the level of accidents along that stretch is extremely high. The road remains a single carriageway, however sections of the journey are now undertaken on the new road that runs adjacent to the old road. There is some optimism that the road will be completed in time for elections.

Chingola itself is well served by buses to and from other towns in the Copperbelt and as far as both Solwezi and Lusaka. For details see under *Kitwe*, page 396.

If you're driving yourself, note that several of the town's side streets are blocked at one end, making the concept of 'driving round the block' somewhat challenging! Note, too, that development of the KCM mine to the north of town has resulted in changes in the road layout from that shown on many maps.

WHERE TO STAY While a few visitors choose to stay overnight at the Chimfunshi Wildlife Orphanage (pages 405–6), most opt to base themselves in Chingola, either at the new Protea or at one of the guesthouses, and visit the orphanage as a day trip. The quality of guesthouses in Chingola has become rather hit and miss and we have had conflicting reports but you could try New Hibiscus or Mica's.

In town

Protea Hotel Chingola [404 D4] (40 rooms) Kabundi Rd; 0212 312810; e reservations@ phchingola.co.zm; www.proteahotel.com/chingola. This L-shaped building, all blues & terracottas, is set in an open position just outside town, fronted by trees & a large parking area. From its cool blue reception area it is modern, light & very well kept, with plenty of solid wood furnishings. Rooms have en-suite bath & separate shower, AC, armchair, kettle, TV, desk & Wi-Fi. They are set out in 2 wings either side of an apex formed by a pool & terrace, & backed by a smart but comfortable restaurant (06.00–22.00). Here, à-la-carte menus offer everything from light meals to pastas to grills. Alongside the conference rooms are a business centre with internet (*office hours only*), & a steel-&-chrome bar with upstairs lounge that can be heaving at w/ends. **$$$–$$$$**

Mokorro Hotel [404 B4] (30 rooms) 514 Kabundi Rd; 0212 310079; m 0968 123190; e mokorro@mokorro.co.zm; www.mokorrohotel. com. Far from the informal establishment of yore, the Mokorro Grill has evolved into a sizeable hotel with a range of rooms decorated in muted greys & white. AC, TV & Wi-Fi come as standard. The grill itself (08.00–23.00 daily, **$$$$**) still has sports TV in the outside *lapa*, with a broad-ranging menu from pizzas & grills to seafood. **$$$**

New Hibiscus Guest House [404 C5] (9 rooms) 33 Katutwa Rd; 0212 313635; m 0966 781045; e hibiscus@copperbeltlodging. com. Under new ownership and located just south of the roundabout, Hibiscus is set in attractive gardens with a small pool. All rooms are en suite with DSTV & a fridge. Wi-Fi. **$$**

Mica's Guesthouse [404 C2] (12 rooms) 59 5th St; 0212 313653; m 0977 188782. Close to the hospital, Mica's has clean dbl & family rooms, each with TV, fan, mosi net, & en-suite bath or shower & toilet. There's a bar in the entrance, & meals can be provided on request. **$$**

Out of town

Nabona Estate & River Lodge [map, page 382] (10 rooms, 4 2-bed cottages) Chililabombwe Rd; m 0966 992900, 0969 302424; e nabonalodge@yahoo.com. Set on a farm on the banks of the Kafue River, Nabona is 16km from the centre of Chigala, off the Kasumbalesa road. All rooms are en suite. Guests have the use of a bar with games area, a dining room, & a lounge with TV & internet access, plus a braai area in the garden. **$$**

Riverbend Campsite [map, page 382] (3 tents, camping) m 0966 997410/990251; e reevo.chas@gmail.com. On a 4km stretch of the Kafue River, Riverbend is situated amidst large, shady trees on a farm some 35km west of Chingola – approx 10km from the chimp orphanage. As well as the campsite, with an ablution block & hot showers, there are simple en-suite walk-in tents. Each has twin beds, a table, chairs & chest of drawers, & a firepit; linen can be supplied but bring your own towels. Campers share a kitchen, plus 2 thatched *lapas* with tables & benches. Firewood is supplied, with an attendant on hand to light fires, & portable braais are available but otherwise you'll need to be totally self sufficient. There are paraffin lamps in the ablution & kitchen blocks, & battery-operated lamps in the tents, but no other power. As well as graded tracks for walking or bikes (bring your own), there are a couple of 2-man canoes & a small children's play area. *Tent without/with linen. Camping K40 per tent. Day visitor K25 (children free).*

The Copperbelt CHINGOLA

13

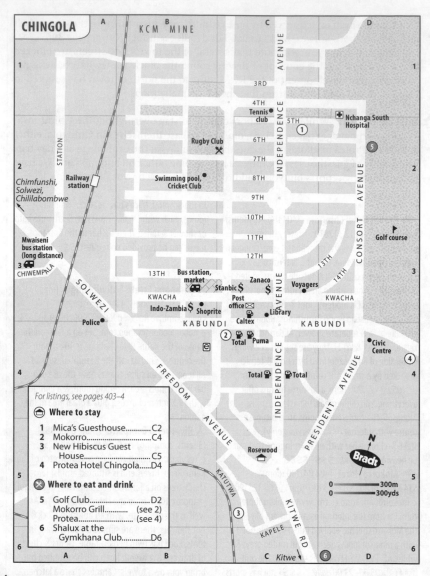

CHINGOLA

KCM MINE

STATION

Chimfunshi,
Solwezi,
Chililabombwe

Railway
station

Mwaiseni
bus station
(long distance)
CHIWEMPALA

SOLWEZI

Police

FREEDOM AVENUE

KATUTWA

3RD

4TH

Tennis
club

5TH

6TH

Rugby Club

7TH

Swimming pool,
Cricket Club

8TH

9TH

10TH

11TH

12TH

13TH

Bus station,
market

KWACHA

Indo-Zambia

Shoprite

Stanbic

Post
office

Caltex

KABUNDI

Zanaco

Library

KABUNDI

INDEPENDENCE AVENUE

AVENUE

13TH

14TH

CONSORT AVENUE

Nchanga South
Hospital

Golf course

Voyagers

KWACHA

Total
Puma

Civic
Centre

Total

Total

INDEPENDENCE AVENUE

PRESIDENT AVENUE

Rosewood

KITWE RD

KAPELE

Kitwe

Bradt

N

0   300m
0   300yds

For listings, see pages 403–4

🛏 **Where to stay**
1   Mica's Guesthouse.............C2
2   Mokorro.................................C4
3   New Hibiscus Guest
     House.................................C5
4   Protea Hotel Chingola......D4

✗ **Where to eat and drink**
5   Golf Club................................D2
     Mokorro Grill............ (see 2)
     Protea............................ (see 4)
6   Shalux at the
     Gymkhana Club...............D6

✗ **WHERE TO EAT AND DRINK** Until recently, Chingola wasn't well endowed with places to eat, but things are slowly changing. The restaurant at the **Protea** (see page 403) is popular for both formal and poolside dining, as is the Mokorro Grill at the **Mokorro Hotel** (page 403).

✗ **Shalux at the Gymkhana Club**
[404 D6] Kitwe Rd; \ 0212 311346; m 0966 781955/908124, 0955 263090; ⊕ all day Mon–Sat, 1st & last Sun of month). Chingola's best Indian restaurant is to the south of town, & also serves Chinese, steaks & fish. $$$$

✗ **Golf Club** [404 D2] \ 0212 311179;
⊕ 10.00–20.00 daily. A good place to come for lunch or an early dinner, the restaurant at the golf club is also open for b/fast. $$

OTHER PRACTICALITIES There is a new mall close to the Boma, adjacent to the roundabout where you leave Chingola for Solwezi and Chililabombwe. For now, Chingola's best shop for **supplies** is Shoprite. Otherwise there are plenty of small shops catering to everyday needs.

Health The place to head for in case of a medical emergency is the well-staffed and well-equipped **Nchanga South Hospital** [404 D2] (*4th St*; ☎ *0212 351018*), which is run by the mine.

Travel agents and car hire
Voyagers [404 C3] 14th St; ☎ 0212 311642/
311722/312195; m 0977 860648;
e ct@voyagerszambia.com; www.
voyagerszambia.com

WHAT TO SEE AND DO Chimfunshi Wildlife Orphanage is the greatest draw in an area whose attractions are otherwise linked to the town's sports clubs. There is also **Hippo Pool**, a designated national monument and a favoured picnic spot, a few kilometres outside the town.

Chimfunshi Wildlife Orphanage (*PO Box 11190 Chingola;* ☎ *0212 311293;* m *0966 208405; www.chimfunshi.de/en/; admission*) Probably the most popular excursion from Chingola is to Chimfunshi Wildlife Orphanage. This refuge for some of Africa's great apes is very much a working wildlife sanctuary. Although tourists are welcome to watch the chimps being fed and at play, it is not specifically geared to visitors. It's well off the main Zambian tourist trail and, aside from a number of dedicated supporters, is virtually unknown outside the country.

Chimfunshi started off as a normal 4,000ha cattle farm beside the banks of the Kafue River, close to the border with the DRC (formerly Zaire). It was run by Sheila Siddle and her late husband, David. Over the years, the Siddles established a reputation for rescuing wild animals in need. Then, in October 1983, Sheila's son-in-law brought her an orphaned chimpanzee, named Pal, who had been confiscated

---

INDIGENOUS CHIMPS?

Chimpanzees are not generally thought to be indigenous to Zambia. Currently the southernmost population of wild chimps is thought to live in a remote (and relatively little-documented) corner of the Rukwa Region of Tanzania – around the Loasi River Forest Reserve on the eastern shore of Lake Tanganyika.

Chimpanzee distribution in the wild is limited by suitable habitat, and especially by the distribution of suitable vegetation and the wild fruit on which they live. Although there are remaining populations in woodland areas, most occur in moister, thicker forests – where the availability of wild fruits is higher. The relatively open, dry miombo woodlands in northern Zambia wouldn't be a typical habitat, although in some areas chimps do inhabit more arid woodland areas.

Sheila Siddle maintains that chimps could have once lived in Zambia. She cites oral evidence, reported from older local people in Mbala, just south of Lake Tanganyika, who refer to a species of animal which is now extinct in the area as *socamuntu*, meaning 'like a man' in the Bemba language.

from Zairean poachers. Pal was sick and malnourished, and had been physically abused, yet against the odds Sheila eventually nursed him back to health.

It had been known for some time that Zambia was a conduit for the illegal export of chimps from Zaire, but as the authorities had nowhere practicable to release any confiscated animals, they had not been over-zealous in trying to stop the trade. Gradually they confiscated more chimps; and, by mid 1988, the Siddles had 19 chimps at Chimfunshi. At first, all were kept in cages, but taken out for regular forest walks. Then, as sending rehabilitated chimps back to Zaire wasn't a safe option, the Siddles decided to build a large enclosure at Chimfunshi. With minimal backing, they built a 4m-high wall around 2.8ha of their own forest land, and gradually introduced a group of chimps into the area. Unexpectedly, these chimps eventually melded into a coherent family-type group, which was clearly a great success. By this time orphaned chimps were being sent here from many corners of the globe, so in 1991 a second, 5.6ha enclosure surrounded by a solar-powered electric fence was constructed to accommodate another group of chimps.

A few years later, the Siddles acquired an adjacent 5,400ha farm, and made over the land to the Chimfunshi Wildlife Orphanage Trust, ensuring that the chimps would have a permanent home – something that is particularly important for animals whose lifespan in captivity mirrors that of humans. The northern boundary of the farm is the Kafue River, which butts onto 1,000ha of dense forest, with large grassy areas of river floodplain and several small tributaries of the Kafue River. There is also a particularly beautiful patch of tropical forest, which follows a narrow gorge. Generous donations enabled the construction of two large 500ha enclosures with plenty of mature *musambya* (*Chrysophyllum magalismontanum*) trees, followed by two smaller enclosures of 200ha each. Each of these has a concrete 'feeding centre' – essentially a building with a door onto the open enclosure, and bars for windows, and the larger two have a rooftop observation area.

In 2000, Sheila and David were jointly awarded the MBE for their work with the chimps, and travelled to London where their medals were presented at Buckingham Palace by the Queen.

Chimfunshi today Today there are 132 chimps on the property and more enclosures are being built. Over the years, several chimps have been born on the farm, but several of the animals are now fitted with contraceptive implants. Most of the chimpanzees live in four large, forested enclosures. A herd of impala grazes the land between the two larger enclosures.

The chimps spend almost all of their time outside, coming inside only at feeding times, which means that they are close enough to be inspected by the keepers for any health problems.

Each of the 'family' groups is made up of animals that have been gradually introduced to each other until they become a cohesive unit, and only then can they be allowed into one of the large enclosures together. Those whose social groups are as yet incomplete live in a variety of pens and large cages near the house, with space at the back where they are free to roam for part of the day, when the keepers are around. Inevitably, there are a few chimps for whom socialising is a step too far, or who have escaped once too often, and these problem animals remain caged for safety's sake. It's not pretty, but the animals are well cared for, and the cages are almost certainly better than where the animals were before coming here; active fundraising is taking place to help improve their lot.

In addition to the chimps, Chimfunshi also rehabilitates various other orphaned animals. At any one time, you're likely to find a menagerie of furry, feathered and warm-blooded beings here, all either being nursed back to health, or being kept on after recovering. A typical story is that of Billy, the hippo, who joined the family in 1992. At ten days old, she was discovered on the bank of the Kafue, next to the body of her dead mother. She was adopted by Sheila, who kept her in the house when small. When, at well over 1,500kg, she was fully grown, she still came to the house each morning for her bottles of milk and wanders around the campsite and the farm with nonchalant disregard for her bulk – and anything that got in the way of it.

The orphanage is supported by a trust. If you would like to help, contact www.chimfunshi.de/en/support/). And to find out more, get hold of a copy of Sheila's book, *In My Family Tree* (page 529). Volunteers are also welcome through African Impact (*www.africanimpact.com/volunteer-projects/zambia/chimpanzee-sanctuary wildlife-orphan-care*).

Getting there It takes about an hour and a quarter to drive to Chimfunshi from Chingola. Take the tar road towards Solwezi for about 42km until you come to a sign pointing right (◈ TUCHIM 12°28.476'S, 27°29.150'E) to the orphanage. If you're coming from Solwezi, it's around 118km to this signpost. From the turn-off it's a further 18km along a reasonably good farm track to the orphanage (◈ CHIMFU 12°21.460'S, 27°33.242'E), taking about 40 minutes to drive in the dry season. There are no buses to the orphanage itself, but plenty of transport plies the route between Solwezi and Chingola, so it would be easy to be dropped at the turning, although hitching (or walking) along the access road could take some time.

Where to stay Chimfunshi was not designed with the tourist in mind, so forget all ideas of upmarket lodge-style accommodation. Those wishing to stay at the sanctuary have the choice of simple, dormitory-style rooms or a riverside campsite. Either way, you'll need to come with all your own food; meals are not provided. Do note, too, that communications out in the bush can be very poor, so if you're planning to stay, you need to allow plenty of time to set up your visit.

Education centre This modern centre is about 12km from the main farmhouse & incorporates accommodation for 20–30 people. It is used mainly for school classes, youth groups & undergraduate students from overseas, but when it is empty, private visitors are welcome to use the facilities. The buildings are simple modern prefabs, with small dormitory-style rooms, some with 7 beds, others with 2; bedding & towels are provided. All are clean, & are set around an open courtyard, with a large braai area, communal kitchens, & separate buildings with hot showers & long-drop toilets. Water is supplied from the site's own borehole. A cheerful classroom features posters showing the chimp 'family' groups, complete with individual portraits, while outside, each of the trees is labelled with both its Bemba & scientific names. *US$20 pp.*

Campsite [map, page 382] Set on a gently sloping bank of grass leading down to the river, the campsite is close to the house owned by Sheila's daughter, Sylvia. Campers share old but hot showers & long-drop toilets, & it's usually possible to borrow a few pots & pans if you need them. Those without their own tent can make use of the (very basic) caravan that's parked at the educational centre. *Camping US$10 pp.*

What to see and do Some visitors prefer to spend a few days here, taking advantage of the freedom to explore the farm's extensive walks and excellent birding (more than 350 species have been recorded), and affording the time to watch the chimps at leisure. Most, though, come for just a half day, or perhaps bring a picnic and spend the day here.

The chimps are divided between the two main enclosures, and a variety of large cages and smaller enclosures near the farmhouse. These, the educational centre and the campsite are a considerable distance apart, making some form of vehicle very useful; you can walk between places, but it takes a while! Visitors can drive themselves, or you can arrange to be collected from the educational centre or campsite to go to the farmhouse, where the bush walks and feeding of the baby chimps takes place.

The chimps follow a straightforward routine, which makes it relatively easy to plan a day out. Feeding times are at 08.00, when the babies are fed their milk in bottles, and balls of nshima are shared out among the older animals. Visitors are welcome to visit for the 11.30 feed of fruit and vegetables, and more milk for the whole group, or at 13.30 for the day's final offering of milk. (Milk provides the chimps with their protein requirement, substituting for the meat which would form a small part of their diet in the wild.) Outside of feeding time, when one of the keepers will explain something of the chimps' behaviour and routine, there are two options. Individual visitors are welcome to explore the enclosures themselves, observing the animals at tree level from the roof of the feeding centres, which makes for some excellent photographic opportunities.

Those staying overnight may have the opportunity to take part in a 2-hour morning bush walk with some of the younger chimps (in the company of one of the keepers. If the idea of a baby chimp jumping into your arms or riding piggyback across the bush to a natural playground appeals, then don't think twice. Just remember that this is no place for smart clothes, and remove any jewellery or other items before the chimps do it for you.

SOLWEZI

There has been a history of copper mining from the Kansanshi Hills north of Solwezi for hundreds of years, but commercial mining started only in the 20th century. Riding on the success of the Kansanshi Mine, Solwezi has evolved in just a few decades from a small village to a busy little town – and is still growing. While it's not an attraction in itself, it is useful for supplies if you're coming from Lusaka and heading west, or driving into Kafue from the north.

GETTING THERE AND AWAY The main 'tarred' road leading from Chingola to Solwezi (⊕ SOLWEZ 12°10.931'S, 26°23.960'E) covers the 180km distance in a series of pot-holes that could well cause the unwary to roll their vehicle. Treat it with caution, and watch out, too, for other road users: goats, pigs and cyclists.

By air Solwezi's airstrip is west of the town. Proflight operates flights to and from Lusaka daily. With so much industrial development in the area it's no surprise that there are plans to upgrade the airstrip to take regular international flights although at the moment it is only possible to charter flights in and out.

By bus Regular buses link Solwezi with Chingola, Kitwe and Lusaka, with departures from Solwezi usually in the early morning and early afternoon. Expect to pay from K80 to Lusaka. The bus station straddles the main road, next to and opposite the market, at the western end of town.

⌂ **WHERE TO STAY** Like so many of Zambia's northern towns, Solwezi has benefited from the resurgence in the mining industry. Now, in addition to several larger, old-style motels, and an ever-increasing variety of small guesthouses, there are one or two entirely different places to stay, from the upmarket Royal Solwezi to the simple but well-run Floriana. Of the rest, most are reasonable – and reasonably accessible from the main tar road through town.

🏠 **Kansanshi Hotel** [off map, 410] (38 rooms) 📞 0218 821221; 📱 0965 611611; e info. kansanshihotel@gmail.com; www.kansanshi-hotel.com. In a forested location about 2km from the main road, this hotel is some 10mins both from town & from the Kansanshi Mine. Its thatched buildings incorporate rooms of various standards, all en suite with internet access & DSTV; there are self-catering villas too. Guests can dine à la carte in the restaurant, or eat in the pizzeria & sports bar near the pool. **$$$–$$$$**

🏠 **Floriana Lodge Trust** [map, page 410] (41 rooms) 📞 0218 821130; 📱 09/3 566937/ 0968 163967. At the eastern entrance to the town, this much-expanded lodge is named after an Italian nun & missionary who spent much of her life working in Zambia before tragically being shot dead by bandits. Its en-suite rooms, each with a TV, phone, fan, fridge & tea/coffee facilities, have been built in blocks around 3 sides of a grassy, tree-shaded area, where thatched gazebos offer plenty of shade (& shelter) for a cool drink. Rates include a full English b/fast served in their restaurant, in which they also conjure up Chinese, Indian, English & Zambian dishes, with the local dish of Solwezi beans, *kingovwa* sweet potatoes, honey & mushroom – all sourced locally – a speciality that's available on request. **$$$**

🏠 **Royal Solwezi** [map, page 410] (48 rooms) 147 Old Chingola Rd; 📞 0211 821620; 📱 0966 271422; e reservations@solwezi.com; www. solwezi.com. Set on a low hill on the eastern edge of town, about 0.5km from the main road, the Royal Solwezi occupies a prime spot, with good views to the east. Rooms are huge – sgls have a dbl bed; dbls have 2 of them – with ultra-modern bathroom fittings, a TV & safe as standard. Bright splashes of colour & trendy photos documenting the hotel's phases of construction enliven tinted cement floors & bed plinths, & solid mukwa-wood desks. The rooms are built in 2-storey blocks, 2 each side of the cavernous central area. Patio doors from each lead onto a balcony or straight out to wide lawns stretching across to the pool & a sports bar with plasma TV screens – sufficiently far away for noise not to be an issue. Towards the bottom of the plot, 10 2-bedroom villas cater to long-stay visitors. The veranda is an attractive & relaxed place for a drink, contrasting with the formality of the modern restaurant. There's Wi-Fi throughout, a business centre & conference facilities, & secure parking. Despite the attractions, the hotel has had long-term problems with retaining management, so standards may not always be as high as they should. **$$$**

🏠 **Crossroads Lodge** [off map, 410] (48 rooms) 📞 0218 821390. About 1.6km from the Royal Solwezi heading northeast along the Old Chingola Road. A reasonable-cost alternative with functional en-suite rooms with fridge, mosi net, TV. **$$**

🏠 **Mwaaka Lodge** [map, page 410] (20 rooms) 📞 0218 821248. Right next to the main road, opposite the Changa Changa Motel (which isn't one we'd recommend!), this little guesthouse, with its slightly jaunty crazy-paving & stone look, seems to promise more than it delivers. Outside, a thatched bar & separate restaurant bode well, & there's secure parking, but the bedrooms are typical of guesthouse bedrooms anywhere, & could do with a bit of care. A TV, fridge & en-suite bath or shower come as standard, while the more expensive also have a sofa. **$$**

✗ **WHERE TO EAT AND DRINK** The Royal Solwezi is a relaxing place for a drink or two and has a smart restaurant, but there are alternatives, including the Kansanshi Hotel and the established Floriana. Smaller eateries – and nightclubs – come and go. For more varied (if not inspiring) fare, there's also:

✗ **Kilimanjaro** [map, page 410] 🕐 06.00– 22.00 daily. Towards the western end of town, the Kilimanjaro has a garden setting, with individual thatched rondavels & an indoor bar/restaurant. It offers an eclectic mix of pasta, grills, Indian, Chinese & Zambian specials. **$$**

COMMUNICATIONS Mobile phone coverage is good in Solwezi. The main **post office** is just off the main road near Shoprite, behind the Puma garage.

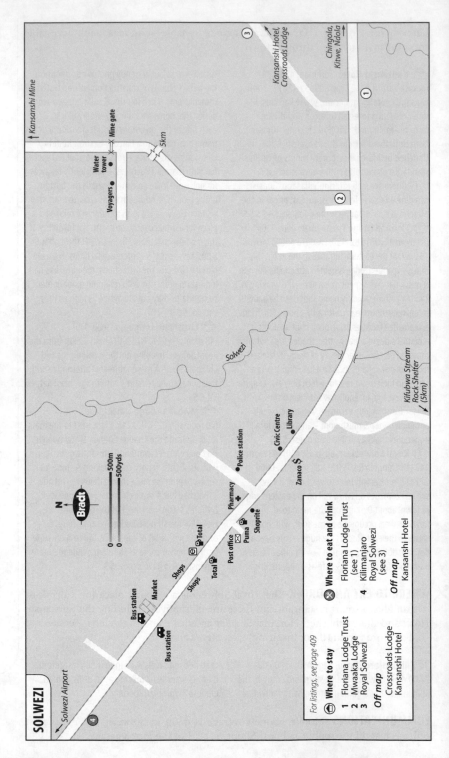

SOLWEZI

↑ Solwezi Airport

Kansanshi Mine ↑

Mine gate

Water tower ●

Voyagers ●

5km

⊗ Kansanshi Hotel, Crossroads Lodge ③

↓ Chingola, Kitwe, Ndola ①

②

Bus station

Market

Shops

Shops

Bus station

Total ⛽

Post office ⊠

Puma ⛽ 🏪

Shoprite

Pharmacy ✚

● Police station

● Civic Centre

● Library

Zanaco $

Total ⛽ @

Solwezi

Kifubwa Stream Rock Shelter (5km) ↓

N Bradt

0   500m
0   500yds

For listings, see page 409

🛏 **Where to stay**

1 Floriana Lodge Trust
2 Mwaaka Lodge
3 Royal Solwezi

Off map
Crossroads Lodge
Kansanshi Hotel

⊗ **Where to eat and drink**

Floriana Lodge Trust
  (see 1)
4 Kilimanjaro
Royal Solwezi
  (see 3)

Off map
Kansanshi Hotel

OTHER PRACTICALITIES Solwezi is basically a linear town, with most shops and offices concentrated along the tarred road. Of greatest practical use to most visitors is the branch of **Shoprite** supermarket, which has a prominent place on the main through road. It's by far the best shop in the region, and a good place to stock up, especially if you're heading south or west. The long-rumoured shopping centre along the road to Kansanshi Mine has yet to materialise.

There are several **fuel** stations; indeed, the town is generally a reliable place to refuel, and you should fill up completely if you're heading west or south from here. There are also several large branches of **banks**, Finance Bank, Barclays, FNB, and Stanbic all have ATMS.

In an emergency, there's a 24-hour Medical Centre (↳ *0218 821225*). For other medical issues, the best place to go is Hilltop Hospital (↳ *0218 821707)*), just off the main road through town.

Travel agents, car hire and vehicle repairs

Voyagers [map, page 410] Stand 5707, off Kansanshi Rd, near Kansanshi main gate; m 0966 400534, 0977 860648; e st@voyagerszambia.com.

In addition to their standard service, Voyagers in Solwezi will carry out minor vehicle repairs, subject to availability of parts.

WHAT TO SEE AND DO Solwezi may not be a tourist mecca but there are still one or two places that offer an interesting diversion if you're passing through. Those visiting Kansanshi Mine may spot the odd herd of impala in the immediately vicinity, though many of them have been relocated further south.

Kifubwa Stream Rock Shelter (*US$15 pp;* ⊕ *09.00–18.00 daily*) Quite close to the centre of Solwezi, where the Kifubwa Stream runs through a narrow gorge, there's a series of enigmatic engravings under an overhanging rock, dating to the late Stone Age. Although these had been known to local people for many years, they were first brought to wider attention in 1928. Subsequent archaeological surveys uncovered evidence of both quartz tools and charcoal fires, giving a clear indication of the site's provenance. Unfortunately, the engravings themselves have suffered at the hands of vandals.

To get there, turn off the main road to the south, towards the Teachers' College; it's signposted 'National Monument'. After about 3km, you'll come to the college; continue for a further 3km or so to a boom across the road. Stop here to pay the entrance fee, then you can either walk or drive the last couple of hundred metres down towards the river. Here, well-marked trails lead to the engravings, and interpretive signboards explain how they were discovered. It's an attractive picnic spot, but don't try swimming; there are some serious undercurrents.

Mutanda Falls (*US$10/5 pp; vehicle US$5/day*) About 36km from town is the Mutanda River, where there's a series of attractive rapids, the Mutanda Falls. To get here, follow the tar road west out of town, go past the airport, and continue almost to the river. Just before this, take a left turning off the road and follow this track for about 1km.

The Mutanda Leisure Resort here has some basic chalets and a bar area with superb views of the rapids, though the standard of food seems to be very hit and miss.

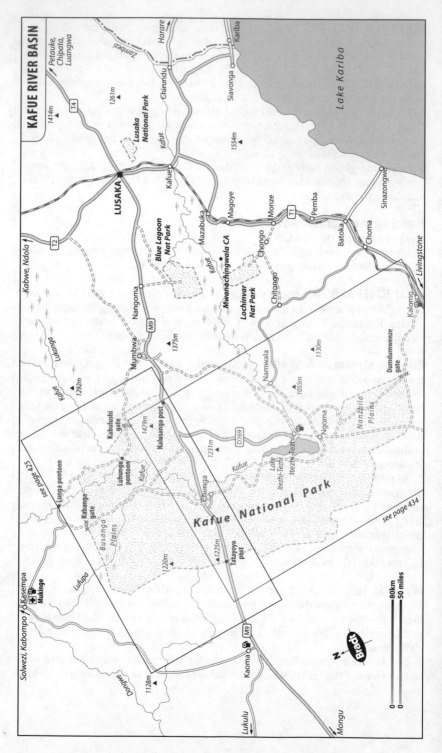

KAFUE RIVER BASIN

Petauke, Chipata, Luangwa

Zambezi

Harare

T4

1414m

1261m

Lusaka National Park

Chirundu

Kafue

Siavonga

Kariba

1554m

Lake Kariba

LUSAKA

Kafue

Magoye

Monze

Pemba

Sinazongwe

Kabwe, Ndola

T2

Mazabuka

Blue Lagoon Nat Park

Kafue

Chongo

T1

Batoka

Choma

Nangoma

Mwanachingwala CA

Chitongo

Livingstone

M9

Mumbwa

1375m

Lochinvar Nat Park

Namwala

1130m

Kalomo

Kgbwe, Ndola

Lukanga

Kafue

1292m

Kabulushi gate

1479m

Nalusanga post

1231m

D769

1055m

Dumdumwenze gate

Nanzhila Plains

Ngoma

Kafue

Lunga pontoon

Kabanga gate

Lubungu pontoon

Chunga

Lake Itezhi-Tezhi

Itezhi-Tezhi

Busanga Plains

1225m

Tatayoyo post

Kafue National Park

see page 434

Solwezi, Kabompo

Kasempa

Mukinge

Lufupa

1220m

1128m

Dongwe

Kaoma

M9

Lukulu

Mongu

see page 425

80km

50 miles

0

0

N

Bradt

The Kafue River Basin

Southwest of the Copperbelt, the Kafue River Basin covers a large swathe of central Zambia stretching almost from the DRC to the west of Lusaka. It encompasses large areas of very sparsely populated bush as well as the Kafue, Blue Lagoon and Lochinvar national parks.

Much of this region of Zambia is difficult to visit, consisting of endless seasonal bush tracks which link occasional farming settlements. At its heart lies the huge Kafue National Park, which has some superb game-viewing areas within its boundaries. The best of these, the Busanga Plains, is not the most accessible, but at times it ranks with the subcontinent's most impressive game areas.

East of the park, there are seasonal floodplains that sustain game and attract a rich variety of birdlife – like the Lukanga Swamps and the Kafue Flats. Part of the latter is in theory protected by two small national parks – Blue Lagoon and Lochinvar – but most such areas remain outside the parks. The Kafue River Basin is a wild area, with some excellent game and endless possibilities for exploring, but very little development.

TOWNS AROUND KAFUE NATIONAL PARK

Southern Kafue is relatively near to Livingstone, and usually accessed from Kalomo or one of the other towns on the Livingstone–Lusaka road (pages 209–14). Northern Kafue has three towns around it which aren't usually destinations in their own right, but may be useful jumping-off points for the northern side of the park: Kasempa in the north, Mumbwa to the east, and Kaoma in the west.

KASEMPA The small town of Kasempa is set in the midst of rolling, hilly country. Although there are many villages in the surrounding bush, the overall population density doesn't feel very high, as much of the area seems to be miombo woodland. The only **fuel** station is closed, but black-market fuel is available here – for a price. Better is to head southeast for 5km to the Mukinge Hospital (see box, page 414), which offers both petrol and diesel for sale to the public.

Getting there and away Three roads run into Kasempa, meeting at a T-junction. To the north is an excellent, tarred road from Solwezi. That meets two reasonably good gravel roads: one just north of town (✪ TUKAOM 13°27.388'S, 25°49.771'E), heading southwest to Kaoma; the other heading southeast towards Mumbwa, with a turn-off to the Kafue National Park's Kabanga gate. For detailed directions on this route, see *Driving from Kasempa to Mumbwa*, pages 414–15.

There's a direct **bus** between Kasempa and Lusaka, via Solwezi. Buses stop in the square.

From Solwezi The good tar road southwest from Solwezi passes the airport then continues in a more southerly direction towards Kasempa, passing close to the Mutanda Falls. After some 140km, at ⊕ TUKALU 13°3.302'S, 25°59.199'E, the M11 from Kalulushi joins this road from the west, then a few kilometres further on there's another junction (⊕ TUKASE 13°6.226'S, 25°52.252'E). The road straight on, heading west, is the good M8 to Kabompo. For Kasempa, turn left and follow the tarred D181 for 43km to the small town (⊕ KASEMP 13°27.404'S, 25°49.779'E). Solwezi is the last reliable fuelling point, as fuel is not always available in Kasempa, so it's advisable to fill up before you depart.

🏠 **Where to stay** There are a few basic guesthouses in town, most of which tend to be fairly rundown, but the quality does tend to improve as you move away from the centre.

Other practicalities Most of the town's shops and other facilities form a square just off the main road. There are a few banks with **ATMs** here, and other amenities include a **post office**, a Catholic church and a few very basic **shops**.

Driving from Kasempa to Mumbwa This once-difficult dirt road has been graded in recent years, although you'll still need to watch out for some large potholes, and the road deteriorates considerably towards Mumbwa. It's easily navigable though, skirting round the eastern edge of the national park. Along the way, the road is lined with a few small rural settlements and a lot of open areas. After 4km, you'll pass the turning to Mukinge Mission, then a further 75km brings

---

MUKINGE MISSION HOSPITAL

Mukinge Mission (*www.mukinge.com*) started around 1925 when the Rev C S Foster came to this area as an evangelical missionary. His son, Bob, was born here, studied medicine in Toronto, and then returned in 1950 to found a mission hospital – even supervising its construction.

Today, Mukinge Hospital serves a huge area that can result in patients travelling on foot or by bike for up to five days. With about 200 beds, it cares for around 140 in-patients a day (including three or four births on average) as well as 160–180 outpatients. The seven in-patient wards include one for malnutrition and another for isolation. There are also two operating theatres, a new eye clinic, a laboratory, a range of X-ray equipment, a physiotherapy department, a training school for nurses and a pharmacy with basic drug supplies. In short, it's the best hospital for a very long way.

Mukinge is supported by the World Medical Mission, a wing of the missionary organisation Samaritan's Purse, as well as the Evangelical Church in Zambia, and the government. However funds for day-to-day expenses such as food and equipment are tight. To this end, the hospital has its own **fuel station**, with both diesel and petrol sold from large drums. Prices are on a par with black-market outlets, around K10 per litre in 2011, but there are no issues about the quality here, and you have the added feel-good factor of knowing that you have contributed to a worthy cause.

To get to the hospital (⊕ MUKING 13°28.894's, 25°51.409'E), head south of Kasempa for about 4km, and then turn right (⊕ TUMUKI 13°28.264'S, 25°51.902'E), following the signs for a further 1km. There are buses between here and Kasempa.

you to a right-hand fork signposted to the Kabanga gate (⊕ TUKABA 13°57.930'S, 26°11.858'E), on the northern border of Kafue National Park. The gate itself (⊕ KABANG 14°5.808'S, 26°7.036'E) is some 19km along a bumpy, sandy track. For Mumbwa, however, continue straight along the graded road, passing through lush green woodland and the occasional village, and keeping right where there's a fork in the road after 11km (⊕ KAFORK 13°57.905'S, 26°17.459'E). A total of almost 28km will bring you to the Lunga pontoon (⊕ FERRYL 13°58.984'S, 26°20.784'E; ⊕ 06.00–18.00 daily; K75 per vehicle).

About 3km before the pontoon is a turning to Lunga River Lodge (⊕ TULUNG 13°58.626'S, 26°20.076'E). This is the start of a very bumpy, black-cotton soil track that shadows the east bank of the Lunga River for around 25km to a currently closed hunting lodge, on the boundary of the park. A continuation then heads northwest to the Kabanga gate (⊕ KABANG 14°5.808'S, 26°7.036'E). Most drivers, however, cross the Lunga River, then continue for another 70km along a good, but winding road to the Lubungu River (⊕ LUBUNG 14°33.750'S, 26°27.250'E); watch out for fallen trees and other debris *en route*. Note that the pontoon here (⊕ 06.00–18.00 daily; K75 per vehicle) is smaller than its counterpart over the Lunga, so not capable of taking large vehicles.

From the Lubungu River, it's another 75km or so to Mumbwa, the first 10km of which are in good condition, but rapidly deteriorates into large potholes and loose dirt after passing through the Kabulushi gate. Until this road is improved this journey will take 2½ to 3 hours.

For directions in reverse on this section, see *Driving north from Mumbwa*, page 416.

Note that the southern parts of this route, from around the Lunga pontoon, are within a GMA, so you are not free to camp – or indeed to do anything other than simply pass through.

MUMBWA Mumbwa's proximity to Lusaka gives it a palpable urban buzz, entirely different from the rural feel of small towns further west. The presence of a large mosque with a dominant minaret only serves to enhance this feel.

The town is 4km north of the main tar road between Lusaka and Mongu, and is the last place for anyone heading into the Kafue National Park to change money or stock up on fuel. That said, you'd be wise not to bank on either of these amenities.

Getting there

By bus Between the town's two roundabouts, in the bustling market area, is the local bus station, where buses between Mongu and Lusaka stop in both directions. It's a relatively busy route, with arrivals and departures at all times of day, though the highest frequency is the middle of the day, when buses that left from Lusaka or Mongu in the morning pass through the town. One-way fares to Lusaka are around K100.

Driving from Lusaka About 3 hours' drive from Lusaka (148km), on the Great West Road towards Mongu, a large modern factory looms next to the road, and orderly warehouses stand behind well-watered lawns. This is perhaps the country's biggest cotton ginnery. A few kilometres further west is a turning off the road to the north, which leads – after about 4km of pot-holed tar – to the thriving town of Mumbwa.

Where to stay There are a couple of overnight choices in Mumbwa, of which the best is the Hacienda. Alternatively, the cheaper Mumbwa Motel is on the right as you drive into town.

Hacienda Hotel (7 rooms, 6 chalets)
m 0978 393838/0962 199624; e mail.ahacienda@
zambia.co.zm; ⊕ HACIEN 14°59.041'S, 27°03.720'E.
This old but refurbished hotel has a quiet location
set in gardens with a pool. To find it, turn left off
the main road at the 2nd roundabout heading
north, then it's on the left. Rooms are en suite with
tiled floors, mosi nets over the beds, AC, fridges &

DSTV. The foyer leads to a separate bar with TV, & a
restaurant ($). **$$**

Mumbwa Motel (22 rooms) m 0977
494400/0966; ⊕ MUMBMO 14°59.710'S,
27°03.622'E. Mumbwa's other option, on the
right as you drive into town, is cheaper, tatty &
less welcoming. Small rondavels are en suite, &
for amenities it boasts a bar & restaurant. **$**

Other practicalities The Total **fuel** station (⊕ TOTALM 14°59.451'S,
27°03.642'E) on the main roundabout into town is the last place to fill up before
heading into the park, but it's unreliable. Opportunities to buy black-market fuel
for a higher price are plentiful. Ask around plainly but politely, and you should be
directed to a suitable source, though it's wise to check with other buyers to ensure
you are purchasing from an untampered supply. Using this fuel in your vehicle is
always a risk, though. In addition to the town's **market**, located between the two
roundabouts, there are endless small local **shops**. Opposite the market is a branch
of Barclays Bank (⊕ 08.30–14.30 Mon–Fri) with a useful **ATM**. Again, it's not
entirely reliable, so don't run your cash too low.

Driving north from Mumbwa

To the Lubungu pontoon From the tarred Great West Road, there is a road of
variable quality along the eastern side of the park to the Lubungu pontoon via the
Kabulushi gate, and on to Kasempa. A high-clearance vehicle remains advisable,
however, and if you're heading for Hippo Lodge or McBrides' Camp (pages 430–2),
then a 4x4 is essential in the rainy season. Note that it is no longer possible to drive
due north into the park from the Nalusanga scout post.

To access this eastern road from the Great West Road, turn north into Mumbwa,
then left at the first roundabout by the Total garage (⊕ TOTALM 14°59.457'S,
27°03.617'E). Continue through a market and after about 1.1km, at the top of the next
rise, take a right turn onto the Kasempa road, a bumpy dirt road that goes to Lubungu
pontoon. The 66km stretch from here to the Kabulushi gate (⊕ KABULU 15°07.947'S,
27°21.881'E) passes through wooded areas and some farmland. The surface here
is incredibly bumpy and slow going, and you can expect it to take approximately
2 hours to get to the gate. No fees are payable at the gate by those just driving through;
if you're staying at Hippo Lodge or McBrides' Camp, park fees should be paid at the
lodges themselves.

After passing through the gate the road improves to a more solid gravel
track, which passes through forested areas with huge rounded boulders. A fork
(⊕ TUHIPP 14°37.866'S, 26°29.659'E) to the left, clearly signposted from the south
(but not from the north) leads to Hippo Lodge and McBrides' Camp – and also
the old Hippo Mine (box, page 431). For the Lubungu pontoon (⊕ LUBUNG
14°33.750'S, 26°27.250'E; ⊕ 06.00–18.00 daily; K75 per vehicle or US$20 if foreign
registered; 12 ton limit) continue on the main road for a further 10km – and note
that this pontoon is smaller than its Lunga counterpart.

If you're driving to Lunga (which very few people do) you could alternatively
take the longer route through the park which, although significantly slower than
this one, is likely to offer some good game sightings.

From the Lubungu pontoon to the Lunga pontoon See *4x4 routes within
and around northern Kafue*, pages 424–7, for directions along this route.

KAOMA Kaoma is a small district town about 3km north of the Great West Road between Kafue and Mongu, and about 76km west of Kafue National Park. Though not close to Kafue, it's on the edge of the Western Province, so is very much a gateway to the area. Whichever way you're travelling, it's wise to fill your fuel tank (and spare fuel drums) here.

If you have space in your vehicle, you'll find no shortage of people wanting to share the journey. Given the shortage of transport, and the insight that hitchhikers can give to visitors, don't appear rude to the locals by refusing a lift.

Getting there and away
By bus All the buses stop at the bus station behind the Total filling station in the centre of town. Buses to/from Lusaka take about 5½ hours; those to/from Mongu about 2 hours.

Driving
From Kaoma to Lukulu If you're heading west to Lukulu, take the tar road towards Mongu for about 25km, then there's a gravel road on the right, signposted as 195km to Lukulu. After 16km on this road it forks: keep to the right. Later there's a sign heralding a turn to the right, to the M8, which leads to the Watopa pontoon (⊕ FERRY4 14°2.338'S, 23°37.744'E).

Lining this road are small villages, each consisting of thatched huts built in varying sizes. Oxcarts are also a frequent sight, straight out of a biblical scene.

From Kaoma to Kasempa From the Great West Road at Kaoma, there's a reasonable gravel road that heads north and then northeast to Kasempa.

Where to stay and eat There's a choice of small local guesthouses in Kaoma, all of which are fairly clean and may be able to arrange simple meals. The best is the Kaoma Cheshire Orphanage, which assists in raising funds for Zambia's AIDS orphans. There are also several places to eat, drink and chat along the main street, typically serving local dishes such as nshima, chips or rice, with beef, chicken or occasionally fish.

Other practicalities Kaoma has a **post office**, a Finance **Bank**, numerous **shops** (of which the best stocked is Cheap & Best along the main road) and local eateries, and two vital **fuel** stations: vital to anyone travelling west, that is. The most reliable of these is the Puma station on the main road, but as always, don't run your supplies too low.

KAFUE NATIONAL PARK

(Park fees US$20 pp/day; vehicle US$15/day or K17 if Zambian registered. Fees payable at Hook Bridge, Dumdumwenze, Kabanga & Musa gates, & at some lodges. ⊙ 06.00–18.00) Kafue is a huge national park, two-and-a-half times the size of South Luangwa. Sadly, in the 1980s and early '90s, few resources were devoted to its upkeep and anti-poaching efforts were left to a couple of dedicated souls from the few safari lodges that remained in the park.

Now the situation is better. A steady trickle of visitors, supported by improving infrastructure and access to the park, have added weight (and finance) to the on-going effort to build the park back up to its former glory. Even the park's elephants are visibly recovering (both in number and in terms of losing some of their shyness), although it will be a while before they return to their former strength. It is very heartening to see that the rest of the game is thriving, and occurring in a volume and variety that bodes well for the future. While the game viewing may not rival that of the South Luangwa or Lower Zambezi, the wilderness experience in the Kafue is greatly heightened when compared to these comparatively busy parks. That said, in Kafue's best areas the game can be very good. In particular, game viewing on and around the Busanga Plains can be stunning, so don't visit the park without at least a side trip into this remarkable area.

Unlike the other national parks in Zambia, the majority of the camps in the Kafue have remained owner-run operations, giving each an individual character. They may not be as plush or well-oiled as their counterparts in other parks, but the owners' passion for the park and its conservation is invariably immediately apparent, and new guiding standards and exams introduced in 2015 are ensuring that guiding standards match those in the Luangwa.

GEOGRAPHY Established in 1924, the Kafue National Park covers some 22,400km^2 (about the size of Wales, or Massachusetts) of very varied terrain and is one of the world's largest national parks. Naturally, its geography varies considerably. Throughout the park, the permanent Kafue River follows a well-defined course, and widens in a few places where barriers of harder rocks near the surface force it into shallow, rocky rapids – Kafwala and the area beside KaingU Safari Lodge being the obvious examples. Bordering the eastern side of southern Kafue is Lake Itezhi-Tezhi – a large, manmade lake that was created in 1977. The primary function of its dam is to regulate the water levels experienced by the Kafue Gorge Hydro-electric Dam, further downstream, although it also generates some electricity.

The map clearly shows that the tarred Great West Road between Lusaka and Mongu bisects the park. This road provides the easiest route into the park, and also a convenient split that allows me to refer to 'northern' and 'southern' Kafue as simply meaning the areas to the north and the south of the road. These have slightly different habitats and species, and also very different access routes. As far as casual visitors are concerned, they could almost be two separate parks.

Surrounding the whole are no fewer than eight game management areas (GMAs), which provide a valuable buffer zone for the park's wildlife.

FLORA AND FAUNA
Flora Most of Kafue is an undulating mosaic of miombo woodlands and dambos, within which you'll find smaller patches of munga woodland, and bands of riparian forest and thickets along the larger rivers.

In the extreme northwest of the park are the permanently wet **Busanga Swamps**, surrounded by adjacent floodplains and now a designated Ramsar site. These are dotted with raised 'tree islands' (a stand of trees rising above an expanse of lower-level vegetation), notable for some mammoth specimens of sycamore figs (*Ficus sycomorus*) amongst other vegetation. The floodplains are ringed by a 'termitaria zone' of grasslands.

Northern Kafue receives slightly more rain than the south, resulting in richer, taller vegetation. In many areas such woodland is dominated by the large-leafed munondo tree (*Julbernardia paniculata*), though you'll also find 'Prince of Wales feathers' (*Brachystegia boehmii*) and the odd mobola plum (*Parinari curatellifolia*).

Southern Kafue is dominated by areas of Kalahari sand, and also has a slightly lower rainfall than the north. Large stretches of Kalahari woodland are the norm here, typified by silver-leaf terminalia (*Terminalia sericea*), poison-pod albizia (*Albizia versicolor*), and *Combretum* species. Within this there are a few patches of mature teak forest – the Ngoma Forest being one of the most spectacular examples – whilst further south, on patches of alluvial clay, are some beautiful groves of cathedral mopane (*Colophospermum mopane*).

In the far south of the park, the **Nanzhila Plains** are a fascinating area. Wide expanses of grassland are dotted with islands of vegetation and large termitaria – often with baobabs (*Adansonia digitata*) or ebony trees (*Diospyros mespiliformis*) growing out of them.

The flora of the park is heavily affected by yearly burning, which is most apparent between June and October. Some of this burning, particularly early in the year, is part of a management regime by ZAWA, but much of it is caused by poachers burning for better visibility, out of control agricultural fires, and general carelessness of people around the park. The debate about the necessity of burning is fierce, with touted benefits including stimulating growth of new grass to attract antelope. However, repeated fires can reduce the variety of plants in the ecosystem, and have a big impact on the aesthetics of the park.

Fauna Covering such a large area, with a variety of habitats, Kafue is rich in wildlife and many of its species seem to exhibit strong local variations in their distribution. This is a reflection of the wide variety of habitats in such a large park.

Antelope Kafue has a superb range of antelope, but you will have to travel throughout the park if you wish to see them all.

The **Busanga Swamps**, in the far north of the park, are permanently flooded and home to the secretive sitatunga, which is uniquely adapted to swamp life. These powerful swimmers will bound off with a series of leaps and plunges when disturbed, aided by their enlarged hooves which have evolved for walking around on floating papyrus islands. They will then stand motionless until the danger passes, or even submerge themselves leaving just their nostrils above the water for breathing.

The **Busanga Plains**, a little further south, is a much larger area that is seasonally inundated. This only starts to dry out around June (it's totally impassable by vehicle until then), when it's possible to visit and see large herds of red lechwe and puku, with smaller groups of zebra and blue wildebeest. Oribi are found throughout the park, but are particularly common here, and you also have a good chance of seeing roan and the beautiful sable antelope.

Across the rest of the northern half of the park, there's a good range of mixed bush environments, and here kudu, bushbuck, eland, reedbuck, common duiker, grysbok and defassa waterbuck (a subspecies without the distinctive white ring on the rump) are all frequently seen. Even within this there are local differences; the Kafwala area, for example, is notable for good numbers of Lichtenstein's hartebeest and sable. Numerically, puku dominate most of the northern side of the park, though they gradually cede to impala as you move further south.

On the south side of Kafue, the game has been more patchy. Generally it thrives in areas around lodges, which provide some sanctuary from poaching, but away from these it can be scarce. However, the success of anti-poaching measures, the presence of three lodges in the GMA, and two new lodges on the western side of the river are certainly having an impact, and the game is improving as a result. The area around Mufungata and KaingU Safari Lodge is particularly rich in impala and bushbuck, and the game is fairly relaxed.

The area from Itezhi-Tezhi south to Ngoma has Kafue's densest elephant population, with some groups also frequenting the Chunga area. In addition there are some larger herds of buffalo in this area, as well as plenty of impala and puku, family groups of Lichtenstein's hartebeest and waterbuck, and numerous bushbuck, warthog and baboons.

South of Ngoma, the picture is improving too. When I first visited in the early 2000s, the game was sparse indeed, and skittish. It was interesting that the only really good sightings that we had of large animals were around the Chilenje Pools loop and what is now Nanzhila Plains Safari Camp – so once again the animals were congregating in areas associated with visitors. Now we're getting credible reports that numbers are increasing, with species ranging from blue wildebeest and eland to roan and sable antelope, as well as waterbuck, kudu and impala.

Large predators Lion are relatively widespread all over the park, but the larger males are increasingly uncommon, with inevitable consequences for numbers as a whole. On the Busanga Plains, prides – including the so-called Busanga pride, notable for climbing trees – stalk through nervous herds of puku and lechwe nightly, using the natural drainage ditches for cover with deadly efficiency.

Leopard remain very common throughout the main forested areas of park, though they are seldom seen on the open plains. They are most easily observed on night drives, and continue with their activities completely unperturbed by the presence of a spotlight trained upon them. In particular, Lufupa has a reputation for great leopard sightings, although this may have been as a result of a few particularly good guides.

Spotted hyena are seen regularly, though not often, throughout the park. They appear to occur in smaller numbers than either lions or leopards. Cheetah are not common anywhere, but they're most frequently seen in the north of the park, and around the Nanzhila/Konkamoya area to the south. It's certainly the best place in Zambia to look for cheetah.

Although wild dog remain uncommon in any locale, occasional sightings occur all over the park (though fewer around the road on the east side), which is one of their strongholds in Zambia. The park's huge size suits their wide-ranging nomadic habits and I have had a number of reports of them being seen on the north side of the park in the last few years. Areas around the Busanga Plains seem a particular favourite.

Other large animals Elephants occur throughout Kafue, though overall their numbers are still recovering from intensive poaching during the 1970s, and their density varies hugely within the park. Just south of Lake Itezhi-Tezhi, around Chunga and, especially, Ngoma, there are large herds and a thriving population – though they're not always relaxed, so drivers there need to be very wary of getting too close to them. South of Ngoma, the situation was much gloomier, although anti-poaching measures have resulted in a resurgence in the elephant population.

On the north side of the park elephant densities are lower than around Ngoma, but they have improved a lot. When I first visited Lufupa in 1995, a few elephants spotted a kilometre from the lodge were a reason for excitement, causing us to leave dinner and jump into a vehicle. Now family groups are commonly seen in the Lufupa and Lunga areas, and are a lot less skittish than they used to be. Visiting in 2015, we saw some very relaxed elephants on the Busanga Plains.

Buffalo, common in the 1970s and '80s, are rarely seen nowadays, though herds do frequent the Busanga Plains. Sadly, black rhino have been completely poached out of the park, and until protection can be improved there's little chance of reintroductions.

The Kafue River and its larger tributaries like the Lunga are fascinating tropical rivers – full of life and infested with hippo and crocodile, which occur in numbers to rival the teeming waters of the Luangwa. Vervet monkeys and yellow (*not* chacma) baboons are common almost everywhere, and you'll usually find porcupines, mongooses, civets and a wide variety of small mammals on night drives. One other curious but interesting fact: there seem to be more pangolins than aardvarks in North Kafue, which is a very unusual situation indeed!

Birds The birding in Kafue is very good. There have been about 495 species recorded here, suggesting that the park has probably the richest birdlife of any Zambian park. This reflects Kafue's wide range of habitats, because in addition to extensive miombo woodlands (quite a Zambian speciality!), Kafue has plenty of rivers, extensive wetlands and – in the north – seasonal floodplains.

The wetlands and floodplains have the full range of herons (including the black heron), storks and ibises, plus crowned and wattled cranes, Denham's (or Stanley's) and kori bustards, secretary birds, and geese (spur-winged and Egyptian) by the thousand.

In the long, verdant stretches of riverine vegetation you're likely to spot Ross's turaco, Narina trogons, MacClounie's (black-backed) barbet, olive woodpecker, brown-headed apalis and the yellow-throated leaflove. Pel's fishing owl is also found here, with birding expert Bob Stjernstedt noting that there are pairs around Ntemwa, and African finfoot frequent the shady fringes of the slower rivers, swimming under the overhanging trees with part of their body submerged.

Kafue's extensive miombo woodlands have endemics such as pale-billed hornbill, miombo pied barbet, grey tit, miombo rock thrush, Sousa's shrike, chestnut-mantled sparrow-weaver, spotted creeper, and three species of eremomela. In the south, on the Nanzhila Plains, the black-cheeked lovebird – near-endemic to southern Zambia – is relatively common.

HUNTING AND POACHING During the 1980s and early '90s there were few efforts or government resources devoted to protecting Kafue, and poaching was rife. This ensured the extermination of black rhino, and a sharp reduction in elephant numbers at the hands of organised commercial poachers. Fortunately the park is massive, surrounded by GMAs, and not easily accessible. So although the smaller game was hunted for meat, this was not generally on a large enough scale to threaten their populations. Nor did it adversely affect the environment.

Organised commercial poaching is now relatively rare, and the remaining incidence of smaller-scale poaching by locals (for food) is being tackled by a number of initiatives. The ZAWA team protecting the park has become much more active in recent years, having received a lot of training and more resources.

Some of these initiatives concentrate on increasing the physical policing of the park, the most obvious being anti-poaching patrols, which have been partially funded by some of the lodges. Others try to tackle the underlying reason for this poaching, and attempt to offer practical alternatives for the local people of the surrounding areas that are more attractive than shooting the game. For example, one such project allows local people in neighbouring areas to come into the park to collect natural honey. Both types of initiatives work with the help and support of some of the more enlightened local safari operators.

GETTING THERE AND AROUND To get to Kafue, and to get around once there, you have three choices. First, you can fly or bus in and stay at one of the better camps or lodges – and the team from the camp will walk, drive and boat you around their

14

area of the park. Second, you can drive yourself into and around the park in a 4x4. Or third, you can arrange for a company from outside to drive you in, and around the park.

By air or scheduled transfer This is certainly the most relaxing way to get to the park, especially if your time is relatively limited, or you like the idea of a holiday here rather than an expedition. There are various airstrips dotted around the park and some are in good repair. There are no scheduled flights into the park, but several charter companies in Lusaka will fly you in or out on request and Wilderness Safaris usually transport their guests by air.

Wilderness Safaris \+27 702 7500; e enquiry@wilderness.co.za; www.wilderness-safaris.com. Compared to Namibia & South Africa, Wilderness has a much smaller presence in Zambia, mostly confined to the northern Kafue, although they do also own Toka Leya (page 165) in Livingstone. Wilderness deals only with agents, so reservations for their lodges should be made through a tour operator (pages 43–5).

Driving If you want to drive within the park, then think of it as an expedition. You will need a 4x4 vehicle with good ground clearance, spare tyre, and enough fuel for your planned trip (bearing in mind that the fuel supplies in the towns surrounding Kafue can be unreliable). Cell phone coverage is limited across the park so taking a satellite phone for emergencies is advisable, but even so if you have problems, you must be able to solve them yourself, as you can expect little help. Although there are many camps listed in the sections below, only a handful would be able to offer aid in an emergency.

However, if you come well equipped then the park is wonderful. Several operators – especially in the east and south of the park – also have excellent campsites. If you do come, then you can be assured of seeing very few other vehicles during your stay in this stunning area.

Arrive with the best maps of the place you can find, and use them in conjunction with those in this book. Do bring a GPS; you will need one. Note that the speed limit within the body of the park is 40km/h – though in reality you'd often be hard pressed to come even close to that.

For those just bisecting the northern and southern areas along the tarred Lusaka–Mongu road, there's no need for a 4x4. However, aside from the obvious danger of colliding with an animal in this area, there are several speed bumps and these – together with the odd pot-hole – mean that sticking to the 80km/h limit is essential.

As a much cheaper, but considerable less convenient and comfortable option, you can easily catch a bus from Lusaka to Kafue. The buses depart between 09.30 and 13.30, with the safest and most reliable buses being run by Shalom and Juldan. You will need to purchase a fare from Koama (*K120*), but let the driver know to drop you off at Hook Bridge, which should take approximately 3 hours from Lusaka. The camps in the central area, the southern half of the park down to KaingU, and Musekese can all pick you up from Hook Bridge (you will need to arrange a time with them in advance), with transfers to camp costing between US$30–80 per vehicle depending on the distance from camp. You can also get on the buses from the Hook Bridge area, but it's best to purchase a ticket as you get on the bus rather than buying a return ticket in advance.

Budget safari operators The Lusaka-based Bongwe Safaris runs 4-day/3-night trips (*US$960 pp/max 7*) into the private and well-stocked Mushingashi

Conservancy, bordering the park's secluded northeast, where you can expect to see no other vehicles. Groups are based in rustic chalets at Bongwe Bush Camp, run exclusively for the trips (page 433) within the Mushingashi Conservancy. For more details, see page 430.

Mobile operators in Kafue Due to its proximity to Livingstone, several safari operators and overlanders run mobile trips into the Kafue, though without a long-term presence in the park they don't know the ground as well as the established camps, they seldom have the logistical support to solve their own problems (There are tales of one inexperienced company that recently came up into the Busanga Plains too early, and ended up with its vehicle stuck in mud for 2 days), and they contribute little to the vital work of preserving the area.

As Kafue starts to receive a few more visitors, the Busanga Plains (especially) is becoming better known and the focus for more attention from small mobile operators. However, if you want to get the very best from it, and effectively contribute to the work to preserve the area, then I recommend that you support the area's permanent operators, of which there are only two running an adequately experienced mobile safari:

Jeffery & McKeith Safaris ☎ +44 (0) 287 83006; m 0976 215426/0974 173403; e info@ jefferymckeith.com; www.jmsafaris-zambia.com. Jeffery & McKeith Safaris run a 3-night fully mobile safari (although this can easily be extended) in the northern area of the park, a trip which is usually bookended by a few nights at their basecamp Musekese (pages 429–30).

The fly-camp consists of safari dome tents with comfortable bedding & mattresses, solar lighting, bucket showers & a short-drop toilet, & accommodates up to 6 people. A mess tent is also set up for meals & drinks, although dinner is usually eaten out under the stars. All of this is set up from scratch at the southern tip of the Busanga Plains, meaning guests can enjoy the prolific birdlife & varied walking in the Moshi/Musanza area, but can also easily access the Busanga Plains on game drives.

While the camping is basic, with few luxuries, it's still perfectly comfortable, & allows small groups to access remote areas of the park. The guides are excellent, & it provides a cheaper option for visiting the Busanga Plains than the permanent camps in the area. *US$590 pp per night at mobile camp, plus costs at Musekese. Min 3 nts at mobile camp. FBA inc park transfers & fees.* ☉ *Jul–Oct.* **LLL**

Mbizi West Safaris m 0978 016191; e paul@ pioneercamp.com; www.kafueriver.com. Starting in 2016, Mbizi West Safaris will be running a 3-night mobile safari based at the northwestern tip of the Busanga Plains. The trips have set departures from Aug to Oct, starting and ending the trip with a night at their main property, Kafue River Lodge (page 432).

The small mobile camp consists of 3 small dome tents, with bucket showers & a short-drop toilet. With few luxuries, the emphasis of the camp is very much on exploring a wilderness area of the park through game drives & walking safaris. *US$1,300 pp for 5nt package (3nts mobile safari, 2nts Kafue River Camp) FBA inc park transfers & fees;* ☉ *15 Aug–20 Oct.* **LLL**

NORTHERN KAFUE The northern section of the park is a slightly undulating plateau, veined by rivers – the Lufupa, the Lunga, the Ntemwa, the Mukombo, the Mukunashi, and the Lubuji – which are all tributaries of the main Kafue, whose basin extends to the border with DRC.

The main Kafue River is already mature by the time it reaches the park, though it has over 400km further to flow before discharging into the Zambezi. Thus within the park its permanent waters are wide, deep and slow-flowing, to the obvious pleasure of large numbers of hippo and crocodile. Tall, shady hardwoods overhang its gently curving banks, and the occasional islands in the stream are favourite feeding places for elephant and buffalo. In short, it is a typically beautiful, large African river.

Occasionally it changes, as at Kafwala. Here, there is a stretch of gentle rapids for about 7km. The river is up to about 1,000m wide and dotted with numerous islands, all supporting dense riverine vegetation – making a particularly good spot for birdwatching.

Most of the park's northern section, between the rivers, is a mosaic of miombo and mopane woodlands, with occasional open grassy pans known as dambos. The edges of the main rivers are lined with tall hardwood trees. Raintrees (*Lonchocarpus capassa*), knobthorns (*Acacia nigrescens*), jackalberries (*Diospyros mespiliformis*), leadwoods (*Combretum imberbe*), and especially sausage trees (*Kigelia africana*) are all very common.

The Kafue's tributaries are smaller, but the larger of these are still wide and permanent. The Lufupa is probably the most important. It enters the park from the Kasonso-Busanga GMA in the north, and immediately feeds into a permanent wetland in the far north of the park: the Busanga Swamps. In the wet season these waters flood out over a much larger area, across the whole Busanga Plains, before finally draining back into the river, which then continues its journey on the south side of the plains.

The swamp and seasonal floodplain together cover about 750km², and are a superb area for game. The seasonal floodwaters on the plains are shallow, but enough to sustain a healthy growth of grasses throughout the year on the mineral-rich black-cotton soil. These open plains are dotted with numerous small 'islands' of wild date palms (*Phoenix reclinata*), and wild fig trees (various *Ficus* species).

The area is perfect for huge herds of water-loving lechwe and puku, which are joined by large numbers of zebra, wildebeest and other plains grazers as the waters recede at the end of the wet season. However, the Busanga Plains are very remote, and normally impossible to reach by vehicle until about July. Until recently, few people (even in the safari business) had heard about them, let alone visited them, but now this remarkable area is firmly on the map.

4x4 routes within and around northern Kafue You really need a high-clearance 4x4 for any of the routes within the park. Despite that, you'll have problems on all of them during the rains, and anything close to the Busanga Plains is impassable between about November and July.

From the north via the Kabanga gate The Kabanga gate (⊕ KABANG 14°5.808'S, 26°7.036'E) is the park's most northerly entrance point, affording access for those coming from Kasempa and the Copperbelt. For directions to the gate, see *Driving from Kasempa to Mumbwa*, pages 414–15.

From the gate, the clear, largely sandy track that proceeds southwards into the park is considerably better than the approach road to the gate from Kasempa. The track keeps east of the Ntemwa River, passing the site of the old Moshi Camp (⊕ MOSHI 14°24.348'S, 26°09.474'E),

NORTHERN KAFUE
For listings, see pages 427–33 & 442

⊖ ⊛ **Where to stay and eat**
1 Bongwe Bush Camp
2 Busanga Bushcamp
3 Busanga Plains Camp
4 Dalai Camp
5 Hippo Lodge
6 Kabalushi
7 Kafue River Camp
8 Kafwala Camp
9 Kalonga Waloba
10 Khosikoto Camp
11 Leopard Lodge
12 Lufupa River Camp
13 Lufupa Tented Camp
14 McBrides' Camp
15 Mayukuyuku Bush Camp
16 Mukambi Safari Lodge
17 Musanza Tented Camp
18 Musekese
19 Mushingashi Conservancy
20 Shumba Camp

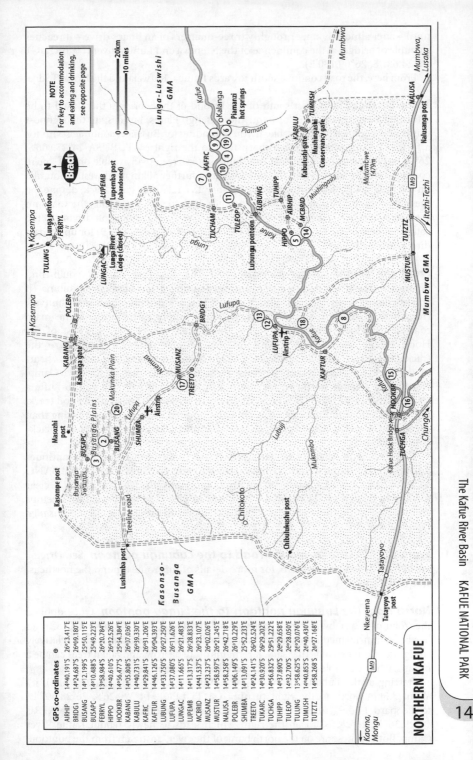

NORTHERN KAFUE

GPS co-ordinates ⊕

AIRHIP	14°40.191'S	26°3.417'E
BRIDG1	14°24.687'S	26°9.180'E
BUSANG	14°2.199'S	25°0.115'E
BUSAPC	14°10.488'S	25°9.223'E
FERRYL	13°58.984'S	26°20.784'E
HIPPO	14°40.610'S	26°22.526'E
HOOKBR	14°56.477'S	25°54.384'E
KABANG	14°05.808'S	26°37.036'E
KABULU	14°40.731'S	26°31.206'E
KAFRC	14°29.841'S	26°31.206'E
KAFTUR	14°46.126'S	26°94.393'E
LUBUNG	14°33.750'S	26°27.250'E
LUFUPA	14°37.080'S	26°11.626'E
LUNGAC	14°11.665'S	26°21.483'E
LUPEMB	14°13.317'S	26°23.107'E
MCBRID	14°41.537'S	26°28.833'E
MUSANZ	14°23.237'S	26°02.026'E
MUSTUR	14°58.597'S	26°21.245'E
NALUSA	14°58.258'S	26°42.718'E
POLEBR	14°06.149'S	26°10.229'E
SHUMBA	14°13.091'S	25°52.233'E
TREETO	14°24.141'S	26°02.524'E
TUKARC	14°30.920'S	26°29.202'E
TUCHGA	14°56.832'S	25°51.222'E
TUHIPP	14°37.890'S	26°29.658'E
TULEOP	14°32.700'S	26°28.050'E
TULUNG	13°58.625'S	26°20.076'E
TUMUSH	14°40.853'S	26°40.430'E
TUTZTZ	14°58.268'S	26°27.168'E

NOTE
For key to accommodation and eating and drinking, see opposite page

until – after almost 39km, or roughly three-quarters of an hour's drive – it reaches a couple of bridges at the confluence of the Ntemwa and Lufupa rivers (⊕ BRIDG1 14°24.687'S, 26°09.180'E).

From here, the road continue south towards Lufupa, Kafwala and the Hook Bridge.

To the Busanga Plains Just south of the second of these bridges there used to be a turning west towards Treetops and the Busanga Plains, but despite the signpost this is now completely impassable. If you're heading for Busanga, continue south for a further 2.5km, where there's a sharp turn to the right (⊕ TUBUSA 14°25.806'S, 26°08.967'E). Note, however, that the signpost (to Treetops) is visible only if you're coming from the south. From this junction, it's a further 50km northwest to Shumba on the Busanga Plains. During the dry season, it's a relatively good track, despite the inevitable bumps, pot-holes and sand patches. Due to yearly flooding, the roads on the plains themselves are rather ephemeral, so if you are planning on driving to the camps up here it's best to contact them individually (see pages 427–9) for up-to-date directions in advance.

From the south: Lusaka–Mongu road The last fuel stations you'll find before you reach the park are at Mumbwa (coming from Lusaka) or Kaoma (if you're coming from Mongu). Either way, if you are driving north into the park from here, to Lufupa or the Busanga Plains, simply turn north off the main road at the Hook Bridge gate beside the Kafue's west bank, just west of the Hook Bridge itself (⊕ HOOKBR 14°56.477'S, 25°54.384'E). From here the track (⊕ KAFTUR 14°46.126'S, 26°4.393'E) heads northeast through the heart of the park for about 44km, where a right turn leads east to Kafwala Camp. Continuing roughly northeast for about a further 26km will lead you to Lufupa (⊕ LUFUPA 14°37.080'S, 26°11.626'E). In the dry season it's basically a good track, fine for a 2WD with high clearance, though designed more for game viewing than speed. In the wet it is impassable due to the toffee-like consistency of the black-cotton soil.

This track is the main vehicular artery through northern Kafue, and continues north over the Lufupa and Ntemwa rivers to the Kabanga gate (⊕ KABANG 14°5.808'S, 26°7.036'E). About 82km from the Hook Bridge, you'll pass a clear turning to the left (⊕ TUBUSA 14°25.806'S, 26°08.967'E) signposted to Treetops and leading to the Busanga Plains. For details of this route, see *To the Busanga Plains*, above.

From the M9 Lusaka–Mongu road to the Lubungu pontoon See *Driving north from Mumbwa*, page 416, for more details of this route around the northeast side of the park.

North from the Lubungu pontoon to the Lunga pontoon Once dubbed the 'road of death' by one very experienced old hand, this 75km stretch of road has been transformed into a good, graded road that makes for pleasant, relatively straightforward driving. That said, it remains quite narrow, and fallen trees can be a hazard, while pot-holes could well materialise in the rainy season.

Starting at the Lubungu pontoon (⊕ LUBUNG 14°33.750'S, 26°27.250'E), it's about 3.5km north to the right turning (⊕ TULEOP 14°32.426'S, 26°28.597'E) to Leopard Lodge. About 6.5km beyond that is another turning (⊕ KAFRC 14°29.367'S, 26°28.583'E) on the right which leads to newly rebuilt Kafue River Camp. Both of these are on the north bank of the river, upstream from the pontoon.

From this second turning, it's some 70km to the Lunga pontoon (✪ FERRYL 13°58.984'S, 26°20.784'E; ⊕ *06.00–18.00 daily; K75 per vehicle*), north of which the road continues as far as Kasempa (see *Driving from Kasempa to Mumbwa*, pages 414–5, for details).

As you cross on the pontoon, you might wish to reflect that the journey that took you just a couple of hours would all too recently have taken at least eight, and required at least two very sturdy vehicles.

🏠 Where to stay

Though the range of camps listed here appears to be long, most non-Zambian visitors are probably best to choose a combination of one of the camps on the Busanga Plains, with a second in the central area of the park, and perhaps one or two camps in the southern half of the park such as KaingU or Konkamoya, in order to see the changing scenery throughout the park. While many of these camps have been here for years, several have been completely rebuilt and some are brand new. Each offers a different experience, yet all are closely involved with the park and its conservation.

Camping is easily arranged at camps throughout the majority of the park, apart from on the Busanga Plains where there are no campsites, and you are not allowed to just camp anywhere. This rule is both wise and effectively enforced.

Busanga Plains With the exception of Mukambi's Busanga Plains Camp, Wilderness Safaris currently has a monopoly here, typically flying their guests into Busanga airstrip before driving them to camp, although in wetter years this final part of the transfer sometimes requires the use of mokoros. Camps in this area are featured largely heading from east to west.

🏠 **Musanza Tented Camp** [map, page 425] (9 tents) Wilderness Safaris, page 422. ✪ MUSANZ 14°23.237'S, 26°02.026'E. Musanza under Wilderness ownership has been moved south to the site of the former Ntemwa Camp, a lovely leafy spot right on the Lufupa River, beloved of kingfishers, paradise flycatchers & the resident hippos. While Musanza was briefly open for independent visitors in 2011, it's now reserved for groups on set tours with the American operator OAT.

Green canvas tents with coir matting & twin beds set the scene, with outdoor bathrooms enclosed by thatching grass & equipped with plumbed-in showers, flushing toilets & a canvas basin. Sand paths lead to a tented awning shading a large circular table, a small seating area & a bar/coffee station. Beyond lies the river, where directors' chairs are set beneath a huge ebony tree entwined with a strangler fig. While this is a more basic camp, it's attractive, & manages to retain a sense of wilderness. A range of activities is offered at the lodge, including game drives, safari walks across the river, & river cruises. Fishing with spinners is also available for a small extra cost (US$10). **LLL**

🏠 **Shumba Camp** [map, page 425] (6 chalets) Wilderness Safaris, page 422. ✪ SHUMBA 14°13.091'S, 25°52.233'E. Set in the middle of the plains on an 'island' of large fig trees, some 15–20 mins' drive south of the base of the permanent swamps, Shumba is probably the smartest camp in northern Kafue. With wooden decks & walkways raised some 2m off the ground, the camp is relatively safe for older children – & the height makes for some interesting wildlife possibilities, too: serval cats in particular seem to favour the longer grass around the camp.

The camp is arranged in a wide semi-circle, with both its wide, rectangular chalets & the main area looking out over the plains. The chalets are constructed from tented walls with gauze panels topped with a mop of thatch, while a larger family room also has a set of large glazed sliding doors. Inside, all is space & light, the wooden floors offset by white linen & neutral décor. As well as twin 4-poster beds enveloped in white mosquito netting, there's a sofa or armchairs, a writing desk & ample storage space with a safe – not to mention a sherry decanter & glasses. The bathroom area, with twin basins,

14

shower & separate toilet, leads through to an outdoor shower. Solar panels heat the water & there's 24hr electricity. Running the length of each chalet is a split-level wooden deck with a table & chairs, & cushioned seating.

Large glass panels mostly surround the main area to offer protection from the wind that whistles across the plains, without obstructing the panoramic view. Central to this area is an open bar fronted by bar stools, around which several 'rooms' are kitted out with comfy seating & a long dining table. There's also a small shop stocking safari clothes & a few curios. An extensive split-level deck incorporates an outdoor eating area with a fire & a small infinity pool. Meals can be taken as a group or at individual tables – the food is very good & there's an impressive selection of drinks on offer.

Activities revolve around day & night game drives, & boat trips (May–Sep, water permitting). Guests who stay at least 3 nights are treated to a hot-air balloon flight, offering a wholly different perspective on the plains & the animals that make it home. *US$1,066/1,310 pp sharing/ sgl FBA, inc local drinks, park fees, laundry; exc transfers. No children under 8.* ☺ Jun–Oct. **LLLLL**

🏠 **Busanga Bush Camp** [map, page 425] (4 tents) Wilderness Safaris, page 422. ✪ BUSANG 14°12.199'S, 25°50.115'E. This deceptively simple camp is on a small tree island in the middle of the plains, & offers a more rustic alternative to its sister camp Shumba, just a short distance away. The camp lacks the elevated walkways of Shumba, with sand paths winding around several fig & palm trees connecting the rooms & the main area instead. As such Busanga feels more like a traditional bushcamp, & is much more mixed in with its surroundings.

Accommodation is in walk-in tents on polished concrete floors, each with comfortable twin beds with white linen, & red throws & cushions adding some colour. A wooden trunk at the end of the beds & a writer's desk also furnish the room, which is lit with solar-power lights. A shaded wooden deck extends from the front of the tent with a couple of wicker armchairs, as well as a suspended chair. Curtains separate the bedroom from an en-suite hot shower & flush toilet, plus a dressing area. It's well equipped, but not luxurious.

An open-sided main area is shaded by a suspended canvas roof, which covers comfortable leather & wicker furniture, a reasonably stocked bar, & several wooden tables where lunch is served, allowing you to eat whilst looking over the plains. Evening meals are usually served in a boma nearby, where an impressive chandelier made from storm lanterns is suspended from the overhanging trees. An isolated wooden deck, a short walk from the main area, faces east, so is a great spot to have a morning coffee & watch the sun rise, or watch herds of antelope in the afternoon.

Activities offered from the camp are game drives, boat trips during wetter years, & balloon flights for guests staying at least 3 nights. *US$890/1,115 pp sharing/sgl FBA, inc local drinks, laundry, park fees.* ☺ Jun–Oct. **LLLL**

✳ 🏠 **Busanga Plains Camp** [map, page 425] (4 tents) Contact via Mukambi, pages 440–1. ✪ BUSAPC 14°10.488'S, 25°49.223'E. This intimate tented camp is also known as Mukambi Plains Camp, & is not to be confused with Busanga Bushcamp. It lies on the eastern side of the Lufupa River & is the northernmost camp in the park, relatively close to the permanent papyrus swamps at the northern end of the plains, making this one of the best camps to spot the incredibly shy sitatunga antelope. To reach the camp itself you must cross a wooden walkway over a plain of floating grass, before finding the camp hidden among wild date palms on a photogenic tree island. It's a relaxed, welcoming place, a shady oasis with its main living area set beneath an extensive mobola tree (*Parinari curatellifolia*) overlooking the plains. Here, red lechwe are in their element, regularly seen from the open deck.

The 4 tented rooms are scattered around the island, hidden behind fig trees & fan palms, & feel incredibly private. The rooms aren't overly large, but they can comfortably accommodate twin or dbl beds, a couple of bedside tables & a small canva wardrobe. The front of the tents can be rolled up to provide views of the plains, & there are also a couple of wooden chairs under a canopy at the front. Bathrooms are surrounded by reed & canvas screens, but are otherwise completely open & are just a couple of steps from the tents. Each is equipped with flush toilets, basins & bucket showers. There is solar lighting in the rooms, while paraffin storm lanterns along the paths & in the main area lend the camp a back-to-nature-feel.

With no more than 8 guests at a time, activities can be flexible – with both game drives & walks around Kapinga Island an option. Busanga Plains Camp combines well with either of its sister camps, Mukambi or Fig Tree, both just south of the Lusaka–Mongu road. The camps can arrange transfers either along the eastern boundary road

(approx 4 hours), or the more scenic but slightly longer road through the park (approx 6 hours). *US$780/1,014 pp sharing/sgl FBA, inc drinks, inter-camp transfers, laundry.* ⊕ *15 Jul–Oct.* **LLLL**

Centre of the park and northeast As on the Busanga Plains, several of the camps in this area are operated by Wilderness Safaris, all of which are reserved for groups on set tours with the American operator OAT (page 45). However, there are also several alternatives available for independent booking. Access is simplest from the Hook Bridge gate: simply turn north from the Great West Road to the west of the bridge, then follow the road north. Camps are listed here from south to north, with road distances given from the gate.

🏠 **Mayukuyuku Bush Camp** [map, page 434] For details of this camp, which lies in the northern Kafue but within easy reach of the main Lusaka–Mongu road, see page 440. **LLL**

🏠 **Kafwala Camp** [map, page 425] (2 chalets, 2 rondavels) m 0966 457133/0977 811717; e busangatrails@gmail.com, sunshineseedlings@gmail.com, wescz@coppernet.zm; www.conservationzambia.org. ⊕ KAFWAL 14°48.090'S, 26°11.177'E. This camp is built on the bank of the Kafue River in a stunning location, about 700m below the start of the Kafwala Rapids. To get there, follow the road through the park northeast for about 44km, then take the right turn to Kafwala.

The camp is only open to WECSZ members (page 51), so if you're thinking of staying here then join the society in Lusaka: it does a lot of good & is deserving of more support. As the camp is popular among society members it would still require booking in advance. Accommodation comprises 2 simple 3-bed chalets that are linked by a walkway with 2 more beds, & 2 rondavels, 1 with a dbl bed, & 1 twin. Toilets, shower & bathroom are communal, as are the lounge, dining & BBQ area. Deep freezes, fridges, lamps, crockery, cutlery & bedding are provided – but you must bring all your own food & drink. In addition, you'll need a decent torch. The staff will also service the rooms, do the washing, & help with anything else that is reasonable. (You should tip them at the end of your stay.)

The area around camp is good for birdlife, & there are some productive game loops, & if you bring your own tackle, fishing from boats on the river is possible. However, guided activities from camp are limited. ⊕ *All year. US$300 up to 12 people.*

✳🏠 **Musekese** [map, page 425] (4 tents) Jeffery & McKeith Safaris, page 423. ⊕ MUSEKE 14°39.052'S, 26°09.136'E. A small intimate camp, Musekese is isolated in its own section of northern Kafue, & is one of the few camps on the eastern side of the Kafue in this area of the park. To get here, continue along the M9 from Mumbwa until you reach a lay-by 10.5km from the Itezhi–Tezhi road (⊕ MUSTUR 14°58.597.S, 26°21.245'E). Drive north along the winding dirt road, keeping left at the fork at 40km, & taking a sharp left after another 3.2km. Continue for 5km before turning right at a T-junction, & follow the track to camp. From the M9 the drive to camp should take around 1½ hours. To fly in you can land at Lufupa airstrip, followed by a 25-min boat transfer & 10-min drive to camp.

The camp takes its name from the local Kaonde name for the monkey bread tree, which is particularly common in the area. Run by owners Phil Jeffery & Tyron McKeith, both of whom have been visiting & working in the park since they were teenagers. Not only do they give the camp a personal, characterful atmosphere, but also provide excellent guiding skills, with a real passion for the conservation of the area & its wildlife.

The camp itself is small, with just 4 canvas tents that can comfortably sleep 2 people, with an open-air bathroom surrounded by reed screens accessed through a zip at the back of the tent. Each is equipped with a flush toilet, plumbed-in sinks & bucket showers. The main area is a thatched, covered wooden deck with a long dining table, small lounge & modest bar, with a sandy firepit nearby. All of this overlooks a large, seasonal riverbed that attracts large amounts of birdlife & game, allowing for some excellent wildlife viewing from camp.

14

Activities at the camp have an emphasis on walking, often starting with a transfer across the river in order to explore terrain inaccessible by car, which highlights the isolation of the area. With 3 qualified guides, though, there's a good deal of flexibility. Day & night game drives in the area are possible, & as this is one of the few areas with little-to-no burning, the scenery is beautiful, with large swathes of tall golden grass. On the river fishing is possible, as well as boat trips that allow viewing of a nest of African skimmers on an island in the middle of the river. Day trips to the Busanga Plains are also possible for an additional cost (*US$150*), but this is a long day & you'll miss the best wildlife viewing hours. A better way to see the plains from Musekese is to go on the camp's mobile safari. US$520/676 pp sharing/sgl FBA, inc local drinks, park fees, laundry; exc transfers. ⏁ Jun–Nov. **LLL**

🏠 **Lufupa River Camp** [map, page 425] (9 tents) Wilderness Safaris, page 422. ✆ LUFUPA 14°37.080'S, 26°11.626'E. Overlooking the confluence of the Lufupa & Kafue rivers, Lufupa River Camp is in an isolated area of miombo woodland with good wildlife, about halfway between the main road & the Busanga Plains. Since 2011, like Musanza (page 427), the camp has been reserved for groups travelling with OAT, who fly guests into the airstrip only a few km from camp. There is currently no way to book this camp on an individual basis.

Accommodation is in spacious safari tents that face the Kafue River, each with en-suite shower, toilet & washbasin. Meals are served in the central dining area & there's a comfortable bar where you can always help yourself to tea & coffee. There is also a swimming pool, disappointingly set behind the camp without views of the river. The atmosphere is friendly, casual & very unpretentious. Most activities from the camp are game drives & boat trips, though walks can be organised on request. **LLL**

🏠 **Lufupa Tented Camp** [map, page 425] (9 tents) Wilderness Safaris, page 422. ✆ LUFUTC 14°36.832'S, 26°11.285'E. Located right next door to Lufupa River Camp, Lufupa Tented Camp is similar in design, with identical rooms, but a slightly more exclusive air. However, like its neighbour & Musanza to the north, it is also reserved for groups on set tours. **LLL**

The Lubungu pontoon area Of the lodges and camps in this area, two – Hippo Lodge and McBrides' – are south of the pontoon, near the old Hippo Mine, and most of the others just to the north, outside the park boundary.

Getting to Hippo and McBrides'
From the main road between Mumbwa and Kasempa, about 10km south of the Lubungu pontoon, take the fork to the west (✆ TUHIPP 14°37.866'S, 26°29.659'E). Although this is clearly signposted from the south, it's easy to miss if you're coming from the north. For Hippo Lodge, follow this road, passing through a gate (✆ MINEGT 14°39.169'S, 26°25.025'E) after 5km, and later turning left at the remains of the whitewashed buildings of the old Hippo Mine (✆ HIPMIN 14°39.169.S, 26°25.025'E; see box page 431). Continue for a further 4km to the airstrip (✆ AIRHIP 14°40.191'S, 26°23.417'E). From here, it's barely 2km to Hippo Lodge (✆ HIPPO 14°40.610'S, 26°22.526'E) – or 3km to McBrides'.

For the more direct route to McBrides', take the same fork off the main road, but after 4.5km turn left (✆ TUMCBR 14°39.158'S, 26°27.871'E), as signposted. Follow the yellow arrows both here and after a further 5.2km (✆ T2MCBR 14°41.512'S, 26°26.775'E), then continue for another 7km or so until you reach the camp (✆ MCBRID 14°41.537'S, 26°23.107'E).

🏠 **Hippo Lodge** [map, page 425] (5 cottages, 2 tents) m 0977 774520; e hippolodgeinfo@gmail.com; www.hippolodge.com. ✆ HIPPO 14°40.610'S, 26°22.526'E. This well-established lodge is located along a tranquil stretch of the Kafue River, and while it started as more of a traditional, basic, bushcamp, it has grown over the years into a more substantial lodge. Hippo airstrip is only 2km away from the camp, making flying in on a chartered flight a very easy option, but the lodge also caters well to self-drives. Access directions for the more adventurous are above.

Zambia's first commercial copper mine was discovered in 1903 by Jacob Elliott – though how he got here, in an area infested with tsetse flies and therefore inaccessible on horseback, remains a mystery. Elliott died only a couple of years later, killed by a hippo, it is said – hence the name of the mine. His grave at the site is marked by a marble gravestone.

Operations at the mine itself commenced in 1911, and it remained active until 1971. The mine acts as an interesting monument to Zambia's mining history, although all that's left is old machinery, rusting vehicles, and the ruins of the white buildings that marked the entrance to the mine on the track leading to Hippo Lodge (⊕ HIPMIN 14°39.169.S, 26°25.025'E), which can arrange visits.

Quirky stone-&-thatch cottages are scattered along the riverbank, & have large unconventional baths & en-suite showers & toilets, yet each is different. Nestled between large riverine trees are 3 dbl chalets with A-frame designs, 2 of which have good views of the river, while a more conventional family chalet has a lower roof & both dbl & twin rooms. The largest, Stony House, comes with a dbl room, a twin loft room, & a spacious kitchen/living area with 2 sgl beds. Set slightly back from the river, simpler are twin-bedded safari tents under thatch, each with a small veranda &, at the back, a large stone-walled bathroom that's partially open to the sky. The main lounge/dining area overlooks the river, with a separate bar to one side. Alongside, sunloungers are set around an attractive stone pool. There is no electricity, but a combination of solar lights & paraffin lamps light the lodge, & there is a charging point in the main area for batteries.

Just 1km from camp is a marvellous natural hot spring, where hot air bubbles up from the sandy bottom, giving the water the appearance of champagne. A rough stone wall has been built to create a swimming area, although this is always carefully checked for hippos before anyone gets in. This is just one of several possible guided walks, either close to camp or across the river, whilst the energetic can arrange a rendezvous with one of the lodge's boats. Whilst the game isn't quite as prolific or varied as further west, what's around is becoming increasingly relaxed, with elephant regularly seen in & around camp, & the shy sitatunga occasionally spotted. With 70km of navigable waterways, boat trips are a major feature, where fishing & birdwatching from

the river can be combined with an island b/fast or lunch. Also on offer are guided day & night drives, & for self drivers, there's a 40-km network of game-viewing loops that has been graded. If you want to continue to Musekese, some 35km downstream, after staying here, a boat transfer can be arranged, as can trips to the Busanga Plains. *US$200/320 pp FB/FBA, exc park fees & drinks; Stony House US$455 (6 people, house only).* ⊕ *Mar–Nov.* **LL–LLL**

🏠 **McBrides' Camp** [map, page 425] (7 chalets, camping) e mcbrides.camp@uuplus. net; www.mcbridescamp.com. ⊕ MCBRID 14°41.537'S, 26°23.107'E. Informality sets the tone at this personal & isolated camp (to get here, see page 430), which has an incredibly rustic & eccentric feel to it. The basic camp was started in 2002 by Chris & Charlotte McBride, who have spent most of their lives in the bush, often with an academic focus; indeed, Chris's MSc thesis was on lions, & he went on to write 3 books on the subject, including *The White Lions of Timbavati*. They are knowledgeable & engaging hosts, who know the area incredibly well, even down to the individual animals frequently seen in camp.

Dotted around the grassy site are some rather quirky reed-&-thatch chalets; they have none of the 'design' element that is common to many safari lodges, but they are comfortable, & the large open windows allow you to experience the sights & sounds of the bush while lying in bed. Six have a dbl & a sgl bed, while the others are smaller, with just a dbl or twin beds. All have mosi nets over the beds, skins or rugs on the floor, a solid wooden chest of drawers, & chairs & a table on a small veranda. Attached to each is a large bathroom, with hot shower, basin, & flush toilet, partially sheltered under a strip of thatch. Lighting is a mix of candlelight, paraffin lanterns & solar power, & batteries can be charged in the main area. There's also a simple campsite, with toilets, basins & hot showers in 2 open-air ablution blocks, but no marked pitches. Campers are welcome to eat at the main camp (*dinner US$20 pp*), & to take part in activities (*from US$15–40 pp, depending on activity*).

Set back from the Kafue River is an open-fronted lounge & dining room. While this couldn't be described as stylish, it's certainly homely with throws & cushions on the old squashy sofas, & slightly cluttered with plenty of books & artefacts.

Moored close by are the camp's boats, including a 2-storey aluminium craft, which are used for river cruises, fishing, & transfers to the western bank of the river so that guests can walk in a pristine area with no roads. Game drives on the eastern side are also possible. Alternatively you can make a trip to their fly-camp, 14km downstream. *US$271/317 Jun–16 Nov &17 Nov–May pp sharing FBA, exc transfers, bar, park fees. Camping US$20 pp & park fees.* ☺ *All year.* **LLL**

🏠 **Kafue River Lodge** [map, page 425] (4 tents) Mbizi West Safaris, page 423. m 0978 016191; e paul@pioneercamp.com; www.kafueriver.com. ⊕ KAFRC 14°29.841'S, 26°31.206'E. Having been taken over by Paul Barnes, the owner of Pioneer Lodge and Camp in Lusaka (pages 131–2), in 2014, Kafue River Camp was undergoing major renovations when we visited in 2015, with the old tents having been knocked down, to be replaced by more substantial chalets. The new camp is being constructed on the old site in the GMA on the northeastern border of the park. To get here from the south cross over the Lubungu pontoon & continue along the main road for about 20km before taking the left turn to camp (⊕ KRCTUR 14°31.039'S, 26°29.144'E), although the camp will easily be able to arrange transfers from Lusaka.

There are 4 new chalets being constructed along a picturesque section of the Kafue River, overlooking several small islands & large granite boulders in the river. The plan is for each to have 2 queen-sized beds, polished wooden floors & fireplaces to help keep the rooms cosy during the winter months. The chalets will also have an indoor & an outdoor bathroom, & a private deck extending from the front towards the river.

The open-sided main area to the side of the camp is being kept, but a wooden deck is being extended over the river, with plans for a wooden walkway to be constructed along the riverbank connecting it to the main area.

The aim of the camp is to focus on drives & walking safaris, both in the GMA & in the park to the south of the Kafue River, although there will also be water-based activities, including boat cruises & fishing. There are also plans to operate mobile safaris to the Busanga Plains, providing 2 full days on the plains whilst camping in dome tents. *US$90/350 pp room only/FBA inc bar, park fees; exc transfers. Camping US$50.* ☺ *All year.* **LLL**

🏠 **Leopard Lodge** [map, page 425] (5 chalets, camping) 📞+27 82 416 5894; e info@leopard-lodge.com; www.leopard-lodge.com. ⊕ LEOPLO 14°32.823'S, 26°28.960'E. Just before Kafue River Camp, & reached by turning off the main track at ⊕ TULEOP 14°32.426'S, 26°28.597'E, the family-run Leopard Lodge lies on a grassy section of the riverbank within the Lunga-Luswishi GMA This allows good views of the river itself, & the opposite bank where puku, impala & elephants can often be seen coming down to drink.

The camp's modern en-suite chalets are well spaced, & set back from the river, each with thatched roofs & cream paintwork. They are spacious, well equipped & comfortable, but they do have some confusing design choices, such as bedrooms at the back of the chalet, overlooking the bland scenery behind camp, & an unusual porch area which is incorporated into the chalets themselves rather than being outside.

A small way downstream there's an excellent campsite, where each stand has its own private shower block with hot water from wood-fired boilers, a braai area, & ample space for camping. The pitches are well hidden from the others by trees & reed screens, giving a good sense of privacy.

Being on the river, Leopard Lodge is able to offer a variety of activities inc boat trips, canoeing & fishing, as well as the usual walking & driven safaris in the GMA, & across the river in the national park. Like all of the staff at the camp, the guides are experienced & incredibly pleasant. *US$300/375, Apr–10 Jun, US$400/500 11 Jun–20 Nov pp sharing/sgl, all FBA, inc park fees, exc drinks. Camping US$25 inc firewood.* ☺ *Apr–20 Nov.* **LLL**

🏠 **Mushingashi Conservancy** [map, page 425] (1 house, 3 camps; camping) m 0977 846978;

e darrellwatt@yahoo.com, darrellwatt7@gmail.com; www.mushingashi.com. ✪ TUMUSH 14°40.853'S, 26°40.430'E. About 65km from Mumbwa, the unfenced 405km² Mushingashi Conservancy runs for 18km along the Kafue River & shares a 37km boundary with the national park. The conservancy has seen an impressive recovery in wildlife over the last few decades under the management of conservationist Darrell Watt, who lives in the area, & it now boasts wildlife, including elephant, sable, eland & roan, predators such as lion & cheetah, & more than 400 bird species. Although used as a hunting concession, there are self-drive game loops, & guided walks can be arranged.

From the road, it's 30km to the main Kabalushi Camp, with well-marked turnings to this & other simple, self-catering camps in the conservancy (bring *all* your own supplies). All are located on the river & with en-suite facilities. **Delai** & **Khosikoto** camps each have 6 rustic thatched chalets & a campsite; then there's **Kalonga Waloba** (14 chalets), & **Kabalushi** (8-bed & 2-bed houses). Bongwe Safaris (page 422) also own **Bongwe Bush Camp**, reserved for their 3-night set trips. Most guests bring their own boats, but there are fully equipped boats for hire, too (*US$100 per day & fuel*). Nearby are the Piamanzi (or Mutoyi) hot springs, bubbling out of black-cotton soil – so not suitable for swimming. *US$50 pp; camping US$25 pp.* **L**

SOUTHERN KAFUE Stretching about 190km southwards from the main road, the southern part of the park is long and thin, only about 85km wide at its broadest point. On its eastern boundary are the Kafue River and the Itezhi-Tezhi Dam: 300km² of water. Itezhi-Tezhi differs from many dams as, apparently, it is not made of continuous concrete, but instead is filled with earth, in order to render it less vulnerable to tremors and minor earthquakes.

The vegetation and geography are broadly similar to the north – see *Geography* and *Flora and fauna*, pages 418–21 – although there's more Kalahari sand in the south. Other noticeable differences are landmarks such as the impressive granite hills rising from the miombo forest as you drive south past KaingU, and a few really beautiful teak forests to the south of the lake.

4x4 routes within and around southern Kafue
Mukambi and Mayukuyuku are very close to the main road and don't require a 4x4. They are clearly signposted around the main bridge over the Kafue in the centre of the park. The completion of the new spinal road down the western side of the Kafue river in 2013 has greatly improved access to the southern half of the park, and is a good quality gravel road negating the need for a 4x4 during the dry season. Alternatively, you can take one of the routes through the GMA, or approach from the south from Monze, Choma or Kalmomo on the Lusaka–Livingstone road, but at the moment these routes are of much poorer quality, with a 4x4 being essential at all times of year.

From the M9 Lusaka–Mongu road to Lake Itezhi-Tezhi Heading west from Luska, the road bypasses Mumbwa after some 150km, then another 37km brings you to the Nalusanga scout post (✪ NALUSA 14°58.258'S, 26°42.718'E) at the entrance to the Kafue National Park. The road then bisects the park before exiting on the western side, and there are several opportunities to turn south into the park along the way. With the completion of the spinal road, access into the park from the Lusaka–Mongu road is now possible from both the eastern and western side of the Kafue River and Lake Itezhi-Tezhi, either through the Mumbwa and Namwala GMAs or through the park itself, with the wildlife being fairly comparable on both sides.

The spinal road on the western side, and the D769 on the eastern are all-season, while an alternative 'river route' on the eastern side is dry season only, being impassable in the rains. (There is also a third route between the two eastern roads, known as the 'hunters' road', which is used by local people, but is not a right of way.)

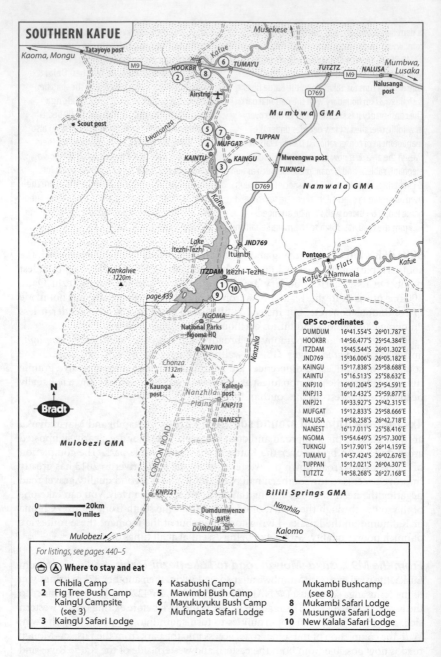

SOUTHERN KAFUE

Kaoma, Mongu
Tatayoyo post
Musekese
Kafue
M9
HOOKBR
6
TUMAYU
TUTZTZ
M9
NALUSA
Mumbwa, Lusaka
2
8
Nalusanga post
Airstrip
D769

Scout post
Lwansanza
M u m b w a   G M A

5   7
4   MUFGAT
TUPPAN
KAINTU
3
KAINGU
Mweengwa post
TUKNGU

D769
N a m w a l a   G M A

Kafue

Lake Itezhi-Tezhi
Itumbi
JND769
Pontoon
Kafue
Flats
Kafue
Kankalwe 1220m
ITZDAM Itezhi-Tezhi
Namwala
1   10
9
page 439

NGOMA
National Parks Ngoma HQ
KNPJIO
Nanzhila

Chonza 1132m
Kaunga post
Nanzhila Plains
Kalenje post
KNPJ13

N
Bradt

NANEST

Mulobezi GMA

CORDON ROAD

Bilili Springs GMA

GPS co-ordinates ⊕

DUMDUM	16°41.554'S	26°01.787'E
HOOKBR	14°56.477'S	25°54.384'E
ITZDAM	15°45.544'S	26°01.302'E
JND769	15°36.006'S	26°05.182'E
KAINGU	15°17.838'S	25°58.688'E
KAINTU	15°16.513'S	25°58.632'E
KNPJ10	16°01.204'S	25°54.591'E
KNPJ13	16°12.432'S	25°59.877'E
KNPJ21	16°33.927'S	25°42.315'E
MUFGAT	15°12.833'S	25°58.666'E
NALUSA	14°58.258'S	26°42.718'E
NANEST	16°17.011'S	25°58.416'E
NGOMA	15°54.649'S	25°57.300'E
TUKNGU	15°17.901'S	26°14.159'E
TUMAYU	14°57.424'S	26°02.676'E
TUPPAN	15°12.021'S	26°04.307'E
TUTZTZ	14°58.268'S	26°27.168'E

KNPJ21

Dumdumwenze gate
DUMDUM

Mulobezi
Nanzhila
Kalomo

0   20km
0   10 miles

For listings, see pages 440–5

⊕ Ⓐ **Where to stay and eat**

1	Chibila Camp	4	Kasabushi Camp		Mukambi Bushcamp
2	Fig Tree Bush Camp	5	Mawimbi Bush Camp		(see 8)
	KaingU Campsite	6	Mayukuyuku Bush Camp	8	Mukambi Safari Lodge
	(see 3)	7	Mufungata Safari Lodge	9	Musungwa Safari Lodge
3	KaingU Safari Lodge			10	New Kalala Safari Lodge

The Spinal Road to Itezhi-Tezhi The turning left onto the southern heading D769 (⊕ TUTZTZ 14°58.268'S, 26°27.168'E) is approximately 28km from the Nalusanga scout post. If you're approaching from the west, that's a fraction more than 51km from the main Hook Bridge over the Kafue River. It is clearly signposted to Itezhi-Tezhi and – in the rainy season – is the only viable road south on the eastern side of the river.

This road has been appalling for years, with the remains of a badly deteriorated tar road impeding progress rather than helping. However, after years of broken promises the government has finally started work on re-tarring the road, starting from the Itezhi-Tezhi side. By late 2015 they had made it almost halfway, with completion tentatively planned for 2016. This work should greatly improve this route, halving the 5–6 hour journey time, although concerns about the quality of the tar suggests that the life cycle of this road might be a quick one. Be aware, too, that whole sections are popular with tsetse flies, making air conditioning a valuable accessory for your vehicle.

About 45km after the turning, you will pass the Mweengwa scout checkpoint (✥ MWEENG 15°16.539'S, 26°14.950'E), where you must stop to sign in. About 2km south of that, there's a turning clearly marked for KaingU Safari Lodge and Mufungata (✥ TUKNGU 15°17.901'S, 26°14.159'E).

About 39km from the scout post you'll stop at a veterinary control post; then a further 22km and you reach **Itezhi-Tezhi village** (✥ ITEZHI 15°44.252'S, 26°2.202'E). This is about 106km from the main Lusaka–Mongu road. Continue for about 2km, bearing left and uphill until you reach a ZESCO checkpoint. At this point, a right turning takes you into the village (page 436) where you can organise fuel and take in some commanding views of the lake. To continue straight to the southern section of the park then drive on, below the dam wall (✥ ITZDAM 15°45.544'S, 26°1.302'E). You'll pass three lodges, which are well signposted on the right-hand side of the road, then it's just a couple of kilometres further to the Musa gate (✥ MUSAGA 15°47.802'S, 25°59.938'E). This is where you pay your park fees into the southern section of Kafue National Park, and connect onto the southern tip of the spinal road. Interestingly, the gate itself is located outside the park boundary, which you'll cross (albeit without any sign) just before Lake View Drive.

The river route to Itezhi-Tezhi Between June and November, there's an altogether more scenic, albeit longer alternative to the D769, following a series of tracks along the Kafue River and passing close to both Mufungata and KaingU safari lodges. The route crosses the Mumbwa GMA, and is absolutely legal, but note that this is also a hunting concession – so safari-goers may not always be welcome. That said, when we asked directions of a hunter, we were treated with absolute courtesy and shown the right turning without any fuss.

To find the river route, leave the M9 Lusaka–Mongu road opposite the turning to Mayukuyuku (✥ TUMAYU 14°57.424'S, 26°02.676'E), signposted to Kafumbakwale (a very underused community campsite). Follow this narrow but good gravel track more or less southwest for about 5km, keeping an eye out for a track to your left into the bush (✥ RR1 14°59.603'S, 26°01.020'E). There's no signpost, and it's not terribly clear, but if you overshoot it you'll soon get to the river so just retrace your steps. The correct, sandy track winds southeast through the bush for about 4km until, at ✥ RR2 14°59.584'S, 26°01.031'E, you come to a confusing medley of tracks in a rough clearing. It's easy to become disorientated here, but continue broadly south, bearing slightly left in the clearing, then right into a steep gully at ✥ RR3 15°00.604'S, 26°02.666'E, and emerging into a thick patch of sand. From here, the track continues roughly south, through bush and across open plains, crossing several river beds, and sometimes with glimpses of the river to your right. Precise route directions are of little help, but the following GPS co-ordinates mark some of the riverbeds and other landmarks *en route* to KaingU Safari Lodge:

14

RR4	15°01.884'S, 26°02.283'E	Riverbed; graveyard termitaria both sides; river on right
RR5	15°03.934'S, 26°01.525'E	Riverbed
RR6	15°05.394'S, 25°59.764'E	Riverbed
+RR7	15°05.997'S, 25°59.302'E	Ignore track to left
RR8	15°06.788'S, 25°58.971'E	Ignore track to right along river
RR9	15°07.905'S, 25°58.488'E	Hunting camp to right on river
RR10	15°10.734'S, 25°58.973'E	Take right fork
RR11	15°12.199'S, 25°58.748'E	Keep right at fork
TUPPN2	15°12.389'S, 25°58.708'E	T-junction with good gravel track; turn right for Puku Pan and to continue south
TUKAI2	15°13.877'S, 25°59.484'E	Take right fork to KaingU and south
POLEBR	15°17.306'S, 25°59.130'E	Cross the pole bridge and turn immediately left (continue straight on for KaingU Safari Lodge)

Continuing south from the pole bridge (and the turning to KaingU), you'll cross several more riverbeds and – after around 21km – you will pass the palace of Chief Kaingu to your left, followed 7km later by Bushinga village. From the pole bridge to the junction with the D769 (⊕ JND769 15°36.006'S, 26°05.182'E) is around 43km. From here, you turn right towards Itezhi-Tezhi village. Useful GPS co-ordinates along this stretch include:

RR12	15°21.495'S, 25°59.695'E	Dip, and pool to left
RR13	15°22.469'S, 25°59.866'E	Double river crossing
RR14	15°25.006'S, 26°00.286'E	Take left fork
RR15	15°25.760'S, 26°00.064'E	Deep river crossing
RR16	15°29.762'S, 26°00.436'E	Stone bridge
RR16	15°34.815'S, 26°03.240'E	Bear left at fork

Itezhi-Tezhi village For those heading into the park, the village is an invaluable source of both fuel and supplies. Instead of following the main road south, turn right and you'll pass a police station immediately on your left, followed by a **post office** and a branch of the Zanaco **Bank**. Pass the school and you'll get to the ZESCO offices (⊕ *08.00–12.30 & 14.00–16.30*), by which point you'll be high up and overlooking the lake. Fuel is paid for and arranged at the ZESCO offices, but collected back on the main road, on the way towards the dam wall. Be aware though that the fuel station is closed at lunch (noon–14.00) and on Sundays, even though you can still pay at the ZESCO offices.

From the south
Kalomo to Dumdumwenze gate The small town of Kalomo (pages 209–10) is about 126km from Livingstone on the way to Lusaka, and marks the turning towards the southern section of the Kafue. There's a **fuel** station here (⊕ KAFUEL 17°01.673'S, 26°29.259'E) which can be useful for a top-up, but it's unreliable and it would be wise to have all the fuel required before you leave Livingstone or Lusaka. Just north of this, a clear sign points west to the Dumdumwenze gate. Almost immediately the road becomes a dirt track, passing through a busy **market** (a good place for supplies) to a T-junction. Turn right here and follow the road as it curves left (ignoring right-hand turn-off).

Continue over a railway bridge, followed shortly afterwards by a river bridge (⊕ KALBRI 17°0.915'S, 26°29.468'E), then take the next left fork. Continue following the main track, ignoring any turnings and keeping left at forks. After a few kilometres you should cross another river bridge (⊕ KLOBRI 16°59.331'S, 26°27.876'E) before travelling northwest, passing through the occasional village. About 40km from the main road, you will start leaving the villages behind to climb through some hills. Eventually, after about 74km, the road drops down gradually to Dumdumwenze gate (⊕ DUMDUM 16°41.554'S, 26°1.787'E), where the game scouts will sign you into the park. (Note that Dumdumwezi is the local spelling and pronunciation.)

The road is generally good with some rough patches, but watch out for some particularly vicious speed bumps which materialise before and after both villages and river bridges, often with no warning signposts. Watch out, too, for goats, cattle and hens along the road.

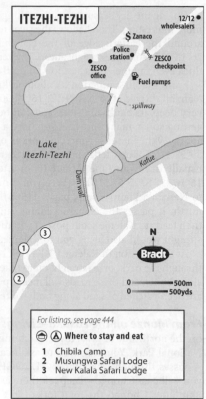

For listings, see page 444

⊖ ⓐ **Where to stay and eat**
1 Chibila Camp
2 Musungwa Safari Lodge
3 New Kalala Safari Lodge

North from Dumdumwenze There are two main routes leading north from the gate, both of which are affected by the yearly rains and sporadically graded, meaning the easiest route switches regularly. You should check with your planned camp when booking for advice, and let them know which route you plan to take – they aren't tricky routes, but they are long and see little traffic. Alternatively ask the scouts at the gate for advice. Whichever route you take, drive north into the park for 2.3km to the first junction (⊕ KNPJ20 16°40.332'S, 26°1.722'E).

Between about December and June, there's little choice: you will have to take the **Cordon route**, which skirts around the southwest side of the park through woodlands. This gets to Ngoma without crossing any substantial rivers, and so while it does have the odd sticky dambo, an experienced driver with a 4x4 should be able to get through even in the rains. Note, however, that high sand can pile up in the centre of the road, so a high-clearance 4x4 is as essential for this route as for any other within the park.

For this route you go into the park, heading north for about 2.3km, then take a left turn at your first junction (⊕ KNPJ20 16°40.332'S, 26°1.722'E). From here you proceed about 40km, through fairly thick forest, heading slightly north of west, until you reach a junction (⊕ KAFU01 16°33.927'S, 25°42.314'E), which indicates the southwestern tip of the park. There you turn right, to head north and slightly east on a basically straight road that passes through the heart of the southern end of the park. This ultimately meets other roads near Ngoma at a junction ⊕ KNPJ10 16°1.204'S, 25°54.591'E.

During the dry season, consider taking the **Nanzhila River route**, which is much more interesting. This shadows the river north, crossing it several times and skirting around the eastern edge of the Nanzhila Plains. From ⊕ KNPJ20 16°40.332'S, 26°1.722'E, continue straight ahead. The vegetation along this route can be exceedingly thick even in June, so it's best to wait until at least July to drive along here.

From that first junction it's about 19km until you cross to the east bank of the Nanzhila River at ⊕ NANRV2 16°30.905'S, 26°0.164'E. Although the river isn't very deep, its banks are steep and can be slippery, so if there's any danger of you getting stuck, make sure that you have a back-up plan. Continue north, and after about 29km there's a concrete marker on a junction at ⊕ NANEST 16°17.011'S, 25°58.416'E. Turn left, and in about 2km you'll reach a river crossing which is usually dry from June. About 100m afterwards there's a crossroads (⊕ KNPJ16 16°16.497'S, 25°57.318'E) where you'll need to turn right (straight on takes you to Nanzhila Plains Camp, pages 445–6). This takes you onto a really lovely road north. It passes the Nanzhila Plains, and bends east at the Chilenje Pools, and then leads to Kalenje scout post. If you didn't go west at NANEST, then continuing straight would also bring you to Kalenje.

At the junction in Kalenje (⊕ KLJJNC 16°12.430'S, 25°59.878'E) you can turn left through the park, or go straight on to take the eastern boundary road. Head straight along either, and these roads will meet up with the cordon road at the airstrip. There are deep patched of sand along both routes, so take extra care.

From Monze on the Lusaka–Livingstone road
From Monze take a turning on the north side of town towards Chongo, heading northwest towards Lochinvar National Park. You may need to ask local directions to get on the right track, but it passes through waypoint ⊕ TULOCH 16°15.465'S, 27°28.632'E. After 7–8km you will pass Chongo – keep left there as the track divides after the village. About 8km after Chongo the road forks (⊕ T2LOCH 16°10.054'S, 27°23.610'E): right leads to Lochinvar National Park; left leads to Namwala and thence the Ngoma area of Kafue.

About 35km later, on a dusty (or, if wet, muddy) and rather pot-holed track, you will reach Chitongo, and a T-junction. Here you find an implausibly good tarred road! (If you turned left onto this, you would find that the tar turned into poor gravel about 60km before Choma.) For the Kafue turn right at Chitongo, and follow this heading slightly west of north, then due west. About 50km after Chitongo you will reach the larger village of Namwala, on the southern edge of the Kafue's floodplain (where, incidentally, there's a pontoon over the Kafue). From Namwala, the track leads about 60km southwest, into the park. This is bumpy and pot-holed gravel, but is passable during the rains. It enters the park past the site of the old Nkala Mission, joining the road network at ⊕ TUNAMW 15°53.894'S, 25°57.854'E, about 2km north of Ngoma.

🏠 **Where to stay** If you're just passing through the park on the main Lusaka–Mongu road, consider stopping for a night or two in the area around Mukambi – but if you have more time, it's well worth penetrating deeper into the park. The southern Itezhi-Tezhi area, and around Ngoma, has impressive game and the most spectacular scenery in this part of the park, whilst KaingU Safari Lodge is built beside a unique and very lovely part of the river.

If you're driving and taking camping kit, there is plenty of choice, even though both the national parks' campsites in the southern Kafue have closed. You can probably afford to turn up at the lodges along the Lusaka road and those around

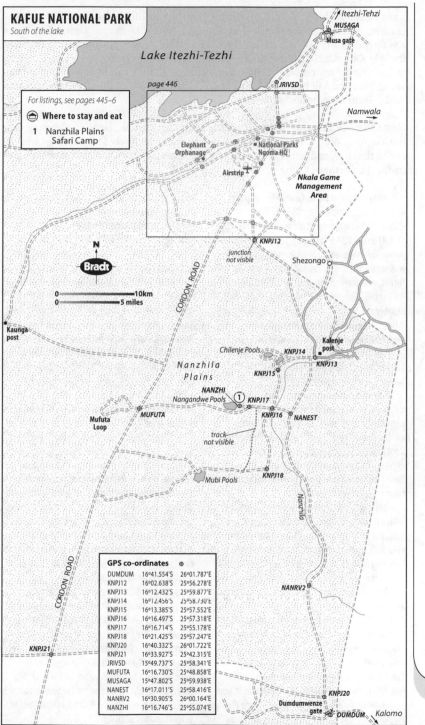

KAFUE NATIONAL PARK
South of the lake

Lake Itezhi-Tezhi

Itezhi-Tehzi
MUSAGA
Musa gate

page 446

JRIVSD

Namwala

For listings, see pages 445–6

🏠 **Where to stay and eat**

1 Nanzhila Plains
Safari Camp

Elephant
Orphanage

National Parks
Ngoma HQ

Airstrip

**Nkala Game
Management
Area**

N

Bradt

KNPJ12

*junction
not visible*

Shezongo

| 0 | 10km |
| 0 | 5 miles |

Kaunga
post

Chilenje Pools   **KNPJ14**

Kalenje
post

KNPJ13

*Nanzhila
Plains*

KNPJ15

NANZHI
Nangandwe Pools   **①** **KNPJ17**

CORDON ROAD

KNPJ16   **NANEST**

Mufuta
Loop   **MUFUTA**

*track
not visible*

Mubi Pools   **KNPJ18**

Nanzhila

NANRV2

CORDON ROAD

KNPJ21

GPS co-ordinates	⊕
DUMDUM	16°41.554'S	26°01.787'E
KNPJ12	16°02.638'S	25°56.278'E
KNPJ13	16°12.432'S	25°59.877'E
KNPJ14	16°12.456'S	25°58.730'E
KNPJ15	16°13.385'S	25°57.552'E
KNPJ16	16°16.497'S	25°57.318'E
KNPJ17	16°16.714'S	25°55.178'E
KNPJ18	16°21.425'S	25°57.247'E
KNPJ20	16°40.332'S	26°01.722'E
KNPJ21	16°33.927'S	25°42.315'E
JRIVSD	15°49.737'S	25°58.341'E
MUFUTA	16°16.730'S	25°48.858'E
MUSAGA	15°47.802'S	25°59.938'E
NANEST	16°17.011'S	25°58.416'E
NANRV2	16°30.905'S	26°00.164'E
NANZHI	16°16.746'S	25°55.074'E

KNPJ20

Dumdumwenze
gate   **DUMDUM**   *Kalomo*

Lake Itezhi-Tezhi, and even at Hippo Bay, but would be advised to book the smaller, more remote campsites at KaingU, Nanzhila Plains Safari Camp and Kasabushi. For those on a fly-in trip, on a flexible budget, the options in this area include KaingU, Nanzhila Plains Safari Camp and Konkamoya.

For ease of reference, I've split the southern Kafue's camps into three distinct areas: 'Near the M9 Lusaka–Mongu road', 'Further south in the GMA' and 'Around Itezhi-Tezhi Dam and south'.

Near the M9 Lusaka–Mongu road There are several places to stay very near the M9 road, but for most people those listed here are likely to be the best bet. All are on the river, and either in or opposite the national park – with Mayukuyuku just inside the northern Kafue.

🛖 **Mayukuyuku Bush Camp** [map, page 434] (4 tents, camping) m 0972 179266; e info@kafuecamps.com; www.kafuecamps.com. ✪ MAYUKU 14°54.975'S, 26°03.925'E. Small, personal & welcoming, Mayukuyuku Bush Camp was set up in 2006 by Patrick Moyo & Pippa Turner, who worked together at Lufupa for years. It's a small, rustic place, more camp than lodge, & capably run by an almost entirely Zambian team. It lies 5.7km north of the main Lusaka–Mongu road, from where it is clearly signposted (✪ TUMAYU 14°57.424'S, 26°02.676'E), some 107km west of Mumbwa. It's positioned just within the national park.

Walk-in tents under shaggy thatch are set on a sandy, tree-shaded site by the river, opposite a small tree-clad island surrounded by water-eroded granite rocks. Each has dbl or twin beds, floor mats, solar lighting, an open-air reed-enclosed bathroom with hot shower & separate flush toilet – & a shady verandah with chairs & table plus its own hammock.

A little way upstream is a separate campsite with 4 pitches; campers can be collected at Hook Bridge (*US$30 per vehicle*). There is a reception area with small curio shop, library, battery charging & Wi-Fi. Closer to the camp are a simple lounge/bar/dining shelter – with meals available to allcomers with advance notice – & a reception area with small shop.

As well as offering fully inclusive packages, both guests & day visitors can book activities like boat cruises, fishing, walking safaris & game drives on an individual basis (*all US$45 pp*). The camp also caters well to self-drivers as it is possible to hire a guide to accompany you in your own vehicle (*from US$30/3hrs*). *US$475 pp FBA inc park fees; US$335 FB; no sgl suppt. Camping*

US$25 pp. Transfers extra. ⊕ *All year.* **LLL** See ad in 3rd colour section.

🛖 **Mukambi Safari Lodge** [map, page 434] (9 chalets, 4 tents, 1 villa) ☎ 0211 840953; m 0974 424013; e info@mukambi.com; www. mukambi.com. ✪ MUKAMB 14°58.656'S, 25°59.599'E. In the capable hands of Linda & Jacques van Heerden, Mukambi is a well-built, comfortable lodge in the GMA, with consistently high standards. It is clearly signposted from the main Lusaka–Mongu tar road (✪ TUMUKA 14°57.584'S, 25°59.721'E), about 9km east of the Hook Bridge over the Kafue. The camp is 2km from the main road – easily accessed in a 2WD.

Thatched, cream-painted chalets (4 twin, 4 dbl, 1 family, & a family villa) are solidly built with beautifully carved wooden doors. There's no AC or fan, but the circular shape, tree shade & netted windows help to keep them cool, & each has a small veranda with chairs. Inside are 4-poster beds under mosquito nets, the neutral décor enlivened by ethnic wall hangings & wood carvings. Stone-tiled showers in the bathrooms are solar-heated, with a geyser in the villa.

The multi-levelled wooden central area, overlooking the Kafue River to the national park, brings an open & relaxed feeling to the lodge. A resident hippo often spends his afternoons sleeping in this area, although a member of staff is always present to keep an eye on him when he's about. The food, from a set menu, is good, served in the substantial restaurant area, while lower down is a relaxed seating area over the river. There's a swimming pool with a deck, & a cosy lounge/bar with a fire for the winter months. Day visitors are welcome & can join in activities subject to availability.

A range of boating & 4x4 game-viewing trips is available, with no more than 8 guests in each safari vehicle. Overall game densities in the Chunga area (where they usually drive) have improved considerably since the camp was opened in 1997 & anti-poaching measures put in place. In addition to some lovely herds of elephant & buffalo, there are now regular sightings of lion, leopard, cheetah & wild dog. Guests may also visit the local primary school, which is supported by the lodge. *US$265/320 pp sharing FB, US$400/460 pp sharing FBA, Nov–Jun/Jul–Oct, exc park fees. 30% sgl suppt* ⏰ *All year.* **LLL**

⚎ Mukambi Bushcamp [map, page 434] Contact via Mukambi, above. Mukambi Safari Lodge did have a well-run campsite associated with the lodge, with 7 pitches with pre-erected tents, bedding, & useful camp staff on hand to help with fires & food preparation. While this was closed to make room for more permanent accommodation at the lodge, there are plans to rebuild the campsite 700m upstream from the old site, to be run much in the same way as the last camp.

⌂ Fig Tree Bush Camp [map, page 434] (4 tents) Contact via Mukambi, above. ✥ FIGTRE 15°00.045'S, 25°49.062'E. Owned by Mukambi Safaris, & sister camp to Mukambi Plains Camp & Mukambi Safari Lodge, Fig Tree is the newest of the 3 having been built in 2015. Located west of the

Kafue River in the national park, it's just 6km south of the main Lusaka–Mongu road. To get here, turn off the main road at ✥ CHUNRD 14°56.834'S, 25°51.220'E to join the start of the road towards Chunga, & drive 2km before taking a left turn at ✥ FIGTUR 14°57.848'S, 25°51.398'E. Follow this winding track for 8km down to Fig Tree.

Completely contrasting in style to Mukambi Safari Lodge, Fig Tree is a small & intimate camp with only 4 tented rooms, each suspended on 3m high platforms, giving them the feeling of rather smart tree houses. A wooden staircase leads up to a polished stone platform, where a small section protrudes from the front of the tent with views of a permanent lagoon or patch of miombo woodland. Large gauze windows allow the breeze into the cream canvas tents, & each is furnished with twin or dbl beds, wicker chairs & a wooden storage unit. Head-height reed screens, shaded by a canvas canopy, surround en-suite bathrooms at the back of the tent, each with flushing toilets & hot showers.

Sandy paths lead to the simple main area, where a canvas canopy shades a long dining table, lounge & small library. It's completely open sided, allowing views of the beautiful beach created by the dried sand banks of the Shishamba River. The camp offers both game drives & walking safaris in the surrounding areas of miombo woodland. *US$460/598 pp sharing/sgl FBA, inc local drinks, inter-camp transfers; exc park fees.* ⏰ *Jun–Oct.* **LLL**

Further south in the Namwala GMA There are four more southerly lodges on the eastern and western banks of the river, which are too far from the Lusaka–Mongu road to be mere stopovers. Several have campsites, which are best booked in advance. The camps on the eastern bank are accessible from the spinal road, but you will have to leave any vehicles on the western side of the river, so if you're camping it's advisable to approach these camps using the D769. There has long been game in this area, effectively protected from poaching by the presence of the lodges. That said, although the game is building up, it isn't as good as in the park's best corners – but the river here is stunning!

⚹⌂ KaingU Safari Lodge [map, page 434] (6 tented chalets, 1 family chalet) e lodgemanager@kaingu-lodge.com, reservations@kaingu-lodge.com; www.kaingu-lodge.com. ✥ KAINGU 15°17.838'S, 25°58.688'E. KaingU stands in an idyllic setting on the east bank of the Kafue; as the bee-eater flies it's about 40km from the M9, or 10km south of Mufungata. To get here from the D769 (pages 435–6) turn

west at the signpost to KaingU ✥ TUKNGU 15°17.901'S, 26°14.159'E. This bush track twists & winds through dense miombo woodland for about 23.5km until you fork left at ✥ TUPPAN 15°12.021'S, 26°4.307'E. From there it's just under 18km to the lodge, during which you cross a small pole bridge (✥ POLEBR 15°17.306'S, 25°59.130'E). An alternative approach is to drive down the spinal road for 33km before turning

right (⊕ KAINTU 15°16.513'S, 25°58.632'E).
Follow this track towards the river for 700m until
you reach a small grass car park. You will need to
arrange with the lodge a time to meet you here in
advance so that they can boat you the rest of the
way to camp.

The lodge is broadly traditional in design, &
finished with a high degree of care. Two of its large,
cream Meru-style tents are raised on polished
wooden decking under thatch, with a proper wood
& gauze door leading to a large veranda facing
the river. Large, high-quality beds stand on hand-
woven rugs, & it's possible to open up the whole of
the front of the tent to be one big mesh window.
At the back, an attractive stone bathroom, with
green bottles cleverly built into the walls, has an
indoor & outdoor shower (or bath), & individual
touches like a towel rail of knurled wood. There's
hot water aplenty & small 12V solar-powered
lights. The 4 older rooms are broadly similar but are
slightly larger, the beds face sideways rather than
towards the river, & the bathrooms are at the back
without a view. There are plans to replace these
rooms over the coming years. Finfoot cottage is a
properly constructed house rather than a tent, &
works well for families. It has 2 en-suite rooms,
each with outdoor showers, either side of a central
living area.

The lodge is owner-run by a small group
of incredibly passionate & personable
individuals, virtues that are shared by the camp's
knowledgeable guides. Activities at the camp
include game drives on either side of the river,
walking safaris – walking up some of the large
granite hills is in the area is particularly
enjoyable – fishing excursions, & visits to one
of their photographic hides overlooking a
waterhole & on an island in the river. For the
more adventurous it's possible to go on overnight
camping trips in basic dome tents. With such a
small lodge, & a high degree of enthusiasm, there's
plenty of flexibility.

The river beside the lodge is as lovely as any
stretch of African river that I know: it's worth
coming here just to spend a few days afloat.
KaingU stands beside an area where the river
broadens to accommodate a scattering of small
islands, each consisting of vegetated sandy banks
& huge granite rocks interspersed with rapids.
Imagine someone throwing half of Zimbabwe's
Matobo Hills into a wide, shallow river & you'll

get the picture. So to potter round here in a boat,
inflatable canoe or even just to go fishing is a real
journey of discovery. With endless side channels
& islands to explore, there's something different
around every corner, plenty of vegetation
everywhere – & birds all around. When the
water's low it's even possible to swim in the
pools above the rapids. It's a real gem of an area.
*US$425/484 pp Jun–Dec/Mar–May, FBA, inc park
fees & local drinks.* ☺ *Mar–Dec.* **LLL**

⚊ KaingU Campsite [map, page 434] (3 private
campsites, 1 shared site) Contact KaingU Safari
Lodge, page 441. KaingU has 3 private riverside
pitches next to the rapids with space for 6 people
(2 cars max), as well as one shared site in the bush
that can accommodate up to 8 people (4 cars max).
Each has its own spotless & very well-designed
reed-walled ablutions (flush toilet, hot shower
& washbasin), a cooking grid, a fireplace, a tap &
a table for washing up. All the sites are pleasant
& grassy, under trees, & firewood is provided.
However, you must bring all your food, as meals
are available at the lodge only if you've arranged
them well in advance. The communal facilities at
the lodge are generally off limits to campers. You
must bring all your own equipment, so you must
approach from the eastern side of the river along
the D769. *US$22 pp.* ☺ *Mar–Dec.*

⌂ Mufungata Safari Lodge [map, page
434] (7 chalets, 2 tents, camping) m 0977
600538/0967 977356; e mufungata@gmail.com;
www.mu-fungata.net. ⊕ MUFGAT 15°12.833'S,
25°58.666'E. Formerly known as Puku Pan Safari
Lodge, this camp was taken over by new owners,
fully refurbished, & renamed to Mufungata
in 2014. It's still on the same 200m stretch of
the Kafue River, overlooking the park from the
GMA & as the fish eagle flies about 10km north
of KaingU. Though it's possible to fly in, most
people drive. By road, follow the directions for
KaingU (pages 435–6) to ⊕ TUPPAN 15°12.021'S,
26°4.307'E. Fork right here, & it's just under 14km
to the lodge, passing the airstrip (⊕ AIRPUK
15°12.202'S, 26°1.989'E). Alternatively you can
approach from the spinal road, turning towards
the river at ⊕ MUFTUR 15°13.236'S, 25°58.155'E
& continuing until you reach a small grass car
park. The lodge is on the opposite side of the
river, so if you beep your horn someone will come
to collect you by boat, but it's best to advise the
lodge what time you expect to arrive.

Seven of the lodges are original cottages, built from mud-finished blocks of wood under thatch, 2 of which are slightly larger 'luxury rooms', & one which is a family unit, with 3 bedrooms sleeping up to 8 people. Each has a veranda overlooking the river, plus flush toilet & bath or shower with hot water; there is solar power. Newly constructed are 2 tented rooms under thatched roofs, with a communal ablutions block. There's also a large if basic campsite with shared ablutions, including hot showers, & a couple of simple tented chalets. A combined dining area, lounge & bar has open sides & views of the river, & has recently been joined by a swimming pool & entertainment area, with a dartboard & pool table, which overlooks a waterhole at the back of camp.

Guests & day visitors can take part in boat trips & day or night game drives (*US$50 pp*), fishing trips (*US$120 pp ½ day*) & game walks (*US$30 pp*). Activities are carried out in the park & the GMA. *US$250/200/150 pp luxury/standard/tented rooms FBA, inc park fees, exc drinks. Camping US$20 pp.* ⊕ *All year.* **LL**

⌂ **Kasabushi Camp** [map, page 434] (4 chalets, camping) e info@undiscoveredafrica. com; www.kasabushi.wordpress.com. ✿ KASABU 15°15.475'S, 25°58.493'E. One of the few camps on the western bank of the Kafue River within the park itself, Kasabushi is a brand new camp that was under construction at time of research in 2015. Owners Andy & Lib Wilson are constructing 4 wood-framed, tented chalets perched on a steep section of the riverbank, with wooden decks extending out over the river. Only the frames & decks were completed when we visited, but the plan is for the chalets to have quite contemporary furnishings.

The plans for the main area are unusual, & if followed, should provide something quite different in the park. The main building will be a red-brick roundhouse (made using mud from termite mounds), with a self-supported roof made from twisted local timber & canvas sails. A lounge area nearby will also be shaded by canvas sails, but will otherwise be completely open, with lovely views of a rocky section of the river filled with tree-clad islands. There are also ambitious plans to convert a large depression in the rocks near the river into a semi-natural swimming pool.

Kasabushi also has a functioning campsite a short distance from camp that opened for business in 2014. To get here, drive along the spinal road until you reach the turning at ✿ KASCTU 15°16.059'S, 25°58.114'E. To get to the main lodge, take the signposted turning at ✿ KASLTU 15°16.059'S, 25°58.396'E. The campsite has 4 separate pitches shaded by trees along the riverbank, each with its own braai area, for which firewood is provided. Shared ablutions include flushing toilets & waterfall showers, all excellently maintained, & built with ferro walls in a style reminiscent of Chongwe River Camp in the Lower Zambezi (pages 238–9). *US$350 pp FBA, inc park fees & local drinks. Camping US$18 p.* ⊕ *Mar–Nov.* **LLL**

⌂ **Mawimbi Bush Camp** [map, page 434] (3 tents) ✆ +263 486 1286; m +263 772 357376, 772 261831; e info@mawimbibushcamp.com; www.mawimbibushcamp.com. ✿ MAWIMB 15°09.937'S, 25°57.630'E. Originally a small fly-camp associated with KaingU Safari Lodge, Mawimbi is now its own independent operation, with a permanent camp constructed in 2014. Located on the western bank of the Kafue River, Mawimbi can be reached via the spinal road. Take the signposted turning at ✿ MAWITU 15°10.598'S, 25°57.062'E & drive approximately 1km to camp.

Accommodation, inside the national park, is in 3 large canvas tents with concrete bases, each with twin or dbl beds & decorated in subtle African themes. Each has an en-suite bathroom at the back, surrounded by reed screens & completely open to the sky. They are equipped with bucket showers & a dry toilet. A veranda at the front, with a couple of armchairs, has views over a picturesque section of the river. Meals are typically served outside, or under the basic, open-sided main area.

Activities focus on canoeing here, led by camp owner Bernard Calonne. Several stretches of the river offer peaceful wildlife viewing & some stunning scenery, as well as a few technical rapids (although these can easily be avoided with alternate routes). There are several trails, & it's possible to paddle the inflatable canoes as far as the Itezhi-Iezhi Dam. Safari walks are also available, but the canoeing is the real highlight at this camp. *US$290–400 pp/night FBA, depending on numbers.* **LL–LLL**

Around Itezhi-Tezhi Dam and south Grouped in the GMA to the southeast of Lake Itezhi-Tezhi, and just south of the dam wall, are three fairly old-style camps catering more to Zambian tastes than to overseas visitors. They're relatively inexpensive – and some would regard them as good value. There's also the option of a small new lodge in Itezhi-Tezhi village.

In the national park itself, Konkamoya offers a unique setting right on the lake, while further south, Nanzhila Plains Safari Camp has made this remote area of the park accessible once again to adventurous visitors. Although both national parks' campsites have been closed, most of the lodges offer camping, and there's also the simple Shiluwe Hill site near the Musa gate.

🏠 **New Kalala Safari Lodge** [map, page 437] (13 chalets, camping) ☎0213 263179, 0211 290914; e info@newkalala.com; www. newkalala.com. ◈ NEWKAL 15°46.583'S, 26°00.538'E. Well signposted south of the dam wall, New Kalala overlooks the lake from a stunning perch on a granite kopje where you'll see the odd rock dassie scurrying about. The large chalets, dotted around well-tended gardens above the lake, are clean & well maintained, although they remain rather stark. All have en-suite bathrooms, fridge & AC. It is also possible to camp on the lake shore. Overlooking the lake, the restaurant/bar serves lunch (*K75*) & dinner (*K100*). Guests can take part in game drives (*K200 pp & park fees*); boat cruises (*K170 pp, or boat hire from K700/½ day, plus fuel*); & a hot-springs tour (*K70 pp*), & there's a nice pool here, too. *Chalet K600/900/1,000 dbl B&B/HB/FB. Camping K70 pp.* **$$$$–$$$$$**

🏕 **Chibila Camp** [map, page 437] (3 chalets, camping) ☎0211 251630; e wecsz@ coppernet.zm, wecsz@zamnet.zm; www. conservationzambia.org. ◈ CHIBIL 15°46.638'S, 26°00.407'E. Almost next door to New Kalala, Chibila (or Chibala – formerly the David Shepherd Camp) stands between large granite boulders on the shores of the lake. It was built for members of the Wildlife Conservation Society of Zambia (the present WECSZ, page 51), although unlike their other camps in the park it's available for independent booking, on the condition that you join once you reach the camp. Each chalet has 4 beds, en-suite shower & toilet, & a private veranda. It's a self-catering camp, but staff are on hand to help cook & there's a fully equipped kitchen & BBQ area. Limited camping is available, but you must come fully equipped. *K600 per chalet; camping K50 per group.* **$$$$**

🏠 **Musungwa Safari Lodge** [map, page 437] (24 chalets, camping) ☎0211 273493; e zamker@zamnet.zm; www.musungwalodge.

co.za. ◈ MUSUNG 15°46.987'S, 26°00.329'E. On the shore of Lake Itezhi-Tezhi, Musungwa is about 5km south of the dam wall, & just 2km north of the Musa gate. This is the largest lodge in the area, & after some much-needed refurbishments, it's looking rather smart; more like a small hotel than a safari lodge. Twin & 3-bed en-suite chalets have tiny private verandas overlooking the lake. Housed in 4 large rondavels are the reception, bar, restaurant & conference centre, open to day visitors. Just below is a swimming pool commanding a stunning view of the lake & surrounded by pleasant gardens, complete with grass, bamboo, bougainvillea & the odd palm. There are tennis & squash courts, too. Activities include boat cruises, game drives &, of course, fishing, with the lodge being a popular base for local fishing competitions. **$$$**

🏠 **Konkamoya Lodge** [map, page 446] (4 tents) ☎0211 213362; m 962 841364; e info@ konkamoya.com; www.konkamoya.com. ◈ KONKAM 15°52.040'S, 25°52.976'E. With a prime position on the lake shore, Konkamoya has a truly unique & picturesque location in the park. Many visitors fly in to Ngoma, a ½-hr game drive to the south. If you're driving yourself, follow the main track from the Musa gate, turning right after 5km on to Lake View Drive. From here, keep to the lake shore until after 18km you come to a crossroads (◈ TUKONK 15°53.061'S, 25°52.671'E). Turn right & the lodge is within 2.5km.

Konkamoya sits at the end of a grassy peninsula, fronted by drowned trees & a small island rising from the lake. With such excellent views, improving levels of game & stunning birdlife in the area it remains a surprise that this is still the only lodge right on the lake. The lodge is run by Andrea Porro, an eccentric Italian expat who brings a good deal of character to the camp, as well as a few Italian home comforts such as excellent coffee, & jars of biscotti in the rooms.

The lodge has 4 elevated tents, which, despite being huge, are discretely tucked into the riparian vegetation, each with wooden decks facing the lake. They are well furnished with dbl beds, a sitting room & an outdoor bathroom with hot & cold running showers & flush toilet. Unfortunately, the tents have no shadecloths or thatch covering, so they get incredibly hot during the day. Luckily the thatched main area is completely open sided to allow a cooling breeze & views of the lake while guests are relaxing in the lounge, or eating at the large dining table. It's tastefully decorated with wooden furniture & old dugout canoes. Close by, steps lead up to the old main area which is currently disused, although there are plans to renovate it into an airy bar.

Activities focus on game drives around the lake area. As the lake waters recede towards the dry season mud flats are exposed that are quickly grassed over, providing ample grazing. The waters also leave residual pools that are prolific breeding grounds for fish, amphibians & invertebrates, which in turn attracts a plethora of birdlife. A drive around this section of the lake bed is fascinating both in terms of the scenery & diversity of wildlife, & at the end of the dry season you can see herds of elephants numbering in their hundreds coming down to drink at the lake. While the guiding can be erratic, Andrea is intensely passionate about the area & its wildlife. Safari walks are also available, but unfortunately activities on the lake itself aren't currently offered. *From US$400 pp FBA, inc park fees & airstrip transfers, exc bar.* ⊕ *15 Jun – 15 Nov.* **LLL** See ad in 3rd colour section.

Ⅹ Hippo Bay Campsite [map, page 446] Contact via Konkamoya, above. Well away from the lodge, Konkamoya's no-frills campsite is set back from the lake & comfortably has space for 12 people. There's a good solid ablution block with hot water, plus a supply of firewood & – a real bonus – drinking water, but otherwise campers need to be entirely self sufficient. They can, though, join in lodge activities for US$35 pp. *US$25 pp.*

🏠 Nanzhila Plains Safari Camp [map, page 439] (6 chalets, camping) ☏ +267 721 23002; e info@nanzhila.com; www.nanzhila.com. ✿ NANZHI 16°16.746'S, 25°55.074'E. In the remote south of the park, this comfortable family-run camp is surrounded by woodland & plains. To the front, the large, grass-fringed Nangandwe Pool attracts good herds of game, including roan & sable antelope, defassa waterbuck, Lichtenstein's

hartebeest & eland – which in turn draw predators such as wild dog & cheetah. Birdlife is good year round; look out in camp for paradise flycatchers & red-headed weaver birds, while the near-endemic black-cheeked lovebird is regularly spotted on game drives.

Most visitors arrive by air at Ngoma, followed by a 2-hr game drive. A new airstrip is being constructed a short distance from camp, but this is work in progress & unlikely to be finished soon. To drive in you'll need a 4x4, & plenty of time. From the Musa gate, continue 22km to the park HQ at Ngoma, then follow the Cordon Rd to the airstrip. Here you can carry straight on down the cordon road, before turning left at the junction at MUFUTA 16°16.730'S, 25°48.858'E. Alternatively, you can turn left just after the airstrip for a further 35km to the Kalenji scout post, then right for a further 15km to camp. The conditions of these roads changes rapidly, so it's best to check with the camp which is currently in the best condition. From the Dumdumwenze gate, follow the track for 3km to a fork; if it's dry, continue straight ahead to the east of the river, but when wet you *must* turn left & head north for 65km on the Cordon Rd, before turning right to the camp.

Facing the pool is an open-fronted thatched boma, raised up beneath a mature ebony tree (*Diospyros mespiliformisi*). With a lounge, dining area & extensive wooden deck, this is the focal point of the camp, its largely wicker furniture offset by comfy cushions & a selection of books. In the evenings, guests congregate by the firepit, before adjourning to a communal table for dinner.

To one side of the pool are 3 solidly built thatched chalets, each with an en-suite shower, toilet & twin washbasins, & a combination of netted windows & doors to allow a through breeze. Although not very spacious, they're furnished with care, to include dbl or twin hardwood beds & matching bedside tables under wraparound mosi nets, & good storage space. Opposite, 3 twin Meru-style tents under shadecloths offer a simpler alternative, with partially open en-suite facilities at the back, & the bonus of a small veranda overlooking the pool. Donkey boilers heat the water, & paraffin lamps add a slightly romantic touch, with a solar-powered generator useful for charging camera batteries etc – usually when guests are out of camp.

14

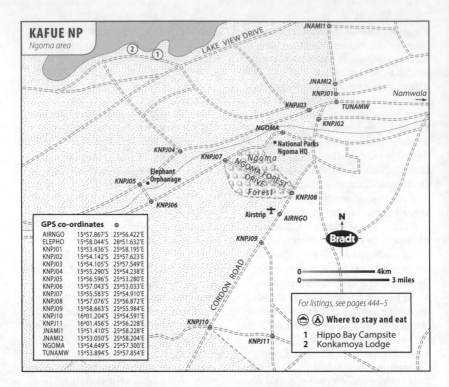

KAFUE NP
Ngoma area

LAKE VIEW DRIVE

JNAMI1
JNAMI2
KNPJ01
KNPJ03
TUNAMW
Namwala
KNPJ02
NGOMA
National Parks
Ngoma HQ
KNPJ04
KNPJ07
Ngoma
NGOMA FOREST DRIVE
KNPJ05
Elephant
Orphanage
Forest
KNPJ08
KNPJ06
Airstrip
AIRNGO
N
KNPJ09
Bradt

CORDON ROAD

GPS co-ordinates	⊕	
AIRNGO	15°57.867'S	25°56.422'E
ELEPHO	15°58.044'S	28°51.632'E
KNPJ01	15°53.436'S	25°58.195'E
KNPJ02	15°54.142'S	25°57.623'E
KNPJ03	15°54.105'S	25°57.549'E
KNPJ04	15°55.290'S	25°54.238'E
KNPJ05	15°56.596'S	25°53.280'E
KNPJ06	15°57.043'S	25°53.033'E
KNPJ07	15°55.583'S	25°54.910'E
KNPJ08	15°57.076'S	25°56.872'E
KNPJ09	15°58.663'S	25°55.984'E
KNPJ10	16°01.204'S	25°54.591'E
KNPJ11	16°01.456'S	25°56.228'E
JNAMI1	15°51.410'S	25°58.228'E
JNAMI2	15°53.050'S	25°57.300'E
NGOMA	15°54.649'S	25°57.300'E
TUNAMW	15°53.894'S	25°57.854'E

KNPJ10

KNPJ11

0 ———— 4km
0 ———— 3 miles

For listings, see pages 444–5

Where to stay and eat

1   Hippo Bay Campsite
2   Konkamoya Lodge

The campsite, with flush toilets & proper showers, lies away from the chalets. By arrangement, campers can sometimes join in meals or activities at the lodge, but otherwise need to be entirely self sufficient, except for firewood.

Flexibility is the key here, with a series of loops for day & night drives, plus guided walks, & trips to Lake Itezhi-Tezhi or – by arrangement – to Shezongo village, the Elephant Orphanage or Ngoma Forest. In the winter months, Jul–Sep, bush b/fasts can also be organised. *US$300 15 May–Jun & Nov, US$350 Jul–Oct pp sharing FBA, inc local drinks, park fees. Camping US$15 pp & park fees.* ⊕ *May–Nov.* **LLL**

Places to visit in Southern Kafue
Southern Kafue suits exploration in your own 4x4 well, so to concentrate on a few places to visit is really to miss the point. However, a few notable highlights are:

Lake View Drive This area is home to some of the best game in the south, enticed in the dry season by lush grassy plains next to the lake. Protection of the game is afforded both by the presence of Konkamoya, and the proximity of the national park's Ngoma headquarters (⊕ NGOMA 15°54.649'S, 25°57.300'E), about 20km from the Itezhi-Tezhi Dam wall. At Ngoma itself, there are various offices and houses for the park's staff, and you can drop in, but it's not in great condition, and isn't really set up for visitors. About 5km south of here is an all-weather airstrip (⊕ AIRNGO 15°57.867'S, 25°56.422'E).

Ngoma Forest In the Ngoma area of the park's southern section, between two junctions (⊕ KNPJ07 15°55.583'S, 25°54.910'E and ⊕ KNPJ08 15°57.076'S, 25°56.872'E), is a fairly clearly signposted track that is seldom driven. This is a shame, as it weaves its way through the beautiful and intriguing Ngoma Forest which, when devoid of leaves at the end of the dry season, is decidedly eerie. It is made up of a dense stand of mature trees which are largely Zambezi teak (*Baikiaea plurijuga*); see box, below.

Camp Phoenix Elephant Orphanage (e *rachael@gamerangersinternational. org; www.gamerangersinternational.org; entry K50/20 adult/child;* ⊕ *guided tour 11.30 daily;* ✪ ELEPHO 15°58.044'S, 25°51.632'E) Named for the first elephant rescued, Camp Phoenix is a key part of the Elephant Orphanage Project (see box, page 448) located just a few kilometres from the ZAWA headquarters at Ngoma,

THE DEMISE OF THE TEAK FORESTS

In the past, stands of teak forest probably covered fairly large areas of the Kalahari, and certainly of southwestern Zambia. They are comprised largely of Zambezi teak (*Baikiaea plurijuga*), previously called Rhodesian teak – a tree that occurs only in undisturbed areas of Kalahari sand in northern Botswana, northern Namibia, southern Angola and western Zambia. Now, however, this tree is severely threatened, its demise typical of that of several other hardwood species that were once common here, like *mukwa* (*Pterocarpus angolensis*), and rosewood (*Guibourtia coleosperma*).

Zambezi teak trees reach up to 20m in height, with a dense, spreading crown of leaves, and smooth, grey-brown bark. The trees flower from December to March, bearing lovely pinky-mauve flowers. Seedpods follow, from June to September, cracking open explosively to catapult their seeds a distance to the ground.

The tree's wood is dense and hard, but also very even grained and strong. Although it has never had many traditional uses, as it was too hard to cut, it was a sought-after timber that was (and sadly is) commercially very valuable. It's been widely used for bridge-building and railway sleepers, and Coates Palgrave (page 528) reports that 'when the London corn exchange was rebuilt in 1952 a special grooved floor was designed to take the grain thrown down by the merchants, and *B. plurijuga* was selected for the parquet blocks because of its ability to withstand abrasion without splintering'.

Baikiaea plurijuga has been commercially logged in Zambia since around the start of the 20th century. Zambian timber production probably peaked in the 1930s, but by the 1960s huge tracts of teak forest had been lost. Now, although the export of *Baikiaea* logs is banned, export licences are still being issued for *Baikiaea* timber, predicated on (difficult-to-enforce) promises to leave a minimum number of the trees, and then not log the same area for 20 years.

Meanwhile, experts suggest that a 300-year cycle would be needed to allow the forests to regenerate. They note that fire is often used as a tool by loggers, to open up the dense under-storey of vegetation (known as *mutemwa*) in *B. plurijuga* forests, and that the debris left behind after logging will often lead to fires. *B. plurijuga* is particularly sensitive because its thin bark renders it very susceptible to fire; once burnt, these forests degrade forever and don't recover.

In recent years the poverty in the area, combined with major commercial pressures, has led to many of Zambia's remaining 'forest reserves' being degazetted, which then opens them up for commercial logging. So, sadly, a beautiful teak forest like Ngoma is an increasingly rare sight.

14

Established in 2001 with the aim to 'rescue, rehabilitate and release' elephants orphaned as a result of human actions, such as poaching, the Elephant Orphanage Project is based on a similar model in Kenya run by Daphne Sheldrick. Under the auspices of the Zambian NGO Game Rangers International, and with the support of the David Shepherd Foundation (*www.davidshepherd.org/project/zambia-elephant-orphanage-project/*), it is one aspect of three elephant-focused projects, which also include park protection and training, plus – crucially – education and awareness. In the long term, it is hoped to extend the remit to include both research and community development.

By mid 2015, the unit comprised ten elephants, from the youngest, three-year-old Mphamvu, to the oldest, eleven-year-old Chodoba. They, like the others, were traumatised on arrival, having lost not just their mothers but also their social bonds within the herd, but with time and care they adapt to both their new companions and the strange environment. The little ones in particular receive protection from Chamilandu, who until recently was the only female here before she was joined by Kavalamanja. Their keepers – ten of them working on a 24-hour rota – form part of a wider 'family' network, bottle-feeding the babies every 3 hours until they are weaned at around two–three years.

The elephants are split into two groups, with six still living within the facility, sleeping within a boma where an electric fence keeps them safe from lions. These elephants are up early, heading out into the bush at 06.00 with two keepers and a ZAWA scout, and returning only at lunchtime. The afternoon routine is similar, leaving at around 14.30 and returning at 18.00, which allows time for regular monitoring, ranging from measuring the orphans to checking the colour of their tongues as a guide to appetite.

The rest of the herd are currently in the release phase, and while they do return to visit the orphan herd, they largely live away from the facility and the keepers. Already, they are interacting with the wild population, although it is not until they reach maturity – and full independence – that they have a hope of being accepted into the herd. With an average maturation of around 15 years for males, and from nine to 15 for the females, this is a long-haul project, with each elephant expected to stay at the orphanage for at least ten years.

For those interested in helping, there's a programme (*US$2,250 pp FB*) through which volunteers spend a month working in pairs in the areas of community development, education, research, and may be required to assist with the elephant husbandry including feedings and support during rescues. The project runs during the dry season only, between April and November.

an area that has an established population of around a thousand wild elephants. It offers visitors the opportunity to watch and take photographs through viewing holes in a fence as the young herd returns to their 'boma' for lunch and a bathe. This isn't a place to get up close and personal with the elephants. Indeed, human contact is kept to an absolute minimum, in order to give the animals the best chance of survival when they are eventually returned to the wild. But if you'd like an opportunity to find out a little about the social systems of elephants, and the complexities of raising orphaned elephants with a view to releasing them back into the wild, then it's an interesting place to spend an hour or so. Note that it's important to arrive promptly at 11.00, so that you have time for a briefing and to don the regulation green coat before the elephants return from the bush.

Chilenje Pools Further south, several pools lie at the heart of two large, neighbouring grassy dambos which are a major attraction for game during the drier months. In theory there's a track going round this area; in practice you may have to make your own across a bumpy expanse of solidified mud.

Mufuta Loop West of Nanzhila Plains Safari Camp, this is another interesting game-drive loop that takes in more undulating terrain, fringed by woodland and dotted with pools that attract numerous waterbirds. Keep an eye out in particular for the magnificent sable antelope.

Nanzhila Plains If you're travelling through the south of the park, then two tracks run east–west. Take these towards the start of the dry season, and you'll often find yourself in plains with grass several metres tall, which is lovely but doesn't make for good game viewing. It's also surprisingly easy to get lost here! (Beware of inflammable seeds in your radiator – see pages 99–100.) Later in the year, when the grass dies back, visibility is excellent.

Within this area you'll also find woodland sections, tree-islands and even the odd lone baobab tree (*Adansonia digitata*). There are several pools here, too, which attract relatively large herds of game and some wonderful birdlife.

South of Nanzhila, however, the lack of wildlife tells a sorrier tale, with just the odd reedbuck putting in an appearance among the tree squirrels and hornbills; poaching in this area of the Kafue is a serious problem.

FURTHER INFORMATION The Kafue Trust sponsored publication of *The Kafue National Park, Zambia*, by Ashley Nikki. For details, see page 530.

LOCHINVAR AND BLUE LAGOON NATIONAL PARKS

Further down the Kafue's course, east of Ngoma, are two small national parks that encompass opposite sides of the Kafue River's floodplain. Their geography and ecosystems are very similar, but despite continuing efforts to rejuvenate both parks, their infrastructure has all but collapsed and wildlife has suffered heavily from poaching in the last few years.

Historically, both Blue Lagoon and Lochinvar have had populations of people living and farming around their borders, and often inside the park. Most are poor cattle herders, and probably aren't averse to supplementing their diets with (technically illegal) subsistence hunting. Their ancestors probably hunted here before these areas were either taken over as farms, or declared national parks; hence it could easily be argued that these lands belong more to these people than they do to ZAWA. Clearly any long-term solution needs to include these people – which is not an easy task.

Neither park receives many visitors, and those who do visit should arrive with their own supplies; there is currently no lodge accommodation or camping facilities here.

GEOGRAPHY Both parks are very flat, and the sections nearer the river are seasonally flooded. The resulting watery grassland reflects the sky like a mirror, for as far as you can see. It is quite a sight, and a remarkable environment for both animals and waterfowl.

In both parks you'll find a variety of quite clearly defined environments, as you move away from the waterways to the dry, permanent woodlands. Immediately beside the water, you'll find very large areas of open grassland which are seasonally flooded – a classic **floodplain** environment. On the drier side of this, where the grassland does not receive a regular annual flooding, termitaria can exist – with high solid mounds (often looking like chimneys) to keep their occupants safe from drowning in the occasional exceptional flood. This is a very distinct area in the grasslands, known as the **termitaria zone**.

Further away still, where there's absolutely no risk of flooding, you'll find a variety of trees in the woodlands which extend across the south of Lochinvar and the north of Blue Lagoon.

FLORA AND FAUNA

Flora The landscapes in both parks change with proximity to the river, especially above the 'high flood' line. Within parts of the termitaria zone you'll find some low bushes like the paperbark acacias (*Acacia sieberana*), zebrawoods (*Dalbergia melanoxylon*), fever trees (*Acacia xanthophloea*) and rough-leaved raisin bushes (*Grewia flavescens*). Drier patches here, such as the area around the tented camp, often have pretty acacia glades with large and shady white thorns (*Acacia polyocantha*) and smaller blue thorns (*Acacia erubescens*).

As the plains gradually merge into woodland, you'll find some of the typical species from munga woodlands (page 30) including sickle-leafed albezias (*Albezi harveyi*), pepper-leafed commiphoras (*Commiphora mossambicensis*) and the distinctive woolly caper-bushes (*Caparis tormentosa*).

Slightly higher and further from the water, the tree-belt becomes more established and varied, containing different bands of mixed woodlands. The belts of mopane woodland are particularly distinctive, dominated by *Colophospermum mopane*, but also including leadwoods (*Combretum imberbe*), raintrees (*Lonchocarpus capassa*), and even the occasional knobthorn (*Acacia negrescens*).

Finally, well away from the water, you find stands of classic miombo woodland becoming the dominant environment – for example, as you travel south out of Lochinvar. (As an aside, it was interesting to see some notable specimens of Natal mahogany, *Trichilia emetica*, in this particular woodland.)

Fauna The very different bands of vegetation in these parks give rise to a wide variety of birds and animals – although this also means that some of the species found here are restricted to fairly small areas of the parks and so you need to move around if you're to have a chance of seeing a good range of them.

Animals Traditionally, the parks have been home to huge herds of Kafue lechwe – a little-known subspecies of the red lechwe, endemic to the Kafue's floodplain. The Kafue lechwe used to occur here in enormous numbers, with population estimates in the 1930s suggesting about 250,000 lived across the whole Kafue Flats area. By the 1950s an aerial survey put the population at about 95,000 lechwe, which continued to decline to 38,000 in 2005. Little data has been collected on their populations since, but they remain threatened by poaching, and increasing pressure from cattle grazing by local communities; we have to move swiftly to conserve them, and their habitat.

Alongside the Kafue lechwe, many other species occur here – although all have reduced in numbers drastically over the last few decades. Typical of this area are buffalo, eland, roan, plains zebra, Lichtenstein's hartebeest, blue wildebeest, puku, reedbuck and the delightful, diminutive oribi antelope; whilst in the thickets on the edge of the plains you'll find kudu, baboon and vervet monkeys. That said, last reports were that reedbuck had disappeared from Blue Lagoon, and that bushbuck numbers were in single digits.

Birds The best season for birds on the Kafue's floodplain is probably around April/May, when the waters are at their highest levels. Then the resulting lagoons attract a great variety of migrant birds – giving a staggering spectacle of waterfowl. Often you'll find large numbers of just a couple of species in one area. This may be dominated by fulvous ducks, pratincoles, sandgrouse, or waders like sandpipers, avocets, ruff, Kittlitz's plovers, little stints and black-winged stilts. In the last ten years, Lochinvar has become a major wintering ground for black-tailed godwits, 3,000 or more of them. Lapwings – or plovers – are usually plentiful, including long-toed, crowned, white-crowned and the ubiquitous blacksmith.

Pelicans are always around, both white and pink backed, and sometimes so are small numbers of flamingos. Cranes, both wattled and crowned, are there, usually in flocks of a hundred or more, plus spoonbills and a variety of storks and ibises (notably sacred and glossy). In both parks the best areas for watching waterbirds are unpredictable. They depend on the water levels, which in turn depend on the flood regime of the Itezhi-Tezhi Dam upstream.

However, during the early rains, the grasslands are always full of harlequin quails, Luapula cisticolas, Ethiopian snipe, yellow-crowned bishops and a sprinkling of streaky-breasted flufftails. Later in the season when the plains are dry, secretary birds pace around in pairs, whilst in the air are plenty of raptors – bateleur, martial and African hawk eagles, plus brown and black-breasted snake eagles. Amongst the thousands of lechwe there are always recent deaths, so there are four species of vulture present, plus large numbers of marabou storks.

LOCHINVAR NATIONAL PARK *(Park fees US$10 pp/day; vehicle US$15/day)*
Lochinvar's northern boundary is the Kafue River. The land on which the park stands was originally obtained from the local Chief Hamusende in around 1908 by a Mr Horne, a man known locally as 'the Major'. Horne was a Scottish cattle farmer from Botswana who registered the land on behalf of the British South Africa Company, and built the old Lochinvar Lodge as his farmhouse.

Previously little of this land had been used for farming because of the game here, including lion and leopard. To convert the land into a cattle ranch, Horne set about exterminating these. In a ruthless programme of annihilation, populations of sable, roan, eland, warthog and wildebeest were wiped out, as well as lion – the last of which is thought to have been killed in 1947.

However, in 1966 Lochinvar Ranch (as it was then called) was bought by the Zambian government with the help of a grant from the WWF, and converted into a GMA; but the extra protection afforded to the wildlife by this designation was not enough to prevent its numbers from diminishing further, and so in 1972 Lochinvar was upgraded to a national park.

Subsequently the park has been designated as a 'wetland of international importance', and at one point a WWF team was working with the local people to help manage the park on a sustainable basis.

There are a lot of settlements around Lochinvar, and local people still come into the park – as they have done for centuries. Many were unhappy with Lochinvar Ranch – and have always felt that this is their land. They come to gather wild foods and fish, and even to drive their cattle from one side to the other; so although major

14

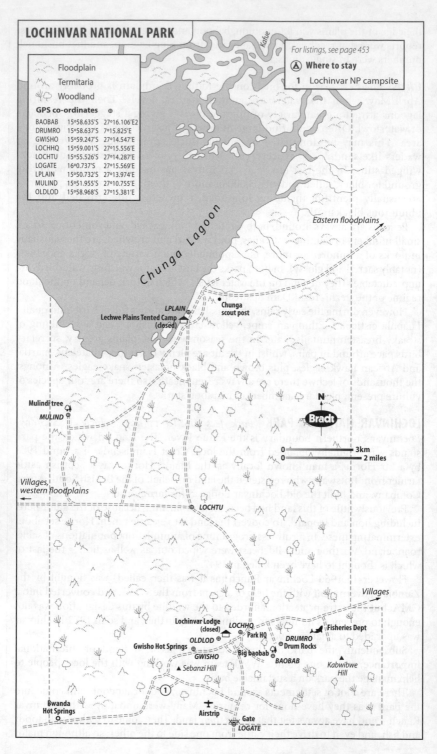

LOCHINVAR NATIONAL PARK

Floodplain

Termitaria

Woodland

GPS co-ordinates ⊕

BAOBAB	15°58.635'S	27°16.106'E2
DRUMRO	15°58.637'S	7°15.825'E
GWISHO	15°59.247'S	27°14.547'E
LOCHHQ	15°59.001'S	27°15.556'E
LOCHTU	15°55.526'S	27°14.287'E
LOGATE	16°0.737'S	27°15.569'E
LPLAIN	15°50.732'S	27°13.974'E
MULIND	15°51.955'S	27°10.755'E
OLDLOD	15°58.968'S	27°15.381'E

For listings, see page 453

Ⓐ **Where to stay**

1 Lochinvar NP campsite

Kafue

Eastern floodplains →

Chunga Lagoon

LPLAIN ⊕
Lechwe Plains Tented Camp (closed) ▫
● **Chunga scout post**

N

Bradt

0		3km
0		2 miles

Mulindi tree
MULIND ⊕

← *Villages, western floodplains*

⊕ LOCHTU

Villages →

Lochinvar Lodge (closed) 🏠
Gwisho Hot Springs ⊕
GWISHO
OLDLOD 🏠
LOCHHQ ⊕ Park HQ
Big baobab ⊕
DRUMRO ⊕ **Drum Rocks**
⊕ BAOBAB
↟ **Fisheries Dept**
▲ *Sebanzi Hill*
▲ *Kabwibwe Hill*

Bwanda Hot Springs ♨
①
✈ **Airstrip**
Gate
🚻 *LOGATE*

conservation efforts are being made in Lochinvar, building up the diversity and number of game species here is not an easy task.

Getting there Lochinvar is easiest to approach from Monze, on the Livingstone–Lusaka road – about 287km from Livingstone and 186km from Lusaka. The road that heads northwest from Monze, signposted for Namwala, is just north of the grain silos on the Lusaka side of town. From town head for the point ⊕ TULOCH 16°15.465'S, 27°28.632'E.

It passes Chongo village and forks (⊕ T2LOCH 16°10.054'S, 27°23.610'E) about 8km afterwards. Ask local advice to find this junction if necessary. Take the right fork, or you will end up in Kafue. Follow this road for about 10km and then turn left at another sign (⊕ TULV14 16°3.718'S, 27°22'E). It is then about 14km to the park gate. This last section of the track twists and turns, but all the tracks that split off eventually rejoin each other and lead to the park. There are also a few more signs so, if you become unsure, ask a local person and they'll show you the way. The gate to Lochinvar (⊕ LOGATE 16°0.737'S, 27°15.569'E) is about 48km from Monze.

🏠 **Where to stay** The original red-brick Lochinvar Lodge (⊕ OLDLOD 15°58.968'S, 27°15.381'E) was used as a farmhouse until 1966, before being sold to the government, and then the private safari operator Star of Africa, who built a new tented camp (⊕ LPLAIN 15°50.732'S, 27°13.974'E) rather than renovating the building. Both then passed to Sanctuary Retreats in 2007, but they have remained closed since then, leaving no accommodation options in the park. There are occasional mumblings about renovating the dilapidated farmhouse, but until the park has the infrastructure and interest to make even the tented camp economically viable, it's likely to remain an evocative old ruin.

Camping Until Lechwe Plains Tented Camp is re-opened, your only option is to camp, for which you will need all your own supplies. There have been several sites here, but it's best to ask the scouts at the gate for the latest news. To reach what was the official campsite, drive about 2km past the gate into the park, and take the second left turning. Continue for about 5km. This site in theory has water, a long-drop toilet and a simple cold shower, with firewood and a barbecue provided. It is close to the hot springs at Bwanda, near the old Lupanda Wildlife Camp. If you wish to pick up a scout from the gate to guide you, then it's advisable to arrange this in advance.

What to see and do With the rapid depletion of the game, the birds are the main attraction at Lochinvar. The best birding is generally close to the water, on the floodplain. For this it's probably best to walk north and east from Mulindi Tree or north of Chunga towards Hippo Corner. It's vital to avoid driving anywhere that's even vaguely damp on the floodplain as your vehicle will just slip through the crust and into the black-cotton soil – which will probably spoil and extend your stay in equal measure. A few sites to note include:

Gwisho Hot Springs (⊕ GWISHO 15°59.247'S, 27°14.547'E) Gwisho Hot Springs are near the southern edge of the park. To get here drive from the main gate to the old lodge, and then turn sharp left immediately in front of the old lodge's gates. From the campsite, drive north out of the camp and turn right towards Sebanzi Hill, following the edge of the plain. After about 2.5km turn left at a stone cairn and palms. The springs are signposted, and just a few kilometres further on, about 2km west of the old lodge.

The Kafue River was dammed in two stages. Initially, in 1971, a dam was built in the Kafue Gorge, just south of Lusaka, which permanently flooded 800–1,100km² of land on the eastern side of the Kafue Flats. However, the gradient of the river above this point had always been very low (about 8m drop in over 200km of river), so the result was a huge, shallow reservoir with a relatively low volume (785 million cubic metres). The Kafue Dam's primary purpose was to provide hydro-electric power: it supplies up to 75% of Zambia's electricity. To guarantee this it needed a reservoir which was effectively larger than this.

Thus a second dam was built and closed in 1977: the Itezhi-Tezhi Dam. This is about 450km upstream of the Kafue Dam, and flooded only 300km² of land with a much deeper lake – holding about 4,925 million cubic metres of water. Hence the flow from Itezhi-Tezhi could be regulated to provide the constant flow needed by the Kafue Dam to generate electricity. When the dams were constructed, ZESCO (Zambia Electricity Supply Corporation) was obliged to ensure that there was a continuous flow out of Itezhi-Tezhi, in order to preserve the Kafue Flats habitat, and service the other users of the water. (The largest of these are the sugar industry around Mazabuka, and the municipality of Lusaka, which extracts water for the city.) However, this was a very difficult task – made all the more complex because the flood takes about six weeks to get from Itezhi-Tezhi to the Kafue Dam.

Before the dams, the river's flow varied enormously with the season: the Kafue Flats flooded every year and the floodplains experienced a long dry season. Since the dams, ZESCO has released a four-week artificial 'flood' in March, but clearly it has failed to simulate the natural situation. The UK's Department for International Development (DFID) reported in 2001 on *Managed Flood Releases from the Itezhi-Tezhi Reservoir*, and within that noted:

> Since the dams, the flooding pattern has changed considerably. There has been a reduction in the seasonal fluctuations. The annual minimum flood area has increased from about 300km² to approximately 1,500km². In places permanent lagoons have formed where ephemeral aquatic habits had existed before. In broad terms, the western half of the Flats is drier, whilst the eastern half is wetter than they were prior to dam construction.

This altered flood pattern has knock-on effects to the whole ecosystem. Old-time visitors to Lochinvar will tell you that the vegetation there has changed enormously over the last 30 years, and not for the better. With the change in vegetation come changes in the grazing – for both wildlife and cattle. Then, of course, the breeding cycles of the fish are affected and there's no longer any movement of fish upriver past the dams. When fish populations change, so do those of many bird species.

There is much further research to be done, and the WWF is involved in a project to simulate the river's old flood regime using new computer models to control the Itezhi-Tezhi Dam outflow. Many people are now starting to make strenuous efforts to ensure that whilst maximising the benefits provided by these dams, they also minimise the inevitable environmental problems caused by them.

The springs were formed by a geological fault which stretches along the southern end of the park, on the edge of the Kafue Flats Basin. Associated with this is a deposit of gypsum, the mineral used to make plaster of Paris, which was mined at Gwisho from 1973 to 1978. You can follow the white rocks which mark this fault from Bwanda Hot Springs past the old campsite and Sebanzi Hill through Gwisho Hot Springs to the lodge, and past Drum Rocks.

The water which wells up into these springs has been heated far below the surface, and thus is independent of the rainfall or local surface water conditions. It varies from about 60°C to 94°C, and contains a high concentration of sodium, chlorine, calcium and sulphates.

The thick vegetation around the springs is surrounded by a picturesque stand of real fan palms (*Hyphaene petersiana*), whose small fruits, when opened, are seen to have a hard kernel known as 'vegetable ivory'. In the thick, wet vegetation here keep a lookout for birding 'specials' including black coucal and Fülleborn's longclaw. Also look out for the stand of gnarled old trees on the rocks at the top of the small rise beside the springs. These may look a little like deformed baobabs, but they are in fact African star-chestnut trees (*Sterculia africana*).

In the early 1960s, when the remains of late Stone-Age settlements were excavated here, it was described as one of the best-preserved and oldest sites in southern Africa. Among the findings were Arab-style trading beads, suggesting that the local inhabitants had traded the salt collected here far and wide, possibly as far as east Africa. Some artefacts discovered here are on display at Livingstone Museum.

Talk to the local people and they will tell you that the Gwisho area was the location of several fierce battles between the Tonga/Ila people and the Batwa, with hundreds of men being killed at a time – hence the existence of several mass burial sites nearby.

Bwanda Hot Springs Bwanda Hot Springs lie in the southwest of the park, surrounded by a large area of reed beds. They're quite close to Limpanda scout camp, and so are often used for bathing and washing by the local people – and even sometimes as a place to water their cattle.

Sebanzi Hill This national monument marks the position of an Iron-Age village on the top of the hill, which was excavated during the 1960s. Archaeologists say it has been inhabited for most of the last millennium. Originally known as Ko-Banza, the village continued to exist right up to the first half of the 20th century when the villagers were evicted, presumably by the ranch owners. Looking out from this site you have an excellent view over the park and the springs, and hence realise why it was a strategically important site in times of turmoil.

The giant baobab on Sebanzi is said to be 2,500 years old, and is often used by nesting white-backed vultures. There are also said to be some caves in the side of the hill, though these are now hidden behind deep, impenetrable thicket. The hill is still probably home to some threatened southern African species, including pangolin and aardvark, as well as hyenas, jackals, bush pig, bushbuck and small wildcats. Notable birds often seen here include the African broadbill.

Drum Rocks Close to the lodge, in the south of the park, is an outcrop of rocks (✪ DRUMRO 15°58.635'S, 27°16.106'E) that echo when tapped, producing a curious, resonant, almost metallic sound. These are the Drum Rocks, or Ibbwe Lyoombwa in the local language. Ask the scouts to direct you to these: they are fascinating. (Similar rocks, on the farm called Immenhof, in Namibia, were originally discovered by San/Bushmen and are now known locally as the 'singing rocks'.)

14

Considered sacred by the locals, these rocks are actually just the remnants of much larger boulders that were dynamited by the ranch's owners, curious to know the secret of their sound. They play an important part in the local religious calendar. As part of an elaborate rite of passage, it is traditional for a young man to come with his cattle to the rocks, chant '*Ibbwe Lyoombwa*' and then perform a dance and various rituals designed to prove his manliness. At the end, he should leave with his cattle without turning back, for fear of seeing his dead ancestors, and then stay away from his village until the beginning of the rains. If he has proved himself sufficiently, he will then be considered an adult and will be able to take a bride on his return. Even today, visitors are supposed to chant '*Ibbwe Lyoombwa*' to prevent bad luck befalling them.

Nearby is a large baobab (⊕ BAOBAB 15°58.637'S, 27°15.825'E) with a completely hollow trunk that can be entered from a crack in the side (which is the size of a small doorway). According to Chief Hamusende, the hollow was formed by an old man who, given a magic club, decided to try it out by bashing it against a nearby baobab; a broken tree and the formation of the hollow were the result of his experiment. It was actually used as a shelter by the district commissioner during the 1800s, and local legend has it that anybody who refuses to believe in the customs and beliefs of the villagers will enter into the hollow and never return, the tree sealing up and closing behind them.

Mwanachingwala Conservation Area Although east of the national park boundary, Mwanachingwala lies in a similar environment to Lochinvar National Park, but is normally accessed from Mazabuka. For details, see page 213.

BLUE LAGOON NATIONAL PARK (*US$10 pp/day; vehicle US$15/day*) Blue Lagoon is on the north side of the Kafue River. It was originally owned by a farming couple turned conservationists, the Critchleys, but more recently, especially during KK's reign, the Ministry of Defence restricted access to the military, plus a few privileged politicians and generals who used the old farmhouse intermittently as a hunting retreat – with predictable impact on the local wildlife.

Despite being declared a Ramsar site, along with Lochinvar, and the WWF drawing up conservation plans for the area, nothing was ever finalised, and no practical management takes place. While it's feasible that the area could be rejuvenated, it would require significant private investment, which is not forthcoming. The park's Nakeenda Lodge has been closed since 2007, so the future remains uncertain. Reports suggest that many of the park's trails are very overgrown and that, while the birding is excellent, and antelope are to be seen near the lagoons, other wildlife is little in evidence.

Getting there Blue Lagoon is reasonably well signposted, and there are several ways to reach it. Note, however, that it's not possible to reach it from the south, unless you're arriving by boat during the floods!

From Lusaka The easiest route from Lusaka is to take the Great West Road towards Mumbwa, then turn left after about 22km, opposite the filling station. There is a faded sign for the park here, but a much clearer one for Nampundwe Mine. This all-weather gravel road leads to the national park's scout camp at Naleeza. If you're heading for Nakeenda Lodge (currently closed) then follow the sign left.

From the west From the west, pass through Kafue's Nalusanga scout post and about 81km from here, beyond Mumbwa, look for a Lushomo garage near Nangoma. Fill up here if they have fuel, then continue towards Lusaka for a few

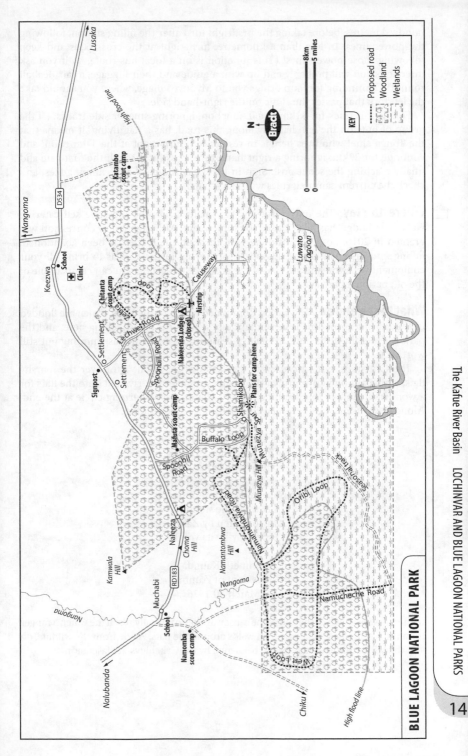

BLUE LAGOON NATIONAL PARK

KEY
Proposed road
Woodland
Wetlands

0 ____ 5 miles
0 ____ 8km

N

Bradt

Lusaka

Nangoma

High flood line

Keezwa

D534

School
Clinic

Katambo
scout camp

Chitanta
scout camp

Settlement
Settlement

Luwato
Lagoon

Zebra Loop
Lechwe Road
Causeway
Airstrip
Nakeenda Lodge
(closed)

Signpost

Spoonbill Road

Shamikoba
Plans for camp here

Matuta scout camp

Buffalo Loop

Spoonbill
Road

Munezya Spur
Munezya Hill

Oribi Loop

Kamwala
Hill

Najeeza

Chona
Hill

Namantombwa Road

Namantombwa Hill

Cheetah track

Muchabi

RD183

School

Nangoma

Namucheche Road

West Loop

Namomba
scout camp

Nalubanda

Nangoma

Chiku

High flood line

hundred metres, before taking the first right turn after the filling station, following the power lines. In less than a kilometre, turn right at the crossroads and keep following those power lines! (This junction is on a local bus route, so if you ask directions you will probably end up with a guide and their luggage; a fair deal all round!) Continuing for 9km brings you to Myooye village, where you should take the left fork that passes the clinic on the right-hand side.

Follow this track for 31km to a T-junction, ignoring smaller side tracks. (If the group of huts on the left, halfway along this road, has a flag flying, it means that the Tonga chief who lives here is in residence.) Turn right at the T-junction, and continue for 22km, ignoring a right-hand turn, passing through the first gate and finally reaching the scout post. Sign in here, pay the park and camping fees, and check the current camping rules with the scouts.

Where to stay The only place to stay in the park, the old-style self-catering Nakeenda Lodge, has been closed for some years. Although a new concession was granted in 2010, nothing was done with this and the lodge has been abandoned, falling into disrepair. The only option for staying in the park is to bring all your equipment with you and ask one of the scouts at the gate if you can camp at one of the old national park sites.

What to see and do The park is dominated by the Kafue Flats, which are flooded in the rainy season. This is certainly the best time for birdwatching here, and the park is generally at its best. In the dry season the view is not as stunning but still worth a visit.

The Critchleys built a causeway that extends for about 5km over the marshy flats, which although overgrown still enables vehicles to drive out onto the flats for a wonderful view of the stunning birdlife; there's even a turning circle at the end. Along the causeway are several memorial stones, one reading:

Erica Critchley 1910–1976
To the memory of the
one who loved Zambia
so much she cared for
human and natural resources.
Let what she stood for
not be forgotten by Zambians
especially by its youth.

Kenneth Kaunda
President of Zambia
March 30 1976

In the dry season, when the end of the causeway doesn't usually reach the water, a ranger from the scout post will take you on walks around the flats. Aside from the wildlife, do visit the old farmhouse that used to be owned by the Critchleys. It's fascinating.

Western Zambia

This remote area of western Zambia is difficult to visit but can reward intrepid travellers with some of the country's most interesting experiences. The Barotse floodplains, near Mongu, offer a glimpse of rural Zambian life that is still largely untouched by the 21st century, while Liuwa Plain National Park has excellent game and few visitors. It may be the venue for one of Africa's last great wildlife migrations, or 'gatherings', which has remained largely unknown because of the difficulty of getting into the area. Other parks, Sioma Ngwezi and West Lunga, do not have the same reputation for wildlife, but Sioma Ngwezi at least is still a very wild place to explore with a well-prepared group of 4x4 vehicles.

Common to almost the whole area are the related problems of supplies and transport. Much of the region stands on deep Kalahari sand where vehicles need a high-clearance 4x4 capability. If you are going off the main roads, then a small expedition is needed consisting of several vehicles, in case one runs into problems. During the rainy season, many of the roads are impassable, and even the pontoons (ferries) across the rivers will often stop working. Being stranded is a very real possibility. Thus the area's paucity of visitors is largely explained by the sheer difficulty of getting around.

The Christian missions have a very well-established network here. On the whole, these do remarkable work for the communities in the area, being involved with schools, hospitals, churches, development projects and many other aspects of local life. The courteous traveller can learn a lot about the region from these missions, and they are also good places to find English-speaking guides to accompany you on your travels – who will prove invaluable for just a few dollars per day.

I've divided this chapter into three sections: southwestern Zambia, Barotseland and northwestern Zambia. These don't slavishly follow provincial divisions; rather they reflect the differences between the areas as I understand them and are a convenient way to organise the text. I have also written the first part of the chapter, through southwestern Zambia, as a tour, starting from the border towns of Kazungula and Sesheke, and continuing north up the Zambezi to Mongu.

SOUTHWESTERN ZAMBIA

Compared with the rest of Zambia, the southwest of the country has been largely neglected, with few roads (which are generally poor) and no major towns. This does mean that its sights, like the marvellous Ngonye Falls, are very quiet. However, with the arrival of the long-awaited tar road running parallel to the Upper Zambezi and investment in Sioma Ngwezi National Park this region is set to see an increase in visitors.

The big draw of the Upper Zambezi, and the *raison d'être* of the camps along the river, has always been fishing – for bream and tiger fish. While an increasing

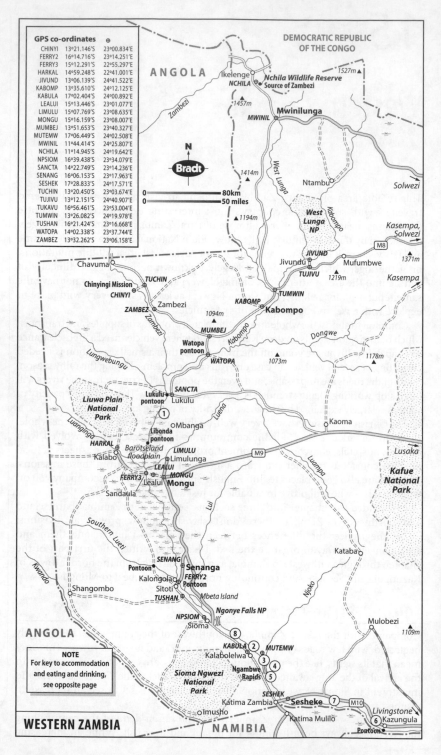

GPS co-ordinates ⊕

CHINYI	13°21.146'S 23°00.834'E
FERRY2	16°14.716'S 23°14.251'E
FERRY3	15°12.291'S 22°55.297'E
HARKAL	14°59.248'S 22°41.001'E
JIVUND	13°06.139'S 24°41.522'E
KABOMP	13°35.610'S 24°12.125'E
KABULA	17°02.404'S 24°00.892'E
LEALUI	15°13.446'S 23°01.077'E
LIMULU	15°07.769'S 23°08.635'E
MONGU	15°16.159'S 23°08.007'E
MUMBEJ	13°51.653'S 23°40.327'E
MUTEMW	17°06.449'S 24°02.508'E
MWINIL	11°44.414'S 24°25.807'E
NCHILA	11°14.945'S 24°19.642'E
NPSIOM	16°39.438'S 23°34.079'E
SANCTA	14°22.749'S 23°14.236'E
SENANG	16°06.153'S 23°17.963'E
SESHEK	17°28.833'S 24°17.571'E
TUCHIN	13°20.450'S 23°03.674'E
TUJIVU	13°12.151'S 24°40.907'E
TUKAVU	16°56.461'S 23°53.004'E
TUMWIN	13°26.082'S 24°19.978'E
TUSHAN	16°21.424'S 23°16.668'E
WATOPA	14°02.338'S 23°37.744'E
ZAMBEZ	13°32.262'S 23°06.158'E

DEMOCRATIC REPUBLIC
OF THE CONGO

ANGOLA

Ikelenge
NCHILA
Nchila Wildlife Reserve
Source of Zambezi
1527m

1457m

MWINIL
Mwinilunga

West Lunga

Ntambu

Solwezi

Zambezi

N
Bradt

1414m

West
Lunga
NP

Kasempa,
Solwezi

0   80km
0   50 miles

1194m

M8

1371m

Jivundu
JIVUND   Mufumbwe
TUJIVU
1219m   Kasempa

Chavuma

Chinyingi Mission   TUCHIN
CHINYI
Zambezi
ZAMBEZ

1094m
MUMBEJ

Watopa
pontoon
WATOPA

TUMWIN
KABOMP   Kabompo

Kabompo

Dongwe

1073m   1178m

Lungwebungu

Liuwa Plain
National
Park

Lukulu
pontoon   Lukulu
SANCTA

Luanginga   ①

Libonda
pontoon

HARKAL
Kalabo   Barotseland
floodplain   LIMULU
LIMULU   Limulunga
LEALUI   M9
FERRY3   MONGU
Lealui   Mongu
Sandaula

Luena

Kaoma

Lusaka

Kafue
National
Park

oMbanga

Luampa

Southern Lueti

Lui

Kwando   SENANG
Pontoon   Senanga
Kalongola   FERRY2
Sitoti   Pontoon
Shangombo   TUSHAN   Mbeta Island

Kataba

Njoko

Ngonye Falls NP

NPSIOM
Sioma   ⑧
KABULA   ②   MUTEMW
Kalabolelwa   ③   ④
Ngambwe   ⑤
Rapids

Mulobezi
1109m

ANGOLA

Sioma Ngwezi
National
Park

Katima Zambia   SESHEK   Sesheke   ⑦   M10
Imusho   Livingstone
Katima Mulilo   ⑥   Kazungula
Pontoon

NOTE
For key to accommodation
and eating and drinking,
see opposite page

WESTERN ZAMBIA

NAMIBIA

number of visitors are coming for other attractions, such as Ngonye Falls and the excellent birdlife, it is fishing that retains the greatest appeal.

HIGHLIGHTS
Fishing on the Upper Zambezi
The Zambezi River here is generally wide, although in parts of its course between Sesheke and Senanga it becomes shallow, broken by forested islands and rocky outcrops, and you'll also find waterfalls and rapids. So there are conditions suitable for challenging fly-fishing and spinning.

Tiger fish are the most sought-after challenge, whilst various bream species, particularly the predatory yellow-belly and the thin-face breams, make good sport fishing in the faster sections. In the slower sections, fishermen find the more sedentary three-spot, red-breast and greenhead bream.

Birdlife
For a more gentle interaction with some of the wildlife, this area offers some excellent, undisturbed birdwatching – with various species frequenting different areas of the river and the surrounding vegetation. A few of the river's 'specials' include rock pratincoles, seen darting about the rocks of many sections of rapids; African finfoots, which lurk at the water's edge in areas of thick, overhanging vegetation; African skimmers, which nest on some of the river's exposed sandbanks; and Pel's fishing owls resting in some of the old riverine trees. You'll also have the chance to spot Schalow's and Lady Ross's turacos, yellow-spotted nicator, narina trogon and wood owls (the Mutemwa Lodge area is particularly good for these).

WEST TO SESHEKE
There's an excellent tarred road, the M10, running parallel to the Zambezi from Livingstone to Sesheke. After 63km, a turning left leads after nearly 3km to the small border town of Kazungula. Continuing past this turning brings you to Sesheke, where there's a bridge over the Zambezi, and a border post with Namibia. The Livingstone to Kazungula section of this road is still excellent but at the time of going to press there are more potholes than tarmac on the 40km section to Sesheke from Kazungula. The 190km journey from Livingstone to Sesheke takes about 2½ hours.

Kazungula
This small town marks the location of a **ferry** over the Zambezi into Botswana (⏰ *06.00–18.00*). This can take just one truck and two or three cars at a time, so can get very busy. As well as a fee of around US$30 per vehicle, depending on size, there are all sorts of other paperwork (and payment) required – insurance, immigration, car import permit, carbon and road tax, police levy – so it's often worth enlisting the help of one of the many 'agents' who are likely to hassle you. And be prepared with plenty of cash.

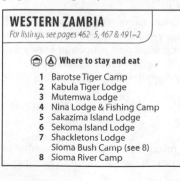

WESTERN ZAMBIA
For listings, see pages 462–5, 467 & 491–2

🏨 Ⓐ **Where to stay and eat**
1 Barotse Tiger Camp
2 Kabula Tiger Lodge
3 Mutemwa Lodge
4 Nina Lodge & Fishing Camp
5 Sakazima Island Lodge
6 Sekoma Island Lodge
7 Shackletons Lodge
   Sioma Bush Camp (see 8)
8 Sioma River Camp

On the main M10 road, just before the turn-off, the Kazungula Reststop offers snacks and more substantial dishes to passing travellers. Then, just before the ferry itself, there are a few **shops**, a small **market** (⏰ *early–18.00 daily*) and a simple **restaurant**. This is also where local buses stop.

Getting there and away A twice-daily bus service run by Mazhandu Family Bus links Livingstone with

Sesheke. If you're heading for Botswana, then hop on one of these and get off at Kazungula; you can expect to pay around K50 from Livingstone, or K60 from Sesheke. The ferry to Botswana is a good place to hitchhike. After that, to get into Kasane or to head for Nata, you should walk the short distance to the disease control post, which makes a perfect hitchhiking spot as vehicles have to stop here anyway.

Where to stay Kazungula itself has nowhere of note to stay, but there are a couple of fishing lodges to the west that welcome visitors:

Sekoma Island Lodge [map, page 460] (9 tents) m +27 83 708 3787; e info@sekoma. co.za, sekoma.island@gmail.com; www.sekoma. co.za. ◈ SEKOMA 17°44.900'S, 25°10.533'E. Set on an island of the Zambezi near the Mambova Rapids, Sekoma is well placed for the angler in search of tiger fish or Zambezi catfish (all catch & release), while outside the fishing season it attracts keen birders, with walks & boat trips available. The lodge is accessible only by boat from Mambova village; to drive to the jetty, turn off the main road about 5km west of Kazungula & follow this for about 5.5km. Safari-style tents sleep either 2 or 4 guests, are right on the river, each with a small decked porch, & a tiled bathroom at the back, & – during the fishing season (May–Sep) – each allocated a speedboat & guide. There's a riverside deck, too, & a boma with bar & large, cool dining room. *R1,980 pp (SA rand) FBA, exc bar, fishing tackle & transfers.* ⊕ *mid May–mid Jan.* **LL**

Shackletons Lodge [map, page 460] (6 chalets); ☎ +27 83 251 7257; e info@

shackletons.co.za; www.shackletons.co.za. ◈ SOKACA 17°29.793'S, 24°46.519'E. Around 170km from Livingstone, or 55km east of Sesheke, Shackletons lies 3.5km down an easily navigable sandy track (turn-off ◈ TUSOKA 17°28.010'S, 24°46.948'E), overlooking an island beside the Zambezi. Beyond are wide floodplains, typical of the seasonally flooded eastern end of Namibia's Caprivi Strip.

En-suite twin chalets with netted windows are solidly built under thatch & overlook the river from their wooden verandas. At the heart of the lodge, the split-level main building incorporates a lounge, dining area & riverside bar, with a firepit & small pool nearby & a deck over the river shaded by an ebony tree. It's a relaxed, unpretentious place, with the emphasis firmly on fishing, but there are river cruises & plenty of birding opportunities, too. *Chalet US$320 pp sharing FB, inc fishing (20 litres fuel), exc drinks & transfers; tent US$75 pp DBB.* ⊕ *Apr–Dec, depending on floods.* **LL**

Sesheke

Sesheke sits on the eastern side of the Zambezi River, linked by a 900m bridge to a smaller town on the other side, known locally as Katima Zambia. The bridge, financed largely by Germany, was opened in 2004 by the presidents of Zambia and Namibia. It lies about 5km inside Zambian territory, and was only the fifth bridge to span the width of the Zambezi – the others being the road bridges at Chirundu, Tete and Livingstone, and the footbridge at Chinyingi Mission. (A sixth bridge, just south of Ngonye Falls, has now reached the drawing board, and a seventh – at Kazungula – is also in the pipeline.)

Sesheke itself (◈ 17°28.599'S, 24°17.208'E), has a few **stores**, a small branch of the Finance **Bank**, a simple hospital, a police station (listen for their early-morning marching songs if you're staying overnight!), a **post office** and a few small **guesthouses**. There's also a **fuel** station here – although fuel is considerably cheaper across the border in Namibia's Katima Mulilo. Supplies are more plentiful there, too, so Sesheke can be very quiet.

The smaller Katima Zambia, right next to the border with Namibia, has just a police post, a small market and a few local stores.

Getting there and away Sesheke is easily reached from either Livingstone or Katima Mulilo, in Namibia, on tarred roads. Note that the section from Kazungula to Sesheke has deteriorated badly. There's a twice-daily bus service from Livingstone, costing K70 one way, with onward connections to Lusaka (*K120*) and Kitwe.

If you're driving from Livingstone to Sesheke, read *Driving* in Chapter 8, page 155. Access to or from the north, until recently, was challenging, but with tarring of the road, this is set to improve dramatically.

Where to stay Sesheke's limited accommodation options are both unsophisticated and correspondingly inexpensive, with the best being Brenda's Baobab. If you're driving yourself, you'll find several lodges along the river, both to the east of town (page 462) and on the way north to Ngonye Falls (below).

Brenda's Best Baobab Tree (4 chalets, camping) Mulambwe St; m 0963 786882; ◈ SESHES 17°28.833'S, 24°17.571'E. Popular with backpackers, this unexpected gem is just over 1km east of the town centre, opposite the hospital, & accessed down a drive between the civic centre & St Kizito Roman Catholic Church. It's owned by Brenda & her husband, a Dutch GP, who travel regularly to Europe, & their en-suite chalets under high thatch have a fridge, TV & fan. Down by the river are grassy lawns dotted with shady picnic tables & a campsite. Nearby are clean toilets & showers, & an expanse of wooden decking around a large central baobab. They'll serve food, drinks, & an eclectic range of beers drawn from Namibia, Zambia & South Africa. **$$**

Sisheke Lodge (9 rooms) 0211 481086. On the left as you drive into Sesheke from Kazungula, & just before the fuel station, this friendly place has simple but clean en-suite rooms. There's a lounge, porch area & dining room, with a self-catering kitchen a useful add-on. **$**

DRIVING NORTH FROM SESHEKE TO NGONYE FALLS The recently tarred road northwest from Sesheke follows the western bank of the river for 139km to Ngonye/Sioma. As you might expect, it is in excellent condition, and as yet it carries scarcely any traffic.

Construction has started on a new bridge over the Zambezi just south of Ngonye Falls, taking the road over to the eastern bank at that point, then continuing north to meet the tar road at Senanga. It is unlikely to be finished, though, before the end of 2016.

Aside from the perennial appeal of the fishing, and other river-based excursions, the main reasons for visiting this area of southwest Zambia are the Ngonye Falls (often referred to as the Sioma Falls; see pages 467–9) and the Sioma Ngwezi National Park, which lies to the west of the river, and is expected to be encompassed within the new KAZA park (pages 465–7). With travel further north often being very slow, this is also a good area to break the journey for a few days on your way north or south.

Where to stay Along the Upper Zambezi, between Sesheke and Ngonye Falls, you'll pass signposts to several places to stay – primarily fishing camps. The following are listed in the order in which they are encountered when driving north from Sesheke. Note that about 17km north of Sesheke bridge you'll come to a fork in the road (◈ RDFORK 17°21.956'S, 24°09.064'E); keep to the left – unless you're heading for the sawmill!

Sakazima Island Lodge [map, page 460] (7 chalets, camping) +264 66252739; m +264 811 246696; www.sakazima.co.za. ◈ TUSAKA 17°17.868'S, 24°08.230'E. Some 2hrs' drive from Livingstone, down a 2.5km track about 26km north of Sesheke, this small, peaceful fishing camp is built on a group of 5 islands in the Zambezi, with its own campsite on the mainland. The original owners were careful not to remove any of the island's trees when building the lodge, & there's still a lush, tropical feel about the place – lots of wild date palms (*Phoenix* *reclinata*), African mangosteens (*Garcinia livingstonei*), ebonies (*Diospyros mespiliformis*), knobthorns (*Acacia nigrescens*) & the occasional pod mahogany (*Afzelia quanzensis*). Whole groups can book the lodge on a self-catering basis.

Each of the reed-&-brick rustic chalets has a wooden deck above the river, & an en-suite shower, washbasin & separate toilet at the back, with water heated by individual gas boilers. The main dining area & bar are entirely of wood, with a small river-water plunge pool on the deck in front, plus a firepit & a couple of shaded hammocks. The lodge offers great fly-fishing opportunities on the rapids & the birding is good, too. Mokoro trips, short nature drives in the nearby bush, guided birding walks & day trips to Ngonye Falls & Livingstone can be booked in advance. *R1,100 pp sharing FB inc sunset cruise. Self catering R550 pp. Camping R100 pp (all rates in South African rand).* ☺ *All year.* **L**

🏠 **Nina Lodge & Fishing Camp** [map, page 460] (6 rooms, 2 houses, camping) m 0979 571407; e ninafishing@gmail.com; www.ninafishing.com. ✆ TUNINA 17°12.340'S, 24°05.387'E. Some 43.5km from Sesheke, or 11km north of Lusu Mission, Nina's overlooks the Lusu Rapids within the proposed KAZA park. Owned & run by Nicky & Dalene Rossouw, it's a self-catering camp, with a range of good-value accommodation & a bar, plus a simple restaurant. Over the rapids are 2 stone-built rooms with gauzed windows, homemade furniture & contemporary bedding, & sharing a kitchen. In addition there are 2 houses, one 2-bedroom & a 3-bedroom family house with 2 bathrooms & a deck, & a self-contained fishing camp – with its own kitchen & 4 bedrooms. Most guests come for the fishing (tackle can be hired), but there's good birding, too; other activities include bush walks & mokoro excursions with members of the local community (*US$50 pp).* **$$**

🏠 **Mutemwa Lodge** [map, page 460] (6 tents) ✆(Namibia) +27 (72) 536 1337; e james@wildmansafaris.com; www.mutemwa. co.za. ✆ MUTEMW 17°6.449'S, 24°2.508'E. About 55km north of Sesheke, Mutemwa has been owned & run by Gavin Johnson, the former Springbok rugby player, & his wife, Penny, since 1996, & is home to their 3 daughters. From the neatly signposted turn-off (✆ TUMUTE 17°7.056'S, 24°1.861'E), it is just 2km to the

lodge. (It is easily accessed by road transfer from Livingstone – a 3-hr drive on mostly tarred roads.)

Although the best lodge in the area, it retains a simplicity that – coupled with a family atmosphere – is particularly appealing. Meru-style twin tents are spread out along the river, shaded by the remaining tall trees in the riverine forest – mostly pale-bark waterberries, as well as pod mahogany, jackalberries & sausage trees – & backed by an expanse of cropped grass. Each tent has a basin, flush toilet & heated shower behind a reed screen, & a small deck overlooking a channel of the Zambezi. A large central thatched roof shelters a bar, lounge & dining area, & there's a small pool nearby. The food is good, wholesome fare, with b/fast & lunch served on the lower deck overlooking the river, & dinner at individual tables arranged around a fire. Lighting comes from paraffin lamps; the camp has no electricity save for a generator that is handy for charging batteries.

Guests, from independent self-drivers to larger, fly-in groups (the lodge has its own landing strip), come primarily for the fishing; the camp has 6 good motorboats & several guides. More broadly, birding trips & sundowner cruises are also on the menu, as are canoeing excursions, perhaps followed by a champagne b/fast on an island in the river, & guided walks on a 1km-long island opposite the lodge. During the winter months, keen anglers can choose between 3 Barotse rivers in Mutemwa's annual Barotse Floodplain Fishing Safaris: the Lungwebungu, the Zambezi & the Kwamashi floodplain. *R2,720 (South African rand) pp sharing FBA inc unlimited guided fishing with unlimited fuel, canoeing, day trips to Sioma Falls (exc drinks & lost or broken fishing tackle).* ☺ *Closed during heavy rains (Jan–Feb).* **LL**

🏠 **Kabula Tiger Lodge** [map, page 460] (7 chalets, camping) ✆ +27 82 550 8642, +27 82 672 5168, +27 82 569 2998; e info@ kabulalodge.com; www.kabulalodge.com. ✆ KABULA 17°02.404'S, 24°00.892'E. This self-catering lodge is primarily geared to families coming in search of fishing & birding, though with high open decks it's not ideal for younger children. It is clearly signposted at ✆ TUKBTL 17°03.363'S, 23°59.706'E, about 10km north of Mutemwa; it also has its own airstrip.

Simple, thatched dbl or 4-bed reed chalets are en suite & most have decks overlooking the river. Light in the chalets is from the lodge's solar power. Two communal kitchens are equipped with gas fridges, a cooker & basic utensils. For campers, there's a tree-shaded campsite with 6 pitches & ablution facilities in individual rondavels rather than a block. Each pitch has a tap & its own washing-up area, with wood-fired boilers for hot water, & there's a thatched *lapa* with tables & benches beneath a venerable pod mahogany.

In addition to guided fishing trips (*R220/hr 3 people*), there are opportunities for walking & birding on Kabula Island, just upstream of the lodge, where over 200 species of birds have been recorded. *Chalet R595/925 twin/4 bed; camping R115pp (South African rand)* ☺ *All year.* **L**

🏠 **Sioma River Camp** [map, page 460] (10 tents, 2 chalets, camping) m 0977 771098; e siomacamp@gmail.com. ⊕ SIOMRC 16°42.525'S 023°38.571'E. At his desk in the Danish embassy in Lusaka, Hans Aaskov dreamed of establishing a lodge – & this is it. Just 11km south of Ngonye Falls, or 115km north of Sesheke, Sioma River

Camp occupies a hilly site that overlooks a narrow but deep stretch of the Zambezi, where in the dry season sculpted sandbanks are exposed on both sides. It's a simple, no-frills place, ideal for self-drive visitors & within easy reach of the falls.

As well as simple dome tents, there are walk-in tents with open-air bathrooms set on elevated wooden decks, some under thatch. The narrow main building, with half walls to allow a through breeze, incorporates a restaurant/bar with a lounge area overlooking the river. On the hill above sits a stone-built library with comfy chairs, a cosy fire – & a selection of single malt whiskies. Well away from the camp, in the woods above the river, the campsite overlooks a broad sandbank. A simple ablution block is set higher up still, secure from any flooding after the rains.

A highlight here is a boat trip upstream to Ngonye Falls. Other activities include fishing trips to the Lumbe River where it's possible to swim & to a village. *Chalet US$75/110 pp B&B/FB; dome tent US$40 pp. Camping US$10 pp.* **L**

SIOMA NGWEZI NATIONAL PARK (*US$5 pp/day, vehicle US$15/day*) Of all Zambia's remote and seldom-visited parks, Sioma Ngwezi would probably be one of the easiest to regenerate. It is really very close to the Victoria Falls/Livingstone area, which has a huge reservoir of visitors keen to do short safari trips. Tourism to Namibia's Caprivi Strip is rapidly taking off, and with the main road between Sesheke and Senanga now being tarred, access to the vicinity of the park is very good.

Against this background, the park has been incorporated into a new 'peace park' (*www.peaceparks.org*), the Kavango-Zambezi Transfrontier Conservation Area. Known locally as KAZA, it covers around 287,132km², connecting Sioma Ngwezi and the surrounding GMAs with protected areas in neighbouring Botswana, Zimbabwe, Angola and northern Namibia – and notably including the Okavango Delta and Victoria Falls. As with all the peace parks, the primary aim is to create a corridor to allow migratory animals to move freely between the various reserves, unencumbered by manmade boundaries. In particular, this would be a step towards ending the absurd situation where Chobe has too many elephants … yet this corner of Zambia, just over the border, has too few!

Although Sioma Ngwezi's tourist infrastructure is still very rudimentary, rough tracks are being cut so that self-drive visitors can explore the park, provided that they take a game scout to show the way.

Geography Positioned in the far southwestern corner of Zambia, Sioma Ngwezi National Park covers 5,000km², making it the third largest of Zambia's national parks. It shares a long border with Angola, along the Kwando (or Cuando) River, and a short border with Namibia in the south. This corner is less than 50km from northern Botswana, and its vegetation and landscape owe much to the Kalahari sand that lies beneath it.

Most of the park is flat, dry and quite densely wooded – covered with a mosaic of miombo and acacia woodland, with the occasional area of teak forest. There are a

15

few open dambos and sometimes these surround the occasional pool in the bush – but surface water is rare here during the dry season.

Geographical problems Bordering both Angola and Namibia's Caprivi Strip, Sioma Ngwezi was always going to be a difficult park to keep secure and well managed. Following years of civil war, Angola has only recently started on the long road back to peace, let alone prosperity. Namibia's Caprivi Strip, too, had security problems in recent years, but these are now thankfully resolved. Sioma Ngwezi itself was a stronghold of Namibia's SWAPO fighters in the early years – and later of the Angolan rebels.

While cross-border poaching is rarely as prevalent as many in Africa will claim (people from 'over there' always make easy scapegoats for crimes), it certainly is a problem in this area.

Looking at the park's geography, you'll realise that most of the animals must either survive entirely without surface water, or need to drink from one of the two rivers nearby: the Kwando on the western border, or the Zambezi which is east, outside of the park. Study a detailed map and you'll realise that what settlements there are in this area are strung out on the banks of these same rivers. So after around July, by which time the park's few dambos have dried out, much of the game needs to run a daily (or more likely, nightly) gauntlet of the riverside villages to drink.

A further problem is how much the logging, which has decimated the oldest hardwood trees in most of Zambia's western provinces, has encroached illegally into this park.

Flora and fauna Sioma Ngwezi is the only Zambian park, outside the Luangwa Valley and the Mosi-oa-Tunya National Park, where giraffe have historically been found. It is claimed that rather than being the same subspecies as those in Luangwa (Thornicroft's giraffe), these are an 'Angolan' subspecies, which is different again from the normal 'southern' variety found throughout the subcontinent. Native antelope species include roan, sable, eland, tsessebe, blue wildebeest, zebra, reedbuck, kudu, steenbok, oribi and possibly lechwe on the Kwando River. The major predators are lion, leopard and spotted hyena, and there have been occasional sightings of wild dog, although these are quite possibly packs visiting from the strong population in northern Botswana. Small numbers of elephant, too, frequent the park, especially in the dry season.

Current game populations Sioma Ngwezi's game populations have taken a battering in recent years. Poaching (aka subsistence hunting) is common, and made much easier by the trek to water that much of the game makes – thus bringing it into close contact with the settlements beside the two main rivers. The predators have also suffered, as they're attracted to the easy meat of grazing cattle from nearby local villages, which then bring them into direct conflict with the local people.

Thus, although small populations of most of the main game species still occur here, it was both scarce and skittish. That said, indications are that the wildlife is recovering slowly and that species like sable, roan, tsessebe, eland and reticulated giraffe are increasingly being spotted. Elephants too are returning and are visible, having re-established an old migration route in the southeast border of the park.

When to go The best time to visit Sioma Ngwezi is probably just after the end of the rains, between May and November, when the dambos inside the park still have a little water and are attracting game. Alternatively, spend time beside the Kwando later in the year, when it's the only water source around.

Getting there and getting organised There is a track leading to the eastern corner of the park and around the boundary from the Sesheke–Ngonye Falls road, about 16km south of Mutemwa Lodge – although I couldn't find this when I last passed this way. A second, 51km further north at Silumbu (⊕ TUSNNP 16°54.674'S, 23°51.117'E), close to Sioma, is clearly signposted. This heads southwest around the perimeter of the park to the Kwando River. Here it joins up with a track that runs parallel to the river from Shangombo in the northwest almost to the park's southern boundary. However, the track across the park that links these two access points has been inaccessible for many years. On the plus side, a new border post with Namibia along the Kwando River is expected to open soon, making it considerably easier to travel between the Zambezi and Kwando rivers.

Driving is difficult and requires the backing of a couple of 4x4s. The Kalahari sand can be slow going, and is also very heavy on fuel – so remember that this is available only at Sesheke or Katima Mulilo in the south, or Senanga and Mongu to the north.

Permits for the park are available from the national park office at Ngonye Falls (⊕ NGOFNP 16°39.820'S, 23°34.264'E). If you intend to explore this area independently, then get a scout from the office to guide you, and perhaps show you to a good spot for camping. There are, as yet, no designated campsites within the park. Alternatively, you can take a two-night guided trip to the park with Mutemwa Lodge (page 464), and day or overnight trips can be organised by Hans Aaskov at Sioma River Camp (page 465).

Security note Note that there is some question over the precise location of the border, as pre-1970s it used to be the eastern edge of the Kwando floodplain. Then Zambia 'moved' it to the middle of the river. Wherever it is, you don't want to stray over it accidentally.

Where to stay Aside from two-night camping trips organised by Mutemwa Lodge, there is a simple camp near the park boundary:

⋀ Sioma Bush Camp [map, page 460] (4 tents) m 0977 771098; e siomacamp@gmail. com;[⊕ SIOMBC 16°45.074'S, 23°25.246'E. Some 35km from its parent Sioma River Camp, the Bush Camp is in the GMA, near the border of the national park & next to a couple of waterholes. Campers can take their own kit, but there are also simple 3x3m dome tents under thatch. In addition, there's a basic bush kitchen with a thatched dining shelter overlooking 1 of the waterholes, & a couple of viewing platforms. Full board 2-night packages (*US$300 pp*) & bush walks/drives can be arranged (*US$15/30 pp plus park fees*), with transfers from Sioma River Camp *Dome tent US$50 pp sharing; own tent US$10 pp.*

NGONYE FALLS NATIONAL PARK (*US$5 pp; vehicle US$15;* ⏱ *06.00–18.00*) One of the newest of Zambia's national parks, Ngonye Falls was gazetted in December 2009. Conceived in partnership with the local community, it lies about 127km north of Sesheke and covers just 200ha on each side of the river, although it is envisaged that it will eventually encompass a total of 1,760ha. The park is centred on the spectacular Ngonye Falls (often referred to as the Sioma Falls), and the surrounding land has been fenced off in order to start restocking it with game.

Livingstone passed this way, having come north through what is now Botswana. He noted:

30th November, 1853 – At Gonye Falls. No rain has fallen here, so it is excessively hot. The trees have put on their gayest dress, and many flowers adorn the landscape, yet the heat makes all the leaves droop at mid-day and look languid for want of rain. If the country increases as much in beauty in front, as it has done within the last four degrees of latitude, it will indeed be a lovely land.

For many miles below, the river is confined in a narrow space of not more than one hundred yards wide. The water goes boiling along, and gives the idea of great masses of it rolling over and over, so that even the most expert swimmer would find it difficult to keep on the surface. Here it is that the river when in flood rises fifty or sixty feet in perpendicular height. The islands above the falls are covered with foliage as beautiful as can be seen anywhere. Viewed from the mass of rock which overhangs the fall, the scenery was the loveliest I had seen.

This was about two years before Livingstone journeyed further down the Zambezi and saw the Victoria Falls for the first time.

Flora and fauna Now that the fences are in place, initial plans to stock the park with the introduction of both zebra and several species of antelope – impala, kudu, bushbuck and sitatunga – as well as warthog and bushpig have started. As the park boundaries are widened, so the number of species will be increased.

Back on the river, one of the wildlife highlights is the presence of cape clawless otters, which cavort in the fast-running waters and rest on the sandbanks.

Getting there and away The park entrance (⊕ NGOFNP 16°39.820'S, 23°34.264'E), is about 127km north of Sesheke, or 57km southeast of the Sitoti pontoon, and is clearly signposted to the east of the road. Here you can pay your entry fees, leave your vehicle safely, and find a guide to take you down to the falls themselves.

Where to stay There are plans to open a lodge near the falls, but for the moment the only accommodation on site is for well-equipped campers. Also worth consideration is Sioma River Camp (page 465), just south of the falls.

⚔ **Campsite** The basic campsite here is close to the river, a short walk from a beautiful sandy beach (strictly no swimming!) & the falls themselves. Its 2 large pitches each have a firepit at the front, with a bucket shower & separate composting toilet; it's all very environmentally friendly. A semi-sheltered camp kitchen offers a food-preparation area, useful if the heavens open at the critical time. Firewood is available, but you need to bring all other food & supplies. *US$10 pp.*

What to see and do Although nothing like as high as Victoria Falls, the Ngonye Falls are still impressive, and if the former didn't exist then they would certainly draw visitors. The geology of the area is the same as that of Victoria Falls, and these falls were formed by a similar process, with erosion taking advantage of cracks in the area's basalt rock.

Ngonye's main falls form a rather spectacular semicircle of water, with lots of smaller streams and falls around the edges. Some of these create little pools, ideal for bathing, though be careful to remain at this point as the main river has too many crocodiles to be safe. The Falls are at their most beautiful during the dry season, from July to December, when the drop is at its greatest. Earlier in the year, the Zambezi floods, so the drop between the falls and the next stage of the river can all but disappear.

Seeing the falls from the western bank is easy – it's a 15-minute walk from the park gate, just beyond the campsite. However, most of the main falls cannot be seen from the bank, and you certainly won't appreciate them fully. To get a really good view, you must cross onto an island in the river in front of the falls. At low water, the park scouts can organise a mokoro to take you across (*US$5 pp, inc guide*), although when the river is in flood, this becomes too dangerous.

Nearby, Sioma River Camp has motorboats that they use for trips to the falls. For notes on birdwatching in this area, see page 461.

DRIVING NORTH FROM NGONYE TO SENANGA

From Ngonye to Sitoti From the park's office at Ngonye Falls it's about 61km northwest to the Sitoti pontoon, or Kalongola on the M10, but it is better to cross over the river on the Sioma pontoon until the new bridge has been built just upriver from the falls. There is a brand new tarmac road on the eastern side of the Zambezi and it is an easy drive to Senanga and on to Mongu. The road signs to the bridge are already in place, though, which can be confusing. Until the bridge is completed don't follow the signs to Senanga (as they lead you along the new road spur to the bridge) but instead stick to the older M10 for a couple of km to Sioma. In the village there is a small road to the river where the pontoon still takes you across for now.

The village of Sioma, where the presence of a tyre repair place could well prove welcome, is also where you turn off for Sioma Ngwezi National Park. If you are sticking to the M10 on the western side of the Zambezi you will come to Nangweshi (⊕ NANGWE 16°23.787'S, 23°19.465'E), which boasts a handful of guesthouses and where you can stock up on drinks and snacks.

About 45km north of Ngonye, and 16km south of Sitati pontoon along this route, there's a substantial road junction (Rd 463 – ⊕ TUSHAN 16°21.424'S, 23°16.668'E) with a sign pointing west to **Cuando Lodge** (which proudly advertises that it has 'showers and lights'), and the Shangombo Mission (140km) on the Kwando (or Cuando) River. This turning is beside a small settlement known as Matebele, where there's a bridge over a tributary to the Zambezi.

Just north of this, the road forks (⊕ TUSITO 16°21.085'S, 23°16.498'E). The right fork drops down onto the lower-lying grasslands of the Zambezi's floodplains – and thence to the Sitoti pontoon. The left fork probably leads to what, in theory, is a very difficult and sandy track along the western side of the Zambezi floodplain to Kalabo; see *Driving from Kalabo to Sitoti*, page 478 for details.

Sitoti pontoon The pontoon across the Zambezi (⊕ FERRY2 16°14.716'S, 23°14.251'E; ⊕ *06.00–18.00*), at Kalongola, is a little over 20km south of Senanga, and 9km north of Sitoti village. The pontoon was closed in early 2016 but it was difficult to ascertain whether this was because of high water or whether it had been abandoned permanently. If it is still operating, though, it's a good, large pontoon which can take several vehicles at a time, setting off when it's full; there's no set schedule. In the wet season, when the crossing is longer, the fare is considerably higher.

When the new bridge across the Zambezi near Ngonye Falls is finally finished, the pontoon will almost certainly close.

SENANGA Coming from the south, Senanga is the first 'proper' town since Sesheke. On the eastern bank of the Zambezi, it's a pleasant place, linear in layout with trees lining the main road and a tall radio mast near the centre. Here you'll find a vital

Puma **fuel** station (which usually even has fuel), a **hospital** (almost opposite the Puma garage), a **post office**, a **market** and a handful of **shops** and small bottle stores – but you still can't shake off the feeling that it's out on a limb.

Getting there and away The 104km stretch of road from Senanga to Mongu east of the Zambezi is good tarmac all the way. From the south, see *From Ngonye to Sitoti*, page 469. If you're heading south, you have to cross to the west bank on the Sioma pontoon – at least until the advent of the promised bridge and take the M10; there is no navigable road on the east side of the Zambezi beyond here.

There are buses as far as Senanga from Mongu, but as yet none heading further south although this may change with the new road.

Where to stay and eat There are several basic guesthouses, of which the Greenrite is not untypical, or you could try Senanga Safaris Lodge although we have had mixed reports recently. You can eat there, too, or perhaps at the very basic restaurant on the opposite side of the road.

BAROTSELAND

The heartland of the former British protectorate of Barotseland, now the Western Province, covers the floodplains which surround some of the upper reaches of the Zambezi. It is the homeland of the Lozi king, the Litunga, and his people – a group who have retained much of their cultural heritage despite the ravages of the past century. They were granted more autonomy by the colonial authorities than most of the ethnic groups in Zambia's other regions, and perhaps this has helped them to preserve more of their culture. The Litunga has winter and summer palaces nearby, and a hunting lodge in Liuwa Plain. (Chapter 47 of John Reader's excellent *Africa: A Biography of the Continent* covers some of the history of this area in fascinating detail. See page 527 for details.)

For the traveller this means that some aspects of life here have altered relatively little since pre-colonial times. Most of the local people still follow lifestyles of subsistence farming, hunting and gathering, and when rains are good they must still move to higher ground to escape the floodwaters. Be aware, though, that political feelings occasionally run high over the level of autonomy that is permitted by the government.

BAROTSE FLOODPLAINS The area bordering the Zambezi River as it runs west of Mongu represents the second-largest wetland in Zambia, and was designated as a Ramsar site in 2007. After the rains, the Barotse or Zambezi floodplains are transformed with small islands of vegetation dotted through the expanse of water. Ramsar (*www.ramsar.org*) notes that 'there is sparse riparian vegetation, small stands of *Acacia albida* in the floodplains, *Syzygium guineens* along the main river channel and patches of *Diplorhynchus* scrub and *Borassus* forest in the northern areas. Semi-evergreen woodlands found on the Kalahari sands have economically important species like *Baikiaea plurijuga* and *Pterocarpus angolensis*'.

MONGU Perched high on a ridge overlooking the eastern edge of the Barotse Plains, Mongu is the provincial centre for western Zambia – and the only large town this side of Livingstone or Lusaka. In the past, very few tourists came here, so there are few people who aren't Zambian, and almost all of those work with or for the fairly permanent contingent of NGO personnel. The areas around Mongu are amongst Zambia's poorest and many are still isolated by seasonal floods, so there is often need for relief workers here. However, the new causeway crossing the floodplain means that Mongu is expanding rapidly, not only as a hub for NGOs, but as a rudimentary tourist destination.

The town is easily reached from Lusaka and Senanga, and is the best place in the region to get **fuel** or **supplies**. Otherwise for the moment there is little to attract visitors, apart perhaps from the good **baskets** to be found here. Make the most of the amenities and relative comforts here – as there are precious few of these to the north or west.

Mongu has long had a bad reputation for theft, but perhaps police vigilance over the years has paid off, since there was little hint of this on our last visit. Indeed, the town may well develop into a new tourist jumping-off point for trips to Ngonye Falls, fishing camps along the river and year-round access to Liuwa.

Geography Mongu is about 25km from the dry-season course of the Zambezi, or immediately adjacent to the water when the river is in full flood. The town is spread out on a ridge above the plains, with no real centre but several quite different busy areas. Small villages and cattle dot the dusty plains during the dry season, but when wet it is all transformed into a haze of green grass on a mirror of water that reflects the sky. Then, when the water is fairly high, the views west over the floodplain are spectacular: myriad channels snaking through apparently endless flat plains.

Orientation The tarred M9 from Lusaka meets the tar road heading south to Senanga at a central roundabout (✥ MONGU 15°16.159'S, 23°08.007'E). North of this is a vibrant, packed old town area with shops, a heaving market, a bus station and an army barracks; if you pass these, then ultimately you'll find a tar road north to Limulunga. West of the roundabout lies a small hill, upon which you'll find most of the government buildings. Beyond, on the other side of this hill, you drop down to the harbour, and to the road across the floodplain which leads to the Zambezi, Kalabo and Liuwa Plain.

Getting there and away Good tar roads link Mongu to Lusaka (638km) and Senanga (103km) and the new causeway to Kalabo to the northwest will also mean that Liuwa Plain National Park will become more accessible, but vehicular access to the north is seriously challenging.

By air Proflight flies twice weekly (on Wednesdays and Thursdays) between Lusaka and Mongu Airport (✥ AIRMON 15°15.227'S, 23°9.376'E). Chartering a plane, although possible (Livingstone or northern Kafue are closest), would be very expensive.

By bus Several buses link Lusaka to Mongu every day – expect a minibus to cost around K100 and a coach about K155. The bus station is beside the old market, while long-distance coaches stop behind the Catholic church on the main road.

Hitchhiking Hitching to Mongu along the Great West Road is possible for the determined. Hitching to get around the surrounding countryside is very slow and difficult – but it is how most of the local population travel.

Driving west to Sanduula on the Zambezi The Chinese have just completed a long causeway/bridge that crosses the floodplain between Mongu and Kalabo.

NYAMINYAMI AND THE MONGU–KALABO ROAD

Contracts signed in March 2002 started the construction of a 74km tar road from Mongu, via Kalabo, to the Angolan border which, it was envisaged, would completely open up wet-season access to impoverished areas west of the Zambezi and a new trade route into Angola.

The project planned to connect Mongu and Kalabo, and ultimately Lusaka, with Angola – spanning not only the Zambezi River, but also the width of the Zambezi floodplain. This entailed 35km of raised causeway above low-lying plains that are seasonally inundated when the river breaks its banks. Initially it was scheduled for completion in 2004, but exceptional flooding washed away part of the structure, prompting a major reassessment of the design. By then, funds for the project were starting to run seriously short, and a hydrologists' report suggested that the section of causeway east of the Zambezi River (from the Zambezi to the canal at Mongu) wasn't strong enough to support a road.

Despite these problems, the 22km section of tar road running from the western edge of the floodplain to Kalabo was eventually opened, but the rest of the original project was abandoned. Today, despite all the challenges, the road has been completed, including the bridge across the Zambezi (and is due to open officially in late spring 2016). Perhaps Nyaminyami, the old river god of the Zambezi Valley's Tonga people, has finally mellowed since the days of building Kariba Dam.

Until the road officially opens you may have to stop at the local police station and get a permit to drive on it, but this is free and easy to obtain. It has been a major project in difficult terrain with 26 bridges (see box, above). It'd be wise to ask around in Mongu about the road's current state before you leave, but if there are any temporary diversions expect them to be largely impassable when the plains are flooded, between about December and July. Even in the dry season, the sand can be very deep and troublesome – so a high-clearance 4x4 remains essential until the road is finished.

To get to this road, head west over the hill from the main Mongu roundabout, pass the post office, then turn left down towards the harbour (⊕ HARMON 15°16.293'S, 23°07.180'E). There you'll clearly see a road to the right dropping down onto the Barotse floodplain. Remember to fill up with fuel in Mongu before you leave; there are no fuel stations west of here.

The road heads roughly northwest, so it's difficult to get lost. About 14km from Mongu's harbour, you'll reach the village of Lealui (⊕ LEALUI 15°13.446'S, 23°1.077'E; page 476). Lealui itself is the location of the isolated summer palace of the Litunga, the Lozi king, and a centre for the Lozi administration. Visitors are advised to show courtesy and respect, even if it doesn't appear to be different from any other small African village.

A little over 10km northwest of Lealui, you'll reach the ferry across the Zambezi, at Sandaula (⊕ FERRY3 15°12.291'S, 22°55.297'E). This may have been superseded by the new road bridge across the Zambezi. See *Kalabo*, pages 477–8 for details of the route continuing to the west.

Driving north to Lukulu There's a good tarred road for 15km north of Mongu, basically as far as the Litunga's winter palace at Limulunga. Then there's nothing more than vanishing local tracks across the Barotse floodplains between there and

Lukulu. These are passable in the dry season – see *Lukulu*, pages 487–8 for directions – but otherwise consider driving to Lukulu on all-weather (albeit relatively poor) roads via Kaoma.

Getting around The Mongu police appear to be vigilant, and there are often roadblocks around town where they will check your vehicle and its papers. If you're driving, make sure that you're wearing your seatbelt and moving slowly. The taxi rank and bus station are located between the market and the Puma garage.

Driving Apart from the main tar roads to Lusaka, Senanga and the new causeway to Kalabo, most of the area's roads are little more than vehicle tracks, and they degenerate into patches of deep sand quite frequently. A 4x4 is essential here, even in the dry season, and the worst of these tracks will require almost constant low-range driving through long sections of Kalahari sand.

During the wet season, from around December to July, the whole area north of Ngonye Falls is subject to flooding. Then the Barotse floodplain becomes a large, shallow lake. Much of the population moves to higher ground to live, and boats are the only option for getting around. Don't even think about trying to drive anywhere off the tarred roads then. The new causeway does make it in theory easier to cross the floodplain, even in high water, and you can now drive year-round to villages such as Lealui (page 476) which could formerly only be reached by boat during the floods.

By boat For much of the year, boat transport has always been the best way to see the immediate area around Mongu, and used to be the only way if the flood was high. The causeway has changed this. The best way to find a suitable boat is to ask at the harbour office in Mongu.

For a few dollars you can hire a mokoro to take you out on the waterways, and – except at the end of the dry season – perhaps down towards Lealui and the main channel. Spend a few hours like this, on the water, and you will appreciate how most of the locals transport themselves around. You will see everything from people to household goods, supplies, live animals and even the occasional bicycle loaded onto boats and paddled or poled (punted) from place to place.

For rather more, there are two larger ferries with outboard motors that will take 20 or so people on longer journeys; once the floods start, there's typically at least one of these per day between Mongu and Kalabo. This may change now the causeway across the Barotse floodplain has been completed.

There is also a privately run postboat on the Zambezi that carries passengers, the mail and cargo, including the occasional vehicle – but note that ferrying a vehicle is likely to be a very expensive option.

Where to stay There's a choice of accommodation in Mongu, much of it of fairly poor quality. Both of the relatively large, old-style hotels are in dire need of refurbishment, leaving a gap filled by a rash of small, private guesthouses. These cater mainly to top local businesspeople, foreign aid workers and expats, so standards of accommodation and security among the best are reasonable, if nothing special. Note that price is seldom a useful guide to quality here – and as new places spring up they will often be better than the older establishments. Try to book accommodation in advance, too, as the better places are often full – especially around the time of the Kuomboka ceremony (pages 24–6). That said, many won't take reservations unless you pay at the time of booking.

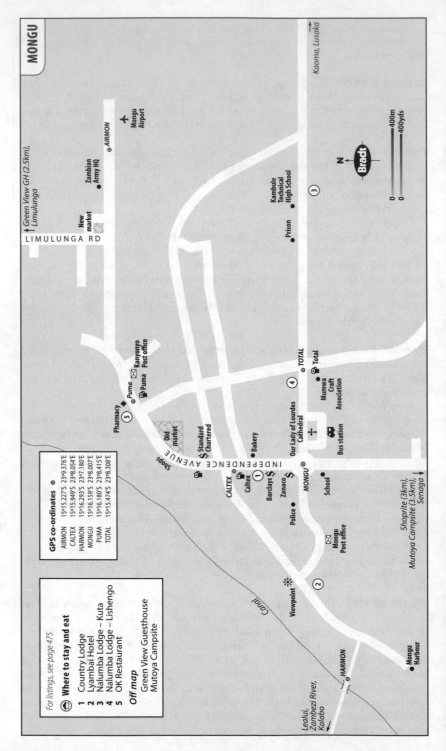

MONGU

For listings, see page 475

Where to stay and eat

1 Country Lodge
2 Lyambai Hotel
3 Nalumba Lodge – Kuta
4 Nalumba Lodge – Lishengo
5 OK Restaurant

Off map
Green View Guesthouse
Mutoya Campsite

GPS co-ordinates ⊕

AIRMON	15°15.227'S	23°9.376'E
CALTEX	15°15.949'S	23°8.054'E
HARMON	15°16.293'S	23°7.180'E
MONGU	15°16.159'S	23°8.007'E
PUMA	15°16.180'S	23°8.415'E
TOTAL	15°15.474'S	23°8.308'E

LIMULUNGA RD

↑ Green View GH (2.5km),
Limulunga

→ Kaoma, Lusaka

New market

Zambian Army HQ ⊕ AIRMON

Mongu Airport

Kambule Technical High School

Prison ●

③

N Bradt

0 ⊢ 400m
0 ⊢ 400yds

Kanyonyo Post office

Puma
⊞ Puma

Pharmacy ⊕
⑤

⊕ TOTAL
● Total

Mumwa Craft Association

④

Old market

⊞ Standard Chartered

● Bakery

Our Lady of Lourdes Cathedral ✝

🚌 Bus station

Shops

INDEPENDENCE AVENUE

⊞ CALTEX
● Caltex ①

Bardays ⊞

Zanaco ⊞

MONGU ⊕

● School

Police ●

Mongu Post office ⊠

Canal

Viewpoint ✳
②

Shoprite (3km),
Mutoya Campsite (3.5km),
Senaga →

Lealui,
Zambezi River,
Kalabo ←

⊕ HARMON

● Mongu Harbour

474

In the past, Mongu has had a bad reputation for theft, so it's wise to take maximum precautions against losing your belongings, even in the hotels. If you can't make it into town, but need to stay in the area, then it's better to ask at a village than to camp alone.

⌂ **Country Lodge** [map, page 474] (20 rooms) 3066 Independence Av; m 0977 222216, 0966 222216; www.countrylodgezambia. com. Close to Barclays Bank in the centre of town, this well-placed lodge was originally recommended by Sister Pat from Lukulu's Catholic mission. En-suite rooms have DSTV, Wi-Fi, fridge & AC, & the food, she tells us, is both good & plentiful if a little slow in arriving. Safe parking. **$–$$$**

⌂ **Nalumba Lodges** [map, page 474] (13 rooms) ☎0217 221199; ⊕ NALUMB 15°15.939'S, 23°09.118'E. Number 2 of 3 Nalumba Lodges in Mongu, this one is on the site of the old Crossroads Lodge, on the south side of Kaoma–Lusaka road, about 2km from the main roundabout. It has small but clean rooms – all with en-suite shower & flush toilet, TV, fridge, kettle, mosi nets & AC. There's a small dining room, & a pleasant bar in the courtyard with seating in individual gazebos. Parking is very secure behind an electric gate. **$–$$**

⌂ **Green View Guesthouse** (23 rooms, camping) Limulunga Rd; ☎0217 221029; m 0967 405551; e mongu@limagarden.com; www.limagarden.com. ⊕ GREENV 15°13.960'S, 23°8.721'E. One of the better options near Mongu, this small, quiet guesthouse is a 15-min drive from the Litunga's winter palace. To reach it head north on the tarred Limulunga Rd for about 2.5km, where there's a sign to the left, behind the New Apostolic Church. It's far enough

from town for security to be less of an issue. Enlargement in 2011 resulted in 16 new twin or dbl chalets, each en suite & with AC. The older twin rondavels, with a fridge, kettle, TV, fan & mosi nets, are also en suite. Camping is a further option, but facilities for campers are limited. *B/fast & dinner are available on request.* **$–$$** *exc b/fast; Camping K70 pp.*

⌂ **Lyambai Hotel** [map, page 474] (17 rooms) ☎0217 221138; lyambai@zamtel.zm. Mongu's oldest hotel, fairly near the harbour, has en-suite rooms laid out in 2 long rows across a courtyard. It's desperately in need of renovation, but the views from its cool courtyard make up for a lot. There's also a restaurant & bar, & secure parking. **$**

Å **Mutoya Campsite** m 0975 627320; e info@zam.co.za; www.zam.co.za. ⊕ MUTOYA 15°18.337'S, 23°08.900'E. About 3.5km south of the roundabout, there's a clearly signposted turning (⊕ TUMUTO 15°17.778'S, 23°08.870'E) to the west to this pleasant, well-kept campsite with a strong Christian foundation. You'll need a 4x4 for the steep, sandy access road, but once at the bottom it opens out into a series of grassy, level pitches, with fresh water from a borehole, electric hook-ups, & – higher up – clean ablution blocks. If you don't have your own tent, you might be able to use one of the pre-erected dome tents on site. The site shares its grounds with a school for orphaned children, for whom it doubles as a place to explore. *K40 pp.*

✗ **Where to eat** Some of the hotels have restaurants and others serve meals on request, or you could put together a picnic from Shoprite. For something a little different try the OK Restaurant.

Other practicalities There are three main **fuel** stations: Caltex just 400m north of the roundabout; Puma another kilometre further on, past the old market; and Total just 700m east of the roundabout.

For banks, there's an ATM at Zanaco beside the roundabout, and another at the adjacent Barclays; both are reasonably reliable. On the other side of the road, further up, is a Standard Chartered Bank. The main **post office** (⊕ POMONG 15°16.256'S, 23°07.566'E) is to the west, high on the hill above the harbour; it is also an agent for Western Union. The town also has an **internet** café opposite Barclays Bank.

Shopping Mongu is the obvious place in the Western Province to buy **supplies** and get organised. The best place to head for is the large and well-stocked Shoprite

(⊕ SHOPRT 15°17.186'S, 23°09.047'E; ⊕ *08.00–18.00 Mon–Fri, 08.00–17.00 Sat, 09.00–13.00 Sun & public holidays*), by far the biggest and best store in town. It is reached by heading about 3km south of town towards Senanga, then turning left (signposted to Lusaka along the M9) for around 0.8km.

The huge old **market** in town is a good place to buy locally produced fresh fruit and vegetables (and, I'm told, bread also).

For **crafts**, take the main road to Lusaka from the roundabout, and on the south side, just before the Total (⊕ TOTAL 15°16.180'S, 23°08.415'E), you will find the Mumwa Craft Association (📞 *0217 221263;* e *mundiakk@yahoo.com;* ⊕ *08.00–17.00 Mon–Sat, or by appointment*). This non-profit-making society was established in 1994 to improve the economic, social and cultural well-being of the local communities by representing a network of several hundred local producers throughout the Western Province. They concentrate on good basket weaving, as well as woodcarvings, pottery and metalwork. Items on sale vary according to the season but may include the large and very beautiful linen baskets that are woven using skills developed over the centuries by the Lozi people in making their fishing traps. You won't find better baskets supporting a more worthy cause, or at lower prices. During and after the rains, when many of the craftsmen gather here during the day, you can also watch them at work.

What to see and do Aside from wandering around the old market or visiting the craft association (above), there are no specific sights in Mongu. You may, though, like to visit the lively and very traditional **harbour** (⊕ HARMON 15°16.293'S, 23°07.180'E). The two main attractions, however – the Litunga's summer and winter palaces – are both excursions from town.

The greatest of Zambia's cultural festivals, the **Kuomboka** (pages 24–6), is the tradition of moving the Litunga, the Lozi king, plus his court and his people, away from the floodwaters and onto higher ground. If the rains have been good and the floodwaters are rising, this spectacular ceremony takes place around February or March, often on a Thursday, just before full moon. It involves a flotilla of boats for most of the day, plus an impromptu orchestra of local musicians and much celebration. Don't miss it if you are travelling in western Zambia at the time.

The Litunga's summer palace at Lealui
About 13km west of Mongu, amidst the floodplains, the Litunga's summer palace (⊕ LEALUI 15°13.637'S, 23°01.107'E) is set in a large grove of trees that is easily seen from the escarpment on which Mongu stands.

Don't expect a Western-style palace; this appears to be a normal small African village with thatched huts. However, it is not only the king's summer residence, but also the main Lozi administration centre. Visitors are warmly welcomed, though are strongly advised to show the utmost courtesy and respect to their hosts. Indeed, until very recently it was normal to introduce yourself to the Kuta (the traditional court) as a courtesy, especially if you planned to continue on to Liuwa. See page 477 for directions of how to get here from Mongu.

The Litunga's winter palace and the Nayuma Museum and Heritage Centre
(⊕ *08.00–17.00 Mon–Fri*) North of Mongu, next to the Litunga's main winter palace, this museum houses some interesting exhibits on the history and culture of the Lozi people, with a strong focus on conserving and promoting the region's heritage. A small craft shop sells some really beautiful basketwork from the area, at very reasonable prices.

To get here, take the tarred Limulunga Road north from Mongu's new market for around 15km, then turn left down a tarred side road opposite the water tower at the centre of Limulunga. Follow this round and after a kilometre or so you reach a barrier, with the museum on the left, and the Lozi palace on the right. This royal complex is all fairly grand and impressive, complete with keen security guards from about March to June, when the Litunga is in residence.

KALABO This small, rambling town by the Luanginga River is the gateway to Liuwa Plain National Park. The name is derived from the Lozi word *silambo*, meaning 'paddling stick'.

Coming from Mongu, you'll arrive at a T-junction where you turn right into a wide main street lined by grand old buildings with verandas, most in various states of decay. It's usually very quiet, though clearly the shopkeepers have active imaginations with the 'Just Imagine' and 'Hard Work Makes Dreams Come True' restaurants.

Continue down this main road to reach the **harbour**, where there is a small pontoon (⊕ HARKAL 14°59.248'S, 22°41.001'E) over the Luanginga.

Getting there and away Now that the long causeway and tarred road from Mongu is complete, Kalabo has become much easier to reach. Off the causeway, anywhere west of the Zambezi remains expedition territory at any time. 'Roads' here are usually just tracks in the Kalahari sand, which need days of low-range driving. They require not only a 4x4 (preferably several, in case of emergency), but also large quantities of fuel. This can be replenished only in Mongu, so long-range fuel tanks and lots of jerrycans are vital. See pages 95–101 for more advice – and note especially the points on higher fuel consumption and misleading milometer readings.

Water is also a problem, as it tends to seep through the Kalahari sand rather than forming pans on the surface. Hence no potable water can be relied upon, even in Kalabo, so if you're heading west, take some good containers and fill up in Mongu.

Kalabo has its own airstrip (⊕ KALAIR 14°59.501'S, 22°38.484'E), so it is possible – albeit very expensive – to charter a plane into the area.

Driving from Mongu via Sandaula See the directions for *Driving west to Sandaula on the Zambezi* on pages 471–2, for the route from Mongu to the pontoon across the Zambezi.

The Sandaula pontoon (⊕ FERRY3 15°12.291'S, 22°55.297'E; ☉ *06.00–18.00*) is large enough for three vehicles – although it will often leave with just one or two. During the dry season, when the Zambezi is confined within its banks, the crossing is only a hundred metres or so, and the ferry is about 27km from Mongu. Once the area is flooded, the pontoon ceases to operate.

From the pontoon, Kalabo (⊕ KALABO 14°59.820'S, 22°39.602'E) is about a 46km drive in the dry season, taking about 90 minutes when road conditions are good. The new tar road is now complete and drivers won't have to take the pontoon in the dry season, but check with the Park for latest information before travelling (e *liuwatourism@african-parks.org*). At the T-junction, turn right; it's then just 2.9km to the harbour, and the pontoon across the river to Liuwa Plain National Park.

Driving from Mongu via the Libonda pontoon In theory it should be possible in the dry season to cross the Zambezi higher up the river, at the Libonda pontoon – and then to head westwards, and slightly south, on small paths and tracks across the floodplains. However, we have reports that the pontoon is no longer operational, presumably put out of business by the new road.

15

If you do try this way, then you should certainly take a local guide (hitchhiker) to help you navigate – and you will see plenty of these throughout the area. You will pass men, women and children carrying everything from luggage to mattresses and supplies on their heads. Given the area's lack of transport, if you have room in your vehicle then you should offer lifts whenever possible.

Driving to Liuwa See *Getting there and away*, under *Liuwa Plain National Park*, page 482, for details.

Driving from Kalabo to Sitoti There is a track on the western side of the Zambezi between Kalabo and Sitoti, but it is thick sand with no fuel (or much else) on the way. You'd probably be wise to take local hitchhikers as guides. The route heads south and slightly west (average bearing of about 157°) from Kalabo to the Sitoti pontoon (page 469); aim for ⊕ TUSHAN 16°21.424'S, 23°16.668'E.

This is 164km as the heron flies, and a lot more on the ground. I haven't driven this route, but am reliably informed that it's about 12 hours of driving. If you were forced to do this, it would take much more time and fuel than going via Mongu and Senanga. So if you cross from Mongu west of the Zambezi during the wet season, bear in mind that this could be your only way out.

Other practicalities There is **no fuel** available in Kalabo – and although you can get the basics in the market or in local shops, you'd be well advised to buy all your **supplies** in Mongu before you arrive. There are, though, often people selling fish along the roadside, and there are a few general stores close to the harbour. There's also a basic **café** there – ideal if you have to wait for someone to fetch the pontoon for you! And if you've longer to spare, the **market** is well worth a visit in its own right.

Kalabo has a mission with a large **hospital** (⊕ HOSPKA 14°59.111'S, 22°40.654'E), and a basic government **resthouse**.

The **immigration** office is behind some of the shops near the harbour, on the left of the Luanginga pontoon.

Liuwa Plain National Park Tourism Centre Of vital importance to most visitors is the tourism centre for Liuwa Plain National Park, which is conveniently located on the left just before the harbour, next to the park's headquarters. This is where you get permits for Liuwa Plain National Park, book your campsites, and get directions for the park. It's also the place where you can organise a guide to accompany you, if required.

LIUWA PLAIN NATIONAL PARK (m *0977 158733, 0977 758603; reservations* e *liuwatourism@african-parks.org, information* e *liuwa@african-parks.org; www. african-parks.org. Park fees US$40 pp per day; camping US$15/7 adult/child/day. Guide fee US$20/day. ⊕ Self-drive 06.00–18.00 May/Jun–Dec)* Liuwa Plain is as wild and remote as virtually any park in Africa; at the right time of year, its game is also as good as most of the best. The cliché 'best-kept secret' is applied with nauseating frequency to many places in Africa by copywriters who can't think of anything original; this is perhaps one of the few places that would deserve it.

Liuwa Plain has long been a very special place. It was declared a 'game reserve' as early as the 19th century by the king of Barotseland, and subsequently administered by the Litunga, or Lozi king. Traditionally, the park was the Litunga's private hunting ground, and the people whose villages were located around the land were charged with looking after the animals for him. Then in 1972 it became a national park, and its management was taken over by central government. Although the local people retained utilisation rights of the park, grazing their animals, fishing in the rivers and pools, and harvesting plants for use in traditional crafts, their cultural connection with the land was broken, and poaching became rife. It was not until 2003, when the park was taken over by African Parks and the link with the Litunga reinstated, that the villagers regained stewardship. Now, in addition to their utilisation rights, they run campsites for visitors, and once more have an interest in the preservation of the wildlife.

The word *liuwa* means 'plain' in the local Lozi language. Legend relates how one Litunga planted his walking stick here on the plain, where it grew into a large *mutata* tree. The tree in question can still be seen from the track which leads from Minde to Luula: after leaving the first tree belt, look in the distance on your left side when you are halfway to the next tree belt.

Liuwa Plain is certainly the most fascinating park in the region, but getting here almost always requires an expedition. For this reason, visitor numbers are tiny but increasing due to improved facilities and infrastructure: in 2014 fewer than 800 visitors entered the park. Yet even these figures dwarf those in some of the previous years: only 50 tourists visited in the whole of 2000.

Geography Although a network of sand game-viewing tracks has been established in the 3,662km² park, it remains largely untouched. Most of it is a vast honey-coloured grass plain, stretching about 70km long and 30km wide. Within this there's just the occasional open pan, cluster of raffia palms, or small tree-island interrupting the flatness. In places you can look 360° around you and see nothing but a flat expanse. The environment is unlike any other park in Zambia – the most similar places are probably Katavi, in western Tanzania, and, possibly, the much smaller Kazuma Pan in Zimbabwe.

Large areas of this plain are totally flooded from around December to April, with the waters rising in the northwest and spreading southeastwards. It's this flooding which drives the wildebeest migration, or 'gathering', as the herds move in search of new, fresh grazing.

In the centre, and especially the southern side, of this enormous grassy plain, you'll find a scattering of open pans, many of which hold their water well into the dry season. These are well worth investigating. Although in the dry season some will appear almost lifeless, others will have great concentrations of birds or antelope.

Flora and fauna

Flora Liuwa Plain's main plant life, on first glance, appears to be vast areas of grasslands, within which species like *Vossia cuspidate* and *Echinocloa stagnina* are amongst the most important for the herds of grazing herbivores. On tree-islands, and around the edges of the plain, you'll find the small false mopane, or copalwood (*Guibourtia coleosperma*); the silver cluster-leaf (*Terminalia sericea*), which is so typical of the Kalahari; stands of Zambezi teak (*Baikiaea plurijuga*) and weeping wattle (*Peltophorum africanum*), while around the pans are occasional stands of palms including the odd tall *Hyphaene*.

Mammals and reptiles As is common in vast open areas, many of Liuwa's larger mammals tend to group together into great herds when on the plain – and these are much of the park's attraction. The 1991 wildlife census estimated populations at 30,000 blue wildebeest, 8,000 tsessebe, 1,000 zebra and 10,000 other large mammals which would have included herds of buffalo, red lechwe, eland, Lichtenstein's

African Parks (*www.african-parks.org*) was founded by a group of businesspeople and conservationists who recognised that African governments had limited resources to pay for conservation or the social development which is needed to accompany it. Their first major venture required about US$15 million to buy the land for, and completely redevelop, Marakele National Park, in South Africa's Waterberg Mountain – in an amazingly short time.

Backed by finance and expertise from a multi-millionaire Dutch businessman, the late Paul Fentener van Vlissingen, that first project was a huge success. Van Vlissingen's family own the multi-national SHV – one of the Netherlands' largest companies. (It controls numerous companies worldwide, including the Makro chain of wholesale stores.)

African Parks, now fully based in South Africa, is concerned with the long-term sustainability of some of Africa's national parks by forming agreements with governments to manage and finance national parks. They aim to work with the inclusion of local communities, to safeguard the flora and fauna and to relieve local poverty. Ultimately, they aim to make their parks into sustainable, self-financing business units. However, they are willing to provide substantial funds to 'kick start' failing parks and areas – and also act as a channel for grants received for this from other donors.

The initial lease agreement for Liuwa Plain National Park was finally signed in Lusaka on 31 May 2004. The event was attended by the Litunga, the Ngambela, other representatives from the Barotse Royal Establishment, the minister of tourism, ZAWA representatives and the ambassadors of the USA and Netherlands. This agreement extends to 2024, with a possibility of renewal for a further 20 years if all partners agree.

Initially, African Parks committed US$2 million to Liuwa Plain over a five-year period, but a total of US$9 million has been invested since 2004. Signs that poaching was coming under control (for example, wildebeest meat is no longer available in the local markets) have been swift to follow.

Communities have benefitted too. African Parks have built wells, clinics, campsites, school classrooms and computer labs, and teachers' housing. They've established conservation clubs focusing on the environment and employment; and sponsor children to secondary school. They also contribute monthly payments to Community Development Funds linked to poaching levels, rewarding reductions.

Now, at last, the picture for the park's wildlife and communities is beginning to look more positive.

hartebeest and roan antelope as well as assorted pairs of reedbuck and the delightful, diminutive oribi which are so common here.

Later surveys suggested that game numbers had declined by around a third, with buffalo, eland, Lichtenstein's hartebeest and roan antelope possibly wiped out completely. However, with more active protection, numbers are building up again; the 2011 count revealed 42,700 wildebeest, around 4,400 zebra and increasing populations of all herbivore species. Both roan antelope and wild dogs have returned to the park, and the population of red lechwe is recovering well. Eland and buffalo have been re-introduced, and the scouts say that sitatunga are still found in some of the rivers on the edge of the park.

The largest herds currently seen in the park are the blue wildebeest which mass here in their thousands during the rains. Amongst them, you'll find zebra and tsessebe. Though widely regarded as a 'migration', some suggest that it may in fact just be a gathering on the plain of all the game that has previously been in the surrounding bush, rather than an actual migration from, say, Angola. Regardless, if you can catch it at the right time, it's a stunning sight: flat, open plain with animals as far as the eye can see.

That said, I think it's quite wrong to concentrate on the sights in November and, in effect, dismiss the rest of the year. I last visited for a few days in the month of September which yielded plenty of wildebeest on the plain, including one herd of over a thousand; several smaller herds of zebra, tsessebe and red lechwe, one of the last numbering over 120 individuals; and some of the most spectacular birding that I'd ever seen in southern Africa.

Predators have also been well represented in Liuwa, with lion, leopard, cheetah, wild dog and hyena all occurring here. By 2007 there was just one remaining lioness, popularly known as Lady Liuwa, whose story of survival was made famous by a National Geographic documentary in 2010. Two male lions had been brought in to join her in 2009. They moved on to Angola, where one was killed. The other, Nakawa, returned to Liuwa. In 2011, two females were reintroduced from Kafue National Park only for one of them to die in a snare. The surviving lioness, Sepo, headed to Angola but was recaptured and airlifted back to Liuwa. There, she bonded with Lady, who took the young lioness under her wing and they have remained together ever since. Nakawa successfully mated with Sepo and in December 2013, three cubs were born, a male and two females. In unexplained circumstances, their father was found dead the following September believed to have been poisoned. In 2015, there were several sightings of an unknown lion in the park, causing much excitement.

Wild dogs were recovering in the park, with two different packs breeding successfully here although sightings are very erratic and in late 2014 it was thought that there were none remaining, probably due to their vast home ranges. However, approximately 20 wild dogs were seen at Makalabumbu in the northeast of the park in mid 2015. Leopard occur within the national park, though the surrounding forest is a better habitat for them than the plain itself. Unusually, hyenas are the apex predators here, rather than scavengers, and are fairly commonly seen: some 700 skulk around these plains, and are cheeky enough to come to the edge of your firelight's glow.

With sharp eyes you're also likely to spot smaller curious omnivores like side-striped jackal, troops of banded mongooses, and possibly porcupines. I've had reports of some particularly large snakes living here – though (thankfully) been unable to verify these.

Birds Liuwa boasts a total of about 334 bird species which, even when I visited during a dry month like September, were amazing: spectacular groups of crowned cranes often numbered several hundred birds; wattled cranes, so endangered in many places, thrive here with numerous pairs and smaller groups of up to 30 individuals; while one particular flock of pelicans included several hundred birds. I saw all of these in just a few days in early September – and so when it rains, the park's birding must be quite unbelievable.

Then, when the pans fill up, open-billed, yellow-billed, marabou and saddle-billed storks arrive, with spoonbills, grey herons, egrets, three-banded and lots of blacksmith's plovers, pygmy and spur-winged geese, and many other waterbirds. Slaty egrets are seen in groups, a rare occurrence elsewhere.

The late Bob Stjernstedt, a Zambian birding expert, commented that Liuwa is relatively rarely visited, and so many more birds are sure to be added to this list. Secretary birds and Denham's and white-bellied bustards are common; and the park is famous for thousands of the migrant black-winged pratincoles, a finely-marked swift-like bird which is rare further east. Other 'specials' here include the pink-billed and clapper larks, rosy-breasted longclaw, swamp boubou, long-tailed widow, sharp-tailed starling and white-cheeked bee-eater. The plain is also a great area for raptors from the greater kestrel to bateleur and martial eagles, fish eagles and palmnut vultures. Pel's fishing owl is found along the rivers, the Luanginga to the south and the Luambimba to the north.

When to go With the exception of guided fly-in trips, the park is open to independent visitors only between May/June and December, depending on the rains: if you want to travel during May/June, contact the park beforehand to check on conditions and opening dates. For many people, Liuwa is at its best during November, when the gathering of wildebeest on the plains reaches its peak. That said, the park is worth visiting whenever you can get there – there's always some amazing wildlife to be seen!

Before you visit it's important to understand the weather and the usual game movements in the park.

From **January to about May**, a large area of the plain is covered in shallow water, and all the pans in the south of the park are full. Although the park is closed to visitors until mid April, these conditions are perfect for the large herds of herbivores which gather there, and the large numbers of birds which also arrive. However, **around June/July** the plains dry up, the waters recede northwards, and gradually the herds move that way also. They desert the waterholes of the southern side of the plain, and move back northwest, eventually melting back into the woodlands which surround the park. Plenty of resident wildlife remains, relying on a scattering of pans which retain their water for most of the year.

From **August to October** the herds start drifting southwards again. At first, in September, you'll find just a few herds, typically just a few hundred wildebeest, venturing south onto the northern areas of the plain – but gradually as the rains approach these increase in number and move further south into the park.

In **November and December** the first rains are falling, and the plains are teeming with game, including young animals, for this is also the calving period. November is classically the best time to visit the park – a balance between catching the best of the game, and ensuring that you can get out rather than getting stuck.

Getting there and away Until recently, driving yourself was the only means of exploring Liuwa Plain, but a couple of interesting options are now available. If you'd like to explore independently, you can hire a vehicle with driver from African Parks (*US$166/day including rescue plus driver, fuel extra*). They will also arrange transfers from Kalabo airport (*US$10 pp*) or Mongu (*US$170 per vehicle dry season; US$360–440 per boat depending on load wet season*). The only camp in the park, Matamanene, now offers 4- and 5-day packages including return flights to Kalabo from late April–mid June and late October–mid December – see page 486.

Self driving For independent drivers (4x4 only), access to the park is technically from May/June to 15 December only; either side of this and you would stand a strong chance of getting completely stuck in deep mud. In May/June, however, it's important to check the state of the Zambezi River well in advance, as if this is too

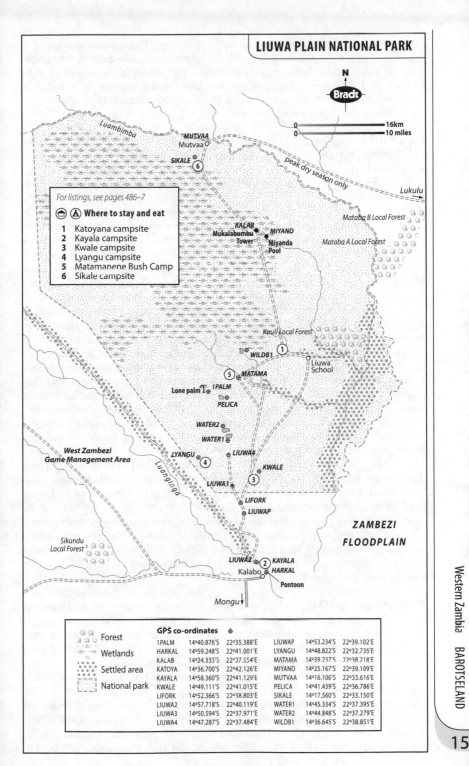

LIUWA PLAIN NATIONAL PARK

N

Bradt

0 ——————— 16km
0 ——————— 10 miles

Luambimbu

MUTVAA
Mutvaa

SIKALE ⊕
6

peak dry season only

Lukulu

Mataba B Local Forest

For listings, see pages 486–7

🏠 Ⓐ Where to stay and eat

1 Katoyana campsite
2 Kayala campsite
3 Kwale campsite
4 Lyangu campsite
5 Matamanene Bush Camp
6 Sikale campsite

KALAB
Mukalabumbu
Tower

MIYAND
Miyanda
Pool

Mataba A Local Forest

Kuuli Local Forest

WILDB1 ⊕ 1
5 MATAMA

Liuwa
School

Lone palm 🌴 1PALM ⊕
⊕ PELICA

WATER2 ⊕
WATER1 ⊕

LYANGU ⊕ ⊕ LIUWA4
4 3 KWALE

**West Zambezi
Game Management Area**

Luanginga

LIUWA3 ⊕

⊕ LIFORK
⊕ LIUWAP

**ZAMBEZI
FLOODPLAIN**

*Sikundu
Local Forest*

LIUWA2 ⊕ 2 KAYALA
Kalabo ⊕ HARKAL

Pontoon

Mongu↓

🌿 Forest
〰️ Wetlands
▓ Settled area
☐ National park

GPS co-ordinates ⊕				
1PALM	14°40.876'S	22°35.388'E	LIUWAP	14°53.234'S	22°39.102'E
HARKAL	14°59.248'S	22°41.001'E	LYANGU	14°48.822'S	22°32.735'E
KALAB	14°24.335'S	22°37.554'E	MATAMA	14°39.237'S	22°38.218'E
KATOYA	14°36.700'S	22°42.126'E	MIYAND	14°25.167'S	22°39.109'E
KAYALA	14°58.360'S	22°41.129'E	MUTVAA	14°16.106'S	22°33.616'E
KWALE	14°49.111'S	22°41.015'E	PELICA	14°41.439'S	22°36.786'E
LIFORK	14°52.366'S	22°38.803'E	SIKALE	14°17.560'S	22°33.150'E
LIUWA2	14°57.718'S	22°40.119'E	WATER1	14°45.334'S	22°37.395'E
LIUWA3	14°50.594'S	22°37.971'E	WATER2	14°44.848'S	22°37.279'E
LIUWA4	14°47.287'S	22°37.484'E	WILDB1	14°36.645'S	22°38.851'E

high, then it cannot be crossed. In some years it is late July before the crossing is possible. Contact the Park for information if you plan to come early in the season. You will also need to check whether a trailer is permitted: this was under review because of the environmental damage they cause and a decision is expected in 2016. A GPS is essential – and indeed may soon be mandatory. Note that there is no mobile phone signal within the park.

From Kalabo First head to the tourism centre on the 'harbour' (✣ HARKAL 14°59.248'S, 22°41.001'E) to get your permits, then take the pontoon across the Luanginga River.

From the pontoon, there are multiple tracks heading to and around the park; it's very confusing. You should head for route markers ✣ LIUWA1 14°59.044'S, 22°40.900'E, which you'll pass after barely 500m, and then ✣ LIUWA2 14°57.718'S, 22°40.119'E, which is a further 3km away. From here, take the right track. Beneath you is deep Kalahari sand, and the driving is a very steady, slow plod in low-range third or fourth gear, with an average speed of about 15km/h. There are a few small villages, but little game along the early part of the drive, although here and there lilac-breasted rollers brighten up the tops of trees along the roadside with dazzling flashes of blue as they fly.

There's no 'official' park entrance, though there used to be a signboard at ✣ LIUWAP 14°53.234'S, 22°39.102'E. One way into the park is to head about 13km north and slightly west of the pontoon. Shortly afterwards there is a small fork in the track at ✣ LIFORK 14°52.366'S, 22°38.803'E, from which both branches continue into the park. The right-hand track continues all the way to Matamanene Camp – and given the higher level of traffic that is likely to travel this way, this might be the best one to follow. However, on my last visit I took the left branch, which continues towards waypoint ✣ LIUWA3 14°50.594'S, 22°37.971'E.

As you get further into the park the trees start to spread out, grouping themselves into small, slightly raised islands, surrounded by a sea of knee-to-thigh-deep golden grass. Carry on for a further 10km or so after ✣ LIUWAP to ✣ LIUWA4 14°47.287'S, 22°37.484'E, by which time you're basically out of the trees, and onto the southern edge of the plain. Here, the track into the park starts to become much less distinct – and ultimately vanishes. (If you're coming back out of the park, then head for this point to pick up the track out.)

Whichever fork you take, you should expect 2 or 3 hours of rough, sandy driving after you leave the pontoon before you are well into the park. The good news is that although getting into the park is a slow slog through deep sand, most of the tracks within the park are generally much firmer, easier and more pleasant to drive. Do keep to these tracks – and enjoy!

North and east to Lukulu While almost all visitors to Liuwa enter and leave via Kalabo, it is nevertheless possible in the peak of the dry season to drive out of the north of the park, crossing the Luambimba River before turning east towards Lukulu. Note that it can't be done in reverse, since both entry permits and campsite bookings for the national park can be organised only at Kalabo.

If you're considering this route, you'll need at least one self-contained 4x4 vehicle (and preferably two), and the services of a local guide (ask at Sikale campsite) in order to negotiate the Luambimba River, since it's a tortuous route that changes according to the level of the river and the time of year. A GPS is also essential.

From Sikale (✣ SIKALE 14°17.933'S, 22°33.226'E), head due north to Mutvaa village (✣ MUTVAA 14°16.106'S, 22°33.616'E). Just after the village, turn right at

✦ MUTVA2 14°15.884'S, 22°33.437'E onto a narrow track through the trees, emerging after 0.5km back on to the plain. Shortly after this, at ✦ MUTVA3 14°15.761'S, 22°33.655'E, take the left fork towards the woodland, following a sandy track with the trees on your right. At ✦ LUAMBI 14°15.524'S, 22°33.842'E, descend through the trees to fiddle your way through deep sand across a series of channels that make up the Luambimba River. At ✦ LUAMB2 14°15.380'S, 22°34.068'E, emerge from the wood and cross to two wooden stakes; go left, keeping the stakes on your right, into more woods. At ✦ LUAMB3 14°15.027'S, 22°34.322'E, there's a junction; turn right here, still in the woodland, on to a good track – well used by oxcarts – with the plain on your right. About 10km from Sikale (40 minutes' drive), or 4.6km from the river, you'll come to the village of Silange (✦ SILANG 14°15.201'S, 22°35.951'E). Bear left into the woodland once more, then follow this track eastwards for close on 77km to the Zambezi River, opposite Lukulu (✦ LUKZAM 14°22.410'S, 23°13.933'E). For details of crossing the river, see page 490. Approaching the river, the woodlands thin out, the number of villages increases, and isolated fan palms dot the plains. Significant landmarks along the way include:

✦ TOLUK1 14°14.166'S, 22°43.125'E	Village on right; bear left just after village, keeping in woodland
✦ TOLUK2 14°14.896'S, 22°46.927'E	Take right fork
✦ TOLUK3 14°15.130'S, 22°47.949'E	Continue straight on at crossroads in small village, across a riverbed, then into woodland
✦ TOLUK4 14°16.912'S, 23°00.060'E	Track diverts around a pool then returns on other side across the plain, keeping village on right
✦ TOLUK5 14°19.045'S, 23°03.899'E	Take left fork

Getting around The only means to explore the park, unless you're on an organised safari (page 482), is by private 4x4. (For local vehicle hire, see *Getting there and away*, pages 69–70) Game-drive loops have been designated for independent visitors, who are provided with a simple map of the park at the tourism centre in Kalabo. Staff here can advise on getting around the park, too. A 30km/h speed limit is largely self-policing; you'd rarely be in a position to drive faster than this anyway.

There's no real need to take a scout as a guide – provided that you're fully equipped with a reliable GPS and have a back-up plan in case of an emergency (see *Safety Precautions*, below). However, if you do take a guide (*US$20 per day, inc food*), then you may learn quite a bit from him or her, as well as helping the park with a valuable extra source of employment. The scout also carries a radio that can be used to communicate with the park headquarters in case of emergency.

Safety precautions A GPS system is essential for anyone planning to visit the park as landmarks are few and the tall grass can obscure views. Early in the season it's essential to have netting on your vehicle to stop grass seeds which will clog up your radiator and may combust (see *Driving through high grass*, on page 99). It's also wise in a park that's this remote to travel in convoy, with a reliable satphone in case of emergency bearing in mind the lack of available mobile phone signals.

Should an emergency arise, African Parks may be able to help, either by supplying fuel (*K1,500/litre surcharge*), or with the rescue of a vehicle (*US$215 exc fuel*). Do note, however, that availability of fuel cannot be relied on; this is absolutely a last resort.

Where to stay

Several campsites have been established as a joint venture between the community and African Parks, thus making the park accessible if you are in a position to drive yourself in a small expedition. Remember, though, that – aside from water and firewood – you must be totally self-sufficient.

Over the years, attempts to set up permanent camps in Liuwa, had all failed; it's just too remote. However, in May 2015, Norman Carr Safaris began operating a lodge from Matamanene Camp, formerly run by African Parks. This is an interim measure until NCS' new luxury camp opens late in 2016 or early 2017, which promises to be an exciting development for the park. Norman Carr Safaris are also working in conjunction with Robin Pope to guide seasonal walking trips out of Matamanene Camp and with Ed Selfe (www.edwardselfephotography.com), a wildlife and photographic guide, on safaris with an emphasis on photography: the park's endless plains, lily-strewn ponds and prolific wildlife make this a photographer's dream.

With the advent of flights between Lusaka and Mongu in 2011, access to this area has improved.

Matamanene Bush Camp [map, page 483] (5 tents) \0216 246015; e bookings@ normancarrsafaris.com; www.normancarrsafaris. com. ✛ MATAMA 14°39.272'S, 22°38.188'E. Visible for its radio mast from some distance across the plains, Matamanene used to be a fully equipped self-catering camp but was transformed in early 2015 into a comfortable & stylish tented camp (*max 8 guests*). At certain times of the year, it is used exclusively for walking safaris guided by Robin Pope or photography safaris with Ed Selfe, operating on set departures during Apr–Jun, & later in Nov & Dec. At the edge of woodland overlooking the plain are en-suite Meru tents under a canvas fly sheet. They're not excessively luxurious but have all you need including en-suite shower rooms. A large central tent shelters a relaxing lounge area, so relaxing even the lion cubs have been seen dozing & playing on the sofas. The dining area is adjacent to the lounge & meals are a delight, with well-presented, inventive dishes.

The camp is adjacent to the base camp of the Liuwa Carnivore Project, a joint research effort by African Parks & the Zambian Carnivore Programme (ZCP) that focuses on wild dog, cheetah, lion & hyena within the park & their main prey, the numerous wildebeest. Activities at Matamanene include an evening presentation by a ZCP researcher & an afternoon accompanying the researchers in their work, tracking the carnivores &/or the wildebeest. This shouldn't be missed – it provides a fascinating insight into the conservation work that goes on behind the scenes of one of Africa's wildest parks. Other activities inc game drives & guided walks across the plains. *Standard 4/5 night FBA packages from US$4,640/5,250 pp minimum 3 people per departure, inc return flights from Lusaka to Kalabo, road transfers to & from Kalabo airport, game-viewing activities, most drinks, laundry & service charge. 5-night specialist walking safaris with Robin Pope Safaris (pages 264–5) from US$5,500 pp sharing; 4-day guided photographic safaris with Ed Selfe from US$4,400 pp sharing plus US$1,000 flights from/to Lusaka.* **LLLLL**

Campsites (m *0977758603*; e *liuwatourism@african-parks.org*; *US$15 pp*) There are four community campsites around the park, three of them within a 15km radius of Matamanene Camp, along the wildebeest migration route, and the fourth in the north of the park. A fifth site, Kayala, is located 2km from Kalabo, south of the park entrance. Note that the camping fee goes to the Liuwa Community Development Fund, administered by African Parks and the area chiefs. Some of this goes towards running the camp; the rest is used for community projects such as schools and teachers' housing.

No more than five vehicles can be accommodated on each site at any one time. Each campsite has five pitches with a maximum of four people allowed per pitch.

With the exception of Sikale, where facilities are more basic, each of the sites has two (cold) showers, two flush toilets, a washbasin and water from a well (not recommended for drinking unless treated). You're not allowed to collect firewood in the park, but it's supplied for a small fee by the attendant at each campsite; better still, bring your own fuel.

It is sometimes possible to arrange with the campsite attendant to be shown a range of local crafts, or for traditional dances to take place at the campsites or to be invited to a nearby village. Similarly, for those interested in fishing, traditional techniques can be demonstrated or even taught, while other options may include boat trips or guided walks, the latter with an armed scout.

Ă Kayala [map, page 483] ⊕ KAYALA 14°58.360'S, 22°41.129'E. Opened in 2010, Kayala is just 2km north of Kalabo, so ideally placed for those arriving later in the day or travelling with a trailer or caravan.

Ă Kwale [map, page 483] ⊕ KWALE 14°49.111'S, 22°41.015'E. Situated in the southeast of the park, 19km (1hr) from Kalabo, Kwale is a shady site bordering open grassland. Buffalo are seen here throughout the year & the wildlife is at its best from the end of Oct.

Ă Lyangu [map, page 483] ⊕ LYANGU 14°46.822'S, 22°32.735'E. 26.4km (1½hrs) from Kalabo, in the southwest of the park, this is a woodland site with plenty of indigenous flora. It is within easy distance of the Lone Palm & several self-drive loops affording excellent birding & game viewing.

Ă Katoyana [map, page 483] ⊕ KATOYA 14°36.700'S, 22°42.126'E. With a central location about 42km (2½hrs) from Kalabo, Katoyana occupies a peaceful wooded site on the edge of the plain, not far from Liuwa School. The eastern area of the park is easily accessible from here. Hyenas den nearby.

Ă Sikale [map, page 483] ⊕ SIKALE 14°17.560'S, 22°33.150'E. Just 78km (3½hrs) from Kalabo, the most isolated of the park's campsites – & consequently less frequented, Sikale is in a wooded glade overlooking the plain at the northern edge of the park, close to the route taken by local fishermen as they return with their evening catch. Immaculately maintained, it has a long-drop toilet & 2 washing enclosures, with water drawn from a waterhole & heated by the camp attendant.

Places to visit Liuwa is all about exploring on your own, although there are a few spots worth noting, some of which are highlighted below. Wherever you go, it's important to stick to the existing roads; the vegetation is extremely fragile and easily damaged. Note, too, that drivers found off road could well incur a fine.

- ⊕ WATER1 14°45.334'S, 22°37.395'E This great waterhole seemed to be a magnet for cranes, with a huge flock of crowned cranes always around it, augmented by parties of wattled cranes.
- ⊕ WATER2 14°44.848'S, 22°37.279'E Another lovely spot which was generally quieter, though did seem to be visited daily by a herd of red lechwe.
- ⊕ 1PALM 14°40.876'S, 22°35.388'E This is the spot known as 'Lone Palm', for obvious reasons. There's also a huge waterhole here where the general birding was excellent.
- ⊕ MIYAND14°25.167'S, 22°39.109'E Miyanda Pool, one of the park's larger pools, close to the Mukalabumbu Tower. Even when devoid of water in mid October, a thousand or so wildebeest formed a cordon around the lake, interspersed with up to a hundred zebra, numerous waders, and a fair few scavengers – vultures and marabou storks – anticipating their dinner.

LUKULU The riverside town of Lukulu is the main town in the district, with a collection of government and local council offices in the boma, or central area.

Supplies of **fuel**, from a drum rather than a pump, are both expensive and not terribly reliable, although at least the quality is considered to be acceptable. As always in outlying areas, you'd be wise not to run your tank too low.

The town, with its primary school, two high schools and a district hospital (now with very limited facilities), was founded as a Catholic mission, and remains typical of rural Zambia; visitors – especially those with fair skins – are something of a novelty. It has a public water pumping and distribution system, which means running (drinkable) water most of the time, but despite the presence of a ZESCO plant (Zambia's electricity supply company), supplies of electricity are erratic. Lukulu is also notable for having a **post office**, but no vehicle, so post to or from Lukulu is often transported by one of the Catholic nuns who work at the mission!

Getting there and away
There are good all-weather roads linking Lukulu (⊕ SANCTA 14°22.749'S, 23°14.236'E) with Kaoma, which is just off the Lusaka–Mongu road, Kabompo and Zambezi. Despite the proximity of Mongu, the route between the two towns is nothing but a series of inter-village footpaths

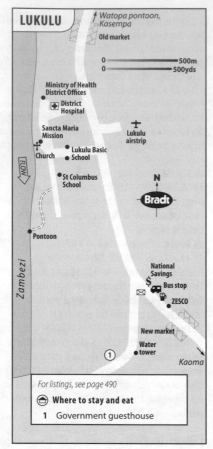

across the Barotse floodplain; it is usually faster to travel via Kaoma. There are no reliable roads on the west side of the Zambezi, though crossing the river and finding a route through to Liuwa Plain is possible in the height of the dry season.

From Mongu across the Barotse floodplain
By far the quickest and best route to Lukulu starts near the Kaoma turn-off, on the Lusaka–Mongu road. However, if it is well into the dry season, then there is another possibility described here: heading cross country across the floodplains.

Leaving Mongu past the new market, the tar ends after the shops at Limulunga (⊕ LIMULU 15°7.769'S, 23°8.635'E) and shortly the track forks. Head down the hill, towards the small river. Fording the first shallow channel of this, take a hard right onto a motorable track and follow this. There are lots of people down here, and if you can pick up a hitchhiker to guide you, then do so. You'll probably give lifts to several before the day is out!

As you head north the tracks split and fork, getting smaller all the time, until about midway to Lukulu. Then there appear to be no good tracks. However, gradually, as you continue, they get clearer again as you approach Lukulu. Think about it and you'll realise that they are all made by the local people, travelling from village to village, and (crucially) to their nearest town – so they radiate out from the towns. This is the typical pattern made by the smallest thoroughfares in most rural areas.

There's little point my trying to describe the precise route here, as every vehicle will end up on a slightly different track – which is half the fun! Instead I'll list a few waypoints, south to north, so that those travelling with a GPS can keep track that they're heading roughly in the right general direction:

- ✪ NANGIL 14°52.659'S, 23°4.478'E Nangili School where an engaging headteacher presides over about 350 children, from grades one to nine.
- ✪ AIRNGU 14°36.687'S, 23°6.977'E Ngulwana Airstrip, which is occasionally used by fishermen coming on private trips up to this corner of the Zambezi.
- ✪ KAWYA 14°28.827'S, 23°13.999'E Near the school at Kawaya. If coming south towards Mongu, this point marks where you deviate from the track to Mbanga, turning right down a steep bank. Coming north, you join a better track here.
- ✪ TUMONG 14°24.515'S, 23°15.588'E Where the bush track from Mongu/Mbanga meets the reasonable Kaoma–Lukulu road.
- ✪ SANCTA 14°22.749'S, 23°14.236'E The Sancta Maria Mission at Lukulu.

The countryside is lovely, with open fields and plenty of patches of various interesting palm trees. You'll pass through a variety of tiny villages and settlements – mostly subsistence farming of rice and maize. On very rural routes like this it's important that you give lifts to other travellers; they're often poor people for whom there probably isn't any other form of transport. Conveniently, they'll often be able to direct you to the nearest town, too, making the second half of your journey much easier than the first. It's about 99km as the stork flies between Mongu and Lukulu, and going over the floodplains will take you about 5 to 6 hours.

From Kaoma to Lukulu The bumpy gravel road between Kaoma and Lukulu offers year-round access to the town. When the Barotse Plains are flooded, it is also the only access route for vehicles from Mongu, which must head east to Kaoma along the tar road, then northwest to Lukulu; the alternative is to go by boat.

Buses ply between Kaoma and Lukulu a couple of times a week. VSO worker Karun Thanjavur described the road as 'an axle breaker … the buses creak and groan from abuse' and that probably still rings true. She advised travellers coming this way on public transport to travel with a good stock of food and water (at least for two days), and a sleeping bag (with mosquito net/coils), etc – just in case the bus breaks down.

From Lukulu to Kasempa Heading north-northwest you pass the school and then the old market before leaving town. This is a reasonable gravel road for which a high-clearance 4x4 would be wise in the rains – but otherwise it is a main artery by local standards on which you can reach 50–60km/h. Traffic is light, primarily oxcarts, as the road undulates past a mix of bush and settlements, with plenty of mango trees and cassava crops being grown.

It's about 63km to the Watopa pontoon (✪ WATOPA 14°02.338'S, 23°37.744'E), where there are a few small shops. If you were to follow the road southeast from the ferry you'd get back to meet the road to Kaoma. For Kasempa, however, take the pontoon across the Kabompo River and follow the similarly good gravel road for almost 22km, heading slightly east of north until you come to a T-junction with the east–west M8. This is Mumbeji (✪ MUMBEJ 13°51.653'S, 23°40.327'E), notable only for a range of small stalls and grocery shops with names such as 'God's Chance' and the 'Work like a Slave'.

From here the good all-weather M8 gravel road (50–60km/h when dry!) goes west to the town of Zambezi (⊕ ZAMBEZ 13°32.262'S, 23°06.158'E), and east about 67km to Kabompo (⊕ KABOMP 13°35.610'S, 24°12.125'E). Although there has clearly been some logging here, much of this road goes through thick woodland with very few settlements.

Without your own vehicle, the only means of public transport around these areas are private local 4x4s, assorted lorries and vans. The charge varies (depending whether you wish to ride in the cab or in the open back, braving the elements) but you can get from Lukulu to Watopa or Kabompo, for example, for about US$10/ K75. Some drivers will inevitably charge more if you are fair-skinned, as you are perceived to be a wealthy *makuwa* (white person). On average, this is probably a fair assumption – so pay and smile, and don't complain!

From the west There is a pontoon crossing at Lukulu, but it's by no means regular, and there are no real roads on the other side – just a series of paths that link the small villages there.

Crossing here and then driving south to Liuwa and/or Kalabo is possible in the height of the dry season, but a GPS and a local guide are essential. Kalabo is much easier to reach by crossing the river further south.

If you do want to use the pontoon at Lukulu, you'll need both plenty of time and, quite possibly, some local help, since even if the pontoon is on your side of the river (it's usually on the Lukulu side), the chances of it being manned are slim. The fare is a matter of local negotiation with the pontoon operator. You will be charged each way – if the pontoon is on the 'wrong' side of the river and has to cross to fetch you. There's room for only one car on the pontoon and as the riverbanks are steep and sandy on both sides, you'll need to reverse onto it in order to be in a position to drive off in forward gear.

🏠 **Where to stay** Basic accommodation comes in the form of a **government guesthouse** [map, page 488] (**$** *exc b/fast*), reached by turning southwest off the main road near the post office, then following it round to the right.

There are no campsites, but if you ask permission you may be able to **camp** in front of the Sancta Maria Mission. The mission itself has rooms, although these are usually occupied by local people working in the town. Either way, the sound of children singing at the local school is likely to be balanced by that of late-night revelry from across the river! If you'd prefer to camp out of town, there are many lovely spots along the river, especially just across from Lukulu on the far bank, where a well-equipped traveller can camp in peace in the dry season. Ask whoever owns the nearest homestead for permission.

For details of fishing camps in the area, see pages 491–2.

✖ **Where to eat** There are several basic restaurants, mostly in the old and new markets. All usually offer rather meagre fare of nshima and some form of relish (**$**).

If you're self catering, it's wise to arrive with a good stock of food and drink. The shops in the old and new markets have only the most basic essentials, and the chances of finding even canned food are not great. Both soft drinks and beer depend on a truck supplying them from Lusaka; news of its arrival spreads like wildfire through the town.

The local people live by subsistence farming and fishing, eating just what they cultivate or catch, so not much fresh produce reaches the market either. That said,

The peaceful Sancta Maria Catholic Mission (✪ SANCTA 14°22.749'S, 23°14.236'E) at Lukulu was founded in the 1930s by Father Phelem O'Shea, later Bishop of Livingstone. Painted a dark pink, it has a stunning setting high on one bank of the Zambezi, overlooking palm-fringed woodlands opposite, and is a beautiful place from which to watch the sunset.

Over the years, several different Catholic missionaries have worked here, including the Sisters of the Holy Cross, who established the girls' school. The sisters tell of one day, in the 1950s, when the bell in the tower started ringing wildly. On investigation the bell ringer proved to be a spotted hyena – probably from Liuwa – which had seized the rawhide rope in its jaws, and was trying to pull it off and eat it.

The building itself now functions as a community guesthouse, but the mission continues its community and social work, particularly in the areas of schools, welfare and health.

There is a Sunday service in Lozi that offers a fascinating blend of Catholicism and Lozi culture – with lots of singing and dancing.

you'll probably find one or two varieties of seasonal fruits and vegetables, plus dried fish, eggs and roller meal for nshima and a butcher in the old market for meat. Bread supplies are erratic, but scones are sometimes available as an alternative. As to the wares at the Ziba Zako Endless Love Shop, who knows?

What to see and do Lukulu doesn't have many obvious attractions, though the nearby Zambezi River and floodplains are very scenic, with excellent views from the Sancta Maria Mission (see box, above). As in many of the area's smaller places, privacy can be a problem as an outsider is regarded as a source of free entertainment by some of the local community. Karun, a VSO volunteer living here, commented, 'If the visitor is willing to offer to the local people the same right to watch that s/he has assumed, then we have a happy relationship; if not, we have an unhappy visitor but content locals. Except for an occasional visit by a group of Makishi dancers, there are no other festivals that take place in Lukulu.'

Fishing camps around Lukulu In the early 1990s several fishing camps started up between Mongu and Lukulu, focusing on the superb tiger fishing in the area. However, it proved a difficult and expensive place to run a camp and several failed.

During July and August, there are fully catered five-night fishing camps on the Lungwebungu River, northwest of Lukulu on the western side of the Zambezi River, run by Mutemwa Lodge (page 464).

🏠 **Barotse Tiger Camp** [map, page 460] (6 tents) 📞0213 327489; m 0977 707829/586353; e anglezam@microlink.zm; www.zambezifishing. com. Some 20km south of Lukulu, this classy fishing lodge under the ownership of the Livingstone-based Angle Zambia is on a stretch of river where numerous fishing world records have been attained over the years. Guests fly in to Lukulu airport &

transferred to the camp by vehicle & boat. There is no vehicular access to the camp itself.

This is a traditional tented camp, spread out along the river. Tents have dbl or twin beds under mosi nets, & en-suite facilities with flush toilets & outdoor showers. At the heart of the camp are 2 large mess tents: 1 with a bar & lounge, comfortably kitted out with sofas & armchairs;

the other the dining area (gourmet picnic lunches are on offer, too). A swimming pool overlooks the Zambezi. As for the fishing, with waters teeming with fish & 18ft aluminium boats with GPS fish-finding technology, anglers will be in their element. *US$450/585 pp sharing/sgl FB, inc laundry, fishing, exc drinks & fuel.* ⊕ *Apr–Oct.* **LLL**

NORTHWESTERN ZAMBIA

West of the Copperbelt, squeezed between Angola and DRC, this area is distant from most of Zambia. This is reflected in its flora and fauna which, in parts, are much more like those of the wet tropical forests which occur to the north than those of the drier areas of the Kalahari to the south.

Despite being out on a limb, the roads here generally work well, with a tar road from the Copperbelt to Mwinilunga and another being constructed over the top of the good gravel road known as the M8, which links Solwezi with Zambezi via Mufumbwe and Kabompo.

MUFUMBWE Once little more than a dot on the map, the linear town of Mufumbwe (⊕ MUFUMB 13°08.212'S, 25°00.251'E), 108km west of the turn-off to Kasempa and 121km east of Kabompo, is growing rapidly. For those driving through on the M8, it's notable for a reasonably reliable if very expensive **fuel** station (diesel only at the time of research) and a **tyre-repair** place. These, as well as a **bakery** and a small **market**, are invaluable if you're planning a detour into West Lunga National Park.

WEST LUNGA NATIONAL PARK (*Park fees US$10 pp/day; vehicle US$15/day or K17 if Zambian registered;* ⊕ *Jun–Oct*) Some 150km northwest of Kafue, as the pied crow flies, West Lunga is another of Zambia's parks which is both very wild and little visited. It was originally gazetted as a game reserve in the late 1940s, mainly to preserve its population of yellow-backed duiker. Then elephants were also abundant, along with a multitude of antelope species including Angolan (giant) sable and Lichtenstein's hartebeest. There was big game here – including buffalo, lion and leopard – but probably never in the volumes found in the Luangwa or Kafue. However, in the last few decades it's been used very little, except for hunting and fishing by the local communities. As a result, the game has been seriously depleted, and vegetation overgrown.

Despite signs during the last decade that, possibly, with a lot of dedication and hard work, it might be coming back to life, there is as yet little evidence of this on the ground. One positive move has been the formation of the West Lunga Trust, to try to conserve some of this pristine corner of Zambia. The surrounding population density here is relatively low, and almost entirely adjacent to the main roads. Thus, with the help and drive of the local chiefs, they've been able to mobilise many of the local communities to help patrol and monitor the environment. Community Resource Boards (CRBs) have been introduced with a view to controlling the natural resources in each of the surrounding areas, and derive a financial benefit from any operations there. It is to be hoped that the willingness of the park's staff, which is considerable, and their tough approach to poaching, will in time translate into improvements in both the infrastructure and environment within the park itself.

Geography, flora and fauna West Lunga National Park covers 1,684km² of forests, dambos, open grasslands and papyrus swamps. It is bounded by the Kabompo River to the east and south (adjacent to which are most of the park's swamps) and by the West Lunga River to the west. The environment is still pristine

CRYPTOSEPALUM FORESTS AND THE WHITE-CHESTED TINKERBIRD

Almost exclusive to Zambia, *Cryptosepalum* forests are distinctive dry evergreen forests which occur in the area of the Kabompo River. They are regarded by botanists as forming the largest area of tropical evergreen forest in Africa outside the equatorial zone.

Dominating these forests is the *mukwe* tree (*Cryptosepalum pseudotaxus*), which grows on relatively infertile Kalahari sand where there is no permanent surface water. This lack of water means that these areas remain relatively uninhabited. Other trees often found here include the much-exploited rosewood (*Guibourtia coleosperma*). Further south, the character of these forests gradually changes and they become dominated by Zambezi teak trees (*Baikiaea plurijuga*; see box, *The demise of the teak forests*, page 447). Hence logging is a serious threat to them.

The under-storey in *Cryptosepalum* forests is usually dense and tangled, including *Liana* and *Combretum* species which form impenetrable thickets. Epiphytic lichens are common, and the forest floor is mainly covered in mosses. It's very difficult to walk through unless a path has already been cleared.

The avifauna is usually particularly rich, with a mixture of bird species which frequent moist evergreen forests, woodlands and riverine forests. Amongst specials found in these forests are gorgeous bush shrikes, crested guineafowls, purple-throated cuckoo-shrikes, Margaret's batises and square-tailed drongos. However, the area is famous amongst ornithologists for the controversy surrounding its one and only endemic species: the white-chested tinkerbird. Just one of these birds has ever been found, and that was the 'type specimen' netted in 1964. Numerous subsequent attempts to find more have failed.

Some feel that they have simply been defeated by the dense foliage, and that a population of these birds exists deep within the thickets. Others argue that the one specimen found was probably an aberrant individual of the similar golden-rumped tinkerbird, which also occurs in these forests. Whatever the truth, it makes these forests a magnet for birdwatchers, all keen to catch a glimpse of the world's second white-chested tinkerbird!

miombo, interspersed with large grassland plains, flooded dambos and some particularly attractive *Cryptosepalum* forests. It's very beautiful and wild, but the grass and vegetation are thick and difficult even to walk through. The rivers that flow through the park are great for canoeing and boating – with some sections of rapids, and some where you canoe beside rock walls.

Buk's 1993–94 survey (page 261) reported two sightings of wild dog in West Lunga, although noted that poaching remained heavy and the species was probably declining here. Rob Munro reports that he saw buffalo, impala, puku and warthog in the park on a trip in mid-1999.

Ten years later, Dorian Tilbury (a first-class guide with a long history in Zambia's more remote areas) confirmed sightings of puku, hippo, crocodile, vervet monkey, yellow baboon and numerous excellent sightings of samango monkey, plus spoor of bushbuck, bush pig, cane rat, thick-tailed bushbaby, civet and genet. There are certainly still puku, vervet monkey, hippo and crocodile here, and the scouts at Jivundu claim recent sightings of elephant, defassa waterbuck, hartebeest, sable and blue duiker. In the north of the park there is talk of buffalo, bushbuck, reedbuck,

BREAKING THE GIRL

A personal view of canoeing the West Lunga, from Dorian Tilbury

> Twisting and turning, your feelings are burning,
> You're breaking the girl … she loves no one else…

The song rolls around my head like the incessant chant of some rhythmic revolution; and it's not from listening to the Red Hot Chili Peppers either. We've been on the road around Zambia for some time and a Peace Corps volunteer in a village outside Kasempa played us a tune one night … strummed his guitar around the dancing firelight and sang the Chili Peppers song. It stuck.

This mission is an odd one. There are two girls involved, one whom I would love to break, the other I would most definitely not. The latter is my wife, newly wed and the single most important person in my life; the former is the West Lunga River down which we are canoeing for the next six days … twisting and turning … my fears are returning … I'm breaking the girl …

There is no road for resupply or extraction, no radio communication, no boat, no village, no Burger King drive-through if it all gets too much. Once we launch our canoe we are committed to the river, to the exit point six days and more than 70km away. But we are well prepared and once we're in and drifting with the oscillating current, we're twisting and turning … our senses enduring … we're breaking the girl …

The water is crystal clear, cutting its snaking path through this emphatic and wild terrain. The banks are high, sometimes even carved from black rock, sheer and straight, almost overbearing in grace and stature. Freaky euphorbias and silver figs emerge from the granite, their roots entwined through crags and crevices, creeping and drifting down secret passages until somewhere their food source is found. When there are no rocks, the banks bulge and swell with matted trees all clambering for a front-row seat, a room with a view, a perch on the edge of this marvellous show. Everything, it seems, was caught suspended in time making a rush for this river.

We cannot see through the trees. We creep down this mystic rhythm with just the noise of our paddles gliding the surface and a multitude of birds flashing blues and yellows, scarlets and purples, every colour of every rainbow on temporary display. Schalow's lourie, half-collared kingfisher, African finfoot and black saw-wing swallows provide the entertainment and make up the pixels within this big picture charade. And all the while, pyjama-clad samango monkeys dance through the trees, turn and look, then sheepishly disappear.

We don't know what awaits us with this girl … we hit rapids and rock pools, hippos and croc dives. We catch glimpses of memories … just a flash then they're gone … evidence of poachers in the shadows of a distant past, long since departed along with the game. There are times when it is almost silent and eerie, the forgotten relic of a time gone by, a time of animal crowding. One day perhaps the forests will again echo and cry with the howl of territory calls, the crack of feeding branches, the whistles of alarm. But for now, the silent majesty flows her irrefutable path down a million years of creation. She carries her life blood and snakes her course, relinquishing the secrets of her past, oblivious to the prospect of her future … twisting and turning … her feelings are burning … we're breaking the girl …

civet and bushpig, too. It's also quite likely that there will be a few sitatunga around, plus common and yellow-backed duiker. There are probably no lion or leopard remaining, though both certainly used to occur here.

Of course with an untouched environment, the birding remains excellent – and even a short visit along the rivers should yield sightings of half-collared kingfishers, African finfoots and large numbers of black saw-wing swallows amongst many more common species. Zambia's turacos do well here, with Schalow's and Ross's more common than the grey lourie or go-away bird.

Getting there West Lunga is still exceptionally wild – so you will require an independent streak both to get here, and to get around.

The park's main entrance, near the village of Jivundu (⊕ JIVUND 13°06.139'S, 24°41.522'E), is accessed from the main M8 road, 64km east of Kabompo, and 41km west of Mufumbwe. There's no signpost here, so it's easy to miss the turning (⊕ TUJIVU 13°12.151'S, 24°40.907'E). This leads on to a sandy track, which runs through woodland for 11.5km to the ZAWA scout post on the south bank of the Kabompo River. Here you pay your entrance and campsite fees, and can arrange for a scout to accompany you across the river into the park.

The easiest ways to get to West Lunga are either from the Copperbelt or from Kafue National Park's eastern boundary, via Kasempa. Approaching from Lukulu is straightforward, but from Mongu is very time-consuming – whether via Kaoma or across the plains, when a good 4x4 is essential even in the dry season.

From the Copperbelt Take the tar road through Kitwe and Chingola to Solwezi (⊕ SOLWEZ 12°10.931'S, 26°23.960'E), from where it turns south until crossing the Mutanda River at Mwelemu (⊕ MWELEM 12°23.661'S, 26°14.276'E). On the other side of the river, there's a good tar road on the right, which heads west to Mwinilunga. For West Lunga, continue on the road south, towards Kabompo and Kasempa. After almost 90km it is joined from the east by a road from Kitwe (which would have made a shorter, but more time-consuming, approach), via the village of Ingwe.

About 16km later there is a road left to Kasempa, and one straight on to Kabompo (⊕ KABOMP 13°35.610'S, 24°12.125'E). Take the road going straight. This is a super tarred road – though you still need to watch out for pedestrians and animals. After 140km you'll come to the turning off the M8, above.

From Kafue Follow the directions in *Chapter 14*, page 416, to approach Kasempa from Mumbwa via the Lubungu and Lunga pontoons, stopping at Mukinge Hospital for fuel, then head north from Kasempa onto the road from Mwelemu to Kabompo. Alternatively, take the tar road to Kitwe and Solwezi, and then cut southwest; this is likely to be easier and probably faster.

➤ **Where to stay**

🏠 **Kabompo River Lodge & Campsite**
m 0955 441567, 0966 441567; e info@ kitebesafaris.com; www.kabomporiverlodge. com. The lodge has 7 chalets with verandas overlooking the park across the Kabompo River
(max 14 guests) & a campsite with ablutions blocks & showers; the generator is on in the evenings & tents can be hired if needed. *Chalet K400/500 sgl/sharing, K600/900 2 people FB; camping K150 pp, tent hire K100* **L**

What to see and do A vehicle pontoon across the river was installed a few years ago and ZAWA's stated aim was to clear the road through the park from Jivundu to Ntambu in the north, making it within reach of the Solwezi–Mwinilunga road. However, when last we heard even the first few kilometres were sufficiently overgrown to make access all but impossible. Until the track through the park has been properly cut, then, it's best to leave your vehicle at Jivundu, under the watchful eyes of the scouts, and take a scout/guide from there to walk with you into the park, returning to camp in the evening.

If you'd like to go out on the river, boat trips can be arranged, provided that fuel is available to Mabongo Hot Springs or Mulongwanyimu Swamp. Thus these are best booked in advance. Similarly, fishing – with your own kit (or hiring – is another option. Boats and mokoros can be launched from the campsite. Note that ZAWA collects park entry fees and/or angling fees from anyone who goes boat cruising, canoeing or fishing in addition to the hire costs.

KABOMPO This small town beside the surging Kabompo River, in the sparsely populated northwest, is at the centre of Zambia's remaining teak forests – and 121km from Mufumbwe. There is a long-established Catholic mission here, as well as a **market**, a hospital, a **post office**, a branch of the Finance **Bank**, several small **shops** and a handful of guesthouses. **Fuel**, supplied from drums, is not guaranteed, although diesel is more reliable than petrol; ask around near the restaurant opposite the water tower for a dealer.

Getting there and away Navigating to and from Kabompo (⊕ KABOMP 13°35.610'S, 24°12.125'E) is very easy, as it's on the main M8 road.

From Mwinilunga The turning northwards to Mwinilunga (⊕ TUMWIN 13°26.082'S, 24°19.978'E) is 25km east of Kabompo, and although it's signposted, is easily missed. After about 4.5km this road splits; the road to Mwinilunga takes the right fork over the tributary, and then bends back to the left, heading roughly north-northwest with the Manyinga River on its left. See the section on getting to Mwinilunga, page 501, for more about this road.

Just 2km east of the turning is the busy roadside town of **Manyinga** (⊕ MANYIN 13°25.095'S, 24°19.901'E), spread out between two bridges – over the Kabompo River on the east side, and the scenic Manyinga River to the west.

By bus Buses to and from Zambezi stop every day except Sunday outside the Big Tree Restaurant on the main road, almost opposite the water tower. There are also three buses a week between Chavuma and Solwezi, and on to Kitwe all stopping in Kabompo.

🏠 **Where to stay and eat** A clutch of simple guesthouses (**$**) is signposted off the main road towards the river. To get there, turn off the main road at ⊕ TUGSTH 13°35.618'S, 24°12.156'E, continue over a rather incongruous but neatly planted roundabout, and you will find them on the left-hand side.

ZAMBEZI Like many regional centres in Zambia, Zambezi is referred to locally as 'the boma'. It's a small town with a few very basic **shops**, a **post office**, a Catholic mission and a small local **market**. Most of its amenity buildings, including the police station and government offices, are situated just off the main road, behind the 'new' **fuel** station (⊕ ZAMBEZ 13°32.262'S, 23°06.158'E), which when we visited was showing no signs of opening. In fact, if you're driving into this area, do so with very large reserves of fuel. The town's old fuel station closed some time

Driving around the Kabompo area, you'll often see what look like hollow logs, suspended high in the trees. These are beehives, and beekeeping has long been a tradition in these forests, with fathers handing down to their sons not only the skills, but also traditional hives of grass, bark and hollow tree trunks.

Now this traditional process has developed into a thriving industry with global reach. This started as a Zambian government initiative, initially supported by funding from the German Technical Development Agency, to improve the marketing of the local honey that was produced here, and thus increase the income of the rural population. Then there were only a few hundred local producers, but in 1979 North Western Bee Products was established.

Now this company is owned by the producers and it buys honey and beeswax from about 3,000 traditional bark hive beekeepers in Zambia. It supplies almost half the African honey exported to the EU, at prices typically 50% above the average price paid for other imported honey, and this was the first honey to be certified organic by the Soil Association.

It exports most of its wax and honey to Tropical Forest Products, in the UK (*www.tropicalforest.com*), which then markets and distributes it as a premium product to shops such as Fortnum & Mason, Sainsbury's, the Body Shop and others.

See their website for more about this model of sustainable development.

ago, leaving drivers dependent on black-market fuel. Supplies of this are erratic, but diesel is more reliable than petrol, albeit very expensive. Do be aware that watered-down petrol from illicit sources – known as 'bush fuel' – is sometimes sold to unsuspecting travellers, so ask locally for a reliable source.

Getting there and away The road west from Kabompo, the M8, is a remarkably good gravel road (gradually being tarred), that continues north to the Angolan border at Chavuma. Along the road are relatively few villages and lots of thick teak forests. In the dry season the smoke from occasional bush fires will be seen drifting in the sky, above areas of scorched and blackened ground. It's a measure of the improvements in the road infrastructure that the journey to Lusaka that used to take five days can now be completed, via Lukulu and Kaoma, in around 10 hours.

There's a pontoon across the river just below Water View Lodge, although most people pay just to be ferried over by mokoro. Few visitors have any reason to cross here, though it's worth noting that there is talk of prospecting for oil to the west.

From Lukulu See *From Lukulu to Kasempa*, on pages 489–9, for the road to Watopa pontoon (✪ FERRY4 14°02.338'S, 23°37.744'E), and note that this pontoon is incorrectly marked on the ITM map of Zambia. Then it is nearly 22km north to Mumbeji (✪ MUMBEJ 13°51.653'S, 23°40.327'E), where you turn left on to the good M8 for a further 75km west and northwest to Zambezi (✪ ZAMBEZ 13°32.262'S, 23°06.158'E).

⌂ **Where to stay and eat** *Map, page 498.*
Perhaps unexpectedly, Zambezi has a handful of guesthouses, including **Ndeke Guesthouse** [off map, 498], and those below – both of which have restaurants.

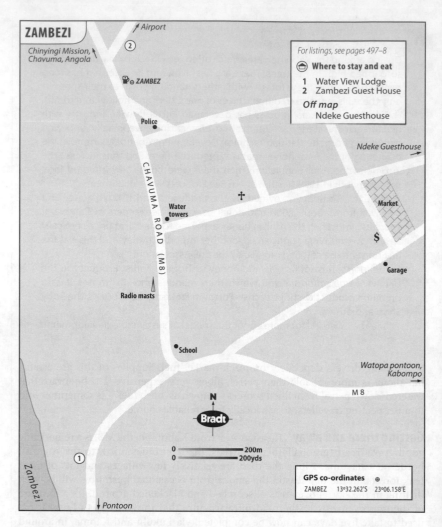

For listings, see pages 497–8

Where to stay and eat

1 Water View Lodge
2 Zambezi Guest House

Off map
Ndeke Guesthouse

GPS co-ordinates ⊕
ZAMBEZ 13°32.262'S 23°06.158'E

🏠 **Water View Lodge** (14 rooms) m 0979 379449. Perched high above the Zambezi, & clearly signposted from the main road, this pleasant guesthouse has 3 types of room, with en-suite shower, TV, fridge, fan & b/fast included. Meals of nshima with chicken or fish are served in a thatched restaurant overlooking the river, where there's also an open rondavel, ideal for sunset drinks. **$**

🏠 **Zambezi Guest House** (25 rooms, camping) off Chavuma Rd; ☎ 0218 371124; m 0978 642882; e zambezi@limagarden.com; www.limagarden.com. En-suite brick-&-thatch chalets with TV, fridge, AC & dbl/twin beds. **$**

What to see and do

Traditional dancing About 17km north of town are the palaces of the Lunda and the Luvale senior chiefs, on the east and west sides of the road respectively – as you might predict from the rough distribution of languages mapped out in *Chapter 2*, pages 19–22. The Luvale chief's palace is the venue for the Likumbi Lya Mize (page 26), as well as for traditional dancing which is held here several times a week.

Chinyingi Mission About 23km north of Zambezi, just after the Makondu River, is a sandy track heading west (⊕ TUCHIN 13°20.450'S, 23°03.674'E). It's signposted to Chinyingi Mission, which is a further 8km along this track, for which a high-clearance 4x4 is essential.

The mission (⊕ CHINYI 13°21.146'S, 23°00.834'E), which stands on the western bank of the Zambezi, was founded in 1953 by a group of Capuchin brothers. It is perhaps most famous for the Chinyingi suspension bridge – one of only four bridges to span the width of the Zambezi at the time of its construction (see box, page 500), though now bridges at Sesheke, Ngonye Falls and Kazungula, have since been built, or are currently being constructed. If you walk across the bridge to the mission (you can park by the bridge), you get a real feel for its 300m span, and some beautiful views along the river, too.

Although the mission is not currently inhabited, the school and a rural health centre are still operational, as is the mission church, and visitors are welcome to look around. It's a tranquil spot, lit up by frangipani and flame trees. The church itself is simple but light and spacious, drums at the ready for the next service, and notable for its cross of scaffolding bars.

CHAVUMA Some 80km north of Zambezi, or 6km south of the Angolan border, Chavuma lies at the point where the Zambezi re-enters Zambia. The land around here is arid, and the soil mostly grey in colour, which makes villages in this area

| MAKISHI DANCERS | *Judi Helmholz* |

Sometimes in Mongu, or whilst travelling in the north of the western provinces, you will encounter colourfully clad characters adorned with fearsome costumes – Makishi dancers. For the uninitiated (defined as women and children in Luvale society), these are traditionally believed to be female spirits from the dead, and most will talk in high voices and even have 'breasts' made of wire.

The creative and artistic skills of the Luvale people are reflected in the wide variety of mask styles worn by the Makishi. These are huge constructions, often made of bark and wood and frequently coloured with red, white and black. Even helicopter blades are sometimes spotted in the designs – a memory of the war in Angola.

Each Likishi (the singular of Makishi) dancer is distinctive and plays a specific role within the various ceremonies and festivals. For example, the Mungali, or hyena, depicts menacing villains, whilst the Chikishikishi, a monster with a boiling pot, represents discipline – and will consume mischievous members of society.

Apart from their occasional appearances throughout the land, the Makishi dancers play central roles during two of the most important ceremonies of Luvale culture: the Mukanda and the Wali. These are the initiation rites for boys and girls respectively.

The Mukanda, also known as circumcision camps, are traditional 'schools' for local boys, normally aged from 12 to 17, but sometimes as young as five. Here, they are introduced to adult life and circumcised. The dancer known as Chileya cha Mukanda, which literally means 'the fool of the school', serves as a jester by mimicking the participants so as to relieve tension and anxiety before the circumcision ceremony. The girls attend a similar ceremony, though there is no physical clitoridectomy operation, as occurs in other cultures.

Western Zambia NORTHWESTERN ZAMBIA

15

CHINYINGI SUSPENSION BRIDGE

With thanks to Richard Miller, Cheshire, Connecticut, USA

The Chinyingi Mission was founded in 1953 to minister to villagers on both sides of the Zambezi, bringing them education and healthcare. However, at this point the river is over 210m wide, very deep, and subject to annual flooding, yet the only means of crossing it in the early days of the mission was by dugout canoe.

When he first arrived at the mission, Brother Crispin was responsible for transport, maintenance and cooking, and in order to help bring heavy supplies as well as people over the river he introduced a pontoon ferry. However, in 1971 four people were drowned while bringing a woman to hospital in a dug-out canoe, and he vowed to prevent any further accident by building a bridge over the river. While his was an unlikely background for the engineering feat he had undertaken, Brother Crispin didn't lack faith. From a picture of a suspension bridge in Nepal that he had seen in *National Geographic*, he set to work, identifying people who could help him in the design of the bridge, sourcing the materials, and securing funds to pay for the project. He pulled together a team of just five young labourers, then spent all his free time working alongside them; for safety reasons, no work was undertaken unless he was present.

The project was not without significant setbacks. At just 6m high, the original towers at each end of the bridge proved to be too low for the cables to span the river at the right height, and had to be rebuilt twice to reach the necessary 18m. The suspension cables, when first hung, swung wildly, until Brother Crispin was advised to install guy wires to hold them in place. And every element of the supplies had to be trucked up to 800km across unforgiving terrain in all weathers. Little wonder that it took over five years for the bridge to be completed.

The result, though, has stood the test of time. Since its opening in 1977, the 300m bridge has continued to provide a lifeline to people on the opposite side of the river to the mission, and a supply line for the mission itself. While Brother Crispin has now returned to his native Italy, as many as 500 people a day continue to cross the 1m-wide metal walkway (the original wood was replaced by Brother Crispin before he left), that he and his team suspended some 13m above the waters. They come on foot, on bicycles, and even on mopeds, up to 60 at a time, taking for granted the work of a Capuchin monk who built their bridge on faith.

look dull compared with those further south. Proximity to the border means that the town has attracted a number of illegal Angolan diamond sellers.

The Brethren Missionaries, who live in a large compound up on the hill by the town, have their own camping spot by the river, which they may allow you to use, or they may be able to direct you to other suitable places to stay.

Fuel supplies are very intermittent, so it's important not to rely on filling up here.

Getting there The M8 here from Solwezi via Kabompo and Zambezi is a decent gravel road. If you're approaching from the south via Lukulu then it's best to cross the Kabompo River at the Watopa pontoon (⊕ FERRY4 14°02.338'S, 23°37.744'E), then join this road from there (page 417).

What to see and do

Chavuma Falls This is not nearly as spectacular as the Zambezi's drops at Ngonye and Victoria Falls, but makes a good picnic site for an afternoon. The falls are found by taking the footpath near the pontoon.

No-man's-land Every morning there is a small market in no-man's-land, between the territories of Zambia and Angola. Both Zambians and Angolans come to barter for goods, under the watchful eyes of the armed border guards. It is a fascinating occurrence. As a foreigner, make sure you have very clear permission from the border guards before you even consider joining in, and don't take any photographs without permission.

MWINILUNGA

Mwinilunga is a large, thriving outpost of a town, raised up in the remote northwest corner of Zambia. The town isn't on the national grid, and there's no fuel station (you might be able to get fuel from drums, but don't rely on it). On the plus side, there are shops with basic supplies and a sizeable local **market**, plus several **banks**, a large **post office** and a small Franciscan mission.

Getting there and away By far the easiest way to get to Mwinilunga is via the Copperbelt, Chingola and Solwezi. To reach it, travel through Chingola and then take the turn to Solwezi. This is tarmac, but in a variable state of repair.

About 28km after Solwezi there's a junction at Mwelemu (⊕ MWELEM 12°23.661'S, 26°14.276'E). Mwinilunga is signposted to the right, and from there it's about 288km of largely reasonable tarmac away. Eventually you'll descend a hill, cross the West Lunga River, and drive into town. Beyond the tar, a good gravel road leads north into the DRC via Ikelenge. Alternatively, head for Angola via Kalene Hill, and the border at Jimbe Bridge just over 100km away.

From Kabompo See Kabompo's section on *Getting there and away* (pages 496–7) to locate the turn-off for Mwinilunga from the M8 (⊕ TUMWIN 13°26.082'S, 24°19.978'E). Then after 4.5km, take the right fork, and bend around left. It's a beautiful drive along a good but narrow road on which you can average about 30–40km/h in the dry season. On either side are occasional subsistence farming communities, and large areas of forest. It does cross one or two large dambos, which could be very sticky during the rainy season. Note that this route goes relatively close to Angola, and you'd be well advised to check the security situation locally before coming this way. Equally, don't be tempted to divert off to the west of the road unless you know exactly where you're going.

After about 49km you'll pass the village of Lunsongwe (⊕ LUNSON 13°02.068'S, 24°13.385'E) – spelled 'Lusongwa' on some maps – where there's a school and a small grocery shop. Around 54km later, you pass the very spread-out village of Kanyilambi, notable mainly for its church and beautiful silvery fields of rice – and then you're almost halfway to Mwinilunga.

Continuing north, the forests and other vegetation start to get thicker whilst the atmosphere becomes perceptibly warmer and more humid – despite the slight but steady rise in altitude. In places the forest is thick enough for the canopy of trees over the track to interlock – and for some of the birding 'specials' found in Mwinilunga to occur here too.

Eventually you reach a T-junction (⊕ TUKABO 11°45.158'S, 24°26.114'E) with the main Mwinilunga–Solwezi tar road, and the centre of town is a few kilometres west. In the dry season it takes about 5 hours to cover the 219km from Kabompo.

🏠 **Where to stay** Mwinilunga has an assortment of largely unremarkable places to sleep and/or eat, all fairly inexpensive, but the following are among the better choices. Many visitors will proceed straight to Hillwood Farm and Nchila Reserve, and campers might do better to head for the campsite at the source of the Zambezi (page 506).

🏠 **Kakuwahi Lodge** (3 rooms) In an attractive setting on the banks of the Lunga River, this lodge is owned by a Christian husband-&-wife team, Roma & Catherine Nyukambumba. Its neat chalets are backed by manicured lawns dotted with trees & shrubs. Inside, clean en-suite rooms come with queen or dbl beds, AC, DSTV, radio & fridge – & (very welcome) hot water. There's a modern lounge & the food is reasonable. **$$**

🏠 **Elidos** On the main street through town, Elidos is popular with backpackers & volunteers, either for a bite to eat or as an overnight stop. **$**

HILLWOOD FARM AND NCHILA WILDLIFE RESERVE Hillwood Farm is an improbable place. It's an oasis of peace and order in a corner of Zambia which the world's media might expect, given its position between Angola and the DRC, to be under permanent siege. What's more, within its bounds, Hillwood has a very special reserve, Nchila, which has flora and fauna that are unique to Zambia: it contains a slice of equatorial forest that's been preserved and nurtured. The family who own this farm, the Fishers, have been working in close partnership with the local communities here for generations.

In recent years the family has placed an increasing emphasis on hunting, and – since hunting and photographic guests don't mix – there are very few weeks of the year that are available for other guests. That said, they still welcome campers, ornithologists and photographers whenever they can.

So while it's exceedingly 'out of the way' by anyone's standards, and there are restrictions on the times when non-hunting guests can stay, Hillwood remains a totally fascinating place that's delightful to visit and contains some amazing wildlife. If you're anywhere near here, do contact them to see if you can stay.

Getting there and away To reach here from Mwinilunga, continue through town on the main road, past the turn-off to the airport. After about 7km, the road changes from tar to well-maintained gravel road. Over its course it then crosses a series of rivers, and you'll drive over four bridges. (Whilst you don't need a 4x4 for this in the dry season, there are several steep sections that could become tricky in the wet season.) In sequence, the rivers include Luakela, the Chitunta and the Kaseki.

About 47km from Mwinilunga there's a right turn that is clearly marked (✪ TUZAMB 11°23.321'S, 24°16.632'E). After about 4.6km, this leads to the source of the Zambezi (see page 506 for details). Then about 3km after that turning, you cross the final river, the Sakeji. About 9km after this there is a clear signpost to the right (✪ TUHILL 11°17.040'S, 24°16.663'E) proclaiming that Hillwood Farm and Nchila Wildlife Reserve are about 7km away. This final road felt a little like a local footpath through a village to us, but eventually you do reach Hillwood Farm (✪ HILLWO 11°14.989'S, 24°18.852'E) – an oasis of order.

Note that on the way from Mwinilunga to Hillwood you pass (although may not notice) the Luakela Forest Reserve and later Chitunta Plain, both of which have some of the birds which attract ornithologists to this corner of the country. Luakela Forest Reserve is noted for lots of bar-winged weavers, whilst Chitunta Plain is very important for many species, including the Angola lark, Grimwood's longclaw, the dambo (black-tailed) cisticola, the black and rufous swallows and short-tailed pipits. Venture several kilometres up the stream there, and you've a good chance of seeing another very uncommon bird, Bocage's weaver.

Hillwood is about 68km from Mwinilunga and, if you don't stop for any birdwatching, will take a bit less than 2 hours to drive. Alternatively, Nchila can be reached by a short (though not very cheap) charter flight from Lusaka or (marginally less costly) from Lunga River Lodge in northern Kafue.

What to see and do Although most people will stay on the reserve (page 505), there is lots to see around the farm. Most people will also detour to the source of the Zambezi, and keen ornithologists will frequently head into the surrounding area in search of the 'specials' found in this corner of Zambia.

Hillwood Farm Zambian farms don't come much more remote or well established than Hillwood. Relatively speaking, it's had a lot of time to build up a very self-sufficient yet interdependent community of people.

Of interest here is the farm itself, which these days relies on beef and dairy cows, cereal and, increasingly, tourism to generate income. The orphanage and the school are also fascinating; the boarding school is used by some of Zambia's more affluent residents, so it's not at all impoverished by local standards.

If you have the opportunity to chat with Pete, Lynn or Pete's father, Paul – do so. You'll get an intriguing insight into the area's past and present. They have always worked closely with the surrounding communities – Pete meets with the local village headmen once a month to inform, involve and share out the maintenance and development work on the reserve fairly between the villages. Roads, bridges, fences and shelters are all built and maintained with local labour and materials wherever possible. This 'Nchila Committee' also helps a great deal to prevent poaching, kept to a minimum thanks to the excellent rapport within the community as a whole. This is built on many years of talking together, mutual trust and help.

Nchila Wildlife Reserve (*www.nchilawildlifereserve.com*; ⊕ *15 May–15 Nov; entrance US$10 pp*). Nchila Wildlife Reserve is a 40km² area of virgin bush within the boundaries of Hillwood Farm. It's a great area for game drives and walks, always accompanied by a guide from Nchila (hence the need to book in advance). See below for more on the flora and fauna, but note that even if you're not a keen 'twitcher', the rolling country is very pleasant walking, with patches of evergreen forests adding a welcome touch of shade.

The prime time to visit is August to end-October for the birding.

Flora and fauna Nchila attracts a steady stream of ornithologists, herpetologists, zoologists and other keen observers of the natural world. Most come for the reserve's pockets of pristine wet, evergreen forest (rainforest). These are typical of large areas of its neighbouring countries – so you'll find species here which you can't see anywhere else, unless you're prepared to brave the instability of either Angola or the DRC.

Note that you'll find some exceedingly comprehensive details of Nchila's flora and fauna on the reserve's website so here I'll just mention a few of the more obvious highlights.

Flora This beautiful, rolling and hilly area has large areas of moist open plains dotted with termitaria. These are veined by miombo woodland and, in the lower areas, patches of wet, evergreen (mishutu) forest which surround many permanent streams.

Animals The larger wildlife here includes possibly Zambia's largest herd of sable antelope (some of which appear to have some genes in common with Angolan giant sables, given their appearance), and very good numbers of roan and eland that are

15

generally very relaxed and approachable. In addition, there are plains zebra, defassa waterbuck, impala, Lichtenstein's hartebeest, Kafue lechwe, puku and kudu. Oribi are very common on the plains, warthog are sometimes seen grubbing around, and there's a herd of blue wildebeest.

Sitatunga frequent the denser, wetter patches of forest – and, like the bushbuck which are found here, sometimes venture out along the edge of the open plains; it's here that I had one of the clearest sightings of these shy antelope that I've ever

THE FISHER FAMILY

Pete Fisher is Zambian – part of the fourth generation of Fishers in Zambia. Lynn, his wife, is Californian, but has always lived in Zambia. They live in the oldest house on Hillwood Farm with their two sons, Sonny and Christopher. Pete's father, Paul Fisher, and his sister Melanie and her family, also live and work at Hillwood.

The history of the Fisher family is an interesting one, and inextricably linked with the development of the local area. The story begins in the late 19th century. Inspired by David Livingstone's and Fred Arnott's aspirations to end the slave trade in Africa by establishing Christianity and legitimate commerce in its place, Walter Fisher was a willing recruit to the missionary quest. In 1889, freshly qualified as a doctor and with a gold medal for surgery at Guy's Hospital, Walter Fisher left the UK with a party of seven other men and women, bound for the Angolan coast. Suffering from various hardships on arrival, the party moved out of Portuguese territory to Kalene Hill in Northern Rhodesia. Indeed, the ruins of the houses and store rooms they built in the Angolan style, with bricks made of baked anthill, can still be found there.

Kalene Hill eventually became the home of a mission hospital and an orphanage after Walter's wife, Anna Fisher, rescued a newborn baby. She found the child after it had been lying on its mother's grave for two days – where it had been placed as it was believed to have caused her death (the mother had died in childbirth). The orphanage is now on Hillwood Farm, in the care of Paul and Eunie Fisher, and its emphasis is on keeping a traditional African way of life so that the children can return to their village at about six years old. Until then, they are taught, fed and clothed to give them a good start. As has always been the case here, each baby comes with a female family member to assist with its care. There are currently 30 orphans; visitors are warmly welcomed. Esther Townsend and Helen Finney, two English orphanage mothers, currently manage the day-to-day needs of the orphanage.

In addition to the orphanage, Anna Fisher was also responsible for establishing the Nyamuweji village for old ladies, where they cultivated the land and were protected by the Fishers from customary witch-hunts. Such women, too old to work hard, often came for refuge. There remain six to eight women at Kalene, and they are more or less self-supporting.

Sakeji School started in 1925, next to Hillwood. It has a very wide catchment area for its size, made possible by road links and the well-maintained Sakeji airstrip. The school teaches Grades 1 to 7 (Junior) and is funded and staffed by mainly Canadian and American missionary workers from an organisation called 'Christian Churches in Many Lands' (CCML). In 1962 the Bible was translated into Lunda by Singleton Fisher. A new version by Paul Fisher and Joan Hoyt is under way for the Zambian Bible House.

experienced. The Nchila team say that there are two different subspecies of sitatunga here: 'normal' sitatunga such as are found to the south in Zambia and the rest of southern Africa, and an 'Angolan' subspecies.

In the forest patches you'll find vervet and blue monkeys, as well as common and blue duiker. (With some luck and much skill, the guides can sometimes call the curious blue duiker in to approach you!)

Birdlife The birdlife here is a real draw; it's a very special place. The forests contain 30 species not found anywhere outside of the DRC, Angola and this area – most of which do not even occur around Mwinilunga (only 70km south of Nchila). However, for some of this area's 'specials' you may have to go a further 50km north to the very tip of Zambia – around the source of the Salujinga and the Jimbe. The borders with Angola and the DRC are very sensitive – so take local advice before you venture that far.

The source of the Zambezi and the Sakeji River, which runs through Hillwood, is a microcosm of the DRC forests. Many of the birds which occupy ecological niches south of here are replaced by different, but closely related, species. The area's 'specials' often need work to spot, and a fair amount of searching with one of Nchila's guides who knows where to look. They include afep and bronze-naped pigeons; black-collared bulbuls; grey-winged robins; rufous ant thrushes; Fülleborne's and rosy-breasted longclaws; honeyguide greenbuls; shining blue, white-bellied and blue-breasted kingfishers; olive long-tailed cuckoos; orange-tufted, green-throated and Bates' sunbirds; buff-throated apalises; Laura's and bamboo warblers; white-cheeked bee-eaters; red-bellied paradise flycatchers; and splendid glossy starlings.

Where to stay

Both the bushcamp and the campsite are on the Nchila reserve, and reservations for both are essential, since hunters are never mixed with other guests In addition, they may not otherwise have the space, staff or supplies to accommodate you. Clients are now also flown by helicopter to a remote second tented camp on Nkwaji Reserve high on the bank of the Lunga river for specific hunts:

Nchila Camp (3 chalets) e nchila@ nchilawildlifereserve.com, nchilawildlife@ iwayafrica.com; www.nchilawildlifereserve.com. ⊕ NCHILA 11°14.945'S, 24°19.642'E. Nchila's small bushcamp overlooks a large plain & dambo from the edge of riverine forest & miombo woodland. It can take a max of 6 people (8 if squeezed!) in well-furnished chalets with solid wooden furniture, stylish fabrics & imaginative touches & you can relax in a swimming pool & jacuzzi a short walk away. One stunning chalet has a king-size bed & a big en-suite bathroom, incorporating a large, slightly sunken bath beside the window, & a good shower. A good 2nd chalet has 2 twin rooms which share a flush toilet, shower & a bath with another shower over it. Both are spacious, built of stone with thatched roofs, & with water heated by wood-fired boilers. A smaller chalet (comfortable for 1 person, or 'cosy' for 2) has its own en-suite shower & toilet.

At the camp's heart is a thatched dining & lounge area, the 2 separated by a large log fire. With a lovely view over the dambo, it makes a pleasant place to sit & watch the wildlife. The food is good but simple: very fresh wholesome farm fare *US$1,500 pp FBA, inc entry fee.* ⊕ *15 May–15 Nov.* **LLLL**

Nchila Campsite Nchila's campsite, in a lovely shady spot next to the Sakeji River, has an ablution block with showers & flush toilets. There's also a dining area & a kitchen with a small wood stove & hot water. Lighting is courtesy of a connection to your car battery. Firewood is provided & a staff member is available to draw & heat water for showers. You'll need to come with all your own camping kit & most of your food, although limited amounts of fresh produce may sometimes be available from the farm. It's best to agree this in advance with Nchila. *US$25 pp plus entry fee US$10 pp.* ⊕ *15 May–15 Nov.*

Excursions from Hillwood and Nchila The **Zambezi rapids** near to Hillwood are a very popular day trip – as a lovely spot to play in the water and float down on inflatable inner tubes. This is a particularly good place for birdwatchers to search for the rare Forbes plover, which hunts for insects on the bare rocks.

Further north, around the **source of the Jimbe River**, is the best place to look for the compact weaver and white-spotted flufftails; a recent sighting of the shrike flycatcher was a new discovery for Zambia.

Source of the Zambezi About 12km south of the entrance road to Nchila is a turn-off (⊕ TUZAMB 11°23.321'S, 24°16.632'E) to the official spot at Kalene Hill where the mighty Zambezi begins its 2,700km journey to the Indian Ocean. Protected both as a national monument and a World Heritage Site, the site itself is unexceptional, but the surrounding dense forest canopy, part of a 36.8ha reserve, is impressive.

A copper plaque, unveiled in 1964 to celebrate Zambia's independence, marks the site, at an altitude of about 1,500m. There's a good thatched shelter here, ideal for picnics, and it takes about half an hour to walk to the source. Note that the short access road is, in part, the boundary between Zambia and the DRC.

If you would like information about advertising in
Bradt Travel Guides please contact us on
+44 (0)1753 893444 or email info@bradtguides.com

Appendix 1

WILDLIFE GUIDE

This wildlife guide is designed in a manner that should allow you to name most large mammals that you see in Zambia. Less common species are featured under the heading *Similar species* beneath the animal to which they are most closely allied, or bear the strongest resemblance.

CATS AND DOGS

Lion *Panthera leo* Shoulder height 100–120cm. Weight 150–220kg.

Africa's largest predator, the lion is the animal that everybody hopes to see on safari. It is a sociable creature, living in prides of five to ten animals and defending a territory of 20–200km². Lions often hunt at night, and their favoured prey is large or medium antelope such as wildebeest and impala. Most of the hunting is done by females, but dominant males normally feed first after a kill. Rivalry between males is intense and takeover battles are frequently fought to the death, so two or more males often form a coalition. Young males are forced out of their home pride at three years of age, and cubs are usually killed after a successful takeover.

When not feeding or fighting, lions are remarkably indolent – they spend up to 23 hours of any given day at rest – so the anticipation of a lion sighting is often more exciting than the real thing. Lions naturally occur in any habitat, except desert or rainforest. They once ranged across much of the Old World, but these days they are all but restricted to the larger conservation areas in sub-Saharan Africa (one residual population exists in India).

Lions occur throughout Zambia, and are very common in the larger parks with better game densities – Luangwa (North and South), Kafue and Lower Zambezi. Spend a week in any of these with a good guide and you'd be unlucky not to see at least some lion! They occur in smaller numbers in the more marginal parks and GMAs, and more sparsely in areas with more human population.

Leopard *Panthera pardus* Shoulder height 70cm. Weight 60–80kg.

The powerful leopard is the most solitary and secretive of Africa's big cats. It hunts at night, using stealth and power, often getting to within 5m of its intended prey before pouncing. If there are hyenas and lions around then leopards habitually move their kills up into trees to safeguard them. The leopard can be distinguished from the cheetah by its rosette-like spots, lack of black 'tearmarks' and more compact, low-slung, powerful build.

The leopard is the most common of Africa's large felines. Zambia's bush is perfect for leopard, which are common throughout the country, as they favour habitats with plenty of cover, like riverine woodlands. Despite this, a good sighting in the wild during the day is unusual. In fact there are many records of individuals living for years, undetected, in close proximity to humans.

Leopard

Sightings at night are a different story and, because Zambia's national parks allow night drives, it's probably Africa's best country for seeking leopard.

South Luangwa National Park was chosen by the BBC for the filming of their remarkable documentary, *Night of the Leopard*. Leopard sightings often become the main goal of night drives there. Your chances of spotting them are equally good in the Lower Zambezi, whilst consistently first-class sightings are also reported from the Lufupa area in Kafue. Remarkably they usually seem unperturbed by the presence of a vehicle and spotlight, and will often continue whatever they are doing regardless of an audience. Watching a leopard stalk is captivating viewing.

Cheetah   *Acynonix jubatus* Shoulder height 70–80cm. Weight 50–60kg.

This remarkable spotted cat has a greyhound-like build, and is capable of running at over 70km/h in bursts, making it the world's fastest land animal. Despite superficial similarities, you can easily tell a cheetah from a leopard by the former's simple spots, disproportionately small head, streamlined build, diagnostic black 'tearmarks', and preference for relatively open habitats. It is often seen pacing the plains restlessly, either on its own or in a small family group consisting of a mother and her offspring. Diurnal hunters, cheetah favour the cooler hours of the day to hunt smaller antelope, like steenbok and duiker, and small mammals like scrub hares.

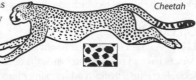

Cheetah

Zambia has a small but growing population of cheetah, centred on Kafue National Park and Liuwa Plain. They've had a historical presence in the Luangwa, although they are likely now absent from the area. Re-introduction attempts were made in the Lower Zambezi, but these were unsuccessful.

Similar species   The **serval** (*Felis serval*) is smaller than a cheetah (shoulder height 55cm) but has a similar build and black-on-gold spots giving way to streaking near the head. Seldom seen, it is widespread and quite common in moist grassland, reed beds and riverine habitats throughout Africa, including Zambia. It does particularly well in some of the swampier areas. Servals prey on mice, rats and small mammals, but will sometimes take the young of small antelope.

Caracal   *Felis caracal* Shoulder height 40cm. Weight 15–20kg.

The caracal resembles the European lynx with its uniform tan coat and tufted ears. It is a solitary and mainly nocturnal hunter, feeding on birds, small antelope and young livestock. Found throughout the subcontinent, it easily adapts to a variety of environments and even occurs in some of Zambia's populated areas. Despite this, being nocturnal it is rarely seen. Caracals normally stalk their prey as closely as possible, before springing with surprise.

Caracal

Similar species   The smaller **African wild cat** (*Felis sylvestris*) is found from the Mediterranean to the Cape of Good Hope, and is similar in appearance to the domestic tabby cat and a little larger. It has an unspotted torso, a ringed tail and a reddish-brown tinge to the back of its ears. Wild cats are generally solitary and nocturnal, often utilising burrows or termite mounds as daytime shelters. They prey upon reptiles, amphibians and birds as well as small mammals.

African wild dog *Lycaon pictus* Shoulder height 70cm. Weight 25kg.

Also known as the **painted hunting dog**, the wild dog is distinguished from other African dogs by its large size and mottled black, brown and cream coat. Highly sociable, living in packs of up

African wild dog

to 20 animals, wild dogs are ferocious hunters that literally tear apart their prey on the run. They are now threatened with extinction, the most endangered of Africa's great predators. This is the result of relentless persecution by farmers, who often view the dogs as dangerous vermin, and their susceptibility to diseases spread by domestic dogs. Wild dogs are now extinct in many areas where they were formerly abundant, like the Serengeti, and they are common nowhere. The global population of fewer than 3,000 is concentrated in southern Tanzania, Zambia, Zimbabwe, Botswana, South Africa and Namibia.

Wild dogs prefer open savannah with only sparse tree cover, if any, and packs have enormous territories, typically covering 400km² or more. They travel huge distances in search of prey and so few parks are large enough to contain them. In Zambia wild dogs have their strongest base in Kafue, closely followed by the Luangwa, though even in these parks they are regarded as an uncommon sight. They are sometimes seen in Liuwa, Lower Zambezi and Nsumbu areas. Elsewhere their existence is less certain.

NILE CROCODILE   *Mike Unwin*

NILE CROCODILE (*Crocodylus niloticus*) Length over 5m. Weight over 1,000kg.
Few visitors to Zambia's mighty rivers will want to miss the opportunity to see this antediluvian creature. With its powerful serrated tail, horny plated skin and up to 100 peg-like teeth crammed into a long, sinister smile, the Nile crocodile is the stuff of nightmares and action movies. Contrary to the more lurid myths, crocodiles generally avoid people (understandably, given the slaughter they have suffered). Yet while they will not usually launch themselves into boats or come galloping after you on land, humans are still potential prey for a big one, and tragedies do occasionally occur. When in crocodile country, it is sensible to keep your distance from the water's edge.

Crocodiles can live up to 100, but reach sexual maturity at 12–15 years. They inhabit lakes, rivers and swamps. Whereas youngsters are boldly marked in black and green, adults are generally a muddy grey-brown colour – usually lighter in rivers than in lagoons. Theirs is an amphibious life: basking on land, jaws agape to lose heat, or cruising the waters, raised eyes and nostrils allowing them to see and breathe undetected. As well as eating fish such as bream and barbel, adult crocs will ambush mammals up to the size of buffalo, grabbing them with an explosive sideways lunge from the water, before dragging them under to drown. Large numbers of crocodiles gather to scavenge big carcasses, churning up the water as they thrash and spin to dislodge chunks of flesh. They will even leave the water to steal a nearby lion kill.

SIMILAR SPECIES The endangered **slender-snouted crocodile** (*Crocodylus cataphractus* or *Mecistops cataphractus*) occurs in Zambia only in isolated instances. In Lake Tanganyika, it is largely confined to the quieter sections of the lake around Nsumbu National Park. Historically it is also said to occur in the upper streams of the Congo basin around Kasanka, although there have been no reliable sightings reported for many years.

Side-striped jackal *Canis adustus* Shoulder height 35–40cm. Weight 8–12kg.
Despite its prevalence in other areas of Africa, the side-striped jackal is common nowhere in Zambia, although it occurs throughout the country. It is greyish in colour and has an indistinct pale horizontal stripe on each flank and often a white-tipped tail. These jackals are most often seen singly or in pairs at dusk or dawn. They are opportunistic feeders, taking rats, mice, birds, insects, wild fruits and even termites. The side-striped jackal is Zambia's only species of jackal.

Spotted hyena *Crocuta crocuta* Shoulder height 85cm. Weight 70kg.
Hyenas are characterised by their bulky build, sloping back, rough brownish coat, powerful jaws and dog-like expression. Contrary to popular myth, spotted hyenas are not exclusively scavengers; they are also adept hunters, which hunt in groups and kill animals as large as wildebeests. Nor are they hermaphroditic, an ancient belief that stems from the false scrotum and penis covering the female hyena's vagina. Sociable animals, hyenas live in loosely structured clans of about ten animals, led by females who are stronger and larger than males, based in a communal den.

Spotted hyena

Hyenas utilise their kills far better than most predators, digesting the bones, skin and even teeth of antelope. This results in the distinctive white colour of their faeces – which is an easily identified sign of them living in an area.

The spotted hyena is the largest hyena, identified by its light brown, blotchily spotted coat. It is found throughout Zambia, though is increasingly restricted to the national parks and GMAs. Although mainly nocturnal, spotted hyenas can often be seen around dusk and dawn in the Luangwa, Kafue and Lower Zambezi, with particularly large clans being found in Liuwa. Their distinctive, whooping calls are a spine-chilling sound of the African night. Note that neither of the spotted hyena's close relatives, the brown hyena and aardwolf, are thought to occur in Zambia.

PRIMATES
Baboon *Papio cynocephalus* Shoulder height 50–75cm approx. Weight male 16–29kg, female 10–16kg.
This powerful terrestrial primate, distinguished from any other monkey by its much larger size, inverted U-shaped tail and distinctive canines, is fascinating to watch from a behavioural perspective. It lives in large troops that boast a complex, rigid social structure characterised by a matriarchal lineage and plenty of inter-troop movement by males seeking social dominance.

Common baboon

Omnivorous and at home in almost any habitat, the baboon is the most widespread primate in Africa, frequently seen in most game reserves. With their highly organised defence system, the only predator that seriously affects baboons is the leopard, which will try to pick them off at night whilst they are roosting in trees.

There are as many as nine types of baboon ranging in Africa and Saudi Arabia, of which three species live in Zambia: the **yellow baboon** (*Papio cynocephalus*) in the east, the grey-footed **chacma baboon** (*Papio ursinus*) in the south, and the **Kinda baboon** (*Papio kindae*) in the north – which some consider to be a subspecies of the yellow baboon (hence *Papio cynocephalus kindae*). Both yellow and chacma baboons have large ranges in Africa. More of a rarity is the Kinda baboon, which is found only in northern Zambia, Angola and parts of the DRC. In Zambia, it is readily seen in Kasanka National Park, Lavushi Manda and the Kafue. Smaller than other baboons, Kindas have softer coats and are generally lighter in colour. Socially, research by the Kasanka Baboon Project (*http://kasankababoonproject.com*) suggests that Kinda males and females have stronger bonds with each other than females have with other females, which is strikingly different to other baboon species.

Vervet monkey *Cercopithecus aethiops* Length (excluding tail) 40–55cm. Weight 4–6kg.
Also known as the green or grivet monkey, the vervet is probably the world's most numerous
monkey and certainly the most common and widespread representative of the
Cercopithecus guenons, a taxonomically controversial genus associated
with African forests. An atypical guenon in that it inhabits savannah and
woodland rather than true forest, the vervet spends a high proportion of
its time on the ground. It occurs throughout Zambia, preferring belts
of tall trees and thicker vegetation within easy reach of water.

The vervet's light grey coat, black face and white forehead
band are distinctive – as are the male's garish blue genitals.
Vervets live in troops averaging about 25 animals; they
are active during the day and roost in trees at night. They
eat mainly fruit and vegetables, though are opportunistic and will take
insects and young birds, and even raid tents at campsites (usually where ill-informed visitors
have previously tempted them into human contact by offering food).

Vervet monkey

Blue monkey *Cercopithecus mitis* Length (excluding tail) 50–60cm. Weight 5–8kg.
The blue monkey is known also as **moloney's monkey** in Zambia,
the **samango monkey** throughout southern Africa, the
golden monkey in southwest Uganda, **Sykes' monkey**
in Kenya and the **diademed** or **white-throated** guenon
in some field guides. This most variable monkey is
divided by some authorities into several species. It is
unlikely to be confused with the vervet monkey, as blue
monkeys have a dark blue-grey coat, which becomes reddish towards
its tail. Its underside is lighter, especially its throat.

Blue monkey

These monkeys live in troops of up to ten animals and associate with other
primates where their ranges overlap. They live in evergreen forests, and so are most likely to
be seen around the Copperbelt and North Western Provinces, or north of Kasanka. However,
they occur as far south as the Lower Zambezi National Park and are resident along the
Luangwa's Muchinga escarpment.

Angola black-and-white colobus monkey *Colobus angolensis* Length (excluding
tail) 65cm. Weight 12kg.
This beautiful jet black monkey has bold white facial markings, a long white tail and white
sides and shoulders. Almost exclusively arboreal, it is capable of jumping up to 30m, a
spectacular sight with its white tail streaming behind. Several races have been described, and
most authorities recognise this Angolan variety as a distinct species. In Zambia they are very
rare, but have been reported from the forests north of Mwinilunga.

Bushbaby *Galago crassicaudatus* Length (excluding tail) 35cm. Weight 1–1.5kg.
The bushbaby is Zambia's commonest member of a group of small and generally indistinguishable
nocturnal primates, distantly related to the lemurs of Madagascar. In Zambia they
occur throughout the country, though are very seldom seen during the day. At night
their wide, endearing eyes are often caught in the spotlight during night drives,
Bushbabies are nocturnal and even around safari camps they can
sometimes be seen by tracing a cry to a tree and shining a torch into the
branches; their eyes reflect as two red dots. These eyes are designed to
function in what we would describe as total darkness, and they feed
on insects – some of which are caught in the air by jumping – and
also by eating sap from trees, especially acacia gum.

Bushbaby

They inhabit wooded areas, and prefer acacia trees or riverine forests. I remember once being startled, whilst lighting a barbecue, by a small family of bushbabies. They raced through the trees above us, bouncing from branch to branch whilst chattering and screaming out of all proportion to their modest size.

Similar species
Lesser bushbaby *Galago senegalensis* Length (excluding tail) 17cm. Weight 150g. The lesser bushbaby, or **night ape**, is half the size of the bushbaby and seems to be less common than its larger cousin. Where it is found, it is often amongst acacia or terminalia vegetation, rather than mopane or miombo bush.

LARGE ANTELOPE
Sable antelope *Hippotragus niger* Shoulder height 135cm. Weight 230kg.

Sable antelope

The striking male sable is jet black with a distinct white face, underbelly and rump, and long decurved horns – a strong contender for the title of Africa's most beautiful antelope. The female is chestnut brown and has shorter horns, whilst the young are a lighter red-brown colour. Sable are found throughout the wetter areas of southern and east Africa.

They are not common in Zambia. However, Kafue is probably the best park for sable, with Kasanka also worthy of note. In the Luangwa, they're confined to the foothills of the Muchinga Escarpment, so very rarely seen by visitors. Nsumbu has a small population, and there have been reports of sable in Sioma Ngwezi and West Lunga.

Sable are normally seen in small herds: either bachelor herds of males, or breeding herds of females and young which are often accompanied by the dominant male in that territory. The breeding females give birth around February or March; the calves remain hidden, away from the herd, for their first few weeks. Sable are mostly grazers, though will browse, especially when food is scarce. They need to drink at least every other day, and seem especially fond of low-lying dewy vleis in wetter areas.

Roan antelope *Hippotragus equinus* Shoulder height 120–150cm. Weight 250–300kg.

Roan antelope

This handsome horse-like antelope is uniform fawn-grey with a pale belly, short decurved horns and a light mane. It could be mistaken for the female sable antelope, but this has a well-defined white belly, and lacks the roan's distinctive black-and-white facial markings. The roan is a relatively rare antelope; common almost nowhere in Africa (the Nyika Plateau being one obvious exception to this rule). In Zambia small groups of roan are found in South Luangwa, Kafue, Kasanka, Nsumbu, Liuwa Plains and (probably) Sioma Ngwezi.

Roan need lots of space if they are to thrive and breed; they don't generally do well where game densities are high. Game farms prize them as one of the most valuable antelope (hence expensive to buy). They need access to drinking water, but are adapted to subsist on relatively high plateaux with poor soils.

Waterbuck *Kobus ellipsiprymnus* Shoulder height 130cm. Weight 250–270kg.
The waterbuck is easily recognised by its shaggy brown coat and the male's large lyre-shaped horns. The **common race** of southern Africa (*K. e. ellipsiprymnus*) and areas east of the Rift Valley has a distinctive white ring around its rump, seen on the left of the sketch. The **defassa**

race (known as *K. e. defassa* or *K. e. crawshayi*) of the Rift Valley and areas further west has a full white rump, as indicated on the right.

Waterbuck

In Zambia, the common waterbuck populates the Luangwa and Lower Zambezi valleys, whilst the defassa race occurs throughout most of the rest of the country, including Kafue National Park. They need to drink very regularly, so usually stay within a few kilometres of water, where they like to graze on short, nutritious grasses. At night they may take cover in adjacent woodlands. It is often asserted that waterbuck flesh is oily and smelly, which may discourage predators.

Blue wildebeest
Connochaetes taurinus Shoulder height 130–150cm. Weight 180–250kg.
This ungainly antelope, also called the **brindled gnu**, is easily identified by its dark coat and bovine appearance. The superficially similar buffalo is far more heavily built. When they have enough space, blue wildebeest can form immense herds – as perhaps a million do for their annual migration from Tanzania's Serengeti Plains into Kenya's Masai Mara. In Zambia,

Blue wildebeest

one such gathering occurs on the Liuwa Plains around November, when tens of thousands of animals congregate here as the rains arrive.

Elsewhere, wildebeest naturally occur from around the Kafue National Park area westwards, to Angola. There's also a subspecies, **Cookson's wildebeest**, *Connochaetes taurinus cooksoni*, which is endemic to the Luangwa Valley. It's found commonly on the north side, in North Luangwa, but only rarely further south. It differs from the main species by having cleaner colours including slightly reddish bands and being a little smaller and more compact.

Lichtenstein's hartebeest
Alcelaphus lichtensteini Shoulder height 125cm. Weight 120–150kg.
Hartebeests are awkward antelopes, readily identified by the combination of large shoulders, a sloping back, a smooth coat and smallish horns in both sexes. Numerous subspecies are recognised, all of which are generally seen in small family groups in reasonably open country. Though once hartebeest were found from the Mediterranean to the Cape, only isolated populations still survive. Hartebeests are almost exclusively grazers and they like access to water.

The only one native to Zambia is Lichtenstein's hartebeest, which used to be found throughout the country, except for the extreme south and west. They are seen frequently in Kafue, and also occur in Nsumbu and Kasanka. The Luangwa has a good population, but they generally stay away from the river, and so remain out of view for most visitors.

Similar species The **tsessebe** (*Damaliscus lunatus*) is basically a darker version of the hartebeest with striking yellow lower legs. (A closely related subspecies is known as *topi* in east Africa.) These are very sparsely distributed in Zambia, occurring in the Kasanka–Bangweulu area, and to the far west of the Zambezi, in Liuwa and Sioma Ngwezi. Its favourite habitat is open grassland, where it is a selective grazer, eating the younger, more nutritious grasses. The tsessebe is one of the fastest antelope species, and jumps very well.

Kudu
Tragelaphus strepsiceros Shoulder height 140–155cm. Weight 180–250kg.
The kudu (or, more properly, the greater kudu) is the most frequently observed member of the genus *Tragelaphus*. These medium-size to large antelopes are characterised by their grey-brown coats and up to ten stripes on each side. The male has magnificent double-spiralled corkscrew

horns. Occurring throughout Mozambique, Zimbabwe, Zambia, Botswana and Namibia, kudu are widespread and common, though not in dense forests or open grasslands. They are normally associated with well-wooded habitats. These browsers thrive in areas with mixed tree savannah and thickets, and the males will sometimes use their horns to pull down the lower branches of trees to eat, with mahogany (*Trichelia emetica*), being a particular favourite.

In Zambia they occur throughout the country except for the far northern areas. Normally they're seen in small herds, consisting of a couple of females and their offspring, sometimes accompanied by a male. Otherwise the males occur either singly, or in small bachelor groups.

Eland   *Taurotragus oryx* Shoulder height 150–175cm. Weight 450–900kg.

Eland

Africa's largest antelope, the eland is light brown in colour, sometimes with a few faint white vertical stripes. Relatively short horns and a large dewlap accentuate its somewhat bovine appearance. It was once widely distributed in east and southern Africa, though the population has now been severely depleted. Small herds of eland frequent grasslands and light woodlands, often fleeing at the slightest provocation. (They have long been hunted for their excellent meat, so perhaps this is not surprising.)

Eland are opportunist browsers and grazers, eating fruit, berries, seed pods and leaves as well as green grass after the rains, and roots and tubers when times are lean. They run slowly, though can trot for great distances and jump exceedingly well. In Zambia they occur widely but sparsely, and are largely confined to the country's protected areas.

MEDIUM AND SMALL ANTELOPE

Bushbuck   *Tragelaphus scriptus* Shoulder height 70–80cm. Weight 30–45kg.

Bushbuck

This attractive antelope, a member of the same genus as the kudu, is widespread throughout Africa and shows great regional variation in its colouring. It occurs in forest and riverine woodland, where it is normally seen singly or in pairs. The male is dark brown or chestnut, while the much smaller female is generally a pale reddish brown. The male has relatively small, straight horns and both sexes are marked with white spots and sometimes stripes, though the stripes are often indistinct.

Bushbuck tend to be secretive and very skittish, except when used to people. They depend on cover and camouflage to avoid predators, and are often found in the thick, herby vegetation around rivers. They will freeze if disturbed, before dashing off into the undergrowth. Bushbuck are both browsers and grazers, choosing the more succulent grass shoots, fruit and flowers. In Zambia they are very widely distributed and fairly common.

Impala   *Aepeceros melampus* Shoulder height 90cm. Weight 45kg.

Impala

This slender, handsome antelope is superficially similar to the springbok, but in fact belongs to its own separate family. Chestnut in colour, and lighter underneath than above, the impala has diagnostic black-and-white stripes running down its rump and tail, and the male has large lyre-shaped horns. One of the most widespread and successful antelope species in east and southern Africa, the impala is normally seen in large herds in wooded savannah habitats. It is the most common antelope in the Luangwa Valley, and throughout much of the central and southern areas of Zambia.

However, in more northerly areas, puku are sometimes more common. As expected of such a successful species, it both grazes and browses, depending on what fodder is available.

Reedbuck
Redunca arundinum Shoulder height 80–90cm. Weight 45–65kg.

Sometimes referred to as the **southern reedbuck** (as distinct from mountain and Bohor reedbucks, found further east), these delicate antelope are uniformly fawn or grey in colour, and lighter below than above. They are generally found in reedbeds and tall grasslands, often beside rivers, and are easily identified by their loud, whistling alarm call and distinctive bounding running style. In Zambia they occur widely, though seem absent from the very bottom of the Zambezi and Luangwa valley floors. (They do occur in both Luangwa and Lower Zambezi national parks, but usually on slightly higher ground, away from the rivers.)

Reedbuck

Klipspringer
Oreotragus oreotragus Shoulder height 60cm. Weight 13kg.

The klipspringer is a strongly built little antelope, normally seen in pairs, and easily identified by its dark, bristly grey-yellow coat, slightly speckled appearance and unique habitat preference. Klipspringer means 'rock jumper' in Afrikaans and it is an apt name for an antelope which occurs exclusively in mountainous areas and rocky outcrops from Cape Town to the Red Sea.

Klipspringer

They occur throughout most of Zambia, except for the extreme western areas, but only where rocky hills or kopjes are found. Given Zambia's generally rolling topography, this means only the odd isolated population exists. They are seen occasionally on the escarpments of the main valleys, but usually away from the main game areas. Klipspringers are mainly browsers, though they do eat a little new grass. When spotted they will freeze, or bound at great speed across the steepest of slopes.

Lechwe
Kobus leche Shoulder height 90–100cm. Weight 80–100kg.

Lechwe are sturdy, shaggy antelope with beautiful lyre-shaped horns, adapted to favour the seasonal floodplains that border lakes and rivers. They need dry land on which to rest, but otherwise will spend much of their time grazing on grasses and sedges, standing in water if necessary. Their hooves are splayed, adapted to bounding through their muddy environment when fleeing from the lion, hyena and wild dog that hunt them, making them the most aquatic of antelope after sitatunga.

Lechwe are found in DRC, Angola, northern Botswana and Namibia's Caprivi Strip, but their stronghold is Zambia. Wherever they occur, the males are generally larger and darker than the females, and in Zambia there are three subspecies (though none occurs in the Luangwa or Lower Zambezi valleys).

The **red lechwe** (*K. l. leche*) is the most widespread subspecies. It's the only one found outside Zambia and has a chestnut-reddish coat, darker on the back and much lighter (almost white) underneath. Its legs have black markings, as does the tip of its tail. Inside Zambia red lechwe are found in large numbers (about 5,000 probably) on the Busanga Plains, with smaller populations in the Western Province and the Lukanga Swamps.

Lechwe

The **Kafue lechwe** (*K. l. kafuensis*) are slightly larger animals, with bigger horns, and are restricted to the Kafue Flats area, between Lake Itezhi-Tezhi and Lusaka. This race is more light brown than red, with black patches on their shoulders that run into the black on their legs. Most of the 40,000–50,000 that remain are confined to the Lochinvar and Blue Lagoon national parks.

The **black lechwe** (*K. l. smithemani*) used to occur in huge numbers, perhaps as many as half a million animals, centred on the plains to the south of the Bangweulu Swamps. They are now restricted to about 30,000–40,000 animals in the same area, and a small population have been re-introduced into the Nashinga Swamps to the west of Chinsali. Black lechwe are much darker and the older males have almost black backs and brownish undersides.

Puku   *Kobus vardoni* Shoulder height 80cm. Weight 60–75kg.

Unless you see them beside each other, puku can be hard to distinguish from red lechwe – though the adults are generally slightly smaller than the lechwe. They are also stocky, orangey-red antelope with shaggy coats. Male pukus have stout, ribbed horns which curve forwards at the tips, though are shorter and spread out less than a lechwe's horns.

Puku are grazers, typically inhabiting open plains adjacent to rivers or marshes, or woodland fringes. They are always found close to water, although are not as fond of completely flooded areas as lechwe. Puku usually feed early or late in the day, and will often lie down in the shade when the sun is at its highest.

They are one of Zambia's most common antelope, found throughout western and northern Zambia, and the Luangwa Valley, although they are noticeably absent from the Lower Zambezi Valley. In the south of Zambia, puku are exceedingly rare, occurring only in one small corner of northern Chobe; to the north they are native to areas of Malawi and the DRC, and common in Tanzania.

Young males form bachelor groups, from which prime animals break away to form territories. The more dominant the buck, the more attractive are the feeding resources within these territories, into which they attract females. Breeding takes place between April and July and thus calves are born in the green season when food resources are abundant.

Sitatunga   *Tragelaphus spekei* Shoulder height 85–90cm. Weight 105–115kg.

The semi-aquatic antelope is a widespread but infrequently observed inhabitant of west and central African papyrus swamps from the Okavango in Botswana to the Sudd in Sudan. In Zambia sitatunga are very widespread. Good populations are found in Bangweulu, the Busanga Swamps, Nsumbu and Kasanka.

Sitatunga

Because of its preferred habitat, the sitatunga is very elusive and seldom seen, even in areas where it is relatively common. They are also less easy to hunt/poach than many other species, although they are exceedingly vulnerable to habitat destruction. Kasanka National Park is one of Africa's very best places to see these antelope; its tree hide provides more agile visitors with a superb vantage point above a small section of papyrus swamp, where sightings are virtually guaranteed in the early morning or late afternoon. Sitatunga are noted for an ability to submerse themselves completely, with just their nostrils showing, when pursued by a predator.

Steenbok   *Raphicerus cempestris* Shoulder height 50cm. Weight 11kg.

Steenbok

This rather nondescript small antelope has red-brown upper parts and clear white underparts, and the male has short straight horns. It is very common south of the Zambezi, but only occurs in southwestern Zambia (Mazabuka seems to be about the limit of their distribution). They like grasslands and open country with a scattering of cover, and seem to do very well in the drier areas. Like most other small antelopes, the steenbok is normally encountered singly or in pairs and tends to 'freeze' when disturbed, before taking flight.

Similar species Sharpe's grysbok (*Raphicerus sharpei*) is similar in size and appearance, though it has a distinctive white-flecked coat. It occurs widely throughout Zambia, and appears to be absent only from the far northwest (Liuwa/Mwinilunga area). It is almost entirely nocturnal in its habits and so very seldom seen.

The **oribi** (*Ourebia ourebi*) is also a widespread but generally uncommon antelope. It is usually found only in large, open stretches of dry grassland, with the termitaria zones of the Busanga Plains, Lochinvar and Bangweulu area standing out as good places to spot them. It looks much like a steenbok but stands about 10cm higher at the shoulder and has an altogether more upright bearing.

Common duiker *Sylvicapra grimmia* Shoulder height 50cm. Weight 20kg.

This anomalous duiker holds itself more like a steenbok or grysbok and is the only member of its (large) family to occur outside of forests. Generally grey in colour, the common duiker can most easily be separated from other small antelopes by the black tuft of hair that sticks up between its horns. They occur throughout Zambia, and tolerate most habitats except for true forest and very open country. They are even found near human settlements, where shooting and trapping is a problem, and are usually mainly nocturnal. Duikers are opportunist feeders, taking fruit, seeds and leaves, as well as crops, small reptiles and amphibians.

Common duiker

OTHER LARGE HERBIVORES
African elephant *Loxodonta africana* Shoulder height 2.3–3.4m. Weight up to 6,000kg.

The world's largest land animal, the African elephant is intelligent, social and often very entertaining to watch. Female elephants live in close-knit clans in which the eldest female plays matriarch over her sisters, daughters and granddaughters. Their lifespans are comparable to those of humans, and mother–daughter bonds are strong and may last for up to 50 years. Males generally leave the family group at around 12 years to roam singly or form bachelor herds. Under normal circumstances, elephants range widely in search of food and water, but when concentrated populations are forced to live in conservation areas their habit of uprooting trees can cause serious environmental damage.

Elephants are widespread and common in habitats ranging from desert to rainforest. In Zambia they were common everywhere except for the Upper Zambezi's floodplains, but have now become more restricted by human expansion. However, individuals often wander widely, turning up in locations from which they have been absent for years.

African elephant

Zambia's strongest population is in the Luangwa, where there are now about 15,000. As recently as 1973 estimates put the Luangwa's population at more than 100,000, but the late 1970s and '80s saw huge commercial poaching for ivory, which wiped out a large proportion of this. Outside of a small, protected area in South Luangwa National Park, Zambia's elephants fared even worse. The populations in Kafue and even North Luangwa are still small, and the individuals are very nervous and skittish near people. (The exception here is possibly the Lower Zambezi, where the elephants regularly swim between Zimbabwe and Zambia, because the

Zimbabwean parks were, on the whole, better protected from poaching than the Zambian parks. Hence the Lower Zambezi's elephant population is also fairly relaxed and numerous.)

Black rhinoceros   *Diceros bicornis* Shoulder height 160cm. Weight 1,000kg.

This is the more widespread of Africa's two rhino species, an imposing and rather temperamental creature. (White rhino are not thought to have been native to Zambia.) In the 1960s, the black rhino was recorded in the Kafue, Luangwa, Lower Zambezi and in the far north around Nsumbu and Mweru Wantipa. However, by the late 1990s it had probably been poached to extinction in Zambia, whilst becoming highly endangered in many of the other countries within its range. (There were a handful of reports of isolated individual animals existing in very remote areas; none was ever confirmed.) However, reintroductions have established a breeding population in a subsection of North Luangwa National Park, with the population standing at 34 in 2015.

Black rhinoceros

Black rhinos exploit a wide range of habitats from dense woodlands and bush, and are generally solitary animals. They can survive without drinking for four to five days. However, their territorial behaviour and regular patterns of movement make them an easy target for poachers. Black rhinos can be very aggressive when disturbed and will charge with minimal provocation. Their hearing and sense of smell are acute, whilst their eyesight is poor (so they often miss if you keep a low profile and don't move).

Hippopotamus   *Hippopotamus amphibius* Shoulder height 150cm. Weight 2,000kg.

Characteristic of Africa's large rivers and lakes, this large, lumbering animal spends most of the day submerged but emerges at night to graze. Strongly territorial, herds of ten or more animals are presided over by a dominant male who will readily defend his patriarchy to the death. Hippos are abundant in most protected rivers and water bodies and are still quite common outside of reserves.

Hippos are widely credited with killing more people than any other African mammal, but I know of no statistics to support this. John Coppinger (one of the Luangwa Valley's most experienced guides) suggests that crocodile, elephant and lion all account for more deaths in that area than hippos – despite the valley having one of Africa's highest concentrations of hippos. So whilst undoubtedly dangerous, perhaps they don't quite deserve their reputation.

In Zambia they are exceptionally common in most of the larger rivers, where hunting is not a problem. The Kafue, the Luangwa and the Zambezi all have large hippo populations.

Buffalo   *Syncerus caffer* Shoulder height 140cm. Weight 700kg.

Frequently and erroneously referred to as a **water buffalo** (an Asian species), the African, or Cape, buffalo is a distinctive, highly social ox-like animal that lives as part of a herd. It prefers well-watered savannah, though also occurs in forested areas. Common and widespread in sub-Saharan Africa, in Zambia it is widely distributed. The Luangwa, and especially the north park, seems to have some particularly large herds, hundreds of animals strong. Buffalo are primarily grazers and need regular access to water, where they swim readily. They smell and hear well, and it's often claimed that they have poor eyesight. This isn't true, though when encountered during a walking safari, they won't be able to discern your presence if you keep still and the wind is right.

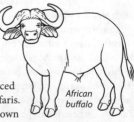

African buffalo

Huge herds are generally fairly peaceful, and experienced guides will often walk straight through them on walking safaris. However, small bachelor herds, or even single old bulls (known in the Luangwa as 'kakuli'), can be very nervous and aggressive. They have a reputation for charging at the slightest provocation, often in the midst of thick bush, and are exceedingly dangerous if wounded. Lion often follow herds of buffalo, their favourite prey.

Giraffe   *Giraffa camelopardis* Shoulder height 250–350cm. Weight 1,000–1,400kg.

The world's tallest and longest-necked land animal, a fully grown giraffe can measure up to 5.5m high. Quite unmistakable, giraffe live in loosely structured herds of up to 15, though herd members often disperse, when they may be seen singly or in smaller groups. Formerly distributed throughout east and southern Africa, these great browsers are now found only in the southern side of the Luangwa Valley and the far southwest of Zambia.

About eight subspecies of giraffe have been identified in Africa, and the Luangwa Valley contains one such distinct population, **Thornicroft's giraffe** (*G. c. thornicroftii*). These are generally regarded as having dark body patches and lighter neck patches than the normal 'southern' race of giraffe, and their colour patches don't normally extend below the knees, leaving their lower legs almost white. Their faces are also light or white. The vast majority of these live on the east side of the Luangwa River, in the GMA outside the park. They have been protected from hunting by a local taboo.

Much further west, the pocket of giraffe which are thought to still survive around the Sioma Ngwezi National Park are **Angolan giraffe** (*G. c. angolensis*), although so little is known of what survives in Sioma Ngwezi that their current status there is uncertain.

Plains zebra   *Equus quagga* Shoulder height 130cm. Weight 300–340kg.

Also known as common zebra, this attractive striped horse is widespread throughout most of east and southern Africa, where it is often seen in large herds alongside wildebeest. It is common in most conservation areas from northern South Africa all the way up to the southeast of Ethiopia.

Most southern races, although not those found in Zambia, have paler brownish 'shadow-stripes' between their bold black stripes. In Zambia, the subspecies in the Luangwa Valley is **Crawshay's zebra** (*E. q. crawshaii*), which also occurs on Nyika Plateau and possibly in Malawi's Vwaza Marsh. Norman Carr comments in his book on the Luangwa's wildlife (page 530) that the zebra found to the west of the Muchinga escarpment belong to the *E. q. zambeziensis* subspecies. In the Kafue's Busanga Plains, the subspecies is known as **Grant's or Boehm's zebra** (*Equus q. boehmii*).

Plains zebra

Regardless of these minor taxonomic differences, zebra are widely distributed throughout Zambia, though they tend to be restricted by human activity to the more remote or protected areas. They lack the brown shadow-stripes of their cousins further south, but otherwise are very similar.

Warthog   *Phacochoerus aethiopicus* Shoulder height 60–70cm. Weight up to 100kg.

This widespread and often conspicuously abundant resident of the African savannah is grey in colour with a thin covering of hairs, wart-like bumps on its face, and rather large upward-curving tusks. Africa's only diurnal swine, the warthog is often seen in family groups, trotting around with its tail raised stiffly (a diagnostic trait) and a determinedly nonchalant air. They occur in most areas of Zambia, except in the extreme northwest, and are very common in most of the national parks. They don't usually fare well near settlements, as they are very susceptible to subsistence hunting/poaching. Wherever they occur, you'll often see them grazing beside the road, on bended knee, with their tails held high in the air as soon as they trot away.

Warthog

Similar species Bulkier, hairier and browner, the **bushpig** (*Potomochoerus larvatus*) is known to occur throughout Zambia, and even in the vicinity of cultivated land where it can do considerable damage to crops. However, it is very rarely seen due to its nocturnal habits and preference for dense vegetation.

SMALL MAMMALS
African civet *Civettictis civetta* Shoulder height 40cm. Weight 10–15kg.
This bulky, long-haired, rather feline creature of the African night is primarily carnivorous, feeding on small animals and carrion, but will also eat fruit. It has a similar-coloured coat to a leopard: densely blotched with large black spots becoming stripes

African civet

towards the head. Civets are widespread and common throughout Zambia in many habitats, and make frequent cameo appearances on night drives. Though occasionally called 'civet cats', this is misleading because they are far more closely related to the mongooses than the felines.

Similar species The smaller, more slender **tree civet** (*Nandinia binotata*) is an arboreal forest animal with a dark brown coat marked with black spots. It is really a resident of the equatorial forests, although is found in a few mountain areas on Zambia's Malawi border (including Nyika) as well as north of Mwinilunga. It is nocturnal, solitary and largely arboreal – and so is very seldom seen.

The **small-spotted genet** (*Genetta genetta*), **large-spotted genet** (*Genetta tigrina*) and **rusty-spotted genet** (*Genetta rubignosa*) are the most widespread members in Zambia of a large group of similar small predators (which even the experts often can't tell apart without examining their skins by hand). All the genets are slender and rather feline in appearance (though they are not cats), with a grey to gold-brown coat marked with black spots (perhaps combining into short bars) and a long ringed tail.

You're most likely to see them on nocturnal game drives or occasionally scavenging around game reserve lodges. They are found all over Zambia, even in urban areas if there is a plentiful supply of rodents. They are excellent climbers and opportunists, eating fruit, small birds, termites and even scorpions.

Banded mongoose *Mungos mungo* Shoulder height 20cm. Weight around 1kg.
The banded mongoose is probably the most commonly observed member of a group of small, slender, terrestrial carnivores. Uniform dark grey-brown except for a dozen black stripes across its back, it is a diurnal mongoose occurring in playful family groups, or troops, in most habitats throughout Zambia. It feeds on insects, scorpions, amphibians, reptiles and even carrion and bird's eggs, and can move through the bush at quite a pace.

Banded mongoose

Similar species Another eight or so mongoose species occur in Zambia; some are social and gather in troops, others are solitary. Several are too scarce and nocturnal to be seen by casual visitors. Of the rest, the **water** or **marsh mongoose** (*Atilax paludinosus*) is large, normally solitary and has a very scruffy brown coat; it's widespread in the wetter areas. The **white-tailed mongoose** (*Ichneumia albicauda*), or white-tailed ichneumon, is a solitary, large brown mongoose with long, coarse, woolly hair. It is nocturnal and easily identified by its bushy white tail if seen crossing roads at night. It's not uncommon in cattle-ranching areas, where it eats the beetle-grubs found in the manure.

The **slender mongoose** (*Galerella sanguinea*) is as widespread and also solitary, but it is very much smaller (shoulder height 10cm) and has a uniform brown or reddish coat and blackish tail tip. Its tail is held up when it runs, and it is common throughout Zambia where there is lots of cover for it. The **dwarf mongoose** (*Helogate parvula*) is a diminutive (shoulder height 7cm), highly sociable light brown mongoose often seen in the vicinity of the termite mounds where it nests. This is Africa's smallest carnivore, occurring in a higher density than any other, and is widespread throughout Zambia. Groups of 20 to 30 are not unknown, consisting of a breeding pair and subordinate others. These inquisitive little animals can be very entertaining to watch.

The **large grey mongoose** (*Herpestes ichneumon*), also called the Egyptian mongoose, is a large mongoose with coarse, grey-speckled body hair, black lower legs and feet, and a black tip to its tail. It's found all over Zambia, but is common nowhere, is generally diurnal and is solitary or lives in pairs. It eats small rodents, reptiles, birds and also snakes – generally killing rather than scavenging. The **bushy-tailed mongoose** (*Bdeogale crassicaude*) is a small, predominantly nocturnal species that looks mainly black, especially its legs and tail. It is found throughout Zambia, though appears relatively uncommon south of the Zambezi.

Meller's mongoose (*Rhynchogale melleri*) is a variable shaggy, grey colour with dark legs and a large muzzle. Its distribution is patchy and somewhat uncertain, but it is thought to occur throughout western Zambia and the Luangwa, but not north of the Serenje–Mbala road. It is solitary and nocturnal, eating a large proportion of termites as well as reptiles, amphibians and fruit. **Selous's mongoose** (*Paracynictis selousi*) is smaller, with fine, speckled grey fur, and a white tip at the end of its tail. It likes open country and woodlands, occurring in many areas of southern and western Zambia, even including the Luangwa. It is nocturnal and solitary, eating mainly insects, grubs, small reptiles and amphibians – it seems especially fond of the larvae of dung beetles, and so is sometimes found in cattle country.

Honey badger *Mellivora capensis* Shoulder height 30cm. Weight 12kg.

Also known as the ratel, the honey badger is black with a puppyish face and grey-white back. It is an opportunistic feeder best known for its allegedly symbiotic relationship with a bird called the honeyguide which leads it to a beehive, waits for it to tear it open, then feeds on the

scraps. The honey badger is among the most widespread of African carnivores, and also amongst the most powerful and aggressive for its size; it occurs all over Zambia. However, it is thinly distributed and infrequently seen, except when it has lost its fear of people and started to scavenge from safari camps.

Honey badger

Similar species Several other mustelids occur in the region, including the **striped polecat** (*Ictonyx striatus*), a widely distributed but rarely seen nocturnal creature which has black underparts and a bushy white back, and the similar but much scarcer **striped weasel** (*Poecilogale albincha*). This has been reported from several locations in Zambia, but only rarely.

The **Cape clawless otter** (*Aonyx capensis*) is a brown freshwater mustelid with a white collar, whilst the smaller **spotted-necked otter** (*Lutra maculicollis*) is darker with light white spots on its throat. Both occur fairly commonly throughout the rivers, swamps and lakes of Zambia.

Aardvark (*Orycteropus afer*) Shoulder height 60cm. Weight up to 70kg.

This singularly bizarre nocturnal insectivore is unmistakable with its long snout, huge ears and powerful legs, adapted to dig up the nests of termites, on which it feeds. Aardvarks occur throughout southern Africa, except the driest western areas of the Namib. Though their distinctive three-toed tracks are often seen, and they are not uncommon animals, sightings of them are rare.

Aardvarks prefer areas of grassland and sparse scrub, rather than dense woodlands. They are absent from Zambia's

Aardvark

floodplains and marshes, but otherwise occur throughout the country where termites are found.

Pangolin *Manis temmincki* Total length 70–100cm. Weight 8–15kg.

Sharing the aardvaak's diet of termites and ants, the pangolin is another very unusual nocturnal insectivore – with distinctive armour plating and a tendency to roll up in a ball when disturbed. (Then it can swipe its tail from side to side – inflicting serious damage on its aggressor.) Sometimes known as **Temminck's pangolins**, or **scaly anteaters**, these strange animals walk on their hindlegs, using their tail and front legs for balance. They are both nocturnal and rare – so sightings are exceedingly unusual and their distribution is uncertain. However, they are thought to occur in Kafue National Park and southern Zambia, as well as in the Luangwa Valley. (Evidence of their occurrence in the Luangwa is limited to about two sightings over the last few decades.)

In some areas further south, particularly Zimbabwe, local custom is to make a present of any pangolin found to the paramount chief (often taken to mean the president). This has caused great damage to their population.

Porcupine *Hystrix africaeaustralis* Total length 80–100cm. Weight 15–25kg.

This is the largest rodent found in the region, and occurs throughout Zambia and all over southern Africa. It easily identified by its black-and-white striped quills, generally black hair, and shambling gait. If heard in the dark, then the slight rattle of its quills augments the rustle of its foraging. These quills drop off fairly regularly, and are often found in the bush.

The porcupine's diet is varied, and they are fairly opportunistic when it comes to food. Roots and tubers are favourites, as is the bark of certain trees; they will also eat meat and small reptiles or birds if they have the chance.

Similar species Also spiky, the **southern African hedgehog** (*Erinaceus frontalis*) has been recorded in a few locations in Zambia, including the Lusaka, Mumbwa and Chipata areas. It's likely to occur elsewhere, though is small and nocturnal, so rarely seen even where it does occur. Hedgehogs are about 20cm long (much smaller than porcupines), omnivorous and uncommon.

Yellow-spotted rock hyrax *Heterohyrax brucei* Length 35–50cm. Weight 2.5–3.5kg.

Rodent-like in appearance, hyraxes (also known as **dassies**) are claimed to be the closest living relative of elephants. Yellow-spotted rock hyraxes are often seen sunning themselves in rocky habitats, and become tame when used to people.

They are social animals, living in large groups, and largely herbivores, eating leaves, grasses and fruits. Where you see lots of dassies, watch out for black eagles and other raptors which prey extensively on them.

Similar species Very similar, the **tree hyrax** (*Dendrohyrax arboreus*) has been recorded in a few locations on the eastern side of the country, including South Luangwa.

Scrub hare *Lepus saxatilis* Shoulder height 45–60cm. Weight 1–4.5kg.

This is the largest and commonest African hare, occurring throughout Zambia. In some areas a short walk, or drive, at dusk or after nightfall might reveal three or four scrub hares. They tend to freeze when disturbed.

Tree squirrel *Paraxerus cepapi* Total length 35cm. Weight 100–250g.

This common rodent is a uniform grey or buff colour, with a long tail that is furry but not bushy. It's widely distributed all over southern and east Africa, and occurs throughout Zambia in most woodland habitats, although not wet evergreen or montane forests. It's often so common in mopane woodlands that it can be difficult to avoid seeing it, hence its other common name – the mopane squirrel.

Tree squirrels can live alone, in pairs or in small family groups, usually nesting in a drey of dry leaves, in a hole in a tree. They are diurnal and venture down to the ground to feed on seeds, fruit, nuts, vegetable matter and small insects. When alarmed they will usually bolt up the nearest tree, keeping on the side of the trunk away from the threat and so out of sight as much as possible. If they can attain a safe vantage point with a view of the threat, then they'll sometimes make a loud clicking alarm call.

Similar species The **sun squirrel** (*Heliosciurus rufobrachium*) is the largest of Zambia's squirrels, and is found everywhere north of a rough line between Kabwe and Lukulu. It has similar habits to those of the more common tree squirrel, though will lie in the sun more often. Its colour varies considerably between individuals, and seasons, from light fawn to greyish brown, though its long bushy tail is consistently crossed by numerous whitish, longitudinal stripes.

The **red-and-black squirrel** (*Heliosciurus lucifer*) is a very pretty species with flame-red upper parts, a black patch in the middle of its back, and whitish underside. It occurs only in montane forest and in Zambia is thought to be restricted to the Nyika Plateau.

Boehm's squirrel (*Paraxerus boehmi*) has a similar size, shape and greyish colouring to the tree squirrel. However, it has two very distinct white stripes, bordered by black, down the side of its back from nape to tail. It inhabits riverine evergreen forest, and has a limited distribution in Zambia, restricted to the country's far north, around the Nsumbu and Lusenga Plain areas.

The **flying squirrel** (*Anomalurus derbianus*) is quite unmistakable as there's a membrane of skin linking the fore and hind legs, and also the base of the tail. It uses this to glide with, when jumping from a higher branch to a lower one. It's a solitary, arboreal species that prefers miombo woodlands. It occurs from the Liuwa area east across Mwinilunga and the Copperbelt, and into the western side of northern Zambia, but is seldom seen.

UPDATES WEBSITE

You can post your comments and recommendations, and read the latest feedback and updates from other readers, online at www.bradtupdates.com/zambia.

Appendix 2

LANGUAGES

Zambia's main language groups are briefly outlined in *Chapter 2*, pages 19–23. This section will try to note down just a few useful phrases, and give their local translations in six of the most frequently encountered languages: Nyanja, Bemba, Lozi, Lunda, Tonga and Luvale. The visitor will probably find Nyanja or Bemba the most useful of these: Nyanja is the language that visitors are most likely to hear in the parks, while Bemba is more widely spoken countrywide. However, in the more remote areas – like the Western Province – where Nyanja and Bemba are not spoken, the other languages will prove invaluable.

Space is too short here, and my knowledge too limited, to give a detailed pronunciation guide to these six languages. However, all are basically phonetic and by far the best way to learn the finer nuances of pronouncing these phrases is to find some Zambians to help you as soon as you arrive. Asking a Zambian to help you with a local language is also an excellent way to break the ice with a new local acquaintance, as it involves them talking about a subject that they know well, and in which they are usually confident.

There may be several ways of saying goodbye, depending on the circumstances. In Nyanya, for example, one form may be said by the person leaving, and the other by the person staying behind – translating as 'go well' and 'stay well'. An alternative is to use the more informal 'see you later'.

Note that there is no specific word for 'please'; rather the meaning is incorporated into the word structure, so in Lozi, for example, 'please' is expressed by adding an 'a' to the subjunctive of the verb.

As noted in *Cultural guidelines*, pages 79–80, learning a few simple phrases in the local language will go a long way towards helping the independent traveller to have an easy and enjoyable time in Zambia. Just remember to laugh at yourself, and have fun. Most Zambians will be very impressed and applaud your efforts to speak their language, no matter how hard they may laugh!

	Nyanja	Bemba	Lozi
Good morning;	*Muli bwanji?* (formal)	*Mwashibukeni?* (formal)	*Muzuhile cwani?* (formal)
How are you?	*Muli shani?* (informal)	*Muzuhile?* (informal)	*Mucwani?* (informal)
I am fine	*Nile bwino* (formal) *Bwino* (informal)	*Eyamukwayi,* *Ndifye bwino* (formal) *Bwino* (informal)	*Lu zuhile hande* (formal) *Hande* (informal)
Goodbye	*Salani bwino*	*Shaaleenipo*	*Muzamave hande*
See you later (*ciao*)	*Tisau onana*	*Twalaamonana*	*Lukabonana*
yes	*inde*	*eya ye*	*kimona*
no	*iyayi*	*awe*	*baatili*
thank you	*zikomo*	*twa to te la*	*nitumezi*

Judi Helmholz

During your travels you may have the good fortune to meet a Wireless, a Handbrake or an Engine. If you are really lucky, you may encounter a Cabbage. These are names of people I have met in Zambia.

Looking for Fame and Fortune? Look no further than twin boys living in the Western Province. Beware of Temptation though, he is a money-changer known for calculating exchanges solely to his advantage.

Working with Sunday and Friday got rather amusing, 'Sunday, can you work on Saturday with Friday?' Working with Trouble was another matter entirely, as we had frequently to enquire, 'Where can I find Trouble?' Gift, true to his namesake, felt compelled to ask for one, while Lunch took on a whole new meaning and Clever is a friend who is true to his name.

Unusual names aren't limited solely to English. For example, there is Mwana Uta which literally means 'son of a gun', and Saka Tutu meaning 'father of an insect'. Pity the local man named Mwana Ngombe or 'child of a cow'!

	Nyanja	**Bemba**	**Lozi**
hey you!	*iwe!*	*iwe!*	*wena!*
I want	*ndifuna*	*ndefwaya*	*nabata*
there	*kunja*	*kulya* (also 'food')	*kwale*
here	*apa*	*hapa* (silent 'h')	*faa*
stop	*imilira*	*yema*	*iminina*
let's go	*tiyeni* or *tye*	*aluye*	*natuleya*
help me	*niyetizipita*	*ngafweniko*	*nituse kwteni*
how much?	*zingati?*	*shinga?*	*kibukayi?*
it is too much!	*yadula!*	*fingi!*	*kihahulu!*
where can I find… ?	*alikuti…?*	*kwisa…?*	*uinzi kai…?*
the doctor	*sing'ang'a doctoro*	*shinganga*	*mualafi*
the police	*kapokola*	*kapokola*	*mupokola*
the market	*kumusika*	*ekobashita fyakulya*	*kwamusika*
drinking water	*mazi akumwa*	*amenshi ayakunwa*	*mezi u kunwa*
some food	*chakudya*	*ichakulya*	*sakuca*

	Lunda	**Tonga**	**Luvale**
Good morning;	*Mudi nahi?*	*Mwabuka buti?*	*Ngacili?*
How are you?		*Muli buti?*	
I am fine	*Cha chiwahi*	*Kabotu*	*Kanawa*
Goodbye	*Shalenuhu*	*Muchale kabotu*	*Salenuho mwane*
See you later (*ciao*)	*Tuualimona*	*Tulabonana*	*Natulimona*
yes	*ena*	*inzya*	*eawa*
no	*inehi*	*pepe*	*kugule*
thank you	*kusakililaku*	*twalumba*	*gunasakulila*
hey, you!	*enu!*	*yebo!*	*enu!*
I want	*nakukena*	*ndiyanda*	*gikutonda*
there	*kuna*	*okuya*	*haaze*
here	*kunu*	*aano* or *awa*	*kuno*
stop	*imanaku*	*koyima* or *ima*	*imana*
let's go	*tuyena*	*atwende*	*tuyenga*
help me	*kwashiku*	*ndigwashe*	*gukafweko*

	Lunda	**Tonga**	**Luvale**
how much?	*anahi?*	*ongaye?*	*jingayi?*
it is too much!	*yayivulu!*	*chadula! or zinji!*	*yayivulu!*
where can I find…?	*kudihi….?*	*ulikuli…?*	*ali kuli…?*
the doctor	*ndotolu*	*mun'ganga*	*ndotolo*
the police	*kapokola*	*kappokola*	*kapokola*
the market	*chisakanu*	*musika*	*mushika*
drinking water	*meji akunwa*	*maanzi akunywa*	*meya a kunwa*
some food	*chakuda*	*chakulya*	*kulya*

Wanderlust travel magazine

Wanderlust offers a unique mix of inspiration and practical advice, making it the ultimate magazine for independent-minded, curious travellers.

For more about *Wanderlust* and for travel inspiration visit www.wanderlust.co.uk

Appendix 3

FURTHER INFORMATION

BOOKS

History, politics and economy

Bigland, Eileen *The Lake of the Royal Crocodiles* Hodder and Stoughton, London, 1939.

Clark, John *Zambia: Debt & Poverty* Oxfam, Oxford, 1989. This slim volume looks with clarity at Zambia's international debt, its causes and its consequences.

Hobson, Dick *Tales of Zambia* Zambia Society Trust, London, 1996. This is a lovely book, cataloguing big moments in Zambia's history, as well as some of its quirkier incidents and characters. It has sections on legends, mining and the country's flora and fauna and is very readable. Dick Hobson's knowledge and love of Zambia shine through.

Lamb, Christine *The Africa House* Viking, London, 2nd edition 2004. This fascinating book pieces together the life and times of Sir Stewart Gore-Browne from diaries, correspondence and memories. It's a spellbinding tale, eloquently told. If this can't convey the fascination of Shiwa, and make you want to see it, then nothing can.

Livingstone, David *Missionary Travels and Researches in Southern Africa* 1857. Over a century after it was written, this classic still makes fascinating reading.

Macmillan, Hugh *An African Trading Empire: the story of Susman Brothers & Wulfsohn, 1901–2005* I B Tauris, London, 2005.

Macmillan, Hugh, and Shapiro, Frank *Zion In Africa: the Jews of Zambia* I B Tauris and the Council for Zambia Jewry, London and Lusaka, 1999.

Reader, John *Africa: A Biography of the Continent* Penguin Books, London, 1997. Over 700 pages of highly readable history, interwoven with facts and statistics, make a remarkable overview of Africa's past. Given that Zambia's boundaries were imposed from Europe, its history must be looked at from a pan-African context to be understood. This book can show you that wider view; it is compelling and essential reading. Chapter 47 is largely devoted to the Lozi people.

Roberts, Andrew *A History of Zambia* Africana Publishing, New York, 1976. A detailed and complete history of Zambia, from prehistory to 1974.

Rotberg, Robert I *Black Heart: Gore-Browne and the Politics of Multiracial Zambia* University of California Press, Berkeley, 1977.

Williams, Geoffrey J (ed) *Lusaka and its Environs* ZGA Handbooks, Lusaka.

David Livingstone and the Victorian Encounter with Africa National Portrait Gallery, London, 1996. Six essays on Livingstone's life, concentrating on not only what he did, but also on how he was perceived in the UK.

Zambia: Condemned to Debt World Development Movement (*www.wdm.org.uk*), London, May 2004. The WDM is a charity which researches into global trade and debt trends, and campaigns for policies to reduce injustice and tackle poverty.

Wildlife and natural history   Books published by the Wildlife and Environmental Conservation Society of Zambia (WECSZ) and the Zambian Ornithological Society

(ZOS), are usually obtainable from bookshops in Lusaka, or direct from the WECSZ office (page 51).

Aspinwall, Dylan, and Beel, Carl *A Field Guide to Zambian Birds not found in Southern Africa* Zambian Ornithological Society, Lusaka, 1998. This excellent small guide is designed to complement a book covering Africa south of the Zambezi, such as Newman's guide, by describing only the birds occurring in Zambia which aren't included in Newman's guide. It's available in Zambia, but difficult to find elsewhere.

Bolnick, Doreen *A Guide to the Common Wild Flowers of Zambia and Neighbouring Regions* Macmillan Educational, London, 1995. This is a good small field guide to the more common species. A revised edition was published in 2007 by WECSZ.

Buk, Kenneth (Zoological Museum, University of Copenhagen) 'African Wild Dog Survey in Zambia', *Canid News*, vol 3, 1995. This piece of academic research looked at the distribution of wild dogs in Zambia in 1994, the reasons for their decline, and their possibilities for long-term survival.

Carr, Norman *A Guide to the Wildlife of the Luangwa Valley* Montford Press, Malawi, 3rd edition 1997. This small paperback (70 pages) was written by the valley's most famous guide and conservationist. It's not comprehensive, but is fascinating for the author's personal insights into the Luangwa area and its wildlife.

Coates Palgrave, Keith and Meg (eds) *Trees of Southern Africa* Struik, South Africa, 2003.

Cooray, Gerald, and Lane, Andrew *Minerals of Zambia* Nchanga Consolidated Copper Mines Ltd.

Hide, Phil *Birds of the Luangwa Valley* Zambian Ornithological Society, Lusaka, 2008.

Jackman, Brian, Scott, Jonathan & Angela *The Marsh Lions: The Story of an African Pride* Bradt Travel Guides, 2012

Jackman, Brian *Savannah Diaries* Bradt Travel Guides, 2014

Konings, Ad *Tanganyika Cichlids in their Natural Habitat* Cichlid Press (*www.cichlidpress.com*), El Paso, 1998.

Leonard, Peter *Important Bird Areas in Zambia* Zambian Ornithological Society, Lusaka, 2005. The most comprehensive survey of the country's top birding areas – complete with a lot of other useful detail about Zambia's ecology, flora and fauna.

Newman, Kenneth *Newman's Birds of Southern Africa* Southern Books, South Africa, 1st edition 1988. This has been republished numerous times since its first edition and has become the standard field guide to birds in southern Africa, south of the Kunene and Zambezi rivers. It also covers most species found in Zambia.

Nyerenda, Patrick *A Guide to the Snakes of the Luangwa Valley* WECSZ, reprint 2007.

Scott, Jonathan & Angela *The Leopard's Tale* Bradt Travel Guides, 2013

Sinclair, Ian, and Ryan, Peter *Birds of Africa south of the Sahara* Struik, Cape Town, 2003. The field guide used by many of Zambia's birders as it incorporates both central African and southern African species, though it's a hefty tome to cart around.

Sinclair, Ian, Hockey, Phil, Tarboton, Warwick, and Ryan, Peter *Sasol Birds of Southern Africa*, Penguin Random House, South Africa 4th edition. Although it doesn't cover Zambia, it includes all species found in the country, bar a few endemics. Used by many of the camps guides.

Smith, P P *Common Trees, Shrubs and Grasses of the Luangwa Valley* Trendrine Press, Cornwall, 1995. This small, practical field guide has pictures to aid identification at the back, and includes a small section on the value to wildlife of the various plants.

Solomon, Derek *Animals in Action: a guide to the common mammals of South Luangwa National Park* 2005.

van Perlo, Ber *Birds of Southern Africa* Collins Illustrated Checklist, 1999. The only concise field guide that covers both Zambia and the rest of the region.

A *Guide to Common Wild Mammals of Zambia* WECSZ, 1991. A small field guide to the more common species.

A *Guide to Reptiles, Amphibians & Fishes of Zambia* Wildlife Conservation Society of Zambia, Lusaka, 1993. Another good guide to the more common species.

Common Birds of Zambia Zambian Ornithological Society, Lusaka, revised 1993. A good small field guide to the more common species.

Art and culture

Jordan, Manuel *Makishi: Mask Characters of Zambia* Fowler Museum of Cultural History, Los Angeles, 2007.

Phillipson, D W, revised by Katanekwa, N M *National Monuments of Zambia* National Heritage Conservation Commission, Livingstone, 1972 (4th printing 1992). Look for this small, green paperback around Lusaka, and buy it if you see one as they're quite scarce. It describes all of Zambia's national monuments, including many historical monuments, archaeological sites and even places of great scenic beauty – with some great old black-and-white photos.

Smith, Benjamin W *Zambia's Ancient Rock Art: The Paintings of Kasama* National Heritage Conservation Commission, Livingstone, 1997.

Coffee-table books

d'Elbée, François *Bush and Eye* Editions de la Martinière, Paris, 2002, and *Busanga: The Northern Plains of the Kafue National Park* 2004. D'Elbée's illuminating photographs focused first on the Lower Zambezi National Park, and then on the northern Kafue – with stunning results.

Travelogues and biography

Carr, Norman *Kakuli: A Story about Wild Animals* CBC Publishing, Harare, 1996. A collection of Norman Carr's tales from his time in the Luangwa Valley. Excellent light reading whilst on safari.

Owens, Mark and Delia *Survivor's Song: Life and Death in an African Wilderness* HarperCollins, London, 1993. Published as *The Eye of the Elephant* in the USA. This relates the authors' struggles to protect the wildlife of North Luangwa National Park from poachers, and their efforts to develop viable alternatives to poaching for the local people. It is excellent reading, though insiders complain of sensationalism, and that it ignores valuable contributions made by others.

Palin, Michael *Pole to Pole* BBC Consumer Publishing, London, 1999. This has an excellent section on Zambia, and Shiwa Ng'andu in particular is covered well.

Quarmby, C A *Just Driving Around in the North* Health Rescue International, Zambia.

Siddle, Sheila *Billy The Hippo* Mission Press, Ndola, 2006. A children's book telling the story of an orphaned hippo raised by the author at Chimfunshi.

Siddle, Sheila, with Cress, Doug *In My Family Tree: A Life with Chimpanzees* Grove/Atlantic, New York, 2002, and Double Storey, Cape Town, 2004. Sheila Siddle's story of the establishment of Chimfunshi Wildlife Orphanage makes inspirational – if sometimes shocking – reading.

Guidebooks

Allen, Quentin, Mwanza, Ilse and Chalcraft, Heather *A Guide to Little-Known Waterfalls of Zambia* Published privately, Lusaka, 2005. A mine of useful information, this detailed guide offers an excuse to head off the beaten track as well as detailed information relating to Zambia's innumerable waterfalls. Illustrated with line drawings, paintings and photographs, it also has plenty of practical information, including GPS co-ordinates.

Ashley, Nikki *The Kafue National Park, Zambia* CBC Publishing, Harare, 2012. This detailed guide to the national park is written by a biologist but also incorporates visitor information and a species list, with photographs by Ian Murphy.

Johnson, Sigrid Anna *A Visitor's Guide to Nyika National Park, Malawi* Mbabazi Book Trust, Blantyre. Sadly out of print, but worth buying if you can find a copy, this book provides a detailed historical and ecological background to Nyika, 20 pages of special-interest sites and notes on recommended walks and hikes, as well as complete checklists of all mammals, birds, butterflies and orchids that are known to occur in the park.

Rattray, Gordon *Access Africa: Safaris for People with Limited Mobility* Bradt Travel Guides, UK, 2009. Written by Bradt's consultant on disabilities, this is an invaluable guide to taking a safari for travellers with limited mobility, and includes a section on Livingstone.

Atlas of the National Parks of Zambia ZAWA, Chilanga, 2009. Available only at ZAWA's Chilanga HQ, near Lusaka, this useful atlas presents the country's national parks through a series of helpful maps.

Welcome to Lusaka – a guide for newcomers Diplomatic Spouses Association, Lusaka, 2011

Health

Wilson-Howarth, Dr Jane *The Essential Guide To Travel Health: don't let Bugs, Bites and Bowels spoil your trip* Cadogan Books, London, 2009. An amusing and erudite overview of the hazards of tropical travel which is small enough to take with you.

Wilson-Howarth, Dr Jane, and Ellis, Dr Matthew *Your Child Abroad: A Travel Health Guide* Bradt Travel Guides, Chalfont St Peter, 3rd edition (eBook) 2014. An invaluable resource for all those travelling with children.

Novels

Banda-Aaku, Ellen *Patchwork* Penguin, South Africa, 2011. Banda-Aaku's award-winning novel of a child growing up in Lusaka gives an insight into Zambian life in the late 1970s. In so doing, it touches on issues as wide ranging as wealth and poverty, cultural evolution and post-independence politics.

Children's books

Griffiths, Meg *Wonky Tusk* Muddy Boots, Zambia, 2008. A children's story about a naughty elephant whose mother has a wonky tusk. The 'Wonky Tusk' of the title refers to the elephant matriarch who annually leads her family through Mfuwe Lodge in the South Luangwa in search of ripe mangoes.

WEBSITES
Website addresses seem to change frequently, especially in Zambia, but some of the more interesting ones include:

Tourist information
https://zambia.co.zm Called 'The National Homepage of Zambia', with some useful links.
www.zambiatourism.com The official website of the Zambia National Tourist Board.

Media

www.lowdownzambia.com An electronic version of *The Lowdown*, Lusaka's monthly magazine – although no longer up to date.

www.postzambia.com For an independent view of Zambian affairs, look at this site from *The Post* newspaper. It usually takes a more objective, critical and questioning approach than the rival *Times of Zambia*.

www.times.co.zm The site of the *Times of Zambia*. Features the main stories of the day and a searchable (but not listed) archive containing stories from June 2001 to the present day.

Index

Page numbers in **bold** indicate main entries; those in *italics* indicate maps

537

INDEX TO ADVERTISERS